Everyday Spelling

Teacher's Edition
Grade 4

Scott Foresman
Addison Wesley

Editorial Offices: Glenview, Illinois • New York, New York
Sales Offices: Reading, Massachusetts • Duluth, Georgia • Glenview, Illinois • Carrollton, Texas • Menlo Park, California
http://everydayspelling.com

Authors

James Beers, Ph.D.
College of William and Mary
Williamsburg, Virginia

Ronald Cramer, Ph.D.
Oakland University
Rochester, Michigan

W. Dorsey Hammond, Ph.D.
Oakland University
Rochester, Michigan

Consultants

Research Consultant
James F. Cipielewski, Ph.D.
Western Michigan University
Kalamazoo, Michigan

Multicultural Consultant
Alice A. Deck, Ph.D.
University of Illinois
Urbana, Illinois

ESL Specialists

Jean Aupont
Haitian Creole

Marcel Hull
Pilipino

S. Patricia Kim
Korean

Huong Banh
Mandarin Chinese

Sundary Khem
Cambodian

Ngoc-Diep Thi Nguyen
Vietnamese

Eugenia de Hoogh
Spanish

Teacher Reviewers

Mary Anderson
Hamilton, OH

Marilyn Harrer
Scottsdale, AZ

Janice Lombardi
Dallas, TX

Rosie Peace
Chicago, IL

Marthella Trueba
El Paso, TX

Sister Sheila Conley
Brooklyn, NY

Sandy Jernberg
Minneapolis, MN

Lynn Mauch
Gahanna, OH

Elizabeth Rodriguez
Sugar Land, TX

Ruth Van Horn
Signal Mountain, TN

Dr. Vivian Dillihunt
Memphis, TN

Jetta Johnson
Cut Bank, MT

Lynn Mekkers
McMinnville, OR

Susan Schiavone
Chicago, IL

Helena Van Rooyen
Hacienda Heights, CA

Dr. Pat Finger
Greensboro, NC

Cathy Kinzer
Las Cruces, NM

Judy Myers
Punxsutawney, PA

Sharon Searcy
Jacksonville, FL

Pam Wert
Carterville, MO

Everyday Spelling

Target the Words Kids Use and Misspell in Everyday Writing

- Words most frequently misspelled at each grade
- Special lessons on high-frequency errors
- Spelling strategies that last a lifetime

Build Vocabulary and Writing Skills

- Weekly vocabulary and writing activities
- Content-area vocabulary lessons
- Built-in dictionary, thesaurus, and writer's handbook

Make Everyone a Better Speller

- Phonics, structure, and meaning-based spelling patterns
- Modified and challenge word lists
- Resources for visual, auditory, and kinesthetic learners
- Bilingual/ESL instructional strategies

Scott Foresman
Addison Wesley

Target Words Kids Use and Misspell

9. our ✳
10. outside ✳

Kids can easily spot words often misspelled

■ **INTRODUCTION**

Vowel Sounds in *boy* and *out*

SPELLING FOCUS

The vowel sound /oi/ can be spelled **oi** and **oy**: **ch<u>oi</u>ce**, **l<u>oy</u>al**. The vowel sound /ou/ can be spelled **ow** and **ou**: **t<u>ow</u>el**, **<u>ou</u>r**.

■ **STUDY** Say the words and read the sentences. Lo for the letters that spell the vowel sounds in **boy** and **ou**

1.	choice	You have a **choice** of two soups.
2.	noisy	Folding chairs is a **noisy** job.
3.	loyal	The fans are **loyal** to their team.
4.	destroy	A tornado can **destroy** homes.
5.	powder	I sprinkled **powder** on the baby.
6.	towel	We used a **towel** to dry the car.
7.	downtown	I like to shop **downtown**.
8.	amount	She saved a small **amount** of mone
9.	our ✳	We found **our** coats, but not theirs.
10.	outside ✳	They played **outside** in the park.

11.	spoil	Milk left out too long may **spoil**.
12.	poison	The bleach label warned of **poison**.
13.	Illinois	Soybeans and corn grow in **Illinois**.
14.	annoy	The loud jets overhead **annoy** us.
15.	oyster	This beach has many **oyster** shells.
16.	voyage	Our sea **voyage** will last one week.
17.	drown	One can **drown** in shallow water.
18.	growl	The dog's low **growl** frightened me.
19.	couch	This leather **couch** stains easily.
20.	surround	I built a fence to **surround** the pool.

■ **PRACTICE** Sort the words by writing
■ ten words with a vowel sound /oi/

What words should be taught in a spelling program?

The answer sounds simple. A good spelling curriculum should teach the words students use and misspell. Traditional spelling lists are often based solely on high-frequency usage and on content-area reading and literature. Only *Everyday Spelling* teaches the words students at each grade level actually write and misspell most frequently.

Everyday Spelling is based on the Research in Action project—the most comprehensive study of children's writing ever completed. More than 250 teachers participated. Over 18,000 student compositions were analyzed to identify the words students misspelled most frequently—and the types of errors most often made. These findings were incorporated into *Everyday Spelling*, making it the first spelling program to teach the words and strategies today's students absolutely need to know.

Lessons on common spelling errors and hard-to-spell words

Strategy workshops develop spelling skills that last a lifetime

PREDICTABLE LESSON FORMAT

PREDICTABLE LESSON FORMAT

Encourages Independent Learning

DAY 1
**Pretest and the
lesson generalization**

DAY 2
**Meaningful practice
plus strategic spelling**

INTRODUCTION

THINK AND PRACTICE

Vowel Sounds in

SPELLING FOCUS

The vowel sound /oi/ can b
ch<u>oi</u>ce, l<u>oy</u>al. The vowel sour
ow and **ou**: t<u>ow</u>el, <u>ou</u>r.

STUDY Say the words and r
for the letters that spell the vowel

1. *choice* — You have a c
2. *noisy* — Folding chair
3. *loyal* — The fans are l
4. *destroy* — A tornado car
5. *powder* — I sprinkled **pow**
6. *towel* — We used a **tow**
7. *downtown* — I like to shop **do**
8. *amount* — She saved a sm
9. *our* ✱ — We found **our** co
10. *outside* ✱ — They played **out**

11. *spoil* — Milk left out too lo
12. *poison* — The bleach label v
13. *Illinois* — Soybeans and cor
14. *annoy* — The loud jets overh
15. *oyster* — This beach has ma
16. *voyage* — Our sea **voyage** will
17. *drown* — One can **drown** in sh
18. *growl* — The dog's low **growl**
19. *couch* — This leather **couch** sto
20. *surround* — I built a fence to **surro**

✱ H OUT FOR
QUENTLY
SPELLED
ORDS!

GE!

PRACTICE Sort the words by writing
- ten words with a vowel sound /oi/
- ten words with a vowel sound /ou/

ANALOGIES Write the list word that completes each
analogy.

1. A hike is to land as a ___ is to sea.
2. Rind is to orange as shell is to ___.
3. Nourishing is to food as deadly is to ___.
4. Scrub is to brush as dry is to ___.
5. Bench is to park as ___ is to living room.
6. Floor is to inside as sidewalk is to ___.
7. Nation is to United States as state is to ___.
8. Picnicking is to park as shopping is to ___.

WORD MATH Write the list word that completes each
equation.

9. voice + animal + threat = ___
10. underwater + suffocate + sink = ___
11. harsh + sounds + loud = ___
12. my + your = ___
13. dusty + sprinkle + a puff = ___
14. count + add + sum = ___
15. decision + pick + one = ___
16. trouble + behavior + bother = ___
17. protect + fence in + enclose = ___

Take a Hint
To spell *poison*, re
poison **is on** the

PROO

The kids p
ideas in t
but they
punctua
this is a
need ch

Write the list word that completes each sentence. The
underlined word is a clue. Circle the letters in each word
that are the same as those in the underlined word.

18. You can't ___ something that is <u>indestructible</u>.
19. Visitors who litter this <u>unspoiled</u> beach will ___ it.

DAY 3
Skill building application in writing

PROOFREADING AND WRITING

PROOFREAD A L
column in a nature n
received this letter. Fi
mistakes and three pu

Dear Al,

My brother an

beutiful and we w

see some. But are fr

ugly. They annoiy .

WRITE A LETTER Be the editor a
se two list words and one personal

Word List

powder	amount	loyal
drown	outside	spoil
towel	growl	oyster

DAY 4
Vocabulary and language development

VOCABULARY BUILD

Review

OPPOSITES Write the words from the box that complete
the phrases.

1. not inside, but ___
2. not quiet, but ___
3. not uptown, but ___
4. not their turn, but ___ turn
5. not to build, but to ___

CLASSIFYING Write the
list word that belongs in
each group.

1. true, faithful, ___
2. selection, option, pick, ___
3. washcloth, bath mat, ___
4. ashes, dust, ___
5. sum, quantity, ___

Word Study

ONOMATOPOEIA What sound do s n ang
make? You could say *growl*. You cou ctually
the dog when you say it. Try it. *Gr-r-r-owl!*

Words like *growl*, *screech*, and *oink* e examp
onomatopoeia. The word imitates th sund t
trying to describe.

Write words that describe the soun s these o
make. Use a word that actually im tates the
little silver bell

DAY 5
Testing Options

- Traditional posttest
- Dictation sentences
- Standardized test format
- Auditory test on CD-ROM

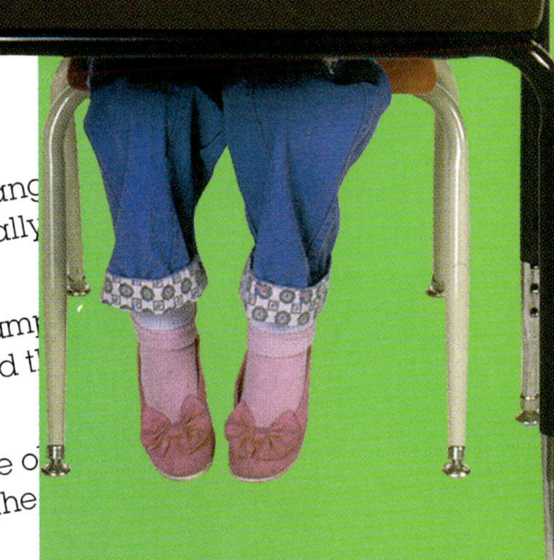

Build Vocabulary and Writing Skills

Word study to extend language learning

Content-area vocabulary pages for every lesson
- Mathematics • Social Studies
- Health   • Reading • Science

VOCABULARY BUILDING

Review

OPPOSITES Write the words from the box that complete the phrases.

1. not inside, but ___
2. not quiet, but ___
3. not uptown, but ___
4. not their turn, but ___ turn
5. not to build, but to ___

CLASSIFYING Write the list word that belongs in each group.

1. true, faithful, ___
2. selection, option, pick

ch___
no.
loy
des
pow
towe
down
amou
our
outside

invertebrates
vertebrates
sponge
jellyfish
tentacles
backbone
mollusks
fish
alligator
gills

SCIENCE

Invertebrates and Vertebrates

The words in the list are about two groups of animals and their differences. Use the Spelling Dictionary if you need to. Add other words to the list.

■ GETTING AT MEANING

Captions Read the paragraph below. Then write the list words to complete the captions about each picture.

Scientists divide all animals into **invertebrates** and **vertebrates**. Animals without **backbones** are invertebrates; animals with backbones are vertebrates. **Jellyfish** and **mollusks**, such as clams and oysters, are invertebrates. Some vertebrates, like the **alligator**, live on the land and breathe air. Others, like **fish**, live underwater and take oxygen from water through **gills**.

■ SPELL WELL

Including All the Letters Sometimes we spell words w because we say them wrong. Say each word below it. Be sure to pronounce the sounds of the underlined

tentacles   mollusks

Did You Know? All **tomato clown fish** are male whe hatched! Later the ones that grow larger and more d turn into females. The males are red-orange except fo white stripe around the middle. The females are blac

The animals below have no backbones. They are all __(1)__.

These animals have backbones. They are all __(6)__.

This invertebrate can grab food with its __(2)__. It is called a __(3)__.

This __(7)__ is d took an X r see its __(8)__.

This animal is called a __(4)__. People use it for scrubbing.

Clams and oysters are also known as __(5)__.

Water passes through the __(9)__ of a __(10)__ so that it can get oxygen.

Using spelling as a writing skill

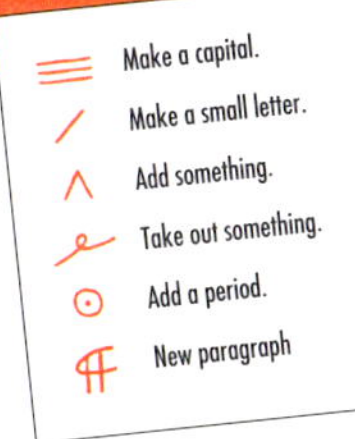

Reinforce grammar, mechanics, and proofreading skills

Real-world writing contexts

Extra process-writing practice with every lesson

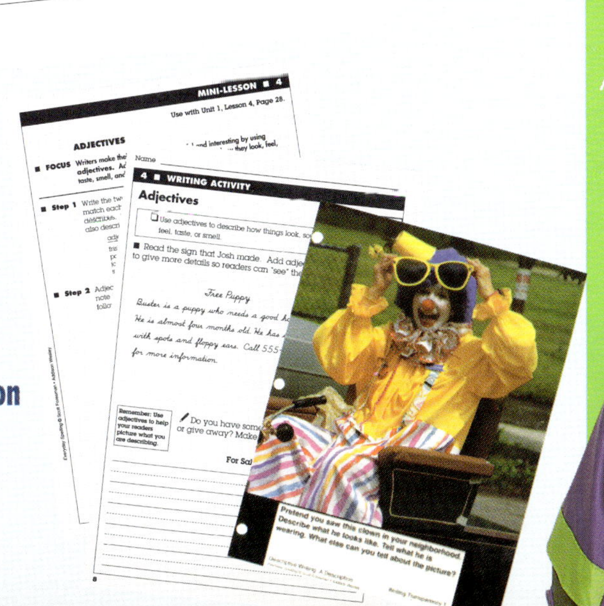

Help Everyone Be a Better Speller

Daily Warm-Up
Write the following word forms on
the board and have children add
ay, **ai**, or **a** and **e** to make long **a**
words: tr ___ n; d ___ ___;
l ___ k ___. **Phonics**

wait	may	mail
make	away	ate
take	paint	baseball

Adding the missing letters **ai** or **ay**.
and for the **long a** sound.

3. aw _ _

aw|ay

6. w _ _ t

w|ai|t

that means   7.   baseball

ym class.   8.   ate

e boxes.

ool?   9.   make

10.   take

11.   way

ections

at is part   12.   rain
box.

ences with   13.   raindrop

(13) fall on   14.   raincoat
on my (14).

THINK AND PRACTICE

Substituting
Meaning Match Children
can substitute list words for
the underlined clue until
they find the correct word.

**MEETING THE NEEDS
OF ALL CHILDREN**

Kinesthetic Learners
Missing Letters Have chil-
dren write **a**, **i**, and **y** on
cards and place **ai** and **ay**
with each set of letters to
identify the correct word.

Bilingual/ESL
Matching Patterns Write
play, came, and train on
the board. Ask children to
write the list words under
the appropriate word and
underline the letters that
stand for the vowel sound.

Modified List
Practice Children studying
the first six words may
complete the Think and
Practice Master instead of
this page.

Additional Practice
Think and Practice Master 21
Extra Practice Master 21
Everyday Spelling CD-ROM
Everyday Spelling Game
Software

Additional Practice

**Think and Practice Master 21
Extra Practice Master 21
Everyday Spelling CD-ROM
Everyday Spelling Game
Software**

Extra practice for
homework and fun

Help all students
succeed every day

Teaching resources for
every learning style

Visual Learners

- Spelling posters

- Word list charts

- Interactive CD-ROM

- Splat! game software

- *Everyday Spelling* Web site

- Four-color writing transparencies

- Daily teaching suggestions

Auditory Learners

- Audiotapes

- Interactive CD-ROM

- Daily teaching suggestions

Kinesthetic Learners

- Word builder tiles (1–3)

- Punch-out letters and words (1)

- Daily teaching suggestions

Bilingual/ESL Learners

- Mini-lessons with activity sheets

- English/Spanish word list in
  the Student Edition

- English/Spanish dictionary
  on CD-ROM

- Audiotapes

- Auditory CD-ROM activities

- Daily and weekly teaching suggestions

Make Spelling Make Sense

Phonics for Beginning Spellers

- Readiness lessons in Grade 1

- Phonics focus all year long in Grade 1

- Phonics-based word lists begin Grade 2

- Daily warmups for phonics

- Weekly Phonics Connections

Phonics Practice Book

- Extra practice for every lesson in Grades 1–3

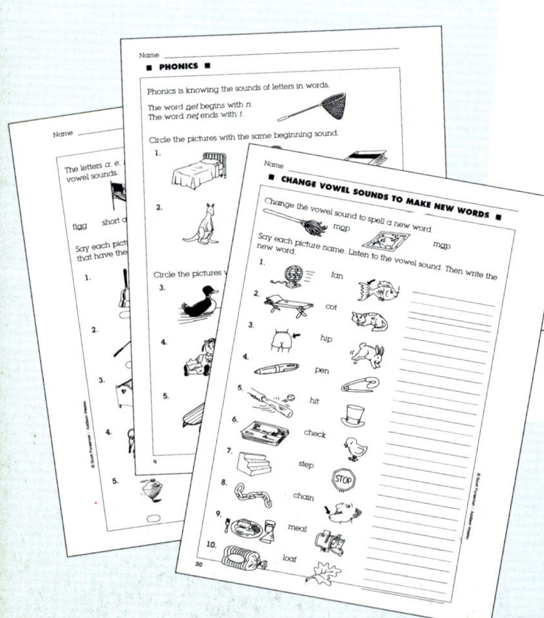

Name

Words with Short e

Look at each word. **Say** it.
Listen for the **short e** sound in
Write each word. **Check** it.

8

bed
led
met
get
pen
ten

1. bed
2. led
3. met
4. get
5. pen
6. ten

Everyday Words

yes
then

7. yes
8. then

Spell each list word aloud and ask your child to say the word. Then say each word and ask your child to spell it.

Grade 1

69

T12

Special lessons on hard-to-spell words

Research shows children misspell the same words repeatedly. Unique lessons target these troublesome words year after year.

- Homophones
- Getting Letters in Correct Order
- Including All Letters
- Using Just Enough Letters
- Words with No Sound Clues

Word Structure for Intermediate Spellers

- **Emphasis on word-structure generalizations**
- **Development of visual awareness of patterns**
- **More complex phonics combinations**

Meaning for More Advanced Spellers

- **Meaning-based/derivational word lists**
- **More complex structural patterns**
- **Complex phonics strategies**

■ INTRODUCTION

Adding -ed and -ing

SPELLING FOCUS

When adding **-ed** and **-ing**, some base words do not change. Others do change.
- In words that end with **consonant-e**, the **e** is dropped.
- In words that end in **y**, the **y** is changed to **i** when adding **-ed** but kept when adding **-ing**.
- In one-syllable words that end with **consonant-vowel-consonant**, the final consonant is doubled.

■ STUDY Read the words in each row. Notice what happens when **-ed** and **-ing** are added.

start	1. started ✳	2. starting
smile	3. smiled	4. smiling
cry	5. cried	6. crying
plan	7. planned	8. planning

hope	9. hoped	10. hoping
fry	11. fried	12. frying
hop	13. hopped	14. hopping

■ PRACTICE Sort these words by writing
- four words in which final **e** is dropped
- four words with no spelling change
- two words in which **y** is changed to **i**
- four words in which the final consonant is doubled

CHALLENGE!
...azed
...nazing
...igged
...gging

■ WRITE Choose seven words to write in sentences.

Grade 3

17

■ INTRODUCTION

Related Words 1

SPELLING FOCUS

Related words often have parts that are spelled the same but pronounced differently: **human, humane.**

■ STUDY Say each word. Then read the sentence.

1. human	It's only **human** to make mistakes.
2. humane	Animals deserve **humane** treatment.
3. clean	We **clean** house on Saturdays.
4. cleanse	Use alcohol to **cleanse** the cut.
5. nature	Forest rangers protect **nature**.
6. natural	He is a **natural** athlete.
7. major	She is a **major** writer of our time.
8. majority	I won with a **majority** of the vo...
9. poem	We like a **poem** that rhymes.
10. poetic	The song's words are **poetic**.

11. equal	Divide the pie into **equal** a...
12. equation	Solve the **equation** for math...
13. unite	A common cause will **unite** u...
14. unity	An experienced team has un...
15. bomb	The **bomb** exploded violentl...
16. bombard	Cannon will **bombard** the fo...
17. muscle	Lifting can cause **muscle** pain.
18. muscular	A weight lifter is **muscular**.
19. resign	My boss said he will **resign**.
20. resignation	We must accept his **resignation**.

CHALLENGE!
haste
hasten
heir
inherit
harmony
harmonious

■ PRACTICE Sort the words by writing
- three pairs of words in which **g**, **c**, or **b** changes from silent to sounded
- seven pairs of words in which a vowel sound changes

■ WRITE Choose two sentences to include in a paragraph.

82

Grade 6

INFORMATION AT YOUR FINGERTIPS

Saves You Time and Effort

Daily options to simplify time management

Phonics, word structure, or meaning connections

Suggestions for using a modified list

Lesson plans for every day of the week

DAY 1 Introduction

LESSON
20

- Pretest and Self-Check
- Spelling Focus and Word List
- Challenge Words
- Modified List

● Core ○ Optional ✓ Assess

INTRODUCTION

Phonics

Vowel Sounds in *boy* and *out* Ask students to write *boy* and *out* as heads, write the appropriate list words under them, and circle the vowel letters that spell /oi/ and /ou/. Point out the two spellings for each vowel sound.

MEETING THE NEEDS OF ALL STUDENTS

Modified List

Practice Students studying only the high-frequency words in the top box write

- three words with a vowel sound spelled **ow**
- three words with a vowel sound spelled **ou**
- two words with a vowel sound spelled **oi**
- two words with a vowel sound spelled **oy**

Visual Learners

Highlighting Have students write the **w, u, i,** or **y** in each vowel pair in a second color.

Additional Practice

Challenge Master 20
Home-School Master 20
Audiotape B, Side 2

1.	choice
2.	noisy
3.	loyal
4.	destroy
5.	spoil
6.	poison
7.	Illinois
8.	annoy
9.	oyster
10.	voyage
11.	powder
12.	towel
13.	downtown
14.	amount
15.	our
16.	outside
17.	drown
18.	growl
19.	couch
20.	surround

CHALLENGE

turmoil
exploit
employer
cauliflower
foundation

WEEK-AT-A-GLANCE
LESSON
20

Generalization

Spelling Focus: The vowel sound /oi/ can be spelled **oi** or **oy**. The vowel sound /ou/ can be spelled **ow** or **ou**.

● Core ○ Optional ✓ Assessment

DAILY PLAN	CORE OBJECTIVES	NOTES
DAY 1 Introduction Pretest and Self-Check, p. 96B Spelling Focus and Word List, p. 96 Challenge Words, p. 96 Challenge Master 20 Home-School Master 20	✓ Take and self-check Pretest • Spell words with the vowel sounds in *boy* and *out;* classify and write the list words	
DAY 2 Think and Practice Analogies; Word Math, p. 97 Strategic Spelling; *Seeing Meaning Connections,* p. 97 Think and Practice Master 20 Extra Practice Master 20 Cross-Curricular Lesson: Introduce, p. 172	• Complete practice activities for words with the vowel sounds in *boy* and *out* • Recognize meaning connections between list words and other words related to them	
DAY 3 Proofreading and Writing Proofread a Letter, p. 98 Proofreading Tip: Punctuation, p. 98 Write a Letter, p. 98 Cooperative Midweek Test Hardbound Book Master 20 Writing Mini-Lesson Master 20 Writing Activity Master 20 Second Language Support Master 20	• Proofread for spelling and punctuation errors • Integrate spelling and writing in a personal writing response ✓ Take and check midweek test	
DAY 4 Vocabulary Building Review: Opposites; Classifying, p. 99 Word Study: Onomatopoeia, p. 99 Cross-Curricular Lesson: Follow-Up, p. 172 Review Master 20	• Complete review activities for words with the vowel sounds in *boy* and *out* • Study and use onomatopoeia	
DAY 5 Assessment Posttest, p. 96B Standardized Test Master 20	✓ Take Posttest	

96A

Daily spelling reviews

DAY 4 Vocabulary Building

- Review: Opposites and Classifying
- Word Study: Onoma-
- Crea-

SPELLING REVIEW

...een we carved a
...nd made *carmel* apples.

...in   caramel

DAILY SPELLING REVIEW

The *racoon* hunted for food scraps
around the fishing *loge*.

raccoon   lodge

DAY 5 Assessment

- Posttest
- Dictation Sentences
- Standardized Test Master 20
- Auditory Test on *Everyday Spelling*
  CD-ROM

ON

...nds in *boy* and *out*

...OCUS

...nd /oi/ can be spelled **oi** and **oy**:
...The vowel sound /ou/ can be spelled
...wel, our.

...the words and read the sentences. Look
...at spell the vowel sounds in **boy** and **out**.

You have a **choice** of two soups.
Folding chairs is a **noisy** job.
The fans are **loyal** to their team.
A tornado can **destroy** homes.
I sprinkled **powder** on the baby.
We used a **towel** to dry the car.
I like to shop **downtown**.
She saved a small **amount** of money.
We found **our** coats, but not theirs.
They played **outside** in the park.

Milk left out too long may **spoil**.
The bleach label warned of **poison**.
Soybeans and corn grow in **Illinois**.
The loud jets overhead **annoy** us.
This beach has many **oyster** shells.
Our sea **voyage** will last one week.
One can **drown** in shallow water.
The dog's low **growl** frightened me.
This leather **couch** stains easily.
I built a fence to **surround** the pool.

...RACTICE Sort the words by writing
...words with a vowel sound /oi/
...words with a vowel sound /ou/
...er of words within groups may vary.

...RITE Choose two sentences to use in a paragraph.

...WATCH OUT FOR FREQUENTLY MISSPELLED WORDS!

VOCABULARY BUILDING

...mplete

choice	towel
noisy	downtown
loyal	amount
destroy	our
powder	outside

1. **outside**
2. **noisy**
3. **downtown**
4. **our**
5. **destroy**

1. **loyal**
2. **choice**
3. **towel**
4. **powder**
5. **amount**

Answers will vary.

99

VOCABULARY BUILDING

Literature Connection

Onomatopoeia in Poetry
Students can identify sound
words in poems from
*Munching: Poems About
Eating* by Lee Bennett
Hopkins (Little, 1985).

MEETING THE NEEDS OF ALL STUDENTS

Modified List

Review Students studying
high-frequency words
complete this page.

Bilingual/ESL

Language Comparisons
Onomatopoeia may be
easier for ESL students if
they are asked to give the
equivalent in their native
language for words such
as *meow, moo,* and *buzz.*

Enrichment

Sound Effects Invite students to use "sound effect"
words as they write about
something they have seen
and heard or read about.

Additional Practice
Review Master 20
Standardized Test Master 20
Everyday Spelling **CD-ROM**

Literature references
to build vocabulary

Strategies to meet
individual needs

Additional practice
at point of use

Powerful Resources and New Technologies

Help Students Be Successful Spellers

Student Edition

- Consumable, 1–8
- Nonconsumable, 2–8
- D'Nealian® editions, 1–3

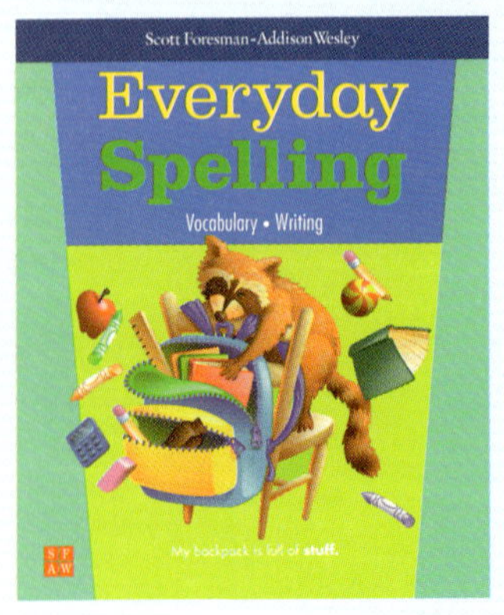
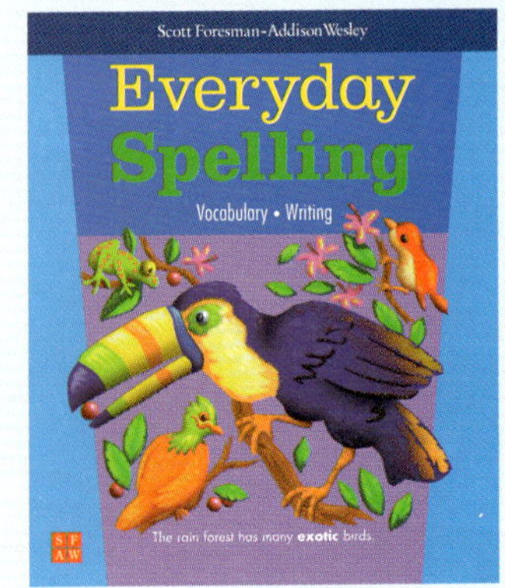

Teacher's Edition

- Clear, easy format
- Strategies for meeting individual needs
- Ready-made lesson plans

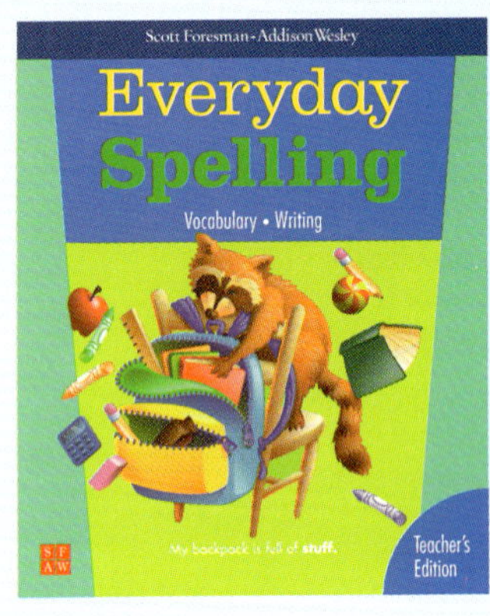

Phonics

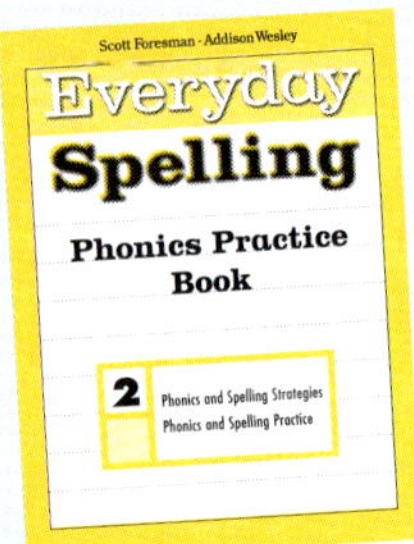

Phonics Practice Book
Extra practice with phonics patterns and spelling strategies. Grades 1–3.

Word List Charts
Weekly charts display phonics-based word lists. Grades 1–3.

Word Builder Tiles
Soft foam manipulative letters teach letter sounds and build phonemic awareness. Grades 1–3.

Little Celebrations®
Easy-to-read mini books reinforce phonics and language skills. Grades 1–2.

PRACTICE

Practice Masters

- Extra Practice
- Review
- Think and Practice
- Challenge

Standardized Tests

Weekly and unit practice in standardized test formats

Second Language Support Package

- Mini-lessons
- Student Activity Masters
- Audiotapes with words, context, and stories
- Teaching Strategies

Home-School Activities

Worksheets and parent letters for at-home learning

TECHNOLOGY

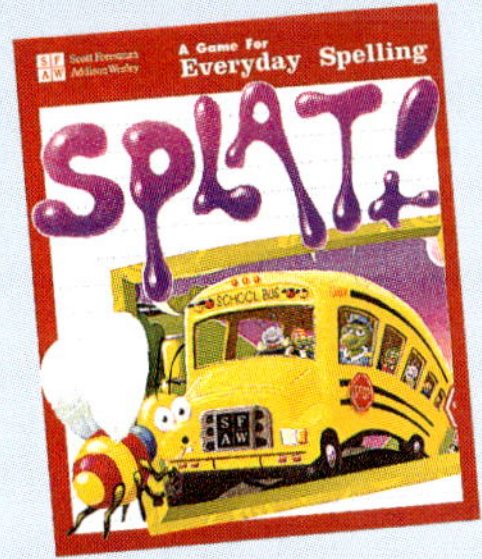

Splat! Software Game

An animated, action-packed game that tests children's spelling savvy. Grades 1–6.

Everyday Spelling CD-ROM

An interactive way for children to practice spelling words and build language skills. Grades 1–6.

- Writing and proofreading
- Vocabulary practice
- Challenge activities
- Splat! spelling game
- Auditory spelling tests

World Wide Web Site

Connects spelling to a world of words on the Web!

WRITING AND VOCABULARY

Proofreading and Writing

Weekly proofreading and writing activities on overhead transparencies

Spelling and Writing

Grammar mini-lessons, activity masters, and writing transparencies to add depth to weekly lessons

Spelling Posters

Frequently misspelled words, spelling tips, and proofreading strategies for teaching and display

Teaching the Program

EVERYDAY SPELLING SIMPLIFIES SPELLING INSTRUCTION THROUGH A CONSISTENT, PREDICTABLE LESSON ORGANIZATION.

The Grade One Program

Unit Structure

Grade One of *Everyday Spelling* has one readiness unit and five spelling units with word lists. Each spelling unit contains these week-long lessons:

▼ 4 phonics-based spelling lessons

▼ 1 theme-based spelling and vocabulary lesson

▼ 1 review lesson

Readiness

A complete readiness unit is included for students who are not yet ready for formal spelling instruction. The six-week unit covers a range of readiness, phonemic awareness, and word-development skills and gives you tools to deal with whatever levels of language experience the children bring with them on the first day of school. The readiness unit builds the foundation emerging readers and writers need for learning to spell.

Lesson Highlights

Word Lists

There are six list words in each weekly spelling lesson. You can choose to use two additional words, called Everyday Words—high-frequency words often misspelled by first graders. For children who can learn extra words, there are two Additional Words in the Teacher's Edition. This gives you the possibility of teaching 6, 8, or 10 words each week depending on the needs of the children. These words are tied to the lesson generalization or theme. All words are listed together in the Unit Overview.

Spelling and Phonics

Twenty week-long lessons teach common spelling generalizations. In Grade One the focus is on phonics. As children begin to write, phonics not only helps them spell the words they want to write, it also gives them important word information that helps them read more fluently. Phonics advances students' general language development at the same time it helps them progress through the appropriate developmental stages of spelling. In Grade One other types of generalizations are also introduced to facilitate children's writing efforts. Word-list generalizations are based on

- phonics *(man, pan, can)*
- structure *(hop, hopped, hope, hoping)*
- Words to Know (sight words)

Writing

On Day 3 of each weekly lesson first graders work on language arts skills and sentence writing and collect personal words for writing. Options to extend the writing experience include a Writing Mini-Lesson and a Writing Activity Master. Review lessons provide language arts activities and writing games plus a Writing Prompt and Writing Model Transparency. The Spelling Dictionary, Writing Journal, Word Place, and *Everyday Spelling* CD-ROM offer additional writing support.

Vocabulary

Each unit contains one theme lesson, which provides the vocabulary development emerging writers need. Because a rich language environment is essential for spelling growth, the theme lessons begin with a poem. Discussion about the poem leads to the introduction of the spelling words grouped around the theme. Themes include number, color, animal, family, and place words.

Weekly Lessons

A familiar lesson structure each week builds students' confidence and gets them started as independent learners.

Day 1	Pretest Lesson Introduction
Day 2	Practice the Words
Day 3	Write
Day 4	Review
Day 5	Test

Further vocabulary development is offered on Bonus Pages, which contain activities that build vocabulary in science, math, art, and social studies, plus special holiday words. Children use Word Place to collect their personal words.

Test-Study-Test

Research shows the test-study-test method to be the single most effective technique for teaching spelling.

The Pretest

Begin teaching spelling each week by giving the pretest. It is important to get Grade One children off to a good start by using this metacognitive strategy to focus their attention on the spelling generalization for the week. See page T20 for information on giving the pretest.

Study

Once you have introduced the spelling concepts for the week, students take over responsibility for their own learning. They think critically, practice, write, extend vocabulary, and develop their spelling savvy with motivating activities that lead to mastery of the week's words.

The Posttest

In Grade One, a traditional posttest can be given to the class using the context sentences that appear in the Teacher's Edition Week-at-a-Glance or individually with an auditory test available on the *Everyday Spelling* CD-ROM.

Teacher's Edition

The Teacher's Edition for Grade One provides everything you need to teach *Everyday Spelling*. Its structure is the same as the Teacher's Editions for Grades 2–8. For a description, see page T22.

The Developmental Spelling Handbook on page T27 is of special interest to Grade One teachers. The handbook describes the stages of spelling development and suggests activities for guiding students through these stages.

The Program for Grades 2 to 8

Unit Structure

Each of six units contains:

▼ 1 strategy workshop

▼ 5 spelling lessons

▼ 5 vocabulary lessons

▼ 1 review lesson

Spelling Strategies

Strategy Workshops teach lifelong spelling skills—skills students can use in all their writing. Strategies help students spell words not typically found on grade-level word lists. Examples of strategies taught in *Everyday Spelling* include:

- Steps for Spelling
- Problem Parts
- Divide and Conquer
- Pronouncing for Spelling
- Memory Tricks
- Meaning Helpers
- Choosing the Best Strategy

Lesson Highlights

Word Lists

The word lists in *Everyday Spelling* teach the words students use and misspell most frequently in their writing. The words are listed in the front of each Student Edition, marked with an asterisk in the lesson word lists, and retaught, recycled, and reviewed throughout the grade and often throughout the program.

Spelling Generalizations

There are thirty week-long lessons. Each is organized around a common spelling generalization. Phonics, so strongly emphasized in Grade One, is the focus of the early part of Grade Two. Then, structural spelling concepts are introduced. As the grades advance, the generalizations change to coincide with students' developing spelling understanding. Phonics concepts become more complex; visual awareness of spelling patterns is developed; and word meanings and derivations are explored in greater depth. Students progress through the developmental stages of spelling by studying generalizations that are:

- phonics-based (*man, pan, can*)
- structural (*hop, hopped, hopping*)
- meaning-based (*nation, national*)

Weekly Lessons

The familiar lesson structure each week motivates students, builds confidence, and encourages independent learning.

Day 1   Pretest
Lesson Introduction

Day 2   Think and Practice
Introduce Cross-Curricular Vocabulary

Day 3   Proofreading and Writing

Day 4   Vocabulary Building

Day 5   Test

Writing

Writing is an integral part of the *Everyday Spelling* program. Both core and optional writing activities encourage students to use words they are learning to spell. Day 3 of each weekly lesson contains both writing and proofreading practice. Options to extend the writing experience include a Writing Mini-Lesson, a Writing Activity Master, and a Proofreading and Writing Transparency.

Writing in the content areas is a key activity of the review lesson in each unit. There is a Writing Prompt on a full-color transparency plus a Writing Model Transparency. A Writer's Handbook, a Spelling Dictionary, and a Writer's Thesaurus in the Student Edition support student writers, and the *Everyday Spelling* CD-ROM provides additional writing support with interactive writing practice and a word processing program.

Vocabulary

Day 4 of each lesson focuses on vocabulary development. Additional vocabulary lessons teach words from the content areas. Each vocabulary lesson is paired with a weekly spelling lesson, but the lessons can also stand alone. Because these cross-curricular lessons are self-contained, they may be taught in whatever sequence best coordinates with the timing of topics in your district's curriculum. For this reason, these lessons are grouped at the end of the book in the cross-curricular vocabulary section. The lessons introduce key words and concepts in science, social studies, mathematics, reading, health, and work and play.

Review Lessons

The final lesson in each six-week unit reviews the spelling generalizations in that unit. Emphasis is on students' use of the unit words in real-world writing contexts, giving teachers a chance to be sure everybody's "got it."

Test-Study-Test

Research shows the test-study-test method to be the single most effective technique for teaching spelling. The test-study-test method is outlined below.

Pretest

Begin each week with a pretest. The pretest is a metacognitive strategy that focuses the students' attention on the words they can't spell. Teacher-guided self-correction of the pretest helps students understand the spelling generalization, discover which words are difficult, locate troublesome parts of words, and zero in on their learning goals for the week.

Giving the Pretest

1. Have the students number a sheet of paper (or use the Pretest Form).
2. Sentences for the pretest appear on the Week-at-a-Glance page of each lesson.

Read aloud the underlined list word, then read the sentence, and finally repeat the word. The students write the word only.
3. Have the students put a question mark beside each word they are not sure they spelled correctly.
4. Say each word and then spell it aloud. As you spell, have students touch their pencils to each letter, circle the part of the word they misspelled, and then write the word correctly beside each misspelled word.

Study

Following teacher-guided self-correction of the pretest, introduce the spelling generalization for the week. Then assign the words students will be responsible for on the posttest. It is likely you will find diverse pretest results and a range of language abilities among your students.

Meeting the Needs of All Students

To meet the needs of all students while teaching a single generalization each week, *Everyday Spelling* offers three levels of spelling instruction in each lesson.

- *For Most Students*
  The word list and all activities on the Student Edition pages are appropriate.

Assigning Activities

	For most students Follow weekly lesson plans	For students who need fewer words Replace core activities as indicated	For students who need challenge Add to core activities
Day 1	Core activities	Modify practice per teaching notes	Challenge Master
Day 2	Core activities	Assign Think and Practice Master	Cross-curricular vocabulary
Day 3	Core activities	Use core activities	CD-ROM writing
Day 4	Core activities	Use core activities	CD-ROM vocabulary
Day 5	Test all list words	Test modified list only	Posttest for all list, challenge, and cross-curricular vocabulary words

- *For Students Who Need Fewer Words* A modified, or shorter, word list limits the words studied to those most frequently misspelled. The modified list, indicated by color, is the first half of the weekly word list.
- *For Students Who Need Extra Challenge* Additional Challenge Words are provided. In addition, the cross-curricular vocabulary words may be assigned as part of the weekly word list.

Everyday Spelling provides teaching suggestions and activities for auditory, visual, and kinesthetic learners; ESL and bilingual students; and students who need extra support. Optional components such as audiotapes and "built-in" features such as an English-Spanish word list make meeting the needs of all students possible.

Assigning Words

There are no rigid guidelines for deciding who will use the modified list or the Challenge Words, but there are several indicators worth considering.

- Pretest performance is one indication teachers have about which students will benefit from using a modified list and which ones will require extra challenge.
- Teachers sometimes recognize that certain students will simply work more

effectively with a modified list. For example, those students subject to over-loading are likely to do well with fewer words to study.

- Some students who are easily distracted may benefit from an increased rather than a decreased workload.
- Students who consistently score 100% on the pretest may benefit from additional challenge.

Posttest

Four options are available for administering the posttest:

Traditional Posttest

Context sentences for each lesson

appear in the Teacher's Edition Week-at-a-Glance.

Standardized Test Masters

The posttest can be given in formats commonly used in standardized tests.

Dictation Sentences

Sentences containing several list words are found on pages T37–T42 in the back of the Teacher's Edition. All words used in these sentences have been taught previously in the program.

Auditory Test

The *Everyday Spelling* CD-ROM has an auditory test for each weekly lesson.

Q: How much time should we spend on spelling each week?

A: A good starting place would be 60–75 minutes per week. Divide that up so students dedicate themselves to spelling for a fraction of an hour every day. One plan might look like this:

Day 1	Pretest, correction, and discussion of the generalization. 20 minutes.
Days 2, 3, 4	Students work on their own doing activities that provide varied contexts for using the words. 15 minutes per day.
Day 5	Posttest. 10 minutes.

Teacher's Edition Resources

Unit Overview

The Unit Overview shows exactly what students will be learning and what activities will solidify their learning during the coming weeks. The Overview also shows the entire range of program resources available to help you meet individual needs, references to literature to help you extend the language arts connection, and cross-curricular vocabulary lessons to support an integrated curriculum.

Lesson Plans

A few minutes with Week-at-a-Glance will take care of your spelling lesson plans for the week. Its easy-access format keeps details to a minimum while offering options for your students. In Week-at-a-Glance you'll find:

- daily lesson plans with core and optional activities
- objectives
- ways to modify the word list to meet the needs of all students
- page references for the cross-curricular vocabulary lessons
- assessment resources, including pretest and posttest sentences

Additional Resources

Easily readable reproductions of the ancillary pages are pictured, with answers, after the Week-at-a-Glance lesson plans. A key to multimedia resources is given here. All these resources are also listed day by day at point of use.

Teaching Notes

Teaching notes offer a rich tapestry of teaching ideas to extend and enrich the lessons. The following are a few of the nuggets you will find.

Introduction helps introduce the lesson generalization by highlighting phonics, word structure, or meaning elements that show how the list words are related.

Meeting the Needs of All Students addresses a wide range of student needs and abilities. Included are suggestions for working with bilingual and ESL learners, students with varied learning styles (visual, auditory, kinesthetic), students using the modified list, and students needing extra support or challenge. This section also contains activities for students who work best in cooperative situations as well as enrichment suggestions—those fun extras everybody enjoys.

Critical Thinking Skills are reinforced as students practice spelling with analogies, synonyms and antonyms, categorizing, and drawing conclusions in the widely varied activities on Days 2, 3, and 4.

Study Skills such as alphabetizing, using the dictionary, and using a thesaurus are integrated into the weekly activities on Day 2 and Day 4.

Grammar, Usage, and Mechanics are a part of the editing process on Day 3.

Literature Connection extends the lesson with quality literature. Literary skills such as simile, metaphor, and onomatopoeia are part of the language-building activities on Day 4.

Multicultural Connection extends language learning around the globe.

Developmental Spelling Handbook

This professional resource assists you in teaching children at various levels of their development in spelling. To help you analyze students' spelling errors, the handbook describes each stage of spelling development and suggests activities for guiding students to the next level of spelling understanding. (See page T27.)

Research in Action

RESEARCH IN ACTION IS THE MOST COMPREHENSIVE STUDY EVER COMPLETED OF HOW CHILDREN SPELL AND MISSPELL WHEN THEY WRITE.

The goal of the study was to discover which words children misspell most often and which linguistic features cause them the most spelling problems. As a result of the study, we created a spelling program that really works. That program, *Everyday Spelling*, is based on the data from the Research in Action study.

Research Findings

Students misspell the same words over and over, week after week, year after year.

Certain common kinds of errors occur at each grade and across the grades.

There are several error types that have not been categorized and taught previously in the traditional spelling curriculum.

Inattention and hurrying cause "slips" in "spelling consciousness."

Spelling instruction is most effective when it is appropriate for the child's developmental stage of spelling.

Students need a repertoire of strategies they can call upon as they tackle the spelling of new words in their ever-widening vocabularies.

Everyday Spelling Strategies

Frequently misspelled words are
- identified for each grade level
- shown in the front of the Student Edition
- flagged on the student's word list
- the subject of hints and reminders in every lesson
- recycled, retaught, and reviewed across several grade levels

Lessons and practice activities that address the most common kinds of spelling problems, such as homophones and apostrophe usage, are repeated across the grade levels where they are found to be the most troublesome.

Six lessons at each grade focus attention on this new category of spelling errors. These lessons on spelling problems include omitted letters, scrambled letters, repeated letters, and incorrect word separation and joining.

Proofreading and writing on Day 3 of each weekly lesson focus students' attention on this type of error.

- The focus of instruction in the early grade levels is on simple sound patterns, moving to more difficult blends and variations that can be generalized to a large number of words.
- Spelling structure, such as forming plurals and adding affixes, is emphasized for students in the middle levels.
- Meaning relationships that affect spelling, such as Greek and Latin roots, receive greater emphasis in lessons at the upper levels.

Every unit begins with a Strategy Workshop that teaches strategies to attack nonlist words. Weekly lessons reinforce previously taught strategies to help students put them to work in their writing.

For a thorough discussion of the findings of Research in Action see Spelling Research & Information: An Overview of Current Research and Practices published by Scott Foresman - Addison Wesley.

Research Highlights

The word lists in *Everyday Spelling* are based on the findings of Research in Action. Hundreds of teachers and their students participated in the Research in Action project. Grades 1–8 in urban, suburban, and rural districts in all fifty states were represented in the study. A total of 18,599 compositions were collected and analyzed for misspellings, and these misspellings were categorized by grade according to error types.

Words Children Should Study

What words should children study? In an effective spelling program, word selection is critical. Some spelling programs base word lists solely on the frequency of word occurrence in children's reading material. Others focus exclusively on words from outdated studies of children's writing—when writing was not a focal point of the curriculum and students' vocabularies were significantly different.

Such programs, based on dated research, oftentimes omit words students misspell most frequently or present words at inappropriate grade levels. A few programs attach primary importance to a limited word list that does not begin to address the broad vocabulary of today's readers and writers.

Everyday Spelling teaches the words children need to learn based on the comprehensive findings of Research in Action. Interestingly, Research in Action revealed an overlap of no more than 4 percent between the 100 **most frequently used words** at any given grade level and the 100 **most frequently misspelled words** at that level.

This puts to rest the myth that words children study in a spelling program should be solely those most frequently used. What must be taught are the words students frequently misspell in their writing. Furthermore, the Research in Action study shows the words children *misspell* most often can be predicted; therefore, these words can be retaught, reviewed, and recycled throughout several grade levels.

Q: What words should children study? Words they read? Words they write? How do we decide?

A: Research in Action has shown what must be taught are the words students frequently misspell in their writing. Furthermore, the study shows the words students misspell most often can be predicted, and therefore, can be retaught and reviewed throughout the grades.

Everyday Spelling puts this compelling research into action by teaching the words students misspell most frequently in their writing. Word lists clearly highlight the most frequently misspelled words in each lesson, so children can concentrate on these troublesome words. (A complete list of frequently misspelled words appears in the front of the Student Edition!) Special spelling hints and tips in each lesson also focus on frequently misspelled words, and these words are retaught and reviewed across grade levels to reinforce them over and over. In addition, high-frequency words from classic word studies make the *Everyday Spelling* word lists the most developmentally appropriate in a spelling program today.

Word List Sources

- *Research in Action,* Ronald Cramer, James F. Cipielewski, James Beers, W. Dorsey Hammond.
- *The American Heritage Word Frequency Book,* John Carroll, Peter Davies, and Barry Richmond.
- "A Basic Sight Vocabulary," Edward Dolch.
- "The 2,000 Commonest Words for Spelling," Edward Dolch.
- *A Basic Life Spelling Vocabulary,* James Fitzgerald.
- *Basic Reading Vocabularies,* Albert J. Harris and Milton D. Jacobson.
- *A Basic Writing Vocabulary,* Ernest Horn.
- *A Basic Vocabulary of Elementary School Children*, Henry Rinsland.
- *3000 Instant Words,* Elizabeth Sakiey and Edward Fry.

Look for this symbol.

You'll find it in the word list! The asterisk indicates the most frequently misspelled words in children's writing. Make sure students zero in on these spelling problems. For added reinforcement, frequently misspelled words are retaught and reviewed across the grades.

Top 100 Misspelled Words

This list shows the top 100 words misspelled across all grade levels. Each level of *Everyday Spelling* provides special treatment for the words most frequently misspelled at that grade.

1. too	27. people	46. and	65. Easter	84. was
2. a lot	28. until	47. Halloween	66. what	85. which
3. because	29. with	48. house	67. there's	86. stopped
4. there	30. different	49. once	68. little	87. two
5. their	31. outside	50. to	69. doesn't	88. Dad
6. that's	32. we're	51. like	70. usually	89. took
7. they	33. through	52. whole	71. clothes	90. friend's
8. it's	34. upon	53. another	72. scared	91. presents
9. when	35. probably	54. believe	73. everyone	92. morning
10. favorite	36. don't	55. I'm	74. have	93. are
11. went	37. sometimes	56. thought	75. swimming	94. could
12. Christmas	38. off	57. let's	76. about	95. around
13. were	39. everybody	58. before	77. first	96. buy
14. our	40. hear	59. beautiful	78. happened	97. maybe
15. they're	41. always	60. everything	79. Mom	98. family
16. said	42. I	61. very	80. especially	99. pretty
17. know	43. something	62. into	81. school	100. tried
18. you're	44. would	63. caught	82. getting	
19. friend	45. want	64. one	83. started	
20. friends				
21. really				
22. finally				
23. where				
24. again				
25. then				
26. didn't				

Spelling Errors in Children's Writing

Welcome to the "twilight zone." Research in Action identified a major type of error that accounts for a significant number of misspellings in students' writing. Designated as "twilight zone" errors because they could not be categorized into traditional groupings, these spelling mistakes have generally been overlooked in traditional programs.

"Twilight Zone" Errors

- added letters, as in *athalete*
- omitted letters, as in *probly*
- repeated letters, as in *rememember*
- scrambled/reversed letters, as in *feild*
- truncated words, as in *bcz*
- mispronounced/misinterpreted words, as in *wanna*

As a teacher, you'll probably recognize these types of errors from your students' writing. But what can you do to help children avoid these common pitfalls? *Everyday Spelling* is the first spelling program that specifically addresses "twilight zone" errors. Specially created lessons focus directly on problems such as omitted letters, repeated letters, and incorrect word separation and joining.

Research in Action further reveals that the types of mistakes students are likely to make can be anticipated, so word features that tend to generate errors can be the focus of both spelling instruction and practice. For example, according to the Research in Action study, homophone usage accounts for a full 20% of spelling mistakes across all eight grades. Armed with this data, the authors and editors of *Everyday Spelling* included instruction and strategies on homophones and other predictable types of spelling errors in addition to "twilight zone" lessons.

Research in Action also demonstrates how children's vocabularies are richer today than in the past. This ever-widening vocabulary has created new kinds of spelling errors for students as they write. *Everyday Spelling* includes strategy workshops, weekly vocabulary activities, and complete cross-curricular vocabulary lessons to provide students with a full repertoire of spelling skills and strategies to attack unfamiliar vocabulary words in their writing. It's just one more way *Everyday Spelling* puts research into action.

Summing Up

Confirming and extending what is already known about the developmental nature of learning to spell and the predictability of the English spelling system on one hand and its frequent irregularity on the other hand, the Research in Action study makes clear which words children need to be taught. It also points out what kinds of problems teachers need to deal with in helping children learn to spell. *Everyday Spelling* is the only program that translates the findings of this comprehensive study into real, concrete spelling strategies and instruction that benefit every student at every grade level.

Top Ten Categories of Errors

Primary Grades 1–3	Intermediate Grades 4–6	Upper Grades 7–8
1. Consonant substitution	1. Omitted letters	1. Homophones
2. Omitted letters	2. Homophones	2. Omitted letters
3. Short *e*	3. Consonant substitution	3. Schwa
4. Consonant blends	4. Scrambled letters	4. Scrambled letters
5. Long *e*	5. Schwa	5. Consonant substitution
6. Scrambled letters	6. Long *e*	6. Words run together/separated
7. Schwa in final syllable	7. Words run together/separated	7. Apostrophe with contraction
8. Homophones	8. Short *e*	8. Compounds separated wrongly
9. Schwa	9. Schwa in final syllable	9. Long *e*
10. Inflected endings	10. Added letters	10. Schwa in final syllable

Developmental Spelling Handbook

by James W. Beers

**Why does a first grader omit a vowel in *kt* for *cat* or a
second grader spell *kickt* for *kicked* or a fifth grader spell
nashunal for *national*?**

Learning to spell is a long-term developmental process. Research has
identified five stages in this process that can be seen in students'
invented spellings at each grade. This handbook describes each stage
and suggests developmentally appropriate activities. Analyzing spelling
errors from a developmental standpoint provides more information
about spelling abilities than simply looking at the number of misspelled
words in children's writing. It also helps explain individual differences
in spelling abilities at each grade.

Stages in Learning to Spell

- Prephonetic
- Early Phonetic
- Phonetic
- Structural
- Meaning/Derivational

James W. Beers

James W. Beers is Professor of Reading and Language
Arts at the College of William and Mary in
Williamsburg, Virginia. An internationally recognized
authority on spelling development and instruction, Dr.
Beers has conducted extensive research that has led to a
better understanding of how children use their knowledge
of sounds as they learn to read, write, and spell. He has
produced numerous publications, including *Developmental and Cognitive Aspects of
Learning to Spell*, coedited with Edmund H. Henderson. It is generally considered
one of the most significant pieces of spelling research ever published. Dr. Beers is
an author of *Everyday Spelling* and *Scott Foresman Reading*.

Prephonetic

Prephonetic spelling shows no connection between letters, or letter-like marks on the paper, and words the child says have been written. Letters may be grouped or separated in writing. Prephonetic spellers need to develop the concept of a written word, learn a one-to-one correspondence between written and spoken words, and build phonemic awareness.

This first grader intends to say: "We went to Yorktown to watch the fireworks on the Fourth of July. It was loud and had lots of colors. It was fun." The letters are written on two lines and some are repeated, but there's no relationship between the letters and what the child said was written.

Activities for Prephonetic Spellers
- Teach letter names with an alphabet song
- Label objects around the classroom
- Use and make pattern books and poems
- Read big books and point to the words as you read
- Do choral readings of big books or dictated stories
- Sort pictures according to initial or final consonant sounds
- Match picture cards with initial or final consonant sounds
- Draw and then write about the drawing

Early Phonetic

Early phonetic spellers are developing phonemic awareness. They're learning that letters and sounds are linked in written words. Within this stage, children progress from beginning consonant spelling to ending consonant spelling to middle vowel spelling.

In this example, the child says, "I take the bus to school," and writes the beginning sound for each word.

The beginning and ending sounds are spelled for each word in "Daddy painted the house."

Middle consonants and two vowels are spelled when a young child writes, "Dinosaur walking."

Activities for Early Phonetic Spellers

- Match beginning and final consonants to picture names
- Sort pictures or words by beginning and ending sounds
- Change beginning or ending consonants in simple word families
- Play rhyming games with word families
- Read and write rhyming pattern poems
- Create word walls for writing

Phonetic

With the appearance of vowels in words, children arrive at the phonetic stage. This is an important stage because the spelling represents most, if not all, sounds or syllables heard in words. Much more of each word is spelled, and most words tend to be spelled phonetically.

Letter name spelling is often used, because it sounds like the sound being spelled. Here, letter name *a* is used for short *e: dras* for *dress*.

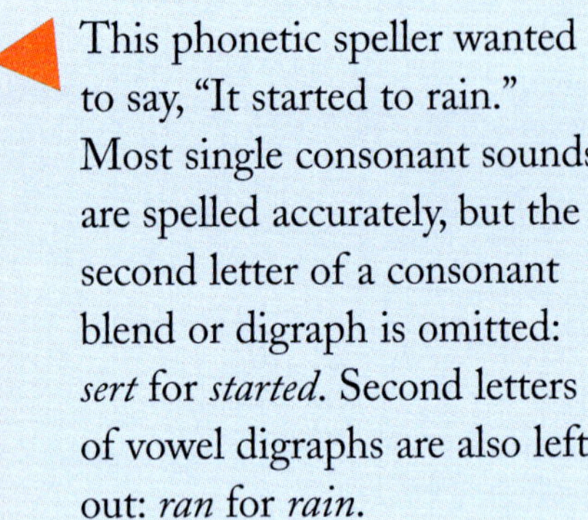

This phonetic speller wanted to say, "It started to rain." Most single consonant sounds are spelled accurately, but the second letter of a consonant blend or digraph is omitted: *sert* for *started*. Second letters of vowel digraphs are also left out: *ran* for *rain*.

"I like fishing. I fish with my dad. It is fun to go fishing." Long vowels frequently appear without final *e* as in this example: *lik* for *like*. Endings are also spelled phonetically at this stage (e.g., *askt* for *asked*).

Activities for Phonetic Spellers

- Contrast single consonant words with words that have consonant blends or digraphs *(pan/plan)*
- Sort short and long vowel words by vowel sound
- Pronounce and spell words with identical endings that are pronounced differently *(stopped, rolled, patted)*
- Contrast short and long vowel sounds
- Contrast *r* blend words with *r* vowel words
- Create personal dictionaries

Structural

The fourth spelling stage is called structural because spellings demonstrate students are trying to deal with key structural elements in words, such as syllables and endings.

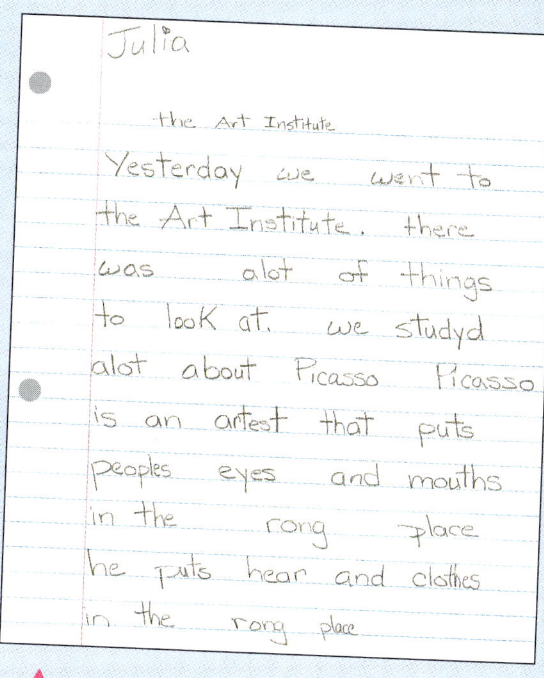

Short vowels are often spelled correctly, but long vowel spellings remain a problem: *complet* for *complete*.

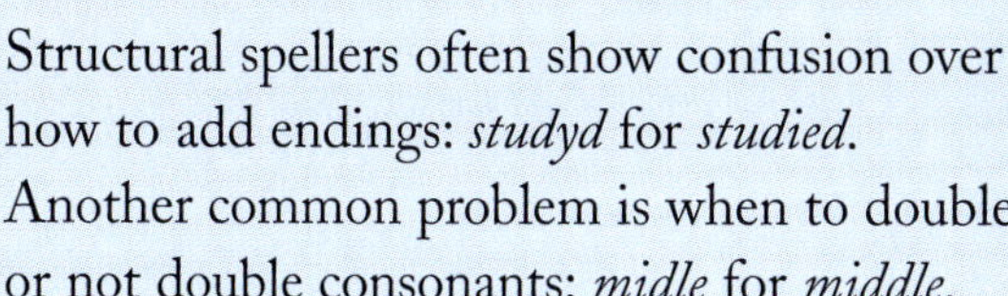

Structural spellers often show confusion over how to add endings: *studyd* for *studied*. Another common problem is when to double or not double consonants: *midle* for *middle*.

Activities for Structural Spellers

- Sort base words that do not change when endings are added
- Sort base words that are modified when endings are added
- Contrast words by how adding endings affects the spelling of base words
- Expand personal dictionaries to include problem words or word categories
- Develop word trees from base words
- Let students serve as spelling editors for other writers

Meaning/Derivational

In the last stage of spelling development, children spell the majority of words correctly in their writing, although they have occasional difficulty with double consonants and the phonetic spelling of alternate forms of words. For example, a child may spell the word *nature* correctly but spell *natteral* for *natural*.

Brennan Williams
Room 104

THE TREATY OF VERSAILLES

The final signiture on the treaty was the signal that war was over. A nashunal holiday was declared so that the entire nation could celebrate the end of World War I.

In this example, one form of a word is spelled correctly and the other is not: *signal* and *nation* are correct, but *signature* is *signiture* and *national* is *nashunal*.

Activities for Meaning/Derivational Spellers

- Collect sets of meaning-related words in which the pronunciation does not change
- Expand the lists to include related words in which the pronunciation changes
- Study related words to deduce how knowing the spelling of one of the words might help with the spelling of others
- Investigate word derivations

Everyday Spelling

Authors

James Beers • **Ronald L. Cramer** • **W. Dorsey Hammond**

Scott Foresman
Addison Wesley

Editorial Offices: Glenview, Illinois • Menlo Park, California
Sales Offices: Reading, Massachusetts • Duluth, Georgia • Glenview, Illinois
Carrollton, Texas • Menlo Park, California

1-800-552-2259

http://www.sf.aw.com

■ ACKNOWLEDGMENTS

TEXT
p. 133: Untitled haiku by Kikaku from *Word Works* by Cathryn Berger Kaye; illustrated by Martha Weston. Copyright © 1985 by the Yolla Bolly Press. By permission of Little, Brown and Company.

ILLUSTRATIONS
p. 11: Seitu Hayden; **pp. 12-33:** Susan Swan; **pp. 12, 38, 64, 81, 90, 116, 129, 132:** Marla Rubin; **pp. 23, 24, 28:** Linda Kinnamon; **pp. 38-59:** Mary Grand Pre; **pp. 40, 44, 47, 48, 51, 52, 55, 56, 59, 60:** John Manders; **pp. 60-62, 86-89, 112-115, 138-141, 164, 165, 167, 184-187, 189, 195, 197, 199, 201, 205-207, 210-213, 215, 219-221, 225-227:** Beth Herman Design Associates; **pp. 60, 63, 88, 210, 211:** Slug Signorino; **pp. 61, 89:** Patti Green; **pp. 62, 113, 166:** Fran Lee; **pp. 63, 86, 87, 89, 115, 139, 165, 204, 207-209, 220, 221:** B.J. Johnson; **pp. 64-85:** Kathy Petrauskas; **pp. 66, 69, 70, 73, 74, 77, 78, 81, 82, 85, 86:** Margaret Spengler; **pp. 87, 114, 140, 141, 202, 203:** Donna Reynolds; **pp. 90-111:** Marianne Wallace; **pp. 113-115, 139, 167, 184, 185, 222, 223:** Linda Kelen; **pp. 115, 138, 166, 192, 193, 214:** Carl Kock; **pp. 116-137:** Darryl Goudreau; **pp. 140, 193, 195, 209, 224, 225, 227:** Tom Herzberg; **pp. 142-163:** Linda Helton; **pp. 148, 152, 156, 164:** Joe Rogers; **pp. 189, 200, 201:** Leon Bishop; **pp. 190, 191:** David Uhl; **pp. 194, 195, 198, 199, 216, 217, 228, 229:** Jacque Auger; **p. 297:** Don Wilson; **p. 304:** Christine Mortensen

PHOTOGRAPHS
pp. 16, 42, 84, 162: Marilyn Meyerhofer; **pp. 77TL,BR, 246B, 261T:** Hans Reinhard/Bruce Coleman, Inc.; **p. 77TR:** Michael & Patricia Fogden; **p. 77BL:** Belinda Wright/DRK Photo; **p. 109L:** Grant Heilman/Grant Heilman Photography, Inc.; **p. 109R:** Jane Grushow/Grant Heilman Photography, Inc.; **p. 131:** Connie Geocaris/Tony Stone Images; **pp. 153, 271T:** Lawrence Migdale; **pp. 167T, 256B:** Don & Pat Valenti; **p. 167C:** "Life on the Prairie, The Buffalo Hunt" by Currier & Ives, 1862, Library of Congress; **p. 182TR:** Steve McCutcheon; **p. 182TL:** Fred Bruemmer; **p. 182BL:** Francois Gohier/Photo Researchers; **pp. 182BR, 183TL, 183TC, 183TR:** Johnny Johnson/ AlaskaStock; **p. 183BR:** Chris Arend/AlaskaStock; **p. 201:** Dwight R. Kuhn/DRK Photo; **p. 203:** Library of Congress; **p. 210:** Vic Thomasson/Tony Stone Images; **p. 211:** Chris Haigh/Tony Stone Images; **p. 211:** Editions Houvet; **p. 213:** R. Maiman/Sygma; **p. 225L:** Ray Amati/Focus On Sports; **p. 225CL:** Focus on Sports; **p. 225CR:** J. Daniel/ ALLSPORT USA; **p. 225R:** Stephen Dunn/ALLSPORT USA; **p. 247:** Dr. Ralph Buchbaum/ Department of Zoology, University of Chicago; **pp. 248T, 274:** Courtesy NASA; **p. 250T:** James L. Ballard/ScottForesman & Co.; **p. 252T:** Robert B. Tolchin/ScottForesman & Co.; **p. 252B:** Michael & Patricia Fogden; **p. 256T:** J. Pickerell/The Image Works; **p. 260:** Miami Seaquarium; **p. 266B:** Cy Furlan; **p. 268B:** J.C. Stevenson/ Animals, Animals; **p. 270T:** Florida Division of Tourism; **p. 270B:** GemMedia; **p. 273T:** Belinda Wright/DRK Photo; **p. 277:** M. Austerman/Animals, Animals; **p. 278:** Raymond Schoder; **p. 280B:** Arizona State Museum, University of Arizona, Helga Teiwes, Photographer; **p. 284T:** Jurg Klages; **p. 284B:** Camermann International, Ltd.; **p. 286B:** Lorraine Rorke/The Image Works; **p. 287:** Geo. T. Hillman; **p. 290T:** Daniel L. Feicht; **p. 291:** Carmen Morrison/ScottForesman & Co.; **p. 292:** American Museum of Natural History, New York; **p. 293:** Michael Heron; **p. 299TL:** Robert Frerck/Odyssey/Chicago; **p. 299TR:** Robert Frerck/Odyssey/Chicago; **p. 299B:** Marianne von Meerwall; **p. 300:** Dr. E. R. Degginger; **p. 306:** Jeff Foott; **p. 308:** The Kobal Collection.

All photographs not specifically credited are Scott Foresman Addison Wesley photographs.

UNIT 2

4

UNIT 3

UNIT 5

UNIT 6

8

Cross-Curricular Lessons

Lots of words on your spelling lists are marked with green asterisks ✳. These are the words that are misspelled the most by students your age.*

Pay special attention to these frequently misspelled words as you read, write, and practice your spelling words.

too	again	everybody	happened	would
a lot	they	off	heard	are
because	Christmas	through	I	enough
there	went	friends	whole	except
their	until	swimming	didn't	friend's
favorite	outside	want	first	probably
that's	said	you're	watch	upon
our	we're	another	people	vacation
when	sometimes	beautiful	always	brought
really	different	I'm	took	house
they're	where	let's	everyone	might
were	caught	then	morning	myself
it's	chocolate	believe	school	basketball
know	friend	cousin	something	hospital
finally	into	especially	with	opened

* **Research in Action** is a research project conducted in 1990–1993. This list of frequently misspelled words is one result of an analysis of 18,599 unedited compositions. Words are listed in the order of their frequency of misspelling.

UNIT 1

SCOPE AND SEQUENCE: LESSONS 1–6

Lesson	Generalization	Think and Practice	Proofreading and Writing
1 pp. 14–17	Letter combinations like **thr**, **scr**, **str**, and **squ** are called consonant blends.	Draw Your Own Conclusion Words in Context Strategic Spelling: Using the Problem Parts Strategy	Proofread a Sign • misspelled words Create a Sign
2 pp. 18–21	The consonant pairs **kn**, **gn**, **wr**, and **mb** have only one sound.	Rhyme Time Defining Words Strategic Spelling: Seeing Meaning Connections	Proofread a Note • misspelled words • capitalization errors Answer the Note
3 pp. 22–25	Consonant sound /k/ can be spelled **c**, **k**, or **ck**. Consonant sound /f/ can be spelled **ff**, **gh**, or **ph**.	Poetry in Motion Classifying Who Am I? Strategic Spelling: Seeing Meaning Connections	Proofread a Self-Portrait • misspelled words • incorrect pronoun Create a Self-Portrait
4 pp. 26–29	When **-ed** or **-ing** is added to a base word, its spelling may change.	Context Clues Add Endings Strategic Spelling: Building New Words	Proofread a Blurb • misspelled words • handwriting errors Write a Blurb
5 pp. 30–33	When **-er** or **-est** is added to a base word, its spelling may change.	Antonym Alert Happy Endings Strategic Spelling: Building New Words	Proofread an Invitation • misspelled words • incorrect comparisons Write an Invitation

	Concepts for Review	Unit 1 Activities	Integrating Spelling
Review 6 pp. 34–37	Words with **thr, scr, str, squ** Words with **kn, gn, wr, mb** Consonant Sounds /k/ and /f/ Adding **-ed** and **-ing** Adding **-er** and **-est**	Newspaper Ad News Article Book Review Project Descriptions Words and Pictures Announcement Science Fiction Plots	**Language Arts:** Newspaper Ad, Book Review, Announcement **Health:** Safety Rules **Art:** A Project **Social Studies:** Geography **Science:** Research

Vocabulary Building	**Meeting the Needs of All Students**	**Cross-Curricular Lessons***
Review Puzzle It Out **Using a Dictionary** Guide Words	**Visual** A Special Letter **Auditory** Words in Context **Bilingual/ESL** Draw Your Own Conclusion **Enrichment** Evaluating Messages; Who's Who	**Work and Play:** Swimming, pp. 222–223
Review Word Associations **Word Study** Hink-Pinks	**Visual** Picturing the Concept **Auditory** Reinforcing Meaning **Bilingual/ESL** Defining Words **Enrichment** Writing Notes	**Reading:** Looking at the World in New Ways, pp. 210–211
Review Defining Words **Multicultural Connection** Languages	**Auditory** Poetry in Motion **Kinesthetic** Hold Up **Bilingual/ESL** Who Am I? **Enrichment** Creating a Self-Portrait	**Social Studies:** Deserts and Forests, pp. 172–173
Review Words in Context **Using a Thesaurus** Entry Words	**Visual** Decorated Letters **Auditory** Syllables **Bilingual/ESL** Synonyms **Enrichment** Personal Writing	**Reading:** Tales of Courage, pp. 212–213 **Connections to BookFestival:** ■ *Willie Mays: Young Superstar* by Louis Sabin
Review Analogies **Word Study** Exaggeration	**Auditory** Syllables **Kinesthetic** Writing Invitations **Bilingual/ESL** Word Study **Enrichment** Exaggerating	**Mathematics:** Measurement, pp. 216–217

CONSONANT ERRORS

Information from *Research in Action* shows that consonants are a major source of spelling errors for fourth graders, especially single consonant sounds that can be spelled many different ways, such as /k/ and /f/, silent consonants, blends, and digraphs.

TYPICAL MISSPELLINGS:

- *reck* for *wreck*
- *attak* for *attack*
- *elefant* for *elephant*
- *skary* for *scary*

Helpful strategies include focusing on how words look, particularly the problem parts.

ADDITIONAL RESOURCES

For Every Weekly Lesson

- **Think and Practice Master**
- **Challenge Master**
- **Extra Practice Master**
- **Review Master**
- **Second Language Support Master**
- **Home-School Activity Master**
- **Writing Mini-Lesson**
- **Writing Activity Master**
- **Standardized Test Master**
- **Proofreading and Writing Transparency**

Technology

- **Audiotape**
- *Everyday Spelling* **CD-ROM**
- *Everyday Spelling* **Game Software**

Unit Review

- **Standardized Test Masters**
- **Writing Prompt Transparency**
- **Writing Model Transparencies**
- *Everyday Spelling* **CD-ROM**

* The cross-curricular lessons are optional. You may, however, wish to teach the cross-curricular lesson that has been paired with the weekly lesson shown in the chart.

OBJECTIVES

- Learn and practice the Problem Parts strategy
- Apply the Problem Parts strategy to list words in Unit 1
- Review the steps for learning to spell new words
- Start a spelling notebook

STEPS FOR SPELLING

This six-step strategy is basic to spelling all new words. It calls upon all the major learning modalities: visual, auditory, and kinesthetic.

PROBLEM PARTS

This strategy helps students figure out what makes a particular word difficult for them to spell. It calls upon use of the visual modality by suggesting that the user focus on the problem part and commit to visual memory the correct spelling of that part.

Additional Resources

Steps for Spelling Poster
Frequently Misspelled Words Poster
Spelling Tool Kit Poster

■ **LEARNING HOW TO LEARN**

Steps for Spelling Problem Parts

REVIEW THE STEPS FOR SPELLING Here is the spelling strategy you should use when learning to spell a new word. Read it over step by step.

1. **Look** at the word. **Say** it and listen to the sounds.
2. **Spell** the word aloud.
3. **Think** about the spelling. Do you notice anything special that you need to remember?
4. **Picture** the word with your eyes shut.
5. **Look** at the word and **write** it.
6. **Cover** the word and picture it. **Write** the word again and **check** its spelling.

DISCOVER THE PROBLEM PARTS STRATEGY If some words are still hard for you to spell, try the Problem-Parts Strategy.

TRY IT OUT Practice the Problem-Parts Strategy with words that gave another writer problems. Follow the directions on the next page.

To promote personal responsibility for students' spelling development, help them start a spelling notebook. You may wish to have students divide the notebook into three sections.

- The first section can be used for personal words students want to learn to spell. Have them use one page for each letter of the alphabet.
- The second section can be used for words students misspell on their pretests.
- The third section can be used for activities from their spelling books. Throughout the year, encourage students to carefully rewrite the correct spelling of the words they have written in their spelling notebooks.

Work with a partner or group. Find the four misspelled words in the description below and write them correctly. Underline the part of each word that gave the writer problems. Use a dictionary if you need help.

I was down on one nee picking up mangoes when the squrrel saw me. It wiggled its nose at me. I bit into a mango and lafed. It turned and ran throgh the trees.

1. **knee**
2. **squirrel**
3. **laughed**
4. **through**

Now practice the Problem-Parts Strategy with your own personal words.

List four words you sometimes misspell. Be sure to spell them right. Underline the part of each word that gives you a problem. Picture the words. Focus on the problem parts.

Have a partner quiz you on your words. Then check the results. How did you do?

5. **Answers will vary.**
6.
7.
8.

LOOK AHEAD Look at the next five lessons. Write four list words that look hard to spell. Underline the part of each word that you think might give you a problem.

1. **Answers will vary.**
2.
3.
4.

13

FREQUENTLY MISSPELLED WORDS

To help students complete the second half of the Try It Out activity, have them consider the words listed in the Frequently Misspelled Words list on page 11 in their books and on the poster.

MEETING THE NEEDS OF ALL STUDENTS

Modified List

Have students learning just the Modified Lists look at spelling words 1–10 only as they complete the Look Ahead activity.

Challenge

Encourage students to consider words appearing in the challenge box, in addition to spelling words 1–20, as they complete the Look Ahead activity.

Bilingual/ESL

Nonnative speakers of English may have difficulty completing the activities on page 13. For the second half of the Try It Out activity, have students choose English words that they use in speaking and writing. For the Look Ahead activity, more fluent English-speaking students can help the nonnative speakers write their words correctly and give help as needed.

13

1

Generalization

Spelling Focus: Letter combinations like **thr, scr, str,** and **squ** are called consonant blends.

● Core ○ Optional ✓ Assessment

DAILY PLAN | CORE OBJECTIVES | NOTES

DAY 1 Introduction

● Strategy Workshop, p. 12
✓ Pretest and Self-Check, p. 14B
● Spelling Focus and Word List, p. 14
○ Challenge Words, p. 14
○ Challenge Master 1
○ Home-School Master 1

- Learn and practice the strategy Problem Parts
✓ - Take and self-check Pretest
- Spell words with the consonant blend **thr, scr, str,** or **squ;** classify and write the list words

DAY 2 Think and Practice

● Draw Your Own Conclusion; Words in Context, p. 15
● Strategic Spelling: *Using the Problem Parts Strategy,* p. 15
○ Think and Practice Master 1
○ Extra Practice Master 1
○ Cross-Curricular Lesson: Introduce, p. 222

- Complete practice activities for words with consonant blends
- Identify and study problem parts of list words

DAY 3 Proofreading and Writing

● Proofread a Sign, p. 16
● Proofreading Tip: Spelling Errors, p. 16
● Create a Sign, p. 16
✓ Cooperative Midweek Test
○ Writing Mini-Lesson Master 1
○ Writing Activity Master 1
○ Second Language Support Master 1

- Proofread for spelling errors
- Integrate spelling and writing in a personal writing response
✓ - Take and check midweek test

DAY 4 Vocabulary Building

● Review: Puzzle It Out, p. 17
● Using a Dictionary: Guide Words, p. 17
○ Hardbound Book Master 1
○ Cross-Curricular Lesson: Follow-Up, p. 222
○ Review Master 1

- Complete review activity for words beginning with the consonant blends **thr, scr, str,** and **squ**
- Group list words between guide words

DAY 5 Assessment

✓ Posttest, p. 14B
○ Standardized Test Master 1

✓ - Take Posttest

Cross-Curricular Lessons

Use the Spelling Focus (consonant blends **thr, scr, str, squ**) to introduce the Work and Play lesson, *Swimming,* page 222, or choose a lesson that correlates with a topic you're currently teaching.

MEETING THE NEEDS OF ALL STUDENTS

The Word List

For students studying 20 words, assign pages 14–17 and Extra Practice and Review masters.

Modified List For students studying 10 words, modify Practice on page 14, and assign Think and Practice Master 1 and pages 16–17.

Challenge For students studying 25 words, assign pages 14–17, Challenge, Extra Practice, and Review masters.

Bilingual/ESL

The blends **sk, sq,** and **st** are not familiar to speakers of Pilipino, who may add an initial vowel to some words: *scrub/iskrab; square/iskuwer.*

Personal Words

Students add to Personal Words lists by looking at work in their writing portfolios and words they want to remember from their reading.

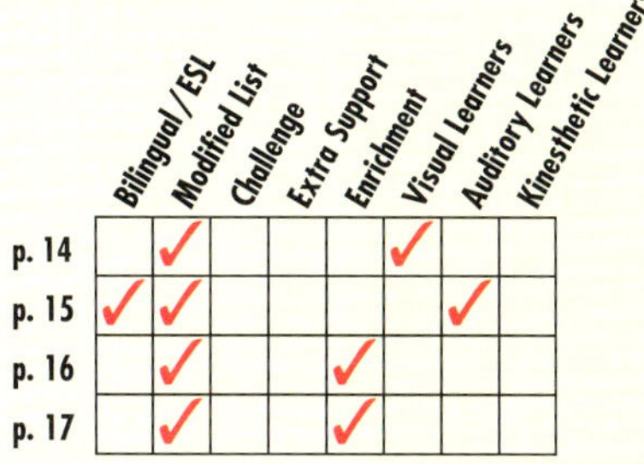

	Bilingual/ESL	Modified List	Challenge	Extra Support	Enrichment	Visual Learners	Auditory Learners	Kinesthetic Learners
p. 14		✓				✓		
p. 15	✓	✓					✓	
p. 16		✓			✓			
p. 17		✓			✓			

ASSESSMENT*

Pretest

Read the underlined word, read the sentence, and then repeat the underlined word. Guide students in self-correcting their pretests and correcting any misspellings.

1. Shouting hurts your <u>throat</u>.
2. Joey swam <u>through</u> water.
3. Close the <u>screen</u> door.
4. The bushes will <u>scratch</u> you.
5. I will <u>scream</u> with laughter.
6. The sky looks very <u>strange</u>.
7. Elsa rides in the <u>street</u>.
8. The batter won't <u>strike</u> out.
9. Fold the paper into a <u>square</u>.
10. <u>Squeeze</u> lemons for juice.
11. Smoking is a health <u>threat</u>.
12. He has <u>thrown</u> three pitches.
13. Fireworks are a <u>thrill</u>.
14. Please <u>scrub</u> the windows.
15. The city has a <u>skyscraper</u>.
16. She made <u>strawberry</u> pie.
17. Horses have great <u>strength</u>.
18. The pigs <u>squeal</u> in the yard.
19. Tickling makes me <u>squirm</u>.
20. <u>Squirt</u> water on the plants.

Posttest

Read aloud the sentences below. These sentences may be used for dictation.

1. Did he walk <u>through</u> here?
2. I walked across the <u>street</u>.
3. I saw a <u>strange</u> animal.
4. Look for a <u>square</u> box.
5. The man at bat made a third <u>strike</u>.
6. My <u>throat</u> hurts today.
7. Please <u>squeeze</u> the orange.
8. Tired babies will <u>scream</u>.
9. The kitten will <u>scratch</u> you.
10. The <u>screen</u> kept the bug out.
11. The frog made me <u>squirm</u>.
12. We saw a tall <u>skyscraper</u>.
13. He has great <u>strength</u>.
14. Halloween night was a <u>thrill</u>.
15. <u>Squirt</u> the glue into the hole.
16. City dirt is a <u>threat</u> to trees.
17. <u>Scrub</u> the mud off.
18. The puppies <u>squeal</u> a lot.
19. They like <u>strawberry</u> jam.
20. Was the ball <u>thrown</u> far?

Challenge Words

1. Grandma has <u>arthritis</u>.
2. He wrote a <u>description</u>.
3. She plays that <u>instrument</u>.
4. An <u>astronaut</u> was on the moon.
5. A lemon is <u>squeezable</u>.

Additional Assessment

Standardized Test Master 1
Dictation Sentences, p. T37
Everyday Spelling CD-ROM

A TOUGH SPELLING
Point out that *through* can be a tough word to spell. It has the homophone *threw* and the sound /ü/ spelled **ough.** Help students remember how to spell *through* by offering this tip: *Through* means "in and **ou**t of."

* See pp. T20 and T33 for test-study-test information.

DAY 1 — CHALLENGE MASTER

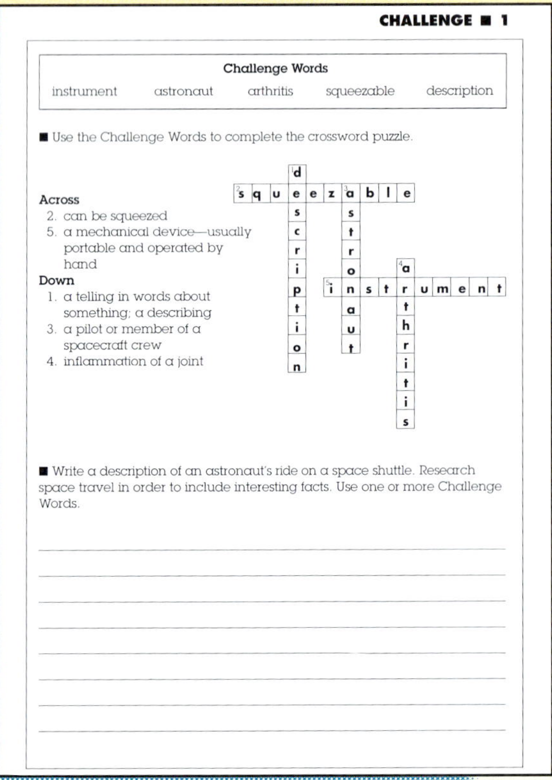

CHALLENGE ■ 1

Challenge Words

instrument   astronaut   arthritis   squeezable   description

■ Use the Challenge Words to complete the crossword puzzle.

Across
2. can be squeezed
5. a mechanical device—usually portable and operated by hand

Down
1. a telling in words about something; a describing
3. a pilot or member of a spacecraft crew
4. inflammation of a joint

(Crossword answers: 2 Across = squeezable; 5 Across = instrument; 1 Down = description; 3 Down = astronaut; 4 Down = arthritis)

■ Write a description of an astronaut's ride on a space shuttle. Research space travel in order to include interesting facts. Use one or more Challenge Words.

Practice Masters, p. 7

DAY 1 — HOME-SCHOOL MASTER

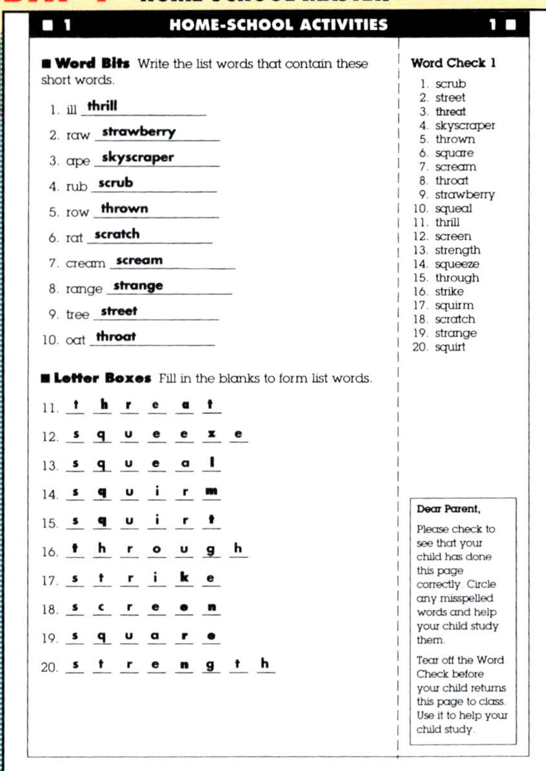

■ 1   HOME-SCHOOL ACTIVITIES   1 ■

■ **Word Bits** Write the list words that contain these short words.

1. ill **thrill**
2. raw **strawberry**
3. ape **skyscraper**
4. rub **scrub**
5. row **thrown**
6. rat **scratch**
7. cream **scream**
8. range **strange**
9. tree **street**
10. oat **throat**

■ **Letter Boxes** Fill in the blanks to form list words.

11. **t h r e a t**
12. **s q u e e z e**
13. **s q u e a l**
14. **s q u i r m**
15. **s q u i r t**
16. **t h r o u g h**
17. **s t r i k e**
18. **s c r e e n**
19. **s q u a r e**
20. **s t r e n g t h**

Word Check 1
1. scrub
2. street
3. threat
4. skyscraper
5. thrown
6. square
7. scream
8. throat
9. strawberry
10. squeal
11. thrill
12. screen
13. strength
14. squeeze
15. through
16. strike
17. squirm
18. scratch
19. strange
20. squirt

Dear Parent,

Please check to see that your child has done this page correctly. Circle any misspelled words and help your child study them.

Tear off the Word Check before your child returns this page to class. Use it to help your child study.

Home-School Activities, p. 1

DAY 2 — THINK AND PRACTICE MASTER

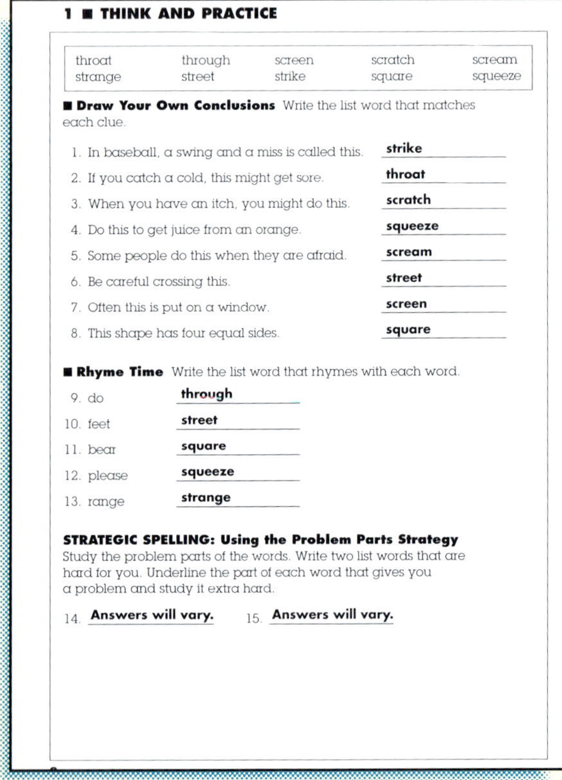

1 ■ THINK AND PRACTICE

throat	through	screen	scratch	scream
strange	street	strike	square	squeeze

■ **Draw Your Own Conclusions** Write the list word that matches each clue.

1. In baseball, a swing and a miss is called this. **strike**
2. If you catch a cold, this might get sore. **throat**
3. When you have an itch, you might do this. **scratch**
4. Do this to get juice from an orange. **squeeze**
5. Some people do this when they are afraid. **scream**
6. Be careful crossing this. **street**
7. Often this is put on a window. **screen**
8. This shape has four equal sides. **square**

■ **Rhyme Time** Write the list word that rhymes with each word.

9. do **through**
10. feet **street**
11. bear **square**
12. please **squeeze**
13. range **strange**

STRATEGIC SPELLING: Using the Problem Parts Strategy
Study the problem parts of the words. Write two list words that are hard for you. Underline the part of each word that gives you a problem and study it extra hard.

14. **Answers will vary.**   15. **Answers will vary.**

Practice Masters, p. 8

DAY 2 — EXTRA PRACTICE MASTER

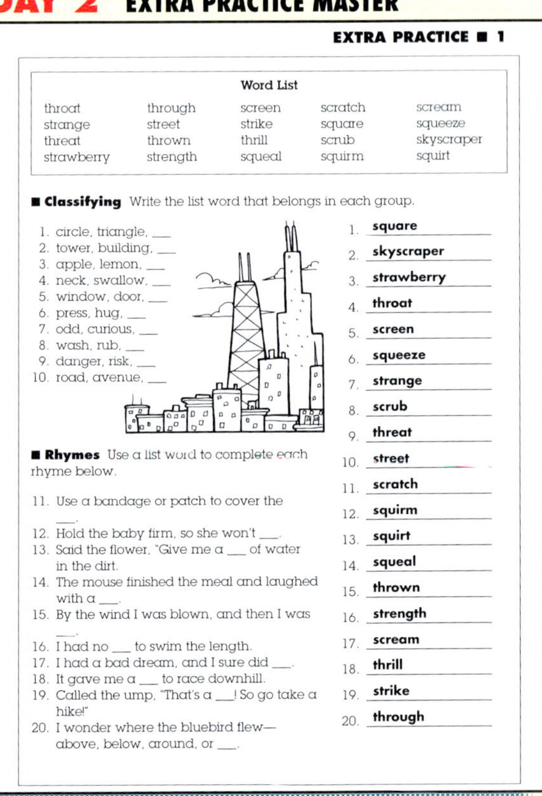

EXTRA PRACTICE ■ 1

Word List

throat	through	screen	scratch	scream
strange	street	strike	square	squeeze
threat	thrown	thrill	scrub	skyscraper
strawberry	strength	squeal	squirm	squirt

■ **Classifying** Write the list word that belongs in each group.

1. circle, triangle, ___ — **square**
2. tower, building, ___ — **skyscraper**
3. apple, lemon, ___ — **strawberry**
4. neck, swallow, ___ — **throat**
5. window, door, ___ — **screen**
6. press, hug, ___ — **squeeze**
7. odd, curious, ___ — **strange**
8. wash, rub, ___ — **scrub**
9. danger, risk, ___ — **threat**
10. road, avenue, ___ — **street**

■ **Rhymes** Use a list word to complete each rhyme below.

11. Use a bandage or patch to cover the ___. — **scratch**
12. Hold the baby firm, so she won't ___. — **squirm**
13. Said the flower, "Give me a ___ of water in the dirt." — **squirt**
14. The mouse finished the meal and laughed with a ___. — **squeal**
15. By the wind I was blown, and then I was ___. — **thrown**
16. I had no ___ to swim the length. — **strength**
17. I had a bad dream, and I sure did ___. — **scream**
18. It gave me a ___ to race downhill. — **thrill**
19. Called the ump, "That's a ___! So go take a hike!" — **strike**
20. I wonder where the bluebird flew—above, below, around, or ___. — **through**

Practice Masters, p. 9

TECHNOLOGY AND VISUAL SUPPORT	 Use Audiotape A, Side 1, Lesson 1  Use Proofreading and Writing Transparency 1	 For additional practice use *Everyday Spelling* Game Software, Lesson 1	 Additional resources on *Everyday Spelling* CD-ROM: proofreading and writing, modified list and challenge words, auditory test

DAY 3 SECOND LANGUAGE SUPPORT MASTER

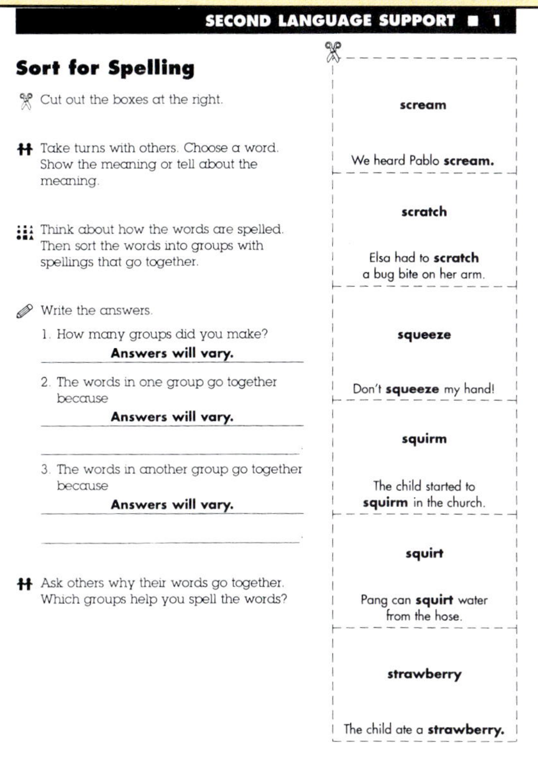

Second Language Support, p. 27

DAY 3 WRITING ACTIVITY MASTER

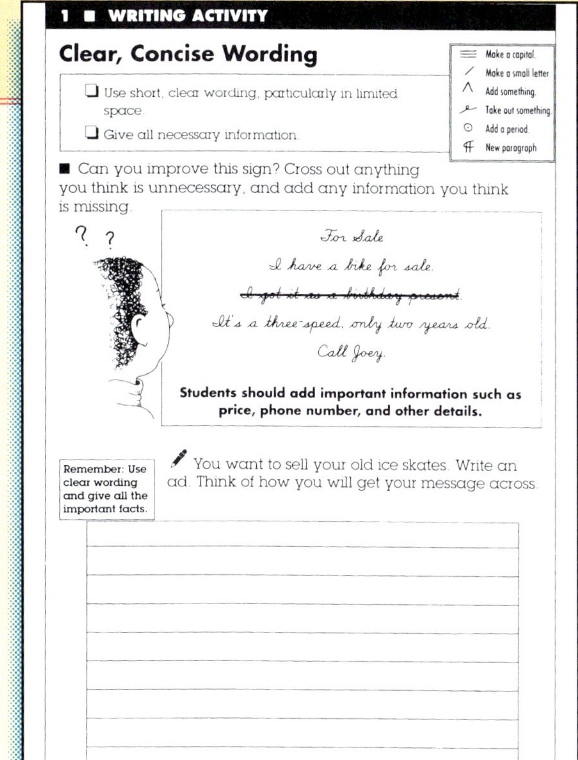

Spelling and Writing, p. 2

DAY 4 REVIEW MASTER

1 ■ REVIEW

Word List

throat	through	screen	scratch	scream
strange	street	strike	square	squeeze
threat	thrown	thrill	scrub	skyscraper
strawberry	strength	squeal	squirm	squirt

■ **Rhyme Time** Write the list word that rhymes with each word below.

1. peel, ___ — squeal
2. tweet, ___ — street
3. worm, ___ — squirm
4. blown, ___ — thrown
5. hatch, ___ — scratch
6. note, ___ — throat
7. length, ___ — strength
8. flypaper, ___ — skyscraper

■ **Making Connections** Write the list word that answers each question.

9. What's red, juicy, and good to eat? — strawberry
10. What can you use a cloth, brush, or mop to do? — scrub
11. Where do you go when you can't go around something? — through
12. What's the shape of a checkerboard? — square
13. What can an elephant do with water in its trunk? — squirt
14. What is it called when you swing and miss? — strike
15. How do you get lemon juice? — squeeze
16. What keeps bugs out of the house? — screen

■ **Base Words** Write the list word that is the base word for each word below.

17. threats — threat
18. stranger — strange
19. screaming — scream
20. thriller — thrill

Practice Masters, p. 10

DAY 5 STANDARDIZED TEST MASTER

LESSON TEST ■ 1

■ Find the word in each group that is spelled correctly. Fill in the letter for the correct word on the answer strip.

Sample:
- a. visiter   c. vizitor
- b. visetor   d. visitor   (a)(b)(c)●

1. a. stret   c. steet   b. street   d. stree — ①(a)●(c)(d)
2. a. stawbary   c. stawberry   b. stawbrrry   d. strawberry — ②(a)(b)(c)●
3. a. throught   c. throat   b. throut   d. throt — ③(a)(b)●(d)
4. a. skrub   c. scrube   b. scrub   d. scrrub — ④(a)●(c)(d)
5. a. thret   c. thraet   b. threat   d. threet — ⑤(a)●(c)(d)
6. a. squar   c. square   b. squrare   d. sqaare — ⑥(a)(b)●(d)
7. a. strang   c. strage   b. strange   d. straing — ⑦(a)●(c)(d)
8. a. through   c. throgh   b. throught   d. throu — ⑧●(b)(c)(d)
9. a. strengh   c. strenth   b. streught   d. strength — ⑨(a)(b)(c)●
10. a. skren   c. skreen   b. screen   d. screan — ⑩(a)●(c)(d)
11. a. squeez   c. squeeze   b. skwezz   d. squesse — ⑪(a)(b)●(d)
12. a. squirm   c. skwirm   b. swerm   d. sqirm — ⑫●(b)(c)(d)
13. a. squail   c. squeal   b. skweel   d. squeel — ⑬(a)(b)●(d)
14. a. throu   c. throughn   b. thrown   d. throwen — ⑭(a)●(c)(d)
15. a. strik   c. strike   b. strick   d. sticke — ⑮(a)(b)●(d)
16. a. treal   c. thril   b. thill   d. thrill — ⑯(a)(b)(c)●
17. a. scach   c. scrach   b. scratch   d. scrath — ⑰(a)●(c)(d)
18. a. skwert   c. squert   b. skwirt   d. squirt — ⑱(a)(b)(c)●
19. a. screem   c. screm   b. scream   d. screme — ⑲(a)●(c)(d)
20. a. skyscrapper   c. skyscraper   b. skyscraper   d. skiscraper — ⑳(a)(b)●(d)

Practice for Standardized Tests, p. 1

INTRODUCTION

Phonics

Words with thr, scr, str, squ Have students pronounce the list words, listen for the beginning consonant blends, and then tell how each blend is spelled.

MEETING THE NEEDS OF ALL STUDENTS

Modified List

Practice Students studying only the high-frequency words in the top box write
- two words beginning with **thr**
- three words with **scr**
- three words with **str**
- two words with **squ**

Visual Learners

A Special Letter Ask students to name the list words that begin with **squ.** Then ask them to think of other words beginning with **q.** Ask students what they notice about the letter that follows **q.** (The letter **u** always follows **q** in English words.)

Additional Practice

Challenge Master 1
Home-School Master 1
Audiotape A, Side 1

1. **throat**
2. **through**
3. **threat**
4. **thrown**
5. **thrill**
6. **screen**
7. **scratch**
8. **scream**
9. **scrub**
10. **skyscraper**
11. **strange**
12. **street**
13. **strike**
14. **strawberry**
15. **strength**
16. **square**
17. **squeeze**
18. **squeal**
19. **squirm**
20. **squint**

CHALLENGE!

arthritis
description
instrument
astronaut
squeezable

14

■ INTRODUCTION

Words with thr, scr, str, squ

SPELLING FOCUS

Some words have consonant blends with three letters pronounced together: **throat**, **screen**, **street**, **square**.

■ STUDY Say each word. Then read the sentence.

1. *throat* — Her cold began with a sore **throat**.
2. *through* ✱ — People strolled **through** the park.
3. *screen* — The window **screen** has a hole.
4. *scratch* — An itch will make you **scratch**.
5. *scream* — Did I hear a **scream** for help?
6. *strange* — The man wore a **strange** pink hat.
7. *street* — She drove the car down the **street**.
8. *strike* — The pitcher threw another **strike**.
9. *square* — The bowl fits in a **square** box.
10. *squeeze* — You **squeeze** a lemon to get juice.

11. *threat* — All nations fear the **threat** of war.
12. *thrown* — That ball was **thrown** too hard.
13. *thrill* — Skydiving gives me a **thrill**.
14. *scrub* — Use this pad to **scrub** the pan.
15. *skyscraper* — The **skyscraper** has 62 stories.
16. *strawberry* — The red fruit is a **strawberry**.
17. *strength* — Gymnasts have great **strength**.
18. *squeal* — I heard the **squeal** of a pig.
19. *squirm* — The puppies **squirm** in their box.
20. *squirt* — Water will **squirt** through a tube.

■ PRACTICE Sort the list words by writing
- five words with **thr**
- five words with **scr**
- five words with **str**
- five words with **squ**

Order of words in each group may vary.

■ WRITE Choose two sentences to write a riddle.
Riddles will vary.

✱ **WATCH OUT FOR FREQUENTLY MISSPELLED WORDS!**

- Practice: Draw Your Own Conclusion and Words in Context
- Strategic Spelling:
  Using the Problem Parts Strategy
- Cross-Curricular Lesson: Introduce
- Modified List

DAILY SPELLING REVIEW

Do you want *leman* and *suger* in your drink?

lemon   sugar

THINK AND PRACTICE ■

DRAW YOUR OWN CONCLUSION   Write the list word that matches each clue.

1. You might clear this when you begin to speak.
2. A piglet might make this sound if you chase it.
3. Never cross this without looking both ways.
4. A box often has this shape.
5. This is a delicious red fruit.
6. You do this to a match when starting a fire.
7. This is what you might call something odd or unusual.
8. An elevator is necessary if you live or work here.
9. Using soap, do this to get a floor clean.
10. If you have poison ivy, you'll feel the urge to do this.
11. Do this loudly if you are frightened and need help.
12. Sledding down a steep hill may give you this.
13. Little children may do this if they have to sit quietly.
14. An elephant might do this with the water in its trunk.
15. This keeps bugs from flying through an open window.

WORDS IN CONTEXT   Write the list word that is missing from each animal's statement.

16. **Monkey:** I swing ___ the jungle from tree to tree.
17. **Zebra:** I was ___ to the ground by a lion, but I escaped.
18. **Gorilla:** I have the ___ of ten men.
19. **Boa:** I wrap around my prey and ___ very hard.
20. **Mongoose:** I'm so quick, even a cobra is no ___ to me.

1.	**throat**
2.	**squeal**
3.	**street**
4.	**square**
5.	**strawberry**
6.	**strike**
7.	**strange**
8.	**skyscraper**
9.	**scrub**
10.	**scratch**
11.	**scream**
12.	**thrill**
13.	**squirm**
14.	**squirt**
15.	**screen**
16.	**through**
17.	**thrown**
18.	**strength**
19.	**squeeze**
20.	**threat**

Study the problem parts of words. Write two list words that are hard for you. Underline the part of each word that gives you the problem, and study it extra hard.

21. **Answers will vary.**   22. **Answers will vary.**

Take a Hint
This sentence may help you remember the difference between *throne* and *thrown*.
The king was thr**ow**n from the throne he once **ow**ned.

THINK AND PRACTICE

Word Meaning

Using a Dictionary Suggest that students use a dictionary if they are unfamiliar with the meaning of *poison ivy* in sentence 10.

MEETING THE NEEDS OF ALL STUDENTS

Modified List

Review Students studying high-frequency words complete Think and Practice Master 1.

Bilingual/ESL

Draw Your Own Conclusion Group together students of varying language ability. Have group members take turns acting out each clue as the others find the matching list word.

Auditory Learners

Words in Context Read each sentence aloud. Have a volunteer suggest the missing list word and tell why it makes sense.

Additional Practice

Think and Practice Master 1
Extra Practice Master 1
Everyday Spelling **CD-ROM**
Everyday Spelling **Game Software**

- Proofread a Sign
- Proofreading Tip: Spelling Errors
- Create a Sign
- ✓ Cooperative Midweek Test

DAILY SPELLING REVIEW

Thats my favorite *acter*.

That's   *actor*

● Core   ○ Optional   ✓ Assessment

PROOFREADING AND WRITING

Spelling

Proofread a Sign To help students focus on correct spelling, have them first write the words for their sign on a sheet of paper and proofread for correct spelling.

MEETING THE NEEDS OF ALL STUDENTS

Modified List

Proofreading Students studying high-frequency words complete this page or the proofreading activity on the *Everyday Spelling* CD-ROM.

Enrichment

Evaluating Messages Discuss using strong, attention-getting words in a sign. Have students read their signs aloud and identify the most effective words.

Additional Practice

Second Language Master 1
Writing Mini-Lesson Master 1
Writing Activity Master 1
Proofreading Transparency 1
Everyday Spelling **CD-ROM**

■ **PROOFREADING AND WRITING**

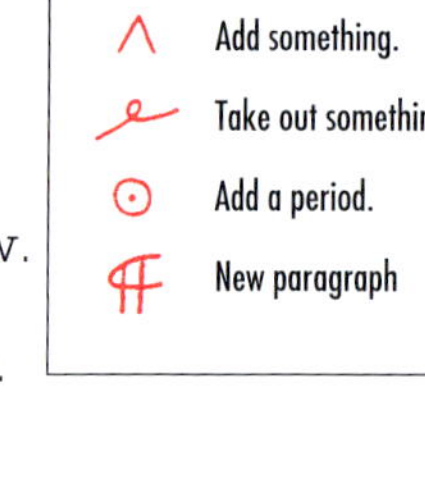

PROOFREAD A SIGN Find the misspelled word in the photograph below. Why do you think it is misspelled in this particular way? Write the word correctly.

strawberry

Word List

scrub	thrill
street	screen
threat	strength
skyscraper	squeeze
thrown	through
square	strike
scream	squirm
throat	scratch
strawberry	strange
squeal	squirt

Personal Words

1. **Words will**
2. **vary.**

CREATE A SIGN Now it's your turn to try to get a message across. Imagine you own The Gyros Stand and want customers to try your exciting new dessert. Use list words to create a sign with a short, sweet message.

Responses will vary. Sign should include list words.

16

VOCABULARY BUILDING

Review

PUZZLE IT OUT   We are a collection of plans you will use for learning to spell new words. What are we? When you write the boxed words that match the definitions, the answer to the riddle will appear in the box.

throat	strange
through	street
screen	strike
scratch	square
scream	squeeze

1. rub to get rid of an itch
2. odd; unusual
3. a passage from the mouth to the stomach or the lungs
4. having four equal sides and four right angles
5. a road
6. press hard
7. from one side to the other
8. set on fire by rubbing
9. a loud cry for help
10. a glass surface on which information or pictures appear

1. s c r a t c h
2. s t r a n g e
3. t h r o a t
4. s q u a r e
5. s t r e e t
6. s q u e e z e
7. t h r o u g h
8. s t r i k e
9. s c r e a m
10. s c r e e n

Using a Dictionary

GUIDE WORDS   At the top of each dictionary page are two guide words in dark type. The first guide word is the first entry word on the page. The second guide word is the last entry word on the page. If the word you are looking for falls alphabetically between these two words, you are on the right page.

When words begin with the same letter, you must look at the second letter, third letter, and so on to alphabetize them. For example, look on page 284 in your Spelling Dictionary. Notice that the word *screen* follows *scream* and comes before *scrub*.

Now, look at each pair of guide words to the right. Which of the boxed words fall between these guide words alphabetically? Write those words.
Order of words in columns may vary.

thought
threat
throat
thrifty
thresh
spray
squirt
squeeze
squeak
squash

thrash/thrill	square/squirm
threat	squeeze
thrifty	squeak
thresh	squash

2

Generalization

Spelling Focus: The consonant pairs **kn**, **gn**, **wr**, and **mb** have only one sound.

● Core   ○ Optional   ✓ Assessment

DAILY PLAN	CORE OBJECTIVES	NOTES

DAY 1 Introduction

✓ Pretest and Self-Check, p. 18B
● Spelling Focus and Word List, p. 18
○ Challenge Words, p. 18
○ Challenge Master 2
○ Home-School Master 2

✓ ▪ Take and self-check Pretest
▪ Spell words with consonant combinations **kn**, **gn**, **wr**, or **mb**; classify and write the list words

DAY 2 Think and Practice

● Rhyme Time; Defining Words, p. 19
● Strategic Spelling: *Seeing Meaning Connections*, p. 19
○ Think and Practice Master 2
○ Extra Practice Master 2
○ Cross-Curricular Lesson: Introduce, p. 210

▪ Complete practice activities for words with **kn**, **gn**, **wr**, or **mb**
▪ Recognize meaning connections between list words and other words related to them

DAY 3 Proofreading and Writing

● Proofread a Note, p. 20
● Proofreading Tip: Capitalization, p. 20
● Answer the Note, p. 20
✓ Cooperative Midweek Test
○ Hardbound Book Master 2
○ Writing Mini-Lesson Master 2
○ Writing Activity Master 2
○ Second Language Support Master 2

▪ Proofread for spelling and capitalization errors
▪ Integrate spelling and writing in a personal writing response
✓ ▪ Take and check midweek test

DAY 4 Vocabulary Building

● Review: Word Associations, p. 21
● Word Study: Hink-Pinks, p. 21
○ Cross-Curricular Lesson: Follow-Up, p. 210
○ Review Master 2

▪ Complete review activity for words with consonant combinations **kn**, **gn**, **wr**, and **mb**
▪ Answer riddles with rhyming words

Day 5 Assessment

✓ Posttest, p. 18B
○ Standardized Test Master 2

✓ ▪ Take Posttest

Cross-Curricular Lessons

Use the Spelling Focus (words with **kn, gn, wr,** or **mb**) to introduce the Reading lesson, *Looking at the World,* page 210, or choose a lesson that correlates with a topic you're currently teaching.

MEETING THE NEEDS OF ALL STUDENTS

The Word List

For students studying 20 words, assign pages 18–21 and Extra Practice and Review masters.

Modified List For students studying 10 words, modify Practice on page 18, and assign Think and Practice Master 2 and pages 20–21.

Challenge For students studying 25 words, assign pages 18–21, Challenge, Extra Practice, and Review masters.

Bilingual/ESL

Vietnamese has no silent **k,** as in *knot* and *knit.* Vietnamese-speaking students may thus omit the **k** when writing.

Personal Words

Students add to Personal Words lists by looking at work in their writing portfolios and words they want to remember from their reading.

	Bilingual/ESL	Modified List	Challenge	Extra Support	Enrichment	Visual Learners	Auditory Learners	Kinesthetic Learners
p. 18		✓				✓		
p. 19	✓	✓					✓	
p. 20		✓			✓			
p. 21		✓	✓	✓				

ASSESSMENT

Pretest

Read the underlined word, read the sentence, and then repeat the underlined word. Guide students in self-correcting their pretests and correcting any misspellings.

1. Pat tied a <u>knot</u> in the rope.
2. That boy is <u>unknown</u> to me.
3. We <u>know</u> the fifty states.
4. Juan made a funny <u>sign</u>.
5. Did he <u>design</u> the house?
6. Rita is <u>writing</u> a letter.
7. Carlos sprained his <u>wrist</u>.
8. Bad driving caused a <u>wreck</u>.
9. Ben will <u>climb</u> a mountain.
10. Press it with your <u>thumb</u>.
11. Mom will <u>knit</u> a sweater.
12. The <u>knob</u> would not turn.
13. Amy will <u>kneel</u> on the floor.
14. Mr. Gomez will <u>assign</u> math.
15. Jan made a pine <u>wreath</u>.
16. He used a big <u>wrench</u>.
17. We saw a <u>wren</u> and a robin.
18. He hung a rope on a <u>limb</u>.
19. Al put a <u>comb</u> in his pocket.
20. The <u>lamb</u> had white fur.

Posttest

Read aloud the sentences below. These sentences may be used for dictation.

1. Do you <u>know</u> who she is?
2. He was in a <u>wreck</u>.
3. She made a <u>sign</u> for class.
4. That actor is <u>unknown</u>.
5. Put a <u>knot</u> in the scarf.
6. He wanted to <u>climb</u> a tree.
7. He hit his <u>thumb</u>.
8. His shirt had a new <u>design</u>.
9. We are <u>writing</u> a story.
10. Bend the <u>wrist</u> like this.
11. <u>Kneel</u> to dig in the dirt.
12. The <u>wren</u> flew to the tree.
13. I will learn to <u>knit</u>.
14. Did she <u>comb</u> her hair?
15. A <u>lamb</u> lived on the farm.
16. A <u>wreath</u> is round.
17. Is there a <u>wrench</u> in the box?
18. Who will <u>assign</u> the work?
19. A squirrel sat on a <u>limb</u>.
20. Turn the <u>knob</u> to the left.

Challenge Words

1. I ate <u>bologna</u> and bread.
2. Grandma made <u>lasagna</u>.
3. <u>Align</u> ten pennies.
4. Mom's <u>cologne</u> has a good smell.
5. Which <u>wrestler</u> won?

Additional Assessment

Standardized Test Master 2
Dictation Sentences, p. T37
Everyday Spelling CD-ROM

Challenge students to solve this puzzle: What two sounds can you add to the ends of **bo-, to-,** and **co-** to make three words in which the vowel **o** is pronounced differently? (Answer: **mb**—*bomb, tomb,* and *comb*)

* See pp. T20 and T33 for test-study-test information.

DAY 1   CHALLENGE MASTER

CHALLENGE ■ 2

Challenge Words

bologna   lasagna   align   wrestler   cologne

■ Write the Challenge Word for each definition.

1. a fragrant liquid, not as strong as
   perfume   **cologne**

2. a large sausage usually made of beef,
   veal, and pork   **bologna**

3. bring into line; arrange in a straight line
   align

4. a person who wrestles   **wrestler**

5. a dish made of noodles, chopped meat, cheese,
   and tomato sauce   **lasagna**

■ Do you like lasagna, pizza, or other Italian foods? Write a paragraph
telling about foods you like or dislike. Use one or more Challenge Words.

Practice Masters, p. 11

DAY 1   HOME-SCHOOL MASTER

■ 2   **HOME-SCHOOL ACTIVITIES**   2 ■

Word Check 2
1. wrist
2. know
3. thumb
4. sign
5. unknown
6. wreck
7. limb
8. wrench
9. knit
10. comb
11. wreath
12. assign
13. knot
14. lamb
15. design
16. knob
17. wren
18. writing
19. climb
20. kneel

■ **Word Cousins** Write a list word to complete each
group of words.

1. finger, toe, **thumb**

2. poster, billboard, **sign**

3. hammer, saw, **wrench**

4. walk, hike, **climb**

5. knee, elbow, **wrist**

6. colt, calf, **lamb**

7. twig, branch, **limb**

8. sew, stitch, **knit**

9. reading, arithmetic, **writing**

10. robin, sparrow, **wren**

■ **Silly Words** Circle the list word in each silly word.
Write the word on the line.

11. opassignit **assign**

12. zcombish **comb**

13. nidesignrge **design**

14. epkneelpe **kneel**

15. foknobi **knob**

16. isknotto **knot**

17. butknowry **know**

18. qunknownz **unknown**

19. sewreathie **wreath**

20. ekwreckdek **wreck**

Dear Parent,

Please check to
see that your
child has done
this page
correctly. Circle
any misspelled
words and help
your child study
them.

Tear off the Word
Check before
your child returns
this page to class.
Use it to help your
child study.

Look at your answer words. What do you notice about
the order in which they are written?

They are in alphabetical order.

Home-School Activities, p. 2

DAY 2   THINK AND PRACTICE MASTER

2 ■ **THINK AND PRACTICE**

| knot | unknown | know | sign | design |
| writing | wrist | wreck | climb | thumb |

■ **Classifying** Write the list word that belongs in each group.

1. elbow, knee, **wrist**

2. reading, spelling, **writing**

3. shape, pattern, **design**

4. hand, finger, **thumb**

5. run, jump, **climb**

6. tie, lace, **knot**

■ **Defining Words** Write the list word that means the same as
the underlined word or words.

7. Do you have the facts about who broke the window? **know**

8. Write your name at the bottom of the letter. **sign**

9. Let's go up the tree. **climb**

10. The song was not familiar, so we didn't sing. **unknown**

11. Did the dog ruin your model plane? **wreck**

12. The short thick finger of the hand helps you pick up things.
    thumb

STRATEGIC SPELLING: Seeing Meaning Connections
Write the list word that completes each sentence. The underlined
word is a clue.

13. The designer will **design** a dress for her.

14. Was the answer known or **unknown**?

15. Write the list words that are related to the words you wrote above.
    sign   **know**

Practice Masters, p. 12

DAY 2   EXTRA PRACTICE MASTER

EXTRA PRACTICE ■ 2

Word List

knot	unknown	know	sign	design
writing	wrist	wreck	climb	thumb
knit	knob	kneel	assign	wreath
wrench	wren	limb	comb	lamb

■ **Analogies** Use a list word to complete
each analogy.

1. Easter is to egg as Christmas is to ___.
2. Tree is to oak as tool is to ___.
3. Dog is to puppy as sheep is to ___.
4. Foot is to toe as hand is to ___.
5. Ocean is to swim as mountain is to ___.
6. Leg is to ankle as arm is to ___.
7. Bricks are to build as yarn is to ___.
8. Flower is to petal as tree is to ___.
9. Fish is to trout as bird is to ___.
10. Clothing is to iron as hair is to ___.
11. Happy is to glad as understand is to ___.
12. Hoe is to farming as pen is to ___.

1. **wreath**
2. **wrench**
3. **lamb**
4. **finger**
5. **climb**
6. **wrist**
7. **knit**
8. **limb**
9. **wren**
10. **comb**
11. **know**
12. **writing**
13. **kneel**
14. **sign**
15. **knob**
16. **wreck**
17. **unknown**
18. **design**
19. **assign**
20. **knot**

■ **Meaning Clues** Write the list word that fits
each clue.

13. what your knees help you to do
14. where you often see the word STOP
15. what is found on each side of a door
16. what happens if a train goes off the track
17. how you describe something that is a
    mystery
18. the regular pattern on your wallpaper
19. what your teacher does with homework
20. what you can get in a shoelace if you tie
    it too fast

Practice Masters, p. 13

18C

TECHNOLOGY AND VISUAL SUPPORT	 Use Audiotape A, Side 1, Lesson 2	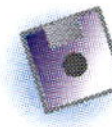 For additional practice use *Everyday Spelling* Game Software, Lesson 2	 Additional resources on *Everyday Spelling* CD-ROM: proofreading and writing, modified list and challenge words, auditory test
	 Use Proofreading and Writing Transparency 2		

DAY 3   SECOND LANGUAGE SUPPORT MASTER

2 ■ SECOND LANGUAGE SUPPORT

About Me

Read what Oren wrote.

> My cat, Mittens, was stuck in a tree. My new friend brought a ladder. He decided to *climb* the ladder to save her. Suddenly he fell! He broke his *wrist* and hurt his *thumb*. I feel that this was my fault.

Write some spelling words that tell about you. Then draw a picture of your ideas.

Words will vary.

Write about your picture.

Answers will vary.

Look over your paper. Talk with a partner about your picture and writing.

Second Language Support, p. 28

DAY 3   WRITING ACTIVITY MASTER

2 ■ WRITING ACTIVITY

Capital Letters

- ☐ Use capital letters for proper nouns
- ☐ Use capital letters for all words in the greeting and the closing
- ☐ Use capital letters to begin all sentences

☰	Make a capital
/	Make a small letter
∧	Add something
↜	Take out something
⊙	Add a period
¶	New paragraph

■ Read the note that Amy wrote to her uncle. Check to see if capital letters were used correctly. Fix any mistakes.

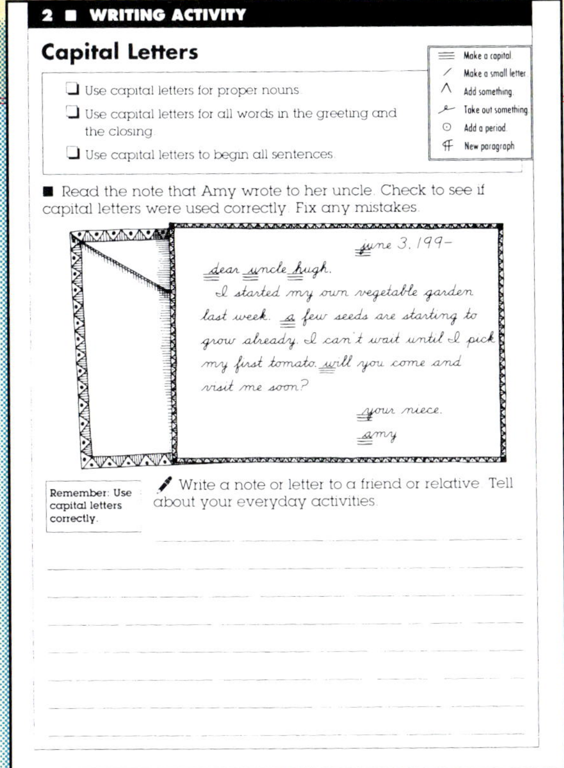

Remember: Use capital letters correctly.

Write a note or letter to a friend or relative. Tell about your everyday activities.

Spelling and Writing, p. 4

DAY 4   REVIEW MASTER

2 ■ REVIEW

Word List

knot	unknown	know	sign	design
writing	wrist	wreck	climb	thumb
knit	knob	kneel	assign	wreath
wrench	wren	limb	comb	lamb

■ Buried Words Each word below is hidden in a list word. Write the list word.

1. eat **wreath**
2. own **unknown**
3. am **lamb**
4. is **wrist**
5. knee **kneel**
6. as **assign**
7. now **know**
8. wren **wrench**

■ Word Plays Write the list words to complete the sentences.

9. A jewelry box opens with a latch. A door opens with a ___. — **knob**
10. To make a dress, sew. To make a sweater, ___. — **knit**
11. A rose is a flower. A branch is a ___. — **limb**
12. Teeth need a toothbrush. Hair needs a ___. — **comb**
13. You have four fingers per hand. You have one ___ per hand. — **thumb**
14. When you make pictures you are drawing. When you make letters you are ___. — **writing**
15. Tie a ribbon in a bow. Tie a string in a ___. — **knot**

■ Words in Context Write the word that completes each sentence.

16. The woodworker carved a **design** into the cabinet.
17. A little bird with a sweet song is the **wren**.
18. After staying up, John looked like a **wreck**.
19. It's healthier to **climb** the stairs than take the elevator.
20. A billboard is a **sign** along a road.

Practice Masters, p. 14

DAY 5   STANDARDIZED TEST MASTER

2 ■ LESSON TEST

■ Find the word in each group that is spelled correctly. Fill in the letter for the correct word on the answer strip.

Sample:

	a.		c.	Answer
Sample	a. visiter / c. vizitor	b. visetor / d. visitor		ⓐ ⓑ ⓒ ●
1.	a. kown / c. nkow	b. nowe / d. know		1. ⓐ ⓑ ⓒ ●
2.	a. clim / c. climb	b. cline / d. climbe		2. ⓐ ⓑ ● ⓓ
3.	a. coum / c. coom	b. comb / d. com		3. ⓐ ● ⓒ ⓓ
4.	a. limb / c. limm	b. lim / d. limd		4. ● ⓑ ⓒ ⓓ
5.	a. lamd / c. lamb	b. lammb / d. laam		5. ⓐ ⓑ ● ⓓ
6.	a. thum / c. thumb	b. thumm / d. thumd		6. ⓐ ⓑ ● ⓓ
7.	a. neel / c. kneal	b. knel / d. kneel		7. ⓐ ⓑ ⓒ ●
8.	a. knitt / c. knette	b. knit / d. knite		8. ⓐ ● ⓒ ⓓ
9.	a. knote / c. knotte	b. knot / d. knoot		9. ⓐ ● ⓒ ⓓ
10.	a. unknowen / c. unknown	b. unown / d. unknow		10. ⓐ ⓑ ● ⓓ
11.	a. reck / c. reack	b. wreck / d. wrech		11. ⓐ ● ⓒ ⓓ
12.	a. sighn / c. sign	b. sihn / d. sihgn		12. ⓐ ⓑ ● ⓓ
13.	a. designh / c. desine	b. disign / d. design		13. ⓐ ⓑ ⓒ ●
14.	a. assign / c. assighn	b. asign / d. assihn		14. ● ⓑ ⓒ ⓓ
15.	a. rench / c. rentch	b. wrentch / d. wrench		15. ⓐ ⓑ ⓒ ●
16.	a. wrene / c. wreen	b. wren / d. wern		16. ⓐ ● ⓒ ⓓ
17.	a. reaf / c. wret	b. wreath / d. reath		17. ⓐ ● ⓒ ⓓ
18.	a. writting / c. wrighting	b. riting / d. writing		18. ⓐ ⓑ ⓒ ●
19.	a. risck / c. wrist	b. rist / d. wrisit		19. ⓐ ⓑ ● ⓓ
20.	a. nob / c. knobe	b. knob / d. knab		20. ⓐ ● ⓒ ⓓ

Practice for Standardized Tests, p. 2

DAY 1 Introduction

✓ Pretest and Self-Check	**DAILY SPELLING REVIEW**
● Spelling Focus and Word List	Anita planted a *gardin* in her *back*
○ Challenge Words	*yard.*
○ Modified List	*garden* *backyard*

● **Core**   ○ **Optional**   ✓ **Assessment**

INTRODUCTION

Phonics

Silent Letters Students can sort the list words into two groups: those with two consonants at the beginning, one of which is silent, and those with two consonants at the end, one of which is silent. They can identify the silent letter in each word.

MEETING THE NEEDS OF ALL STUDENTS

Modified List

Practice Students studying only the high-frequency words in the top box write
- three words with **kn**
- two words with **gn**
- three words with **wr**
- two words with **mb**

Visual Learners

Picturing the Concept

Have students draw and label pictures to illustrate six list words. They can use special colors to highlight the silent-letter combinations.

Additonal Practice

Challenge Master 2
Home-School Master 2
Audiotape A, Side 1

1. knot
2. unknown
3. know
4. knit
5. knob
6. kneel
7. sign
8. design
9. assign
10. writing
11. wrist
12. wreck
13. wreath
14. wrench
15. wren
16. climb
17. thumb
18. limb
19. comb
20. lamb

CHALLENGE!

bologna
lasagna
align
cologne
wrestler

■ INTRODUCTION

Words with kn, gn, wr, mb

SPELLING FOCUS

The underlined consonants stand for only one sound: k<u>n</u>ot, si<u>gn</u>, <u>wr</u>ist, cli<u>mb</u>.

■ **STUDY** Say each word. Then read the sentence.

1.	knot	I have a **knot** in my shoelace.
2.	unknown	The book's author is **unknown.**
3.	know ✳	I **know** the answer to the question.
4.	sign	The **sign** said "Big Sale Today."
5.	design	The wallpaper has a striped **design.**
6.	writing	She is **writing** a book about cats.
7.	wrist	I wear a watch on my **wrist.**
8.	wreck	The car is a rusty old **wreck.**
9.	climb	Cats sometimes **climb** trees.
10.	thumb	The baby sucks his **thumb.**
11.	knit	Who **knit** that pretty sweater?
12.	knob	The **knob** fell off the door.
13.	kneel	My knees hurt when I **kneel.**
14.	assign	She will **assign** homework later.
15.	wreath	He hung a **wreath** on the door.
16.	wrench	Use a **wrench** to tighten the bolts.
17.	wren	A **wren** is a small, brown bird.
18.	limb	A tree **limb** fell to the ground.
19.	comb	I need to **comb** my hair.
20.	lamb	Watch that frisky little **lamb.**

■ **PRACTICE** Sort the words by writing
- six words with **kn**
- three words with **gn**
- six words with **wr**
- five words with **mb**

Order of words in each group may vary.

■ **WRITE** Choose two sentences to include in a paragraph.
Paragraphs will vary.

✳ **WATCH OUT FOR FREQUENTLY MISSPELLED WORDS!**

THINK AND PRACTICE ■

RHYME TIME   Write the list word that rhymes with each word below.

1. teeth
2. snow
3. biting
4. hum
5. rim
6. bench
7. list
8. clam
9. roam
10. peel
11. when
12. deck

1. wreath
2. know
3. writing
4. thumb
5. limb
6. wrench
7. wrist
8. lamb
9. comb
10. kneel
11. wren
12. wreck
13. unknown
14. knit
15. climb
16. knot
17. knob

DEFINING WORDS   Write the list word that means the same as the underlined words.

13. The explorers traveled to a land that was <u>not familiar</u> to them.
14. I like to <u>make clothing by looping yarn.</u>
15. We had to <u>use hands and feet to go over</u> the fence to get into our yard.
16. Please <u>tie the ends of</u> this rope tightly.
17. I caught my coat on the <u>handle on a door.</u>

Write the list word that completes each sentence. The underlined word is a clue.

18. The <u>designer</u> will ______**design**______ a dress for her.
19. Please don't ______**assign**______ another <u>assignment</u>.
20. Write the list word that both of the words you wrote above are related to: ______**sign**______.

✳ FREQUENTLY MISSPELLED WORDS ✳

Know is a frequently misspelled word because it is a word many students misspell. Remember that if you **know** something, you have **know**ledge.

THINK AND PRACTICE

Rhyme Time
Creating Rhymes To help students who have difficulties with near-rhymes, such as *hum/comb* or *roam/thumb*, have volunteers make up simple rhymes, such as "I *roam* and *roam* to find my *comb.*"

MEETING THE NEEDS OF ALL STUDENTS

Modified List
Review Students studying high-frequency words complete Think and Practice Master 2.

Bilingual/ESL
Defining Words Pair ESL students with more fluent English speakers to act out the underlined phrases.

Auditory Learners
Reinforcing Meaning Have each student say aloud an "I know" sentence with a list word, such as "I know how to *design* a card."

Additional Practice

Think and Practice Master 2
Extra Practice Master 2
Everyday Spelling **CD-ROM**
Everyday Spelling **Game Software**

DAY 3 Proofreading and Writing

- Proofread a Note
- Proofreading Tip: Capitalization
- Answer the Note
- ✓ Cooperative Midweek Test

DAILY SPELLING REVIEW

The *vistor* brought *choclate*.

visitor   *chocolate*

● Core   ○ Optional   ✓ Assessment

PROOFREADING AND WRITING

Capitalization
Proofreading a Note
Suggest that students proofread a draft of a note several times, looking only for capitalization errors in one of those readings.

MEETING THE NEEDS OF ALL STUDENTS

Modified List
Proofreading Students studying the high-frequency words complete this page or the proofreading activity on the *Everyday Spelling* CD-ROM.

Enrichment
Writing Notes Point out that notes are brief and focus on a single purpose. Have students brainstorm occasions when they might write notes. Then have them write notes to a partner.

Additional Practice

Hardbound Book Master 2
Second Language Master 2
Writing Mini-Lesson Master 2
Writing Activity Master 2
Proofreading Transparency 2
Everyday Spelling **CD-ROM**

■ PROOFREADING AND WRITING

≡	Make a capital.
/	Make a small letter.
∧	Add something.
℮	Take out something.
⊙	Add a period.
⌗	New paragraph.

PROOFREAD A NOTE Read the thank-you note that Pat wrote her aunt. Find three misspelled words and three capitalization errors. Write them correctly.

PROOFREADING TIP
Pat is guilty of three "Capital Crimes"—mistakes with capital letters. Did you find them? If not, check the beginnings of sentences, the names of people, and the opening and closing of her note.

October 10, 19--

Dear aunt Sally,

Thank you for the sweater. I love the desine, [design] especially the lamb on the pocket. did you knitt [knit] it yourself? I no [know] I will wear it a lot.

love,
Pat

ANSWER THE NOTE Imagine that you are Pat's aunt. Answer the note above. Use some of your spelling words and personal words in your reply.

Responses will vary. Note should include spelling words and personal words.

Word List

wrist	wreath
know	assign
thumb	knot
sign	lamb
unknown	design
wreck	knob
limb	wren
wrench	writing
knit	climb
comb	kneel

Personal Words

1. **Words will**
2. **vary.**

20

VOCABULARY BUILDING

Review

WORD ASSOCIATIONS Write the boxed word that you would associate with each situation described below.

1. a motorist stopping at an intersection
2. bystanders observing the scene of an automobile accident
3. a child making a birthday party list
4. a girl spotting her friend across a crowded room of strangers
5. a team of explorers hiking across a mountain range
6. a Boy Scout tying two pieces of rope together
7. a mother pulling her young son's hand from his mouth to keep him from sucking
8. astronauts exploring a strange planet
9. a jeweler measuring a customer for a new watch
10. an architect creating a floor plan for a new house

knot
unknown
know
sign
design
writing
wrist
wreck
climb
thumb

1. **sign**
2. **wreck**
3. **writing**
4. **know**
5. **climb or unknown**
6. **knot**
7. **thumb**
8. **unknown**
9. **wrist**
10. **design**

Word *Study*

HINK-PINKS Have you ever played the rhyming game called *Hink-Pink?* Now is your chance. First, you read a question. Then, you answer it with two rhyming words. Here's an example:

Q: What do you call damage done to a pack of playing cards?
A: a deck wreck

Now try to answer the questions below. Hint: One of the words is always a list word.

1. **Q:** What do you call an excellent drawing?
   A: a **fine** **design**

2. **Q:** What do you call a thin leg?
   A: a **slim** **limb**

3. **Q:** What would you call a fastening made with rope that is lying on a heated stove?
   A: a **hot** **knot**

Literature Connection

More Rhymes A good source of additional poems is *The Random House Book of Poetry for Children* edited by Jack Prelutsky (Random House, 1983).

MEETING THE NEEDS OF ALL STUDENTS

Modified Word List

Review Students studying high-frequency words complete this page.

Extra Support

Picture Hink-Pinks Have students work with a partner to use list words in Hink-Pinks of their own. Have them write the questions and then draw pictures that show the answers.

Challenge

Hink-Pinks Have students make up lists of rhyming words, such as *wreath/ teeth* and *thumb/hum.* Encourage students to turn word pairs into Hink-Pinks.

Additional Practice

Review Master 2
Standardized Test Master 2
Everyday Spelling **CD-ROM**

LESSON

3

Generalization

Spelling Focus: Consonant sound /k/ can be spelled **c**, **k**, or **ck**. Consonant sound /f/ can be spelled **ff**, **gh**, or **ph**.

● Core ○ Optional ✓ Assessment

DAILY PLAN

DAY 1 Introduction

✓ Pretest and Self-Check, p. 22B
● Spelling Focus and Word List, p. 22
○ Challenge Words, p. 22
○ Challenge Master 3
○ Home-School Master 3

DAY 2 Think and Practice

● Poetry in Motion; Classifying; Who Am I?, p. 23
● Strategic Spelling: *Seeing Meaning Connections*, p. 23
○ Think and Practice Master 3
○ Extra Practice Master 3
○ Cross-Curricular Lesson: Introduce, p. 172

DAY 3 Proofreading and Writing

● Proofread a Self-Portrait, p. 24
● Proofreading Tip: Personal Pronouns, p. 24
● Create a Self-Portrait, p. 24
✓ Cooperative Midweek Test
○ Hardbound Book Master 3
○ Writing Mini-Lesson Master 3
○ Writing Activity Master 3
○ Second Language Support Master 3

DAY 4 Vocabulary Building

● Review: Defining Words, p. 25
● Multicultural Connection: Languages, p. 25
○ Cross-Curricular Lesson: Follow-Up, p. 172
○ Review Master 3

DAY 5 Assessment

✓ Posttest, p. 22B
○ Standardized Test Master 3

CORE OBJECTIVES

✓ ▪ Take and self-check Pretest
▪ Spell words with the consonant sounds /k/ and /f/; classify and write the list words

▪ Complete practice activities for words with consonant sounds /k/ and /f/
▪ Recognize meaning connections between list words and other words related to them

▪ Proofread for spelling and grammar errors
▪ Integrate spelling and writing in a personal writing response
✓ ▪ Take and check midweek test

▪ Complete review activity for words with the consonant sounds /k/ and /f/
▪ Extend knowledge of words from different languages

✓ ▪ Take Posttest

NOTES

Cross-Curricular Lessons

Use the Spelling Focus (consonant sounds /k/ and /f/) to introduce the Social Studies lesson, *Deserts and Forests,* page 172, or choose a lesson that correlates with a topic you're currently teaching.

MEETING THE NEEDS OF ALL STUDENTS

The Word List

For students studying 20 words, assign pages 22–25 and Extra Practice and Review masters.

Modified List For students studying 10 words, modify Practice on page 22, and assign Think and Practice Master 3 and pages 24–25.

Challenge For students studying 25 words, assign pages 24–25, Challenge, Extra Practice, and Review masters.

Bilingual/ESL

In Korean, no consonant clusters or blends appear in the initial position in a syllable. Students may insert a vowel between consonants since they are used to c-v-c syllables: *track/tarack.*

Personal Words

Students add to Personal Words lists by looking at work in their writing portfolios and words they want to remember from their reading.

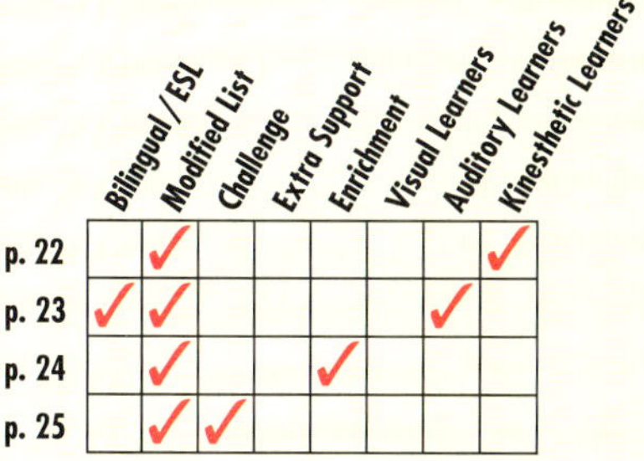

	Bilingual/ESL	Modified List	Challenge	Extra Support	Enrichment	Visual Learners	Auditory Learners	Kinesthetic Learners
p. 22		✓						✓
p. 23	✓	✓					✓	
p. 24		✓			✓			
p. 25		✓	✓					

ASSESSMENT*

Pretest

Read the underlined word, read the sentence, and then repeat the underlined word. Guide students in self-correcting their pretests and correcting any misspellings.

1. Nurses <u>care</u> for sick people.
2. I cried <u>because</u> I was sad.
3. Nina used the <u>brake</u> to stop.
4. We ran laps around the <u>track</u>.
5. Tia put a pen in her <u>pocket</u>.
6. Starch makes a shirt <u>stiff</u>.
7. Do you have <u>enough</u> paper?
8. Pedro <u>laughed</u> at my joke.
9. Gina took a <u>photo</u> of clouds.
10. Ryan can say the <u>alphabet</u>.
11. <u>Cover</u> up if you are cold.
12. William broke the <u>record</u>.
13. A big storm struck <u>Kansas</u>.
14. Ted had a <u>snack</u> after class.
15. Will a brown bear <u>attack</u>?
16. Jim ate a <u>muffin</u> for lunch.
17. The <u>giraffe</u> had big spots.
18. The sandpaper felt <u>rough</u>.
19. A <u>dolphin</u> swam in a show.
20. The <u>elephant</u> ate peanuts.

Posttest

Read aloud the sentences below. These sentences may be used for dictation.

1. Pull the <u>brake</u> on the bus.
2. He took a <u>photo</u> of his dog.
3. They <u>laughed</u> at the clown.
4. The cold made her <u>stiff</u>.
5. You must <u>care</u> for a pet.
6. My cap is in my <u>pocket</u>.
7. He cried <u>because</u> he was lost.
8. Do you know the <u>alphabet</u>?
9. I have had <u>enough</u> candy.
10. He ran down the <u>track</u>.
11. Lions may <u>attack</u> a person.
12. See the <u>elephant</u> at the zoo.
13. A <u>giraffe</u> has a long neck.
14. The <u>dolphin</u> did a trick.
15. The <u>cover</u> is on the bed.
16. <u>Kansas</u> is a pretty state.
17. The ball game was <u>rough</u>.
18. I ate an orange <u>muffin</u>.
19. An apple is a good <u>snack</u>.
20. We played an old <u>record</u>.

Challenge Words

1. The <u>cuckoo clock</u> goes off every hour.
2. He has <u>freckles</u> on his face.
3. The <u>sheriff</u> gave us a ticket.
4. I got his <u>autograph</u>.
5. May I use the <u>headphones</u>?

Additional Assessment

Standardized Test Master 3
Dictation Sentences, p. T37
Everyday Spelling CD-ROM

KIDSPELLING

Lee's uncle was uncomfortable from open-heart surgery. Lee wrote in his journal, *I wish Uncle Fred didn't have that "hard a tack."* Discuss the exact meaning of such phrases. For example, you might ask, "It's a heart problem, so what would make sense with *heart?*"

* See pp. T20 and T33 for test-study-test information.

DAY 1 CHALLENGE MASTER

CHALLENGE ■ 3

Challenge Words

freckles   sheriff   autograph   headphones   cuckoo clock

■ Write the Challenge Words in which two letters spell /f/. Write the letters that spell the sound after the word.

1. **headphones**   ph
2. **autograph**   ph
3. **sheriff**   ff

■ Write the Challenge Words in which two letters spell /k/. Write the letters that spell the sound after the word.

4. **freckles**   ck
5. **cuckoo clock**   ck

■ Sounds are all around. Write about the sounds you might hear from a cuckoo clock, a sheriff's car, or headphones. Use one or more Challenge Words.

Practice Masters, p. 15

DAY 1 HOME-SCHOOL MASTER

■ 3   HOME-SCHOOL ACTIVITIES   3 ■

■ **Relationships** Write a list word to complete each word group below.

1. country and Canada, state and **Kansas**
2. car and road, train and **track**
3. land and dog, ocean and **dolphin**
4. lunch and sandwich, breakfast and **muffin**
5. VCR and videotape, phonograph and **record**
6. long tail and monkey, long neck and **giraffe**
7. start and engine, stop and **brake**
8. nose and person, trunk and **elephant**

■ **How Do You Spell It?** Write each of the other list words on the line under its correct spelling.

/f/ spelled gh
9. **rough**
10. **enough**
11. **laughed**

/f/ spelled ph
12. **alphabet**
13. **photo**

/f/ spelled ff
14. **stiff**

/k/ speeled ck
15. **snack**
16. **attack**
17. **pocket**

/k/ spelled c
18. **care**
19. **cover**
20. **because**

Word Check 3

1. care
2. snack
3. attack
4. cover
5. pocket
6. Kansas
7. brake
8. track
9. because
10. record
11. stiff
12. dolphin
13. rough
14. elephant
15. muffin
16. enough
17. photo
18. laughed
19. alphabet
20. giraffe

Dear Parent,

Please check to see that your child has done this page correctly. Circle any misspelled words and help your child study them.

Tear off the Word Check before your child returns this page to class. Use it to help your child study.

Home-School Activities, p. 3

DAY 2 THINK AND PRACTICE MASTER

3 ■ THINK AND PRACTICE

care   because   brake   track   pocket
stiff   enough   laughed   photo   alphabet

■ **Context** Write the list word that completes each sentence.

1. Maria **laughed** when I told her my newest joke.
2. I lost my key because of a hole in my **pocket**.
3. Jake did not have a **care** in the world.
4. Do you have **enough** money to buy a ticket?
5. Tori pulled hard on the **brake** to stop the wagon.
6. We stood clear of the **track** as the train pulled in.
7. The bread is dry **because** Dad baked it too long.
8. Kieran is only two, but he knows the letters of the **alphabet**.
9. My jeans were so **stiff** that I could not sit down!
10. Aunt Kate took a **photo** of the whole family.

■ **Classifying** Write the list word that belongs in each group.

11. camera, film, **photo**
12. train, rails, **track**
13. rigid, unbending, **stiff**
14. smiled, giggled, **laughed**
15. car, stop, **brake**
16. worry, concern, **care**

STRATEGIC SPELLING: Seeing Meaning Connections

careless   careful   caring

17. Write a list word that is related to the words above. **care**

Write the words that fit the definitions.

18. done with thought   19. feeling concern about   20. not watching out
    careful   **caring**   **careless**

Practice Masters, p. 16

DAY 2 EXTRA PRACTICE MASTER

EXTRA PRACTICE ■ 3

Word List

care   because   brake   track   pocket
stiff   enough   laughed photo   alphabet
cover   record   Kansas   snack   attack
muffin giraffe   rough   dolphin elephant

■ **Characters** Use a list word to help identify each person or animal below.

1. an ___: "I always have to carry my own trunk."
2. a farmer in ___: "It's kind of corny."
3. a ___ coach: "I seem to run around in circles."
4. a ___ repair mechanic: "There's no stopping me!"
5. a ___: "My head is swimming."
6. a ___ developer: "I have nothing negative to say."
7. a clerk at a ___ bar: "It's a piece of cake."
8. a ___ producer: "It is music to my ears."
9. a ___ maker: "It's crummy."
10. a ___: "I'm sick of sticking my neck out."

1. **elephant**
2. **Kansas**
3. **track**
4. **brake**
5. **dolphin**
6. **photo**
7. **snack**
8. **record**
9. **muffin**
10. **giraffe**

■ **Context** Write the list word that completes each sentence.

11. That's **enough** potato salad for me.
12. My little sister is learning the **alphabet**.
13. They **laughed** so hard at the movie that their sides hurt.
14. I was **stiff** and sore after my fall.
15. The power is off **because** of the violent storm.
16. The high winds make the lake **rough**.
17. **Cover** the baby with a blanket.
18. Do you have any change in your **pocket**?
19. The general planned to **attack** the enemy at dawn.
20. Sue loves the rain and does not **care** if she gets wet.

Practice Masters, p. 17

22C

TECHNOLOGY AND VISUAL SUPPORT	 Use Audiotape A, Side 1, Lesson 3  Use Proofreading and Writing Transparency 3	 For additional practice use *Everyday Spelling* Game Software, Lesson 3	 Additional resources on *Everyday Spelling* CD-ROM: proofreading and writing, modified list and challenge words, auditory test

DAY 3 SECOND LANGUAGE SUPPORT MASTER

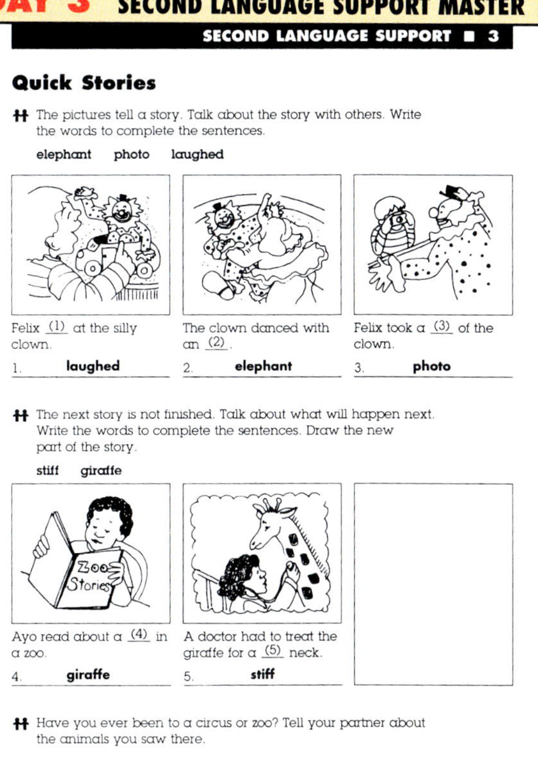

SECOND LANGUAGE SUPPORT ■ 3

Quick Stories

The pictures tell a story. Talk about the story with others. Write the words to complete the sentences.

elephant   photo   laughed

Felix __(1)__ at the silly clown.
1. **laughed**

The clown danced with an __(2)__.
2. **elephant**

Felix took a __(3)__ of the clown.
3. **photo**

The next story is not finished. Talk about what will happen next. Write the words to complete the sentences. Draw the new part of the story.

stiff   giraffe

Ayo read about a __(4)__ in a zoo.
4. **giraffe**

A doctor had to treat the giraffe for a __(5)__ neck.
5. **stiff**

Have you ever been to a circus or zoo? Tell your partner about the animals you saw there.

Second Language Support, p. 29

DAY 3 WRITING ACTIVITY MASTER

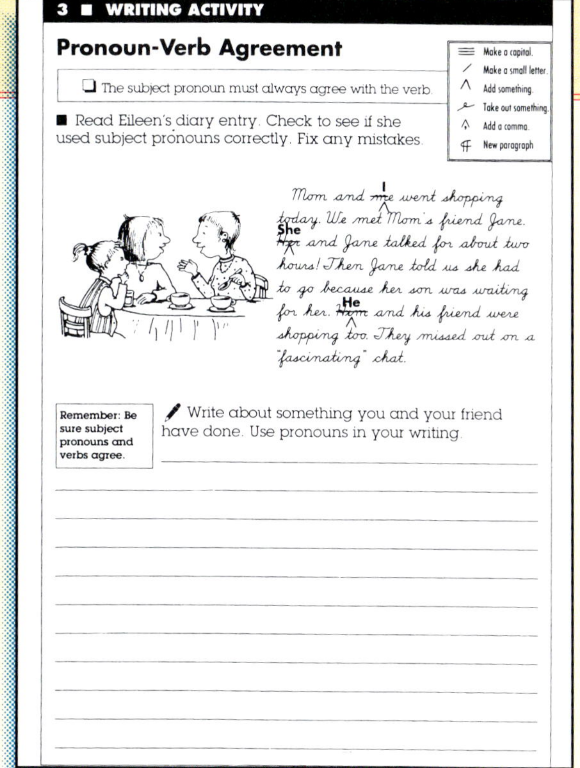

3 ■ WRITING ACTIVITY

Pronoun-Verb Agreement

The subject pronoun must always agree with the verb.

Read Eileen's diary entry. Check to see if she used subject pronouns correctly. Fix any mistakes.

= Make a capital.
/ Make a small letter.
∧ Add something.
⌁ Take out something.
∧ Add a comma.
¶ New paragraph.

Mom and I went shopping today. We met Mom's friend Jane. She and Jane talked for about two hours! Then Jane told us she had to go because her son was waiting for her. He and his friend were shopping too. They missed out on a "fascinating" chat.

Remember: Be sure subject pronouns and verbs agree.

Write about something you and your friend have done. Use pronouns in your writing.

Spelling and Writing, p. 6

DAY 4 REVIEW MASTER

3 ■ REVIEW

Word List

care	because	brake	track	pocket
stiff	enough	laughed	photo	alphabet
cover	record	Kansas	snack	attack
muffin	giraffe	rough	dolphin	elephant

Making Associations Write the list word that you might associate with each word or phrase below.

1. camera **photo**
2. letters **alphabet**
3. rock star **record**
4. long neck **giraffe**
5. popcorn **snack**
6. blueberry **muffin**
7. wheat fields **Kansas**
8. bumpy **rough**
9. fight **attack**
10. coins **pocket**

Draw Your Own Conclusions
Write the list word that matches each clue.

11. an animal with a trunk for a nose
12. this helps stop a bike
13. spies are "under" this
14. what you did when you heard a joke
15. what a starched shirt is
16. what you have had when you will not take any more
17. what to "take" when you cross the street
18. a word that starts an explanation

11. **elephant**
12. **brake**
13. **cover**
14. **laughed**
15. **stiff**
16. **enough**
17. **care**
18. **because**

Tongue Twisters Write the list word that would best complete each tongue twister.

19. Doxie Dachshund didn't doubt Dogface Doogie ___.
20. Two trash trucks tried to take two tramps to the ___.

19. **Dolphin**
20. **track**

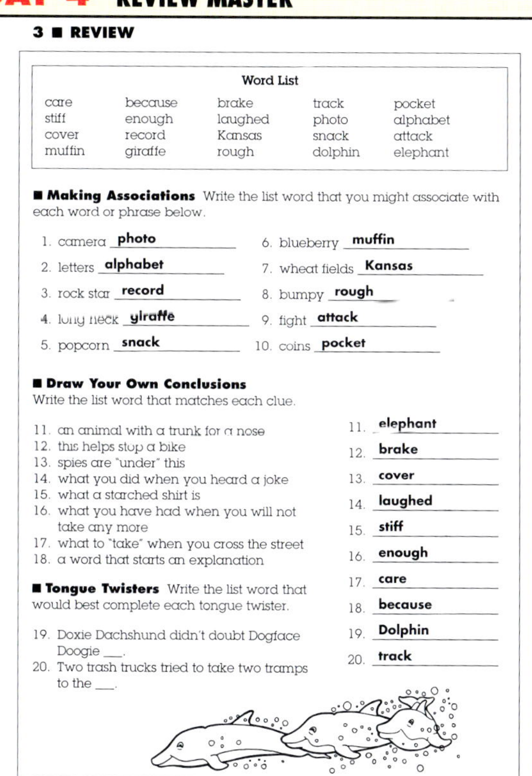

Practice Masters, p. 18

DAY 5 STANDARDIZED TEST MASTER

LESSON TEST ■ 3

Find the word in each group that is spelled correctly. Fill in the letter for the correct word on the answer strip.

Sample
a. visiter   c. vizitor
b. visetor   d. visitor   (a)(b)(c)●

1. a. Kansis   c. Kansas
   b. Kassas   d. kansas   1. (a)(b)●(d)
2. a. brak   c. braek
   b. brake   d. breake   2. (a)●(c)(d)
3. a. trak   c. track
   b. treke   d. tracke   3. (a)(b)●(d)
4. a. attack   c. attak
   b. attac   d. attack   4. (a)(b)(c)●
5. a. snack   c. snalt
   b. snank   d. snac   5. ●(b)(c)(d)
6. a. poket   c. pocet
   b. pocket   d. poctet   6. (a)●(c)(d)
7. a. kare   c. ker
   b. care   d. carr   7. (a)●(c)(d)
8. a. cuver   c. cover
   b. covir   d. covere   8. (a)(b)●(d)
9. a. becuse   c. becouse
   b. becaus   d. because   9. (a)(b)(c)●
10. a. reckord   c. rocord
    b. record   d. recerd   10. (a)●(c)(d)
11. a. anof   c. enough
    b. anough   d. enoug   11. (a)(b)●(d)
12. a. rugh   c. rough
    b. ruf   d. rofe   12. (a)(b)●(d)
13. a. laught   c. laghed
    b. laughed   d. laght   13. (a)●(c)(d)
14. a. elefaut   c. elephent
    b. elaphant   d. elephant   14. (a)(b)(c)●
15. a. stif   c. stife
    b. stiph   d. stiff   15. (a)(b)(c)●
16. a. dolphin   c. dofin
    b. dolfin   d. dophine   16. ●(b)(c)(d)
17. a. mufine   c. mufin
    b. muffin   d. muffen   17. (a)●(c)(d)
18. a. foto   c. fotoe
    b. photow   d. photo   18. (a)(b)(c)●
19. a. alfabet   c. alfabit
    b. alphabet   d. alphbet   19. (a)●(c)(d)
20. a. girafe   c. giraffe
    b. giraff   d. girrafe   20. (a)(b)●(d)

Practice for Standardized Tests, p. 3

22D

LESSON 3

INTRODUCTION

Phonics

Consonant sounds /k/ and /f/ Write /k/ and /f/ on the board. Have students pronounce each list word and write it in the appropriate column. Have students discuss patterns they notice in the spellings.

MEETING THE NEEDS OF ALL STUDENTS

Modified List

Practice Students studying only the high-frequency words in the top box write two words with /k/ spelled **c**, two words with /f/ spelled **ph**, three words with /k/ spelled **k** or **ck**, and three words with /f/ spelled **ff** or **gh**.

Kinesthetic Learners

Hold Up Have students write the letters **c, ck, ff, gh,** and **ph** on index cards. Pronounce the words with /k/. Have students hold up the card that shows the /k/ spelling for each word. Repeat with /f/.

Additional Practice

Challenge Master 3
Home-School Master 3
Audiotape A, Side 1

Word List

1. care
2. because
3. cover
4. record
5. brake
6. Kansas
7. track
8. pocket
9. snack
10. attack
11. photo
12. alphabet
13. dolphin
14. elephant
15. stiff
16. muffin
17. giraffe
18. enough
19. laughed
20. rough

CHALLENGE!

cuckoo clock
freckles
sheriff
autograph
headphones

22

■ INTRODUCTION

Consonant Sounds /k/ and /f/

SPELLING FOCUS

Usually the sound /k/ is spelled **c**, **k**, or **ck**: <u>c</u>are, bra<u>k</u>e, tra<u>ck</u>. The sound /f/ can be spelled **ff**, **gh**, or **ph**: sti<u>ff</u>, lau<u>gh</u>ed, <u>ph</u>oto.

■ **STUDY** Say each word. Then read the sentence.

1. care — Parents **care** about their children.
2. because ✻ — I fell asleep **because** I was tired.
3. brake — You use the **brake** to stop a car.
4. track — Runners often use this **track**.
5. pocket — Put the quarter in your **pocket**.
6. stiff — The leather boots are new and **stiff**.
7. enough ✻ — Have you had **enough** to eat?
8. laughed — The audience **laughed** at the jokes.
9. photo — He took a **photo** of his family.
10. alphabet — The **alphabet** has 26 letters.

11. cover — Use a quilt to **cover** the bed.
12. record — I found an old phonograph **record**.
13. Kansas — **Kansas** is a state in the Midwest.
14. snack — An apple is my after-school **snack**.
15. attack — The enemy will **attack** at dawn.
16. muffin — She bought a blueberry **muffin**.
17. giraffe — A **giraffe** has a long neck.
18. rough — The road is **rough** and rocky.
19. dolphin — A **dolphin** is not a fish.
20. elephant — He rode on the big, gray **elephant**.

■ **PRACTICE** Sort the words by writing
- four words with **c**
- two words with **k**
- four words with **ck**
- four words with **ph**
- three words with **ff**
- three words with **gh**

Order of words in each group may vary.

■ **WRITE** Choose ten words to write in sentences.
Sentences will vary.

✻ **WATCH OUT FOR FREQUENTLY MISSPELLED WORDS!**

THINK AND PRACTICE ■

POETRY IN MOTION   Complete the poem by writing list words.

Sitting by the TV eating a (1).
Watching a train smoking down the (2).
Energetic engineer pulling on the (3).
The gear is (4), so it doesn't take.
I (5) at his antics, sure enough.
Stopping that train was going to be (6).
Cow on the track without a (7).
Train finally stopped without a second to spare.

CLASSIFYING   Write the list word that fits in each group.

8. snapshot, picture, ___
9. Iowa, Nebraska, ___
10. pouch, clothes, ___
11. tape, CD, ___
12. letters, *a* to *z*, ___
13. set upon, fight, ___
14. roll, cupcake, ___
15. since, on account of, ___
16. plenty, full, ___

WHO AM I?   Write the list word naming each speaker.

17. "I love to swim and dive. I'm a ___**dolphin**___."

18. "My sore throats are endless. I'm a ___**giraffe**___."

19. "I fill my trunk with water. I'm an ___**elephant**___."

1. **snack**
2. **track**
3. **brake**
4. **stiff**
5. **laughed**
6. **rough**
7. **care**
8. **photo**
9. **Kansas**
10. **pocket**
11. **record**
12. **alphabet**
13. **attack**
14. **muffin**
15. **because**
16. **enough**

cover
scover
verlet

20. Write a list word that is related to the words in the box.   ___**cover**___

Write words from the box that fit the definitions.

21. to find out   22. to get back a lost item   23. a covering for a bed

___**discover**___   ___**recover**___   ___**coverlet**___

THINK AND PRACTICE

Poetry in Motion
Using a Dictionary Students may have to look up the words *gear* and *antics*.

MEETING THE NEEDS OF ALL STUDENTS

Modified List
Review Students studying high-frequency words complete Think and Practice Master 3.

Bilingual/ESL
Who Am I? Have ESL students look for the three animal names from the word list in a picture dictionary. They can then match each animal to its clue.

Auditory Learners
Poetry in Motion To help students who have difficulty with rhyming words, ask volunteers to identify the list words that rhyme. Write those words on the board and focus students on the rhyming parts.

Additional Practice

Think and Practice Master 3
Extra Practice Master 3
Everyday Spelling **CD-ROM**
Everyday Spelling **Game Software**

LESSON 3

- Proofread a Self-Portrait
- Proofreading Tip: Personal Pronouns
- Create a Self-Portrait
- ✓ Cooperative Midweek Test

DAILY SPELLING REVIEW

How does a *caterpiller* turn into a *butterfly*?

caterpillar   *butterfly*

● Core   ○ Optional   ✓ Assessment

PROOFREADING AND WRITING

Usage

Personal Pronouns

Explain that *I* is used when you're telling about something you do; *me* is used when you're telling about something done to you or for you. Students can proofread a recent piece of personal writing for correct usage of *I* and *me*.

MEETING THE NEEDS OF ALL STUDENTS

Modified List

Proofreading Students studying high-frequency words complete this page or the proofreading activity on the *Everyday Spelling* CD-ROM.

Enrichment

Creating a Self-Portrait

Suggest that students use pictures and words in a mural about a real or an imaginary experience.

> **Additional Practice**
>
> **Hardbound Book Master 3**
> **Second Language Master 3**
> **Writing Mini-Lesson Master 3**
> **Writing Activity Master 3**
> **Proofreading Transparency 3**
> *Everyday Spelling* CD-ROM

■ PROOFREADING AND WRITING

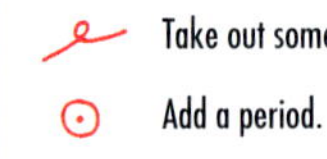

PROOFREAD A SELF-PORTRAIT

Julio's class is drawing self-portraits and writing short descriptions of them. Find four misspelled words and one incorrect pronoun in Julio's writing. Correct them.

PROOFREADING TIP

Would you ever say "Me go to the zoo"? Well, that's really what Julio did in his sentence. Drop "Mom and ..." to be sure the personal pronoun is correct.

CREATE A SELF-PORTRAIT

Draw a picture of yourself doing something you enjoy. Write a description of where you are and what you're doing. Use some of your list words.

Responses will vary. Self-portrait should include some list words.

Word List

care	stiff
snack	dolphin
attack	rough
cover	elephant
pocket	muffin
Kansas	enough
brake	photo
track	laughed
because	alphabet
record	giraffe

Personal Words

1. **Words will**
2. **vary.**

24

VOCABULARY BUILDING

Review

DEFINING WORDS Write the boxed word that means the same as the underlined words.

care	stiff
because	enough
brake	laughed
track	photo
pocket	alphabet

1. After the accident, my neck was <u>hard to move</u>.
2. At age three, Mira can already recite the <u>letters of the English language arranged in their usual order</u>.
3. Many people <u>are concerned</u> about the future of our planet.
4. Do we have <u>a sufficient amount</u> of food for the party?
5. I went shopping <u>for the reason that</u> I needed new shoes.
6. My best <u>picture made with a camera</u> is the one of my dog.
7. I ran five laps around the race <u>course for running or racing</u>.
8. Della slammed on her <u>device for slowing down the motion of wheels or vehicles</u> pedal to avoid hitting the ducks.
9. Mr. Carter <u>made happy sounds and movements</u> when we explained what had happened on our way to school.
10. I put my lunch money into my <u>pouch sewed into clothing for carrying small items</u>, and now my money is gone.

1. **stiff**
2. **alphabet**
3. **care**
4. **enough**
5. **because**
6. **photo**
7. **track**
8. **brake**
9. **laughed**
10. **pocket**

Multicultural *Connection*

LANGUAGES Julio saw these signs at the zoo. Each animal is named in English, Swahili, Spanish, and Japanese.

Complete each sentence. Write the missing word in a different language each time.

1. Count the eight legs of the ___.
2. Can you tell the difference between an alligator and a ___?
3. The roaring of the ___ scared the baby.
4. The ___ can reach the treetop.

1. **a word from column 4**
2. **a word from column 3**
3. **a word from column 2**
4. **a word from column 1**

VOCABULARY BUILDING

Literature Connection

Street Rhymes A fun resource for extending students' knowledge of words from other languages is *Street Rhymes from Around the World,* edited by Jane Yolen (Boyds Mills Press, 1992).

MEETING THE NEEDS OF ALL STUDENTS

Modified List

Review Students studying high-frequency words complete this page.

Challenge

Money Around the World

The dollar is the basic unit of money in the United States. Have students use an encyclopedia to find the names of the basic units of money in Ecuador, Japan, Kenya, and France. Suggest they include the names as part of a chart called *Money Around the World.*

Additional Practice

Review Master 3
Standardized Test Master 3
Everyday Spelling CD-ROM

LESSON

4

Generalization

Spelling Focus: When **-ed** or **-ing** is added to a base word, its spelling may change.

● Core　　○ Optional　　✓ Assessment

DAILY PLAN	CORE OBJECTIVES	NOTES

DAY 1 Introduction

✓ Pretest and Self-Check, p. 26B
● Spelling Focus and Word List, p. 26
○ Challenge Words, p. 26
○ Challenge Master 4
○ Home-School Master 4

✓ ▪ Take and self-check Pretest
▪ Spell words that end with **-ed** or **-ing;** classify and write the list words

DAY 2 Think and Practice

● Context Clues; Add Endings, p. 27
● Strategic Spelling:
　Building New Words, p. 27
○ Think and Practice Master 4
○ Extra Practice Master 4
○ Cross-Curricular Lesson: Introduce, p. 212

▪ Complete practice activities for words ending in **-ed** or **-ing**
▪ Apply spelling rules for adding **-ed** and **-ing** to additional words

DAY 3 Proofreading and Writing

● Proofread a Blurb, p. 28
● Proofreading Tip: Handwriting, p. 28
● Write a Blurb, p. 28
✓ Cooperative Midweek Test
○ Hardbound Book Master 4
○ Writing Mini-Lesson Master 4
○ Writing Activity Master 4
○ Second Language Support Master 4

▪ Proofread for spelling and handwriting errors
▪ Integrate spelling and writing in a personal writing response
✓ ▪ Take and check midweek test

DAY 4 Vocabulary Building

● Review: Words in Context, p. 29
● Using a Thesaurus: Entry Words, p. 29
○ Cross-Curricular Lesson: Follow-Up, p. 212
○ Review Master 4

▪ Complete review activity for words ending in **-ed** and **-ing**
▪ Find an entry word in a thesaurus and list its synonyms

DAY 5 Assessment

✓ Posttest, p. 26B
○ Standardized Test Master 4

✓ ▪ Take Posttest

Cross-Curricular Lessons

Use the Spelling Focus (**-ed** and **-ing** endings) to introduce the Reading lesson, *Tales of Courage*, page 212, or choose a lesson that correlates with a topic you're currently teaching.

MEETING THE NEEDS OF ALL STUDENTS

The Word List

For students studying 20 words, assign pages 26–29 and Extra Practice and Review masters.

Modified List For students studying 10 words, modify Practice on page 26, and assign Think and Practice Master 4 and pages 28–29.

Challenge For students studying 25 words, assign pages 26–29, Challenge, Extra Practice, and Review masters.

Bilingual/ESL

As Vietnamese does not contain suffixes, students may be confused by the **-ed** and **-ing** endings. They will benefit from extra help in understanding suffixes.

Personal Words

Students add to Personal Words lists by looking at work in their writing portfolios and words they want to remember from their reading.

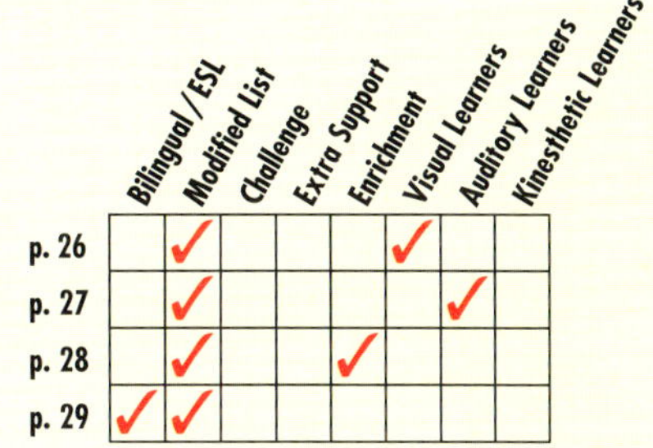

	Bilingual/ESL	Modified List	Challenge	Extra Support	Enrichment	Visual Learners	Auditory Learners	Kinesthetic Learners
p. 26		✓				✓		
p. 27		✓					✓	
p. 28		✓			✓			
p. 29	✓	✓						

ASSESSMENT*

Pretest

Read the underlined word, read the sentence, and then repeat the underlined word. Guide students in self-correcting their pretests and correcting any misspellings.

1. What happened at school?
2. What is happening here?
3. Rob opened the candy box.
4. Yolanda is opening the door.
5. Alicia danced on the stage.
6. Do you like dancing?
7. Jan and I studied science.
8. Tina is studying a lot.
9. Coach stopped the game.
10. He is stopping at our house.
11. The dog chased a squirrel.
12. The boys were chasing us.
13. He worried about the time.
14. Dad is always worrying.
15. Pat dried her hair outside.
16. The plants are drying up.
17. The thief robbed the store.
18. Were they robbing a bank?
19. Diane slipped on the ice.
20. He is slipping his shoes on.

Posttest

Read aloud the sentences below. These sentences may be used for dictation.

1. He stopped at the store.
2. What is happening today?
3. He opened the presents.
4. They are dancing together.
5. The train is stopping here.
6. She is opening a can.
7. We studied for the test.
8. What happened to him?
9. Our class is studying trees.
10. She danced in the play.
11. Mom is drying our clothes.
12. The man robbed a bank.
13. We were slipping on the wet grass.
14. Worrying will not help.
15. She dried the dishes.
16. He slipped on the ground.
17. Is the dog chasing a car?
18. They were robbing a store.
19. The cat chased its tail.
20. I am worried about her.

Challenge Words

1. They skied in the winter.
2. Skiing is a lot of fun.
3. He argued with his sister.
4. Why are they arguing?
5. What occurred last Tuesday?
6. A strange thing is occurring.

Additional Assessment

Standardized Test Master 4
Dictation Sentences, p. T37
Everyday Spelling CD-ROM

WHAT'S THE BIG IDEA?
In *Research in Action*, omitting the **e** accounted for almost 66% of the spelling errors with **-ed** at fourth grade. Remind students of this as they study this list. Suggest they check for this error in a piece of recent writing in their portfolios.

* See pp. T20 and T33 for test-study-test information.

LESSON 4

DAY 1 CHALLENGE MASTER

CHALLENGE ■ 4

Challenge Words

occurred	occurring	argued
arguing	skied	skiing

■ Write the Challenge Word which completes each sentence.

1. **Skiing** is Susan's favorite sport.
2. Last year, she **skied** in Colorado.
3. Every morning, the sisters **argued** about sharing their clothes.
4. This morning, they are **arguing** about a red sweater.
5. Sunset **occurred** at 5:45 P.M. last Friday.
6. This Friday, it will be **occurring** at 5:47 P.M.

■ Imagine skiing down a steep slope. What do you think it feels like? Describe the experience that you imagine. Use one or more Challenge Words.

Practice Masters, p. 19

DAY 1 HOME-SCHOOL MASTER

■ 4 HOME-SCHOOL ACTIVITIES 4 ■

Word Check 4
1. opened
2. opening
3. happened
4. happening
5. chased
6. chasing
7. danced
8. dancing
9. worried
10. worrying
11. studied
12. studying
13. dried
14. drying
15. stopped
16. stopping
17. slipped
18. slipping
19. robbed
20. robbing

Dear Parent,
Please check to see that your child has done this page correctly. Circle any misspelled words and help your child study them.

Tear off the Word Check before your child returns this page to class. Use it to help your child study.

■ **Word Forms** Write the list word that means the same as each word or phrase below.

1. unlocked **opened**
2. occurring **happening**
3. running after **chasing**
4. bothered **worried**
5. stealing **robbing**
6. falling **slipping**
7. reviewed **studied**
8. waltzed **danced**

■ **Add Endings** Write the list word that you form by adding the ending to each word below.

-ed
9. dry **dried**
10. slip **slipped**
11. chase **chased**
12. rob **robbed**
13. stop **stopped**
14. happen **happened**

-ing
15. open **opening**
16. stop **stopping**
17. worry **worrying**
18. dance **dancing**
19. dry **drying**
20. study **studying**

Home-School Activities, p. 4

DAY 2 THINK AND PRACTICE MASTER

4 ■ THINK AND PRACTICE

happened	happening	opened	opening	danced
dancing	studied	studying	stopped	stopping

■ **Context Clues** Use the list words to finish the sentences.

1. The student **studied** for the test.
2. Five ballerinas **danced** onto the stage.
3. My aunt is **studying** to be a doctor.
4. My watch **stopped** at two o'clock.
5. I saw you **opening** my box of bugs!
6. What is **happening** over there?

■ **Word Forms** Write a list word with the same ending as the underlined ending.

7. At the party, there was dining and **dancing**.
8. Are you playing games or **studying** your lessons?
9. A cat walked in when the door was **opened**.
10. We laughed when we saw what had **happened**.
11. He was planning on **stopping** in the next town.
12. I worried about passing, so I **studied** hard.

STRATEGIC SPELLING: Building New Words
Use the rules you learned to complete the chart.

Base word	Add -ed	Add -ing
13. scrub	**scrubbed**	**scrubbing**
14. cause	**caused**	**causing**
15. cry	**cried**	**crying**

Practice Masters, p. 20

DAY 2 EXTRA PRACTICE MASTER

EXTRA PRACTICE ■ 4

Word List

happened	happening	opened	opening	danced
dancing	studied	studying	stopped	stopping
chased	chasing	worried	worrying	dried
drying	robbed	robbing	slipped	slipping

■ **Word Forms** Complete each sentence by writing a form of the word that is in parentheses at the end of the sentence.

1. I ___ all day for the test. (study)
2. Everybody else was ___, too. (study)
3. The ice skaters were ___ on the ice. (slip)
4. I almost ___ and fell myself. (slip)
5. The dog ___ the cat outside. (chase)
6. Now they are ___ each other all across the lawn. (chase)
7. It seemed as if nothing was ___ on that boring day. (happen)
8. Finally, something ___ when the storm hit suddenly. (happen)
9. Two thieves ___ the video store last night. (rob)
10. While they were ___ it, the police sneaked in on them. (rob)
11. Cora ___ the dishes after her brother washed them. (dry)
12. Cora hates ___ dishes. (dry)
13. All the traffic has ___ coming up the steep hill. (stop)
14. The police are ___ people because power lines are down. (stop)
15. Reggie watched the bedroom door slowly ___. (open)
16. Suddenly it ___ wide and his dog Tank came in. (open)
17. Most people at the party were ___. (dance)
18. Some people ___ for hours and became tired. (dance)
19. Last year she ___ about her grandfather's health. (worry)
20. Now he is fine, so she can stop ___. (worry)

1. **studied**
2. **studying**
3. **slipping**
4. **slipped**
5. **chased**
6. **chasing**
7. **happening**
8. **happened**
9. **robbed**
10. **robbing**
11. **dried**
12. **drying**
13. **stopped**
14. **stopping**
15. **opening**
16. **opened**
17. **dancing**
18. **danced**
19. **worried**
20. **worrying**

Practice Masters, p. 21

<table>
<tr><td rowspan="2">TECHNOLOGY AND VISUAL SUPPORT</td><td> Use Audiotape A, Side 1, Lesson 4</td><td rowspan="2"> For additional practice use Everyday Spelling Game Software, Lesson 4</td><td rowspan="2"> Additional resources on Everyday Spelling CD-ROM: proofreading and writing, modified list and challenge words, auditory test</td></tr>
<tr><td> Use Proofreading and Writing Transparency 4</td></tr>
</table>

DAY 3 SECOND LANGUAGE SUPPORT MASTER

4 ■ SECOND LANGUAGE SUPPORT

About Me

📖 Read what Mina wrote about herself.

> I have been _studying_ hard for my first math test at my new school. I was _worried_ that I might not do well. Today something good _happened_. I took the test and I got a good grade!

1.	3,889 + 1,650 5,539	2.	5,324 + 3,485 8,809
3.	8,722 − 2,199 6,523	4.	7,570 − 4,935 2,635

✏ Write some spelling words that tell about you. Then draw a picture of your ideas.

Words will vary. ________________

✏ Write about your picture.

Answers will vary.

____
____
____

🙌 Look over your paper. Talk with a partner about your picture and writing.

Second Language Support, p. 30

DAY 3 WRITING ACTIVITY MASTER

4 ■ WRITING ACTIVITY

Vivid Details

▭ Use vivid details to grab the reader's attention

≡	Make a capital.
/	Make a small letter
∧	Add something.
﹂	Take out something
⊙	Add a period.
¶	New paragraph

■ Read the blurbs about the movie *Home Alone.* Can you improve them by using more vivid words?

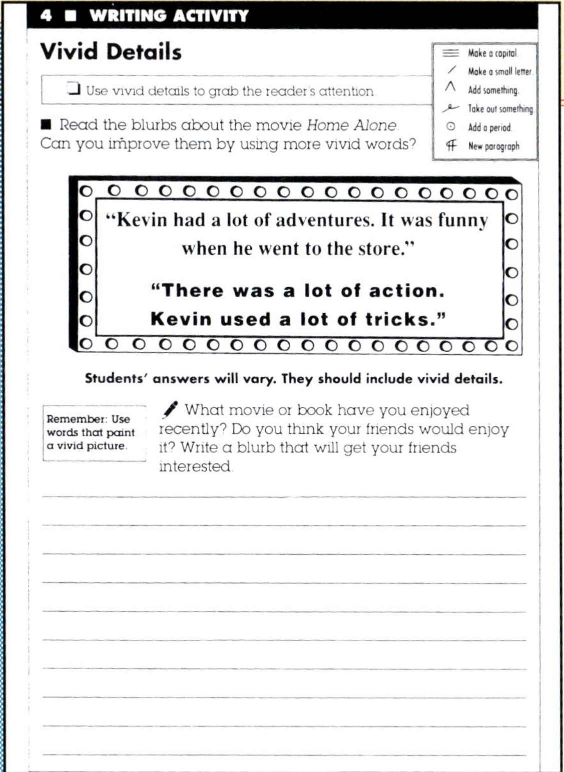

Students' answers will vary. They should include vivid details.

Remember: Use words that paint a vivid picture.

✏ What movie or book have you enjoyed recently? Do you think your friends would enjoy it? Write a blurb that will get your friends interested.

Spelling and Writing, p. 8

DAY 4 REVIEW MASTER

4 ■ REVIEW

Word List

happened	happening	opened	opening	danced
dancing	studied	studying	stopped	stopping
chased	chasing	worried	worrying	dried
drying	robbed	robbing	slipped	slipping

■ **Rhyme Time** Write the list word that rhymes with each word below.

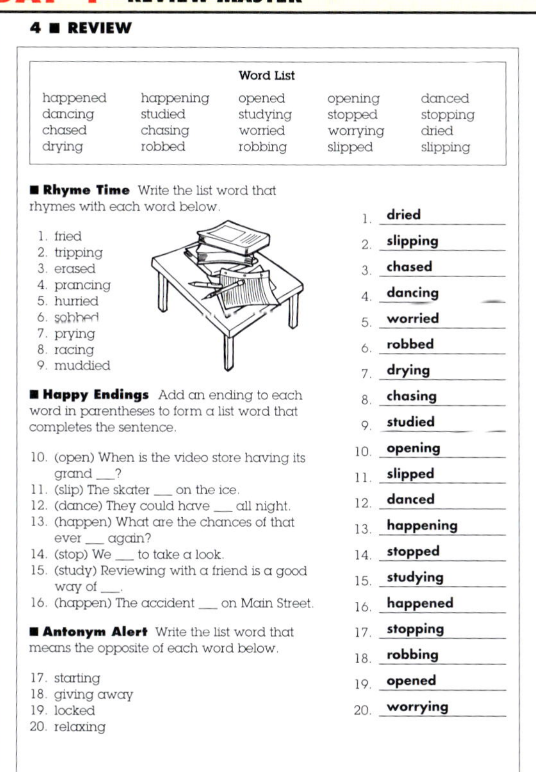

1. fried
2. tripping
3. erased
4. prancing
5. hurried
6. sobbed
7. prying
8. racing
9. muddled

1. **dried**
2. **slipping**
3. **chased**
4. **dancing**
5. **worried**
6. **robbed**
7. **drying**
8. **chasing**
9. **studied**

■ **Happy Endings** Add an ending to each word in parentheses to form a list word that completes the sentence.

10. (open) When is the video store having its grand ___?
11. (slip) The skater ___ on the ice.
12. (dance) They could have ___ all night.
13. (happen) What are the chances of that ever ___ again?
14. (stop) We ___ to take a look.
15. (study) Reviewing with a friend is a good way of ___.
16. (happen) The accident ___ on Main Street.

10. **opening**
11. **slipped**
12. **danced**
13. **happening**
14. **stopped**
15. **studying**
16. **happened**

■ **Antonym Alert** Write the list word that means the opposite of each word below.

17. starting
18. giving away
19. locked
20. relaxing

17. **stopping**
18. **robbing**
19. **opened**
20. **worrying**

Practice Masters, p. 22

DAY 5 STANDARDIZED TEST MASTER

4 ■ LESSON TEST

■ Find the word in each group that is spelled correctly. Fill in the letter for the correct word on the answer strip.

Sample:

a. visiter	c. vizitor	Ⓐ Ⓑ Ⓒ ●
b. visetor	d. visitor	

1. a. opend	c. opened	1. Ⓐ Ⓑ ● Ⓓ
b. opned	d. oppend	
2. a. chast	c. chaced	2. Ⓐ ● Ⓒ Ⓓ
b. chased	d. chasted	
3. a. stuting	c. studing	3. Ⓐ ● Ⓒ Ⓓ
b. studying	d. steding	
4. a. danceing	c. dancing	4. Ⓐ Ⓑ ● Ⓓ
b. dansing	d. dancen	
5. a. stopping	c. stoping	5. ● Ⓑ Ⓒ Ⓓ
b. stoppin	d. stopeing	
6. a. happened	c. happend	6. ● Ⓑ Ⓒ Ⓓ
b. hapend	d. happed	
7. a. openin	c. oppening	7. Ⓐ Ⓑ Ⓒ ●
b. openning	d. opening	
8. a. studyed	c. sutdid	8. Ⓐ Ⓑ Ⓒ ●
b. stueyded	d. studied	
9. a. woried	c. worryed	9. Ⓐ ● Ⓒ Ⓓ
b. worried	d. weried	
10. a. robbert	c. robbed	10. Ⓐ Ⓑ ● Ⓓ
b. robbid	d. robbet	
11. a. dring	c. drying	11. Ⓐ Ⓑ Ⓒ ●
b. drieing	d. dryying	
12. a. stoped	c. stopt	12. Ⓐ Ⓑ Ⓒ ●
b. stoppet	d. stopped	
13. a. sliping	c. slipeing	13. Ⓐ ● Ⓒ Ⓓ
b. slipping	d. slippeing	
14. a. robbering	c. robben	14. Ⓐ ● Ⓒ Ⓓ
b. robbing	d. robbinng	
15. a. danst	c. danced	15. Ⓐ Ⓑ ● Ⓓ
b. dansed	d. danct	
16. a. happening	c. happing	16. ● Ⓑ Ⓒ Ⓓ
b. hapining	d. happining	
17. a. dryed	c. dreyed	17. Ⓐ Ⓑ Ⓒ ●
b. dryied	d. dried	
18. a. chaseing	c. chacing	18. Ⓐ ● Ⓒ Ⓓ
b. chasing	d. chaesing	
19. a. sliped	c. slipped	19. Ⓐ Ⓑ ● Ⓓ
b. sleped	d. slep	
20. a. worring	c. worring	20. Ⓐ ● Ⓒ Ⓓ
b. worrying	d. worryiing	

Practice for Standardized Tests, p. 4

DAY 1 Introduce

✓ Pretest and Self-Check
● Spelling Focus and Word List
○ Challenge Words
○ Modified List

DAILY SPELLING REVIEW

Rosa *dosen't* want the dog in her *wagen.*

doesn't   *wagon*

● Core   ○ Optional   ✓ Assessment

INTRODUCTION

Word Structure

Adding Endings Let students decide the best way to study words with **-ed** and **-ing.** For example, some learners may make up a chant: "Drop the **e** when you are dancing."

MEETING THE NEEDS OF ALL STUDENTS

Modified List

Practice Students studying only the high-frequency words in the top box write
- two words in which the final **e** is dropped
- five words with no spelling changes
- two words in which the final consonant is doubled
- one word in which the **y** changes to **i**

Visual Learners

Decorated Letters Visual learners may write the list words using decorated letters.

> **Additional Practice**
>
> **Challenge Master 4**
> **Home-School Master 4**
> **Audiotape A, Side 1**

1. **danced**
2. **dancing**
3. **chased**
4. **chasing**
5. **happened**
6. **happening**
7. **opened**
8. **opening**
9. **studying**
10. **worrying**
11. **drying**
12. **stopped**
13. **stopping**
14. **robbed**
15. **robbing**
16. **slipped**
17. **slipping**
18. **studied**
19. **worried**
20. **dried**

CHALLENGE!

skied	skiing
argued	arguing
occurred	occurring

■ INTRODUCTION

Adding -ed and -ing

SPELLING FOCUS

Here are four things to remember when adding **-ed** and **-ing:**
- Some base words are not changed: **happen, happened, happening.**
- In words that end with **consonant-e**, the e is dropped: **dance, danced, dancing.**
- In words that end in **y**, the **y** is changed to **i** when adding **-ed**, but kept when adding **-ing**: **study, studied, studying.**
- In one-syllable words that end with **consonant-vowel-consonant**, the final consonant is doubled: **stop, stopped, stopping.**

■ **STUDY** Look at each base word. Notice whether the spelling changes when **-ed** and **-ing** are added.

happen	1. *happened* ✳	2. *happening*	
open	3. *opened* ✳	4. *opening*	
dance	5. *danced*	6. *dancing*	
study	7. *studied*	8. *studying*	
stop	9. *stopped*	10. *stopping*	
chase	11. *chased*	12. *chasing*	
worry	13. *worried*	14. *worrying*	
dry	15. *dried*	16. *drying*	
rob	17. *robbed*	18. *robbing*	
slip	19. *slipped*	20. *slipping*	

■ **PRACTICE** Sort the list words by writing
- four words in which the final **e** is dropped
- seven words with no spelling changes
- six words in which the final consonant is doubled
- three words in which **y** changes to **i**

Order of words in each group may vary.

■ **WRITE** Choose three words to write a paragraph about a memorable event in your school or community. **Paragraphs will vary.**

✳ **WATCH OUT FOR FREQUENTLY MISSPELLED WORDS!**

THINK AND PRACTICE

CONTEXT CLUES   Use list words to finish the sentences.

1. The party-goers were **dancing** to the music.
2. The thief **robbed** the man of his wallet.
3. Is she **opening** her present now?
4. Dad was very **worried** when I was late.
5. The clown **slipped** on a banana peel.
6. We washed and **dried** the dishes.
7. I was **studying** for my history test all night.
8. The lion **chased** the monkey up a tree.
9. What **happened** to the injured ape?
10. We **stopped** talking to listen to the bird sing.

Did You Know?
The fastest rate ever measured for tap **dancing** is 32 taps per second.

ADD ENDINGS   Complete each group with a list word.

11. worry, worried, ___
12. rob, robbed, ___
13. slip, slipped, ___
14. chase, chased, ___
15. open, ___, opening
16. study, ___, studying
17. dry, dried, ___
18. happen, happened, ___
19. stop, stopped, ___
20. dance, ___, dancing

11. **worrying**
12. **robbing**
13. **slipping**
14. **chasing**
15. **opened**
16. **studied**
17. **drying**
18. **happening**
19. **stopping**
20. **danced**

Use the rules you learned to complete the chart.

Base word	Add -ed	Add -ing
21. scrub	scrubbed	scrubbing
22. cause	caused	causing
23. cry	cried	crying

LESSON 4

- ● Proofread a Blurb
- ● Proofreading Tip: Handwriting
- ● Write a Blurb
- ✓ Cooperative Midweek Test

DAILY SPELLING REVIEW

Wont Jaime like her new *cloths?*

Won't   *clothes*

● Core   ○ Optional   ✓ Assessment

PROOFREADING AND WRITING

Handwriting

Partner Proofing Suggest that partners exchange a piece of recent writing and check each other's work. They can point out illegible letters that make the handwriting difficult to read.

MEETING THE NEEDS OF ALL STUDENTS

Modified List

Proofreading Students studying high-frequency words complete this page or the proofreading activity on the *Everyday Spelling* CD-ROM.

Enrichment

Personal Writing Encourage students to start a logbook of blurbs about their favorite books, movies, and music. Point out that it is a fun, quick way to keep a personal record.

Additional Practice

Hardbound Book Master 4
Second Language Master 4
Writing Mini-Lesson 4
Writing Activity Master 4
Proofreading Transparency 4
***Everyday Spelling* CD-ROM**

■ PROOFREADING AND WRITING

═	Make a capital.
/	Make a small letter.
∧	Add something.
ℓ	Take out something
⊙	Add a period.
¶	New paragraph

PROOFREAD A BLURB   A **blurb** is a short, favorable description written on the jacket of a book or CD. The blurbs below were written about the book *Night of the Twisters*. Find four misspellings and two handwriting errors and write them correctly.

PROOFREADING TIP
Jodie knows how to spell the words, but her handwriting looks as though she doesn't. Not closing letters like **d** and **o** will really frustrate your reader.

"From the moment I *opened* opend this book I never *stopped* stopt reading it!" – Jodie

"Frightening things kept *happening* hapeneng. I *worried* worried about Dan and Art." – Dana

WRITE A BLURB   Write blurbs about two of the following: a favorite book, an enjoyable movie, or a good compact disc or tape. Try to use your list words.

Responses will vary. Blurbs should include list words.

Word List

opened	opening
happened	happening
chased	chasing
danced	dancing
worried	worrying
studied	studying
dried	drying
stopped	stopping
slipped	slipping
robbed	robbing

Personal Words

1. **Words will**
2. **vary.**

28

**

- Review: Words in Context
- Using a Thesaurus: Entry Words
- Cross-Curricular Lesson: Follow-Up

DAILY SPELLING REVIEW

That *squirel* is *bieng* a real pest.

squirrel   being

- ✓ Posttest
- ✓ Dictation Sentences
- Standardized Test Master 4
- ✓ Auditory Test on *Everyday Spelling* CD-ROM

VOCABULARY BUILDING ■

Review

WORDS IN CONTEXT Write the boxed words to complete Terry's story about a strange happening at a carnival.

happened	happening
opened	opening
danced	dancing
studied	studying
stopped	stopping

A strange event (1) on the night the carnival (2). After Darren and I bought our tickets, we couldn't help (3) to admire the bright lights, rides, exhibits, and games. Teenagers were (4) to rock music pouring from huge speakers. Children were eating the usual carnival treats. Suddenly, the carnival lights dimmed, the music (5), and the rides slowly came to a halt. "What's (6)?" Darron asked. I (7) his face and could see he was worried. "Look there!" a man shouted as he pointed at the sky. Darren and I peered upward through the (8) between two booths and saw a huge metallic object in the sky. We were (9) its unusual shape and lights that (10) in rhythmic patterns when the object took a sharp turn, shot upward, and disappeared. Then the lights shone brightly again, rides restarted, and everything was just as it had been before, except for one thing—the crowd had just witnessed the most amazing carnival act ever!

1. **happened**
2. **opened**
3. **stopping**
4. **dancing**
5. **stopped**
6. **happening**
7. **studied**
8. **opening**
9. **studying**
10. **danced**

Using a *Thesaurus*

ENTRY WORDS Imagine that you are writing about the time you attended a game played by your favorite sports team. Your team won, and the game was the best you had ever seen. You want to express the excitement you felt, but the word *exciting* does not seem quite strong enough to you. You can look up *exciting* in a thesaurus to find synonyms, or other words with similar meanings.

A thesaurus provides a list of **entry words** in alphabetical order. The Writer's Thesaurus on pages 296–309 of your spelling book shows the entry words in color and in large type at the left of the pages.

Find the entry word *worried* in your Writer's Thesaurus. Notice the three synonyms for *worried.* Write the synonyms.

1. **nervous**
2. **uneasy**
3. **anxious**

Order of answers may vary.

Literature Connection

Build a Synonym Bank

Ask students to contribute pairs of synonyms to the bank. Also, lists of synonyms can be found in books such as *The Reading Teacher's Book of Lists* (Third Edition) by Edward Fry et al. (Prentice-Hall, 1993).

MEETING THE NEEDS OF ALL STUDENTS

Modified List

Review Students studying high-frequency words complete this page.

Bilingual/ESL

Synonyms Nonnative speakers of English may have difficulty with the concept of synonyms. Help them collect pairs of synonyms in word or picture form on cards. These can be used to play games in which students match the pairs of synonyms.

Additional Practice

Review Master 4
Standardized Test Master 4
***Everyday Spelling* CD-ROM**

5

Generalization

Spelling Focus: When **-er** or **-est** is added to a base word, the spelling of the base word may change.

● Core ○ Optional ✓ Assessment

DAILY PLAN	CORE OBJECTIVES	NOTES

DAY 1 Introduction

✓● Pretest and Self-Check, p. 30B
● Spelling Focus and Word List, p. 30
○ Challenge Words, p. 30
○ Challenge Master 5
○ Home-School Master 5

✓ ▪ Take and self-check Pretest
▪ Spell words that end with **-er** or **-est;** classify and write the list words

DAY 2 Think and Practice

● Antonym Alert; Happy Endings, p. 31
● Strategic Spelling: *Building New Words,* p. 31
○ Think and Practice Master 5
○ Extra Practice Master 5
○ Cross-Curricular Lesson: Introduce, p. 216

▪ Complete practice activities for words with **-er** or **-est**
▪ Build new words with **-er** and **-est**

DAY 3 Proofreading and Writing

● Proofread an Invitation, p. 32
● Proofreading Tip: Comparisons, p. 32
● Write an Invitation, p. 32
✓ Cooperative Midweek Test
○ Hardbound Book Master 5
○ Writing Mini-Lesson Master 5
○ Writing Activity Master 5
○ Second Language Support Master 5

▪ Proofread for spelling and grammar errors
▪ Integrate spelling and writing in a personal writing response
✓ ▪ Take and check midweek test

DAY 4 Vocabulary Building

● Review: Analogies, p. 33
● Word Study: Exaggeration, p. 33
○ Cross-Curricular Lesson: Follow-Up, p. 216
○ Review Master 5

▪ Complete review activity for words that end with **-er** and **-est**
▪ Practice using exaggeration

Day 5 Assessment

✓ Posttest, p. 30B
○ Standardized Test Master 5

✓ ▪ Take Posttest

Cross-Curricular Lessons

Use the Spelling Focus (**-er** and **-est** endings) to introduce the Mathematics lesson, *Measurement*, page 216, or choose a lesson that correlates with a topic you're currently teaching.

MEETING THE NEEDS OF ALL STUDENTS

The Word List

For students studying 20 words, assign pages 30–33 and Extra Practice and Review masters.

Modified List For students studying 10 words, modify Practice on page 30, and assign Think and Practice Master 5 and pages 32–33.

Challenge For students studying 25 words, assign pages 30–33, Challenge, Extra Practice, and Review masters.

Bilingual/ESL

Chinese-speaking students may need extra help with adding suffixes, since suffixes do not exist in their native language.

Personal Words

Students add to Personal Words lists by looking at work in their writing portfolios and words they want to remember from their reading.

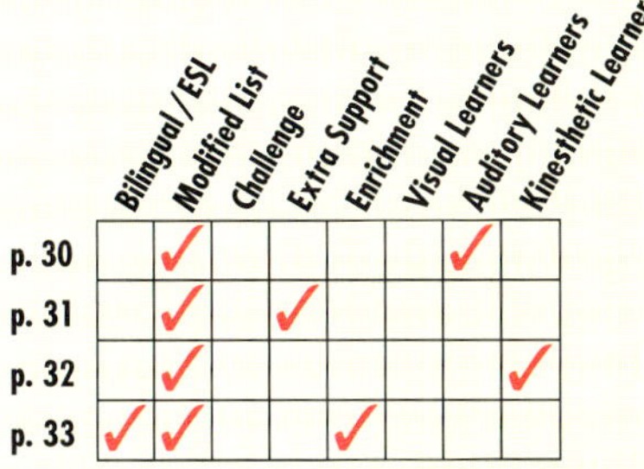

	Bilingual/ESL	Modified List	Challenge	Extra Support	Enrichment	Visual Learners	Auditory Learners	Kinesthetic Learners
p. 30		✓					✓	
p. 31		✓		✓				
p. 32		✓						✓
p. 33	✓	✓			✓			

ASSESSMENT*

Pretest

Read the underlined word, read the sentence, and then repeat the underlined word. Guide students in self-correcting their pretests and correcting any misspellings.

1. Peter found a <u>smaller</u> bug.
2. Lee grew the <u>smallest</u> plant.
3. Can you make a <u>larger</u> kite?
4. Rosa has the <u>largest</u> doll.
5. Miguel is <u>happier</u> today.
6. Ann is the <u>happiest</u> girl.
7. It is even <u>hotter</u> in July.
8. When was the <u>hottest</u> day?
9. Tom wrote a <u>sadder</u> story.
10. Bobo is the <u>saddest</u> clown.
11. The lake is <u>deeper</u> here.
12. Fred dove the <u>deepest</u>.
13. Sit <u>closer</u> to the window.
14. Dan is <u>closest</u> to the door.
15. Michael has a <u>scarier</u> mask.
16. We saw the <u>scariest</u> movie.
17. Carol made a <u>funnier</u> face.
18. It is the <u>funniest</u> cartoon.
19. The baby bear got <u>fatter</u>.
20. Poky was the <u>fattest</u> puppy.

Posttest

Read aloud the sentences below. These sentences may be used for dictation.

1. I got the <u>smallest</u> box.
2. It is <u>hotter</u> at the beach.
3. He had the <u>saddest</u> face.
4. That star is the <u>largest</u> one.
5. Which movie is <u>sadder</u>?
6. She is the <u>happiest</u> baby.
7. The bird is getting <u>larger</u>.
8. Last summer was the <u>hottest</u>.
9. I am <u>happier</u> camping.
10. The <u>smaller</u> rabbit is his.
11. I caught the <u>fattest</u> frog.
12. He has a <u>deeper</u> voice.
13. Pull the chair <u>closer</u>.
14. He is the <u>funniest</u> clown.
15. They are the <u>closest</u> friends.
16. They know the <u>scariest</u> stories.
17. My joke is <u>funnier</u>.
18. I want a <u>scarier</u> book.
19. The shirt is the <u>deepest</u> blue.
20. Is the puppy <u>fatter</u>?

Challenge Words

1. He wrote a <u>weirder</u> story.
2. That was the <u>weirdest</u> movie!
3. Be <u>gentler</u> with the kitten.
4. Is the lamb the <u>gentlest</u>?
5. Work made Mom <u>angrier</u>.
6. Who was the <u>angriest</u>?

Additional Assessment

Standardized Test Master 5
Dictation Sentences, p. T37
Everyday Spelling CD-ROM

WHAT'S THE BIG IDEA?

Fourth graders seem to have a tough time remembering to change **y** to **i** before adding **-er** and **-est.** Suggest students create posters illustrating the rules. Display the posters to serve as reminders.

*** See pp. T20 and T33 for test-study-test information.

ADDITIONAL RESOURCES (OPTIONAL PRACTICE)

LESSON 5

DAY 1 CHALLENGE MASTER

CHALLENGE ■ 5

Challenge Words

gentler	gentlest	weirder
weirdest	angrier	angriest

■ Write the Challenge Words to complete each tongue twister.

1. The giant is **gentler** than the **gentlest** giraffe in the jungle.

2. Angry Ann is **angrier** than Andy and the **angriest** of all the antelopes.

3. A walrus is **weirder** than a wallaby, but a wombat is the **weirdest**.

■ Write a tongue twister for each pair of Challenge Words. Then underline all the beginning letters that are the same sound in each tongue twister.

Practice Masters, p. 23

DAY 1 HOME-SCHOOL MASTER

■ 5 HOME-SCHOOL ACTIVITIES 5 ■

■ Word Relatives Write the list word that completes each group below.

1. scary, scariest, **scarier**
2. deep, deeper, **deepest**
3. happy, happiest, **happier**
4. small, smaller, **smallest**
5. hot, hotter, **hottest**
6. sad, saddest, **sadder**
7. fat, fatter, **fattest**
8. large, larger, **largest**
9. close, closest, **closer**
10. funny, funniest, **funnier**

■ Word Forms Write the list word that you form when you add the ending to each word below.

-er
11. hot **hotter**
12. large **larger**
13. small **smaller**
14. fat **fatter**
15. deep **deeper**

-est
16. sad **saddest**
17. happy **happiest**
18. close **closest**
19. scary **scariest**
20. funny **funniest**

Word Check 5

1. deeper
2. deepest
3. smaller
4. smallest
5. closer
6. closest
7. larger
8. largest
9. scarier
10. scariest
11. funnier
12. funniest
13. happier
14. happiest
15. hotter
16. hottest
17. fatter
18. fattest
19. sadder
20. saddest

Dear Parent,

Please check to see that your child has done this page correctly. Circle any misspelled words and help your child study them.

Tear off the Word Check before your child returns this page to class. Use it to help your child study.

Home-School Activities, p. 5

DAY 2 THINK AND PRACTICE MASTER

5 ■ THINK AND PRACTICE

smaller	smallest	larger	largest	happier
happiest	hotter	hottest	sadder	saddest

■ Antonyms Write the list word that completes each phrase.

1. not colder but **hotter**
2. not the largest but the **smallest**
3. not happier but **sadder**
4. not the tiniest but the **largest**
5. not sadder but **happier**
6. not the coldest but the **hottest**

■ Adding Endings Write a list word by adding the ending shown beside each word.

7. sad (est) **saddest**
8. large (er) **larger**
9. happy (est) **happiest**
10. small (er) **smaller**
11. large (est) **largest**
12. hot (er) **hotter**

STRATEGIC SPELLING: Building New Words
Write the words that complete the chart. Remember what you learned.

Base word	Add -er	Add -est
13. busy	**busier**	**busiest**
14. big	**bigger**	**biggest**
15. strange	**stranger**	**strangest**

Practice Masters, p. 24

DAY 2 EXTRA PRACTICE MASTER

EXTRA PRACTICE ■ 5

Word List

smaller	smallest	larger	largest	happier
happiest	hotter	hottest	sadder	saddest
deeper	deepest	closer	closest	scarier
scariest	funnier	funniest	fatter	fattest

■ Word Forms Write a list word that means the same as each word below with the ending added.

1. nearby + er = **closer**
2. glad + est = **happiest**
3. unhappy + est = **saddest**
4. unhappy + er = **sadder**
5. nearby + est = **closest**
6. plump + est = **fattest**
7. warm + est = **hottest**
8. glad + er = **happier**
9. plump + er = **fatter**
10. big + er = **larger**
11. big + est = **largest**
12. tiny + er = **smaller**
13. warm + er = **hotter**
14. tiny + est = **smallest**

■ Picture Clues Look at each picture. Then look at the word under the picture. Write the list words that are related to the word.

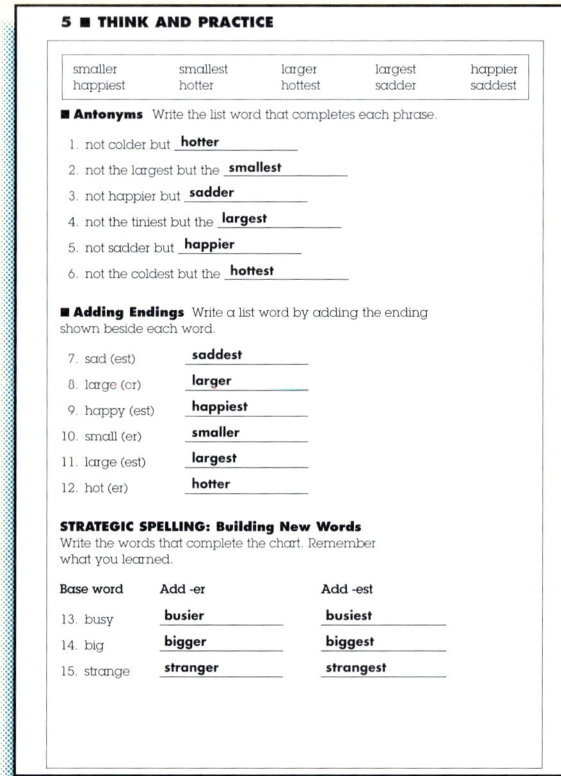

deep

funny

scary

15. **deeper**
16. **deepest**
17. **funnier**
18. **funniest**
19. **scarier**
20. **scariest**

Practice Masters, p. 25

30C

TECHNOLOGY AND VISUAL SUPPORT	 Use Audiotape A, Side 1, Lesson 5 Use Proofreading and Writing Transparency 5	 For additional practice use *Everyday Spelling* Game Software, Lesson 5	 Additional resources on *Everyday Spelling* CD-ROM: proofreading and writing, modified list and challenge words, auditory test

DAY 3 SECOND LANGUAGE SUPPORT MASTER

SECOND LANGUAGE SUPPORT ■ 5

Quick Stories

✚✚ The pictures tell a story. Talk about the story with others. Write the words to complete the sentences.

largest   closer   deepest

Pilar swam in a deep part of the lake. It was the (1) part.

1. **deepest**

She saw a large fish. It was the (2) fish she had ever seen.

2. **largest**

The fish came (3) to her. Pilar got out of the water!

3. **closer**

✚✚ The next story is not finished. Talk about what will happen next. Write the words to complete the sentences. Draw the new part of the story.

scariest   funniest

Sophan likes to write stories. His (4) story is about a scary house.

4. **scariest**

His (5) story is about monkeys doing funny things.

5. **funniest**

✚✚ Have you ever written a story? Talk to your partner about what you wrote.

Second Language Support, p. 31

DAY 3 WRITING ACTIVITY MASTER

5 ■ WRITING ACTIVITY

Adjectives That Compare

☐ Use the ending -er to compare two things.

☐ Use the ending -est to compare more than two things.

≡	Make a capital.
/	Make a small letter.
∧	Add something.
ℰ	Take out something.
⊙	Add a period.
¶	New paragraph.

■ Read the paragraph that Sam wrote about the cheetah. Fix the mistakes he made in using adjectives that compare.

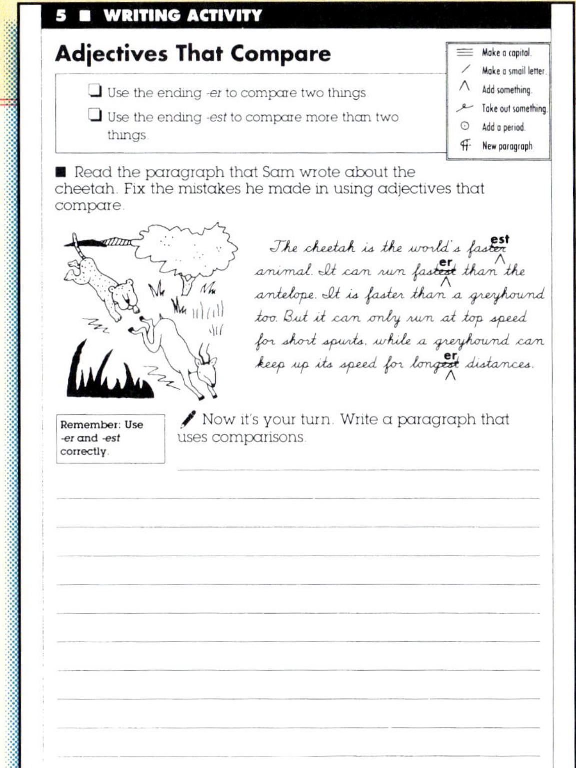

Remember: Use -er and -est correctly.

✐ Now it's your turn. Write a paragraph that uses comparisons.

Spelling and Writing, p. 10

DAY 4 REVIEW MASTER

5 ■ REVIEW

Word List				
smaller	smallest	larger	largest	happier
happiest	hotter	hottest	sadder	saddest
deeper	deepest	closer	closest	scarier
scariest	funnier	funniest	fatter	fattest

■ **Add Endings** Complete each group with a list word.

1. deep, ___, deepest
2. close, closer, ___
3. scary, ___, scariest
4. funny, funnier, ___
5. hot, hotter, ___
6. fat, ___, fattest

■ **Defining Words** Write the list word that means the same as the underlined words.

7. My story was <u>more comical</u> than yours.
8. That TV thriller was <u>the most frightening</u> I have ever seen.
9. Is Canada <u>bigger</u> than the United States?
10. The <u>littlest</u> animal can be seen only through a microscope.
11. The audience was <u>more pleased</u> than anyone expected.
12. His voice is the <u>lowest</u> in the class.
13. She was even <u>more miserable</u> when Martha moved away.

■ **Context Clues** Write a list word to complete each sentence.

14. These two turkeys are fat, but this one is the ___.
15. The elephant is the ___ animal on land.
16. What is ___, a mouse or a kitten?
17. The ___ time was when we said good-by to everyone.
18. This car is ___ to the curb than that one.
19. The American desert is hot, but the African desert is ___.
20. The healthiest people are often the ___.

1. **deeper**
2. **closest**
3. **scarler**
4. **funniest**
5. **hottest**
6. **fatter**
7. **funnier**
8. **scariest**
9. **larger**
10. **smallest**
11. **happier**
12. **deepest**
13. **sadder**
14. **fattest**
15. **largest**
16. **smaller**
17. **saddest**
18. **closer**
19. **hotter**
20. **happiest**

Practice Masters, p. 26

DAY 5 STANDARDIZED TEST MASTER

LESSON TEST ■ 5

■ Find the word in each group that is spelled correctly. Fill in the letter for the correct word on the answer strip.

Sample:
		Answer
a. visiter	**c.** vizitor	ⓐ ⓑ ⓒ ●
b. visetor	**d.** visitor	

1. **a.** scarrier   **c.** scareier   **b.** scarier   **d.** scaryer — 1. ⓐ ● ⓒ ⓓ
2. **a.** saddest   **c.** saddist   **b.** sadest   **d.** saidest — 2. ● ⓑ ⓒ ⓓ
3. **a.** hoter   **c.** hotter   **b.** hodder   **d.** hoder — 3. ⓐ ⓑ ● ⓓ
4. **a.** smalest   **c.** smaliest   **b.** smalliest   **d.** smallest — 4. ⓐ ⓑ ⓒ ●
5. **a.** happiest   **c.** happest   **b.** happist   **d.** happyest — 5. ● ⓑ ⓒ ⓓ
6. **a.** clocer   **c.** closr   **b.** closer   **d.** closser — 6. ⓐ ● ⓒ ⓓ
7. **a.** scaryest   **c.** scariest   **b.** scarriest   **d.** scarest — 7. ⓐ ⓑ ● ⓓ
8. **a.** fater   **c.** fatter   **b.** fadder   **d.** fader — 8. ⓐ ⓑ ● ⓓ
9. **a.** funiest   **c.** funnyest   **b.** funniest   **d.** funyest — 9. ⓐ ● ⓒ ⓓ
10. **a.** lardgest   **c.** larjest   **b.** largest   **d.** lardjest — 10. ⓐ ● ⓒ ⓓ
11. **a.** deapest   **c.** deeppest   **b.** deipest   **d.** deepest — 11. ⓐ ⓑ ⓒ ●
12. **a.** hotest   **c.** hoddest   **b.** hottest   **d.** hotst — 12. ⓐ ● ⓒ ⓓ
13. **a.** lardger   **c.** lardjer   **b.** larjer   **d.** larger — 13. ⓐ ⓑ ⓒ ●
14. **a.** funnyer   **c.** funneyer   **b.** funnier   **d.** funier — 14. ⓐ ● ⓒ ⓓ
15. **a.** satter   **c.** sadder   **b.** sader   **d.** sadter — 15. ⓐ ⓑ ● ⓓ
16. **a.** fattest   **c.** fatest   **b.** fattes   **d.** faddest — 16. ● ⓑ ⓒ ⓓ
17. **a.** happyer   **c.** hapier   **b.** happer   **d.** happier — 17. ⓐ ⓑ ⓒ ●
18. **a.** smoler   **c.** smoller   **b.** smaler   **d.** smaller — 18. ⓐ ⓑ ⓒ ●
19. **a.** closest   **c.** closes   **b.** clost   **d.** closesed — 19. ● ⓑ ⓒ ⓓ
20. **a.** deeppr   **c.** deepr   **b.** deepre   **d.** deeper — 20. ⓐ ⓑ ⓒ ●

Practice for Standardized Tests, p. 5

INTRODUCTION

Word Structure

Adding Endings Have students pronounce the words in groups of three: *deep, deeper, deepest.* Have them identify the words that change spelling when endings are added.

MEETING THE NEEDS OF ALL STUDENTS

Modified List

Practice Students studying only the high-frequency words in the top box write
- two words in which the final **e** is dropped
- two words in which the base word does not change
- four words in which the final consonant is doubled
- two words in which **y** changes to **i**

Auditory Learners

Syllables Have students carefully pronounce words, such as *happier* and *scariest,* listening for all three syllables.

Additional Practice

Challenge Master 5
Home-School Master 5
Audiotape A, Side 1

1. **larger**
2. **largest**
3. **closer**
4. **closest**
5. **smaller**
6. **smallest**
7. **deeper**
8. **deepest**
9. **hotter**
10. **hottest**
11. **sadder**
12. **saddest**
13. **fatter**
14. **fattest**
15. **happier**
16. **happiest**
17. **scarier**
18. **scariest**
19. **funnier**
20. **funniest**

CHALLENGE!

weirder	weirdest
gentler	gentlest
angrier	angriest

30

■ INTRODUCTION

Adding *-er* and *-est*

SPELLING FOCUS

Here are four things to remember when adding **-er** and **-est**:
- Some base words do not change: **small, smaller, smallest.**
- In words that end with **consonant-e**, the **e** is dropped: **large, larger, largest.**
- In words that end in **y**, the **y** is changed to **i**: **happy, happier, happiest.**
- In one-syllable words that end with **consonant-vowel-consonant**, the final consonant is doubled: **hot, hotter, hottest.**

■ **STUDY** Look at each base word. Notice whether the spelling changes when **-er** and **-est** are added.

small	1. *smaller*	2. *smallest*	
large	3. *larger*	4. *largest*	
happy	5. *happier*	6. *happiest*	
hot	7. *hotter*	8. *hottest*	
sad	9. *sadder*	10. *saddest*	

deep	11. *deeper*	12. *deepest*	
close	13. *closer*	14. *closest*	
scary	15. *scarier*	16. *scariest*	
funny	17. *funnier*	18. *funniest*	
fat	19. *fatter*	20. *fattest*	

■ **PRACTICE** Sort the list words by writing
- four words in which the final **e** is dropped
- four words in which the base word does not change
- six words in which the final consonant is doubled
- six words in which **y** changes to **i**

Order of words in each group may vary.

■ **WRITE** Choose ten words to write in sentences.
Sentences will vary.

THINK AND PRACTICE ■

ANTONYM ALERT Write the list word that means the opposite of each word below.

1. larger
2. skinnier
3. smallest
4. colder
5. shallower
6. saddest
7. coldest
8. largest
9. farther
10. happiest
11. skinniest

1. **smaller**
2. **fatter**
3. **largest**
4. **hotter**
5. **deeper**
6. **happiest**
7. **hottest**
8. **smallest**
9. **closer**
10. **saddest**
11. **fattest**

HAPPY ENDINGS Add an ending to each word in parentheses to form a list word that completes the sentence.

12. (scary) This is the **scariest** thriller I've read.
13. (funny) Your skit was **funnier** than mine.
14. (deep) Pike Lake is the **deepest** lake around.
15. (close) Morgan is my very **closest** friend.
16. (sad) Was *Sounder* **sadder** than *Old Yeller*?
17. (large) A gorilla is **larger** than a gibbon.
18. (funny) Ribsy is the **funniest** dog of all time.
19. (happy) Al was **happier** with the gift than Di.
20. (scary) I think snakes are **scarier** than lizards.

Did You Know?
The **smallest** horse ever recorded, Little Pumpkin, stood only fourteen inches tall and weighed twenty pounds.

Building New Words

Write the words that complete the chart. Remember what you learned.

Base word	Add -er	Add -est
21. busy	**busier**	**busiest**
22. big	**bigger**	**biggest**
23. strange	**stranger**	**strangest**

31

LESSON 5

- Proofread an Invitation
- Proofreading Tip: Comparisons
- Write an Invitation
- ✓ Cooperative Midweek Test

DAILY SPELLING REVIEW

My *cosin* brought *pop corn*.

cousin   *popcorn*

● Core   ○ Optional   ✓ Assessment

PROOFREADING AND WRITING

Comparisons

Double-check Have students trade corrected invitations with a partner and decide whether the right changes were made.

MEETING THE NEEDS OF ALL STUDENTS

Modified List

Proofreading Students studying high-frequency words complete this page or the proofreading activity on the *Everyday Spelling* CD-ROM.

Kinesthetic Activity

Writing Invitations Have students work in small groups to create invitations to a real or imaginary class event: a party, display, or program to which others are invited.

Additional Practice

Hardbound Book Master 5
Second Language Master 5
Writing Mini-Lesson 5
Writing Activity Master 5
Proofreading Transparency 5
Everyday Spelling **CD-ROM**

■ PROOFREADING AND WRITING

Make a capital.
Make a small letter.
Add something.
Take out something.
Add a period.
New paragraph

PROOFREAD AN INVITATION Lizzy is having a party. Below is the first draft of her invitation. Correct three misspellings and one incorrect comparison.

PROOFREADING TIP
Remember to use **-er** when you compare two things. Use **-est** when comparing more than two.

COME TO A HALLOWEEN PARTY!!!

PLACE: Lizzy's house —202 Lake St.

TIME: October 31 from 3:00 to 6:00 P.M.

Wear your scaryest [scariest] costume. We'll carve the fatest [fattest] pumpkins and drink the hotest [hottest] cider. I'll be the sadder [saddest] ghoul in town unless you come!

WRITE AN INVITATION What kind of party would you like to give? Write an invitation for it. Use list words.

Word List

deeper	deepest
smaller	smallest
closer	closest
larger	largest
scarier	scariest
funnier	funniest
happier	happiest
hotter	hottest
fatter	fattest
sadder	saddest

Personal Words

1. **Words will**
2. **vary.**

COME TO A ________________**PARTY!!!**
PLACE: ________________________________
TIME: ________________________________
Invitations will vary.
____
____
____

32

VOCABULARY BUILDING

Review

ANALOGIES   Write the boxed word that completes each analogy.

smaller	smallest
larger	largest
happier	happiest
hotter	hottest
sadder	saddest

1. Saddest is to unhappiest as merriest is to ___ .
2. Smaller is to littler as bigger is to ___ .
3. Loudest is to quietest as biggest is to ___ .
4. Tightest is to loosest as happiest is to ___ .
5. Nicest is to meanest as coldest is to ___ .
6. Quicker is to faster as cheerier is to ___
7. Closer is to nearer as littler is to ___ .
8. Thinner is to slimmer as unhappier is to ___ .
9. Smallest is to biggest as littlest is to ___ .
10. Cooler is to colder as warmer is to ___ .

1. **happiest**
2. **larger**
3. **smallest**
4. **saddest**
5. **hottest**
6. **happier**
7. **smaller**
8. **sadder**
9. **largest**
10. **hotter**

Word *Study*

EXAGGERATION   Liz read a book in which a character "had eyes as large and brown as a coconut." She liked this exaggerated wording and was eager to try it out herself. Exaggeration is often used to emphasize, amuse, or surprise.

Liz practiced using exaggeration in her diary but left a few words out. Choose list words to finish the sentences.

October 31 My party was the (1) I've ever given— spilling over into five states. People came in costumes that were (2) than a barrel of comedians. One tiny kid dressed as a peanut and was (3) than one too! We drank cocoa that was (4) than an oven, and we ate so much that we felt (5) than an overweight elephant. Then we told stories that were (6) than a haunted hotel. It was the (7) time of my life!

1. **largest**
2. **funnier**
3. **smaller**
4. **hotter**
5. **fatter**
6. **scarier**
7. **happiest**

6

Unit Review Concepts
Words with thr, scr, str, squ
Words with kn, gn, wr, mb
Consonant Sounds /k/ and /f/
Adding -ed and -ing
Adding -er and -est

● Core   ○ Optional   ✓ Assessment

DAILY PLAN	CORE OBJECTIVES	NOTES

DAY 1
Review Activity:
●   Bakery Specials, p. 34
✓ Self-Assessment:
  How Am I Doing?, p. 34
Integrating Spelling:
○   Language Arts, p. 34
○ Review Master 6A

- Use review words to complete a newspaper advertisement
- ✓ Assess their own progress in the spelling of words in Unit 1

DAY 2
Review Activities:
●   Bicycles, p. 35
●   Fairy Tales, p. 35
Integrating Spelling:
○   Health, p. 35
○   Language Arts, p. 35

- Use review words to complete a class news bulletin article
- Use review words to complete a book review

DAY 3
Review Activities:
●   Crafts, p. 36
●   Pairing Things and Places, p. 36
Integrating Spelling:
○   Art, p. 36
○   Social Studies, p. 36
○ Review Master 6B

- Use review words to complete project descriptions
- Identify review words that relate to given words and pictures

DAY 4
Review Activities:
●   Water Park, p. 37
●   Science Fiction, p. 37
Integrating Spelling:
○   Language Arts, p. 37
○   Science, p. 37
○ Standardized Test Masters 6A–6D

- Use review words to complete an announcement
- Use review words to complete plots for a science fiction skit

DAY 5
✓ Unit Review Test
✓ Writing Test
○ Writing Prompt Transparency 1
○ Writing Model Transparencies
  1A, 1B

- ✓ Assess review words
- ✓ Assess narrative writing

MEETING THE NEEDS OF ALL STUDENTS

Modified List

For students studying only the high-frequency words in each lesson, assign Review Masters 6A–6B for unit review. Use the Modified Dictation Sentences for assessment.

Bilingual/ESL

Second-language learners might benefit from making flashcards of words and their definitions for future review.

Spelling Conferences

Conduct individual spelling conferences to discuss each student's spelling progress during Unit 1. You might want to take this opportunity to remind students to add words to their personal dictionaries.

ASSESSMENT

Dictation Sentences

1. Be careful walking on the rough track.
2. I always carry a snack in my pocket.
3. Don't squirt paint on that sign.
4. We didn't climb high enough to see the top.
5. An angry elephant might attack a person.
6. We are writing the alphabet letter by letter.
7. Do you know where Kansas is?
8. You must kneel to scrub the chair.
9. If I worried about the unknown, I would never travel.
10. Why would you squeeze a strawberry?
11. I scream because I'm scared.
12. That squeal was made by the brake on a train.
13. After the game, people danced in the street.
14. A wren flew through the trees.
15. He must be worrying about the wreck.
16. Please hand me the smallest wrench.
17. On the screen, a dolphin is swimming by.
18. Who can design a skyscraper that tall?
19. The shirt has a square opening at the neck.
20. Do you care if I knit?
21. I'm stopping to take a photo.
22. We always assign the scariest story to him.
23. Mom made a dried wreath for my room.
24. Studying about such a large star is a thrill.
25. I didn't scratch the cover of the book.

Writing Test

Writing Prompt Transparency 1 and Writing Model Transparencies 1A and 1B will help students prepare for holistic writing tests. Helpful information relating to narrative writing tests is provided in the Writer's Handbook on page 235.

Everyday Spelling CD-ROM

An auditory test is available as an alternate testing format.

Modified Dictation Sentences

1. Mother is happiest when she is dancing.
2. The man studied the photo.
3. The knot in her hair looks strange.
4. Did he scream when he hit his thumb?
5. I don't care if you strike out.
6. I put my pennies in the smallest pocket.
7. You made me sadder when you laughed at me.
8. The cat will climb the larger tree.
9. You might wreck the bike if you don't use the brake.
10. People were stopping to look at the design.
11. It happened on the hottest day last summer.
12. Can the dog squeeze through the opening?

DAY 1 REVIEW MASTER A

REVIEW ■ 6A

Lesson 1

| through | scream | strange | strike | squeeze |

■ **Synonyms** Write the list word that means the same as each word or phrase.

1. yell — **scream**
2. hit — **strike**
3. odd — **strange**
4. in and out — **through**
5. compress — **squeeze**

Lesson 2

| knot | design | wreck | climb | thumb |

■ **Definitions** Write the list word that is missing from each statement.

1. Artist: "I will add more color to my **design** ."
2. Police Officer: "Who caused this **wreck** ?"
3. Scout: "I will learn to tie a square **knot** ."
4. Jack Horner: "There is a plum on my **thumb** !"
5. Adventurer: "I will **climb** that high mountain."

Lesson 3

| care | brake | pocket | laughed | photo |

■ **Puzzles** Write the list word that matches each clue. The message in the circles answers the riddle "What might a train jump?"

1. comes from a camera — p (h) (o) (t) o
2. use this to stop a car — b (r) a k e
3. what people did after a joke — l (a) u g h e d
4. what you do for a sick friend — (c) a r e
5. a place to keep keys and coins — p o c (k) e t

Practice Masters, p. 27

DAY 3 REVIEW MASTER B

6B ■ REVIEW

Lesson 4

| dancing | opening | happened | stopping | studied |

■ **Word Forms** Write the list word that completes each group.

1. dance, danced, **dancing**
2. study, **studied** , studying
3. happen, **happened** , happening
4. stop, stopped, **stopping**
5. open, opened, **opening**

Lesson 5

| hottest | happiest | larger | smallest | sadder |

■ **Word Equations** Write the list word that completes the equation.

1. happy + est = **happiest**
2. sad + er = **sadder**
3. small + est = **smallest**
4. large + er = **larger**
5. hot + est = **hottest**

Practice Masters, p. 28

DAY 4 STANDARDIZED TEST MASTER A

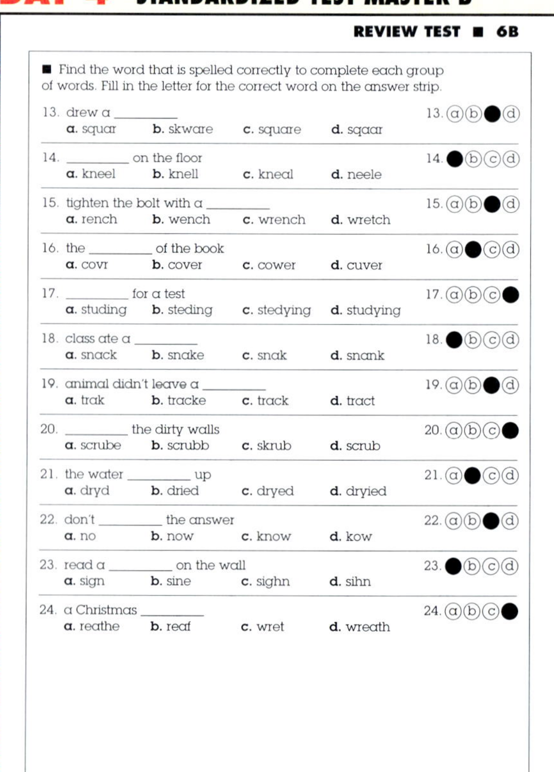

6A ■ REVIEW TEST

■ Find the word that is spelled correctly to complete each group of words. Fill in the letter for the correct word on the answer strip.

Sample:

_______ to the field — **a.** cum **b.** kume **c.** come **d.** comm — (a)(b)●(d)

1. the _______ of winning — **a.** trill **b.** threal **c.** thrill **d.** thril — 1. (a)(b)●(d)
2. the _______ on the road — **a.** wrech **b.** reck **c.** reack **d.** wreck — 2. (a)(b)(c)●
3. let out a _______ — **a.** screem **b.** scream **c.** screm **d.** sream — 3. (a)●(c)(d)
4. _______ over the wall — **a.** climb **b.** clim **c.** clime **d.** climbe — 4. ●(b)(c)(d)
5. a _______ landing — **a.** ruf **b.** ruff **c.** rouph **d.** rough — 5. (a)(b)(c)●
6. to _______ the work — **a.** assine **b.** assign **c.** assighn **d.** asine — 6. (a)●(c)(d)
7. likes to _______ — **a.** knit **b.** knette **c.** nit **d.** knitt — 7. ●(b)(c)(d)
8. is _______ a letter — **a.** writeing **b.** wrighting **c.** writing **d.** righting — 8. (a)(b)●(d)
9. the _______ TV show — **a.** scariest **b.** scaryest **c.** scarriest **d.** scaries — 9. ●(b)(c)(d)
10. the farms in _______ — **a.** Kansis **b.** Kansas **c.** kansace **d.** kansas — 10. (a)●(c)(d)
11. take _______ of him — **a.** car **b.** kare **c.** carr **d.** care — 11. (a)(b)(c)●
12. read _______ the book — **a.** though **b.** through **c.** threw **d.** throw — 12. (a)●(c)(d)

Practice for Standardized Tests, p. 6

DAY 4 STANDARDIZED TEST MASTER B

REVIEW TEST ■ 6B

■ Find the word that is spelled correctly to complete each group of words. Fill in the letter for the correct word on the answer strip.

13. drew a _______ — **a.** squar **b.** skware **c.** square **d.** sqaar — 13. (a)(b)●(d)
14. _______ on the floor — **a.** kneel **b.** knell **c.** kneal **d.** neele — 14. ●(b)(c)(d)
15. tighten the bolt with a _______ — **a.** rench **b.** wench **c.** wrench **d.** wretch — 15. (a)(b)●(d)
16. the _______ of the book — **a.** covr **b.** cover **c.** cower **d.** cuver — 16. (a)●(c)(d)
17. _______ for a test — **a.** studing **b.** steding **c.** stedying **d.** studying — 17. (a)(b)(c)●
18. class ate a _______ — **a.** snack **b.** snake **c.** snak **d.** snank — 18. ●(b)(c)(d)
19. animal didn't leave a _______ — **a.** trak **b.** tracke **c.** track **d.** tract — 19. (a)(b)●(d)
20. _______ the dirty walls — **a.** scrube **b.** scrubb **c.** skrub **d.** scrub — 20. (a)(b)(c)●
21. the water _______ up — **a.** dryd **b.** dried **c.** dryed **d.** dryied — 21. (a)●(c)(d)
22. don't _______ the answer — **a.** no **b.** now **c.** know **d.** kow — 22. (a)(b)●(d)
23. read a _______ on the wall — **a.** sign **b.** sine **c.** sighn **d.** sihn — 23. ●(b)(c)(d)
24. a Christmas _______ — **a.** reathe **b.** reaf **c.** wret **d.** wreath — 24. (a)(b)(c)●

Practice for Standardized Tests, p. 7

TECHNOLOGY — Additional test on *Everyday Spelling* CD-ROM

DAY 4 STANDARDIZED TEST MASTER C

6C ■ REVIEW TEST

■ Find the word that is spelled correctly to complete each sentence. Fill in the letter for the correct word on the answer strip.

25. She couldn't go _______ she was sick.
   a. because **b.** becuse **c.** cause **d.** becouse
   25. ● b c d

26. We watched the movie on the _______.
   a. skren **b.** screen **c.** skreen **d.** scream
   26. a ● c d

27. I took a _______ of the mountain.
   a. phoeto **b.** photo **c.** foeto **d.** foto
   27. a ● c d

28. Stop _______ about what might happen.
   a. worriing **b.** worrieing **c.** worrying **d.** worring
   28. a b ● d

29. That small bird is a _______.
   a. renn **b.** wrean **c.** ren **d.** wren
   29. a b c ●

30. The child gave a _______ of happiness.
   a. squeal **b.** squail **c.** squeel **d.** skueel
   30. ● b c d

31. The _______ didn't stop the car in time.
   a. braek **b.** brake **c.** brak **d.** break
   31. a ● c d

32. Watch out when you cross the _______.
   a. stret **b.** steet **c.** street **d.** sreet
   32. a b ● d

33. They _______ until the clock struck midnight.
   a. danced **b.** dance **c.** danst **d.** dancied
   33. ● b c d

34. Some _______ person did a good deed.
   a. unknow **b.** unknown **c.** unown **d.** un knowen
   34. a ● c d

35. She ran the whole way without _______.
   a. stopping **b.** stopeing **c.** stopped **d.** stoping
   35. ● b c d

36. Don't _______ that water!
   a. squirred **b.** squiret **c.** squirt **d.** skwirt
   36. a b ● d

Practice for Standardized Tests, p. 8

DAY 4 STANDARDIZED TEST MASTER

REVIEW TEST ■ 6D

■ Find the word in each group that is spelled correctly. Fill in the letter for the correct word on the answer strip.

37. **a.** attak **b.** attack **c.** atach **d.** attach
   37. a b c ●

38. **a.** dolfin **b.** dolphin **c.** dofin **d.** dolphine
   38. a ● c d

39. **a.** scach **b.** scrach **c.** scratch **d.** scrath
   39. a b ● d

40. **a.** stawberry **b.** strawbery **c.** stawbary **d.** strawberry
   40. a b c ●

41. **a.** alphabet **b.** alfabet **c.** alfabit **d.** alphbet
   41. ● b c d

42. **a.** enought **b.** enough **c.** a nuf **d.** enuf
   42. a ● c d

43. **a.** openning **b.** opning **c.** openin **d.** opening
   43. a b c ●

44. **a.** elephant **b.** elaphant **c.** elefant **d.** elafent
   44. ● b c d

45. **a.** squeez **b.** skweez **c.** squeeze **d.** squize
   45. a b ● d

46. **a.** desine **b.** designh **c.** dezine **d.** design
   46. a b c ●

47. **a.** sky skraper **b.** skyscraper **c.** skyscrapper **d.** sky scrapper
   47. a ● c d

48. **a.** smalliest **b.** smallist **c.** smallest **d.** smalest
   48. a b ● d

49. **a.** pokket **b.** poket **c.** pocet **d.** pocket
   49. a b c ●

50. **a.** worried **b.** worryed **c.** woried **d.** weread
   50. ● b c d

Practice for Standardized Tests, p. 9

DAY 5 WRITING PROMPT TRANSPARENCY

Spelling and Writing, Transparency 1

LESSON 6

SELF-ASSESSMENT

How Am I Doing?

Talk with students about why it is helpful to think about their progress in spelling. Raise issues such as

1. The hardest words to spell were ___.
2. I learned to spell a hard word by ___.
3. An interesting word I learned in this unit was ___.
4. When a word I write looks wrong, I ___.
5. I try to use spelling words in my writing.

INTEGRATING SPELLING

Language Arts

Newspaper Ad Provide newspapers and have students cut out an ad that catches their eye. Have them circle interesting, vivid words that make the ad appealing.

> **Additional Resources**
> Review Master 6A

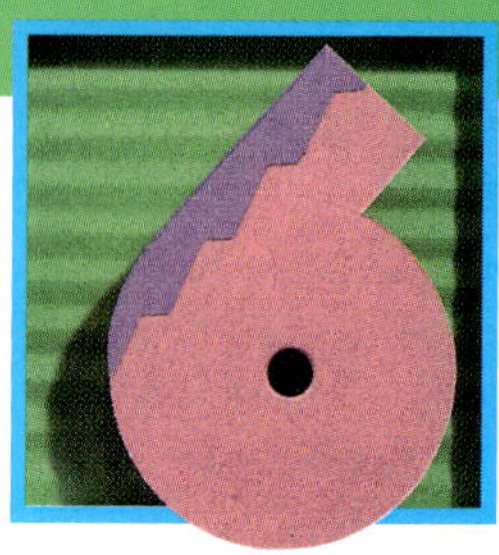

Review

Lesson 1: Words with thr, scr, str, squ
Lesson 2: Words with kn, gn, wr, mb
Lesson 3: Consonant Sounds /k/ and /f/
Lesson 4: Adding -ed and -ing
Lesson 5: Adding -er and -est

REVIEW WORD LIST

1. scratch	11. street	21. unknown	31. care	41. track
2. scream	12. thrill	22. wreath	32. cover	42. danced
3. screen	13. through	23. wreck	33. dolphin	43. dried
4. scrub	14. assign	24. wren	34. elephant	44. opening
5. skyscraper	15. climb	25. wrench	35. enough	45. stopping
6. square	16. design	26. writing	36. Kansas	46. studying
7. squeal	17. kneel	27. alphabet	37. photo	47. worried
8. squeeze	18. knit	28. attack	38. pocket	48. worrying
9. squirt	19. know	29. because	39. rough	49. scariest
10. strawberry	20. sign	30. brake	40. snack	50. smallest

BAKERY SPECIALS

Use the list words to complete the newspaper advertisement.

strawberry
scratch
snack
worrying
alphabet

1. **scratch**
2. **strawberry**
3. **worrying**
4. **alphabet**
5. **snack**

34

get out and have fun

Where do you usually ride your bike? Do you ride all **through** _____ town or just on the **street** _____ you live on? Do you **climb** _____ hills or bounce along on **rough** _____ trails? Maybe your town has a racing **track** _____. No matter where you ride, you should remember these two tips. ❶ Always wear a helmet. ❷ Keep your bike in good repair, especially the **brake** _____ system. Good brakes make **stopping** _____ safe. Take good **care** _____ of your bike, and it will take good care of you.

Bret writes articles about outdoor activities for the class news bulletin. Use each list word once to complete this article.

stopping   **care**   **rough**   **brake**   **track**   **through**   **street**   **climb**

Lindy doesn't like fairy tales, but she had to read one. Use the list words to complete her book review.

know
scrub
scariest
danced
wren
scream
kneel
because
knit

1. **scariest**
2. **scrub**
3. **scream**
4. **kneel**
5. **because**
6. **know**
7. **danced**
8. **knit**
9. **wren**

The Sweetest Princess
A Book Review by Lindy Grach

This is another one of those stories about a sweet princess and the (1) old queen you could ever imagine. Every day, the princess has to (2) the hard marble floor until it shines. Not a day goes by that the queen doesn't (3) at the princess for some little thing, and the queen demands that the princess curtsey and (4) before her friends. The queen wants the princess to marry a neighboring king (5) he is rich. You probably (6) who the princess wants to marry. Right! A poor young man she (7) with at the fair. The only surprise in the book is that there is no fairy godmother, just a troll who asks the princess to (8) him a sweater from her golden hair. In return, he turns the queen into a (9), and the princess locks her safely in a bird cage. The princess marries the young man, and lives . . . well, you know the rest.

Health
Safety Rules Have students write two additional rules for bicycle safety. As a group, they can combine their rules to make a bicycle safety poster.

Language Arts
Book Review Have students discuss whether they've ever read a book or story that they did not enjoy. In small groups, have them give a short oral book review, explaining why they did not like a particular piece of literature.

35

LESSON 6

INTEGRATING SPELLING

Art
A Project Have students write step-by-step directions for an art project. Remind students to include every step and make their directions easy to follow.

Social Studies
Geography Divide the class into four groups and a U.S. map into quadrants. Each group studies the quadrant assigned to it and makes a list of words group members associate with their "share" of the United States.

Additional Resources
Review Master 6B

Crafts

Complete the descriptions of the three projects below. Use each list word once.

I. Make an outline picture of a city in winter. Cut squares and rectangles out of newspapers and make a (1) and other such buildings. Glue the buildings along the bottom of a piece of black construction paper. For snow, fill a spray bottle with water and white paint and (2) your paper. Then, (3) your name to your art work.

II. Shape grapevines into a ring to make a festive (4) for your front door. Decorate it with bunches of (5) flowers.

III. Make a picture frame in the shape of a (6). Collect buttons of all sizes and colors. Make sure there are (7) buttons to cover the frame. Arrange them in an interesting (8) and then glue them on the frame.

sign
dried
design
square
squirt
skyscraper
wreath
enough

1. **skyscraper**
2. **squirt**
3. **sign**
4. **wreath**
5. **dried**
6. **square**
7. **enough**
8. **design**

Pairing Things and Places

Write the list word that relates to each shape.

1. **elephant**
2. **Kansas**
3. **pocket**
4. **wrench**
5. **dolphin**

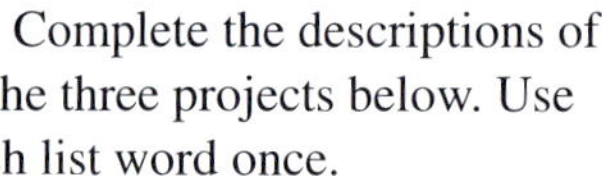

36

WATER PARK

Complete the announcement below.
Use each list word once.

opening
squeal
cover
thrill
assign
worried
photo

1. **opening**
2. **squeal**
3. **photo**
4. **thrill**
5. **worried**
6. **cover**
7. **assign**

Hey Scouts!

Troop #116 is going to the grand (1) of Rocky Valley Water Park on Saturday, August 10. Imagine us as we holler and (2), sliding down the new water slide! Included will be a souvenir (3) of our group for us to take home. So, get ready for the (4) of your life! If you are (5) about how much the trip will cost, here's some good news. The park will (6) the cost for each scout who has earned a service badge. We plan to (7) seats on the bus, so tell Mr. Sato whom you'd like to sit with.

Science Fiction

Jason's writing group invented two plots for a science fiction skit. Complete them using each list word once.

squeeze studying smallest screen writing attack wreck unknown

The skit might be about alien creatures who come to Earth in a battered (1) of a spaceship plastered with bumper stickers.

They have come in the hopes of (2) the human sense of humor.

In one scene, the very (3) alien, measuring 2 feet, 6 inches, says, "Take me to your ladder!"

He uses it to climb up to the TV (4) so he can watch old Marx Brothers reruns.

The skit could be about time travel. Six students (5) into a small time machine and visit the year 2096.

Their Time-Travel Guide tells them that they will go to a distant place, but the exact location is (6).

In one scene, forces on Planet Circon prepare to (7) Mars with high-impact squirt guns.

When the kids return, they begin (8) a tell-all documentary of their amazing adventure.

1. **wreck**
2. **studying**
3. **smallest**
4. **screen**
5. **squeeze**
6. **unknown**
7. **attack**
8. **writing**

Language Arts

Announcement Have students write an announcement for a school, community, or family event. Point out that a good announcement serves both to inform and to interest a reader in an event.

Science

Research Have students brainstorm items they use that their grandparents would have thought belonged only in science fiction. They might then research the history of one item (cable TV, microwave ovens, video cameras, space travel).

Additional Resources
Standardized Test Masters 6A–6D
Writing Prompt Transparency 1
Writing Model Transparencies 1A, 1B
Everyday Spelling **CD-ROM**

STRATEGY WORKSHOP

Introduces the metacognitive strategy **Divide and Conquer:** 1. Divide long words into syllables, 2. Separate them into prefixes, suffixes, and base words, 3. Divide them into base words if they are compounds.

SCOPE AND SEQUENCE: LESSONS 7–12

Lesson	Generalization	Think and Practice	Proofreading and Writing
7 pp. 40–43	Some words have consonant combinations, such as **sh, ch, tch,** and **wh,** that are pronounced as one sound.	Buried Words Making Associations Strategic Spelling: The Divide and Conquer Strategy	Proofread a Sign ■ misspelled words Create a Sign
8 pp. 44–47	Sometimes double consonants, such as **ff, pp,** and **rr,** stand for one sound.	Antonym Argument Words in Context Strategic Spelling: Building New Words	Proofread a Message ■ misspelled words ■ careless errors Write a Message
9 pp. 48–51	Short **e** is often spelled **e.** Long **e** can be spelled **ea** and **ey.**	Words in Context Definitions Strategic Spelling: Seeing Meaning Connections	Proofread a Letter ■ misspelled words ■ punctuation errors Answer a Letter
10 pp. 52–55	Short **a** is usually spelled **a,** short **i** is usually spelled **i,** and short **o** is usually spelled **o.** Short **u** is usually spelled **u,** but it is often spelled **ou.**	Definitions Vowel Trade Base Words Strategic Spelling: Seeing Meaning Connections	Proofread a Message ■ misspelled words ■ handwriting errors Write a Message
11 pp. 56–59	Long vowels are often spelled with one letter. They can also be spelled **vowel-consonant-e.**	Compare Vowel Trade Strategic Spelling: Using the Rhyming Helper Strategy	Proofread a Summary ■ misspelled words ■ run-on sentences Write a Summary

	Concepts for Review	Unit 2 Activities	Integrating Spelling
Review 12 pp. 60–63	Words with **sh, ch, tch, wh** Words with Double Consonants Short **e** and Long **e** Short Vowels **a, i, o, u** Long Vowels **a, i, o**	Contest Directions Story Summary Postcard List of Chores Story Description Conversation	**Social Studies:** Trip Description, Postcard **Language Arts:** Story Summary, Calendar, Journal Entry, Announcement **Science:** Facts for Camping

VOWEL ERRORS

Vowel sounds continue to cause spelling problems for students in fourth grade, accounting for more than one-third of their spelling errors. The more spelling variations a vowel sound has, the more difficult it is for students to spell correctly.

TYPICAL MISSPELLINGS:

- *trete* for *treat*
- *mony* for *money*
- *troble* for *trouble*
- *behinde* for *behind*

Helpful strategies include having students examine any spelling errors from their pretest and focusing on the problem parts of those words.

ADDITIONAL RESOURCES

For Every Weekly Lesson

- **Think and Practice Master**
- **Challenge Master**
- **Extra Practice Master**
- **Review Master**
- **Second Language Support Master**
- **Home-School Activity Master**
- **Writing Mini-Lesson**
- **Writing Activity Master**
- **Standardized Test Master**
- **Proofreading and Writing Transparency**

Technology

- **Audiotape**
- *Everyday Spelling* **CD-ROM**
- *Everyday Spelling* **Game Software**

Unit Review

- **Standardized Test Masters**
- **Writing Prompt Transparency**
- **Writing Model Transparencies**
- *Everyday Spelling* **CD-ROM**

Vocabulary Building	Meeting the Needs of All Students	Cross-Curricular Lessons*
Review Rhymes **Using a Thesaurus** Parts of an Entry	**Visual** Buried Words **Auditory** Oral Sentences **Bilingual/ESL** Show to Tell **Enrichment** Class Signs	**Reading:** How Families Matter, pp. 206–207 **Connections to BookFestival:** ■ *Sarah, Plain and Tall* by Patricia McLachlan
Review Context Clues **Word Study** Acrostics	**Visual** Say It with Pictures **Kinesthetic** Home Town Acrostics **Bilingual/ESL** Past Tense **Enrichment** Message Writing	**Science:** The Eyes and Ears, pp. 200–201 **Connections to BookFestival:** ■ *From Anna* by Jean Little
Review Crossword Puzzle **Multicultural Connection** Proverbs	**Visual** Labeling **Auditory** Rhyming Words **Bilingual/ESL** Definitions; Proverbs **Enrichment** Wise Sayings	**Mathematics:** The Calculator, pp. 214–215
Review Context Clues **Using a Dictionary** Pronunciation	**Visual** Highlight Letters **Kinesthetic** Phone Message **Bilingual/ESL** Using Prepositions **Enrichment** Symbols	**Health:** Your Body, pp. 188–189
Review Analogies **Word Study** Idioms	**Auditory** Pronunciation **Kinesthetic** Act It Out **Bilingual/ESL** Multicultural Idioms **Enrichment** Anatomy of an Idiom	**Work and Play:** Reporter, pp. 226–227 **Connections to BookFestival:** ■ *The Case of the Sabotaged School Play* by Marilyn Singer

***** The cross-curricular lessons are optional. You may, however, wish to teach the cross-curricular lesson that has been paired with the weekly lesson shown in the chart.

OBJECTIVES

- Learn and practice the Divide and Conquer strategy
- Apply the Divide and Conquer strategy to list words in Unit 2

DIVIDE AND CONQUER

Students are encouraged to use this strategy with words that are long and hard to spell. It calls for students to use the auditory modality to determine where syllables fall and then listen for the sounds they hear in each syllable. Using this strategy with compound and multisyllabic words calls upon use of the visual modality.

Additional Resources

Frequently Misspelled Words Poster
Spelling Tool Kit Poster

Divide and Conquer

DISCOVER THE STRATEGY Do long words give you spelling problems? Help is on the way. It's the Divide and Conquer Strategy, and it consists of the following three ways to divide long words:

Use the way that works best for you to divide each long word. Then study the word part by part.

TRY IT OUT Now practice the Divide and Conquer Strategy yourself. Follow the directions on the next page.

1. Divide into Syllables Use this method with any long word. Remember: A syllable is a word or part of a word that you say as a unit: **(choc/o/late)**.

Write *America, alphabet,* and *elephant.* Listen for the syllables and draw lines between them. Check a dictionary for any words you're not sure of.

1. A/mer/i/ca
2. al/pha/bet
3. el/e/phant

2. Divide into Prefixes, Suffixes, and Base Words This method will help you see the parts of the word with a prefix or suffix. You will also see if adding a suffix changes the spelling of the base word.

Write *unhappy, beautiful,* and *rewrite.* Draw lines between each base word and any prefix or suffix.

Look back at the words you wrote. Underline the base word in which the spelling changed when the suffix was added.

4. un/happy
5. beauti/ful
6. re/write

3. Divide Compounds This method will show you that two words have been put together with no letters lost.

Write *everybody, afternoon,* and *something.* Draw a line between the two base words in each compound.

7. every/body
8. after/noon
9. some/thing

LOOK AHEAD Look ahead at the next five lessons. Write two list words that are long and look hard to spell. Divide each word to make it easier to study.

1. Words will vary.
2. Words will vary.

39

LESSON

7

Generalization

Spelling Focus: Some words have consonant combinations, such as **sh**, **ch**, **tch**, and **wh**, that are pronounced as one sound.

● Core   ○ Optional   ✓ Assessment

DAILY PLAN	CORE OBJECTIVES	NOTES

DAY 1 Introduction

● Strategy Workshop, p. 38
✓ Pretest and Self-Check, p. 40B
● Spelling Focus and Word List, p. 40
○ Challenge Words, p. 40
○ Challenge Master 7
○ Home-School Master 7

- Learn and practice the strategy Divide and Conquer
✓ - Take and self-check Pretest
- Spell words with consonant combination **sh**, **ch**, **tch**, or **wh**; classify and write the list words

DAY 2 Think and Practice

● Buried Words; Making Associations, p. 41
● Strategic Spelling: *The Divide and Conquer Strategy*, p. 41
○ Think and Practice Master 7
○ Extra Practice Master 7
○ Cross-Curricular Lesson: Introduce, p. 206

- Complete practice activities for words with consonant combinations **sh**, **ch**, **tch**, and **wh**
- Apply the Divide and Conquer Strategy to list words

DAY 3 Proofreading and Writing

● Proofread a Sign, p. 42
● Proofreading Tip: Dictionary Check, p. 42
● Create a Sign, p. 42
✓ Cooperative Midweek Test
○ Writing Mini-Lesson Master 7
○ Writing Activity Master 7
○ Second Language Support Master 7

- Proofread for spelling errors
- Integrate spelling and writing in a personal writing response
✓ - Take and check midweek test

DAY 4 Vocabulary Building

● Review: Rhymes, p. 43
● Using a Thesaurus: Parts of an Entry, p. 43
○ Cross-Curricular Lesson: Follow-Up, p. 206
○ Review Master 7

- Complete review activity for words with **sh**, **ch**, **tch**, and **wh**
- Study and use the parts of a thesaurus entry

DAY 5 Assessment

✓ Posttest, p. 40B
○ Standardized Test Master 7

✓ - Take Posttest

Cross-Curricular Lessons

Use the Spelling Focus (consonant combinations **sh**, **ch**, **tch**, and **wh**) to introduce the Reading lesson, *How Families Matter*, page 206, or choose a lesson that correlates with a topic you're currently teaching.

MEETING THE NEEDS OF ALL STUDENTS

The Word List

For students studying 20 words, assign pages 40–43 and Extra Practice and Review masters.

Modified List For students studying 10 words, modify Practice on page 40, and assign Think and Practice Master 7 and pages 42–43.

Challenge For students studying 25 words, assign pages 40–43, Challenge, Extra Practice, and Review masters.

Bilingual/ESL

In Spanish, the sound /ch/ is never found in final position and is never spelled **tch**. Spanish-speaking students might write *pich* instead of *pitch*.

Personal Words

Students add to Personal Words lists by looking at work in their writing portfolios and words they want to remember from their reading.

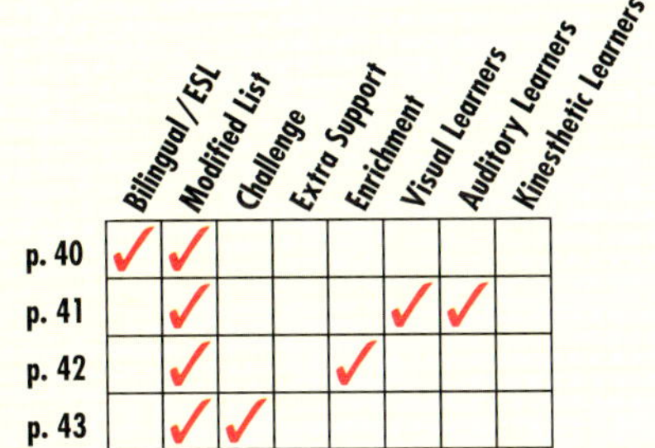

	Bilingual/ESL	Modified List	Challenge	Extra Support	Enrichment	Visual Learners	Auditory Learners	Kinesthetic Learners
p. 40	✓	✓						
p. 41		✓				✓	✓	
p. 42		✓			✓			
p. 43		✓	✓					

ASSESSMENT*

Pretest

Read the underlined word, read the sentence, and then repeat the underlined word. Guide students in self-correcting their pretests and correcting any misspellings.

1. I was <u>shown</u> to the room.
2. The class read a <u>short</u> poem.
3. Mom will not <u>punish</u> him.
4. <u>March</u> was a windy month.
5. The first <u>chapter</u> is great.
6. <u>Watch</u> the teacher carefully.
7. John cleaned the <u>kitchen</u>.
8. Buy <u>whatever</u> you want.
9. I couldn't find it <u>anywhere</u>.
10. Go <u>whenever</u> you like.
11. The trees will <u>shelter</u> you.
12. Use a <u>flashlight</u> at camp.
13. Put the <u>trash</u> by the curb.
14. Becky loves <u>chocolate</u> cake.
15. Julio sings in <u>church</u>.
16. The <u>pitcher</u> hit a batter.
17. Matt threw to the <u>catcher</u>.
18. The farmer planted <u>wheat</u>.
19. Sit down and rest <u>awhile</u>.
20. Gold is hidden <u>somewhere</u>.

Posttest

Read aloud the sentences below. These sentences may be used for dictation.

1. Will you <u>watch</u> the dog?
2. Dad will mop the <u>kitchen</u>.
3. Reread the last <u>chapter</u>.
4. Winter ends in <u>March</u>.
5. They will <u>punish</u> the robber.
6. A visitor took a <u>short</u> walk.
7. Have you <u>shown</u> her the city?
8. You may travel <u>anywhere</u>.
9. Go <u>whenever</u> you want.
10. Buy <u>whatever</u> you need.
11. The <u>catcher</u> got the ball.
12. Put the drink in a <u>pitcher</u>.
13. Let's have hot <u>chocolate</u>.
14. People met in the <u>church</u>.
15. Please take the <u>trash</u> out.
16. A <u>flashlight</u> is helpful.
17. The boys made a <u>shelter</u>.
18. Let's take a trip <u>somewhere</u>.
19. Bread is made from <u>wheat</u>.
20. Rest <u>awhile</u> before swimming.

Challenge Words

1. We ate yellow <u>squash</u>.
2. The player is a <u>champion</u>.
3. A player can score a <u>touchdown</u>.
4. Grandma must use <u>crutches</u>.
5. My dog goes <u>wherever</u> I go.

Additional Assessment

Standardized Test Master 7
Dictation Sentences, p. T38
Everyday Spelling CD-ROM

WHAT'S THE BIG IDEA?
Since there are no sound clues to distinguish words that begin with **w** and **wh**, encourage students to exaggerate the sound /hw/ when they say **wh** words.

* See pp. T20 and T33 for test-study-test information.

DAY 1 CHALLENGE MASTER

CHALLENGE ■ 7

Challenge Words

champion touchdown squash crutches wherever

■ Unscramble the Challenge Words to complete each puzzle. Then unscramble the circled letters to answer the riddle.

1. ccurtehs — c r u t c h e s
2. qhasus — s q u a s h
3. ioamnchp — c h a m p i o n
4. reerevhw — w h e r e v e r
5. dthoncuow — t o u c h d o w n

What an artichoke and a human have in common. h e a r t

■ Have you seen a football game? Have you seen a team score a winning touchdown? Write a description of a sports event that you like. Use one or more Challenge Words.

Practice Masters, p. 29

DAY 1 HOME-SCHOOL MASTER

■ 7 HOME-SCHOOL ACTIVITIES 7 ■

Word Check 7
1. watch
2. anywhere
3. punish
4. church
5. wheat
6. kitchen
7. shown
8. awhile
9. pitcher
10. flashlight
11. somewhere
12. short
13. catcher
14. whatever
15. chapter
16. whenever
17. shelter
18. chocolate
19. trash
20. March

■ **Relationships** Write a list word to complete each sentence below.

1. sleeping and bedroom, cooking and **kitchen**
2. day and Saturday, month and **March**
3. play and act, book and **chapter**
4. soup and bowl, juice and **pitcher**
5. roof and house, steeple and **church**
6. fruit and orange, candy and **chocolate**
7. high and low, tall and **short**
8. soccer and goalie, baseball and **catcher**
9. day and night, nowhere and **somewhere**
10. electricity and light bulb, battery and **flashlight**

■ **Letter Circles** Fill in the blanks to form list words. Then write the circled letters to solve the riddle.

11. t r a s h
12. w h e n e v e r
13. s h o w n
14. a w h i l e
15. w h e a t
16. s h e l t e r
17. w a t c h
18. w h a t e v e r
19. a n y w h e r e
20. p u n i s h

In these spelling words, some single sounds are spelled with
t w o   l e t t e r s

Dear Parent,

Please check to see that your child has done this page correctly. Circle any misspelled words and help your child study them.

Tear off the Word Check before your child returns this page to class. Use it to help your child study.

Home-School Activities, p. 6

DAY 2 THINK AND PRACTICE MASTER

7 ■ THINK AND PRACTICE

shown	short	punish	March	chapter
watch	kitchen	whatever	anywhere	whenever

■ **Find the Sound** Write the list words that answer the questions.

Which two words begin with *wh*?
1. **whatever** 2. **whenever**

Which two words begin with *sh*?
3. **shown** 4. **short**

Which word has *wh* in the middle?
5. **anywhere**

What word has *tch* at the end?
6. **watch**

■ **Making Associations** Write the list word that you would associate with each word.

7. stove and **kitchen**
8. bad and **punish**
9. February and **March**
10. book and **chapter**
11. hidden and **shown**

STRATEGIC SPELLING: The Divide and Conquer Strategy
Study long words piece by piece. Write *anywhere, whatever, kitchen,* and *whenever.* Draw lines to break each word into smaller parts. Study the parts.

12. **any/where** 14. **kitch/en**
13. **what/ever** 15. **when/ever**

Practice Masters, p. 30

DAY 2 EXTRA PRACTICE MASTER

EXTRA PRACTICE ■ 7

Word List

shown	short	punish	March	chapter
watch	kitchen	whatever	anywhere	whenever
shelter	flashlight	trash	chocolate	church
pitcher	catcher	wheat	awhile	somewhere

■ **Classifying** Write the list word that belongs in each group.

1. May, July, ___
2. temple, chapel, ___
3. bedroom, living room, ___
4. book, section, ___
5. dessert, candy, ___
6. garbage, waste, ___
7. lantern, candle, ___
8. observe, stare, ___
9. corn, oats, ___
10. safety, protection, ___
11. fielder, shortstop, ___
12. vase, jug, ___

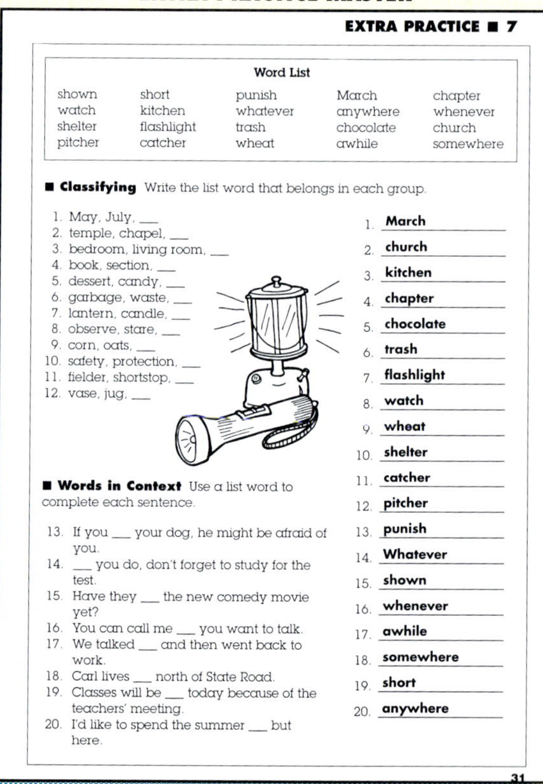

1. **March**
2. **church**
3. **kitchen**
4. **chapter**
5. **chocolate**
6. **trash**
7. **flashlight**
8. **watch**
9. **wheat**
10. **shelter**
11. **catcher**
12. **pitcher**

■ **Words in Context** Use a list word to complete each sentence.

13. If you ___ your dog, he might be afraid of you.
14. ___ you do, don't forget to study for the test.
15. Have they ___ the new comedy movie yet?
16. You can call me ___ you want to talk.
17. We talked ___ and then went back to work.
18. Carl lives ___ north of State Road.
19. Classes will be ___ today because of the teachers' meeting.
20. I'd like to spend the summer ___ but here.

13. **punish**
14. **Whatever**
15. **shown**
16. **whenever**
17. **awhile**
18. **somewhere**
19. **short**
20. **anywhere**

31

Practice Masters, p. 31

TECHNOLOGY AND VISUAL SUPPORT	 Use Audiotape A, Side 2, Lesson 7	 For additional practice use *Everyday Spelling* Game Software, Lesson 7	 Additional resources on *Everyday Spelling* CD-ROM: proofreading and writing, modified list and challenge words, auditory test
	Use Proofreading and Writing Transparency 7		

DAY 3 SECOND LANGUAGE SUPPORT MASTER

7 ■ SECOND LANGUAGE SUPPORT

More Than One Meaning

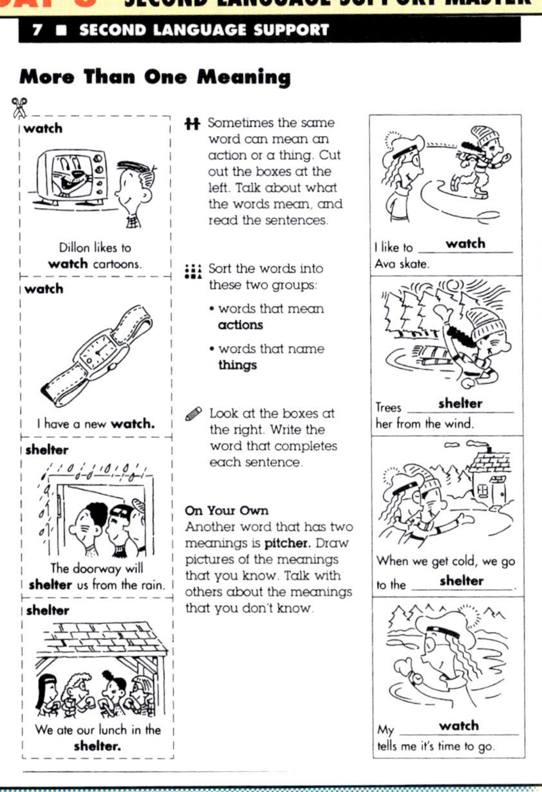

Second Language Support, p. 32

DAY 3 WRITING ACTIVITY MASTER

7 ■ WRITING ACTIVITY

Rhymes

❑ Rhymes sound the same at the end.

■ Here is a cheer Bonnie started to write for her soccer team, the Haddonfield Tigers. Help her complete it by writing the lines that rhyme with *roar* and *play*.

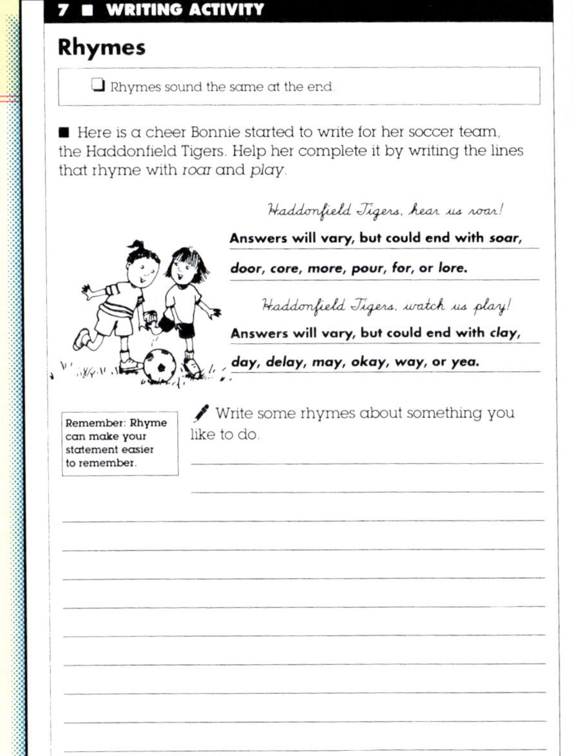

Remember: Rhyme can make your statement easier to remember.

✎ Write some rhymes about something you like to do.

Spelling and Writing, p. 12

DAY 4 REVIEW MASTER

7 ■ REVIEW

Word List

shown	short	punish	March	chapter
watch	kitchen	whatever	anywhere	whenever
shelter	flashlight	trash	chocolate	church
pitcher	catcher	wheat	awhile	somewhere

■ **Words in Context** Write the list word that is missing from each person's statement.

1. Farmer: "I am harvesting the ___ fields."
2. Baker: "The ___ cake was just frosted."
3. Jeweler: "Would you like to see a ___ ?"
4. Sports doctor: "A baseball ___ needs to wear a face mask."
5. Veterinarian: "There are many kittens for adoption at the animal ___."
6. Minister: "Many members of the ___ came to the picnic."
7. Writer: "I just finished my last ___."
8. Interior decorator: "What colors do you like best for your ___?"
9. Waiter: "Let me refill the ___ of water."
10. Child: "I always have to take out the ___."
11. Parent: "I never ___ my child."

1. **wheat**
2. **chocolate**
3. **watch**
4. **catcher**
5. **shelter**
6. **church**
7. **chapter**
8. **kitchen**
9. **pitcher**
10. **trash**
11. **punish**
12. **anywhere**
13. **short**
14. **March**
15. **whenever**
16. **shown**
17. **somewhere**
18. **whatever**
19. **awhile**
20. **flashlight**

■ **Sentence Clues** Write the list word that means the same as the underlined word or words. Use the Spelling Dictionary for help.

12. My dog follows me <u>anyplace</u> I go.
13. Mabel is rather <u>small</u>—about five feet.
14. The <u>third month</u> comes in like a lion.
15. Call me <u>anytime</u> you need me.
16. Charles hasn't <u>let me see</u> his pictures.

■ **Syllable Scramble** Match one syllable from each column to make list words.

17. some	light
18. what	while
19. a	where
20. flash	ever

Practice Masters, p. 32

DAY 5 STANDARDIZED TEST MASTER

7 ■ LESSON TEST

■ Find the word in each group that is spelled correctly. Fill in the letter for the correct word on the answer strip.

Sample:
a. crowde   c. croud
b. croued   d. crowd   ● (d)

1. a. wach   c. whatch
   b. watch   d. wath   ● (b)
2. a. watever   c. wutever
   b. whetever   d. whatever   ● (d)
3. a. awill   c. awhile
   b. awile   d. awille   ● (c)
4. a. kichen   c. kitchen
   b. kithen   d. kitohin   ● (c)
5. a. wenever   c. wanever
   b. whenever   d. when evere   ● (b)
6. a. cacher   c. catcher
   b. cather   d. checher   ● (c)
7. a. punish   c. punsh
   b. punnish   d. punishe   ● (a)
8. a. tash   c. tras
   b. trach   d. trash   ● (d)
9. a. weat   c. wheet
   b. whaet   d. wheat   ● (d)
10. a. pitcher   c. picher
    b. pichter   d. picther   ● (a)
11. a. flachlight   c. flashlight
    b. flashelite   d. flashlite   ● (c)
12. a. showne   c. shown
    b. showin   d. showen   ● (c)
13. a. short   c. shrot
    b. schort   d. shorte   ● (a)
14. a. choclate   c. cholate
    b. chocolate   d. chocalate   ● (b)
15. a. cherch   c. chruch
    b. church   d. chrch   ● (b)
16. a. capter   c. chaptir
    b. chapder   d. chapter   ● (d)
17. a. anywere   c. anywar
    b. anywear   d. anywhere   ● (d)
18. a. somewhere   c. somewere
    b. somwhere   d. somewear   ● (a)
19. a. chelter   c. shiler
    b. shelter   d. schelter   ● (b)
20. a. marc   c. March
    b. Marche   d. marche   ● (c)

Practice for Standardized Tests, p. 10

40D

DAY 1 Introduction

✓ Pretest and Self-Check
● Spelling Focus and Word List
○ Challenge Words
○ Modified List

DAILY SPELLING REVIEW

That is the *fatest stawbary* I ever saw.

fattest   *strawberry*

● Core   ○ Optional   ✓ Assessment

INTRODUCTION

Phonics

Words with sh, ch, tch, wh Have students write a sentence that combines all the words with **ch** or **tch**, for example, *We watch the catcher and pitcher from the kitchen.*

MEETING THE NEEDS OF ALL STUDENTS

Modified List

Practice Students studying only the high-frequency words in the top box write
- three words with **sh**
- two words with **ch**
- two words with **tch**
- three words with **wh**

Bilingual/ESL

Show to Tell To help clarify the meanings of the words *somewhere, anywhere, whenever,* and *whatever,* use props (pictures, a map, a clock) and sentences, such as "There is a rabbit *somewhere* in this picture."

Additional Practice

Challenge Master 7
Home-School Master 7
Audiotape A, Side 2

1. shown
2. short
3. punish
4. shelter
5. flashlight
6. trash
7. watch
8. kitchen
9. pitcher
10. catcher
11. March
12. chapter
13. chocolate
14. church
15. whatever
16. anywhere
17. whenever
18. wheat
19. awhile
20. somewhere

CHALLENGE!

squash
champion
touchdown
crutches
wherever

■ INTRODUCTION

Words with sh, ch, tch, wh

SPELLING FOCUS

Words can have two or three consonants together that are pronounced as one sound: **punish, chapter, watch, whenever.**

■ **STUDY**   Say each word. Then read the sentence.

1. *shown* — That movie was **shown** last week.
2. *short* — My aunt came for a **short** visit.
3. *punish* — They will **punish** the criminal.
4. *March* — Does winter end in **March?**
5. *chapter* — I read a **chapter** of the book.
6. *watch* ✳ — Children **watch** the juggler.
7. *kitchen* — Who will clean the **kitchen?**
8. *whatever* — My sister does **whatever** I do.
9. *anywhere* — I can't find my shoe **anywhere.**
10. *whenever* — Visit me **whenever** you can.

11. *shelter* — We found **shelter** in a barn.
12. *flashlight* — Use a **flashlight** when it is dark.
13. *trash* — Don't put cans in the **trash.**
14. *chocolate* ✳ — Dad made a **chocolate** cake.
15. *church* — The **church** bell rings on Sundays.
16. *pitcher* — He is a **pitcher** on a baseball team.
17. *catcher* — He threw the ball to the **catcher.**
18. *wheat* — Is that white or **wheat** bread?
19. *awhile* — Can you stay **awhile?**
20. *somewhere* — She is **somewhere** in the house.

■ **PRACTICE**   Sort the words by writing
- six words with **sh**   ■ four words with **ch**
- four words with **tch**   ■ six words with **wh**

Order of words in each group may vary.

■ **WRITE**   Choose two sentences to include in a paragraph.

Questions and answers will vary.

✳ **WATCH OUT FOR FREQUENTLY MISSPELLED WORDS!**

- Practice: Buried Words and Making Associations
- Strategic Spelling:
  The Divide and Conquer Strategy
- Cross-Curricular Lesson: Introduce
- Modified List

DAILY SPELLING REVIEW

Do you *no* how to *clime* a tree?

know   *climb*

THINK AND PRACTICE

BURIED WORDS Each word below is hidden in a list word. Write the list word.

1. eat
2. pitch
3. what
4. pun
5. arch
6. or
7. rash
8. own
9. chap
10. catch

MAKING ASSOCIATIONS Write the list word that you would associate with each word or phrase below.

11. protection ____
12. a short time ____
13. worship ____
14. clock ____
15. dark candy ____
16. cook's place ____

1. **wheat**
2. **pitcher**
3. **whatever**
4. **punish**
5. **March**
6. **short**
7. **trash**
8. **shown**
9. **chapter**
10. **catcher**
11. **shelter**
12. **awhile**
13. **church**
14. **watch**
15. **chocolate**
16. **kitchen**

The Divide and Conquer Strategy

Study long words piece by piece. Write *flashlight, somewhere, anywhere, whenever, chocolate,* and *pitcher.* Draw lines to break each word into smaller parts. Study the parts.

17. **flash/light**
18. **some/where**
19. **any/where**
20. **when/ever**
21. **choc/o/late**
22. **pitch/er**

Did You Know?
The word **chocolate** was borrowed from Mexican Spanish. It came from *chocolatl,* a word in Nahuatl, the language of the Aztecs and Toltecs.

THINK AND PRACTICE

Making Associations

Using a Dictionary Explain that a clue may be a synonym, a definition, or a word with a related meaning. Encourage students to use a dictionary as needed.

MEETING THE NEEDS OF ALL STUDENTS

Modified List

Review Students studying high-frequency words complete Think and Practice Master 7.

Visual Learners

Buried Words Students may work with a partner to find the "buried words," such as *own* within *shown.*

Auditory Learners

Oral Sentences Auditory learners might work with a partner to make up and repeat sentences for each buried word, such as "I had an *itch* in the *kitchen.*"

Additional Practice

Think and Practice Master 7
Extra Practice Master 7
Everyday Spelling CD-ROM
Everyday Spelling Game Software

LESSON

7

- Proofread a Sign
- Proofreading Tip: Dictionary Check
- Create a Sign
- ✓ Cooperative Midweek Test

DAILY SPELLING REVIEW

John's money fell *threw* his *poket*.

through   *pocket*

● Core ○ Optional ✓ Assessment

PROOFREADING AND WRITING

Checking Spelling
Real-World Spelling Errors
Give students a week to look for spelling errors on outdoor signs. Have them write down and bring in the misspelled words they find and then correct those misspellings.

MEETING THE NEEDS OF ALL STUDENTS

Modified List
Proofreading Students studying high-frequency words complete this page or the proofreading activity on the *Everyday Spelling* CD-ROM.

Enrichment
Class Signs Have students work in small groups to create signs announcing a class activity. Encourage students to divide up the tasks, such as rough-draft writer, proofreader, and sign letterer.

Additional Practice

Second Language Master 7
Writing Mini-Lesson Master 7
Writing Activity Master 7
Proofreading Transparency 7
Everyday Spelling CD-ROM

■ **PROOFREADING AND WRITING**

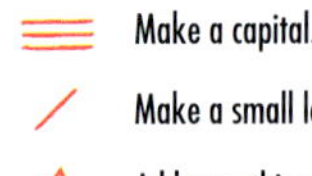

PROOFREAD A SIGN A spelling error on a large outdoor sign really stands out. Find the two mistakes in the photograph below, and spell the words correctly.

PROOFREADING TIP
Watch out! Don't be caught making a big mistake. Keep a dictionary handy when you write signs.

watch, jewelry

CREATE A SIGN Think of one of your favorite stores. Create a sign for an item that is sold there. Try to use words from your spelling list. Check your sign for careless errors.

Responses will vary. Sign should include list words.

Word List

watch	somewhere
anywhere	short
punish	catcher
church	whatever
wheat	chapter
kitchen	whenever
shown	shelter
awhile	chocolate
pitcher	trash
flashlight	March

Personal Words

1. Words will vary.

2. ___________

VOCABULARY BUILDING

Review

RHYMES   Write the boxed word that rhymes with the underlined word and makes sense in the sentence.

shown	watch
short	kitchen
punish	whatever
March	anywhere
chapter	whenever

1. Meet me at the <u>arch</u> on the last day in ___
2. The pilot was ___ where the plane had <u>flown</u>.
3. The <u>men</u> placed the groceries on the table in the ___.
4. The librarian said, "Choose ___ books you like, but <u>never</u> forget to return them."
5. My time visiting the old frontier <u>fort</u> was much too ___.
6. Did you see a <u>bear</u> ___ in Yellowstone National Park?
7. Just ___ me make this <u>blotch</u> disappear from your shirt sleeve.
8. In this ___, I learned that a bird of prey is called a <u>raptor</u>.
9. That <u>clever</u> comedian has his audiences howling with laughter ___ he performs.
10. Carl's parents won't ___ him for breaking the <u>dish</u> accidentally.

1. **March**
2. **shown**
3. **kitchen**
4. **whatever**
5. **short**
6. **anywhere**
7. **watch**
8. **chapter**
9. **whenever**
10. **punish**

Using a *Thesaurus*

PARTS OF AN ENTRY   To make your *Writer's Thesaurus* a useful resource, it is important to know all the parts of a thesaurus entry. Study the parts of the entry for the word *show*. Then answer the questions.

1. What part of speech is *show*?
2. Which synonym would you use to tell about a friend who showed you how to make a kite?
3. Which synonym would you use to tell about a boy who showed his kindness by helping an injured child?
4. What cross-references would lead you to other words with related meanings?
5. Write one antonym for *show*.

1. **verb**
2. **demonstrate**
3. **point out**
4. **guide**
5. **turn up**
6. **conceal or hide**

Part of speech   Definition

Entry Word → **Show** *v.* to cause something to be seen. *Patrick wants to show his new shoes to Saburo.*

Synonyms → **Display** to show things in a way that gets attention. *Thalia yawned widely, displaying her braces.*
Exhibit to show something publicly. *Tara exhibited her paintings at the arts and crafts show.*
Demonstrate to show something in a way that helps people understand. *A company demonstrated its new milking machine at the county fair.*
Point out to show where something is or to call attention to something. *Manuel pointed out all the sights of Chicago.*

Cross-References → SEE *guide* and *turn up* for related words.

VOCABULARY BUILDING

Literature Connection
Another Way to Say . . .
Students can read an essay from *Champions: Stories of Ten Remarkable Athletes* by Bill Littlefield (Little, Brown and Company, 1993) and paraphrase a few sentences, using a thesaurus to find synonyms. Encourage them to share their paraphrases and discuss which are most appropriate.

MEETING THE NEEDS OF ALL STUDENTS

Modified List
Review Students studying high-frequency words complete this page.

Challenge
Round-Robin Rhymes
Have students work with a partner to write a rhyme. One partner writes one line, then passes the paper to his or her partner, who writes a rhyming line. For an extra challenge, encourage students to include list words.

Additional Practice

Review Master 7
Standardized Test Master 7
***Everyday Spelling* CD-ROM**

43

8

Generalization

Spelling Focus: Sometimes double consonants, such as **ff, pp,** and **rr,** stand for one sound.

● Core　○ Optional　✓ Assessment

DAILY PLAN	CORE OBJECTIVES	NOTES

DAY 1 Introduction

✓ Pretest and Self-Check, p. 44B
● Spelling Focus and Word List, p. 44
● Challenge Words, p. 44
○ Challenge Master 8
○ Home-School Master 8

✓ ▪ Take and self-check Pretest
▪ Spell words that have double consonants; classify and write the list words

DAY 2 Think and Practice

● Antonym Argument; Words in Context, p. 45
● Strategic Spelling: *Building New Words,* p. 45
○ Think and Practice Master 8
○ Extra Practice Master 8
○ Cross-Curricular Lesson: Introduce, p. 200

▪ Complete practice activities for words with double consonants
▪ Create new words by adding **-ed** to list words

DAY 3 Proofreading and Writing

● Proofread a Message, p. 46
● Proofreading Tip: Careless Errors, p. 46
● Write a Message, p. 46
✓ Cooperative Midweek Test
○ Hardbound Book Master 8A
○ Writing Mini-Lesson Master 8
○ Writing Activity Master 8
○ Second Language Support Master 8

▪ Proofread for spelling and careless errors
▪ Integrate spelling and writing in a personal writing response
✓ ▪ Take and check midweek test

DAY 4 Vocabulary Building

● Review: Context Clues, p. 47
● Word Study: Acrostics, p. 47
● Hardbound Book Master 8B
○ Cross-Curricular Lesson: Follow-Up, p. 200
○ Review Master 8

▪ Complete review activity for words with double consonants
▪ Study and make an acrostic

DAY 5 Assessment

✓ Posttest, p. 44B
○ Standardized Test Master 8

✓ ▪ Take Posttest

Cross-Curricular Lessons

Use the Spelling Focus (words with double consonants) to introduce the Science lesson, *The Eyes and Ears*, page 200, or choose a lesson that correlates with a topic you're currently teaching.

MEETING THE NEEDS OF ALL STUDENTS

The Word List

For students studying 20 words, assign pages 44–47 and Extra Practice and Review masters.

Modified List For students studying 10 words, modify Practice on page 44, and assign Think and Practice Master 8 and pages 46–47.

Challenge For students studying 25 words, assign pages 44–47, Challenge, Extra Practice, and Review masters.

Bilingual/ESL

In Haitian-Creole, there are no double consonants. Students will tend to omit one of the consonants when writing English words containing double consonants.

Personal Words

Students add to Personal Words lists by looking at work in their writing portfolios and words they want to remember from their reading.

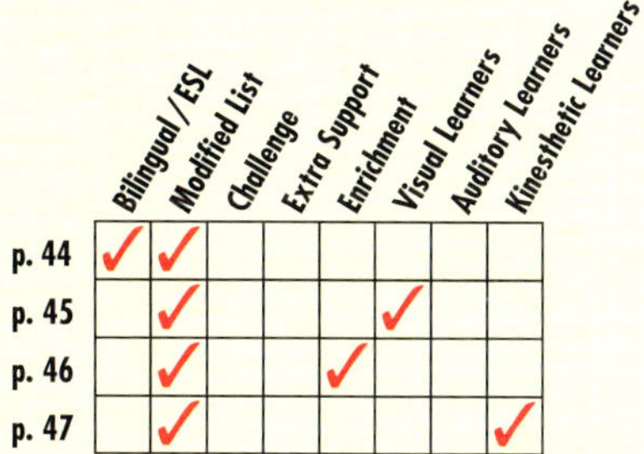

	Bilingual/ESL	Modified List	Challenge	Extra Support	Enrichment	Visual Learners	Auditory Learners	Kinesthetic Learners
p. 44	✓	✓						
p. 45		✓				✓		
p. 46		✓			✓			
p. 47		✓						✓

ASSESSMENT*

Pretest

Read the underlined word, read the sentence, and then repeat the underlined word. Guide students in self-correcting their pretests and correcting any misspellings.

1. It might rain <u>tomorrow</u>.
2. May I <u>borrow</u> your book?
3. Chad wore a <u>different</u> shirt.
4. We had salad for <u>supper</u>.
5. It doesn't <u>matter</u> who wins.
6. Andy has <u>written</u> a letter.
7. Paco drank a <u>bottle</u> of milk.
8. Have you <u>ridden</u> before?
9. That is an <u>odd</u> butterfly.
10. Tara blew a soap <u>bubble</u>.
11. The host will <u>offer</u> you tea.
12. The poor horse will <u>suffer</u>.
13. <u>Slippers</u> keep my feet warm.
14. Liz found a big <u>grasshopper</u>.
15. That problem will <u>worry</u> you.
16. We discussed <u>current</u> events.
17. Ali put <u>lettuce</u> on bread.
18. Put the <u>paddle</u> in the water.
19. I <u>shudder</u> to think of it.
20. Painting is a good <u>hobby</u>.

Posttest

Read aloud the sentences below. These sentences may be used for dictation.

1. We went a <u>different</u> way.
2. Let's go out after <u>supper</u>.
3. The picnic is <u>tomorrow</u>.
4. Have you <u>ridden</u> on a sled?
5. Have you <u>written</u> a story?
6. What is the <u>matter</u> with you?
7. Do you like <u>bubble</u> gum?
8. Did you <u>borrow</u> my pencil?
9. Put the flower in a <u>bottle</u>.
10. We saw an <u>odd</u> black lamb.
11. Don't <u>worry</u> about it.
12. It's fun to <u>paddle</u> a boat.
13. Bird watching is a <u>hobby</u>.
14. <u>Offer</u> the girls a cookie.
15. Wear some warm <u>slippers</u>.
16. The cold made me <u>shudder</u>.
17. The hurt dog will <u>suffer</u>.
18. Is that the <u>current</u> paper?
19. We saw a green <u>grasshopper</u>.
20. I grew <u>lettuce</u> in a garden.

Challenge Words

1. My friend is in <u>Mississippi</u>.
2. Let's swing at <u>recess</u>.
3. That trick is <u>impossible</u>.
4. The house has two <u>antennas</u>.
5. Do you get an <u>allowance</u>?

Additional Assessment

Standardized Test Master 8
Dictation Sentences, p. T38
Everyday Spelling CD-ROM

Tennessee and *committee* have two sets of double consonants in them. Challenge students to find a word with three sets of double letters (possible answer: *Mississippi*).

* See pp. T20 and T33 for test-study-test information.

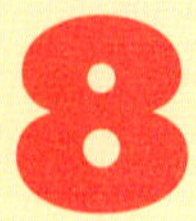

8

DAY 1 CHALLENGE MASTER

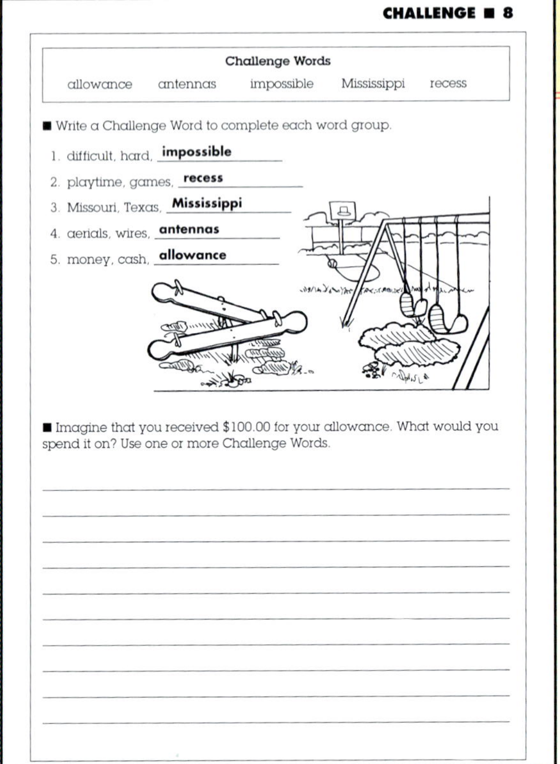

CHALLENGE ■ 8

Challenge Words

allowance   antennas   impossible   Mississippi   recess

■ Write a Challenge Word to complete each word group.

1. difficult, hard, **impossible**
2. playtime, games, **recess**
3. Missouri, Texas, **Mississippi**
4. aerials, wires, **antennas**
5. money, cash, **allowance**

■ Imagine that you received $100.00 for your allowance. What would you spend it on? Use one or more Challenge Words.

Practice Masters, p. 33

DAY 1 HOME-SCHOOL MASTER

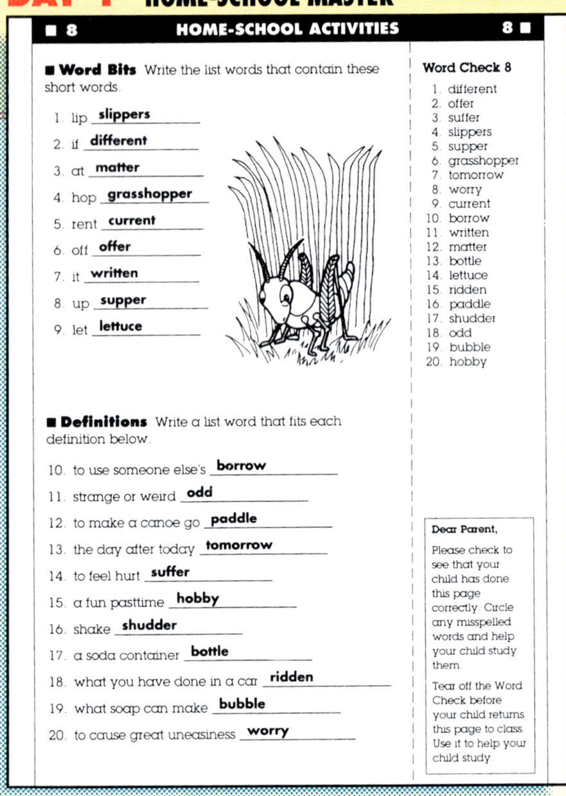

■ 8   HOME-SCHOOL ACTIVITIES   8 ■

■ **Word Bits** Write the list words that contain these short words.

1. lip **slippers**
2. if **different**
3. at **matter**
4. hop **grasshopper**
5. rent **current**
6. off **offer**
7. it **written**
8. up **supper**
9. let **lettuce**

■ **Definitions** Write a list word that fits each definition below.

10. to use someone else's **borrow**
11. strange or weird **odd**
12. to make a canoe go **paddle**
13. the day after today **tomorrow**
14. to feel hurt **suffer**
15. a fun pasttime **hobby**
16. shake **shudder**
17. a soda container **bottle**
18. what you have done in a car **ridden**
19. what soap can make **bubble**
20. to cause great uneasiness **worry**

Word Check 8

1. different
2. offer
3. suffer
4. slippers
5. supper
6. grasshopper
7. tomorrow
8. worry
9. current
10. borrow
11. written
12. matter
13. bottle
14. lettuce
15. ridden
16. paddle
17. shudder
18. odd
19. bubble
20. hobby

Dear Parent,

Please check to see that your child has done this page correctly. Circle any misspelled words and help your child study them.

Tear off the Word Check before your child returns this page to class. Use it to help your child study.

Home-School Activities, p. 7

DAY 2 THINK AND PRACTICE MASTER

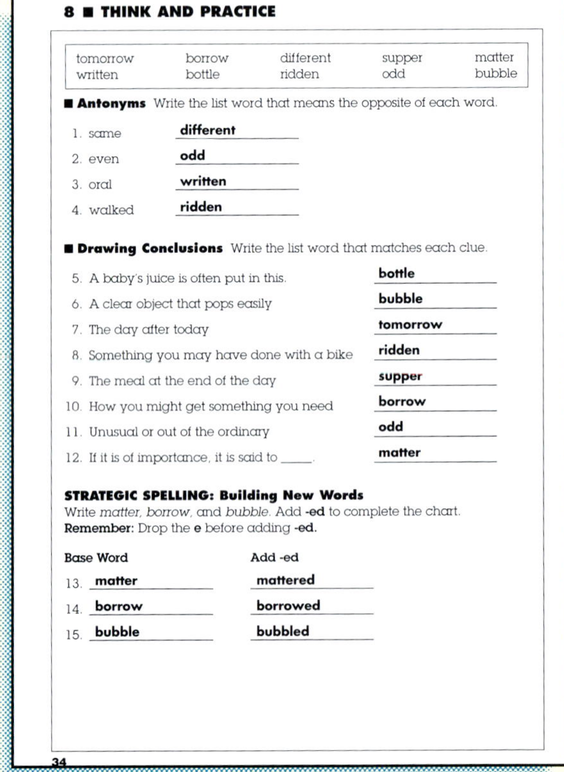

8 ■ THINK AND PRACTICE

| tomorrow | borrow | different | supper | matter |
| written | bottle | ridden | odd | bubble |

■ **Antonyms** Write the list word that means the opposite of each word.

1. same **different**
2. even **odd**
3. oral **written**
4. walked **ridden**

■ **Drawing Conclusions** Write the list word that matches each clue.

5. A baby's juice is often put in this. **bottle**
6. A clear object that pops easily **bubble**
7. The day after today **tomorrow**
8. Something you may have done with a bike **ridden**
9. The meal at the end of the day **supper**
10. How you might get something you need **borrow**
11. Unusual or out of the ordinary **odd**
12. If it is of importance, it is said to ____. **matter**

STRATEGIC SPELLING: Building New Words
Write *matter, borrow,* and *bubble.* Add **-ed** to complete the chart.
Remember: Drop the **e** before adding **-ed.**

Base Word	Add -ed
13. **matter**	**mattered**
14. **borrow**	**borrowed**
15. **bubble**	**bubbled**

Practice Masters, p. 34

DAY 2 EXTRA PRACTICE MASTER

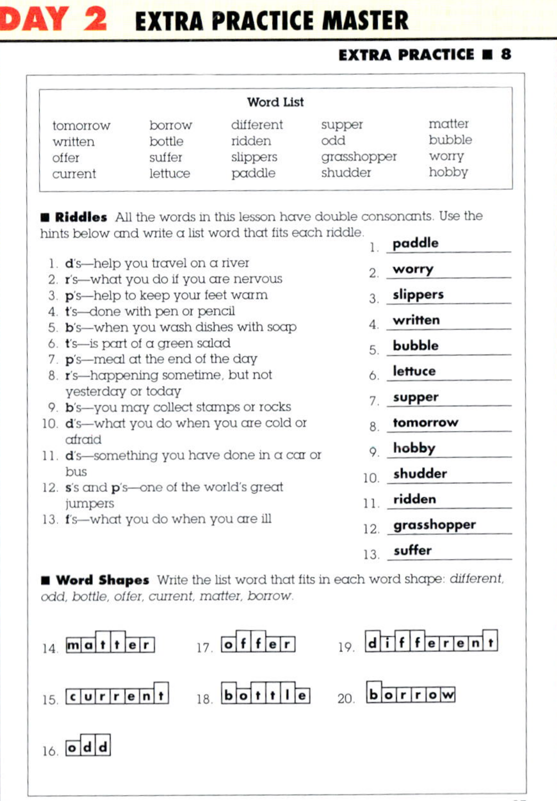

EXTRA PRACTICE ■ 8

Word List

tomorrow	borrow	different	supper	matter
written	bottle	ridden	odd	bubble
offer	suffer	slippers	grasshopper	worry
current	lettuce	paddle	shudder	hobby

■ **Riddles** All the words in this lesson have double consonants. Use the hints below and write a list word that fits each riddle.

1. d's—help you travel on a river
2. r's—what you do if you are nervous
3. p's—help to keep your feet warm
4. t's—done with pen or pencil
5. b's—when you wash dishes with soap
6. t's—is part of a green salad
7. p's—meal at the end of the day
8. r's—happening sometime, but not yesterday or today
9. b's—you may collect stamps or rocks
10. d's—what you do when you are cold or afraid
11. d's—something you have done in a car or bus
12. s's and p's—one of the world's great jumpers
13. f's—what you do when you are ill

1. **paddle**
2. **worry**
3. **slippers**
4. **written**
5. **bubble**
6. **lettuce**
7. **supper**
8. **tomorrow**
9. **hobby**
10. **shudder**
11. **ridden**
12. **grasshopper**
13. **suffer**

■ **Word Shapes** Write the list word that fits in each word shape: *different, odd, bottle, offer, current, matter, borrow.*

14. m a t t e r
15. c u r r e n t
16. o d d
17. o f f e r
18. b o t t l e
19. d i f f e r e n t
20. b o r r o w

Practice Masters, p. 35

44C

TECHNOLOGY AND VISUAL SUPPORT	 Use Audiotape A, Side 2, Lesson 8	 For additional practice use *Everyday Spelling* Game Software, Lesson 8	 Additional resources on *Everyday Spelling* CD-ROM: proofreading and writing, modified list and challenge words, auditory test
	Use Proofreading and Writing Transparency 8		

DAY 3 SECOND LANGUAGE SUPPORT MASTER

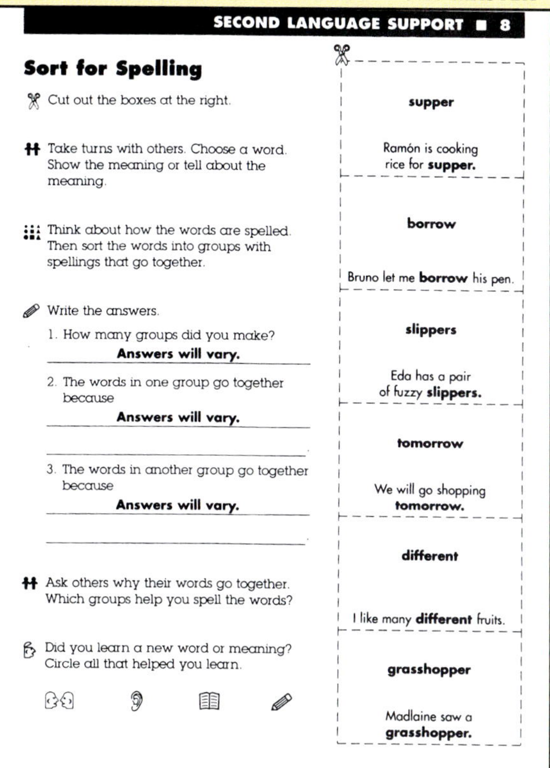

SECOND LANGUAGE SUPPORT ■ 8

Sort for Spelling

✂ Cut out the boxes at the right.

✄ Take turns with others. Choose a word. Show the meaning or tell about the meaning.

⋮ Think about how the words are spelled. Then sort the words into groups with spellings that go together.

✐ Write the answers.

1. How many groups did you make?
   Answers will vary.

2. The words in one group go together because
   Answers will vary.

3. The words in another group go together because
   Answers will vary.

✄ Ask others why their words go together. Which groups help you spell the words?

✍ Did you learn a new word or meaning? Circle all that helped you learn.

supper

Ramón is cooking rice for **supper**.

borrow

Bruno let me **borrow** his pen.

slippers

Eda has a pair of fuzzy **slippers**.

tomorrow

We will go shopping **tomorrow**.

different

I like many **different** fruits.

grasshopper

Madlaine saw a **grasshopper**.

Second Language Support, p. 33

DAY 3 WRITING ACTIVITY MASTER

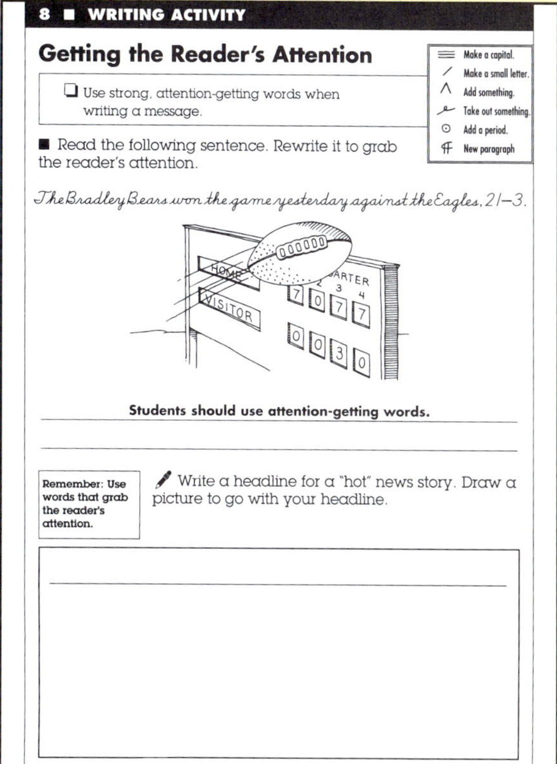

8 ■ WRITING ACTIVITY

Getting the Reader's Attention

= Make a capital.
/ Make a small letter.
∧ Add something.
✄ Take out something.
⊙ Add a period.
¶ New paragraph.

☐ Use strong, attention-getting words when writing a message.

■ Read the following sentence. Rewrite it to grab the reader's attention.

Students should use attention-getting words.

Remember: Use words that grab the reader's attention.

✐ Write a headline for a "hot" news story. Draw a picture to go with your headline.

Spelling and Writing, p. 14

DAY 4 REVIEW MASTER

8 ■ REVIEW

Word List

tomorrow	borrow	different	supper	matter
written	bottle	ridden	odd	bubble
offer	suffer	slippers	grasshopper	worry
current	lettuce	paddle	shudder	hobby

■ **Synonyms** Write the list word that means the same as the underlined word in each sentence.

1. The lion wouldn't have to feel pain.
2. She had composed the letter before lunch.
3. They were an unusual couple.
4. I walked to school three separate ways.
5. The newspaper reported recent events.

1. **suffer**
2. **written**
3. **odd**
4. **different**
5. **current**

■ **Definitions** Answer each question with a list word.

6. Which list word is an insect?
7. Which list word is a vegetable?
8. Which list word is a meal?
9. Which list word goes with coin collecting?
10. Which list word goes with goosebumps?
11. Which list word keeps your feet warm?
12. Which list word is round and floats?
13. Which list word can soda come in?
14. Which list word comes after today?
15. Which list word strokes through the water?

6. **grasshopper**
7. **lettuce**
8. **supper**
9. **hobby**
10. **shudder**
11. **slippers**
12. **bubble**
13. **bottle**
14. **tomorrow**
15. **paddle**

■ **Word Search** Find the five list words in the puzzle below. They may be printed down or across. Write them.

```
w r i d d e n
u b l g m s u
i o r o a y n
t r q f t o d
j r p f t o k
y o x e e l z
l w o r r y v
```

16. **ridden**
17. **borrow**
18. **matter**
19. **worry**
20. **offer**

Practice Masters, p. 36

DAY 5 STANDARDIZED TEST MASTER

LESSON TEST ■ 8

■ Find the word in each group that is spelled correctly. Fill in the letter for the correct word on the answer strip.

Sample:
| a. crowde | c. croud | Ⓐ Ⓑ Ⓒ ● |
| b. croued | d. crowd | |

1. a. diffrent / c. difrent / b. differnt / d. different — 1. Ⓐ Ⓑ Ⓒ ●
2. a. ridden / c. riddin / b. riden / d. ridin — 2. ● Ⓑ Ⓒ Ⓓ
3. a. lettce / c. lettece / b. letes / d. lettuce — 3. Ⓐ Ⓑ Ⓒ ●
4. a. ofer / c. offre / b. offer / d. offir — 4. Ⓤ ● Ⓒ Ⓓ
5. a. botle / c. bottle / b. botel / d. boddle — 5. Ⓐ Ⓑ ● Ⓓ
6. a. sufer / c. suffer / b. suffire / d. sufire — 6. Ⓐ Ⓑ ● Ⓓ
7. a. worrie / c. wory / b. worry / d. woory — 7. Ⓐ ● Ⓒ Ⓓ
8. a. corrent / c. courent / b. curent / d. current — 8. Ⓐ Ⓑ Ⓒ ●
9. a. slipprs / c. slipers / b. slippers / d. sleprs — 9. Ⓐ ● Ⓒ Ⓓ
10. a. padel / c. paddle / b. pattle / d. paddel — 10. Ⓐ Ⓑ ● Ⓓ
11. a. shudder / c. shuder / b. shuttre / d. shuddre — 11. ● Ⓑ Ⓒ Ⓓ
12. a. od / c. odt / b. ood / d. odd — 12. Ⓐ Ⓑ Ⓒ ●
13. a. buble / c. bubbel / b. bouble / d. bubble — 13. Ⓐ Ⓑ Ⓒ ●
14. a. hobbie / c. hoby / b. hobby / d. hobe — 14. Ⓐ ● Ⓒ Ⓓ
15. a. saper / c. supere / b. supr / d. supper — 15. Ⓐ Ⓑ Ⓒ ●
16. a. barow / c. borow / b. borrow / d. borro — 16. Ⓐ ● Ⓒ Ⓓ
17. a. mader / c. matter / b. madar / d. mater — 17. Ⓐ Ⓑ ● Ⓓ
18. a. grasshooper / c. grasshopper / b. grashopper / d. grasshoper — 18. Ⓐ Ⓑ ● Ⓓ
19. a. writen / c. ritten / b. written / d. writon — 19. Ⓐ ● Ⓒ Ⓓ
20. a. tommorow / c. tomorow / b. tomarrow / d. tomorrow — 20. Ⓐ Ⓑ Ⓒ ●

Practice for Standardized Tests, p. 11

LESSON 8

✓ Pretest and Self-Check
● Spelling Focus and Word List
○ Challenge Words
○ Modified List

○ **DAILY SPELLING REVIEW**

We saw a *dolfin* and an *elefant* at the zoo.

dolphin   *elephant*

● Core   ○ Optional   ✓ Assessment

INTRODUCTION

Phonics

One Sound To help students recognize that double consonants can stand for one sound, write *cuff, mitt,* and *odd* on the board. Have students read each word aloud and tell how many consonant sounds they hear at the end of it.

MEETING THE NEEDS OF ALL STUDENTS

Modified List

Practice Students studying only the high-frequency words in the top box write three words with **tt,** two words with **rr,** two words with **dd,** and three other words with double consonants.

Bilingual/ESL

Past Tense Point out that *written* and *ridden* are past tense forms of *write* and *ride.* Help students make sentences with these and with *bitten* and *hidden.*

Additional Practice

Challenge Master 8
Home-School Master 8
Audiotape A, Side 2

1. ___________
2. ___________
3. ___________
4. ___________
5. ___________
6. ___________
7. ___________
8. ___________
9. ___________
10. ___________
11. ___________
12. ___________
13. ___________
14. ___________
15. ___________
16. ___________
17. ___________
18. ___________
19. ___________
20. ___________

CHALLENGE!

Mississippi
recess
impossible
antennas
allowance

44

■ INTRODUCTION

Words with Double Consonants

SPELLING FOCUS

Sometimes double consonants stand for one sound. For example, you hear the sound /f/ one time in **different** and the sound /p/ one time in **supper**.

■ **STUDY** Say each word. Then read the sentence.

1. *tomorrow* — Her birthday is **tomorrow**.
2. *borrow* — May I **borrow** your eraser?
3. *different* ✳ — Painters use **different** brushes.
4. *supper* — We eat **supper** at 5:00.
5. *matter* — It does not **matter** if he comes.
6. *written* — You need **written** permission.
7. *bottle* — Recycle that glass **bottle**.
8. *ridden* — I have **ridden** a horse many times.
9. *odd* — Elves wear **odd** shoes and hats.
10. *bubble* — She blew a huge **bubble**.

11. *offer* — I will **offer** to help them.
12. *suffer* — Some people **suffer** from illness.
13. *slippers* — She put on her robe and **slippers**.
14. *grasshopper* — The **grasshopper** sat on a leaf.
15. *worry* — They **worry** about our safety.
16. *current* — We study **current** events.
17. *lettuce* — He served a **lettuce** salad.
18. *paddle* — Ducks **paddle** with their feet.
19. *shudder* — Thunder makes me **shudder**.
20. *hobby* — Model making is his **hobby**.

■ **PRACTICE** First write the words in the list you think are easy to spell. Then write the words you think are difficult. Underline the double consonants in each word.
Order of words will vary.
■ **WRITE** Choose two sentences to write a rhyme.
Rhymes will vary.

✳ **WATCH OUT FOR FREQUENTLY MISSPELLED WORDS!**

- Practice: Antonym Argument and
  Words in Context
- Strategic Spelling:
  Building New Words
- Cross-Curricular Lesson: Introduce
- Modified List

DAILY SPELLING REVIEW

The *girafe* was *chaseing* its tail.

giraffe   *chasing*

THINK AND PRACTICE

ANTONYM ARGUMENT   Write the list word that is the opposite of the underlined word in each sentence.

1. Mo and Al are as <u>alike</u> as they can be.
2. At <u>breakfast</u> yesterday they didn't even eat.
3. "Why can't I <u>lend</u> your knit hat?" asked Mo.
4. "Because losing hats is a <u>job</u> with you," said Al.
5. "But I like its <u>ancient</u> style," responded Mo.
6. Mo agreed to a <u>spoken</u> contract before wearing the hat.
7. These <u>ordinary</u> fellows enjoy disagreeing.

WORDS IN CONTEXT   Write the list word that completes each sentence.

8. Both of my parents ___ from allergies.
9. Rabbits eat greens such as ___ and spinach.
10. I forgot to do it today, but I will be sure to do it ___.
11. I am learning how to ___ a canoe.
12. After her bath, she put on a robe and ___.
13. What is the ___ with that howling dog?
14. I bought this gum so I could blow a ___.
15. Do you buy apple juice in a can or a ___?
16. I had never ___ on a Ferris wheel before.
17. The ___ jumped from the leaf to the ground.

1. **different**
2. **supper**
3. **borrow**
4. **hobby**
5. **current**
6. **written**
7. **odd**
8. **suffer**
9. **lettuce**
10. **tomorrow**
11. **paddle**
12. **slippers**
13. **matter**
14. **bubble**
15. **bottle**
16. **ridden**
17. **grasshopper**

Building New Words

Write *worry*, *offer*, and *shudder*. Add **-ed** to complete the chart. Remember: Change the **y** to **i** before adding **-ed**.

Base word	Add-ed
18. worry	worried
19. offer	offered
20. shudder	shuddered

FREQUENTLY MISSPELLED WORDS

To spell **different** correctly, be sure to pronounce every syllable: **dif fer ent.**

THINK AND PRACTICE

Words in Context
How-to Tip Suggest that students go through items 8–17 once and first fill in all the words they're sure of. Then they can go through a second time to fill in the rest.

MEETING THE NEEDS OF ALL STUDENTS

Modified List
Review Students studying high-frequency words complete Think and Practice Master 8.

Visual Learners
Say It with Pictures Have students fold three sheets of drawing paper in half and then write and illustrate each word of three antonym pairs on its own half of the paper.

Additional Practice

Think and Practice Master 8
Extra Practice Master 8
Everyday Spelling CD-ROM
Everyday Spelling Game Software

45

DAY 3 Proofreading and Writing

- Proofread a Message
- Proofreading Tip: Careless Errors
- Write a Message
- ✓ Cooperative Midweek Test

DAILY SPELLING REVIEW

We *laught* at what *happend* on the stage.

laughed   *happened*

● Core   ○ Optional   ✓ Assessment

PROOFREADING AND WRITING

Careless Errors

Reading Aloud Reading aloud may be one of the best ways to catch repetition or omission of words. Have students read their writing aloud to themselves.

MEETING THE NEEDS OF ALL STUDENTS

Modified List

Proofreading Students studying high-frequency words complete this page or the proofreading activity on the *Everyday Spelling* CD-ROM.

Enrichment

Message Writing Have students choose two characters from a book or story and then write a message from one character to the other. Remind students to proofread for spelling errors and careless errors.

Additional Practice

Hardbound Book Master 8A
Second Language Master 8
Writing Mini-Lesson Master 8
Writing Activity Master 8
Proofreading Transparency 8
Everyday Spelling **CD-ROM**

PROOFREADING AND WRITING

PROOFREADING TIP

Lucas is careless with the same word twice. He repeats it in one place, and leaves it out in another. These mistakes are easy to catch if you proofread.

PROOFREAD A MESSAGE Lucas read about someone finding an important message in a bottle. He wrote a message of his own. Find four spelling errors and two careless errors and correct them.

Make a capital.
Make a small letter.
Add something.
Take out something.
Add a period.
New paragraph

different
Dare to be diffrent!
paddle
If you padel your own canoe today, you
tomorrow
you may captain the ship tommorow.
bubble   **you**
If your buble bursts, can blow another one.

WRITE A MESSAGE Pretend you are writing a message for a bottle. Tell someone what you think is important in life. Use list words and personal words.

Responses will vary. Message should include list words and personal words.

Word List

different	written
offer	matter
suffer	bottle
slippers	lettuce
supper	ridden
grasshopper	paddle
tomorrow	shudder
worry	odd
current	bubble
borrow	hobby

Personal Words

1. **Words will vary.**

2. _______________

46

VOCABULARY BUILDING

Review

CONTEXT CLUES Use the context in each sentence to help you write the correct boxed word.

1. Whenever I ___ something, I try to return it as soon as possible.
2. Have you ___ on the new roller coaster at the amusement park?
3. A soap ___ floated up from the dishwater and hit me right in the eye.
4. What's the ___ with Tony? He seems upset about something.
5. My friend takes a ___ route to school than I do.
6. I thought it was ___ that the store was closed in the middle of the afternoon.
7. I would have ___ you a note, but I couldn't find a pencil.
8. I tipped over a ___ of juice and it spilled on the floor.
9. I'm busy today, but maybe we can go to a movie ___.
10. In our house, we must be ready to sit down for ___ promptly at 6:00.

tomorrow
borrow
different
supper
matter
written
bottle
ridden
odd
bubble

1. **borrow**
2. **ridden**
3. **bubble**
4. **matter**
5. **different**
6. **odd**
7. **written**
8. **bottle**
9. **tomorrow**
10. **supper**

Word *Study*

ACROSTICS An **acrostic** is a way of connecting letters to spell different words, often about a particular subject. To make an acrostic, write a noun across or down the page. Then connect words that describe that noun. Try it with *grasshopper*. Use the words shown and add your own, or make up a new acrostic with a noun of your own.

Words added will vary.

VOCABULARY BUILDING

Literature Connection

Word Play Students interested in word play will enjoy *Word Works* by Cathryn Berger Kaye (Little, Brown and Company, 1985).

MEETING THE NEEDS OF ALL STUDENTS

Modified List

Review Students studying high-frequency words complete this page.

Kinesthetic Learners

Home Town Acrostics

Suggest that students pair up to make home town acrostics. Students use large pieces of paper to write the name of their town in large, colorful letters, and then add the words that tell about the town.

Additional Practice

Hardbound Book Master 8B
Review Master 8
Standardized Test Master 8
***Everyday Spelling* CD-ROM**

LESSON

9

Generalization

Spelling Focus: Short **e** is often spelled **e**. Long **e** can be spelled **ea** and **ey**.

● Core   ○ Optional   ✓ **Assessment**

DAILY PLAN	CORE OBJECTIVES	NOTES

DAY 1 Introduction

✓ Pretest and Self-Check, p. 48B
● Spelling Focus and Word List, p. 48
○ Challenge Words, p. 48
○ Challenge Master 9
○ Home-School Master 9

✓ ▪ Take and self-check Pretest
▪ Spell words with short **e** and long **e** sounds; classify and write the list words

DAY 2 Think and Practice

● Words in Context; Definitions, p.49
● Strategic Spelling: *Seeing Meaning Connections,* p. 49
○ Think and Practice Master 9
○ Extra Practice Master 9
○ Cross-Curricular Lesson: Introduce, p. 214

▪ Complete practice activities for words with short **e** and long **e** sounds
▪ Recognize meaning connections between list words and other words related to them

DAY 3 Proofreading and Writing

● Proofread a Letter, p. 50
● Proofreading Tip: Punctuation, p. 50
● Answer a Letter, p. 50
✓ Cooperative Midweek Test
○ Hardbound Book Master 9A
○ Writing Mini-Lesson Master 9
○ Writing Activity Master 9
○ Second Language Support Master 9

▪ Proofread for spelling and punctuation errors
▪ Integrate spelling and writing in a personal writing response
✓ ▪ Take and check midweek test

DAY 4 Vocabulary Building

● Review: Crossword Puzzle, p. 51
● Multicultural Connection: Proverbs, p. 51
○ Hardbound Book Master 9B
Cross-Curricular Lesson: Follow-Up, p. 214
○ Review Master 9

▪ Complete review activity for words with short **e** and long **e** sounds
▪ Study and use proverbs

DAY 5 Test

✓ Posttest
○ Standardized Test Master 9

✓ ▪ Take Posttest

Cross-Curricular Lessons

Use the Spelling Focus (**long e** spelled **ea** and **ey**) to introduce the Mathematics lesson, *The Calculator,* page 214, or choose a lesson that correlates with a topic you're currently teaching.

MEETING THE NEEDS OF ALL STUDENTS

The Word List

For students studying 20 words, assign pages 48–51 and Extra Practice and Review masters.

Modified List For students studying 10 words, modify Practice on page 48, and assign Think and Practice Master 9 and pages 50–51.

Challenge For students studying 25 words, assign pages 48–51, Challenge, Extra Practice, and Review masters.

Bilingual/ESL

Spanish does not contain the short **e** sound, and the sound of long **e** is written as **i**. Watch for misspellings by Spanish-speaking students that are rooted in these differences.

Personal Words

Students add to Personal Words lists by looking at work in their writing portfolios and words they want to remember from their reading.

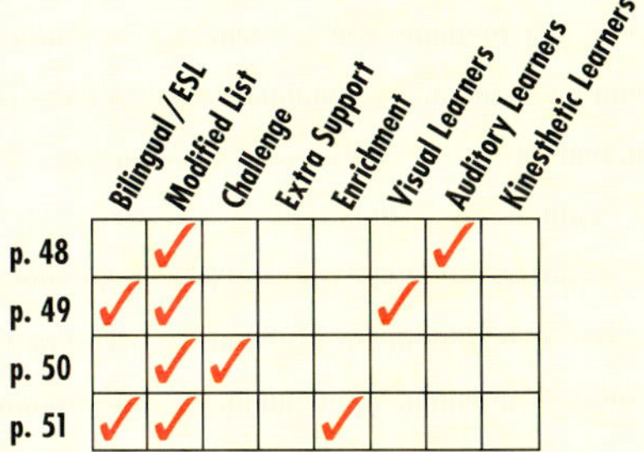

	Bilingual / ESL	Modified List	Challenge	Extra Support	Enrichment	Visual Learners	Auditory Learners	Kinesthetic Learners
p. 48		✓					✓	
p. 49	✓	✓				✓		
p. 50		✓	✓					
p. 51	✓	✓			✓			

ASSESSMENT*

Pretest

Read the underlined word, read the sentence, and then repeat the underlined word. Guide students in self-correcting their pretests and correcting any misspellings.

1. We will meet <u>them</u> later.
2. The family <u>went</u> to America.
3. A <u>fence</u> kept the dog out.
4. Can you <u>speak</u> French?
5. I have a <u>reason</u> to go.
6. Sue <u>beat</u> Adam in the race.
7. Spend your <u>money</u> wisely.
8. Jaime lives in a <u>valley</u>.
9. Ava put <u>honey</u> in her tea.
10. A <u>monkey</u> made faces at us.
11. Dad has <u>credit</u> at the store.
12. The tractor has an <u>engine</u>.
13. Kate won a spelling <u>contest</u>.
14. Joe liked that game <u>least</u>.
15. A robber could <u>steal</u> a bike.
16. Candy is a special <u>treat</u>.
17. Spring is a rainy <u>season</u>.
18. You need skates for <u>hockey</u>.
19. A truck parked in the <u>alley</u>.
20. The <u>donkey</u> carried a pack.

Posttest

Read aloud the sentences below. These sentences may be used for dictation.

1. Take <u>money</u> to the store.
2. We saw a lively <u>monkey</u>.
3. Do you like <u>honey</u> on bread?
4. I <u>beat</u> an egg for muffins.
5. He gave <u>them</u> popcorn.
6. The <u>valley</u> has many trees.
7. I will <u>speak</u> to Grandma.
8. I can paint the <u>fence</u> red.
9. Grandma <u>went</u> to Maine.
10. Do you have a <u>reason</u> to go?
11. Did you ever ride a <u>donkey</u>?
12. We can dance in the <u>contest</u>.
13. The <u>engine</u> had died.
14. Put the boxes in the <u>alley</u>.
15. They play <u>hockey</u> in winter.
16. Summer is a great <u>season</u>.
17. It's my <u>least</u> favorite gift.
18. A fox will <u>steal</u> an apple.
19. We got <u>credit</u> for the photo.
20. <u>Treat</u> him with kindness.

Challenge Words

1. The animal <u>escaped</u>.
2. <u>Celery</u> is a good snack.
3. The wheel <u>squeaked</u>.
4. We sat on hard <u>bleachers</u>.
5. The player had a red <u>jersey</u>.

Additional Assessment

Standardized Test Master 9
Dictation Sentences, p. T38
Everyday Spelling CD-ROM

KIDSPELLING
Misspellings sometimes show what a child knows about spelling. When Annie wrote about the *canapea* over her bed, we knew she was using a familiar way to spell long **e**. Review spellings of long **e** for students making similar errors.

* See pp. T20 and T33 for test-study-test information.

ADDITIONAL RESOURCES (OPTIONAL PRACTICE)
LESSON 9

DAY 1 CHALLENGE MASTER

CHALLENGE ■ 9

Challenge Words

bleachers   squeaked   celery   escaped   jersey

■ Write a Challenge Word that finishes each phrase.

1. the crunch of fresh **celery**
2. the roar from the crowd in the **bleachers**
3. wore a **jersey** to play soccer
4. the mouse that scurried and **squeaked**
5. the last of the prisoners who **escaped**

■ Do you know where to find bleachers? Write an imaginary detective story called "The Bleachers of . . ." Use one or more Challenge Words.

Practice Masters, p. 37

DAY 1 HOME-SCHOOL MASTER

■ 9   HOME-SCHOOL ACTIVITIES   9 ■

Word Check 9

1. credit
2. speak
3. alley
4. fence
5. least
6. hockey
7. went
8. contest
9. beat
10. honey
11. reason
12. valley
13. money
14. engine
15. them
16. steal
17. monkey
18. treat
19. season
20. donkey

■ **Word Cousins** Write a list word to complete each group of words below.

1. baseball, soccer, **hockey**
2. ape, gorilla, **monkey**
3. sugar, syrup, **honey**
4. canyon, ravine, **valley**
5. coins, cash, **money**
6. race, relay, **contest**
7. rob, cheat, **steal**
8. horse, mule, **donkey**
9. us, you, **them**
10. passage, pathway, **alley**
11. say, talk, **speak**
12. stir, mix, **beat**

■ **Vowel Sounds** Using words that you did not use above, write each list word in the column under its vowel sound.

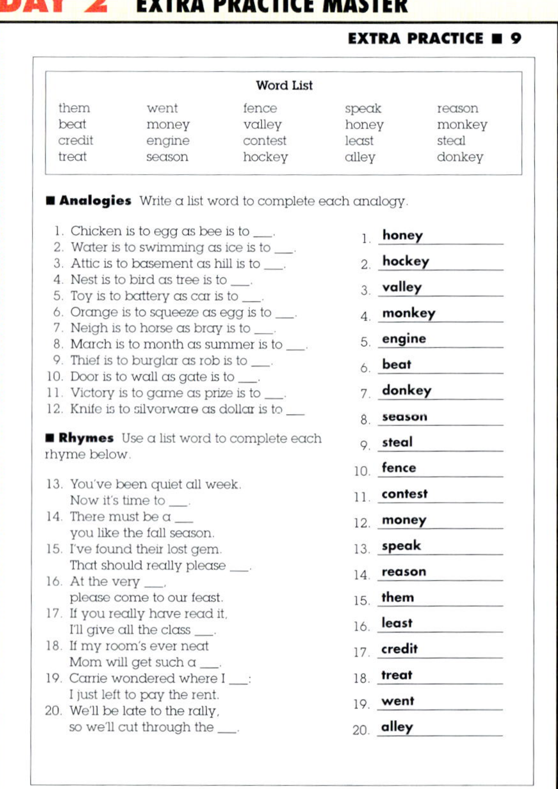

short e

13. **credit**
14. **fence**
15. **went**
16. **engine**

long e

17. **least**
18. **reason**
19. **treat**
20. **season**

Dear Parent,

Please check to see that your child has done this page correctly. Circle any misspelled words and help your child study them.

Tear off the Word Check before your child returns this page to class. Use it to help your child study.

Home-School Activities, p. 8

DAY 2 THINK AND PRACTICE

9 ■ THINK AND PRACTICE

| them | went | fence | speak | reason |
| beat | money | valley | honey | monkey |

■ **Words in Context** Write the list word that completes each sentence.

1. What **reason** did he give for being late?
2. The **monkey** hung by its tail.
3. Our team **beat** their team.
4. An astronaut will **speak** to our class.
5. Cows are grazing in the **valley**.
6. The bees were busy making **honey**.
7. We will paint the **fence** white.

■ **Vowel Sorting** Write the list words that have these sounds.

/ē/ as in least

8. **speak**
9. **reason**
10. **beat**

/ē/ as in donkey

11. **money**
12. **valley**
13. **honey**
14. **monkey**

/e/ as in contest

15. **went**
16. **them**
17. **fence**

STRATEGIC SPELLING: Seeing Meaning Connections

unbeaten   unbeatable

18. Write the list word related in spelling and meaning to the boxed words.
beat

Complete the sentences using the words in the box.

The _(19)_ football team is very good. Some people say the team is _(20)_.

19. **unbeaten**   20. **unbeatable**

Practice Masters, p. 38

DAY 2 EXTRA PRACTICE MASTER

EXTRA PRACTICE ■ 9

Word List

them	went	fence	speak	reason
beat	money	valley	honey	monkey
credit	engine	contest	least	steal
treat	season	hockey	alley	donkey

■ **Analogies** Write a list word to complete each analogy.

1. Chicken is to egg as bee is to ___.
2. Water is to swimming as ice is to ___.
3. Attic is to basement as hill is to ___.
4. Nest is to bird as tree is to ___.
5. Toy is to battery as car is to ___.
6. Orange is to squeeze as egg is to ___.
7. Neigh is to horse as bray is to ___.
8. March is to month as summer is to ___.
9. Thief is to burglar as rob is to ___.
10. Door is to wall as gate is to ___.
11. Victory is to game as prize is to ___.
12. Knife is to silverware as dollar is to ___.

■ **Rhymes** Use a list word to complete each rhyme below.

13. You've been quiet all week.
    Now it's time to ___.
14. There must be a ___
    you like the fall season.
15. I've found their lost gem.
    That should really please ___.
16. At the very ___,
    please come to our feast.
17. If you really have read it,
    I'll give all the class ___.
18. If my room's ever neat
    Mom will get such a ___.
19. Carrie wondered where I ___;
    I just left to pay the rent.
20. We'll be late to the rally,
    so we'll cut through the ___.

1. **honey**
2. **hockey**
3. **valley**
4. **monkey**
5. **engine**
6. **beat**
7. **donkey**
8. **season**
9. **steal**
10. **fence**
11. **contest**
12. **money**
13. **speak**
14. **reason**
15. **them**
16. **least**
17. **credit**
18. **treat**
19. **went**
20. **alley**

Practice Masters, p. 39

TECHNOLOGY AND VISUAL SUPPORT	 Use Audiotape A, Side 2, Lesson 9	 For additional practice use *Everyday Spelling* Game Software, Lesson 9	 Additional resources on *Everyday Spelling* CD-ROM: proofreading and writing, modified list and challenge words, auditory test
	 Use Proofreading and Writing Transparency 9		

DAY 3 SECOND LANGUAGE SUPPORT MASTER

9 ■ SECOND LANGUAGE SUPPORT

Words Around You

Think about where you have seen the words you learned in Lesson 9.

Write some of the words in the chart. Then write about the words. One word has been done for you.

A word I saw	Where or when I saw it	How the word was used
season	in the newspaper	The team has won four games this season.
Answers will vary.		

Second Language Support, p.34

DAY 3 WRITING ACTIVITY MASTER

9 ■ WRITING ACTIVITY

Correct Punctuation

☐ Use a comma between the date and year.

☐ Use a comma after the greeting and the closing in a letter

≡	Make a capital.
/	Make a small letter.
∧	Add something
✗	Take out something
⊙	Add a period.
¶	New paragraph

■ Here is a thank-you note that Claudia wrote to her cousin. She made some mistakes with commas. Fix the errors.

Remember: Use commas correctly in a letter.

Pretend you have a pen pal. Write a letter to your pen pal. Tell about something fun or interesting that you did this week.

Spelling and Writing, p. 16

DAY 4 REVIEW MASTER

9 ■ REVIEW

Word List

them	went	fence	speak	reason
beat	money	valley	honey	monkey
credit	engine	contest	least	steal
treat	season	hockey	alley	donkey

■ **Poetry** Complete the poem by writing list words.

The chattering (1) ___ and braying (2) ___
Loved warm (3) ___ served on their meat.
They did for a (4) ___: No matter the (5) ___,
It made every meal a sweet (6) ___!

■ **You Can Quote Me** Write the list words that help the famous characters below complete their sentences.

7. Bugs Bunny: "How about letting me buy some carrots with my ___ card?"
8. Little Mermaid: "I wasn't able to ___ for a while, but my dreams finally came true."
9. Batman: "Let's rev up the Batmobile's ___ and catch that Penguin!"
10. Beauty: "I ___ into a strange house but found a perfect beast!"
11. Tramp: "Lady and I look for food in trash cans in the ___."
12. Fairy Godmother: "Cinderella, you must ___ the clock to get home on time."
13. Sleepy: "I won the ___ to see who could sleep longest."
14. Charlie Brown: "Snoopy, don't dig holes to get under the ___."
15. Alice in Wonderland: "Cheshire Cat, at ___ let me see all of you at the same time."
16. Popeye to Bluto: "You have a face like a ___ puck!"
17–18. Wicked Witch of the West: "Dorothy, did you ___ my sister's ruby slippers and then put ___ on?"
19–20. Superman: "I'll search every mountain and ___ to recover the stolen ___."

1. **monkey**
2. **donkey**
3. **honey**
4. **reason**
5. **season**
6. **treat**
7. **credit**
8. **speak**
9. **engine**
10. **went**
11. **alley**
12. **beat**
13. **contest**
14. **fence**
15. **least**
16. **hockey**
17. **steal**
18. **them**
19. **valley**
20. **money**

Practice Masters, p. 40

DAY 5 STANDARDIZED TEST MASTER

9 ■ LESSON TEST

■ Find the word in each group that is spelled correctly. Fill in the letter for the correct word on the answer strip.

Sample:

		Answer
a. crowde	**c.** croud	ⓐ ⓑ ⓒ ●
b. croued	**d.** crowd	
1. **a.** speek	**c.** speeck	1. ⓐ ● ⓒ ⓓ
b. speak	**d.** spek	
2. **a.** dongcke	**c.** donkey	2. ⓐ ⓑ ● ⓓ
b. donkie	**d.** donke	
3. **a.** leest	**c.** leste	3. ⓐ ⓑ ⓒ ●
b. leist	**d.** least	
4. **a.** vally	**c.** vallie	4. ⓐ ● ⓒ ⓓ
b. valley	**d.** valle	
5. **a.** bete	**c.** baet	5. ⓐ ● ⓒ ⓓ
b. beat	**d.** beyt	
6. **a.** tham	**c.** them	6. ⓐ ⓑ ● ⓓ
b. thim	**d.** tem	
7. **a.** reson	**c.** reason	7. ⓐ ⓑ ● ⓓ
b. reasen	**d.** resen	
8. **a.** steal	**c.** steil	8. ⓐ ● ⓒ ⓓ
b. steal	**d.** stell	
9. **a.** treet	**c.** trete	9. ⓐ ⓑ ⓒ ●
b. tret	**d.** treat	
10. **a.** mony	**c.** moeny	10. ⓐ ● ⓒ ⓓ
b. money	**d.** moniey	
11. **a.** monky	**c.** mokey	11. ⓐ ⓑ ⓒ ●
b. munky	**d.** monkey	
12. **a.** whent	**c.** wint	12. ⓐ ⓑ ⓒ ●
b. wnt	**d.** went	
13. **a.** fance	**c.** fence	13. ⓐ ⓑ ● ⓓ
b. fense	**d.** fens	
14. **a.** cradit	**c.** creidt	14. ⓐ ● ⓒ ⓓ
b. credit	**d.** credt	
15. **a.** engin	**c.** engine	15. ⓐ ⓑ ● ⓓ
b. engen	**d.** ingen	
16. **a.** seson	**c.** seesin	16. ⓐ ● ⓒ ⓓ
b. season	**d.** sesan	
17. **a.** hocky	**c.** hockey	17. ⓐ ⓑ ● ⓓ
b. hocye	**d.** hokee	
18. **a.** alley	**c.** aley	18. ● ⓑ ⓒ ⓓ
b. allie	**d.** alleye	
19. **a.** hony	**c.** hoeny	19. ⓐ ⓑ ⓒ ●
b. heney	**d.** honey	
20. **a.** coutist	**c.** cotest	20. ⓐ ⓑ ⓒ ●
b. contist	**d.** contest	

Practice for Standardized Tests, p. 12

LESSON 9

✓ Pretest and Self-Check
● Spelling Concept and Word List
○ Challenge Words
○ Modified List

DAILY SPELLING REVIEW

Jerry *studied cause* the test is on Friday.

studied   because

● Core   ○ Optional   ✓ Assessment

INTRODUCTION

Phonics

Long e spelled ea, ey
Have students pronounce the list words, listen for the long **e** sound, and identify the spelling of long **e** in each word.

MEETING THE NEEDS OF ALL STUDENTS

Modified List

Practice Students studying only the high-frequency words in the top box write
- three words with short **e**
- three words with long **e** spelled **ea**
- four words with long **e** spelled **ey**

Auditory Learners

Rhyming Words Auditory learners might make up and share rhyming couplets for the words.

Additional Practice

Challenge Master 9
Home-School Master 9
Audiotape A, Side 2

INTRODUCTION

Short e and Long e

SPELLING FOCUS

Short e is often spelled **e**: w<u>e</u>nt. **Long e** can be spelled **ea** and **ey**: sp<u>ea</u>k, mon<u>ey</u>.

■ STUDY   Say each word. Then read the sentence.

1. them — Let's share our food with **them**.
2. went ✳ — Our class **went** to the museum.
3. fence — My father put up an iron **fence**.
4. speak — Actors must **speak** clearly.
5. reason — Dogs have a **reason** for barking.
6. beat — Use a whisk to **beat** the eggs.
7. money — You need **money** to buy food.
8. valley — Cows graze down in the **valley**.
9. honey — Bees make **honey**.
10. monkey — The **monkey** swung on a vine.

11. credit — She bought new clothes on **credit**.
12. engine — Can you fix the car **engine**?
13. contest — I won a prize in a poetry **contest**.
14. least — Which shirt is the **least** expensive?
15. steal — Thieves **steal** from others.
16. treat — I want to **treat** you to lunch.
17. season — Spring is my favorite **season**.
18. hockey — Ice **hockey** is popular in Canada.
19. alley — The trash cans are in the **alley**.
20. donkey — The gray **donkey** brayed loudly.

Word List

1. speak
2. reason
3. beat
4. least
5. steal
6. treat
7. season
8. money
9. valley
10. honey
11. monkey
12. hockey
13. alley
14. donkey
15. them
16. went
17. fence
18. credit
19. engine
20. contest

CHALLENGE!

escaped
celery
squeaked
bleachers
jersey

■ PRACTICE   Sort the words by writing
- seven words with **long e** spelled **ea**
- seven words with **long e** spelled **ey**
- six words with **short e** spelled **e**

Order of words in each group may vary.

■ WRITE   Choose two sentences to include in a paragraph.
Paragraphs will vary.

✳ **WATCH OUT FOR FREQUENTLY MISSPELLED WORDS!**

- Practice: Words in Context and Definitions
- Strategic Spelling:
  Seeing Meaning Connections
- Cross-Curricular Lesson: Introduce
- Modified List

DAILY SPELLING REVIEW

Use the *smallist* bag for your *snak*.

smallest   *snack*

THINK AND PRACTICE

WORDS IN CONTEXT   Write the list word that completes each sentence.

1. I can't hear you. Please ___ up.
2. Bees were in the hive making ___.
3. The necklace cost a great deal of ___.
4. Around the yard was a picket ___.
5. She had the most homework and I had the ___.
6. The king gave ___ all silver swords.
7. The child sat upon a long-eared ___.
8. The peasants farmed the fertile ___.
9. The cook ___ the eggs for the omelet.
10. She hid the gold so no one would ___ it.
11. The knight ___ riding off.

DEFINITIONS   Answer each question with a list word.

12. Which list word is a sport?
13. What can you use to buy things if you have no cash?
14. What animal chatters and often lives in trees?
15. Which word means to think and understand?
16. Which names a narrow driveway behind a building?
17. What piece of machinery gives a car power?
18. Which word describes what winter is?
19. Which names something special that gives pleasure?

1. **speak**
2. **honey**
3. **money**
4. **fence**
5. **least**
6. **them**
7. **donkey**
8. **valley**
9. **beat**
10. **steal**
11. **went**
12. **hockey**
13. **credit**
14. **monkey**
15. **reason**
16. **alley**
17. **engine**
18. **season**
19. **treat**

STRATEGIC SPELLING

Seeing Meaning Connections

| contestant |
| uncontested |

Write the list word related in spelling and meaning to the boxed words.

20. **contest**

Complete the sentences using the words in the box.

Mai was a (21) on a new TV quiz show. All of her answers were correct, so her victory was (22) by her opponent.

21. **contestant**
22. **uncontested**

Take a Hint

Do you have trouble remembering how to spell **beat** and **beet**? This riddle may help: What do you do when you can't **beat the heat**? Eat a cool **treat**!

LESSON 9

- Proofreading a Letter
- Proofreading Tip: Punctuation
- Answering a Letter
- ✓ Cooperative Midweek Test

DAILY SPELLING REVIEW

Miguel wants to *desine* a *skyscrapper*.

design   *skyscraper*

● Core   ○ Optional   ✓ Assessment

PROOFREADING AND WRITING

Punctuation

Punctuating Letters Have students bring letters from home. Find commas in greetings and closings of those letters.

MEETING THE NEEDS OF ALL STUDENTS

Modified List

Proofreading Students studying high-frequency words complete this page or the proofreading activity on the *Everyday Spelling* CD-ROM.

Challenge

Letter Writing Extend the writing activity by having students write a letter of their own to Ms. Understanding, describing any problem they wish.

Additional Practice

Hardbound Book Master 9A
Second Language Master 9
Writing Mini-Lesson 9
Writing Activity Master 9
Proofreading Transparency 9
Everyday Spelling CD-ROM

■ PROOFREADING AND WRITING

Make a capital.
Make a small letter.
Add something.
Take out something.
Add a period.
New paragraph

PROOFREAD A LETTER Find the four misspelled words in this letter to an advice columnist. Write them correctly and add the two missing punctuation marks.

May 8, 19--

Dear Ms. Understanding,
   Michelle and I have practiced all **season** for the dance **contest**. We **went** to the finals last year, but Michelle dropped out at the last second. We didn't **speak** for weeks! How can I help her?

     Yours truly,

     Riana

PROOFREADING TIP
Don't forget what you know about the parts of a letter. What punctuation is needed at the end of the greeting and closing?

Word List

credit	reason
speak	valley
alley	money
fence	engine
least	them
hockey	steal
went	monkey
contest	treat
beat	season
honey	donkey

Personal Words

1. **Words will vary.**

2.

ANSWER A LETTER Pretend you are Ms. Understanding. Answer Riana's letter. Use spelling words.

Responses will vary. Letters should include spelling words.

50

VOCABULARY BUILDING

Review

CROSSWORD PUZZLE Fill in the crossword puzzle by writing the boxed word that matches each definition.

them
went
fence
speak
reason
beat
money
valley
honey
monkey

Across

3. low land between hills or mountains
5. past tense of go
6. the people being spoken about
9. explanation

Down

1. mix by stirring rapidly with a fork or spoon
2. a wall put around a yard
4. a mammal with a long tail; one of the most intelligent animals
7. a golden liquid that bees make out of nectar
8. coins
10. say with words; talk

Multicultural Connection

PROVERBS A **proverb** is a short, wise saying. People everywhere use proverbs to pass along common beliefs.

The Chinese proverb **Talk does not cook rice** is much like the English proverb **Actions speak louder than words.**

Write a proverb from the banner that has a similar meaning to these proverbs.

People from Thailand say:

1. You don't force a buffalo to eat grass.

The Senegalese say:

2. To catch a monkey requires patience.

The Iranians say:

3. One finger cannot lift a pebble.

1. You can lead a horse to water, but you can't make it drink.
2. Good things come to those who wait.
3. In unity there is strength.

VOCABULARY BUILDING

Literature Connection

More Proverbs *First Things First: An Illustrated Collection of Sayings Useful and Familiar for Children*, Betty Fraser (Harper & Row, 1990).

MEETING THE NEEDS OF ALL STUDENTS

Modified List

Review Students studying high-frequency words complete this page.

Enrichment

Wise Sayings Have students explore other short, thought-provoking sayings, such as epigrams and maxims.

Bilingual/ESL

Proverbs Students can ask parents or grandparents for a saying from another language or culture, or a particular region of the United States. Create a bulletin board with the proverbs.

Additional Practice

Hardbound Book Master 9B
Review Master 9
Standardized Test Master 9
Everyday Spelling **CD-ROM**

LESSON
10

Generalization

Spelling Focus: Short a is usually spelled **a**, **short i** is usually spelled **i**, and **short o** is usually spelled **o**. **Short u** is usually spelled **u**, but it is often spelled **ou**.

● Core   ○ Optional   ✓ Assessment

DAILY PLAN	CORE OBJECTIVES	NOTES

DAY 1 Introduction

✓ Pretest and Self-Check, p. 52B
● Spelling Focus and Word List, p. 52
● Challenge Words, p. 52
○ Challenge Master 10
○ Home-School Master 10

✓ ▪ Take and self-check Pretest
▪ Spell words with the short vowel sounds **a, i, o,** and **u**; classify and write the list words

DAY 2 Think and Practice

● Definitions; Vowel Trade; Base Words, p. 53
● Strategic Spelling: *Seeing Meaning Connections,* p. 53
○ Think and Practice Master 10
○ Extra Practice Master 10
○ Cross-Curricular Lesson: Introduce, p. 188

▪ Complete practice activities for words with the short vowel sounds **a, i, o,** and **u**
▪ Recognize meaning connections between list words and other words related to them

DAY 3 Proofreading and Writing

● Proofread a Message, p. 54
● Proofreading Tip: Numbers, p. 54
● Write a Message, p. 54
✓ Cooperative Midweek Test
○ Hardbound Book Master 10
○ Writing Mini-Lesson Master 10
○ Writing Activity Master 10
○ Second Language Support Master 10

▪ Proofread for spelling and hand-writing errors
▪ Integrate spelling and writing in a personal writing response
✓ ▪ Take and check midweek test

DAY 4 Vocabulary Building

● Review: Context Clues, p. 55
● Using a Dictionary: Pronunciation, p. 55
○ Cross-Curricular Lesson: Follow-Up, p. 188
○ Review Master 10

▪ Complete review activity for words with short vowel sounds **a, i, o,** and **u**
▪ Study and use pronunciation key symbols

DAY 5 Assessment

✓ Posttest, p. 52B
○ Standardized Test Master 10

✓ ▪ Take Posttest

Cross-Curricular Lessons

Use the Spelling Focus (short vowels **a, i, o,** and **u**) to introduce the Health lesson, *Your Body*, page 188, or choose a lesson that correlates with a topic you're currently teaching.

MEETING THE NEEDS OF ALL STUDENTS

The Word List

For students studying 20 words, assign pages 52–55 and Extra Practice and Review masters.

Modified List For students studying 10 words, modify Practice on page 52, and assign Think and Practice Master 10 and pages 54–55.

Challenge For students studying 25 words, assign pages 52–55, Challenge, Extra Practice, and Review masters.

Bilingual/ESL

In Haitian Creole, there are no short or long vowels. Every letter has one sound and is pronounced distinctly. Students may write only the sounds they hear: *young/yung.*

Personal Words

Students add to Personal Words lists by looking at work in their writing portfolios and words they want to remember from their reading.

	Bilingual/ESL	Modified List	Challenge	Extra Support	Enrichment	Visual Learners	Auditory Learners	Kinesthetic Learners
p. 52	✓	✓						
p. 53		✓			✓			
p. 54		✓						✓
p. 55		✓		✓				

ASSESSMENT*

Pretest

Read the underlined word, read the sentence, and then repeat the underlined word. Guide students in self-correcting their pretests and correcting any misspellings.

1. William heard a great <u>band</u>.
2. You can pay <u>cash</u> for a car.
3. Mary put water <u>into</u> the jar.
4. We go fishing in the <u>river</u>.
5. The boys will sit <u>with</u> us.
6. The farm has a little <u>pond</u>.
7. The church is on our <u>block</u>.
8. Meg <u>forgot</u> her homework.
9. Rita had car <u>trouble</u>.
10. A <u>young</u> sheep is a lamb.
11. <u>January</u> was snowy.
12. The baby likes his <u>blanket</u>.
13. Don't forget your <u>backpack</u>.
14. Judy's <u>finger</u> is swollen.
15. Look out the <u>window</u>.
16. The skis are in the <u>closet</u>.
17. <u>Chop</u> carrots for dinner.
18. Jorge is my <u>cousin</u>.
19. Lyn took a <u>couple</u> of photos.
20. The meat was too <u>tough</u>.

Posttest

Read aloud the sentences below. These sentences may be used for dictation.

1. Camping is a lot of <u>trouble</u>.
2. The <u>young</u> lions grew fast.
3. The boy went <u>into</u> his fort.
4. I made a picture <u>with</u> chalk.
5. We had a picnic by a <u>river</u>.
6. Take enough <u>cash</u> for the trip.
7. The girls led the <u>band</u>.
8. A park is on our <u>block</u>.
9. I <u>forgot</u> my baseball cap.
10. A big frog lived in a <u>pond</u>.
11. My <u>cousin</u> lived in Kansas.
12. Take a <u>blanket</u> to the game.
13. We played a <u>couple</u> of games.
14. A bug flew in the <u>window</u>.
15. Dad hurt his <u>finger</u>.
16. It's a cold day in <u>January</u>.
17. Put a book in the <u>backpack</u>.
18. It was a <u>tough</u> race.
19. <u>Chop</u> up an apple.
20. Keep your shoes in a <u>closet</u>.

Challenge Words

1. Help me wrap the <u>package</u>.
2. <u>Pilgrims</u> came to America.
3. The class <u>ignored</u> the noise.
4. The party is at two <u>o'clock</u>.
5. I came from a <u>southern</u> city.

Additional Assessment

Standardized Test Master 10
Dictation Sentences, p. T38
Everyday Spelling CD-ROM

TAKE A CLOSER LOOK
Help students to notice all the different sound combinations in these common words with **ough** by having them say each word aloud, followed by another word that rhymes with it.

tough   cough   drought
dough   through

* See pp. T20 and T33 for test-study-test information.

DAY 1 CHALLENGE MASTER

CHALLENGE ■ 10

Challenge Words

southern   ignored   Pilgrims   package   o'clock

■ Use the clues to write Challenge Words.

1. pay no attention to + ed = **ignored**
2. put things together + age = **package**
3. o + ' + timepiece = **o'clock**
4. a direction + ern = **southern**
5. Puritan settler + s = **pilgrims**

■ Write an article about being on time. Convince people of the importance of being on time. Use one or more Challenge Words.

Practice Masters, p. 41

DAY 1 HOME-SCHOOL MASTER

■ 10   HOME-SCHOOL ACTIVITIES   10 ■

■ **Relationships** Write a list word to complete each sentence below.

1. Foot is to hand as toe is to **finger**
2. Actor is to play as drummer is to **band**
3. Bird is to tree as frog is to **pond**
4. Summer is to June as winter is to **January**
5. Car is to garage as clothes are to **closet**
6. Last is to first as old is to **young**.
7. Comb is to purse as books are to **backpack**
8. Swim is to swam as forget is to **forgot**
9. Hammer is to pound as ax is to **chop**
10. One is to single as two is to **couple**

Word Check 10

1. cousin
2. cash
3. into
4. closet
5. with
6. couple
7. block
8. January
9. river
10. young
11. chop
12. finger
13. blanket
14. forgot
15. band
16. trouble
17. window
18. backpack
19. tough
20. pond

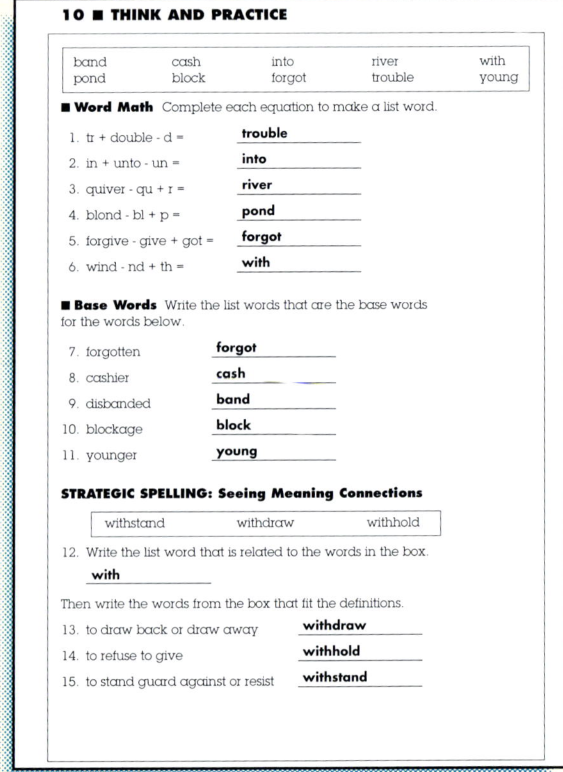

■ **Puzzle** Fill in the blanks to form list words. HINT: Try filling in the words in alphabetical order.

11. **b l a n k e t**
12. **b l o c k**
13. **c a s h**
14. **c o u s i n**
15. **i n t o**
16. **r i v e r**
17. **t o u g h**
18. **t r o u b l e**
19. **w i n d o w**
20. **w i t h**

Dear Parent,

Please check to see that your child has done this page correctly. Circle any misspelled words and help your child study them.

Tear off the Word Check before your child returns this page to class. Use it to help your child study.

Home-School Activities, p. 9

DAY 2 THINK AND PRACTICE MASTER

10 ■ THINK AND PRACTICE

| band | cash | into | river | with |
| pond | block | forgot | trouble | young |

■ **Word Math** Complete each equation to make a list word.

1. tr + double - d = **trouble**
2. in + unto - un = **into**
3. quiver - qu + r = **river**
4. blond - bl + p = **pond**
5. forgive - give + got = **forgot**
6. wind - nd + th = **with**

■ **Base Words** Write the list words that are the base words for the words below.

7. forgotten — **forgot**
8. cashier — **cash**
9. disbanded — **band**
10. blockage — **block**
11. younger — **young**

STRATEGIC SPELLING: Seeing Meaning Connections

| withstand | withdraw | withhold |

12. Write the list word that is related to the words in the box.
with

Then write the words from the box that fit the definitions.

13. to draw back or draw away — **withdraw**
14. to refuse to give — **withhold**
15. to stand guard against or resist — **withstand**

Practice Masters, p. 42

DAY 2 EXTRA PRACTICE MASTER

EXTRA PRACTICE ■ 10

Word List

band	cash	into	river	with
pond	block	forgot	trouble	young
January	blanket	backpack	finger	window
closet	chop	cousin	couple	tough

■ **Classifying** Write the list word that completes each sentence.

1. You can pay with ___ or a credit card.
2. Would you prefer to go to Canada in May, June, or ___?
3. Do you want a quilt, a sheet, or a ___?
4. I'd like you to meet my aunt, uncle, and ___.
5. My great-grandmother is old, but I am ___.
6. My father uses an ax to ___ wood.
7. The baby likes to play with my thumb or my ___.
8. This store will sell you a purse, a bookbag, or a ___.
9. Please open the ___ and let in some air.
10. He plays the guitar in the ___.
11. Because of the rain, the ___ was overflowing.
12. Rita likes to look at the frogs and lily pads in the ___.

1. **cash**
2. **January**
3. **blanket**
4. **cousin**
5. **young**
6. **chop**
7. **finger**
8. **backpack**
9. **window**
10. **band**
11. **river**
12. **pond**

■ **Definitions** Write a list word that fits each definition.

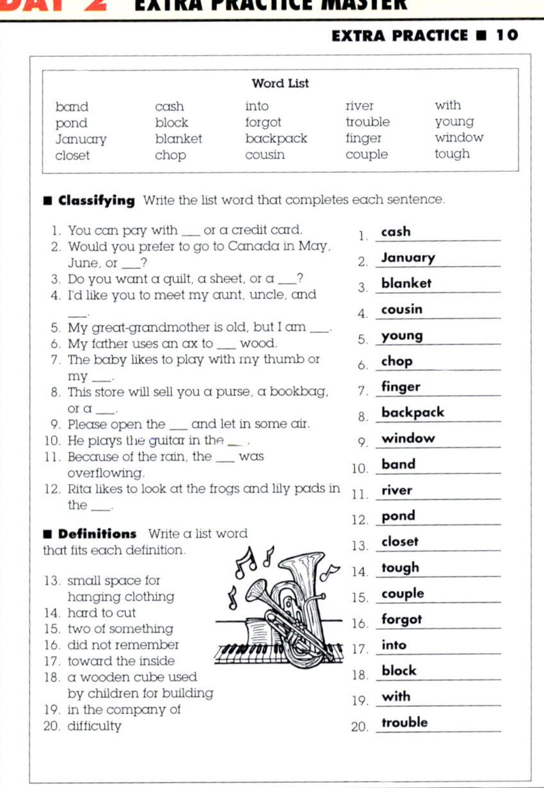

13. small space for hanging clothing
14. hard to cut
15. two of something
16. did not remember
17. toward the inside
18. a wooden cube used by children for building
19. in the company of
20. difficulty

13. **closet**
14. **tough**
15. **couple**
16. **forgot**
17. **into**
18. **block**
19. **with**
20. **trouble**

Practice Masters, p. 43

TECHNOLOGY AND VISUAL SUPPORT	 Use Audiotape A, Side 2, Lesson 10  Use Proofreading and Writing Transparency 10	 For additional practice use *Everyday Spelling* Game Software, Lesson 10	 Additional resources on *Everyday Spelling* CD-ROM: proofreading and writing, modified list and challenge words, auditory test

DAY 3 — SECOND LANGUAGE SUPPORT MASTER

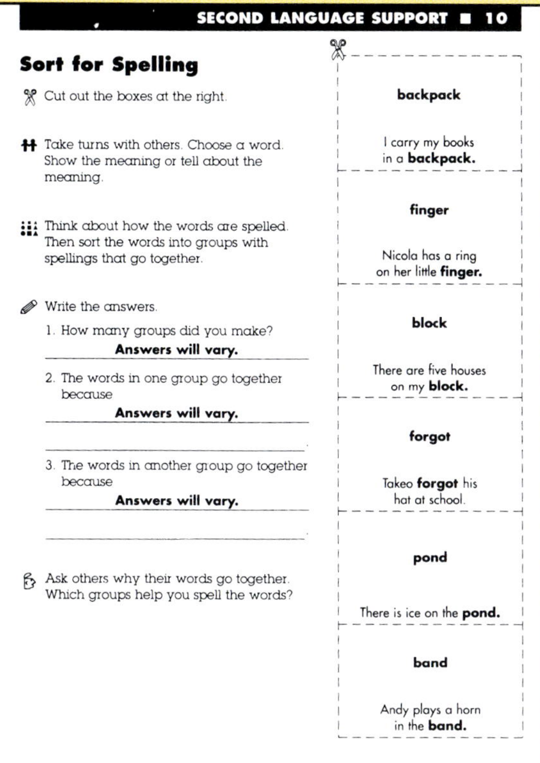

SECOND LANGUAGE SUPPORT ■ 10

Sort for Spelling

Cut out the boxes at the right.

Take turns with others. Choose a word. Show the meaning or tell about the meaning.

Think about how the words are spelled. Then sort the words into groups with spellings that go together.

Write the answers.

1. How many groups did you make?
   Answers will vary.

2. The words in one group go together because
   Answers will vary.

3. The words in another group go together because
   Answers will vary.

Ask others why their words go together. Which groups help you spell the words?

backpack

I carry my books in a **backpack.**

finger

Nicola has a ring on her little **finger.**

block

There are five houses on my **block.**

forgot

Takeo **forgot** his hat at school.

pond

There is ice on the **pond.**

band

Andy plays a horn in the **band.**

Second Language Support, p. 35

DAY 3 — WRITING ACTIVITY MASTER

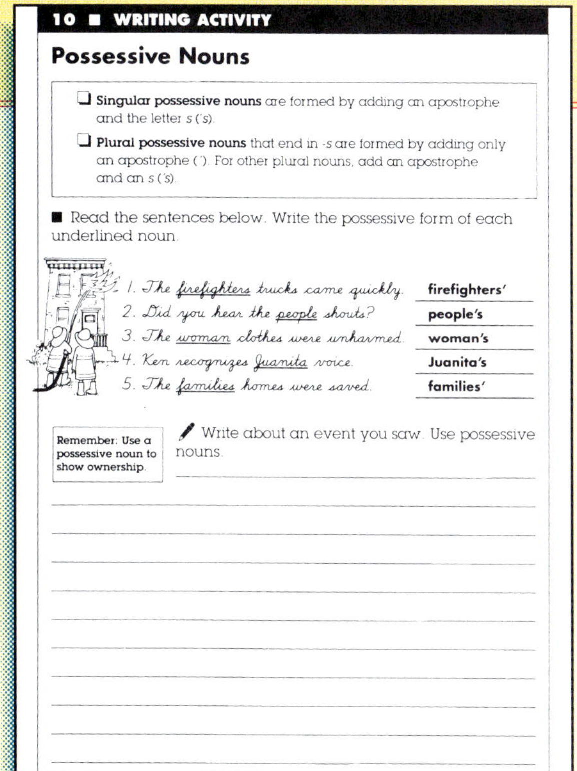

10 ■ WRITING ACTIVITY

Possessive Nouns

- **Singular possessive nouns** are formed by adding an apostrophe and the letter *s* (*'s*).
- **Plural possessive nouns** that end in *-s* are formed by adding only an apostrophe (*'*). For other plural nouns, add an apostrophe and an *s* (*'s*).

Read the sentences below. Write the possessive form of each underlined noun.

1. The firefighters trucks came quickly.   **firefighters'**
2. Did you hear the people shouts?   **people's**
3. The woman clothes were unharmed.   **woman's**
4. Ken recognizes Juanita voice.   **Juanita's**
5. The families homes were saved.   **families'**

Remember: Use a possessive noun to show ownership.

Write about an event you saw. Use possessive nouns.

Spelling and Writing, p. 18

DAY 4 — REVIEW MASTER

10 ■ REVIEW

Word List				
band	cash	into	river	with
pond	block	forgot	trouble	young
January	blanket	backpack	finger	window
closet	chop	cousin	couple	tough

Antonym Argument Write the list word that is the opposite of the underlined word or words in each sentence.

1. Who remembered to lock the door?
2. Lora is old enough to be my sister.
3. Being in charge of a party can be a lot of fun.
4. Billy wants his banana without peanut butter.
5. When did you see them walk out of the house?
6. The steak is tender.

What Am I? Write the list word naming each speaker.

7. I hold clothes, and I'm usually in the dark.
8. I am on your hand, and I help you grab.
9. I am a body of water much smaller than a lake.
10. You can count me and put me in the bank.
11. I start the new year.
12. You might put your school books in me.
13. Music comes from me.
14. When it's chilly, you might snuggle under me.

Making Associations Write the list word that you might associate with each word or phrase below.

15. Mississippi
16. around the
17. pork
18. stained-glass
19. second
20. two of a kind

1. **forgot**
2. **young**
3. **trouble**
4. **with**
5. **into**
6. **tough**
7. **closet**
8. **finger**
9. **pond**
10. **cash**
11. **January**
12. **backpack**
13. **band**
14. **blanket**
15. **river**
16. **block**
17. **chop**
18. **window**
19. **cousin**
20. **couple**

Practice Masters, p. 44

DAY 5 — STANDARDIZED TEST MASTER

LESSON TEST ■ 10

Find the word in each group that is spelled correctly. Fill in the letter for the correct word on the answer strip.

Sample:
- **a.** crowde   **c.** croud
- **b.** croued   **d.** crowd   → ⓐ ⓑ ⓒ ●

1. **a.** cusin   **c.** cosin / **b.** cousin   **d.** cousen   1. ⓐ ● ⓒ ⓓ
2. **a.** cople   **c.** couple / **b.** cuple   **d.** coupel   2. ⓐ ⓑ ● ⓓ
3. **a.** touf   **c.** tuf / **b.** tuff   **d.** tough   3. ⓐ ⓑ ⓒ ●
4. **a.** troble   **c.** trouble / **b.** truble   **d.** trowbl   4. ⓐ ⓑ ● ⓓ
5. **a.** yong   **c.** yung / **b.** young   **d.** younge   5. ⓐ ● ⓒ ⓓ
6. **a.** intoo   **c.** itto / **b.** into   **d.** ento   6. ⓐ ● ⓒ ⓓ
7. **a.** wiht   **c.** with / **b.** weth   **d.** whith   7. ⓐ ⓑ ● ⓓ
8. **a.** windo   **c.** wendow / **b.** winddow   **d.** window   8. ⓐ ⓑ ⓒ ●
9. **a.** river   **c.** rivier / **b.** niver   **d.** riveer   9. ● ⓑ ⓒ ⓓ
10. **a.** figer   **c.** finger / **b.** firger   **d.** fingrer   10. ⓐ ⓑ ● ⓓ
11. **a.** Janurary   **c.** January / **b.** january   **d.** Januwary   11. ⓐ ⓑ ● ⓓ
12. **a.** blanet   **c.** blankete / **b.** blanket   **d.** blankt   12. ⓐ ● ⓒ ⓓ
13. **a.** cach   **c.** cash / **b.** casch   **d.** cashe   13. ⓐ ⓑ ● ⓓ
14. **a.** band   **c.** baned / **b.** bandt   **d.** bannd   14. ● ⓑ ⓒ ⓓ
15. **a.** blok   **c.** bloce / **b.** block   **d.** balch   15. ⓐ ● ⓒ ⓓ
16. **a.** bakpack   **c.** backpack / **b.** backpac   **d.** backepack   16. ⓐ ⓑ ● ⓓ
17. **a.** chopp   **c.** chape / **b.** chope   **d.** chop   17. ⓐ ⓑ ⓒ ●
18. **a.** forgot   **c.** fogot / **b.** fergot   **d.** foregot   18. ● ⓑ ⓒ ⓓ
19. **a.** pand   **c.** ponned / **b.** ponde   **d.** pond   19. ⓐ ⓑ ⓒ ●
20. **a.** closit   **c.** clocet / **b.** closet   **d.** closted   20. ⓐ ● ⓒ ⓓ

Practice for Standardized Tests, p. 13

LESSON
10

INTRODUCTION

Phonics

Short u spelled ou Have students pronounce the list words, listen for the short vowel sound of **u**, and identify the spelling of the short **u** sound in each word.

MEETING THE NEEDS OF ALL STUDENTS

Modified List

Practice Students studying only the high-frequency words in the top box write
- two words with short **a** spelled **a**
- two words with short **u** spelled **ou**
- three words with short **o** spelled **o**
- three words with short **i** spelled **i**

Bilingual/ESL

Using Prepositions Point out the words *into* and *with*. Have volunteers use each word in a sentence and demonstrate its meaning. (I pour water *into* a bottle. We walk *with* friends.)

Additional Practice

Challenge Master 10
Home-School Master 10
Audiotape A, Side 2

10

1. **band**
2. **cash**
3. **January**
4. **blanket**
5. **backpack**
6. **trouble**
7. **young**
8. **cousin**
9. **couple**
10. **tough**
11. **pond**
12. **block**
13. **forgot**
14. **closet**
15. **chop**
16. **into**
17. **river**
18. **with**
19. **finger**
20. **window**

Order of words in each group may vary.

CHALLENGE!

package
Pilgrims
ignored
o'clock
southern

■ INTRODUCTION

Short Vowels a, i, o, u

SPELLING FOCUS

Short **a** is usually spelled **a**: b**a**nd. Short **i** is usually spelled **i**: **i**nto. Short **o** is usually spelled **o**: p**o**nd. Short **u** is usually spelled **u**, but it is also often spelled **ou**: tr**ou**ble.

■ **STUDY** Say each word. Then read the sentence.

1. *band* — Do you like that rock **band**?
2. *cash* — She took the **cash** to the bank.
3. *into* ❋ — Come **into** the kitchen.
4. *river* ❋ — The **river** flows down to the sea.
5. *with* ❋ — Let's go **with** the hikers.
6. *pond* — Fish live in this **pond**.
7. *block* — He ran around the **block**.
8. *forgot* — Dad **forgot** to pack my lunch.
9. *trouble* — Does being late **trouble** you?
10. *young* — She is too **young** to see that movie.

11. *January* — A new year begins in **January**.
12. *blanket* — Put the wool **blanket** on the bed.
13. *backpack* — Her **backpack** is full of books.
14. *finger* — He pointed his **finger** at me.
15. *window* — I looked out the **window**.
16. *closet* — Coats hang in the **closet**.
17. *chop* — She will **chop** these carrots.
18. *cousin* ❋ — My aunt's son is my **cousin**.
19. *couple* — He will be gone a **couple** of days.
20. *tough* — An overcooked roast is **tough**.

■ **PRACTICE** Sort the list words by writing
- five words with **short a** spelled **a**
- five words with **short o** spelled **o**
- five words with **short u** spelled **ou**
- five words with **short i** spelled **i**

Advertisements will vary. ■ **WRITE** Use two sentences in an advertisement.

❋ **WATCH OUT FOR FREQUENTLY MISSPELLED WORDS!**

52

- Practice: Definitions, Vowel Trade, and Base Words
- Strategic Spelling:
  Seeing Meaning Connections
- Cross-Curricular Lesson: Introduce
- Modified List

DAILY SPELLING REVIEW

Julie *stoped* playing to *coam* her hair.

stopped   comb

THINK AND PRACTICE ■

DEFINITIONS   Write the list word that fits each definition. Use the Spelling Dictionary if you need to.

1. the first month of the year
2. one of the five slender parts on a hand
3. to the inside of
4. water that flows into a lake or ocean
5. a small room for storing clothes or supplies
6. a group of musicians performing together
7. didn't remember
8. money in the form of coins and bills

VOWEL TRADE   Change the vowel in each word to make a list word with the **short o** sound.

9. black   10. chap   11. pend

BASE WORDS   Write the list words that are the base words for the words below.

12. coupled   15. cousins   18. untroubled
13. toughness   16. youngster   19. windowless
14. blanketed   17. backpacking

STRATEGIC SPELLING

Seeing Meaning Connections

withstand
withdraw
withhold

20. Write the list word that is related to the words in the box.   **with**

Then write the words from the box that fit the definitions.

21. to draw back or draw away   **withdraw**

22. to refuse to give   **withhold**

23. to stand against or resist   **withstand**

1. **January**
2. **finger**
3. **into**
4. **river**
5. **closet**
6. **band**
7. **forgot**
8. **cash**
9. **block**
10. **chop**
11. **pond**
12. **couple**
13. **tough**
14. **blanket**
15. **cousin**
16. **young**
17. **backpack**
18. **trouble**
19. **window**

Did You Know?
The word **couple** comes from the Old French word *cople. Cople* came from the Latin word *copula,* meaning "bond." A married couple is thought to be bonded together.

THINK AND PRACTICE

Definitions

Demonstrate Definitions
Have small groups think of ways to draw or act out each definition. For example, they could draw and label a hand (finger), and act out "a group of musicians . . ." (band).

MEETING THE NEEDS OF ALL STUDENTS

Modified List

Review Students studying high-frequency words complete Think and Practice Master 10.

Visual Learners

Highlight Letters Have students read the list words, listening for words with the short **u** sound. They can write these words on cards and highlight the letters (**ou**) that stand for the short **u** sound.

Additional Practice

Think and Practice Master 10
Extra Practice Master 10
Everyday Spelling **CD-ROM**
Everyday Spelling **Game Software**

53

LESSON 10

- Proofread a Message
- Proofreading Tip: Numbers
- Write a Message
- ✓ Cooperative Midweek Test

DAILY SPELLING REVIEW

Ronald looks *happyest* in that *foto*.

happiest   *photo*

● **Core**   ○ **Optional**   ✓ **Assessment**

PROOFREADING AND WRITING

Numbers

Checking Accuracy A good strategy to use after writing down a phone message is to read back the given phone number to the caller. Have students practice this with a partner.

MEETING THE NEEDS OF ALL STUDENTS

Modified List

Proofreading Students studying high-frequency words complete this page or the proofreading activity on the *Everyday Spelling* CD-ROM.

Kinesthetic Learners

Phone Message Have pairs of students role-play one person leaving a phone message with another about a homework assignment. Partners can take turns acting as the caller and the message taker.

Additional Practice

Hardbound Book Master 10
Second Language Master 10
Writing Mini-Lesson Master 10
Writing Activity Master 10
Proofreading Transparency 10
***Everyday Spelling* CD-ROM**

■ **PROOFREADING AND WRITING**

=== Make a capital.
/ Make a small letter.
∧ Add something.
⌎ Take out something.
⊙ Add a period.
⌗ New paragraph

PROOFREAD A MESSAGE Jane took a message for her cousin, Hiro, from his teacher, Ms. Cortez. Find four spelling errors and one handwriting error.

PROOFREADING TIP
Did Jane write "7279" or "1219"? When you take a phone message, be sure to write the phone number carefully.

You Have a Message!!!

To: _Hiro_   Date: _January 5_ (January)

Time: _4_ A.M. (P.M.)   From: _Ms. Cortez_

Phone #: _555-1219_ (7279)   Taken by: _Jane_

Message

She has the bagpack you left at school. She will drop it off here tomarrow. It's no troble. (backpack) (tomorrow) (trouble)

WRITE A MESSAGE Read the following telephone message. Write down only the important information.

"Hello, is Jane there? No? Well, this is Hiro, her cousin. I'm calling from a pay phone. Tell her I won't be there until 5:00. I'm at school, looking for my backpack."

Responses will vary.

You Have a Message!!!

To: ___________   Date: ___________

Time: _4:15_ A.M. (P.M.)   From: ___________

Phone #: ___________   Taken by: ___________

Message

____

Word List

cousin	chop
cash	finger
into	blanket
closet	forgot
with	band
couple	trouble
block	window
January	backpack
river	tough
young	pond

Personal Words

Words will vary.

1.

2.

54

VOCABULARY BUILDING ■

Review

band	pond
cash	block
into	forgot
river	trouble
with	young

CONTEXT CLUES Write the missing boxed words to complete the announcement below.

In case you (1), Fairview's summer festival will be held on July 2–4 at Merritime Park, just one (2) south of Lakeside Road and Briar Street. Here's just a sample of the wonderful entertainment at this year's festival.
- Afternoon and evening performances by the *Romper-Stompers* rock-and-roll (3).
- Lovely boat rides on the (4) that flows (5) our beautiful Lake Opeka.
- A fishing (6) with poles and prizes for (7) children.
- Food and game booths galore!

Bring your friends (8) you.
Admission is $5.00. Bring (9) only please.
Avoid (10) parking by driving directly to Lot 57.

1. **forgot**
2. **block**
3. **band**
4. **river**
5. **into**
6. **pond**
7. **young**
8. **with**
9. **cash**
10. **trouble**

Using a *Dictionary*

PRONUNCIATION Dictionaries include a **pronunciation key** on every other page in the book. It helps you pronounce the symbols in the dictionary. It might look like this:

a	hat	i	ice	u̇	put	ə stands for	
ā	age	o	not	ü	rule	a	in about
ä	far, calm	ō	open	ch	child	e	in taken
âr	care	ȯ	saw	ng	long	i	in pencil
e	let	ô	order	sh	she	o	in lemon
ē	equal	oi	oil	th	thin	u	in circus
ė	term	ou	out	ᵺ	then		
i	it	u	cup	zh	measure		

Each word in the dictionary is followed by its **pronunciation** in parentheses. The entry for the word *window* might look like this:

win•dow (win′dō), an opening in an outer wall or roof of a building, or in a vehicle, that lets in air or light. It is usually a wooden or metal frame that surrounds panes of glass or plastic. *n.*

Using the pronunciation key, you see the **i** is pronounced like the **i** in *it,* and the **ow** is pronounced like the **o** in *open.*

The dot between **win** and **dow** tells you that *window* has two syllables. The **accent mark** (′) tells you to say the first syllable in *window* with more force than the second.

Read each pronunciation below. Write the word that each pronunciation stands for. In each two-syllable word, underline the syllable you would say with more force.

1. (tuf)
2. (kloz′it)
3. (fər got′)
4. (kash)
5. (kuz′n)
6. (trub′əl)

1. **tough**
2. **closet**
3. **forgot**
4. **cash**
5. **cousin**
6. **trouble**

55

11

Generalization

Spelling Focus: Long vowels are often spelled with one letter. They can also be spelled **vowel-consonant-e.**

● Core   ○ Optional   ✓ Assessment

DAILY PLAN	CORE OBJECTIVES	NOTES

DAY 1 Introduction

✓ Pretest and Self-Check, p. 56B
● Spelling Focus and Word List, p. 56
● Challenge Words, p. 56
○ Challenge Master 11
○ Home-School Master 11

✓ ■ Take and self-check Pretest
■ Spell words with the long vowel sounds **a, i,** and **o;** classify and write the list words

DAY 2 Think and Practice

● Compare; Vowel Trade, p. 57
● Strategic Spelling: *Using the Rhyming Helper Strategy,* p. 57
○ Think and Practice Master 11
○ Extra Practice Master 11
○ Cross-Curricular Lesson: Introduce, p. 226

■ Complete practice activities for words with long vowel sounds
■ Apply the Rhyming Helper Strategy to list words

DAY 3 Proofreading and Writing

● Proofread a Summary, p. 58
● Proofreading Tip: Run-ons, p. 58
● Write a Summary, p. 58
✓ Cooperative Midweek Test
○ Hardbound Book Master 11
○ Writing Mini-Lesson Master 11
○ Writing Activity Master 11
○ Second Language Support Master 11

■ Proofread for spelling and grammar errors
■ Integrate spelling and writing in a personal writing response
✓ ■ Take and check midweek test

DAY 4 Vocabulary Building

● Review: Analogies, p. 59
● Word Study: Idioms, p. 59
● Cross-Curricular Lesson: Follow-Up, p. 226
○ Review Master 11

■ Complete review activity for words with long vowel sounds **a, i,** and **o**
■ Study and use idioms

DAY 5 Assessment

✓ Posttest, p. 56B
○ Standardized Test Master 11

✓ ■ Take Posttest

Cross-Curricular Lessons

Use the Spelling Focus (long vowels **a**, **i**, and **o**) to introduce the Work and Play lesson, *Reporter*, page 226, or choose a lesson that correlates with a topic you're currently teaching.

MEETING THE NEEDS OF ALL STUDENTS

The Word List

For students studying 20 words, assign pages 56–59 and Extra Practice and Review masters.

Modified List For students studying 10 words, modify Practice on page 56, and assign Think and Practice Master 11 and pages 58–59.

Challenge For students studying 25 words, assign pages 56–59, Challenge, Extra Practice, and Review masters.

Bilingual/ESL

Because the English long **i** sound is represented in Spanish by the diphthong **ai**, Spanish-speaking students may misspell *lion/laion* and *wild/waild*.

Personal Words

Students add to Personal Words lists by looking at work in their writing portfolios and words they want to remember from their reading.

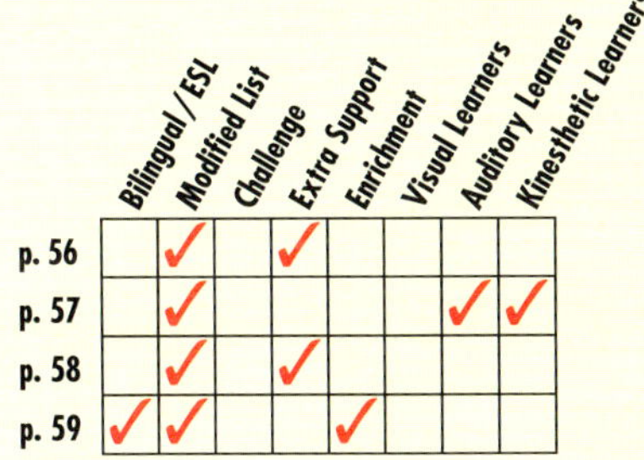

	Bilingual / ESL	Modified List	Challenge	Extra Support	Enrichment	Visual Learners	Auditory Learners	Kinesthetic Learners
p. 56		✓		✓				
p. 57		✓					✓	✓
p. 58		✓		✓				
p. 59	✓	✓			✓			

ASSESSMENT*

Pretest

Read the underlined word, read the sentence, and then repeat the underlined word. Guide students in self-correcting their pretests and correcting any misspellings.

1. A bus came into the <u>station</u>.
2. Thin ice is a <u>danger</u>.
3. Tulips bloom in <u>April</u>.
4. Wolves are <u>wild</u> animals.
5. Kelly hid <u>behind</u> the bush.
6. Gina ate a <u>whole</u> sandwich.
7. Anthony <u>broke</u> his foot.
8. The family <u>drove</u> to a city.
9. The dog will <u>hide</u> its bone.
10. <u>Decide</u> between the two.
11. We took a <u>vacation</u>.
12. They put in a new <u>cable</u>.
13. <u>Bacon</u> is good for breakfast.
14. We ate a <u>pint</u> of yogurt.
15. A <u>lion</u> growled at us.
16. <u>Smoke</u> came from a bonfire.
17. He lives on a <u>remote</u> island.
18. A dog <u>stole</u> the boy's sock.
19. Did you <u>invite</u> a friend?
20. The bus will <u>arrive</u> on time.

Posttest

Read aloud the sentences below. These sentences may be used for dictation.

1. There was sunshine in <u>April</u>.
2. Dad <u>drove</u> us to the movie.
3. A train <u>station</u> is so busy.
4. A cat sat <u>behind</u> the barn.
5. Is a fox a <u>wild</u> animal?
6. I will <u>decide</u> which is best.
7. It's hard to <u>hide</u> a monster.
8. We lost a <u>whole</u> pack of gum.
9. <u>Watch</u> for unknown <u>danger</u>.
10. She <u>broke</u> her blue crayon.
11. We bought a <u>pint</u> of jelly.
12. A <u>lion</u> is in the cat family.
13. <u>Smoke</u> came from the trees.
14. A <u>cable</u> goes into the house.
15. A beach <u>vacation</u> is fun.
16. Did you <u>invite</u> your cousin?
17. We will <u>arrive</u> early.
18. I ate <u>bacon</u> and an egg.
19. We played on a <u>remote</u> beach.
20. The fox <u>stole</u> the peaches.

Challenge Words

1. Grandma had an <u>operation</u>.
2. His <u>behavior</u> is very good.
3. This is a <u>private</u> place.
4. <u>Rhode Island</u> is in America.
5. <u>Apologize</u> for getting angry.

Additional Assessment

Standardized Test Master 11
Dictation Sentences, p. T38
Everyday Spelling CD-ROM

KIDSPELLING

Research in Action found it refreshing to see how Mona drew on what she knew about the spelling of English to write about her favorite food—*canaty* and *bachon* (Canadian bacon). Remind yourself to recognize what your students' writing reveals about their application of spelling principles.

* See pp. T20 and T33 for test-study-test information.

LESSON 11

DAY 1 CHALLENGE MASTER

CHALLENGE ■ 11

Challenge Words

behavior　operation　private　apologize　Rhode Island

■ Use the clues to complete the crossword puzzle.

Across
2. way of acting
5. not for the public; personal

Down
1. the smallest state in the United States
3. make a statement saying one is sorry
4. the way something works

■ Although it is small, there are many things to see and many things to do in Rhode Island. Research to find information, then write a report persuading people to visit the state. Use one or more Challenge Words.

Practice Masters, p. 45

DAY 1 HOME-SCHOOL MASTER

■ 11　HOME-SCHOOL ACTIVITIES　11 ■

Word Check 11
1. smoke
2. cable
3. whole
4. invite
5. April
6. behind
7. remote
8. lion
9. vacation
10. pint
11. broke
12. station
13. stole
14. arrive
15. danger
16. drove
17. hide
18. bacon
19. wild
20. decide

■ **Base Words** Write the list word that is the base word for each word below.

1. lions **lion**
2. remotely **remote**
3. decided **decide**
4. arriving **arrive**
5. invited **invite**
6. hiding **hide**
7. stationed **station**
8. unbroken **broke**
9. vacationed **vacation**
10. pints **pint**
11. wildness **wild**
12. wholesome **whole**
13. smoking **smoke**

■ **Vowel Sound Puzzle** Fill in the blanks to form list words. Then write the letters from the circles to complete the riddle.

14. c a b l e
15. d r o v e
16. b a c o n
17. d a n g e r
18. A p r i l
19. b e h i n d
20. s t o l e

The vowel sounds in these list words are **long a i**, and **o**.

Dear Parent,
Please check to see that your child has done this page correctly. Circle any misspelled words and help your child study them.
Tear off the Word Check before your child returns this page to class. Use it to help your child study.

Home-School Activities, p. 10

DAY 2 THINK AND PRACTICE MASTER

11 ■ THINK AND PRACTICE

| station | danger | April | wild | behind |
| whole | broke | drove | hide | decide |

■ **Making Comparisons** Write a list word that begins with the same first letter and has the same vowel sound as the underlined letter in each word.

1. date **danger**
2. wide **wild**
3. define **decide**
4. high **hide**
5. brocade **broke**

■ **Classifying Words** Write the list word that belongs in each group.

6. airport, wharf, **station**
7. biked, flew, **drove**
8. all, complete, **whole**
9. February, March, **April**
10. last, in back of, **behind**
11. conceal, put out of sight, **hide**

STRATEGIC SPELLING: Using the Rhyming Helper Strategy
A rhyming helper rhymes with a word and is the same at the end. Write *hide, drove, broke,* and *wild.* Write a rhyming helper next to each word. Underline the matching letters. Be sure your helper is spelled right.

List Word	Rhyming Helper
12. _______	ride, slide, wide, etc.
13. _______	cove, stove, wove, etc.
14. _______	choke, joke, woke, etc.
15. _______	child, mild

Practice Masters, p. 46

DAY 2 EXTRA PRACTICE MASTER

EXTRA PRACTICE ■ 11

Word List

station	danger	April	wild	behind
whole	broke	drove	hide	decide
vacation	cable	bacon	pint	lion
smoke	remote	stole	invite	arrive

■ **Words in Context** Use a list word to complete each person's statement below.

1. A retired person: "I plan to go on a long ___."
2. A TV installer: "Most people here have ___ TV service."
3. A firefighter: "We saw ___ coming from the building."
4. A gardener: "___ is my favorite month."
5. A train conductor: "We will get to the ___ at 4:00 P.M."
6. A wildlife photographer: "We are filming a ___ family that just had cubs."
7. A baby-sitter: "I play a lot of ___ and seek."
8. A restaurant worker: "We have a special on ___, lettuce, and tomato sandwiches."
9. A long-distance trucker: "I ___ 600 miles today."
10. A mountain climber: "We always use safety equipment to lessen our ___ of falling."

1. **vacation**
2. **cable**
3. **smoke**
4. **April**
5. **station**
6. **lion**
7. **hide**
8. **bacon**
9. **drove**
10. **danger**

■ **Long Vowel Sounds** Write the unused list words in their correct column.

Long i		Long o	
11. **decide**		17. **broke**	
12. **behind**		18. **remote**	
13. **invite**		19. **whole**	
14. **arrive**		20. **stole**	
15. **wild**			
16. **pint**			

Practice Masters, p. 47

TECHNOLOGY AND VISUAL SUPPORT	 Use Audiotape A, Side 2, Lesson 11  Use Proofreading and Writing Transparency 11	 For additional practice use *Everyday Spelling* Game Software, Lesson 11	 Additional resources on *Everyday Spelling* CD-ROM: proofreading and writing, modified list and challenge words, auditory test

DAY 3 SECOND LANGUAGE SUPPORT MASTER

11 ■ SECOND LANGUAGE SUPPORT

Words Around You

Think about where you have seen the words you learned in Lesson 11.

Write some of the words in the chart. Then write about the words. One word has been done for you.

A word I saw	Where or when I saw it	How the word was used
vacation	classroom calendar	Winter vacation begins.
Answers will vary.		

Second Language Support, p. 36

DAY 3 WRITING ACTIVITY MASTER

11 ■ WRITING ACTIVITY

Combining Sentences

	Make a capital.
	Make a small letter.
∧	Add something.
	Take out something.
⊙	Add a period.
¶	New paragraph.

☐ One way to combine two related sentences is to join them with the word *and*.

■ Tim wrote the following announcement for his scout troop. Combine some sentences.

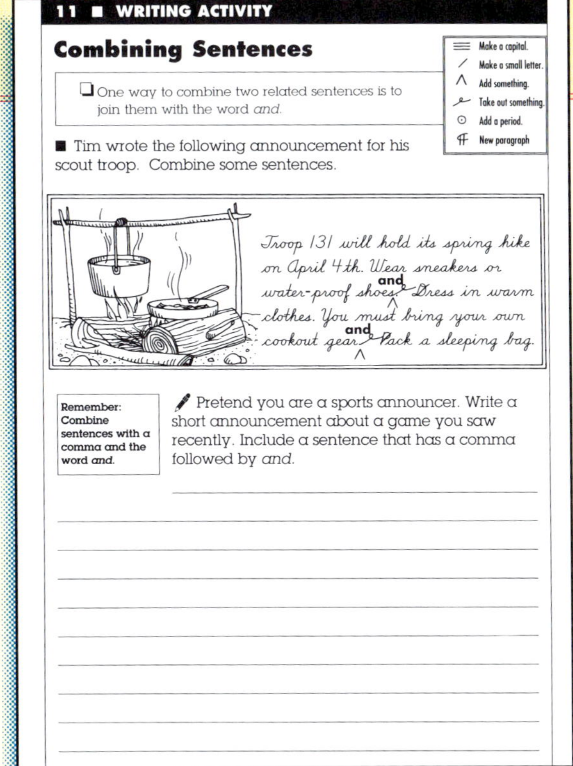

Remember: Combine sentences with a comma and the word *and*.

Pretend you are a sports announcer. Write a short announcement about a game you saw recently. Include a sentence that has a comma followed by *and*.

Spelling and Writing, p. 20

DAY 4 REVIEW MASTER

11 ■ REVIEW

	Word List			
station	danger	April	wild	behind
whole	broke	drove	hide	decide
vacation	cable	bacon	pint	lion
smoke	remote	stole	invite	arrive

■ **Word Equations** Write each list word using the math clues.

1. bent - nt + hind = **behind**
2. invest - est + ite = **invite**
3. scab - s + le = **cable**
4. back - k + on = **bacon**
5. dangerous - ous = **danger**
6. Apron - on + il = **April**
7. remove - ve + te = **remote**
8. state - e + ion = **station**
9. vacant -nt + tion = **vacation**
10. decision - sion + de = **decide**

■ **Synonyms** Write the list word that means the same as the underlined word or words. Use the Spelling Dictionary.

11. John <u>took the car</u> to the grocery store.
12. No one can eat that <u>entire</u> large pizza!
13. The police caught the robber who <u>took</u> our car.
14. The glass <u>shattered</u>.
15. When will the train <u>get here</u>?
16. Alice bought the <u>two-cup</u> container of milk.
17. The black <u>cloud</u> rose from the ashes.
18. Did you ever try to <u>conceal</u> balloons?
19. The <u>king of beasts</u> wears a golden mane.
20. <u>Untamed</u> horses couldn't stop me.

11. **drove**
12. **whole**
13. **stole**
14. **broke**
15. **arrive**
16. **pint**
17. **smoke**
18. **hide**
19. **lion**
20. **Wild**

Practice Masters, p. 48

DAY 5 STANDARDIZED TEST MASTER

11 ■ LESSON TEST

■ Find the word in each group that is spelled correctly. Fill in the letter for the correct word on the answer strip.

Sample:
- **a.** crowde
- **b.** croued
- **c.** croud
- **d.** crowd — ⓐⓑⓒ●

1. **a.** broke **b.** brok **c.** brock **d.** brouk — 1. ●ⓑⓒⓓ
2. **a.** vaction **b.** vacatoin **c.** vacation **d.** vacaition — 2. ⓐⓑ●ⓓ
3. **a.** drov **b.** drove **c.** drivd **d.** droove — 3. ⓐ●ⓒⓓ
4. **a.** cable **b.** cabel **c.** cabble **d.** cabbel — 4. ●ⓑⓒⓓ
5. **a.** stoll **b.** stoled **c.** stole **d.** stolle — 5. ⓐⓑ●ⓓ
6. **a.** staition **b.** stason **c.** staion **d.** station — 6. ⓐⓑⓒ●
7. **a.** remot **b.** remote **c.** romote **d.** remotte — 7. ⓐ●ⓒⓓ
8. **a.** bacon **b.** baccon **c.** backon **d.** baken — 8. ●ⓑⓒⓓ
9. **a.** smouk **b.** smok **c.** smoke **d.** smoek — 9. ⓐⓑ●ⓓ
10. **a.** Apirl **b.** april **c.** April **d.** Aprail — 10. ⓐⓑ●ⓓ
11. **a.** wole **b.** whole **c.** whle **d.** whol — 11. ⓐ●ⓒⓓ
12. **a.** behind **b.** behide **c.** behinde **d.** be hind — 12. ●ⓑⓒⓓ
13. **a.** hie **b.** hidde **c.** hied **d.** hide — 13. ⓐⓑⓒ●
14. **a.** willd **b.** wyel **c.** wild **d.** wayld — 14. ⓐⓑ●ⓓ
15. **a.** decide **b.** deside **c.** desid **d.** dicide — 15. ●ⓑⓒⓓ
16. **a.** lione **b.** lion **c.** lino **d.** linoe — 16. ⓐ●ⓒⓓ
17. **a.** arive **b.** arivve **c.** arrive **d.** arrieve — 17. ⓐⓑ●ⓓ
18. **a.** pinnt **b.** pinte **c.** pinet **d.** pint — 18. ⓐⓑⓒ●
19. **a.** invite **b.** invit **c.** ivite **d.** envite — 19. ●ⓑⓒⓓ
20. **a.** dager **b.** dannger **c.** danger **d.** dangger — 20. ⓐⓑ●ⓓ

Practice for Standardized Tests, p. 14

DAY 1 Introduction

- ✓ Pretest and Self-Check
- ● Spelling Focus and Word List
- ○ Challenge Words
- ○ Modified List

DAILY SPELLING REVIEW

The *lamm danst* around the yard.

lamb   *danced*

● Core   ○ Optional   ✓ Assessment

INTRODUCTION

Phonics

Vowel-consonant-e Have students write the list words that end in **e**. Help them note that, aside from *cable*, the words all end in **vowel-consonant-e**; the preceding vowel sound is always long, and the final **e** is always silent.

MEETING THE NEEDS OF ALL STUDENTS

Modified List

Practice Students studying only the high-frequency words in the top box write
- three words with long **a**
- four words with long **i**
- three words with long **o**

Extra Support

Homophones Make sure students don't confuse the word *whole* with its homophone *hole.* Illustrate the two words with a picture or sentences: Here is the *whole* pie. There is a *hole* in the pie.

Additional Practice

Challenge Master 11
Home-School Master 11
Audiotape A, Side 2

---

1. station
2. danger
3. April
4. vacation
5. cable
6. bacon
7. wild
8. behind
9. hide
10. decide
11. pint
12. lion
13. invite
14. arrive
15. whole
16. broke
17. drove
18. smoke
19. remote
20. stole

CHALLENGE!

operation
behavior
private
Rhode Island
apologize

56

■ INTRODUCTION

Long Vowels a, i, o

SPELLING FOCUS

Long vowels are often spelled with one letter: **station**, **wild**. They can also be spelled **vowel-consonant-e**: **whole**, **hide**.

STUDY Say each word. Then read the sentence.

1. station — Visitors arrive at the bus **station.**
2. danger — Dogs can sense **danger.**
3. April — **April** weather is often wet.
4. wild — Lions are **wild** cats.
5. behind — He is **behind** in his work.
6. whole ✦ — I could eat that **whole** pie.
7. broke — The cat **broke** the glass vase.
8. drove — Our friends **drove** to Florida.
9. hide — Close your eyes and I'll **hide.**
10. decide — Did you **decide** to join us?

11. vacation ✦ — They took a **vacation** by the sea.
12. cable — Wind tore down the power **cable.**
13. bacon — Dad cooked **bacon** and eggs.
14. pint — Will you buy me a **pint** of milk?
15. lion — A male **lion** has a mane.
16. smoke — They saw **smoke** from a campfire.
17. remote — She sailed to a **remote** island.
18. stole — A spy **stole** valuable papers.
19. invite — Let's **invite** them to dinner.
20. arrive — The plane will **arrive** at noon.

PRACTICE Sort the list words by writing
- six words with **long a**
- eight words with **long i**
- six words with **long o**

Order of words in each group may vary.

WRITE Choose ten words to write in sentences.
Sentences will vary.

✦ **WATCH OUT FOR FREQUENTLY MISSPELLED WORDS!**

- Practice: Compare and Vowel Trade
- Strategic Spelling: *Using the Rhyming Helper Strategy*
- Cross-Curricular Lesson: Introduce
- Modified List

DAILY SPELLING REVIEW

Darlene *sliped* and got a *scrach.*

slipped   scratch

THINK AND PRACTICE

COMPARE   Write a list word that has the same first letter, last letter, <u>and number of syllables</u> as each word below.

1. lotion
2. beacon
3. stallion
4. Abdul
5. ramble
6. veteran
7. drier
8. divide
9. pant
10. wood
11. beyond
12. inside

VOWEL TRADE   Change the vowel in each word to make a list word with the **long o** sound.

13. whale   14. brake   15. drive   16. stale

STRATEGIC SPELLING

Using the Rhyming Helper Strategy

A rhyming helper rhymes with a word and is spelled the same at the end. Write *hide, cable, arrive,* and *smoke.* Write a rhyming helper alongside each word. Underline the matching letters. Be sure your helper is spelled right.

Answers will vary.

List Word	Rhyming Helper
17. hide	<u>ri</u>de, <u>gli</u>de, <u>pri</u>de, etc.
18. cable	<u>a</u>ble, <u>fa</u>ble, <u>ta</u>ble, etc.
19. arrive	f<u>ive</u>, str<u>ive</u>, der<u>ive</u>, etc.
20. smoke	p<u>oke</u>, j<u>oke</u>, str<u>oke</u>, etc.

1. lion
2. bacon
3. station
4. April
5. remote
6. vacation
7. danger
8. decide
9. pint
10. wild
11. behind
12. invite
13. whole
14. broke
15. drove
16. stole

FREQUENTLY MISSPELLED WORDS

Can't remember when to use **whole** or **hole**? Remember this: A complete **whole** has a wide **w**, while **hole** has just an empty middle.

THINK AND PRACTICE

Compare

Say Aloud Students can say each word aloud in order to match the beginning and ending sounds with those of list words.

MEETING THE NEEDS OF ALL STUDENTS

Modified List

Review Students studying high-frequency words complete Think and Practice Master 11.

Kinesthetic Learners

Act It Out Have students work in groups to act out the context phrases for the word list. They may use props as needed.

Auditory Learners

Pronunciation Have students say aloud each word in items 13–16. Point out that the beginning sound of the first word is pronounced one way with an **a** and another way with an **o**.

Additional Practice

Think and Practice Master 11
Extra Practice Master 11
Everyday Spelling **CD-ROM**
Everyday Spelling **Game Software**

57

LESSON 11

- Proofread a Summary
- Proofreading Tip: Run-ons
- Write a Summary
- ✓ Cooperative Midweek Test

DAILY SPELLING REVIEW

The pitcher had *thron* a *strik*.

thrown   *strike*

● Core   ○ Optional   ✓ Assessment

PROOFREADING AND WRITING

Run-ons
Proofreading Technique
Inform students that a good strategy for detecting run-on sentences is to read a passage aloud.

MEETING THE NEEDS OF ALL STUDENTS

Modified List
Proofreading Students studying high-frequency words complete this page or the proofreading activity on the *Everyday Spelling* CD-ROM.

Extra Support
Group Effort Students may work together on summaries in two ways. They may meet in groups to discuss films as a pre-writing exercise. They also may exchange papers at the proofreading stage to check for clarity.

Additional Practice

Hardbound Book Master 11
Second Language Master 11
Writing Mini-Lesson Master 11
Writing Activity Master 11
Proofreading Transparency 11
Everyday Spelling **CD-ROM**

■ PROOFREADING AND WRITING

═	Make a capital.
/	Make a small letter.
∧	Add something.
ℰ	Take out something.
⊙	Add a period.
⁋	New paragraph

PROOFREAD A SUMMARY
Shanieka's class enjoyed a documentary film about Africa. Shanieka wrote a summary of what she saw. Correct four misspellings and one run-on sentence.

Africa has deserts, jungles, and large cities It is a place where **wild** willd animals roam and buildings touch the sky. A **lion** line roars loudly **, and smoke** smock floats from a house. It would be a wonderful place to **vacation** vacashun.

WRITE A SUMMARY Think of an interesting film you saw lately. Write a summary of the film. Try to use some of your list words and personal words.

Responses will vary. Summaries should include list words and personal words.

Word List

smoke	broke
cable	station
whole	stole
invite	arrive
April	danger
behind	drove
remote	hide
lion	bacon
vacation	wild
pint	decide

Personal Words

1. **Words will vary.**

2.

58

VOCABULARY BUILDING

Review

ANALOGIES   Write the boxed word that completes each analogy.

station	whole
danger	broke
April	drove
wild	hide
behind	decide

1. Rider is to rode as driver is to ___.
2. Some is to all as part is to ___.
3. Pardon is to blame as show is to ___.
4. Ship is to port as bus is to ___.
5. Study is to examine as determine is to ___.
6. Wednesday is to Thursday as March is to ___.
7. Here is to there as front is to ___.
8. Kind is to cruel as calm is to ___.
9. Swim is to swam as break is to ___.
10. Rough is to bumpy as hazard is to ___.

1. **drove**
2. **whole**
3. **hide**
4. **station**
5. **decide**
6. **April**
7. **behind**
8. **wild**
9. **broke**
10. **danger**

Word *Study*

IDIOMS   An **idiom** is a word picture that means something more than the words in it would suggest. One idiom has an interesting history.

Long ago in France, the people of Paris did not want Henry IV as their king. Henry decided to make war on them to "teach them a lesson." A wise counselor said to Henry, "If you destroy Paris, you will be king of a dead city. Would you chop off your nose to teach your face a lesson?" Henry spared Paris, became a popular king, and helped coin the idiom **cut off one's nose to spite one's face.**

Use the phrases in the box to help you write the meaning of each idiom below.

| praise oneself; boast |
| earn a living |
| have control over |
| get excited |

1. bring home the bacon
2. blow one's own horn
3. lose one's head
4. lead by the nose

1. **earn a living**
2. **praise oneself; boast**
3. **get excited**
4. **have control over**

LESSON
12

Unit Review Concepts

Words with sh, ch, tch, wh
Words with Double Consonants
Short e and Long e
Short Vowels: a, i, o, u
Long Vowels: a, i, o

● Core ○ Optional ✓ Assessment

DAILY PLAN	CORE OBJECTIVES	NOTES

DAY 1

● Review Activity: Win a Trip, p. 60
✓ Self-Assessment:
  How Am I Doing?, p. 60
○ Integrating Spelling:
  Social Studies, p. 60
○ Review Master 12A

- Use review words to complete an entry form
✓ ▪ Assess their own progress in the spelling of words in Unit 2

DAY 2

Review Activities:
● Nat's Story, p. 61
● Postcard from L.A., p. 61
Integrating Spelling:
○ Language Arts, p. 61
○ Social Studies, p. 61

- Use review words to complete a story summary
- Use review words to complete a postcard

DAY 3

Review Activities:
● Household Chores, p. 62
● The Big Game, p. 62
Integrating Spelling:
○ Language Arts, p. 62
○ Language Arts, p. 62
○ Review Master 12B

- Use review words to complete a work calendar
- Use review words to complete a story

DAY 4

Review Activities:
● A Family Meal, p. 63
● Camping Out, p. 63
Integrating Spelling:
○ Language Arts, p. 63
○ Science, p. 63
○ Standardized Test Masters 12A–12D

- Use review words to complete an announcement
- Use review words to complete a conversation

DAY 5

✓ Unit Review Test
✓ Writing Test
○ Writing Prompt Transparency 2
○ Writing Model Transparencies
  2A, 2B

✓ ▪ Assess review words
✓ ▪ Assess descriptive writing

MEETING THE NEEDS OF ALL STUDENTS

Modified List

For students studying only the high-frequency words in each lesson, assign Review Masters 12A–12B for unit review. Use the Modified Dictation Sentences for assessment.

Bilingual/ESL

Bilingual and ESL students might benefit from working with a partner. The partners can help each other review the meanings of words that they find difficult.

Spelling Conferences

Conduct individual spelling conferences to discuss each student's spelling progress during Unit 2. You might want to take this opportunity to remind students to add words to their personal dictionaries.

ASSESSMENT

Dictation Sentences

1. What will we have for supper tomorrow?
2. A young couple may move into the house.
3. What did he see out the kitchen window?
4. Watch that pitcher throw the ball.
5. Hot chocolate is a treat.
6. Can you chop up a head of lettuce?
7. Let's invite them to our Halloween party.
8. Beat one egg into the drink.
9. The dog stole the bacon right off the table.
10. We found shelter by a river.
11. She drove the truck to a remote spot.
12. I forgot to bring my flashlight.
13. April is part of the spring season.
14. Smoke came from the police station.
15. Who will offer to help at the church?
16. I put the bottle in the trash can.
17. He had trouble with the puppy.
18. I'll do whatever you decide.
19. I left my backpack somewhere.
20. The catcher had to make a tough play.
21. An odd dog was in the alley.
22. Our whole vacation was great.
23. Each person will speak in the contest.
24. Can you wear those slippers anywhere?
25. Dry the blanket on the fence.

Writing Test

Writing Prompt Transparency 2 and Writing Model Transparencies 2A and 2B will help students prepare for holistic writing tests. Helpful information relating to descriptive writing tests is provided in the Writer's Handbook on page 236.

Everyday Spelling CD-ROM

An auditory test is available as an alternate testing format.

Modified Dictation Sentences

1. Tomorrow is March third.
2. My sister broke the bottle.
3. Did he hide the money?
4. Watch the monkey do tricks.
5. Do you have enough cash to pay for the honey?
6. Dad will punish me for getting into trouble.
7. He gave them a different reason.
8. We drove to the river.
9. There is a fence near the pond.
10. The big danger is from wild animals.
11. That band will play anywhere!
12. I had written my short story before supper.

LESSON
12

DAY 1 REVIEW MASTER A

REVIEW ■ 12A

Lesson 7

| short | punish | watch | March | anywhere |

■ Antonyms Write the list word that means the opposite of each word.

1. nowhere — **anywhere**
2. long — **short**
3. ignore — **watch**
4. reward — **punish**
5. September — **March**

Lesson 8

| different | written | supper | tomorrow | bottle |

■ Analogies Write the list word that completes each phrase.

1. cardboard and carton, glass and **bottle**
2. light and dark, same and **different**
3. take and taken, write and **written**
4. past and yesterday, future and **tomorrow**
5. breakfast and brunch, dinner and **supper**

Lesson 9

| reason | money | honey | monkey | fence |

■ Seeing Relationships Write the list word that tells what each person might need.

1. A banker might need **money** to invest.
2. A rancher might need a **fence** to keep the cattle in.
3. A lawyer might need a **reason** to argue in court.
4. A baker might need **honey** for bread and cookies.
5. A zookeeper might need a **monkey** for the Ape House.

Practice Masters, p. 49

DAY 3 REVIEW MASTER B

12B ■ REVIEW

Lesson 10

| band | cash | pond | trouble | river |

■ Drawing Conclusions Write the list word that completes each phrase.

1. Use **cash** to pay for the groceries.
2. Misbehave and get into **trouble**
3. Play a trumpet in a **band**
4. Ride a steamboat up a **river**
5. See a tadpole in a **pond**

Lesson 11

| danger | wild | hide | broke | drove |

■ Rhymes Complete each sentence by writing a list word that rhymes with the underlined word.

1. We tried to <u>decide</u> where to **hide**
2. A park <u>ranger</u> watches for **danger**
3. It was no <u>joke</u> when the window **broke**
4. That little <u>child</u> acts very **wild**
5. Down to the <u>cove</u> was where we **drove**

Practice Masters, p. 50

DAY 4 STANDARDIZED TEST MASTER A

REVIEW TEST ■ 12A

■ Find the word that is spelled correctly to complete each group of words. Fill in the letter for the correct word on the answer strip.

Sample:
face in the ________
a. crowde   b. croude   c. crowd   d. croud   ⓐⓑ●ⓓ

1. cans in the ________
a. alley   b. allie   c. aley   d. ally   1. ●ⓑⓒⓓ

2. the ________ apple
a. wole   b. hole   c. whole   d. holl   2. ⓐⓑ●ⓓ

3. took it to ________
a. tham   b. then   c. theme   d. them   3. ⓐⓑⓒ●

4. ________ the money
a. stold   b. stoll   c. stooled   d. stole   4. ⓐⓑⓒ●

5. can't ________ what to do
a. desid   b. decide   c. dicide   d. deside   5. ⓐ●ⓒⓓ

6. ________ to bring it
a. forgot   b. fergot   c. foregot   d. for got   6. ●ⓑⓒⓓ

7. flowers in ________
a. april   b. aprill   c. April   d. Apirl   7. ⓐⓑ●ⓓ

8. put on her ________
a. slippers   b. sleprs   c. slipprs   d. slipers   8. ●ⓑⓒⓓ

9. took out the ________
a. trass   b. trash   c. trach   d. tash   9. ⓐ●ⓒⓓ

10. the ________ in the wall
a. windo   b. widow   c. wendow   d. window   10. ⓐⓑⓒ●

11. came ________ the news
a. weth   b. whith   c. with   d. whit   11. ⓐⓑ●ⓓ

12. you can go ________
a. anywhere   b. anywere   c. eny where   d. any where   12. ●ⓑⓒⓓ

Practice for Standardized Tests, p. 15

DAY 4 STANDARDIZED TEST MASTER B

12B ■ REVIEW TEST

■ Find the word that is spelled correctly to complete each group of words. Fill in the letter for the correct word on the answer strip.

13. to ________ the drum
a. beet   b. bet   c. beat   d. bete   13. ⓐⓑ●ⓓ

14. ________ and tomato
a. ledis   b. lettuce   c. lettce   d. lettece   14. ⓐ●ⓒⓓ

15. went to ________
a. chruch   b. cherch   c. chourch   d. church   15. ⓐⓑⓒ●

16. ________ from the rain
a. shiler   b. shelter   c. chelter   d. shelleder   16. ⓐ●ⓒⓓ

17. turned on the ________
a. flash light   b. flachlight   c. flashlight   d. flase light   17. ⓐⓑ●ⓓ

18. ________ the car slowly
a. drivd   b. drove   c. drov   d. drived   18. ⓐ●ⓒⓓ

19. ducks on the ________
a. river   b. wever   c. rivier   d. rever   19. ●ⓑⓒⓓ

20. ________ where you go
a. whatch   b. wach   c. wath   d. watch   20. ⓐⓑⓒ●

21. to ________ my friends
a. invit   b. envite   c. invite   d. envit   21. ⓐⓑ●ⓓ

22. a pie-eating ________
a. cotest   b. contest   c. contist   d. countis   22. ⓐ●ⓒⓓ

23. saw an ________ thing
a. awd   b. od   c. ode   d. odd   23. ⓐⓑⓒ●

24. went ________ the store
a. in two   b. into   c. intoo   d. in to   24. ⓐ●ⓒⓓ

Practice for Standardized Tests, p. 16

DAY 4 STANDARDIZED TEST MASTER C

REVIEW TEST ■ 12C

■ Find the word that is spelled correctly to complete each sentence. Fill in the letter for the correct word on the answer strip.

25. I had my friends here for ________.
   a. supper   **b.** supr   **c.** saper   **d.** super
   25. ● b c d

26. My friend is the ________ in the game today.
   a. pichter   **b.** picher   **c.** pitcher   **d.** pither
   26. a b ● d

27. They can't go for a ________ of hours.
   a. cuple   **b.** couple   **c.** coupel   **d.** cople
   27. a ● c d

28. The ________ from the fire was quite dense.
   a. smock   **b.** smouk   **c.** smoke   **d.** smok
   28. a b ● d

29. You should ________ small pets gently.
   a. thret   **b.** treet   **c.** trete   **d.** treat
   29. a b c ●

30. Dad sent me out to ________ wood.
   a. chop   **b.** chohped   **c.** chopp   **d.** chope
   30. ● b c d

31. Can you ________ slowly, please?
   a. speck   **b.** speek   **c.** speeck   **d.** speak
   31. a b c ●

32. That was a ________ job to do!
   a. tuf   **b.** tough   **c.** tuff   **d.** touf
   32. a ● c d

33. He can do ________ you ask him to do.
   a. wate ever   **b.** what ever   **c.** whatever   **d.** watever
   33. a b ● d

34. The woman at the store made me a good ________.
   a. offer   **b.** ofer   **c.** awfer   **d.** oufer
   34. ● b c d

35. Kim threw the ball to the ________.
   a. cacher   **b.** cather   **c.** checher   **d.** catcher
   35. a b c ●

36. Take your books out of your ________.
   a. bagepack   **b.** backpack   **c.** backpak   **d.** back pack
   36. a ● c d

Practice for Standardized Tests, p. 17

DAY 4 STANDARDIZED TEST MASTER D

12D ■ REVIEW TEST

■ Find the word in each group that is spelled correctly. Fill in the letter for the correct word on the answer strip.

37. **a.** baccon   **c.** bacon
    b. backon   **d.** baken
    37. a b ● d

38. **a.** re moat   **c.** remot
    b. romote   **d.** remote
    38. a b c ●

39. **a.** young   **c.** younge
    b. yong   **d.** yung
    39. ● b c d

40. **a.** fence   **c.** fince
    b. fons   **d.** fense
    40. ● b c d

41. **a.** botel   **c.** botle
    b. bottle   **d.** bottal
    41. a ● c d

42. **a.** staition   **c.** steshin
    b. stason   **d.** station
    42. a b c ●

43. **a.** tomarrow   **c.** tomorrow
    b. tommorrow   **d.** tommorow
    43. a b ● d

44. **a.** kithen   **c.** kitchin
    b. kitchen   **d.** kichen
    44. a ● c d

45. **a.** chocalate   **c.** choclet
    b. choclate   **d.** chocolate
    45. a b c ●

46. **a.** vacation   **c.** vaction
    b. vacaition   **d.** vacatoin
    46. ● b c d

47. **a.** seesin   **c.** season
    b. seson   **d.** sesand
    47. a b ● d

48. **a.** blankit   **c.** blaket
    b. banket   **d.** blanket
    48. a b c ●

49. **a.** som were   **c.** some where
    b. somewhere   **d.** somwhere
    49. a ● c d

50. **a.** trouble   **c.** trobel
    b. troble   **d.** truble
    50. ● b c d

Practice for Standardized Tests, p. 18

DAY 5 WRITING PROMPT TRANSPARENCY

Spelling and Writing, Transparency 2

LESSON
12

SELF-ASSESSMENT

How Am I Doing?

Talk with students about why it is helpful to think about their progress in spelling. Raise issues such as

1. I learned to spell a hard word by ___.
2. I spell spelling words correctly when I write.
3. I am a good speller for my age.
4. I try to use spelling words in my writing.
5. A word that is hard for me to spell is ___.

INTEGRATING SPELLING

Social Studies

Trip Description Have students write an answer for the contest describing in about fifty words where they would go if they could go anywhere in the world.

Additional Resources
Review Master 12A

Review

Lesson 7: Words with sh, ch, tch, wh
Lesson 8: Words with Double Consonants
Lesson 9: Short e and Long e
Lesson 10: Short Vowels a, i, o, u
Lesson 11: Long Vowels a, i, o

REVIEW WORD LIST

1. anywhere	11. watch	21. beat	31. couple	41. bacon
2. catcher	12. whatever	22. contest	32. forgot	42. decide
3. chocolate	13. bottle	23. fence	33. into	43. drove
4. church	14. lettuce	24. season	34. river	44. invite
5. flashlight	15. odd	25. speak	35. tough	45. remote
6. kitchen	16. offer	26. them	36. trouble	46. smoke
7. pitcher	17. slippers	27. treat	37. window	47. station
8. shelter	18. supper	28. backpack	38. with	48. stole
9. somewhere	19. tomorrow	29. blanket	39. young	49. vacation
10. trash	20. alley	30. chop	40. April	50. whole

60

Nat's Story

Nat is telling the story of *Aladdin* to his classmates, but he has forgotten a few of the details. Use the list words to complete his story.

ALADDIN AND THE MAGIC LAMP

Aladdin is a (1) man who finds a magic lamp. He rubs the lamp and an (2) fellow, called a genie, floats out in a puff of (3). The genie gives Aladdin (4) he asks for. Aladdin falls in love with the Emperor's daughter and must (5) how to win her. The genie helps (6), and the happy (7) are finally married.

couple   young   odd
them   decide   whatever
smoke

1. **young**
2. **odd**
3. **smoke**
4. **whatever**
5. **decide**
6. **them**
7. **couple**

Language Arts

Story Summary Have students write a summary of a story they have read recently. Point out that they should include the most important things that happened in the story and omit unnecessary details.

Social Studies

Postcard Have students write a postcard from the wished-for destination they wrote about in Win a Trip on page 60. Encourage them to describe what they might see and do at the place they have chosen.

While in Los Angeles, Aponi sent her friend Ray this postcard. Use the list words to complete her message.

church   river   season
April   speak   station
window

1. **April**
2. **station**
3. **season**
4. **speak**
5. **church**
6. **window**
7. **river**

POSTCARD FROM L.A.

Dear Ray,

April 3, 19--

We arrived in Los Angeles on the first of (1). Our train pulled into the (2) at midnight. It's supposed to be the rainy (3), but each day is sunny. It's fun to (4) Spanish with my friend Carlota. Today we visited Watts Towers. They look like steeples on a (5). I can see them from my bedroom (6). Tomorrow we will find a (7) and do some fishing. Have fun.

Aponi

61

LESSON 12

Language Arts

Calendar Have students list their household chores for a week. They might wish to put the information in calendar form and illustrate it.

Language Arts

Journal Entry Have students write a journal entry describing a sports event that they have seen, participated in, or imagined. Point out that vivid verbs add excitement to sports writing.

Additional Resources

Review Master 12B

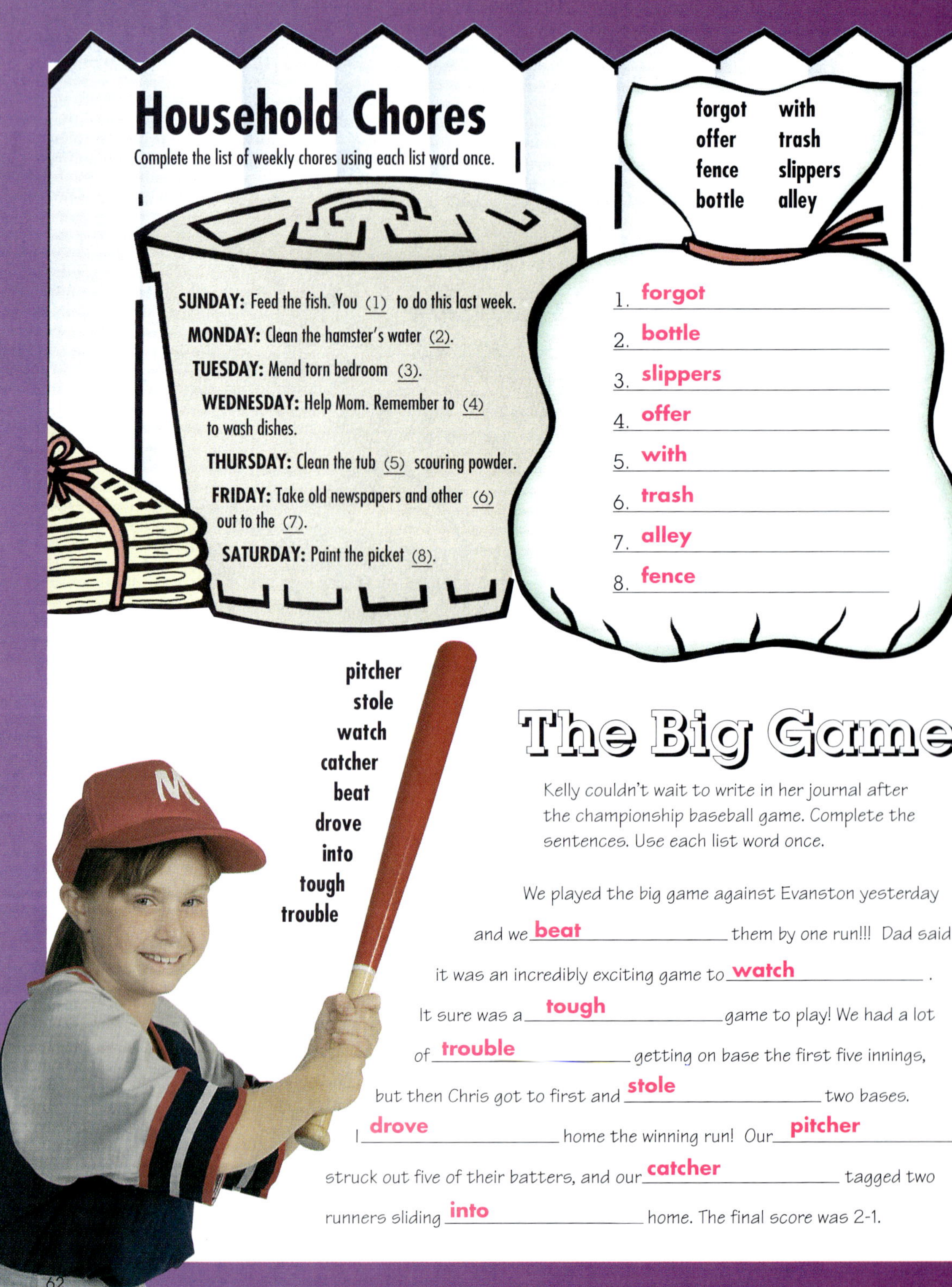

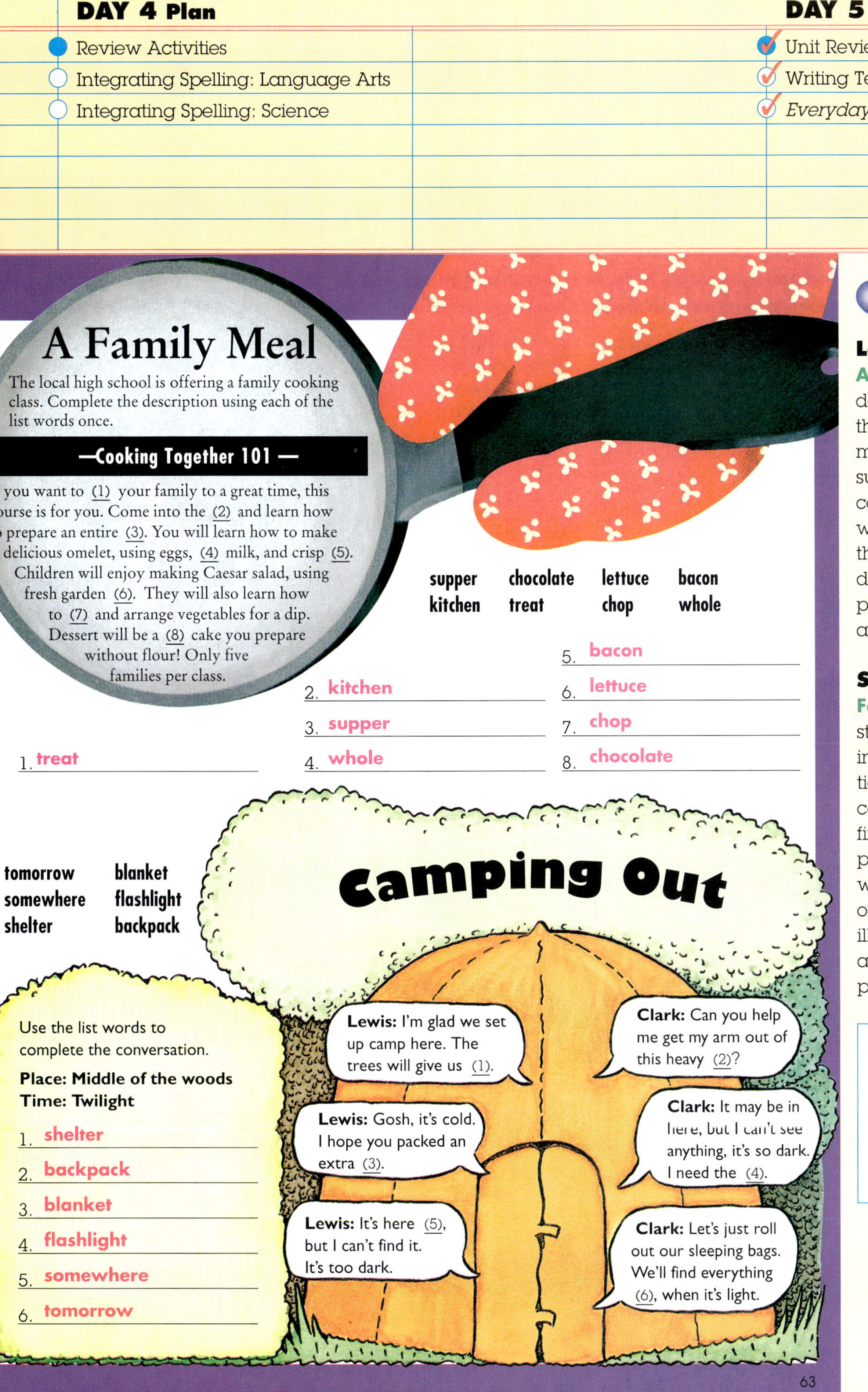

A Family Meal

The local high school is offering a family cooking class. Complete the description using each of the list words once.

—Cooking Together 101 —

If you want to (1) your family to a great time, this course is for you. Come into the (2) and learn how to prepare an entire (3). You will learn how to make a delicious omelet, using eggs, (4) milk, and crisp (5). Children will enjoy making Caesar salad, using fresh garden (6). They will also learn how to (7) and arrange vegetables for a dip. Dessert will be a (8) cake you prepare without flour! Only five families per class.

supper   chocolate   lettuce   bacon
kitchen   treat   chop   whole

1. treat
2. kitchen
3. supper
4. whole
5. bacon
6. lettuce
7. chop
8. chocolate

Camping Out

tomorrow   blanket
somewhere   flashlight
shelter   backpack

Use the list words to complete the conversation.

Place: Middle of the woods
Time: Twilight

1. shelter
2. backpack
3. blanket
4. flashlight
5. somewhere
6. tomorrow

63

Language Arts

Announcement Have students imagine a class that their family members might like to take together, such as one in camping or computer use. Have them write an announcement for the class, including a short description and other important information, such as time and costs.

Science

Facts for Camping Have students brainstorm ways in which science information can be helpful on camping trips (building fires, avoiding poisonous plants, preparing for weather conditions, and so on). Students may wish to illustrate camping scenes and label them with appropriate scientific facts.

Additional Resources

Standardized Test Masters 12A–12D
Writing Prompt Transparency 2
Writing Model Transparencies 2A, 2B
Everyday Spelling **CD-ROM**

OVERVIEW

UNIT 3

Introduces the metacognitive strategy **Meaning Helpers** to relate new words to words whose spelling students already know. Often the simpler word is hidden within the related word.

SCOPE AND SEQUENCE: LESSONS 13–18

Lesson	Generalization	Think and Practice	Proofreading and Writing
13 pp. 66–69	Some words have parts that are spelled the same but pronounced differently.	Contrasts Synonyms Strategic Spelling: Using the Meaning Helper Strategy	Proofread a Persuasive Paragraph ■ misspelled words Write a Persuasive Paragraph
14 pp. 70–73	The consonant sound /j/ can be spelled **ge** and **dge**; the consonant sound /ks/ can be spelled **xc** and **x**; the consonant sound /kw/ is usually spelled **qu**.	Tongue Twisters Word Search Strategic Spelling: Seeing Meaning Connections	Proofread a Recipe ■ misspelled words ■ usage errors Write a Recipe
15 pp. 74–77	Add **-s** to form plurals of words that end in a **vowel** and **y** and to most other words. Change **y** to **i** and add **-es** to words that end in a **consonant** and **y**. Add **-es** to words that end with **sh, ch, s, ss,** or **x**.	Making Comparisons Word Associations Strategic Spelling: Building New Words	Proofread a Description ■ misspelled words ■ incorrect pronoun Write a Description
16 pp. 78–81	Visualizing a word as you pronounce it helps you to use just enough letters.	Classifying Words in Context Strategic Spelling: Using the Meaning Helper Strategy	Proofread a Warning ■ misspelled words ■ punctuation errors Write a Warning
17 pp. 82–85	In contractions, words are combined and shortened, and an apostrophe replaces the letters that are left out.	Homophones Creating Contractions Don't Quote Me Strategic Spelling: Building New Words	Proofread a Sign ■ misspelled words ■ punctuation errors Write a Sign

	Concepts for Review	Unit 3 Activities	Integrating Spelling
Review 18 pp. 86–89	Related Words Consonant sounds /j/, /ks/, /kw/ Adding **-s** and **-es** Using Just Enough Letters Contractions	Good Health Rules Daily Record Statements Advertising Blurbs Interview Speech Posters	**Health:** Good Health Rules **Language Arts:** Daily Record, Advertising Jingle **Physical Education:** Research **Music:** Research **Social Studies:** Map Talk **Art:** Poster

RESEARCH IN ACTION

ADDED LETTERS

Research in Action notes that students often add extra letters to words. A word might be mispronounced, or single letters might spell more than one sound, such as /ks/ in *extra*.

TYPICAL MISSPELLINGS:
* *exstra* for *extra*
* *hampster* for *hamster*
* *missted* for *missed*
* *durring* for *during*

Helpful strategies include using the Divide and Conquer strategy to break words into syllables. Students can then focus on the configuration of each syllable to get the right number of letters.

ADDITIONAL RESOURCES

For Every Weekly Lesson
* **Think and Practice Master**
* **Challenge Master**
* **Extra Practice Master**
* **Review Master**
* **Second Language Support Master**
* **Home-School Activity Master**
* **Writing Mini-Lesson**
* **Writing Activity Master**
* **Standardized Test Master**
* **Proofreading and Writing Transparency**

Technology
* **Audiotape**
* *Everyday Spelling* **CD-ROM**
* *Everyday Spelling* **Game Software**

Unit Review
* **Standardized Test Masters**
* **Writing Prompt Transparency**
* **Writing Model Transparencies**
* *Everyday Spelling* **CD-ROM**

Vocabulary Building	Meeting the Needs of All Students	Cross-Curricular Lessons*
Review Context Clues **Word Study** Triplets	**Visual** Partner Words **Auditory** Brainstorming **Bilingual/ESL** Comparing Sounds **Enrichment** Triplet Trade-Off	**Social Studies:** Using Natural Resources, pp. 176–177
Review Context Clues **Using a Dictionary** Finding the Right Meaning	**Visual** Illustrating Meanings **Auditory** Twisting Words **Bilingual/ESL** Word Search **Enrichment** Writing Measurements	**Science:** Landforms, pp. 198–199
Review Word Associations; Categorizing **Multicultural Connection** Environment	**Visual** Singular or Plural? **Kinesthetic** Acting Out Details **Bilingual/ESL** Flower Details **Enrichment** Flower Symbols	**Social Studies:** Global Grid, pp. 170–171
Review Antonyms; Draw Your Own Conclusions **Word Study** Word Play	**Visual** Syllables **Auditory** Warning Signs **Bilingual/ESL** Words with **-ing** **Enrichment** Antonym Analysis	**Mathematics:** Division, pp. 218–219
Review Context Clues **Word Study** Pyramid Sentences	**Visual** Creating Contractions **Auditory** Don't Quote Me **Bilingual/ESL** Contraction Match **Enrichment** Upside-Down Pyramid	**Work and Play:** Basketball, pp. 224–225

* The cross-curricular lessons are optional. You may, however, wish to teach the cross-curricular lesson that has been paired with the weekly lesson shown in the chart.

OBJECTIVES

- Learn and practice the Meaning Helpers strategy
- Apply the Meaning Helpers strategy to list words in Unit 3

MEANING HELPERS

This strategy encourages students to relate words they are learning to shorter words that are hidden in the longer words and whose spellings they already know.

Illustrate the strategy by pronouncing and then writing examples, such as *child/children, hear/heard,* and *invite/invitation,* on the board. Call on volunteers to explain how knowing the spelling of the first word in each pair helps them spell the second word.

Additional Resources

Frequently Misspelled Words Poster
Spelling Tool Kit Poster

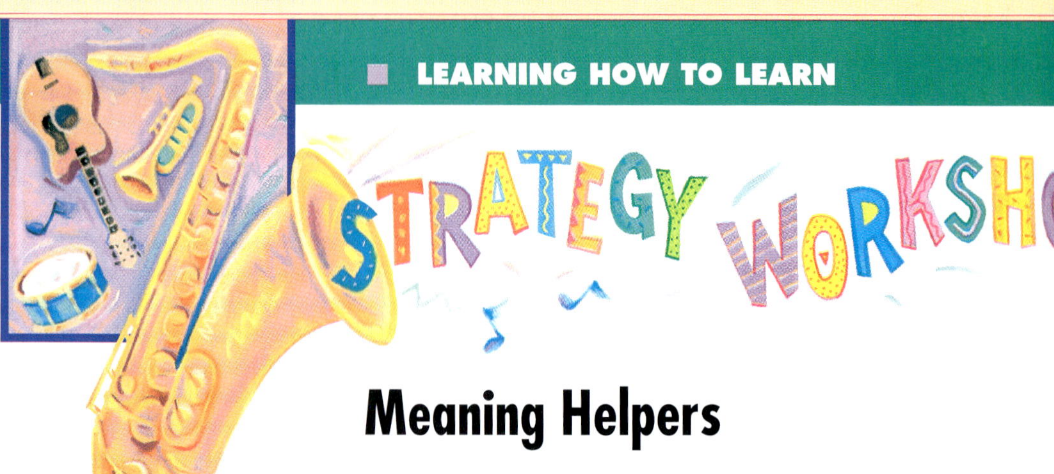

Meaning Helpers

DISCOVER THE STRATEGY Even a short word like **every** can be hard to spell—until you discover where it comes from.

You don't hear the second **e** when you say **every,** but you *do* hear it when you say **ever.** **Ever** is a meaning helper for **every** because a sound clue in **ever** helps you spell *every*.

TRY IT OUT Now try the Meaning Helper Strategy yourself. Follow the directions on the next page.

Work with a partner to figure out what sound clue in the top word helps you spell the bottom word. The first two pairs are done for you.

major
majority

The **long a** in **major** reminds me that **majority** is spelled with an **a** too. The sound of **a** is different in the two words, but the spelling of that sound is the same.

act
action

The sound of **t** in **act** reminds me that **action** is spelled with a **t** too.

1. press
   pressure

   The double s in *press* reminds me that *pressure* has two s's.

2. fast
   fasten

   The t in *fast* reminds me that *fasten* is spelled with a t also.

Write a meaning helper of your own for each word below. Mark the letter or letters that give the sound clue.

3. national

   nation

4. election

   elect

5. confession

   confess

LOOK AHEAD Look ahead at the next five lessons. Write two list words and the helpers that you could use with this strategy. Underline the letters that give the sound clues.

1. **Words will vary.**

2. **Words will vary.**

65

Modified List

Have students learning just the Modified Lists look at spelling words 1–10 only as they complete the Look Ahead activity.

Challenge

Encourage students to consider words appearing in the challenge box, in addition to spelling words 1–20, as they complete the Look Ahead activity.

Bilingual/ESL

Nonnative speakers may have difficulty identifying meaning helpers within words, especially in cases such as *invite/invitation*. Help students identify the meaning helper in such cases by circling it and identifying the base word.

Visual Learners

Visual learners might extend their study of meaning-related words by creating word webs. In the center, they write a list word; around the list word, they write words related in meaning. For example, a web for *composition* might include *compose*, *composed*, *composer*, and *composure*.

LESSON

13

Generalization

Spelling Focus: Some words have parts that are spelled the same but pronounced differently.

● Core ○ Optional ✓ Assessment

DAILY PLAN	CORE OBJECTIVES	NOTES

DAY 1 Introduction

● Strategy Workshop, p. 64
✓ Pretest and Self-Check, p. 66B
● Spelling Focus and Word List, p. 66
○ Challenge Words, p. 66
○ Challenge Master 13
○ Home-School Master 13

- Learn and apply the Meaning Helpers strategy
✓ ▪ Take and self-check Pretest
- Spell words related in meaning; classify and write the list words

DAY 2 Think and Practice

● Contrasts; Synonyms, p. 67
● Strategic Spelling: *Using the Meaning Helpers Strategy,* p. 67
○ Think and Practice Master 13
○ Extra Practice Master 13
○ Cross-Curricular Lesson: Introduce, p. 176

- Complete practice activities for related words
- Use the Meaning Helpers strategy to help spell words

DAY 3 Proofreading and Writing

● Proofread a Persuasive Paragraph, p. 68
● Proofreading Tip: Incorrect Words, p. 68
● Write a Persuasive Paragraph, p. 68
✓ Cooperative Midweek Test
○ Hardbound Book Master 13
○ Writing Mini-Lesson Master 13
○ Writing Activity Master 13
○ Second Language Support Master 13

- Proofread for spelling errors
- Integrate spelling and writing in a personal writing response
✓ ▪ Take and check midweek test

DAY 4 Vocabulary Building

● Review: Context Clues, p. 69
● Word Study: Triplets, p. 69
○ Cross-Curricular Lesson: Follow-Up, p. 176
○ Review Master 13

- Complete review activity for related words
- Learn a word association game

DAY 5 Assessment

✓ Posttest, p. 66B
○ Standardized Test Master 13

✓ ▪ Take Posttest

Cross-Curricular Lessons

Use the Spelling Focus (related words) to introduce the Social Studies lesson, *Using Natural Resources,* page 176, or choose a lesson that correlates with a topic you're currently teaching.

MEETING THE NEEDS OF ALL STUDENTS

The Word List

For students studying 20 words, assign pages 66–69 and Extra Practice and Review masters.

Modified List For students studying 10 words, modify Practice on page 66, and assign Think and Practice Master 13 and pages 68–69.

Challenge For students studying 26 words, assign pages 66–69, Challenge, Extra Practice, and Review masters.

Bilingual/ESL

Many words are spelled similarly in English and Spanish, for example, *sign/signo.* Spanish-speaking students may confuse the spelling of such words.

Personal Words

Students add to Personal Words lists by looking at work in their writing portfolios and words they want to remember from their reading.

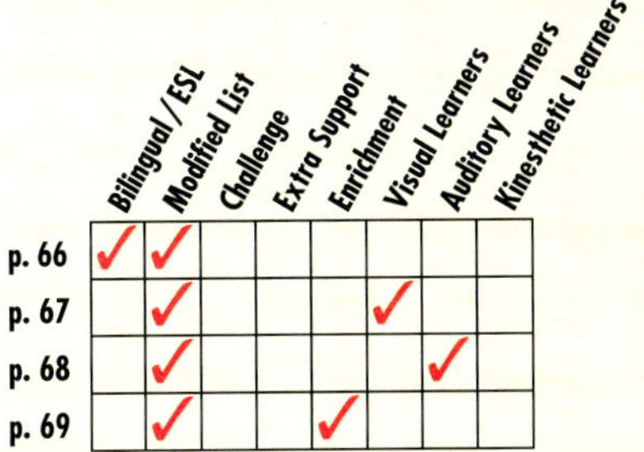

	Bilingual/ESL	Modified List	Challenge	Extra Support	Enrichment	Visual Learners	Auditory Learners	Kinesthetic Learners
p. 66	✓	✓						
p. 67		✓				✓		
p. 68		✓					✓	
p. 69		✓			✓			

ASSESSMENT*

Pretest

Read the underlined word, read the sentence, and then repeat the underlined word. Guide students in self-correcting their pretests and correcting any misspellings.

1. Ava is <u>able</u> to jump rope.
2. He has the <u>ability</u> to run.
3. Alex put a <u>sign</u> up.
4. The coach gave a <u>signal</u>.
5. What did you <u>mean</u>?
6. Julio <u>meant</u> to be on time.
7. Whose turn is it to <u>deal</u>?
8. Ed <u>dealt</u> all the cards.
9. The kitten has <u>soft</u> fur.
10. First, <u>soften</u> the butter.
11. She can <u>relate</u> to animals.
12. Juan visited a <u>relative</u>.
13. The cut will <u>heal</u> quickly.
14. Exercise for good <u>health</u>.
15. The desk is a <u>meter</u> long.
16. I know the <u>metric</u> system.
17. Dee will <u>compose</u> music.
18. Sue sang her <u>composition</u>.
19. A <u>crumb</u> fell on the floor.
20. Don't <u>crumble</u> the cracker.

* See pp. T20 and T33 for test-study-test information.

Posttest

Read aloud the sentences below. These sentences may be used for dictation.

1. What does she <u>mean</u>?
2. She can <u>deal</u> with the cat.
3. This bed is too <u>soft</u>.
4. Are you <u>able</u> to dance?
5. Stop at the red <u>sign</u>.
6. They <u>dealt</u> with the money.
7. Rain will <u>soften</u> dirt.
8. An <u>ability</u> can be a gift.
9. The girl <u>meant</u> to be nice.
10. A red light is a <u>signal</u>.
11. They played a <u>composition</u>.
12. The mouse ate a <u>crumb</u>.
13. I <u>relate</u> to people.
14. His leg will <u>heal</u> soon.
15. Did you <u>crumble</u> the bread?
16. We can <u>compose</u> a story.
17. What is a <u>metric</u> foot?
18. Eat right for good <u>health</u>.
19. My <u>relative</u> was an actor.
20. A frog can jump a <u>meter</u>.

Challenge Words

1. The police can <u>direct</u> you.
2. Which <u>direction</u> did he go?
3. That letter is <u>personal</u>.
4. He has a good <u>personality</u>.
5. Foxes <u>invade</u> my garden.
6. I watched the <u>invasion</u>.

Additional Assessment

Standardized Test Master 13
Dictation Sentences, p. T39
Everyday Spelling CD-ROM

WHAT'S THE BIG IDEA?
It's interesting that /m/ spelled **mb** is found only in the middle or at the end of a word: *plumber, crumb.* But /n/ spelled **gn** may appear anywhere: *gnat, designer, sign.* Challenge students to think of other unusual consonant spellings, such as /n/ spelled **kn** and /r/ spelled **wr.**

LESSON 13

DAY 1 CHALLENGE MASTER

CHALLENGE ■ 13

Challenge Words

direct	direction	personal
personality	invade	invasion

■ Use these math clues to spell the Challenge Words.

1. r e p r e s e n t – r, e, e, t + o, a, l spells **personal**
2. s p i r i t e d – s, p, i + c spells **direct**
3. n o i s i e s t – s, s + d, r, c spells **direction**
4. b a n i s h – b, s, h + v, d, e spells **invade**
5. p a t r o l l i n g – l, g + e, s, y spells **personality**
6. S p a n i s h – p, S, h + v, i, o, n spells **invasion**

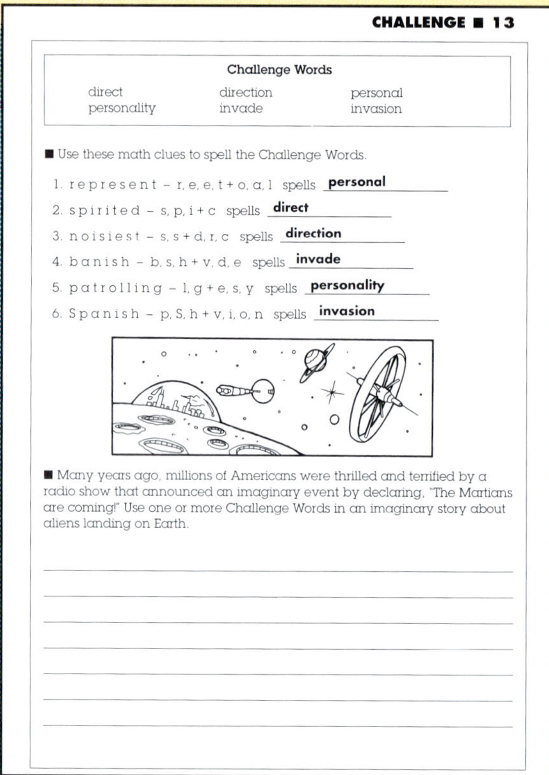

■ Many years ago, millions of Americans were thrilled and terrified by a radio show that announced an imaginary event by declaring, "The Martians are coming!" Use one or more Challenge Words in an imaginary story about aliens landing on Earth.

Practice Masters, p. 51

DAY 1 HOME-SCHOOL MASTER

■ 13   HOME-SCHOOL ACTIVITIES   13 ■

■ **Word Pictures** Write the two list words that you think of when you look at each picture.

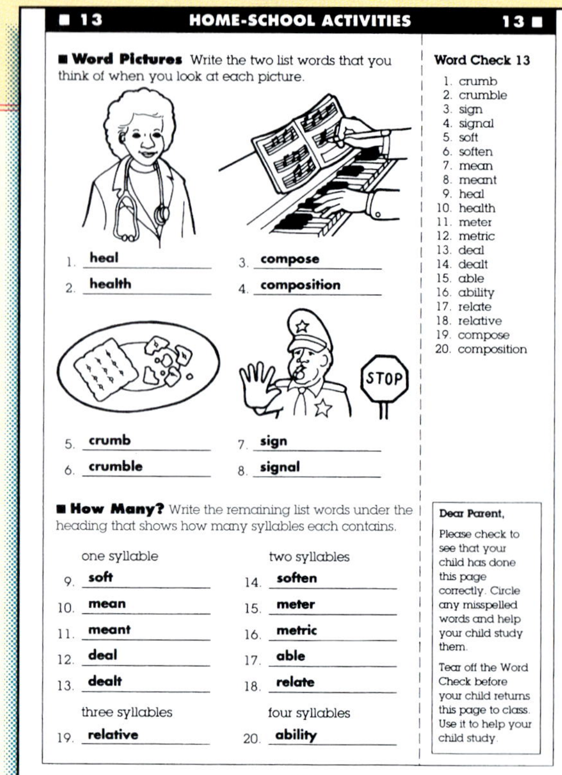

1. **heal**
2. **health**
3. **compose**
4. **composition**

5. **crumb**
6. **crumble**
7. **sign**
8. **signal**

Word Check 13

1. crumb
2. crumble
3. sign
4. signal
5. soft
6. soften
7. mean
8. meant
9. heal
10. health
11. meter
12. metric
13. deal
14. dealt
15. able
16. ability
17. relate
18. relative
19. compose
20. composition

■ **How Many?** Write the remaining list words under the heading that shows how many syllables each contains.

one syllable	two syllables
9. **soft**	14. **soften**
10. **mean**	15. **meter**
11. **meant**	16. **metric**
12. **deal**	17. **able**
13. **dealt**	18. **relate**
three syllables	four syllables
19. **relative**	20. **ability**

Dear Parent,

Please check to see that your child has done this page correctly. Circle any misspelled words and help your child study them.

Tear off the Word Check before your child returns this page to class. Use it to help your child study.

Home-School Activities, p. 11

DAY 2 THINK AND PRACTICE MASTER

13 ■ THINK AND PRACTICE

able	ability	sign	signal	mean
meant	deal	dealt	soft	soften

■ **Alphabetical Order** Write the list word that fits alphabetically between the two words in each group.

1. ability	**able**	about
2. sock	**soft**	soften
3. dead	**deal**	dealt
4. mean	**meant**	meat
5. sight	**sign**	signal
6. softball	**soften**	software
7. abide	**ability**	able
8. deal	**dealt**	dear

■ **Synonyms** Write the list word that means the same as the underlined word or words.

9. Did you <u>intend</u> to miss the bus? **mean**
10. Give a <u>warning</u> before you turn. **Signal**
11. Does she have the <u>skill</u> to swim a lap? **ability**
12. <u>Write</u> your name here. **Sign**

STRATEGIC SPELLING: Using the Meaning Helper Strategy
Meaning helpers can help you spell words. Write the list words related to *soft*, *sign*, and *deal*. Mark the letters that match the underlined letters in the helpers.

13. **soften**
14. **signal**
15. **dealt**

Practice Masters, p. 52

DAY 2 EXTRA PRACTICE MASTER

EXTRA PRACTICE ■ 13

Word List

able	ability	sign	signal	mean
meant	deal	dealt	soft	soften
relate	relative	heal	health	meter
metric	compose	composition	crumb	crumble

■ **Word Forms** Use a pair of related words to complete each pair of sentences.

1a. I will slow down the car and put on the turn **signal**
  b. Yes, we need to turn left at the stop **sign**.
2a. Is one **meter** longer than one yard?
  b. Let's find out on this chart of **metric** measurements.
3a. I don't **relate** well to my cousin on my mother's side.
  b. Well, you can't make every **relative** your best friend.
4a. After your fall, you look in the best of **health** to me.
  b. If only I could get the blisters on my foot to **heal**.
5a. Did you **mean** what you said about your brother?
  b. Yes, I **meant** exactly what I said.
6a. My dog likes for me to **crumble** up her dog-food burger.
  b. Then she eats every last **crumb** and looks for more.
7a. Mrs. Taylor has **dealt** with many car salespeople.
  b. She always gets a very good **deal** on a new car.
8a. Do you **compose** classical music?
  b. Yes, this song is my seventh **composition**.
9a. I have little **ability** to throw a ball.
  b. I am **able** to hit the ball out of the park, however!
10a. Don't let the ice cream **soften** outside the refrigerator.
  b. If it gets too **soft**, the container will leak.

Practice Masters, p. 53

| TECHNOLOGY AND VISUAL SUPPORT |   Use Audiotape B, Side 1, Lesson 13 / Use Proofreading and Writing Transparency 13 |  For additional practice use *Everyday Spelling* Game Software, Lesson 13 |  Additional resources on *Everyday Spelling* CD-ROM: proofreading and writing, modified list and challenge words, auditory test |

DAY 3 — SECOND LANGUAGE SUPPORT MASTER

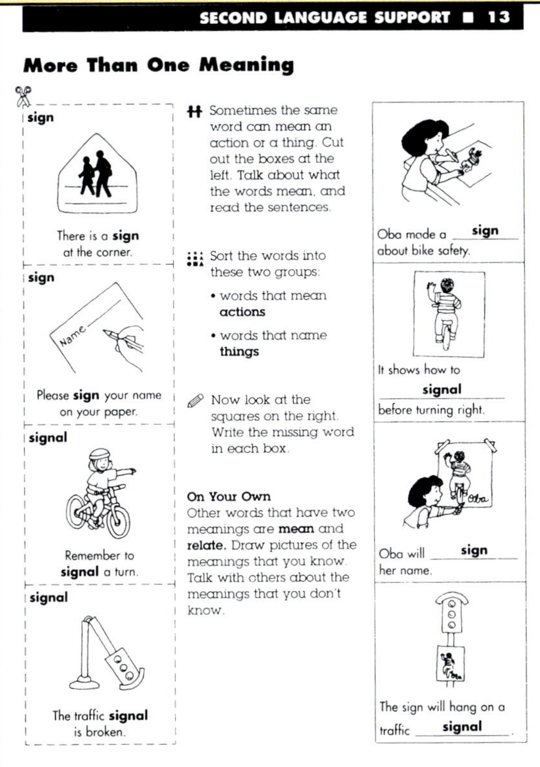

SECOND LANGUAGE SUPPORT ■ 13

More Than One Meaning

There is a **sign** at the corner.

Please **sign** your name on your paper.

Remember to **signal** a turn.

The traffic **signal** is broken.

Sometimes the same word can mean an action or a thing. Cut out the boxes at the left. Talk about what the words mean, and read the sentences.

Sort the words into these two groups:
- words that mean **actions**
- words that name **things**

Now look at the squares on the right. Write the missing word in each box.

On Your Own
Other words that have two meanings are **mean** and **relate**. Draw pictures of the meanings that you know. Talk with others about the meanings that you don't know.

Oba made a ____ **sign** about bike safety.

It shows how to **signal** before turning right.

Oba will ____ **sign** her name.

The sign will hang on a traffic ____ **signal**.

Second Language Support, p. 37

DAY 3 — WRITING ACTIVITY MASTER

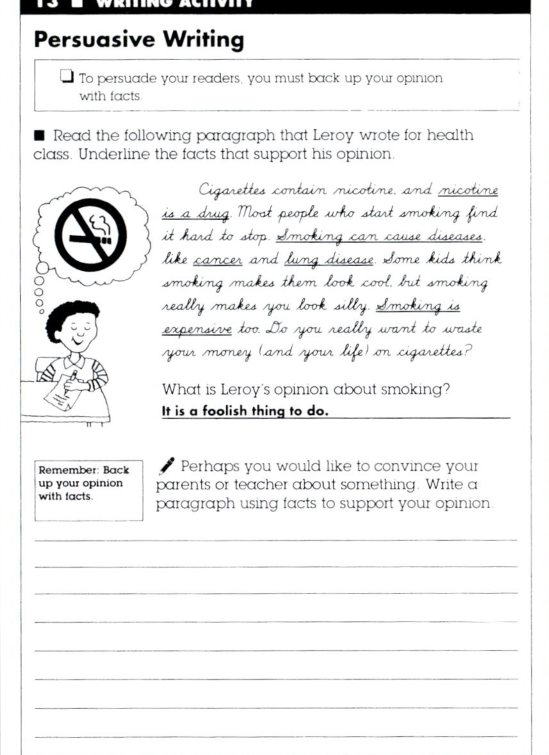

13 ■ WRITING ACTIVITY

Persuasive Writing

☐ To persuade your readers, you must back up your opinion with facts.

■ Read the following paragraph that Leroy wrote for health class. Underline the facts that support his opinion.

Cigarettes contain nicotine, and nicotine is a drug. Most people who start smoking find it hard to stop. Smoking can cause diseases like cancer and lung disease. Some kids think smoking makes them look cool, but smoking really makes you look silly. Smoking is expensive too. Do you really want to waste your money (and your life) on cigarettes?

What is Leroy's opinion about smoking?
It is a foolish thing to do.

Remember: Back up your opinion with facts.

Perhaps you would like to convince your parents or teacher about something. Write a paragraph using facts to support your opinion.

Spelling and Writing, p. 22

DAY 4 — REVIEW MASTER

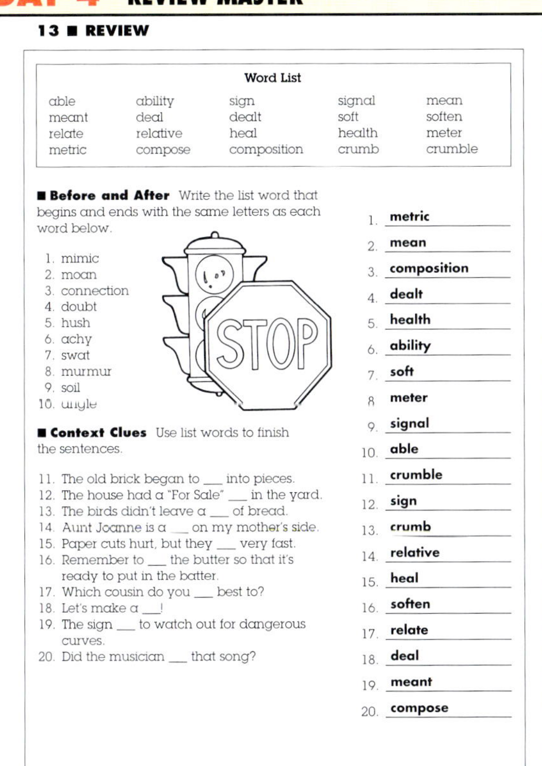

13 ■ REVIEW

Word List

able	ability	sign	signal	mean
meant	deal	dealt	soft	soften
relate	relative	heal	health	meter
metric	compose	composition	crumb	crumble

■ **Before and After** Write the list word that begins and ends with the same letters as each word below.

1. mimic
2. moan
3. connection
4. doubt
5. hush
6. achy
7. swat
8. murmur
9. soil
10. angle

1. **metric**
2. **mean**
3. **composition**
4. **dealt**
5. **health**
6. **ability**
7. **soft**
8. **meter**
9. **signal**
10. **able**

■ **Context Clues** Use list words to finish the sentences.

11. The old brick began to ___ into pieces.
12. The house had a "For Sale" ___ in the yard.
13. The birds didn't leave a ___ of bread.
14. Aunt Joanne is a ___ on my mother's side.
15. Paper cuts hurt, but they ___ very fast.
16. Remember to ___ the butter so that it's ready to put in the batter.
17. Which cousin do you ___ best to?
18. Let's make a ___!
19. The sign ___ to watch out for dangerous curves.
20. Did the musician ___ that song?

11. **crumble**
12. **sign**
13. **crumb**
14. **relative**
15. **heal**
16. **soften**
17. **relate**
18. **deal**
19. **meant**
20. **compose**

Practice Masters, p. 54

DAY 5 — STANDARDIZED TEST MASTER

LESSON TEST ■ 13

■ Find the word in each group that is spelled correctly. Fill in the letter for the correct word on the answer strip.

Sample:
a. lione	c. linoe	
b. lino	d. lion	ⓐⓑⓒ●

1.	a. sihgn / b. sign	c. sighn / d. sihn	1. ⓐ●ⓒⓓ
2.	a. able / b. abel	c. abol / d. abl	2. ●ⓑⓒⓓ
3.	a. meetir / b. meater	c. meter / d. metere	3. ⓐⓑ●ⓓ
4.	a. dael / b. deel	c. deal / d. deil	4. ⓐⓑ●ⓓ
5.	a. soften / b. soffen	c. sofen / d. softin	5. ●ⓑⓒⓓ
6.	a. meant / b. ment	c. mant / d. maent	6. ●ⓑⓒⓓ
7.	a. cumpose / b. compoze	c. cumpoze / d. compose	7. ⓐⓑⓒ●
8.	a. sof / b. soft	c. saft / d. solf	8. ⓐ●ⓒⓓ
9.	a. relate / b. reelate	c. relat / d. reluyle	9. ●ⓑⓒⓓ
10.	a. metrik / b. metrick	c. metric / d. meetric	10. ⓐⓑ●ⓓ
11.	a. hael / b. heal	c. heale / d. heele	11. ⓐ●ⓒⓓ
12.	a. dealt / b. dealet	c. delt / d. deallt	12. ●ⓑⓒⓓ
13.	a. ability / b. abity	c. abillity / d. abilitie	13. ●ⓑⓒⓓ
14.	a. relative / b. reletive	c. releteve / d. relitive	14. ●ⓑⓒⓓ
15.	a. croumble / b. crummble	c. crumble / d. crummbel	15. ⓐⓑ●ⓓ
16.	a. compotison / b. compisition	c. compsition / d. composition	16. ⓐⓑⓒ●
17.	a. mean / b. meen	c. maen / d. mene	17. ●ⓑⓒⓓ
18.	a. hellth / b. helth	c. health / d. halth	18. ⓐⓑ●ⓓ
19.	a. signil / b. signal	c. signol / d. singnal	19. ⓐ●ⓒⓓ
20.	a. croumb / b. crumb	c. crum / d. crumm	20. ⓐ●ⓒⓓ

Practice for Standardized Tests, p. 19

LESSON 13

INTRODUCTION

Word Meaning
Comparing Meanings
Help students understand differences in parts of speech and meaning between words that are related in spelling. For example, *crumb* is a noun and *crumble* is a verb. Demonstrate the meanings with a cracker.

MEETING THE NEEDS OF ALL STUDENTS

Modified List
Practice Students studying only the high-frequency words in the top box write
- the word in each pair that is easier to spell
- the related word

Bilingual/ESL
Comparing Sounds Discuss the related spellings and the pronunciation changes in the word pairs. For example, the **b** is silent in *crumb* but not in *crumble*. Continue with other word pairs.

> **Additional Practice**
>
> **Challenge Master 13**
> **Home-School Master 13**
> **Audiotape B, Side 1**

1. able
2. ability
3. sign
4. signal
5. mean
6. meant
7. deal
8. dealt
9. soft
10. soften
11. relate
12. relative
13. heal
14. health
15. meter
16. metric
17. compose
18. composition
19. crumb
20. crumble

CHALLENGE!

direct	direction
personal	personality
invade	invasion

66

■ INTRODUCTION

Related Words

SPELLING FOCUS

Related words often have parts that are spelled the same but pronounced differently: <u>able</u>, <u>a</u>bility; <u>sign</u>, <u>sign</u>al.

■ **STUDY**   Say each word. Then read the sentence.

1. able — Is anyone **able** to do a flip?
2. ability — Gymnasts have that **ability**.
3. sign — The **sign** said "Railroad crossing."
4. signal — You must **signal** when you turn.
5. mean — Did you **mean** to make me laugh?
6. meant — I **meant** what I said about leaving.
7. deal — Will you **deal** the number cards?
8. dealt — She **dealt** six math fact cards.
9. soft — We play **soft**, relaxing music.
10. soften — Lotion will **soften** dry skin.

11. relate — Dogs **relate** well to people.
12. relative — My cousin is my **relative.**
13. heal — A cut will **heal** in time.
14. health — Good **health** is important.
15. meter — A **meter** is about 39 inches.
16. metric — Do you have a **metric** ruler?
17. compose — He can **compose** piano music.
18. composition — He wrote a piano **composition.**
19. crumb — You ate every **crumb** of the cake!
20. crumble — Sandcastles quickly **crumble.**

■ **PRACTICE**   Write the related word pairs. For each pair, first write the word that is easier for you to spell. The easier word should help you spell the related word.
Order of paired words may vary.

■ **WRITE**   Choose two sentences to write an advertisement, slogan, or saying.
Responses will vary.

THINK AND PRACTICE ■

CONTRASTS Write list words to complete the sentences.

1. A small bit of water is a drop.
   A small bit of bread is a ___.
2. Lack of rest and a virus may cause sickness.
   Rest and medicine may bring about ___.
3. If you fail at something, you are unable to do it.
   If you finally succeed, you are ___ to do it.
4. A person who helps you is kind.
   A person who harms you is ___.
5. You use your voice in spoken language.
   You use your hands in ___ language.
6. Apples should be sweet and hard.
   Raisins should be sweet and ___.

SYNONYMS Write the list word that means the same as the underlined word or words. Use the Spelling Dictionary.

7. I wrote a <u>short essay</u> about my dog.
8. Please shuffle and <u>pass out</u> the division fact cards.
9. The <u>arrangement of beats</u> in a polka is very quick.
10. Mozart was able to <u>put together</u> twenty-two operas.
11. She was able to <u>tell</u> the exact details of the event.
12. Is that what you <u>intended</u> to say?
13. The cut will <u>become well</u> in a few days.
14. Dogs have the <u>power</u> to hear high-pitched sounds.
15. A red light is a <u>sign giving notice</u> to stop.
16. The old wall was beginning to <u>decay.</u>
17. Asia uses the <u>measurement-that-counts-by-tens</u> system.

1. **crumb**
2. **health**
3. **able**
4. **mean**
5. **sign**
6. **soft**
7. **composition**
8. **deal**
9. **meter**
10. **compose**
11. **relate**
12. **meant**
13. **heal**
14. **ability**
15. **signal**
16. **crumble**
17. **metric**

STRATEGIC SPELLING
Using the Meaning Helper Strategy

18.–20. Meaning helpers can help you spell words. Write the list words related to *soft, relate,* and *deal.* Mark the letters that match the underlined letters in the helpers.

18. **sof<u>t</u>en**
19. **rela<u>t</u>ive**
20. **dealt**

LESSON 13

- Proofread a Persuasive Paragraph
- Proofreading Tip: Incorrect Words
- Write a Persuasive Paragraph
- ✓ Cooperative Midweek Test

DAILY SPELLING REVIEW

Wach out for storms in the *vally.*

Watch   *valley*

● Core   ○ Optional   ✓ Assessment

PROOFREADING AND WRITING

Incorrect Words

Wrong Meaning Encourage students to proofread for sense. They can ask, "Did I write what I meant to say?" Reading aloud is a helpful proofreading technique.

MEETING THE NEEDS OF ALL STUDENTS

Modified List

Proofreading Students studying high-frequency words complete this page or the proofreading activity on the *Everyday Spelling* CD-ROM.

Auditory Learners

Brainstorming Before students write their paragraphs, lead them in suggesting persuasive topics and discussing reasons they could use to persuade their readers.

Additional Practice

Hardbound Book Master 13
Second Language Master 13
Writing Mini-Lesson Master 13
Writing Activity Master 13
Proofreading Transparency 13
Everyday Spelling **CD-ROM**

■ PROOFREADING

	Make a capital.
/	Make a small letter.
∧	Add something.
	Take out something.
⊙	Add a period.
	New paragraph

PROOFREAD A PERSUASIVE PARAGRAPH Min and her friends are trying to convince their principal to allow music during lunch. They are writing their reasons on index cards to be delivered on a cafeteria tray. Correct the five spelling errors Min has made.

PROOFREADING TIP
Min wrote *brother* when she meant to write something else. Always proofread your writing for words that are spelled correctly but have the wrong meaning.

It is ~~meen~~ **mean** not to let us listen to music at lunch. Good music is good for our ~~helth~~ **health**. It helps us relax and be ~~abel~~ **able** to face the next class. We will only play sof music. It won't ~~brother~~ **bother** anyone.

Min Yi

WRITE A PERSUASIVE PARAGRAPH Think of something you would like to persuade someone to do or to allow you to do. Write about it. Try to use list words and a personal word.

Responses will vary. Paragraph should include a list word and a personal word.

Word List

crumb	meter
crumble	metric
sign	deal
signal	dealt
soft	able
soften	ability
mean	relate
meant	relative
heal	compose
health	composition

Personal Words

1. **Words will vary.**

2.

VOCABULARY BUILDING

Review

CONTEXT CLUES Mr. Chambers asked his students to list their talents and good qualities. One of his students made the list below. Write the boxed word that completes each sentence in the list.

able	ability
sign	signal
mean	meant
deal	dealt
soft	soften

My Talents and Good Qualities

I have the (1) to make friends easily.
I am never (2) or spiteful towards anyone.
I have (3), shiny hair.
When I am misunderstood, I always take the time to explain what I (4).
I am (5) to do a cartwheel and a handstand.
I have helped my mother the times she has (6) out food at the homeless shelter. I spend a good (7) of my free time doing volunteer work like that.
I obey every street (8) and traffic (9) when riding my bike.
I know how to (10) the hurt feelings of others with kind words.

1. **ability**
2. **mean**
3. **soft**
4. **meant**
5. **able**
6. **dealt**
7. **deal**
8. **sign**
9. **signal**
10. **soften**

Word Study

TRIPLETS Here's a challenging vocabulary game called **Triplets.** It's a game in which you supply the one word that is often associated with three others. For example, what list word would you associate with the three words below?

post   language   up

The answer is **sign,** as in **signpost, sign language,** and **sign up.** Here are more for you to try. Remember, the missing word always goes in front. Use the boxed words for help.

soft	night	whole	music	dry

1. drink	boiled	soap
2. cleaner	run	ice
3. gown	crawler	mare
4. video	hall	box
5. milk	note	wheat

1. **soft**
2. **dry**
3. **night**
4. **music**
5. **whole**

LESSON

14

Generalization

Spelling Focus: The consonant sound /j/ can be spelled **ge** and **dge**; the consonant sound /ks/ can be spelled **xc** and **x**; the consonant sound /kw/ is usually spelled **qu**.

● Core ○ Optional ✓ Assessment

DAILY PLAN	CORE OBJECTIVES	NOTES

DAY 1 Introduction

✓ Pretest and Self-Check, p. 70B
● Spelling Focus and Word List, p. 70
○ Challenge Words, p. 70
○ Challenge Master 14
○ Home-School Master 14

✓ Take and self-check Pretest
▪ Spell words with the consonant sound /j/, /ks/, or /kw/; classify and write the list words

DAY 2 Think and Practice

● Tongue Twisters; Word Search, p. 71
● Strategic Spelling: *Seeing Meaning Connections*, p. 71
○ Hardbound Book Master 14A
○ Think and Practice Master 14
○ Extra Practice Master 14
○ Cross-Curricular Lesson: Introduce, p. 198

▪ Complete practice activities for words with the consonant sound /j/, /ks/, or /kw/
▪ Recognize meaning connections between list words and other words related to them

DAY 3 Proofreading and Writing

● Proofread a Recipe, p. 72
● Proofreading Tip: *Good* and *Well*, p. 72
● Write a Recipe, p. 72
✓ Cooperative Midweek Test
○ Hardbound Book Master 14B
○ Writing Mini-Lesson Master 14
○ Writing Activity Master 14
○ Second Language Support Master 14

▪ Proofread for spelling and usage errors
▪ Integrate spelling and writing in a personal writing response
✓ ▪ Take and check midweek test

DAY 4 Vocabulary Building

● Review: Context Clues, p. 73
● Using a Dictionary: Finding the Right Meaning, p. 73
○ Cross-Curricular Lesson: Follow-Up, p. 198
○ Review Master 14

▪ Complete review activity for the consonant sound /j/, /ks/, or /kw/
▪ Use a dictionary to find the right meaning of a word

DAY 5 Assessment

✓ Posttest, p. 70B
○ Standardized Test Master 14

✓ ▪ Take Posttest

Cross-Curricular Lessons

Use the Spelling Focus (consonant sounds /j/, /ks/, /kw/) to introduce the Science lesson, *Landforms*, page 198, or choose a lesson that correlates with a topic you're currently teaching.

MEETING THE NEEDS OF ALL STUDENTS

The Word List

For students studying 20 words, assign pages 70–73 and Extra Practice and Review masters.

Modified List For students studying 10 words, modify Practice on page 71, and assign Think and Practice Master 14 and pages 72–73.

Challenge For students studying 25 words, assign pages 70–73, Challenge, Extra Practice, and Review masters.

Bilingual/ESL

The letters **q** and **x** do not exist in one of the languages used in the Philippines. The letters **k** and **ks** may be substituted for them. Students who speak this language may spell *quilt/kuwilt* and *relax/relaks*.

Personal Words

Students add to Personal Words lists by looking at work in their writing portfolios and words they want to remember from their reading.

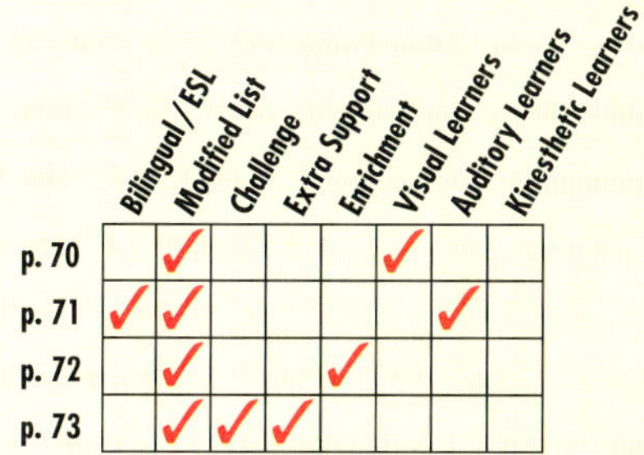

	Bilingual/ESL	Modified List	Challenge	Extra Support	Enrichment	Visual Learners	Auditory Learners	Kinesthetic Learners
p. 70		✓				✓		
p. 71	✓	✓					✓	
p. 72		✓			✓			
p. 73		✓	✓	✓				

ASSESSMENT*

Pretest

Read the underlined word, read the sentence, and then repeat the underlined word. Guide students in self-correcting their pretests and correcting any misspellings.

1. <u>Change</u> your clothes.
2. Aston is the next <u>village</u>.
3. The knife <u>edge</u> is sharp.
4. Everyone went <u>except</u> Jack.
5. She sounded <u>excited</u>.
6. Can you <u>explain</u> the noise?
7. I <u>expect</u> to be home then.
8. Summers are hot in <u>Texas</u>.
9. Donna made a <u>quick</u> trip.
10. The pie is in <u>equal</u> parts.
11. Did Dad use a <u>charge</u> card?
12. Cars crossed the <u>bridge</u>.
13. Raul makes good <u>fudge</u>.
14. Tom is an <u>excellent</u> actor.
15. Alicia can <u>relax</u> later.
16. Do you have an <u>extra</u> pen?
17. Mom felt like a <u>queen</u>.
18. Buy a <u>quart</u> of milk.
19. Water is a <u>liquid</u>.
20. Lisa made a warm <u>quilt</u>.

Posttest

Read aloud the sentences below. These sentences may be used for dictation.

1. Don't stand on the <u>edge</u>!
2. Is <u>Texas</u> a large state?
3. I can't <u>explain</u> my dream.
4. They are <u>equal</u> in ability.
5. That player is <u>quick</u>.
6. Did he <u>change</u> his mind?
7. Who lived in that <u>village</u>?
8. Everyone smiled <u>except</u> me.
9. I'm <u>excited</u> about camping.
10. Do you <u>expect</u> a visitor?
11. The <u>queen</u> has a castle.
12. Watch how much you <u>charge</u>.
13. Did you do <u>extra</u> work?
14. Put the <u>liquid</u> in a cup.
15. <u>Relax</u> and enjoy the ride.
16. <u>Fudge</u> is a kind of candy.
17. A van went over a <u>bridge</u>.
18. That's an <u>excellent</u> idea.
19. I bought a big, red <u>quilt</u>.
20. Bring a <u>quart</u> bottle.

Challenge Words

1. The dark was an <u>advantage</u>.
2. I made a <u>pledge</u> to help.
3. She took the <u>excess</u> food.
4. Did you see the <u>explosion</u>?
5. Ask me any <u>question</u>.

Additional Assessment

Standardized Test Master 14
Dictation Sentences, p. T39
Everyday Spelling CD-ROM

TAKE A CLOSER LOOK
Fourth graders often confuse *except* and *accept*, but it is more common for them to misspell *except* by omitting the **c.** Remind students that *except* is most often used as a preposition and *accept* as a verb, or action word. Share this memory trick: Both *accept* and *action* begin with the letter **a.**

** See pp. T20 and T33 for test-study-test information.*

DAY 1 CHALLENGE MASTER

CHALLENGE ■ 14

Challenge Words

pledge   explosion   question   advantage   excess

■ Use the Challenge Words to complete the puzzle. What mystery word appears?

1. a bursting with a loud noise
2. more than enough
3. something asked
4. a promise
5. a benefit or help

(crossword puzzle)

e x p l o s i o n
e x c e s s
q u e s t i o n
p l e d g e
a d v a n t a g e

■ All scientists have had surprises in their work. Use one or more Challenge Words to write about an experiment that had an unexpected result. Your story could be funny.

Practice Masters, p. 55

DAY 1 HOME-SCHOOL MASTER

■ 14   HOME-SCHOOL ACTIVITIES   14 ■

Word Check 14
1. bridge
2. queen
3. except
4. change
5. relax
6. quart
7. edge
8. extra
9. village
10. liquid
11. expect
12. quick
13. explain
14. Texas
15. charge
16. equal
17. excellent
18. quilt
19. excited
20. fudge

■ **Relationships** Write a list word to complete each sentence.

1. River is to Hudson as state is to __Texas__
2. Oxygen is to gas as water is to __liquid__
3. Bad is to awful as good is to __excellent__
4. Table is to cloth as bed is to __quilt__
5. Unlike is to different as same is to __equal__
6. School is to student as castle is to __queen__
7. Sour is to lemon as sweet is to __fudge__
8. Inch is to foot as pint is to __quart__
9. Large is to city as small is to __village__
10. Up is to down as slow is to __quick__
11. Less is to few as more is to __extra__
12. Happy is to sad as bored is to __excited__

■ **Rhymes** Write the list word that rhymes with each word below.

13. barge __charge__
14. accept __except__
15. range __change__
16. complain __explain__
17. tax __relax__
18. reject __expect__
19. ridge __bridge__
20. ledge __edge__

Dear Parent,

Please check to see that your child has done this page correctly. Circle any misspelled words and help your child study them.

Tear off the Word Check before your child returns this page to class. Use it to help your child study.

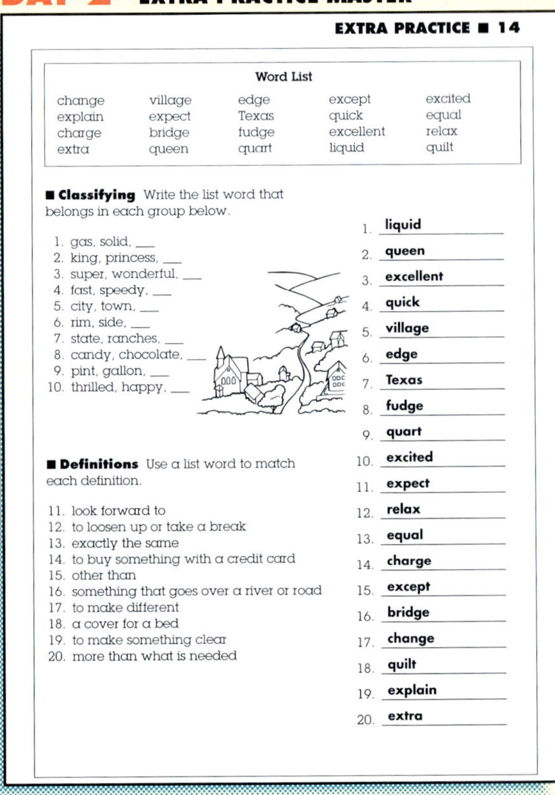

Home-School Activities, p. 12

DAY 2 THINK AND PRACTICE MASTER

14 ■ THINK AND PRACTICE

| change | village | edge | except | excited |
| explain | expect | Texas | quick | equal |

■ **Making Inferences** Write the list word that answers each question.

1. What is the name of a large state?
2. What might a small town be called?
3. How might you feel on your birthday?
4. What do you do to tell someone how to cook?
5. If your clothes are wet, what might you do?
6. If you are tense, where might you sit on a chair?

1. __Texas__
2. __village__
3. __excited__
4. __explain__
5. __change__
6. __edge__

■ **Word Search** Circle the list words in the puzzle. Look across and down. Write the words.

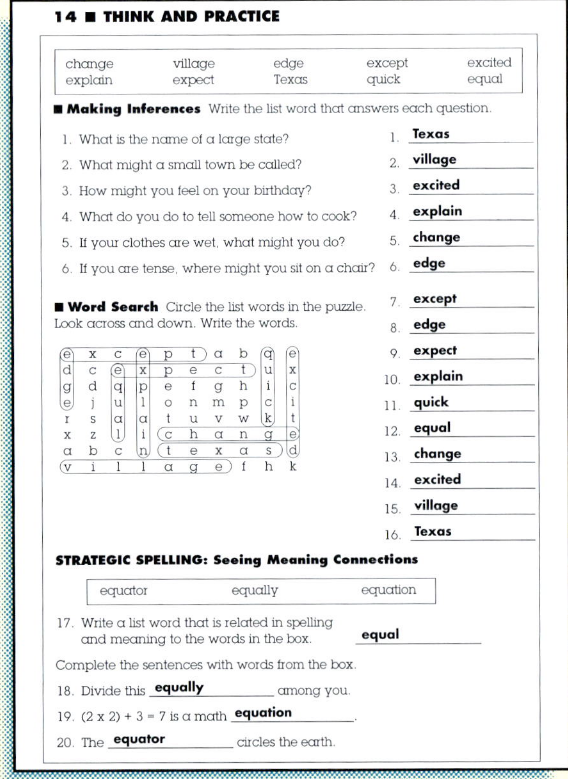

7. __except__
8. __edge__
9. __expect__
10. __explain__
11. __quick__
12. __equal__
13. __change__
14. __excited__
15. __village__
16. __Texas__

STRATEGIC SPELLING: Seeing Meaning Connections

| equator | equally | equation |

17. Write a list word that is related in spelling and meaning to the words in the box. __equal__

Complete the sentences with words from the box.

18. Divide this __equally__ among you.
19. (2 x 2) + 3 = 7 is a math __equation__
20. The __equator__ circles the earth.

Practice Masters, p. 56

DAY 2 EXTRA PRACTICE MASTER

EXTRA PRACTICE ■ 14

Word List

change	village	edge	except	excited
explain	expect	Texas	quick	equal
charge	bridge	fudge	excellent	relax
extra	queen	quart	liquid	quilt

■ **Classifying** Write the list word that belongs in each group below.

1. gas, solid, ___
2. king, princess, ___
3. super, wonderful, ___
4. fast, speedy, ___
5. city, town, ___
6. rim, side, ___
7. state, ranches, ___
8. candy, chocolate, ___
9. pint, gallon, ___
10. thrilled, happy, ___

1. __liquid__
2. __queen__
3. __excellent__
4. __quick__
5. __village__
6. __edge__
7. __Texas__
8. __fudge__
9. __quart__
10. __excited__

■ **Definitions** Use a list word to match each definition.

11. look forward to
12. to loosen up or take a break
13. exactly the same
14. to buy something with a credit card
15. other than
16. something that goes over a river or road
17. to make different
18. a cover for a bed
19. to make something clear
20. more than what is needed

11. __expect__
12. __relax__
13. __equal__
14. __charge__
15. __except__
16. __bridge__
17. __change__
18. __quilt__
19. __explain__
20. __extra__

Practice Masters, p. 57

70C

TECHNOLOGY AND VISUAL SUPPORT			
	Use Audiotape B, Side 1, Lesson 14	For additional practice use *Everyday Spelling* Game Software, Lesson 14	Additional resources on *Everyday Spelling* CD-ROM: proofreading and writing, modified list and challenge words, auditory test
	Use Proofreading and Writing Transparency 14		

DAY 3 SECOND LANGUAGE SUPPORT MASTER

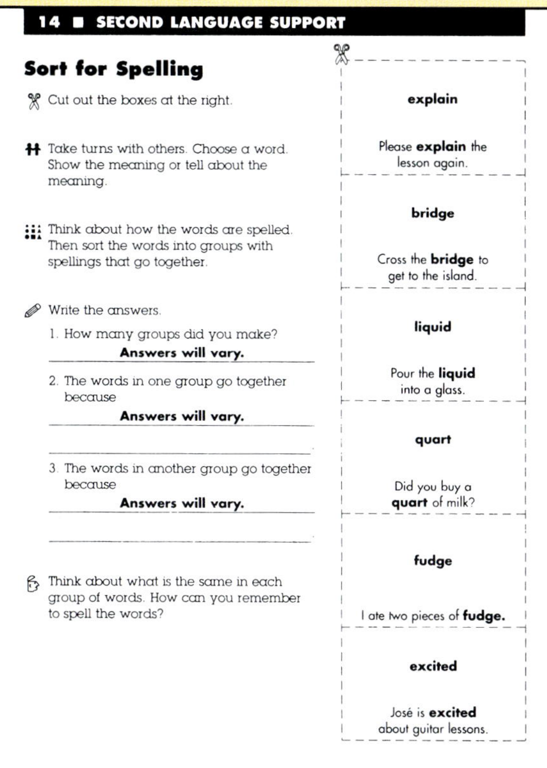

14 ■ SECOND LANGUAGE SUPPORT

Sort for Spelling

Cut out the boxes at the right.

Take turns with others. Choose a word. Show the meaning or tell about the meaning.

Think about how the words are spelled. Then sort the words into groups with spellings that go together.

Write the answers.

1. How many groups did you make?
   Answers will vary.
2. The words in one group go together because
   Answers will vary.
3. The words in another group go together because
   Answers will vary.

Think about what is the same in each group of words. How can you remember to spell the words?

explain Please **explain** the lesson again.
bridge Cross the **bridge** to get to the island.
liquid Pour the **liquid** into a glass.
quart Did you buy a **quart** of milk?
fudge I ate two pieces of **fudge.**
excited José is **excited** about guitar lessons.

Second Language Support, p. 38

DAY 3 WRITING ACTIVITY MASTER

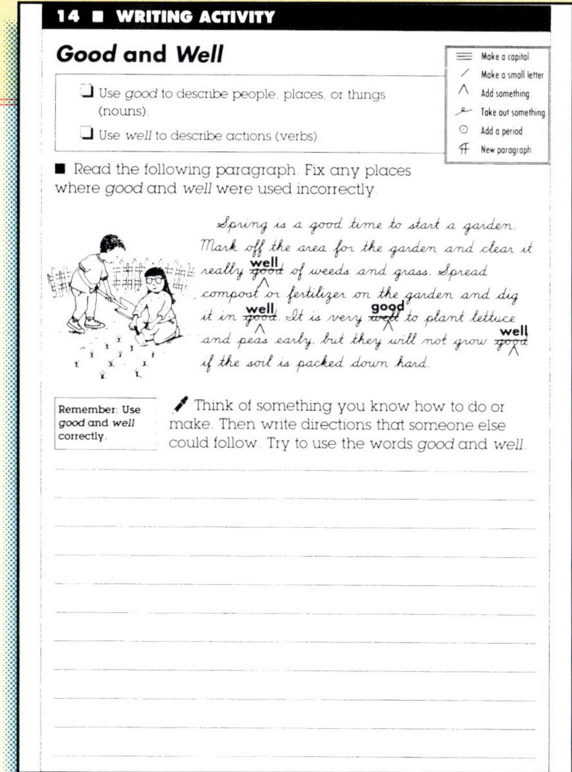

14 ■ WRITING ACTIVITY

Good and *Well*

❑ Use *good* to describe people, places, or things (nouns).
❑ Use *well* to describe actions (verbs).

Proofreading Marks
≡ Make a capital
/ Make a small letter
∧ Add something
Take out something
⊙ Add a period
¶ New paragraph

■ Read the following paragraph. Fix any places where *good* and *well* were used incorrectly.

Spring is a good time to start a garden. Mark off the area for the garden and clear it really ~~good~~ well of weeds and grass. Spread compost or fertilizer on the garden and dig it in ~~good~~ well. It is very ~~well~~ good to plant lettuce and peas early, but they will not grow ~~good~~ well if the soil is packed down hard.

Remember: Use *good* and *well* correctly.

Think of something you know how to do or make. Then write directions that someone else could follow. Try to use the words *good* and *well*.

Spelling and Writing, p. 24

DAY 4 REVIEW MASTER

14 ■ REVIEW

Word List

change	village	edge	except	excited
explain	expect	Texas	quick	equal
charge	bridge	fudge	excellent	relax
extra	queen	quart	liquid	quilt

■ Analogies Write the list word that completes each analogy.

1. A male ruler is a king. A female ruler is a ___.
2. Information will inform. An explanation will ___.
3. Sweetened dough makes cookies. Sweetened chocolate makes ___.
4. Ice is a solid. Water is a ___.
5. Two cups are a pint. Two pints are a ___.
6. Minnesota is often cold. ___ is often hot.
7. Bored people are tired. Interested people are ___.
8. A small city is a town. A small town is a ___.
9. Tortoises are slow. Rabbits are ___.
10. On weekdays, people work. On weekends, people ___.

■ Making Connections Write the list word that answers each question.

11. What connects two sides of a river?
12. What is better than good?
13. What's the very end of a ledge?
14. What do you do when you use a credit card?
15. What's a patchwork blanket?
16. What is an additional amount?
17. What are two identical objects?
18. What do the seasons do?
19. What do you do when you anticipate?
20. What is all but one?

1. **queen**
2. **explain**
3. **fudge**
4. **liquid**
5. **quart**
6. **Texas**
7. **excited**
8. **village**
9. **quick**
10. **relax**
11. **bridge**
12. **excellent**
13. **edge**
14. **charge**
15. **quilt**
16. **extra**
17. **equal**
18. **change**
19. **expect**
20. **except**

Practice Masters, p. 58

DAY 5 STANDARDIZED TEST MASTER

14 ■ LESSON TEST

■ Find the word in each group that is spelled correctly. Fill in the letter for the correct word on the answer strip.

	a./b.	c./d.	Answer strip
Sample:	a. lione b. lino	c. linoe d. lion	ⓐ ⓑ ⓒ ●
1.	a. quart b. qwart	c. kourt d. qourt	1. ● ⓑ ⓒ ⓓ
2.	a. eksplain b. explain	c. eksplane d. explane	2. ⓐ ● ⓒ ⓓ
3.	a. excellent b. exellent	c. excelent d. ecxellent	3. ● ⓑ ⓒ ⓓ
4.	a. villige b. villiage	c. villege d. village	4. ⓐ ⓑ ⓒ ●
5.	a. quick b. quik	c. qwick d. quike	5. ● ⓑ ⓒ ⓓ
6.	a. Texes b. Texses	c. texas d. Texas	6. ⓐ ⓑ ⓒ ●
7.	a. exitra b. exdra	c. extra d. exster	7. ⓐ ⓑ ● ⓓ
8.	a. liquid b. liqid	c. liqiud d. likwid	8. ● ⓑ ⓒ ⓓ
9.	a. kwilt b. quilt	c. qwill d. quilet	9. ⓐ ● ⓒ ⓓ
10.	a. qeen b. gueen	c. queen d. qeene	10. ⓐ ⓑ ● ⓓ
11.	a. chang b. chage	c. change d. chanj	11. ⓐ ⓑ ● ⓓ
12.	a. exspect b. exepct	c. expet d. expect	12. ⓐ ⓑ ⓒ ●
13.	a. bridge b. brige	c. brigde d. bringe	13. ● ⓑ ⓒ ⓓ
14.	a. fudge b. fuje	c. fudje d. fugde	14. ● ⓑ ⓒ ⓓ
15.	a. except b. exept	c. exsept d. execpt	15. ● ⓑ ⓒ ⓓ
16.	a. relaxe b. relax	c. relacks d. realaxe	16. ⓐ ● ⓒ ⓓ
17.	a. exsited b. exicted	c. excited d. exscited	17. ⓐ ⓑ ● ⓓ
18.	a. charg b. chare	c. charnge d. charge	18. ⓐ ⓑ ⓒ ●
19.	a. equal b. ecqule	c. ekwil d. eqaul	19. ● ⓑ ⓒ ⓓ
20.	a. ege b. edge	c. eage d. edger	20. ⓐ ● ⓒ ⓓ

Practice for Standardized Tests, p. 20

DAY 1 Introduction

LESSON 14

- ✓ Pretest and Self-Check
- ● Spelling Focus and Word List
- ○ Challenge Words
- ○ Modified List

● Core ○ Optional ✓ Assessment

DAILY SPELLING REVIEW

What time did you *arive* at *cherch?*

arrive *church*

INTRODUCTION

Phonics

Consonant Sounds /j/, /ks/, and /kw/ Have students label a sheet of paper with the headings /j/, /ks/, and /kw/. Ask them to write each list word under the appropriate heading and circle the letters that spell the sound.

MEETING THE NEEDS OF ALL STUDENTS

Modified List

Practice Students studying only the high-frequency words in the top box write

- three words with /j/ spelled **ge** or **dge**
- two words with /ks/ spelled **xc**
- three words with /ks/ spelled **x**
- two words with /kw/ spelled **qu**

Visual Learners

Illustrating Meanings Have students illustrate the meaning of list words, such as *bridge*, *village*, and *quilt*.

Additional Practice

Challenge Master 14
Home-School Master 14
Audiotape B, Side 1

14

1. except
2. excited
3. explain
4. expect
5. Texas
6. excellent
7. relax
8. extra
9. change
10. village
11. edge
12. charge
13. bridge
14. fudge
15. quick
16. equal
17. queen
18. quart
19. liquid
20. quilt

CHALLENGE!

advantage
pledge
excess
explosion
question

INTRODUCTION

Consonant Sounds /j/, /ks/, /kw/

SPELLING FOCUS

The sound /j/ can be spelled **ge** and **dge: change, edge.** The sounds /ks/ and /kw/ can be spelled **xc, x,** and **qu: except, explain, quick.**

STUDY Say each word. Then read the sentence.

1. *change*	Leaves **change** colors in autumn.
2. *village*	The country **village** was quiet.
3. *edge*	He stood at the **edge** of the cliff.
4. *except* ✻	Everyone **except** me went home.
5. *excited*	She is **excited** about the trip.
6. *explain*	Can a book **explain** how to draw?
7. *expect*	Scientists **expect** an earthquake.
8. *Texas*	Alaska is larger than **Texas.**
9. *quick*	We enjoy a **quick** morning jog.
10. *equal*	Give them **equal** shares.
11. *charge*	Plumbers **charge** by the hour.
12. *bridge*	The **bridge** crosses the river.
13. *fudge*	Smooth, rich **fudge** is a treat.
14. *excellent*	The concert was **excellent.**
15. *relax*	Try to **relax** and go to sleep.
16. *extra*	He did the work for **extra** credit.
17. *queen*	That country is ruled by a **queen.**
18. *quart*	This bottle holds one **quart.**
19. *liquid*	Cough syrup is in **liquid** form.
20. *quilt*	The **quilt** is made of cloth scraps.

PRACTICE Sort the list words by writing

- eight words with the sound /ks/ spelled **x** or **xc**
- six words with the sound /j/ spelled **ge** or **dge**
- six words with the sound /kw/ spelled **qu**

Order of words in each group may vary.

WRITE Use two sentences in a paragraph.
Paragraphs will vary.

✻ **WATCH OUT FOR FREQUENTLY MISSPELLED WORDS!**

THINK AND PRACTICE

TONGUE TWISTERS   Write the list word that would best complete each tongue twister.

1. Fran fasts Fridays, frequently forgetting flavorful ____.
2. The ____ quickly quashed the quarrelsome quibbler.
3. Tula took trips to ____ a total of ten times.
4. Beside the bay ____, Binita built a bungalow.
5. Running relentlessly, Russ will rarely ____ or rest.
6. Chang's chum can ____ cheese into cheesecake.
7. This Vermont ____ is veiled in the vast verdant valley.
8. Lassie lapped at the ____ in the ladle.
9. Ed is edgy at the ____ of the edifice.

WORD SEARCH   Find the ten list words in the puzzle below. They may be printed down or across. Write them.

```
c e x c e l l e n t e e
h x e q u a r t e a x x
a p e x t r a q u i c k
r e x p l a i n q u e e
g c e x c i t e d e p e
e t q u i l q u i l t x
```

Order of words from 10 to 19 may vary.

20. Write a list word that is related in spelling and meaning to the words in the box.

equal

equator
equally
equation

Finish the sentences with words from the box.

21. Divide this **equally** among you.

22. (2 x 2) + 3 = 7 is a math **equation** .

23. The **equator** circles the earth.

1. **fudge**
2. **queen**
3. **Texas**
4. **bridge**
5. **relax**
6. **change**
7. **village**
8. **liquid**
9. **edge**
10. **excellent**
11. **charge**
12. **quart**
13. **quilt**
14. **excited**
15. **expect**
16. **except**
17. **extra**
18. **quick**
19. **explain**

FREQUENTLY MISSPELLED WORDS

Because they sound alike, *except* and *accept* are often confused. Make an **ex**tra effort to remember the **ex** in **ex**cept.

THINK AND PRACTICE

Tongue Twisters
Finding the Right Word
Tell students to first find list words with the same beginning letter as in the tongue twister. Then they can decide which word best fits the context.

MEETING THE NEEDS OF ALL STUDENTS

Modified List
Review Students studying high-frequency words complete Think and Practice Master 14.

Auditory Learners
Twisting Words Have students make up additional tongue twisters and record them on tape. Place the tapes in a learning center.

Bilingual/ESL
Word Search Suggest that ESL students use a piece of paper to cover puzzle lines and then scan for list words.

Additional Practice

Hardbound Book Master 14A
Think and Practice Master 14
Extra Practice Master 14
Everyday Spelling **CD-ROM**
Everyday Spelling **Game Software**

LESSON 14

- Proofread a Recipe
- Proofreading Tip: *Good* and *Well*
- Write a Recipe
- ✓ Cooperative Midweek Test

DAILY SPELLING REVIEW

We had *troble* with the *engin.*

trouble   *engine*

● Core   ○ Optional   ✓ Assessment

PROOFREADING AND WRITING

Usage

Good and **Well** Have students make up sentences using *good* and *well* for a classmate to complete, such as: *That is a* (good, well) *recipe. He bakes bread* (good, well).

MEETING THE NEEDS OF ALL STUDENTS

Modified List

Proofreading Students studying high-frequency words complete this page or the proofreading activity on the *Everyday Spelling* CD-ROM.

Enrichment

Writing Measurements

Explain that recipes often use abbreviations for measurements. Have students look in a cookbook for the abbreviations for *cup, teaspoon, tablespoon, pound, ounce,* and *quart.*

Additional Practice

Hardbound Book Master 14B
Second Language Master 14
Writing Mini-Lesson Master 14
Writing Activity Master 14
Proofreading Transparency 14
Everyday Spelling **CD-ROM**

■ PROOFREADING AND WRITING

Make a capital. ≡
Make a small letter. /
Add something. ∧
Take out something. ℮
Add a period. ⊙
New paragraph. ¶

PROOFREAD A RECIPE   Read the following recipe. Correct four misspellings and one place where *good* is used incorrectly.

PROOFREADING TIP
Good food, good kids, good home are good ways to use the word good. Good describes a person, place, or thing. Use well to describe how you do something: cook well.

Here's a recipe for very good **fudge** fuge.

In a pan over low heat mix together good **well**:

2 tablespoons butter

2 cups marshmallows

2 cups **excellent** exellent chocolate

2 cups sugar

Pour **liquid** liqid into pan. Allow to cool. Cut into bars. For a good snack, freeze **extra** exdra pieces.

WRITE A RECIPE   Think of something you enjoy eating. Find out how to make it and write the recipe. You might want to make the dish and share it with your classmates.

Responses will vary.

Word List

bridge	expect
queen	quick
except	explain
change	Texas
relax	charge
quart	equal
edge	excellent
extra	quilt
village	excited
liquid	fudge

Personal Words

1. **Words will vary.**

2. _______________

72

VOCABULARY BUILDING

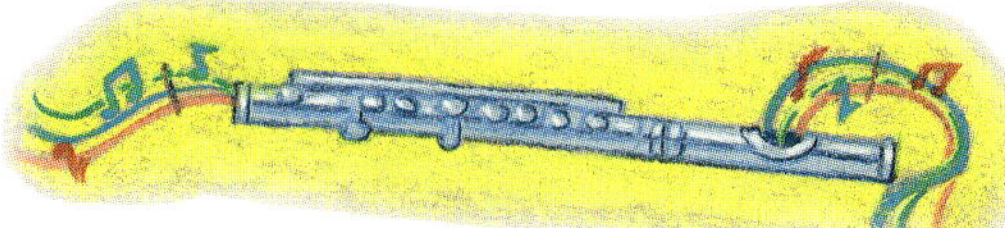

review

CONTEXT CLUES   Isabella was in a hurry when she wrote this letter to her friend. Write the missing boxed words to complete her letter.

change	explain
village	expect
edge	Texas
except	quick
excited	equal

Dear Nina,

I'm having a great time on my trip in the southwest. The weather here has been a nice (1) from the cold weather we left in Minnesota. Temperatures have been in the nineties every day (2) one day when it was over one hundred. Standing on the (3) of the Grand Canyon was awesome! Nothing is (4) to its beauty. I saw a Pueblo Indian (5) where the people live in houses called adobes. When I see you I'll (6) how they are made. Tomorrow we make a (7) stop in Santa Fe where we catch a flight to Dallas, (8). We (9) to see a rodeo there. I'm (10) about that! I'll write again soon.

Love,
Isabella

1. **change**
2. **except**
3. **edge**
4. **equal**
5. **village**
6. **explain**
7. **quick**
8. **Texas**
9. **expect**
10. **excited**

Using a *Dictionary*

FINDING THE RIGHT MEANING   If someone said, "I can't eat without my bridge," would you understand the person? *Bridge* has many meanings. If you look it up in a dictionary, you might find these definitions.

bridge (brij), **1** something built over a river, road, or railroad, so that people can get across. **2** to build a bridge over: *The engineers bridged the river.* **3** the false tooth or teeth in a mounting fastened to natural teeth. **4** a thin, arched piece over which the strings of a violin and other stringed instruments are stretched. 1, 3–4 *n.,* 2 *v.,* **bridged, bridg•ing.**

The second definition is followed by a **sentence.** This sentence helps you to see how the word is used.

At the end of the entry, each definition is identified by its **part of speech** (whether noun, verb, adjective, etc.). These are called part-of-speech labels.

Look at the entry for *bridge* again. Write the number of the definition that answers each question below.

1. Which definition of *bridge* fits the meaning, "I can't eat without my bridge"? ___
2. Which definition of *bridge* is part of a stringed instrument? ___
3. Which definition is a verb? ___

1. **3**
2. **4**
3. **2**

LESSON
15

Generalization

Spelling Focus: Add **-s** to form plurals of words that end in a **vowel** and **y** and to most other words. Change **y** to **i** and add **-es** to words that end in a **consonant** and **y.** Add **-es** to words that end with **sh, ch, s, ss,** or **x.**

● Core ○ Optional ✓ Assessment

DAILY PLAN	CORE OBJECTIVES	NOTES

DAY 1 Introduction

✓ Pretest and Self-Check, p. 74B
● Spelling Focus and Word List, p. 74
○ Challenge Words, p. 74
○ Challenge Master 15
○ Home-School Master 15

✓ ▪ Take and self-check Pretest
▪ Spell words that end in **-s** and **-es;** classify and write the list words

DAY 2 Think and Practice

● Making Comparisons: Word Associations, p. 75
● Strategic Spelling: *Building New Words,* p. 75
○ Think and Practice Master 15
○ Extra Practice Master 15
○ Cross-Curricular Lesson: Introduce, p. 170

▪ Complete practice activities for words with the ending **-s** or **-es**
▪ Recognize that new words can be formed by adding endings to words

DAY 3 Proofreading and Writing

● Proofread a Description, p. 76
● Proofreading Tip: Redundant Pronouns, p. 76
● Write a Description, p. 76
✓ Cooperative Midweek Test
○ Hardbound Book Master 15
○ Writing Mini-Lesson Master 15
○ Writing Activity Master 15
○ Second Language Support Master 15

▪ Proofread for spelling and usage errors
▪ Integrate spelling and writing in a personal writing response
✓ ▪ Take and check midweek test

DAY 4 Vocabulary Building

● Review: Word Associations and Categorizing, p. 77
● Multicultural Connection: Environment, p. 77
○ Cross-Curricular Lesson: Follow-Up, p. 170
○ Review Master 15

▪ Complete review activity for words that end in **-s** and **-es**
▪ Expand knowledge of other cultures through the study of flower names

DAY 5 Assessment

✓ Posttest, p. 74B
○ Standardized Test Master 15

✓ ▪ Take Posttest

Cross-Curricular Lessons

Use the Spelling Focus (words ending with **-s** and **-es**) to introduce the Social Studies lesson, *Global Grid,* page 170, or choose a lesson that correlates with a topic you're currently teaching.

MEETING THE NEEDS OF ALL STUDENTS

The Word List

For students studying 20 words, assign pages 74–77 and Extra Practice and Review masters.

Modified List For students studying 10 words, modify Practice on page 74, and assign Think and Practice Master 15 and pages 76–77.

Challenge For students studying 25 words, assign pages 74–77, Challenge, Extra Practice, and Review masters.

Bilingual/ESL

Suffixes do not exist in the Khmer language. A noun is usually made plural by using numbers, but not inflecting the noun. For example, Cambodian students speaking Khmer would say *one box, two box, three box.*

Personal Words

Students add to Personal Words lists by looking at work in their writing portfolios and words they want to remember from their reading.

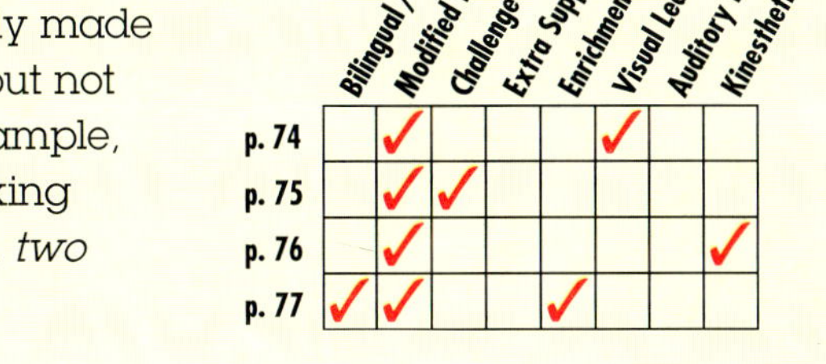

	Bilingual / ESL	Modified List	Challenge	Extra Support	Enrichment	Visual Learners	Auditory Learners	Kinesthetic Learners
p. 74		✓				✓		
p. 75		✓	✓					
p. 76		✓						✓
p. 77	✓	✓			✓			

ASSESSMENT*

Pretest

Read the underlined word, read the sentence, and then repeat the underlined word. Guide students in self-correcting their pretests and correcting any misspellings.

1. Jenny likes toy <u>monkeys</u>.
2. Juan gave his mom <u>flowers</u>.
3. Eli visited his <u>friends</u>.
4. Put away the <u>supplies</u>.
5. Most animals have <u>enemies</u>.
6. Do dogs have <u>eyelashes</u>?
7. Florida has many <u>beaches</u>.
8. <u>Circuses</u> have animals.
9. All <u>classes</u> were tested.
10. Our parents pay <u>taxes</u>.
11. <u>Tigers</u> live in the jungle.
12. I go to Ohio for <u>holidays</u>.
13. The traffic caused <u>delays</u>.
14. It's fun to have <u>hobbies</u>.
15. Write down your <u>memories</u>.
16. Police solve <u>mysteries</u>.
17. <u>Ashes</u> filled the grill.
18. Carrots come in <u>bunches</u>.
19. Maria got new <u>glasses</u>.
20. Those words have <u>suffixes</u>.

Posttest

Read aloud the sentences below. These sentences may be used for dictation.

1. The <u>friends</u> had a picnic.
2. <u>Monkeys</u> swing in trees.
3. She has long <u>eyelashes</u>.
4. The man has many <u>enemies</u>.
5. We go swimming at <u>beaches</u>.
6. The <u>classes</u> will do math.
7. Children like <u>circuses</u>.
8. Buy new school <u>supplies</u>.
9. In America we pay <u>taxes</u>.
10. I picked seven <u>flowers</u>.
11. We like school <u>holidays</u>.
12. The <u>ashes</u> were still hot.
13. The train had many <u>delays</u>.
14. I have <u>bunches</u> of boxes.
15. <u>Tigers</u> are a kind of cat.
16. <u>Glasses</u> can help you see.
17. What are her <u>hobbies</u>?
18. Does that word have <u>suffixes</u>?
19. Grandma has good <u>memories</u>.
20. I like to read <u>mysteries</u>.

Challenge Words

1. The van had two <u>accidents</u>.
2. Take <u>skis</u> on the trip.
3. A fall can cause <u>injuries</u>.
4. I like to visit <u>libraries</u>.
5. <u>Couches</u> must be soft.

Additional Assessment

Standardized Test Master 15
Dictation Sentences, p. T39
Everyday Spelling CD-ROM

FREQUENT MISSPELLINGS
The list word *friends* is the eighth most frequently misspelled word by fourth graders. Provide this mnemonic: We will be fri**end**s to the **end**.

* See pp. T20 and T33 for test-study-test information.

DAY 1 — CHALLENGE MASTER

CHALLENGE ■ 15

Challenge Words

| couches | accidents | skis | injuries | libraries |

■ Use the Challenge Words to complete the categories.

Living Room Furniture	Sports Equipment	1. **Injuries**
chairs lamps 2. **couches**	bats rackets 3. **skis**	sprains bruises breaks

Places with Books		4. **Accidents**
stores waiting rooms 5. **libraries**	spilled milk auto crash broken plate	

■ Sometimes a vacation can turn out much differently than planned. Use one or more Challenge Words to write about a surprising vacation you have taken, heard about, or imagined.

Practice Masters, p. 59

DAY 1 — HOME-SCHOOL MASTER

■ 15   HOME-SCHOOL ACTIVITIES   15 ■

■ **Word Cousins** Write the list word that completes each group of words.

1. puzzles, riddles, **mysteries**
2. roses, violets, **flowers**
3. lions, leopards, **tigers**
4. Fourth of July, Halloween, **holidays**
5. batches, bundles, **bunches**
6. pals, buddies, **friends**
7. coastlines, shores, **beaches**
8. clowns, trapeze artists, **circuses**

■ **Plurals** Write the list word that is the plural of each word below.

9. class **classes**
10. enemy **enemies**
11. monkey **monkeys**
12. eyelash **eyelashes**
13. supply **supplies**
14. suffix **suffixes**
15. delay **delays**
16. memory **memories**
17. tax **taxes**
18. hobby **hobbies**
19. ash **ashes**
20. glass **glasses**

Word Check 15

1. friends
2. tigers
3. flowers
4. holidays
5. delays
6. monkeys
7. ashes
8. eyelashes
9. beaches
10. bunches
11. circuses
12. glasses
13. classes
14. taxes
15. suffixes
16. hobbies
17. enemies
18. memories
19. mysteries
20. supplies

Dear Parent,

Please check to see that your child has done this page correctly. Circle any misspelled words and help your child study them.

Tear off the Word Check before your child returns this page to class. Use it to help your child study.

Home-School Activities, p. 13

DAY 2 — THINK AND PRACTICE MASTER

15 ■ THINK AND PRACTICE

| monkeys | flowers | friends | supplies | enemies |
| eyelashes | beaches | circuses | classes | taxes |

■ **Making Comparisons** Complete each comparison using a list word.

1. The fireworks looked like exploding **flowers**
2. Children scampered up and down the slide like **monkeys**
3. The two rams charged like **enemies** attacking.
4. These dog acts are as lively as three-ring **circuses**
5. The strangers smiled at each other like two old **friends**

■ **Adding Endings** Add -s or -es to form a list word that completes each sentence.

6. (tax) Do you think **taxes** are too high?
7. (class) Two **classes** went to the museum.
8. (supply) Mom bought school **supplies** for me.
9. (eyelash) The baby has long **eyelashes**
10. (beach) Some **beaches** are rocky.
11. (monkey) Two **monkeys** chased each other.
12. (circus) I have seen two **circuses**

STRATEGIC SPELLING: Building New Words
Write the plural form of each word. Remember what you learned.

13. scratch **scratches**
14. guess **guesses**
15. play **plays**

Practice Masters, p. 60

DAY 2 — EXTRA PRACTICE MASTER

EXTRA PRACTICE ■ 15

Word List

monkeys	flowers	friends	supplies	enemies
eyelashes	beaches	circuses	classes	taxes
tigers	holidays	delays	hobbies	memories
mysteries	ashes	bunches	glasses	suffixes

■ **Words in Context** Write a list word to complete each sentence

1. The beautiful ___ in the garden bloomed all summer long.
2. You go to the eye doctor to be fitted for ___.
3. Some ___ have better clowns than others.
4. Those rival teams have been ___ for years.
5. The program showed lions and ___ in a zoo.
6. After the storms, the ___ were full of shells.
7. My ___ in math and art are in the morning.
8. St. Patrick's Day is one of my favorite ___.
9. You can make verb forms with ___ -ed and -ing.
10. Things you enjoy doing in your spare time are ___.

■ **Riddles** Each riddle tells you about a list word. Write each word.

11. They swing in the trees and eat bananas.
12. These people like you and will always be true.
13. These are left over at dawn, after the firewood's gone.
14. Clusters, batches, if you please, bananas and grapes come in these.
15. Solve the clues, or sing the blues!
16. Some are short and some are long. When you blink, you can't go wrong.
17. Buy notebooks, pencils, and a pen—you are ready for school then.
18. These must be paid, after money has been made.
19. A trip to camp, a favorite doll, these things help you recall.
20. Slow bus or slow train, they are a pain.

1. **flowers**
2. **glasses**
3. **circuses**
4. **enemies**
5. **tigers**
6. **beaches**
7. **classes**
8. **holidays**
9. **suffixes**
10. **hobbies**
11. **monkeys**
12. **friends**
13. **ashes**
14. **bunches**
15. **mysteries**
16. **eyelashes**
17. **supplies**
18. **taxes**
19. **memories**
20. **delays**

Practice Masters, p. 61

TECHNOLOGY AND VISUAL SUPPORT	 Use Audiotape B, Side 1, Lesson 15	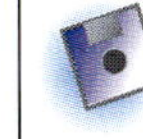 For additional practice use *Everyday Spelling* Game Software, Lesson 15	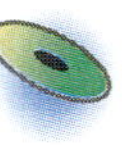 Additional resources on *Everyday Spelling* CD-ROM: proofreading and writing, modified list and challenge words, auditory test
	Use Proofreading and Writing Transparency 15		

DAY 3 SECOND LANGUAGE SUPPORT MASTER

SECOND LANGUAGE SUPPORT ■ 15

Quick Stories

The pictures tell a story. Talk about the story with others. Write the words to complete the sentences.

friends   flowers   hobbies

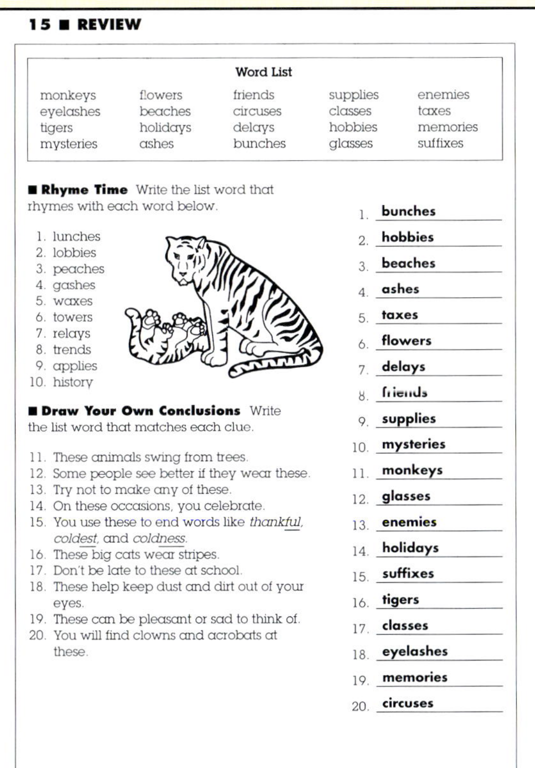

My (1) and I are planning a show.

1. **friends**

We will tell about our (2).

2. **hobbies**

Haidar's hobby is growing (3).

3. **flowers**

The next story is not finished. Talk about what will happen next. Write the words to complete the sentences. Draw the new part of the story.

ashes   mysteries

Hwon and Diva like to solve (4).

4. **mysteries**

One day they found some (5) on the rug.

5. **ashes**

Have you ever solved a mystery? Tell your partner what you did.

Second Language Support, p. 39

DAY 3 WRITING ACTIVITY MASTER

15 ■ WRITING ACTIVITY

Descriptive Language

Words that appeal to the senses will make your writing descriptive.

■ Mr. Chambers wrote this newspaper ad to advertise the specials at his restaurant. Add descriptions to the menu items.

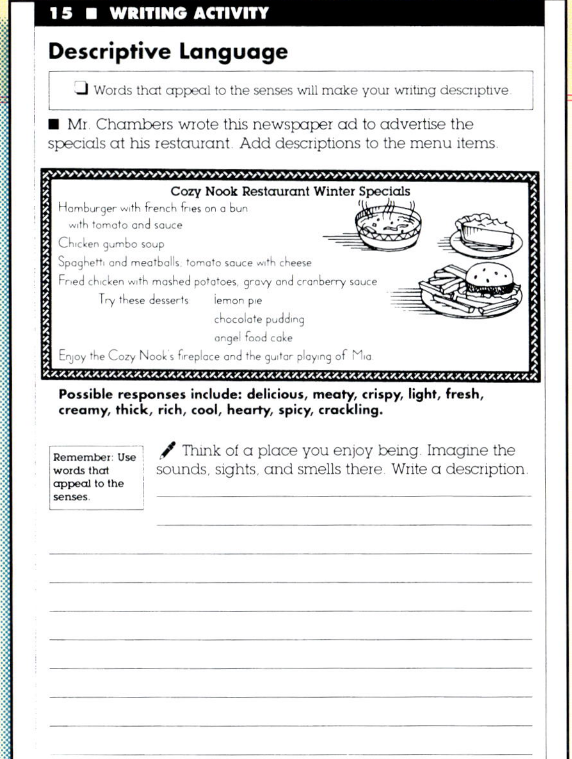

Possible responses include: delicious, meaty, crispy, light, fresh, creamy, thick, rich, cool, hearty, spicy, crackling.

Remember: Use words that appeal to the senses.

Think of a place you enjoy being. Imagine the sounds, sights, and smells there. Write a description.

Spelling and Writing, p. 26

DAY 4 REVIEW MASTER

15 ■ REVIEW

Word List

monkeys	flowers	friends	supplies	enemies
eyelashes	beaches	circuses	classes	taxes
tigers	holidays	delays	hobbies	memories
mysteries	ashes	bunches	glasses	suffixes

■ **Rhyme Time** Write the list word that rhymes with each word below.

1. lunches
2. lobbies
3. peaches
4. gashes
5. waxes
6. towers
7. relays
8. trends
9. applies
10. history

1. **bunches**
2. **hobbies**
3. **beaches**
4. **ashes**
5. **taxes**
6. **flowers**
7. **delays**
8. **friends**
9. **supplies**
10. **mysteries**

■ **Draw Your Own Conclusions** Write the list word that matches each clue.

11. These animals swing from trees.
12. Some people see better if they wear these.
13. Try not to make any of these.
14. On these occasions, you celebrate.
15. You use these to end words like *thankful, coldest,* and *coldness.*
16. These big cats wear stripes.
17. Don't be late to these at school.
18. These help keep dust and dirt out of your eyes.
19. These can be pleasant or sad to think of.
20. You will find clowns and acrobats at these.

11. **monkeys**
12. **glasses**
13. **enemies**
14. **holidays**
15. **suffixes**
16. **tigers**
17. **classes**
18. **eyelashes**
19. **memories**
20. **circuses**

Practice Masters, p. 62

DAY 5 STANDARDIZED TEST MASTER

LESSON TEST ■ 15

■ Find the word in each group that is spelled correctly. Fill in the letter for the correct word on the answer strip.

Sample:
- **a.** lione   **c.** linoe
- **b.** lino   **d.** lion   — ⓐⓑⓒ●

1. **a.** freinds   **c.** friends   **b.** frends   **d.** frinds — 1. ⓐⓑ●ⓓ
2. **a.** curuses   **c.** surcuses   **b.** sircuses   **d.** circuses — 2. ⓐⓑⓒ●
3. **a.** supplies   **c.** suplise   **b.** suplies   **d.** supplys — 3. ●ⓑⓒⓓ
4. **a.** bunches   **c.** bunchis   **b.** buches   **d.** bunchs — 4. ●ⓑⓒⓓ
5. **a.** deelays   **c.** delayes   **b.** delays   **d.** delaies — 5. ⓐ●ⓒⓓ
6. **a.** eyelasches   **c.** eyelashes   **b.** eyelasses   **d.** eyelashs — 6. ⓐⓑ●ⓓ
7. **a.** hoildays   **c.** holidays   **b.** hollidays   **d.** holadays — 7. ⓐⓑ●ⓓ
8. **a.** hobbys   **c.** hobbiez   **b.** hobies   **d.** hobbies — 8. ⓐⓑⓒ●
9. **a.** tatoos   **c.** taksas   **b.** tackses   **d.** taxses — 9. ●ⓑⓒⓓ
10. **a.** meomories   **c.** memeries   **b.** memories   **d.** menrogies — 10. ⓐ●ⓒⓓ
11. **a.** glases   **c.** glasses   **b.** glasis   **d.** glassis — 11. ⓐⓑ●ⓓ
12. **a.** classes   **c.** clasis   **b.** clases   **d.** classis — 12. ●ⓑⓒⓓ
13. **a.** monkys   **c.** mokeys   **b.** mankes   **d.** monkeys — 13. ⓐⓑⓒ●
14. **a.** beachs   **c.** beechez   **b.** beaches   **d.** baeches — 14. ⓐ●ⓒⓓ
15. **a.** enemies   **c.** enimes   **b.** enemys   **d.** enimies — 15. ●ⓑⓒⓓ
16. **a.** mystries   **c.** mysteries   **b.** mysterys   **d.** mistrys — 16. ⓐⓑ●ⓓ
17. **a.** sufixes   **c.** sufickses   **b.** suffickses   **d.** suffixes — 17. ⓐⓑⓒ●
18. **a.** ashes   **c.** ashs   **b.** ases   **d.** ahses — 18. ●ⓑⓒⓓ
19. **a.** fowers   **c.** flowers   **b.** flowes   **d.** floweres — 19. ⓐⓑ●ⓓ
20. **a.** tigirs   **c.** tigirs   **b.** tigers   **d.** tigeres — 20. ⓐ●ⓒⓓ

Practice for Standardized Tests, p. 21

LESSON

15

INTRODUCTION

Phonics

Word Structure Have students list the words ending in **y** whose plurals are formed by adding **-s** and those whose plurals are formed by changing the **y** to **i** and adding **-es**. Have students circle the letter that comes before the letters **-ys** and **-ies**.

MEETING THE NEEDS OF ALL STUDENTS

Modified List

Practice Students studying only the high-frequency words in the top box write two words in which **y** has been changed to **i**, five other words in which **-es** is added, and three words in which **-s** is added.

Visual Learners

Singular or Plural? Have students illustrate the singular and plural list words, showing that the **-s** and **-es** endings mean "more than one."

Additional Practice

Challenge Master 15
Home-School Master 15
Audiotape B, Side 1

1. **supplies**
2. **enemies**
3. **hobbies**
4. **memories**
5. **mysteries**
6. **eyelashes**
7. **beaches**
8. **circuses**
9. **classes**
10. **taxes**
11. **ashes**
12. **bunches**
13. **glasses**
14. **suffixes**
15. **monkeys**
16. **flowers**
17. **friends**
18. **tigers**
19. **holidays**
20. **delays**

Order of words in each group may vary.

CHALLENGE!

accidents
skis
injuries
libraries
couches

Sentences will vary.

74

INTRODUCTION

Adding -s and -es

SPELLING FOCUS

Add **-s** to words ending in a **vowel** and **y** and to most words: **monkeys, flowers**. Change **y** to **i** and add **-es** to words ending in a **consonant** and **y**: **supplies**. Add **-es** to words ending in **sh, ch, s, ss, x**: **beaches**.

STUDY See whether **-s** or **-es** is added to each list word.

monkey	1. *monkeys*
flower	2. *flowers*
friend	3. *friends* ✳
supply	4. *supplies*
enemy	5. *enemies*
eyelash	6. *eyelashes*
beach	7. *beaches*
circus	8. *circuses*
class	9. *classes*
tax	10. *taxes*

tiger	11. *tigers*
holiday	12. *holidays*
delay	13. *delays*
hobby	14. *hobbies*
memory	15. *memories*
mystery	16. *mysteries*
ash	17. *ashes*
bunch	18. *bunches*
glass	19. *glasses*
suffix	20. *suffixes*

PRACTICE Sort the words by writing
- five words in which **y** has been changed to **i**
- nine other words in which **-es** is added
- six words in which **-s** is added

WRITE Choose ten words to write in sentences.

✳ **WATCH OUT FOR FREQUENTLY MISSPELLED WORDS!**

THINK AND PRACTICE

MAKING COMPARISONS   Complete each comparison using a list word.

1. The children chattered like ____ in a tree.
2. Her sweet perfume smelled like fresh ____.
3. The long threads were as thin and dark as ____.
4. Their faces were as dry and gray as ____.
5. The play had more problems than one of my math ____.
6. The two round puddles shined like a pair of ____.
7. The floor was as sandy as ten ____.
8. Deep-sea photography is like having two ____ in one.
9. They ate the roast like ferocious, snarling ____.

WORD ASSOCIATIONS   Write the list word that you would associate with the words or phrases below. Use the Spelling Dictionary for help.

10. stops along the way
11. grapes in groups
12. July 4, Thanksgiving
13. groups at war
14. clowns and acrobats
15. money citizens pay
16. sleeping bags, canteens
17. good pals
18. puzzling secrets
19. -ment, -ly, -ous
20. things remembered

1. **monkeys**
2. **flowers**
3. **eyelashes**
4. **ashes**
5. **classes**
6. **glasses**
7. **beaches**
8. **hobbies**
9. **tigers**
10. **delays**
11. **bunches**
12. **holidays**
13. **enemies**
14. **circuses**
15. **taxes**
16. **supplies**
17. **friends**
18. **mysteries**
19. **suffixes**
20. **memories**

Write the plural form of each word. Remember what you learned.

21. scratch — **scratches**
22. guess — **guesses**
23. play — **plays**

Take a Hint
Here's another way to remember when to add **-es:**
Say the plural form aloud. If the ending you hear adds a syllable, the ending you add is **-es:**
watch•es   tax•es

THINK AND PRACTICE

Making Comparisons
Word Study Some students may have difficulty with comparisons. Have them work with a partner. Suggest that they try different list words in each sentence until they find one that makes sense.

MEETING THE NEEDS OF ALL STUDENTS

Modified List
Review Students studying high-frequency words complete Think and Practice Master 15.

Challenge
Play It Again Have students create their own word associations for list words, such as swimming, soccer, and stamp collecting for *hobbies.* Then they can exchange with a partner and play the word association game.

Additional Practice
Think and Practice Master 15
Extra Practice Master 15
Everyday Spelling CD-ROM
Everyday Spelling Game Software

LESSON 15

- Proofread a Description
- Proofreading Tip:
  Redundant Pronouns
- Write a Description
- Cooperative Midweek Test

DAILY SPELLING REVIEW

Can we have *baken* for *super*?

bacon   *supper*

○ **Core**   ○ **Optional**   ✓ **Assessment**

PROOFREADING AND WRITING

Usage

Redundant Pronouns Use sentences like the following to give students practice in deleting redundant pronouns: *Sue and Ana they like rock music. Sasha he plays the guitar.*

MEETING THE NEEDS OF ALL STUDENTS

Modified List

Proofreading Students studying high-frequency words complete this page or the proofreading activity on the *Everyday Spelling* CD-ROM.

Kinesthetic Learners

Acting Out Details Have students act out their favorite sport or hobby. Then have them write a short paragraph in which they describe their own or another student's performance.

Additional Practice

Hardbound Book Master 15
Second Language Master 15
Writing Mini-Lesson Master 15
Writing Activity Master 15
Proofreading Transparency 15
Everyday Spelling **CD-ROM**

■ PROOFREADING AND WRITING

PROOFREADING TIP
My friends and I means the same thing as we. Byron should use one or the other, never both.

PROOFREAD A DESCRIPTION
Byron wrote this description of reggae, his favorite music. Read what he wrote, and then correct three misspellings and one pronoun error.

In Jamaica, my homeland, my **friends** freinds and I we listen to reggae music. Reggae has a strong beat, like rock music. It is not as hard as rock, though, because it was born on island beach**es** (**beaches**). It is like the blues, but brighter. It has the sound of sunshine and flowe**rs** (**flowers**).

Make a capital.
Make a small letter.
Add something.
Take out something.
Add a period.
New paragraph

Word List

friends	circuses
tigers	glasses
flowers	classes
holidays	taxes
delays	suffixes
monkeys	hobbies
ashes	enemies
eyelashes	memories
beaches	mysteries
bunches	supplies

Personal Words

1. **Words will vary.**

2. _______________

WRITE A DESCRIPTION   Write a description of your favorite music. Use list words and personal words.

Responses will vary. Description should contain list words and personal words.

76

VOCABULARY BUILDING

Review

WORD ASSOCIATIONS Write the boxed word that belongs in each group.

1. leopards, zebras, ___
2. chin, nose, ___
3. students, learning, ___
4. foes, rivals, ___
5. allowances, wages, ___
6. carnivals, fairs, ___
7. buddies, pals, ___
8. sunbathers, lifeguards, ___

CATEGORIZING Write the boxed word that is a name you would give to each group.

9. pens, paper, ruler
10. roses, daisies, petunias

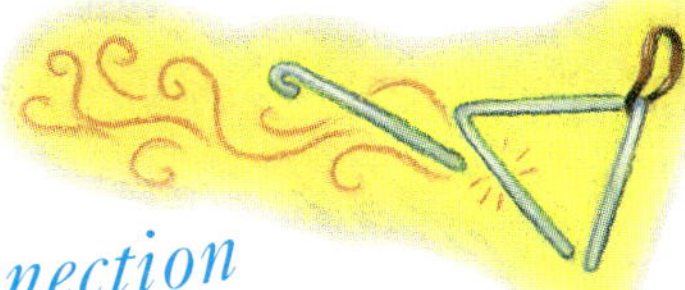

Multicultural *Connection*

ENVIRONMENT People of all nations use flowers to express feelings and to symbolize love. The flowers pictured below are national flowers. Write the boxed word that matches each description. Use your Spelling Dictionary to look up the flowers you don't know.

monkeys	eyelashes
flowers	beaches
friends	circuses
supplies	classes
enemies	taxes

1. monkeys
2. eyelashes
3. classes
4. enemies
5. taxes
6. circuses
7. friends
8. beaches
9. supplies
10. flowers

1. a small flower that grows in Austria, made famous in a song

2. a bright, showy flower that grows in the tropics of Costa Rica

3. a kind of water lily found in India

4. the flower of the almond tree, often seen in Israel

lotus
almond blossom
cattleya orchid
edelweiss

1. edelweiss
2. cattleya orchid
3. lotus
4. almond blossom

VOCABULARY BUILDING

Literature Connection

Your Own Environment
A wildflower handbook or a local expert can give students the names and descriptions of wildflowers that grow locally.

MEETING THE NEEDS OF ALL STUDENTS

Modified List

Review Students studying high-frequency words complete this page.

Enrichment

Flower Symbols Have students select a flower as their symbol. Invite them to write a paragraph telling why they would choose this flower.

Bilingual/ESL

Flower Details Encourage ESL students to describe familiar flowers so that other students can visualize them.

Additional Practice

Review Master 15
Standardized Test Master 15
***Everyday Spelling* CD-ROM**

LESSON
16

Generalization

Spelling Focus: Visualizing a word as you pronounce it helps you to use just enough letters.

● Core ○ Optional ✓ Assessment

DAILY PLAN	CORE OBJECTIVES	NOTES

DAY 1 Introduction
✓ Pretest and Self-Check, p. 78B
● Spelling Focus and Word List, p. 78
○ Challenge Words, p. 78
○ Challenge Master 16
○ Home-School Master 16

✓ • Take and self-check Pretest
• Spell words using pronunciation and visualization; classify and write the list words

DAY 2 Think and Practice
● Classifying; Words in Context, p. 79
● Strategic Spelling: *Using the Meaning Helpers Strategy*, p. 79
○ Think and Practice Master 16
○ Extra Practice Master 16
○ Cross-Curricular Lesson: Introduce, p. 218

• Complete practice activities for words using just enough letters
• Use the Meaning Helpers Strategy to find words related to a list word

DAY 3 Proofreading and Writing
● Proofread a Warning, p. 80
● Proofreading Tip: *It's* and *Its,* p. 80
● Write a Warning, p. 80
✓ Cooperative Midweek Test
○ Hardbound Book Master 16
○ Writing Mini-Lesson Master 16
○ Writing Activity Master 16
○ Second Language Support Master 16

• Proofread for spelling usage and punctuation errors
• Integrate spelling and writing in a personal writing response
✓ • Take and check midweek test

DAY 4 Vocabulary Building
● Review: Antonyms; Draw Your Own Conclusions, p. 81
● Word Study: Word Play, p. 81
○ Cross-Curricular Lesson: Follow-Up, p. 218
○ Review Master 16

• Complete review activity for words using just enough letters
• Explore language through word play

DAY 5 Assessment
✓ Posttest, p. 78B
○ Standardized Test Master 16

✓ • Take Posttest

Cross-Curricular Lessons

Use the Spelling Focus (using just enough letters) to introduce the Mathematics lesson, *Division*, page 218, or choose a lesson that correlates with a topic you're currently teaching.

MEETING THE NEEDS OF ALL STUDENTS

The Word List

For students studying 20 words, assign pages 78–81 and Extra Practice and Review masters.

Modified List For students studying 10 words, modify Practice on page 78, and assign Think and Practice Master 16 and pages 80–81.

Challenge For students studying 25 words, assign pages 78–81, Challenge, Extra Practice, and Review masters.

Bilingual/ESL

Because the Spanish language has only one vowel per syllable, Spanish-speaking students may omit the **e** in spelling the **-ed** ending: *washed/washd; missed/missd.*

Personal Words

Students add to Personal Words lists by looking at work in their writing portfolios and words they want to remember from their reading.

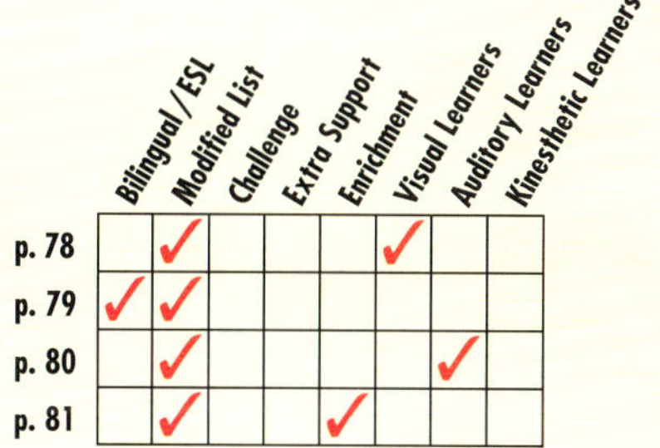

	Bilingual / ESL	Modified List	Challenge	Extra Support	Enrichment	Visual Learners	Auditory Learners	Kinesthetic Learners
p. 78		✓				✓		
p. 79	✓	✓						
p. 80		✓					✓	
p. 81		✓			✓			

ASSESSMENT*

Pretest

Read the underlined word, read the sentence, and then repeat the underlined word. Guide students in self-correcting their pretests and correcting any misspellings.

1. He is <u>coming</u> to visit.
2. Alan is <u>always</u> in a hurry.
3. The cake is <u>almost</u> ready.
4. The radio <u>didn't</u> work.
5. Put the top <u>upon</u> the jar.
6. She <u>wasn't</u> at the party.
7. We played ball <u>until</u> six.
8. He works <u>during</u> the day.
9. Do you <u>want</u> another apple?
10. Carolina helps her <u>father</u>.
11. A <u>hamster</u> is a cute pet.
12. Camping was <u>a lot</u> of fun.
13. I saw an <u>ugly</u> bug.
14. Evie <u>washed</u> the clothes.
15. Nico stayed at a <u>hotel</u>.
16. We <u>missed</u> the last bus.
17. Ryan will be <u>eleven</u> soon.
18. The dog did <u>crazy</u> tricks.
19. Our cat is very <u>lazy</u>.
20. She hurt my <u>feelings</u>.

Posttest

Read aloud the sentences below. These sentences may be used for dictation.

1. His <u>father</u> is an actor.
2. Mom will <u>always</u> help me.
3. He woke <u>during</u> the night.
4. Do you <u>want</u> some popcorn?
5. I can't wait <u>until</u> summer.
6. We <u>didn't</u> have homework.
7. Put the pen <u>upon</u> the desk.
8. Spring is <u>coming</u> soon.
9. Is the game <u>almost</u> over?
10. The apple <u>wasn't</u> ripe.
11. That is an <u>ugly</u> smell!
12. A <u>hamster</u> has soft fur.
13. The city has a big <u>hotel</u>.
14. We were <u>lazy</u> on Saturday.
15. We <u>missed</u> our friends.
16. She had a <u>crazy</u> idea.
17. We saw <u>eleven</u> puppies.
18. I wrote about my <u>feelings</u>.
19. They <u>washed</u> the dishes.
20. We ate <u>a lot</u> of peaches.

Challenge Words

1. Mail <u>delivery</u> is at three.
2. Can you use a <u>magnet</u>?
3. He <u>replied</u> to my letter.
4. The dog almost <u>drowned</u>.
5. Put <u>mustard</u> on a hot dog.

Additional Assessment

Standardized Test Master 16
Dictation Sentences, p. T39
Everyday Spelling CD-ROM

WHAT'S THE BIG IDEA?
This may be a good time to review contractions. *Research in Action* discovered that it's common to add a vowel before the contracted part: *didint.* Review contractions by writing *did not* and *was not* on the board and asking volunteers to show how to form the contractions *didn't* and *wasn't*.

* See pp. T20 and T33 for test-study-test information.

DAY 1 CHALLENGE MASTER

CHALLENGE ■ 16

Challenge Words

delivery	drowned	magnet	mustard	replied

■ Unscramble and write the Challenge Words on the lines. Use the circled letters to answer the riddle.

1. r i d e l p e
   r e p (l) i e d

2. t a m e g n
   m a (g) n e t

3. d r u m s a t
   m u s (t) a r d

4. r e v l y i e d
   d e (l) i v e r y

5. r e d w o n d
   d r (o) w n e d

I am used in an "enlightened" kind of surgery. What am I?
l a s e r

■ The answer to the riddle has many uses. Use one or more Challenge Words to describe one way it is used now or might be used in the future.

Practice Masters, p. 63

DAY 1 HOME-SCHOOL MASTER

■ 16 HOME-SCHOOL ACTIVITIES 16 ■

Word Check 16
1. hamster
2. a lot
3. ugly
4. washed
5. hotel
6. always
7. father
8. missed
9. until
10. coming
11. eleven
12. upon
13. crazy
14. didn't
15. lazy
16. almost
17. wasn't
18. want
19. feelings
20. during

■ **Word Bits** Find the list word in each letter puzzle. Write the word.

1. tbelevenwors **eleven**
2. wawasheddoby **washed**
3. urduringomtz **during**
4. sterhamsterh **hamster**
5. utuponotrzob **upon**
6. oferfeelings **feelings**
7. alallalwaysu **always**
8. smmissededod **missed**

■ **Words in Context** Write a list word to complete each sentence.

9. The plane **wasn't** ready to board.
10. One friend **didn't** want to see that movie.
11. Wait **until** I say "Go!"
12. We stayed overnight at a **hotel**.
13. I think that is an **ugly** color!
14. Joe felt **lazy** and wanted to relax.
15. There are **a lot** of beans in that jar.
16. Do you **want** some juice with your lunch?
17. My little brother is **crazy** about collecting baseball cards.
18. My **father** works for the railroad.
19. It's **almost** time to eat.
20. Are you **coming** to our party?

Dear Parent,

Please check to see that your child has done this page correctly. Circle any misspelled words and help your child study them.

Tear off the Word Check before your child returns this page to class. Use it to help your child study.

Home-School Activities, p. 14

DAY 2 THINK AND PRACTICE MASTER

16 ■ THINK AND PRACTICE

coming	always	almost	didn't	upon
wasn't	until	during	want	father

■ **Antonyms** Write the list word that means the opposite of each word.

1. going **coming**
2. mother **father**
3. never **always**
4. under **upon**
5. did **didn't**
6. have **want**
7. was **wasn't**

■ **Words in Context** Write the missing list words to complete the paragraph.

"You'll have to wait _(8)_ you grow up." That's what everyone _(9)_ tells me. Then one night I dreamed I was all grown up and a _(10)_ with a boy my age. I learned that it _(11)_ as much fun as I had thought. I had _(12)_ no time to myself. _(13)_ the day, I had to work. After _(14)_ home, there was more work. And my kid—he _(15)_ stop asking me to do things. Of course, you know what I told him—"If you _(16)_ to do that, you'll have to wait until you grow up."

8. **until**
9. **always**
10. **father**
11. **wasn't**
12. **almost**
13. **During**
14. **coming**
15. **didn't**
16. **want**

STRATEGIC SPELLING: Using the Meaning Helper Strategy

outcome	homecoming	overcome

17. Write a list word that is related to the words in the box.
    coming

Now write words from the box that fit the clues.

18. What you have to do if you have a problem **overcome**
19. You have this upon returning to the place where you live **homecoming**
20. How an event turns out **outcome**

Practice Masters, p. 64

DAY 2 EXTRA PRACTICE MASTER

EXTRA PRACTICE ■ 16

Word List

coming	always	almost	didn't	upon
wasn't	until	during	want	father
hamster	a lot	ugly	washed	hotel
missed	eleven	crazy	lazy	feelings

■ **Which Word Is It?** Write the list word that:

1. has double consonants
2. has the **sh** sound
3. has the word *way* in it
4. is made up of two separate words
5. is a plural form
6. names an animal
7. is a compound word
8. names a number
9. has the base word *come*
10. names a family member
11. describes something that is not pretty

1. **missed**
2. **washed**
3. **always**
4. **a lot**
5. **feelings**
6. **hamster**
7. **upon**
8. **eleven**
9. **coming**
10. **father**
11. **ugly**

■ **Keep Choosing** Now look at the list words that are left. Write the **two** words that:

have the long a sound
12. **crazy**
13. **lazy**

have the long o sound
14. **almost**
15. **hotel**

are contractions
16. **wasn't**
17. **didn't**

■ **Leftovers** Use the remaining list words to complete the sentences.

18. I have some leftover words. Do you **want** them?
19. Wait **until** tomorrow. Then I can use them in a report.
20. Maybe you can also use them **during** social studies class.

Practice Masters, p. 65

TECHNOLOGY AND VISUAL SUPPORT	 Use Audiotape B, Side 1, Lesson 16  Use Proofreading and Writing Transparency 16	 For additional practice use *Everyday Spelling* Game Software, Lesson 16	 Additional resources on *Everyday Spelling* CD-ROM: proofreading and writing, modified list and challenge words, auditory test

DAY 3 SECOND LANGUAGE SUPPORT MASTER

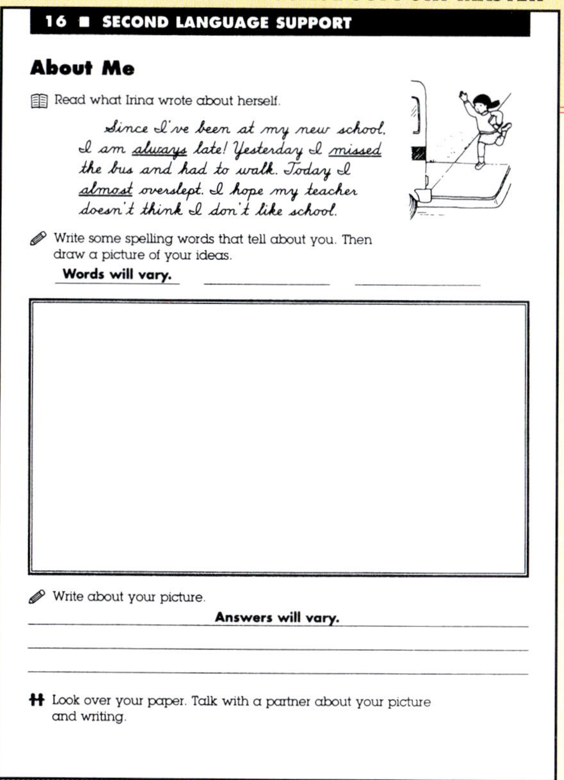

16 ■ SECOND LANGUAGE SUPPORT

About Me

Read what Irina wrote about herself.

Since I've been at my new school, I am *always* *late! Yesterday I* *missed* *the bus and had to walk. Today I* *almost* *overslept. I hope my teacher doesn't think I don't like school.*

Write some spelling words that tell about you. Then draw a picture of your ideas.

Words will vary.

Write about your picture.

Answers will vary.

Look over your paper. Talk with a partner about your picture and writing.

Second Language Support, p. 40

DAY 3 WRITING ACTIVITY MASTER

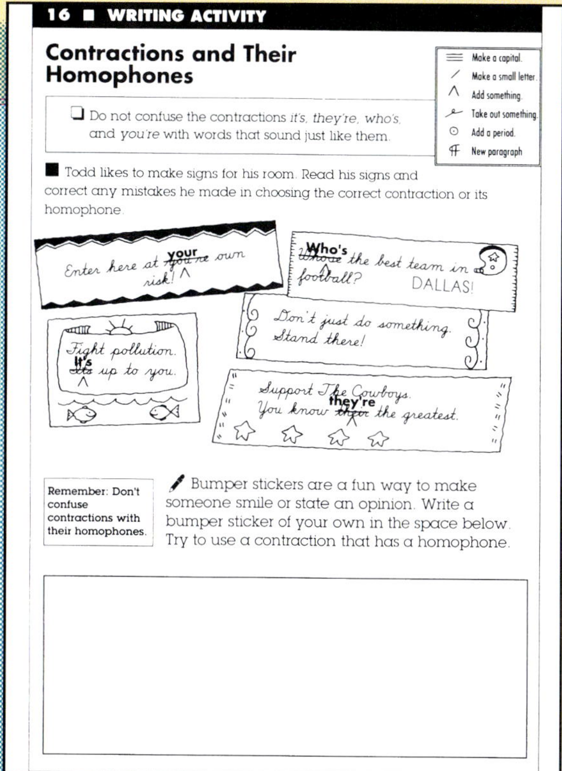

16 ■ WRITING ACTIVITY

Contractions and Their Homophones

Do not confuse the contractions *it's, they're, who's,* and *you're* with words that sound just like them.

Todd likes to make signs for his room. Read his signs and correct any mistakes he made in choosing the correct contraction or its homophone.

Remember: Don't confuse contractions with their homophones.

Bumper stickers are a fun way to make someone smile or state an opinion. Write a bumper sticker of your own in the space below. Try to use a contraction that has a homophone.

Spelling and Writing, p. 28

DAY 4 REVIEW MASTER

16 ■ REVIEW

		Word List		
coming	always	almost	didn't	upon
wasn't	until	during	want	father
hamster	a lot	ugly	washed	hotel
missed	eleven	crazy	lazy	feelings

■ Buried Words Each word below is hidden in a list word. Write the list word.

1. eel
2. ham
3. even
4. ways
5. most
6. ant
7. her
8. ash
9. ring
10. on
11. hot

1. **feelings**
2. **hamster**
3. **eleven**
4. **always**
5. **almost**
6. **want**
7. **father**
8. **washed**
9. **during**
10. **upon**
11. **hotel**

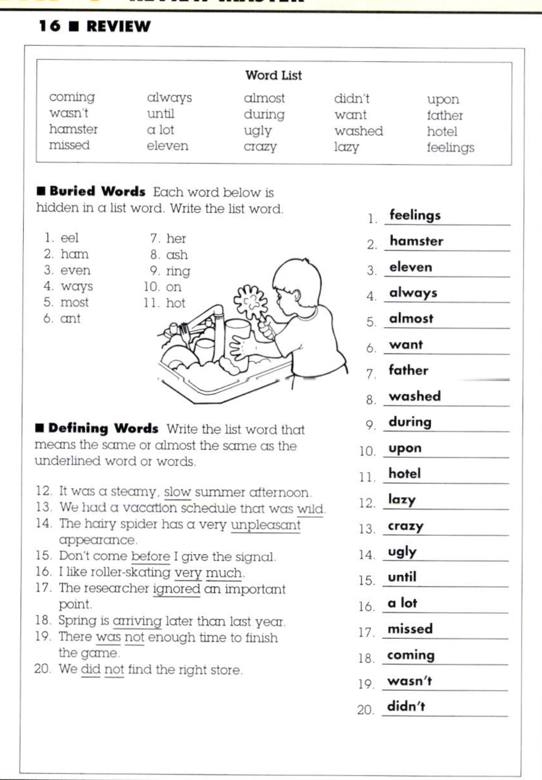

■ Defining Words Write the list word that means the same or almost the same as the underlined word or words.

12. It was a steamy, <u>slow</u> summer afternoon.
13. We had a vacation schedule that was <u>wild</u>.
14. The hairy spider has a very <u>unpleasant</u> appearance.
15. Don't come <u>before</u> I give the signal.
16. I like roller-skating very <u>much</u>.
17. The researcher <u>ignored</u> an important point.
18. Spring is <u>arriving</u> later than last year.
19. There <u>was not</u> enough time to finish the game.
20. We <u>did not</u> find the right store.

12. **lazy**
13. **crazy**
14. **ugly**
15. **until**
16. **a lot**
17. **missed**
18. **coming**
19. **wasn't**
20. **didn't**

Practice Masters, p. 66

DAY 5 STANDARDIZED TEST MASTER

16 ■ LESSON TEST

■ Find the word in each group that is spelled correctly. Fill in the letter for the correct word on the answer strip.

Sample:
- **a.** lione
- **b.** lino
- **c.** linoe
- **d.** lion

1. **a.** carzy **b.** crazzy **c.** crazey **d.** crazy
2. **a.** father **b.** fother **c.** fathere **d.** fater
3. **a.** comeing **b.** comming **c.** coming **d.** cuming
4. **a.** fellings **b.** fealings **c.** feelings **d.** felings
5. **a.** mised **b.** missed **c.** misst **d.** missd
6. **a.** washt **b.** washed **c.** wost **d.** washd
7. **a.** ugly **b.** ugley **c.** ulgy **d.** ugle
8. **a.** apon **b.** opon **c.** upon **d.** apone
9. **a.** intill **b.** untill **c.** intell **d.** until
10. **a.** didn't **b.** didnt **c.** dident **d.** did'nt
11. **a.** lazzy **b.** lazey **c.** lasse **d.** lazy
12. **a.** eleven **b.** elleven **c.** elevalon **d.** elevan
13. **a.** wont **b.** want **c.** whant **d.** wan't
14. **a.** a lot **b.** alot **c.** alote **d.** alott
15. **a.** hotel **b.** holtel **c.** hotell **d.** hotle
16. **a.** allmost **b.** omost **c.** almost **d.** almosd
17. **a.** during **b.** durring **c.** doring **d.** dering
18. **a.** wasnt **b.** wasn't **c.** wasen't **d.** wasent
19. **a.** allways **b.** allway **c.** alway **d.** always
20. **a.** hampster **b.** hamstr **c.** hamster **d.** hammster

Practice for Standardized Tests, p. 22

78D

DAY 1 Introduction

✓ Pretest and Self-Check
● Spelling Focus and Word List
○ Challenge Words
○ Modified List

○ **DAILY SPELLING REVIEW**

Roberto put a *hole* jar of *hony* in the sauce.

whole   *honey*

● Core   ○ Optional   ✓ Assessment

INTRODUCTION

Phonics

One Sound, One Letter
Explain that several list words have middle or final consonant sounds that are often incorrectly spelled with a double letter. Write *always, almost,* and *until* on the board as examples.

MEETING THE NEEDS OF ALL STUDENTS

Modified List

Practice Students studying only the high-frequency words in the top box write
- one word that has one syllable
- nine words that have two syllables

Visual Learners

Syllables Students can learn to visualize the single letters in the list words by looking at their separate syllables. Write *coming, always, almost, upon, until,* and *during* in syllables on the board.

Additional Practice

Challenge Master 16
Home-School Master 16
Audiotape B, Side 1

1. a lot
2. eleven
3. want
4. washed
5. missed
6. coming
7. always
8. almost
9. didn't
10. upon
11. wasn't
12. until
13. during
14. father
15. hamster
16. ugly
17. hotel
18. crazy
19. lazy
20. feelings

CHALLENGE!

delivery
magnet
replied
drowned
mustard

78

■ **INTRODUCTION**

Using Just Enough Letters

SPELLING FOCUS

Pronouncing a word correctly and picturing how it looks can help you avoid writing too many letters.

■ **STUDY** Say each word. Then read the sentence.

1. coming — He is **coming** to my house.
2. always ✻ — Jokes **always** make me laugh.
3. almost — Our team **almost** lost the game.
4. didn't ✻ — You **didn't** wash your hands.
5. upon ✻ — Birds perch **upon** the fence.
6. wasn't — Dinner **wasn't** ready yet.
7. until ✻ — Can you wait **until** later?
8. during — Bears hibernate **during** the winter.
9. want ✻ — Do you **want** this sweater?
10. father — The **father** played with his son.

11. hamster — Her pet is a furry, little **hamster**.
12. a lot ✻ — Our family likes to ski **a lot**.
13. ugly — What an **ugly**, old car!
14. washed — The floor needs to be **washed**.
15. hotel — We stayed at a **hotel** in the city.
16. missed — I think we **missed** the bus.
17. eleven — The carton has only **eleven** eggs.
18. crazy — Stunt people do **crazy** things.
19. lazy — She felt **lazy** all day.
20. feelings — I may have hurt his **feelings**.

■ **PRACTICE** Sort the list words by writing
- the only two-word form
- one word that has three syllables
- three words that have one syllable
- fifteen words that have two syllables

Order of words in each group may vary.

■ **WRITE** Choose two sentences to write a riddle.
Riddles will vary.

✻ **WATCH OUT FOR FREQUENTLY MISSPELLED WORDS!**

- Practice: Classifying and Words in Context
- Strategic Spelling: *Using the Meaning Helpers Strategy*
- Cross-Curricular Lesson: Introduce
- Modified List

DAILY SPELLING REVIEW

The Reeds took a *vaction* in a *remot* place.

vacation   remote

THINK AND PRACTICE

CLASSIFYING   Write the list word that fits in each group.

1. sister, mother, ____
2. ten, ____, twelve
3. inn, resort, ____
4. wish, desire, ____
5. in the course of, at the time, ____
6. foolish, nutty, ____
7. emotions, thoughts, ____
8. careless, not working, ____
9. guinea pig, gerbil, ____

WORDS IN CONTEXT   Write the missing list words to complete the paragraph below.

Once (10) a time, there was a little boy who thought of himself as an (11) duckling, although his grandmother always told him, "You're truly a handsome fellow." She (12) kidding, but the boy (13) believe her. He would frown at himself in a mirror (14) his face would begin to hurt. Other children would ask him to play quite (15), but he would (16) find an excuse to smile and say, "Not today, thanks." One day a little girl invited him to a party. He (17) didn't go, but his grandmother convinced him that the girl would feel hurt if he stayed home. When he finally arrived at the party, his friend rushed to him, saying, "I was worried you weren't (18)! We would have (19) your friendly face!"

1.	**father**
2.	**eleven**
3.	**hotel**
4.	**want**
5.	**during**
6.	**crazy**
7.	**feelings**
8.	**lazy**
9.	**hamster**
10.	**upon**
11.	**ugly**
12.	**wasn't**
13.	**didn't**
14.	**until**
15.	**a lot**
16.	**always**
17.	**almost**
18.	**coming**
19.	**missed**

| wishy-washy |
| washable |
| washcloth |

20. Write a list word that is related to the words in the box. **washed**

Now write words from the box that fit the clues.

21. Use it when you take a bath. **washcloth**

22. If asked an opinion, don't be this. **wishy-washy**

23. Your play clothes should definitely be this. **washable**

FREQUENTLY MISSPELLED WORDS

The two-word form **a lot** is misspelled a lot! Remember, **a lot** is NEVER one word. It is NEVER more than four letters.

THINK AND PRACTICE

Classifying

Things in Common

Remind students to consider what the words in each group have in common. For example, a sister and a mother are both family members. A list word that names another family member is *father*.

MEETING THE NEEDS OF ALL STUDENTS

Modified List

Review Students studying high-frequency words complete Think and Practice Master 16.

Bilingual/ESL

Words with -ing Explain that although many **-ing** words are action words (*coming*), some name things (*feelings*) or begin a phrase (*during* a storm). Have pairs of students write each **-ing** word in a sentence.

Additional Practice

Think and Practice Master 16
Extra Practice Master 16
Everyday Spelling CD-ROM
Everyday Spelling **Game Software**

LESSON 16

- Proofread a Warning
- Proofreading Tip: *It's* and *Its*
- Write a Warning
- ✓ Cooperative Midweek Test

DAILY SPELLING REVIEW

Please put your *bakpack* in the *closit.*

backpack   *closet*

● Core   ○ Optional   ✓ Assessment

PROOFREADING AND WRITING

Spelling

It's and Its To provide practice with *it's* and *its*, use the following sentences and make up others like them: *The dog scratched* (it's, its) *ear.* (It's, Its) *time to go.*

MEETING THE NEEDS OF ALL STUDENTS

Modified List

Proofreading Students studying high-frequency words complete this page or the proofreading activity on the *Everyday Spelling* CD-ROM.

Auditory Learners

Warning Signs To spark ideas for places where a warning sign would be useful, create or play sound effects. Sounds might include a train whistle (railroad crossing) and an ambulance siren (hospital).

Additional Practice

Hardbound Book Master 16
Second Language Master 16
Writing Mini-Lesson Master 16
Writing Activity Master 16
Proofreading Transparency 16
Everyday Spelling **CD-ROM**

■ PROOFREADING AND WRITING

≡	Make a capital.
/	Make a small letter.
∧	Add something.
ℓ	Take out something.
⊙	Add a period.
¶	New paragraph.

PROOFREAD A WARNING One morning the sign below appeared beside the cage of Scratch the Hamster. Correct four misspellings and one place where the punctuation is wrong.

PROOFREADING TIP
Remember that *it's* has an apostrophe because it's short for *it is*. Say *it is* aloud when you write *it's* or *its*. If *it is* doesn't fit, take out the apostrophe.

WRITE A WARNING Think of a warning sign you would like to write. Try to use your list words and your personal words.

Word List

hamster	eleven
a lot	didn't
ugly	upon
washed	crazy
hotel	lazy
always	wasn't
father	almost
missed	want
until	feelings
coming	during

Personal Words

1. **Words will vary.**

2. _______________

Responses will vary. Warning signs should use list words and personal words.

80

VOCABULARY BUILDING

Review

ANTONYMS Complete each phrase by writing the boxed word that means the opposite of the underlined word.

coming	wasn't
always	until
almost	during
didn't	want
upon	father

1. not a <u>mother</u>, but a ___   2. not <u>going</u>, but ___

DRAW YOUR OWN CONCLUSIONS Write the boxed word that matches each clue.

3. before, ___, after
4. This word is used in the following phrase that starts many fairy tales: *Once ___ a time.*
5. This word means the same as *nearly.*
6. was + not = ___
7. ___, sometimes, never
8. This word means the same as *desire.*
9. did + not = ___
10. This word means "up to the time when."

1. **father**
2. **coming**
3. **during**
4. **upon**
5. **almost**
6. **wasn't**
7. **always**
8. **want**
9. **didn't**
10. **until**

Word *Study*

WORD PLAY Janna thinks that the word *ugly* looks just like what it means. "It's an ugly word," she says. "Just look at that open, gaping **u** and the hanging **g** and **y.** It just says 'ugly' to me!" Janna drew the word *ugly* to illustrate her point.

Lee had other ideas. "That's a neat drawing, Janna," he said, "but I don't see it that way. I think there's some beauty to be found in the word *ugly.*" Lee drew the word his way.

Now it's your turn. Find a way to make a word look like what it means. You might want to take Lee's approach and do the opposite. **Words and drawings will vary.**

VOCABULARY BUILDING

Literature Connection

More Word Play *Word Works* by Catherine Berger Kaye (Little, Brown and Company, 1985) contains many types of word play, including word pyramids and illustrated words.

MEETING THE NEEDS OF ALL STUDENTS

Modified List

Review Students studying high-frequency words complete this page.

Enrichment

Antonym Analysis Invite students to work with a partner to choose an antonym pair, such as *loud* and *soft,* and to write each word in a way that suggests what the word means.

Additional Practice

Review Master 16
Standardized Test Master 16
Everyday Spelling **CD-ROM**

81

LESSON
17

Generalization

Spelling Focus: In contractions, words are combined and shortened, and an apostrophe replaces the letters that are left out.

● Core   ○ Optional   ✓ Assessment

DAILY PLAN	CORE OBJECTIVES	NOTES

DAY 1 Introduction

✓ Pretest and Self-Check, p. 82B
● Spelling Focus and Word List, p. 82
○ Challenge Words, p. 82
○ Challenge Master 17
○ Home-School Master 17

✓ Take and self-check Pretest
■ Spell words that are contractions; classify and write the list words

DAY 2 Think and Practice

● Homophones; Creating Contractions; Don't Quote Me, p. 83
● Strategic Spelling: *Building New Words,* p. 83
○ Think and Practice Master 17
○ Extra Practice Master 17
○ Cross-Curricular Lesson: Introduce, p. 224

■ Complete practice activities for contractions
■ Create new words by forming contractions

DAY 3 Proofreading and Writing

● Proofread a Sign, p. 84
● Proofreading Tip: Apostrophes, p. 84
● Write a Sign, p. 84
✓ Cooperative Midweek Test
○ Writing Mini-Lesson Master 17
○ Writing Activity Master 17
○ Second Language Support Master 17

■ Proofread for spelling and punctuation errors
■ Integrate spelling and writing in a personal writing response
✓ Take and check midweek test

DAY 4 Vocabulary Building

● Review: Context Clues, p. 85
● Word Study: Pyramid Sentences, p. 85
○ Cross-Curricular Lesson: Follow-Up, p. 224
○ Review Master 17

■ Complete review activity for contractions
■ Study and write pyramid sentences

DAY 5 Assessment

✓ Posttest, p. 82B
○ Standardized Test Master 17

✓ Take Posttest

Cross-Curricular Lessons

Use the Spelling Focus (contractions) to introduce the Work and Play lesson, *Basketball*, page 224, or choose a lesson that correlates with a topic you're currently teaching.

MEETING THE NEEDS OF ALL STUDENTS

The Word List

For students studying 20 words, assign pages 82–85 and Extra Practice and Review masters.

Modified List For students studying 10 words, modify Practice on page 82, and assign Think and Practice Master 17 and pages 84–85.

Challenge For students studying 25 words, assign pages 82–85, Challenge, Extra Practice, and Review masters.

Bilingual/ESL

Contractions do not exist in Haitian Creole. Therefore, students who speak this language may omit the apostrophes when writing contractions.

Personal Words

Students add to Personal Words lists by looking at work in their writing portfolios and words they want to remember from their reading.

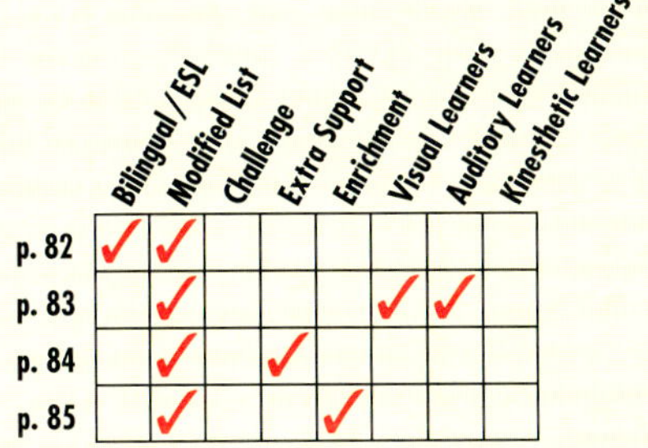

	Bilingual/ESL	Modified List	Challenge	Extra Support	Enrichment	Visual Learners	Auditory Learners	Kinesthetic Learners
p. 82	✓	✓						
p. 83		✓				✓	✓	
p. 84		✓		✓				
p. 85		✓			✓			

ASSESSMENT*

Pretest

Read the underlined word, read the sentence, and then repeat the underlined word. Guide students in self-correcting their pretests and correcting any misspellings.

1. We'll go to the zoo soon.
2. I'm opening the package.
3. I'd like to watch a video.
4. You'd better be careful.
5. I'll study at the library.
6. We've repainted the house.
7. It's a beautiful morning.
8. That's not fair to her.
9. What's your name?
10. Kim doesn't like spiders.
11. He'll be back next week.
12. She'll be tired tomorrow.
13. They'll show us the house.
14. I wish they'd leave.
15. He'd been there before.
16. I would've liked to go.
17. He could've been an actor.
18. The horse wouldn't jump.
19. People shouldn't smoke.
20. Let's go swimming.

Posttest

Read aloud the sentences below. These sentences may be used for dictation.

1. She doesn't like the cold.
2. It's fun to travel.
3. That's a caterpillar.
4. You'd better go now.
5. What's for supper?
6. I'm chasing a butterfly.
7. We've been to a farm.
8. I'll rewrite the story.
9. We'll unpack tomorrow.
10. I'd like to be helpful.
11. She'll keep a secret.
12. You shouldn't carry that.
13. Let's pick a flower.
14. You could've been hurt.
15. They'd like to fly kites.
16. He'll like that movie.
17. That wouldn't surprise me.
18. I would've written before.
19. He'd tried to be careful.
20. They'll be looking for us.

Challenge Words

1. It'll just take a second.
2. Who'll bring the food?
3. He might've tripped.
4. You mustn't talk here.
5. We'd walked too far.

Additional Assessment

Standardized Test Master 17
Dictation Sentences, p. T39
Everyday Spelling CD-ROM

WHAT'S THE BIG IDEA?
Research in Action found that four contractions (it's, that's, let's, I'm) were misspelled 1141 times. The error was a missing apostrophe 1049, or 92%, of those times. Help students see that if letters have been dropped, an apostrophe must show where the letters used to be.

* See pp. T20 and T33 for test-study-test information.

ADDITIONAL RESOURCES (OPTIONAL PRACTICE)

LESSON 17

DAY 1 CHALLENGE MASTER

CHALLENGE ■ 17

Challenge Words

we'd	mustn't	it'll	might've	who'll

■ Use the Challenge Words to complete the following conversations.

1. "**Who'll** help me with my chores?" called my brother.

   "Who will help me with my homework?" I replied.

2. "Do you really think **it'll** rain?" he asked.

   "Yes, Jorge," she answered. "I think it will."

3. "Tommy **mustn't** touch the vase," Mama said.

4. "We had better look for the will," said the lawyer.

   "And **we'd** better find it," growled the banker.

5. "I **might've** finished second, if I were luckier," Amy said.

   "If you had practiced, you might have won," scolded the coach.

■ Conversations can be the most interesting part of a story. Use some of
more Challenge Words in a conversation between two characters.

Practice Masters, p. 67

DAY 1 HOME-SCHOOL MASTER

■ 17 HOME-SCHOOL ACTIVITIES 17 ■

■ **Contractions** Write the list word that contains
each of the words below.

1. you **you'd**
2. she **she'll**
3. let **let's**
4. does **doesn't**
5. what **what's**
6. could **could've**
7. that **that's**
8. it **it's**

■ **Making New Words** Write the
list word that is a contraction of each
pair of words below.

9. I will **I'll**
10. would have **would've**
11. we have **we've**
12. he would **he'd**
13. they will **they'll**
14. I would **I'd**
15. should not **shouldn't**
16. would not **wouldn't**
17. he will **he'll**
18. I am **I'm**
19. we will **we'll**
20. they would **they'd**

Word Check 17

1. I'm
2. I'd
3. you'd
4. they'd
5. he'd
6. I'll
7. he'll
8. she'll
9. we'll
10. they'll
11. it's
12. that's
13. what's
14. let's
15. wouldn't
16. shouldn't
17. doesn't
18. we've
19. would've
20. could've

Dear Parent,

Please check to
see that your
child has done
this page
correctly. Circle
any misspelled
words and help
your child study
them.

Tear off the Word
Check before
your child returns
this page to class.
Use it to help your
child study.

Home-School Activities, p. 15

DAY 2 THINK AND PRACTICE MASTER

17 ■ THINK AND PRACTICE

we'll	I'm	I'd	you'd	I'll
we've	it's	that's	what's	doesn't

■ **Creating Contractions** Write the contractions for each pair of words.

1. I am — **I'm**
2. does not — **doesn't**
3. I would — **I'd**
4. what is — **what's**
5. I will — **I'll**
6. we will — **we'll**

■ **Writing Contractions** Find the words in each sentence that could be
made into a contraction. Write the contractions on the lines.

7. That is a beautiful painting. — **that's**
8. I think you would like my friends. — **you'd**
9. What is in that big box? — **What's**
10. I would like to try to play a guitar. — **I'd**
11. If it is raining, call for a ride. — **it's**
12. We have just bought a new car. — **We've**
13. I am a shy person. — **I'm**

STRATEGIC SPELLING: Building New Words
Add the contraction for _will_ to the base words. Remember
what you learned.

Base Word	Contraction with -'ll
14. you	**you'll**
15. who	**who'll**

Practice Masters, p. 68

DAY 2 EXTRA PRACTICE MASTER

EXTRA PRACTICE ■ 17

Word List

we'll	I'm	I'd	you'd	I'll
we've	it's	that's	what's	doesn't
he'll	she'll	they'll	they'd	he'd
would've	could've	wouldn't	shouldn't	let's

■ **Turn It Around** Use a list word contraction to answer each question.
HINT: Look at the underlined words in each sentence.

1. Would they like the movie? I'm sure ___ love it!
2. Could you have jumped that high? I think I ___.
3. Will she be ready for the test? Oh, yes, I think ___ pass.
4. Would you ever climb Mt. Everest? Knowing you, ___ do it.
5. Will they ever get off of the phone? No, ___ talk forever!
6. Is that what you bought at the store? Yes, ___ it!
7. Will I ever get up on time? No, ___ always be late.
8. Is it time for the show? Yes, ___ almost 8:00.
9. Will he win the election? No, ___ lose.
10. Have we met before? No, ___ never been introduced.
11. Am I in good enough shape to run this race? Well, ___ faster than I was last time.
12. Would he come to visit? Yes, ___ be happy to come.
13. Would you like to help me clean, or not? Frankly, I ___.
14. Does this bus go to T Road, or not? Sorry, it ___.

■ **Words in Context** Write one of the remaining
list words to complete each sentence.

15. You ___ swim just after eating.
16. Hurry, or ___ be late for the movie.
17. ___ the name of that book?
18. I ___ liked to meet the mayor.
19. She likes to bicycle but ___ like to roller skate.
20. ___ get together to study tonight.

1. **they'd**
2. **could've**
3. **she'll**
4. **you'd**
5. **they'll**
6. **that's**
7. **I'll**
8. **it's**
9. **he'll**
10. **we've**
11. **I'm**
12. **he'd**
13. **wouldn't**
14. **doesn't**
15. **shouldn't**
16. **we'll**
17. **What's**
18. **would've**
19. **I'd**
20. **Let's**

Practice Masters, p. 69

<table>
<tr><td>TECHNOLOGY AND VISUAL SUPPORT</td><td> Use Audiotape B, Side 1, Lesson 17
 Use Proofreading and Writing Transparency 17</td><td> For additional practice use Everyday Spelling Game Software, Lesson 17</td><td> Additional resources on Everyday Spelling CD-ROM: proofreading and writing, modified list and challenge words, auditory test</td></tr>
</table>

DAY 3 — SECOND LANGUAGE SUPPORT MASTER

SECOND LANGUAGE SUPPORT ■ 17

Words Around You

Think about where you have seen the words you learned in Lesson 17.

Write some of the words in the chart. Then write about the words. One word has been done for you.

A word I saw	Where or when I saw it	How the word was used
it's	newspaper headline	Brrr, it's cold outside!
Answers will vary.		

Second Language Support, p. 41

DAY 3 — WRITING ACTIVITY MASTER

17 ■ WRITING ACTIVITY

End Punctuation

Make a capital.
Make a small letter.
Add something.
Take out something.
Add a period.

☐ Use a **period** (.) to end a sentence that makes a statement or gives a command

☐ Use a **question mark** (?) to end a sentence that asks a question

☐ Use an **exclamation mark** (!) to end a sentence that shows strong feeling

■ Anita's class made posters of famous Americans. Read her poster. Fix any errors in end punctuation.

Remember: Use end punctuation correctly.

The FBI prints posters too—of the most wanted criminals. Write your own wanted poster using a pet or family member as the subject.

Spelling and Writing, p. 30

DAY 4 — REVIEW MASTER

17 ■ REVIEW

Word List

we'll	I'm	I'd	you'd	I'll
we've	it's	that's	what's	doesn't
he'll	she'll	they'll	they'd	he'd
would've	could've	wouldn't	shouldn't	let's

■ **Words in Context** Write the list word that is missing from each animal's statement.

1. Cheetah: "Hunters will chase me, but ___ never catch me!"
2. Elephant: "We may seem slow to you, but ___ be surprised how fast we are."
3. Monkey: "If we all get together, ___ have a barrel of fun!"
4. Dolphin: "Since everyone is here, ___ take a swim!"
5. Mouse: "You see, ___ little things that count."
6. Hyena: "___ laughing my head off!"
7. Blue whale: "My species is heavy, but ___ 200 tons between friends?"
8. Skunk: "I ___ be rude if I were you!"
9. Owl: "It ___ take much light for me to see."
10. Rabbit: "Today I will look for the carrots, and ___ buy two bunches."

1. they'll
2. you'd
3. we'll
4. let's
5. it's
6. I'm
7. what's
8. wouldn't
9. doesn't
10. I'll

■ **Contractions** Write the contractions for the underlined phrases below.

11. I <u>would</u> rather eat an early dinner.
12. Back home, <u>they would</u> be surprised that I became a teacher.
13. If Jerry sells his bike, <u>he will</u> regret it.
14. Unfortunately, <u>that is</u> my only clean outfit.
15. <u>We have</u> always had a Labor Day picnic.
16. It <u>should not</u> take long to do the dishes.
17–18. John and Mary agreed that <u>he would</u> wash the car and <u>she will</u> wax it.
19–20. I <u>would have</u> done so if I <u>could have</u>.

11. I'd
12. they'd
13. he'll
14. that's
15. We've
16. shouldn't
17. he'd
18. she'll
19. would've
20. could've

Practice Masters, p. 70

DAY 5 — STANDARDIZED TEST MASTER

LESSON TEST ■ 17

■ Find the word in each group that is spelled correctly. Fill in the letter for the correct word on the answer strip.

Sample:
a. lione   c. linoe
b. lino   d. lion — **d**

1. a. weve   c. we've   b. we'v   d. wev'e — **c**
2. a. we'll   c. wel'l   b. whill   d. wei'll — **a**
3. a. wouldn't c. would'nt b. wouldent d. wouldnt — **a**
4. a. I'ed   c. i'd   b. I'd   d. I'de — **b**
5. a. les   c. let's   b. le'ts   d. lets' — **c**
6. a. hed   c. hed'   b. hee'd   d. he'd — **d**
7. a. he'll   c. hel   b. he'l   d. hee'l — **a**
8. a. yo'd   c. youd   b. you'd   d. you'dd — **b**
9. a. cood've c. could'ev b. couldv'e d. could've — **d**
10. a. i'll   c. I'le   b. I'll   d. I'l — **b**
11. a. Im   c. I'am   b. I'm   d. i'm — **b**
12. a. what's c. wats   b. whats   d. waht's — **a**
13. a. dosen't c. doesn't b. dosn't d. doesnt — **c**
14. a. it's   c. it'se   b. i'ts   d. its'e — **a**
15. a. that's c. thats' b. thats d. thas — **a**
16. a. she'l c. she'll b. shee'll d. sh'll — **c**
17. a. the'll c. they'll b. theill d. they'l — **c**
18. a. shouldnt c. shoulden't b. shouldn't d. should't — **b**
19. a. would've c. would'ev b. wood've d. would'v — **a**
20. a. they'd c. theyd   b. theyed d. they'de — **a**

Practice for Standardized Tests, p. 23

LESSON 17

INTRODUCTION

Word Structure

Contractions Have students write list words 1–10 and underline the word that comes before the apostrophe. Then help them to identify the letters the apostrophe replaces.

MEETING THE NEEDS OF ALL STUDENTS

Modified List

Practice Students studying only the high-frequency words in the top box write
- two words ending in -'ll
- two words ending in -'d
- four words ending in either -'t or -'s
- two words with other contraction endings

Bilingual/ESL

Contraction Match Have pairs of students make two sets of word cards, one for each contraction and one for the two words that make up the contraction. Partners lay the cards face-down and turn over two at a time to find the matches.

Additional Practice

Challenge Master 17
Home-School Master 17
Audiotape B, Side 1

1.	**we'll**
2.	**I'll**
3.	**he'll**
4.	**she'll**
5.	**they'll**
6.	**I'm**
7.	**we've**
8.	**would've**
9.	**could've**
10.	**I'd**
11.	**you'd**
12.	**they'd**
13.	**he'd**
14.	**it's**
15.	**that's**
16.	**what's**
17.	**doesn't**
18.	**wouldn't**
19.	**shouldn't**
20.	**let's**

Order of words in each group may vary.

CHALLENGE!

it'll
who'll
might've
mustn't
we'd

Sentences will vary.

■ INTRODUCTION

Contractions

SPELLING FOCUS

In contractions, an apostrophe replaces omitted letters. **We will** becomes **we'll**; **I am** becomes **I'm**.

■ **STUDY** A **contraction** is a shortened form of two words. Say each pair of words and then say its contraction.

we + will	=	1. *we'll*
I + am	=	2. *I'm* ✳
I + would	=	3. *I'd*
you + would	=	4. *you'd*
I + will	=	5. *I'll*
we + have	=	6. *we've*
it + is	=	7. *it's* ✳
that + is	=	8. *that's* ✳
what + is	=	9. *what's*
does + not	=	10. *doesn't*

he + will	=	11. *he'll*
she + will	=	12. *she'll*
they + will	=	13. *they'll*
they + would	=	14. *they'd*
he + would	=	15. *he'd*
would + have	=	16. *would've*
could + have	=	17. *could've*
would + not	=	18. *wouldn't*
should + not	=	19. *shouldn't*
let + us	=	20. *let's* ✳

■ **PRACTICE** Sort the list words by writing
- five words ending in -'ll
- four words ending in either -'ve or -'m
- four words ending in -'d
- seven words ending either in -'t or -'s

■ **WRITE** Choose ten words to write in sentences.

✳ **WATCH OUT FOR FREQUENTLY MISSPELLED WORDS!**

THINK AND PRACTICE

HOMOPHONES   Write the contraction that sounds just like each word below.

1. heed
2. weave
3. aisle
4. eyed
5. heel
6. lets

CREATING CONTRACTIONS   Write the contractions for the words below.

7. they will
8. we will
9. what is
10. they would
11. that is
12. could have
13. would have
14. she will

DON'T QUOTE ME   Write list words to help the famous people below complete sentences they might have said.

15. Nathan Hale: "____ sorry I have but one life to give."
16. Rosa Parks: "Would I give up my seat on the bus? I ____!"
17. Mohandas Gandhi: "One should resist oppression, but one ____ use violence to do so."
18. Pablo Picasso: "Painting isn't beautiful, ____ magical."
19. Confucius: "Do to others what ____ want done to you."
20. Amelia Earhart: "Peace comes with courage. It ____ come easily."

1. **he'd**
2. **we've**
3. **I'll**
4. **I'd**
5. **he'll**
6. **let's**
7. **they'll**
8. **we'll**
9. **what's**
10. **they'd**
11. **that's**
12. **could've**
13. **would've**
14. **she'll**
15. **I'm**
16. **wouldn't**
17. **shouldn't**
18. **it's**
19. **you'd**
20. **doesn't**

Add the contraction for *will* to the base words. Remember what you learned.

Base word	Contraction with '11
21. you	**you'll**
22. who	**who'll**

> **Did You Know?**
> *I* is a capital because in old handwritten manuscripts, a small *i* would often be lost or attached to a neighboring word. A capital *I* helped separate it.

THINK AND PRACTICE

Homophones

Word Study Have students read the words aloud slowly before deciding which are homophones.

MEETING THE NEEDS OF ALL STUDENTS

Modified List

Review Students studying high-frequency words complete Think and Practice Master 17.

Visual Learners

Creating Contractions

Some students may find it easier to remember where to place the apostrophe if they write out the two words and draw a delete mark through the letter or letters being dropped.

Auditory Learners

Don't Quote Me Ask students to read each quote aloud with appropriate expression to help identify the missing words.

> **Additional Practice**
>
> **Think and Practice Master 17**
> **Extra Practice Master 17**
> *Everyday Spelling* **CD-ROM**
> *Everyday Spelling* **Game Software**

LESSON 17

- Proofread a Sign
- Proofreading Tip: Apostrophes
- Write a Sign
- ✓ Cooperative Midweek Test

○ **DAILY SPELLING REVIEW**

The robber will *still* the *mony*.
steal   *money*

● Core   ○ Optional   ✓ Assessment

PROOFREADING AND WRITING

Punctuation

Punctuating Sentences

Have students add the missing end punctuation and apostrophes in the following sentences:
- *Doesnt Carla have a cat*
- *The car wouldve started if it had gas in it*

MEETING THE NEEDS OF ALL STUDENTS

Modified List

Proofreading Students studying high-frequency words complete this page or the proofreading activity on the *Everyday Spelling* CD-ROM.

Extra Support

Proofreading Signs Have students work in pairs to proofread each other's signs. Remind them to check for words that need apostrophes.

Additional Practice

Second Language Master 17
Writing Mini-Lesson Master 17
Writing Activity Master 17
Proofreading Transparency 17
Everyday Spelling **CD-ROM**

■ PROOFREADING AND WRITING

═ Make a capital.
╱ Make a small letter.
∧ Add something.
℮ Take out something
⊙ Add a period.
╫ New paragraph

PROOFREAD A SIGN The photograph below contains a misspelled word. Since a question is being asked, the punctuation is also incorrect. Write the word correctly as well as the punctuation mark.

PROOFREADING TIP
When making a sign, it's easy to make a mistake in a word. Be sure you carefully proofread your sign before others see it.

wouldn't   ?

WRITE A SIGN Isn't there a question you'd like to ask in a big way? Use a few list words to create your message.

Responses will vary. Sign should include list words.

Word List

I'm	it's
I'd	that's
you'd	what's
they'd	let's
he'd	wouldn't
I'll	shouldn't
he'll	doesn't
she'll	we've
we'll	would've
they'll	could've

Personal Words

1. **Words will vary.**

2. ___________

84

VOCABULARY BUILDING ■

Review

CONTEXT CLUES   Write the missing boxed words to complete the paragraph below.

(1) convinced that my dog Rusty is the world's naughtiest dog! That (2) mean I don't love him. After all, (3) been great pals ever since he was a pup, and (4) always be the best of friends. But (5) rather he didn't get into so much mischief! (6) never forget the time he saw the kid across the street with a big ice cream cone. There isn't any treat that Rusty loves more than ice cream, (7) for sure! Well, he ran lickety-split toward that kid, jumped all over him and started licking his cone. Then there was the time that Rusty jumped into the bathtub when Dad was giving my younger brother Joel a bath. I bet (8) have laughed like I did though if you saw how Dad couldn't get ahold of Rusty. What a mess! You never know (9) going to happen next with Rusty around, but you can bet (10) going to be BIG TROUBLE!

we'll	we've
I'm	it's
I'd	that's
you'd	what's
I'll	doesn't

1. **I'm**
2. **doesn't**
3. **we've**
4. **we'll**
5. **I'd**
6. **I'll**
7. **that's**
8. **you'd**
9. **what's**
10. **it's**

Word *Study*

PYRAMID SENTENCES   **Pyramid sentences** start with one word, the subject, and get longer and longer. Each word that is added must begin with the same letter. Arranged one atop the other, the sentences look like a pyramid. Here's an example:

Subject word: *she'll*

> She'll sing.
> She'll sing songs.
> She'll sing six songs.
> Shelly says she'll sing six silly songs.

Now you try writing your own pyramid sentences. Begin with one of these words: *They'll, I'm, It's, He'd,* or *We'll.*

Sentences will vary.

LESSON

18

Unit Review Concepts
Related Words
Consonant Sounds /j/, /ks/, /kw/
Endings -s and -es
Using Just Enough Letters
Contractions

● Core ○ Optional ✓ Assessment

DAILY PLAN	CORE OBJECTIVES	NOTES

DAY 1
Review Activity:
●   RX for Good Health, p. 86
✓ Self-Assessment:
  How Am I Doing?, p. 86
Integrating Spelling:
○   Health, p. 86
○ Review Master 18A

- Use review words to complete rules for good health
✓ - Assess their own progress in the spelling of words in Unit 3

DAY 2
Review Activities:
●   Daily Record, p. 87
●   Good Sports, p. 87
Integrating Spelling:
○   Language Arts, p. 87
○   Physical Education, p. 87

- Use review words to complete a daily record
- Use review words to complete athletes' statements

DAY 3
Review Activities:
●   Off the Shelf, p. 88
●   Interview, p. 88
Integrating Spelling:
○   Language Arts, p. 88
○   Music, p. 88
○ Review Master 18B

- Use review words to complete advertising blurbs
- Use review words to complete an interview

DAY 4
Review Activities:
●   Visiting the Lone Star State, p. 89
●   School Fund-Raiser, p. 89
Integrating Spelling:
○   Social Studies, p. 89
○   Art, p. 89
○ Standardized Test Masters 18A–18D

- Use review words to complete a speech
- Use review words to complete posters

DAY 5
✓ Unit Review Test
✓ Writing Test
○ Writing Prompt Transparency 3
○ Writing Model Transparencies
  3A, 3B

✓ - Assess review words
✓ - Assess expository writing

MEETING THE NEEDS OF ALL STUDENTS

Modified List

For students studying only the high-frequency words in each lesson, assign Review Masters18A–18B for unit review. Use the Modified Dictation Sentences for assessment.

Bilingual/ESL

For picturable review words, second-language learners might draw their own pictures to help them remember the meanings of those words.

Spelling Conferences

Conduct individual spelling conferences to discuss each student's spelling progress during Unit 3. You might want to take this opportunity to remind students to add to their personal dictionaries.

ASSESSMENT

Dictation Sentences

1. Drink a quart of liquid when it is hot outside.
2. Our cat is quick but lazy.
3. Texas has many excellent beaches.
4. His visitor was a relative from Kansas.
5. I'll get washed and change my clothes.
6. Do you want some fudge?
7. We'll eat every crumb of the bread.
8. This quilt is nice and soft.
9. He will always wear glasses.
10. They went into the village for extra food.
11. Eleven friends came over to my house.
12. My father is in good health.
13. I'm so excited about the trip.
14. He's in charge of the fair.
15. Do you have happy memories of that vacation?
16. She missed a lot at school while she was away.
17. He didn't have the ability to break the record.
18. The little wagon is a meter long.
19. It's a beautiful composition to listen to.
20. I shouldn't sit on the edge of the table.
21. They picked bunches of flowers for their mother.
22. This can help a burn heal.
23. Let's compose a funny story.
24. I want to relax and enjoy the holidays.
25. She can't explain her feelings about that picture.
26. He doesn't know the signal for that throw.
27. She will be able to give classes this summer.

Writing Test

Writing Prompt Transparency 3 and Writing Model Transparencies 3A and 3B will help students prepare for holistic writing tests. Helpful information relating to expository writing tests is provided in the Writer's Handbook on page 237.

Everyday Spelling CD-ROM

An auditory test is available as an alternate testing format.

Modified Dictation Sentences

1. I meant to stop in Texas.
2. I always soften the dirt first.
3. I have the ability to pay my taxes.
4. He doesn't want to deal the math cards.
5. Once upon a time we were enemies.
6. Where does he sit during his morning classes?
7. We've been friends for a year.
8. We'll be coming soon.
9. I'm not sure what's there.
10. She made a quick change to her homework.
11. There is a sign at the edge of the street.
12. I'm excited about my new school supplies.

LESSON 18

DAY 1 REVIEW MASTER A

REVIEW ■ 18A

Lesson 13

| sign | soften | meant | deal | ability |

■ **Context** Write the list word that completes each sentence.

1. Lotion will **soften** your skin.
2. **Deal** four cards to each player.
3. A stop **sign** has eight sides.
4. Luis has the **ability** to become a great soccer player.
5. Ann **meant** to be on time, but the bus was late.

Lesson 14

| change | edge | excited | Texas | quick |

■ **Riddles** Write a list word that answers each riddle.

1. Which word has a /ks/ sound and names a large state? **Texas**
2. Which word has a /j/ sound and means "to become different"? **change**
3. Which word has a /kw/ sound and means "fast"? **quick**
4. Which word has a /ks/ sound and names a feeling? **excited**
5. Which word has a /j/ sound and is a synonym for *rim*? **edge**

Lesson 15

| supplies | enemies | classes | friends | taxes |

■ **Word Forms** Write the list word that is the plural of each word.

1. friend **friends**
2. class **classes**
3. supply **supplies**
4. tax **taxes**
5. enemy **enemies**

Practice Masters, p. 71

DAY 3 REVIEW MASTER B

18B ■ REVIEW

Lesson 16

| always | coming | upon | want | during |

■ **Making Inferences** Write the list word that completes each phrase.

1. not going or staying but **coming**
2. not before or after but **during**
3. not sometimes or never but **always**
4. not under or beside but **upon**
5. not need or have but **want**

Lesson 17

| we'll | I'm | we've | what's | doesn't |

■ **Contractions** Write the contraction that contains each word.

1. is **what's**
2. am **I'm**
3. will **we'll**
4. not **doesn't**
5. have **we've**

Practice Masters, p. 72

DAY 4 STANDARDIZED TEST MASTER A

18A ■ REVIEW TEST

■ Find the word that is spelled correctly to complete each group of words. Fill in the letter for the correct word on the answer strip.

Sample:
my favorite _______
a. trete b. treet c. treat d. tret — c

1. enjoy music _______
a. allots b. a lot c. allot d. alot — c

2. the cut will _______
a. heel b. heil c. heal d. heele — c

3. six _______ at lunch
a. class'es b. classes c. class's d. classes' — b

4. the beautiful _______
a. flowers b. flowrs c. fowers d. flawrs — a

5. he _______ class
a. mised b. mist c. misted d. missed — d

6. _______ the dishes
a. wost b. washt c. washed d. warshed — c

7. she _______ see
a. didn't b. dident c. dint d. didnt — a

8. _______ have done it
a. all ways b. alwas c. allways d. always — d

9. making a _______
a. quit b. quilt c. quillet d. qwilt — b

10. moved to _______
a. Texes b. texas c. Texas d. Texses — c

11. a little bit _______
a. extra b. exter c. exdra d. exitra — a

12. a _______ in the country
a. village b. villiage c. villege d. villige — a

Practice for Standardized Tests, p. 24

DAY 4 STANDARDIZED TEST MASTER B

REVIEW TEST ■ 18B

■ Find the word that is spelled correctly to complete each group of words. Fill in the letter for the correct word on the answer strip.

13. to _______ a song
a. compoze b. compoz c. cumpoze d. compose — d

14. must _______ the baby
a. chage b. chansce c. change d. chang — c

15. you _______ have gone
a. shouldnt b. shouldn't c. shoulden't d. shount — b

16. one _______ long
a. mitre b. metre c. meter d. meeter — c

17. a _______ of the cake
a. crumb b. crumm c. crum d. crume — a

18. a _______ in the air
a. signol b. singnal c. signil d. signal — d

19. my _______ and mother
a. fother b. father c. farther d. fatter — b

20. cannot _______ the problem
a. explain b. explane c. explan d. esplane — a

21. now _______ a big job
a. its b. it's c. it's d. its' — b

22. showed her _______
a. fealings b. feelings c. fellings d. felings — b

23. sandy _______ along the ocean
a. beeches b. beachs c. beatchs d. beaches — d

24. a _______ of milk
a. cort b. quort c. quart d. quorte — c

Practice for Standardized Tests, p. 25

DAY 4 STANDARDIZED TEST MASTER C

18C ■ REVIEW TEST

■ Find the word that is spelled correctly to complete each sentence. Fill in the letter for the correct word on the answer strip.

25. She was _______ to do the work easily. 25. (a) ● (c) (d)
   a. abol   **b.** able   **c.** abel   **d.** abell

26. Do you _______ more carrots? 26. (a) (b) (c) ●
   a. whant   **b.** wont   **c.** what   **d.** want

27. _______ all get on the bus. 27. ● (b) (c) (d)
   a. Let's   **b.** Les   **c.** Lets   **d.** Lest

28. She sat on the _______ of the bed. 28. (a) ● (c) (d)
   a. eje   **b.** edge   **c.** eage   **d.** ege

29. We all were _______ when our team won. 29. (a) (b) ● (d)
   a. exsited   **b.** exited   **c.** excited   **d.** excided

30. We need to work on a _______ project. 30. ● (b) (c) (d)
   a. health   **b.** halth   **c.** heath   **d.** helth

31. Who is in _______ of your work? 31. (a) (b) (c) ●
   a. charnge   **b.** carger   **c.** charje   **d.** charge

32. Soon _______ be going to the show. 32. (a) (b) ● (d)
   a. well   **b.** will   **c.** we'll   **d.** whill

33. At cold temperatures, water is no longer a _______. 33. (a) (b) (c) ●
   a. liqid   **b.** licquid   **c.** likuid   **d.** liquid

34. His eyes are weak and he must wear _______. 34. (a) ● (c) (d)
   a. glass'es   **b.** glasses   **c.** glases   **d.** glass's

35. Dad makes the best _______! 35. ● (b) (c) (d)
   a. fudge   **b.** fujje   **c.** fudje   **d.** fudj

36. He _______ go to hockey games. 36. (a) (b) ● (d)
   a. dosen't   **b.** dosn't   **c.** doesn't   **d.** doesnt

Practice for Standardized Tests, p. 26

DAY 4 STANDARDIZED TEST MASTER D

REVIEW TEST ■ 18D

■ Find the word in each group that is spelled correctly. Fill in the letter for the correct word on the answer strip.

37. **a.** memerys   **c.** meomories   37. (a) ● (c) (d)
   b. memories   **d.** memeries

38. **a.** excellent   **c.** exalent   38. ● (b) (c) (d)
   b. exellent   **d.** excelent

39. **a.** abilty   **c.** abelity   39. (a) (b) (c) ●
   b. abilaty   **d.** ability

40. **a.** relative   **c.** releteve   40. ● (b) (c) (d)
   b. reletive   **d.** relitive

41. **a.** solf   **c.** saft   41. (a) ● (c) (d)
   b. soft   **d.** sof

42. **a.** elleven   **c.** a liven   42. (a) (b) (c) ●
   b. elavaion   **d.** eleven

43. **a.** buches   **c.** bunches   43. (a) (b) (c) ●
   b. bunchs   **d.** buntches

44. **a.** relacks   **c.** relax   44. (a) (b) (c) ●
   b. relaxe   **d.** ralax

45. **a.** composition   **c.** compisition   45. ● (b) (c) (d)
   b. compotision   **d.** compsition

46. **a.** lazey   **c.** lazzy   46. (a) (b) (c) ●
   b. lassey   **d.** lazy

47. **a.** I'am   **c.** i'm   47. (a) ● (c) (d)
   b. I'm   **d.** Im

48. **a.** quick   **c.** quik   48. ● (b) (c) (d)
   b. qwick   **d.** cwick

49. **a.** frends   **c.** friends   49. (a) (b) ● (d)
   b. freinds   **d.** frinds

50. **a.** hollidays   **c.** holadays   50. (a) (b) (c) ●
   b. hoildays   **d.** holidays

Practice for Standardized Tests, p. 27

DAY 5 WRITING PROMPT TRANSPARENCY

Spelling and Writing, Transparency 3

LESSON 18

SELF-ASSESSMENT

How Am I Doing?

Talk with students about why it is helpful to think about their progress in spelling. Raise issues such as

1. The word I am proudest about learning to spell is ___.
2. I learned to spell a hard word by ___.
3. When I just can't figure out the spelling, I ___.
4. A word that is hard for me to spell is ___.
5. I try to use spelling words in my writing.

INTEGRATING SPELLING

Health

Good Health Rules Have small groups of students write four additional rules for good health. After the groups present their rules to the class, have the class choose the most useful rules and use them to make a health poster.

Additional Resources
Review Master 18A

Review

Lesson 13: Related Words
Lesson 14: Consonant Sounds /j/, /ks/, /kw/
Lesson 15: Adding -s and -es
Lesson 16: Using Just Enough Letters
Lesson 17: Contractions

REVIEW WORD LIST

1. ability	11. soft	21. quart	31. friends	41. missed
2. able	12. change	22. quick	32. glasses	42. want
3. compose	13. charge	23. quilt	33. holidays	43. washed
4. composition	14. edge	24. relax	34. memories	44. didn't
5. crumb	15. excellent	25. Texas	35. a lot	45. doesn't
6. heal	16. excited	26. village	36. always	46. I'm
7. health	17. explain	27. beaches	37. eleven	47. it's
8. meter	18. extra	28. bunches	38. father	48. let's
9. relative	19. fudge	29. classes	39. feelings	49. shouldn't
10. signal	20. liquid	30. flowers	40. lazy	50. we'll

R℞ for Good Health

excellent   lazy   we'll   heal   charge   health

The students in health class put together the rules below. Supply the missing words and see how the rules apply to you.

Take (1) of your own life. Eat sensibly! Exercise!

To maintain good (2), always get plenty of rest.

Don't be (3)! Get out and do things!

Exercise is an (4) way to reduce stress.

If a sore doesn't (5), see your doctor.

If we follow these simple rules, (6) all stay healthy.

1. **charge**
2. **health**
3. **lazy**
4. **excellent**
5. **heal**
6. **we'll**

- Review Activities
- Integrating Spelling: Language Arts
- Integrating Spelling: Physical Education

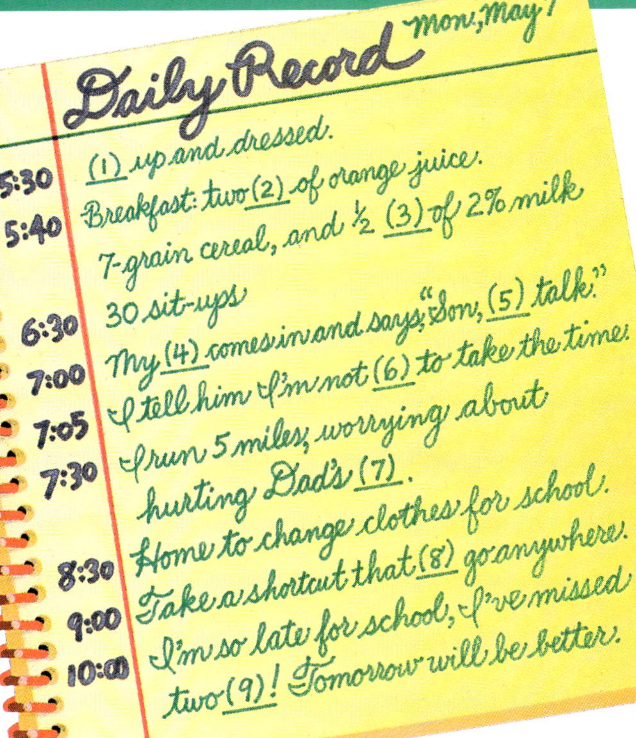

Daily Record Mon., May 7

5:30 (1) up and dressed.
5:40 Breakfast: two (2) of orange juice,
      7-grain cereal, and ½ (3) of 2% milk
6:30 30 sit-ups
7:00 My (4) comes in and says, "Son, (5) talk."
7:05 I tell him I'm not (6) to take the time.
7:30 I run 5 miles, worrying about
      hurting Dad's (7).
8:30 Home to change clothes for school.
9:00 Take a shortcut that (8) go anywhere.
10:00 I'm so late for school, I've missed
      two (9)! Tomorrow will be better.

N'Jabi decided to keep a record of his daily routine. Complete the entry for Monday, May 7.

quart	glasses	father
able	feelings	classes
I'm	doesn't	let's

1. **I'm**
2. **glasses**
3. **quart**
4. **father**
5. **let's**
6. **able**
7. **feelings**
8. **doesn't**
9. **classes**

GOOD SPORTS

Use the words below to complete each person's statement.

1. **missed**
2. **beaches**
3. **signal**
4. **always**

signal
missed
beaches
always

Language Arts

Daily Record Have students write a daily record of a real or an imaginary day. Remind them to write the day and date at the top of the page and to use correct punctuation when writing times.

Physical Education

Research Divide students into groups based on their sport of choice. Have them research the origin of the sport, equipment used, and number of players needed.

87

INTEGRATING SPELLING

Language Arts
Advertising Jingle Have students work in small groups to make up a product, such as a new video game or piece of athletic equipment, and write an advertising jingle for it.

Music
Research Have students work with a partner. The partners can choose a classical composer or rock musician they would like to interview and write questions they would ask.

Additional Resources
Review Master 18B

Off the Shelf

a lot   extra   change
quick   shouldn't   want

The items below are missing words.
Complete each item with a list word.

1. **quick**
2. **change**
3. **a lot**
4. **want**

5. **extra**
6. **shouldn't**

Interview

Karli loves music and wondered what it would be like to discuss it with a famous composer. She wrote this imaginary interview with J. S. Bach.

KARLI: Mr. Bach, can you ___explain___ why you became a composer?

J. S.: Yes. I ___didn't___ want to do anything in my life but ___compose___ music.

KARLI: Did you have musical ___ability___ at a young age?

J. S.: I believe so. I wrote my first ___composition___ as a young man.

didn't
meter
ability
compose
excited
it's
explain
soft
composition

KARLI: What was it about music that ___excited___ you?

J. S.: Everything! The notes, the ___meter___, the harmonies!

KARLI: You write music that is loud and triumphant or ___soft___ and romantic. Which do you prefer?

J. S.: I think ___it's___ all a challenge. Music is my life.

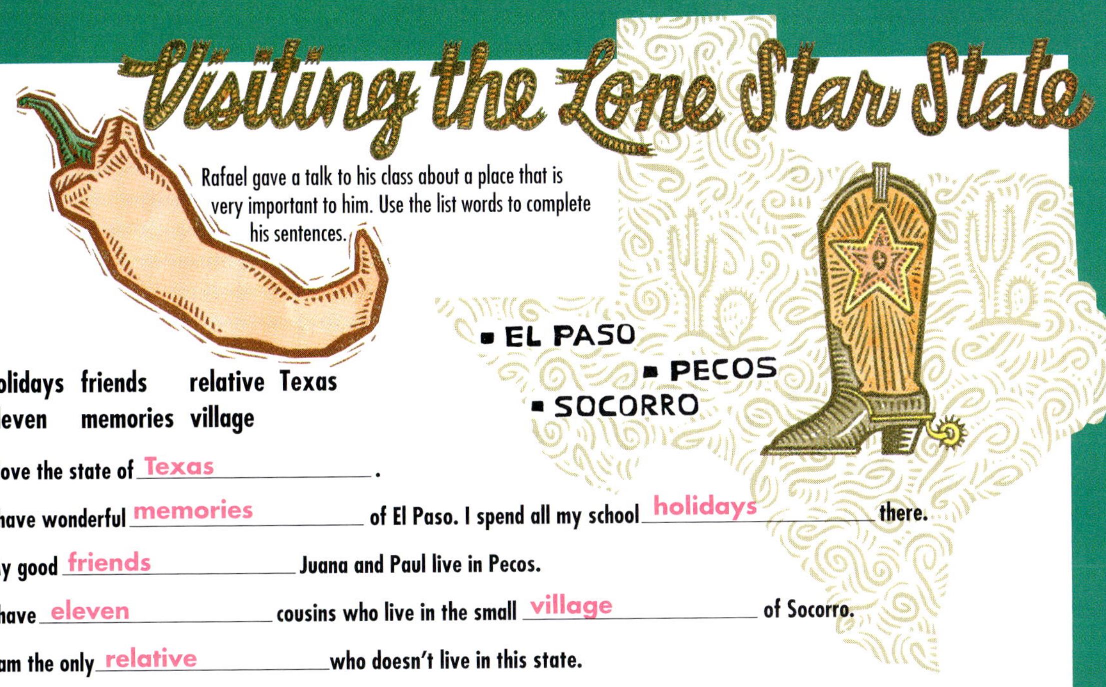

Rafael gave a talk to his class about a place that is very important to him. Use the list words to complete his sentences.

holidays   friends   relative   Texas
eleven   memories   village

I love the state of **Texas**.

I have wonderful **memories** of El Paso. I spend all my school **holidays** there.

My good **friends** Juana and Paul live in Pecos.

I have **eleven** cousins who live in the small **village** of Socorro.

I am the only **relative** who doesn't live in this state.

School Fund-Raiser

Martin Luther King, Jr. School is having its annual fund-raiser. Use the list words to finish the posters.

fudge   washed   liquid
quilt   bunches   edge
flowers   crumb   relax

1. **quilt**
2. **edge**
3. **fudge**
4. **crumb**
5. **flowers**
6. **bunches**
7. **washed**
8. **relax**
9. **liquid**

Social Studies

Map Talk Have students think of a city, state, or country that is important to them and draw a simple map of that place. They can then write a paragraph explaining why the place is meaningful to them and read the paragraph aloud to the class.

Art

Posters Have students make a poster for a family, school, or community event. Encourage them to use vivid words and art work to capture attention.

Additional Resources

Standardized Test Masters 18A–18D
Writing Prompt Transparency 3
Writing Model Transparencies 3A, 3B
Everyday Spelling CD-ROM

STRATEGY WORKSHOP

Introduces the metacognitive strategy **Memory Tricks** to create mnemonics for difficult words: 1. Mark the problem part, 2. Find words with the same letters, 3. Use the problem word and the word you know in a sentence.

SCOPE AND SEQUENCE: LESSONS 19–24

Lesson	Generalization	Think and Practice	Proofreading and Writing
19 pp. 92–95	Some words contain letter combinations that are hard to keep in order.	Equations Homophones Strategic Spelling: Using the Memory Tricks Strategy	Proofread a Description ■ misspelled words ■ careless errors Write a Description
20 pp. 96–99	The vowel sound /ôr/ can be spelled **our** or **or**. The vowel sound /ėr/ can be spelled **er** or **ir**.	Making Connections Poetry Strategic Spelling: Building New Words	Proofread an Advertisement ■ misspelled words ■ usage errors Write an Advertisement
21 pp. 100–103	The vowel sound in *put* is spelled **oo** and **u**; the vowel sound in *out* is spelled **ow** and **ou**.	Syllable Scramble Rhyme Time Strategic Spelling: Seeing Meaning Connections	Proofread a List ■ misspelled words ■ capitalization errors Write a List
22 pp. 104–107	The vowel sound in *few* can be spelled **u-consonant-e**, **ew**, or **u**. The vowel sound in *moon* can be spelled **oo** or **ui**.	Analogies Tongue Twisters Strategic Spelling: Seeing Meaning Connections	Proofread Directions ■ misspelled words ■ punctuation errors Write Directions
23 pp. 108–111	A **homophone** is a word that sounds exactly like another word but has a different spelling and meaning.	Homophone Photos Homophone Quotes Strategic Spelling: Using the Memory Tricks Strategy	Proofread an Outline ■ misspelled words ■ capitalization errors Write an Outline

	Concepts for Review	Unit 4 Activities	Integrating Spelling
Review 24 pp. 112–115	Getting Letters in Correct Order Vowels with **r** Vowel Sounds in *put* and *out* Vowel Sounds in *few* and *moon* Homophones	Letter of Complaint Labels Descriptive Riddles Comic Strip Pen Pal Card Poems Shopping List	**Language Arts:** Writing a Letter of Complaint, Choral Reading **Science:** Making Labels, Descriptions **Health:** Safety Rules, Shopping List **Social Studies:** Pen Pals

Vocabulary Building	Meeting the Needs of All Students	Cross-Curricular Lessons*
Review Words in Context **Word Study** Affixes	**Visual** Write the Equations **Kinesthetic** Using the Senses **Bilingual/ESL** Homophone Posters **Enrichment** New Words	**Science:** Weather, pp. 196–197
Review Words in Context **Word Study** Onomatopoeia	**Auditory** Share Aloud **Kinesthetic** Phrase Charades **Bilingual/ESL** Animal Sounds **Enrichment** Sounds on the Way	**Work and Play:** Photography, pp. 228–229 **Connections to BookFestival:** ▪ *Night Markets: Bringing Food to a City* by Joshua Horwitz
Review Crossword Puzzle **Multicultural Connection** Sports	**Auditory** Focus on the Rhyme **Kinesthetic** Share a Sport **Bilingual/ESL** Visual Definitions **Enrichment** Playing the Field	**Reading:** Your Own Universe, pp. 208–209 **Connections to BookFestival:** ▪ *Staying Nine* by Pam Conrad
Review Words in Context **Word Study** Collective Nouns	**Visual** Collective Phrases **Auditory** Tongue Twisters **Bilingual/ESL** Word Clues **Enrichment** Animal Groups	**Science:** Plant Reproduction, pp. 190–191
Review Poetry **Using a Dictionary** Homographs	**Visual** Flashcards **Auditory** Homographs Aloud **Bilingual/ESL** Homophone Photos **Enrichment** Using Outlines	**Social Studies:** Arctic Life, pp. 182–183

* The cross-curricular lessons are optional. You may, however, wish to teach the cross-curricular lesson that has been paired with the weekly lesson shown in the chart.

RESEARCH IN ACTION

LETTER ORDER

According to *Research in Action*, reversing and scrambling letters is another common spelling problem. This is especially true in two-letter spellings of vowel sounds but is also seen in vowel-consonant combinations, blends, and digraphs.

TYPICAL MISSPELLINGS:

- *feild* for *field*
- *olny* for *only*
- *frist* for *first*
- *briuse* for *bruise*

Helpful strategies include the Memory Tricks strategy, to make up a sentence that helps with the order: Don't bel*ie*ve a l*ie*.

ADDITIONAL RESOURCES

For Every Weekly Lesson

- **Think and Practice Master**
- **Challenge Master**
- **Extra Practice Master**
- **Review Master**
- **Second Language Support Master**
- **Home-School Activity Master**
- **Writing Mini-Lesson**
- **Writing Activity Master**
- **Standardized Test Master**
- **Proofreading and Writing Transparency**

Technology

- **Audiotape**
- ***Everyday Spelling* CD-ROM**
- ***Everyday Spelling* Game Software**

Unit Review

- **Standardized Test Masters**
- **Writing Prompt Transparency**
- **Writing Model Transparencies**
- ***Everyday Spelling* CD-ROM**

OBJECTIVES

- Learn and practice the Memory Tricks strategy
- Apply the Memory Tricks strategy to list words in Unit 4

MEMORY TRICKS

This strategy suggests to students that creating mnemonics for difficult words can make them easier to spell. A mnemonic works best if it is amusing, perhaps even rhyming, and focuses on the part of the word that is a problem.

Direct students' attention to the three pictures. Have them read the steps that the girl follows to create the mnemonic for *pocket.* Tell them that they will be creating some mnemonics of their own in the activities in this Strategy Workshop.

Additional Resources

Frequently Misspelled Words Poster
Spelling Tool Kit Poster

Memory Tricks

DISCOVER THE STRATEGY Some words seem so tricky to spell that we need to outsmart them with tricks of our own. Follow these steps.

1. Mark the letters that give you a problem.

2. Find words you know with those same letters.

3. Use your problem word and the word you know in a phrase or sentence.

Your memory trick might be more than one word. It might rhyme. Just be sure you can spell the helping word and that the problem letters match. Here are more memory tricks.

wheat—Heat the wheat.

liquid—quick liquid
young—You are young.
bubbles— big beautiful bubbles

TRY IT OUT Now practice the Memory Tricks Strategy yourself. Follow the directions on the next page.

Complete each memory
trick using a word from the box to the right.

1. Ride **on** the lion.

2. A couple is **plenty**.

3. Flick the kitchen **switch**.

4. Give **Bruce** lettuce.

With a partner, write your own memory tricks for each pair
of words below. It's all right if they sound silly. The point is to
find ways to remember how to spell tricky words. Underline
the matching letters.

5. hotel—Elvis **the hotel where Elvis stayed (or similar answer)**

6. blanket—thank **Thank you for the blanket (or similar answer).**

7. window—down **Pull the window down (or similar answer).**

Make a memory trick for one of the words in the box to the
right. Follow steps 2 and 3 on page 90. Mark the matching
letters.

8. **Memory tricks will vary.**

LOOK AHEAD Look ahead at the next five lessons. Find
one list word that looks hard to spell and write a memory
trick for it. Share your trick with the class.

Memory tricks will vary.

MEETING THE NEEDS OF ALL STUDENTS

Modified List
Have students learning just the Modified Lists look at spelling words 1–10 only as they complete the Look Ahead activity.

Challenge
Encourage students to consider words appearing in the challenge box, in addition to spelling words 1–20, as they complete the Look Ahead activity.

Bilingual/ESL
More fluent English-speaking students can help nonnative speakers of English understand and create mnemonics. Suggest that native speakers help nonnative speakers with the mnemonics in the first activity by identifying the trick in each sentence. Then have pairs work together to create mnemonics in the remaining activities.

Kinesthetic Learners
Explain that some memory tricks lend themselves to performances. Ask kinesthetic learners to choose one of the memory tricks that they think might be especially useful. Suggest that they practice the mnemonic with a partner and present it as a rap before their classmates.

19

Generalization

Spelling Focus: Some words contain letter combinations that are hard to keep in order.

● Core   ○ Optional   ✓ Assessment

DAILY PLAN	CORE OBJECTIVES	NOTES

DAY 1 Introduction

● Strategy Workshop, p. 90
✓ Pretest and Self-Check, p. 92B
● Spelling Focus and Word List, p. 92
○ Challenge Words, p. 92
○ Challenge Master 19
○ Home-School Master 19

- Learn and practice the Memory Tricks strategy
✓ - Take and self-check Pretest
- Spell words by remembering the order of certain letter combinations; classify and write the list words

DAY 2 Think and Practice

● Equations; Homophones, p. 93
● Strategic Spelling: *Using the Memory Tricks Strategy*, p. 93
○ Think and Practice Master 19
○ Extra Practice Master 19
○ Cross-Curricular Lesson: Introduce, p. 196

- Complete practice activities for words with tricky letter combinations
- Use memory tricks to help spell list words

DAY 3 Proofreading and Writing

● Proofread a Description, p. 94
● Proofreading Tip: Omitted Words p. 94
● Write a Description, p. 94
✓ Cooperative Midweek Test
○ Hardbound Book Master 19
○ Writing Mini-Lesson Master 19
○ Writing Activity Master 19
○ Second Language Support Master 19

- Proofread for spelling and careless errors
- Integrate spelling and writing in a personal writing response
✓ - Take and check midweek test

DAY 4 Vocabulary Building

● Review: Words in Context, p. 95
● Word Study: Affixes, p. 95
○ Cross-Curricular Lesson: Follow-Up, p. 196
○ Review Master 19

- Complete review activity for words with tricky letter combinations
- Study and use affixes

DAY 5 Assessment

✓ Posttest, p. 92B
○ Standardized Test Master 19

✓ - Take Posttest

Cross-Curricular Lessons

Use the Spelling Focus (getting letters in correct order) to introduce the Science lesson, *Weather*, page 196, or choose a lesson that correlates with a topic you're currently teaching.

MEETING THE NEEDS OF ALL STUDENTS

The Word List

For students studying 20 words, assign pages 92–95 and Extra Practice and Review masters.

Modified List For students studying 10 words, modify Practice on page 92, and assign Think and Practice Master 19 and pages 94–95.

Challenge For students studying 25 words, assign pages 92–95, Challenge, Extra Practice, and Review masters.

Bilingual/ESL

In one of the languages used in the Philippines, there are no silent letters. All vowels are pronounced separately. Students who speak this language may spell words exactly as they are pronounced.

Personal Words

Students add to Personal Words lists by looking at work in their writing portfolios and words they want to remember from their reading.

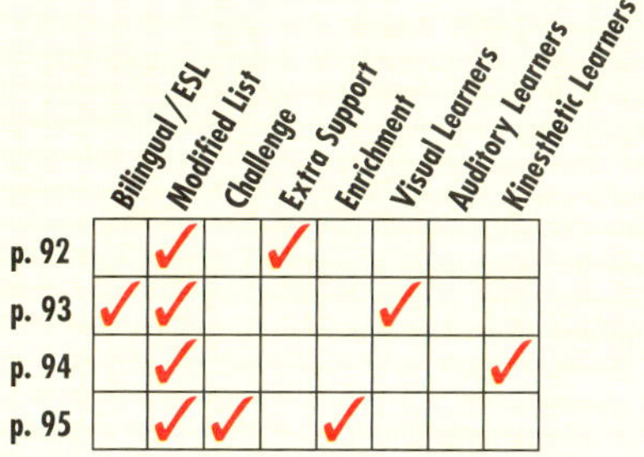

	Bilingual/ESL	Modified List	Challenge	Extra Support	Enrichment	Visual Learners	Auditory Learners	Kinesthetic Learners
p. 92		✓		✓				
p. 93	✓	✓				✓		
p. 94		✓						✓
p. 95		✓	✓		✓			

ASSESSMENT*

Pretest

Read the underlined word, read the sentence, and then repeat the underlined word. Guide students in self-correcting their pretests and correcting any misspellings.

1. I ate a big piece of cake.
2. Invite your friend over.
3. A farmer plowed the field.
4. They said I was late.
5. Let's sing that song again.
6. Carlo asked for water.
7. I saw the movie only once.
8. Elisa brought her umbrella.
9. Jan heard a train whistle.
10. The boys can build a fort.
11. Do you believe his tales?
12. Luz drew a red heart.
13. We saw a weird animal.
14. What is the tree's height?
15. The box's weight is a ton.
16. Our neighbor has a garden.
17. The motor had a rattle.
18. I'd like a sweet pickle.
19. We got sand on our toes.
20. Dr. Yu works in a hospital.

Posttest

Read aloud the sentences below. These sentences may be used for dictation.

1. She brought the cat food.
2. He said the trip was long.
3. Draw on a piece of paper.
4. She heard a strange sound.
5. Always swim with a friend.
6. Let's play ball again.
7. Wheat grew in that field.
8. Only one place is left.
9. I asked a friend to visit.
10. She can build a house.
11. I believe that's our bus.
12. I shall work in a hospital.
13. What is that weird noise?
14. Did you eat the pickle?
15. He can't carry the weight.
16. My neighbor will help me.
17. Grandma has a kind heart.
18. The baby shook his rattle.
19. The height is five feet.
20. Don't step on my toes!

Challenge Words

1. Mom had a job interview.
2. My hobby is writing poetry.
3. The knight took his sword.
4. It was sweet on my tongue.
5. His story was unusual.

Additional Assessment

Standardized Test Master 19
Dictation Sentences, p. T40
Everyday Spelling CD-ROM

TAKE A CLOSER LOOK

The short **e** sound can be spelled at least eleven ways, but the **ai** spelling is found in only a few words. Two of them are on this list. Challenge students to think of another (*against*).

* See pp. T20 and T33 for test-study-test information.

ADDITIONAL RESOURCES (OPTIONAL PRACTICE)

LESSON 19

DAY 1 CHALLENGE MASTER

CHALLENGE ■ 19

Challenge Words

tongue unusual interview sword poetry

■ Use the Challenge Words to solve the riddles.

1. I am not as mighty as a pen, but I am often sharper: **sword**
2. I don't have notes, but I have rhythm and rhyme: **poetry**
3. I am not your run-of-the-mill clue: **unusual**
4. I am always in good taste: **tongue**
5. This should answer some questions: **interview**

■ Use one or more Challenge Words to write the beginning of a story set in the Middle Ages. You might write about a queen, a knight, a king, a dragon, or any characters from medieval times.

Practice Masters, p. 73

DAY 1 HOME-SCHOOL MASTER

■ 19 HOME-SCHOOL ACTIVITIES 19 ■

Word Check 19

1. believe
2. friend
3. piece
4. field
5. weird
6. height
7. weight
8. neighbor
9. said
10. again
11. heard
12. heart
13. rattle
14. pickle
15. brought
16. asked
17. toes
18. build
19. only
20. hospital

Dear Parent,

Please check to see that your child has done this page correctly. Circle any misspelled words and help your child study them.

Tear off the Word Check before your child returns this page to class. Use it to help your child study.

■ **Rhymes** Write a list word to complete each rhyme below. Each word you write should rhyme with the underlined word.

1. In his new beard, he looks so **weird**!
2. Pay the freight, based on its **weight**.
3. I have such woes, someone stood on my **toes**.
4. You hurt your head? That's what I **said**!
5. The tomato that she peeled was grown in a **field**.
6. Her fancy kite, has reached a **height**!
7. After we **build**, the hole will be filled.
8. She heard the beating of her **heart**, when she learned she got the part!

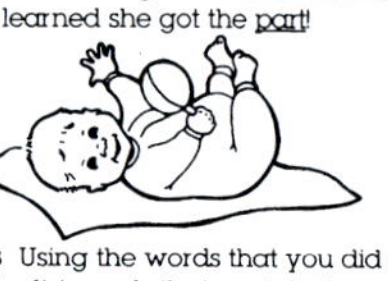

■ **Word Bits** Using the words that you did not use above, write the list words that contain these short words.

9. end **friend**
10. pie **piece**
11. gain **again**
12. pick **pickle**
13. be **believe**
14. on **only**
15. at **rattle**
16. neigh **neighbor**
17. pit **hospital**
18. as **asked**
19. ear **heard**
20. ought **brought**

Home-School Activities, p. 16

DAY 2 THINK AND PRACTICE MASTER

19 ■ THINK AND PRACTICE

piece asked friend only field brought said heard again build

■ **Word Equations** Complete each equation to make a list word.

1. hearing - ing + d = **heard**
2. as + k + ed = **asked**
3. say - y + id = **said**
4. bright - ight + ought = **brought**
5. once - ce + ly = **only**
6. ahead - head + gain = **again**

■ **Drawing Conclusions** Write the list word that matches each clue.

7. someone you like **friend**
8. part of a jigsaw puzzle **piece**
9. place where a farmer works **field**
10. the last one left **only**
11. what a carpenter will do **build**
12. when you do something over **again**

STRATEGIC SPELLING: Using the Memory Tricks Strategy
Use memory tricks to help you spell. Write a list word to complete each trick. Underline the matching letters.

13. gain **again**
14. I eat a **piece** of pie.
15. I **brought** grapes, honey, and tea to the party.

Practice Masters, p. 74

DAY 2 EXTRA PRACTICE MASTER

EXTRA PRACTICE ■ 19

Word List

piece	friend	field	said	again
asked	only	brought	heard	build
believe	heart	weird	height	weight
neighbor	rattle	pickle	toes	hospital

■ **Puzzle** Write a list word that matches each definition to complete the puzzle. The words in the dark boxes tell you how to arrange the vowels when you write the list words.

1. a pal or buddy
2. a place that treats sick people
3. once more
4. a major body organ
5. the ends of the feet
6. by itself; single
7. strange
8. past tense of *hear*
9. requested
10. the person next door

■ **Rhymes** Write the list word that rhymes with each pair of words.

11. battle, tattle, ___ **rattle**
12. date, gate, ___ **weight**
13. lease, grease, ___ **piece**
14. tickle, nickel, ___ **pickle**
15. head, red, ___ **said**
16. right, flight, ___ **height**
17. fought, bought, ___ **brought**
18. shield, yield, ___ **field**
19. receive, sleeve, ___ **believe**
20. chilled, spilled, ___ **build**

Practice Masters, p. 75

TECHNOLOGY AND VISUAL SUPPORT	 Use Audiotape B, Side 2, Lesson 19	 For additional practice use *Everyday Spelling* Game Software, Lesson 19	 Additional resources on *Everyday Spelling* CD-ROM: proofreading and writing, modified list and challenge words, auditory test
	 Use Proofreading and Writing Transparency 19		

DAY 3 SECOND LANGUAGE SUPPORT MASTER

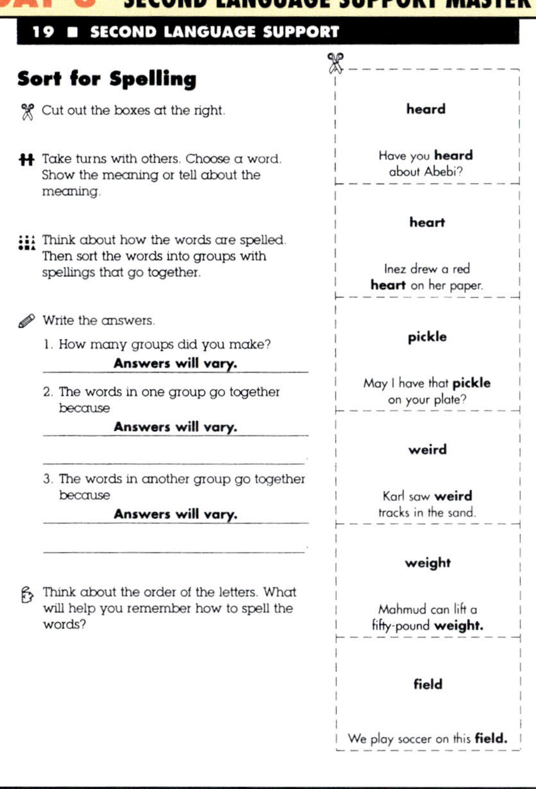

19 ■ SECOND LANGUAGE SUPPORT

Sort for Spelling

✂ Cut out the boxes at the right.

�hↃ Take turns with others. Choose a word. Show the meaning or tell about the meaning.

⋮⋮⋮ Think about how the words are spelled. Then sort the words into groups with spellings that go together.

✎ Write the answers.

1. How many groups did you make?
   Answers will vary.

2. The words in one group go together because
   Answers will vary.

3. The words in another group go together because
   Answers will vary.

♗ Think about the order of the letters. What will help you remember how to spell the words?

heard
Have you **heard** about Abebi?
heart
Inez drew a red **heart** on her paper.
pickle
May I have that **pickle** on your plate?
weird
Karl saw **weird** tracks in the sand.
weight
Mahmud can lift a fifty-pound **weight**.
field
We play soccer on this **field**.

Second Language Support, p. 42

DAY 3 WRITING ACTIVITY MASTER

19 ■ WRITING ACTIVITY

Figurative Language

☐ Use **figurative language** to make a description more interesting.

☐ Create a **simile** by using the words *like* or *as* to make a comparison.

☐ Create a **metaphor** by using the words *is* or *was* to make a comparison.

■ Shannade left out some words in her description of her cat. Complete one simile and one metaphor.

My cat, Boots, runs through the house like a funny wind-up toy. Then he jumps, straight up off the ground like a _____________. Sometimes my cat is a porpoise. That's when he jumps and twists at the same time. When he's hunting, he is a _____________ arching his back like a bridge.

Accept any logical answers.

Remember: Use similes or metaphors in your descriptions.

✐ Have you ever wished you could zoom off in a rocket ship? Pretend you are on a space flight. Use similes and metaphors to describe Earth as seen from above.

Spelling and Writing, p. 32

DAY 4 REVIEW MASTER

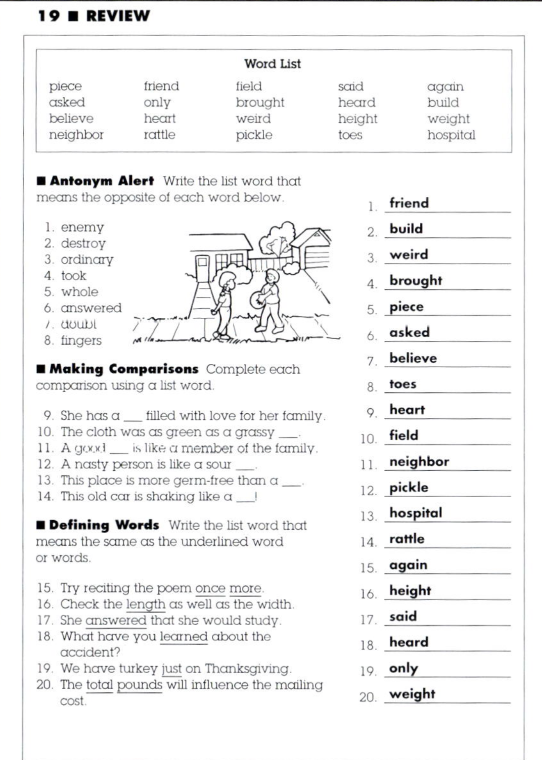

19 ■ REVIEW

Word List				
piece	friend	field	said	again
asked	only	brought	heard	build
believe	heart	weird	height	weight
neighbor	rattle	pickle	toes	hospital

■ Antonym Alert Write the list word that means the opposite of each word below.

1. enemy
2. destroy
3. ordinary
4. took
5. whole
6. answered
7. doubt
8. fingers

■ Making Comparisons Complete each comparison using a list word.

9. She has a ___ filled with love for her family.
10. The cloth was as green as a grassy ___.
11. A good ___ is like a member of the family.
12. A nasty person is like a sour ___.
13. This place is more germ-free than a ___.
14. This old car is shaking like a ___!

■ Defining Words Write the list word that means the same as the underlined word or words.

15. Try reciting the poem <u>once more</u>.
16. Check the <u>length</u> as well as the width.
17. She <u>answered</u> that she would study.
18. What have you <u>learned</u> about the accident?
19. We have turkey <u>just</u> on Thanksgiving.
20. The <u>total</u> <u>pounds</u> will influence the mailing cost.

1. **friend**
2. **build**
3. **weird**
4. **brought**
5. **piece**
6. **asked**
7. **believe**
8. **toes**
9. **heart**
10. **field**
11. **neighbor**
12. **pickle**
13. **hospital**
14. **rattle**
15. **again**
16. **height**
17. **said**
18. **heard**
19. **only**
20. **weight**

Practice Masters, p. 76

DAY 5 STANDARDIZED TEST MASTER

19 ■ LESSON TEST

■ Find the word in each group that is spelled correctly. Fill in the letter for the correct word on the answer strip.

Sample:
- **a.** kwilt   **c.** qwilt
- **b.** quilet   **d.** quilt   → ⓐ ⓑ ⓒ ●

1. **a.** nieghbor   **c.** nabor
   b. neighbor   **d.** neibor   1. ⓐ ● ⓒ ⓓ
2. **a.** belive   **c.** believe
   b. beleive   **d.** beleave   2. ⓐ ⓑ ● ⓓ
3. **a.** brout   **c.** brought
   b. brot   **d.** broght   3. ⓐ ⓑ ● ⓓ
4. **a.** siad   **c.** sed
   b. said   **d.** sead   4. ⓐ ● ⓒ ⓓ
5. **a.** pickel   **c.** picel
   b. pickle   **d.** pickol   5. ⓐ ● ⓒ ⓓ
6. **a.** heart   **c.** haert
   b. hart   **d.** harte   6. ● ⓑ ⓒ ⓓ
7. **a.** wierd   **c.** weird
   b. weard   **d.** werd   7. ⓐ ⓑ ● ⓓ
8. **a.** hospitle   **c.** hospetal
   b. hospitol   **d.** hospital   8. ⓐ ⓑ ⓒ ●
9. **a.** teos   **c.** tous
   b. tose   **d.** toes   9. ⓐ ⓑ ⓒ ●
10. **a.** agin   **c.** agian
    b. again   **d.** agen   10. ⓐ ● ⓒ ⓓ
11. **a.** hurd   **c.** hered
    b. heared   **d.** hoard   11. ⓐ ⓑ ⓒ ●
12. **a.** piece   **c.** pice
    b. peice   **d.** peece   12. ● ⓑ ⓒ ⓓ
13. **a.** olny   **c.** onley
    b. only   **d.** onle   13. ⓐ ● ⓒ ⓓ
14. **a.** friend   **c.** frend
    b. freind   **d.** frind   14. ● ⓑ ⓒ ⓓ
15. **a.** rattel   **c.** rattle
    b. raddel   **d.** raddle   15. ⓐ ⓑ ● ⓓ
16. **a.** ast   **c.** asked
    b. askt   **d.** aksed   16. ⓐ ⓑ ● ⓓ
17. **a.** feild   **c.** fild
    b. feld   **d.** field   17. ⓐ ⓑ ⓒ ●
18. **a.** weight   **c.** wate
    b. wieght   **d.** weihgt   18. ● ⓑ ⓒ ⓓ
19. **a.** biuld   **c.** bild
    b. build   **d.** billd   19. ⓐ ● ⓒ ⓓ
20. **a.** hieght   **c.** height
    b. hight   **d.** highth   20. ⓐ ⓑ ● ⓓ

Practice for Standardized Tests, p. 28

LESSON 19

✓ Pretest and Self-Check
● Spelling Focus and Word List
○ Challenge Words
○ Modified List

DAILY SPELLING REVIEW

Everyone is *comeing exept* Alex.

coming   *except*

● Core   ○ Optional   ✓ Assessment

INTRODUCTION

Phonics

Words with ie and ei
Have students say aloud the words with the vowel combinations **ie** and **ei**. Ask students to name the vowel sounds that **ie** stands for (long **e**, short **e**) and the vowel sounds that **ei** stands for (long **e**, long **i**, long **a**).

MEETING THE NEEDS OF ALL STUDENTS

Modified List

Practice Students studying only the high-frequency words in the top box write
- the five list words they use most in their writing
- the five list words they use least

Extra Support

Past Tense Ask students to name the list words that are the past tense forms of verbs. *(said, heard, brought, asked)* Have students write a sentence using each verb in the past tense.

Additional Practice

Challenge Master 19
Home-School Master 19
Audiotape B, Side 2

1. _______________
2. _______________
3. _______________
4. _______________
5. _______________
6. _______________
7. _______________
8. _______________
9. _______________
10. _______________
11. _______________
12. _______________
13. _______________
14. _______________
15. _______________
16. _______________
17. _______________
18. _______________
19. _______________
20. _______________

CHALLENGE!

interview
poetry
sword
tongue
unusual

92

INTRODUCTION

Getting Letters in Correct Order

SPELLING FOCUS

Watch for letter combinations that are hard to keep in order, and pay special attention to those parts: **friend**, **said**.

STUDY Say each word. Then read the sentence.

1. *piece*   He took the last **piece** of pie.
2. *friend* ✳   She always helps a **friend**.
3. *field*   Wheat grows in this **field**.
4. *said* ✳   Who **said** it was going to snow?
5. *again* ✳   I'd like to see that movie **again**.
6. *asked*   No one **asked** for my opinion.
7. *only*   She works **only** on Tuesdays.
8. *brought* ✳   He **brought** chips to the party.
9. *heard* ✳   Have you **heard** this song?
10. *build*   Birds **build** nests in trees.

11. *believe* ✳   Do you **believe** her story?
12. *heart*   My uncle has a kind **heart**.
13. *weird*   Elves wear **weird** hats.
14. *height*   He's a boy of average **height**.
15. *weight*   Lift that ten-pound **weight**.
16. *neighbor*   I haven't met my new **neighbor**.
17. *rattle*   Shake the baby's **rattle**.
18. *pickle*   A good **pickle** tastes sour.
19. *toes*   The baby grabbed her **toes**.
20. *hospital* ✳   Nurses work at the **hospital**.

PRACTICE Decide which of the list words you use most in your writing. Then write them in order, from the ones you use most to the ones you use least. Underline any letter combinations that are hard for you to keep in order.
Order of words and underlined letters will vary.

WRITE Use two sentences in a paragraph.
Paragraphs will vary.

✳ **WATCH OUT FOR FREQUENTLY MISSPELLED WORDS!**

- Practice: Equations and Homophones
- Strategic Spelling: *Using the Memory Tricks Strategy*
- Cross-Curricular Lesson: Introduce
- Modified List

DAILY SPELLING REVIEW

We wrote about our happy *memeries* of *hoildays*.

memories   holidays

EQUATIONS   Write each list word using the math clues.

1. a + gain =
2. on + lye - e =
3. we + bird - b =
4. ask + led - l =
5. rat + tile - i =
6. fried - d + nd =
7. is - i + aid =
8. pick + led - d =
9. outfield - out =
10. built - t + d =
11. be + lie - e + eve =
12. neigh + born - n =

HOMOPHONES   Write the list word that sounds like each word below.

13. herd
14. peace
15. wait
16. tows
17. hart

Use memory tricks to help you spell. Write a list word to complete each trick. Underline the matching letters.

18. eight feet in **height**

19. patients in traction in a **hospital**

20. I **brought** grapes, honey, and tea to the party.

1.	**again**
2.	**only**
3.	**weird**
4.	**asked**
5.	**rattle**
6.	**friend**
7.	**said**
8.	**pickle**
9.	**field**
10.	**build**
11.	**believe**
12.	**neighbor**
13.	**heard**
14.	**piece**
15.	**weight**
16.	**toes**
17.	**heart**

Take a Hint
Is it **peace** or **piece**?
Just remember:
Slice a **piece** of **pie.**

LESSON 19

- Proofread a Description
- Proofreading Tip: Omitted Words
- Write a Description
- ✓ Cooperative Midweek Test

DAILY SPELLING REVIEW

Is a *qart* a *metrik* measurement?

quart   metric

● Core   ○ Optional   ✓ Assessment

PROOFREADING AND WRITING

Careless Errors

Omitted Words Have students exchange descriptions and check each other's writing for omission of small words. Students should use proofreading marks to make corrections.

MEETING THE NEEDS OF ALL STUDENTS

Modified List

Proofreading Students studying high-frequency words complete this page or the proofreading activity on the *Everyday Spelling* CD-ROM.

Kinesthetic Learners

Using the Senses Have students examine their object again, without the blindfold, using as many of their senses as possible. Then have them revise their descriptions by adding sensory details.

Additional Practice

Hardbound Book Master 19
Second Language Master 19
Writing Mini-Lesson Master 19
Writing Activity Master 19
Proofreading Transparency 19
Everyday Spelling **CD-ROM**

■ PROOFREADING AND WRITING

═	Make a capital.
/	Make a small letter
∧	Add something.
ℓ	Take out something
⊙	Add a period.
⌗	New paragraph

PROOFREAD A DESCRIPTION

While blindfolded, Bria felt an object and then wrote a description of it. First correct three misspellings and two careless errors in her description below. Then write the name of the object. Hint: It's a list word.

PROOFREADING TIP
Bria tried so hard to get the description right that small words were left out. Such mistakes are easy to catch if you proofread.

It is a long **piece** peice of plastic with a round part on top.

Its weight is about two ounces.

Its **height is** hight about five inches.

It makes **a weird** wierd sound when you shake it.

What is it? **rattle**

WRITE A DESCRIPTION

Play this guessing game with your classmates. While blindfolded, each player feels a different object and writes a description of that object. After everyone has written descriptions, read them aloud one by one and guess the names of the objects.

Responses will vary.

Word List

believe	heard
friend	heart
piece	rattle
field	pickle
weird	brought
height	asked
weight	toes
neighbor	build
said	only
again	hospital

Personal Words

1. **Words will vary.**

2.

94

VOCABULARY BUILDING

Review

WORDS IN CONTEXT Write the missing boxed words to complete the dialogue below.

piece	asked
friend	only
field	brought
said	heard
again	build

"Have you (1)?" (2) Louie. "There's a new pizza place called Pepe's Premium Pizza Palace across from the baseball (3) on Fifth Street. You can get a (4) of pizza there for (5) seventy-five cents."

"Oh, I bet that's the place that Ramon was telling me about," Ricky replied. "He (6) the pizza is great and he can hardly wait to get back there (7). I heard that the owners are planning to (8) a video arcade right next door too."

"Let's go over there for lunch," said Louie. "I (9) some money with me. It'll be my treat."

"Thanks! You're a great (10)!" Ricky said, just as his stomach let out an approving growl. "My stomach thanks you too."

1. **heard**
2. **asked**
3. **field**
4. **piece**
5. **only**
6. **said**
7. **again**
8. **build**
9. **brought**
10. **friend**

Word *Study*

AFFIXES **Affixes** are added to words to change their meanings. An affix added to the beginning of a word is called a **prefix.** An affix added to the end of a word is called a **suffix.** Look at the table below.

PREFIXES			SUFFIXES		
	Meaning	Example		Meaning	Example
un-	not	(unhappy = not happy)	**-less**	without	(hopeless = without hope)
re-	again	(replay = play again)	**-ly**	in a ___ way	(slowly = in a slow way)
mis-	badly	(misbehave = behave badly)	**-ness**	being ___	(happiness = being happy)

Use the list words below and the affixes in the chart to make new words that will finish the sentences. One sentence will need a word with two affixes.

  build   friend   heard   weight

1. The cat's noisy meowing was ___ by its sleeping owner.
2. The astronauts floated around in a ___ state.
3. The beavers were able to ___ their home after it was destroyed by a flood.
4. I backed away from the growling, ___ dog.

1. **unheard**
2. **weightless**
3. **rebuild**
4. **unfriendly**

20

Generalization

Spelling Focus: The vowel sound /ôr/ can be spelled **our** or **or**. The vowel sound /ėr/ can be spelled **er** or **ir**.

● Core   ○ Optional   ✓ Assessment

DAILY PLAN	CORE OBJECTIVES	NOTES

DAY 1 Introduction

✓ Pretest and Self-Check, p. 96B
● Spelling Focus and Word List, p. 96
○ Challenge Words, p. 96
○ Challenge Master 20
○ Home-School Master 20

✓ ▪ Take and self-check Pretest
▪ Spell words with the vowel sound /ėr/ or /ôr/; classify and write the list words

DAY 2 Think and Practice

● Making Connections; Poetry, p. 97
● Strategic Spelling: *Building New Words,* p. 97
○ Think and Practice Master 20
○ Extra Practice Master 20
○ Cross-Curricular Lesson: Introduce, p. 228

▪ Complete practice activities for words with the vowel sound /ėr/ or /ôr/
▪ Apply guidelines for adding **-er** and **-est** to words

DAY 3 Proofreading and Writing

● Proofread an Advertisement, p. 98
● Proofreading Tip: Verb Tenses, p. 98
● Write an Advertisement, p. 98
✓ Cooperative Midweek Test
○ Hardbound Book Master 20
○ Writing Mini-Lesson Master 20
○ Writing Activity Master 20
○ Second Language Support Master 20

▪ Proofread for spelling and usage errors
▪ Integrate spelling and writing in a personal writing response
✓ ▪ Take and check midweek test

DAY 4 Vocabulary Building

● Review: Words in Context, p. 99
● Word Study: Onomatopoeia, p. 99
○ Cross-Curricular Lesson: Follow-Up, p. 228
○ Review Master 20

▪ Complete review activity for words with the vowel sound /ėr/ or /ôr/
▪ Study and use onomatopoeia

DAY 5 Assessment

✓ Posttest, p. 96B
○ Standardized Test Master 20

✓ ▪ Take Posttest

Cross-Curricular Lessons

Use the Spelling Focus (vowels with **r**) to introduce the Work and Play lesson, *Photography*, page 228, or choose a lesson that correlates with a topic you're currently teaching.

MEETING THE NEEDS OF ALL STUDENTS

The Word List

For students studying 20 words, assign pages 96–99 and Extra Practice and Review masters.

Modified List For students studying 10 words, modify Practice on page 96, and assign Think and Practice Master 20 and pages 98–99.

Challenge For students studying 25 words, assign pages 96–99, Challenge, Extra Practice, and Review masters.

Bilingual/ESL

Vowels in English are very difficult for Chinese-speaking students to hear because the vowel sounds blend in with the consonants. Students will find it especially difficult to determine whether to write **l** or **r**.

Personal Words

Students add to Personal Words lists by looking at work in their writing portfolios and words they want to remember from their reading.

	Bilingual/ESL	Modified List	Challenge	Extra Support	Enrichment	Visual Learners	Auditory Learners	Kinesthetic Learners
p. 96		✓						✓
p. 97		✓	✓	✓				
p. 98		✓					✓	
p. 99	✓	✓			✓			

ASSESSMENT*

Pretest

Read the underlined word, read the sentence, and then repeat the underlined word. Guide students in self-correcting their pretests and correcting any misspellings.

1. Shannon is in <u>fourth</u> grade.
2. Dad took a cooking <u>course</u>.
3. We are expecting a <u>storm</u>.
4. Birds sing in the <u>morning</u>.
5. Animals live in the <u>forest</u>.
6. Who will <u>serve</u> dinner?
7. Jo made the dress <u>herself</u>.
8. Lee is <u>certain</u> she can go.
9. Wash the <u>dirty</u> clothes.
10. Vhin was <u>first</u> in line.
11. <u>Pour</u> the tea into a cup.
12. Juan is <u>fourteen</u> years old.
13. We play tennis on a <u>court</u>.
14. Have you visited <u>Florida</u>?
15. I filled out a health <u>form</u>.
16. He has a lot of <u>nerve</u>.
17. That is a <u>perfect</u> rose.
18. My <u>girlfriend</u> is visiting.
19. I was hot and <u>thirsty</u>.
20. Sue wore a red <u>skirt</u>.

Posttest

Read aloud the sentences below. These sentences may be used for dictation.

1. I woke early this <u>morning</u>.
2. Deer lived in that <u>forest</u>.
3. The <u>storm</u> blew trees down.
4. He is in the <u>fourth</u> grade.
5. I caught my <u>first</u> fish.
6. Mom will <u>serve</u> a snack.
7. He wanted a <u>certain</u> house.
8. She played by <u>herself</u>.
9. Try not to get <u>dirty</u>.
10. The ship stayed on <u>course</u>.
11. The walk made us <u>thirsty</u>.
12. Please sign this <u>form</u>.
13. It's a <u>perfect</u> party.
14. We can play on that <u>court</u>.
15. Don't <u>pour</u> the drink out.
16. It took <u>nerve</u> to jump.
17. I picked <u>fourteen</u> flowers.
18. My <u>girlfriend</u> saw him.
19. <u>Florida</u> has many beaches.
20. I'll wear my new <u>skirt</u>.

Challenge Words

1. We care for <u>resources</u>.
2. <u>Unfortunately</u>, it may rain.
3. I saw a good <u>commercial</u>.
4. I will <u>determine</u> the cause.
5. My head is in a <u>whirl</u>.

Additional Assessment

Standardized Test Master 20
Dictation Sentences, p. T40
Everyday Spelling CD-ROM

RHYMING WORDS

Try this with vowels with **r**: Have students fill in the first letter of these one-syllable words to make four words that rhyme: **-erd, -ird, -ord, -urd (h, b, w, c).**

* See pp. T20 and T33 for test-study-test information.

LESSON 20

DAY 1 CHALLENGE MASTER

CHALLENGE ■ 20

Challenge Words

whirl   commercial   determine   unfortunately   resources

■ Unscramble the Challenge Words to complete the puzzles. Use the circled letters to answer the riddle.

1. sourseerc   r e s o u r c e s
2. climmecaro   c o m m e r c i a l
3. timereedn   d e t e r m i n e
4. rihlw   w h i r l
5. flyroutenatnu

u n f o r t u n a t e l y

I have a voice but no face. I am a

r a d i o

■ Use one or more Challenge Words to write a radio commercial. Remember that your audience will only be able to hear your words.

Practice Masters, p. 77

DAY 1 HOME-SCHOOL MASTER

■ 20   HOME-SCHOOL ACTIVITIES   20 ■

■ **Base Words** Write the list word that is the base word for each word below.

1. perfectly   **perfect**
2. formed   **form**
3. server   **serve**
4. pouring   **pour**
5. nerveless   **nerve**
6. firsthand   **first**
7. courting   **court**
8. courses   **course**

■ **Word Cousins** Using the words that you did not use above, write a list word to complete each group of words.

9. evening, afternoon,   **morning**
10. twelve, thirteen,   **fourteen**
11. hungry, parched,   **thirsty**
12. jungle, woods,   **forest**
13. Alabama, Georgia,   **Florida**
14. dress, blouse,   **skirt**
15. yourself, himself,   **herself**
16. second, third,   **fourth**
17. messy, grubby,   **dirty**
18. wind, rain,   **storm**
19. boyfriend, partner,   **girlfriend**
20. sure, definite,   **certain**

Word Check 20

1. pour
2. morning
3. course
4. Florida
5. storm
6. fourth
7. forest
8. fourteen
9. form
10. court
11. nerve
12. dirty
13. first
14. serve
15. girlfriend
16. certain
17. thirsty
18. perfect
19. skirt
20. herself

Dear Parent,

Please check to see that your child has done this page correctly. Circle any misspelled words and help your child study them.

Tear off the Word Check before your child returns this page to class. Use it to help your child study.

Home-School Activities, p. 17

DAY 2 THINK AND PRACTICE MASTER

20 ■ THINK AND PRACTICE

fourth	course	storm	morning	forest
serve	herself	certain	dirty	first

■ **Context** Write the list word that completes each sentence.

1. You can see trees in a   **forest**
2. You get out of bed in the   **morning**
3. I was not last in line but   **first**
4. Race cars drive on a race   **course**
5. To know for a fact is to be   **certain**
6. A waiter or waitress will   **serve**
7. Hands that are not clean are   **dirty**

■ **Classifying** Write the list word that belongs in each group.

8. myself, himself,   **herself**
9. daybreak, sunrise,   **morning**
10. tornado, hurricane,   **storm**
11. beginning, start,   **first**
12. sixth, fifth,   **fourth**
13. positive, sure,   **certain**

STRATEGIC SPELLING: Building New Words
Write *dirty* and *stormy*. Write the forms of these words that complete the chart. **Remember:** In words that end in **y**, change the **y** to **i** before adding **-er** or **-est**.

Spelling Word	Add -er	Add -est
14. **dirty**	dirtier	dirtiest
15. **stormy**	stormier	stormiest

Practice Masters, p. 78

DAY 2 EXTRA PRACTICE MASTER

EXTRA PRACTICE ■ 20

Word List

fourth	course	storm	morning	forest
serve	herself	certain	dirty	first
pour	fourteen	court	Florida	form
nerve	perfect	girlfriend	thirsty	skirt

■ **Word Clues** Use a list word to complete each analogy below.

1. France is a country. ___ is a state.
2. Z is a letter. ___ is a number.
3. You bowl in an alley. You play tennis on a ___.
4. You eat food when you are hungry. You drink water when you are ___.
5. Sunset occurs in the evening. Sunrise occurs in the ___.
6. Corn grows in a field. Trees grow in a ___.
7. A mountain is a landform. A hurricane is a ___.
8. Wednesday is the third day of the school week. April is the ___ month of the year.
9. A silver medal means second place. A gold medal means ___ place.
10. A pronoun for a boy is *himself*. A pronoun for a girl is ___.

1. **Florida**
2. **Fourteen**
3. **court**
4. **thirsty**
5. **morning**
6. **forest**
7. **storm**
8. **fourth**
9. **first**
10. **herself**

■ **Before and After** Write the list word that begins and ends with the same letters as each word below.

11. project
12. pear
13. foam
14. grandad
15. sport
16. dusky
17. chance
18. native
19. curtain
20. shave

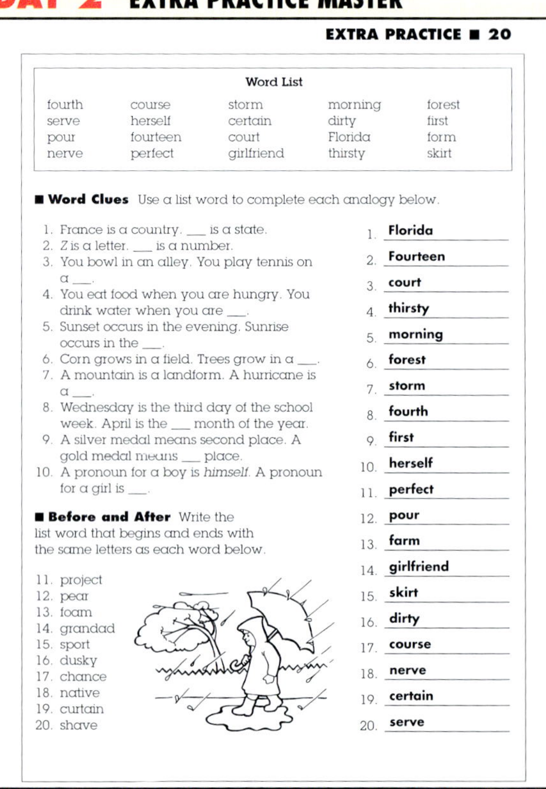

11. **perfect**
12. **pour**
13. **farm**
14. **girlfriend**
15. **skirt**
16. **dirty**
17. **course**
18. **nerve**
19. **certain**
20. **serve**

Practice Masters, p. 79

TECHNOLOGY AND VISUAL SUPPORT	 Use Audiotape B, Side 2, Lesson 20	 For additional practice use *Everyday Spelling* Game Software, Lesson 20	 Additional resources on *Everyday Spelling* CD-ROM: proofreading and writing, modified list and challenge words, auditory test
	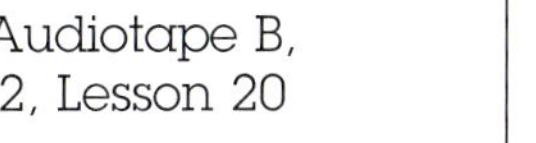 Use Proofreading and Writing Transparency 20		

DAY 3 SECOND LANGUAGE SUPPORT MASTER

SECOND LANGUAGE SUPPORT ■ 20

About Me

Read what Javier wrote about himself.

Yesterday I was the first one awake. It was early morning and everything was quiet. Then I heard a crash of thunder! I was certain that a storm was on the way.

Write some spelling words that tell about you. Then draw a picture of your ideas.

Words will vary.

Write about your picture.

Answers will vary.

Look over your paper. Talk about your picture and writing with a partner.

Second Language Support, p. 43

DAY 3 WRITING ACTIVITY MASTER

20 ■ WRITING ACTIVITY

Irregular Verbs with *Has* and *Have*

- ☐ Memorize irregular verb forms.
- ☐ Use the helping verb *has* with singular subjects.
- ☐ Use the helping verb *have* with plural subjects.

Proofreading marks:
≡ Make a capital.
/ Make a small letter.
∧ Add something.
✎ Take out something.
⊙ Add a period.
¶ New paragraph.

■ Read Simon's play review. Check to see if he used the past tense of irregular verbs with *have* and *has* correctly. Fix any mistakes.

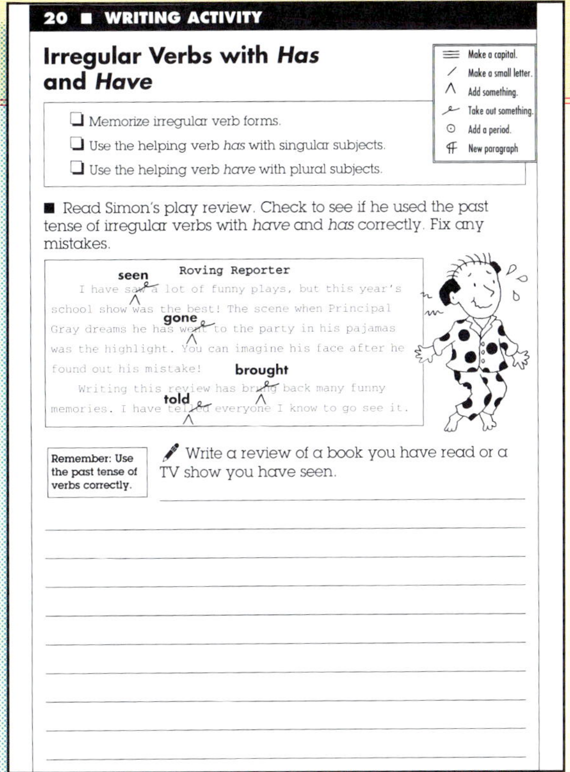

Remember: Use the past tense of verbs correctly.

Write a review of a book you have read or a TV show you have seen.

Spelling and Writing, p. 34

DAY 4 REVIEW MASTER

20 ■ REVIEW

Word List

fourth	course	storm	morning	forest
serve	herself	certain	dirty	first
pour	fourteen	court	Florida	form
nerve	perfect	girlfriend	thirsty	skirt

■ **Base Words** Write the list words that are the base words for the words below.

1. courses
2. courting
3. stormed
4. certainly
5. perfection
6. forests
7. poured
8. nervous

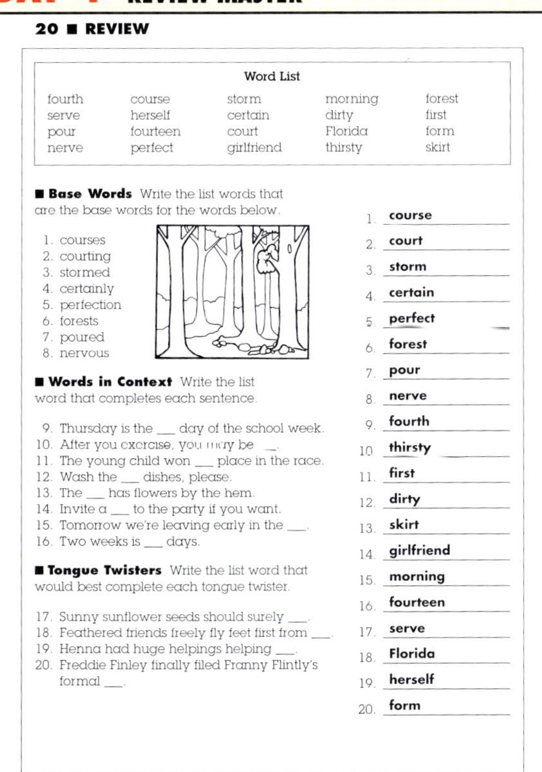

1. **course**
2. **court**
3. **storm**
4. **certain**
5. **perfect**
6. **forest**
7. **pour**
8. **nerve**

■ **Words in Context** Write the list word that completes each sentence.

9. Thursday is the ___ day of the school week.
10. After you exercise, you may be ___.
11. The young child won ___ place in the race.
12. Wash the ___ dishes, please.
13. The ___ has flowers by the hem.
14. Invite a ___ to the party if you want.
15. Tomorrow we're leaving early in the ___.
16. Two weeks is ___ days.

9. **fourth**
10. **thirsty**
11. **first**
12. **dirty**
13. **skirt**
14. **girlfriend**
15. **morning**
16. **fourteen**

■ **Tongue Twisters** Write the list word that would best complete each tongue twister.

17. Sunny sunflower seeds should surely ___.
18. Feathered friends freely fly feet first from ___.
19. Henna had huge helpings helping ___.
20. Freddie Finley finally filed Franny Flintly's formal ___.

17. **serve**
18. **Florida**
19. **herself**
20. **form**

Practice Masters, p. 80

DAY 5 STANDARDIZED TEST MASTER

LESSON TEST ■ 20

■ Find the word in each group that is spelled correctly. Fill in the letter for the correct word on the answer strip.

Sample:
a. kwilt   c. qwilt
b. quilet   d. quilt   — (d)

1. a. hersalf   c. herselve   b. herself   d. hersel — (b)
2. a. four-teen   c. fourteen   b. forteen   d. foteen — (c)
3. a. form   c. fourm   b. foarm   d. forme — (a)
4. a. neve   c. nearve   b. nerve   d. nerv — (b)
5. a. durty   c. derty   b. dirty   d. dirtie — (b)
6. a. surve   c. searve   b. sirve   d. serve — (d)
7. a. perfict   c. perfect   b. perefect   d. pefect — (c)
8. a. storm   c. stom   b. strom   d. storum — (a)
9. a. Florida   c. Flordia   b. florida   d. Florda — (a)
10. a. moring   c. mornig   b. morning   d. moning — (b)
11. a. girlfreind   c. girllfriend   b. girlfrend   d. girlfriend — (d)
12. a. forist   c. forest   b. forset   d. forst — (c)
13. a. thirsty   c. thursty   b. thersty   d. thirstie — (a)
14. a. skert   c. kirt   b. skirt   d. skurt — (b)
15. a. frist   c. first   b. firt   d. frst — (c)
16. a. sertain   c. certian   b. serten   d. certain — (d)
17. a. course   c. couse   b. corse   d. corese — (a)
18. a. cort   c. coort   b. court   d. corte — (b)
19. a. por   c. powr   b. poure   d. pour — (d)
20. a. fouth   c. forthe   b. fourth   d. foorth — (b)

Practice for Standardized Tests, p. 29

LESSON 20

INTRODUCTION

Phonics

Sort by Spelling Pattern

After students have written the list words, help them note that **er** and **ir** spell the vowel sound /ėr/, while **or** and **our** spell the sound /ôr/. Point out that there are no general guidelines for using each spelling.

MEETING THE NEEDS OF ALL STUDENTS

Modified List

Practice Students studying only the high-frequency words in the top box write

- three words with **er**
- two words with **ir**
- three words with **or**
- two words with **our**

Kinesthetic Learners

Phrase Charades Divide the list words among five groups. Students can decide how to act out the context phrases for their words for other groups to guess.

Additional Practice

Challenge Master 20
Home-School Master 20
Audiotape B, Side 2

1. serve
2. herself
3. certain
4. nerve
5. perfect
6. dirty
7. first
8. girlfriend
9. thirsty
10. skirt
11. storm
12. morning
13. forest
14. Florida
15. form
16. fourth
17. course
18. pour
19. fourteen
20. court

CHALLENGE!

resources
unfortunately
commercial
determine
whirl

96

■ **INTRODUCTION**

Vowels with r

SPELLING FOCUS

The vowel sound in **fourth** and **storm** is the same, but it is spelled differently: **our, or**. The same is true of **serve** and **dirty: er, ir.**

■ **STUDY**   Say each word. Then read the sentence.

1. *fourth*   Our team took **fourth** place.
2. *course*   Sign up for a Spanish **course**.
3. *storm*   The **storm** blew down trees.
4. *morning* ✳   I woke up early this **morning**.
5. *forest*   Bears may live in this **forest**.
6. *serve*   You **serve** yourself at a buffet.
7. *herself*   She finished the job **herself**.
8. *certain*   I am **certain** the car will run.
9. *dirty*   We got **dirty** planting flowers.
10. *first* ✳   He wanted to be the **first** in line.

11. *pour*   Let me **pour** you some tea.
12. *fourteen*   This tank has **fourteen** fish.
13. *court*   We waited for a tennis **court**.
14. *Florida*   Hurricanes often hit **Florida**.
15. *form*   Fill out an application **form**.
16. *nerve*   He had the **nerve** to sing a solo.
17. *perfect*   It was **perfect** weather for running.
18. *girlfriend*   She invited a **girlfriend** to stay.
19. *thirsty*   Salty food makes me **thirsty**.
20. *skirt*   She wore a red **skirt** and blouse.

■ **PRACTICE**   Sort the list words by writing
- five words with **er**
- five words with **ir**
- five words with **or**
- five words with **our**

Order of words in each group may vary.

■ **WRITE**   Choose four sentences to rewrite as questions.
Questions and answers will vary.

✳ **WATCH OUT FOR FREQUENTLY MISSPELLED WORDS!**

- Practice: Making Connections and Poetry
- Strategic Spelling:
  Building New Words
- Cross-Curricular Lesson: Introduce
- Modified List

DAILY SPELLING REVIEW

Sarah *allmost* cried *dureing* the movie.

almost   during

THINK AND PRACTICE ■

MAKING CONNECTIONS Write the list word that answers each question.

1. What follows second and third?
2. In what kind of place could you see many trees?
3. What type of clothing is often worn with a blouse?
4. What do you call that special female pal?
5. What does a waiter do with the meal you order?
6. When you play basketball, what do you play it on?
7. What comes next: myself, yourself, himself,____?
8. If something is absolutely wonderful, what is it?

POETRY Write the list words that complete the poem.

Early one (9) in their Michigan dorm,
The students could hear the raging (10).
They hadn't the (11) to go out the door,
Because rain continued to pour and (12).
Then the temperature dropped to a cold (13).
Snow mounds began to (14) all over the green.
Said one, "I'm (15) now of nature's force.
Mother Nature always takes her own (16)."
Well, they did the same—on the (17) bus they could reach.
They arrived in sunny (18) and headed for the beach.

Strategic Spelling

Building New Words

Write *dirty* and *thirsty*. Write the forms of these words that complete the chart. **Remember:** In words that end in **y**, you change the **y** to **i** before adding **-er** or **-est**.

	Spelling Word	Add -er	Add -est
19.	dirty	dirtier	dirtiest
20.	thirsty	thirstier	thirstiest

1. **fourth**
2. **forest**
3. **skirt**
4. **girlfriend**
5. **serve**
6. **court**
7. **herself**
8. **perfect**
9. **morning**
10. **storm**
11. **nerve**
12. **pour**
13. **fourteen**
14. **form**
15. **certain**
16. **course**
17. **first**
18. **Florida**

Take a Hint
If you think it may **rain**,
But you're not quite cert**ain**,
Spare yourself some p**ain**.
Open up the curt**ain**.

THINK AND PRACTICE

Making Connections

Clue Words Encourage students to discuss the clue words in each question with a partner. Suggest that they use a dictionary to look up the words if necessary.

MEETING THE NEEDS OF ALL STUDENTS

Modified List

Review Students studying high-frequency words complete Think and Practice Master 20.

Extra Support

Poetry Have small groups of students read the poem aloud to help them focus on the context clues and the end rhymes.

Challenge

More Poetry Students may write their own poetry with blanks in which to write list words. Partners can complete their poems.

Additional Practice

Think and Practice Master 20
Extra Practice Master 20
Everyday Spelling CD-ROM
Everyday Spelling Game Software

LESSON 20

- Proofread an Advertisement
- Proofreading Tip: Verb Tenses
- Write an Advertisement
- ✓ Cooperative Midweek Test

DAILY SPELLING REVIEW

Id read *mystries* all day long if I could.

I'd   *mysteries*

● Core   ○ Optional   ✓ Assessment

PROOFREADING AND WRITING

Usage

Verb Tenses Use the following sentences for practice with verb tenses:

- I have (*knew, known*) Sally since first grade.
- We have (*went, gone*) camping before.

MEETING THE NEEDS OF ALL STUDENTS

Modified List

Proofreading Students studying high-frequency words complete this page or the proofreading activity on the *Everyday Spelling* CD-ROM.

Auditory Learners

Share Aloud Auditory learners will benefit from reading their ads aloud in small groups. Have the groups discuss whether the ads are effective.

Additional Practice

Hardbound Book Master 20
Second Language Master 20
Writing Mini-Lesson Master 20
Writing Activity Master 20
Proofreading Transparency 20
Everyday Spelling **CD-ROM**

■ PROOFREADING AND WRITING

Make a capital.
Make a small letter.
Add something.
Take out something.
Add a period.
New paragraph

PROOFREAD AN ADVERTISEMENT

The ad below was written for a small travel magazine. Correct four misspelled words and two incorrect verbs.

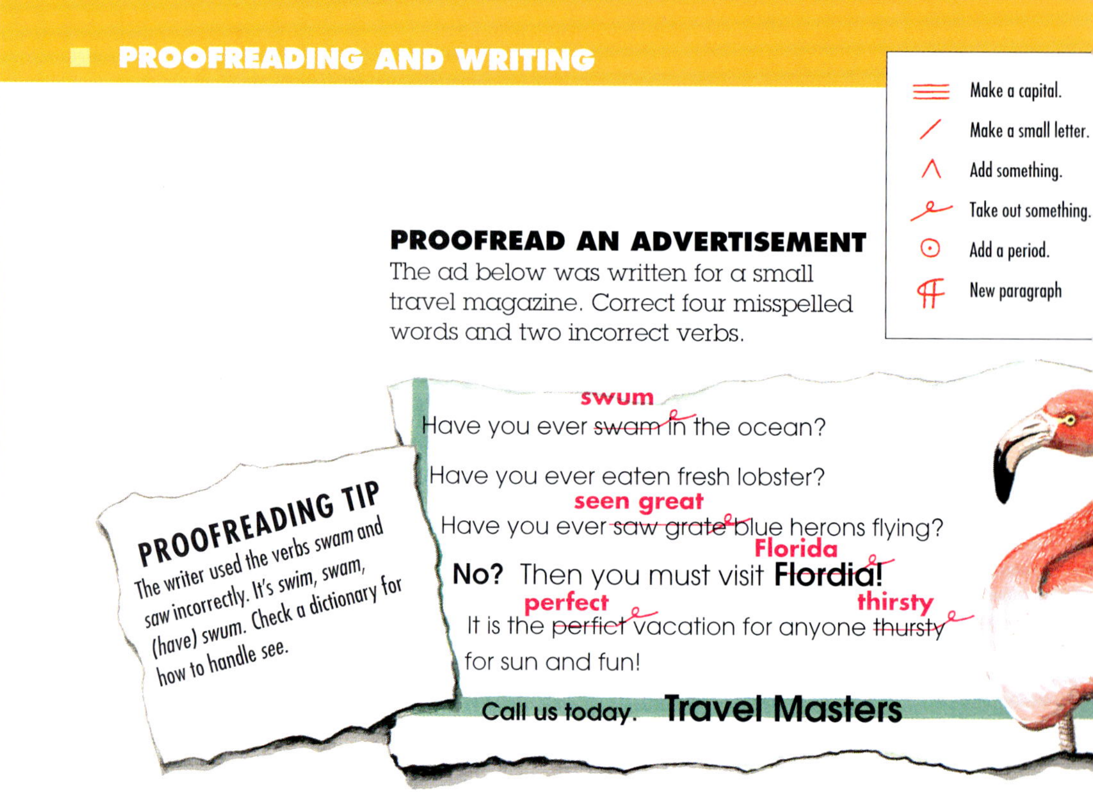

PROOFREADING TIP
The writer used the verbs *swam* and *saw* incorrectly. It's swim, swam, (have) swum. Check a dictionary for how to handle see.

WRITE AN ADVERTISEMENT
Write an advertisement for a place you think others might like to visit. Use a few list words and personal words.

Word List

pour	nerve
morning	dirty
course	first
Florida	serve
storm	girlfriend
fourth	certain
forest	thirsty
fourteen	perfect
form	skirt
court	herself

Personal Words

1. **Words will vary.**
2.

Responses will vary. Advertisements should include a few list words and personal words.

98

VOCABULARY BUILDING ■

Review

WORDS IN CONTEXT   Write the boxed word that completes each person's statement.

fourth	serve
course	herself
storm	certain
morning	dirty
forest	first

1. **TV Weatherman:** "A severe ___ warning is in effect for Greenfield County until 10:00 P.M."
2. **Teacher:** "The ___ and ___ grades will be performing together at this year's fall concert."
3. **Waitress:** "I'm happy to ___ you this evening. May I take your order?"
4. **Softball Coach:** "If Marilyn wants to be on the softball team, she must train ___ to be on time for practice."
5. **News Reporter:** "At the top of the news this ___ is the president's visit to Chicago."
6. **Park Ranger:** "I am ___ that you will enjoy the many hiking trails, plants, and wildlife in the ___."
7. **Student:** "I plan to take a ___ in history at college."
8. **Laundromat Worker:** "Our brand new washing machines will do a good job cleaning those ___ clothes."

1. **storm**
2. **first or fourth**
   fourth or first
3. **serve**
4. **herself**
5. **morning**
6. **certain**
   forest
7. **course**
8. **dirty**

Word *Study*

ONOMATOPOEIA   This big word is pronounced on′ ə mat′ ə pē′ ə. It's what we call words like *buzz, hum,* and *splash.* When you use **onomatopoeia,** the words sound like the sounds they describe. Read the poem aloud. Emphasize the words that are examples of onomatopoeia.

Whack! The tennis ball is served.
It whizzes 'cross the net.
Bing! It bounces on the court.
Wham! It's hard to get.
Then...thud!
Oh...
No!
It's collapsed into the net.

Now use onomatopoeia to write words you might use to describe the sounds of

1. walking on leaves in wet tennis shoes
2. bees building a honeycomb
3. dropping pebbles in a puddle
4. eating soup and salad

1. **Answers will vary.**
2.
3.
4.

99

LESSON
21

Generalization

Spelling Focus: The vowel sound in *put* is spelled **oo** and **u**; the vowel sound in *out* is spelled **ow** and **ou**.

● Core ○ Optional ✓ Assessment

DAILY PLAN	CORE OBJECTIVES	NOTES

DAY 1 Introduction

✓● Pretest and Self-Check, p. 100B
● Spelling Focus and Word List, p. 100
○ Challenge Words, p. 100
○ Challenge Master 21
○ Home-School Master 21

✓ ▪ Take and self-check Pretest
▪ Spell words with the vowel sound /u̇/ or /ou/; classify and write the list words

DAY 2 Think and Practice

● Syllable Scramble; Rhyme Time, p. 101
● Strategic Spelling: *Seeing Meaning Connections,* p. 101
○ Think and Practice Master 21
○ Extra Practice Master 21
○ Cross-Curricular Lesson: Introduce, p. 208

▪ Complete practice activities for words with the vowel sound /u̇/ or /ou/
▪ Recognize meaning connections between list words and other words related to them

DAY 3 Proofreading and Writing

● Proofread a List, p. 102
● Proofreading Tip: Capitalization, p. 102
● Write a List, p. 102
✓ Cooperative Midweek Test
○ Hardbound Book Master 21A
○ Writing Mini-Lesson Master 21
○ Writing Activity Master 21
○ Second Language Support Master 21

▪ Proofread for spelling and capitalization errors
▪ Integrate spelling and writing in a personal writing response
✓ ▪ Take and check midweek test

DAY 4 Vocabulary Building

● Review: Crossword Puzzle, p. 103
● Multicultural Connection: Sports, p. 103
○ Hardbound Book Master 21B
○ Cross-Curricular Lesson: Follow-Up, p. 208
○ Review Master 21

▪ Complete review activity for words with the vowel sound /u̇/ or /ou/
▪ Investigate sports from different cultures

DAY 5 Assessment

✓● Posttest, p. 100B
○ Standardized Test Master 21

✓ ▪ Take Posttest

Cross-Curricular Lessons

Use the Spelling Focus (words with the vowel sound /u̇/ or /ou/) to introduce the Reading lesson, *Your Own Universe*, page 208, or choose a lesson that correlates with a topic you're currently teaching.

MEETING THE NEEDS OF ALL STUDENTS

The Word List

For students studying 20 words, assign pages 100–103 and Extra Practice and Review masters.

Modified List For students studying 10 words, modify Practice on page 100, and assign Think and Practice Master 21 and pages 102–103.

Challenge For students studying 25 words, assign pages 100–103, Challenge, Extra Practice, and Review masters.

Bilingual/ESL

The vowel sound /ou/ in English is similar to the **au** diphthong in Spanish. Spanish-speaking students may misspell *cloud* as *claud.*

Personal Words

Students add to Personal Words lists by looking at work in their writing portfolios and words they want to remember from their reading.

	Bilingual/ESL	Modified List	Challenge	Extra Support	Enrichment	Visual Learners	Auditory Learners	Kinesthetic Learners
p. 100	✓	✓						
p. 101		✓					✓	
p. 102		✓		✓				
p. 103		✓			✓			✓

ASSESSMENT*

Pretest

Read the underlined word, read the sentence, and then repeat the underlined word. Guide students in self-correcting their pretests and correcting any misspellings.

1. A man <u>stood</u> on the corner.
2. We <u>took</u> out our lunches.
3. We got <u>wood</u> for a fire.
4. Flowers grow on the <u>bush</u>.
5. It will be hot in <u>July</u>.
6. A king had great <u>power</u>.
7. Do it <u>however</u> you like.
8. <u>Loud</u> noises scare the dog.
9. We live in that <u>house</u>.
10. The children play <u>outside</u>.
11. The chair has a <u>cushion</u>.
12. The <u>butcher</u> cut our meat.
13. We put milk in the <u>pudding</u>.
14. It's fun to play <u>football</u>.
15. People wade in the <u>brook</u>.
16. Did you take a <u>shower</u>?
17. We were part of the <u>crowd</u>.
18. That <u>mountain</u> is high.
19. We saw a dark storm <u>cloud</u>.
20. Al was <u>proud</u> of his work.

Posttest

Read aloud the sentences below. These sentences may be used for dictation.

1. We played ball <u>outside</u>.
2. The <u>bush</u> is big and green.
3. The chair is made of <u>wood</u>.
4. The <u>house</u> has a big yard.
5. That whistle is <u>loud</u>.
6. I <u>took</u> her to the park.
7. Dress <u>however</u> you want.
8. The player <u>stood</u> alone.
9. We have a holiday in <u>July</u>.
10. The engine has <u>power</u>.
11. Let's climb a <u>mountain</u>.
12. Flowers grow by the <u>brook</u>.
13. The <u>shower</u> won't turn off!
14. The sun is behind a <u>cloud</u>.
15. Mom and Dad will be <u>proud</u>.
16. I like chocolate <u>pudding</u>.
17. A <u>crowd</u> watched the play.
18. The <u>butcher</u> is in his shop.
19. Sit on this soft <u>cushion</u>.
20. Some boys play <u>football</u>.

Challenge Words

1. We go <u>barefoot</u> in summer.
2. The <u>jury</u> will decide.
3. The lion was a <u>coward</u>.
4. We saw a <u>thousand</u> flowers.
5. He <u>announced</u> who won.

Additional Assessment

Standardized Test Master 21
Dictation Sentences, p. T40
Everyday Spelling CD-ROM

WHAT'S THE BIG IDEA?
The vowel sound /ou/ has about the fewest variant spellings of any vowel sound in our language, but it still causes problems, probably because **ou** and **ow** look so much alike. Encourage students to create memory tricks for words in which they misspell the vowel sound /ou/. For example, **Y**o**u** should be pr**ou**d of yourself.

* See pp. T20 and T33 for test-study-test information.

DAY 1 CHALLENGE MASTER

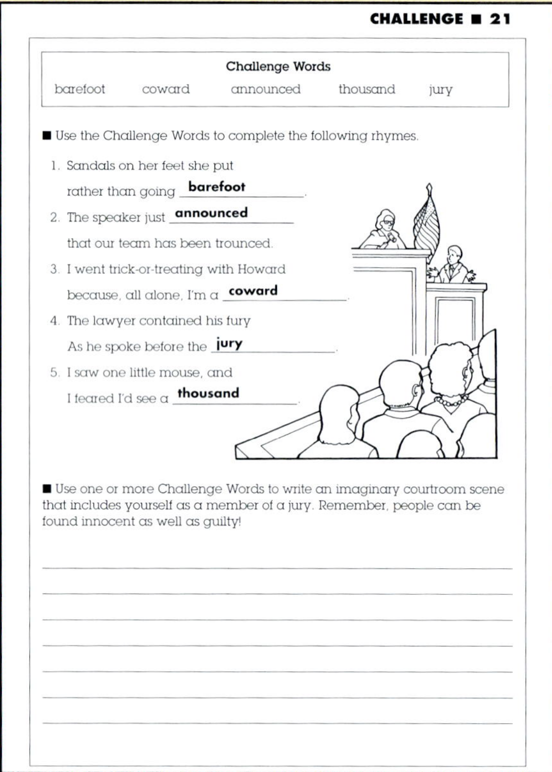

Practice Masters, p. 81

DAY 1 HOME-SCHOOL MASTER

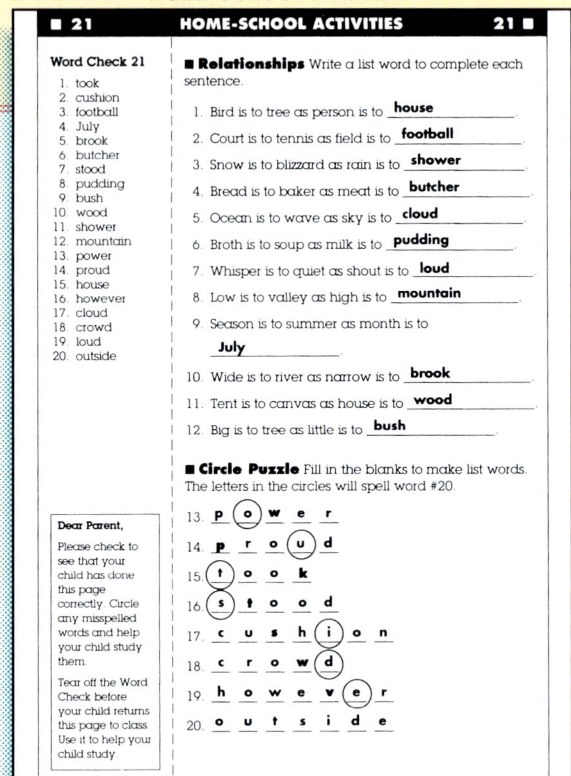

Home-School Activities, p. 18

DAY 2 THINK AND PRACTICE MASTER

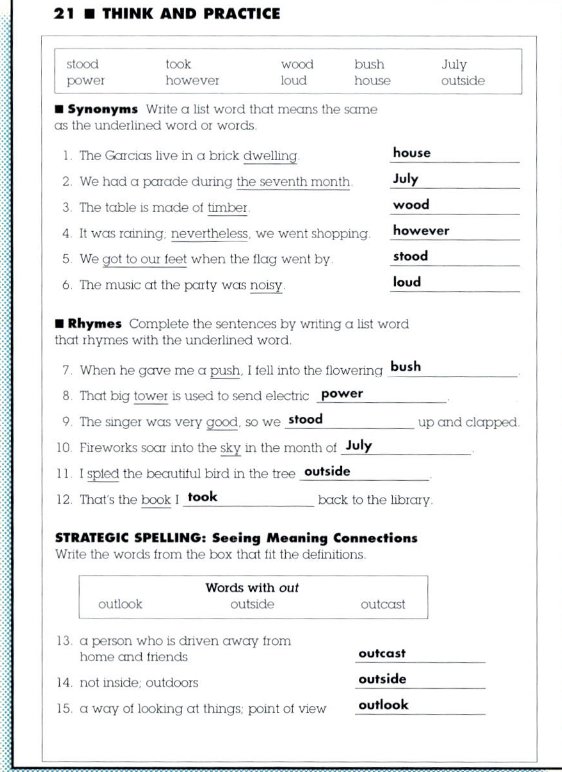

Practice Masters, p. 82

DAY 2 EXTRA PRACTICE MASTER

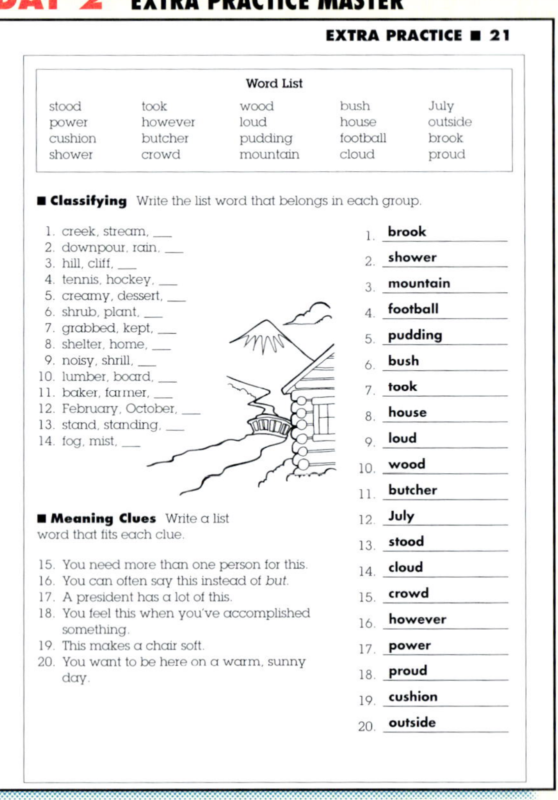

Practice Masters, p. 83

TECHNOLOGY AND VISUAL SUPPORT	Use Audiotape B, Side 2, Lesson 21	For additional practice use *Everyday Spelling* Game Software, Lesson 21	Additional resources on *Everyday Spelling* CD-ROM: proofreading and writing, modified list and challenge words, auditory test
	Use Proofreading and Writing Transparency 21		

DAY 3   SECOND LANGUAGE SUPPORT MASTER

21 ■ SECOND LANGUAGE SUPPORT

Quick Stories

The pictures tell a story. Talk about the story with others. Write the words to complete the sentences.

proud   mountain   took

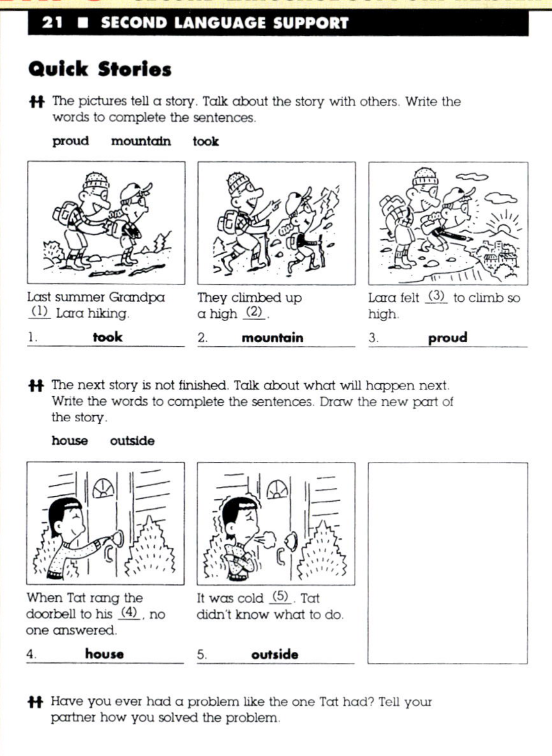

Last summer Grandpa (1) Lara hiking.
1.   **took**

They climbed up a high (2).
2.   **mountain**

Lara felt (3) to climb so high.
3.   **proud**

The next story is not finished. Talk about what will happen next. Write the words to complete the sentences. Draw the new part of the story.

house   outside

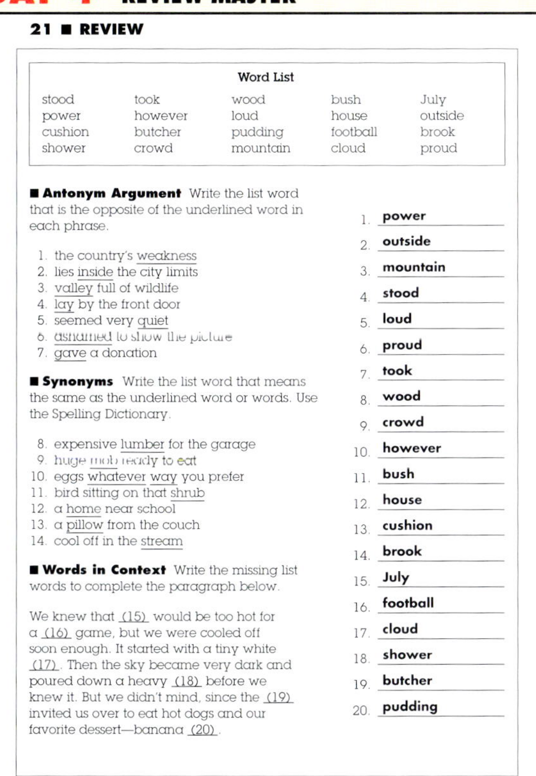

When Tat rang the doorbell to his (4), no one answered.
4.   **house**

It was cold (5). Tat didn't know what to do.
5.   **outside**

Have you ever had a problem like the one Tat had? Tell your partner how you solved the problem.

Second Language Support, p. 44

DAY 3   WRITING ACTIVITY MASTER

21 ■ WRITING ACTIVITY

Capital Letters

☐ Capitalize people's first and last names.
☐ Capitalize days and months.

■ Read Tony's letter. Correct any errors in capitalization.

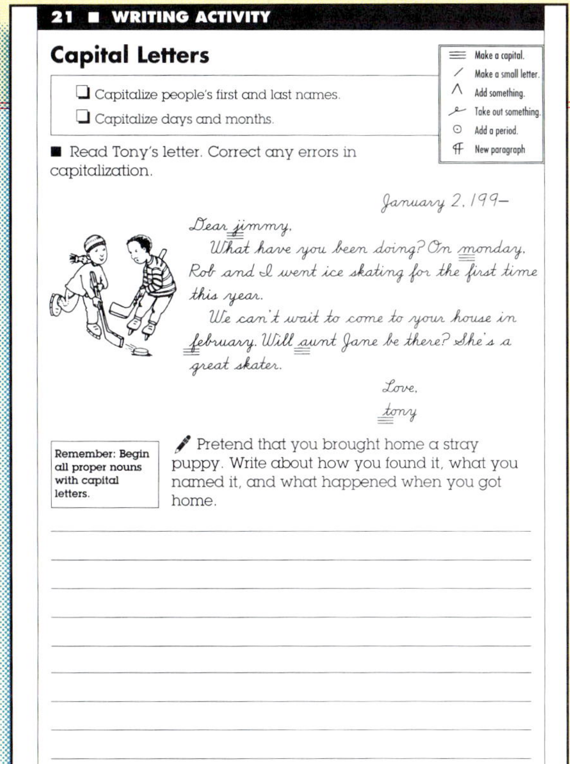

Remember: Begin all proper nouns with capital letters.

Pretend that you brought home a stray puppy. Write about how you found it, what you named it, and what happened when you got home.

Spelling and Writing, p. 36

DAY 4   REVIEW MASTER

21 ■ REVIEW

Word List

stood	took	wood	bush	July
power	however	loud	house	outside
cushion	butcher	pudding	football	brook
shower	crowd	mountain	cloud	proud

■ **Antonym Argument** Write the list word that is the opposite of the underlined word in each phrase.

1. the country's <u>weakness</u>
2. lies <u>inside</u> the city limits
3. <u>valley</u> full of wildlife
4. <u>lay</u> by the front door
5. seemed very <u>quiet</u>
6. <u>ashamed</u> to show the picture
7. <u>gave</u> a donation

1.   **power**
2.   **outside**
3.   **mountain**
4.   **stood**
5.   **loud**
6.   **proud**
7.   **took**

■ **Synonyms** Write the list word that means the same as the underlined word or words. Use the Spelling Dictionary.

8. expensive <u>lumber</u> for the garage
9. huge <u>mob</u> ready to eat
10. eggs <u>whatever way</u> you prefer
11. bird sitting on that <u>shrub</u>
12. a <u>home</u> near school
13. a <u>pillow</u> from the couch
14. cool off in the <u>stream</u>

8.   **wood**
9.   **crowd**
10.   **however**
11.   **bush**
12.   **house**
13.   **cushion**
14.   **brook**

■ **Words in Context** Write the missing list words to complete the paragraph below.

We knew that (15) would be too hot for a (16) game, but we were cooled off soon enough. It started with a tiny white (17). Then the sky became very dark and poured down a heavy (18) before we knew it. But we didn't mind, since the (19) invited us over to eat hot dogs and our favorite dessert—banana (20).

15.   **July**
16.   **football**
17.   **cloud**
18.   **shower**
19.   **butcher**
20.   **pudding**

Practice Masters, p. 84

DAY 5   STANDARDIZED TEST MASTER

21 ■ LESSON TEST

■ Find the word in each group that is spelled correctly. Fill in the letter for the correct word on the answer strip.

Sample:
- a. kwilt   c. qwilt
- b. quilet   d. quilt   → ⓐⓑⓒ●

1. a. besh   c. bush
   b. bish   d. bushsh   → 1. ⓐⓑ●ⓓ
2. a. lowd   c. loud
   b. loude   d. lowde   → 2. ⓐⓑ●ⓓ
3. a. football   c. footboll
   b. foot ball   d. footbal   → 3. ●ⓑⓒⓓ
4. a. shawer   c. shouwer
   b. shower   d. showe   → 4. ⓐ●ⓒⓓ
5. a. pouer   c. prower
   b. power   d. pouwer   → 5. ⓐ●ⓒⓓ
6. a. puding   c. pooding
   b. pudding   d. puddin   → 6. ⓐ●ⓒⓓ
7. a. waud   c. wood
   b. wod   d. wöud   → 7. ⓐⓑ●ⓓ
8. a. bucher   c. buttcher
   b. bucther   d. butcher   → 8. ⓐⓑⓒ●
9. a. however   c. harwever
   b. howeveer   d. howevver   → 9. ●ⓑⓒⓓ
10. a. July   c. july
    b. Juli   d. Jliy   → 10. ●ⓑⓒⓓ
11. a. out side   c. outsyde
    b. outsid   d. outsiae   → 11. ⓐⓑⓒ●
12. a. cluod   c. clould
    b. cloud   d. clouhd   → 12. ⓐ●ⓒⓓ
13. a. brok   c. bruk
    b. brook   d. broock   → 13. ⓐ●ⓒⓓ
14. a. prouhd   c. prawd
    b. prowd   d. proud   → 14. ⓐⓑⓒ●
15. a. hous   c. house
    b. houes   d. howes   → 15. ⓐⓑ●ⓓ
16. a. croud   c. cround
    b. crowd   d. crawd   → 16. ⓐ●ⓒⓓ
17. a. cushion   c. cushen
    b. cushend   d. cushin   → 17. ●ⓑⓒⓓ
18. a. stode   c. stude
    b. stod   d. stood   → 18. ⓐⓑⓒ●
19. a. tolk   c. tuk
    b. took   d. touk   → 19. ⓐ●ⓒⓓ
20. a. mountian   c. mountain
    b. moutain   d. mountnn   → 20. ⓐⓑ●ⓓ

Practice for Standardized Tests, p. 30

LESSON 21

Pretest and Self-Check
Spelling Focus and Word List
Challenge Words
Modified List

DAILY SPELLING REVIEW

We need plenty of exercise for
exellent heath.

excellent   health

● Core ○ Optional ✓ Assessment

INTRODUCTION

Phonics

Sorting by Vowel Sound
Write *put* in blue and *out* in red on two large cards. Read each list word aloud. Ask students to use the appropriate color to underline the spelling pattern for that sound in each word.

MEETING THE NEEDS OF ALL STUDENTS

Modified List

Practice Students studying only the high-frequency words in the top box write
- three words with **ou**
- two words with **ow**
- two words with **u**
- three words with **oo**

Bilingual/ESL

Visual Definitions Assign each student a picturable list word. Students might draw or cut out pictures for *house, cloud, mountain.* For *wood, cushion, football,* props may be used.

Additional Practice

Challenge Master 21
Home-School Master 21
Audiotape B, Side 2

1. loud
2. house
3. outside
4. mountain
5. cloud
6. proud
7. power
8. however
9. shower
10. crowd
11. bush
12. July
13. cushion
14. butcher
15. pudding
16. stood
17. took
18. wood
19. football
20. brook

CHALLENGE!

barefoot
jury
coward
thousand
announced

100

■ INTRODUCTION

Vowel Sounds in *put* and *out*

SPELLING FOCUS

The vowel sound in **put** is spelled **oo** in **took** and **u** in **bush**. The vowel sound in **out** is spelled **ow** in **power** and **ou** in **loud**.

STUDY Say each word. Then read the sentence.

1. stood — A man **stood** at the door.
2. took ✳ — They **took** a nap after lunch.
3. wood — Oak and pine are types of **wood**.
4. bush — The **bush** has shiny leaves.
5. July — It is usually hot in **July**.
6. power — Leaders have a lot of **power**.
7. however — Paint it **however** you wish.
8. loud — Babies don't like **loud** noises.
9. house ✳ — We live in an old brick **house**.
10. outside ✳ — The children played **outside**.

11. cushion — The cat sat on a soft **cushion**.
12. butcher — A **butcher** sells meat.
13. pudding — Vanilla **pudding** tastes good.
14. football — Can you catch a **football?**
15. brook — We waded in the **brook**.
16. shower — Do you take a bath or a **shower?**
17. crowd — A **crowd** of people waited in line.
18. mountain — She climbed the **mountain**.
19. cloud — He drew a white, puffy **cloud**.
20. proud — They are **proud** of their children.

PRACTICE Sort the list words by writing
- six words with **ou**
- five words with **u**
- four words with **ow**
- five words with **oo**

Order of words in each group may vary.

WRITE Choose ten words to write in sentences.
Sentences will vary.

✳ **WATCH OUT FOR FREQUENTLY MISSPELLED WORDS!**

THINK AND PRACTICE ■

SYLLABLE SCRAMBLE   Each group of letters is one syllable of a two-syllable word. Match one from each column to make list words.

1. moun	ball
2. butch	ly
3. foot	er
4. cush	ding
5. Ju	tain
6. pud	ion

1. **mountain**
2. **butcher**
3. **football**
4. **cushion**
5. **July**
6. **pudding**

RHYME TIME   Write the list words that rhyme with the underlined words and make sense in the sentences. Circle the list word that ends differently than its rhyming word.

The tiny <u>mouse</u> crept through the (7).
With one swift <u>push</u> I fell into the (8).
Lee Loud looked up at a fluffy white (9)
The actors <u>bowed</u> before the cheering (10).
"Milk a <u>cow</u>? <u>Never</u>!" "You may have to, (11)."
I (12) a <u>book</u> and read beside the (13).
Tired Ms. <u>Good</u> (14) beside the cut (15).
Gower lacked the (16) to turn off the dripping (17).
Mr. <u>Doud</u> shouted out (18) because he was so (19).

7. **house**
8. **bush**
9. **cloud**
10. (**crowd**)
11. **however**
12. **took**
13. **brook**
14. **stood**
15. **wood**
16. **power**
17. **shower**
18. **loud**
19. **proud**

Strategic Spelling

Seeing Meaning Connections

Write the words from the box that fit the definitions.

words with *out*
look
side
cast

20. a person who is driven away from home and friends   **outcast**

21. not inside; outdoors   **outside**

22. a way of looking at things; point of view   **outlook**

Take a Hint
If you have trouble with **wood** and **would**, remember the two round knotholes in **wood**.

Syllable Scramble
Make a Match Model the activity by writing *moun* on a slip of paper and then trying to match *moun* with each syllable in the other column. Explain that no combination makes sense except *moun* and *tain*.

MEETING THE NEEDS OF ALL STUDENTS

Modified List
Review Students studying high-frequency words complete Think and Practice Master 21.

Auditory Learners
Focus on the Rhyme
Auditory learners might find it helpful to read aloud each sentence in the Rhyme Time activity, stressing the underlined word to help them focus on the rhyme they are looking for.

Additional Practice
Think and Practice Master 21
Extra Practice Master 21
Everyday Spelling **CD-ROM**
Everyday Spelling **Game Software**

101

LESSON
21

- Proofread a List
- Proofreading Tip: Capitalization
- Write a List
- ✓ Cooperative Midweek Test

DAILY SPELLING REVIEW

His *enemys ment* to do him harm.

enemies   *meant*

● Core   ○ Optional   ✓ Assessment

PROOFREADING AND WRITING

Capitalization

Names and Days Use the following sentences for practice with capitalization:

- On wednesday I jumped rope with rita. *(Wednesday, Rita)*
- I saw uncle jim on saturday. *(Uncle Jim, Saturday)*

MEETING THE NEEDS OF ALL STUDENTS

Modified List

Proofreading Students studying high-frequency words complete this page or the proofreading activity on the *Everyday Spelling* CD-ROM.

Extra Support

Proper Nouns Have partners exchange lists and proofread, paying close attention to capital letters in proper nouns.

Additional Practice

Hardbound Book Master 21A
Second Language Master 21
Writing Mini-Lesson Master 21
Writing Activity Master 21
Proofreading Transparency 21
Everyday Spelling **CD-ROM**

■ PROOFREADING AND WRITING

≡	Make a capital.
/	Make a small letter.
∧	Add something.
ℓ	Take out something.
⊙	Add a period.
¶	New paragraph.

PROOFREAD A LIST Lamont has written a list of the things he must do Saturday morning. Correct four misspelled words and two words that should be capitalized.

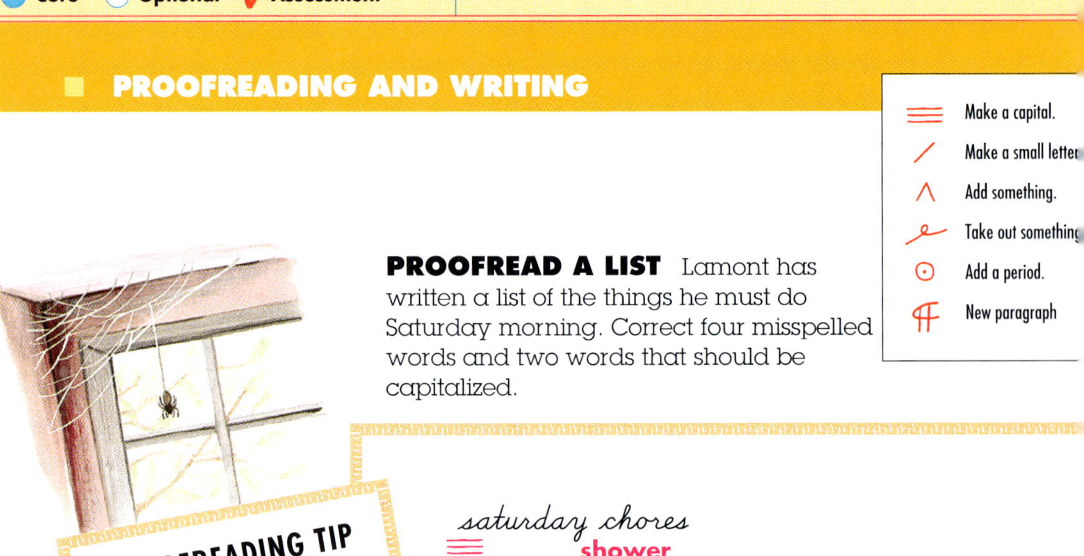

WRITE A LIST Write a list of the things you plan to do this weekend. Use some of your list words and a few personal words.

Responses will vary. Lists should include one or more list words and personal words.

Word List

took	shower
cushion	mountain
football	power
July	proud
brook	house
butcher	however
stood	cloud
pudding	crowd
bush	loud
wood	outside

Personal Words

1. **Words will vary.**

2.

102

VOCABULARY BUILDING ■

Review

CROSSWORD PUZZLE Complete the crossword puzzle by writing the boxed word that matches each definition.

stood	power
took	however
wood	loud
bush	house
July	outside

Across

1. past tense form of the verb *take*
5. a woody plant
7. past tense form of the verb *stand*
8. in whatever way
10. strength

Down

2. outdoors
3. the opposite of quiet
4. the seventh month of the year
6. a building in which people live
9. parts of trees used for building houses and making furniture

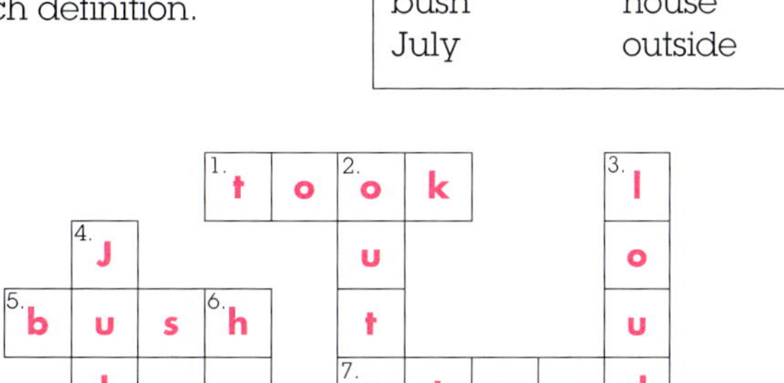

jai alai

Multicultural Connection

SPORTS All over the world, sports are played in which players try to move a ball from one place to another. Use the pictures and the labels at the right to help you name each sport described. Your Spelling Dictionary may also help.

1. North American Indians invented this game. It is played with a small rubber ball and sticks, or "crosses." It is called ___.

2. South Americans play a very fast game using a small, hard ball called a "pelota." Curved baskets are worn on the hands. The game is called ___.

3. This is the most popular game in the world. It is played without using the hands. Most Africans and Europeans call it "football," but you may know it as ___.

lacrosse

soccer

1. **lacrosse**
2. **jai alai**
3. **soccer**

VOCABULARY BUILDING

Literature Connection

World Sports Students can learn more about sports all over the world in the book *Sports* by Melvin Berger (Franklin Watts, 1983).

MEETING THE NEEDS OF ALL STUDENTS

Modified List

Review Students studying high-frequency words complete this page.

Kinesthetic Learners

Share a Sport Assemble students into groups and have them list the sports they enjoy. Then have each group decide on one sport to demonstrate to the class.

Enrichment

Playing the Field Have students explain a game or sport that they enjoy to someone who knows nothing about the game. Students might use a diagram as a visual aid.

Additional Practice

Hardbound Book Master 21B
Review Master 21
Standardized Test Master 21
Everyday Spelling CD-ROM

103

LESSON

22

Generalization

Spelling Focus: The vowel sound in *few* can be spelled **u-consonant-e, ew,** or **u.** The vowel sound in *moon* can be spelled **oo** or **ui.**

● Core   ○ Optional   ✓ Assessment

DAILY PLAN	CORE OBJECTIVES	NOTES

DAY 1 Introduction

✓ Pretest and Self-Check, p. 104B
● Spelling Focus and Word List,
    p. 104
○ Challenge Words, p. 104
○ Challenge Master 22
○ Home-School Master 22

✓ ▪ Take and self-check Pretest
▪ Spell words with the vowel
  sound /yü/ or /ü/; classify
  and write the list words

DAY 2 Think and Practice

● Analogies; Tongue Twisters, p. 105
● Strategic Spelling: *Seeing Meaning
    Connections,* p. 105
○ Think and Practice Master 22
○ Extra Practice Master 22
○ Cross-Curricular Lesson: Introduce,
    p. 190

▪ Complete practice activities for
  words with the vowel sound
  /yü/ or /ü/
▪ Recognize meaning connections
  between list words and other
  words related to them

DAY 3 Proofreading and Writing

● Proofread Directions, p. 106
● Proofreading Tip: End Punctuation,
    p. 106
● Write Directions, p. 106
✓ Cooperative Midweek Test
○ Hardbound Book Master 22
○ Writing Mini-Lesson Master 22
○ Writing Activity Master 22
○ Second Language Support
    Master 22

▪ Proofread for spelling and
  punctuation errors
▪ Integrate spelling and writing
  in a personal writing response
✓ ▪ Take and check midweek test

DAY 4 Vocabulary Building

● Review: Words in Context, p. 107
● Word Study: Collective Nouns,
    p. 107
○ Cross-Curricular Lesson: Follow-Up,
    p. 190
○ Review Master 22

▪ Complete review activity for
  words with the vowel sound
  /yü/ or /ü/
▪ Study and use collective nouns

DAY 5 Assessment

✓ Posttest, p. 104B
○ Standardized Test Master 22

✓ ▪ Take Posttest

Cross-Curricular Lessons

Use the Spelling Focus (vowel sounds in *few* and *moon*) to introduce the Science lesson, *Plant Reproduction*, page 190, or choose a lesson that correlates with a topic you're currently teaching.

MEETING THE NEEDS OF ALL STUDENTS

The Word List

For students studying 20 words, assign pages 104–107 and Extra Practice and Review masters.

Modified List For students studying 10 words, modify Practice on page 104, and assign Think and Practice Master 22 and pages 106–107.

Challenge For students studying 25 words, assign pages 104–107, Challenge, Extra Practice, and Review masters.

Bilingual/ESL

Spanish-speaking students may misspell words in which /yü/ and /ü/ are spelled with vowels other than **yu** and **u.** *Cool* may be misspelled as *cul; few* as *fu.*

Personal Words

Students add to Personal Words lists by looking at work in their writing portfolios and words they want to remember from their reading.

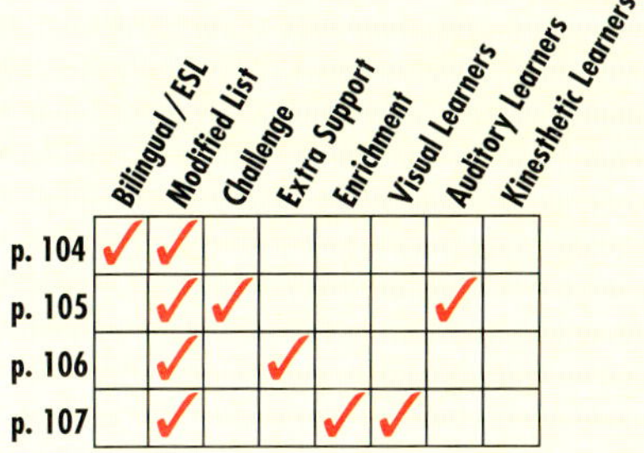

	Bilingual/ESL	Modified List	Challenge	Extra Support	Enrichment	Visual Learners	Auditory Learners	Kinesthetic Learners
p. 104	✓	✓						
p. 105	✓	✓					✓	
p. 106	✓			✓				
p. 107					✓	✓		

ASSESSMENT*

Pretest

Read the underlined word, read the sentence, and then repeat the underlined word. Guide students in self-correcting their pretests and correcting any misspellings.

1. Whales are <u>huge</u> animals.
2. Do you have an <u>excuse</u>?
3. Let's rest a <u>few</u> minutes.
4. I ordered my <u>usual</u> lunch.
5. Each <u>pupil</u> took the test.
6. Rain made the day <u>cool</u>.
7. Jo is in a good <u>mood</u> today.
8. Eat some <u>fruit</u> every day.
9. Mom wore a <u>suit</u> to work.
10. Have <u>juice</u> with breakfast.
11. The noise can <u>confuse</u> you.
12. His <u>nephew</u> went to France.
13. The <u>curfew</u> is at 9:00.
14. Airplanes run on <u>fuel</u>.
15. Are hot dogs on the <u>menu</u>?
16. <u>Shoot</u> a picture at the zoo.
17. We study health in <u>school</u>.
18. That <u>shampoo</u> smells great.
19. Ana got a <u>bruise</u>.
20. A <u>cruise</u> is a fun vacation.

Posttest

Read aloud the sentences below. These sentences may be used for dictation.

1. We can make orange <u>juice</u>.
2. Peaches are a <u>fruit</u>.
3. The <u>suit</u> has a blue jacket.
4. It is <u>cool</u> under the trees.
5. I woke up in a good <u>mood</u>.
6. Let's invite a <u>few</u> people.
7. That dinosaur was <u>huge</u>!
8. We had class as <u>usual</u>.
9. Sickness was her <u>excuse</u>.
10. Each <u>pupil</u> made a sign.
11. Does the <u>bruise</u> hurt?
12. Did the note <u>confuse</u> you?
13. A hunter may <u>shoot</u> a deer.
14. Their <u>curfew</u> is at ten.
15. We work hard at <u>school</u>.
16. We have met her <u>nephew</u>.
17. Oil is a kind of <u>fuel</u>.
18. A <u>cruise</u> ship left at two.
19. Buy <u>shampoo</u> at the store.
20. Fried fish is on the <u>menu</u>.

Challenge Words

1. We <u>commute</u> to work.
2. Earth is in the <u>universe</u>.
3. The friends had a <u>reunion</u>.
4. The money box is <u>fireproof</u>.
5. The police are in <u>pursuit</u>.

Additional Assessment

Standardized Test Master 22
Dictation Sentences, p. T40
Everyday Spelling CD-ROM

FREQUENT MISSPELLINGS
The most frequent misspelling of *school* involves reversing the order of **c** and **h.** To help students remember this order, present this mnemonic: We use **ch**alk in s**ch**ool.

---

* See pp. T20 and T33 for test-study-test information.

ADDITIONAL RESOURCES (OPTIONAL PRACTICE)

LESSON 22

DAY 1 CHALLENGE MASTER

CHALLENGE ■ 22

Challenge Words

reunion   universe   commute   fireproof   pursuit

■ Use the Challenge Words to complete the puzzle.

Across
2. resistant to fire
5. the stars, galaxies, and everything else

Down
1. travel back and forth to work
3. a get-together
4. a chase

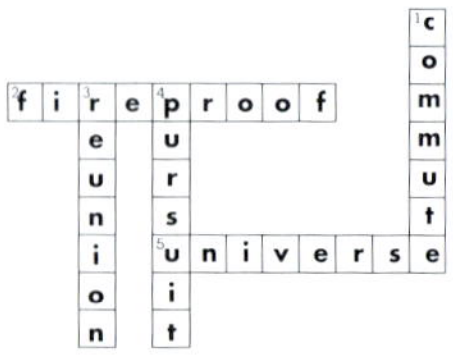

■ Often the most exciting jobs are also the most dangerous. Use one or more Challenge Words to write a paragraph about a day in the life of a firefighter.

Practice Masters, p. 85

DAY 1 HOME-SCHOOL MASTER

■ 22 HOME-SCHOOL ACTIVITIES 22 ■

■ **Riddles** The sentences below should each help you think of one of the list words. HINT: Look at the underlined word in each.

1. Does this person have a pup? **pupil**
2. I like ice in my drink. **juice**
3. Does it look good on me? **suit**
4. "Shoo," she said to the birds. **shoot**
5. Will the men order lunch? **menu**
6. I only have a few minutes left. **curfew**
7. I am washing my hair soon. **shampoo**
8. She had no use for his words. **excuse**
9. She gave me a big hug. **huge**
10. It's just us, as always. **usual**
11. We get mixed up when a fuse blows. **confuse**
12. "Phew, it's hot," said a relative. **nephew**

■ **Base Words** Write the list word that is the base word for each word below.

13. fueled **fuel**
14. cooler **cool**
15. cruises **cruise**
16. fruitless **fruit**
17. fewer **few**
18. schools **school**
19. moody **mood**
20. bruised **bruise**

Word Check 22

1. bruise
2. cool
3. juice
4. school
5. fruit
6. mood
7. suit
8. shoot
9. cruise
10. shampoo
11. pupil
12. few
13. fuel
14. excuse
15. nephew
16. huge
17. curfew
18. confuse
19. usual
20. menu

Dear Parent,

Please check to see that your child has done this page correctly. Circle any misspelled words and help your child study them.

Tear off the Word Check before your child returns this page to class. Use it to help your child study.

Home-School Activities, p. 19

DAY 2 THINK AND PRACTICE MASTER

22 ■ THINK AND PRACTICE

huge	excuse	few	usual	pupil
cool	mood	fruit	suit	juice

■ **Riddles** Write the list word that answers each riddle.

1. What are apples, bananas, and pears? **fruit**
2. Who goes to school to learn? **pupil**
3. What do you offer when you are late? **excuse**
4. What does a businessperson wear? **suit**
5. What is something to drink in the morning? **juice**
6. How big is a blue whale? **huge**
7. What is something if it is not odd? **usual**

■ **Tongue Twisters** Write the list word that would best complete each tongue twister.

8. Fay found a **few** flitting fireflies one fine Friday.
9. The cave in the cove was clammy and **cool**.
10. Paula put a pineapple on the plate of each **pupil**.
11. Mel's mellow **mood** was made by the moving music.
12. The joking jester jumped over the jar of juniper **juice**.

STRATEGIC SPELLING: Seeing Meaning Connections
Write the list word that completes each sentence. The underlined word is a clue.

13. The coolness of the water made it too **cool** to swim in.
14. I am usually on time if I take the **usual** route.
15. She had an unexcused absence because she had no written **excuse**.

Practice Masters, p. 86

DAY 2 EXTRA PRACTICE MASTER

EXTRA PRACTICE ■ 22

Word List

huge	excuse	few	usual	pupil
cool	mood	fruit	suit	juice
confuse	nephew	curfew	fuel	menu
shoot	school	shampoo	bruise	cruise

■ **Making Connections** Write a list in each blank below.

1. We went on a **cruise** on a large ship.
2. My sister's boy is my **nephew**.
3. *Student* is another word for **pupil**.
4. Do you drink **juice** with your breakfast?
5. Each clerk wore a **suit** to work.
6. Apples and oranges are **fruit**.
7. I used a new **shampoo** on my hair.
8. I arrive at **school** at eight o'clock.
9. The city council passed a law with a **curfew**.
10. Everyone should help conserve **fuel**.

■ **Synonyms** Write a list word that means the same as each word or phrase below.

11. food list — **menu**
12. not many — **few**
13. injury — **bruise**
14. large — **huge**
15. customary — **usual**
16. chilly — **cool**
17. feeling — **mood**
18. reason — **excuse**
19. mix up — **confuse**
20. throw — **shoot**

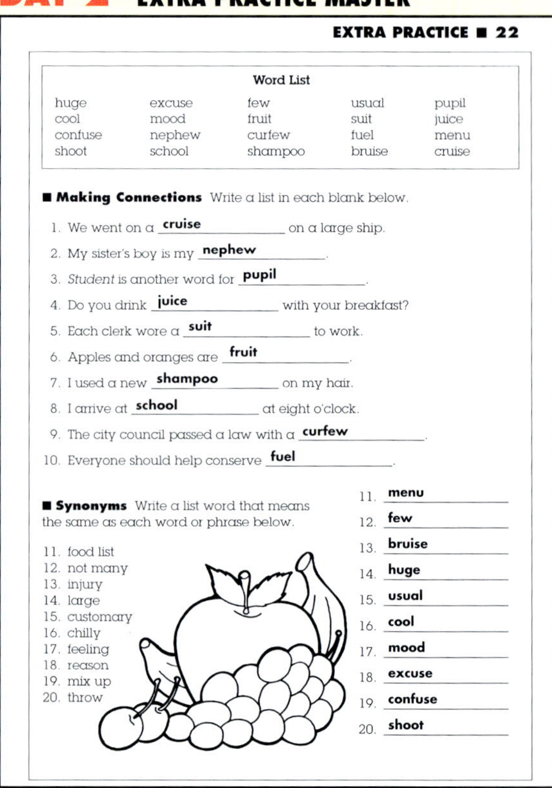

Practice Masters, p. 87

TECHNOLOGY AND VISUAL SUPPORT	 Use Audiotape B, Side 2, Lesson 22	 For additional practice use *Everyday Spelling* Game Software, Lesson 22	 Additional resources on *Everyday Spelling* CD-ROM: proofreading and writing, modified list and challenge words, auditory test
	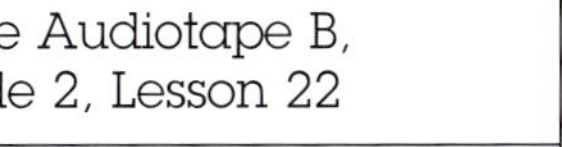 Use Proofreading and Writing Transparency 22		

DAY 3 — SECOND LANGUAGE SUPPORT MASTER

SECOND LANGUAGE SUPPORT ■ 22

Quick Stories

The pictures tell a story. Talk about the story with others. Write the words to complete the sentences.

usual   school   huge

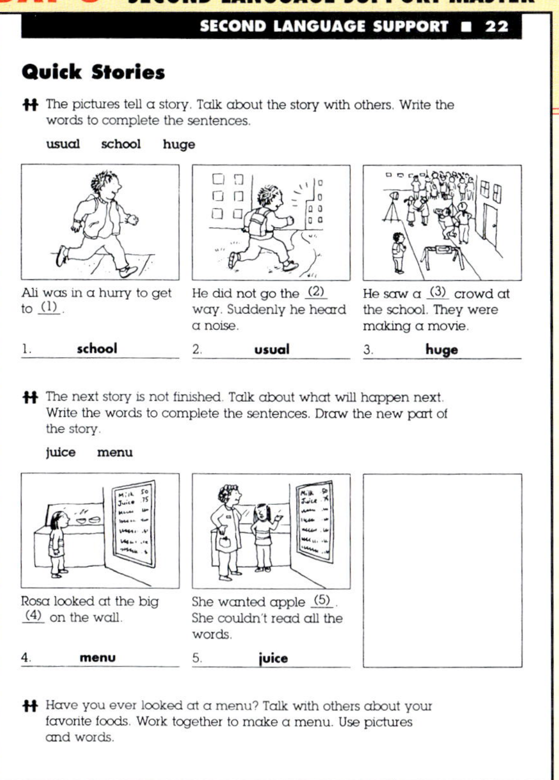

Ali was in a hurry to get to (1).

He did not go the (2) way. Suddenly he heard a noise.

He saw a (3) crowd at the school. They were making a movie.

1. **school**   2. **usual**   3. **huge**

The next story is not finished. Talk about what will happen next. Write the words to complete the sentences. Draw the new part of the story.

juice   menu

Rosa looked at the big (4) on the wall.

She wanted apple (5). She couldn't read all the words.

4. **menu**   5. **juice**

Have you ever looked at a menu? Talk with others about your favorite foods. Work together to make a menu. Use pictures and words.

Second Language Support, p. 45

DAY 3 — WRITING ACTIVITY MASTER

22 ■ WRITING ACTIVITY

Directions in Correct Order

- Write directions in order, step by step.
- You can use numbers to show each step.

Read these directions on how to make a stone sculpture. Write a number from 1 to 4 to show the correct order.

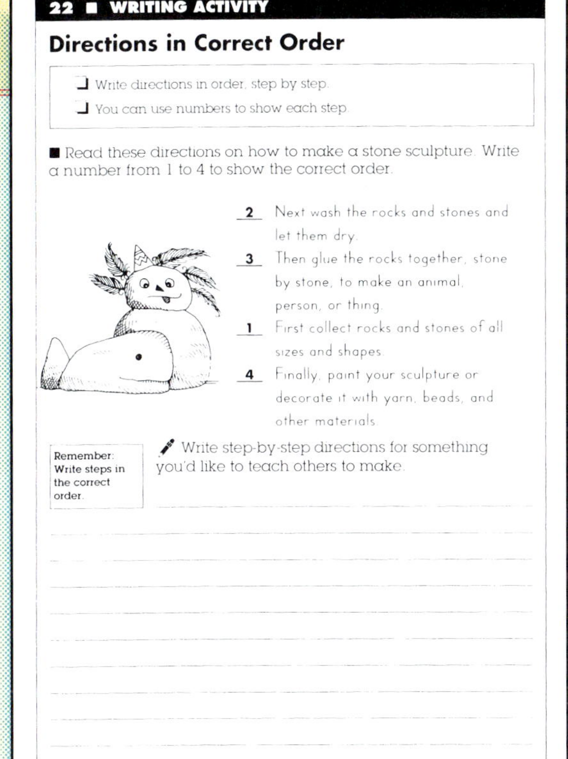

__2__ Next wash the rocks and stones and let them dry.

__3__ Then glue the rocks together, stone by stone, to make an animal, person, or thing.

__1__ First collect rocks and stones of all sizes and shapes.

__4__ Finally, paint your sculpture or decorate it with yarn, beads, and other materials.

Remember: Write steps in the correct order.

Write step-by-step directions for something you'd like to teach others to make.

Spelling and Writing, p. 38

DAY 4 — REVIEW MASTER

22 ■ REVIEW

Word List

huge	excuse	few	usual	pupil
cool	mood	fruit	suit	juice
confuse	nephew	curfew	fuel	menu
shoot	school	shampoo	bruise	cruise

■ Who Am I? Write the list word naming each speaker.

1. "I'm where children learn. I'm a ___."
2. "I show food you can order. I'm a ___."
3. "I clean hair. I'm called ___."
4. "I attend elementary school. I'm a ___."
5. "I am sweet to eat and come in all sizes, colors, and shapes. I'm called ___."
6. "I'm blue and swollen and sore, and I happen when someone gets a bump. I'm a ___."
7. "When you miss school, I'm the note your parents sign when you return. I'm an ___."
8. "Many grownups wear me to work. I'm a ___."
9. "People ride a boat to enjoy me. I'm a ___."
10. "I'm the rules that say when it's time to go home at night. I'm called a ___."
11. "Especially in the morning, you might drink me. I'm called ___."
12. "I have a sister who's a niece, so I'm a ___."

1. **school**
2. **menu**
3. **shampoo**
4. **pupil**
5. **fruit**
6. **bruise**
7. **excuse**
8. **suit**
9. **cruise**
10. **curfew**
11. **juice**
12. **nephew**
13. **cool**
14. **fuel**
15. **few**
16. **mood**
17. **huge**
18. **confuse**
19. **shoot**
20. **usual**

■ Making Associations Write the list word that you might associate with each word or phrase below.

13. as ___ as a cucumber
14. diesel ___
15. in a ___ days
16. in a grumpy ___
17. make a ___ mistake
18. ___ the issue
19. ___ a game of pool
20. as ___

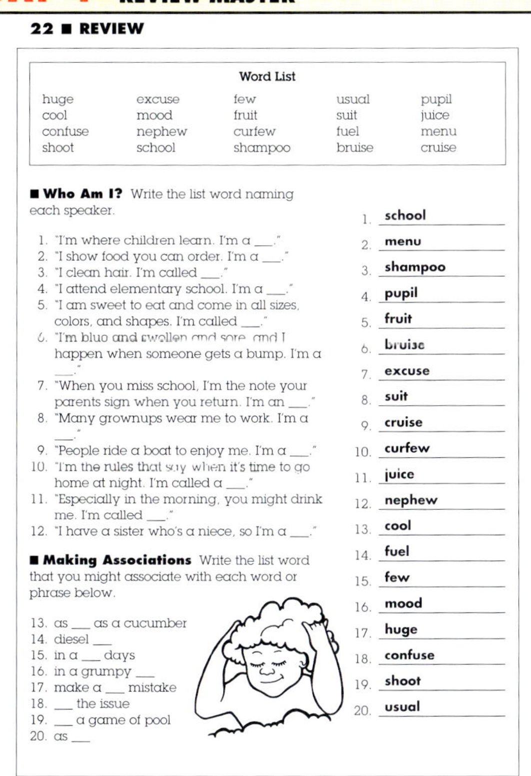

Practice Masters, p. 88

DAY 5 — STANDARDIZED TEST MASTER

LESSON TEST ■ 22

■ Find the word in each group that is spelled correctly. Fill in the letter for the correct word on the answer strip.

Sample:
a. kwilt   c. qwilt
b. quilet   d. quilt   — ⓐ ⓑ ⓒ ●

1. a. huge   c. huje
   b. houge   d. hewge   — 1. ● ⓑ ⓒ ⓓ
2. a. usuall   c. usal
   b. usual   d. ushual   — 2. ⓐ ● ⓒ ⓓ
3. a. exuce   c. excuse
   b. exuse   d. excus   — 3. ⓐ ⓑ ● ⓓ
4. a. cruise   c. cruize
   b. cruse   d. cruze   — 4. ● ⓑ ⓒ ⓓ
5. a. cule   c. cool
   b. coul   d. coole   — 5. ⓐ ⓑ ● ⓓ
6. a. confuse   c. cunfuse
   b. konfuse   d. confuze   — 6. ● ⓑ ⓒ ⓓ
7. a. pewpil   c. pupile
   b. pupil   d. pupul   — 7. ⓐ ● ⓒ ⓓ
8. a. menyou   c. menue
   b. menu   d. meneu   — 8. ⓐ ● ⓒ ⓓ
9. a. nepew   c. nephew
   b. nefyou   d. nphew   — 9. ⓐ ⓑ ● ⓓ
10. a. mood   c. moud
    b. moode   d. moude   — 10. ● ⓑ ⓒ ⓓ
11. a. shoot   c. shoote
    b. shoout   d. shyout   — 11. ● ⓑ ⓒ ⓓ
12. a. shampooh   c. shammpo
    b. shampoo   d. shammpoo   — 12. ⓐ ● ⓒ ⓓ
13. a. jouce   c. juice
    b. juce   d. joos   — 13. ⓐ ⓑ ● ⓓ
14. a. sute   c. suit
    b. sut   d. soit   — 14. ⓐ ⓑ ● ⓓ
15. a. fue   c. few
    b. fyew   d. fews   — 15. ⓐ ⓑ ● ⓓ
16. a. curfew   c. curfyou
    b. cerfew   d. cerfyoo   — 16. ● ⓑ ⓒ ⓓ
17. a. fule   c. feul
    b. fuel   d. feuel   — 17. ⓐ ● ⓒ ⓓ
18. a. frut   c. froot
    b. fruet   d. fruit   — 18. ⓐ ⓑ ⓒ ●
19. a. briuse   c. bruse
    b. brus   d. bruise   — 19. ⓐ ⓑ ⓒ ●
20. a. school   c. scool
    b. shcool   d. sckool   — 20. ● ⓑ ⓒ ⓓ

Practice for Standardized Tests, p. 31

INTRODUCTION

Phonics

Murals for /yü/ and /ü/
Have two groups of students sort the list words by the vowel sounds /yü/ or /ü/. Then have each group make a mural that presents its words.

MEETING THE NEEDS OF ALL STUDENTS

Modified List

Practice Students studying only the high-frequency words in the top box write
- two words with **oo**
- three words with **ui**
- three words with **u-consonant-e** or **ew**
- two words with **u**

Bilingual/ESL

Word Clues Have each student make up a spelling or meaning clue for a list word, such as **U** *and* **I** *drink* juice.

Additional Practice

Challenge Master 22
Home-School Master 22
Audiotape B, Side 2

1. cool
2. mood
3. shoot
4. school
5. shampoo
6. fruit
7. suit
8. juice
9. bruise
10. cruise
11. huge
12. excuse
13. few
14. confuse
15. nephew
16. curfew
17. usual
18. pupil
19. fuel
20. menu

CHALLENGE!

commute
universe
reunion
fireproof
pursuit

104

INTRODUCTION

Vowel Sounds in *few* and *moon*

SPELLING FOCUS

The vowel sound in **few** can be spelled **u-consonant-e, ew,** or **u**: exc**u**se, f**ew**, p**u**pil. The vowel sound in **moon** can be spelled **oo** or **ui**: c**oo**l, j**ui**ce.

STUDY   Say each word. Then read the sentence.

1. huge — Blue whales are **huge** animals.
2. excuse — She had no **excuse** for being late.
3. few — There are a **few** apples left.
4. usual — He took the **usual** route home.
5. pupil — I am a fourth grade **pupil**.
6. cool — Marble feels smooth and **cool**.
7. mood — My dad is in a good **mood**.
8. fruit — Cherries are a kind of **fruit**.
9. suit — The man wore a business **suit**.
10. juice — I drink orange **juice** for breakfast.

11. confuse — I **confuse** pigeons with doves.
12. nephew — My sister's son is my **nephew**.
13. curfew — I must be in by my 9:00 **curfew**.
14. fuel — We need to **fuel** the car with gas.
15. menu — You order food from a **menu**.
16. shoot — They **shoot** baskets at practice.
17. school ✳ — Our **school** is on the corner.
18. shampoo — Should we **shampoo** the rug?
19. bruise — The **bruise** on her leg was purple.
20. cruise — We went on a Caribbean **cruise**.

PRACTICE   Sort the list words by writing
- five words with **oo**
- six words with **u-consonant-e** or **ew**
- five words with **ui**
- four words with **u**

Order of words in each group may vary.

WRITE   Choose two sentences to write an advertisement, slogan, or saying.
Responses will vary.

✳ **WATCH OUT FOR FREQUENTLY MISSPELLED WORDS!**

104

THINK AND PRACTICE ■

ANALOGIES   Write the list word that completes each phrase.

1. hot and warm, cold and ____.
2. most and many, least and ____.
3. aunt and uncle, niece and ____.
4. small and tiny, large and ____.
5. carrot and banana, vegetable and ____.
6. apple and sauce, orange and ____.
7. teeth and toothpaste, hair and ____.
8. train and schedule, restaurant and ____.
9. doctor and patient, teacher and ____.

TONGUE TWISTERS   Write the list word that would best complete each tongue twister.

10. Being bucked by a bronco brought about Brian's ____.
11. The sensational singer sported a silky silver ____.
12. Should Shelly snap the shutter and ____ the shy sheep?
13. Curt's camp counselor calls "Come in!" at ____.
14. Maybe Maya managed to maintain a merry ____.
15. Chemistry quiz questions ____ and confound Cornelius.
16. Chris chartered a craft to ____ the Caribbean.
17. The extravagant explorers had an ____ for the expensive expedition.

Write the list word that completes each sentence. The underlined word is a clue. Circle the letters in each list word that are the same as in the underlined word.

18. The schoolwork at our ____ is very challenging.
19. I am usually on time if I take the ____ route.
20. We had to stop and refuel when we ran out of ____.

1.	cool
2.	few
3.	nephew
4.	huge
5.	fruit
6.	juice
7.	shampoo
8.	menu
9.	pupil
10.	bruise
11.	suit
12.	shoot
13.	curfew
14.	mood
15.	confuse
16.	cruise
17.	excuse
18.	(school)
19.	(usual)
20.	(fuel)

Did You Know?
The word *curfew* comes from the French words *covrir*, to "cover," and *feu*, "fire." When the curfew bell rang, people covered, or put out, their fires each night.

THINK AND PRACTICE

Analogies

Hot Is to Warm   Help students see the relationship between the words *hot* and *warm*. Ask them to find the word that relates in the same way to *cold* (*cool*).

MEETING THE NEEDS OF ALL STUDENTS

Modified List

Review   Students studying high-frequency words complete Think and Practice Master 22.

Auditory Learners

Tongue Twisters   Auditory learners may benefit by reading the tongue twisters aloud.

Challenge

Parts of Speech   Have students write two sentences using the following words both as a verb and as another part of speech: *bruise, suit, shoot, cruise, shampoo, fuel*.

Additional Practice

Think and Practice Master 22
Extra Practice Master 22
Everyday Spelling **CD-ROM**
Everyday Spelling **Game Software**

- Proofread Directions
- Proofreading Tip: End Punctuation
- Write Directions
- ✓ Cooperative Midweek Test

DAILY SPELLING REVIEW

We need *alot* of school *suplies*.

a lot   *supplies*

● **Core**   ○ Optional   ✓ **Assessment**

PROOFREADING AND WRITING

Punctuation

Add It to the End Ask students to add the correct end punctuation to each sentence: *Do you know how to get to Green Street* (?) *Turn left and then right* (.) *Watch out* (!)

MEETING THE NEEDS OF ALL STUDENTS

Modified List

Proofreading Students studying high-frequency words complete this page or the proofreading activity on the *Everyday Spelling* CD-ROM.

Extra Support

Writing Directions Review the importance of sequence when writing directions. Then you might have students help you write directions for such activities as feeding a pet or playing a game.

Additional Practice

Hardbound Book Master 22
Second Language Master 22
Writing Mini-Lesson Master 22
Writing Activity Master 22
Proofreading Transparency 22
Everyday Spelling **CD-ROM**

■ PROOFREADING AND WRITING

PROOFREAD DIRECTIONS The owner of Cozy's Café left these directions for her after-school assistant. Correct four misspelled words and add three missing end marks.

PROOFREADING TIP

Cozy forgot to use an exclamation mark in her final sentence. What other mark did she forget (twice) ?

P. J.,

    How was shcool **school** ? Please squeeze oranges and cut up apples. Type up a new menu to include frut **fruit** salad and fresh orange joos **juice**. Are you in the mude **mood** to make one of your special soups ? They are terrific !

      Cozy

WRITE DIRECTIONS Isn't there something you'd like to ask someone to do in writing? Use spelling words and personal words to write your directions.

Responses will vary. Directions should include at least one list word and one personal word.

Word List

bruise	pupil
cool	few
juice	fuel
school	excuse
fruit	nephew
mood	huge
suit	curfew
shoot	confuse
cruise	usual
shampoo	menu

Personal Words

1. **Words will vary.**

2.

- Review: Words in Context
- Word Study: Collective Nouns
- Cross-Curricular Lesson: Follow-Up

DAILY SPELLING REVIEW

My *hampster* is a *lazzy* pet.

hamster   lazy

- ✓ Posttest
- ✓ Dictation Sentences
- Standardized Test Master 22
- ✓ Auditory Test on *Everyday Spelling* CD-ROM

Review

WORDS IN CONTEXT   Maybe you have seen advertisements for vacation spots much like the one below. Write the boxed words to complete the advertisement.

Is the hot weather putting you in a bad (1)? Do you need to get away for a (2) days? Imagine this:

- Taking a dip in the ocean to (3) off
- Having fresh (4), including slices of watermelon, honeydew, and bananas, with your breakfast every morning
- Sipping a cool fruit (5) as you relax under a palm tree
- Being a (6) in one of Peter Orca's famous scuba diving classes

The Sand and Surf Hotel in southern Florida has a special limited offer. Instead of the (7) tiny rooms you find at other vacation spots, you can stay in a (8) room at a very low cost. So don't make the (9) that you can't afford a vacation. Call a travel agent NOW and make your reservation. See you at the Sand and Surf soon, and don't forget your bathing (10)!

huge	cool
excuse	mood
few	fruit
usual	suit
pupil	juice

1. **mood**
2. **few**
3. **cool**
4. **fruit**
5. **juice**
6. **pupil**
7. **usual**
8. **huge**
9. **excuse**
10. **suit**

Word *Study*

COLLECTIVE NOUNS   You know the phrase, "a herd of elephants," but did you know a group of geese is called a "gaggle"? Words like *herd* and *gaggle* are called **collective nouns.** Sometimes they reflect a quality possessed by the subject. This is why we speak of a *pride* of lions—because they seem proud to us.

Find the collective noun at the right that names each group below. Your Spelling Dictionary will help you.

1. Just one is called a goldfish.
   Two are goldfish or goldfishes.
   As a group, they are called a ___ .
2. One alone is a bee.
   More than one are bees.
   As a group, they are called a ___ .
3. One is called a fox.
   Two or more are called foxes.
   As a group, they are called a ___ .

1. **school**
2. **swarm**
3. **skulk**

Literature Connection

Collective Nouns *A Cache of Jewels and Other Collective Nouns* by Ruth Heller (Putnam, 1989)

MEETING THE NEEDS OF ALL STUDENTS

Modified List

Review Students studying high-frequency words complete this page.

Enrichment

Animal Groups Extend the collective noun activity by having students find out what animal each of the following collective nouns refers to: *gam* (whales), *kindle* (kittens), *parcel* (penguins), *sloth* (bears).

Visual Learners

Collective Phrases Have students draw a picture to illustrate a collective phrase, such as *a gaggle of geese*, or *a swarm of bees*. Have them write the phrase below the picture.

Additional Practice

Review Master 22
Standardized Test Master 22
Everyday Spelling **CD-ROM**

LESSON

23

Generalization

Spelling Focus: A homophone is a word that sounds exactly like another word but has a different spelling and meaning.

● Core ○ Optional ✓ Assessment

DAILY PLAN	CORE OBJECTIVES	NOTES

DAY 1 Introduction

● ✓ Pretest and Self-Check, p. 108B
● Spelling Focus and Word List, p. 108
○ Challenge Words, p. 108
○ Challenge Master 23
○ Home-School Master 23

✓ ▪ Take and self-check Pretest
▪ Spell words that are homophones; classify and write the list words

DAY 2 Think and Practice

● Homophone Photos; Homophone Quotes, p. 109
● Strategic Spelling: *Using the Memory Tricks Strategy*, p. 109
○ Hardbound Book Master 23A
○ Think and Practice Master 23
○ Extra Practice Master 23
○ Cross-Curricular Lesson: Introduce, p. 182

▪ Complete practice activities for words that are homophones
▪ Use memory tricks to help spell homophones

DAY 3 Proofreading and Writing

● Proofread an Outline, p. 110
● Proofreading Tip: Capitalization in Outlines, p. 110
● Write an Outline, p. 110
✓ Cooperative Midweek Test
○ Hardbound Book Master 23B
○ Writing Mini-Lesson Master 23
○ Writing Activity Master 23
○ Second Language Support Master 23

▪ Proofread for spelling and capitalization errors
▪ Integrate spelling and writing in a personal writing response
✓ ▪ Take and check midweek test

DAY 4 Vocabulary Building

● Review: Poetry, p. 111
● Using a Dictionary: Homographs, p. 111
○ Cross-Curricular Lesson: Follow-Up, p. 182
○ Review Master 23

▪ Complete review activity for homophones
▪ Investigate how to use a dictionary to find the right meaning of a homograph

DAY 5 Assessment

● ✓ Posttest, p. 108B
○ Standardized Test Master 23

✓ ▪ Take Posttest

Cross-Curricular Lessons

Use the Spelling Focus (homophones) to introduce the Social Studies lesson, *Arctic Life,* page 182, or choose a lesson that correlates with a topic you're currently teaching.

MEETING THE NEEDS OF ALL STUDENTS

The Word List

For students studying 20 words, assign pages 108–111 and Extra Practice and Review masters.

Modified List For students studying 10 words, modify Practice on page 108, and assign Think and Practice Master 23 and pages 110–111.

Challenge For students studying 26 words, assign pages 108–111, Challenge, Extra Practice, and Review masters.

Bilingual/ESL

Because each Spanish vowel sound is generally represented by the same letter, Spanish-speaking students may have difficulty with homophones that differ in the spelling of the vowel sounds. They may misspell *beat* and *beet* as *bit* and *brake* and *break* as *brek.*

Personal Words

Students add to Personal Words lists by looking at work in their writing portfolios and words they want to remember from their reading.

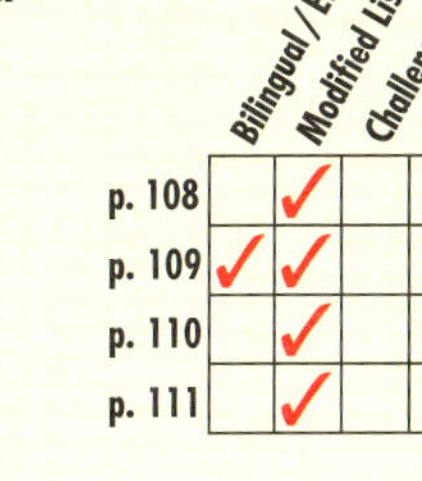

	Bilingual / ESL	Modified List	Challenge	Extra Support	Enrichment	Visual Learners	Auditory Learners	Kinesthetic Learners
p. 108	✓				✓			
p. 109	✓	✓						
p. 110		✓		✓				
p. 111		✓				✓		

ASSESSMENT*

Pretest

Read the underlined word, read the sentence, and then repeat the underlined word. Guide students in self-correcting their pretests and correcting any misspellings.

1. The lamp is made of <u>wood</u>.
2. I <u>would</u> like that balloon.
3. It's <u>too</u> cool for swimming.
4. Please go <u>to</u> the store.
5. There are <u>two</u> books left.
6. The food is over <u>there</u>.
7. <u>Their</u> house has a red door.
8. <u>They're</u> going on vacation.
9. Did you do <u>your</u> homework?
10. <u>You're</u> the first in line.
11. Jon <u>beat</u> me in the race.
12. A <u>beet</u> is actually a root.
13. Did she <u>break</u> her promise?
14. My bike has a hand <u>brake</u>.
15. He bought new <u>clothes</u>.
16. Please <u>close</u> the window.
17. He ate a <u>piece</u> of pie.
18. They work for world <u>peace</u>.
19. The trash was <u>thrown</u> out.
20. A king sat on his <u>throne</u>.

Posttest

Read aloud the sentences below. These sentences may be used for dictation.

1. <u>They're</u> studying math.
2. <u>Their</u> horse won a race.
3. <u>There</u> is no reason to cry.
4. Have you been <u>to</u> a farm?
5. She ate <u>too</u> many peaches.
6. I wrote <u>two</u> stories.
7. <u>You're</u> very careful.
8. Are those <u>your</u> flowers?
9. The fort is made of <u>wood</u>.
10. <u>Would</u> you get the mail?
11. The queen has a <u>throne</u>.
12. The ball was <u>thrown</u> hard.
13. A <u>brake</u> stopped the train.
14. Don't <u>break</u> any dishes.
15. She took a <u>piece</u> of fudge.
16. They want food and <u>peace</u>.
17. I <u>beat</u> her in the contest.
18. Is the <u>beet</u> white or red?
19. Change <u>clothes</u> for class.
20. Who will <u>close</u> the shop?

Challenge Words

1. You <u>guessed</u> my surprise.
2. I will invite a <u>guest</u>.
3. The church has one <u>aisle</u>.
4. An <u>isle</u> may have beaches.
5. Can you bend at the <u>waist</u>?
6. Please don't <u>waste</u> food.

Additional Assessment

Standardized Test Master 23
Dictation Sentences, p. T40
Everyday Spelling CD-ROM

WHAT'S THE BIG IDEA?
Research in Action told us that homophones comprise a major portion of spelling errors at all grades. Encourage students to make up mnemonics, such as *I* **brake** for **cake.**

* See pp. T20 and T33 for test-study-test information.

DAY 1 CHALLENGE MASTER

CHALLENGE ■ 23

Challenge Words

guessed	guest	waste
waist	aisle	isle

■ Use the Challenge Words to answer the following questions.

1. Which one would you sail to? **isle**
2. Which one means you didn't know? **guessed**
3. Which one helps your body bend? **waist**
4. Which one is a bunch of garbage? **waste**
5. Which one do people walk down at a wedding? **aisle**
6. Which one should you treat with special care? **guest**

■ Have you ever had a party? Have you ever been invited to one? Write about the best party—or the worst party—you ever had or attended. Use one or more Challenge Words.

Practice Masters, p. 89

DAY 1 HOME-SCHOOL MASTER

■ 23   HOME-SCHOOL ACTIVITIES   23 ■

Word Check 23
1. beat
2. beet
3. break
4. brake
5. wood
6. would
7. clothes
8. close
9. piece
10. peace
11. your
12. you're
13. thrown
14. throne
15. to
16. too
17. two
18. there
19. their
20. they're

■ **Word Cousins** Write a list word to complete each group of words.

1. castle, crown, **throne**
2. smash, shatter, **break**
3. should, could, **would**
4. zero, one, **two**
5. metal, brick, **wood**
6. here, where, **there**
7. shut, slam, **close**
8. we're, they're, **you're**
9. slice, chunk, **piece**
10. outfits, garments, **clothes**

■ **Word Bits** Write the list words that contain these short words. Use two list words to complete the riddle.

11. rake **brake**
12. you **your**
13. bee **beet**
14. hey **they're**
15. pea **peace**
16. heir **their**
17. eat **beat**
18. row **thrown**

The two last words sound alike and one is found inside the other. Write the words.

19. t o   **t** **o**   20. t o o   **t** **o** **o**

Dear Parent,

Please check to see that your child has done this page correctly. Circle any misspelled words and help your child study them.

Tear off the Word Check before your child returns this page to class. Use it to help your child study.

Home-School Activities, p. 20

DAY 2 THINK AND PRACTICE MASTER

23 ■ THINK AND PRACTICE

wood	would	too	to	two
there	their	they're	your	you're

■ **Homophones** Read each sentence. Then write the homophones under their correct meanings.

They're over there by their car.

they are	belonging to them	at that place
1. **They're**	2. **their**	3. **there**

Your sister said you're not going out.

you are	belonging to you
4. **you're**	5. **Your**

These two people went to the store too.

one more than one	also	in the direction of
6. **two**	7. **too**	8. **to**

■ **Context** Write two list words that sound alike to complete each sentence.

9. **Would** you please bring in some **wood** for the fire?
10. Did you know that **you're** the tallest person at **your** party?
11. Are **there** five people in **their** family?
12. Those **two** dogs belong here **too**
13. I want **to** buy those **two** shirts.

STRATEGIC SPELLING: Using the Memory Tricks Strategy
Use memory tricks to help you spell. Write a list word to complete each trick. Underline the matching letters.

14. two holes in **wood**
15. I **would** if I could.

Practice Masters, p. 90

DAY 2 EXTRA PRACTICE MASTER

EXTRA PRACTICE ■ 23

Word List

wood	would	too	to	two
there	their	they're	your	you're
beat	beet	break	brake	clothes
close	piece	peace	thrown	throne

■ **Which Is Which?** Use the list word homophones to complete the sentences.

1. Are these your ___ scattered all over the bedroom?
2. Yes, but if the mess bothers you, I'll ___ the door.
3. I never thought that team would ___ us!
4. How embarrassing, my face is ___ red!
5. The ___ cousins, Alan and Mike, went to the same school.
6. A third cousin, Sal, went there ___.
7. They all wished they could go ___ different schools.
8. May I have a ___ of the pizza?
9. Yes, if you'll give me some ___ so I can study!
10. The police officer saw a thief about to ___ into a store.
11. She hit the ___ pedal and stopped to make an arrest.
12. I hope ___ going to bring that new CD to the party.
13. I will if you bring ___ guitar.
14. The king sat angrily on his ___.
15. He was angry because the queen had ___ out his old robe.
16. We went to ___ school for a science fair.
17. Cora and June demonstrated a gravity experiment ___.
18. We think ___ the two smartest science students we have.
19. This heavy table is made of ___.
20. ___ you please help me move it?

1. **clothes**
2. **close**
3. **beat**
4. **beet**
5. **two**
6. **too**
7. **to**
8. **piece**
9. **peace**
10. **break**
11. **brake**
12. **you're**
13. **your**
14. **throne**
15. **thrown**
16. **their**
17. **there**
18. **they're**
19. **wood**
20. **Would**

Practice Masters, p. 91

TECHNOLOGY AND VISUAL SUPPORT	 Use Audiotape B, Side 2, Lesson 23	 For additional practice use *Everyday Spelling* Game Software, Lesson 23	 Additional resources on *Everyday Spelling* CD-ROM: proofreading and writing, modified list and challenge words, auditory test
	Use Proofreading and Writing Transparency 23		

DAY 3 SECOND LANGUAGE SUPPORT MASTER

23 ■ SECOND LANGUAGE SUPPORT

About Me

Read what Colette wrote about herself.

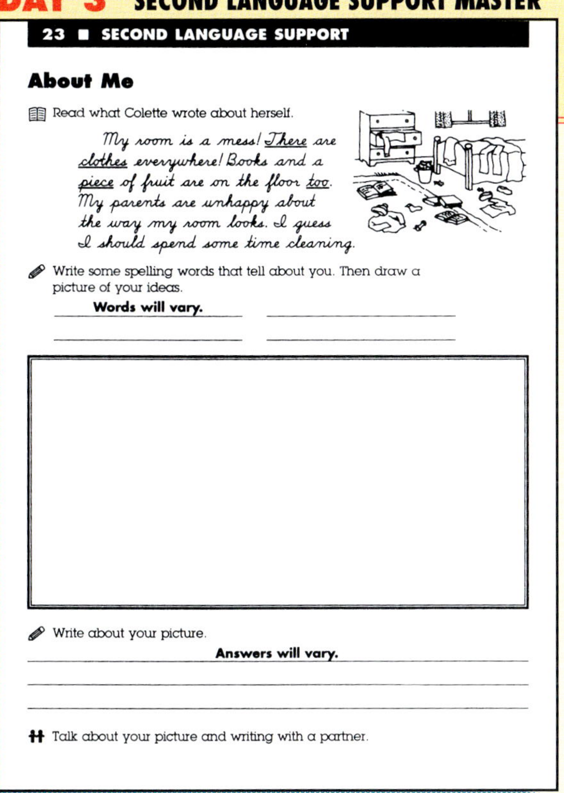

Write some spelling words that tell about you. Then draw a picture of your ideas.

Words will vary.

Write about your picture. **Answers will vary.**

✚ Talk about your picture and writing with a partner.

Second Language Support, p. 46

DAY 3 WRITING ACTIVITY MASTER

23 ■ WRITING ACTIVITY

Capital Letters in an Outline

≡	Make a capital
/	Make a small letter
∧	Add something
⸜	Take out something
⊙	Add a period
¶	New paragraph

⅃ Use capital letters in an outline for the first word of each main topic and subtopic.

■ Read the outline Seamus wrote. Fix any mistakes with capital letters.

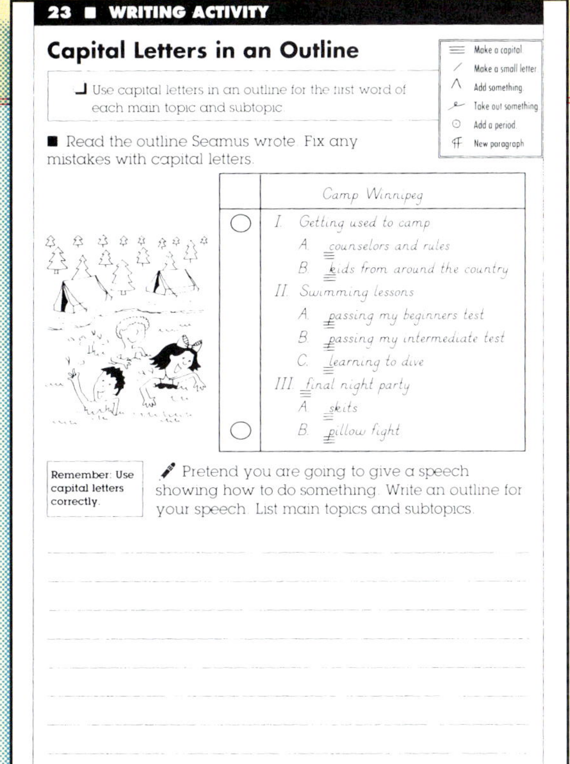

Remember: Use capital letters correctly.

Pretend you are going to give a speech showing how to do something. Write an outline for your speech. List main topics and subtopics.

Spelling and Writing, p. 40

DAY 4 REVIEW MASTER

23 ■ REVIEW

Word List

wood	would	too	to	two
there	their	they're	your	you're
beat	beet	break	brake	clothes
close	piece	peace	thrown	throne

■ **Draw Your Own Conclusions**
Write the list word that matches each clue.

1. a nation's ruler might sit on this
2. where you are when you're not here
3. a vegetable that is round and red
4. what there is when there isn't war
5. a hand pedal on some bikes
6. the sum of one and one
7. what comes from trees
8. models show these off
9. belonging to them
10. a part of something

1. **throne**
2. **there**
3. **beet**
4. **peace**
5. **brake**
6. **two**
7. **wood**
8. **clothes**
9. **their**
10. **piece**

■ **Context Clues** Use list words to complete the sentences below.

11. Double chocolate fudge is ___ sweet for my taste.
12. If it gets cold, ___ the windows.
13. It's a shame not ___ go out on a beautiful night like this.
14. I heard ___ up to your neck in work.
15. The class ___ like to help save the rain forests.
16. Why have you ___ away your book bag?
17. Take care not to ___ any dishes.
18. Carlos and Terry may watch TV when ___ finished with dinner.
19. The ___ of bongo drums can be soft or loud.
20. Mind ___ table manners.

11. **too**
12. **close**
13. **to**
14. **you're**
15. **would**
16. **thrown**
17. **break**
18. **they're**
19. **beat**
20. **your**

Practice Masters, p. 92

DAY 5 STANDARDIZED TEST MASTER

23 ■ LESSON TEST

■ Find the word in each group that is spelled correctly. Fill in the letter for the correct word on the answer strip.

Sample:
- **a.** kwilt **c.** qwilt
- **b.** quilet **d.** quilt   → ⓐⓑⓒ●

1. **a.** thier **b.** their **c.** ther **d.** theer   → 1. ⓐ●ⓒⓓ
2. **a.** there **b.** ther **c.** thar **d.** theer   → 2. ●ⓑⓒⓓ
3. **a.** ther **b.** theyre **c.** they're **d.** theyer   → 3. ⓐⓑ●ⓓ
4. **a.** beat **b.** bete **c.** beate **d.** baet   → 4. ●ⓑⓒⓓ
5. **a.** brak **b.** braek **c.** break **d.** breack   → 5. ⓐⓑ●ⓓ
6. **a.** two **b.** tou **c.** toow **d.** twoo   → 6. ●ⓑⓒⓓ
7. **a.** toow **b.** tooe **c.** too **d.** tou   → 7. ⓐⓑ●ⓓ
8. **a.** beit **b.** beet **c.** beete **d.** bete   → 8. ⓐ●ⓒⓓ
9. **a.** cloes **b.** clohtes **c.** clothse **d.** clothes   → 9. ⓐⓑⓒ●
10. **a.** brake **b.** braek **c.** breake **d.** brayke   → 10. ●ⓑⓒⓓ
11. **a.** wold **b.** woud **c.** wuuld **d.** woode   → 11. ⓐⓑ●ⓓ
12. **a.** klows **b.** close **c.** closse **d.** clos   → 12. ⓐ●ⓒⓓ
13. **a.** peice **b.** piece **c.** pice **d.** peece   → 13. ⓐ●ⓒⓓ
14. **a.** thrown **b.** thron **c.** throwen **d.** throwne   → 14. ●ⓑⓒⓓ
15. **a.** youre **b.** your **c.** yor **d.** yur   → 15. ⓐ●ⓒⓓ
16. **a.** tou **b.** tu **c.** to **d.** toow   → 16. ⓐⓑ●ⓓ
17. **a.** thron **b.** throwne **c.** throne **d.** throon   → 17. ⓐⓑ●ⓓ
18. **a.** woud **b.** wod **c.** wode **d.** wood   → 18. ⓐⓑⓒ●
19. **a.** you're **b.** youre **c.** yor **d.** your'e   → 19. ●ⓑⓒⓓ
20. **a.** pes **b.** peace **c.** peez **d.** peece   → 20. ⓐ●ⓒⓓ

Practice for Standardized Tests, p. 32

LESSON 23

INTRODUCTION

Word Meaning

Context To stress the importance of context in learning to spell homophones, have pairs of students play a game in which one says a sentence using a list word and the other identifies and spells the homophone.

MEETING THE NEEDS OF ALL STUDENTS

Modified List

Practice Students studying only the high-frequency words in the top box write the homophone groups that may be difficult for them. Then they write the rest.

Visual Learners

Flashcards Have students prepare flashcards for picturable homophones, with the word on one card and a picture on another. Students can match the words with the illustrations.

Additional Practice

Challenge Master 23
Home-School Master 23
Audiotape B, Side 2

1. _______________
2. _______________
3. _______________
4. _______________
5. _______________
6. _______________
7. _______________
8. _______________
9. _______________
10. _______________
11. _______________
12. _______________
13. _______________
14. _______________
15. _______________
16. _______________
17. _______________
18. _______________
19. _______________
20. _______________

CHALLENGE!

guessed	guest
aisle	isle
waist	waste

108

■ INTRODUCTION

Homophones

SPELLING FOCUS

A homophone is a word that sounds exactly like another word but has a different spelling and meaning: **wood, would.**

■ **STUDY**   Say each word. Then read the sentence.

1. wood — Put some **wood** on the fire.
2. would ✳ — He asked if I **would** help.
3. too ✳ — She was **too** tired to stay awake.
4. to — Come **to** the meeting at noon.
5. two — He has **two** dogs and a cat.
6. there ✳ — I've never been **there** before.
7. their ✳ — The girls brought **their** guitars.
8. they're ✳ — Ask them if **they're** twins.
9. your — Did you leave **your** bike here?
10. you're ✳ — She asked when **you're** going.

11. beat — The drummer **beat** his drum.
12. beet — You can eat a **beet** cooked or raw.
13. break — Eggs **break** easily.
14. brake — Always **brake** at a stop sign.
15. clothes — He bought some new **clothes.**
16. close — Remember to **close** the window.
17. piece — I cut a **piece** of cheese.
18. peace — People dream of world **peace.**
19. thrown — She was **thrown** from a horse.
20. throne — The queen sat on her **throne.**

■ **PRACTICE**   First write the homophone groups that may be difficult for you to keep straight. Then write the rest of the homophones.
Order of words in each group may vary.

■ **WRITE**   Choose two sentences to write a dialogue, or conversation, between two or more people.
Dialogues will vary.

✳ **WATCH OUT FOR FREQUENTLY MISSPELLED WORDS!**

THINK AND PRACTICE

HOMOPHONE PHOTOS Write the list word that labels each photograph. Below that word, write another list word that sounds just like it.

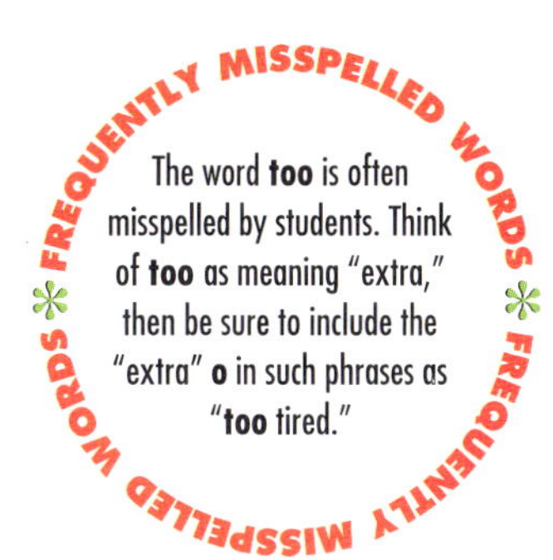

FREQUENTLY MISSPELLED WORDS

The word **too** is often misspelled by students. Think of **too** as meaning "extra," then be sure to include the "extra" **o** in such phrases as "**too** tired."

1. __wood__
2. __would__
3. __clothes__
4. __close__
5. __beet__
6. __beat__

HOMOPHONE QUOTES Complete the statements of the people below by writing list words that sound alike.

King: "I was so unpopular, I was (7) from my (8)."
Teacher: "If they stay (9), I know (10) going to miss (11) bus."
Twins: "The (12) of us would like (13) ride the bus (14)."
Driver: "If I (15) suddenly, the dishes in the back will (16)."
Dentist: "Tino, (17) going to have to brush (18) teeth more."

7. thrown
8. throne
9. there
10. they're
11. their
12. two
13. to
14. too
15. brake
16. break
17. you're
18. your

Strategic Spelling

Using the Memory Tricks Strategy

Use memory tricks to help you spell. Write a list word to complete each trick. Underline the matching letters.

19. a __piece__ of pie
20. __peace__ for people all over

THINK AND PRACTICE

Homophone Quotes

Process of Elimination

Have pairs of students read the statements aloud. Suggest that they read each sentence several times, trying one set of homophones each time until they find the appropriate words.

MEETING THE NEEDS OF ALL STUDENTS

Modified List

Review Students studying high-frequency words complete Think and Practice Master 23.

Bilingual/ESL

Homophone Photos

Focusing on picturable words is a good way for ESL students to learn some sets of homophones. To extend the activity, find and display additional pictures illustrating homophones.

Additional Practice

Hardbound Book Master 23A
Think and Practice Master 23
Extra Practice Master 23
Everyday Spelling **CD-ROM**
Everyday Spelling **Game Software**

LESSON 23

- ● Proofread an Outline
- ● Proofreading Tip: Capitalization in Outlines
- ● Write an Outline
- ✓ Cooperative Midweek Test

DAILY SPELLING REVIEW

Dosen't your sister wear *glass*?

Doesn't   *glasses*

● **Core**   ○ **Optional**   ✓ **Assessment**

PROOFREADING AND WRITING

Punctuation

Capitalization in Outlines

Ask students to capitalize this outline:

Transportation
I. public
  A. Trains
  B. buses
II. personal
  A. Car
  B. bicycle
  C. on foot

MEETING THE NEEDS OF ALL STUDENTS

Modified List

Proofreading Students studying high-frequency words complete this page or the proofreading activity on the *Everyday Spelling* CD-ROM.

Enrichment

Using Outlines Have students exchange and check each other's outlines. Then ask volunteers to give their speeches.

Additional Practice

Hardbound Book Master 23B
Second Language Master 23
Writing Mini-Lesson Master 23
Writing Activity Master 23
***Everyday Spelling* CD-ROM**

■ PROOFREADING AND WRITING

PROOFREAD AN OUTLINE Sara is giving a speech tomorrow. Read her outline. Correct four misspelled words and two errors in capitalization.

PROOFREADING TIP
Sara knows that the first word in each main topic and subtopic of her outline must be capitalized. Proofreading would have helped her do just that.

How to Build a Birdhouse
I. Gather your materials
  A. Seven squares of wod [wood] (sides, bottom, roof)
  B. Hammer and nails
II. assemble you're [your] materials
  A. Cut hole in one peace [piece]
  B. Nail four sides together (opening in front)
  C. nail bottom to sides
  D. Nail the last to [two] pieces on top for roof
III. Paint your birdhouse

WRITE AN OUTLINE Write an outline of a speech you would like to give. Use list words.

Responses will vary. Outlines should include one or more list words.

| Make a capital. |
| Make a small letter |
| Add something. |
| Take out something |
| Add a period. |
| New paragraph |

Word List

beat	your
beet	you're
break	thrown
brake	throne
wood	to
would	too
clothes	two
close	there
piece	their
peace	they're

Personal Words

1. **Words will vary.**
2.

110

VOCABULARY BUILDING

Review

POETRY   Write the boxed words that complete the poem.

Hair, oh hair,
It's just not fair!
Give me (1) hair, (2) hair,
Any hair but MY hair!

I'd say (3) lucky, (4) lucky (5),
To have such a fine-looking, stylish hairdo.
Mine is neither here nor (6),
Usually it's ho-hum hair.

Wait! Look in that window. STOP!
See that head made of (7) with a wig on top?
It's curly! I do declare,
I simply MUST have that hair!

Could you, (8) you spare a dollar or (9),
And help me (10) get a brand-new exciting hairdo?

wood	there
would	their
too	they're
to	your
two	you're

1. **your or their**
2. **their or your**
3. **you're or they're**
4. **they're or you're**
5. **too**
6. **there**
7. **wood**
8. **would**
9. **two**
10. **to**

Using a *Dictionary*

HOMOGRAPHS   If you looked up *brake* in a dictionary, here is what you would find:

There is more than one entry for *brake*. *Brake* is a **homograph.** Homographs are spelled exactly alike, but they have different word histories and different meanings. The raised number alerts you to this.

Study the entries for *brake*. Write *brake¹* or *brake²* to answer each question below.

1. Which entry can be more than one part of speech?
2. Which entry has an example sentence?
3. Which entry would you find in a forest?

brake¹ (brāk), **1** anything used to slow or stop the motion of a wheel or vehicle by pressing or scraping or by rubbing against. **2** show or stop by moving a brake: *The driver braked the speeding car and it slid to a stop. 1 n., 2 v.,* **braked, brak•ing.**

brake² (brāk), **1** a thick growth of bushes; thicket. *n.*

1. **brake¹**
2. **brake¹**
3. **brake²**

111

LESSON

24

Unit Review Concepts
Getting Letters in Correct Order
Vowels with r
Vowel Sounds in *put* and *out*
Vowel Sounds in *few* and *moon*
Homophones

● **Core**   ○ **Optional**   ✓ **Assessment**

DAILY PLAN	CORE OBJECTIVES	NOTES

DAY 1

Review Activity:
●   Clarinetists' Complaint, p. 112
✓ Self-Assessment:
  How Am I Doing?
Integrating Spelling:
○   Language Arts, p. 112
○ Review Master 24A

- Use review words in a letter of complaint
- ✓ Assess their own progress in the spelling of words in Unit 4

DAY 2

Review Activities:
●   Labels, p. 113
●   Description, p. 113
Integrating Spelling:
○   Science, p. 113
○   Science, p. 113

- Use review words to complete labels
- Use review words to answer descriptive riddles

DAY 3

Review Activities:
●   Wally, p.114
●   Pen Pals, p. 114
Integrating Spelling:
○   Health, p. 114
○   Social Studies, p. 114
○ Review Master 24B

- Use review words to complete a comic strip
- Use review words to complete a card to a pen pal

DAY 4

Review Activities:
●   Petite Poems, p. 115
●   Shopping List, p. 115
Integrating Spelling:
○   Language Arts, p. 115
○   Health, p. 115
○ Standardized Test Masters 24A–24D

- Use review words to complete short poems
- Use review words to complete a shopping list

DAY 5

✓ Unit Review Test
✓ Writing Test
○ Writing Prompt Transparency 4
○ Writing Model Transparencies
  4A, 4B

- ✓ Assess review words
- ✓ Assess narrative writing

MEETING THE NEEDS OF ALL STUDENTS

Modified List

For students studying only the high-frequency words in each lesson, assign Review Masters 24A–24B for unit review. Use the Modified Dictation Sentences for assessment.

Bilingual/ESL

Second-language learners might enjoy choosing a review word to copy on a card and then telling what they know about this word. They may offer attributes of nouns, demonstrate the action of a verb, or tell what an adjective describes.

Spelling Conferences

Conduct individual spelling conferences to discuss each student's spelling progress during Unit 4. You might want to take this opportunity to remind students to add to their personal dictionaries.

ASSESSMENT

Dictation Sentences

1. A <u>storm</u> came up while we were walking in the <u>forest</u>.
2. The nurse will go to the <u>hospital</u> as <u>usual</u>.
3. I could never climb that <u>huge</u> <u>mountain</u>!
4. My new <u>neighbor</u> is a <u>butcher</u>.
5. The <u>suit</u> has a short jacket and a long <u>skirt</u>.
6. His <u>nephew</u> is <u>fourteen</u>.
7. Mom put a <u>heart</u> design on the chair <u>cushion</u>.
8. What is the <u>weight</u> of that <u>football</u> player?
9. I will have a <u>piece</u> of <u>fruit</u> with my breakfast.
10. That <u>cloud</u> will cause a rain <u>shower</u>.
11. This <u>shampoo</u> is great for <u>dirty</u> hair.
12. Chocolate <u>pudding</u> is on the <u>menu</u>.
13. I will drink <u>two</u> glasses of <u>juice</u> after the game.
14. A <u>crowd</u> of people stood near the <u>school</u>.
15. It must take a lot of <u>nerve</u> to fly an airplane.
16. What holiday is on <u>July</u> <u>fourth</u>?
17. Did the class <u>believe</u> <u>your</u> story?
18. We <u>heard</u> that loud noise <u>again</u>.
19. The baby tried to hold his <u>toes</u>.
20. My grandfather made the <u>wood</u> into a <u>rattle</u>.
21. Every <u>morning</u> I must decide which <u>clothes</u> to wear.
22. A <u>few</u> people use <u>too</u> much <u>fuel</u>.
23. <u>They're</u> not going to climb to that <u>height</u>.
24. We saw some <u>perfect</u> beaches in Florida.
25. My <u>friend</u> asked me to give her the largest <u>pickle</u>.
26. The most beautiful flowers are over <u>there</u>.

Writing Test

Writing Prompt Transparency 4 and Writing Model Transparencies 4A and 4B will help students prepare for holistic writing tests. Helpful information relating to narrative writing tests is provided in the Writer's Handbook on page 238.

Everyday Spelling CD-ROM

An auditory test is available as an alternate testing format.

Modified Dictation Sentences

1. Did you have <u>juice</u> this <u>morning</u>?
2. My writing <u>course</u> puts me in a good <u>mood</u>.
3. There is a <u>field</u> near our <u>house</u>.
4. I was the <u>first</u> <u>pupil</u> to finish.
5. Are you <u>certain</u> <u>you're</u> ready?
6. My <u>friend</u> <u>said</u> he saw you at the park.
7. <u>Your</u> brother knows a <u>few</u> tricks.
8. <u>Two</u> deer ran through the <u>forest</u>.
9. The <u>power</u> went out <u>again</u>.
10. It's <u>too</u> cold to stay <u>outside</u>.
11. There is a <u>huge</u> <u>bush</u> in our yard.
12. We will use <u>wood</u> <u>to</u> <u>build</u> the fort.

DAY 1 REVIEW MASTER A

REVIEW ■ 24A

Lesson 19

| friend | said | again | field | build |

■ **Definitions** Write the list word that fits the definition.

1. piece of land used for crops — **field**
2. spoke, uttered — **said**
3. make by putting materials together — **build**
4. person who knows and likes another — **friend**
5. once more — **again**

Lesson 20

| certain | first | morning | forest | course |

■ **Synonyms** Write the list word that means the same as each word or phrase.

1. woods — **forest**
2. dawn — **morning**
3. sure — **certain**
4. track — **course**
5. number one — **first**

Lesson 21

| outside | house | power | bush | wood |

■ **Analogies** Write the list word that completes each phrase.

1. ants and anthill, family and **house**
2. in and out, inside and **outside**
3. airplane and jet, shrub and **bush**
4. body builder and strength, leader and **power**
5. window and glass, table and **wood**

Practice Masters, p. 93

DAY 3 REVIEW MASTER B

24B ■ REVIEW

Lesson 22

| mood | juice | few | huge | pupil |

■ **Classifying** Write the list word that has the same spelling and vowel sound as the words in each group.

1. cube, mule, **huge**
2. pool, spoon, **mood**
3. nephew, curfew, **few**
4. cruise, suit, **juice**
5. music, unit, **pupil**

Lesson 23

| too | to | two | your | you're |

■ **Homophones** Write the list word that correctly completes each sentence.

1. What did you get for **your** mom's birthday?
2. There are **too** many people in the small pool.
3. Did you see the **two** baby birds in the nest?
4. Do you want to drive when **you're** old enough?
5. Who went **to** the mall with you?

Practice Masters, p. 94

DAY 4 STANDARDIZED TEST MASTER A

REVIEW TEST ■ 24A

■ Find the word that is spelled correctly to complete each group of words. Fill in the letter for the correct word on the answer strip.

Sample:
smooth and ______
a. sof   b. saft   c. soft   d. solf   — ⓐⓑ●ⓓ

1. put on new ______
   a. cloths   b. clouths   c. close   d. clothes   — ⓐⓑⓒ●
2. one or ______ reasons
   a. two   b. to   c. tou   d. too   — ●ⓑⓒⓓ
3. a hot day in ______
   a. july   b. July   c. Juli   d. Jily   — ⓐ●ⓒⓓ
4. hands are ______
   a. dirtie   b. derty   c. dirty   d. durty   — ⓐⓑ●ⓓ
5. ______ a loud noise
   a. herd   b. heard   c. heared   d. hered   — ⓐ●ⓒⓓ
6. need ______ for the fire
   a. feuel   b. feul   c. fule   d. fuel   — ⓐⓑⓒ●
7. a ______ with rain and wind
   a. storm   b. stom   c. storum   d. strom   — ●ⓑⓒⓓ
8. everyone is going ______
   a. their   b. thar   c. there   d. ther   — ⓐⓑ●ⓓ
9. take ______ pick
   a. you're   b. youre   c. your   d. yor   — ⓐⓑ●ⓓ
10. read the ______
    a. menoo   b. menu   c. menyou   d. minu   — ⓐ●ⓒⓓ
11. is ______ years old
    a. forteen   b. four-teen   c. foteen   d. fourteen   — ⓐⓑⓒ●
12. a hard game of ______
    a. football   b. foutball   c. foot-ball   d. foot ball   — ●ⓑⓒⓓ

Practice for Standardized Tests, p. 33

DAY 4 STANDARDIZED TEST MASTER B

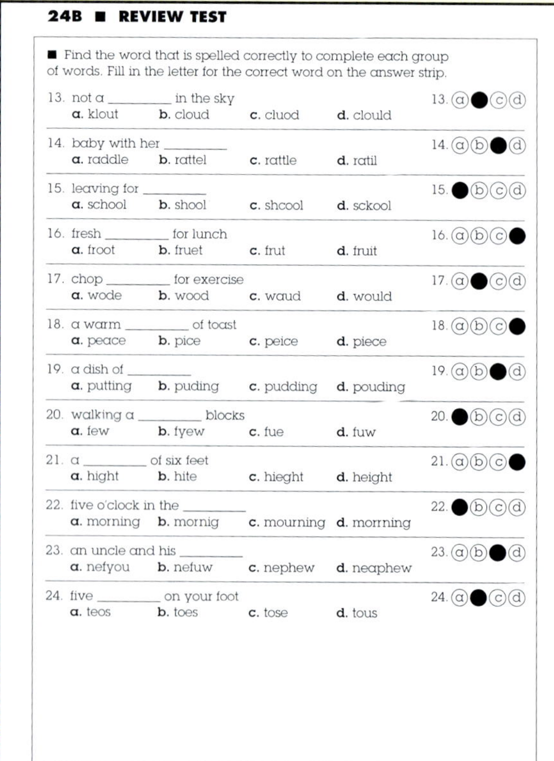

24B ■ REVIEW TEST

■ Find the word that is spelled correctly to complete each group of words. Fill in the letter for the correct word on the answer strip.

13. not a ______ in the sky
    a. klout   b. cloud   c. cluod   d. clould   — 13. ⓐ●ⓒⓓ
14. baby with her ______
    a. raddle   b. rattel   c. rattle   d. ratil   — 14. ⓐⓑ●ⓓ
15. leaving for ______
    a. school   b. shool   c. shcool   d. sckool   — 15. ●ⓑⓒⓓ
16. fresh ______ for lunch
    a. froot   b. fruet   c. frut   d. fruit   — 16. ⓐⓑⓒ●
17. chop ______ for exercise
    a. wode   b. wood   c. waud   d. would   — 17. ⓐ●ⓒⓓ
18. a warm ______ of toast
    a. peace   b. pice   c. peice   d. piece   — 18. ⓐⓑⓒ●
19. a dish of ______
    a. putting   b. puding   c. pudding   d. pouding   — 19. ⓐⓑ●ⓓ
20. walking a ______ blocks
    a. few   b. fyew   c. fue   d. fuw   — 20. ●ⓑⓒⓓ
21. a ______ of six feet
    a. hight   b. hite   c. hieght   d. height   — 21. ⓐⓑⓒ●
22. five o'clock in the ______
    a. morning   b. mornig   c. mourning   d. morrning   — 22. ●ⓑⓒⓓ
23. an uncle and his ______
    a. nefyou   b. nefuw   c. nephew   d. neaphew   — 23. ⓐⓑ●ⓓ
24. five ______ on your foot
    a. teos   b. toes   c. tose   d. tous   — 24. ⓐ●ⓒⓓ

Practice for Standardized Tests, p. 34

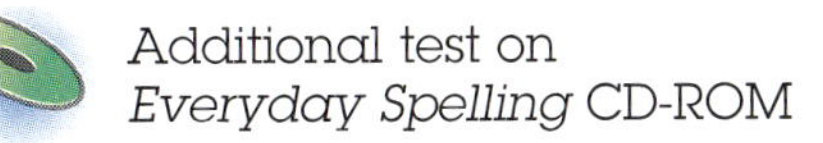

TECHNOLOGY — Additional test on *Everyday Spelling* CD-ROM

DAY 4 — STANDARDIZED TEST MASTER C

REVIEW TEST ■ 24C

■ Find the word that is spelled correctly to complete each sentence. Fill in the letter for the correct word on the answer strip.

25. That family lives in a ________ house.
   a. houge   **b.** huje   **c.** hugde   **d.** huge
   25. ⓐⓑⓒ●

26. She is wearing a pretty ________ today.
   a. skirt   **b.** skart   **c.** skrt   **d.** skert
   26. ●ⓑⓒⓓ

27. I'd like a glass of orange ________, please.
   a. joos   **b.** juice   **c.** jouce   **d.** juce
   27. ⓐ●ⓒⓓ

28. He yelled something about the ________ of that man.
   a. nevre   **b.** nerf   **c.** nerve   **d.** nurve
   28. ⓐⓑ●ⓓ

29. My grandfather had a ________ attack.
   a. heart   **b.** hart   **c.** hrot   **d.** haert
   29. ●ⓑⓒⓓ

30. ________ the best books I have read.
   a. There   **b.** Thier   **c.** They're   **d.** Their
   30. ⓐⓑ●ⓓ

31. A large ________ came to the game.
   a. croud   **b.** crowed   **c.** cround   **d.** crowd
   31. ⓐⓑⓒ●

32. She wanted some water ________.
   a. two   **b.** too   **c.** to   **d.** towo
   32. ⓐ●ⓒⓓ

33. He felt as if a ________ was lifted of his chest.
   a. weight   **b.** wate   **c.** wait   **d.** wieght
   33. ●ⓑⓒⓓ

34. We spent our spring vacation in ________.
   a. Flordia   **b.** florida   **c.** florda   **d.** Florida
   34. ⓐⓑⓒ●

35. That is the ________ eagle I have seen!
   a. four   **b.** fourth   **c.** fouth   **d.** forth
   35. ⓐ●ⓒⓓ

36. He bought a new ________ for the dance.
   a. suite   **b.** sute   **c.** suit   **d.** soot
   36. ⓐⓑ●ⓓ

Practice for Standardized Tests, p. 35

DAY 4 — STANDARDIZED TEST MASTER D

24D ■ REVIEW TEST

■ Find the word in each group that is spelled correctly. Fill in the letter for the correct word on the answer strip.

37. **a.** cushion   **b.** cushun   **c.** cushend   **d.** cution
   37. ●ⓑⓒⓓ

38. **a.** moutain   **b.** mountain   **c.** mountian   **d.** mountan
   38. ⓐ●ⓒⓓ

39. **a.** purfict   **b.** perfict   **c.** perefect   **d.** perfect
   39. ⓐⓑⓒ●

40. **a.** beleave   **b.** beleive   **c.** believe   **d.** belive
   40. ⓐⓑ●ⓓ

41. **a.** hospetal   **b.** hospital   **c.** hospitle   **d.** hospitol
   41. ⓐ●ⓒⓓ

42. **a.** pickle   **b.** pickol   **c.** pickel   **d.** picel
   42. ●ⓑⓒⓓ

43. **a.** freind   **b.** frind   **c.** friend   **d.** frend
   43. ⓐⓑ●ⓓ

44. **a.** shampou   **b.** champoo   **c.** schampoo   **d.** shampoo
   44. ⓐⓑⓒ●

45. **a.** usual   **b.** ushual   **c.** yousuwal   **d.** usuall
   45. ●ⓑⓒⓓ

46. **a.** bootcher   **b.** butcher   **c.** bucher   **d.** butcker
   46. ⓐ●ⓒⓓ

47. **a.** showe   **b.** shawer   **c.** shower   **d.** shouwer
   47. ⓐⓑ●ⓓ

48. **a.** agen   **b.** again   **c.** agian   **d.** agin
   48. ⓐ●ⓒⓓ

49. **a.** forset   **b.** forist   **c.** fourist   **d.** forest
   49. ⓐⓑⓒ●

50. **a.** nieghbor   **b.** neibor   **c.** neighbor   **d.** nabor
   50. ⓐⓑ●ⓓ

Practice for Standardized Tests, p. 36

DAY 5 — WRITING PROMPT TRANSPARENCY

Spelling and Writing, Transparency 4

DAY 1 Plan

- Review Activity
- ✓ Self-Assessment: How Am I Doing?
- Integrating Spelling: Language Arts

● **Core**　○ **Optional**　✓ **Assessment**

How Am I Doing?

Talk with students about why it is helpful to think about their progress in spelling. Raise issues such as

1. I'm learning to spell many new words.
2. When I misspell a word, I usually know it doesn't look correct.
3. When I try to spell a word, I can usually picture it in my head.
4. The hardest word I have learned to spell is ___.
5. I learn to spell a hard word by ___.

Language Arts

Writing a Letter of Complaint Help students think of changes they would like to see take place at school, such as introducing a new food in the cafeteria or making a change in the daily schedule. Have students write a letter explaining their viewpoint.

Additional Resources

Review Master 24A

Review

Lesson 19: Getting Letters in Correct Order
Lesson 20: Vowels with r
Lesson 21: Vowel Sounds in put and out
Lesson 22: Vowel Sounds in few and moon
Lesson 23: Homophones

REVIEW WORD LIST

1. again	11. rattle	21. perfect	31. pudding	41. shampoo
2. believe	12. toes	22. skirt	32. shower	42. suit
3. friend	13. weight	23. storm	33. few	43. usual
4. heard	14. dirty	24. butcher	34. fruit	44. clothes
5. heart	15. Florida	25. cloud	35. fuel	45. there
6. height	16. forest	26. crowd	36. huge	46. they're
7. hospital	17. fourteen	27. cushion	37. juice	47. too
8. neighbor	18. fourth	28. football	38. menu	48. two
9. pickle	19. morning	29. July	39. nephew	49. wood
10. piece	20. nerve	30. mountain	40. school	50. your

CLARINETISTS' COMPLAINT

Band members are filing an official complaint with their leader. Write the words they left out.

usual
suit
clothes
believe
crowd

Dear Mr. Seifworth,

　We, the Woodwind Section, (1) it is unfair that we must wear (2) pants to play in school concerts. The (3) comes to hear us play, not to admire our (4). Please consider letting us wear our (5) school clothes at future concerts.

　　　　Thank you,
　　　　The Woodwinds

1. **believe**
2. **suit**
3. **crowd**
4. **clothes**
5. **usual**

Labels

Tess received a small label maker and went around her house labeling items. Match the name of each item to the number next to it.

1. **shower**
2. **forest**
3. **heart**
4. **cushion**
5. **fourteen**
6. **skirt**
7. **football**

Descriptions

Guess what each person is describing below. Write your answers.

cloud
hospital
wood
storm
nephew

1. **nephew**
2. **cloud**
3. **storm**
4. **wood**
5. **hospital**

113

Science

Making Labels Ask small groups of students to imagine a garden that they would like to plant and care for. Have the groups research the various types of plants in their gardens. Then have them draw a diagram of their garden and label each type of plant.

Science

Descriptions Have students write descriptive clues for weather phenomena, such as thunder, lightning, hail, sleet, blizzard, tornado, and hurricane. Ask volunteers to present their clues to the class and have the class identify the phenomenon.

INTEGRATING SPELLING

Health

Safety Rules Have small groups of students create a strip of three or four panels in which they present rules for a subject, such as bicycle safety or fire prevention.

Social Studies

Pen Pals Students may enjoy having pen pals in other countries. Names may be obtained through clubs, such as Student Letter Exchange, 630 Third Avenue, New York, NY 10017.

Additional Resources

Review Master 24B

Wally
– a cartoon by Sam
Help Sam finish his comic strip about a big baby named Wally.

dirty rattle shampoo friend nerve huge toes

1. **huge**
2. **toes**
3. **rattle**
4. **dirty**
5. **shampoo**
6. **nerve**
7. **friend**

Pen Pals
Read Marissa's card to her pen pal in Moscow, Russia. Supply the missing words.

fourth school height your too they're July weight again

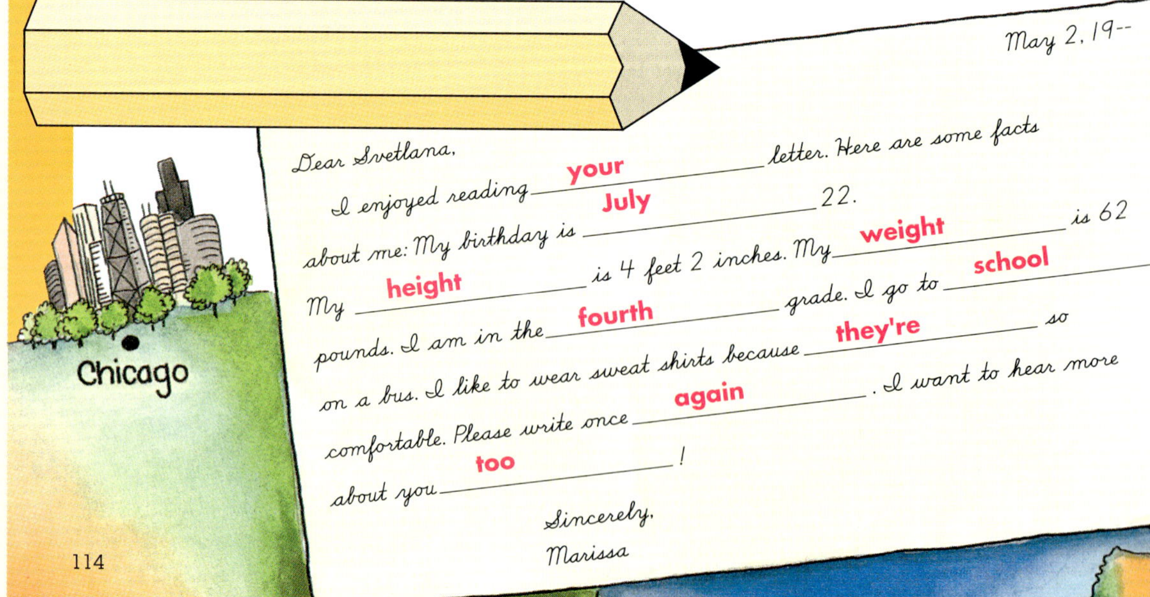

PETITE POEMS

1. **fuel**
2. **there**
3. **heard**
4. **neighbor**
5. **menu**
6. **piece**
7. **morning**
8. **mountain**

Read each short poem below and supply the missing word.

Here's a handy driving rule:
Don't go on the highway
when you're low on (1).

When you've lost something,
you look everywhere.
The last place you look, it's sure
to be (2).

Did I hear the squawks of the
early bird? For an hour and a half
it was all I (3)!

Do yourself a great big favor.
Get to know your next-door (4).

It's easy to order a fine meal when you,
Take a good look at the restaurant's (5).

If this arguing doesn't cease,
The cake will vanish; no one gets a (6).

The storm came up without a warning,
And rocked the city early one (7).

Here's one thing you can always count on:
A hill is never as large as a (8)!

$hopping List

Denzel left this list for Jacqui. Write the missing items.

| few | butcher | fruit | Florida | juice |
| two | pickle | perfect | pudding | |

- fresh orange juice from **Florida**
- a large dill **pickle**
- oranges, apples, bananas, and other **fruit**
- one gallon of sweet apple **juice** —not cider
- six red roses—must be **perfect** !
- one stick of butter and **two** loaves of bread
- just a **few** sprigs of parsley
- ready-made thick chocolate **pudding**
- Have the **butcher** cut up a three-pound chicken.

UNIT 5

Introduces the metacognitive strategy **Pronouncing for Spelling** to show two ways in which pronunciation aids spelling: 1. Pronounce words carefully, listening to each letter's sounds, 2. Exaggerate pronunciation of silent letters.

SCOPE AND SEQUENCE: LESSONS 25–30

Lesson	Generalization	Think and Practice	Proofreading and Writing
25 pp. 118–121	Some words have more letters than expected. To spell these words, pronounce each syllable carefully.	Puzzle It Out Syllable Alert Strategic Spelling: Pronouncing for Spelling	Proofread a Math Problem ■ misspelled words ■ punctuation errors Write a Math Problem
26 pp. 122–125	A compound word is made of two or more words. Keep all the letters when spelling the compounds.	Classifications Joining Words Strategic Spelling: Seeing Meaning Connections	Proofread an Essay ■ misspelled words ■ usage errors Write an Essay
27 pp. 126–129	When adding **-ful**, **-ly**, or **-ion** to most base words, the base stays the same. To words ending in **y**, change the **y** to **i**. To words ending in **e**, drop the **e**.	Suffix Addition Word Forms Strategic Spelling: Using the Meaning Helper Strategy	Proofread Captions ■ misspelled words ■ usage errors Write a Caption
28 pp. 130–133	When **-less**, **-ment** or **-ness** is added to most base words, the base stays the same. If the base word ends in a **consonant** and a **y**, the **y** is changed to **i** before adding the suffix.	Adding Endings Match Up Strategic Spelling: Building New Words	Proofread a Comic Strip ■ misspelled words ■ careless errors Write a Comic Strip
29 pp. 134–137	When prefixes **dis-**, **in-**, **mis-** and **re-** are added to words, make no change in the spelling of the base word.	Super Antonyms Prefix Addition Strategic Spelling: Building New Words	Proofread a Letter ■ misspelled words ■ handwriting errors Write a Letter

	Concepts for Review	Unit 5 Activities	Integrating Spelling
Review 30 pp. 138–141	Including All the Letters Compound Words Suffixes **-ful**, **-ly**, **-ion** Suffixes **-less**, **-ment**, **-ness** Prefixes **dis-**, **in-**, **mis-**, **re-**	Stories Chapter Titles List Newspaper Stories Birthday Card Report	**Health:** Pet Care Poster **Language Arts:** Paragraphs, Dramatizing **Social Studies:** Map Study, Interview **Art:** Birthday Card

OMITTED LETTERS

Leaving letters out of words was the single most common spelling error among fourth graders in *Research in Action*. Silent letters, double letters, and unusual spellings are common culprits, but so are mispronunciation and compound words.

TYPICAL MISSPELLINGS:

- *suprised* for *surprised*
- *ofen* for *often*
- *earings* for *earrings*
- *safly* for *safely*

Helpful strategies include Pronouncing for Spelling.

Vocabulary Building	**Meeting the Needs of All Students**	**Cross-Curricular Lessons***
Review Synonyms; Defining Words **Using a Dictionary** Words That Aren't Entries	**Visual** The Ending Game **Auditory** Mental Math **Bilingual/ESL** Puzzle It Out **Enrichment** Adverbs	**Social Studies:** Our Government, pp. 178–179 **Connections to BookFestival** ■ *Sidewalk Story* by Sharon Bell Mathis
Review Words in Context **Multicultural Connection** Arts	**Visual** Compound Booklets **Auditory** Joining Words **Kinesthetic** Make Jewelry **Bilingual/ESL** Picture Equations **Enrichment** Write a Description	**Health:** Being Safe, pp. 186–187
Review Analogies **Word Study** Codes	**Visual** Find Examples **Auditory** Word Forms **Bilingual/ESL** Context Sentences **Enrichment** Create a Code	**Reading:** Many Ways of Learning, pp. 204–205 **Connections to BookFestival** ■ *There's a Boy in the Girl's Bathroom* by Louis Sachar
Review Puzzle It Out **Word Study** Haiku	**Visual** Compare Base Words **Auditory** Count Syllables **Bilingual/ESL** Focus on Meanings **Enrichment** Draw the Comic Strip	**Reading:** Hopes, Dreams, and Wishes, pp. 202–203 **Connections to BookFestival** ■ *The Mouse and the Motorcycle* by Beverly Cleary
Review Word Associations **Word Study** Synonyms	**Visual** Prefix Addition **Kinesthetic** Prefix Pantomime **Bilingual/ESL** Synonyms **Enrichment** Writing Letters	**Health:** Know Yourself, pp. 184–185 **Connections to BookFestival** ■ *Grandma Moses: Painter of Rural America* by Zibby O'Neal

ADDITIONAL RESOURCES

For Every Weekly Lesson

- **Think and Practice Master**
- **Challenge Master**
- **Extra Practice Master**
- **Review Master**
- **Second Language Support Master**
- **Home-School Activity Master**
- **Writing Mini-Lesson**
- **Writing Activity Master**
- **Standardized Test Master**
- **Proofreading and Writing Transparency**

Technology

- **Audiotape**
- ***Everyday Spelling* CD-ROM**
- ***Everyday Spelling* Game Software**

Unit Review

- **Standardized Test Masters**
- **Writing Prompt Transparency**
- **Writing Model Transparencies**
- ***Everyday Spelling* CD-ROM**

* The cross-curricular lessons are optional. You may, however, wish to teach the cross-curricular lesson that has been paired with the weekly lesson shown in the chart.

5

OBJECTIVES

- Learn and practice the Pronouncing for Spelling strategy
- Apply the Pronouncing for Spelling strategy to list words in Unit 5

PRONOUNCING FOR SPELLING

This strategy suggests that students use pronunciation in two ways to help them spell words. Both ways call upon the use of the auditory modality. The first way calls for students to read a word, pronounce it carefully, and notice how the letters relate to the pronunciation. The second way calls for students to pronounce letters that are usually silent, or not heard clearly in a word, to help them remember the correct spelling.

Additional Resources

Frequently Misspelled Words Poster
Spelling Tool Kit Poster

■ **LEARNING HOW TO LEARN**

Pronouncing for Spelling

DISCOVER THE STRATEGY 1   To avoid making the mistake Josh made in the cartoon below, use this strategy:

1. Pronounce the word carefully and correctly. Listen to the sound of each letter.
2. Pronounce the word again as you write it.

TRY IT OUT   Now practice this strategy yourself.

Pronounce each word in dark type slowly and correctly. Pay special attention to the sounds of the underlined letters. Pronounce each word again as you write it.

1. Say **sur**prise (NOT su-prise) _______ surprise
2. Say **pic**ture (NOT pi-ture) _______ picture
3. Say **streng**th (NOT strenth) _______ strength
4. Say **differ**ent (NOT diff-rent) _______ different
5. Say **chas**ing (NOT chas-in) _______ chasing

DISCOVER THE STRATEGY 2   Pronouncing the word correctly won't work for a word like *thumb*. How can you remember to include the silent **b?** Use the "secret pronunciation" strategy below.

1. Pronounce any silent letters to yourself. Don't worry if the word sounds funny. Say the **b** in *thumb* and the **k** in *knit*. Say "thum-**b**" and "**k**-nit."

2. Exaggerate or change a sound in the word. You might pronounce *million* by exaggerating the smaller word *lion* inside it. Say "mil-**li-on**" to yourself.

TRY IT OUT   Now practice this strategy.

With a partner, make up secret pronunciations for the words below. Pay special attention to the underlined letters. Write each word correctly. Say its secret pronunciation to yourself.

1. lamb		6. talk
2. knit		7. once
3. wrist		8. hour
4. guess		9. clothes
5. everyone		10. movie

1. _____ **lamb** _____
2. _____ **knit** _____
3. _____ **wrist** _____
4. _____ **guess** _____
5. _____ **everyone** _____
6. _____ **talk** _____
7. _____ **once** _____
8. _____ **hour** _____
9. _____ **clothes** _____
10. _____ **movie** _____

LOOK AHEAD   Look ahead at the next five lessons. Write four list words you could use these strategies with. Mark the part of each word that you'll pay special attention to when you pronounce it.

1. _____ **Answers** _____   3. _____ **Answers** _____
2. _____ **will vary.** _____   4. _____ **will vary.** _____

117

117

25

Generalization

Spelling Focus: Some words have more letters than expected. To spell these words, pronounce each syllable carefully.

● Core   ○ Optional   ✓ Assessment

DAILY PLAN	CORE OBJECTIVES	NOTES

DAY 1 Introduction

● Strategy Workshop, p. 116
✓ Pretest and Self-Check, p. 118B
● Spelling Focus and Word List, p. 118
○ Challenge Words, p. 118
○ Challenge Master 25
○ Home-School Master 25

- Learn and practice the strategy Pronouncing for Spelling
✓ Take and self-check Pretest
- Spell words by including all the letters; classify and write the list words

DAY 2 Think and Practice

● Puzzle It Out; Syllable Alert, p. 119
● Strategic Spelling: *Pronouncing for Spelling,* p. 119
○ Hardbound Book Master 25A
○ Think and Practice Master 25
○ Extra Practice Master 25
○ Cross-Curricular Lesson: Introduce, p. 178

- Complete practice activities for words in which it is important to include all the letters
- Pronounce words correctly in order to spell them correctly

DAY 3 Proofreading and Writing

● Proofread a Math Problem, p. 120
● Proofreading Tip: Quotations, p. 120
● Write a Math Problem, p. 120
✓ Cooperative Midweek Test
○ Hardbound Book Master 25B
○ Writing Mini-Lesson Master 25
○ Writing Activity Master 25
○ Second Language Support Master 25

- Proofread for spelling and punctuation errors
- Integrate spelling and writing in a personal writing response
✓ Take and check midweek test

DAY 4 Vocabulary Building

● Review: Synonyms; Defining Words, p. 121
● Using a Dictionary: Words That Aren't Entries, p. 121
○ Cross-Curricular Lesson: Follow-Up, p. 178
○ Review Master 25

- Complete review activities for words that have more letters than expected
- Study inflected forms in dictionary entries

DAY 5 Assessment

✓ Posttest, p. 118B
○ Standardized Test Master 25

✓ Take Posttest

Cross-Curricular Lessons

Use the Spelling Focus (including all the letters) to introduce the Social Studies lesson, *Our Government,* page 178, or choose a lesson that correlates with a topic you're currently teaching.

MEETING THE NEEDS OF ALL STUDENTS

The Word List

For students studying 20 words, assign pages 118–121 and Extra Practice and Review masters.

Modified List For students studying 10 words, modify Practice on page 118, and assign Think and Practice Master 25 and pages 120–121.

Challenge For students studying 25 words, assign pages 118–121, Challenge, Extra Practice, and Review masters.

Bilingual/ESL

In Spanish, the long **e** sound is spelled **i.** Spanish-speaking students may spell the suffix **-ly** as **-li.** For example, they may spell *finally* as *finalli.*

Personal Words

Students add to Personal Words lists by looking at work in their writing portfolios and words they want to remember from their reading.

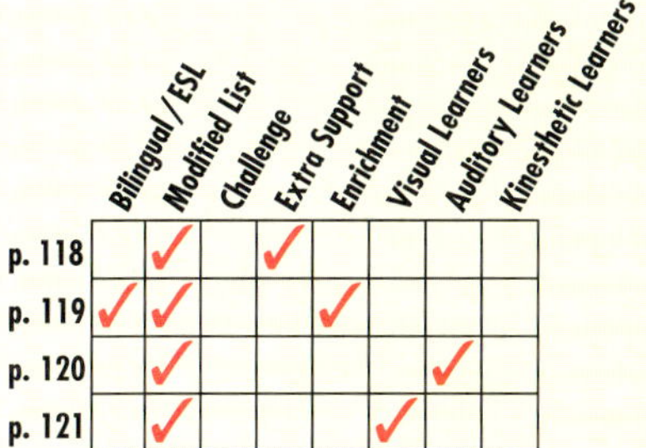

	Bilingual/ESL	Modified List	Challenge	Extra Support	Enrichment	Visual Learners	Auditory Learners	Kinesthetic Learners
p. 118		✓		✓				
p. 119	✓	✓			✓			
p. 120		✓					✓	
p. 121		✓				✓		

ASSESSMENT*

Pretest

Read the underlined word, read the sentence, and then repeat the underlined word. Guide students in self-correcting their pretests and correcting any misspellings.

1. It rains <u>often</u> in the spring.
2. We <u>might</u> go next week.
3. <u>They</u> will march today.
4. Do you <u>remember</u> the date?
5. Kate <u>finally</u> found her shoe.
6. It is <u>really</u> hot today.
7. We saw <u>several</u> planets.
8. <u>Everyone</u> should eat fruit.
9. The zoo is <u>interesting</u>.
10. <u>Everybody</u> liked the play.
11. He is <u>known</u> for his singing.
12. Tom <u>caught</u> a huge fish.
13. The storm <u>surprised</u> us.
14. The hotel was on an <u>island</u>.
15. Who went <u>swimming</u>?
16. Joe bought a <u>camera</u>.
17. I was born in <u>December</u>.
18. I work each <u>evening</u>.
19. He is <u>beginning</u> to cry.
20. <u>February</u> is a short month.

Posttest

Read aloud the sentences below. These sentences may be used for dictation.

1. The team <u>finally</u> won.
2. The sun is <u>really</u> a star.
3. Did <u>everybody</u> dance?
4. <u>Everyone</u> has wishes.
5. <u>They</u> read mysteries.
6. I can't <u>remember</u> that girl.
7. A picnic <u>might</u> be fun.
8. I <u>often</u> visit my cousin.
9. <u>Several</u> people were here.
10. I heard an <u>interesting</u> tale.
11. Bring a <u>camera</u> to the show.
12. The man is <u>known</u> in town.
13. <u>February</u> has holidays.
14. Winter began in <u>December</u>.
15. The loud noise <u>surprised</u> us.
16. The <u>island</u> has a beach.
17. He <u>caught</u> a cold.
18. The <u>evening</u> was beautiful.
19. I took a <u>swimming</u> lesson.
20. It is <u>beginning</u> to rain.

Challenge Words

1. We ate <u>broccoli</u>.
2. She is in <u>kindergarten</u>.
3. The box is in the <u>cabinet</u>.
4. The teacher was <u>serious</u>.
5. I took my <u>temperature</u>.

Additional Assessment

Standardized Test Master 25
Dictation Sentences, p. T41
Everyday Spelling CD-ROM

To help students understand the complexity of English, ask them to write *they* with the sound of long **a** as written in *veil, great, rain,* and *neighbor* (thei, thea, thai, and theigh).

---

* See pp. T20 and T33 for test-study-test information.

DAY 1 CHALLENGE MASTER

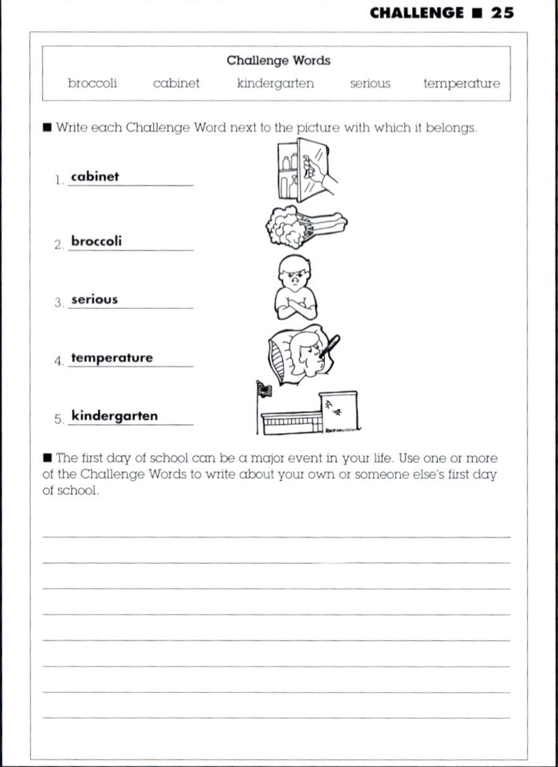

Practice Masters, p. 95

DAY 1 HOME-SCHOOL MASTER

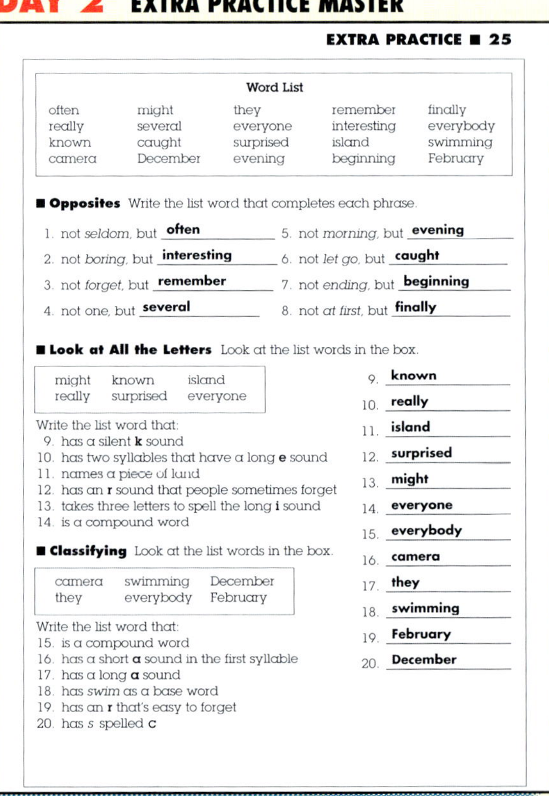

Home-School Activities, p. 21

DAY 2 THINK AND PRACTICE MASTER

25 ■ THINK AND PRACTICE

often	might	they	remember	finally
really	several	everyone	interesting	everybody

■ **Drawing Conclusions** Write the list word or words that match each clue.

1. two words that end in **-ly** — finally / really
2. a word that ends with **-ing** — interesting
3. two compound words — everyone / everybody
4. a word that begins and ends with **r** — remember
5. a word that rhymes with *sight* — might
6. the opposite of *few* — several
7. the opposite of *seldom* — often
8. a word that begins like *that* — they

■ **Syllable Alert** Write the list word that starts and ends with the same letter and has the same number of syllables as each word.

9. try — they
10. reminder — remember
11. fitfully — finally
12. must — might
13. exercise — everyone
14. interlocking — interesting
15. ocean — often
16. rainy — really

STRATEGIC SPELLING: Pronouncing for Spelling
Write *often, finally, interesting,* and *several.* Say each word carefully, pronouncing the underlined letters. It may sound funny, but this strategy will help you spell words.

17. often
18. finally
19. interesting
20. several

Practice Masters, p. 96

DAY 2 EXTRA PRACTICE MASTER

EXTRA PRACTICE ■ 25

		Word List		
often	might	they	remember	finally
really	several	everyone	interesting	everybody
known	caught	surprised	island	swimming
camera	December	evening	beginning	February

■ **Opposites** Write the list word that completes each phrase.

1. not *seldom,* but often
2. not *boring,* but interesting
3. not *forget,* but remember
4. not *one,* but several
5. not *morning,* but evening
6. not *let go,* but caught
7. not *ending,* but beginning
8. not *at first,* but finally

■ **Look at All the Letters** Look at the list words in the box.

might	known	island
really	surprised	everyone

Write the list word that:
9. has a silent **k** sound — known
10. has two syllables that have a long **e** sound — really
11. names a piece of land — island
12. has an **r** sound that people sometimes forget — surprised
13. takes three letters to spell the long **i** sound — might
14. is a compound word — everyone

■ **Classifying** Look at the list words in the box.

camera	swimming	December
they	everybody	February

Write the list word that:
15. is a compound word — everybody
16. has a short **a** sound in the first syllable — camera
17. has a long **a** sound — they
18. has *swim* as a base word — swimming
19. has an **r** that's easy to forget — February
20. has **s** spelled **c** — December

Practice Masters, p. 97

TECHNOLOGY AND VISUAL SUPPORT	 Use Audiotape C, Side 1, Lesson 25  Use Proofreading and Writing Transparency 25	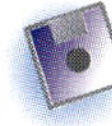 For additional practice use *Everyday Spelling* Game Software, Lesson 25	 Additional resources on *Everyday Spelling* CD-ROM: proofreading and writing, modified list and challenge words, auditory test

DAY 3 SECOND LANGUAGE SUPPORT MASTER

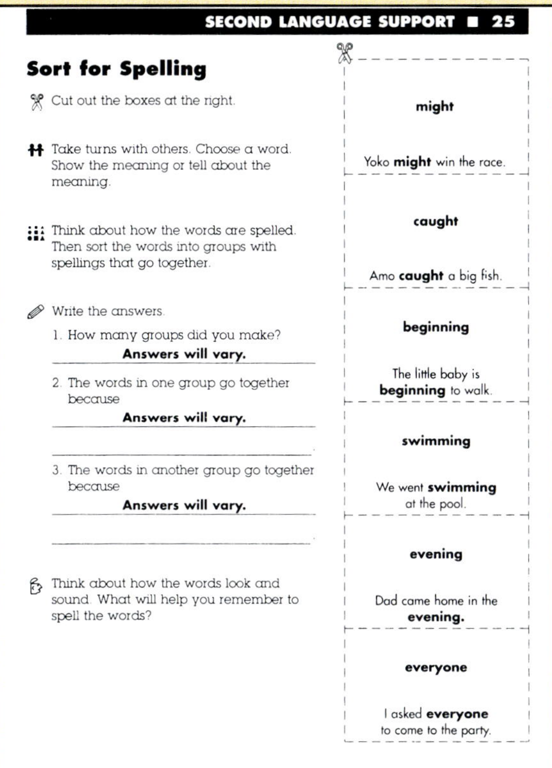

Second Language Support, p. 47

DAY 3 WRITING ACTIVITY MASTER

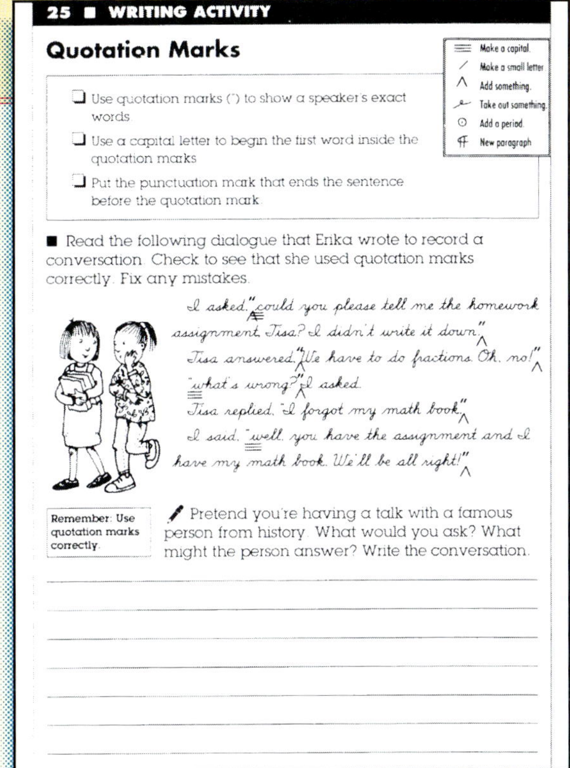

Spelling and Writing, p. 42

DAY 4 REVIEW MASTER

25 ■ REVIEW

Word List

often	might	they	remember	finally
really	several	everyone	interesting	everybody
known	caught	surprised	island	swimming
camera	December	evening	beginning	February

■ **Happy Endings** Add an ending to each word in parentheses to form a list word that completes each question.

1. (begin) When is the fall TV season ___?
2. (know) How long have you ___ Timmy?
3. (final) When are you ___ going to clean up the garage?
4. (interest) Did you find the book ___ or dull?
5. (surprise) Was Beth ___, or did she know about her party?
6. (swim) When will you be well enough to go ___?
7. (real) Do you ___ want to throw out your old dolls?

■ **Word Groups** Write the list word that fits in each group.

8. twilight, nightfall, ___
9. January, ___, March
10. lens, photo, ___
11. October, November, ___
12. anyone, no one, ___
13. some, a few, ___
14. recall, recollect, ___
15. trapped, taken, ___
16. may, is possible, ___
17. somebody, nobody, ___
18. them, those, ___
19. frequently, many times, ___
20. isle, Hawaii, ___

1. **beginning**
2. **known**
3. **finally**
4. **interesting**
5. **surprised**
6. **swimming**
7. **really**
8. **evening**
9. **February**
10. **camera**
11. **December**
12. **everyone**
13. **several**
14. **remember**
15. **caught**
16. **might**
17. **everybody**
18. **they**
19. **often**
20. **island**

Practice Masters, p. 98

DAY 5 STANDARDIZED TEST MASTER

LESSON TEST ■ 25

■ Find the word in each group that is spelled correctly. Fill in the letter for the correct word on the answer strip.

Sample:
- **a.** contes   **c.** cotest
- **b.** contist   **d.** contest   (a)(b)(c)●

1. **a.** camera   **c.** camara
   b. camra   **d.** cammary   1. ●(b)(c)(d)
2. **a.** several   **c.** seral
   b. severel   **d.** sevral   2. ●(b)(c)(d)
3. **a.** iland   **c.** island
   b. ailen   **d.** ilind   3. (a)(b)●(d)
4. **a.** eveing   **c.** evnig
   b. evaning   **d.** evening   4. (a)(b)(c)●
5. **a.** often   **c.** allfin
   b. offen   **d.** ofen   5. ●(b)(c)(d)
6. **a.** thay   **c.** theay
   b. they   **d.** thaiy   6. (a)●(c)(d)
7. **a.** cought   **c.** cauhgt
   b. cout   **d.** caught   7. (a)(b)(c)●
8. **a.** might   **c.** mihgt
   b. myte   **d.** mighte   8. ●(b)(c)(d)
9. **a.** everone   **c.** evryone
   b. everyone   **d.** evrryone   9. (a)●(c)(d)
10. **a.** rember   **c.** remeber
    b. remember   **d.** rememer   10. (a)●(c)(d)
11. **a.** begining   **c.** beginning
    b. beging   **d.** begininng   11. (a)(b)●(d)
12. **a.** swimming   **c.** swmming
    b. swiming   **d.** swimminng   12. ●(b)(c)(d)
13. **a.** suprised   **c.** suprized
    b. surprized   **d.** surprised   13. (a)(b)(c)●
14. **a.** December   **c.** Decmber
    b. Decenber   **d.** december   14. ●(b)(c)(d)
15. **a.** finally   **c.** finly
    b. finaly   **d.** finelly   15. ●(b)(c)(d)
16. **a.** realy   **c.** really
    b. relly   **d.** rilly   16. (a)(b)●(d)
17. **a.** nown   **c.** nowen
    b. known   **d.** knowen   17. (a)●(c)(d)
18. **a.** Febuary   **c.** February
    b. Febrary   **d.** Feburary   18. (a)(b)●(d)
19. **a.** everbody   **c.** everebody
    b. evrybody   **d.** everybody   19. (a)(b)(c)●
20. **a.** intresting   **c.** enterecting
    b. interesting   **d.** interrecting   20. (a)●(c)(d)

Practice for Standardized Tests, p. 37

LESSON 25

✓ Pretest and Self-Check
● Spelling Focus and Word List
○ Challenge Words
○ Modified List

DAILY SPELLING REVIEW

Wood you like a *pickel* with lunch?
Would   *pickle*

● Core   ○ Optional   ✓ Assessment

INTRODUCTION

Phonics

Silent Consonants Have students write the list words with silent consonants and create a mnemonic device for each word (for example, *South Sea island*).

MEETING THE NEEDS OF ALL STUDENTS

Modified List

Practice Students studying only the high-frequency words in the top box write
- two words with one syllable
- one word with two syllables
- five words with three syllables
- two words with four syllables

Extra Support

To Pronounce or Not

Distinguish between words with silent consonants, such as *might,* and those in which pronunciation aids spelling, such as *several.*

Additional Practice

Challenge Master 25
Home-School Master 25
Audiotape C, Side 1

25

1. **might**
2. **they**
3. **caught**
4. **known**
5. **often**
6. **surprised**
7. **island**
8. **swimming**
9. **evening**
10. **remember**
11. **finally**
12. **really**
13. **several**
14. **everyone**
15. **camera**
16. **December**
17. **beginning**
18. **interesting**
19. **everybody**
20. **February**

Order of words in each group may vary.

CHALLENGE!

broccoli
kindergarten
cabinet
serious
temperature

Sentences will vary.

118

■ INTRODUCTION

Including All the Letters

SPELLING FOCUS

Some words have more letters than you might expect. To spell these words, pronounce each syllable carefully.

■ **STUDY** Say each word. Then read the sentence.

1. *often* — Cats **often** sleep most of the day.
2. *might* ✳ — We **might** go fishing next week.
3. *they* ✳ — The girls can go if **they** want to.
4. *remember* — Did he **remember** my name?
5. *finally* ✳ — The package **finally** arrived.
6. *really* ✳ — She sees things as they **really** are.
7. *several* — He invited **several** close friends.
8. *everyone* ✳ — Not **everyone** agreed with me.
9. *interesting* — That's an **interesting** clock.
10. *everybody* ✳ — I saw **everybody** at the party.

11. *known* — Dogs are **known** to be loyal.
12. *caught* ✳ — The player **caught** the ball.
13. *surprised* — He was **surprised** to see her.
14. *island* — Puerto Rico is an **island**.
15. *swimming* ✳ — I went **swimming** in the pool.
16. *camera* — She got film for her **camera**.
17. *December* — Snow may fall in **December**.
18. *evening* — The air cools in the **evening**.
19. *beginning* — The baby is **beginning** to crawl.
20. *February* — **February** 14 is Valentine's Day.

■ **PRACTICE** Sort the list words by writing
- four words with one syllable
- five words with two syllables
- eight words with three syllables
- three words with four syllables

■ **WRITE** Choose ten words to write in sentences.

✳ **WATCH OUT FOR FREQUENTLY MISSPELLED WORDS!**

THINK AND PRACTICE ■

PUZZLE IT OUT   What do you shoot people with that makes them smile? When you write the list words that match the clues, the answer to this riddle will appear in the box.

1. the twelfth month
2. truly; actually
3. call back to mind
4. early part of night
5. astonished; shocked
6. grabbed; took and held
7. The answer to the riddle is a ____.

1. **December**
2. **really**
3. **remember**
4. **evening**
5. **surprised**
6. **caught**

7. **camera**
8. **beginning**
9. **known**
10. **everybody**
11. **they**
12. **swimming**
13. **everyone**
14. **island**
15. **often**
16. **might**

SYLLABLE ALERT   Write the list word that starts and ends with the same letter and has the same number of syllables as each word below.

8. ballooning
9. keen
10. eventfully
11. tray
12. sweeping
13. exercise
14. inward
15. open
16. moat

We sometimes misspell words because we say them wrong. Write *February*, *finally*, *interesting*, and *several*. Now say each word carefully. Be sure to pronounce the underlined syllable.

17. **February**
18. **finally**
19. **interesting**
20. **several**

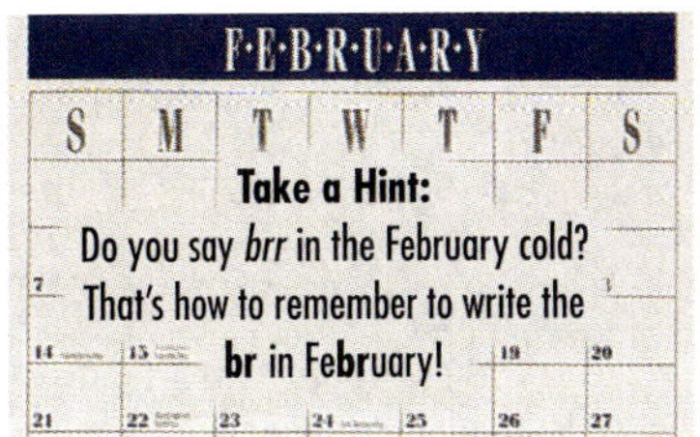

THINK AND PRACTICE

Syllable Alert
Say It Slowly Encourage students to say each word aloud slowly to count the syllables.

MEETING THE NEEDS OF ALL STUDENTS

Modified List
Review Students studying high-frequency words complete Think and Practice Master 25.

Bilingual/ESL
Puzzle It Out Have students of varying language abilities work together on the clues.

Enrichment
Adverbs Have students write sentences using the words *finally*, *really*, and *often*. Point out that the words add meaning to verbs, adjectives, or other adverbs.

Additional Practice
Hardbound Book Master 25A
Think and Practice Master 25
Extra Practice Master 25
Everyday Spelling CD-ROM
Everyday Spelling Game
   Software

LESSON 25

- Proofread a Math Problem
- Proofreading Tip: Quotations
- Write a Math Problem
- ✓ Cooperative Midweek Test

● Core   ○ Optional   ✓ Assessment

PROOFREADING AND WRITING

Punctuation

Quotation Marks Remind students that quotation marks always come in pairs.

MEETING THE NEEDS OF ALL STUDENTS

Modified List

Proofreading Students studying high-frequency words complete this page or the proofreading activity on the *Everyday Spelling* CD-ROM.

Auditory Learners

Mental Math Some students may want to write mental math problems to be read aloud. They can work with a partner to ask and answer the problems orally.

Additional Practice

Hardbound Book Master 25B
Second Language Master 25
Writing Mini-Lesson Master 25
Writing Activity Master 25
Proofreading Transparency 25
Everyday Spelling **CD-ROM**

■ **PROOFREADING AND WRITING**

≡	Make a capital.
/	Make a small letter.
∧	Add something.
ℓ	Take out something.
⊙	Add a period.
¶	New paragraph

PROOFREAD A MATH PROBLEM

Ms. Yasutaki's class is keeping a math journal. Read the journal entry below and correct four misspelled words and add the missing quotation marks.

I multiplied 22 X 15 in 3 seconds! Everyone was **surprised** by my speed. They asked, "How do you do it?" I **finally** told them this secret: "You know 22 X 10 is 220. Half of 220 is 110. So just add them up to get 330." Math is **interesting** if you **know** the shortcuts!

PROOFREADING TIP

A speaker's exact words are called a **quotation.** Quotations begin with a capital letter and have quotation marks at the beginning (") and end (") of the speaker's words.

Word List

camera	surprised
finally	might
really	often
known	island
everybody	caught
everyone	evening
they	swimming
remember	several
February	beginning
December	interesting

Personal Words

1.   **Words will vary.**

2.

WRITE A MATH PROBLEM

You probably have a math shortcut or interesting problem you'd like to share. Use list words as well as personal words.

Responses will vary. Math problems should include list words and personal words.

120

Review

SYNONYMS   Write the two boxed words that have similar meanings.

often	really
might	several
they	everyone
remember	interesting
finally	everybody

1.   **everyone**   2.   **everybody**

DEFINING WORDS   Write the boxed word that means the same as the underlined word or words in each sentence.

3. Our team <u>at last</u> has won a game against the mighty Falcons.
4. Eddie was absent from school for <u>more than two or three</u> days when he had the flu.
5. The program about the grizzly bears in Yellowstone National Park was <u>holding my attention</u>.
6. I <u>frequently</u> stop to talk with Mrs. Griffin when I see her out in her yard.
7. Do you <u>truly</u> think that I bake good cookies?
8. I will <u>possibly</u> want to go bike riding with my friends on Saturday.
9. Do you <u>call back to mind</u> what time the train is due to arrive this evening?
10. The kittens are hungry and <u>the animals spoken about</u> need a good home.

3.   **finally**
4.   **several**
5.   **interesting**
6.   **often**
7.   **really**
8.   **might**
9.   **remember**
10.   **they**

Using a *Dictionary*

WORDS THAT AREN'T ENTRIES   You won't find **inflected forms,** words like *surprised* and *dirtiest,* as entry words in most dictionaries. If a dictionary included words like these as entries, it would be too large and heavy to use! To find inflected forms, look for the base words. You will find *dirtiest* at the end of *dirty* and *surprised* at the end of *surprise.*

Write the entry word you would look for in order to find the definition of each word below.

1. smuggled
2. funnier
3. speeches
4. largest

dirt•y (dėr′tē), **1** soiled by dirt; not clean: *I got dirty emptying the garbage.* **2** not fair or decent: *Fooling me was a dirty trick. adj.,* **dirt•i•er, dirt•i•est.**

sur•prise (sər prīz′), **1** a feeling caused by something that happens suddenly. **2** to cause to feel surprise; astonish: *The news surprised us.* **3** something unexpected: *I have a surprise for you. 1 n., 2,3 v.,* **sur•prised, sur•pris•ing.**

1.   **smuggle**
2.   **funny**
3.   **speech**
4.   **large**

121

LESSON

26

Generalization

Spelling Focus: A compound word is made of two or more words. Keep all the letters when spelling compounds.

● Core ○ Optional ✓ Assessment

DAILY PLAN	CORE OBJECTIVES	NOTES

DAY 1 Introduction

✓● Pretest and Self-Check, p. 122B
● Spelling Focus and Word List, p. 122
○ Challenge Words, p. 122
○ Challenge Master 26
○ Home-School Master 26

✓■ Take and self-check Pretest
■ Spell compound words; alphabetize and write the list words

DAY 2 Think and Practice

● Classifications; Joining Words, p. 123
● Strategic Spelling: *Seeing Meaning Connections*, p. 123
○ Think and Practice Master 26
○ Extra Practice Master 26
○ Cross-Curricular Lesson: Introduce, p. 186

■ Complete practice activities for compound words
■ Recognize meaning connections between list words and other words related to them

DAY 3 Proofreading and Writing

● Proofread an Essay, p. 124
● Proofreading Tip: Comparative Forms, p. 124
● Write an Essay, p. 124
✓○ Cooperative Midweek Test
○ Hardbound Book Master 26
○ Writing Mini-Lesson Master 26
○ Writing Activity Master 26
○ Second Language Support Master 26

■ Proofread for spelling and usage errors
■ Integrate spelling and writing in a personal writing response
✓■ Take and check midweek test

DAY 4 Vocabulary Building

● Review: Words in Context, p. 125
● Multicultural Connection: Arts, p. 125
○ Cross-Curricular Lesson: Follow-Up, p. 186
○ Review Master 26

■ Complete review activity for compound words
■ Study the art of jewelry in different cultures

DAY 5 Assessment

✓● Posttest, p. 122B
○ Standardized Test Master 26

✓■ Take Posttest

Cross-Curricular Lessons

Use the Spelling Focus (compound words) to introduce the Health lesson, *Being Safe,* page 186, or choose a lesson that correlates with a topic you're currently teaching.

MEETING THE NEEDS OF ALL STUDENTS

The Word List

For students studying 20 words, assign pages 122–125 and Extra Practice and Review masters.

Modified List For students studying 10 words, modify Practice on page 122, and assign Think and Practice Master 26 and pages 124–125.

Challenge For students studying 25 words, assign pages 122–125, Challenge, Extra Practice, and Review masters.

Bilingual/ESL

Many English compound words are borrowed into Spanish and changed. Spanish-speaking students may misspell *baseball* as *béisbol.*

Personal Words

Students add to Personal Words lists by looking at work in their writing portfolios and words they want to remember from their reading.

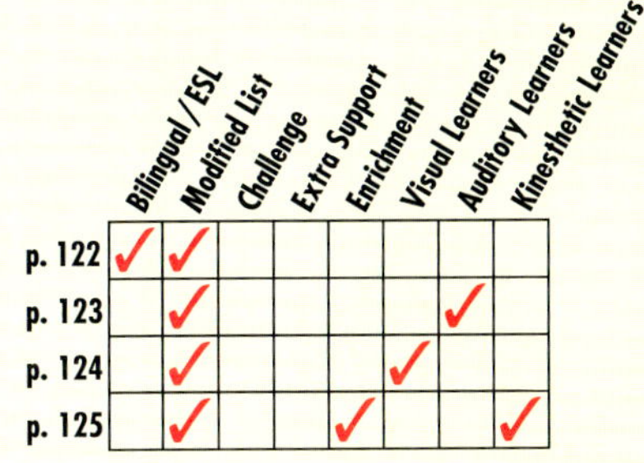

	Bilingual/ESL	Modified List	Challenge	Extra Support	Enrichment	Visual Learners	Auditory Learners	Kinesthetic Learners
p. 122	✓	✓						
p. 123		✓					✓	
p. 124		✓				✓		
p. 125		✓			✓			✓

ASSESSMENT*

Pretest

Read the underlined word, read the sentence, and then repeat the underlined word. Guide students in self-correcting their pretests and correcting any misspellings.

1. My <u>baseball</u> team is ahead.
2. <u>Basketball</u> is a great sport.
3. The bedrooms are <u>upstairs</u>.
4. I hurt <u>myself</u> on the swing.
5. A <u>highway</u> has many lanes.
6. The <u>classroom</u> is noisy.
7. It doesn't matter <u>anyway</u>.
8. I saw it in the <u>newspaper</u>.
9. She has <u>something</u> to say.
10. <u>Sometimes</u> I get lonely.
11. Teachers use a <u>chalkboard</u>.
12. Those <u>earrings</u> are pretty.
13. Cats play in the <u>nighttime</u>.
14. That is a noisy <u>motorcycle</u>.
15. The workshop is <u>downstairs</u>.
16. We play on a <u>softball</u> team.
17. I saw a movie last <u>weekend</u>.
18. A <u>classmate</u> will help you.
19. Visitors ring the <u>doorbell</u>.
20. The car is in the <u>driveway</u>.

Posttest

Read aloud the sentences below. These sentences may be used for dictation.

1. Throw me the <u>basketball</u>.
2. I can make supper <u>myself</u>.
3. <u>Sometimes</u> I eat alone.
4. Dad said <u>something</u> funny.
5. Do you like <u>baseball</u>?
6. We had a party <u>anyway</u>.
7. My bedroom is <u>upstairs</u>.
8. I read the <u>newspaper</u>.
9. That is her <u>classroom</u>.
10. Which way is the <u>highway</u>?
11. He rode a <u>motorcycle</u>.
12. Erase the <u>chalkboard</u>.
13. I gave Mom <u>earrings</u>.
14. We sleep in the <u>nighttime</u>.
15. A <u>weekend</u> trip can be fun.
16. The kitchen is <u>downstairs</u>.
17. She played <u>softball</u>.
18. We stood on the <u>driveway</u>.
19. My <u>classmate</u> is from Ohio.
20. I didn't hear the <u>doorbell</u>.

Challenge Words

1. People sat in the <u>courtroom</u>.
2. We take care of <u>ourselves</u>.
3. The girl was <u>heartbroken</u>.
4. Our <u>teammate</u> will score.
5. A <u>skateboard</u> can go fast.

Additional Assessment

Standardized Test Master 26
Dictation Sentences, p. T41
Everyday Spelling CD-ROM

KIDSPELLING
Research in Action found that a child attempting to spell *newspaper* ended up with "noosepaper." Help students divide compound words into their component parts and discuss their meanings: A *newspaper* is a *paper* on which the *news* is printed.

* See pp. T20 and T33 for test-study-test information.

LESSON 26

DAY 1 CHALLENGE MASTER

CHALLENGE ■ 26

Challenge Words

courtroom heartbroken ourselves teammate skateboard

■ Put these word pairs together to create the Challenge Words listed above.

1. place of law + indoor place = **courtroom**
2. mine and your + individuals = **ourselves**
3. group + partner = **teammate**
4. chest organ + in pieces = **heartbroken**
5. glide + flat wood = **skateboard**

■ Have you ridden on a skateboard? Where did you ride it? Use one or more of the Challenge Words to write about your experience.

Practice Masters, p. 99

DAY 1 HOME-SCHOOL MASTER

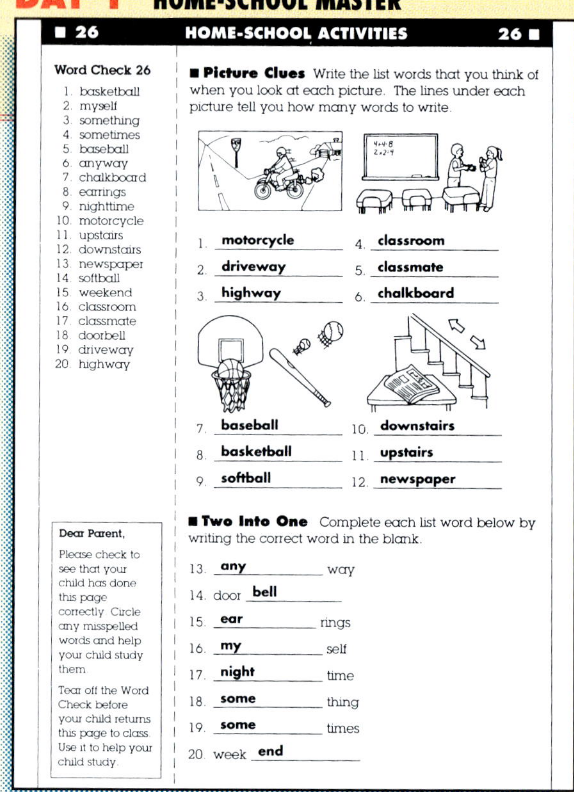

■ 26 HOME-SCHOOL ACTIVITIES 26 ■

Word Check 26
1. basketball
2. myself
3. something
4. sometimes
5. baseball
6. anyway
7. chalkboard
8. earrings
9. nighttime
10. motorcycle
11. upstairs
12. downstairs
13. newspaper
14. softball
15. weekend
16. classroom
17. classmate
18. doorbell
19. driveway
20. highway

■ **Picture Clues** Write the list words that you think of when you look at each picture. The lines under each picture tell you how many words to write.

1. **motorcycle**   4. **classroom**
2. **driveway**   5. **classmate**
3. **highway**   6. **chalkboard**

7. **baseball**   10. **downstairs**
8. **basketball**   11. **upstairs**
9. **softball**   12. **newspaper**

■ **Two Into One** Complete each list word below by writing the correct word in the blank.

13. **any** ________ way
14. door **bell** ________
15. **ear** ________ rings
16. **my** ________ self
17. **night** ________ time
18. **some** ________ thing
19. **some** ________ times
20. week **end** ________

Dear Parent,
Please check to see that your child has done this page correctly. Circle any misspelled words and help your child study them.

Tear off the Word Check before your child returns this page to class. Use it to help your child study.

Home-School Activities, p. 22

DAY 2 THINK AND PRACTICE MASTER

26 ■ THINK AND PRACTICE

baseball basketball upstairs myself highway
classroom anyway newspaper something sometimes

■ **Compounds** Match a word from each column to make a list word. Write the list words.

any   self   1. **anyway**
my   paper   2. **myself**
up   way   3. **upstairs**
news   thing   4. **newspaper**
class   stairs   5. **classroom**
some   room   6. **something**

■ **Joining Words** Find two words in each sentence that can be joined to make a list word. Write the word.

7. The dog sat up when he heard a thump on the stairs.   **upstairs**
8. What news do you have to give to the school paper?   **newspaper**
9. I got to first base before the ball did.   **baseball**
10. Climbing the high hill is the best way to see the town.   **highway**
11. Some of my friends have good times at the beach.   **sometimes**
12. Look in the basket for the ball you want.   **basketball**

STRATEGIC SPELLING: Seeing Meaning Connections
Write the word from the box that answers each question.

Words with ball
baseball   basketball   football

13. What game has a home plate? **baseball**
14. What game uses a ball that is not round? **football**
15. What game has five players on a team? **basketball**

Practice Masters, p. 100

DAY 2 EXTRA PRACTICE MASTER

EXTRA PRACTICE ■ 26

Word List

baseball   basketball   upstairs   myself   highway
classroom   anyway   newspaper   something   sometimes
chalkboard   earrings   nighttime   motorcycle   downstairs
softball   weekend   classmate   doorbell   driveway

■ **Some Words Make Many Compounds** Write the list words that:

use the word *way*
1. **anyway**
2. **driveway**
3. **highway**

use the word *ball*
4. **basketball**
5. **softball**
6. **baseball**

use the word *some*
7. **something**
8. **sometimes**

use the word *class*
9. **classroom**
10. **classmate**

use the word *stairs*
11. **upstairs**
12. **downstairs**

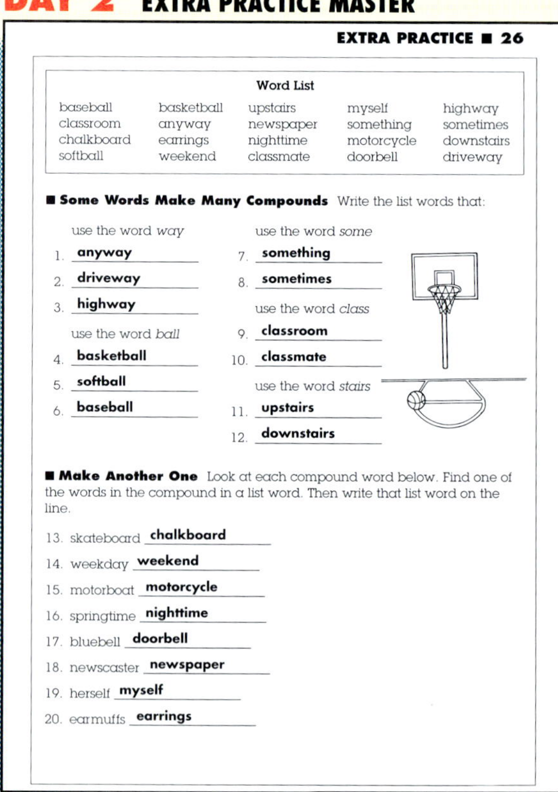

■ **Make Another One** Look at each compound word below. Find one of the words in the compound in a list word. Then write that list word on the line.

13. skateboard **chalkboard**
14. weekday **weekend**
15. motorboat **motorcycle**
16. springtime **nighttime**
17. bluebell **doorbell**
18. newscaster **newspaper**
19. herself **myself**
20. earmuffs **earrings**

Practice Masters, p. 101

TECHNOLOGY AND VISUAL SUPPORT	 Use Audiotape C, Side 1, Lesson 26 Use Proofreading and Writing Transparency 26	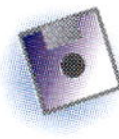 For additional practice use *Everyday Spelling* Game Software, Lesson 26	 Additional resources on *Everyday Spelling* CD-ROM: proofreading and writing, modified list and challenge words, auditory test

DAY 3 SECOND LANGUAGE SUPPORT MASTER

26 ■ SECOND LANGUAGE SUPPORT

About Me

Read what Ulla wrote.

Irene is my best friend. She is also a classmate. She sometimes spends the weekend with me. She helps me speak English. We play games upstairs in my room.

Write some spelling words that tell about you. Then draw a picture of your ideas.

Words will vary.

Write about your picture.

Answers will vary.

Talk about your writing and picture with a partner.

Did you learn a new word or meaning? What helped you to learn it?

Second Language Support, p. 48

DAY 3 WRITING ACTIVITY MASTER

26 ■ WRITING ACTIVITY

Adjectives in Comparisons

	Make a capital.
/	Make a small letter.
∧	Add something.
	Take out something.
⊙	Add a period.
¶	New paragraph.

❑ Use *more* or the ending -er to compare two persons, places, or things.

❑ Use *most* or the ending -est to compare more than two persons, places, or things.

❑ Never use *more* or *most* with adjectives that end in -er or -est.

■ Read Jasmin's journal entry. Check to see that she used adjectives correctly. Fix any mistakes.

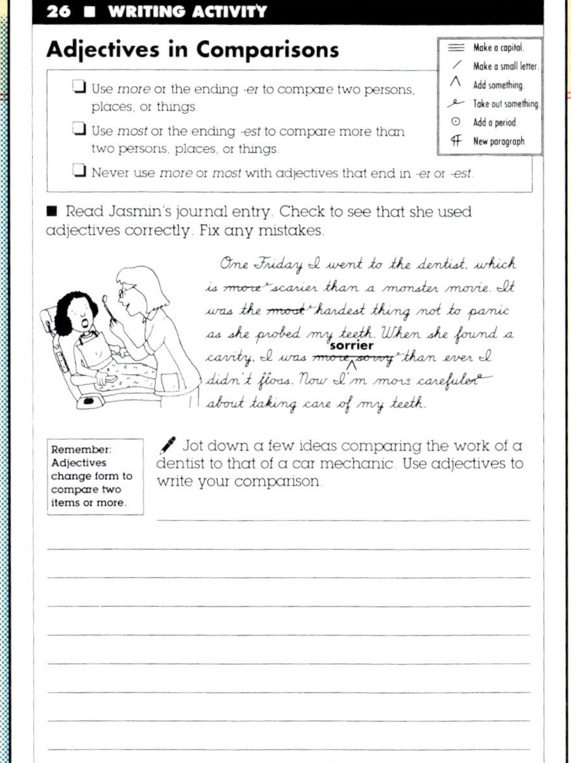

Remember: Adjectives change form to compare two items or more.

Jot down a few ideas comparing the work of a dentist to that of a car mechanic. Use adjectives to write your comparison.

Spelling and Writing, p. 44

DAY 4 REVIEW MASTER

26 ■ REVIEW

Word List

baseball	basketball	upstairs	myself	highway
classroom	anyway	newspaper	something	sometimes
chalkboard	earrings	nighttime	motorcycle	downstairs
softball	weekend	classmate	doorbell	driveway

■ **Rebuses** Write the list word that matches each clue below.

1. [ear] + rings = ___
2. door + [bell] = ___
3. [pail] + ball = ___
4. night + [clock] = ___
5. down + [stairs] = ___
6. soft + [basketball] = ___
7. [car] + cycle = ___

1. **earrings**
2. **doorbell**
3. **basketball**
4. **nighttime**
5. **downstairs**
6. **softball**
7. **motorcycle**
8. **chalkboard**
9. **upstairs**
10. **classroom**
11. **driveway**
12. **myself**
13. **weekend**
14. **sometimes**
15. **baseball**
16. **newspaper**
17. **highway**
18. **classmate**
19. **anyway**
20. **something**

■ **Syllable Scramble** Each group of letters is one syllable of a two-syllable word. Match one from each column to make list words.

8. chalk	end	
9. up	room	
10. class	way	
11. drive	ball	
12. my	board	
13. week	times	
14. some	stairs	
15. base	self	

■ **Buried Words** Each word below is hidden in a list word. Write the list word.

16. new	19. an
17. high	20. thin
18. mat	

Practice Masters, p. 102

DAY 5 STANDARDIZED TEST MASTER

26 ■ LESSON TEST

■ Find the word in each group that is spelled correctly. Fill in the letter for the correct word on the answer strip.

Sample:
a. contes   c. cotest
b. contist   d. contest   ⓐⓑⓒ●

1. a. motorcycle c. motorcicle
b. motercycle d. motercicle   1. ●ⓑⓒⓓ

2. a. anyways c. anyway
b. aneway d. aneyway   2. ⓐⓑ●ⓓ

3. a. classroom c. clasrium
b. clasrom d. classroum   3. ●ⓑⓒⓓ

4. a. drive-way c. drivway
b. driveway d. driveaway   4. ⓐ●ⓒⓓ

5. a. sofball c. soffball
b. sfitball d. softball   5. ⓐⓑⓒ●

6. a. up-stairs c. upstiars
b. upstares d. upstairs   6. ⓐⓑⓒ●

7. a. baseball c. baceball
b. busbull d. barrball   7. ●ⓑⓒⓓ

8. a. earings c. earinngs
b. earrings d. earrinngs   8. ⓐ●ⓒⓓ

9. a. chalkborde c. chockboard
b. chalkboard d. chawkboard   9. ⓐ●ⓒⓓ

10. a. classmat c. classmate
b. classmayte d. classmaet   10. ⓐⓑ●ⓓ

11. a. dorbell c. doorbelle
b. dorebell d. doorbell   11. ⓐⓑⓒ●

12. a. something c. sommthing
b. somthing d. sommething   12. ●ⓑⓒⓓ

13. a. sometimes c. sumtimes
b. somtimes d. sommtimes   13. ●ⓑⓒⓓ

14. a. bascetball c. basetball
b. basketball d. baskitball   14. ⓐ●ⓒⓓ

15. a. myselfe c. mysellf
b. mysilf d. myself   15. ⓐⓑⓒ●

16. a. nightime c. nitetime
b. nithgtime d. nighttime   16. ⓐⓑⓒ●

17. a. newspapper c. newspaper
b. newespaper d. knewspaper   17. ⓐⓑ●ⓓ

18. a. hiway c. haywaye
b. highway d. hieway   18. ⓐ●ⓒⓓ

19. a. wekend c. weakend
b. weekand d. weekend   19. ⓐⓑⓒ●

20. a. downstairs c. down-stairs
b. downstars d. downstares   20. ●ⓑⓒⓓ

Practice for Standardized Tests, p. 38

122D

LESSON 26

DAY 1 Introduction
☑ Pretest and Self-Check
● Spelling Focus and Word List
○ Challenge Words
○ Modified List

DAILY SPELLING REVIEW

I *beleive* Mt. Everest is the tallest *mountian*.

believe   *mountain*

● Core   ○ Optional   ✓ Assessment

INTRODUCTION

Word Structure

Compound Words Emphasize that when two words are joined to make a compound word, each word keeps all its letters. Have each student think of one additional compound word and write it on the chalkboard.

MEETING THE NEEDS OF ALL STUDENTS

Modified List

Practice Students studying only the high-frequency words in the top box write the first ten list words in alphabetical order.

Bilingual/ESL

Picture Equations Have students make picture equations for these compound words: *basketball, baseball, chalkboard, earrings, upstairs, downstairs, newspaper, doorbell.*
For example:

 = earrings

Additional Practice

Challenge Master 26
Home-School Master 26
Audiotape C, Side 1

26

1. anyway
2. baseball
3. basketball
4. chalkboard
5. classmate
6. classroom
7. doorbell
8. downstairs
9. driveway
10. earrings
11. highway
12. motorcycle
13. myself
14. newspaper
15. nighttime
16. softball
17. something
18. sometimes
19. upstairs
20. weekend

CHALLENGE!

courtroom
ourselves
heartbroken
teammate
skateboard

122

■ INTRODUCTION

Compound Words

SPELLING FOCUS

A compound word is made of two or more words. Keep all the letters when spelling compounds:
base + ball = baseball.

■ **STUDY**   Say each word. Then read the sentence.

1. *baseball*   We play **baseball** in the summer.
2. *basketball* ✳   The **basketball** player is very tall.
3. *upstairs*   She's using the **upstairs** phone.
4. *myself* ✳   I saw **myself** on television.
5. *highway*   Traffic on the **highway** is heavy.
6. *classroom*   Students filled the **classroom**.
7. *anyway*   I was late but went **anyway**.
8. *newspaper*   He wrote a **newspaper** article.
9. *something* ✳   You have to eat **something**.
10. *sometimes* ✳   Doctors **sometimes** get sick.

11. *chalkboard*   She wrote on the **chalkboard**.
12. *earrings*   These are real gold **earrings**.
13. *nighttime*   Bats fly during the **nighttime**.
14. *motorcycle*   He rode on a **motorcycle**.
15. *downstairs*   Dad is vacuuming **downstairs**.
16. *softball*   All her friends play **softball**.
17. *weekend*   Do you work this **weekend**?
18. *classmate*   Ask a **classmate** for help.
19. *doorbell*   The **doorbell** rang twice.
20. *driveway*   Park the car in the **driveway**.

■ **PRACTICE**   Write the words in alphabetical order.

■ **WRITE**   Choose two sentences to include in a paragraph.
Paragraphs will vary.

✳ **WATCH OUT FOR FREQUENTLY MISSPELLED WORDS!**

THINK AND PRACTICE

CLASSIFICATIONS Add the list words that belong in each group. The words already listed are clues.

Sports
football
1. basketball
2. baseball
3. softball

School
homeroom
4. classroom
5. classmate
schoolmate

Time
weeknight
6. nighttime
7. weekend
sometime

JOINING WORDS Find two words in each sentence that can be joined to make a list word. Write the word.

8. Because I was so worried, I was not my old self.
9. Were there any sights along the way?
10. The dog ran to the door when the bell rang.
11. The good news is that I got an A on my paper.
12. Here are some crackers for that thing in the cage.
13. I got up and walked to the stairs near the porch.
14. When the sirens blast, my ear always rings.
15. There are some of us who enjoy good times.
16. The chalk was ordered by a member of the board.
17. He fell and went rolling down the stairs.
18. The washer's motor failed, so the cycle didn't finish.

8. myself
9. anyway
10. doorbell
11. newspaper
12. something
13. upstairs
14. earrings
15. sometimes
16. chalkboard
17. downstairs
18. motorcycle

Seeing Meaning Connections

Write the word from the box that answers each question.

…s with
…y
…eway
…ray
…way

19. Where does an airplane take off?   runway
20. Where do cars go whizzing along?   highway
21. Where might a car be parked?   driveway

Did You Know?
Today, basketball players throw a ball through a net to score points. When the game was invented in 1891, they used a real basket. This is how the game got its name.

THINK AND PRACTICE

Joining Words
Reflexive Pronouns Discuss the usage of words made up of a personal pronoun plus *self*. Ask students to name words like myself (himself, yourself, herself, itself, themselves) and to use each in a sentence.

MEETING THE NEEDS OF ALL STUDENTS

Modified List
Review Students studying high-frequency words complete Think and Practice Master 26.

Auditory Learners
Joining Words Point out that the list words should not be inserted in the sentences. Auditory learners may locate the list words more easily if they read each sentence aloud.

Additional Practice
Think and Practice Master 26
Extra Practice Master 26
Everyday Spelling CD-ROM
Everyday Spelling Game
   Software

DAY 3 Proofreading and Writing

- Proofread an Essay
- Proofreading Tip: Comparative Forms
- Write an Essay
- ✓ Cooperative Midweek Test

DAILY SPELLING REVIEW

I'm *sertain* we can play tennis on this *cort*.

certain   court

● Core   ○ Optional   ✓ Assessment

PROOFREADING AND WRITING

Usage

Comparative Forms Have students correct these sentences: *Carla is my most best friend. Jorge is more taller than me.*

MEETING THE NEEDS OF ALL STUDENTS

Modified List

Proofreading Students studying high-frequency words complete this page or the proofreading activity on the *Everyday Spelling* CD-ROM.

Visual Learners

Compound Booklets

Have students illustrate a compound word by folding the ends of a sheet of paper to meet in the middle. On each of the two flaps, they write and illustrate one part of the compound. On the inside, they write and illustrate the entire compound.

Additional Practice

Hardbound Book Master 26
Second Language Master 26
Writing Mini-Lesson Master 26
Writing Activity Master 26
Proofreading Transparency 26
Everyday Spelling **CD-ROM**

■ PROOFREADING AND WRITING

Make a capital.
Make a small letter.
Add something.
Take out something.
Add a period.
New paragraph

PROOFREAD AN ESSAY Nan wrote this essay about an important event in her life. Correct four misspelled words and one incorrectly used adjective.

PROOFREADING TIP

Nan forgot this rule about using the adjectives more and most: Don't use more or most with words that end in -er or -est.

My Proud Moment

I play ~~basket ball~~ **basketball** in the Adapted Athletics Program. At first it was hard dribbling from my wheelchair, but I soon got ~~more~~ better at it. Once, I faked out my ~~classmat~~ **classmate**, Pete. I drove ~~my self~~ **myself** around him and swished the ball ~~trough~~ **through** the net. I felt like Supergirl!

WRITE AN ESSAY Write about one of your proud moments. Use your spelling words and a personal word.

Responses will vary. Essays should include spelling words and a personal word.

Word List

basketball	upstairs
something	downstairs
sometimes	newspaper
baseball	softball
anyway	weekend
chalkboard	classroom
earrings	classmate
nighttime	doorbell
myself	driveway
motorcycle	highway

Personal Words

1. **Words will vary.**
2. _______

124

DAY 4 Vocabulary Building

- Review: Words in Context
- Multicultural Connection: Arts
- Cross-Curricular Lesson: Follow-Up

DAILY SPELLING REVIEW

My *nabor* got the fence *durty*.

neighbor   *dirty*

DAY 5 Assessment

- ✓ Posttest
- ✓ Dictation Sentences
- Standardized Test Master 26
- ✓ Auditory Test on *Everyday Spelling* CD-ROM

VOCABULARY BUILDING ■

Review

WORDS IN CONTEXT Write the missing boxed words to complete the following letter.

baseball	classroom
basketball	anyway
upstairs	newspaper
myself	something
highway	sometimes

Dear Jessica,

It's supposed to rain on Saturday, but I'm glad you're coming for a visit (1). Here are directions to my house.

Go to the intersection of Davis Street and Grant Avenue. Get on the (2) that takes you north to Cedar City. You will be on this road for about thirty miles.
Get off at the Dillard Street exit and turn left at the first stoplight. You will see a park with a (3) court on the corner. That's where I (4) shoot baskets either with a few other kids on my block or all by (5).
My house is the white one across from the (6) field. The Little League will probably be in the middle of a game.

I'll be looking for you from my (7) window. When you get here, we'll check the movie section in the (8) to see what's playing. If you'd rather do (9) else, that's all right. Oh, I almost forgot. My school will be open on Saturday, so I'll show you all the neat stuff in my new (10).

Your friend,
Marguerita

1. **anyway**
2. **highway**
3. **basketball**
4. **sometimes**
5. **myself**
6. **baseball**
7. **upstairs**
8. **newspaper**
9. **something**
10. **classroom**

Multicultural *Connection*

ARTS Throughout history, people have worn jewelry. Read about the handcrafted jewelry pictured at the right. Then complete each description below by writing the name of one of the items pictured.

1. The ancient Egyptians used colored gemstones in jewelry, such as this beautiful pin, or ___.
2. The Greeks valued fine metalwork and often used lacelike *filigree*, or ornamental gold or silver wire, as seen in the center of this ___.
3. Carved jade and metal ornaments like this white jade hanging ornament, or ___, were popular in China.
4. The Inca of South America worked with gold and silver. This ___ shows their craftsmanship in making strings of ornaments for wearing around the neck.

earring

pendant

brooch

necklace

1. **brooch**
2. **earring**
3. **pendant**
4. **necklace**

125

27

Generalization

Spelling Focus: When adding **-ful**, **-ly**, or **-ion** to most base words, the base stays the same. To words ending in **y**, change **y** to **i**. To words ending in **e**, drop the **e** when the suffix begins with a vowel.

● Core ○ Optional ✓ Assessment

DAILY PLAN	CORE OBJECTIVES	NOTES

DAY 1 Introduction

✓ Pretest and Self-Check, p. 126B
● Spelling Focus and Word List, p. 126
○ Challenge Words, p. 126
○ Challenge Master 27
○ Home-School Master 27

✓ • Take and self-check Pretest
• Spell words with the suffix **-ful**, **-ly**, or **-ion**; classify and write the list words

DAY 2 Think and Practice

● Suffix Addition; Word Forms, p. 127
● Strategic Spelling: *Using the Meaning Helper Strategy*, p. 127
○ Think and Practice Master 27
○ Extra Practice Master 27
○ Cross-Curricular Lesson: Introduce, p. 204

• Complete practice activities for words with the suffix **-ful, -ly,** or **-ion**
• Use known words to help spell hard words

DAY 3 Proofreading and Writing

● Proofread Captions, p. 128
● Proofreading Tip: Double Negatives, p. 128
● Write a Caption, p. 128
✓ Cooperative Midweek Test
○ Hardbound Book Master 27
○ Writing Mini-Lesson Master 27
○ Writing Activity Master 27
○ Second Language Support Master 27

• Proofread for spelling and usage errors
• Integrate spelling and writing in a personal writing response
✓ • Take and check midweek test

DAY 4 Vocabulary Building

● Review: Analogies, p. 129
● Word Study: Codes, p. 129
○ Cross-Curricular Lesson: Follow-Up, p. 204
○ Review Master 27

• Complete review activity for words with the suffix **-ful, -ly,** or **-ion**
• Study and use codes

DAY 5 Assessment

✓ Posttest, p. 126B
○ Standardized Test Master 27

✓ • Take Posttest

Cross-Curricular Lessons

Use the Spelling Focus (suffixes **-ful, -ly,** and **-ion**) to introduce the Reading lesson, *Many Ways of Learning,* page 204, or choose a lesson that correlates with a topic you're currently teaching.

MEETING THE NEEDS OF ALL STUDENTS

The Word List

For students studying 20 words, assign pages 126–129 and Extra Practice and Review masters.

Modified List For students studying 10 words, modify Practice on page 126, and assign Think and Practice Master 27 and pages 128–129.

Challenge For students studying 25 words, assign pages 126–129, Challenge, Extra Practice, and Review masters.

Bilingual/ESL

Suffixes do not exist in Vietnamese because it is a monosyllabic language. Students might require extra time and explanation to understand suffixes.

Personal Words

Students add to Personal Words lists by looking at work in their writing portfolios and words they want to remember from their reading.

	Bilingual/ESL	Modified List	Challenge	Extra Support	Enrichment	Visual Learners	Auditory Learners	Kinesthetic Learners
p. 126	✓	✓						
p. 127		✓		✓			✓	
p. 128		✓				✓		
p. 129		✓	✓		✓			

ASSESSMENT*

Pretest

Read the underlined word, read the sentence, and then repeat the underlined word. Guide students in self-correcting their pretests and correcting any misspellings.

1. That engine is <u>powerful</u>.
2. It was a <u>peaceful</u> morning.
3. The trees look <u>beautiful</u>.
4. Time seems to pass <u>slowly</u>.
5. They arrived <u>safely</u>.
6. We go to school <u>daily</u>.
7. A storm came up <u>suddenly</u>.
8. He fed the lion <u>carefully</u>.
9. The army will take <u>action</u>.
10. I don't know its <u>location</u>.
11. She has a <u>cheerful</u> smile.
12. The bruise was <u>painful</u>.
13. That was a <u>thoughtful</u> gift.
14. We take a test <u>weekly</u>.
15. Have you seen him <u>lately</u>?
16. He answered <u>truthfully</u>.
17. She looked up <u>hopefully</u>.
18. One <u>invention</u> is the TV.
19. Make one more <u>correction</u>.
20. The city has air <u>pollution</u>.

Posttest

Read aloud the sentences below. These sentences may be used for dictation.

1. That quilt is <u>beautiful</u>.
2. We walked to school <u>slowly</u>.
3. It has a good <u>location</u>.
4. The big horse is <u>powerful</u>.
5. It's a <u>peaceful</u> place.
6. The van stopped <u>suddenly</u>.
7. Dad drove <u>safely</u>.
8. The movie had <u>action</u>.
9. Carry the baby <u>carefully</u>.
10. Mom read to us <u>daily</u>.
11. This is a <u>weekly</u> newspaper.
12. She is a <u>thoughtful</u> person.
13. I'm <u>cheerful</u> in the morning.
14. He made a new <u>invention</u>.
15. I studied land <u>pollution</u>.
16. Have you written <u>lately</u>?
17. She made a <u>correction</u>.
18. I asked <u>hopefully</u>.
19. A burn can be <u>painful</u>.
20. We will speak <u>truthfully</u>.

Challenge Words

1. He was <u>grateful</u> to her.
2. This story is <u>suspenseful</u>.
3. The box is <u>completely</u> full.
4. He is <u>exactly</u> five feet tall.
5. Their <u>separation</u> was sad.

Additional Assessment

Standardized Test Master 27
Dictation Sentences, p. T41
Everyday Spelling CD-ROM

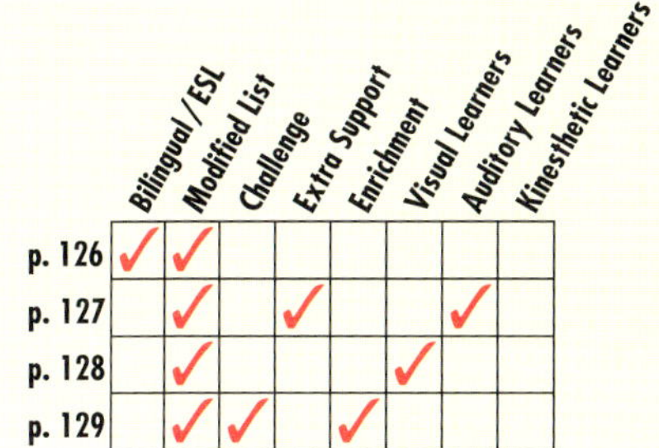

TAKE A CLOSER LOOK
Remind students that *beauty* and *beautiful* are related words and that the **y** to **i** rule applies. They will then be more likely to spell the word correctly.

* See pp. T20 and T33 for test-study-test information.

LESSON 27

DAY 1 CHALLENGE MASTER

CHALLENGE ■ 27

Challenge Words				
grateful	suspenseful	completely	exactly	separation

■ Combine the words listed below and a suffix meaning from the sack to write each Challenge Word. Discard any letters you don't need.

1. gratitude + = **grateful**
2. suspense + = **suspenseful**
3. complete + = **completely**
4. exact + = **exactly**
5. separate + = **separation**

(sack: like / full of / state of being)

■ Detective stories are fun to read because the mysteries create excitement. Use one or more of the Challenge Words to begin your own detective story about a real or imaginary mystery.

Practice Masters, p. 103

DAY 1 HOME-SCHOOL MASTER

■ 27   HOME-SCHOOL ACTIVITIES   27 ■

■ **Base Words** Write the list word that contains the base word given below.

1. slow **slowly**
2. power **powerful**
3. sudden **suddenly**
4. peace **peaceful**
5. cheer **cheerful**
6. week **weekly**
7. day **daily**
8. beauty **beautiful**
9. safe **safely**
10. pain **painful**
11. late **lately**
12. thought **thoughtful**

(calendar: DECEMBER)

Word Check 27
1. peaceful
2. thoughtful
3. powerful
4. cheerful
5. painful
6. beautiful
7. safely
8. slowly
9. weekly
10. suddenly
11. lately
12. daily
13. truthfully
14. carefully
15. hopefully
16. invention
17. correction
18. action
19. pollution
20. location

■ **Words in Context** Write a list word that fits each definition below.

13. in a careful way **c a r e f u l l y**
14. in a truthful manner **t r u t h f u l l y**
15. in a hopeful way **h o p e f u l l y**
16. process of acting **a c t i o n**
17. something corrected **c o r r e c t i o n**
18. something new **i n v e n t i o n**
19. something that dirties **p o l l u t i o n**
20. a position or place **l o c a t i o n**

Dear Parent,
Please check to see that your child has done this page correctly. Circle any misspelled words and help your child study them.

Tear off the Word Check before your child returns this page to class. Use it to help your child study.

Home-School Activities, p. 23

DAY 2 THINK AND PRACTICE MASTER

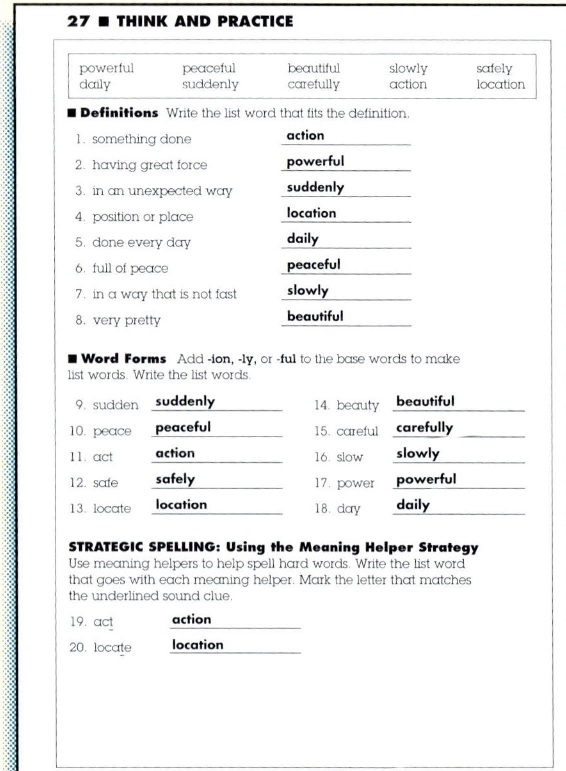

27 ■ THINK AND PRACTICE

| powerful | peaceful | beautiful | slowly | safely |
| daily | suddenly | carefully | action | location |

■ **Definitions** Write the list word that fits the definition.

1. something done — **action**
2. having great force — **powerful**
3. in an unexpected way — **suddenly**
4. position or place — **location**
5. done every day — **daily**
6. full of peace — **peaceful**
7. in a way that is not fast — **slowly**
8. very pretty — **beautiful**

■ **Word Forms** Add -ion, -ly, or -ful to the base words to make list words. Write the list words.

9. sudden — **suddenly**
10. peace — **peaceful**
11. act — **action**
12. safe — **safely**
13. locate — **location**
14. beauty — **beautiful**
15. careful — **carefully**
16. slow — **slowly**
17. power — **powerful**
18. day — **daily**

STRATEGIC SPELLING: Using the Meaning Helper Strategy
Use meaning helpers to help spell hard words. Write the list word that goes with each meaning helper. Mark the letter that matches the underlined sound clue.

19. act — **action**
20. locate — **location**

Practice Masters, p. 104

DAY 2 EXTRA PRACTICE MASTER

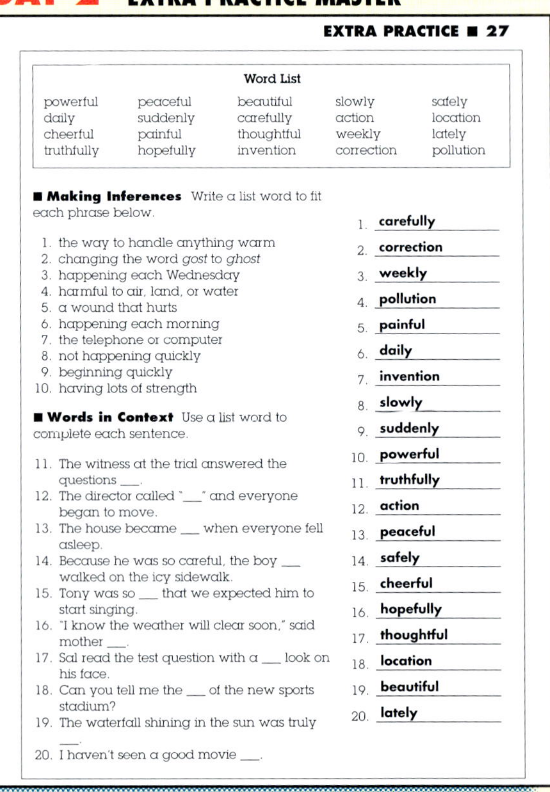

EXTRA PRACTICE ■ 27

Word List				
powerful	peaceful	beautiful	slowly	safely
daily	suddenly	carefully	action	location
cheerful	painful	thoughtful	weekly	lately
truthfully	hopefully	invention	correction	pollution

■ **Making Inferences** Write a list word to fit each phrase below.

1. the way to handle anything warm — **carefully**
2. changing the word *gost* to *ghost* — **correction**
3. happening each Wednesday — **weekly**
4. harmful to air, land, or water — **pollution**
5. a wound that hurts — **painful**
6. happening each morning — **daily**
7. the telephone or computer — **invention**
8. not happening quickly — **slowly**
9. beginning quickly — **suddenly**
10. having lots of strength — **powerful**

■ **Words in Context** Use a list word to complete each sentence.

11. The witness at the trial answered the questions ___. — **truthfully**
12. The director called "___" and everyone began to move. — **action**
13. The house became ___ when everyone fell asleep. — **peaceful**
14. Because he was so careful, the boy ___ walked on the icy sidewalk. — **safely**
15. Tony was so ___ that we expected him to start singing. — **cheerful**
16. "I know the weather will clear soon," said mother ___. — **hopefully**
17. Sal read the test question with a ___ look on his face. — **thoughtful**
18. Can you tell me the ___ of the new sports stadium? — **location**
19. The waterfall shining in the sun was truly ___. — **beautiful**
20. I haven't seen a good movie ___. — **lately**

Practice Masters, p. 105

	Use Audiotape C, Side 1, Lesson 27	 For additional practice use *Everyday Spelling* Game Software, Lesson 27	 Additional resources on *Everyday Spelling* CD-ROM: proofreading and writing, modified list and challenge words, auditory test
TECHNOLOGY AND VISUAL SUPPORT	 Use Proofreading and Writing Transparency 27		

DAY 3 — SECOND LANGUAGE SUPPORT MASTER

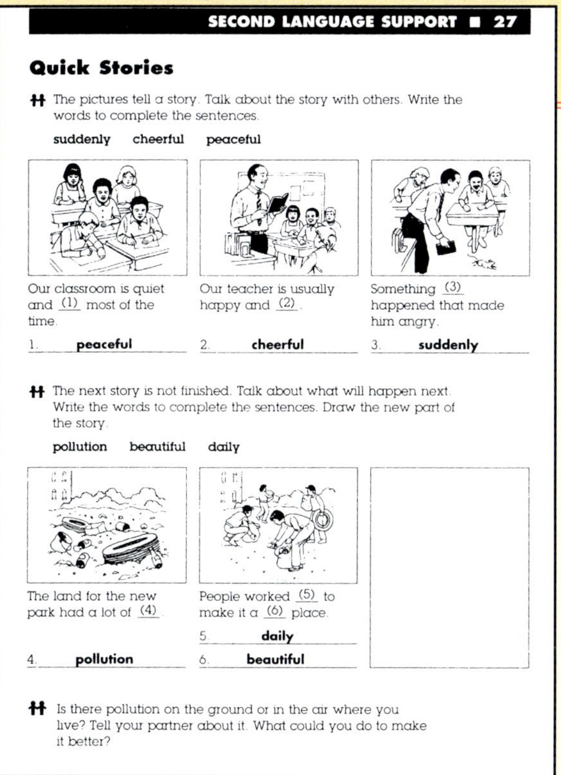

Second Language Support, p. 49

DAY 3 — WRITING ACTIVITY MASTER

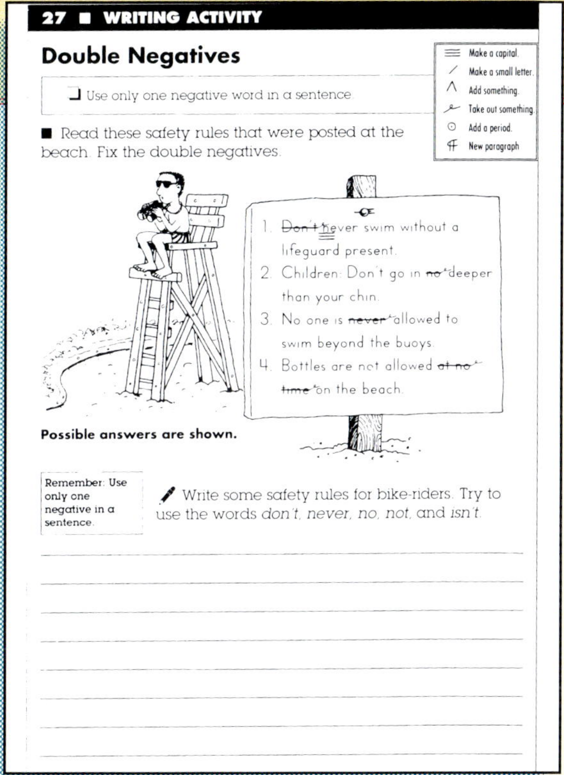

Spelling and Writing, p. 46

DAY 4 — REVIEW MASTER

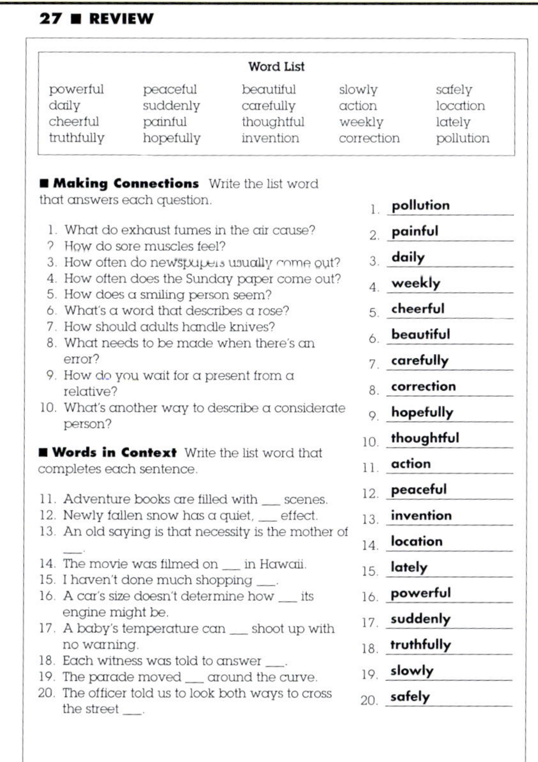

Practice Masters, p. 106

DAY 5 — STANDARDIZED TEST MASTER

LESSON TEST ■ 27

Find the word in each group that is spelled correctly. Fill in the letter for the correct word on the answer strip.

Sample:
a. contes   c. cotest
b. contist   d. contest   (a)(b)(c)●

1. a. cheerful   c. cherful
   b. cheerfull   d. chearful   1. ●(b)(c)(d)
2. a. invition   c. invechen
   b. invention   d. invenchen   2. (a)●(c)(d)
3. a. latly   c. lately
   b. latley   d. lateley   3. (a)(b)●(d)
4. a. carfully   c. careflee
   b. carfuly   d. carefully   4. (a)(b)(c)●
5. a. location   c. locatetion
   b. lowcation   d. loccation   5. ●(b)(c)(d)
6. a. dailey   c. dayley
   b. daily   d. daryly   6. (a)●(c)(d)
7. a. peaceful   c. peacful
   b. peacefull   d. piceful   7. ●(b)(c)(d)
8. a. polution   c. pollution
   b. polition   d. pollotion   8. (a)(b)●(d)
9. a. trewthfully   c. truthfuly
   b. truthfully   d. trueththfully   9. ●(b)(c)(d)
10. a. powerfull   c. powrfel
    b. pwerfull   d. powerful   10. (a)(b)(c)●
11. a. weakley   c. weeklie
    b. weekley   d. weekly   11. (a)(b)(c)●
12. a. slowly   c. slowley
    b. sloly   d. sloely   12. ●(b)(c)(d)
13. a. beatiful   c. butiful
    b. beutiful   d. beautiful   13. (a)(b)(c)●
14. a. corection   c. correcktion
    b. correcttion   d. correction   14. (a)(b)(c)●
15. a. aiction   c. action
    b. aktion   d. acttion   15. (a)(b)●(d)
16. a. painfull   c. panefull
    b. painful   d. paneful   16. (a)●(c)(d)
17. a. safely   c. safley
    b. safly   d. saftly   17. ●(b)(c)(d)
18. a. hopfully   c. hopeforly
    b. hopefuly   d. hopefully   18. (a)(b)(c)●
19. a. sudenly   c. suddly
    b. suddenly   d. sudunly   19. (a)●(c)(d)
20. a. thawtful   c. thoughtful
    b. thoughtfull   d. thaughtful   20. (a)(b)●(d)

Practice for Standardized Tests, p. 39

126D

LESSON

27

✓ Pretest and Self-Check
● Spelling Focus and Word List
○ Challenge Words
○ Modified List

○ **DAILY SPELLING REVIEW**

What is the *hieght* of your *nefuw*?

height   *nephew*

● Core   ○ Optional   ✓ Assessment

INTRODUCTION

Word Structure

Sort by Base Word Have students write four list words in which the base word changes when adding a suffix, and sixteen words in which the base word does not change.

MEETING THE NEEDS OF ALL STUDENTS

Modified List

Practice Students studying only the high-frequency words in the top box write

- five words with the suffix **-ly**
- three words with the suffix **-ful**
- two words with the suffix **-ion**

Bilingual/ESL

Context Sentences Pair ESL students with a native speaker. Assign each pair three list words and have them write a context sentence for each word.

> **Additional Practice**
>
> **Challenge Master 27**
> **Home-School Master 27**
> **Audiotape C, Side 1**

27

1. **slowly**
2. **safely**
3. **daily**
4. **suddenly**
5. **carefully**
6. **weekly**
7. **lately**
8. **truthfully**
9. **hopefully**
10. **powerful**
11. **peaceful**
12. **beautiful**
13. **cheerful**
14. **painful**
15. **thoughtful**
16. **action**
17. **location**
18. **invention**
19. **correction**
20. **pollution**

Order of words in each group may vary.

CHALLENGE!

grateful
suspenseful
completely
exactly
separation

Responses will vary.

■ INTRODUCTION

Suffixes -ful, -ly, -ion

SPELLING FOCUS

When adding **-ful**, **-ly**, or **-ion** to most base words, the base stays the same: **slowly**. To words ending in **y**, change **y** to **i**: **beautiful**. To words ending in **e**, drop the **e** when the suffix begins with a vowel: **location**.

■ STUDY   What happens when each suffix is added?

power + ful =	1.	*powerful*
peace + ful =	2.	*peaceful*
beauty + ful =	3.	*beautiful* ✳
slow + ly =	4.	*slowly*
safe + ly =	5.	*safely*
day + ly =	6.	*daily*
sudden + ly =	7.	*suddenly*
careful + ly =	8.	*carefully*
act + ion =	9.	*action*
locate + ion =	10.	*location*

cheer + ful =	11.	*cheerful*
pain + ful =	12.	*painful*
thought + ful =	13.	*thoughtful*
week + ly =	14.	*weekly*
late + ly =	15.	*lately*
truthful + ly =	16.	*truthfully*
hopeful + ly =	17.	*hopefully*
invent + ion =	18.	*invention*
correct + ion =	19.	*correction*
pollute + ion =	20.	*pollution*

■ PRACTICE   Sort the list words by writing
- nine words with the suffix **-ly**
- six words with the suffix **-ful**
- five words with the suffix **-ion**

■ WRITE   Use three words to write about a friend.

✳ **WATCH OUT FOR FREQUENTLY MISSPELLED WORDS!**

126

- Practice: Suffix Addition and Word Forms
- Strategic Spelling: *Using the Meaning Helper Strategy*
- Cross-Curricular Lesson: Introduce
- Modified List

DAILY SPELLING REVIEW

There are *to* kinds of pie on the menue.

two   menu

THINK AND PRACTICE ■

SUFFIX ADDITION   Write the list word that has each meaning and ending shown below.

1. gladness and joy + ful
2. seven days + ly
3. feeling hope + ly
4. not early + ly
5. quiet and still + ful
6. without warning + ly
7. good looks + ful
8. not fast + ly
9. feeling hurt + ful
10. free from harm + ly
11. strength and might + ful
12. twenty-four hours + ly

1. **cheerful**
2. **weekly**
3. **hopefully**
4. **lately**
5. **peaceful**
6. **suddenly**
7. **beautiful**
8. **slowly**
9. **painful**
10. **safely**
11. **powerful**
12. **daily**

WORD FORMS   Add **-ion**, **-ly**, or **-ful** to the base words below to make list words. Write the list words. Circle the word in which the spelling changed when the suffix was added.

13. act _____ **action**
14. thought _____ **thoughtful**
15. pollute _____ (**pollution**)
16. invent _____ **invention**
17. truthful _____ **truthfully**
18. careful _____ **carefully**

STRATEGIC SPELLING

Using the Meaning Helper Strategy

Use meaning helpers to help spell hard words. Write the list word that goes with each meaning helper. Mark the letter that matches the underlined sound clue.

19. correc<u>t</u>

correc<u>t</u>ion

20. loca<u>t</u>e

loca<u>t</u>ion

Did You Know?
The word *pollution* comes from a Latin word meaning "soiled," "dirty."

THINK AND PRACTICE

Suffix Addition

Using a Dictionary Suggest that students use a dictionary to look up or confirm definitions.

MEETING THE NEEDS OF ALL STUDENTS

Modified List

Review Students studying high-frequency words complete Think and Practice Master 27.

Auditory Learners

Word Forms Auditory learners may want to try each ending in turn orally until they find the correct one for the given word.

Extra Support

Parts of Speech Have students write one sentence using a list word with the suffix **-ful**, one with **-ly**, and one with **-ion**. Help them analyze the function of each list word in its sentence.

Additional Practice

Think and Practice Master 27
Extra Practice Master 27
Everyday Spelling CD-ROM
Everyday Spelling Game Software

127

LESSON 27

- Proofread Captions
- Proofreading Tip: Double Negatives
- Write a Caption
- ✓ Cooperative Midweek Test

DAILY SPELLING REVIEW

The teacher *ast* for my *excus.*

asked   *excuse*

● Core   ○ Optional   ✓ Assessment

PROOFREADING AND WRITING

Usage

Double Negatives Students can correct these sentences:
- I can't find no paper.
- He won't go nowhere.

MEETING THE NEEDS OF ALL STUDENTS

Modified List

Proofreading Students studying high-frequency words complete this page or the proofreading activity on the *Everyday Spelling* CD-ROM.

Visual Learners

Find Examples Have students look through magazines for examples of captioned pictures. Students can display their captions and discuss what they like about them. Ask questions such as: *Are the captions brief and to the point?*

Additional Practice

Hardbound Book Master 27
Second Language Master 27
Writing Mini-Lesson Master 27
Writing Activity Master 27
Proofreading Transparency 27
Everyday Spelling **CD-ROM**

■ PROOFREADING AND WRITING

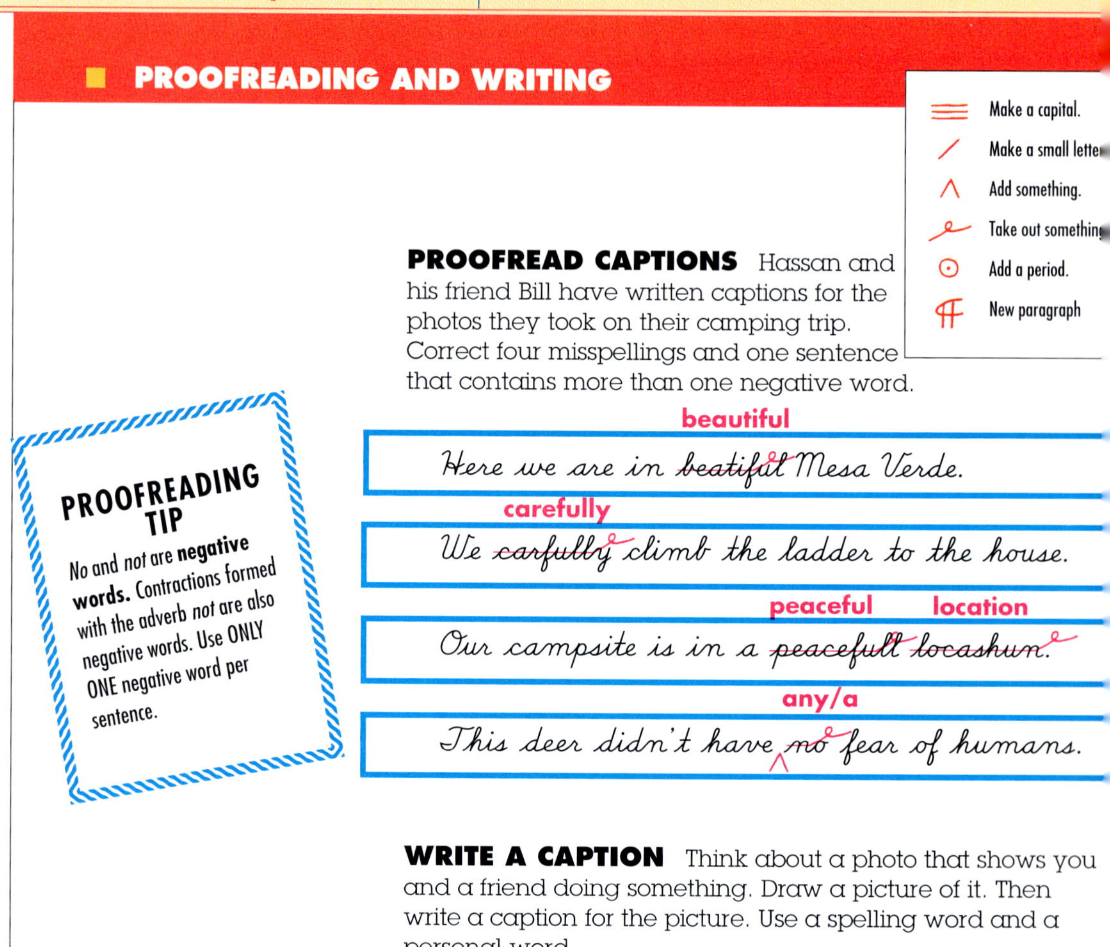

PROOFREAD CAPTIONS Hassan and his friend Bill have written captions for the photos they took on their camping trip. Correct four misspellings and one sentence that contains more than one negative word.

WRITE A CAPTION Think about a photo that shows you and a friend doing something. Draw a picture of it. Then write a caption for the picture. Use a spelling word and a personal word.

Word List

peaceful	lately
thoughtful	daily
powerful	truthfully
cheerful	carefully
painful	hopefully
beautiful	invention
safely	correction
slowly	action
weekly	pollution
suddenly	location

Personal Words

1. **Words will vary.**

2.

Captions should include a spelling word and a personal word.

VOCABULARY BUILDING ■

Review

ANALOGIES   Write the boxed word that completes each analogy.

powerful	daily
peaceful	suddenly
beautiful	carefully
slowly	action
safely	location

1. Eagerly is to anxiously as thoroughly is to ___ .
2. Narrow is to wide as ugly is to ___ .
3. Edge is to rim as place is to ___ .
4. Politely is to courteously as unexpectedly is to ___ .
5. Week is to weekly as day is to ___ .
6. Lazy is to hardworking as hostile is to ___ .
7. Gently is to roughly as swiftly is to ___ .
8. Stillness is to calmness as movement is to ___ .
9. Generously is to selfishly as dangerously is to ___ .
10. Tricky is to clever as mighty is to ___ .

1. **carefully**
2. **beautiful**
3. **location**
4. **suddenly**
5. **daily**
6. **peaceful**
7. **slowly**
8. **action**
9. **safely**
10. **powerful**

Word *Study*

CODES   Many different kinds of codes can be used to disguise what we write. Can you read the message below?

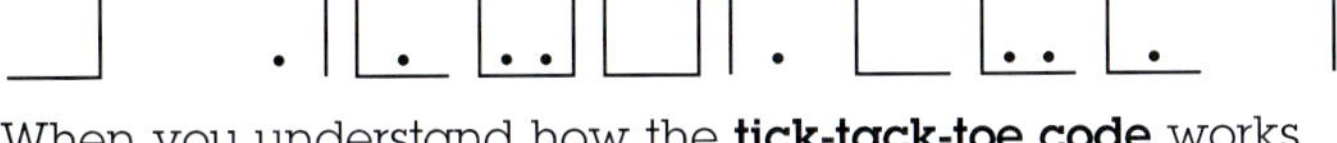

When you understand how the **tick-tack-toe code** works, the message is easy to read.

A	B	C		J	K	L		S	T	U
D	E	F		M	N	O		V	W	X
G	H	I		P	Q	R		Y	Z	

All the letters of the alphabet are on three tick-tack-toe grids. To spell a word in code, look at where the letter is on the grid. Then draw the lines that appear around it. If there are dots, draw those too. So, B = ⌶   M = ⌄   F = ⌐
Now read the words above and write them.

A ___   **POWERFUL** ___   **HERO**

LESSON

28

Generalization

Spelling Focus: When the suffix **-less**, **-ment**, or **-ness** is added to most base words, the base stays the same. If the base word ends in a **consonant** and a **y**, the **y** is changed to **i** before adding the suffix.

● Core   ○ Optional   ✓ Assessment

DAILY PLAN	**CORE OBJECTIVES**	**NOTES**

DAY 1 Introduction

✓ Pretest and Self-Check, p. 130B
● Spelling Focus and Word List, p. 130
○ Challenge Words, p. 130
○ Challenge Master 28
○ Home-School Master 28

- ✓ Take and self-check Pretest
- ▪ Spell words with the suffix **-less**, **-ment**, or **-ness**; classify and write the list words

DAY 2 Think and Practice

● Adding Endings; Match Up, p. 131
● Strategic Spelling: *Building New Words*, p. 131
○ Think and Practice Master 28
○ Extra Practice Master 28
○ Cross-Curricular Lesson: Introduce, p. 202

- ▪ Complete practice activities for words with the suffix **-less**, **-ment**, or **-ness**
- ▪ Apply rules for adding the suffixes **-less**, **-ment**, and **-ness** to make new words

DAY 3 Proofreading and Writing

● Proofread a Comic Strip, p. 132
● Proofreading Tip: Careless Errors, p. 132
● Write a Comic Strip, p. 132
✓ Cooperative Midweek Test
○ Hardbound Book Master 28A
○ Writing Mini-Lesson Master 28
○ Writing Activity Master 28
○ Second Language Support Master 28

- ▪ Proofread for spelling and careless errors
- ▪ Integrate spelling and writing in a personal writing response
- ✓ Take and check midweek test

DAY 4 Vocabulary Building

● Review: Puzzle It Out, p. 133
● Word Study: Haiku, p. 133
○ Hardbound Book Master 28B
○ Cross-Curricular Lesson: Follow-Up, p. 202
○ Review Master 28

- ▪ Complete review activity for words with the suffix **-less**, **-ment**, or **-ness**
- ▪ Study and write haiku

DAY 5 Assessment

✓ Posttest, p. 130B
○ Standardized Test Master 28

- ✓ Take Posttest

Cross-Curricular Lessons

Use the Spelling Focus (suffixes **-less**, **-ment**, and **-ness**) to introduce the Reading lesson, *Hopes, Dreams, and Wishes*, page 202, or choose a lesson that correlates with a topic you're currently teaching.

MEETING THE NEEDS OF ALL STUDENTS

The Word List

For students studying 20 words, assign pages 130–133 and Extra Practice and Review masters.

Modified List For students studying 10 words, modify Practice on page 130, and assign Think and Practice Master 28 and pages 132–133.

Challenge For students studying 25 words, assign pages 130–133, Challenge, Extra Practice, and Review masters.

Bilingual/ESL

As Vietnamese has no suffixes, students may need extra help to understand the function of suffixes such as **-less**, **-ment**, and **-ness**.

Personal Words

Students add to Personal Words lists by looking at work in their writing portfolios and words they want to remember from their reading.

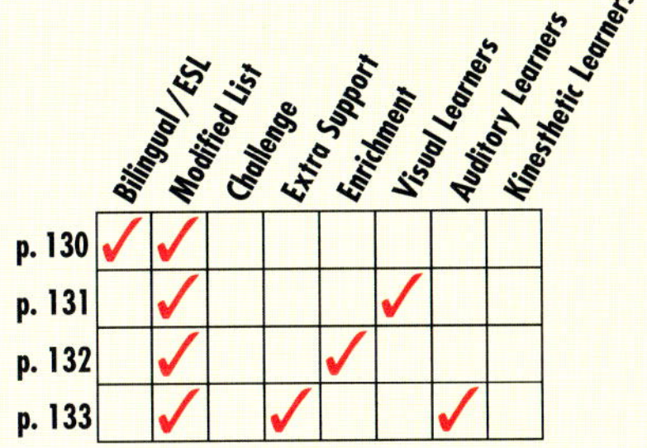

	Bilingual/ESL	Modified List	Challenge	Extra Support	Enrichment	Visual Learners	Auditory Learners	Kinesthetic Learners
p. 130	✓	✓						
p. 131		✓				✓		
p. 132		✓			✓			
p. 133		✓		✓			✓	

ASSESSMENT*

Pretest

Read the underlined word, read the sentence, and then repeat the underlined word. Guide students in self-correcting their pretests and correcting any misspellings.

1. A baby is <u>helpless</u>.
2. That's a <u>careless</u> mistake.
3. Her problem is <u>hopeless</u>.
4. We made a <u>payment</u>.
5. That is a true <u>statement</u>.
6. Her <u>movement</u> was smooth.
7. I admire her <u>goodness</u>.
8. I enjoy the rain's <u>softness</u>.
9. I like red's <u>brightness</u>.
10. Mr. Lee has a car <u>business</u>.
11. The kitchen is <u>spotless</u>.
12. Fear made me <u>breathless</u>.
13. That old thing is <u>worthless</u>.
14. A rusty nail is <u>useless</u>.
15. The <u>pavement</u> is wet.
16. Vi got <u>treatment</u> for a cut.
17. The <u>punishment</u> was no TV.
18. I read of his <u>greatness</u>.
19. She is known for <u>fairness</u>.
20. We played in <u>darkness</u>.

Posttest

Read aloud the sentences below. These sentences may be used for dictation.

1. It's a graceful <u>movement</u>.
2. The house <u>payment</u> is due.
3. Was it a funny <u>statement</u>?
4. My <u>goodness</u>, who is that?
5. Feel the <u>softness</u> of a cat.
6. Mom is never <u>careless</u>.
7. A new kitten is <u>helpless</u>.
8. The chase was <u>hopeless</u>.
9. I'd like to own a <u>business</u>.
10. So much <u>brightness</u> hurts my eyes.
11. The dog got good <u>treatment</u>.
12. Don't fall on the <u>pavement</u>.
13. What is true <u>greatness</u>?
14. That's a fair <u>punishment</u>.
15. He asked for <u>fairness</u>.
16. I'm hot and <u>breathless</u>.
17. I'm scared of the <u>darkness</u>.
18. Our classroom is <u>spotless</u>.
19. This is <u>worthless</u> trash.
20. It's <u>useless</u> to be angry.

Challenge Words

1. What is the <u>assignment</u>?
2. Dad had an <u>appointment</u>.
3. I made an <u>announcement</u>.
4. <u>Homelessness</u> is sad.
5. He lost <u>consciousness</u>.

Additional Assessment

Standardized Test Master 28
Dictation Sentences, p. T41
Everyday Spelling CD-ROM

KIDSPELLING

Sometimes misspellings are because of a misconception. That's how *Research in Action* analyzed a young writer's use of "nice nest" instead of *niceness*. Help students find the base word and then discuss how adding a suffix changes the word's meaning.

* See pp. T20 and T33 for test-study-test information.

LESSON
28

DAY 1   CHALLENGE MASTER

CHALLENGE ■ 28

Challenge Words

assignment	announcement	appointment
homelessness	consciousness	

■ Use Challenge Words to complete the limerick below.

1. The senator kept her **appointment**
2. To make an important **announcement** :
3. She would raise **consciousness**
4. About **homelessness**
5. If the voters gave her the **assignment** .

■ One simple statement can affect your whole day—or even your whole life. Use one or more of the Challenge Words to write about a statement that changed everything.

Practice Masters, p. 107

DAY 1   HOME-SCHOOL MASTER

■ 28   HOME-SCHOOL ACTIVITIES   28 ■

Word Check 28
1. pavement
2. statement
3. movement
4. payment
5. treatment
6. punishment
7. greatness
8. fairness
9. goodness
10. softness
11. darkness
12. brightness
13. business
14. breathless
15. careless
16. spotless
17. helpless
18. useless
19. hopeless
20. worthless

■ **Base Words** Write the list word that contains each base word below.

1. great **greatness**
2. move **movement**
3. busy **business**
4. soft **softness**
5. pay **payment**
6. pave **pavement**
7. bright **brightness**
8. treat **treatment**
9. state **statement**
10. good **goodness**
11. fair **fairness**
12. punish **punishment**
13. dark **darkness**

■ **Add The Ending** Add the suffix **-less** to each word below and write the list word. Then use the letters in the boxes to answer the riddle.

14. care   c a r e l e s s
15. spot   s p o t l e s s
16. worth w o r t h l e s s
17. use   u s e l e s s
18. breath b r e a t h l e s s
19. help   h e l p l e s s
20. hope   h o p e l e s s

What word would you use to describe something with no color?

c o l o r l e s s

Dear Parent,

Please check to see that your child has done this page correctly. Circle any misspelled words and help your child study them.

Tear off the Word Check before your child returns this page to class. Use it to help your child study.

Home-School Activities, p. 24

DAY 2   THINK AND PRACTICE MASTER

28 ■ THINK AND PRACTICE

helpless	careless	hopeless	payment	statement
movement	goodness	softness	brightness	business

■ **Word Forms** Write the list word that is a form of the word in parentheses to complete each sentence.

1. The (care) driver hit a pole. **careless**
2. The (move) of the waves rocked the boat. **movement**
3. A newborn baby is (help). **helpless**
4. I felt the (soft) of the kitten when I touched its fur. **softness**
5. My room is a (hope) mess. **hopeless**
6. Send the (pay) to the bank. **payment**

■ **Match Up** Match each word with one of the suffixes to form a list word. Write each word.

	-less	-ment	-ness
7. care	**careless**		
8. bright	**brightness**		
9. move	**movement**		
10. busy	**business**		
11. state	**statement**		
12. good	**goodness**		

STRATEGIC SPELLING: Building New Words
Add the suffix to each base word to make a new word.

Base Word	Suffix	New Word
13. home	-less	**homeless**
14. enjoy	-ment	**enjoyment**
15. cold	-ness	**coldness**

Practice Masters, p. 108

DAY 2   EXTRA PRACTICE MASTER

EXTRA PRACTICE ■ 28

Word List

helpless	careless	hopeless	payment	statement
movement	goodness	softness	brightness	business
spotless	breathless	worthless	useless	pavement
treatment	punishment	greatness	fairness	darkness

■ **Definitions** Write the list word that means the same as the underlined word or words in each sentence.

1. The bird watcher thought she saw <u>motion</u> in the bushes.   1. **movement**
2. A car skidded along the <u>street's surface</u>.   2. **pavement**
3. The <u>gasping</u> hikers stopped to rest.   3. **breathless**
4. There was a <u>gentle tone</u> to her voice when she spoke of her child.   4. **softness**
5. The jewelry that was stolen turned out to be <u>without value</u>.   5. **worthless**
6. The injured man was <u>without help</u>.   6. **helpless**
7. The mayor gave a prepared <u>speech</u> at the rally.   7. **statement**
8. Ms. Jacobs likes her construction <u>profession</u>.   8. **business**
9. Cal felt <u>like giving up</u> when he lost.   9. **hopeless**
10. The writer had reached a <u>position of high importance</u> in her field.   10. **greatness**
11. We like to be treated with <u>justice</u>.   11. **fairness**
12. The new house was <u>without a stain</u>.   12. **spotless**

■ **Words in Context** Use a list word to complete each sentence.

13. A power failure left us in ___.   13. **darkness**
14. Jack was ___ and kept losing his keys.   14. **careless**
15. We received a bill for the doctor's ___.   15. **treatment**
16. Helen's ___ for being out late was to be home early for a week.   16. **punishment**
17. The matches got wet and were ___ for lighting a fire.   17. **useless**
18. We were impressed by the ___ of the people who stopped to help.   18. **goodness**
19. Did you make a ___ on your account?   19. **payment**
20. The ___ of the exploding star amazed the onlookers.   20. **brightness**

Practice Masters, p. 109

130C

TECHNOLOGY AND VISUAL SUPPORT	 Use Audiotape C, Side 1, Lesson 28 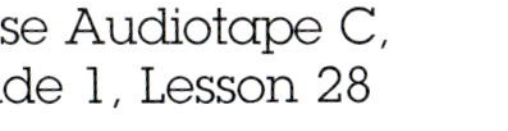 Use Proofreading and Writing Transparency 28	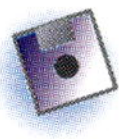 For additional practice use *Everyday Spelling* Game Software, Lesson 28	 Additional resources on *Everyday Spelling* CD-ROM: proofreading and writing, modified list and challenge words, auditory test

DAY 3 SECOND LANGUAGE SUPPORT MASTER

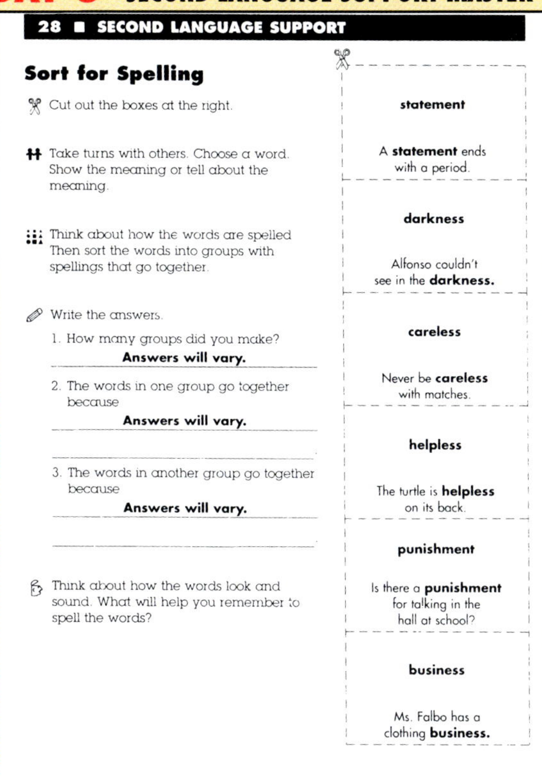

28 ■ SECOND LANGUAGE SUPPORT

Sort for Spelling

Cut out the boxes at the right.

Take turns with others. Choose a word. Show the meaning or tell about the meaning.

Think about how the words are spelled. Then sort the words into groups with spellings that go together.

Write the answers.

1. How many groups did you make?
   Answers will vary.

2. The words in one group go together because
   Answers will vary.

3. The words in another group go together because
   Answers will vary.

Think about how the words look and sound. What will help you remember to spell the words?

statement

A **statement** ends with a period.

darkness

Alfonso couldn't see in the **darkness.**

careless

Never be **careless** with matches.

helpless

The turtle is **helpless** on its back.

punishment

Is there a **punishment** for talking in the hall at school?

business

Ms. Falbo has a clothing **business.**

Second Language Support, p. 50

DAY 3 WRITING ACTIVITY MASTER

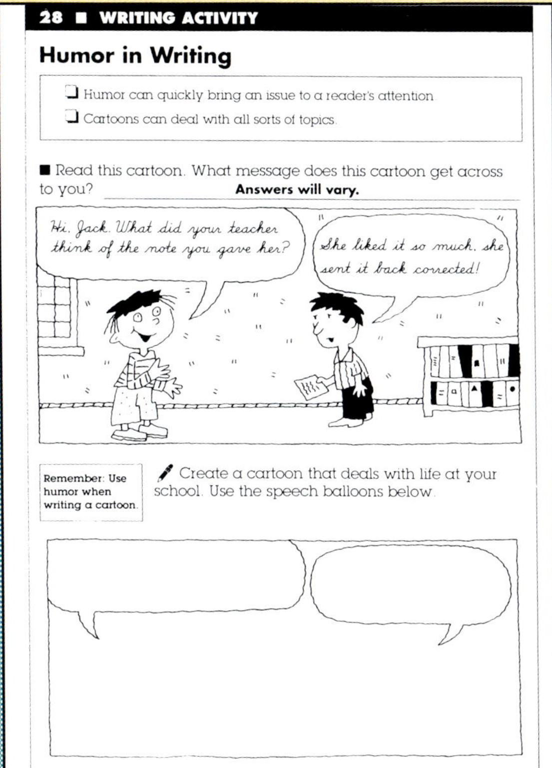

28 ■ WRITING ACTIVITY

Humor in Writing

- Humor can quickly bring an issue to a reader's attention
- Cartoons can deal with all sorts of topics

■ Read this cartoon. What message does this cartoon get across to you? **Answers will vary.**

Remember: Use humor when writing a cartoon.

Create a cartoon that deals with life at your school. Use the speech balloons below.

Spelling and Writing, p. 48

DAY 4 REVIEW MASTER

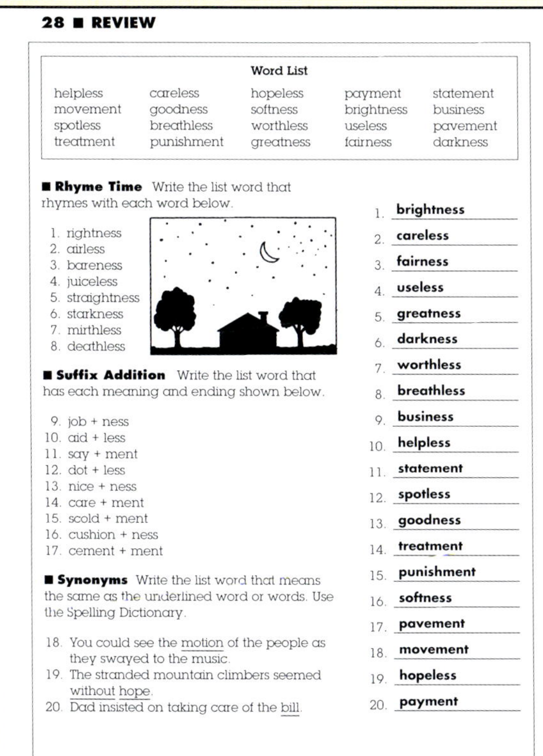

28 ■ REVIEW

Word List

helpless	careless	hopeless	payment	statement
movement	goodness	softness	brightness	business
spotless	breathless	worthless	useless	pavement
treatment	punishment	greatness	fairness	darkness

■ **Rhyme Time** Write the list word that rhymes with each word below.

1. rightness
2. airless
3. bareness
4. juiceless
5. straightness
6. starkness
7. mirthless
8. deathless

■ **Suffix Addition** Write the list word that has each meaning and ending shown below.

9. job + ness
10. aid + less
11. say + ment
12. dot + less
13. nice + ness
14. care + ment
15. scold + ment
16. cushion + ness
17. cement + ment

■ **Synonyms** Write the list word that means the same as the underlined word or words. Use the Spelling Dictionary.

18. You could see the <u>motion</u> of the people as they swayed to the music.
19. The stranded mountain climbers seemed <u>without hope</u>.
20. Dad insisted on taking care of the <u>bill</u>.

1. **brightness**
2. **careless**
3. **fairness**
4. **useless**
5. **greatness**
6. **darkness**
7. **worthless**
8. **breathless**
9. **business**
10. **helpless**
11. **statement**
12. **spotless**
13. **goodness**
14. **treatment**
15. **punishment**
16. **softness**
17. **pavement**
18. **movement**
19. **hopeless**
20. **payment**

Practice Masters, p. 110

DAY 5 STANDARDIZED TEST MASTER

28 ■ LESSON TEST

■ Find the word in each group that is spelled correctly. Fill in the letter for the correct word on the answer strip.

Sample:
- **a.** contes **c.** cotest
- **b.** contist **d.** contest → ⓐⓑⓒ●

1. **a.** movement **c.** movemint **b.** moovement **d.** muvement → 1. ●ⓑⓒⓓ
2. **a.** breethless **c.** breathless **b.** braethless **d.** breatheless → 2. ⓐⓑ●ⓓ
3. **a.** fairness **c.** faireness **b.** fareness **d.** fariness → 3. ●ⓑⓒⓓ
4. **a.** hepless **c.** helpeles **b.** hellpless **d.** helpless → 4. ⓐⓑⓒ●
5. **a.** treatment **c.** treetment **b.** tretment **d.** traetment → 5. ●ⓑⓒⓓ
6. **a.** usless **c.** ussless **b.** useless **d.** useliss → 6. ⓐ●ⓒⓓ
7. **a.** softness **c.** softness **b.** sofness **d.** softnes → 7. ⓐⓑ●ⓓ
8. **a.** hopeless **c.** hopeliss **b.** hoppeless **d.** hopless → 8. ●ⓑⓒⓓ
9. **a.** statment **c.** staytment **b.** statement **d.** stament → 9. ⓐ●ⓒⓓ
10. **a.** wolthes **c.** wurthless **b.** wortless **d.** worthless → 10. ⓐⓑⓒ●
11. **a.** buissness **c.** buisness **b.** bussiness **d.** business → 11. ⓐⓑⓒ●
12. **a.** spatless **c.** spotless **b.** spoless **d.** spotles → 12. ⓐⓑ●ⓓ
13. **a.** briteness **c.** brihgtness **b.** brightness **d.** brightniss → 13. ⓐ●ⓒⓓ
14. **a.** payment **c.** payement **b.** paement **d.** payiment → 14. ●ⓑⓒⓓ
15. **a.** punishment **c.** punisment **b.** punshment **d.** punnishment → 15. ●ⓑⓒⓓ
16. **a.** darknes **c.** darkeness **b.** darkness **d.** darrkness → 16. ⓐ●ⓒⓓ
17. **a.** grateness **c.** greatnes **b.** graetness **d.** greatness → 17. ⓐⓑⓒ●
18. **a.** goodnes **c.** goodness **b.** goodneness **d.** goodeness → 18. ⓐⓑ●ⓓ
19. **a.** pavement **c.** paevment **b.** payvement **d.** pavemment → 19. ●ⓑⓒⓓ
20. **a.** carreless **c.** cairless **b.** careles **d.** careless → 20. ⓐⓑⓒ●

Practice for Standardized Tests, p. 40

DAY 1 Introduction

- ✓ Pretest and Self-Check
- ● Spelling Focus and Word List
- ○ Challenge Words
- ○ Modified List

DAILY SPELLING REVIEW

My *girl friend* fell and hurt *her self.*

girlfriend   *herself*

● Core   ○ Optional   ✓ Assessment

INTRODUCTION

Word Structure

Changing y to i Have students think of words in which the **y** of a base word is changed to **i** before adding **-less**, **-ment**, or **-ness**. Examples are *happiness, laziness,* and *silliness.*

MEETING THE NEEDS OF ALL STUDENTS

Modified List

Practice Students studying only the high-frequency words in the top box write
- four words ending in **-ness**
- three words ending in **-ment**
- three words ending in **-less**

Bilingual/ESL

Focus on Meanings Point out that the meaning of each list word comes from the meaning of the base word. For example, the meaning of *movement* is based on the meaning of *move.*

Additional Practice

Challenge Master 28
Home-School Master 28
Audiotape C, Side 1

28

1. goodness
2. softness
3. brightness
4. business
5. greatness
6. fairness
7. darkness
8. payment
9. statement
10. movement
11. pavement
12. treatment
13. punishment
14. helpless
15. careless
16. hopeless
17. spotless
18. breathless
19. worthless
20. useless

Order of words in each group may vary.

CHALLENGE!

assignment
appointment
announcement
homelessness
consciousness

Sentences will vary.

■ **INTRODUCTION**

Suffixes -less, -ment, -ness

SPELLING FOCUS

When **-less**, **-ment**, or **-ness** is added to most base words, the base stays the same: **goodness**. If the base word ends in a **consonant** and a **y**, the **y** is changed to **i** before adding the suffix: **business**.

■ **STUDY**   What happens when each suffix is added?

help + less =	1.	*helpless*
care + less =	2.	*careless*
hope + less =	3.	*hopeless*
pay + ment =	4.	*payment*
state + ment =	5.	*statement*
move + ment =	6.	*movement*
good + ness =	7.	*goodness*
soft + ness =	8.	*softness*
bright + ness =	9.	*brightness*
busy + ness =	10.	*business*

spot + less =	11.	*spotless*
breath + less =	12.	*breathless*
worth + less =	13.	*worthless*
use + less =	14.	*useless*
pave + ment =	15.	*pavement*
treat + ment =	16.	*treatment*
punish + ment =	17.	*punishment*
great + ness =	18.	*greatness*
fair + ness =	19.	*fairness*
dark + ness =	20.	*darkness*

■ **PRACTICE**   Sort the list words by writing
- seven words ending in **-ness**
- six words ending in **-ment**
- seven words ending in **-less**

■ **WRITE**   Choose ten words to write in sentences.

THINK AND PRACTICE

ADDING ENDINGS Complete each sentence by adding **-less**, **-ment**, or **-ness** to the word in parentheses.

1. (busy)   She was out of town on ___.
2. (pay)   He just made his last car ___.
3. (help)   The trapped fox was ___.
4. (use)   This old map is ___.
5. (move)   I watched the dancer's graceful ___.
6. (great)   The child was destined for ___.
7. (state)   The lawyer began her closing ___.
8. (hope)   Our unfortunate situation looked ___.
9. (good)   He helped us out of the ___ of his heart.
10. (worth)   Throw away that ___ old inner tube.
11. (breath)   I ran so fast I was soon ___.
12. (pave)   We rode our bikes on the concrete ___.
13. (fair)   In all ___, I don't want to take sides.
14. (soft)   The child loved the ___ of the blanket.

MATCH UP Match each word with one of the suffixes below to form a list word. Write each word.

ness	less	ment

15. care   18. spot
16. treat   19. dark
17. bright   20. punish

Building New Words

Add the suffix to each base word to make a new word.

Base word	Suffix	New word
21. home	-less	homeless
22. enjoy	-ment	enjoyment
23. cold	-ness	coldness

1. **business**
2. **payment**
3. **helpless**
4. **useless**
5. **movement**
6. **greatness**
7. **statement**
8. **hopeless**
9. **goodness**
10. **worthless**
11. **breathless**
12. **pavement**
13. **fairness**
14. **softness**
15. **careless**
16. **treatment**
17. **brightness**
18. **spotless**
19. **darkness**
20. **punishment**

Take a Hint
It's easy to leave out the **i** in **business** because you don't say it. Just remember this phrase: Take the **bus in** when you have **busi**ness in town.

131

LESSON 28

- ● Proofread a Comic Strip
- ● Proofreading Tip: Careless Errors
- ● Write a Comic Strip
- ✓ Cooperative Midweek Test

DAILY SPELLING REVIEW

Your an excellent *pupel.*

You're   *pupil*

● Core   ○ Optional   ✓ Assessment

PROOFREADING AND WRITING

Proofreading

Left-Out Words Point out to students that left-out words can usually be discovered by reading copy aloud.

MEETING THE NEEDS OF ALL STUDENTS

Modified List

Proofreading Students studying high-frequency words complete this page or the proofreading activity on the *Everyday Spelling* CD-ROM.

Enrichment

Draw the Comic Strip

After students have written their comic strip dialogues, have them draw the comic strips to accompany the dialogues. These may be displayed in the classroom.

Additional Practice

Hardbound Book Master 28A
Second Language Master 28
Writing Mini-Lesson Master 28
Writing Activity Master 28
Proofreading Transparency 28
Everyday Spelling CD-ROM

■ PROOFREADING AND WRITING

≡	Make a capital.
/	Make a small letter
∧	Add something.
ℒ	Take out something
⊙	Add a period.
¶	New paragraph

PROOFREAD A COMIC STRIP

LaDonna and Jake created a superhero named WizKid, who fights crime by using brain power. Read WizKid's words and correct four misspellings and two careless errors.

PROOFREADING TIP

LaDonna and Jake made a great superhero, but they also made two super errors. Words such as *to* and *for* may be small, but they should never be left out.

WRITE A COMIC STRIP Practice writing your own comic strip dialogue. Use list words.

Word List

pavement	darkness
statement	brightness
movement	business
payment	breathless
treatment	careless
punishment	spotless
greatness	helpless
fairness	useless
goodness	hopeless
softness	worthless

Personal Words

1. **Words will vary.**

2. __________

132

VOCABULARY BUILDING ■

Review

PUZZLE IT OUT What is a name for action figures that are brave, strong, and good? Write the boxed words that match the clues. Then use the numbered letters to solve the riddle.

helpless	movement
careless	goodness
hopeless	softness
payment	brightness
statement	business

1. shininess
2. amount of money paid
3. motion
4. the opposite of badness
5. fluffiness
6. unable to take care of oneself
7. the opposite of confident
8. work; occupation
9. done without enough thought or effort
10. remark; declaration

1. **b r i g h t n e s s**
2. **p a y m e n t**
3. **m o v e m e n t**
4. **g o o d n e s s**
5. **s o f t n e s s**
6. **h e l p l e s s**
7. **h o p e l e s s**
8. **b u s i n e s s**
9. **c a r e l e s s**
10. **s t a t e m e n t**

s u p e r h e r o e s

Word *Study*

HAIKU Long ago in Japan, a contest was held in which competitors added lines to existing poems. Those who created the best lines won. The name **haiku** (hī′kü) comes from this contest. Read the two haiku below.

The falling flower
I saw drift back to the branch
was a butterfly.

Poor crying cricket,
perhaps your little husband
was caught by our cat.

A haiku is usually three lines long and often describes a scene in nature. The first line has five syllables, the second line has seven syllables, and the third line has five syllables.

Write your own haiku. Start with the line at the right. Use a dictionary if you need help counting syllables.

Raindrops on a leaf.

Responses will vary.

LESSON
29

Generalization

Spelling Focus: When prefixes **dis-**, **in-**, **mis-**, and **re-** are added to words, make no change in the spelling of the base word.

● Core ○ Optional ✓ Assessment

DAILY PLAN	CORE OBJECTIVES	NOTES

DAY 1 Introduction

✓ Pretest and Self-Check, p. 134B
● Spelling Focus and Word List, p. 134
○ Challenge Words, p. 134
○ Challenge Master 29
○ Home-School Master 29

- ✓ Take and self-check Pretest
- Spell words with the prefix **dis-**, **in-**, **mis-**, and **re-**; classify and write the list words

DAY 2 Think and Practice

● Super Antonyms; Prefix Addition, p. 135
● Strategic Spelling: *Building New Words,* p. 135
○ Think and Practice Master 29
○ Extra Practice Master 29
○ Cross-Curricular Lesson: Introduce, p. 184

- Complete practice activities for words with the prefix **dis-**, **in-**, **mis-**, and **re-**
- Apply rules for adding prefixes to make new words

DAY 3 Proofreading and Writing

● Proofread a Letter, p. 136
● Proofreading Tip: Handwriting, p. 136
● Write a Letter, p. 136
✓ Cooperative Midweek Test
○ Hardbound Book Master 29
○ Writing Mini-Lesson Master 29
○ Writing Activity Master 29
○ Second Language Support Master 29

- Proofread for spelling and handwriting errors
- Integrate spelling and writing in a personal writing response
- ✓ Take and check midweek test

DAY 4 Vocabulary Building

● Review: Word Associations, p. 137
● Word Study: Synonyms, p. 137
○ Cross-Curricular Lesson: Follow-Up, p. 184
○ Review Master 29

- Complete review activity for words with the prefix **dis-**, **in-**, **mis-**, and **re-**
- Study and use synonyms

DAY 5 Assessment

✓ Posttest, p. 134B
○ Standardized Test Master 29

- ✓ Take Posttest

Cross-Curricular Lessons

Use the Spelling Focus (prefixes **dis-**, **in-**, **mis-**, and **re-**) to introduce the Health lesson, *Know Yourself*, page 184, or choose a lesson that correlates with a topic you're currently teaching.

MEETING THE NEEDS OF ALL STUDENTS

The Word List

For students studying 20 words, assign pages 134–137 and Extra Practice and Review masters.

Modified List For students studying 10 words, modify Practice on page 134, and assign Think and Practice Master 29 and pages 136–137.

Challenge For students studying 25 words, assign pages 134–137, Challenge, Extra Practice, and Review masters.

Bilingual/ESL

Because some Spanish prefixes are similar to their English equivalents, Spanish-speaking students may confuse the two and misspell *disagree* as *desagre* or *distrust* as *destrust*.

Personal Words

Students add to Personal Words lists by looking at work in their writing portfolios and words they want to remember from their reading.

	Bilingual/ESL	Modified List	Challenge	Extra Support	Enrichment	Visual Learners	Auditory Learners	Kinesthetic Learners
p. 134		✓						✓
p. 135		✓				✓		
p. 136		✓			✓			
p. 137	✓	✓	✓					

ASSESSMENT*

Pretest

Read the underlined word, read the sentence, and then repeat the underlined word. Guide students in self-correcting their pretests and correcting any misspellings.

1. Does anyone <u>dislike</u> candy?
2. Why did they <u>disappear</u>?
3. My work is <u>incomplete</u>.
4. My sister is <u>independent</u>.
5. That statement is <u>incorrect</u>.
6. Don't <u>misplace</u> your pen.
7. What did you <u>misspell</u>?
8. The president <u>misled</u> us.
9. We'll <u>rebuild</u> the model.
10. Let's <u>reuse</u> this bag.
11. I <u>distrust</u> the weather.
12. The thief was <u>dishonest</u>.
13. My friend and I <u>disagree</u>.
14. Some pollution is <u>invisible</u>.
15. Mai is <u>inactive</u> in the club.
16. Don't <u>mistreat</u> animals.
17. We wouldn't <u>misbehave</u>.
18. A cat will <u>react</u> to a dog.
19. <u>Replace</u> those cookies.
20. I don't <u>recall</u> your name.

Posttest

Read aloud the sentences below. These sentences may be used for dictation.

1. I'll make that <u>disappear</u>.
2. I <u>dislike</u> planning parties.
3. My math is never <u>incorrect</u>.
4. The picture is <u>incomplete</u>.
5. Don't be <u>misled</u> by anyone.
6. Did I <u>misspell</u> that word?
7. I won't <u>misplace</u> my book.
8. We can <u>reuse</u> this paper.
9. Let's <u>rebuild</u> the shelter.
10. The baby is <u>independent</u>.
11. That answer is <u>dishonest</u>.
12. I <u>distrust</u> an old chair.
13. I read of an <u>invisible</u> man.
14. My grandfather is <u>inactive</u>.
15. It's all right to <u>disagree</u>.
16. We'll <u>replace</u> the tape.
17. They sometimes <u>misbehave</u>.
18. A horse will <u>react</u> to noise.
19. He wouldn't <u>mistreat</u> a fly.
20. Do you <u>recall</u> that story?

Challenge Words

1. <u>Disobedience</u> is wrong.
2. That story is <u>incredible</u>.
3. This room is <u>inconvenient</u>.
4. His <u>misfortune</u> is sad.
5. <u>Recycling</u> is good for us.

Additional Assessment

Standardized Test Master 29
Dictation Sentences, p. T41
Everyday Spelling CD-ROM

WHAT'S THE BIG IDEA?
Research in Action tells us that students at fourth grade have begun to understand that while suffixes sometimes require a spelling change in a word, prefixes do not.

***** See pp. T20 and T33 for test-study-test information.

LESSON
29

DAY 1 CHALLENGE MASTER

CHALLENGE ■ 29

Challenge Words

disobedience   inconvenience   incredible   misfortune   recycling

■ Use these math clues to spell the Challenge Words.

1. r a d i a n c e - a, a + e, i, b, l = **incredible**
2. r e m o r s e f u l - r, e, l + i, t, n = **misfortune**
3. m i d d l i n g - m, l, g + s, o, b, e, e, e, c = **disobedience**
4. n e e d l e p o i n t - d, l, p, t + c, c, v, n, n, i = **inconvenience**
5. c o l o r i n g - o, o + e, c, y = **recycling**

■ Pets are lots of fun, but they can get into trouble sometimes. They often do things no one expects. Use one or more of the Challenge Words to write about a pet that does something unexpected.

Practice Masters, p. 111

DAY 1 HOME-SCHOOL MASTER

■ 29   HOME-SCHOOL ACTIVITIES   29 ■

■ **Meaning Clues** Write the list word that you think of for the underlined words in each sentence.

1. One atom is <u>too small to be seen</u>. **invisible**
2. Joe is <u>relaxing</u> after his work. **inactive**
3. We need to <u>get a new</u> toaster. **replace**
4. Don't <u>yell at</u> your friends. **mistreat**
5. I <u>can go alone</u> to the doctor. **independent**
6. I <u>would argue with</u> your opinion. **disagree**
7. Do you <u>remember</u> my address? **recall**
8. The word knee is <u>not spelled</u> nee. **misspell**
9. The witness <u>told a lie</u>. **dishonest**
10. You <u>gave me the wrong directions</u>. **misled**
11. Hal <u>leaped up</u> when I surprised him. **react**
12. I'm <u>not very fond of</u> Mark. **dislike**

■ **Synonyms** Write the list word that fits each word or phrase below.

13. make again **rebuild**
14. lose **misplace**
15. vanish **disappear**
16. wrong **incorrect**
17. act up **misbehave**
18. use over **reuse**
19. not done **incomplete**
20. doubt **distrust**

Word Check 29

1. disappear
2. distrust
3. dishonest
4. disagree
5. dislike
6. invisible
7. incorrect
8. incomplete
9. inactive
10. independent
11. misplace
12. misspell
13. mistreat
14. misled
15. misbehave
16. react
17. replace
18. recall
19. rebuild
20. reuse

Dear Parent,

Please check to see that your child has done this page correctly. Circle any misspelled words and help your child study them.

Tear off the Word Check before your child returns this page to class. Use it to help your child study.

Home-School Activities, p. 25

DAY 2 THINK AND PRACTICE MASTER

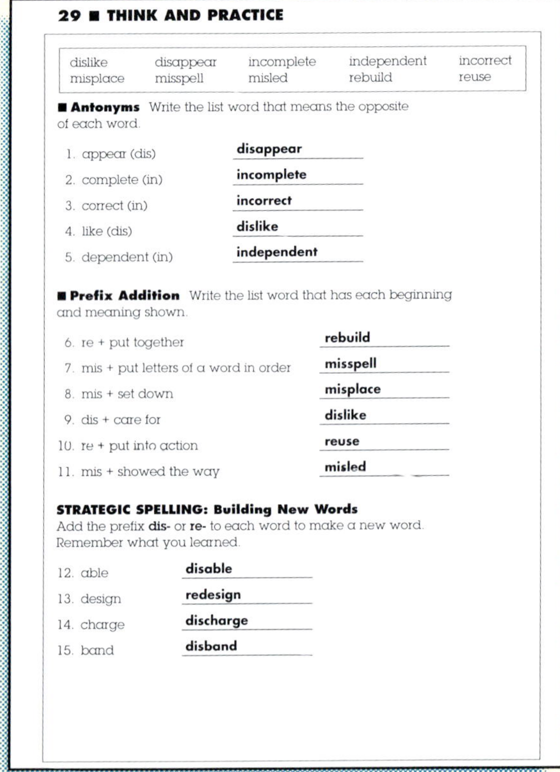

29 ■ THINK AND PRACTICE

| dislike | disappear | incomplete | independent | incorrect |
| misplace | misspell | misled | rebuild | reuse |

■ **Antonyms** Write the list word that means the opposite of each word.

1. appear (dis) **disappear**
2. complete (in) **incomplete**
3. correct (in) **incorrect**
4. like (dis) **dislike**
5. dependent (in) **independent**

■ **Prefix Addition** Write the list word that has each beginning and meaning shown.

6. re + put together **rebuild**
7. mis + put letters of a word in order **misspell**
8. mis + set down **misplace**
9. dis + care for **dislike**
10. re + put into action **reuse**
11. mis + showed the way **misled**

STRATEGIC SPELLING: Building New Words
Add the prefix **dis-** or **re-** to each word to make a new word. Remember what you learned.

12. able **disable**
13. design **redesign**
14. charge **discharge**
15. band **disband**

Practice Masters, p. 112

DAY 2 EXTRA PRACTICE MASTER

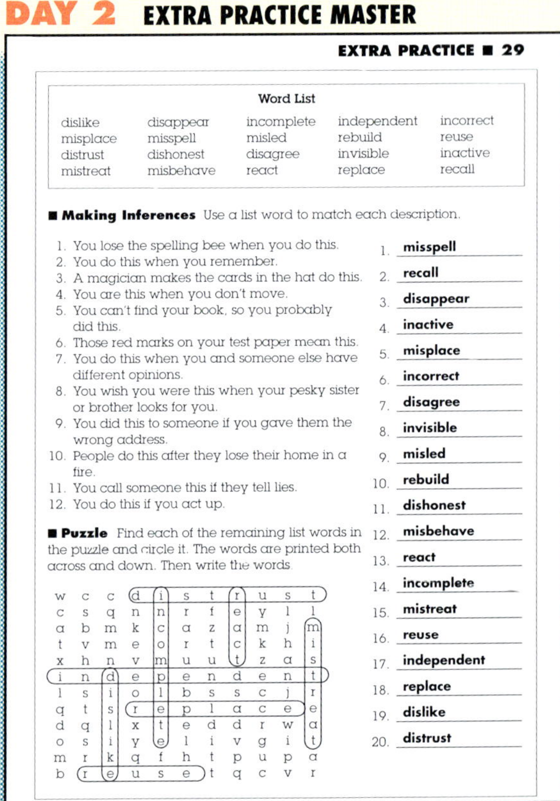

EXTRA PRACTICE ■ 29

Word List

dislike	disappear	incomplete	independent	incorrect
misplace	misspell	misled	rebuild	reuse
distrust	dishonest	disagree	invisible	inactive
mistreat	misbehave	react	replace	recall

■ **Making Inferences** Use a list word to match each description.

1. You lose the spelling bee when you do this.
2. You do this when you remember.
3. A magician makes the cards in the hat do this.
4. You are this when you don't move.
5. You can't find your book, so you probably did this.
6. Those red marks on your test paper mean this.
7. You do this when you and someone else have different opinions.
8. You wish you were this when your pesky sister or brother looks for you.
9. You did this to someone if you gave them the wrong address.
10. People do this after they lose their home in a fire.
11. You call someone this if they tell lies.
12. You do this if you act up.

1. **misspell**
2. **recall**
3. **disappear**
4. **inactive**
5. **misplace**
6. **incorrect**
7. **disagree**
8. **invisible**
9. **misled**
10. **rebuild**
11. **dishonest**
12. **misbehave**
13. **react**
14. **incomplete**
15. **mistreat**
16. **reuse**
17. **independent**
18. **replace**
19. **dislike**
20. **distrust**

■ **Puzzle** Find each of the remaining list words in the puzzle and circle it. The words are printed both across and down. Then write the words.

```
w c c d i s t r u s t
c s q n n r f e y l
a b m k c a z a m j m
t v m e o r t c k h i
x h n v m u u t z a s
i n d e p e n d e n t
l s i o l b s s c j r
q t s r e p l a c e e
d q l x t e d d r w a
o s i y e l i v g i t
m r k q f h t p u p a
b r e u s e t q c v r
```

Practice Masters, p. 113

<table>
<tr><td rowspan="2">TECHNOLOGY AND VISUAL SUPPORT</td><td> Use Audiotape C, Side 1, Lesson 29</td><td rowspan="2"> For additional practice use Everyday Spelling Game Software, Lesson 29</td><td rowspan="2"> Additional resources on Everyday Spelling CD-ROM: proofreading and writing, modified list and challenge words, auditory test</td></tr>
<tr><td>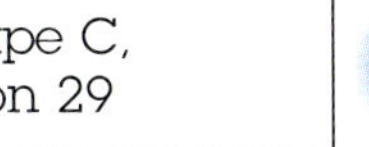 Use Proofreading and Writing Transparency 29</td></tr>
</table>

DAY 3 SECOND LANGUAGE SUPPORT MASTER

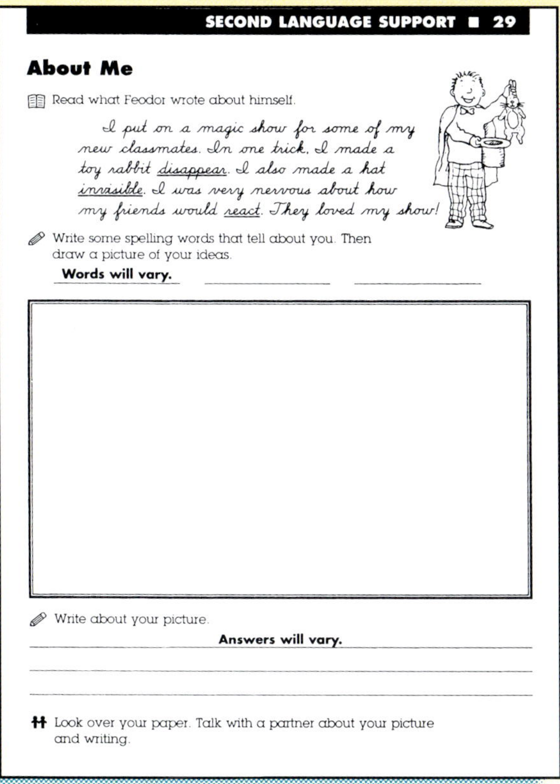

SECOND LANGUAGE SUPPORT ■ 29

About Me

Read what Feodor wrote about himself.

I put on a magic show for some of my new classmates. In one trick, I made a toy rabbit disappear. I also made a hat invisible. I was very nervous about how my friends would react. They loved my show!

Write some spelling words that tell about you. Then draw a picture of your ideas.

Words will vary.

Write about your picture.

Answers will vary.

Look over your paper. Talk with a partner about your picture and writing.

Second Language Support, p. 51

DAY 3 WRITING ACTIVITY MASTER

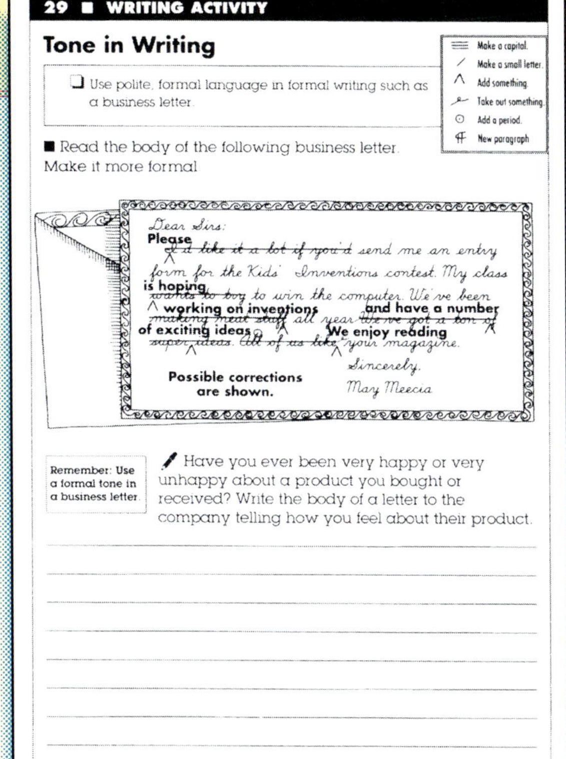

29 ■ WRITING ACTIVITY

Tone in Writing

Use polite, formal language in formal writing such as a business letter.

Read the body of the following business letter. Make it more formal.

Dear Sirs:
Please send me an entry form for the Kids' Inventions contest. My class is hoping to win the computer. We've been working on inventions and have a number of exciting ideas. We enjoy reading your magazine.

Sincerely,
May Meecia

Possible corrections are shown.

Make a capital. / Make a small letter. ∧ Add something. Take out something. Add a period. New paragraph.

Remember: Use a formal tone in a business letter.

Have you ever been very happy or very unhappy about a product you bought or received? Write the body of a letter to the company telling how you feel about their product.

Spelling and Writing, p. 50

DAY 4 REVIEW MASTER

29 ■ REVIEW

Word List

dislike	disappear	incomplete	independent	incorrect
misplace	misspell	misled	rebuild	reuse
distrust	dishonest	disagree	invisible	inactive
mistreat	misbehave	react	replace	recall

■ **Happy Beginnings** Add a beginning to each word in parentheses to form a list word that completes the sentence.

1. (treat) Never ___ small animals.
2. (build) There's so much fire damage, they will have to ___ most of the house.
3. (correct) The answer was ___ because of a misplaced decimal.
4. (agree) It's often easier to ___ than get along.
5. (act) People can ___ badly to drugs that seem harmless.
6. (led) The advertising ___ the shopper.
7. (active) Older people need to fight becoming ___.
8. (trust) Friendship and ___ don't mix.

■ **Antonym Alert** Write the list word that means the opposite of each word below.

9. find
10. enjoy
11. dependent
12. honest
13. take
14. obey
15. seen
16. waste

■ **Tongue Twisters** Write the list word that would best complete each tongue twister.

17. Daily Denny Daley did ___.
18. Richie Roonie regrets rotten ___.
19. Inge Ingall's investigation is ___.
20. Molly mentioned Minnie might ___.

1. mistreat
2. rebuild
3. incorrect
4. disagree
5. react
6. misled
7. inactive
8. distrust
9. misplace
10. dislike
11. independent
12. dishonest
13. replace
14. misbehave
15. invisible
16. reuse
17. disappear
18. recall
19. incomplete
20. misspell

Practice Masters, p. 114

DAY 5 STANDARDIZED TEST MASTER

LESSON TEST ■ 29

■ Find the word in each group that is spelled correctly. Fill in the letter for the correct word on the answer strip.

Sample:
a. contes   c. cotest
b. contist   d. contest → (a)(b)(c)●

1. a. disapear   c. disaper
   b. disappear   d. disepere → 1.(a)●(c)(d)
2. a. reeuse   c. reuze
   b. reuse   d. reeuze → 2.(a)●(c)(d)
3. a. missplace   c. misplase
   b. misplace   d. missplase → 3.(a)●(c)(d)
4. a. inacktive   c. inactive
   b. inaktive   d. innactive → 4.(a)(b)●(d)
5. a. invisable   c. invesble
   b. invisebul   d. invisible → 5.(a)(b)(c)●
6. a. distrust   c. disetrust
   b. disstrust   d. disttrust → 6.●(b)(c)(d)
7. a. replace   c. replac
   b. reeplace   d. roplase → 7.●(b)(c)(d)
8. a. rc build   c. rebuild
   b. rebiuld   d. rebuild → 8.(a)(b)(c)●
9. a. disslike   c. dislike
   b. disleke   d. disliek → 9.(a)(b)●(d)
10. a. missbehave   c. misbehav
    b. misbehave   d. missbehav → 10.(a)●(c)(d)
11. a. incomplete   c. incompplete
    b. incomplete   d. incomplet → 11.(a)●(c)(d)
12. a. disagree   c. disagre
    b. dissagree   d. dissagre → 12.●(b)(c)(d)
13. a. mispell   c. misspell
    b. missppell   d. misspel → 13.(a)(b)●(d)
14. a. mistreat   c. mistreet
    b. misstreat   d. misstreet → 14.●(b)(c)(d)
15. a. react   c. reacked
    b. reeact   d. reactd → 15.●(b)(c)(d)
16. a. recal   c. reecal
    b. reecall   d. recall → 16.(a)(b)(c)●
17. a. independent   c. independent
    b. independant   d. independend → 17.(a)(b)(c)●
18. a. disshonnest   c. disshonest
    b. dishonest   d. dishonnest → 18.(a)●(c)(d)
19. a. misslead   c. misled
    b. mislede   d. misslede → 19.(a)(b)●(d)
20. a. incorrect   c. inncorrect
    b. inncorrecked   d. incorreckt → 20.●(b)(c)(d)

Practice for Standardized Tests, p. 41

LESSON

29

- ✓ Pretest and Self-Check
- ● Spelling Focus and Word List
- ○ Challenge Words
- ○ Modified List

DAILY SPELLING REVIEW

Margo went to the *hospitle* when she was *throne* from a horse.

hospital   *thrown*

● Core   ○ Optional   ✓ Assessment

INTRODUCTION

Word Structure

Sorting by Prefix Create a class chart with the following heads: **dis-, in-, mis-,** and **re-**. Have students write the list words under the appropriate heads. Point out that when these prefixes are added, the spelling of the base word does not change.

MEETING THE NEEDS OF ALL STUDENTS

Modified List

Practice Students studying only the high-frequency words in the top box write
- two words with **dis-**
- two words with **re-**
- three words with **in-**
- three words with **mis-**

Kinesthetic Learners

Prefix Pantomime Have each student choose one list word to act out. Have the other students take turns guessing the word being acted out and writing it on the board.

Additional Practice

Challenge Master 29
Home-School Master 29
Audiotape C, Side 1

29

1. **dislike**
2. **disappear**
3. **distrust**
4. **dishonest**
5. **disagree**
6. **rebuild**
7. **reuse**
8. **react**
9. **replace**
10. **recall**
11. **incomplete**
12. **independent**
13. **incorrect**
14. **invisible**
15. **inactive**
16. **misplace**
17. **misspell**
18. **misled**
19. **mistreat**
20. **misbehave**

CHALLENGE!

disobedience
incredible
inconvenient
misfortune
recycling

134

■ INTRODUCTION

Prefixes dis-, in-, mis-, re-

SPELLING FOCUS

When prefixes **dis-, in-, mis-,** and **re-** are added to words, make no change in the spelling of the base word: **dis + like = dislike**.

■ **STUDY** Notice that each base word below does not change when a prefix is added.

dis + like	=	1. *dislike*
dis + appear	=	2. *disappear*
in + complete	=	3. *incomplete*
in + dependent	=	4. *independent*
in + correct	=	5. *incorrect*
mis + place	=	6. *misplace*
mis + spell	=	7. *misspell*
mis + led	=	8. *misled*
re + build	=	9. *rebuild*
re + use	=	10. *reuse*

dis + trust	=	11. *distrust*
dis + honest	=	12. *dishonest*
dis + agree	=	13. *disagree*
in + visible	=	14. *invisible*
in + active	=	15. *inactive*
mis + treat	=	16. *mistreat*
mis + behave	=	17. *misbehave*
re + act	=	18. *react*
re + place	=	19. *replace*
re + call	=	20. *recall*

■ **PRACTICE** Sort the list words by writing
- five words with **dis-**
- five words with **in-**
- five words with **re-**
- five words with **mis-**

Order of words in each group may vary.

■ **WRITE** Choose ten words to write in sentences.
Sentences will vary.

- Practice: Super Antonyms and Prefix Addition
- Strategic Spelling: *Building New Words*
- Cross-Curricular Lesson: Introduce
- Modified List

DAILY SPELLING REVIEW

The singer made a record when he was *olny forteen*.

only   fourteen

THINK AND PRACTICE ■

SUPER ANTONYMS   Complete each statement with a list word that means the opposite of the underlined word.

1. Superguy said, "I <u>like</u> good guys, but I ___ criminals."
2. Spygirl stated, "I <u>trust</u> that you won't ___ me."
3. X-ray Man boasted, "What is <u>visible</u> to me is ___ to you."
4. Wiseguy said, "<u>Treat</u> others <u>well</u> and they won't ___ you."
5. Plastic Woman asked, "Do you <u>agree</u> or ___ with me?"
6. Supergirl warned, "The <u>honest</u> are rewarded, but the ___ are never happy."

PREFIX ADDITION   Write the list word that has each beginning and meaning indicated below.

7. re + do something
8. dis + come into sight
9. in + without mistakes
10. mis + put down
11. re + put into service
12. in + finished
13. mis + went in front of
14. in + ready to do things
15. re + put down
16. mis + act politely
17. in + needing help
18. re + speak or shout
19. mis + write words
20. re + put pieces together

1. dislike
2. distrust
3. invisible
4. mistreat
5. disagree
6. dishonest
7. react
8. disappear
9. incorrect
10. misplace
11. reuse
12. incomplete
13. misled
14. inactive
15. replace
16. misbehave
17. independent
18. recall
19. misspell
20. rebuild

STRATEGIC SPELLING

Building New Words

Add the prefix **dis-** or **re-** to each word to make a new word. Remember what you learned.

21. able — disable
22. design — redesign
23. charge — discharge
24. band — disband

PROOFREADING AND WRITING

Handwriting

Proofreading Sentences

Have students write a sentence with several **t**'s and **l**'s, such as *Tell Pat to call Dottie*. Have them circle their **t**'s and **l**'s and ask themselves if they have formed the letters correctly.

MEETING THE NEEDS OF ALL STUDENTS

Modified List

Proofreading Students studying high-frequency words complete this page or the proofreading activity on the *Everyday Spelling* CD-ROM.

Enrichment

Writing Letters Students might like to express their opinion to a political leader. Remind them to offer suggestions for improvements as well as positive comments in their letters.

Additional Practice

Hardbound Book Master 29
Second Language Master 29
Writing Mini-Lesson Master 29
Writing Activity Master 29
Proofreading Transparency 29
Everyday Spelling **CD-ROM**

■ **PROOFREADING AND WRITING**

Proofreading marks:
- ═ Make a capital.
- / Make a small letter.
- ∧ Add something.
- Take out something.
- ⊙ Add a period.
- New paragraph

PROOFREAD A LETTER Editors at a textbook publisher received the letter below. Correct four misspellings and four handwriting errors.

PROOFREADING TIP

People appreciate hearing your opinion, but they have to be able to read what you write. Make it easy for them—always cross your *t*'s and loop your *l*'s.

April 8, 19--

Dear Editors,

Your spelling book is fun and sometimes challenging, but we all have certain lessons we dislike. We enjoy finding words other writers misspell.

Sincerely,

Lill School Fourth Graders

WRITE A LETTER Let the editors of one of your textbooks know what you think of their product. Use list words.

Responses will vary. Letters should include list words.

Word List

disappear	misplace
distrust	misspell
dishonest	mistreat
disagree	misled
dislike	misbehave
invisible	react
incorrect	replace
incomplete	recall
inactive	rebuild
independent	reuse

Personal Words

1. Words will vary.
2. ___________

136

VOCABULARY BUILDING ■

Review

WORD ASSOCIATIONS Write the boxed word that you would associate with each situation described below.

dislike	misplace
disappear	misspell
incomplete	misled
independent	rebuild
incorrect	reuse

1. a town repairing buildings that were damaged by a tornado
2. a child choosing activities he likes instead of just doing what everyone else wants to do
3. a student accidentally adding an extra letter as she is writing a word
4. a man saving a piece of paper to write on again
5. a student handing in a written assignment with missing answers
6. a customer discovering that a salesperson directed him to the wrong department
7. a student giving the wrong answer on a math test
8. a child not eating broccoli
9. a child forgetting where she left her library book
10. a boat sinking into a lake

1. **rebuild**
2. **independent**
3. **misspell or incorrect**
4. **reuse**
5. **incomplete**
6. **misled**
7. **incorrect**
8. **dislike**
9. **misplace**
10. **disappear**

Word *Study*

SYNONYMS Words that have the same meanings are called **synonyms**. The words in dark type in the sentences below are synonyms.

When I rub my powerful ring, my assistant will **disappear.**

When I rub my powerful ring, my assistant will **vanish.**

Write the list word that is a synonym for each underlined word below.

1. I'm sorry that the number I gave you was <u>wrong</u>.
2. Doctors often <u>differ</u> about the way to treat patients.
3. You've made a good start, but your work is <u>unfinished</u>.
4. I cannot <u>remember</u> the words to that song.

1. **incorrect**
2. **disagree**
3. **incomplete**
4. **recall**

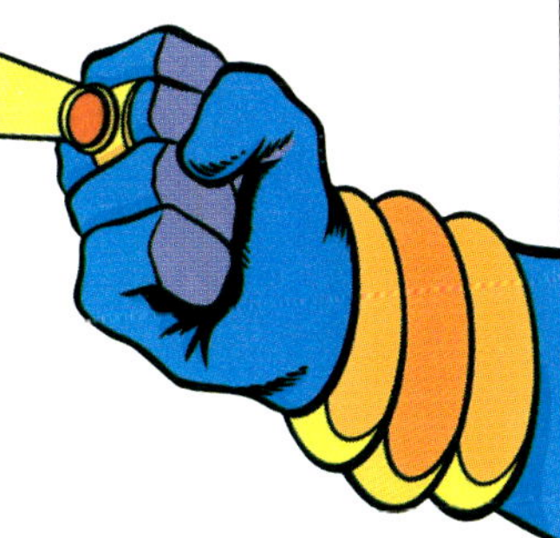

137

30

Unit Review Concepts
Including All the Letters
Compound Words
Suffixes -ful, -ly, -ion
Suffixes -less, -ment, -ness
Prefixes dis-, in-, mis-, re-

● Core   ○ Optional   ✓ Assessment

DAILY PLAN | CORE OBJECTIVES | NOTES

DAY 1

Review Activity:
● Adopt-a-Pet, p. 138
✓ Self-Assessment:
  How Am I Doing?, p. 138
Integrating Spelling:
○ Health, p. 138
○ Review Master 30A

- Use review words to complete stories
✓ - Assess their own progress in the spelling of words in Unit 5

DAY 2

Review Activities:
● Tricks of the Trade, p. 139
● Necessities of Life, p. 139
Integrating Spelling:
○ Language Arts, p. 139
○ Social Studies , p. 139

- Use review words to complete chapter titles
- Use review words to complete a list

DAY 3

Review Activities:
● Story Book Secrets, p. 140
● Birthday Greetings, p. 140
Integrating Spelling:
○ Language Arts, p. 140
○ Art, p. 140
○ Review Master 30B

- Use review words to complete newspaper stories
- Use review words to complete a birthday card

DAY 4

Review Activity:
● Benjamin Banneker—American Genius, p. 141
Integrating Spelling:
○ Social Studies, p. 141
○ Standardized Test Masters 30A–30D

- Use review words to complete a report

DAY 5

✓ Unit Review Test
✓ Writing Test
○ Writing Prompt Transparency 5
○ Writing Model Transparencies 5A, 5B

✓ - Assess review words
✓ - Assess expository writing

MEETING THE NEEDS OF ALL STUDENTS

Modified List

For students studying only the high-frequency words in each lesson, assign Review Masters 30A–30B for unit review. Use the Modified Dictation Sentences for assessment.

Bilingual/ESL

Suggest that second-language learners look through the pages of this review lesson and list the words they think will be hardest for them to spell. Help them review the strategies under items 2 and 3 of How Am I Doing? on page 138, asking them which strategy will work best for them.

Spelling Conferences

Conduct individual spelling conferences to discuss each student's spelling progress during Unit 5. You might want to take this opportunity to remind students to add words to their personal dictionaries.

ASSESSMENT

Dictation Sentences

1. Something strange is swimming in my bathtub.
2. I took a beautiful picture with my camera.
3. Nighttime is a peaceful time in our home.
4. I wrote an interesting story about an invisible dog.
5. She ran fast and caught the baseball.
6. I disagree with your statement.
7. Everybody ran downstairs when we heard the doorbell.
8. They work for an independent newspaper.
9. In December it is often cold.
10. We will rebuild the fence carefully.
11. That classmate is a thoughtful person.
12. Remember to help keep our classroom clean.
13. A powerful storm hit the island.
14. His invention can make trash disappear.
15. We were surprised when rain suddenly began to fall.
16. I dislike spotless rooms.
17. She will finally finish her incomplete story.
18. I want to go into business for myself.
19. He went to the nurse for treatment of a painful cut.
20. Several people think this old desk is worthless.
21. Try to recall who put paint on the pavement.
22. Her fairness to all people is part of her greatness.
23. It is hopeless to try to find my lost homework.
24. Everyone in our family will go to the play this evening.
25. The brightness of the moon kept me from sleeping.
26. Try to think how we can reuse the daily paper.

Writing Test

Writing Prompt Transparency 5 and Writing Model Transparencies 5A and 5B will help students prepare for holistic writing tests. Helpful information relating to expository writing tests is provided in the Writer's Handbook on page 239.

Everyday Spelling CD-ROM

An auditory test is available as an alternate testing format.

Modified Dictation Sentences

1. I don't often misspell words.
2. That was an interesting story in the newspaper.
3. So far the movement has been peaceful.
4. I remember the softness of his fur.
5. Suddenly everything seems hopeless.
6. Everyone went to the basketball game.
7. We will rebuild our house at a different location.
8. We all sat safely in the classroom.
9. The brightness of the stars was beautiful.
10. A storm is something I dislike.
11. I will make the payment myself.
12. His homework might be incorrect and incomplete.

LESSON 30

DAY 1   REVIEW MASTER A

REVIEW ■ 30A

Lesson 25

often	everyone	remember	might	interesting

■ **Antonyms** Write the list word that means the opposite of each word.

1. forget — **remember**
2. boring — **interesting**
3. weakness — **might**
4. no one — **everyone**
5. seldom — **often**

Lesson 26

something	myself	newspaper	classroom	basketball

■ **Compounds** Combine the words in the box with the numbered words to create list words. Write the words.

thing	self	room	ball	paper

1. news   2. class   3. some   4. my   5. basket

1. **newspaper**   4. **myself**
2. **classroom**   5. **basketball**
3. **something**

Lesson 27

suddenly	safely	beautiful	peaceful	location

■ **Context** Add a suffix to each word in parentheses to form a list word and complete each sentence.

1. (safe)   The plane landed **safely**.
2. (peace)   The baby looked **peaceful** as she slept.
3. (locate)   At what **location** was the picture taken?
4. (sudden)   The storm began **suddenly**.
5. (beauty)   Tonight's sunset was **beautiful**.

Practice Masters, p. 115

DAY 3   REVIEW MASTER B

30B ■ REVIEW

Lesson 28

softness	brightness	payment	movement	hopeless

■ **Word Forms** Write the list word with the same suffix as the underlined word that completes each sentence.

1. Struggling through the snow, he felt <u>helpless</u> and **hopeless**.
2. The <u>gentleness</u> and **softness** of her voice put the baby to sleep.
3. The <u>statement</u> showed when the **payment** had been made.
4. My room went from <u>darkness</u> to **brightness** when the moon came out.
5. After <u>treatment</u> the boy had **movement** in his legs again.

Lesson 29

dislike	rebuild	incomplete	incorrect	misspell

■ **Word Equations** Write the list word that completes the equation.

1. re + build = **rebuild**
2. in + complete = **incomplete**
3. dis + like = **dislike**
4. mis + spell = **misspell**
5. in + correct = **incorrect**

116

Practice Masters, p. 116

DAY 4   STANDARDIZED TEST MASTER A

30A ■ REVIEW TEST

■ Find the word that is spelled correctly to complete each group of words. Fill in the letter for the correct word on the answer strip.

Sample:
trees in the ________
a. forist   **b.** farest   **c.** forest   **d.** forrest   ⓐⓑ●ⓓ

1. went into the ________
a. clas rom   **b.** clasrium   **c.** classroom   **d.** class room   ⓐⓑ●ⓓ

2. must ________ after the storm
a. re-build   **b.** rebild   **c.** rebild   **d.** rebuild   ⓐⓑⓒ●

3. small insect seems ________
a. invesble   **b.** invisible   **c.** invisebul   **d.** invisable   ⓐ●ⓒⓓ

4. went to tell ________
a. everyone   **b.** everone   **c.** evryone   **d.** every one   ●ⓑⓒⓓ

5. in ________ to you
a. farness   **b.** fairness   **c.** fareness   **d.** fair ness   ⓐ●ⓒⓓ

6. can't ________ her name
a. rember   **b.** rememer   **c.** remimber   **d.** remember   ⓐⓑⓒ●

7. ________ that kind of thing
a. dislick   **b.** disslike   **c.** dislike   **d.** dis like   ⓐⓑ●ⓓ

8. ________ it in the air
a. coght   **b.** cought   **c.** cot   **d.** caught   ⓐⓑⓒ●

9. landed on an ________
a. island   **b.** ilind   **c.** iland   **d.** ailen   ●ⓑⓒⓓ

10. one time too ________
a. ofen   **b.** all fin   **c.** offen   **d.** often   ⓐⓑⓒ●

11. shirt came out ________
a. spot less   **b.** spotless   **c.** spottless   **d.** spotliss   ⓐ●ⓒⓓ

12. can ________ your paper
a. re-use   **b.** ruse   **c.** reuse   **d.** reyuse   ⓐⓑ●ⓓ

Practice for Standardized Tests, p. 42

DAY 4   STANDARDIZED TEST MASTER B

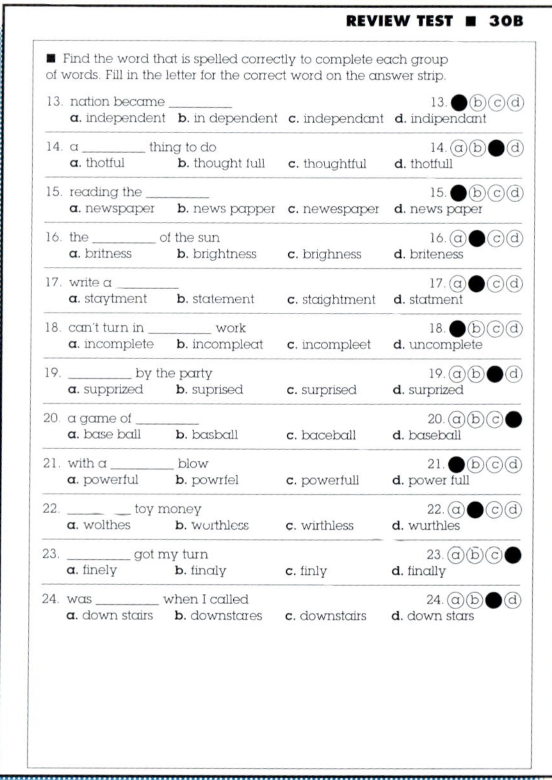

REVIEW TEST ■ 30B

■ Find the word that is spelled correctly to complete each group of words. Fill in the letter for the correct word on the answer strip.

13. nation became ________
a. independent   **b.** in dependent   **c.** independant   **d.** indipendant   ●ⓑⓒⓓ

14. a ________ thing to do
a. thotful   **b.** thought full   **c.** thoughtful   **d.** thotfull   ⓐⓑ●ⓓ

15. reading the ________
a. newspaper   **b.** news papper   **c.** newespaper   **d.** news paper   ●ⓑⓒⓓ

16. the ________ of the sun
a. britness   **b.** brightness   **c.** brighness   **d.** briteness   ⓐ●ⓒⓓ

17. write a ________
a. staytment   **b.** statement   **c.** staightment   **d.** statment   ⓐ●ⓒⓓ

18. can't turn in ________ work
a. incomplete   **b.** incompleat   **c.** incompleet   **d.** uncomplete   ●ⓑⓒⓓ

19. ________ by the party
a. supprized   **b.** suprised   **c.** surprised   **d.** surprized   ⓐⓑ●ⓓ

20. a game of ________
a. base ball   **b.** basball   **c.** baceball   **d.** baseball   ⓐⓑⓒ●

21. with a ________ blow
a. powerful   **b.** powrfel   **c.** powerfull   **d.** power full   ●ⓑⓒⓓ

22. ________ toy money
a. wolthes   **b.** wurthless   **c.** wirthless   **d.** wurthles   ⓐ●ⓒⓓ

23. ________ got my turn
a. finely   **b.** finaly   **c.** finly   **d.** finally   ⓐⓑⓒ●

24. was ________ when I called
a. down stairs   **b.** downstares   **c.** downstairs   **d.** down stars   ⓐⓑ●ⓓ

Practice for Standardized Tests, p. 43

TECHNOLOGY — Additional test on *Everyday Spelling* CD-ROM

DAY 4 STANDARDIZED TEST MASTER C

30C ■ REVIEW TEST

■ Find the word that is spelled correctly to complete each sentence.
Fill in the letter for the correct word on the answer strip.

25. We enjoyed _________ in the pool on the hot day.   25. ● b c d
    a. swimming   b. swing   c. swiming   d. swimmig

26. She invited a _________ of hers to her house.   26. a ● c d
    a. classmat   b. classmate   c. clasemate   d. class mate

27. I don't _________ what we were talking about.   27. a b c ●
    a. recale   b. reicall   c. recal   d. recall

28. This machine is her latest _________.   28. ● b c d
    a. invention   b. invechon   c. invition   d. invenshon

29. My cut is very _________.   29. a b ● d
    a. painfull   b. pain full   c. painful   d. paneful

30. You should take _________ for your cold.   30. a ● c d
    a. somthing   b. something   c. someting   d. some thing

31. People don't like to _________ with him!   31. a b ● d
    a. dissagree   b. disgree   c. disagree   d. disugree

32. This book is for your _________ reading.   32. a b ● d
    a. dailey   b. daley   c. daily   d. dayly

33. There is a gift for _________.   33. a b c ●
    a. evrybody   b. every body   c. everbody   d. everybody

34. The _________ of that woman is clear.   34. ● b c d
    a. greatness   b. grateness   c. great ness   d. graitnes

35. She enjoys listening to _________ music.   35. a ● c d
    a. piceful   b. peaceful   c. peacful   d. peacefull

36. Owls and bats fly in the _________.   36. ● b c d
    a. nighttime   b. nightime   c. nithg time   d. night time

Practice for Standardized Tests, p. 44

DAY 4 STANDARDIZED TEST MASTER D

REVIEW TEST ■ 30D

■ Find the word in each group that is spelled correctly. Fill in the letter for
the correct word on the answer strip.

37. a. cammery   c. camra   37. a b c ●
    b. camara   d. camera

38. a. treatment   c. treat ment   38. ● b c d
    b. tret ment   d. treetment

39. a. my self   c. myself   39. a b ● d
    b. my selfe   d. myslef

40. a. enteresting   c. intresting   40. a ● c d
    b. interesting   d. interresting

41. a. disipear   c. disepere   41. a b c ●
    b. disapear   d. disappear

42. a. careflee   c. carfully   42. a ● c d
    b. carefully   d. carfuly

43. a. pavement   c. paivment   43. ● b c d
    b. pavemunt   d. pavment

44. a. seavral   c. several   44. a b ● d
    b. severel   d. sevrall

45. a. evaning   c. evning   45. a b c ●
    b. eavning   d. evening

46. a. Desembar   c. Decenber   46. a b c ●
    b. Decmber   d. December

47. a. beautiful   c. beutiful   47. ● b c d
    b. butiful   d. beatiful

48. a. sudenly   c. suddenly   48. a b ● d
    b. sundenly   d. suddiy

49. a. bussiness   c. buisness   49. a ● c d
    b. business   d. bissness

50. a. hopless   c. hopeless   50. a b ● d
    b. hope less   d. hoppiless

Practice for Standardized Tests, p. 45

DAY 5 WRITING PROMPT TRANSPARENCY

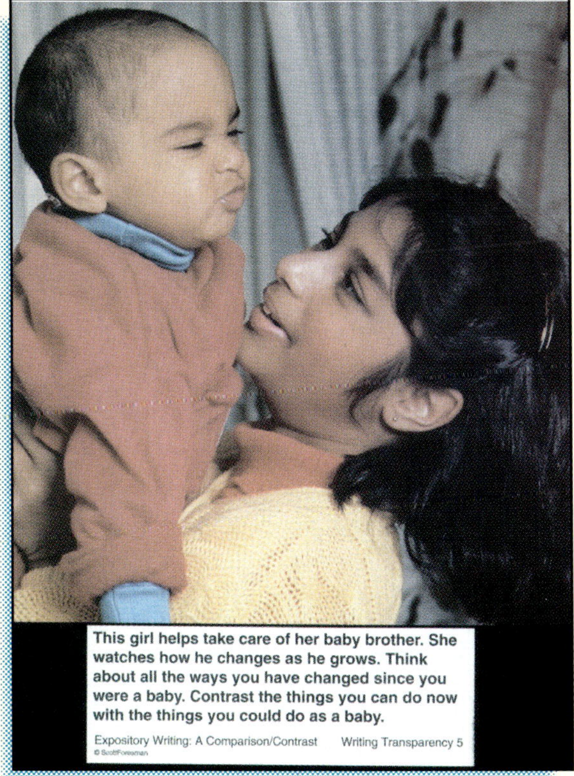

Spelling and Writing, Transparency 5

LESSON

30

● Review Activity
✓ Self-Assessment: How Am I Doing?
○ Integrating Spelling: Health

● Core   ○ Optional   ✓ Assessment

How Am I Doing?

Talk with students about why it is helpful to think about their progress in spelling. Raise issues such as

1. The hardest word I have learned to spell is ___.
2. I learn how to spell hard words by a) pronouncing silent letters secretly, b) thinking of a sound clue from a related word, or c) saying the word as I write it.
3. I make sure I pronounce the spelling words correctly.
4. I try to use spelling words in my writing.

Health

Pet Care Posters Partners can create a poster that lists guidelines for caring for pets. Encourage partners to use reference materials to find information about pet care.

Additional Resources

Review Master 30A

30 Review

Lesson 25: Including All the Letters
Lesson 26: Compound Words
Lesson 27: Suffixes -ful, -ly, -ion

Lesson 28: Suffixes -less, -ment, -ne...
Lesson 29: Prefixes dis-, in-, mis-, re...

REVIEW WORD LIST

1. camera	11. remember	21. nighttime	31. thoughtful	41. worthless
2. caught	12. several	22. something	32. brightness	42. disagree
3. December	13. surprised	23. beautiful	33. business	43. disappear
4. evening	14. swimming	24. carefully	34. fairness	44. dislike
5. everybody	15. baseball	25. daily	35. greatness	45. incomplete
6. everyone	16. classmate	26. invention	36. hopeless	46. independent
7. finally	17. classroom	27. painful	37. pavement	47. invisible
8. interesting	18. downstairs	28. peaceful	38. spotless	48. rebuild
9. island	19. myself	29. powerful	39. statement	49. recall
10. often	20. newspaper	30. suddenly	40. treatment	50. reuse

Adopt-a-Pet

These animals are looking for good homes. Read their stories and supply the words that are missing.

1. **independent**
2. **brightness**
3. **dislike**
4. **rebuild**
5. **daily**
6. **newspaper**

brightness
newspaper
independent
daily
dislike
rebuild

Rico

Rico is a quiet cat. He's a bit of a loner and very (1). The (2) of his wide, green eyes will delight you. Rico likes kids but would (3) living with another cat.

Mim

When Mim first arrived, she distrusted everyone. Help her ( ) her trust by giving her a loving home. Mim must have (5) exer... She loves to fetch the (6)!

Tricks of the Trade

Read the chapter subtitles from the book *Magic to Annoy Those Around You.* Write the words that have been left out.

reuse   downstairs   everybody
invisible   December   caught   disappear

1. **invisible**
2. **reuse**
3. **caught**
4. **disappear**
5. **downstairs**
6. **everybody**
7. **December**

1. Writing on your Grandpa's best shirt with ____ ink
2. New ways to ____ old paper towels
3. Ten foolproof ways to grab cookies without getting ____
4. Making your little sister ____ without a trace
5. Throwing your voice all the way ____ when you are upstairs
6. Convincing ____ at home that you're asleep when you're not
7. Creating ____ snowstorms in July with the spurting whipped-cream trick

classmate
powerful
baseball
island
several
camera
swimming

Use list words to complete the list below.

I would want these things along if I were stranded on a desert **island** :

my **swimming** ________ cap—for cool dips in the sea
my **classmate** ________ Alex—for good company
a **camera** ________ — to capture the sights

• a **baseball** ________ to toss around with Alex
• **several** ________ books—about wilderness camping
• a **powerful** ________ speedboat—for escape— HA HA!

Language Arts

Paragraphs Ask students the following question: *If you had a magic wand that could change things, what would you change?* Have students write about what they would change and why they think the change would be good.

Social Studies

Map Study Ask students to look at a world map and choose an island. Have them prepare a short report about the island. Auditory learners might present their reports orally.

INTEGRATING SPELLING

Language Arts

Dramatizing Ask pairs of students to choose a story villain, such as the Big Bad Wolf. Have them act out a scene in which the villain explains why he or she is "misunderstood."

Art

Birthday Card Invite students to create a birthday card for a pet. Students may want to include a rhyming verse about the pet. If students have no pet, suggest that they "adopt" a zoo animal.

Additional Resources

Review Master 30B

Jack and the Beanstalk and the Three Little Pigs had their sides of the story told, but what do the giant and the wolf have to say? You supply the missing words.

Story Book Secrets

Daily Report ★★★★★★★ Read all about it!

Giant Tells All

Bigtown, Austria—The giant of the beanstalk legend has (1) agreed to share his story. He feels that the (2) the press has given him lacks (3). "I strongly (4) with what's been written about me," he said. "Jack stole my (5) harp and golden eggs! He brought disorder to my once quiet, (6) household. He gets to be the hero, and I'm the (7) one! Well, I'm here to defend (8)!"

disagree	beautiful	fairness
peaceful	treatment	finally
myself	worthless	

1. **finally**
2. **treatment**
3. **fairness**
4. **disagree**
5. **beautiful**
6. **peaceful**
7. **worthless**
8. **myself**

From the Trial of B. B. Wolf

Bailiff: Do you swear that the (1) you are about to give is the whole truth, and nothing but the truth?
Wolf: I do.
Bailiff: Be seated.
Defense Lawyer: Tell us, Mr. Wolf, do you (2) the night of August 6?
Wolf: Yes, I think about it (3). It is the night I huffed and puffed and blew. . . .
Defense Lawyer: To be sure, but how were you feeling that particular (4)?
Wolf: I had a terrible cold. My sinuses were blocked and very (5). Whenever I sneezed, a house fell to the (6)!
Defense Lawyer: So it wasn't your intention to destroy the homes of these squealing piglets?
Wolf: Certainly not! I am a peaceful wolf who minds his own business.

| painful | pavement | statement |
| recall | evening | often |

1. **statement**
2. **recall**
3. **often**
4. **evening**
5. **painful**
6. **pavement**

The Leszczynsky family is celebrating the birthday of their dog, Spot. Supply the words that are missing from the card they wrote.

1. **everyone**
2. **spotless**
3. **surprised**
4. **nighttime**
5. **remember**

140

page 1

Benjamin Banneker— American Genius
By Yael Rubin

Learning about Benjamin Banneker was very (1). He became famous for the (2) of his mathematical abilities.

He was (3) taught to read and write by his grandmother. He was further educated in the (4) of a Quaker school. George Ellicott, who owned a large flour mill (5), also encouraged Benjamin's (6) pursuit of knowledge.

invention   hopeless   suddenly
incomplete   something

7. **invention**
8. **suddenly**
9. **incomplete**
10. **hopeless**
11. **something**

Write the words that are missing from Yael's report on a famous American.

business
carefully
interesting
thoughtful
classroom
greatness

1. **interesting**
2. **greatness**
3. **carefully**
4. **classroom**
5. **business**
6. **thoughtful**

page 2

At the age of 24, Benjamin built a clock that struck the hour. This clock is thought to be the first such (7) made in the United States.

Later, Benjamin was appointed by George Washington to help plan Washington, D.C. The chief architect had (8) left the project, so the work was (9). The architect had taken the plans with him, and re-creating them seemed (10). Benjamin came to the rescue, drawing all the plans from memory. The building of the capital city is (11) people can thank Benjamin Banneker for.

Social Studies

Interviews Ask students to choose a famous person from the past or present whom they would like to know more about. Suggest that they write three interview questions to ask the person. Then allow time for students to research their person, looking for possible answers to their interview questions. Students can share their questions and answers in small groups.

Additional Resources

Standardized Test Masters 30A–30D
Writing Prompt Transparency 5
Writing Model Transparencies 5A, 5B
Everyday Spelling CD-ROM

141

STRATEGY WORKSHOP

Reviews the Steps for Spelling new words and other spelling strategies. Introduces the metacognitive strategy **Choosing the Best Strategy** to help students choose the best approach for spelling specific words.

SCOPE AND SEQUENCE: LESSONS 31–36

Lesson	Generalization	Think and Practice	Proofreading and Writing
31 pp. 144–147	In many words, the vowel sound gives no clue to its spelling.	Drawing Conclusions Synonyms Strategic Spelling: Choosing the Best Strategy	Proofread a Letter • misspelled words Write a Letter
32 pp. 148–151	The vowels in final syllables often sound alike but are spelled differently.	Context Clues Abbreviations Categorizing Strategic Spelling: Seeing Meaning Connections	Proofread a Card • misspelled words • careless errors Write a Card
33 pp. 152–155	Holidays, days and months of the year, titles, and words that are part of an address are always capitalized. Abbreviations should be capitalized and followed by a period.	Abbreviations Identification Strategic Spelling: The Divide and Conquer Strategy	Proofread an Announcement • misspelled words • handwriting errors Write an Announcement
34 pp. 156–159	To form possessives of singular nouns, add an apostrophe and **s**. To form possessives of plural nouns that end in **s**, add only an apostrophe.	Singular Possessives Using Context Clues Plural Possessives Strategic Spelling: Building New Words	Proofread an Opinion • misspelled words • subject-verb agreement Write an Opinion
35 pp. 160–163	Some words are easily confused because they have similar pronunciations and spellings.	Antonyms Context Sentences Alpha Puzzles Strategic Spelling: Choosing the Best Strategy	Proofread a Sign • misspelled words Create a Sign

	Concepts for Review	Unit 6 Activities	Integrating Spelling
Review 36 pp. 164–167	Vowels with No Sound Clues Vowels in Final Syllables Capitalization and Abbreviation Possessives Easily Confused Words	Calendar Greeting Cards Advertising Brochure Sentences About Holidays Labels Paragraph Campaign Slogans	**Art:** Calendar, Greeting Cards **Language Arts:** Recipe, Labels **Mathematics:** Graph **Science:** Research **Social Studies:** Council Jobs

Vocabulary Building	Meeting the Needs of All Students	Cross-Curricular Lessons*
Review Crossword Puzzle **Using a Dictionary** Finding a Word When You Can't Spell It	**Visual** Visual Strategies **Auditory** Reading Drafts **Bilingual/ESL** Picture This; Drawing Conclusions **Enrichment** Spelling English Sounds	**Social Studies:** Southwest American Indians, pp. 180–181
Review Words in Context **Word Study** Word Webs	**Visual** Context Clues **Kinesthetic** Web Mobile **Bilingual/ESL** Double Consonants **Enrichment** Cooperative Writing	**Science:** Electricity and Magnetism, pp. 194–195
Review Making Inferences; Making Associations **Multicultural Connection** Holidays	**Visual** Holiday Calendar **Auditory** Public Address **Bilingual/ESL** Flashcard Abbreviations; Sorting Abbreviations **Enrichment** Researching Holidays; Share a Holiday	**Social Studies:** The Great Lakes, pp. 174–175
Review Context Clues **Word Study** Palindromes	**Visual** Who Owns What? **Kinesthetic** Acting Out Clues **Bilingual/ESL** Pictures and Labels **Enrichment** Crossword Palindrome	**Science:** Living Together, pp. 192–193
Review Words in Context **Word Study** Using Exact Words	**Auditory** Say It Aloud **Kinesthetic** Antonym Action **Bilingual/ESL** Listen for Words **Enrichment** Cooperative Writing	**Mathematics:** Geometry, pp. 220–221

SCHWA

The schwa is a major source of spelling errors at all grade levels because the sound can be spelled with any vowel. Misspellings of schwas are often logical attempts at spelling the words, but students don't have the necessary sound clues to help.

TYPICAL MISSPELLINGS:

- *relitives* for *relatives*
- *faverite* for *favorite*
- *modle* for *model*
- *peopel* for *people*

Helpful strategies include applying Pronouncing for Spelling. The Meaning Helpers strategy may also help with words like *relatives (relate)*.

ADDITIONAL RESOURCES

For Every Weekly Lesson

- **Think and Practice Master**
- **Challenge Master**
- **Extra Practice Master**
- **Review Master**
- **Second Language Support Master**
- **Home-School Activity Master**
- **Writing Mini-Lesson**
- **Writing Activity Master**
- **Standardized Test Master**
- **Proofreading and Writing Transparency**

Technology

- **Audiotape**
- ***Everyday Spelling* CD-ROM**
- ***Everyday Spelling* Game Software**

Unit Review

- **Standardized Test Masters**
- **Writing Prompt Transparency**
- **Writing Model Transparencies**
- ***Everyday Spelling* CD-ROM**

* The cross-curricular lessons are optional. You may, however, wish to teach the cross-curricular lesson that has been paired with the weekly lesson shown in the chart.

6

OBJECTIVES

- Learn and practice Choosing the Best Strategy
- Apply Choosing the Best Strategy to list words in Unit 6
- Review the Steps for Spelling new words

CHOOSING THE BEST STRATEGY

Students are encouraged to recall and use the Steps for Spelling and the spelling strategies they have learned to help them be better spellers.

Review with students the Steps for Spelling new words and the five additional strategies. Then have small groups debate possible strategies to use with such words as *necessary*, *routine*, and *literature*. Encourage students to select the approach that works best for them and to tell why.

Additional Resources

Steps for Spelling Poster
Frequently Misspelled Words
   Poster
Spelling Tool Kit Poster

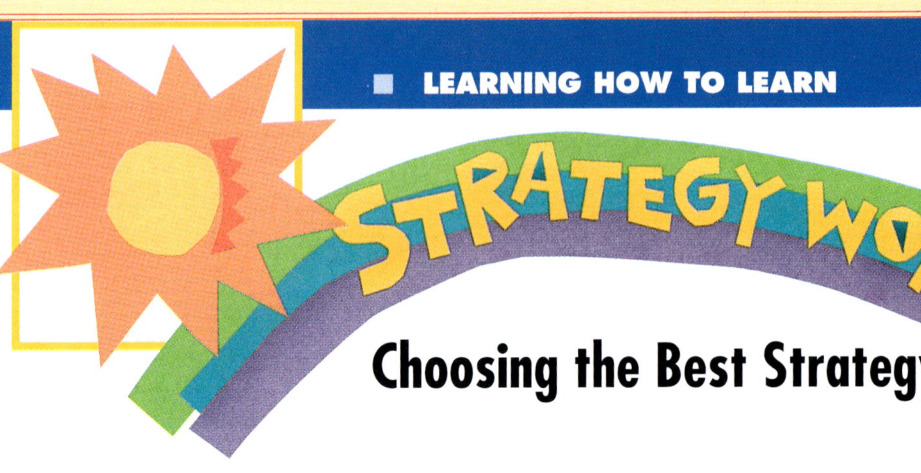

■ **LEARNING HOW TO LEARN**

Choosing the Best Strategy

DISCOVER THE STRATEGY You've learned that it is important to use the Steps for Spelling when studying spelling words. Don't forget to also use the strategies you've learned when a spelling word gives you a problem. Read about the strategies in the chart below.

Steps for Spelling	**Divide and Conquer**	**Memory Tricks**
Use the step-by-step strategy for studying most spelling words. 1. Look. 2. Spell. 3. Think. 4. Picture. 5. Look. 6. Cover and write.	Divide long words into shorter pieces. choc/o/late un/known	Link the tricky word with a helper you can spell. <u>You</u> are <u>you</u>ng. <u>qu</u>ick li<u>qu</u>id
Problem Parts	**Pronouncing for Spelling**	**Meaning Helpers**
Identify the problem part and study it extra hard. <u>wrong</u> lau<u>gh</u>ed	Pronounce the word correctly, say a silent letter, or exaggerate a sound. Say "thum<u>b</u>." Say "mil-<u>li-on</u>."	Find a related word that gives you a sound clue. ev<u>e</u>r—every ac<u>t</u>—action

TRY IT OUT Now it's time to practice choosing the best strategies. Read the exercises below and on the next page. Write the name of each strategy. Use the chart.

1. Which tricky strategy helps you remember the two **r**'s in *arrives?*

   Memory Tricks

142

2. Which strategy helps you conquer a long word like *caterpillar?*

Divide and Conquer

3. Which strategy helps you remember to pronounce the **o** in *favorite?*

Pronouncing for Spelling

4. Name the meaningful strategy that is helpful when trying to remember that *operation* is spelled with a **t.**

Meaning Helpers

5. Which strategy would you use if a certain part of the word were giving you a spelling problem?

Problem Parts

Compare your results with others in your class. It's fine to have different choices as long as you can explain them.

Answers will vary.

LOOK AHEAD Look ahead at the next five lessons. Find three words that look hard to spell. Write the word and the strategy you would use to help spell each word.

1. ______ **Words will** ______ ______ **Strategies will** ______

2. ______ **vary.** ______ ______ **vary.** ______

3. ______ ______

LESSON

31

Generalization

Spelling Focus: In many words, the vowel sound gives no clue to its spelling.

● Core　○ Optional　✓ Assessment

DAILY PLAN	CORE OBJECTIVES	NOTES

DAY 1 Introduction

● Strategy Workshop, p. 142
✓ Pretest and Self-Check, p. 144B
● Spelling Focus and Word List, p. 144
○ Challenge Words, p. 144
○ Challenge Master 31
○ Home-School Master 31

- Learn and choose the best strategy for spelling difficult words
✓ - Take and self-check Pretest
- Spell words that have vowels with no sound clues; classify and write the list words

DAY 2 Think and Practice

● Drawing Conclusions; Synonyms, p. 145
● Strategic Spelling: *Choosing the Best Strategy*, p. 145
○ Think and Practice Master 31
○ Extra Practice Master 31
○ Cross-Curricular Lesson: Introduce, p. 180

- Complete practice activities for words that have vowels with no sound clues
- Choose the best spelling strategy to use with given list words

DAY 3 Proofreading and Writing

● Proofread a Letter, p. 146
● Proofreading Tip: Plurals, p. 146
● Write a Letter, p. 146
✓ Cooperative Midweek Test
○ Hardbound Book Master 31A
○ Writing Mini-Lesson Master 31
○ Writing Activity Master 31
○ Second Language Support Master 31

- Proofread for spelling errors
- Integrate spelling and writing in a personal writing response
✓ - Take and check midweek test

DAY 4 Vocabulary Building

● Review: Crossword Puzzle, p. 147
● Using a Dictionary: Finding a Word When You Can't Spell It, p. 147
○ Hardbound Book Master 31B
○ Cross-Curricular Lesson: Follow-Up, p. 180
○ Review Master 31

- Complete review activity for words that have vowels with no sound clues
- Learn how to find words with unknown spellings in the dictionary

DAY 5 Assessment

✓ Posttest, p. 144B
○ Standardized Test Master 31

✓ - Take Posttest

Cross-Curricular Lessons

Use the Spelling Focus (vowels with no sound clues) to introduce the Social Studies lesson, *Southwest American Indians,* page 180, or choose a lesson that correlates with a topic you're currently teaching.

MEETING THE NEEDS OF ALL STUDENTS

The Word List

For students studying 20 words, assign pages 144–147 and Extra Practice and Review masters.

Modified List For students studying 10 words, modify Practice on page 144, and assign Think and Practice Master 31 and pages 146–147.

Challenge For students studying 25 words, assign pages 144–147, Challenge, Extra Practice, and Review masters.

Bilingual/ESL

Because there are no unstressed vowels in Spanish, Spanish-speaking students may have difficulty choosing the correct vowel in an unstressed syllable. Therefore, *animals* may be misspelled as *anamals,* and *suppose* as *seppose.*

Personal Words

Students add to Personal Words lists by looking at work in their writing portfolios and words they want to remember from their reading.

	Bilingual/ESL	Modified List	Challenge	Extra Support	Enrichment	Visual Learners	Auditory Learners	Kinesthetic Learners
p. 144	✓	✓						
p. 145	✓	✓				✓		
p. 146		✓					✓	
p. 147		✓			✓			

ASSESSMENT*

Pretest

Read the underlined word, read the sentence, and then repeat the underlined word. Guide students in self-correcting their pretests and correcting any misspellings.

1. That <u>machine</u> cuts grass.
2. I <u>especially</u> like apple pie.
3. We <u>usually</u> play together.
4. The train is <u>probably</u> late.
5. The <u>giant</u> chased Jack.
6. This will take a <u>moment</u>.
7. We enjoy the circus <u>animals</u>.
8. Be careful with a hot <u>iron</u>.
9. We'll <u>support</u> the team.
10. Do you <u>suppose</u> it will rain?
11. <u>Buffalo</u> live in the West.
12. <u>Canada</u> is up north.
13. We paddled a <u>canoe</u>.
14. We visit <u>relatives</u> on Sunday.
15. My <u>stomach</u> is sore.
16. The workers poured <u>cement</u>.
17. <u>Yesterday</u> I forgot my lunch.
18. That is my <u>favorite</u> game.
19. Pets are <u>welcome</u> here.
20. <u>August</u> was very dry.

Posttest

Read aloud the sentences below. These sentences may be used for dictation.

1. The class saw farm <u>animals</u>.
2. I am <u>especially</u> happy now.
3. That dinosaur was a <u>giant</u>.
4. Do you <u>suppose</u> that is true?
5. It's <u>usually</u> cold in January.
6. Can you <u>iron</u> your shirt?
7. She fixes any <u>machine</u>.
8. He'll be here in a <u>moment</u>.
9. He'll <u>probably</u> like the book.
10. Thank you for your <u>support</u>.
11. A storm came <u>yesterday</u>.
12. What is your <u>favorite</u> fruit?
13. We took a trip in <u>August</u>.
14. He is from <u>Canada</u>.
15. There's a <u>canoe</u> on the river.
16. I have <u>relatives</u> in Texas.
17. Where can we see <u>buffalo</u>?
18. My <u>stomach</u> hurt today.
19. The driveway is <u>cement</u>.
20. We will <u>welcome</u> them.

Challenge Words

1. A <u>dictionary</u> can be helpful.
2. They have <u>separate</u> rooms.
3. We will learn <u>multiplication</u>.
4. <u>Salmon</u> is a good fish to eat.
5. Do you <u>recognize</u> that actor?

Additional Assessment

Standardized Test Master 31
Dictation Sentences, p. T42
Everyday Spelling CD-ROM

WHAT'S THE BIG IDEA?
Mispronunciation accounts for the misspelling of many words on this list. Have students make a list of words in which mispronunciation causes spelling problems and then develop strategies that will help them.

* See pp. T20 and T33 for test-study-test information.

DAY 1 — CHALLENGE MASTER

CHALLENGE ■ 31

Challenge Words

dictionary   multiplication   salmon   recognize   separate

■ Use Challenge Words to solve the clues below and complete the puzzle. Then use the combined clues to spell vertically the word meaning "a place to look up words."

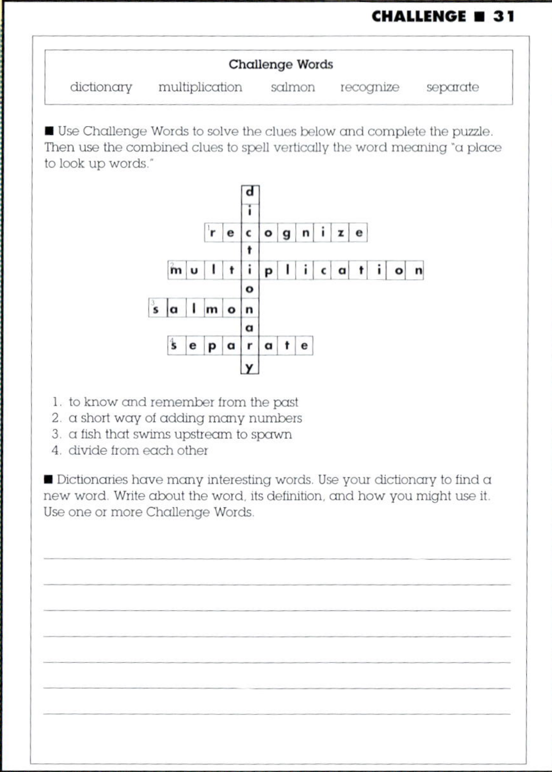

1. to know and remember from the past
2. a short way of adding many numbers
3. a fish that swims upstream to spawn
4. divide from each other

■ Dictionaries have many interesting words. Use your dictionary to find a new word. Write about the word, its definition, and how you might use it. Use one or more Challenge Words.

____

____

____

____

____

____

Practice Masters, p. 117

DAY 1 — HOME-SCHOOL MASTER

■ 31   HOME-SCHOOL ACTIVITIES   31 ■

Word Check 31

1. animals
2. buffalo
3. especially
4. favorite
5. giant
6. August
7. suppose
8. usually
9. iron
10. Canada
11. canoe
12. machine
13. moment
14. relatives
15. stomach
16. cement
17. yesterday
18. probably
19. support
20. welcome

Dear Parent,

Please check to see that your child has done this page correctly. Circle any misspelled words and help your child study them.

Tear off the Word Check before your child returns this page to class. Use it to help your child study.

■ **Riddles** The sentences below should each make you think of one of the list words. HINT: Look at the underlined word or words in each sentence.

1. This creature is bigger than an <u>ant</u>.
   giant

2. Watch out for a stormy <u>gust</u> of wind!
   August

3. Put the hot metal appliance <u>on</u> the shirt.
   iron

4. Which do you like most, milk <u>or</u> juice?
   favorite

5. <u>Come over</u> anytime you want to.   **welcome**

6. The beams hold <u>up</u> the ceiling.   **support**

7. I have a <u>special</u> liking for cats.   **especially**

8. Here is <u>an ad</u> for a trip.   **Canada**

9. Don't hit your <u>chin</u> on the exercise bike.
   machine

■ **Syllables** Write the remaining list words in the column that tells how many syllables it has.

two syllables

10. **suppose**
11. **canoe**
12. **moment**
13. **stomach**
14. **cement**

three syllables

15. **animals**
16. **buffalo**
17. **probably**
18. **relatives**
19. **yesterday**

four syllables

20. **usually**

Home-School Activities, p. 26

DAY 2 — THINK AND PRACTICE MASTER

31 ■ THINK AND PRACTICE

| machine | especially | usually | probably | giant |
| moment | animals | iron | support | suppose |

■ **Drawing Conclusions** Write the list word that fits each clue.

1. Use this to remove wrinkles from clothes.   **iron**
2. This character might be in a make-believe story.   **giant**
3. Dogs and tigers are examples of these.   **animals**
4. This helps us do work.   **machine**
5. This may be needed to help hold up a bridge.   **support**
6. This is a short period of time.   **moment**

■ **Alpha Order** Write the list word that fits alphabetically between the two words in each group.

7. escape   **especially**   eve
8. useless   **usually**   utmost
9. support   **suppose**   surprise
10. macaroni   **machine**   magnet
11. print   **probably**   proud

STRATEGIC SPELLING: Choosing the Best Strategy
Write *especially*, *probably*, *support*, and *animals*. Which strategy could help you spell all four words? Name the strategy and tell why you chose it. Compare choices with a partner. For a list of strategies, see page 142.

12. **especially**   14. **support**
13. **probably**   15. **animals**

Name of strategy: **Answers will vary.**

Why I chose it: _______________________________

____

Practice Masters, p. 118

DAY 2 — EXTRA PRACTICE MASTER

EXTRA PRACTICE ■ 31

Word List

machine	especially	usually	probably	giant
moment	animals	iron	support	suppose
buffalo	Canada	canoe	relatives	stomach
cement	yesterday	favorite	welcome	August

■ **Words in Context** Write the list word that completes each person's statement below.

1. Construction worker: "We'll mix some new ___ for the sidewalk."   **cement**
2. Camp counselor: "Tomorrow we're having ___ races."   **canoe**
3. Soldier: "I had to crawl on my ___ through the mud."   **stomach**
4. Weather forecaster: "Today will be a rainy day, just like ___."   **yesterday**
5. Storyteller: "Paul Bunyan was a friendly ___."   **giant**
6. Hotel clerk: "Your ___ can stay here when they visit."   **relatives**
7. Traveler: "My favorite place to visit is ___."   **Canada**
8. Office worker: "I'll take my vacation in ___."   **August**
9. History teacher: "The ___ is an important animal in our history."   **buffalo**
10. Clothing salesperson: "This is a good material because you don't have to ___ it."   **iron**
11. Sports trainer: "Do you want to use the rowing ___?"   **machine**
12. Pet sitter: "People hire me to care for their ___ when they go away."   **animals**

■ **Definitions** Write the list word that matches each definition.

13. most liked   **favorite**
14. short space of time   **moment**
15. greet kindly   **welcome**
16. chiefly   **especially**
17. ordinarily   **usually**
18. take for granted   **suppose**
19. likely   **probably**
20. hold up   **support**

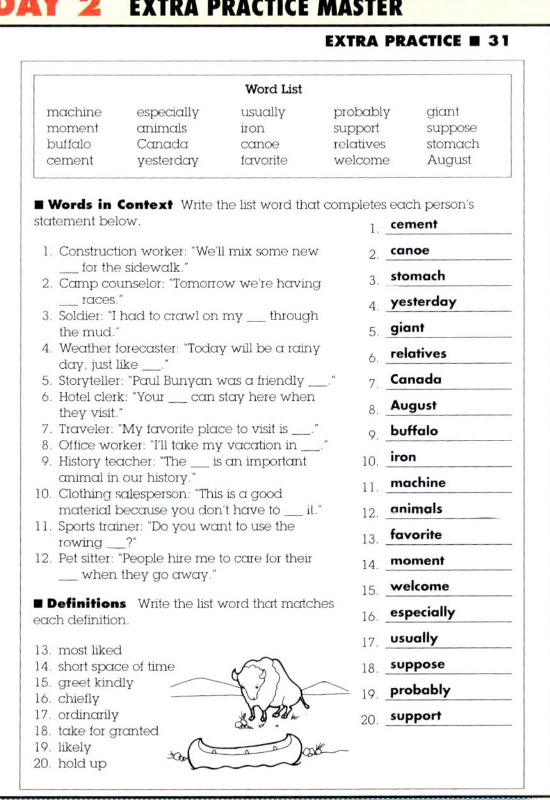

Practice Masters, p. 119

144C

TECHNOLOGY AND VISUAL SUPPORT	 Use Audiotape C, Side 2, Lesson 31  Use Proofreading and Writing Transparency 31	 For additional practice use *Everyday Spelling* Game Software, Lesson 31	 Additional resources on *Everyday Spelling* CD-ROM: proofreading and writing, modified list and challenge words, auditory test

DAY 3 — SECOND LANGUAGE SUPPORT MASTER

31 ■ SECOND LANGUAGE SUPPORT

More Than One Meaning

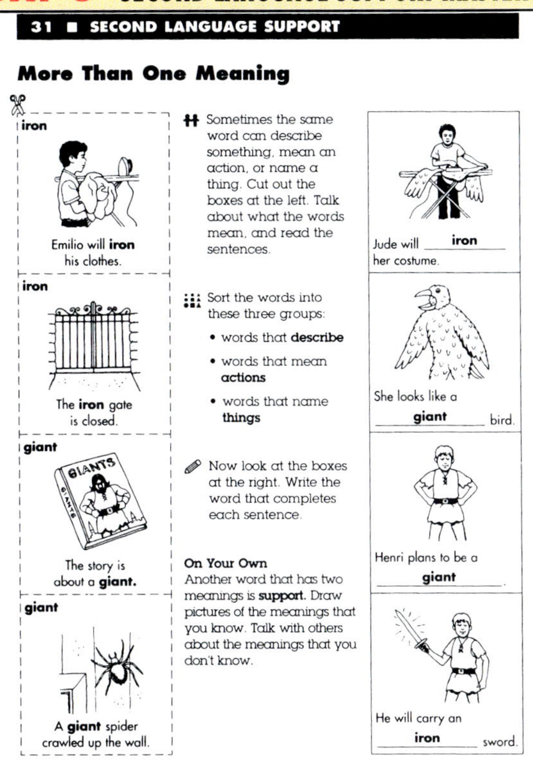

✄ Sometimes the same word can describe something, mean an action, or name a thing. Cut out the boxes at the left. Talk about what the words mean, and read the sentences.

Sort the words into these three groups:
- words that **describe**
- words that mean **actions**
- words that name **things**

✏ Now look at the boxes at the right. Write the word that completes each sentence.

On Your Own
Another word that has two meanings is **support**. Draw pictures of the meanings that you know. Talk with others about the meanings that you don't know.

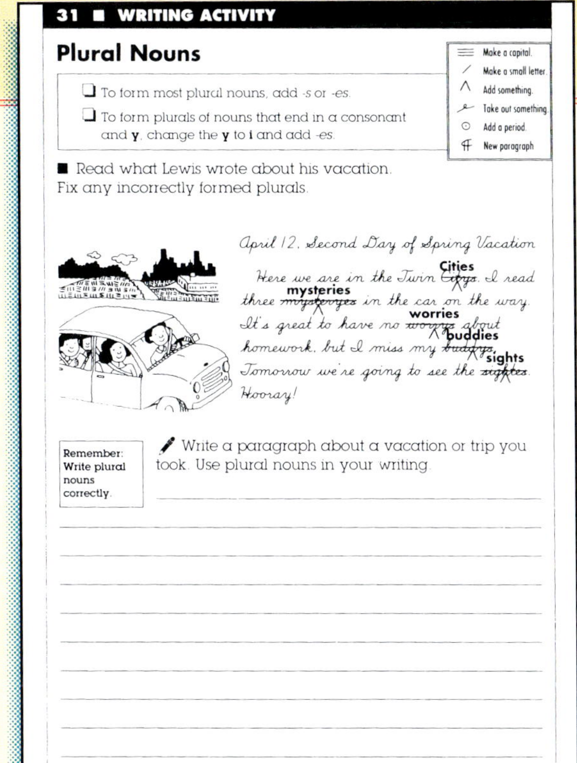

Second Language Support, p. 52

DAY 3 — WRITING ACTIVITY MASTER

31 ■ WRITING ACTIVITY

Plural Nouns

☐ To form most plural nouns, add -s or -es.

☐ To form plurals of nouns that end in a consonant and **y**, change the **y** to **i** and add -es.

≡	Make a capital.
/	Make a small letter.
∧	Add something.
⌒	Take out something.
⊙	Add a period.
⁋	New paragraph

■ Read what Lewis wrote about his vacation. Fix any incorrectly formed plurals.

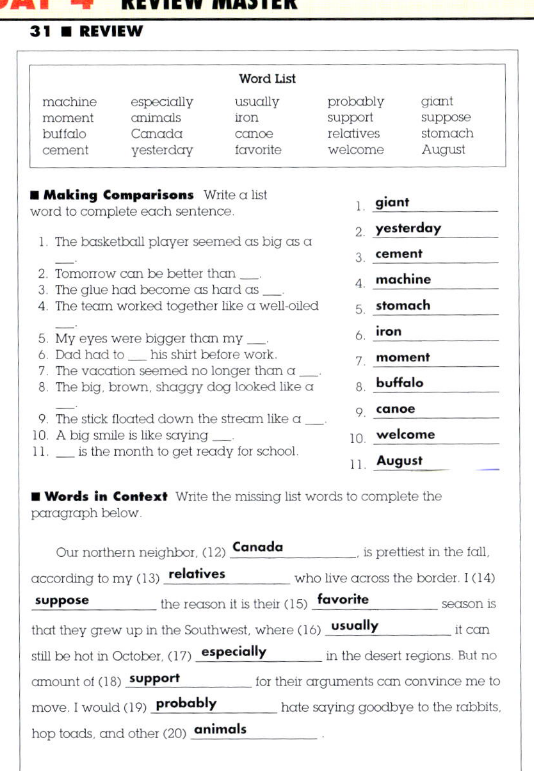

Remember: Write plural nouns correctly.

✏ Write a paragraph about a vacation or trip you took. Use plural nouns in your writing.

Spelling and Writing, p. 52

DAY 4 — REVIEW MASTER

31 ■ REVIEW

Word List

machine	especially	usually	probably	giant
moment	animals	iron	support	suppose
buffalo	Canada	canoe	relatives	stomach
cement	yesterday	favorite	welcome	August

■ **Making Comparisons** Write a list word to complete each sentence.

1. The basketball player seemed as big as a ___.
2. Tomorrow can be better than ___.
3. The glue had become as hard as ___.
4. The team worked together like a well-oiled ___.
5. My eyes were bigger than my ___.
6. Dad had to ___ his shirt before work.
7. The vacation seemed no longer than a ___.
8. The big, brown, shaggy dog looked like a ___.
9. The stick floated down the stream like a ___.
10. A big smile is like saying ___.
11. ___ is the month to get ready for school.

1. **giant**
2. **yesterday**
3. **cement**
4. **machine**
5. **stomach**
6. **iron**
7. **moment**
8. **buffalo**
9. **canoe**
10. **welcome**
11. **August**

■ **Words in Context** Write the missing list words to complete the paragraph below.

Our northern neighbor, (12) **Canada**, is prettiest in the fall, according to my (13) **relatives** who live across the border. I (14) **suppose** the reason it is their (15) **favorite** season is that they grew up in the Southwest, where (16) **usually** it can still be hot in October, (17) **especially** in the desert regions. But no amount of (18) **support** for their arguments can convince me to move. I would (19) **probably** hate saying goodbye to the rabbits, hop toads, and other (20) **animals**.

Practice Masters, p. 120

DAY 5 — STANDARDIZED TEST MASTER

31 ■ LESSON TEST

■ Find the word in each group that is spelled correctly. Fill in the letter for the correct word on the answer strip.

Sample:
a. mihgt   c. mighte
b. myte   d. might   — (a)(b)(c)●

1. a. probly   c. probaly   b. probaly   d. probably — 1. (a)(b)(c)●
2. a. cement   c. sament   b. sement   d. sment — 2. ●(b)(c)(d)
3. a. usually   c. usualy   b. usally   d. usaly — 3. ●(b)(c)(d)
4. a. especially   c. especially   b. exspecially   d. expecially — 4. (a)(b)●(d)
5. a. agust   c. Agust   b. August   d. Augest — 5. (a)●(c)(d)
6. a. anamals   c. animls   b. animals   d. animils — 6. (a)●(c)(d)
7. a. wellcome   c. wellcum   b. wallome   d. welcome — 7. (a)(b)(c)●
8. a. conu   c. canoe   b. canew   d. conew — 8. (a)(b)●(d)
9. a. favorite   c. favrit   b. favorit   d. favrite — 9. ●(b)(c)(d)
10. a. canada   c. Canad   b. Canda   d. Canada — 10. (a)(b)(c)●
11. a. relatives   c. reletives   b. relitives   d. realitives — 11. ●(b)(c)(d)
12. a. suppose   c. soppose   b. supose   d. supposse — 12. ●(b)(c)(d)
13. a. gaint   c. giant   b. gaient   d. jiant — 13. (a)(b)●(d)
14. a. iron   c. iren   b. iorn   d. iern — 14. ●(b)(c)(d)
15. a. suport   c. support   b. soport   d. suporte — 15. (a)(b)●(d)
16. a. stomache   c. stomik   b. stomack   d. stomach — 16. (a)(b)(c)●
17. a. mashine   c. michine   b. machine   d. mosheen — 17. (a)●(c)(d)
18. a. moment   c. momment   b. momat   d. momint — 18. ●(b)(c)(d)
19. a. yesturday   c. yesterday   b. yestarday   d. yestarday — 19. (a)(b)●(d)
20. a. bufflo   c. buffulo   b. buffalo   d. bufalote — 20. (a)●(c)(d)

Practice for Standardized Tests, p. 46

144D

LESSON

31

✔ Pretest and Self-Check
● Spelling Focus and Word List
○ Challenge Words
○ Modified List

○ **DAILY SPELLING REVIEW**

I lost my *earings* when I was *swiming*.

earrings   swimming

● Core ○ Optional ✔ Assessment

INTRODUCTION

Phonics

Sorting by Vowel Have students sort and write the list words according to whether **a, e, i, o,** or **u** is the underlined vowel. Point out that the underlined vowels stand for the same sound.

MEETING THE NEEDS OF ALL STUDENTS

Modified List

Practice Students studying only the high-frequency words in the top box write
- the words they know how to spell
- the words they think are difficult to spell

Bilingual/ESL

Picture This Have ESL students look up these list words in a picture dictionary: *animals, buffalo, giant, iron, canoe, machine, stomach, cement.* Pair them with native speakers to make up context sentences for the rest.

Additional Practice

Challenge Master 31
Home-School Master 31
Audiotape C, Side 2

1.
2.
3.
4.
5.
6.
7.
8.
9.
10.
11.
12.
13.
14.
15.
16.
17.
18.
19.
20.

CHALLENGE!

dictionary
separate
multiplication
salmon
recognize

144

■ INTRODUCTION

Vowels with No Sound Clues

SPELLING FOCUS

In many words, the vowel sound gives no clue to its spelling: m**a**chine, mom**e**nt, **a**nimals, ir**o**n, s**u**pport.

■ **STUDY** Say each word. Then read the sentence.

1.	machine	We need an answering **machine**.
2.	especially ✳	I love fruit, **especially** bananas.
3.	usually	Pandas **usually** eat bamboo.
4.	probably ✳	Prices will **probably** rise.
5.	giant	This **giant** pillow is too big.
6.	moment	Talk to me for just a **moment**.
7.	animals	A zoo has many **animals**.
8.	iron	You must **iron** those pants.
9.	support	He offered her his **support**.
10.	suppose	I **suppose** we'll be invited.
11.	buffalo	We saw **buffalo** on the plains.
12.	Canada	**Canada** is our northern neighbor.
13.	canoe	We often **canoe** down this stream.
14.	relatives	My **relatives** live in the South.
15.	stomach	I hear my **stomach** growling!
16.	cement	The sidewalk is made of **cement**.
17.	yesterday	We did that lesson **yesterday**.
18.	favorite ✳	Blue is my **favorite** color.
19.	welcome	Cities always **welcome** visitors.
20.	August	School may begin in **August**.

■ **PRACTICE** Sort the words by writing those you know how to spell. Then write the ones you think are difficult. You can use a memory trick like this for learning hard words: The **stomach** is an eating **machine**. Tell which strategy you will use for learning the hard words.
Order of words will vary.

■ **WRITE** Choose ten words to write in sentences.
Sentences will vary.

✳ **WATCH OUT FOR FREQUENTLY MISSPELLED WORDS!**

THINK AND PRACTICE

DRAWING CONCLUSIONS   Write a list word that fits the clues below.

1. A bricklayer uses this material to keep things in place.
2. If you want to paddle down a river, do it in this.
3. These people may be your aunts, uncles, and cousins.
4. When friends come to visit, greet them with a big one.
5. This is what you call the one you like more than others.
6. Use this to straighten out a wrinkled shirt.
7. A fairy tale might include one of these large fellows.
8. This is the month before September.
9. To sew a dress quickly, learn to operate one of these.
10. Sit-ups firm up the muscles in this part of your body.
11. This country is the United States neighbor to the north.

SYNONYMS   Write the list word that means the same as each word below. Use the Spelling Dictionary for help.

12. particularly; chiefly
13. assume; believe
14. help; comfort
15. instant; short time
16. normally; customarily

1.	cement
2.	canoe
3.	relatives
4.	welcome
5.	favorite
6.	iron
7.	giant
8.	August
9.	machine
10.	stomach
11.	Canada
12.	especially
13.	suppose
14.	support
15.	moment
16.	usually

Write *yesterday, probably, buffalo,* and *animals.* Which strategy could help you spell all four words? Name the strategy and tell why you chose it. Compare choices with a partner. For a list of strategies, see page 142.

17. yesterday
18. probably
19. buffalo
20. animals

Name of strategy: Answers will vary.

Why I chose it:

FREQUENTLY MISSPELLED WORDS • FREQUENTLY MISSPELLED WORDS

To be an e**special**ly good speller, include the word *special* inside *especially* whenever you write it.

THINK AND PRACTICE

Synonyms
Synonym Clues Students can reinforce the word meanings by making up a context sentence for each synonym clue and then rewriting the sentence using the correct list word.

MEETING THE NEEDS OF ALL STUDENTS

Modified List
Review Students studying high-frequency words complete Think and Practice Master 31.

Bilingual/ESL
Drawing Conclusions ESL students and native English speakers can work in pairs to identify the list words.

Visual Learners
Visual Strategies Review strategies that are most beneficial to visual learners: Divide and Conquer, Memory Tricks, and Problem Parts.

Additional Practice

Think and Practice Master 31
Extra Practice Master 31
Everyday Spelling **CD-ROM**
Everyday Spelling **Game Software**

145

LESSON 31

- Proofread a Letter
- Proofreading Tip: Plurals
- Write a Letter
- ✓ Cooperative Midweek Test

DAILY SPELLING REVIEW

The class thought of an *intresting invenshen.*

interesting   invention

● Core   ○ Optional   ✓ Assessment

PROOFREADING AND WRITING

Plurals
Checking the Endings

Encourage students to look over any writing they have in progress. Suggest that they check the endings on any plural nouns used in their writing.

MEETING THE NEEDS OF ALL STUDENTS

Modified List
Proofreading Students studying high-frequency words complete this page or the proofreading activity on the *Everyday Spelling* CD-ROM.

Auditory Learners
Reading Drafts Students can read the draft of their letters aloud to a partner. Partners should listen to make sure their classmate has included all the parts of a letter and make suggestions for revision.

Additional Practice

Hardbound Book Master 31A
Second Language Master 31
Writing Mini-Lesson Master 31
Writing Activity Master 31
Proofreading Transparency 31
Everyday Spelling **CD-ROM**

■ **PROOFREADING AND WRITING**

PROOFREAD A LETTER Anya wrote this letter home after her first day at camp. Correct five misspelled words, one of which is an incorrectly formed plural.

PROOFREADING TIP

Remember, to make words that end in a consonant and **y** plural, you must change the **y** to **i** and add **-es.**

July 8, 19--

Dear Mom and Aunt Carol,

I arrived ~~yesterday~~ **yesterday**. Flies are everywhere. My canoe tipped over. The food is ~~relly~~ **really** bad. I ~~supose~~ **suppose** one day I'll have fond ~~memorys~~ **memories** of camp, but so far it's not my ~~favrite~~ **favorite** place.

Love,

Tenderfoot

WRITE A LETTER Pretend you are at camp. Write a letter home telling all about your first day. Use list words.

Responses will vary. Letters should include list words.

Word List

animals	canoe
buffalo	machine
especially	moment
favorite	relatives
giant	stomach
August	cement
suppose	yesterday
usually	probably
iron	support
Canada	welcome

Personal Words

1. **Words will**
2. **vary.**

146

VOCABULARY BUILDING

Review

CROSSWORD PUZZLE Complete the crossword puzzle by writing the word that matches each definition.

machine   moment
especially   animals
usually   iron
probably   support
giant   suppose

Across

3. help
5. living things that are not plants
8. likely
9. huge
10. a very short space of time

Down

1. more than others
2. press
4. commonly; ordinarily
6. consider as possible
7. an object for doing work

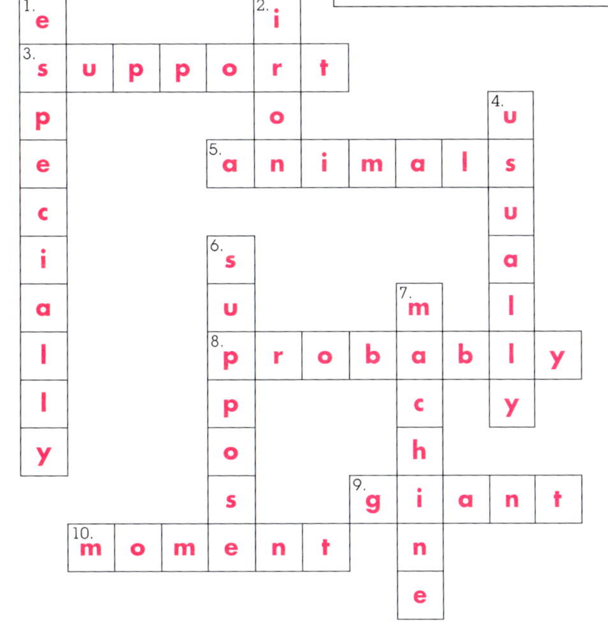

Using a *Dictionary*

FINDING A WORD WHEN YOU CAN'T SPELL IT

Many sounds in the English language can be spelled lots of different ways. Take the sound /s/, for example. It can be spelled **s**upport, **c**ement, **sc**ent, li**st**en, wal**tz**, and about six other ways. So if you wanted to look up *sword* and only knew it began with the sound /s/, what would you do?

You'd check the Spellings of English Sounds chart in your dictionary (and in this book on page 245). It shows you all the ways any given sound in English can be spelled.

Look at each pronunciation below. Write the word you would look up in the dictionary to find its spelling. If you are unsure, check the Spellings of English Sounds chart. Then check your Spelling Dictionary for the correct spelling.

1. (hwēt)   2. (brij)   3. (fō′tō)

1.   **wheat**   2.   **bridge**   3.   **photo**

VOCABULARY BUILDING

Literature Resources

A Sound Idea Encourage students to look in other dictionaries, such as *The American Heritage Children's Dictionary* (Houghton Mifflin, 1994), to see how clues to spelling different English sounds are handled.

MEETING THE NEEDS OF ALL STUDENTS

Modified List

Review Students studying high-frequency words complete this page.

Enrichment

Spelling English Sounds
Write the following pronunciations on the board: *hwėrl, skwosh, pēt′ sə,* and *gest.* Have students use the Spellings of English Sounds chart on page 245 to help them write the word each pronunciation stands for.

Additional Practice

Hardbound Book Master 31B
Review Master 31
Standardized Test Master 31
Everyday Spelling **CD-ROM**

LESSON

32

Generalization

Spelling Focus: The vowels in final syllables often sound alike but are spelled differently.

● Core   ○ Optional   ✓ Assessment

DAILY PLAN	CORE OBJECTIVES	NOTES

DAY 1 Introduction

✓ Pretest and Self-Check, p. 148B
● Spelling Focus and Word List, p. 148
○ Challenge Words, p. 148
○ Challenge Master 32
○ Home-School Master 32

✓ ▪ Take and self-check Pretest
▪ Spell words with vowels in their final syllables; classify and write the list words

DAY 2 Think and Practice

● Context Clues; Abbreviations; Categorizing, p. 149
● Strategic Spelling: *Seeing Meaning Connections*, p. 149
○ Think and Practice Master 32
○ Extra Practice Master 32
○ Cross-Curricular Lesson: Introduce, p. 194

▪ Complete practice activities for words with vowels in their final syllables
▪ Recognize meaning connections between list words and other words related to them

DAY 3 Proofreading and Writing

● Proofread a Card, p. 150
● Proofreading Tip: Omitted Words, p. 150
● Write a Card, p. 150
✓ Cooperative Midweek Test
○ Hardbound Book Master 32A
○ Writing Mini-Lesson Master 32
○ Writing Activity Master 32
○ Second Language Support Master 32

▪ Proofread for spelling and careless errors
▪ Integrate spelling and writing in a personal writing response
✓ ▪ Take and check midweek test

DAY 4 Vocabulary Building

● Review: Words in Context, p. 151
● Word Study: Word Webs, p. 151
○ Hardbound Book Master 32B
○ Cross-Curricular Lesson: Follow-Up, p. 194
○ Review Master 32

▪ Complete review activity for words with vowels in final syllables
▪ Study and make word webs

DAY 5 Assessment

✓ Posttest, p. 148B
○ Standardized Test Master 32

✓ ▪ Take Posttest

Cross-Curricular Lessons

Use the Spelling Focus (words with vowels in their final syllables) to introduce the Science lesson, *Electricity and Magnetism,* page 194, or choose a lesson that correlates with a topic you're currently teaching.

MEETING THE NEEDS OF ALL STUDENTS

The Word List

For students studying 20 words, assign pages 148–151 and Extra Practice and Review masters.

Modified List For students studying 10 words, modify Practice on page 148, and assign Think and Practice Master 32 and pages 150–151.

Challenge For students studying 25 words, assign pages 148–151, Challenge, Extra Practice, and Review masters.

Bilingual/ESL

Chinese-speaking students have a difficult time hearing the schwa sound, particularly after **l, n,** and **r,** because it sounds like either short **e** or **a.** Encourage students to memorize the spellings of words with the schwa sound.

Personal Words

Students add to Personal Words lists by looking at work in their writing portfolios and words they want to remember from their reading.

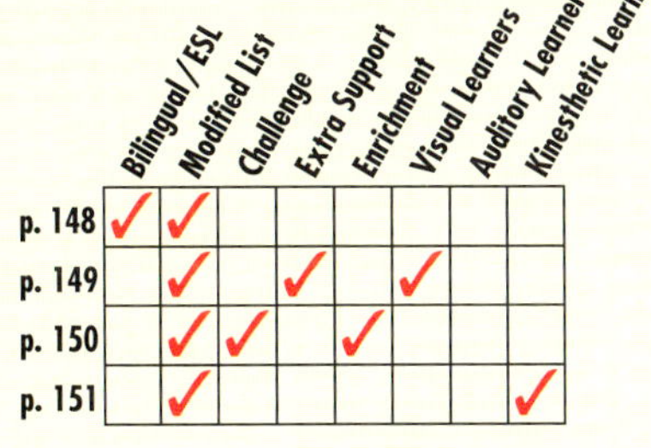

	Bilingual /ESL	Modified List	Challenge	Extra Support	Enrichment	Visual Learners	Auditory Learners	Kinesthetic Learners
p. 148	✓	✓						
p. 149		✓		✓		✓		
p. 150		✓	✓		✓			
p. 151		✓						✓

ASSESSMENT*

Pretest

Read the underlined word, read the sentence, and then repeat the underlined word. Guide students in self-correcting their pretests and correcting any misspellings.

1. The car went the <u>other</u> way.
2. What is your lucky <u>number</u>?
3. Yellow is a cheerful <u>color</u>.
4. A <u>doctor</u> set her leg.
5. Many <u>people</u> enjoy food.
6. Here's a <u>simple</u> problem.
7. Can you build a <u>model</u> car?
8. I picked up the <u>broken</u> glass.
9. All of a <u>sudden</u> he tripped.
10. A daisy is a <u>common</u> flower.
11. Days are cool in <u>October</u>.
12. It's <u>another</u> beautiful day.
13. A <u>motor</u> runs the machine.
14. We can measure an <u>angle</u>.
15. Every book has a <u>title</u>.
16. The apples are in a <u>barrel</u>.
17. She dressed as an <u>angel</u>.
18. Joel put a cake in the <u>oven</u>.
19. We drank a <u>gallon</u> of milk.
20. A <u>button</u> fell off my jacket.

PostTest

Read aloud the sentences below. These sentences may be used for dictation.

1. He made a <u>model</u> airplane.
2. The homework was <u>simple</u>.
3. Many <u>people</u> were there.
4. Two is an even <u>number</u>.
5. They took the <u>other</u> road.
6. A nurse helped the <u>doctor</u>.
7. The little doll was <u>broken</u>.
8. Purple is a rich <u>color</u>.
9. That's a <u>common</u> tree.
10. A <u>sudden</u> noise scared us.
11. What is the movie <u>title</u>?
12. Can you find a right <u>angle</u>?
13. She is as sweet as an <u>angel</u>.
14. Get a pickle from the <u>barrel</u>.
15. Have <u>another</u> apple.
16. Halloween is in <u>October</u>.
17. The train has a <u>motor</u>.
18. There's a muffin in the <u>oven</u>.
19. <u>Button</u> your coat outside.
20. Here's a <u>gallon</u> of juice.

Challenge Words

1. Talk into the <u>receiver</u>.
2. A <u>counselor</u> can help you.
3. I read an <u>article</u> on flowers.
4. He is an excellent <u>citizen</u>.
5. <u>Cinnamon</u> is good on toast.

Additional Assessment

Standardized Test Master 32
Dictation Sentences, p. T42
Everyday Spelling CD-ROM

TAKE A CLOSER LOOK
Research in Action found that *people* is a difficult word to spell because of the unusual spelling of the long **e.** We tried to think of another word in English with that vowel spelling—and failed! Point out this unusual spelling to students.

DAY 1 — CHALLENGE MASTER

CHALLENGE ■ 32

Challenge Words

receiver   counselor   citizen   cinnamon   article

■ Use the Challenge Words to complete the categories. Use your Spelling Dictionary for help with meanings.

Kind of Profession	Stereo Equipment	Kind of Citizen	Reading Material	Kind of Spice
teacher	speaker	lawmaker	book	**cinnamon**
storekeeper	**receiver**	criminal	sign	pepper
counselor	tape player	voter	**article**	ginger

■ Imagine that you are a travel writer who flies to new places and writes about them. Use one or more Challenge Words to write about a new and exciting place you have just visited.

Practice Masters, p. 121

DAY 1 — HOME-SCHOOL MASTER

■ 32   HOME-SCHOOL ACTIVITIES   32 ■

■ **Seeing Relationships** Write the list word that completes each sentence.

1. Labor Day is to September as Halloween is to **October**.

2. Fur is to animals as hair is to **people**.

3. Cold is to freezer as heat is to **oven**.

4. Mark Twain is to author as *Tom Sawyer* is to **title**.

5. A is to letter as 10 is to **number**.

6. Light is to dark as difficult is to **simple**.

7. Flute is to instrument as blue is to **color**.

8. Dish is to plate as container is to **barrel**.

■ **Which Words?** Write list words to answer the questions. Which word or words:

—have double consonants?

9. **button**   11. **sudden**

10. **common**   12. **gallon**

—begin with *an*?

13. **angle**   15. **another**

14. **angel**

—have the long o sound in their first syllables?

16. **broken**   17. **motor**

—begins the same as *off*?

18. **other**

—have the short o sound in their first syllables?

19. **model**   20. **doctor**

Word Check 32

1. people
2. gallon
3. color
4. broken
5. October
6. angle
7. number
8. barrel
9. motor
10. model
11. sudden
12. another
13. button
14. other
15. simple
16. doctor
17. oven
18. title
19. angel
20. common

Dear Parent,

Please check to see that your child has done this page correctly. Circle any misspelled words and help your child study them.

Tear off the Word Check before your child returns this page to class. Use it to help your child study.

Home-School Activities, p. 27

DAY 2 — THINK AND PRACTICE MASTER

32 ■ THINK AND PRACTICE

other	number	color	doctor	people
simple	model	broken	sudden	common

■ **Context Clues** Write the list word that ends like the underlined word and completes each sentence.

1. The **color** of the <u>motor</u> is red.

2. A **sudden** puff of smoke came from the <u>oven</u>.

3. My **doctor** has a sense of <u>humor</u>.

4. She wrote a <u>couple</u> of **simple** rhymes.

5. I think I will <u>order</u> the **other** shirt.

6. It is **common** for pepper to make a <u>person</u> sneeze.

7. Try to <u>fasten</u> the **broken** pieces together.

8. He made sure the **model** in the bottle was <u>level</u>.

■ **Rhymes** Write a list word that rhymes with the underlined word and makes sense in the verse.

9. One little twin <u>brother</u>
   Looks just like the **other**

10. The man on the <u>steeple</u>
    Was watched by some **people**

11. When the words were <u>spoken</u>,
    The promise was **broken**

12. To order some <u>lumber</u>,
    Call this **number**

STRATEGIC SPELLING: Seeing Meaning Connections

13. Write a list word that is related to the words in the box.
    common

Write the words from the box that fit the definitions.

uncommon
commonly

14. usually   **commonly**

15. rare, unusual   **uncommon**

Practice Masters, p. 122

DAY 2 — EXTRA PRACTICE MASTER

EXTRA PRACTICE ■ 32

Word List

other	number	color	doctor	people
simple	model	broken	sudden	common
October	another	motor	angle	title
barrel	angel	oven	gallon	button

■ **Puzzle** Look at the pictured objects. Write the list word that names each object in the correct place in the puzzle.

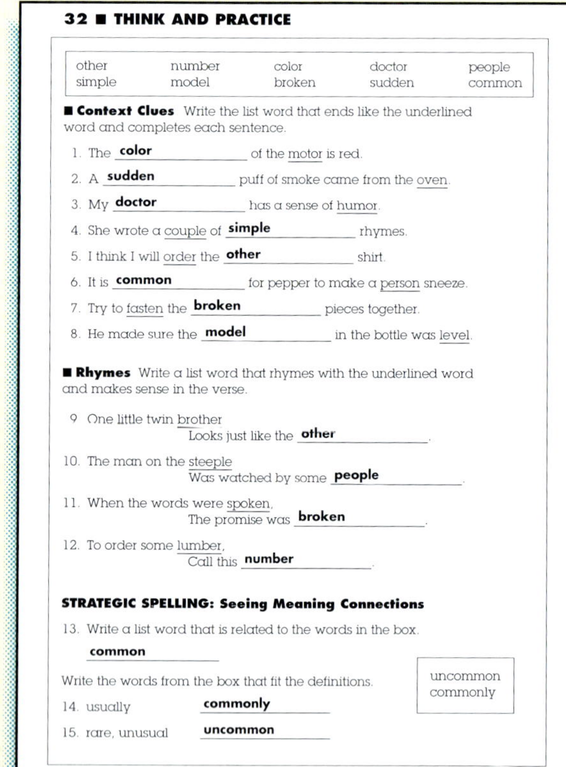

■ **Before and After** Write the list word that begins and ends with the same letters as each word below.

9. neater   **number**

10. born   **broken**

11. purple   **people**

12. alligator   **another**

13. musical   **model**

14. table   **title**

15. opener   **other**

16. salmon   **sudden**

17. ocean   **oven**

18. car   **color**

19. serve   **simple**

20. cannon   **common**

Practice Masters, p. 123

TECHNOLOGY AND VISUAL SUPPORT	 Use Audiotape C, Side 2, Lesson 32  Use Proofreading and Writing Transparency 32	 For additional practice use *Everyday Spelling* Game Software, Lesson 32	 Additional resources on *Everyday Spelling* CD-ROM: proofreading and writing, modified list and challenge words, auditory test

DAY 3 SECOND LANGUAGE SUPPORT MASTER

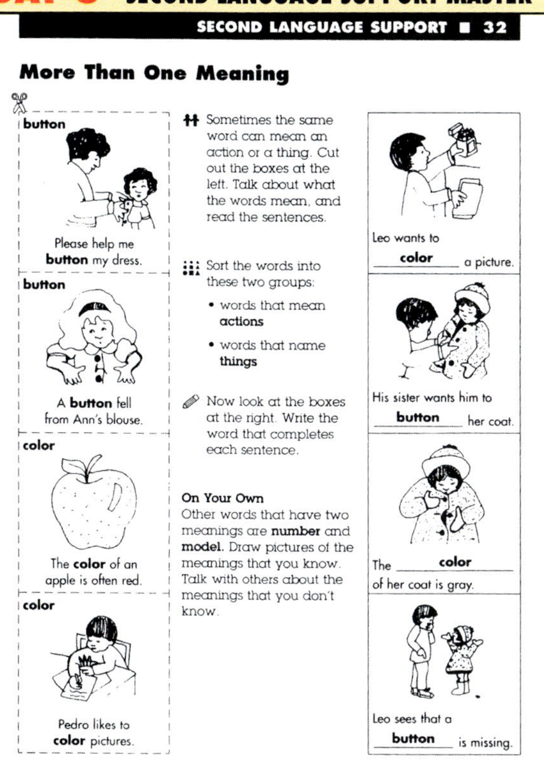

SECOND LANGUAGE SUPPORT ■ 32

More Than One Meaning

Sometimes the same word can mean an action or a thing. Cut out the boxes at the left. Talk about what the words mean, and read the sentences.

Sort the words into these two groups:

- words that mean **actions**
- words that name **things**

Now look at the boxes at the right. Write the word that completes each sentence.

On Your Own
Other words that have two meanings are **number** and **model.** Draw pictures of the meanings that you know. Talk with others about the meanings that you don't know.

Please help me **button** my dress.

A **button** fell from Ann's blouse.

The **color** of an apple is often red.

Pedro likes to **color** pictures.

Leo wants to ____ **color** a picture.

His sister wants him to ____ **button** her coat.

The ____ **color** of her coat is gray.

Leo sees that a ____ **button** is missing.

Second Language Support, p. 53

DAY 3 WRITING ACTIVITY MASTER

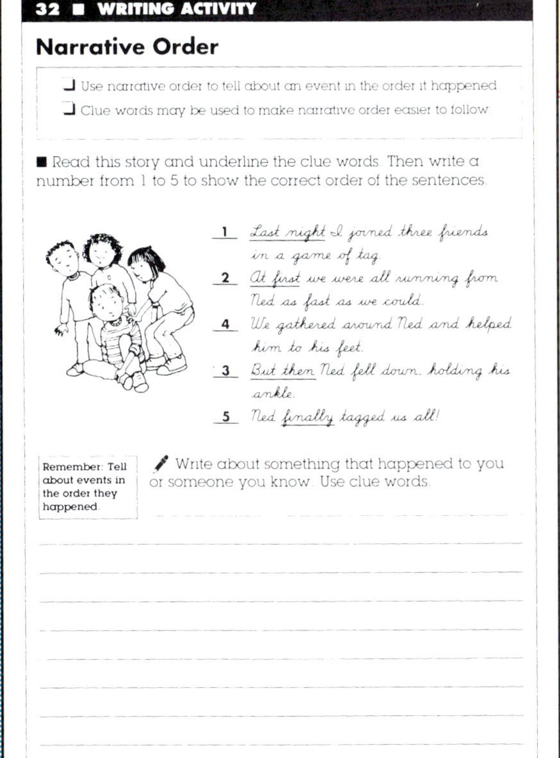

32 ■ WRITING ACTIVITY

Narrative Order

❑ Use narrative order to tell about an event in the order it happened

❑ Clue words may be used to make narrative order easier to follow

■ Read this story and underline the clue words. Then write a number from 1 to 5 to show the correct order of the sentences.

1 Last night I joined three friends in a game of tag.

2 At first we were all running from Ned as fast as we could.

4 We gathered around Ned and helped him to his feet.

3 But then Ned fell down, holding his ankle.

5 Ned finally tagged us all!

Remember: Tell about events in the order they happened.

Write about something that happened to you or someone you know. Use clue words.

Spelling and Writing, p. 54

DAY 4 REVIEW MASTER

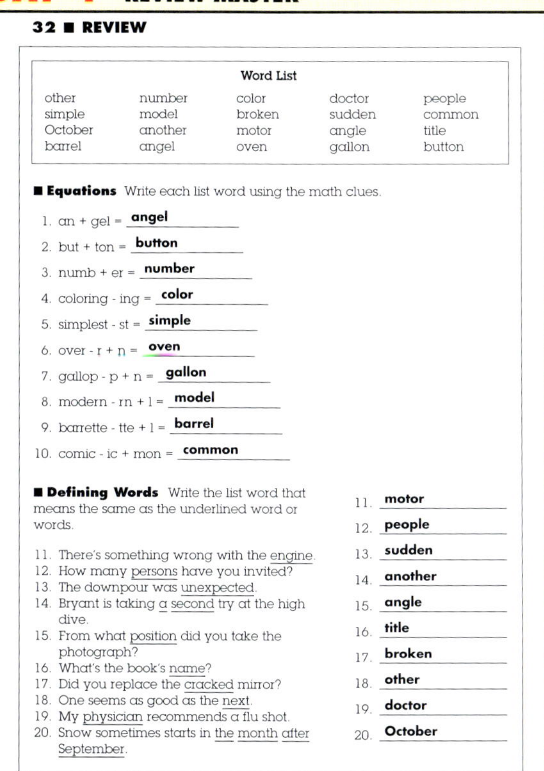

32 ■ REVIEW

Word List

other	number	color	doctor	people
simple	model	broken	sudden	common
October	another	motor	angle	title
barrel	angel	oven	gallon	button

■ **Equations** Write each list word using the math clues.

1. an + gel = **angel**
2. but + ton = **button**
3. numb + er = **number**
4. coloring - ing = **color**
5. simplest - st = **simple**
6. over - r + n = **oven**
7. gallop - p + n = **gallon**
8. modern - rn + l = **model**
9. barrette - tte + l = **barrel**
10. comic - ic + mon = **common**

■ **Defining Words** Write the list word that means the same as the underlined word or words.

11. There's something wrong with the <u>engine</u>.
12. How many <u>persons</u> have you invited?
13. The downpour was <u>unexpected</u>.
14. Bryant is taking <u>a second</u> try at the high dive.
15. From what <u>position</u> did you take the photograph?
16. What's the book's <u>name</u>?
17. Did you replace the <u>cracked</u> mirror?
18. One seems as good as the <u>next</u>.
19. My <u>physician</u> recommends a flu shot.
20. Snow sometimes starts in <u>the month after September</u>.

11. **motor**
12. **people**
13. **sudden**
14. **another**
15. **angle**
16. **title**
17. **broken**
18. **other**
19. **doctor**
20. **October**

Practice Masters, p. 124

DAY 5 STANDARDIZED TEST MASTER

LESSON TEST ■ 32

■ Find the word in each group that is spelled correctly. Fill in the letter for the correct word on the answer strip.

Sample:
- **a.** mihgt   **c.** mighte
- **b.** myte   **d.** might   — (a)(b)(c)●

1. **a.** nomber   **c.** number
   b. numbur   **d.** nuber   — 1. (a)(b)●(d)
2. **a.** comen   **c.** common
   b. coman   **d.** comon   — 2. (a)(b)●(d)
3. **a.** anouther   **c.** anuther
   b. another   **d.** annother   — 3. (a)●(c)(d)
4. **a.** angal   **c.** anggel
   b. anjel   **d.** angel   — 4. (a)(b)(c)●
5. **a.** moter   **c.** morter
   b. motor   **d.** muter   — 5. (a)●(c)(d)
6. **a.** October   **c.** Octber
   b. october   **d.** Octobar   — 6. ●(b)(c)(d)
7. **a.** titel   **c.** titele
   b. tilte   **d.** title   — 7. (a)(b)(c)●
8. **a.** barral   **c.** barl
   b. baral   **d.** barrel   — 8. (a)(b)(c)●
9. **a.** sudden   **c.** sudne
   b. suden   **d.** soden   — 9. ●(b)(c)(d)
10. **a.** gallone   **c.** galon
    b. gaillon   **d.** gallon   — 10. (a)(b)(c)●
11. **a.** brocken   **c.** broken
    b. brokin   **d.** brooken   — 11. (a)(b)●(d)
12. **a.** model   **c.** moddel
    b. madel   **d.** modle   — 12. ●(b)(c)(d)
13. **a.** peopl   **c.** peple
    b. people   **d.** peaple   — 13. (a)●(c)(d)
14. **a.** silple   **c.** simpl
    b. simple   **d.** semple   — 14. (a)●(c)(d)
15. **a.** anggle   **c.** angle
    b. aingel   **d.** angul   — 15. (a)(b)●(d)
16. **a.** outher   **c.** uther
    b. othe   **d.** other   — 16. (a)(b)(c)●
17. **a.** ovin   **c.** ovein
    b. oven   **d.** avin   — 17. (a)●(c)(d)
18. **a.** doctor   **c.** docicter
    b. docter   **d.** dockter   — 18. ●(b)(c)(d)
19. **a.** button   **c.** butten
    b. botton   **d.** buttun   — 19. ●(b)(c)(d)
20. **a.** coler   **c.** collor
    b. colar   **d.** color   — 20. (a)(b)(c)●

Practice for Standardized Tests, p. 47

148D

LESSON

32

✓ Pretest and Self-Check
● Spelling Focus and Word List
○ Challenge Words
○ Modified List

○ **DAILY SPELLING REVIEW**

Febuary is a good time to visit the *iland.*

February   island

● Core   ○ Optional   ✓ Assessment

INTRODUCTION

Phonics

Sounds Alike Have students pronounce these word pairs: *people/model, doctor/number, button/broken.* Guide them to generalize that the final syllable in each pair sounds alike, but is spelled differently.

MEETING THE NEEDS OF ALL STUDENTS

Modified List

Practice Students studying only the high-frequency words in the top box write
- four words that end with **or** and **er**
- three words that end with **el** and **le**
- three words that end with **en** and **on**

Bilingual/ESL

Double Consonants Students can list five words with double consonants and make a poster illustrating and labeling them.

Additional Practice

Challenge Master 32
Home-School Master 32
Audiotape C, Side 2

1. other
2. number
3. color
4. doctor
5. October
6. another
7. motor
8. people
9. simple
10. model
11. angle
12. title
13. barrel
14. angel
15. broken
16. sudden
17. common
18. oven
19. gallon
20. button

CHALLENGE!

receiver
counselor
article
citizen
cinnamon

148

■ INTRODUCTION

Vowels in Final Syllables

SPELLING FOCUS

The vowels in final syllables often sound alike but are spelled differently: **people, model; broken, common.**

■ **STUDY** Say each word. Then read the sentence.

1. *other* — Where's my **other** shoe?
2. *number* — The runner wore the **number** ten.
3. *color* — I painted the room a different **color.**
4. *doctor* — The **doctor** looked at the X ray.
5. *people* ✳ — She loves meeting new **people.**
6. *simple* — Spelling **simple** words is fun.
7. *model* — He is a **model** for all soldiers.
8. *broken* — I threw away the **broken** glass.
9. *sudden* — The siren gave a **sudden** warning.
10. *common* — Cake is a **common** dessert.

11. *October* — **October** evenings are often cool.
12. *another* ✳ — Pass me **another** rye roll, please.
13. *motor* — The **motor** in a car makes it run.
14. *angle* — Set the boards at a right **angle.**
15. *title* — What is the story's **title?**
16. *barrel* — The pickles are stored in a **barrel.**
17. *angel* — She drew wings on the **angel.**
18. *oven* — Cookies are baking in the **oven.**
19. *gallon* — We bought a **gallon** of cider.
20. *button* — Would you **button** my cuffs?

■ **PRACTICE** Sort the list words by writing
- seven words that end with **or** and **er**
- seven words that end with **el** and **le**
- six words that end with **en** and **on**

Order of words in each group may vary.

■ **WRITE** Choose two sentences to include in a paragraph.
Paragraphs will vary.

✳ **WATCH OUT FOR FREQUENTLY MISSPELLED WORDS!**

THINK AND PRACTICE

CONTEXT CLUES   Write the list word that ends like the underlined word and completes the sentence.

1. An ___ with wings was carved into each door <u>panel</u>.
2. Tex was my ___ when I learned how to <u>yodel</u>.
3. The little <u>squirrel</u> jumped into the wooden ___.
4. To cure a <u>pimple</u>, try this ___ solution.
5. No one ___ than <u>Mother</u> will be waiting.
6. The <u>inventor</u> built a new automobile ___.
7. My <u>cotton</u> shirt is missing a ___.
8. I would not <u>bother</u> to look for ___ pen.
9. Drinking tea with <u>lemon</u> is ___ in many countries.
10. A ___ rainstorm will <u>sadden</u> picnickers.
11. The poor little <u>chicken</u> had a ___ wing.

ABBREVIATIONS   Write the list word that corresponds to each abbreviation below. Use the Spelling Dictionary if you need help.

12. Dr.
13. Oct.
14. gal.
15. no.

CATEGORIZING   Write the list word that names the category to which you would assign each group below.

16. men, women, children
17. turquoise, mauve, orange
18. your highness, her majesty
19. gas, electric

1. **angel**
2. **model**
3. **barrel**
4. **simple**
5. **other**
6. **motor**
7. **button**
8. **another**
9. **common**
10. **sudden**
11. **broken**
12. **doctor**
13. **October**
14. **gallon**
15. **number**
16. **people**
17. **color**
18. **title**
19. **oven**
20. **angle**

20. Write a list word that is related to the words in the box.
Write the words from the box that fit the definitions.

21. a three-sided shape _______ **triangle**
22. a four-sided shape _______ **rectangle**

ngle
ngle

Did You Know?
The word *angel* comes from a Greek word meaning "messenger."

THINK AND PRACTICE

Categorizing
Classification Suggest that students name the groups before scanning the list words. Then have them look for a match or a similar word.

MEETING THE NEEDS OF ALL STUDENTS

Modified List
Review Students studying high-frequency words complete Think and Practice Master 32.

Visual Learners
Context Clues Visual learners might find it useful to highlight the ending of each word they write.

Extra Support
Abbreviations Point out that letters in abbreviations are not always in the same order as those of the word. Suggest that students write the word and then circle just the letters used.

Additional Practice

Think and Practice Master 32
Extra Practice Master 32
Everyday Spelling **CD-ROM**
Everyday Spelling **Game Software**

DAY 3 Proofreading and Writing

- Proofread a Card
- Proofreading Tip: Omitted Words
- Write a Card
- ✓ Cooperative Midweek Test

DAILY SPELLING REVIEW

You should read the *daley* paper *carfully.*

daily   *carefully*

● Core   ○ Optional   ✓ Assessment

PROOFREADING AND WRITING

Careless Errors

Omitted Words Give students this tip: Left-out words can often be discovered by reading your writing aloud.

MEETING THE NEEDS OF ALL STUDENTS

Modified List

Proofreading Students studying high-frequency words complete this page or the proofreading activity on the *Everyday Spelling* CD-ROM.

Enrichment

Cooperative Writing Have small groups of students create and illustrate a card for a special occasion.

Challenge

Writing Verse Have students write a short poem to include in their card.

Additional Practice

Hardbound Book Master 32A
Second Language Master 32
Writing Mini-Lesson Master 32
Writing Activity Master 32
Proofreading Transparency 32
Everyday Spelling **CD-ROM**

■ PROOFREADING AND WRITING

═	Make a capital.
/	Make a small letter
∧	Add something.
ℰ	Take out something
⊙	Add a period.
¶	New paragraph

PROOFREAD A CARD Indira received this card from a friend at school. Correct five misspelled words and two careless errors.

PROOFREADING TIP You may leave out words when you're writing a card you're in a hurry to mail. Take a minute to proofread. Your reader will thank you.

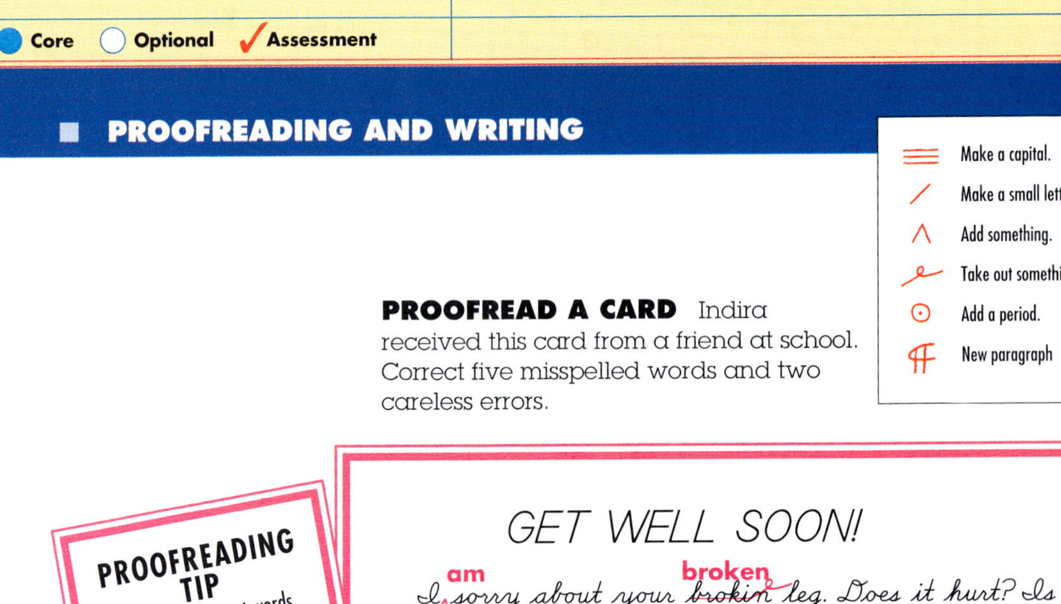

WRITE A CARD Pretend you are Indira. Write a response to your friend's card. Use a few list words and some personal words.

Word List

people	sudden
gallon	another
color	button
broken	other
October	simple
angle	doctor
number	oven
barrel	title
motor	angel
model	common

Personal Words

1. **Words will**
2. **vary.**

Responses will vary, but should include list words and personal words.

VOCABULARY BUILDING

Review

WORDS IN CONTEXT   Write the missing boxed words to complete the following news story.

Jimmy Thundercloud got quite a surprise during his demonstration of a (1) of the new XK-2000 vacuum cleaner at Mulberry's Department Store. "Most vacuum cleaners have a hard time picking up pet hair, but that task is (2) for the XK-2000," Mr. Thundercloud announced to the large (3) of (4) who were admiring the bright red (5) of the machine. Just as Mr. Thundercloud turned on the machine, the loud roar of the motor could be heard in all the (6) departments. All of a (7), the powerful suction turned the hose into a wild monster. It thrashed about wildly and hit Mr. Thundercloud in the arm with a loud *smack.*

"The arm is (8) and will be in a cast for about six weeks," says Mr. Thundercloud's (9).

A (10) reaction might be anger, but in an interview, Mr. Thundercloud chuckled and said, "I guess that machine just doesn't like me!"

Word *Study*

WORD WEBS   Suppose you wanted to write a report about spiders. The first thing you'd want to do is ask yourself what you know about them. "What do they look like? What do they do? What makes them special?" Your next step would be to create a **word web** like the one below.

Now suppose you were a spider, spinning a word web about people. Write the words you would use in your web.

other	simple
number	model
color	broken
doctor	sudden
people	common

1. **model**
2. **simple**
3. **number**
4. **people**
5. **color**
6. **other**
7. **sudden**
8. **broken**
9. **doctor**
10. **common**

1. **Words will vary.**
2.
3.
4.

VOCABULARY BUILDING

Literature Connection

More Word Webs Have students develop a word web for concepts in a non-fiction book, such as *The Great Kapok Tree* by Lynne Cherry (Harcourt Brace Jovanovich, 1990).

MEETING THE NEEDS OF ALL STUDENTS

Modified List

Review Students studying high-frequency words complete this page.

Kinesthetic Learners

Web Mobile Have students work with a partner to make a word web mobile. Have them write the month on a large piece of colored paper and words they associate with that month on smaller pieces of paper. The paper pieces can be attached to a coat hanger and hung up.

Additional Practice

Hardbound Book Master 32B
Review Master 32
Standardized Test Master 32
Everyday Spelling **CD-ROM**

151

151

33

Generalization

Spelling Focus: Holidays, days and months of the year, titles, and words that are part of an address are always capitalized. Abbreviations should be capitalized and followed by a period.

● Core ○ Optional ✓ Assessment

DAILY PLAN	CORE OBJECTIVES	NOTES

DAY 1 Introduction
✓ Pretest and Self-Check, p. 152B
● Spelling Focus and Word List, p. 152
○ Challenge Words, p. 152
○ Challenge Master 33
○ Home-School Master 33

✓ ▪ Take and self-check Pretest
▪ Spell words that are capitalized and/or abbreviated; classify and write the list words

DAY 2 Think and Practice
● Abbreviations; Identification, p. 153
● Strategic Spelling: *The Divide and Conquer Strategy*, p. 153
○ Think and Practice Master 33
○ Extra Practice Master 33
○ Cross-Curricular Lesson: Introduce, p. 174

▪ Complete practice activities for words that are capitalized and/or abbreviated
▪ Study multisyllabic words by breaking them into syllables

DAY 3 Proofreading and Writing
● Proofread an Announcement, p. 154
● Proofreading Tip: Handwriting, p. 154
● Write an Announcement, p. 154
✓ Cooperative Midweek Test
○ Hardbound Book Master 33
○ Writing Mini-Lesson Master 33
○ Writing Activity Master 33
○ Second Language Support Master 33

▪ Proofread for spelling and handwriting errors
▪ Integrate spelling and writing in a personal writing response
✓ ▪ Take and check midweek test

DAY 4 Vocabulary Building
● Review: Making Inferences; Making Associations, p. 155
● Multicultural Connection: Holidays, p. 155
○ Cross-Curricular Lesson: Follow-Up, p. 174
○ Review Master 33

▪ Complete review activity for words that are capitalized and/or abbreviated
▪ Study holidays celebrated around the world

DAY 5 Assessment
✓ Posttest, p. 152B
○ Standardized Test Master 33

✓ ▪ Take Posttest

Cross-Curricular Lessons

Use the Spelling Focus (capitalization and abbreviation) to introduce the Social Studies lesson, *The Great Lakes,* page 174, or choose a lesson that correlates with a topic you're currently teaching.

MEETING THE NEEDS OF ALL STUDENTS

The Word List

For students studying 20 words, assign pages 152–155 and Extra Practice and Review masters.

Modified List For students studying 10 words, modify Practice on page 152, and assign Think and Practice Master 33 and pages 154–155.

Challenge For students studying 25 words, assign pages 152–155, Challenge, Extra Practice, and Review masters.

Bilingual/ESL

Capitalization and abbreviation do not exist in Korean. There are no large and small letters; words are never abbreviated. These features of English should be made clear to Korean-speaking students.

Personal Words

Students add to Personal Words lists by looking at work in their writing portfolios and words they want to remember from their reading.

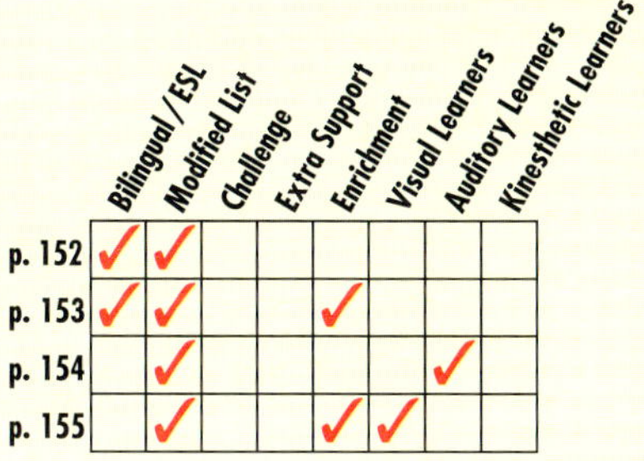

	Bilingual / ESL	Modified List	Challenge	Extra Support	Enrichment	Visual Learners	Auditory Learners	Kinesthetic Learners
p. 152	✓	✓						
p. 153	✓	✓			✓			
p. 154		✓					✓	
p. 155		✓			✓	✓		

ASSESSMENT*

Pretest

Read the underlined word, read the sentence, and then repeat the underlined word. Guide students in self-correcting their pretests and correcting any misspellings.

1. We're off on <u>Memorial Day</u>.
2. We enjoy <u>Christmas</u>.
3. The game was <u>Sun.</u> at one.
4. I planted a garden in <u>May</u>.
5. We go swimming in <u>June</u>.
6. School starts in <u>September</u>.
7. The <u>Dec.</u> snow was heavy.
8. <u>Dr.</u> Baker checks our throats.
9. <u>Mrs.</u> Green can fix the motor.
10. Shady <u>Rd.</u> is a quiet street.
11. Light <u>Hanukkah</u> candles.
12. Do you celebrate <u>Kwanzaa</u>?
13. <u>Chinese New Year</u> was fun.
14. I sent <u>Valentine's Day</u> cards.
15. It is dark in <u>November</u>.
16. Does <u>Feb.</u> have thirty days?
17. We met <u>Wed.</u> night.
18. <u>Ms.</u> Perez teaches sewing.
19. <u>Mr.</u> Shah is a coach.
20. The business is on Lake <u>Ave.</u>

Posttest

Read aloud the sentences below. These sentences may be used for dictation.

1. It was an afternoon in <u>May</u>.
2. <u>Mrs.</u> Green is an inventor.
3. <u>September</u> can be cool.
4. School will be out in <u>June</u>.
5. Our family goes to <u>Dr.</u> Long.
6. Take Beach <u>Rd.</u> to school.
7. The party is <u>Sun.</u> afternoon.
8. Grandma will visit in <u>Dec.</u>
9. That's a huge <u>Christmas</u> tree.
10. Come for <u>Memorial Day</u>.
11. We'll come in <u>November</u>.
12. <u>Ms.</u> Brown wrote a book.
13. My lesson is <u>Wed.</u> night.
14. Texas <u>Ave.</u> is a busy street.
15. <u>Mr.</u> May took us home.
16. I enjoy the <u>Feb.</u> holidays.
17. He got a nice <u>Hanukkah</u> gift.
18. I got <u>Valentine's Day</u> candy.
19. When is <u>Chinese New Year</u>?
20. Let's have a <u>Kwanzaa</u> party.

Challenge Words

1. We like the <u>Fourth of July</u>.
2. <u>St. Patrick's Day</u> is in March.
3. Does she speak <u>English</u>?
4. Forest <u>Blvd.</u> has many trees.
5. Take a pen, paper, <u>etc.</u>

Additional Assessment

Standardized Test Master 33
Dictation Sentences, p. T42
Everyday Spelling CD-ROM

WHAT'S THE BIG IDEA?
The error most students make with the words in this list is forgetting to use a capital letter. Have students write their own names without capitals to see how strange they look.

* See pp. T20 and T33 for test-study-test information.

DAY 1 CHALLENGE MASTER

CHALLENGE ■ 33

Challenge Words

| St. Patrick's Day | Fourth of July | English | Blvd. | etc. |

■ Change words to abbreviations and abbreviations to words in order to write each of the Challenge Words.

1. Saint Pat's Day — **St. Patrick's Day**
2. 4th of July — **Fourth of July**
3. Eng. — **English**
4. Boulevard — **Blvd.**
5. etcetera — **etc.**

■ Holidays are filled with unforgettable sights, smells, and sounds. Use one or more of the Challenge Words to describe the best holiday you have ever had. Remember to describe what you see, smell, taste, touch, and hear.

Practice Masters, p. 125

DAY 1 HOME-SCHOOL MASTER

■ 33 HOME-SCHOOL ACTIVITIES 33 ■

Word Check 33
1. Ms.
2. Mr.
3. Mrs.
4. Dr.
5. Ave.
6. Rd.
7. Sun.
8. Wed.
9. Feb.
10. Dec.
11. Hanukkah
12. Christmas
13. Kwanzaa
14. Chinese New Year
15. Valentine's Day
16. Memorial Day
17. May
18. June
19. September
20. November

■ Abbreviations Write the list word that is the abbreviation for each word or description below.

1. December **Dec.**
2. Mister **Mr.**
3. February **Feb.**
4. Road **Rd.**
5. Sunday **Sun.**
6. Avenue **Ave.**
7. Doctor **Dr.**
8. Wednesday **Wed.**

Write two abbreviations that women use in their names.

9. **Ms.**   10. **Mrs.**

■ Inferences Write the list word that fits each clue below.

11. African-American holiday **Kwanzaa**
12. trees and mistletoe **Christmas**
13. beginning of autumn **September**
14. war heroes' holiday **Memorial Day**
15. Asian holiday **Chinese New Year**
16. beginning of summer **June**
17. Jewish winter holiday **Hanukkah**
18. turkey and pumpkin pie **November**
19. day for hearts and flowers **Valentine's Day**
20. April showers bring flowers this month **May**

Dear Parent,
Please check to see that your child has done this page correctly. Circle any misspelled words and help your child study them.

Tear off the Word Check before your child returns this page to class. Use it to help your child study.

Home-School Activities, p. 28

DAY 2 THINK AND PRACTICE MASTER

33 ■ THINK AND PRACTICE

| Memorial Day | Christmas | Sun. | May | June |
| September | Dec. | Dr. | Mrs. | Rd. |

■ Abbreviations Write the abbreviation in the list that stands for each word.

1. December **Dec.**
2. road **Rd.**
3. doctor **Dr.**
4. Sunday **Sun.**
5. mistress **Mrs.**

■ Classifying Write the list words that belong in each group.

Holidays	Months	Abbreviations for Titles
6. **Christmas**	8. **September**	12. **Mrs.**
7. **Memorial Day**	9. **May**	13. **Dr.**
	10. **June**	
	11. **Dec.**	

■ Making Connections Write the list word that matches each clue.

14. the month before October — **September**
15. holiday honoring those who died for our country — **Memorial Day**
16. abbreviation for the first day of the week — **Sun.**
17. abbreviation for the last month of the year — **Dec.**

STRATEGIC SPELLING: The Divide and Conquer Strategy
Sometimes it helps to study long words piece by piece. Write *September*, *Christmas*, and *Memorial Day*. Draw lines between the syllables. Then study each word syllable by syllable. Use a dictionary if you need help.

18. **Sep/tem/ber**   20. **Me/mo/ri/al Day**
19. **Christ/mas**

Practice Masters, p. 126

DAY 2 EXTRA PRACTICE MASTER

EXTRA PRACTICE ■ 33

Word List

Memorial Day	Christmas	Sun.	May
June	September	Dec.	Dr.
Mrs.	Rd.	Hanukkah	Kwanzaa
Chinese New Year	Valentine's Day	November	Feb.
Wed.	Ms.	Mr.	Ave.

■ Words in Context Write list words to complete the sentences below.

Dear Grandma,
I'm glad you are coming to live with us. You will get here just before *Labor Day*. We go back to school in early (1) ___. Then, in the month of (2) ___, we will celebrate Thanksgiving. Sometime in December, my Jewish friends will celebrate their holiday, (3) ___. Then the whole school will have a holiday for (4) ___ on December 25. Of course, our family will celebrate (5) ___, along with other African Americans. Sometime in January my friend Tsiu Tan and her family will celebrate (6) ___. After that, we will look forward to sending each other cards for (7) ___.
Of course, we will be studying hard when we aren't having holidays. Then, at the end of the month of (8) ___ we will celebrate the holiday for remembering members of the armed services, called (9) ___. Finally, in (10) ___ we will start summer vacation.

Love, Tanya

1. **September**
2. **November**
3. **Hanukkah**
4. **Christmas**
5. **Kwanzaa**
6. **Chinese New Year**
7. **Valentine's Day**
8. **May**
9. **Memorial Day**
10. **June**

■ Who or What? Write the list word that is the abbreviation for each of the following:

11. the second day of the weekend
12. the short roadway where your friend lives
13. the person who treats you for a cold
14. the name for a wide street
15. the shortest month of the year
16. the father of your best friend
17. three-letter title for a woman
18. two-letter title for a woman
19. the day halfway between weekends
20. the month in which winter begins

11. **Sun.**
12. **Rd.**
13. **Dr.**
14. **Ave.**
15. **Feb.**
16. **Mr.**
17. **Mrs.**
18. **Ms.**
19. **Wed.**
20. **Dec.**

Practice Masters, p. 127

TECHNOLOGY AND VISUAL SUPPORT	 Use Audiotape C, Side 2, Lesson 33	 For additional practice use *Everyday Spelling* Game Software, Lesson 33	 Additional resources on *Everyday Spelling* CD-ROM: proofreading and writing, modified list and challenge words, auditory test
	Use Proofreading and Writing Transparency 33		

DAY 3 SECOND LANGUAGE SUPPORT MASTER

33 ■ SECOND LANGUAGE SUPPORT

Words Around You

Think about where you have seen the words you learned in Lesson 33.

Write some of the words in the chart. Then write about the words. One word has been done for you.

A word I saw	Where or when I saw it	How the word was used
September	*calendar*	*name of the month*
Answers will vary.		

Second Language Support, p. 54

DAY 3 WRITING ACTIVITY MASTER

33 ■ WRITING ACTIVITY

Including the Important Facts

☐ Organize facts so they are easy to understand	≡ Make a capital.
☐ Give facts that answer the questions *who,* *when, where, what,* and *why.*	/ Make a small letter.
	∧ Add something
	Take out something
	⊙ Add a period.
	¶ New paragraph

■ Look at the picture of the dog. Then read the announcement. Add any important information that has been left out. Delete information that isn't needed.

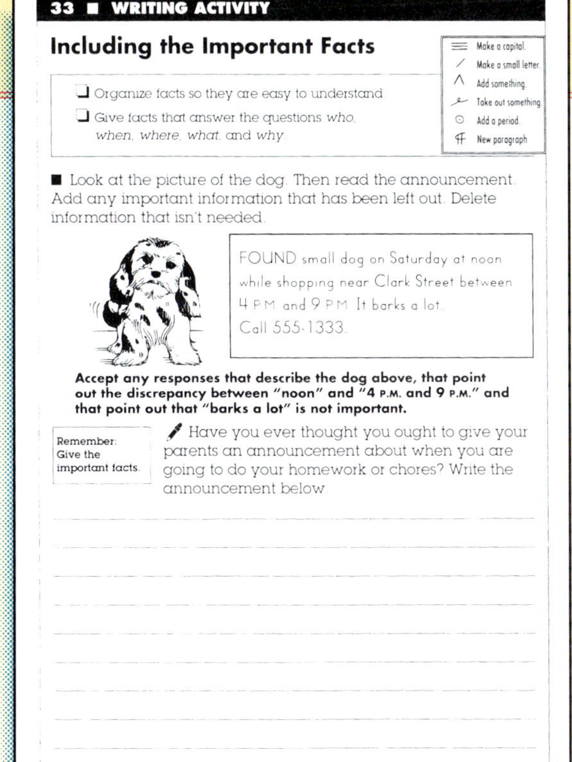

Accept any responses that describe the dog above, that point out the discrepancy between "noon" and "4 P.M. and 9 P.M." and that point out that "barks a lot" is not important.

Remember: Give the important facts.

Have you ever thought you ought to give your parents an announcement about when you are going to do your homework or chores? Write the announcement below.

Spelling and Writing, p. 56

DAY 4 REVIEW MASTER

33 ■ REVIEW

Word List

Memorial Day	Christmas	Sun.	May
June	September	Dec.	Dr.
Mrs.	Rd.	Hanukkah	Kwanzaa
Chinese New Year	Valentine's Day	November	Feb.
Wed.	Ms.	Mr.	Ave.

■ **Making Associations** Write the list abbreviation or word that you might associate with each word or phrase below.

1. shots
2. Thanksgiving
3. cupid
4. married woman
5. holly
6. dragon parade
7. single or married woman
8. African American, candles
9. Labor Day
10. menorah
11. remembering
12. Father's Day
13. Cinco de Mayo

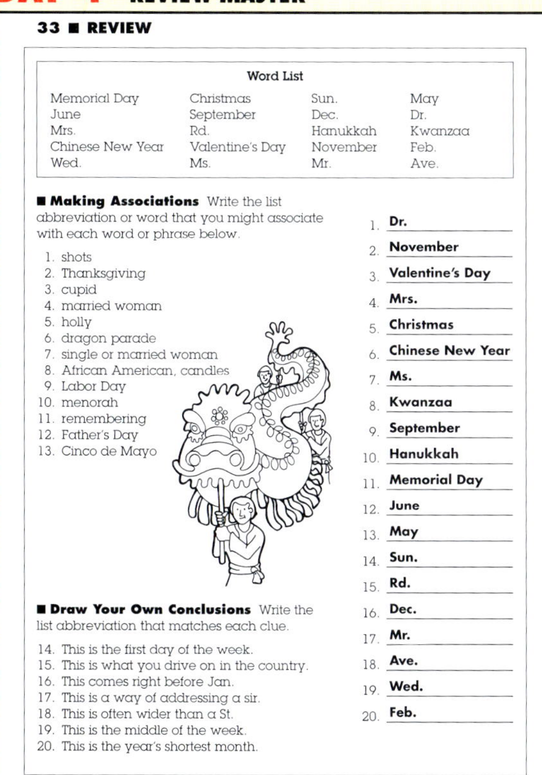

1. **Dr.**
2. **November**
3. **Valentine's Day**
4. **Mrs.**
5. **Christmas**
6. **Chinese New Year**
7. **Ms.**
8. **Kwanzaa**
9. **September**
10. **Hanukkah**
11. **Memorial Day**
12. **June**
13. **May**
14. **Sun.**
15. **Rd.**
16. **Dec.**
17. **Mr.**
18. **Ave.**
19. **Wed.**
20. **Feb.**

■ **Draw Your Own Conclusions** Write the list abbreviation that matches each clue.

14. This is the first day of the week.
15. This is what you drive on in the country.
16. This comes right before Jan.
17. This is a way of addressing a sir.
18. This is often wider than a St.
19. This is the middle of the week.
20. This is the year's shortest month.

Practice Masters, p. 128

DAY 5 STANDARDIZED TEST MASTER

33 ■ LESSON TEST

■ Find the word in each group that is spelled correctly. Fill in the letter for the correct word on the answer strip.

Sample:
a. mihgt   c. mighte
b. myte   d. might — ⓐⓑⓒ●

1. a. christmas c. Chrismas / b. Christmas d. Cristmas — 1. ⓐ●ⓒⓓ
2. a. Mrs. c. Mrss. / b. mrs. d. Mrrs. — 2. ●ⓑⓒⓓ
3. a. november c. November / b. Novemder d. Novenber — 3. ⓐⓑ●ⓓ
4. a. Sun. c. son. / b. sun. d. Sunn. — 4. ●ⓑⓒⓓ
5. a. wed. c. Wen. / b. Wed. d. Wedn. — 5. ⓐ●ⓒⓓ
6. a. hanukkah c. Hanukkah / b. Hannukah d. Hanuka — 6. ⓐⓑ●ⓓ
7. a. Kwannzaa c. Kwonza / b. Kiwanza d. Kwanzaa — 7. ⓐⓑⓒ●
8. a. Mr. c. mr. / b. Mesr. d. Msr. — 8. ●ⓑⓒⓓ
9. a. Aev. c. Avv. / b. Ave. d. Aven. — 9. ⓐ●ⓒⓓ
10. a. dec. c. Dec. / b. Dcr. d. Decm. — 10. ⓐⓑ●ⓓ
11. a. Feb. c. febr. / b. feb. d. Febr. — 11. ●ⓑⓒⓓ
12. a. May c. Maye / b. mae d. Mae — 12. ●ⓑⓒⓓ
13. a. dr. c. Dr. / b. Dtr. d. Dcr. — 13. ⓐⓑ●ⓓ
14. a. Rd. c. Ro. / b. Rde. d. Rod. — 14. ●ⓑⓒⓓ
15. a. Chineese New Year c. chineese new year / b. Chinese New Year d. chinease new year — 15. ⓐ●ⓒⓓ
16. a. September c. Sepptember / b. Septemder d. Septeber — 16. ●ⓑⓒⓓ
17. a. Jume c. June / b. Jun. d. june — 17. ⓐⓑ●ⓓ
18. a. valentine's day c. Valintines Day / b. Valentine's day d. Valentine's Day — 18. ⓐⓑⓒ●
19. a. memorial day c. Mumorial Day / b. Mimorial Day d. Memorial Day — 19. ⓐⓑⓒ●
20. a. Mis. c. Ms. / b. Mes. d. Mz. — 20. ⓐⓑ●ⓓ

Practice for Standardized Tests, p. 48

LESSON 33

DAILY SPELLING REVIEW

The noisy *motor cycle suprised* us.

motorcycle   surprised

● Core   ○ Optional   ✓ Assessment

INTRODUCTION

Word Structure

Abbreviations Have students make a two-column chart with each abbreviation from the list in the first column and the word it stands for in the second.

MEETING THE NEEDS OF ALL STUDENTS

Modified List

Practice Students studying only the high-frequency words write

- two words for holidays
- one word for a day
- four words for months
- two words for people
- one word for a type of street

Bilingual/ESL

Flashcard Abbreviations

Have pairs of students make a flashcard for each abbreviation, with the abbreviation on one side and both the pronunciation and the word that the abbreviation stands for on the other.

> **Additional Practice**
>
> **Challenge Master 33**
> **Home-School Master 33**
> **Audiotape C, Side 2**

1. **Memorial Day**
2. **Christmas**
3. **Hanukkah**
4. **Kwanzaa**
5. **Chinese New Year**
6. **Valentine's Day**
7. **Sun.**
8. **Wed.**
9. **May**
10. **June**
11. **September**
12. **Dec.**
13. **November**
14. **Feb.**
15. **Dr.**
16. **Mrs.**
17. **Ms.**
18. **Mr.**
19. **Rd.**
20. **Ave.**

CHALLENGE!

> Fourth of July
> St. Patrick's Day
> English
> Blvd.
> etc.

152

■ INTRODUCTION

Capitalization and Abbreviation

SPELLING FOCUS

Holidays, days and months of the year, titles, and words that are part of an address are always capitalized: **Christmas, May.** Abbreviations should be capitalized and followed by a period: **Dr., Rd., Sun.**

■ STUDY Notice that these words are capitalized. Some have periods.

1. Memorial Day
2. Christmas ✱
3. Sun.
4. May
5. June
6. September
7. Dec.
8. Dr.
9. Mrs.
10. Rd.
11. Hanukkah
12. Kwanzaa
13. Chinese New Year
14. Valentine's Day
15. November
16. Feb.
17. Wed.
18. Ms.
19. Mr.
20. Ave.

■ PRACTICE Sort the list words by writing

- six words that name holidays
- two words that name days
- six words that name months
- four words that name people
- two words that name types of streets

Order of words in each group may vary.

■ WRITE Choose three words to write an invitation to a holiday party. **Invitations will vary.**

✱ **WATCH OUT FOR FREQUENTLY MISSPELLED WORDS!**

THINK AND PRACTICE ■

ABBREVIATIONS   Write the abbreviation on your spelling list that stands for each word below.

1. doctor
2. avenue
3. December
4. Wednesday
5. February
6. mister
7. Sunday
8. road

IDENTIFICATION   Write the list word that matches each clue below.

9. This is the ninth month of the year.
10. On this day we remember those who have died.
11. This is the fifth month of the year.
12. This is the eleventh month of the year.
13. This is a title put in front of a married woman's name.
14. This is the sixth month of the year.
15. On this day we may send a card to a sweetheart.
16. This is a title put in front of a woman's name, married or unmarried.

1. **Dr.**
2. **Ave.**
3. **Dec.**
4. **Wed.**
5. **Feb.**
6. **Mr.**
7. **Sun.**
8. **Rd.**
9. **September**
10. **Memorial Day**
11. **May**
12. **November**
13. **Mrs.**
14. **June**
15. **Valentine's Day**
16. **Ms.**

Sometimes it helps to study long words piece by piece. Write *Kwanzaa, Hanukkah, Christmas,* and *Chinese New Year*. Draw lines between the syllables. Then study each word syllable by syllable. Use a dictionary if you need help.

17. **Kwan/zaa**
18. **Han/uk/kah**
19. **Christ/mas**
20. **Chi/nese New Year**

Did You Know?
Both **Hanukkah** and **Kwanzaa** can be spelled in different ways. You may also see **Hanukkah** spelled **Chanukah**. **Kwanzaa** may also be spelled **Kwanza**.

THINK AND PRACTICE

Abbreviations

Capitalization Point out to students that although the name for a title or place is not always capitalized, its abbreviation always is.

MEETING THE NEEDS OF ALL STUDENTS

Modified List

Review Students studying high-frequency words complete Think and Practice Master 33.

Bilingual/ESL

Sorting Abbreviations
Pair ESL students with native English speakers. Suggest that students sort the abbreviations into days, titles, months, and places.

Enrichment

Researching Holidays
Have students find out the date of each holiday in the word list. They may also discuss in groups what they know about each holiday.

Additional Practice

Think and Practice Master 33
Extra Practice Master 33
Everyday Spelling CD-ROM
Everyday Spelling Game Software

DAY 3 Proofreading and Writing

- Proofread an Announcement
- Proofreading Tip: Handwriting
- Write an Announcement
- ✓ Cooperative Midweek Test

DAILY SPELLING REVIEW

Everyone *cougt* a bad cold in *Decenber.*

caught   *December*

● Core   ○ Optional   ✓ Assessment

PROOFREADING AND WRITING

Handwriting
Proofreading Papers
Encourage students to exchange papers with a partner for close examination of handwriting errors. Partners should circle errors, such as uncrossed **t**'s.

MEETING THE NEEDS OF ALL STUDENTS

Modified List
Proofreading Students studying high-frequency words complete this page or the proofreading activity on the *Everyday Spelling* CD-ROM.

Auditory Learners
Public Address Partners can pretend to "broadcast" each other's announcements by reading them aloud. Direct students to listen for completeness and revise as needed.

Additional Practice

Hardbound Book Master 33
Second Language Master 33
Writing Mini-Lesson Master 33
Writing Activity Master 33
Proofreading Transparency 33
Everyday Spelling CD-ROM

■ **PROOFREADING AND WRITING**

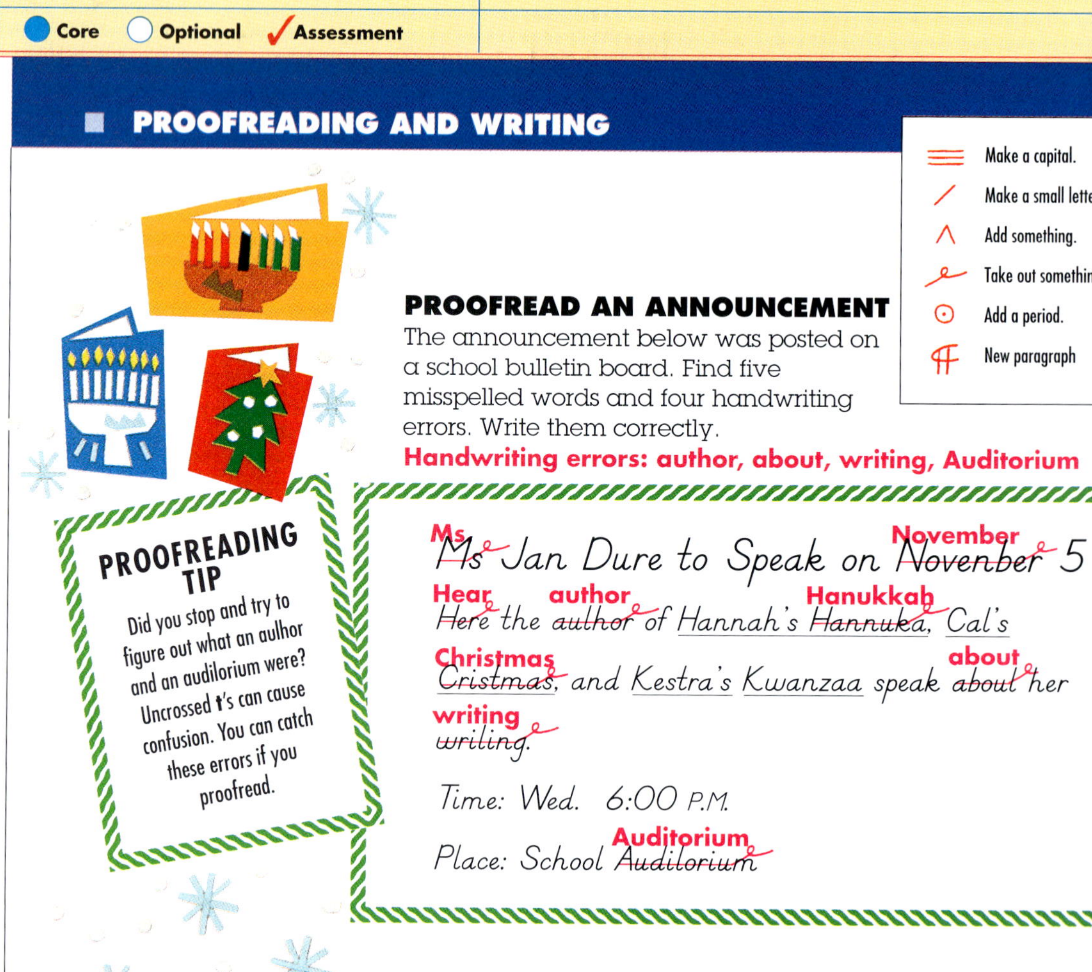

═══	Make a capital.
/	Make a small letter.
∧	Add something.
ℓ	Take out something
⊙	Add a period.
⌗	New paragraph

PROOFREAD AN ANNOUNCEMENT
The announcement below was posted on a school bulletin board. Find five misspelled words and four handwriting errors. Write them correctly.
Handwriting errors: author, about, writing, Auditorium

PROOFREADING TIP
Did you stop and try to figure out what an aulhor and an audilorium were? Uncrossed **t**'s can cause confusion. You can catch these errors if you proofread.

WRITE AN ANNOUNCEMENT Now it's your turn to write an announcement about a visiting author. Use list words and personal words.

Responses will vary.

Announcements should include list

words and personal words.

Word List

Ms.	Hanukkah
Mr.	Christmas
Mrs.	Kwanzaa
Dr.	Chinese New Year
Ave.	Valentine's Day
Rd.	Memorial Day
Sun.	May
Wed.	June
Feb.	September
Dec.	November

Personal Words

1. **Words will**
2. **vary.**

154

- Review: Making Inferences and Making Associations
- Multicultural Connection: Holidays
- Cross-Curricular Lesson: Follow-Up

○ **DAILY SPELLING REVIEW**

The *class room* is *begining* to look cheerful.

classroom *beginning*

✓ Posttest
✓ Dictation Sentences
○ Standardized Test Master 33
✓ Auditory Test on *Everyday Spelling* CD-ROM

VOCABULARY BUILDING ■

Review

MAKING INFERENCES   Complete each group by writing the missing boxed word.

1. April, ___, June
2. Oct., Nov., ___
3. August, ___, October
4. Sat., ___, Mon.
5. May, ___, July

MAKING ASSOCIATIONS   Write the boxed word that you would associate with each group of words below.

6. December, tree, celebration
7. woman, married, title
8. person, professional, medicine
9. street, address, abbreviation
10. holiday, May, remembering

Memorial Day	September
Christmas	Dec.
Sun.	Dr.
May	Mrs.
June	Rd.

1. **May**
2. **Dec.**
3. **September**
4. **Sun.**
5. **June**
6. **Christmas**
7. **Mrs.**
8. **Dr.**
9. **Rd.**
10. **Memorial Day**

Multicultural *Connection*

HOLIDAYS   People everywhere celebrate important occasions. Read the descriptions of the holidays below. Then answer the questions.

Hanukkah celebrates the recapturing of the great temple at Jerusalem over 2,000 years ago. Jewish writings describe how the Jews had barely enough lamp oil for one night in the temple, yet the lamp burned for eight days. Today, the menorah is lit in memory of this. Also called the "Festival of Lights," Hanukkah is celebrated in November or December.

Christmas celebrates the birth of Jesus, also called Christ. According to the Bible, Jesus was born in a stable and welcomed with gifts from wise men and shepherds. Christians believe Jesus is their savior. Small stable scenes are often seen at Christmas. It comes on December 25.

Kwanzaa is a yearly African American holiday created in 1966. It celebrates black people and their history. There are seven principles of Kwanzaa. The kinara, or candle holder, holds seven candles, one for each principle. Kwanzaa lasts from December 26 through January 1.

1. Which holiday celebrates African traditions?
2. Which holiday celebrates the birth of Jesus?
3. Which holiday is also called the "Festival of Lights"?

1. **Kwanzaa**
2. **Christmas**
3. **Hanukkah**

VOCABULARY BUILDING

Literature Connection

Read More About It Suggest that students can find additional information about Kwanzaa in *Kwanzaa* by A. P. Porter (Carolrhoda, 1991).

MEETING THE NEEDS OF ALL STUDENTS

Modified List

Review Students studying high-frequency words complete this page.

Visual Learners

Holiday Calendar Have visual learners make a class calendar of holidays. The calendar should incorporate month and day abbreviations as well as names of holidays.

Enrichment

Share a Holiday Have students write out a plan for a holiday celebration. Plans might include favorite traditions, meals, songs, and games.

Additional Practice

Review Master 33
Standardized Test Master 33
***Everyday Spelling* CD-ROM**

LESSON

34

Generalization

Spelling Focus: To form possessives of singular nouns, add an apostrophe and **s.** To form possessives of plural nouns that end in **s,** add only an apostrophe.

● Core   ○ Optional   ✓ Assessment

DAILY PLAN | CORE OBJECTIVES | NOTES

DAY 1 Introduction

✓ Pretest and Self-Check, p. 156B
● Spelling Focus and Word List, p. 156
○ Challenge Words, p. 156
○ Challenge Master 34
○ Home-School Master 34

✓ ▪ Take and self-check Pretest
▪ Spell possessives; classify and write the list words

DAY 2 Think and Practice

● Singular Possessives; Using Context Clues; Plural Possessives, p. 157
● Strategic Spelling: *Building New Words,* p. 157
○ Think and Practice Master 34
○ Extra Practice Master 34
○ Cross-Curricular Lesson: Introduce, p. 192

▪ Complete practice activities for possessives
▪ Apply guidelines for forming possessives to new words

DAY 3 Proofreading and Writing

● Proofread an Opinion, p. 158
● Proofreading Tip: Subject-Verb Agreement, p. 158
● Write an Opinion, p. 158
✓ Cooperative Midweek Test
○ Hardbound Book Master 34A
○ Writing Mini-Lesson Master 34
○ Writing Activity Master 34
○ Second Language Support Master 34

▪ Proofread for spelling and usage errors
▪ Integrate spelling and writing in a personal writing response
✓ ▪ Take and check midweek test

DAY 4 Vocabulary Building

● Review: Context Clues, p. 159
● Word Study: Palindromes, p. 159
○ Hardbound Book Master 34B
○ Cross-Curricular Lesson: Follow-Up, p. 192
○ Review Master 34

▪ Complete review activity for possessives
▪ Study and use palindromes

DAY 5 Assessment

✓ Posttest, p. 156B
○ Standardized Test Master 34

✓ ▪ Take Posttest

Cross-Curricular Lessons

Use the Spelling Focus (possessives) to introduce the Science lesson, *Living Together,* page 192, or choose a lesson that correlates with a topic you're currently teaching.

MEETING THE NEEDS OF ALL STUDENTS

The Word List

For students studying 20 words, assign pages 156–159 and Extra Practice and Review masters.

Modified List For students studying 10 words, modify Practice on page 156, and assign Think and Practice Master 34 and pages 158–159.

Challenge For students studying 25 words, assign pages 156–159, Challenge, Extra Practice, and Review masters.

Bilingual/ESL

In Spanish, the possessive is formed with a prepositional phrase instead of a suffix. Consequently, Spanish-speaking students may omit the apostrophe when spelling list words.

Personal Words

Students add to Personal Words lists by looking at work in their writing portfolios and words they want to remember from their reading.

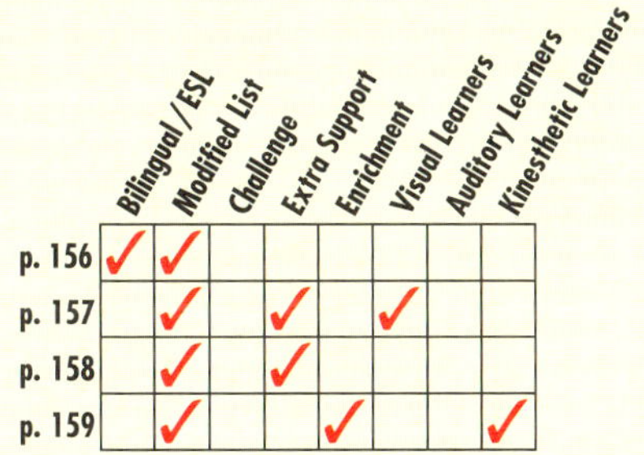

	Bilingual / ESL	Modified List	Challenge	Extra Support	Enrichment	Visual Learners	Auditory Learners	Kinesthetic Learners
p. 156	✓	✓						
p. 157		✓	✓		✓			
p. 158		✓		✓				
p. 159		✓			✓			✓

ASSESSMENT*

Pretest

Read the underlined word, read the sentence, and then repeat the underlined word. Guide students in self-correcting their pretests and correcting any misspellings.

1. We can use <u>Dad's</u> tools.
2. My <u>friend's</u> mom is a nurse.
3. That <u>girl's</u> story is funny.
4. Some <u>girls'</u> moms were there.
5. A <u>teacher's</u> day is busy.
6. Some <u>teachers'</u> pens got lost.
7. The <u>baby's</u> foot is tiny.
8. <u>Babies'</u> clothes are small.
9. I use my <u>family's</u> boat.
10. The <u>families'</u> yards are neat.
11. That is <u>Grandma's</u> house.
12. <u>Grandpa's</u> pies are good.
13. My <u>brother's</u> name is Albert.
14. Both <u>brothers'</u> dogs are fat.
15. The <u>boy's</u> dog is on a leash.
16. All the <u>boys'</u> feet got wet.
17. My <u>aunt's</u> foot was painful.
18. We stay at our <u>aunts'</u> houses.
19. One <u>lady's</u> hat blew away.
20. <u>Ladies'</u> dresses are upstairs.

Posttest

Read aloud the sentences below. These sentences may be used for dictation.

1. I played at a <u>friend's</u> house.
2. <u>Dad's</u> train is coming soon.
3. The store has <u>babies'</u> toys.
4. Some <u>families'</u> cash was lost.
5. The <u>baby's</u> blanket is blue.
6. I made my <u>family's</u> supper.
7. That <u>teacher's</u> class is good.
8. The <u>girls'</u> softball team won.
9. The <u>teachers'</u> games are fun.
10. That <u>girl's</u> dress is bright.
11. Here's my <u>brother's</u> photo.
12. <u>Grandpa's</u> coat is upstairs.
13. We visit our <u>aunts'</u> families.
14. The <u>lady's</u> hand got caught.
15. Is that your <u>aunt's</u> voice?
16. The <u>boy's</u> knee was cut.
17. The <u>ladies'</u> babies came too.
18. My two <u>brothers'</u> room is big.
19. The <u>boys'</u> work was done.
20. I like my <u>grandma's</u> chair.

Challenge Words

1. Here's <u>someone's</u> homework.
2. The <u>boss's</u> child will help.
3. <u>James's</u> frog got lost again.
4. My <u>grandparent's</u> leg is hurt.
5. <u>Grandparents'</u> stories are the best.

Additional Assessment

Standardized Test Master 34
Dictation Sentences, p. T42
Everyday Spelling CD-ROM

WHAT'S THE BIG IDEA?
Once young writers learn about using apostrophes, they begin to use them in places where they don't belong— in plurals, for example. Take time to work with students on this.

* See pp. T20 and T33 for test-study-test information.

DAY 1 — CHALLENGE MASTER

CHALLENGE ■ 34

Challenge Words

someone's   grandparent's   grandparents'   boss's   James's

■ Complete the following sentences with the correct Challenge Word.

1. (belongs to James) I am sure that the red coat is **James's** new coat.

2. (belongs to my grandparents) The **grandparents'** places were decorated with flowers.

3. (belongs to one grandparent) My **grandparent's** new car is blue.

4. (belongs to someone) This lost mitten must be **someone's** .

5. (belongs to the boss) The **boss's** remark made everyone happier.

■ Members of a family can live in different cities—across the country or around the world. It is a special occasion whenever the family gets together. Use one or more Challenge Words to write about a family reunion.

Practice Masters, p. 129

DAY 1 — HOME-SCHOOL MASTER

■ 34   HOME-SCHOOL ACTIVITIES   34 ■

■ **Singular Possessives** Write the list word that matches the clue: belonging to—

1. a young female person **girl's**
2. an infant **baby's**
3. an educator **teacher's**
4. my mother's mother **grandma's**
5. a close buddy **friend's**
6. the son of my parents **brother's**
7. a young male person **boy's**
8. my male parent **Dad's**
9. an adult female person **lady's**
10. the sister of my father **aunt's**
11. a collection of related people **family's**
12. my mother's father **grandpa's**

■ **Plural Possessives** Write a plural possessive list word for each word below.

13. baby **babies'**
14. brother **brothers'**
15. aunt **aunts'**
16. lady **ladies'**
17. boy **boys'**
18. family **families'**
19. teacher **teachers'**
20. girl **girl's**

Word Check 34

1. boy's
2. boys'
3. girl's
4. girls'
5. aunt's
6. aunts'
7. brother's
8. brothers'
9. teacher's
10. teachers'
11. lady's
12. ladies'
13. family's
14. families'
15. baby's
16. babies'
17. grandma's
18. grandpa's
19. Dad's
20. friend's

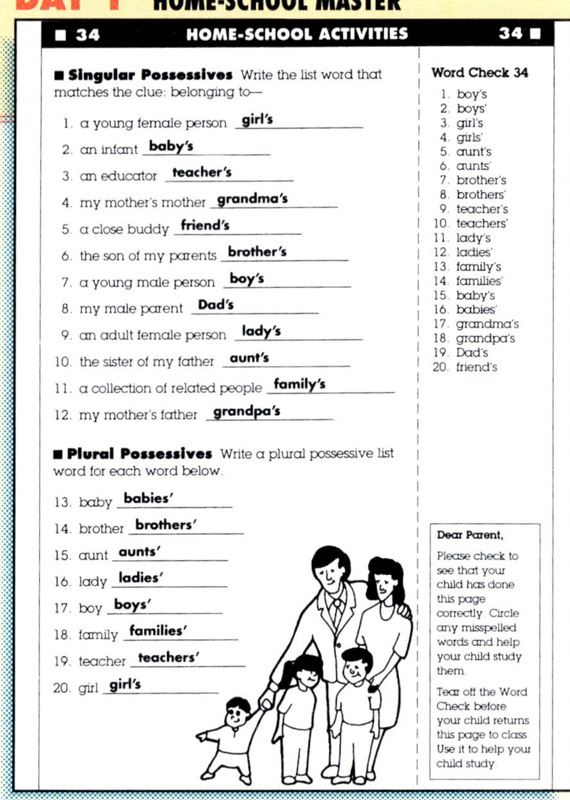

Dear Parent,

Please check to see that your child has done this page correctly. Circle any misspelled words and help your child study them.

Tear off the Word Check before your child returns this page to class. Use it to help your child study.

Home-School Activities, p. 29

DAY 2 — THINK AND PRACTICE MASTER

34 ■ THINK AND PRACTICE

Dad's	friend's	girl's	girls'	teacher's
teachers'	baby's	babies'	family's	families'

■ **Singular Possessives** Write the singular possessive of each word.

1. girl **girl's**
2. family **family's**
3. teacher **teacher's**
4. friend **friend's**

■ **Word Forms** Write the plural possessive form for each singular possessive.

5. teacher's **teachers'**
6. baby's **babies'**
7. girl's **girls'**
8. family's **families'**

■ **Context** Write the list word that is the possessive form of the word in parentheses to complete each sentence.

9. Two (girls) voices were heard outside. **girls'**
10. The (baby) bottle is on the table. **baby's**
11. Ten (families) apartments were destroyed by the fire. **families'**
12. (Dad) truck is used in his business. **Dad's**
13. The (teacher) notebook is on his desk. **teacher's**

Strategic Spelling: Building New Words
Write the words that complete the chart.

Singular	Singular Possessive	Plural Possessive
14. father	**father's**	**fathers'**
15. monkey	**monkey's**	**monkeys'**

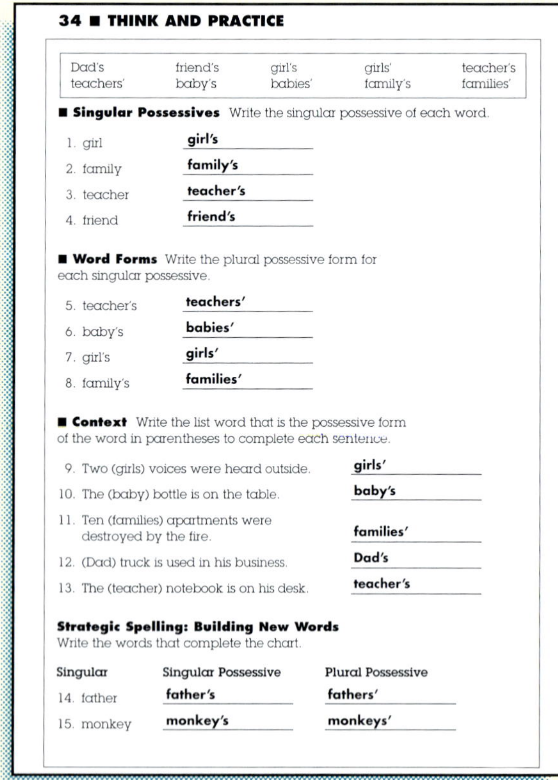

Practice Masters, p. 130

DAY 2 — EXTRA PRACTICE MASTER

EXTRA PRACTICE ■ 34

Word List

Dad's	friend's	girl's	girls'	teacher's
teachers'	baby's	babies'	family's	families'
grandma's	grandpa's	brother's	brothers'	boy's
boys'	aunt's	aunts'	lady's	ladies'

■ **To Whom Does It Belong?** Write the correct list word for each phrase below. Use the underlined words as clues for help.

1. one <u>brother</u> has a jacket — **brother's**
2. one <u>father of a parent</u> has golf clubs — **grandpa's**
3. several <u>adult women</u> have a soccer team — **ladies'**
4. several <u>young males</u> have a club — **boys'**
5. one <u>school employee</u> has a briefcase — **teacher's**
6. several <u>newborn persons</u> have rattles — **babies'**
7. one <u>sister of my father</u> has a farm — **aunt's**
8. two <u>sisters of my father</u> have a hotel — **aunts'**
9. one <u>family</u> has a business — **family's**
10. two <u>young females</u> have a treehouse — **girls'**
11. several <u>brothers</u> have a swim team — **brothers'**
12. several <u>families</u> have summer cottages — **families'**
13. one <u>adult woman</u> has books — **lady's**
14. one <u>male parent</u> has two canoes — **Dad's**
15. one <u>young male</u> has drums — **boy's**
16. one <u>newborn person</u> has a crib — **baby's**
17. one <u>pal</u> has a skateboard — **friend's**
18. one <u>mother of a parent</u> has a store — **grandma's**
19. several <u>school employees</u> have cars — **teachers'**
20. one <u>young female</u> has rollerblades — **girl's**

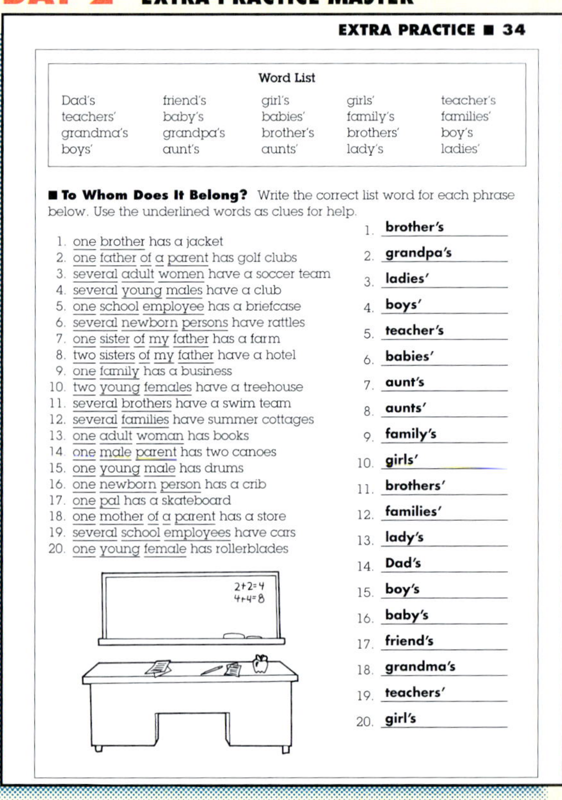

Practice Masters, p. 131

<table>
<tr><td rowspan="2">TECHNOLOGY AND VISUAL SUPPORT</td><td> Use Audiotape C, Side 2, Lesson 34</td><td rowspan="2">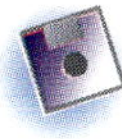 For additional practice use Everyday Spelling Game Software, Lesson 34</td><td rowspan="2"> Additional resources on Everyday Spelling CD-ROM: proofreading and writing, modified list and challenge words, auditory test</td></tr>
<tr><td> Use Proofreading and Writing Transparency 34</td></tr>
</table>

DAY 3 SECOND LANGUAGE SUPPORT MASTER

SECOND LANGUAGE SUPPORT ■ 34

Words Around You

Think about where you have seen the words you learned in Lesson 34.

Write some of the words in the chart. Then write about the words. One word has been done for you.

A word I saw	Where or when I saw it	How the word was used
boy's	bulletin board	Lost: a boy's blue jacket
Answers will vary.		

Second Language Support, p. 55

DAY 3 WRITING ACTIVITY MASTER

34 ■ WRITING ACTIVITY

Subject-Verb Agreement

☐ The subject and verb must agree in a sentence.

☐ Singular verbs in the present tense end in -s.

☐ Plural verbs in the present tense usually do not end in -s.

Proofreading marks:
≡ Make a capital.
/ Make a small letter.
∧ Add something.
⌖ Take out something.
⊙ Add a period.
¶ New paragraph

■ Read the paragraph that Armand wrote about his favorite place. Fix any errors in subject-verb agreement.

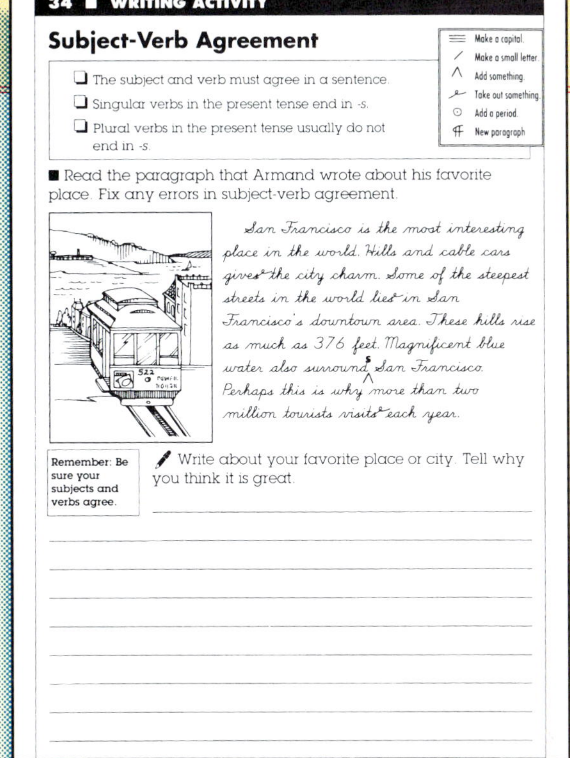

Remember: Be sure your subjects and verbs agree.

Write about your favorite place or city. Tell why you think it is great.

Spelling and Writing, p. 58

DAY 4 REVIEW MASTER

34 ■ REVIEW

Word List

Dad's	friend's	girl's	girls'	teacher's
teachers'	baby's	babies	family's	families'
grandma's	grandpa's	brother's	brothers'	boy's
boys'	aunt's	aunts'	lady's	ladies'

■ **Happy Endings** Add an ending to each word in parentheses to form a list word that completes the sentence.

1. (Dad) See if you may borrow ___ striped tie.
2. (baby) Have you seen the ___ rattle?
3. (families) Which ___ cars are parked the farthest away?
4. (girls) Two ___ raincoats are orange.
5. (teacher) Did you follow the ___ instructions?
6. (ladies) The ___ tickets are in the drawer.
7. (friend) Are you going to your ___ house?
8. (brother) I helped feed my ___ cat.
9. (grandpa) At our ___ house, we always get fudge brownies.
10. (boys) I climbed up to the ___ tree house.
11. (family) The ___ vacation was scheduled for August.
12. (aunts) Where is your ___ condo?

1. **Dad's**
2. **baby's**
3. **families'**
4. **girls'**
5. **teacher's**
6. **ladies'**
7. **friend's**
8. **brother's**
9. **grandpa's**
10. **boys'**
11. **family's**
12. **aunts'**

■ **Making Comparisons** Complete each comparison using a list word.

13. Puppies' diets are as important as ___ diets.
14. Our ___ duties at school are sometimes like our parents' duties at home.
15. The ___ ideas were similar to the gentleman's.
16. Your uncle's pickup is more practical than your ___ sports car.
17. My grandad doesn't have my ___ good health.
18. Which bedroom is your sisters' and which is your ___?
19. The woman's dress is the same material as her little ___.
20. The ___ costume was similar to his dad's.

13. **babies'**
14. **teachers'**
15. **lady's**
16. **aunt's**
17. **grandma's**
18. **brothers'**
19. **girl's**
20. **boy's**

Practice Masters, p. 132

DAY 5 STANDARDIZED TEST MASTER

LESSON TEST ■ 34

■ Find the word in each group that is spelled correctly. Fill in the letter for the correct word on the answer strip.

Sample:
- **a.** mihgt
- **b.** myte
- **c.** mighte
- **d.** might — answer: d

1. **a.** friend's **b.** freind's **c.** friends's **d.** friende's — answer: a
2. **a.** families' **b.** famlies **c.** familyes **d.** familys' — answer: a
3. **a.** girll's **b.** gir'ls **c.** girl's **d.** girrl's — answer: c
4. **a.** bruthers' **b.** bruther'ses **c.** brothers'es **d.** brothers' — answer: d
5. **a.** anut's **b.** ant'se **c.** aunt's **d.** aunt'se — answer: c
6. **a.** boy'se **b.** boy's **c.** bo'ys **d.** boyy's — answer: b
7. **a.** baby's **b.** babey's **c.** babby's **d.** baby'se — answer: a
8. **a.** teechers' **b.** teechers'es **c.** teachers' **d.** teachers's — answer: c
9. **a.** family'se **b.** family's **c.** familie's **d.** familys's — answer: b
10. **a.** dads's **b.** Dads's **c.** Dad'se **d.** Dad's — answer: d
11. **a.** gramas **b.** granma's **c.** grandma's **d.** grandmas's — answer: c
12. **a.** brother's **b.** bruthr **c.** bruther's **d.** bruthr's — answer: a
13. **a.** boys'e **b.** boy'se **c.** boys' **d.** boys'es — answer: c
14. **a.** giles **b.** girls' **c.** girls'es **d.** girls's — answer: b
15. **a.** teacher'se **b.** teachers's **c.** teacher's **d.** teecher's — answer: c
16. **a.** ladies' **b.** landyes **c.** ladies'es **d.** ladyes' — answer: a
17. **a.** babyes **b.** babies' **c.** babbies' **d.** babies's — answer: b
18. **a.** granpa's **b.** grannpa's **c.** grandpas's **d.** grandpa's — answer: d
19. **a.** aunts's **b.** aunts' **c.** aunts'se **d.** aunts'es — answer: b
20. **a.** ladie's **b.** ladys's **c.** lady's **d.** lady'se — answer: c

Practice for Standardized Tests, p. 49

LESSON 34

- ✓ Pretest and Self-Check
- ● Spelling Focus and Word List
- ○ Challenge Words
- ○ Modified List

DAILY SPELLING REVIEW

I can't hear the *door bell up stairs.*

doorbell   *upstairs*

● Core   ○ Optional   ✓ Assessment

INTRODUCTION

Word Structure

Forming Possessives

Explain that students must first decide if a word is possessive by asking themselves if it shows ownership. Next, they must decide which guideline for forming the possessive applies.

MEETING THE NEEDS OF ALL STUDENTS

Modified List

Practice Students studying only the high-frequency words in the top box write

- six singular possessive nouns
- four plural possessive nouns

Bilingual/ESL

Pictures and Labels Have students illustrate and label four sets of possessives from the word list. Pairs used should distinguish between the singular and plural possessive, for example, *the baby's toy,* and *the two babies' beds.*

Additional Practice

Challenge Master 34
Home-School Master 34
Audiotape C, Side 2

1. **Dad's**
2. **friend's**
3. **girl's**
4. **teacher's**
5. **baby's**
6. **family's**
7. **grandma's**
8. **grandpa's**
9. **brother's**
10. **boy's**
11. **aunt's**
12. **lady's**
13. **girls'**
14. **teachers'**
15. **babies'**
16. **families'**
17. **brothers'**
18. **boys'**
19. **aunts'**
20. **ladies'**

CHALLENGE!

someone's
boss's
James's
grandparent's
grandparents'

156

■ INTRODUCTION

Possessives

SPELLING FOCUS

To form possessives of
- singular nouns, add an **apostrophe** and **s: baby's**
- plural nouns that end in **s**, add only an **apostrophe: babies'**

■ STUDY   Say each word. Then read the sentence.

1. *Dad's*   April 25 is **Dad's** birthday.
2. *friend's* ✻   That's my **friend's** book.
3. *girl's*   That **girl's** drawing was good.
4. *girls'*   I can't find the **girls'** bathroom.
5. *teacher's*   I met my **teacher's** mother.
6. *teachers'*   This room is the **teachers'** lounge.
7. *baby's*   Wash the **baby's** bottle.
8. *babies'*   She saw all the **babies'** fathers.
9. *family's*   Look at my **family's** picture.
10. *families'*   We shared our **families'** stories.

11. *grandma's*   I have my **grandma's** ring.
12. *grandpa's*   Show me my **grandpa's** store.
13. *brother's*   He is my older **brother's** friend.
14. *brothers'*   This is my two **brothers'** room.
15. *boy's*   We found that **boy's** bicycle.
16. *boys'*   They are on the **boys'** soccer team.
17. *aunt's*   We're keeping my **aunt's** dog.
18. *aunts'*   These are my **aunts'** cars.
19. *lady's*   He returned the **lady's** purse.
20. *ladies'*   That store sells **ladies'** hats.

■ PRACTICE   Sort the list words by writing
- twelve singular possessive nouns
- eight plural possessive nouns
Order of words in each group may vary.

■ WRITE   Choose four sentences to rewrite as questions.
Questions and answers will vary.

✻ **WATCH OUT FOR FREQUENTLY MISSPELLED WORDS!**

THINK AND PRACTICE ■

SINGULAR POSSESSIVES   Complete each sentence by writing the singular possessive of the underlined word.

1. We found the boy cap under the chair.
2. I enjoyed the girl piano playing very much.
3. I visited my aunt office last Tuesday.
4. I accidentally scratched my brother car.
5. I listened to Dad advice.
6. The children loved their grandma lullabies.
7. She always followed her grandpa directions.
8. I stayed the night at my best friend house.

USING CONTEXT CLUES   Write the list word that is a form of the word in parentheses to complete each sentence.

9. I found a (lady) ring at the bottom of the pool.
10. That makes five (lady) rings I've found this week!
11. My (family) way of spending free time is to go hiking.
12. Other (family) free time activities may differ from ours.
13. My math (teacher) classroom is full of large posters.
14. The other (teacher) classrooms have smaller posters.
15. I put the (baby) little jacket on a hook in the closet.

1.	**boy's**
2.	**girl's**
3.	**aunt's**
4.	**brother's**
5.	**Dad's**
6.	**grandma's**
7.	**grandpa's**
8.	**friend's**
9.	**lady's**
10.	**ladies'**
11.	**family's**
12.	**families'**
13.	**teacher's**
14.	**teachers'**
15.	**baby's**

PLURAL POSSESSIVES   Write the possessive of each word.

16. brothers   **brothers'**
17. boys   **boys'**
18. aunts   **aunts'**
19. babies   **babies'**
20. girls   **girls'**

Take a Hint
Dad's is capitalized only when it is used as a name. *You read Dad's letter, but you borrow your dad's pen.*

STRATEGIC SPELLING

Building New Words

Write the words that complete the chart.

Singular	Singular Possessive	Plural Possessive
21. father	**father's**	**fathers'**
22. monkey	**monkey's**	**monkeys'**

157

DAY 3 Proofreading and Writing

- Proofread an Opinion
- Proofreading Tip: Subject-Verb Agreement
- Write an Opinion
- Cooperative Midweek Test

DAILY SPELLING REVIEW

That *basket ball* player is very well *know.*

basketball   known

● **Core**   ○ **Optional**   ✓ **Assessment**

PROOFREADING AND WRITING

Usage

Subject-Verb Agreement
Have students look at a recent writing sample. To check for subject-verb agreement, they can circle the subject, underline the verb, and draw an arrow between the two.

MEETING THE NEEDS OF ALL STUDENTS

Modified List

Proofreading Students studying high-frequency words complete this page or the proofreading activity on the *Everyday Spelling* CD-ROM.

Extra Support

Writing Opinions Students can check their writing by drawing a single line under their position statement and double lines under their supporting ideas.

Additional Practice

Hardbound Book Master 34A
Second Language Master 34
Writing Mini-Lesson Master 34
Writing Activity Master 34
Proofreading Transparency 34
Everyday Spelling **CD-ROM**

■ PROOFREADING AND WRITING

PROOFREADING TIP
I take, you take, but it takes. Be sure your subject (it) always agrees with your verb (takes).

Make a capital.
Make a small letter
Add something.
Take out somethin
Add a period.
New paragraph

PROOFREAD AN OPINION Find four misspelled words in this opinion. Write them correctly. Fix two places where the subject and verb don't agree.

Opinion Poll: Should Your TV Watching Be Restricted?
☑ Yes   ☐ No

Comments:

Watching *too* much TV is bad for you. It *takes* away from the time you'd be doing important stuff. At my *friend's* house, his family *watches* TV all day! I read, play *baseball*, and help build my *grandpa's* boat instead.

WRITE AN OPINION Do you think that you should restrict the amount of TV you watch? Write the reasons for your opinion. Use list words and personal words.

Responses will vary.

Opinions should include list

words and personal words.

Word List

brother's	lady's
brothers'	ladies'
boy's	family's
boys'	families'
girl's	baby's
girls'	babies'
aunt's	grandma's
aunts'	grandpa's
teacher's	Dad's
teachers'	friend's

Personal Words

1. **Words will**
2. **vary.**

158

VOCABULARY BUILDING

Review

CONTEXT CLUES   Write the list word that completes each *if...then* sentence.

Dad's	teachers'
friend's	baby's
girl's	babies'
girls'	family's
teacher's	families'

1. If a teacher owns a house, then it is the ___ house.
2. If your friend is having a party, then it is your ___ party.
3. If some cars are owned by more than one family, then they are the ___ cars.
4. If a baby has a stuffed animal, then it is the ___ stuffed animal.
5. If some computers are owned by more than one teacher, then they are the ___ computers.
6. If two or more girls have lunches, then they are the ___ lunches.
7. If Dad has his own special chair, then it is ___ chair.
8. If a girl has her own telephone, then it is the ___ telephone.
9. If a family has a vegetable garden, then it is the ___ garden.
10. If several babies have blankets, then they are the ___ blankets.

1. **teacher's**
2. **friend's**
3. **families'**
4. **baby's**
5. **teachers'**
6. **girls'**
7. **Dad's**
8. **girl's**
9. **family's**
10. **babies'**

Word Study

PALINDROMES   Anna, Otto, and Ada have something in common. Their first names are **palindromes**. A palindrome is a word that reads the same backward and forward. To complete the puzzle below, you must write palindromes. You will find the names of the Palindrome Kids hiding in the puzzle.

Across

3. the sound made by a horn or whistle
6. 12 o'clock in the daytime
7. something done; a good ___ should be rewarded
8. a girl's name
9. a young dog

Down

1. a boy's name
2. a short word for *mother*
4. a girl's name
5. the sound made by a young bird

159

159

35

Generalization

Spelling Focus: Some words are easily confused because they have similar pronunciations and spellings.

● Core   ○ Optional   ✓ Assessment

DAILY PLAN	CORE OBJECTIVES	NOTES

DAY 1 Introduction

✓ Pretest and Self-Check, p. 160B
● Spelling Focus and Word List,
   p. 160
○ Challenge Words, p. 160
○ Challenge Master 35
○ Home-School Master 35

✓ ▪ Take and self-check Pretest
▪ Spell easily confused words; classify and write the list words

DAY 2 Think and Practice

● Antonyms; Context Sentences;
   Alpha Puzzles, p. 161
● Strategic Spelling: *Choosing the Best Strategy,* p. 161
○ Think and Practice Master 35
○ Extra Practice Master 35
○ Cross-Curricular Lesson: Introduce,
   p. 220

▪ Complete practice activities for easily confused words
▪ Choose the best spelling strategy to use with given list words

DAY 3 Proofreading and Writing

● Proofread a Sign, p. 162
● Proofreading Tip: Apostrophes,
   p. 162
● Create a Sign, p. 162
✓ Cooperative Midweek Test
○ Writing Mini-Lesson Master 35
○ Writing Activity Master 35
○ Second Language Support
   Master 35

▪ Proofread for spelling errors
▪ Integrate spelling and writing in a personal writing response
✓ ▪ Take and check midweek test

DAY 4 Vocabulary Building

● Review: Words in Context, p. 163
● Word Study: Using Exact Words,
   p. 163
○ Cross-Curricular Lesson: Follow-Up,
   p. 220
○ Review Master 35

▪ Complete review activity for easily confused words
▪ Study and use exact words

DAY 5 Assessment

✓ Posttest, p. 160B
○ Standardized Test Master 35

✓ ▪ Take Posttest

Cross-Curricular Lessons

Use the Spelling Focus (easily confused words) to introduce the Mathematics lesson, *Geometry*, page 220, or choose a lesson that correlates with a topic you're currently teaching.

MEETING THE NEEDS OF ALL STUDENTS

The Word List

For students studying 20 words, assign pages 160–163 and Extra Practice and Review masters.

Modified List For students studying 10 words, modify Practice on page 160, and assign Think and Practice Master 35 and pages 162–163.

Challenge For students studying 26 words, assign pages 160–163, Challenge, Extra Practice, and Review masters.

Bilingual/ESL

The letters **wh** do not appear together in Spanish. Therefore, Spanish-speaking students may need reminders to include both letters when spelling *where, when,* and *whose.*

Personal Words

Students add to Personal Words lists by looking at work in their writing portfolios and words they want to remember from their reading.

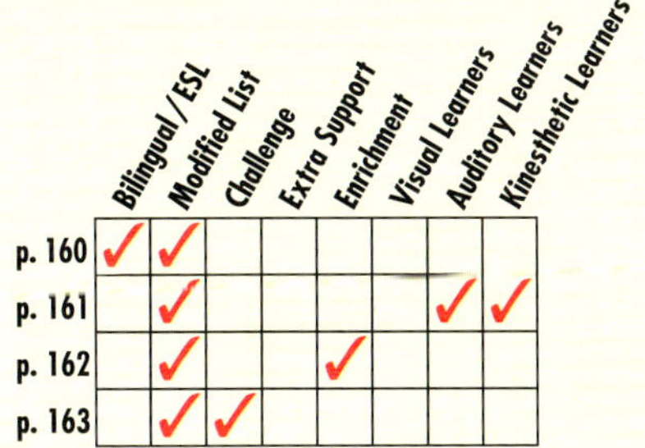

	Bilingual / ESL	Modified List	Challenge	Extra Support	Enrichment	Visual Learners	Auditory Learners	Kinesthetic Learners
p. 160	✓	✓						
p. 161	✓						✓	✓
p. 162	✓			✓				
p. 163	✓	✓						

ASSESSMENT*

Pretest

Read the underlined word, read the sentence, and then repeat the underlined word. Guide students in self-correcting their pretests and correcting any misspellings.

1. <u>Set</u> your books down.
2. I <u>sit</u> at my desk to work.
3. The boys got <u>off</u> the bus.
4. One <u>of</u> the cats ran away.
5. <u>When</u> will the plane land?
6. Did the team <u>win</u> the game?
7. Our flowers <u>are</u> beautiful.
8. The lions <u>are</u> graceful.
9. Sue is taller <u>than</u> you.
10. <u>Then</u> we can go out.
11. Don't <u>lose</u> your lunch money.
12. The snake has gotten <u>loose</u>.
13. The girls <u>were</u> at the park.
14. <u>We're</u> reading the news.
15. <u>Where</u> did you get those?
16. The classroom is very <u>quiet</u>.
17. You have grown <u>quite</u> tall.
18. Mom <u>quit</u> taking the bus.
19. <u>Whose</u> backpack is this?
20. <u>Who's</u> setting the table?

Posttest

Read aloud the sentences below. These sentences may be used for dictation.

1. The babies <u>are</u> crying.
2. What's the title <u>of</u> the book?
3. <u>Our</u> picnic is in April.
4. I got my puppy <u>off</u> the chair.
5. <u>Then</u> the man walked by.
6. July is hotter <u>than</u> May.
7. They will <u>win</u> a game.
8. We can <u>sit</u> on the grass.
9. <u>When</u> is the school fair?
10. <u>Set</u> the flowers on the desk.
11. <u>Who's</u> going to the movie?
12. The animals are <u>quite</u> lively.
13. <u>Whose</u> jacket got lost?
14. We might <u>lose</u> our way.
15. My brother <u>quit</u> his job.
16. <u>We're</u> proud of our invention.
17. The children <u>were</u> hungry.
18. A lion got <u>loose</u> at the zoo.
19. Let's be <u>quiet</u> when we work.
20. <u>Where</u> is everyone going?

Challenge Words

1. This is a <u>recent</u> newspaper.
2. I <u>resent</u> dishonest people.
3. We can <u>pedal</u> fast.
4. The flower has a red <u>petal</u>.
5. Write in your <u>diary</u> daily.
6. This food came from a <u>dairy</u>.

Additional Assessment

Standardized Test Master 35
Dictation Sentences, p. T42
Everyday Spelling CD-ROM

WHAT'S THE BIG IDEA?
The words *were, where,* and *we're* are among the fifty most frequently misspelled words in fourth grade. Their misspellings? One of the other words in the trio, of course! Review how these words differ in meaning and usage.

* See pp. T20 and T33 for test-study-test information.

ADDITIONAL RESOURCES (OPTIONAL PRACTICE)

LESSON 35

DAY 1 CHALLENGE MASTER

CHALLENGE ■ 35

Challenge Words

recent	resent	pedal
petal	diary	dairy

■ Write the Challenge Word for each clue given below.

1. You might do this if someone gets credit for work you did: **resent**

2. You might describe what happened yesterday this way: **recent**

3. You might visit here for a fresh glass of milk: **dairy**

4. You might do this instead of drive: **pedal**

5. You might record your secret thoughts here: **diary**

6. You might see this fall off a flower: **petal**

■ Many people keep all kinds of journals in order to capture their thoughts, ideas, feelings, and observations. Use one or more of the Challenge Words to write an entry for your journal.

Practice Masters, p. 133

DAY 1 HOME-SCHOOL MASTER

■ 35 HOME-SCHOOL ACTIVITIES 35 ■

Word Check 35
1. were
2. we're
3. where
4. quiet
5. quite
6. quit
7. off
8. of
9. our
10. are
11. then
12. than
13. lose
14. loose
15. set
16. sit
17. when
18. win
19. whose
20. who's

■ **Rhymes** Write a list word to rhyme with each word below.

pen
1. **then**

pin
3. **win**

diet
4. **quiet**

kite
5. **quite**

flower
6. **our**

fit
7. **quit**

far
9. **are**

goose
10. **loose**

there
11. **where**

2. **when**

8. **sit**

■ **Which Words Are Which?** Write pairs of confusing words to answer each question below.

Which two pairs of words look like or rhyme with each other?

12. **were**   14. **whose**

13. **we're**   15. **who's**

Which two words have one as part of the other?

16. **off**   17. **of**

Which word is easily confused with *then*?

18. **than**

Which word is like *sit* and tells about placement?

19. **set**

Which word is the opposite of *win*?

20. **lose**

Dear Parent,
Please check to see that your child has done this page correctly. Circle any misspelled words and help your child study them.
Tear off the Word Check before your child returns this page to class. Use it to help your child study.

Home-School Activities, p. 30

DAY 2 THINK AND PRACTICE MASTER

35 ■ THINK AND PRACTICE

set	sit	off	of	when
win	our	are	than	then

■ **Context** Write the list word that completes the sentence.

1. Please **sit** in that chair.

2. That is **our** new car.

3. It is your turn to **set** the table.

4. What happened **then**?

5. There **are** twenty-four hours in a day.

6. Six is greater **than** five.

7. How many **of** the people are going to the picnic?

■ **Alpha Puzzles** Decide what letter of the alphabet comes between each pair of letters. Write the letters to make a list word.

8. r t + d f + s u   **set**
9. v x + h j + m o   **win**
10. n p + e g + e g   **off**
11. r t + h j + s u   **sit**
12. v x + g i + d f + m o   **when**

STRATEGIC SPELLING: Choosing the Best Strategy
Write *set*, *win*, and *than*. Name one strategy that would help you spell all three words. Discuss your choice with a partner. For a list of strategies, see page 142.

13. **set**
14. **win**
15. **than**

Name of Strategy: **Answers will vary.**

Practice Masters, p. 134

DAY 2 EXTRA PRACTICE MASTER

EXTRA PRACTICE ■ 35

Word List

set	sit	off	of	when
win	our	are	than	then
lose	loose	were	we're	where
quiet	quite	quit	whose	who's

■ **Words in Context** Write each pair or group of easily confused list words to complete the sentences below. HINT: Each list word you use rhymes with the underlined word and makes sense in the sentence.

1. He was such a laugh <u>riot</u>, we couldn't be **quiet**.

2. When she lost her <u>mitt</u> she stopped playing and **quit**.

3. I took a <u>bite</u> and it was **quite** good.

4. What's your <u>excuse</u> for why the dog got **loose**.

5. It's no <u>news</u> that the visiting team will **lose**.

6. Please tell me if we **are** going by bus or by <u>car</u>.

7. The <u>power</u> finally came back on **our** street.

8. My <u>pen</u> leaked **when** I tried to write a letter.

9. You'll see my big <u>grin</u> if I **win**.

10. I <u>love</u> this photo **of** Grandma and Grandpa.

11. He started to <u>cough</u> when he took **off** his warm hat.

12. We'll meet you at the <u>fair</u>, but **where**?

13. I asked <u>her</u> if the toys **were** on sale.

14. I hope **we're** good enough to join the team next <u>year</u>.

15. That is the singer **who's** giving the <u>blues</u> concert.

16. Do you know **whose** painting the judges will <u>choose</u>?

17. Don't **sit** on my baseball <u>mitt</u>!

18. Please **set** the book here where I can <u>get</u> it.

19. The <u>men</u> counted three and **then** shouted "Happy New Year!"

20. I am a bigger <u>fan</u> of the team **than** she.

Practice Masters, p. 135

TECHNOLOGY AND VISUAL SUPPORT	 Use Audiotape C, Side 2, Lesson 35	 For additional practice use *Everyday Spelling* Game Software, Lesson 35	 Additional resources on *Everyday Spelling* CD-ROM: proofreading and writing, modified list and challenge words, auditory test
	Use Proofreading and Writing Transparency 35		

DAY 3 SECOND LANGUAGE SUPPORT MASTER

35 ■ SECOND LANGUAGE SUPPORT

Quick Stories

The pictures tell a story. Talk about the story with others. Write the words to complete the sentences.

who's   we're   where

Notice that __(1)__ all wearing T-shirts.

1. __we're__

This is __(2)__ you can get one.

2. __where__

Do you know __(3)__ going to buy this shirt?

3. __who's__

The next story is not finished. Talk about what will happen next. Write the words to complete the sentences. Draw the new part of the story.

whose   were

Hakeem and Kendra __(4)__ walking to the playground.

4. __were__

They saw a little dog. They wondered __(5)__ dog it was.

5. __whose__

Have you ever lost or found something? Tell each other what happened.

Second Language Support, p. 56

DAY 3 WRITING ACTIVITY MASTER

35 ■ WRITING ACTIVITY

Run-on Sentences

☐ Fix a run-on sentence by writing each complete thought as a separate sentence.

☐ Use end punctuation to show the end of a thought.

☐ Begin each new thought with a capital letter.

■ Read each sentence below. If a sentence contains a run-on sentence, correct it. If a sentence is correct, leave it as it is.

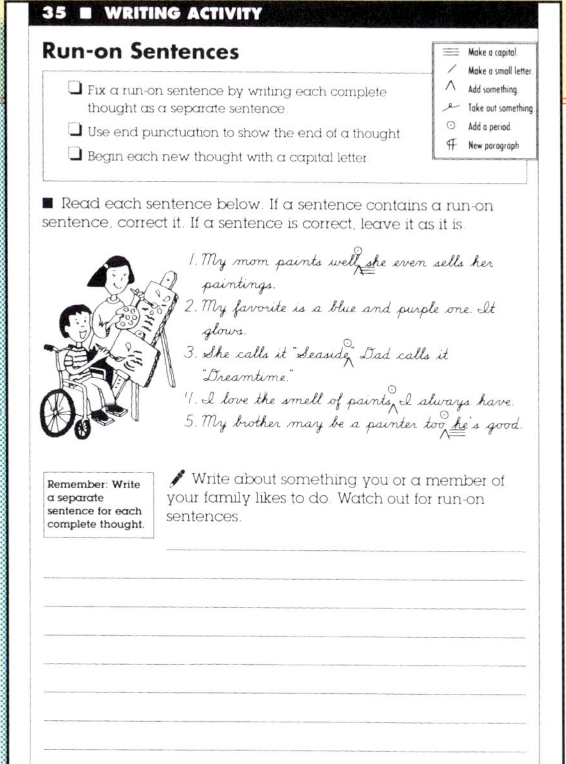

Remember: Write a separate sentence for each complete thought.

Write about something you or a member of your family likes to do. Watch out for run-on sentences.

Spelling and Writing, p. 60

DAY 4 REVIEW MASTER

35 ■ REVIEW

Word List

set	sit	off	of	when
win	our	are	than	then
lose	loose	were	we're	where
quiet	quite	quit	whose	who's

■ **Classifying** Write the list word that belongs in each group below.

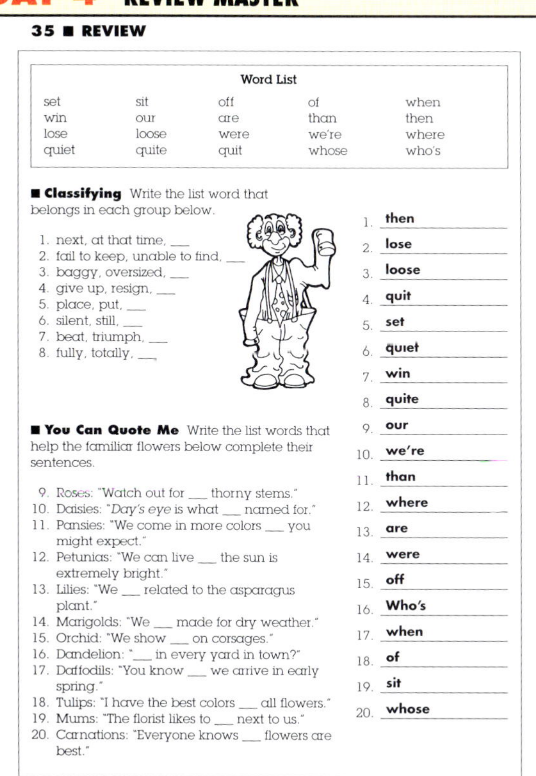

1. next, at that time, ___
2. fail to keep, unable to find, ___
3. baggy, oversized, ___
4. give up, resign, ___
5. place, put, ___
6. silent, still, ___
7. beat, triumph, ___
8. fully, totally, ___

1. __then__
2. __lose__
3. __loose__
4. __quit__
5. __set__
6. __quiet__
7. __win__
8. __quite__
9. __our__
10. __we're__
11. __than__
12. __where__
13. __are__
14. __were__
15. __off__
16. __Who's__
17. __when__
18. __of__
19. __sit__
20. __whose__

■ **You Can Quote Me** Write the list words that help the familiar flowers below complete their sentences.

9. Roses: "Watch out for ___ thorny stems."
10. Daisies: "*Day's eye* is what ___ named for."
11. Pansies: "We come in more colors ___ you might expect."
12. Petunias: "We can live ___ the sun is extremely bright."
13. Lilies: "We ___ related to the asparagus plant."
14. Marigolds: "We ___ made for dry weather."
15. Orchid: "We show ___ on corsages."
16. Dandelion: "___ in every yard in town?"
17. Daffodils: "You know ___ we arrive in early spring."
18. Tulips: "I have the best colors ___ all flowers."
19. Mums: "The florist likes to ___ next to us."
20. Carnations: "Everyone knows ___ flowers are best."

Practice Masters, p. 136

DAY 5 STANDARDIZED TEST MASTER

35 ■ LESSON TEST

■ Find the word in each group that is spelled correctly. Fill in the letter for the correct word on the answer strip.

Sample:
  a. mihgt   c. mighte
  b. myte   d. might   ⓐⓑⓒ●

1. a. sett   c. sete
   b. set   d. sette   1. ⓐ●ⓒⓓ

2. a. than   c. thain
   b. thane   d. thann   2. ●ⓑⓒⓓ

3. a. loos   c. lose
   b. loes   d. lews   3. ⓐⓑ●ⓓ

4. a. qiut   c. kwit
   b. qwit   d. quit   4. ⓐⓑⓒ●

5. a. our   c. owr
   b. ar   d. oure   5. ●ⓑⓒⓓ

6. a. ar   c. are
   b. ur   d. arre   6. ⓐⓑ●ⓓ

7. a. wer   c. wheare
   b. wher   d. where   7. ⓐⓑⓒ●

8. a. win   c. winn
   b. wen   d. wihn   8. ●ⓑⓒⓓ

9. a. whos   c. who's
   b. whos'   d. who'se   9. ⓐⓑ●ⓓ

10. a. queit   c. kwiet
   b. qwiet   d. quiet   10. ⓐⓑⓒ●

11. a. when   c. wene
   b. wen   d. wehn   11. ●ⓑⓒⓓ

12. a. quite   c. quete
   b. queit   d. qwite   12. ●ⓑⓒⓓ

13. a. of   c. av
   b. ov   d. uv   13. ●ⓑⓒⓓ

14. a. seet   c. sitt
   b. sit   d. siht   14. ⓐ●ⓒⓓ

15. a. losse   c. loose
   b. los   d. lews   15. ⓐⓑ●ⓓ

16. a. whos   c. whoze
   b. whoose   d. whose   16. ⓐⓑⓒ●

17. a. then   c. theen
   b. thene   d. thein   17. ●ⓑⓒⓓ

18. a. ovf   c. off
   b. owf   d. awf   18. ⓐⓑ●ⓓ

19. a. we're   c. wer'e
   b. wer   d. weer   19. ●ⓑⓒⓓ

20. a. wer   c. wir
   b. wher   d. were   20. ⓐⓑⓒ●

Practice for Standardized Tests, p. 50

LESSON
35

✓ Pretest and Self-Check
● Spelling Focus and Word List
○ Challenge Words
○ Modified List

DAILY SPELLING REVIEW
I *disslike* people who are not *thougtful.*

dislike   thoughtful

● Core   ○ Optional   ✓ Assessment

INTRODUCTION

Word Meaning
Usage Questions Have students find definitions for these pairs of words: *then/than, lose/loose,* and *set/sit.* Then have them write context sentences for each set of words.

MEETING THE NEEDS OF ALL STUDENTS

Modified List
Practice Students studying only the high-frequency words in the top box write
- the words that they find most confusing
- the rest of the list words

Bilingual/ESL
Listen for Words Have students make a flashcard for each list word. Read each dictation sentence and have students hold up the card with the correct word.

Additional Practice

Challenge Master 35
Home-School Master 35
Audiotape C, Side 2

1. ___________
2. ___________
3. ___________
4. ___________
5. ___________
6. ___________
7. ___________
8. ___________
9. ___________
10. ___________
11. ___________
12. ___________
13. ___________
14. ___________
15. ___________
16. ___________
17. ___________
18. ___________
19. ___________
20. ___________

CHALLENGE!

recent	resent
pedal	petal
diary	dairy

160

■ INTRODUCTION

Easily Confused Words

SPELLING FOCUS

Some words are easily confused because they have similar pronunciations and spellings: **our, are.**

■ **STUDY** Say each word. Then read the sentence.

1. *set* — He **set** the alarm for 6:00.
2. *sit* — May I **sit** on this cushion?
3. *off* ✳ — Please turn **off** the radio.
4. *of* — Half is part **of** a whole.
5. *when* ✳ — Call me **when** you finish.
6. *win* — Not everyone can **win.**
7. *our* ✳ — We love **our** new home.
8. *are* ✳ — They **are** watching television.
9. *than* — Geese are bigger **than** ducks.
10. *then* ✳ — Wash your hair, **then** comb it.

11. *lose* — They didn't **lose** the game.
12. *loose* — My shoelace is coming **loose.**
13. *were* ✳ — I'd stay if I **were** you.
14. *we're* ✳ — She says **we're** not going.
15. *where* ✳ — He doesn't know **where** I live.
16. *quiet* — The woods were dark and **quiet.**
17. *quite* — The cat is not **quite** a year old.
18. *quit* — She **quit** a job that she hated.
19. *whose* — Tell me **whose** voice that was.
20. *who's* — He asked **who's** bringing the food.

■ **PRACTICE** First write the groups of words that are confusing for you. Then write the rest of the words.
Order of words will vary.

■ **WRITE** Choose two sentences to write a rhyme.
Rhymes will vary.

✳ **WATCH OUT FOR FREQUENTLY MISSPELLED WORDS!**

- Practice: Antonyms, Context Sentences, and Alpha Puzzles
- Strategic Spelling:
  Choosing the Best Strategy
- Cross-Curricular Lesson: Introduce
- Modified List

DAILY SPELLING REVIEW

I have a *class mate* who is very *independant.*

classmate   independent

THINK AND PRACTICE

ANTONYMS   Write the list word that means the opposite of the underlined word to complete each phrase.

1. not <u>tight</u>, but ____
2. not <u>noisy</u>, but ____
3. not <u>on</u>, but ____
4. not <u>begin</u>, but ____
5. not <u>stand</u>, but ____
6. not <u>find</u>, but ____

CONTEXT SENTENCES   Write the list word that completes each sentence.

7. Yes, ___ all going camping tomorrow.
8. I'm not sure just ___ we will return.
9. No, I haven't ___ finished packing.
10. I can't remember ___ the camp is located.
11. No, I don't know ___ tent we'll use.
12. No, I'm not sure ___ going to drive.
13. Yes, ___ trip should be full of surprises.

ALPHA PUZZLES   Decide what letter of the alphabet comes between each pair of letters below. Write the letters to make a list word.

14. **n p + e g =**
15. **z b + q s + d f =**
16. **v x + d f + q s + d f =**
17. **s u + g i + d f + m o =**

1.	**loose**
2.	**quiet**
3.	**off**
4.	**quit**
5.	**sit**
6.	**lose**
7.	**we're**
8.	**when**
9.	**quite**
10.	**where**
11.	**whose**
12.	**who's**
13.	**our**
14.	**of**
15.	**are**
16.	**were**
17.	**then**

Write *set, win,* and *than.* Name one strategy that would help you spell all three words. Discuss your choice with a partner. For a list of strategies, see page 142.

18. **set**

19. **win**   Name of Strategy:

20. **than**   **Answer will vary.**

THINK AND PRACTICE

Antonyms

Try It Out Have students come up with opposites for the underlined words and then look through the list words for similar words.

MEETING THE NEEDS OF ALL STUDENTS

Modified List

Review Students studying high-frequency words complete Think and Practice Master 35.

Kinesthetic Learners

Antonym Action Each set of antonyms can be acted out. Kinesthetic learners may find this helpful.

Auditory Learners

Say It Aloud Auditory learners may benefit from reading the Context Sentences aloud, trying different list words In Alpha Puzzles, allow them to read the letters aloud.

Additional Practice

Think and Practice Master 35
Extra Practice Master 35
Everyday Spelling **CD-ROM**
Everyday Spelling **Game Software**

DAY 3 Proofreading and Writing

- Proofread a Sign
- Proofreading Tip: Apostrophes
- Create a Sign
- ✓ Cooperative Midweek Test

DAILY SPELLING REVIEW

The mountain was *realy beatiful.*

really   *beautiful*

● **Core** ○ **Optional** ✓ **Assessment**

PROOFREADING AND WRITING

Spelling
Apostrophe or Not?
Remind students to check possessives by verifying ownership. Suggest that they read their writing aloud without the possessive to see if apostrophes are really needed.

MEETING THE NEEDS OF ALL STUDENTS

Modified List
Proofreading Students studying high-frequency words complete this page or the proofreading activity on the *Everyday Spelling* CD-ROM.

Enrichment
Cooperative Writing
Have students share their signs in small groups. They may also bring in sample food advertisements. Allow students to revise their signs to include new ideas.

Additional Practice

Second Language Master 35
Writing Mini-Lesson Master 35
Writing Activity Master 35
Proofreading Transparency 35
***Everyday Spelling* CD-ROM**

■ **PROOFREADING AND WRITING**

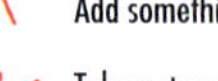
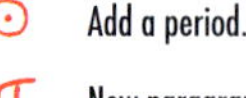

PROOFREAD A SIGN The sign in the photograph below contains a misspelled word. Can you find it? Write the word correctly.

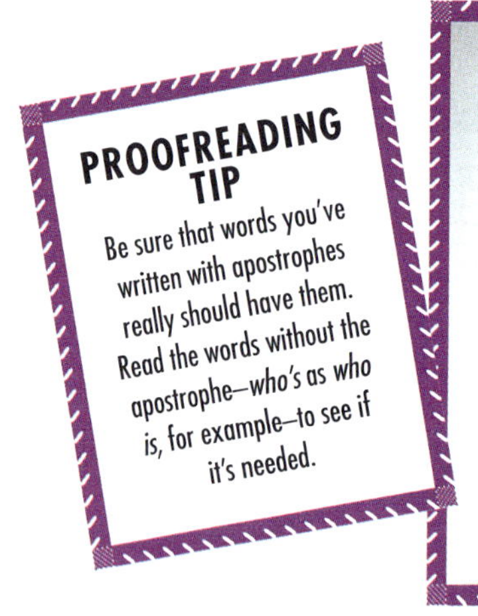

whose

CREATE A SIGN Do you have a favorite snack you'd like to tell everyone about? Draw a picture and use a word or two from the word list. Be sure to proofread your writing.

Signs will vary but should include a list word.

Word List

were	then
we're	than
where	lose
quiet	loose
quite	set
quit	sit
off	when
of	win
our	whose
are	who's

Personal Words

1. **Words will**
2. **vary.**

162

VOCABULARY BUILDING

 Review

WORDS IN CONTEXT   Write the boxed words that complete the following note.

Dear Robert and Carrie,
   I will be a little late getting home this evening. In case you (1) hungry, I (2) a bowl of fruit on the kitchen table. I plan to be home about 6:30, and (3) we will have (4) dinner. Remember, do not (5) in front of the television while you are doing your homework. The TV must be turned (6) until you have finished your work.
   Carrie, did your team (7) the relay race today? You said your team had faster runners (8) the other team. Robert, did you do all right on that math test? I am anxious to see both (9) you (10) I get home.

Love,
Mom

P.S. Don't forget to feed Scuffy.

set	win
sit	our
off	are
of	than
when	then

1. **are**
2. **set**
3. **then**
4. **our**
5. **sit**
6. **off**
7. **win**
8. **than**
9. **of**
10. **when**

Word *Study*

USING EXACT WORDS   *Win* is a perfectly good word to use when describing a victory. But think how boring sportscasts would be if scores from baseball games were read using only *win* or *lose*.

Cozy Cafe had a 10–9 win against Dee's Diner.

Harold's Hardware lost 3–5 to Main St. Lumber.

When sportscasters use words that are more exact and descriptive, we get a better (and more interesting) picture.

Cozy Cafe slapped Dee's Diner with a 10–9 check that was the upset of the season.

Main St. Lumber hammered away at Harold's Hardware to gain a 5–3 victory.

Use your own words to complete the sportscast below.

1. The Hawks' superior pitching _______________ the Pigeons in the first five innings.
2. The Pigeons _______________, but couldn't get a hit.
3. The Pigeons were _______________ by the Hawks 6–0.

Words will vary.

VOCABULARY BUILDING

Literature Connection

Use Precise Language

Encourage students to read more about using exact words in *Sparkle and Spin: A Book About Words* by Ann & Paul Rand (Harry N. Abrams, 1991).

MEETING THE NEEDS OF ALL STUDENTS

Modified List

Review Students studying high-frequency words complete this page.

Challenge

Writing Descriptions

Encourage students to write a paragraph describing a character in a favorite book or the plot of a favorite movie. Then have them go back over their writing to improve their descriptions.

Additional Practice

Review Master 35
Standardized Test Master 35
Everyday Spelling **CD-ROM**

WEEK-AT-A-GLANCE

LESSON

36

Unit Review Concepts
Vowels with No Sound Clues
Vowels in Final Syllables
Capitalization and Abbreviation
Possessives
Easily Confused Words

● Core   ○ Optional   ✓ Assessment

DAILY PLAN	CORE OBJECTIVES	NOTES

DAILY PLAN

DAY 1
Review Activity:
●   Weekly Calendar, p. 164
✓ Self-Assessment:
  How Am I Doing?, p. 164
Integrating Spelling:
○   Art, p. 164
○ Review Master 36A

CORE OBJECTIVES
- Use review words to complete a calendar
✓ Assess their own progress in the spelling of words in Unit 6

DAY 2
Review Activities:
●   Offbeat Greetings, p. 165
●   Being Catered To, p. 165
Integrating Spelling:
○   Art, p. 165
○   Language Arts, p. 165

CORE OBJECTIVES
- Use review words to complete greeting cards
- Use review words to complete an advertising brochure

DAY 3
Review Activities:
●   Happy Holidays, p. 166
●   Moving Out, p. 166
Integrating Spelling:
○   Mathematics, p. 166
○   Language Arts, p. 166
○ Review Master 36B

CORE OBJECTIVES
- Use review words to complete sentences about holidays
- Use review words to complete labels

DAY 4
Review Activities:
●   Where the Buffalo Roam, p. 167
●   Election Time, p. 167
Integrating Spelling:
○   Science, p. 167
○   Social Studies, p. 167
○ Standardized Test Masters 36A–36D

CORE OBJECTIVES
- Use review words to complete a paragraph
- Use review words to complete campaign slogans

DAY 5
✓ Unit Review Test
✓ Writing Test
○ Writing Prompt Transparency 6
○ Writing Model Transparencies
  6A, 6B

CORE OBJECTIVES
✓ Assess review words
✓ Assess persuasive writing

MEETING THE NEEDS OF ALL STUDENTS

Modified List

For students studying only the high-frequency words in each lesson, assign Review Masters 36A–36B for unit review. Use the Modified Dictation Sentences for assessment.

Bilingual/ESL

Students for whom English is a developing language might benefit from choosing those review words they think will be most difficult for them and practicing the words.

Spelling Conferences

Conduct individual spelling conferences to discuss each student's spelling progress during Unit 6. You might want to take this opportunity to remind students to add words to their personal dictionaries.

ASSESSMENT

Dictation Sentences

1. The baby's tooth is loose.
2. Yesterday my stomach hurt, so I stayed home.
3. There were many people at the football game.
4. Dad's favorite shirt is bright red and blue.
5. Our family took a trip to Canada.
6. Did the baseball team win or lose last night?
7. We saw a giant dragon during Chinese New Year.
8. Dr. March set my broken leg.
9. There is an angel on the top of the Christmas tree.
10. Our relatives visit during Hanukkah.
11. Are there any buffalo left in America?
12. On Valentine's Day he gave Ms. Brook some flowers.
13. The iron isn't quite hot enough to use.
14. We will welcome another new girl to our class.
15. Is your birthday in August or November?
16. We're probably going to visit Grandma on Saturday.
17. What is the model number of that stereo?
18. Why did he quit the boys' basketball team?
19. Push that button to restart the machine.
20. Animals are common in this forest.
21. The turkey in the oven will be ready in a moment.
22. Will we go to the movie on Sun. or Wed.?
23. First Ave. is an especially busy street.
24. I am sadder than he is about the sign on Farm Rd.
25. I will support your idea.

Writing Test

Writing Prompt Transparency 6 and Writing Model Transparencies 6A and 6B will help students prepare for holistic writing tests. Helpful information relating to persuasive writing tests is provided in the Writer's Handbook on page 240.

Everyday Spelling CD-ROM

An auditory test is available as an alternate testing format.

Modified Dictation Sentences

1. We usually play baseball on Memorial Day.
2. Our teacher's coat is red.
3. I made a giant model of an airplane.
4. We will probably win.
5. Where can I set the other dishes?
6. I suppose Dr. Brown has left.
7. Two babies' bottles are broken.
8. I like June better than September.
9. Last Sun. the trees were a beautiful color.
10. Those girls' drawings are very simple.
11. The men asked for their families' support.
12. Turn off May Rd. to get to my friend's house.

LESSON 36

DAY 1 REVIEW MASTER A

REVIEW ■ 36A

Lesson 31

| suppose | usually | probably | support | giant |

■ **Synonyms** Write the list word that means the same as each word.

1. assume — **suppose**
2. huge — **giant**
3. commonly — **usually**
4. likely — **probably**
5. help — **support**

Lesson 32

| other | color | model | simple | broken |

■ **Riddles** Write the list word that answers each riddle.

1. I end with **le** and mean "easy." — **simple**
2. I end in **or** and name words such as *red* and *blue*. — **color**
3. I end in **el** and am something you build. — **model**
4. I end in **en** and mean "in pieces." — **broken**
5. I end in **er** and mean "additional." — **other**

Lesson 33

| Memorial Day | Sun. | June | Dr. | Rd. |

■ **Capitals and Abbreviations** Write each word or abbreviation correctly.

1. abbreviation for *doctor* — **Dr.**
2. memorial day — **Memorial Day**
3. june — **June**
4. abbreviation for *road* — **Rd.**
5. abbreviation for *Sunday* — **Sun.**

Practice Masters, p. 137

DAY 3 REVIEW MASTER B

36B ■ REVIEW

Lesson 34

| girls' | families' | babies' | teacher's | friend's |

■ **Word Forms** Complete the chart with list words.

Singular Possessive	Plural Possessive
1. **teacher's**	teachers
2. girl's	**girls'**
3. baby's	**babies'**
4. family's	**families'**
5. **friend's**	friends'

Lesson 35

| win | off | our | than | set |

■ **Analogies** Write a list word that completes each sentence.

1. Defeat is to victory as lose is to **win**.
2. I is to eye as hour is to **our**.
3. Picture is to draw as table is to **set**.
4. Up is to down as on is to **off**.
5. Hem is to ham as then is to **than**.

Practice Masters, p. 138

DAY 4 STANDARDIZED TEST MASTER A

REVIEW TEST ■ 36A

■ Find the word that is spelled correctly to complete each group of words. Fill in the letter for the correct word on the answer strip.

Sample:
been home ______   ⓐⓑ●ⓓ
a. latly   **b.** lateley   **c.** lately   **d.** latley

1. ______ will stay home   1. ●ⓑⓒⓓ
a. probably   **b.** propoly   **c.** propibly   **d.** probbly

2. Stone ______ at two o'clock   2. ⓐ●ⓒⓓ
a. rd.   **b.** Rd.   **c.** rd   **d.** Rod

3. not to ______ before finishing   3. ⓐⓑ●ⓓ
a. quite   **b.** qiut   **c.** quit   **d.** queit

4. they ______ on time   4. ●ⓑⓒⓓ
a. were   **b.** wer   **c.** where   **d.** wear

5. four ______ houses   5. ⓐⓑⓒ●
a. boys   **b.** boy's   **c.** boi'es   **d.** boys'

6. ______ his homework   6. ⓐ●ⓒⓓ
a. loos   **b.** lose   **c.** loes   **d.** loose

7. a useful ______   7. ⓐⓑ●ⓓ
a. michine   **b.** mosheen   **c.** machine   **d.** mashine

8. still planning ______ vacation   8. ⓐⓑⓒ●
a. ar   **b.** owr   **c.** are   **d.** our

9. first snow in ______   9. ⓐ●ⓒⓓ
a. Novemder   **b.** November   **c.** Novenber   **d.** november

10. a pot ______ gold   10. ⓐⓑ●ⓓ
a. fo   **b.** ov   **c.** of   **d.** off

11. come this ______ to a party   11. ●ⓑⓒⓓ
a. Sun.   **b.** S.   **c.** sun.   **d.** sun

12. said it to ______ them   12. ⓐⓑⓒ●
a. well come   **b.** wallcome   **c.** wellcome   **d.** welcome

Practice for Standardized Tests, p. 51

DAY 4 STANDARDIZED TEST MASTER B

36B ■ REVIEW TEST

■ Find the word that is spelled correctly to complete each group of words. Fill in the letter for the correct word on the answer strip.

13. a hard plate made of ______   13. ⓐⓑⓒ●
a. irn   **b.** iorn   **c.** iern   **d.** iron

14. a ______ question   14. ⓐ●ⓒⓓ
a. comen   **b.** common   **c.** coman   **d.** comon

15. classroom of ______ Collins   15. ●ⓑⓒⓓ
a. Ms.   **b.** mis   **c.** ms.   **d.** Ms

16. what ______ you doing   16. ⓐⓑⓒ●
a. or   **b.** our   **c.** ar   **d.** are

17. that team will ______   17. ⓐⓑ●ⓓ
a. wen   **b.** when   **c.** win   **d.** wine

18. older ______ this puppy   18. ⓐ●ⓒⓓ
a. thin   **b.** than   **c.** that   **d.** then

19. an ______ with bright wings   19. ⓐⓑⓒ●
a. angal   **b.** angle   **c.** anjel   **d.** angel

20. went for ______ apple   20. ●ⓑⓒⓓ
a. another   **b.** a nother   **c.** a nuther   **d.** a nuther

21. said to come on ______   21. ⓐⓑ●ⓓ
a. wed   **b.** wed.   **c.** Wed.   **d.** Wead.

22. a ______ from my shirt   22. ⓐⓑ●ⓓ
a. butten   **b.** butin   **c.** button   **d.** botton

23. the ______ first tooth   23. ⓐ●ⓒⓓ
a. babies   **b.** baby's   **c.** babie's   **d.** babys

24. so many ______   24. ●ⓑⓒⓓ
a. people   **b.** peaple   **c.** peple   **d.** peopl

Practice for Standardized Tests, p. 52

<table>
<tr><td>TECHNOLOGY</td><td>Additional test on
Everyday Spelling CD-ROM</td></tr>
</table>

DAY 4   STANDARDIZED TEST MASTER C

REVIEW TEST ■ 36C

■ Find the word that is spelled correctly to complete each sentence. Fill in the letter for the correct word on the answer strip.

25. He is so tall he looks like a _______!
    a. gnat   **b.** giant   **c.** gaint   **d.** gaient   25. (a) ● (c) (d)

26. I have to see _______ Wilson about my teeth.
    a. Dr   **b.** dr.   **c.** Doctor.   **d.** Dr.   26. (a) (b) (c) ●

27. She is my _______ aunt.
    a. favorit   **b.** favrit   **c.** favorite   **d.** favrit   27. (a) (b) ● (d)

28. Last _______ was unusually cool.
    a. Aguist   **b.** August   **c.** augist   **d.** august   28. (a) ● (c) (d)

29. She was not _______ sure what to do.
    a. quiet   **b.** quit   **c.** queit   **d.** quite   29. (a) (b) (c) ●

30. That car is the latest _______.
    a. model   **b.** madel   **c.** modle   **d.** modal   30. ● (b) (c) (d)

31. The invitation said "on Fifth _______ in a red house."
    a. Av.   **b.** ave.   **c.** Ave.   **d.** Avenu   31. (a) (b) ● (d)

32. Chris says that this is _______ hammer.
    a. Dads   **b.** Dad's   **c.** Dades   **d.** dad's   32. (a) ● (c) (d)

33. There is a bolt _______ on the bike.
    a. lose   **b.** los   **c.** luse   **d.** loose   33. (a) (b) (c) ●

34. I said _______ taking it with us!
    a. we're   **b.** where   **c.** were   **d.** wear   34. ● (b) (c) (d)

35. That is a wonderful _______ game!
    a. Hanakah   **b.** Hanukkah   **c.** hanukah   **d.** Hannukkah   35. (a) ● (c) (d)

36. Mom told me to _______ the table for dinner.
    a. set   **b.** site   **c.** sat   **d.** sait   36. ● (b) (c) (d)

Practice for Standardized Tests, p. 53

DAY 4   STANDARDIZED TEST MASTER D

36D ■ REVIEW TEST

■ Find the word in each group that is spelled correctly. Fill in the letter for the correct word on the answer strip.

37. **a.** yesturday   **c.** yesterday   37. (a) (b) ● (d)
    b. yester day   **d.** yestrday

38. **a.** Chinese new year   **c.** Chines new year   38. (a) (b) (c) ●
    b. Chinees New Year   **d.** Chinese New Year

39. **a.** expecially   **c.** exspecially   39. (a) ● (c) (d)
    b. especially   **d.** especialy

40. **a.** number   **c.** nomber   40. ● (b) (c) (d)
    b. nuber   **d.** numbur

41. **a.** anamals   **c.** animls   41. (a) (b) (c) ●
    b. anamils   **d.** animals

42. **a.** momment   **c.** moment   42. (a) (b) ● (d)
    b. momant   **d.** momat

43. **a.** oven   **c.** avin   43. ● (b) (c) (d)
    b. ovin   **d.** ovcin

44. **a.** realitives   **c.** reletives   44. (a) (b) (c) ●
    b. relitives   **d.** relatives

45. **a.** stomache   **c.** stomach   45. (a) (b) ● (d)
    b. stomack   **d.** stomik

46. **a.** buffalo   **c.** bufelo   46. ● (b) (c) (d)
    b. buffulo   **d.** bufflo

47. **a.** soport   **c.** suporte   47. (a) ● (c) (d)
    b. support   **d.** suport

48. **a.** Canada   **c.** canad   48. ● (b) (c) (d)
    b. Canda   **d.** canada

49. **a.** Valentines day   **c.** Valentine's Day   49. (a) (b) ● (d)
    b. Valentine's day   **d.** Valintines Day

50. **a.** brokin   **c.** brokn   50. (a) (b) (c) ●
    b. brocken   **d.** broken

Practice for Standardized Tests, p. 54

DAY 5   WRITING PROMPT TRANSPARENCY

Spelling and Writing, Transparency 6

LESSON 36

SELF-ASSESSMENT

How Am I Doing?

Talk with students about why it is helpful to think about their progress in spelling. Raise issues such as

1. The most unusual word I've learned to spell is ___.
2. I learn to spell hard words by ___.
3. When I encounter a hard spelling word, I ___.
4. I try to use spelling words in my writing.
5. Something new I learned about spelling is ___.

INTEGRATING SPELLING

Art

Calendar Ask students to create a calendar for the upcoming month. They can note birthdays, holidays, school events, and other activities. Encourage students to illustrate their calendars.

Additional Resources

Review Master 36A

Review

Lesson 31: Vowels with No Sound Clues
Lesson 32: Vowels in Final Syllables
Lesson 33: Capitalization and Abbreviation
Lesson 34: Possessives
Lesson 35: Easily Confused Words

REVIEW WORD LIST

1. animals	14. support	27. Chinese New Year	39. are
2. August	15. welcome	28. Dr.	40. loose
3. buffalo	16. yesterday	29. Hanukkah	41. lose
4. Canada	17. angel	30. Ms.	42. of
5. especially	18. another	31. November	43. our
6. favorite	19. broken	32. Rd.	44. quit
7. giant	20. button	33. Sun.	45. quite
8. iron	21. common	34. Valentine's Day	46. set
9. machine	22. model	35. Wed.	47. than
10. moment	23. number	36. baby's	48. were
11. probably	24. oven	37. boys'	49. we're
12. relatives	25. people	38. Dad's	50. win
13. stomach	26. Ave.		

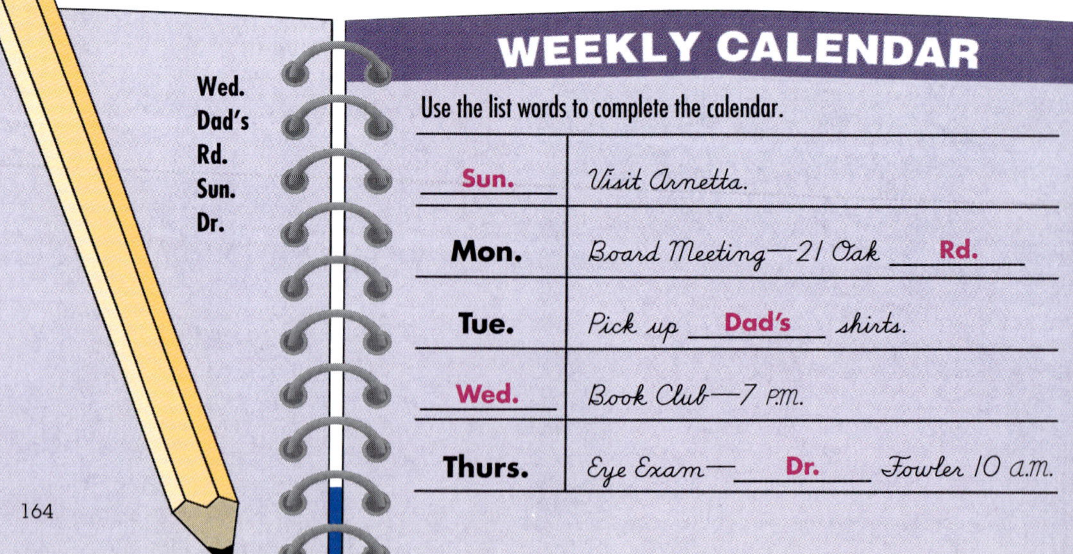

164

Offbeat Greetings

These days, greeting cards say more than just "Happy Birthday" and "Get Well." Supply the missing words in each card below.

baby's   August   probably
iron   Ave.   yesterday
loose   of

Congratulations!
It's your (1) first tooth! Let's hope it stays in there and doesn't get (2) !

HAPPY BIRTHDAY
(in advance)
I know it's July and you were born in (3), but I like to keep ahead (4) things!

Welcome to the Neighborhood!
You have (5) heard the rumors about Maple (6). Well, most of them are true!

DEAR FRIEND,
I'm sorry I didn't call you (7). I had to (8) my best shirt and that takes time. Maybe tomorrow... after I wash my hair.

1. __baby's__
2. __loose__
3. __August__
4. __of__
5. __probably__
6. __Ave.__
7. __yesterday__
8. __iron__

BEING CATERED TO

Jake and Clare make healthy desserts for people giving parties. Supply the list words missing from their advertising brochure.

- Ja'Clare offers your (1) the healthiest and tastiest dessert it's ever had.
- Our treats come direct from our (2) to you!
- Choose from tarts, pies, custards, mousses, and any (3) of your (4) cakes.
- We work seven days a week and (5) always available for consultations.
- You'll find that (6) desserts are (7) the thing for parties, (8) the masterpiece we call Strawberry Rapture.

favorite
number
we're
especially
stomach
oven
our
quite

1. __stomach__
2. __oven__
3. __number__
4. __favorite__
5. __we're__
6. __our__
7. __quite__
8. __especially__

Art

Greeting Cards Ask students to think of an event they would like to celebrate and to make a greeting card for that event. Display the cards on a bulletin board.

Language Arts

Recipe Ask students to think of a favorite dish and to write the steps for making the dish. Students from different ethnic backgrounds might offer dishes unique to their heritage.

LESSON 36

INTEGRATING SPELLING

Mathematics

Graph Students can work in groups to conduct a poll of people's favorite holidays. Each group can decide on the kind of graph they will use to record the results. This kind of activity is helpful for visual learners.

Language Arts

Labels Take students on a tour of their school. Ask them to list things they see that are labeled. Discuss with students why the labels are used.

Additional Resources
Review Master 36B

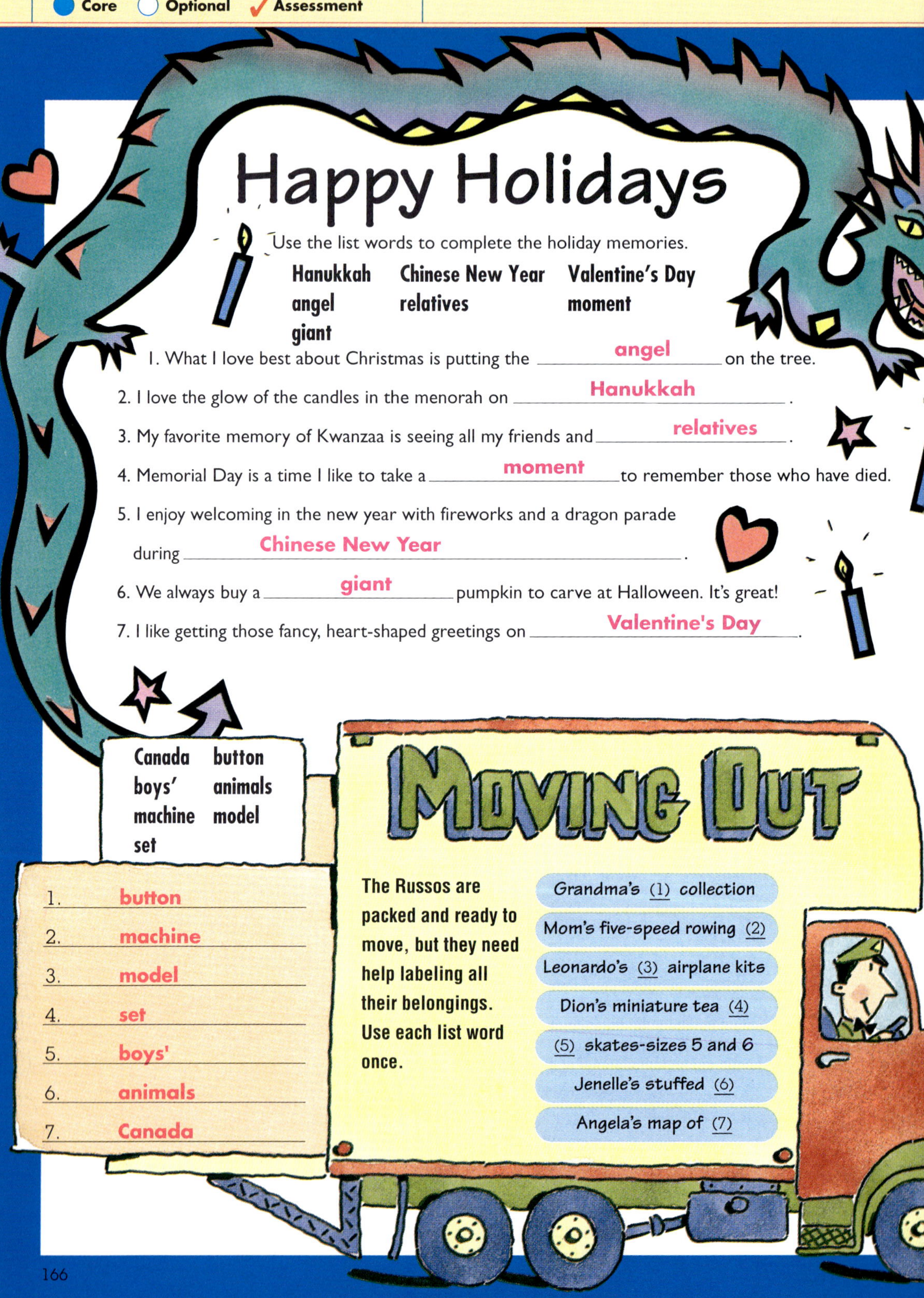

Where the Buffalo Roam

Read the information below and supply the missing list words.

lose	buffalo	are	than
quit	were	common	

The American bison, also called the (1) , once roamed over most of North America. In the 1700s there (2) thirty to sixty million buffalo in North America. A single herd might be twenty miles wide and more (3) fifty miles long. By the 1800s the slaughter of buffalo by the thousands was a (4) occurrence. It looked as though we might (5) the buffalo forever. By 1900 there were only 20 wild bison left in the United States. Laws were passed to ensure that people would (6) hunting them, and there (7) now parks and preserves that protect the buffalo.

1. buffalo
2. were
3. than
4. common
5. lose
6. quit
7. are

Election Time

Lynn Page is running for student council treasurer. Help her finish her campaign slogans.

1. win
2. support
3. people
4. November
5. Ms.
6. broken
7. welcome
8. another

INTEGRATING SPELLING

Science

Research Have small groups of students find out about animals that are in danger of becoming extinct. Ask each group to write a short report about one of the animals and what is being done to save it.

Social Studies

Council Jobs Ask students to choose a student council position, such as president, treasurer, or secretary, and write what they think a person in that position does.

Additional Resources

Standardized Test Masters 36A–36D
Writing Prompt Transparency 6
Writing Model Transparencies 6A, 6B
Everyday Spelling **CD-ROM**

CROSS-CURRICULAR
CONTENTS

Use this contents as a checklist to keep track
of which lessons you've assigned.

INTEGRATING SPELLING:
WORDS ACROSS THE CURRICULUM

Why should cross-curricular lessons be included in a spelling program?

The basic word lists in *Everyday Spelling* are based on research into the words children most frequently use and misspell at each grade level. But while students are learning spelling words, they're also meeting subject-specific vocabulary in all areas of the curriculum. Including cross-curricular lessons reinforces and develops the meanings of key words and concepts in these curriculum areas. It's an added dimension that promotes learning.

How were topics for lessons chosen?

To find topics that truly matched what teachers were teaching, textbooks in all relevant subject areas were studied before lesson topics were finalized. The lessons cover all the major subject areas—social studies, science, mathematics, reading, and health. Within these areas, the lessons expand and integrate curriculum areas with ready-to-use materials. These lessons can be effective adjuncts to daily subject-area teaching.

Why have separate cross-curricular lessons?

In *Everyday Spelling,* cross-curricular lessons are organized so that you can easily correlate them with your teaching plan—in other words, choose lessons that match topics you're teaching *today*. Each lesson promotes vocabulary development through context, through illustrations, and through other visual techniques that clarify word meanings and key concepts.

How can teachers and students benefit from these lessons?

Cross-curricular lessons help students see the "connections" among all subject areas and so expand their view of learning. For teachers, the benefits focus on flexibility and choices. In other words, these separate lessons give you options. Here are some of them:

- The weekly plan for each spelling lesson offers two choices: Use the suggested cross-curricular lesson, or choose one that correlates with a topic you're currently teaching. Remember, these lessons can be used in any order you prefer.
- Because the lessons are self-directed, students can work independently. They can do the lessons alone or with a partner.
- You may decide to have some students master these vocabulary words. It's up to you. You know each student's capabilities.
- You can use the cross-curricular lessons and their brief lesson plans (found on the following pages) as resource and enrichment segments when you teach your regular content lessons.

Why is *Everyday Spelling* the only program that offers separate cross-curricular lessons?

Scott Foresman - Addison Wesley is one publisher that recognizes teachers' superiority in knowing what works in a classroom. *You* know the advantage for students of integrating spelling into the curriculum. *You* know the value of having students make subject-area vocabulary words their own so they can use them in their writing. And *you* know what a pleasure teaching can be when you have materials that give you the flexibility and the choices you need in your classroom. No wonder you've chosen *Everyday Spelling!*

LESSON PLAN

● Building Background
● Developing Concepts
● Practice on pp. 170–171
○ Follow-Up

● **Core**   ○ **Optional**

Link to Weekly Lesson

Before presenting this lesson, you may wish to teach Lesson 15, **Adding -s and -es,** to introduce the spelling patterns that appear in *parallels, degrees, hemispheres, meridians,* and *coordinates.*

BUILDING BACKGROUND

Ask volunteers to tell what they know about finding locations on the earth. Use appropriate words from students' suggestions to build a simple word web like the one shown below. Then display a globe or a world map that has parallels and meridians. Point out the Equator—a parallel, or line of latitude—and the Prime Meridian, a line of longitude going from pole to pole. Explain that latitude and longitude are used to describe the location of all places on Earth.

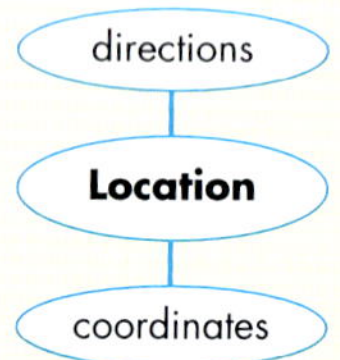

DEVELOPING CONCEPTS

Ask volunteers to help define the remaining list words, using the world map or globe to illustrate them as appropriate. Then allow students to help you expand the word web by adding list words that describe how to use coordinates to locate places on the earth.

Additional Practice
Everyday Spelling CD-ROM, Lesson 15

---

location
latitude
parallels
equator
degrees
hemispheres
longitude
meridians
prime meridian
coordinates

Answers will vary.

1. **latitude**
2. **parallels**
3. **equator**
4. **hemispheres**
5. **longitude**
6. **meridians**
7. **prime meridian**
8. **degrees**
9. **coordinates**
10. **location**

Global Grid

Can you find Ecuador on a map? What about Egypt or Finland? Understanding the words in the list can help you find places in the world. Add your own words to the list. Use your Spelling Dictionary if you need help.

■ GETTING AT MEANING

Locating Places   Look at globes A and B on the next page. Use them to help you complete the sentences.

hemispheres   latitude   equator   parallels

The imaginary east-west lines on a map or globe are used to show (1). They are called (2). The (3) is at 0° latitude. It divides the Earth into two halves, or (4)—the Northern and Southern Hemispheres.

degrees   longitude   meridians   location
prime meridian   coordinates

The imaginary north-south lines that go from pole to pole on a map or globe are used to show (5). They are called (6). The (7) is at 0° longitude. Both latitude and longitude are measured in (8). On a globe showing both parallels and meridians, the intersecting lines 20°S, 20°E that go through Africa are called (9). You can find any (10) on a map or globe when you know its coordinates.

170

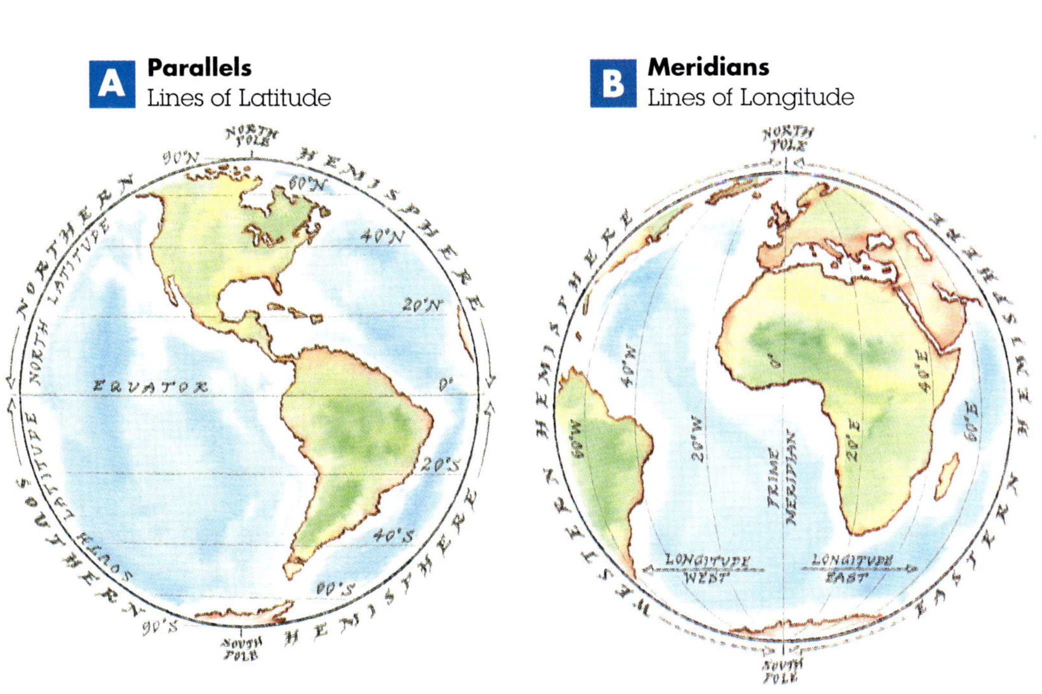

■ SPELL WELL

Double Letters   Sometimes double letters can cause spelling problems. Write the words in the list that have double letters. Underline the double letters.

11. parallels

12. degrees

13. coordinates

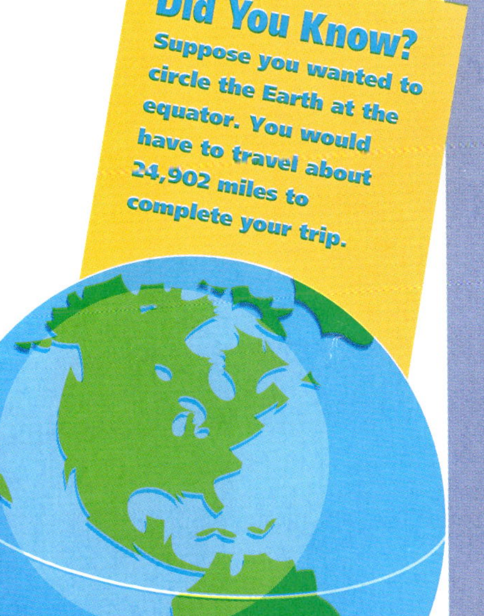

FOLLOW-UP

Critical Thinking

Applying Have students apply what they have learned about finding locations with a grid. Have them use a map of the United States to find the latitude and longitude of the following locations:

- Washington, D.C.
- the capital of their state
- their local community

MEETING THE NEEDS OF ALL STUDENTS

Visual Learners

Using a Map Have students use a map of the world or a globe to find the 40°N parallel. Encourage them to give the names of some of the locations that it passes through or near (Philadelphia, Denver, Beijing, Madrid). Have them do the same with the 20°E meridian (Warsaw, Belgrade, Cape Town).

Bilingual/ESL

Visualizing the Words Students can draw two globes similar to the illustrations. Suggest that they use list words to label the various parts of their drawings.

171

LESSON PLAN

- Building Background
- Developing Concepts
- Practice on pp. 172–173
- Follow-Up

● Core ○ Optional

Link to Weekly Lesson

Before presenting this lesson, you may wish to teach Lesson 3, **Consonant Sounds /k/ and /f/,** to introduce the spelling patterns that appear in *oak* and *cactus*.

BUILDING BACKGROUND

Ask students what they know about forests and deserts. List some of the important characteristics of forests and deserts on the board. Then make a Venn diagram like the one below that shows how the two environments differ and what they have in common.

Deserts
cactus
dry
sand

birds
reptiles
insects
spiders

Forests
trees
streams

DEVELOPING CONCEPTS

Explain that most of the list words have to do with the kinds of plants that live in the forest and desert. Have volunteers read each list word. Ask students whether each word pertains to forests or deserts or both. Then have students add the words to the Venn diagram, using the Spelling Dictionary for any help they might need with word meanings.

> **Additional Practice**
>
> *Everyday Spelling* **CD-ROM,** Lesson 3

---

oak
dune
evergreens
cactus
needleleaf
moisture
forest
broadleaf
desert
sagebrush

Answers will vary.

1. **desert**
2. **dune**
3. **sagebrush**
4. **moisture**
5. **cactus**

Deserts and Forests

What makes a desert? What makes a forest? How are the two alike or different? Use the pictures below to find out. Add your own words to the list. Use the Spelling Dictionary.

■ GETTING AT MEANING

Using Picture Clues   Look at all of the illustrations. Use words from the list to complete each caption.

cactus   desert   sagebrush   dune   moisture

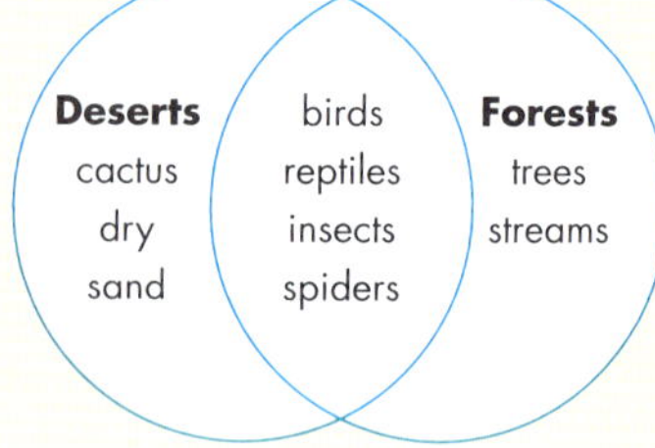

One-seventh of all the Earth's land is dry, sandy (1). The United States has deserts in the Southwest. Strong, dry winds can blow sand into a mounded (2).

The dry, bushy (3) is found on western plains.

Although all living things require (4) to live, a (5) doesn't need much water. It grows in hot, dry regions.

172

evergreens needleleaf oak forest broadleaf	6. **forest**
	7. **broadleaf**
	8. **oak**
	9. **needleleaf**
	10. **evergreens**

A (6) is more than just trees. It includes shrubs, mosses, and flowers. The largest ones in the United States are in the North and East.

Trees with broad, flat leaves are called (7) trees. Their leaves change color and fall off. The (8) is this kind of tree.

Trees with leaves like thin, sharp needles are called (9) trees. These trees are also called (10) because they stay green all year.

■ SPELL WELL

Divide and Conquer   Study long words piece by piece. Draw a line between the two base words in each compound below. Write each word.

11. needleleaf   **needle|leaf**

12. evergreens   **ever|greens**

CREATE A DIORAMA

Make a three-dimensional desert or forest. First, research your chosen area. What kinds of plants and animals are found there? Next, get a shoe box and pictures, sand, clay, branches, and so on. Create the environment inside the box. Label your diorama.

173

FOLLOW-UP

Interpretive Thinking
Compare and Contrast

Have students compare and contrast life in the forest and in the desert. Suggest the following questions:

- What plants and animals live in each place?
- Where do the animals make their homes?
- Where do the animals get food?
- Where do the plants and animals get water?

MEETING THE NEEDS OF ALL STUDENTS

Auditory Learners
Classifying Words Have partners match list words with forest or desert conditions. One can read the list words aloud; the other can tell whether the word relates to the desert or the forest.

Bilingual/ESL
Environmental Posters

Invite students to draw or cut out pictures to create two posters, *Desert* and *Forest*. Students can describe the posters, using appropriate list words.

173

SOCIAL STUDIES
THE GREAT LAKES

LESSON PLAN

- Building Background
- Developing Concepts
- Practice on pp. 174–175
- Follow-Up

● Core ○ Optional

Link to Weekly Lesson

Before presenting this lesson, you may wish to teach Lesson 33, **Capitalization and Abbreviation,** to introduce the capital letters and period that appear in *St. Lawrence Seaway.*

BUILDING BACKGROUND

Display a map of the United States or North America and have a volunteer point out the Great Lakes. On the board, create a word web centered on the term *Great Lakes* by having students name the lakes as you write them.

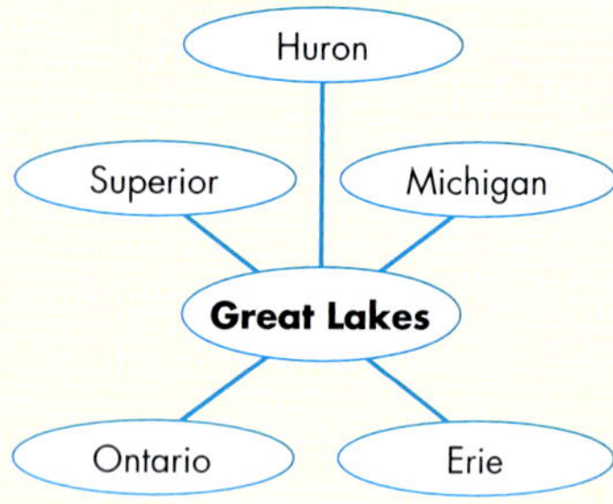

DEVELOPING CONCEPTS

Explain that bodies of water like the Great Lakes can be an important part of a country's transportation system. Help students locate the St. Lawrence Seaway on the map. Show how the seaway links the Great Lakes with the Atlantic Ocean. Discuss students' ideas about how the remaining list words also relate to water transportation.

Additional Practice

***Everyday Spelling* CD-ROM, Lesson 33**

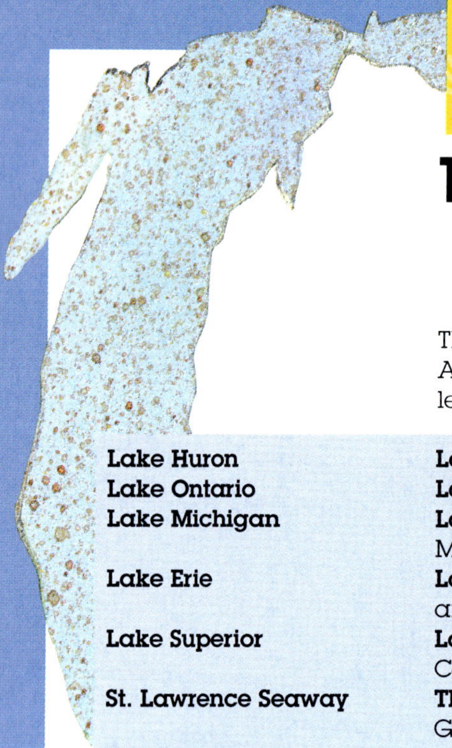

SOCIAL STUDIES

The Great Lakes

The Great Lakes and the St. Lawrence Seaway are North America's major water highways. Read the list below to learn about them. Add your own words and sentences.

Lake Huron	**Lake Huron** borders Michigan and Canada.
Lake Ontario	**Lake Ontario** borders New York and Canada.
Lake Michigan	**Lake Michigan** borders Wisconsin, Illinois, Indiana, and Michigan.
Lake Erie	**Lake Erie** borders Michigan, Ohio, New York, Pennsylvania, and Canada.
Lake Superior	**Lake Superior** borders Michigan, Wisconsin, Minnesota, and Canada.
St. Lawrence Seaway	**The St. Lawrence Seaway** is a waterway that connects the Great Lakes and the Atlantic Ocean.
Atlantic Ocean	**The Atlantic Ocean** is east of North and South America and west of Europe and Africa.
waterway	A **waterway** is a channel through which boats can navigate
canal	An artificial waterway for navigation is a **canal.**
lock	An enclosed section of a canal in which the level of water can be changed is called a **lock.**
Answers will vary. ________	________
________	________

GETTING AT MEANING

Using Written Clues Complete each sentence using either **lock, canal,** or **waterway.**

1. The St. Lawrence Seaway is a major ___waterway___.

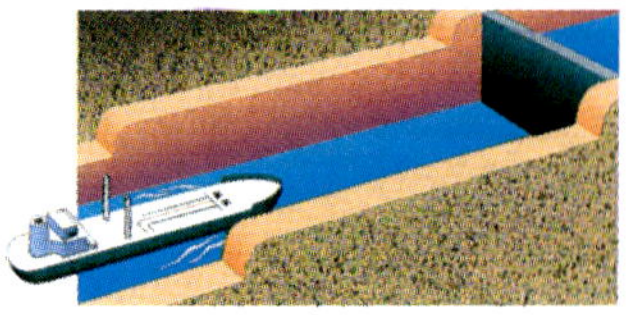

2. The ship at right is sailing through a ___canal___.

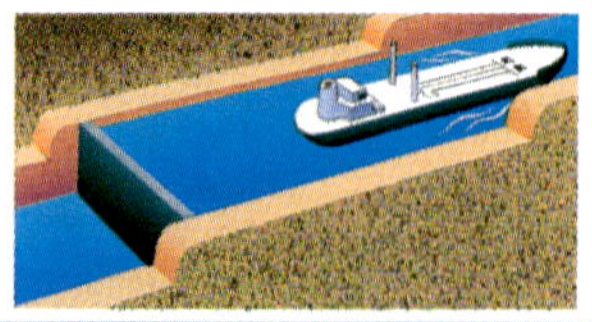

3. The ship at left enters a ___lock___ and the gates ar then closed.

• Lake Superior, the largest of the Great Lakes, is also the largest freshwater lake in the world.
• Lake Huron is the second largest of the Great Lakes.
• Lake Michigan, the third largest of the Great Lakes, is the only one located completely within the United States.
• Lake Erie is the shallowest of the Great Lakes; Lake Ontario is the smallest.

Labeling a Map   Label the Great Lakes, the St. Lawrence Seaway, and the Atlantic Ocean using the map below.

■ SPELL WELL

Divide and Conquer   Study the name of each lake syllable by syllable. Then write the names.

11. Lake Su • per • i • or   **Lake Superior**

12. Lake On • tar • i • o   **Lake Ontario**

Lŏŏk into This

List the names of streams, rivers, lakes, and other bodies of water that influence your environment. Are they natural or made by people? Where do they begin and end? Present your findings in the form of a chart, map, or diagram.

Did You Know?

The first letters of the names of the Great Lakes spell a word that means "places where we live." What is that word? (Once you figure it out, you can use it to help you remember the names of all the Great Lakes!)

FOLLOW-UP

Interpretive Thinking

Determining Cause and Effect   Help students research the pollution of the Great Lakes and the efforts that have been made to make the lakes cleaner. Encourage them to find out about the causes of the pollution and its effects, and to ask why cleaning up the lakes is so important.

MEETING THE NEEDS OF ALL STUDENTS

Auditory Learners

Acronyms   Help students remember the names of the Great Lakes by encouraging them to learn the acronym *HOMES*. Students who want to remember the lakes in size order should think of the acronym *SHMEO*.

Bilingual/ESL

Lakes Around the World   In small groups, students can study a globe or a large map of the world to locate and identify other lakes. Encourage them to compare the size of the Great Lakes with that of other lakes around the world.

175

BUILDING BACKGROUND

Build a word web like the one below on the board. Point out that natural resources are important to our lives every day. Invite students to name some natural resources and tell how they are used.

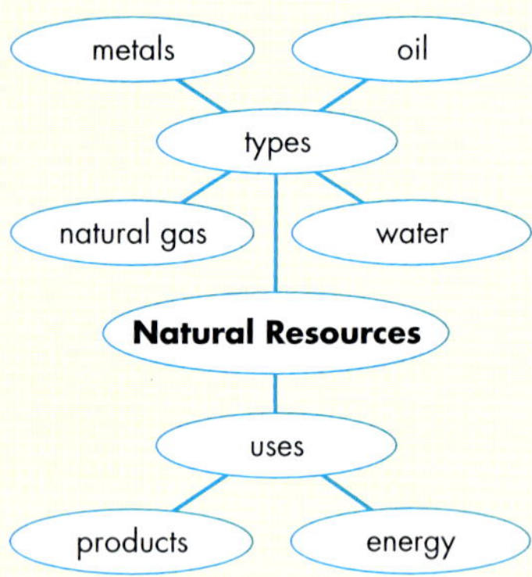

DEVELOPING CONCEPTS

Help students select list words to answer the following questions: *What do we use to fuel automobiles? What do we use to power lights and appliances in our homes? What materials do we use to make machines and buildings?* Point out that the list words are all natural resources or products made with natural resources, and add them to the word web.

Additional Practice

***Everyday Spelling* CD-ROM, Lesson 13**

Using Natural Resources

Our natural resources are very important to our way of living. Read the sentences below to find out why. Add your own related words and phrases to the list.

energy electricity hydroelectric fuels	We use natural resources to create **energy** to do work. **Electricity** is energy that powers lights and machines. **Hydroelectric** plants use water power to make electricity. **Fuels** are resources that are burned to create energy or heat.
oil gasoline natural gas coal steel	**Oil** is our main fuel for running kinds of transportation. By cleaning and breaking down oil, we get **gasoline.** Another fuel, **natural gas,** is used for heating and cooking. We burn **coal** to create heat. **Steel** is a product of iron ore and carbon that is formed into sheets, beams, and other shapes.
products	Steel and gasoline are **products** that are made from natural resources.

Answers will vary.

1. **products**
2. **steel**
3. **fuels**
4. **energy**
5. **natural gas**

■ GETTING AT MEANING

Using Context Clues   Use the clues in the sentences above to help you choose the right list word for each blank below.

1. In manufacturing and industry, natural resources are made into finished ___.
2. Melting down the natural resource of iron ore and mixing it with carbon produces ___.
3. Factories may burn coal, oil, or other ___ to produce energy.
4. Burning coal turns water into steam that generates electrical ___.
5. The Earth's mineral fuels, including coal, oil, and ___, may be used up in the next few centuries.

Using Visual Clues   Write the list word that best corresponds to each picture below.

6. **coal**

7. **electricity**

8. **oil**

9. **hydroelectric**

10. **gasoline**

■ SPELL WELL

Seeing Meaning Connections   The word *electric* is related to two list words. Finish each sentence by writing the correct list word.

11. Without _____**electricity**_____ I couldn't watch TV.

12. Hoover Dam is a _____**hydroelectric**_____ dam.

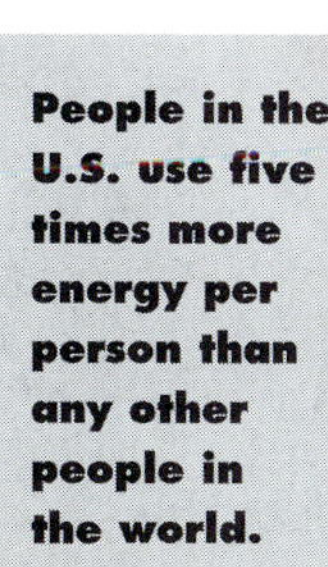

LESSON PLAN

- Building Background
- Developing Concepts
- Practice on pp. 178–179
- Follow-Up

● Core ○ Optional

Link to Weekly Lesson

Before presenting this lesson, you may wish to teach Lesson 25, **Including All the Letters.** Have students exaggerate troublesome sounds to spell words like *federal* (not *fedral*) and *democratic* (not *demcratic*).

BUILDING BACKGROUND

Create a word web on the board centered around the word *Government*. Have students name words that they associate with government. You may wish to remind students that government operates at the local as well as the state and federal levels.

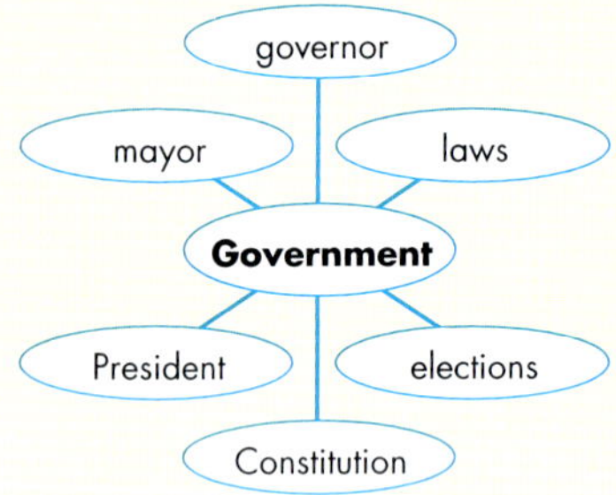

DEVELOPING CONCEPTS

Call students' attention to the word *Constitution.* Point out that the Constitution has the dual purpose of upholding both laws and individual liberties. The words *democratic, participate, elected,* and *represent* are keys to describing how American government operates. Other words name different levels of government. Have volunteers add any missing list words to the web.

Additional Practice

Everyday Spelling **CD-ROM**, Lesson 25

Constitution
republic
democratic
participate
leaders
elected
represent
local
state
federal

Answers will vary.

1. **leaders**
2. **elected**
3. **participate**
4. **democratic**
5. **represent**
6. **republic**

Our Government

What's so special about the United States' government? Plenty! The words in the list will help you find this out. Add more government words to the list. Then do the exercises.

■ GETTING AT MEANING

Context Clues Use the list words to complete what the people below are saying.

democratic   participate   represent   elected
leaders   republic

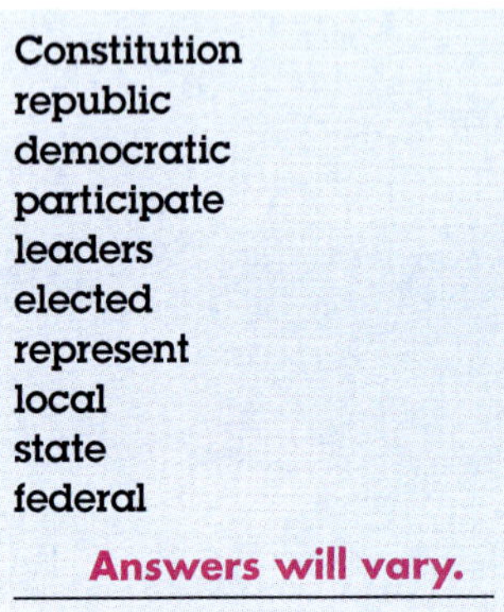

178

FYI

Although the Constitution is a uniquely American document, it is based on ideas from England and France.
• The guarantee that laws should reflect "the consent of the governed" comes from the writings of John Locke, an Englishman.
• The separation of government into three branches—executive, legislative, and judicial—is based on the ideas of a French noble, the Baron de Montesquieu.

State the Facts
Use the list words to answer the questions.

state   federal   local   Constitution

7 What written plan gives Americans their power?

8 Do governors and lieutenant governors work on the state or local level?

9 Do the President and Vice-President work on the federal, state, or local level?

10 Do mayors and city council members work on the federal, state, or local level?

7. **Constitution**

8. **state**

9. **federal**

10. **local**

■ SPELL WELL

Divide and Conquer Some long words are easier to study if you sound them out in syllables. Study each word below, saying it syllable by syllable. Then write the words.

11. Con • sti • tu • tion   **Constitution**

12. par • tic • i • pate   **participate**

CLASSMATE CONSTITUTION

What kind of government would work best in your classroom? Work in small groups to author a "Classroom Constitution" that establishes the kind of government you want. Think about the number of leaders, their powers, limitations, and responsibilities, as well as the role of the rights and responsibilities of classroom citizens. Use the Constitution of the United States as your guide.

Did You Know?

The Constitution of the United States is one of the oldest written constitutions. Many other countries have patterned their constitutions after it.

SOCIAL STUDIES
SOUTHWEST AMERICAN INDIANS

LESSON PLAN

- ● Building Background
- ● Developing Concepts
- ● Practice on pp. 180–181
- ○ Follow–Up

● Core ○ Optional

Link to Weekly Lesson

Before presenting this lesson, you may wish to teach Lesson 31, **Vowels with No Sound Clues,** to introduce words with vowel sounds that give no clues to their spelling, such as *pueblo, ceremony, Navajo, hogans,* and *reservation.*

BUILDING BACKGROUND

Build a word web like the one below on the board. Point out that many American Indians in the Southwest live on reservations in parts of New Mexico, Utah, and Arizona. Ask students to help you expand the web by suggesting words and phrases that fit the six categories shown.

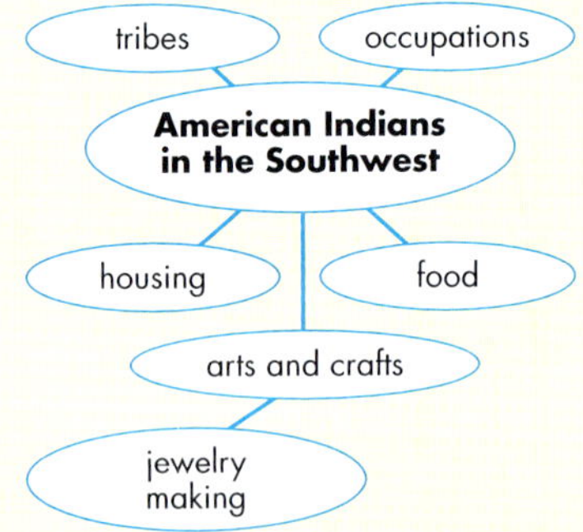

DEVELOPING CONCEPTS

Explain that the list words are related to the Southwest American Indians. Have volunteers say the words. Then ask students to identify any list words that are missing from the web. Volunteers can suggest where and why any of those words can be added.

Additional Practice
Everyday Spelling **CD-ROM,** Lesson 31

pueblo
adobe
corn
ceremony
pottery
Navajo
hogans
silver
weaving
reservation

Answers will vary.

1. **pueblo**
2. **adobe**
3. **ceremony**
4. **pottery**
5. **reservation**

Southwest American Indians

Many Southwest American Indians keep the traditions their ancestors kept hundreds of years ago. The list words reflect their past as well as their present life. Add your own words. Use the Spelling Dictionary as you do the exercises.

■ GETTING AT MEANING

Using Picture Clues   Look at the illustrations. Complete the sentences using words from the list.

adobe   ceremony   pottery   pueblo   reservation

These American Indians of New Mexico and Arizona get their name from the apartmentlike villages in which they live. Each village is called a (1). The pueblos are made of stone or sun-dried (2) bricks. In one religious (3), the Pueblo pray for harmony and order in the universe. The Pueblo make beautiful clay (4), which they sell to tourists who visit the (5).

6. **Navajo**

7. **corn**

8. **weaving**

9. **silver**

10. **hogans**

11. **pottery**

12. **reservation**

silver   hogans   weaving   Navajo   corn

The (6) are also American Indians of the Southwest. Many of them are farmers, growing (7) and raising sheep. Others are gifted at (8) wool into beautiful blankets, while others are engineers, teachers, and technicians. The Navajo are also famous for the artistic turquoise and (9) jewelry they make. A single ring can cost over $20,000. Many Navajo live in (10), shelters made of log frames covered with earth.

■ SPELL WELL

Seeing Meaning Connections Write the list word that completes each sentence. The underlined word is a clue.

11. That beautiful clay <u>pot</u> is just one of a large (11) collection.

12. A parcel of land <u>reserved</u> exclusively for American Indians is a (12).

Design Your Own Pottery
Each Pueblo village creates pottery using its own special design. Draw a pot and decorate it with your own one-of-a-kind design.

181

FOLLOW-UP

Interpretive Thinking
Compare and Contrast
Have students compare and contrast objects of the same craft that their classmates have brought to class. For example, you might ask a student to point out the likenesses and differences between a Southwest American Indian piece of pottery and a piece of pottery from another culture.

MEETING THE NEEDS OF ALL STUDENTS

Visual Learners
Describing Illustrations
Ask students to examine the Southwest American artwork in the illustrations. Students who have Southwest American Indian artwork of their own might create a classroom display.

Bilingual/ESL
Cultural Awareness Invite students to bring to class or create a piece of art that represents their own culture. Have them share their art in small groups, using any list words that apply.

BUILDING BACKGROUND

On a map of the world or a globe, pinpoint the Arctic. Have students volunteer words they associate with this part of the world. Use students' suggestions to build a word web on the board. Point out that the Arctic is associated with Santa Claus and polar bears, but that penguins live in the Southern Hemisphere—in Antarctica.

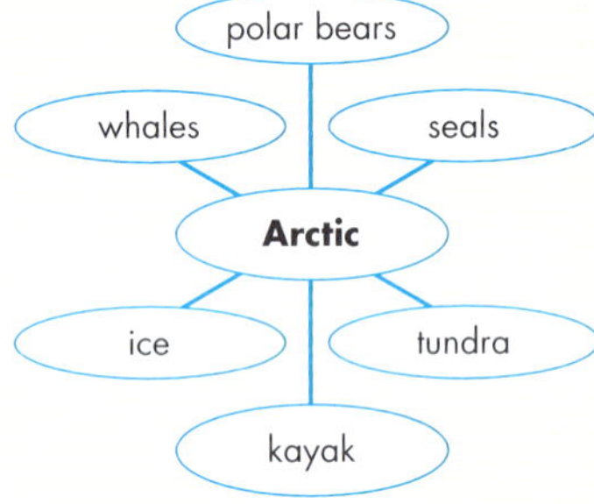

DEVELOPING CONCEPTS

Discuss the list words. Explain that some of the words name animals, while others name a group of people—the Inuit—and things that are part of their daily lives. Invite students to help you add any missing list words to the web.

Additional Practice

Everyday Spelling **CD-ROM, Lesson 23**

Inuit
seal
whale
walrus
polar bear
caribou
blubber
fur
tundra
kayak

Answers will vary.

Arctic Life

The Arctic is quite a place! How do people and animals live and travel there? The list words will help you answer these questions. Add your own Arctic words to the list.

■ GETTING AT MEANING

Using Photographs Use list words to complete the caption for each photograph.

blubber   Inuit   kayak   polar bear   whale

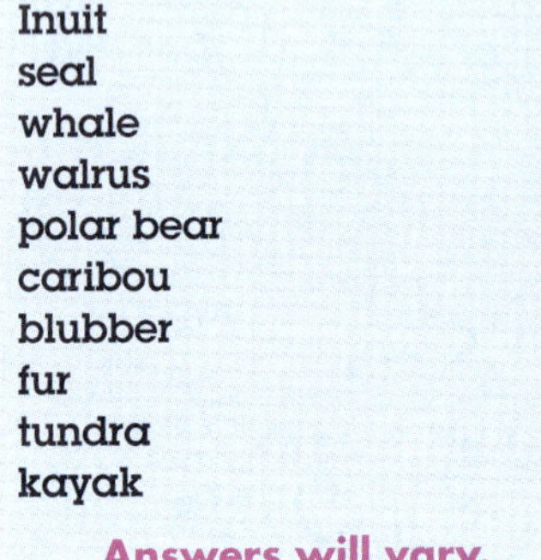

Many of the people who live in the Arctic, such as the (1), zip around in snappy little snowmobiles!

1. **Inuit**
2. **kayak**
3. **polar bear**
4. **whale**
5. **blubber**

When the ice melts, an easy way to get around is to paddle a (2), a special boat.

The huge, snow-colored (3) looks at u as if to say, "Isn't the Arctic wonderful?"

This leaping (4) has a thick layer of fat called (5) that keeps it warm in cold water.

fur   tundra   walrus   caribou   seal

The (6) has two huge teeth called tusks.

A sleek (7) tends to its pup.

This girl will stay warm in a hood trimmed in animal (8).

The reindeer feeding on the grass is also called a (9)!

The caribou stands on the treeless plain, called (10).

6.   **walrus**
7.   **seal**
8.   **fur**
9.   **caribou**
10.   **tundra**

■ SPELL WELL

Rhyming Helpers   The rhyming helpers *meal* and *Mary Lou* can help you spell two list words. Write the list word that rhymes with each rhyming helper.

11. The polar bear
    Sniffs the air,
    Hoping for a meal.
    While diving for a codfish,

    It sees a lively ___**seal**___.

12. "What are you doing,
    Mary Lou?"
    "Reading a book

    About ___**caribou**___."

TRY IT OUT

The Inuit are famous for their sculptures. They use soapstone, whalebone, and other material to carve animals or scenes from their environment. Try it yourself. Use clay or a bar of soap to carve something you see each day.

FOLLOW-UP

Interpretive Thinking

Visualizing Explain to students that in the summer, due to the tilt of the earth's axis, the sun never completely sets in the Arctic. However, in the winter the reverse is true, and the sun never fully rises in the Arctic. Have students visualize what it would be like to spend these two seasons in the Arctic. Ask them to consider how lighting conditions might affect their school life, recreation, and other daily aspects of life.

MEETING THE NEEDS OF ALL STUDENTS

Auditory Learners

Arctic Journeys Have students work with a partner to make a list of supplies they would need for an Arctic expedition. One student can be the recorder, and the other can make an oral report.

Bilingual/ESL

Naming Objects Suggest that students name the illustrated objects and animals in their primary language.

183

LESSON PLAN	Link to Weekly Lesson
● Building Background	Before presenting this lesson,
● Developing Concepts	you may wish to teach Lesson 29,
● Practice on pp. 184–185	**Prefixes dis-, in-, mis-, re-,** to
○ Follow-Up	introduce the spelling pattern
	that appears in _disagree._

● Core ○ Optional

BUILDING BACKGROUND

Ask students to suggest something that makes them happy, something that makes them sad, and something that makes them angry. Ask students to suggest the kinds of things that make each of them unique, or special. Use students' responses to build a word web around the words _Know Yourself._ Afterward, add the word _feelings_ to the chart if it is not already there.

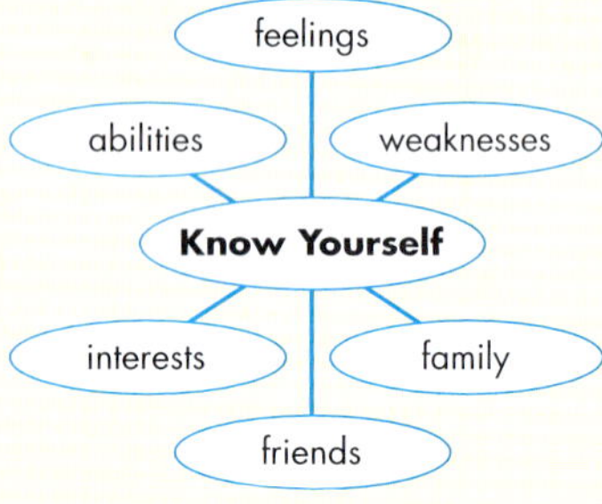

DEVELOPING CONCEPTS

Ask volunteers to read the list words. Discuss how each of the words relates to knowing oneself. Explain that a psychologist is someone who is trained to understand why people think, act, and feel as they do. Volunteers can add any missing words to the web.

Additional Practice

Everyday Spelling **CD-ROM,** Lesson 29

strengths
appreciate
weaknesses
decision
disagree
tears
result
psychologist
special
appearance

Words will vary.

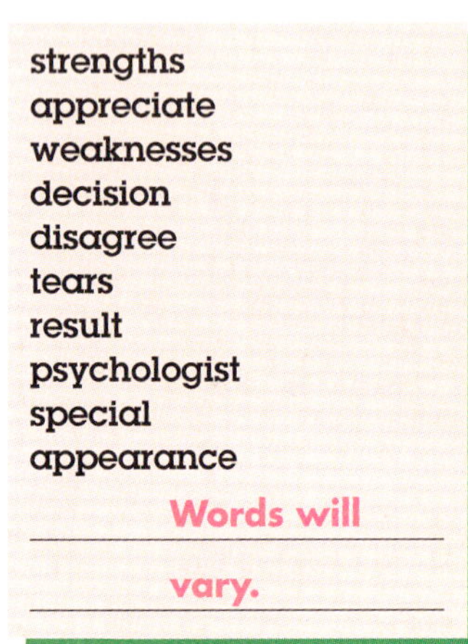

Know Yourself

You are one of a kind. The list words celebrate that. Add your own words to the list. Use the Spelling Dictionary for help.

■ GETTING AT MEANING

Talking About You The friends in the comic strip are eager to share their wisdom with you, but the cartoonist left out words. Use the list words to complete their sentences.

1. **special**
2. **appearance**
3. **strengths**
4. **appreciate**

184

The main site of thought and intelligence in people is the outer layer of the brain's cerebral cortex.
• This layer is gray and 0.12–0.16 inches thick. If laid out flat, the central cortex would cover the area of an office desk.
• The cortex is also the part of the brain that analyzes signals from the senses and initiates movement.

Connections to *BookFestival*

You may wish to recommend that students read *Grandma Moses: Painter of Rural America* by Zibby O'Neal in the Scott Foresman - Addison Wesley *BookFestival* program.

5.	**tears**	8.	**decision**
6.	**disagree**	9.	**psychologist**
7.	**weaknesses**	10.	**result**

Did You Know?

Tears not only help keep eyes moist and clear of dust and grit, they also fight bacteria and other infections.

■ SPELL WELL

Problem Parts Some words cause problems because they are not spelled the way they sound. Write *psychologist* and *appreciate.* Underline any letters in these words that you think might cause spelling problems.

11. **psychologist**   12. **appreciate**

Letters underlined will vary.

decision psychologist disagree result weaknesses

FOLLOW-UP

Interpretive Thinking

Solving Problems Have students discuss the following in pairs or small groups: *Name two strengths and two weaknesses that you have. How might you improve your weaknesses?*

MEETING THE NEEDS OF ALL STUDENTS

Auditory Learners

Reading Aloud Have volunteers read aloud the dialogue in the comic strip. Have them replace the numbers with list words as other students follow along silently. Encourage other pairs to read when the first has finished.

Bilingual/ESL

Everyone Teaches Invite students to become teachers. Assign each student two list words. Each student should explain his or her words using any of the following techniques: sentences, pantomime, or illustration.

BEING SAFE

- Building Background
- Developing Concepts
- Practice on pp. 186–187
- Follow-Up

Before presenting this lesson, you may wish to teach Lesson 26, **Compound Words,** to introduce words that are made of two or more words, such as *crosswalks, first aid, hand signal,* and *jaywalking.*

● Core ○ Optional

BUILDING BACKGROUND

Make a chart on the board titled *Bicycle Safety.* In one column have students list safety equipment. In the other column have them list safe-riding behaviors.

Bicycle Safety	
Equipment	**Behaviors**
helmet	wear helmet
reflectors	watch traffic
brakes	

DEVELOPING CONCEPTS

Point out that everyone who uses the roads—drivers, pedestrians, and cyclists—must follow traffic-safety rules. Introduce the list words and ask volunteers to read them. Ask students to explain how the list words relate to traffic safety and emergencies. Then call on volunteers to add any appropriate words to the *Bicycle Safety* chart.

> **Additional Practice**
> *Everyday Spelling* **CD-ROM,**
> Lesson 26

crosswalks
first aid
pedestrians
rescue
reflector
bicycle
hand signal
jaywalking
emergency
helmet

Words will

vary.

reflector
bicycle
helmet
hand signal

1. **helmet**
2. **hand signal**
3. **bicycle**
4. **reflector**

Being Safe

You've heard the phrase "safety first." Understanding the words in the list can help you put safety first in your life. Add your own words to the list. Use the Spelling Dictionary if you need help.

■ GETTING AT MEANING

Labeling Write a list word from the sign that identifies each numbered part of the picture.

186

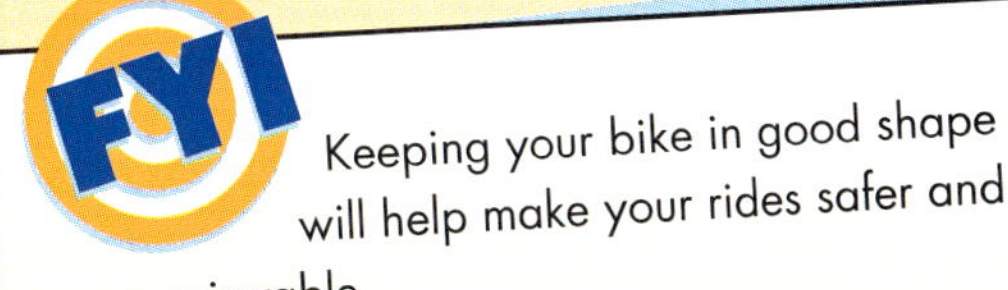

Keeping your bike in good shape will help make your rides safer and more enjoyable.

- Check tire pressure. Make sure tires are inflated and there are no cuts, gravel, or glass in the tires.
- Be sure all cables move easily and don't slip.
- Make sure brake blocks meet the wheel rims accurately and that the blocks aren't worn.
- Lubricate the chain.

Using Context Clues   As Sara rides to school, she is reviewing some of the safety rules she knows. Use the list words on the sign to complete Sara's thoughts.

- People who are walking, or (5), must follow safety rules.
- Pedestrians should cross streets only at (6), or specially marked places.
- Not crossing a street at a crosswalk is called (7).
- If someone is hurt in an accident, call the police and request an ambulance. A paramedic team will come to the (8).
- When driving a car or riding a bike, always pull over to the right side of the road and stop to allow an (9) vehicle to pass.
- Stand back and allow the paramedics to provide (10).

5. **pedestrians**
6. **crosswalks**
7. **jaywalking**
8. **rescue**
9. **emergency**
10. **first aid**

■ **SPELL WELL**

Divide and Conquer   Sometimes it helps to study long words piece by piece. Study the following words syllable by syllable. Then write each one.

11. e • mer • gen • cy _____ **emergency**

12. pe • des • tri • an _____ **pedestrian**

LESSON PLAN

- Building Background
- Developing Concepts
- Practice on pp. 188–189
- Follow-Up

● Core ○ Optional

Link to Weekly Lesson

Before presenting this lesson, you may wish to teach Lesson 10, **Short Vowels a, i, o, u,** to introduce the spelling patterns that appear in *cuspid, incisor, enamel, epidermis,* and *gland.*

BUILDING BACKGROUND

Call students' attention to their skin and teeth, which are parts of their bodies that they may take for granted. Ask why their skin and teeth are important, and list responses on the board in a chart.

Skin	Teeth
protection	talking
perspiration	smiling
appearance	eating
	appearance

DEVELOPING CONCEPTS

Have volunteers read the list words aloud, define any they know, and identify which words are related to teeth and which are related to skin. Then have students add the list words to the chart.

Additional Practice

Everyday Spelling CD-ROM, Lesson 10

bicuspid
cuspid
incisor
molar
enamel
epidermis
dermis
pore
sweat gland
oil gland

Words will

vary.

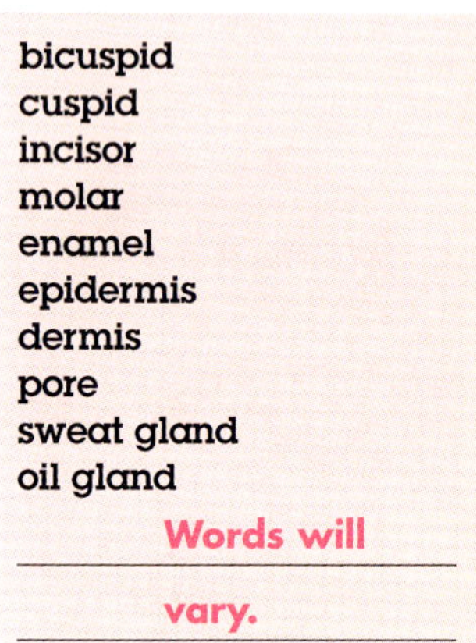

Your Body

■ GETTING AT MEANING

There's more to teeth than a dazzling smile, and more to skin than bone covering. Read about them below. Add more words to the list. Use your Spelling Dictionary for help.

Labeling Diagrams   Read about the teeth and skin. Then use list words to write the parts of each diagram.

The Teeth

The word **cuspid** means "tooth with a sharp point." A **bicuspid,** therefore, is a tooth with two sharp points. An **incisor** is a front tooth, and a **molar** is a back tooth. All of our teeth are protected by hard, white **enamel.**

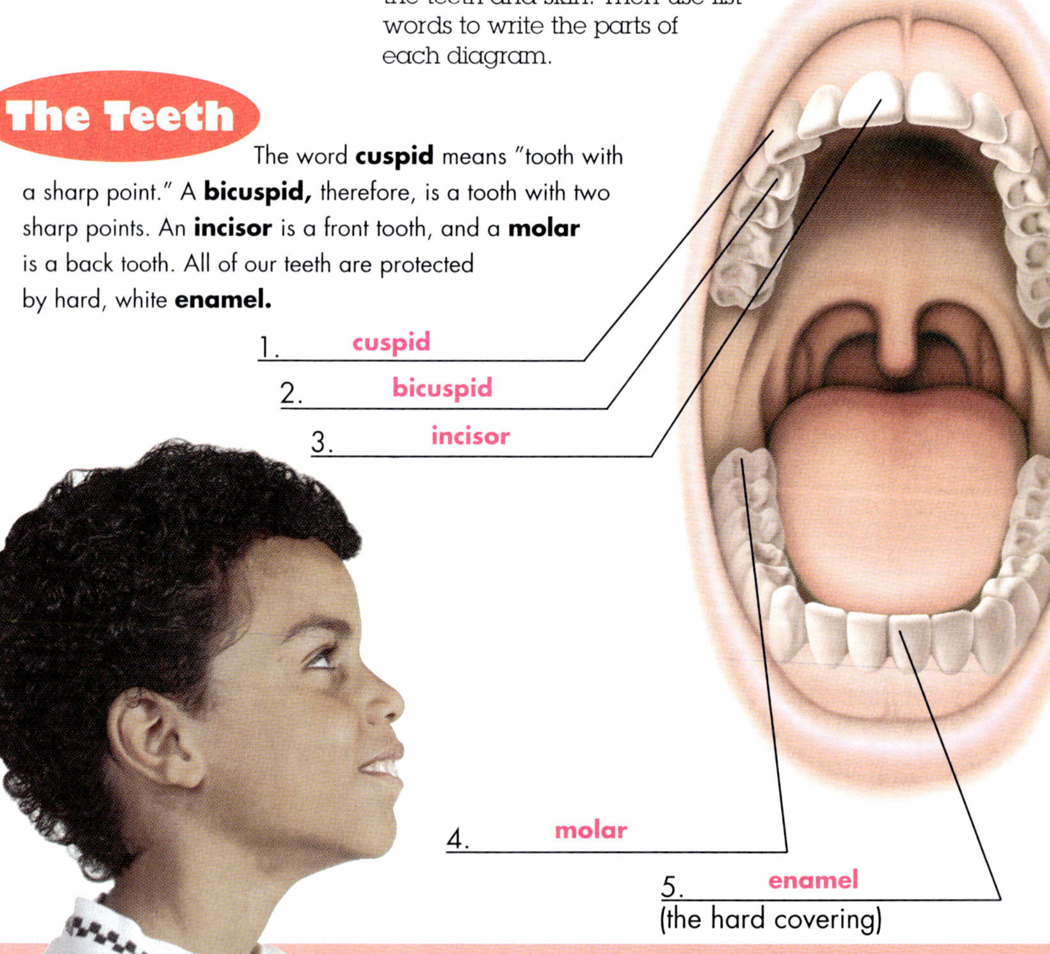

188

The Skin

The **epidermis** is the outer layer of the skin. The **dermis** is the inner layer. Each tiny opening in the skin is called a **pore.** Sweat is released through the **sweat gland,** and oil is released through the **oil gland.**

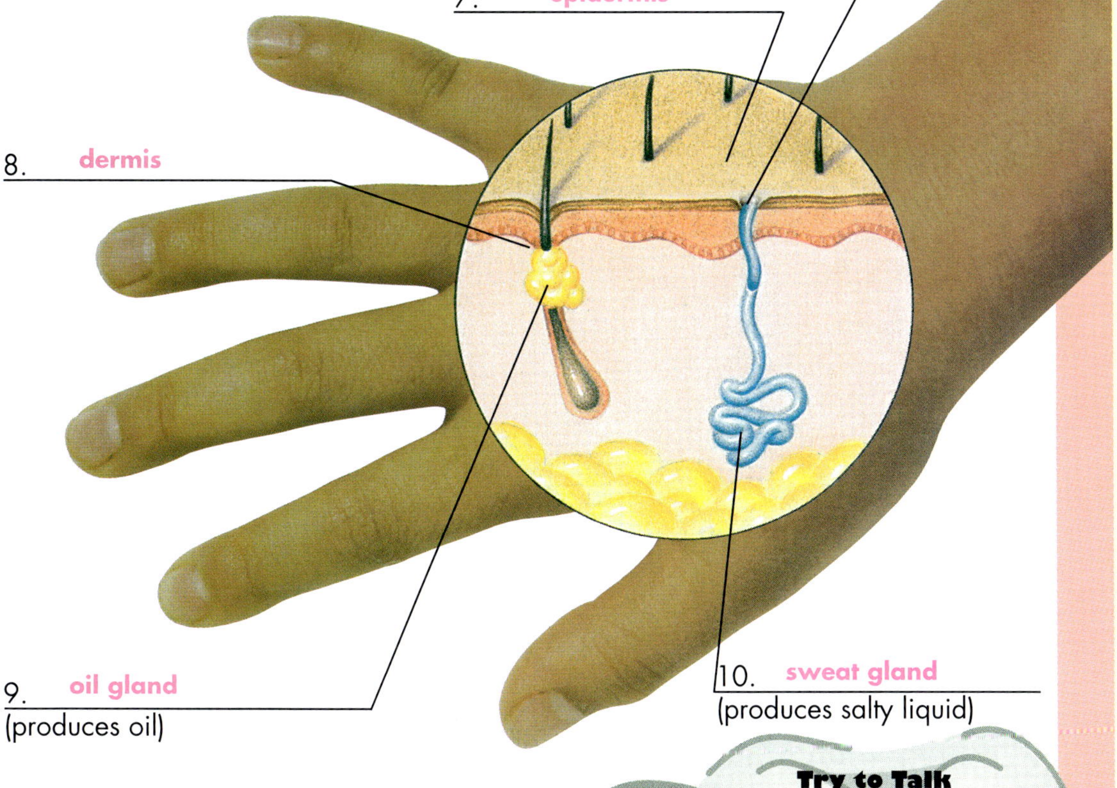

6. pore

7. epidermis

8. dermis

9. oil gland (produces oil)

10. sweat gland (produces salty liquid)

■ SPELL WELL

Root Awareness   Some of your list words come from Greek and Latin words. Often, a word is easier to understand and remember if you look at its root, the word it came from. Complete the chart to create two list words.

Prefix	Root Word	List Word
	derm (skin)	11. dermis
epi (on, upon)	derm (skin)	12. epidermis

Try to Talk Without Teeth!

Not only do we need our teeth to eat, we need them to talk. Slowly read this sentence out loud: The tiny worm sat upon a log. Write down the words in which your tongue touches your teeth. Next to each word, also jot down where your tongue touches your teeth.

189

SCIENCE
PLANT REPRODUCTION

LESSON PLAN

- ● Building Background
- ● Developing Concepts
- ● Practice on pp. 190–191
- ○ Follow-Up

● Core   ○ Optional

Link to Weekly Lesson

Before presenting this lesson, you may wish to teach Lesson 22, **Vowel Sounds in *few* and *moon*,** to introduce the spelling patterns that appear in *fru_it* and *reprod_uce*.

BUILDING BACKGROUND

Ask students to share experiences they have had growing plants from seeds. Explain that different kinds of plants reproduce in different ways; for instance, ferns don't have seeds. Work with students to begin building a word web like the one below about plant reproduction.

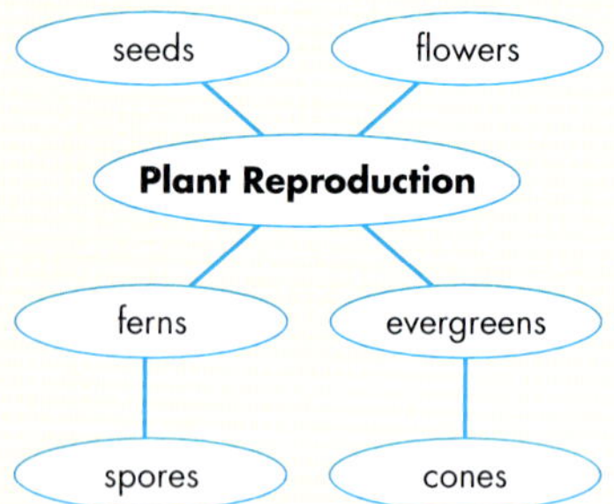

DEVELOPING CONCEPTS

Ask volunteers to read and define the list words. If necessary, explain that the list words can be used to describe how three different kinds of plants—plants from seeds, plants from spores, and plants from cones—reproduce, or make other plants of the same kind. Have students help you add the list words to the web.

Additional Practice

***Everyday Spelling* CD-ROM, Lesson 22**

---

reproduce
seed
conifers
ferns
spores
pollen
stamen
pistil
fertilize
fruit

____
Words will
____
vary.

SCIENCE

Plant Reproduction

How do plants reproduce—that is, make other plants? Use the list words and the diagrams to find the answer. Add your own words to the list. Use the Spelling Dictionary.

■ GETTING AT MEANING

Plants from Seeds   Many plants, like the cherry tree below, reproduce by means of seeds. The diagram will help you complete the sentences.

1. This flower will ______reproduce______ by means of seeds.

2. The tiny grains made by the stamen are called ______pollen______ .

3. The flower's ______stamen______ makes these tiny grains.

4. Bees and butterflies carry pollen from the stamen to the ______pistil______ .

5. The pollen will ______fertilize______ an egg at the bottom of the flower's pistil.

6. The fertilized ______seed______ will grow inside the plant.

7. The ______fruit______ grows around the seed. It is the part we eat.

fertilize
bee carries pollen from flower to flower

pollen combines with egg to make seed

stamen makes tiny grains of pollen

fruit

seed

pistil makes eggs that combine with pollen

190

Plants from Spores and Cones   **Ferns** and mosses reproduce by means of **spores**. **Conifers** such as pine trees reproduce by means of cones. The male cone is smaller and softer. The female cone is larger and harder. Use the diagram to complete the sentences.

8. Unlike flowers, mosses and _____ **ferns** _____ have clusters of tiny cells under their leaves.

9. These cells are called _____ **spores** _____.

10. Spruce and pine are both _____ **conifers** _____. They produce cones.

fern

spores
on the underside of a fern

■ SPELL WELL

Divide and Conquer
Long words are easy to spell if you divide them into smaller parts. Study each word below, syllable by syllable. Then write each word.

11. fer • ti • lize _____ **fertilize**

12. re • pro • duce _____ **reproduce**

13. con • i • fers _____ **conifers**

Plants Aplenty

What's your favorite plant? a garden flower? a wildflower? an exotic tree of the rain forest? Draw and paint or color your favorite plant on a big sheet of paper. Cut it out, and with your classmates' plants, create a classroom "botanical garden" on the wall. For fun, label your plant with its name, where it grows, and some interesting facts about it.

FOLLOW-UP

Critical Thinking

Making Decisions Challenge students with the following: *Suppose you were asked to make decisions about what kinds of plants should be put in a park in your community. What kinds of plants would you choose?* Have students work together to brainstorm a list of possibilities. Then have a general discussion of their choices.

MEETING THE NEEDS OF ALL STUDENTS

Visual Learners

Making a Chart Work with students to make a chart with drawings of a flower, a pine tree, and a fern as headings. They can then write each list word under the heading or headings to which it relates.

Bilingual/ESL

Cultural Awareness Invite students to bring to class pictures of plants that are native to their culture, or make drawings of the plants. Encourage them to label the pictures using appropriate list words.

191

SCIENCE	**LESSON PLAN**	**Link to Weekly Lesson**
LIVING TOGETHER	● Building Background ● Developing Concepts ● Practice on pp. 192–193 ○ Follow-Up ● Core ○ Optional	Before presenting this lesson, you may wish to teach Lesson 34, **Possessives.** Help students practice using possessives by having them write phrases, such as *predator's prey.*

BUILDING BACKGROUND

Discuss the fact that all people and other animals must eat in order to live. Whether they are meat eaters or vegetarians, they depend on life lower in the food chain for their food. Draw a simple food chain on the board indicating that grass is eaten by a rabbit, which is eaten by a fox.

fox
↑
rabbit
↑
grass

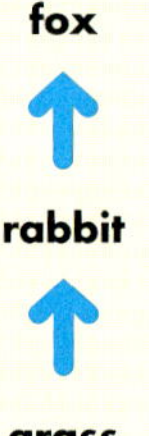

DEVELOPING CONCEPTS

Ask volunteers to read the list words. Explain that the words relate to the way plants and animals live together. Discuss students' ideas about which list words relate to themselves.

> **Additional Practice**
> ***Everyday Spelling* CD-ROM, Lesson 34**

producers
consumers
herbivore
carnivore
omnivore
food chain
food web
predator
prey
decomposer
Words will
vary.

SCIENCE

Living Together

Every living thing—plant and animal—depends in some way on other living things. The list words can help you find out how. Can you add others? Use your Spelling Dictionary.

GETTING AT MEANING

Looking at Pictures **Producers** make their own food. **Consumers** eat other living things.
Look at the picture below. Then answer the questions.

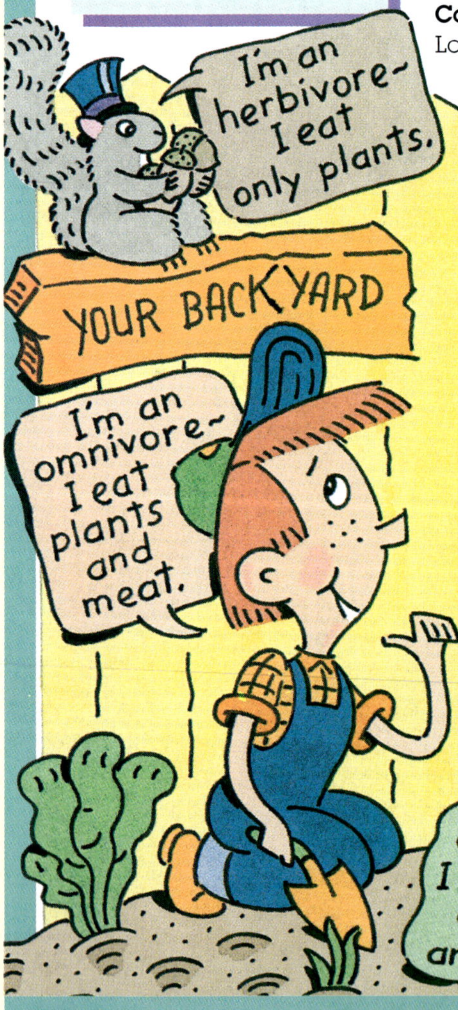

1. The dog, boy, and squirrel all eat food. What are they called? consumers
2. Are plants such as lettuce and carrots producers or consumers? producers
3. What do you call an animal who eats only beef and chicken? carnivore
4. What is an animal who eats only leaves, fruit, and nuts called? herbivore
5. What is an animal who eats both fish and rice called? omnivore
6. What do you call the tiny organism that causes dead plants and animals to crumble and rot? decomposer

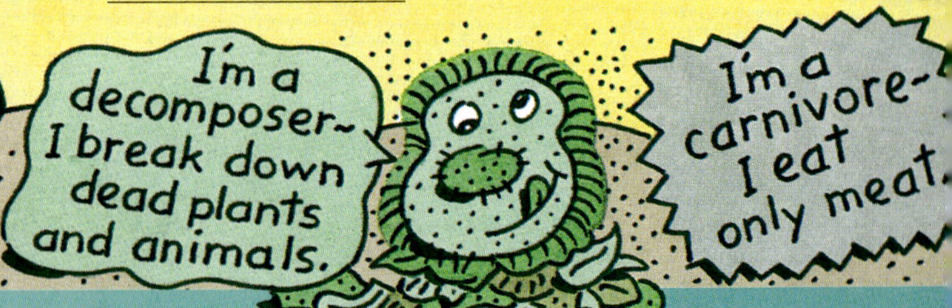

192

Seeing Connections   Animals that are hunted and eaten are called **prey.** Animals that do the hunting and eating are called **predators.** A **food chain** shows a direct link between an animal and the thing it eats and is eaten by. A **food web** is a complex arrangement of food chains. Label each picture either **food chain** or **food web.** Answer the questions that follow.

7. _food chain_

8. _food web_

9. Is the mouse in the food chain predator or prey? _prey_

10. Is the hawk in the food chain predator or prey? _predator_

■ SPELL WELL

Pronouncing Words Carefully   We sometimes spell words wrong because we say them wrong. Say each word below. Be sure to pronounce the sounds of the underlined letters. Write the words.

11. herbivore _herbivore_

12. carnivore _carnivore_

13. omnivore _omnivore_

Draw the Food Chain in Your Yard

Take a good look around your schoolyard or yard at home. Sketch some of the plant and animal life you see. Turn your sketches into an illustration of your yard's food chains. Does your yard also have a food web? Illustrate that too!

LESSON PLAN

- ● Building Background
- ● Developing Concepts
- ● Practice on pp. 194–195
- ○ Follow-Up

● Core   ○ Optional

Link to Weekly Lesson

Before presenting this lesson, you may wish to teach Lesson 32, **Vowels in Final Syllables,** to introduce the spelling patterns that appear in *insulation* and *current*.

BUILDING BACKGROUND

Encourage students to offer their ideas about how they use electricity and magnetism in their daily lives. Then ask them what they know about how these forces work. List their responses in a chart.

Electricity	Magnetism
lights	compass
television	magnets
cooking	attraction
battery	

DEVELOPING CONCEPTS

Tell students that the list words can help explain how electricity and magnetism work. Have volunteers define any of the words they are already familiar with. Then work with students to sort the terms into the appropriate categories in the chart.

Additional Practice

Everyday Spelling CD-ROM, Lesson 32

conduct
insulation
current
series circuit
parallel circuit
magnet
magnetism
poles
magnetic field
compass

Words will

vary.

SCIENCE

Electricity and Magnetism

Electricity and magnetism are forces we use every day. The list words tell about each force. Look up unknown words in the Spelling Dictionary. Add other words to the list.

■ GETTING AT MEANING

Using Diagrams Write the words **current, conduct, insulation, series circuit,** and **parallel circuit** to complete the explanation below the diagrams.

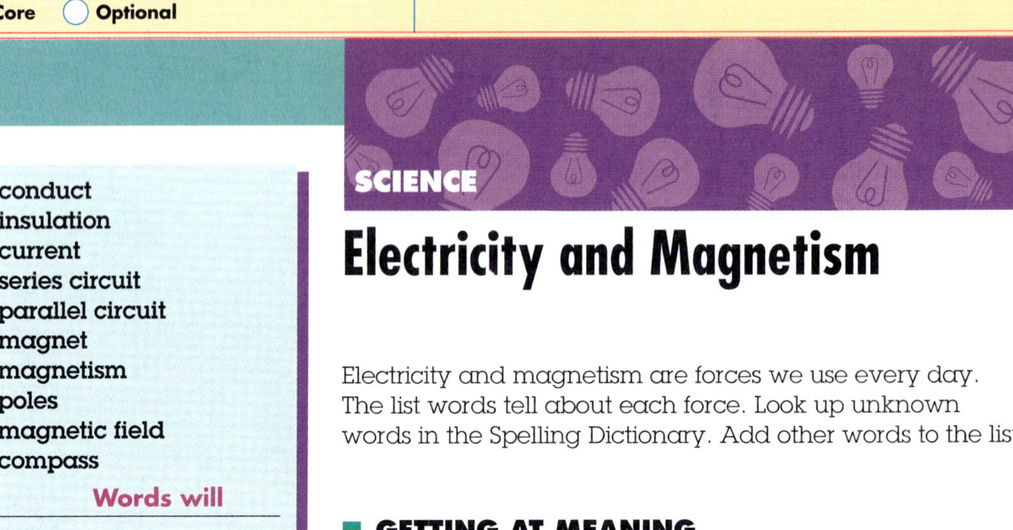

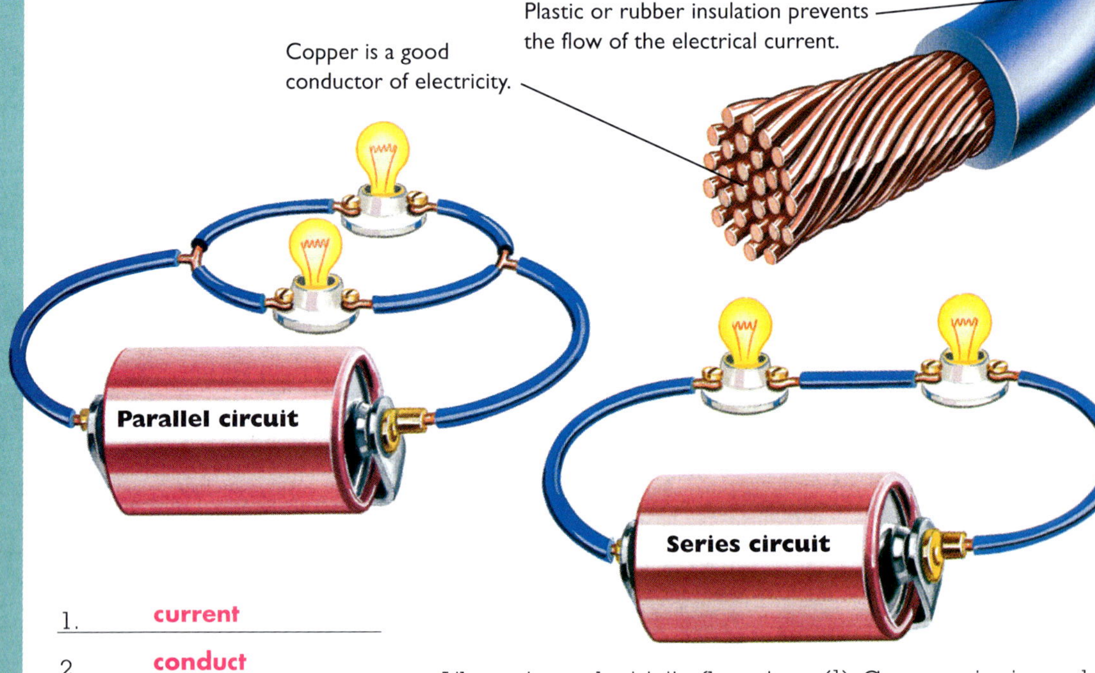

1. **current**
2. **conduct**
3. **insulation**
4. **series circuit**
5. **parallel circuit**

Like a river, electricity flows in a (1). Copper wire is used to (2) the electricity. The wires are wrapped in plastic (3) so that they are safe to touch. When the electricity moves along one path, the circuit is a (4). When the electricity moves along two or more paths, the circuit is a (5).

194

Using Diagrams   Use the words below to complete the sentences.

poles   magnetic field   magnetism   compass   magnet

A __(6)__ is any piece of iron or steel that can pull iron or steel things to it. The magnet's power to attract is called __(7)__. The parts of a magnet where the magnetism is the strongest are called the __(8)__. The magnetic force curves out between a magnet's poles creating what is called a __(9)__. A magnetic __(10)__ helps travelers to find directions. The arrow on the compass will point to the north because the north-seeking pole of the needle is attracted to the magnetic north pole of the earth.

6. **magnet**
7. **magnetism**
8. **poles**
9. **magnetic field**
10. **compass**

Compass

Magnet

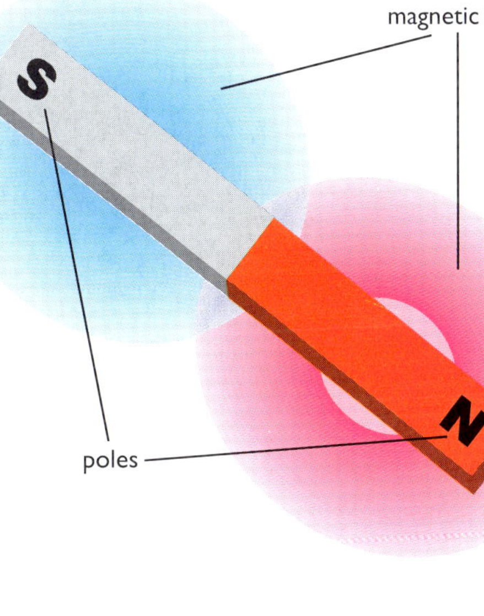

■ **SPELL WELL**

Related Words   Write the two list words that are related in spelling and meaning to *magnet*.

11. **magnetism**
12. **magnetic field**

Did You Know?

About 500 species of fish send out electric charges. Electric eels are the best known. They stun their prey with a 350–650 volt charge!

FOLLOW-UP

Interpretive Thinking

Visualizing Have students discuss the following question in small groups: *How would your life be different if people hadn't discovered electricity?* Encourage students to begin by visualizing all the everyday uses of electricity they listed in their charts.

MEETING THE NEEDS OF ALL STUDENTS

Auditory Learners

Oral Descriptions Have students study the diagrams illustrating electric current and magnetism as you discuss them. After completing the activities, students can use the diagrams to explain the concepts, in their own words, to a partner.

Bilingual/ESL

Flashcard Practice Have students work in pairs. One student can make flashcards for the list words relating to electricity. The partner can do the same for the words relating to magnetism. Students can then practice pronouncing and defining the list words.

195

LESSON PLAN

- ● Building Background
- ● Developing Concepts
- ● Practice on pp. 196–197
- ○ Follow-Up

● Core ○ Optional

Link to Weekly Lesson

Before presenting this lesson, you may wish to teach Lesson 19, **Getting Letters in Correct Order,** to introduce the spelling patterns that appear in *rain, gauge,* and *Fahrenheit.*

BUILDING BACKGROUND

Have students recall weather reports they have heard on television and radio. Using words that students suggest, build a word web around the word *Weather.* Include words that relate to weather forecasting as well as types of weather.

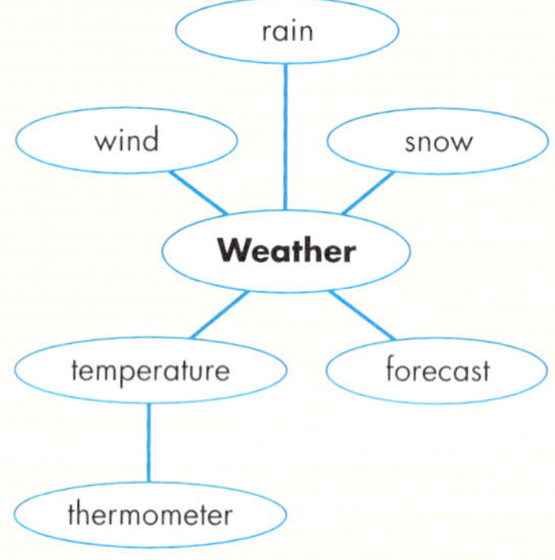

DEVELOPING CONCEPTS

Tell students that the list words include terms that describe how weather conditions are predicted and measured. Read each word and have volunteers tell how it relates to weather. Add any missing words to the web.

Additional Practice

Everyday Spelling **CD-ROM,** Lesson 19

---

meteorologist
forecast
barometer
wind vane
rain gauge
humidity
air mass
front
Fahrenheit
Celsius

Words will

vary.

Weather

The weather's "behavior" tells us how to behave. What we wear and do often depends on the weather. The list words name ways we find out about weather. Look up unfamiliar words in the Spelling Dictionary. Add more weather words to the list.

■ GETTING AT MEANING

Weather Report Finish writing the newscaster's and weather forecaster's cue cards by writing these list words. Use the thermometer on the next page to help you.

humidity
meteorologist
forecast
Celsius
Fahrenheit

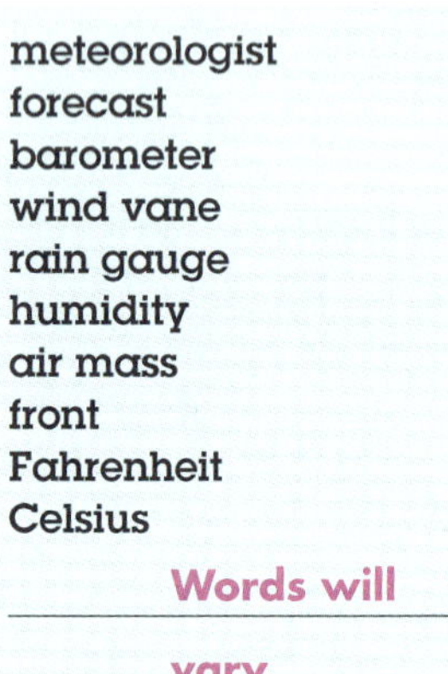

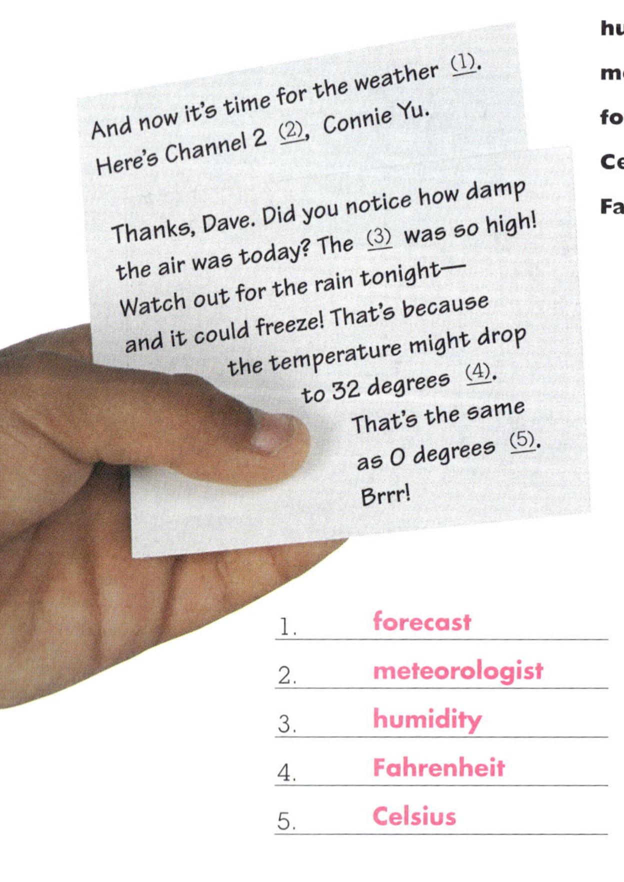

1. **forecast**
2. **meteorologist**
3. **humidity**
4. **Fahrenheit**
5. **Celsius**

196

Related Words Complete each sentence by writing the list word that is related to the underlined word or term.

rain gauge

wind vane

barometer

6. A _____**barometer**_____ measures the <u>barometric</u>, or air, pressure.

7. A _____**rain gauge**_____ measures the amount of <u>rainfall</u>.

8. Both a _____**wind vane**_____ and a <u>wind sock</u> can show wind direction.

Reading a Weather Map An **air mass** is a large body of air pushing into an area. A **front** is where two different air masses meet. Look at the map key. Then label the symbols on the map for **air mass** and **front**.

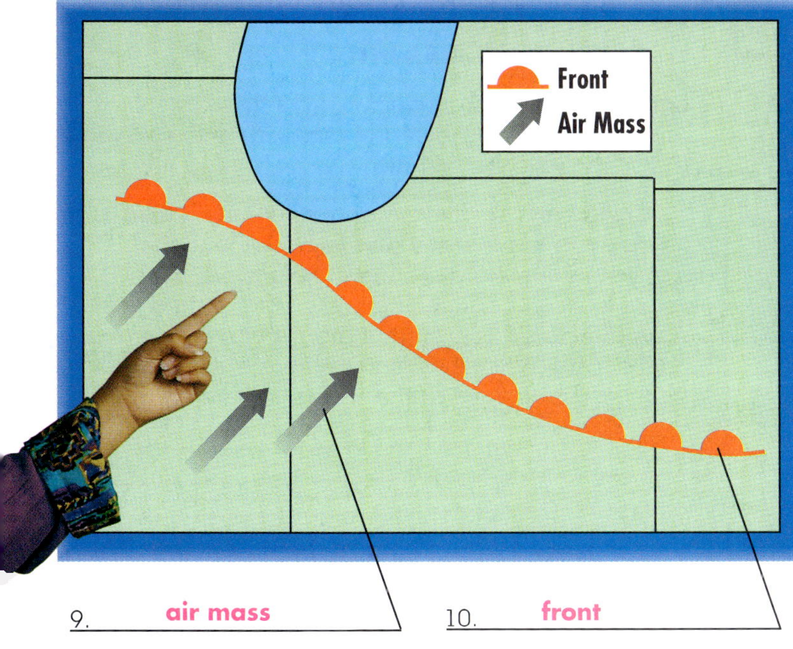

9. _____**air mass**_____

10. _____**front**_____

Weather Records

What's the coldest recorded temperature in your hometown? What's the warmest recorded temperature? Find out and share your information with your classmates.

197

SPELL WELL

Divide and Conquer Study these long words syllable by syllable. Then cover the words and write them.

11. me • te • o • rol • o • gist _____**meteorologist**_____

12. Fahr • en • heit _____**Fahrenheit**_____

FOLLOW-UP

Interpretive Thinking

Compare and Contrast
Divide the class into four groups. Assign each group a season. Have them describe local weather during that season, such as average, high, and low temperatures and amounts and kinds of precipitation. Then have students use their reports to compare and contrast the local weather during different seasons.

MEETING THE NEEDS OF ALL STUDENTS

Auditory Learners

Weather Reports Have students listen to weather reports on television or radio. Encourage them to identify the list words as they are used in the reports.

Bilingual/ESL

Cultural Awareness The weather in students' native countries is often very different from that of their new communities. Invite them to describe the weather in their native countries, using any list words that apply.

197

LANDFORMS

- Building Background
- Developing Concepts
- Practice on pp. 198–199
- Follow-Up

● Core ○ Optional

Before presenting this lesson, you may wish to teach Lesson 14, **Consonant Sounds /j/, /ks/, /kw/,** to introduce the spelling pattern that appears in the word *earthquake.*

BUILDING BACKGROUND

Ask students if they have ever seen a mountain. Point out that this is one kind of landform. Landforms include all the different shapes of the land. Have students volunteer the names of additional landforms and list them in a chart.

Landforms
mountains
hills
valleys
canyons

DEVELOPING CONCEPTS

Explain that some of the list words name landforms. Work with students to add those words to the chart. Other list words—*faults, seismograph,* and *Richter scale*—relate to earthquakes. Point out that earthquakes can create or change the shape of landforms.

Additional Practice

***Everyday Spelling* CD-ROM, Lesson 14**

landforms
mountains
plains
plateau
plates
volcano
faults
earthquake
seismograph
Richter scale

_______________ **Words will**

_______________ **vary.**

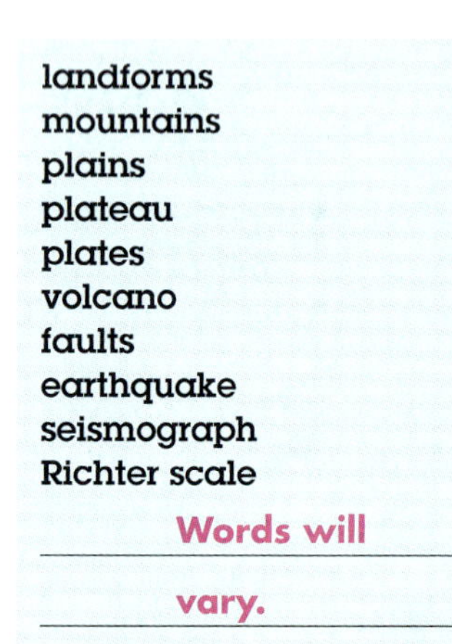

Landforms

Can you describe your natural surroundings? Are there any mountains or plains nearby? The list words will help you talk about landforms and the forces that cause them. Look up unfamiliar words in the Spelling Dictionary. Add two words of your own.

■ GETTING AT MEANING

Labeling   Read the explanations of these list words and look at the numbered pictures. Write the list word that identifies each picture.

Landforms are different shapes of land. **Plains** are flat areas of land, and a **plateau** is flat land that is higher than the land around it. **Mountains** are hills that rise at least 600 meters above the land around them. A **volcano** looks like a mountain with an opening on the top. Lava, ashes, and steam sometimes flow through this opening in the earth's crust.

1.   **mountains**

2.   **plateau**

3.   **plains**

4.   **volcano**

5. These four shapes of land are called
   landforms .

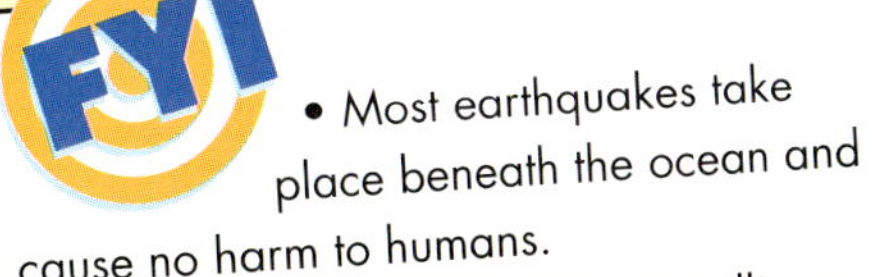

- Most earthquakes take place beneath the ocean and cause no harm to humans.
- There may be as many as one million earthquakes a year.
- Plate movements along faults are a common cause of earthquakes. The largest fault—the Great Rift Valley in Africa—is more than 6,000 miles long.

Scientific Vocabulary   When writers use technical words, they often put clues in the sentences to help you understand what the terms mean. Using the underlined clues, write list words to complete this paragraph about earthquakes.

Earth Notes

When the <u>earth shakes</u>, it is called an (6). An earthquake is caused by the shifting of <u>large sections of rock that make up the earth's surface</u> called (7). The earth's surface has <u>cracks</u> called (8). Earthquakes usually begin along these fault lines. An instrument called a (9) <u>records how strong the earthquake is by drawing lines on graph paper</u>. Scientists report their results using the (10), a <u>scale of measurement</u> that goes from zero for the weakest quake, up to 9 for the very strongest.

6. __earthquake__
7. __plates__
8. __faults__
9. __seismograph__
10. __Richter scale__

■ SPELL WELL

Divide and Conquer   Study these long words syllable by syllable. Then cover the words and write them.

11. earth • quake ___earthquake___
12. seis • mo • graph ___seismograph___

Did You Know?

There are about 1,300 potentially active volcanoes in the world. Many of them lie in what is called "The Ring of Fire" around the Pacific Ocean.

FOLLOW-UP

Critical Thinking

Inferring Have students, in small groups, infer answers to these questions:
What causes danger during an earthquake?
How might an earthquake's dangers be avoided?
Allow time for groups to present their suggestions to the class.

MEETING THE NEEDS OF ALL STUDENTS

Visual Learners

Draw Landforms Have students work together to draw an imaginary landscape that includes as many landforms named in the word list as possible. Have them label each feature. Encourage students to use the imaginary drawing to develop a geography lesson for younger students.

Bilingual/ESL

Cultural Awareness Invite students to bring into class or draw pictures that show the landforms of their native country. Have them label their pictures with appropriate list words and share them in small groups.

LESSON PLAN

- ● Building Background
- ● Developing Concepts
- ● Practice on pp. 200–201
- ○ Follow-Up

● Core ○ Optional

Link to Weekly Lesson

Before presenting this lesson, you may wish to teach Lesson 8, **Words with Double Consonants,** to introduce the spelling patterns that appear in *middle ear* and *inner ear.*

BUILDING BACKGROUND

Ask students to brainstorm a list of things they enjoy seeing every day. Then work with them to list things they enjoy hearing. Write the lists on the board in chart form, as shown below. Title the chart *Things We See and Hear.*

Things We See and Hear	
See	Hear
sunrise	music
television	television

DEVELOPING CONCEPTS

Explain that the list words name parts of our eyes and ears. Work with students to begin to make a chart titled *How We See and Hear.* Have volunteers read the list words, tell any meanings they know, and add the words to the chart.

How We See and Hear	
Eye	Ear
pupil	eardrum
iris	ear canal

Additional Practice

Everyday Spelling CD-ROM, Lesson 8

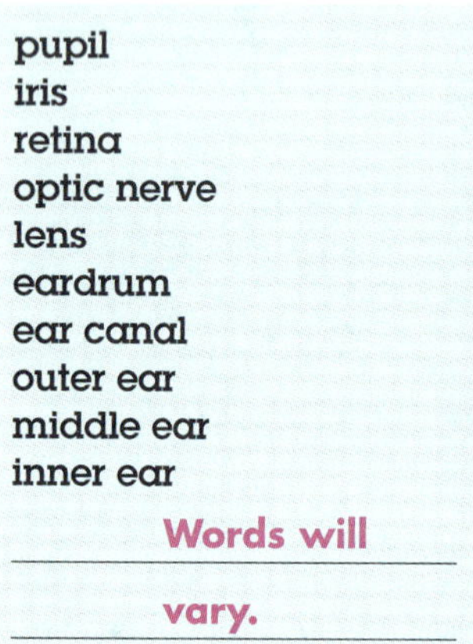

pupil
iris
retina
optic nerve
lens
eardrum
ear canal
outer ear
middle ear
inner ear

Words will

vary.

The Eyes and Ears

Our eyes and ears provide us with two important senses—seeing and hearing. The list words tell about the parts that make up our eyes and ears. Add other related words. Use your Spelling Dictionary for help.

■ GETTING AT MEANING

Labeling Diagrams   Read the paragraphs describing the parts of the eye and the parts of the ear. Write the list word that identifies each numbered part in the diagram.

The Eyes   We can see only certain parts of the eye: the white of the eye and the colored part called the **iris.** The iris has an opening in the middle called the **pupil,** which controls the amount of light that enters the eye. Right behind the iris is the **lens.** The lens works to make sure that the eye gets a sharp picture. The **retina** is the eye's "back wall." The retina changes the light coming in into electric signals. Then the **optic nerve** carries the electric signals to the brain.

1. **pupil**
2. **iris**
3. **lens**
4. **optic nerve**
5. **retina**

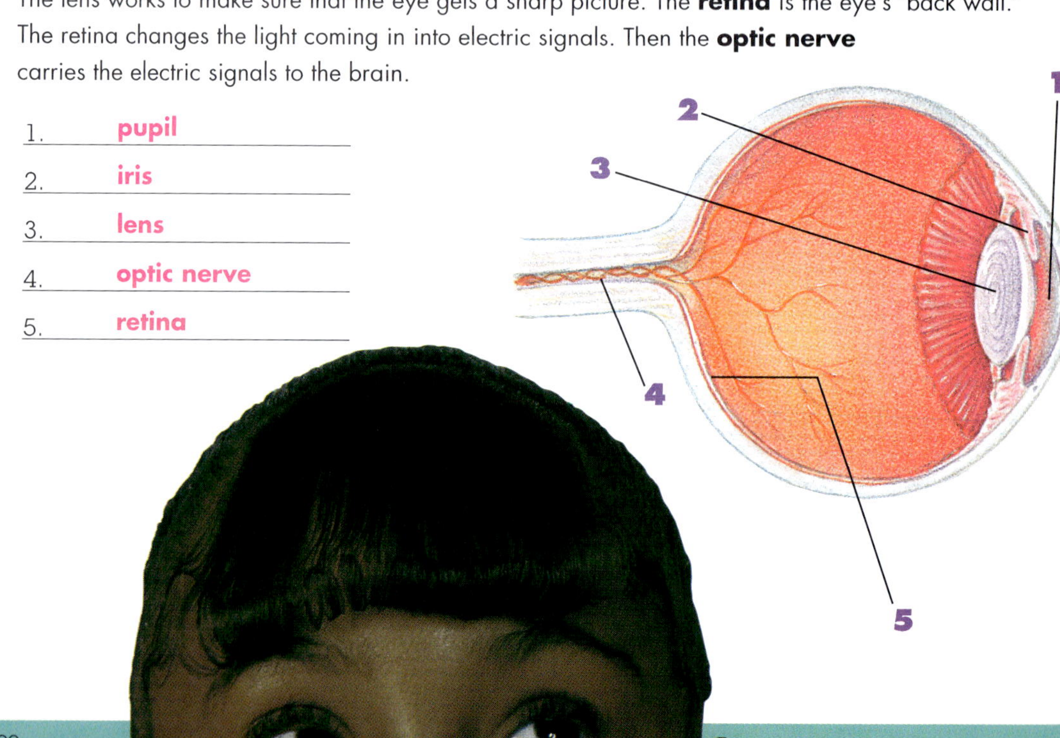

200

FYI

- The human eyeball is about one inch in diameter.
- An average blink lasts one-third of a second.
- The three bones in the middle ear are the smallest bones in the human body. Attached to them are two of the body's smallest muscles.

The Ears

Ears are the sense organs that let us hear. The part of the ear on the outside of the head is part of the **outer ear.** The other part of the outer ear is the **ear canal.** This little "tunnel" leads from the outer ear to the **eardrum,** which separates the outer ear from the **middle ear.** Sound waves make the eardrum vibrate. These vibrations move through the middle ear to the inner ear. The middle ear has three tiny bones that link the eardrum to the **inner ear** deep inside the head. The inner ear is the part of the ear that sends messages to the brain. The brain then "hears" the sounds.

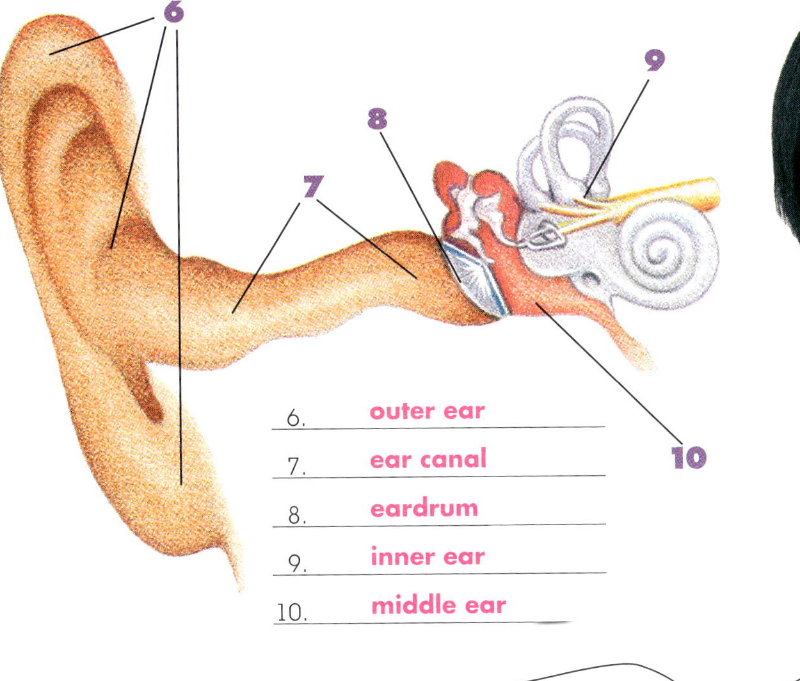

6. **outer ear**
7. **ear canal**
8. **eardrum**
9. **inner ear**
10. **middle ear**

■ SPELL WELL

Pronouncing Words Carefully
Some words are not spelled the way they're pronounced. Exaggerate the sounds of the underlined letters to help you remember them. Write the words.

11. retina **retina**
12. pupil **pupil**

All Eyes and Ears

The animal kingdom is full of amazing eyes and ears. Check out eagles, owls, cats, insects, or lobsters to learn about their eyes. To learn about animals that "get an earful," check out foxes, bats, dogs, or elephants. Share what you find.

FOLLOW-UP

Interpretive Thinking

Classifying In small groups, students can list activities in which they use their ears and eyes. Then have them use a Venn diagram to classify the activities as things they do with their eyes alone, their ears alone, or with both their eyes and ears.

MEETING THE NEEDS OF ALL STUDENTS

Visual Learners

Using Diagrams Help students use the diagrams and the list words to understand how the various parts of the eye and the ear work. Have them follow the numbers to trace the path of light through the eye and sound waves through the ear.

Bilingual/ESL

Cultural Awareness The eye and ear are important symbols in many cultures. For instance, an eye is featured on the back of every U.S. dollar bill. Ask students how eyes and ears may be used as symbols in their culture.

LESSON PLAN

- ● Building Background
- ● Developing Concepts
- ● Practice on pp. 202–203
- ○ Follow-Up

● Core   ○ Optional

Link to Weekly Lesson

Before presenting this lesson, you may wish to teach Lesson 28, **Suffixes -less, -ment, -ness,** to introduce the spelling pattern that appears in *accomplish<u>ment</u>s* and *disappoint<u>ment</u>.*

BUILDING BACKGROUND

Have students think about their goals for the short term (the school year) and the long term (after high school). Point out that writing down goals is one step toward achieving them. Circulate as students make a chart of their short- and long-term goals.

Short-Term Goals	Long-Term Goals
do better at math	go to college
play Little League baseball	get a job
earn some money	buy a car

DEVELOPING CONCEPTS

Have students use the list words to discuss the concept of working for and achieving goals. Students may wish to add other goals to their chart, using list words.

Additional Practice

Everyday Spelling CD-ROM, **Lesson 28**

accomplishments
artist
celebrated
humor
confidence
determination
disappointment
expert
strategy
successful

Words will

vary.

READING

Hopes, Dreams, and Wishes

What goals and achievements do you dream about and wish for? The words in the list will help you understand attitudes and actions that help make dreams come true. Look up unfamiliar words in the Spelling Dictionary. Add your own words to the list.

■ GETTING AT MEANING

Using Context Clues   Write the list words below to complete a recipe for success.

determination
disappointment
accomplishments
humor
expert

1. **accomplishments**
2. **determination**
3. **humor**
4. **disappointment**
5. **expert**

202

Connections to _BookFestival_

You may wish to recommend that students read _The Mouse and the Motorcycle_ by Beverly Cleary in the Scott Foresman - Addison Wesley _BookFestival_ program.

Using Synonyms Write the list word that is similar in meaning to each group of words below.

successful   celebrated   strategy   artist   confidence

6. **artist**
painter, musician, sculptor

7. **celebrated**
famous, well-known

8. **strategy**
method, plan

9. **confidence**
self-trust, self-belief

10. **successful**
triumphant, fortunate, well-off

■ **SPELL WELL**

Double Trouble Double letters can cause spelling problems. Write the words below. Underline the double letters in each word to help you remember them.

11. successful _______ **su<u>cc</u>e<u>ss</u>ful**

12. accomplishments _______ **a<u>cc</u>omplishments**

13. disappointment _______ **disa<u>pp</u>ointment**

Did You Know?

Not all dreams come true overnight. Inventors Wilbur and Orville Wright experimented for about seven years before their first successful airplane flight!

FOLLOW-UP

Critical Thinking

Making Decisions Invite students to review their goals charts from Building Background. Have them select one short-term goal that they particularly want to achieve. After they make the decision of which goal to pursue, encourage them to list the steps that will help them achieve success.

MEETING THE NEEDS OF ALL STUDENTS

Visual Learners

Picturing Yourself
Have students look at the illustrations in the lesson. Discuss how a picture can show a person's goals. Then encourage students to illustrate themselves achieving one of their own goals.

Bilingual/ESL

Language Goals Invite students to share their goals for becoming fluent in a second language. Help them use appropriate list words as they describe the steps in achieving their goals.

MANY WAYS OF LEARNING

LESSON PLAN

- ● Building Background
- ● Developing Concepts
- ● Practice on pp. 204–205
- ○ Follow-Up

Link to Weekly Lesson

Before presenting this lesson, you may wish to teach Lesson 27, **Suffixes -ful, -ly, -ion,** to introduce the spelling pattern that appears in *collections* and *demonstrations*.

● Core ○ Optional

BUILDING BACKGROUND

Work with students to create a word web based on the concept *ways to learn*. Encourage students to name ways they use every day, such as going to school, reading, and listening to teachers. Help students see that they also learn from other sources, such as television, the radio, and their parents.

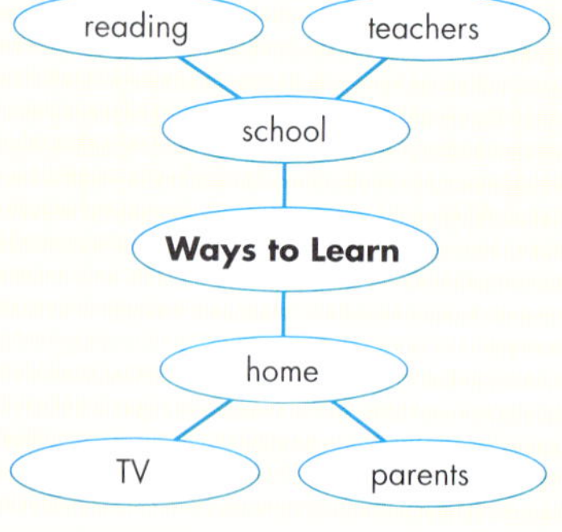

DEVELOPING CONCEPTS

Ask volunteers to read the list words. Point out that the words identify different learning activities. Help students decide where the activities would be likely to take place—in school, at home, at the library, or in a museum. Then ask volunteers to add any missing words to the web.

Additional Practice

Everyday Spelling **CD-ROM,** Lesson 27

---

assignments
collections
counselor
demonstrations
interview
experiment
exhibit
research
librarian
brainstorm

Words will

vary.

READING

Many Ways of Learning

How do we learn new things? We learn in many different ways. The list words name just a few. Use the Spelling Dictionary to look up unknown words. Add your own words.

■ GETTING AT MEANING

Labeling Illustrations   Write the list word that identifies each picture.

interview   brainstorm
exhibit   assignments
experiment

1. **brainstorm**
2. **exhibit**
3. **experiment**
4. **assignments**
5. **interview**

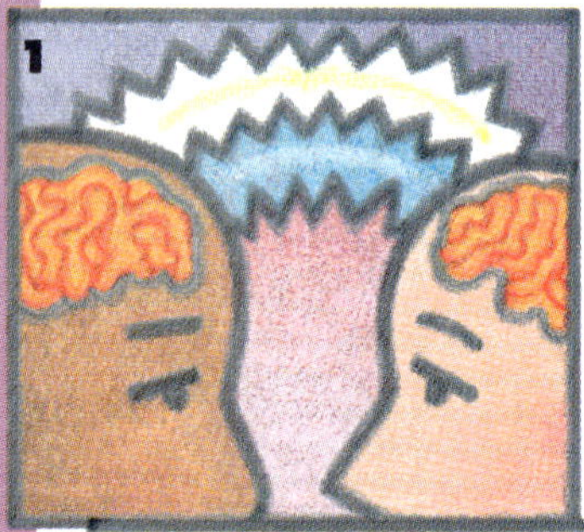

FYI Here are some "brain-teasing" facts about the brain.
- The brain is only one-fiftieth of the body's weight, but it receives one-fifth of the blood supply.
- The brain has about 100 billion nerve cells, which are interlinked via trillions of connections.
- One side of a person's brain usually dominates—the left side dominates in right-handers and the right side in left-handers.

■ **SPELL WELL**

Pronouncing Words Carefully   We sometimes spell words wrong because we say them wrong. Say each word carefully. Be sure to pronounce the sound of each underlined letter. Write each word.

11. experiment ______ experiment
12. counselor ______ counselor

Create the Perfect Learning Environment

Suppose you could create the perfect place where you could learn everything you wanted to know. Where would it be? What would it look like? What would you have there? Who would you have there? Draw or write a description of your "perfect learning place."

205

Link to Weekly Lesson

Before presenting this lesson, you may wish to teach Lesson 7, **Words with sh, ch, tch, wh,** to introduce the spelling patterns that appear in *children, shared, chores,* and *childhood.*

BUILDING BACKGROUND

Have students brainstorm words they associate with families. Put students' contributions in a word web on the board that begins with *Families* in the center.

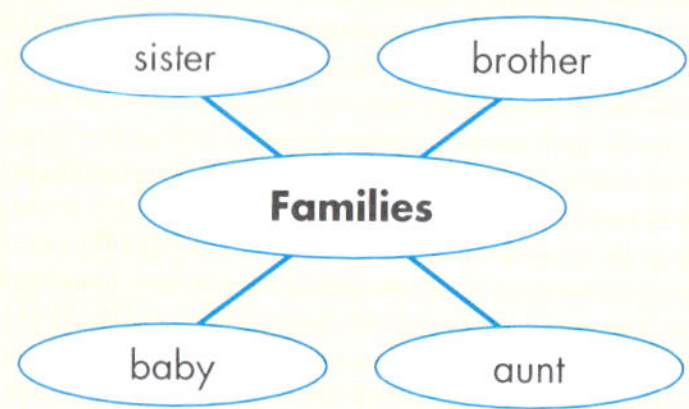

DEVELOPING CONCEPTS

Read each list word and ask a volunteer to explain how it relates to family life. Add to the web any list words that are not already there.

> **Additional Practice**
>
> *Everyday Spelling CD-ROM,* Lesson 7

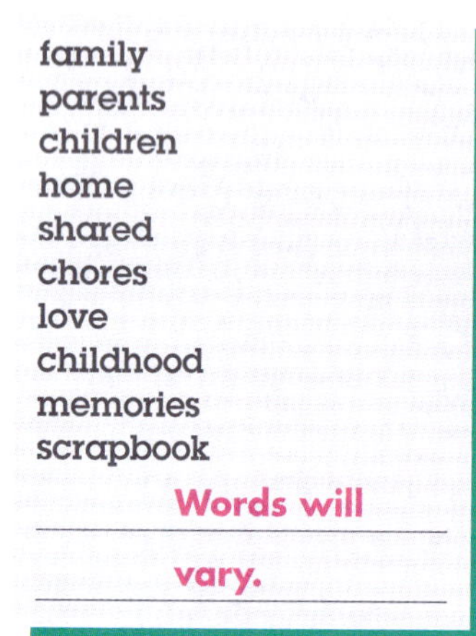

family
parents
children
home
shared
chores
love
childhood
memories
scrapbook

Words will vary.

1. **home**
2. **chores**
3. **children**

206

How Families Matter

What makes families special? Read the list of words, and look up unknown words in the Spelling Dictionary. Add your own family words to the list.

■ GETTING AT MEANING

Labeling Photographs   Everyone's family is different. Using what you know about families, write the list word that describes each photograph in John's scrapbook.

home   family   chores   parents   children

4. **parents**
5. **family**

Connections to *BookFestival*

You may wish to recommend that students read *Sarah, Plain and Tall* by Patricia MacLachlan in the Scott Foresman - Addison Wesley *BookFestival* program.

FYI

• The first prehistoric communities consisted of several families who moved around together, hunting small animals and gathering plants for food.

• About 10,000 years ago, people began to settle in permanent homes in order to raise crops for food. They also began to keep domestic animals.

Using Context Clues Use these list words to complete the note that John's parents wrote to him in the front of his scrapbook.

love	shared	childhood
memories	scrapbook	

6. **childhood**

7. **scrapbook**

8. **memories**

9. **shared**

10. **love**

Dear John,

We can't believe that you are nine years old already! Your (6) is going so quickly! For your birthday we would like you to have this (7). It is full of photos, and it holds (8) of many happy times we have (9) together. Happy 9th birthday! We (10) you!

Mom and Dad

Conduct Interviews

Interview the older members of your family. Ask them to tell you about their early memories of childhood. Take notes as they speak. Share these memories with the class.

■ **SPELL WELL**

Related Words

Write the two list words that are related in spelling and meaning to *child*.

11. **children**

12. **childhood**

FOLLOW-UP

Interpretive Thinking

Questioning Have the class discuss the following statement: *Family members must accept certain responsibilities.* Encourage students to formulate questions. For example, *What are some responsibilities? Why must family members accept responsibilities? Should everyone's responsibilities be the same?*

MEETING THE NEEDS OF ALL STUDENTS

Visual Learners

Family Photo Bulletin Board Ask students to contribute photos of families to a bulletin board. Photos may come from home or from newspapers and magazines. Have students use list words as appropriate to label the photos and items shown in the photos.

Bilingual/ESL

Cultural Awareness Invite students to draw pictures or bring in photos that show their own families in their native country. Help them to describe their pictures, using any list words that apply.

LESSON PLAN

- Building Background
- Developing Concepts
- Practice on pp. 208–209
- Follow-Up

○ Core   ○ Optional

Link to Weekly Lesson

Before presenting this lesson, you may wish to teach Lesson 21, **Vowel Sounds in** *put* **and** *out,* to introduce the spelling pattern that appears in terms such as *water fountain.*

BUILDING BACKGROUND

Work with students to start a chart like the one below on the board. Encourage students to think about all the different aspects of their own universe—the things they do, the places they go, the people they see— as they contribute to the class chart.

My Universe Chart
School
Home
Sports
Hobbies

DEVELOPING CONCEPTS

Have volunteers read the list words and suggest where they belong on the chart (some of the words may fit in more than one place). Encourage students to discuss whether or not the list words fit into their own personal universes.

Additional Practice

Everyday Spelling **CD-ROM, Lesson 21**

cafeteria
concert
curtains
furniture
office
library
orchestra
skateboarding
spider web
water fountain
Words will vary.

____

____

Your Own Universe

The words in the list name just ten of the thousands of things that are part of your universe. Add your own words. Use the Spelling Dictionary if you need help.

■ GETTING AT MEANING

Context Clues   School is a big part of your universe. Look at the bulletin board notices from Maple School. Complete them with list words.

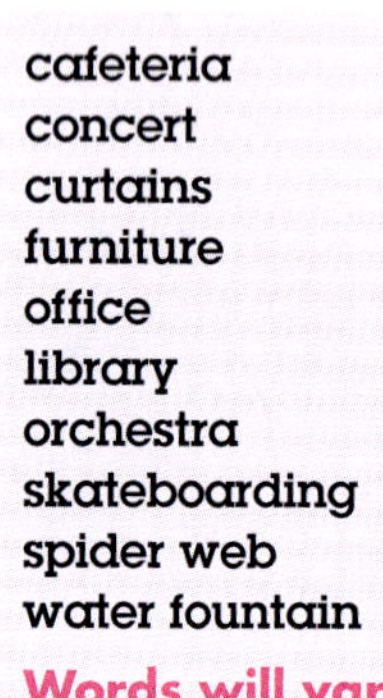

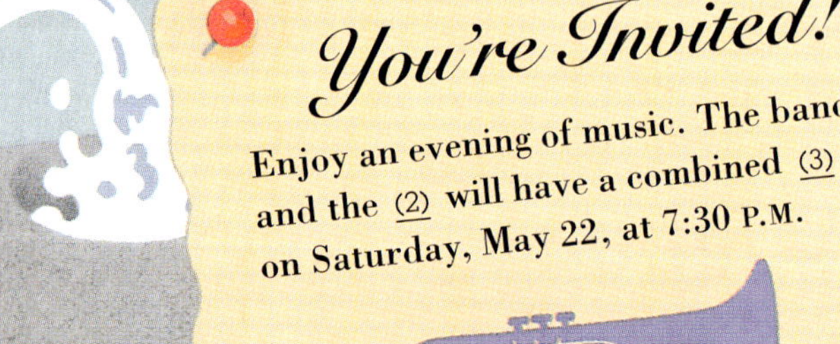

1. **water fountain**

2. **orchestra**

3. **concert**

4. **skateboarding**

208

FYI If you took a trip back in time to a nineteenth-century Native American village, you might be surprised to find children playing these familiar games:
- Stilt-walking and top-spinning
- Playing house with deerskin dolls and miniature tepees or lodges
- One-legged races, wrestling matches, and versions of football and field hockey

5. **curtains**
6. **spider web**
7. **furniture**
8. **library**
9. **office**
10. **cafeteria**

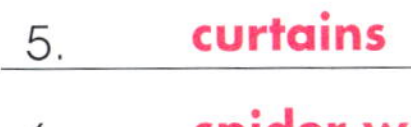

The Student Council will be selling hot dog lunches every Wednesday. Tickets are $1.75 each and may be purchased in the principal's (9) before school or in the (10) during the lunch hour.

■ **SPELL WELL**

Pronouncing for Spelling Some words are not spelled the way they're pronounced. Exaggerate the sounds of the underlined letters in each word below. Then write the words.

11. orchestra   **orchestra**
12. furniture   **furniture**

209

LESSON PLAN

- ● Building Background
- ● Developing Concepts
- ● Practice on pp. 210–211
- ○ Follow-Up

● Core   ○ Optional

Link to Weekly Lesson

Before presenting this lesson, you may wish to teach Lesson 2, **Words with kn, gn, wr, mb,** to introduce the spelling pattern that appears in *tomb.*

BUILDING BACKGROUND

Work with students to brainstorm a list of famous buildings. Write the list on the chalkboard. Then discuss what students know about each building, such as its appearance, location, and purpose. Organize the information into a chart like the one below.

Building	Empire State Building
Location	New York
Purpose	offices
Physical Description	skyscraper

DEVELOPING CONCEPTS

Point out that some list words describe famous buildings—the *Cathedral* of Notre Dame at *Chartres,* the *Parthenon,* and the *Taj Mahal.* Other list words (*church, temple, tomb*) describe the purposes of these buildings. Suggest that students add these words to the chart. Encourage them to discuss how the other list words might relate to famous buildings.

Additional Practice

Everyday Spelling **CD-ROM, Lesson 2**

cathedral
Chartres
church
temple
Parthenon
marble
jewels
tomb
Taj Mahal
honor

Words will vary.

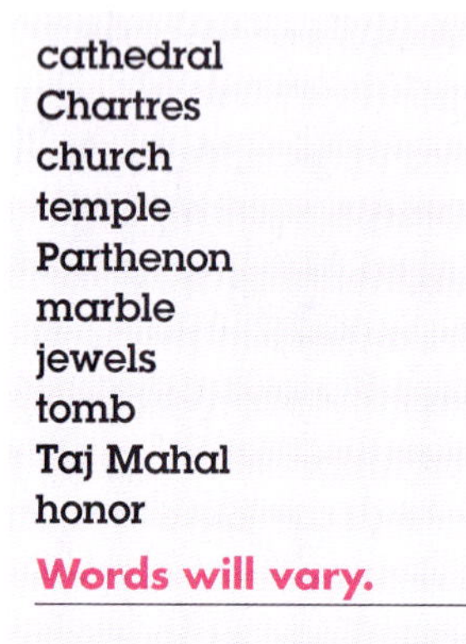

Looking at the World in New Ways

Imagine that you are at the Parthenon, the Cathedral of Notre Dame, or the Taj Mahal. What would you notice about it? The list words tell about these three monuments. Add words about other world-famous buildings. Use your Spelling Dictionary for help.

■ GETTING AT MEANING

Using Photographs   Complete the caption under each postcard. Use the words in the brick.

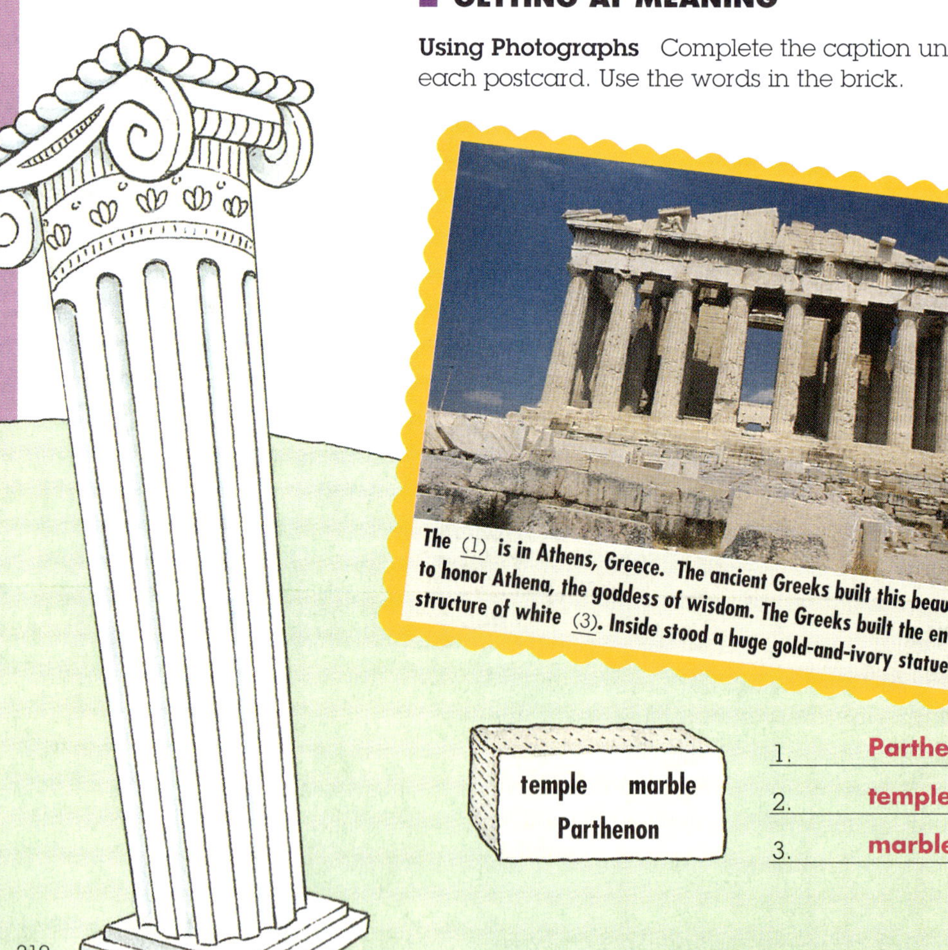

The __(1)__ is in Athens, Greece. The ancient Greeks built this beautiful to honor Athena, the goddess of wisdom. The Greeks built the entire __(2)__ structure of white __(3)__. Inside stood a huge gold-and-ivory statue of Athena.

1. **Parthenon**
2. **temple**
3. **marble**

210

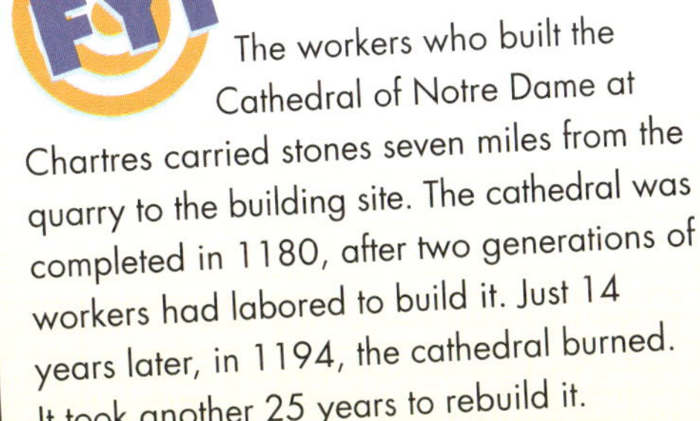

The workers who built the Cathedral of Notre Dame at Chartres carried stones seven miles from the quarry to the building site. The cathedral was completed in 1180, after two generations of workers had labored to build it. Just 14 years later, in 1194, the cathedral burned. It took another 25 years to rebuild it.

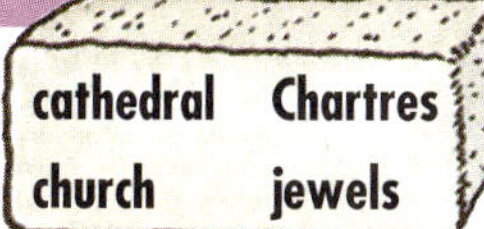

4. **Chartres**

5. **cathedral or church**

6. **church or cathedral**

7. **jewels**

The city of (4) in France is world famous for its (5), called the Cathedral of Notre Dame. The great (6) has more than 100 stained-glass windows so richly colored that they shine like (7).

The (8) is in Agra, India. The Indian ruler Shah Jahan had this beautiful (9) built in the mid-1600s. It was constructed in (10) of his wife, Mumtaz Mahal. It has a domed roof and four prayer towers.

8. **Taj Mahal**

9. **tomb**

10. **honor**

■ SPELL WELL

Capital Letters Three of your list words are proper nouns. Write them. Remember to capitalize the words.

11. **Chartres**

12. **Parthenon**

13. **Taj Mahal**

Design a Monument

The Parthenon was erected to honor Athena. Farmers in Enterprise, Alabama, erected a monument to the boll weevil in 1919. By destroying their crops, the insect forced them to grow new and different crops. As a result, the farmers became richer. Think of someone you'd like to design a monument to honor. Draw the monument and write an inscription.

211.

FOLLOW-UP

Critical Thinking

Making Decisions Have students working in pairs decide where they would go if they could visit one building anywhere in the world. Before finalizing their decision, students should find facts about the building. Afterward, they should present their reasons for deciding to visit it.

MEETING THE NEEDS OF ALL STUDENTS

Visual Learners

Creating a Bulletin Board Create a bulletin board entitled *Famous Buildings Around the World*. Students can add photographs or drawings of famous buildings to the display. Encourage them to label their contributions, using as many list words as possible.

Bilingual/ESL

Cultural Awareness Invite students to bring in pictures of buildings that are important in their culture. They can post these pictures with labels on the bulletin board after sharing them with the class.

TALES OF COURAGE

LESSON PLAN

- ● Building Background
- ● Developing Concepts
- ● Practice on pp. 212–213
- ○ Follow-Up

● Core ○ Optional

Link to Weekly Lesson

Before presenting this lesson, you may wish to teach Lesson 4, **Adding -ed and -ing,** to introduce guidelines for adding endings to *devastate* and *recover.*

BUILDING BACKGROUND

Build a word web on the board like the one below. Help students think about different types of emergencies and the different ways in which people react to them. Expand the web by adding words or phrases that fit the categories shown.

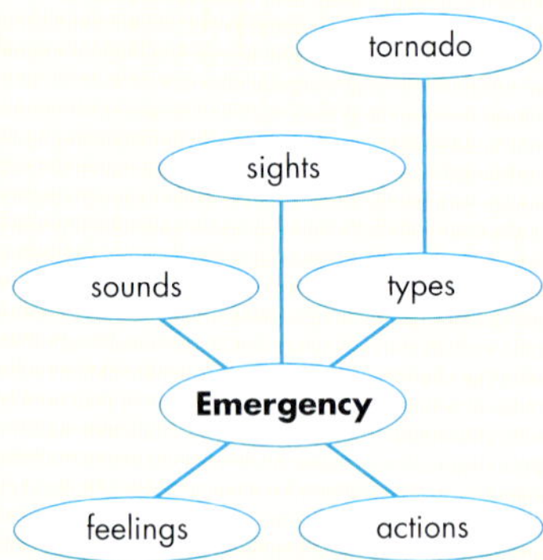

DEVELOPING CONCEPTS

Ask volunteers to read the list words. Point out that some of the words describe how people might feel in an emergency situation, while others describe what people do. Then work with the students to determine which list words might be added to the web.

Additional Practice

Everyday Spelling **CD-ROM,** Lesson 4

compassionate
debris
devastate
emergency
extraordinary
panic
pressure
recover
siren
tremendous

Words will vary.

Tales of Courage

Many situations call for courage. The words in the list bring to mind some sounds, sights, and feelings of such situations. Add some of your own words of courage.

■ GETTING AT MEANING

Using Context Clues Use the list words at the right to complete the phone call.

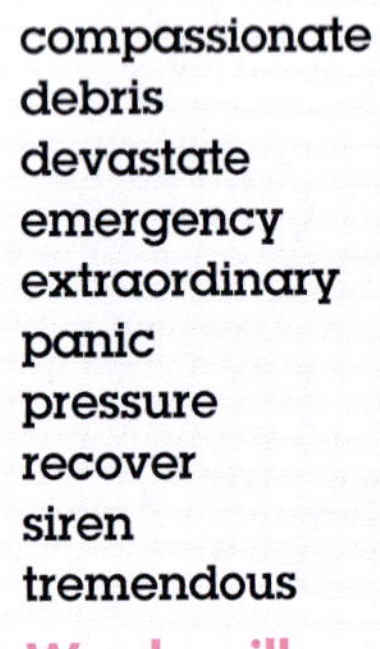

1. emergency
2. panic
3. recover
4. siren
5. pressure

212

Connections to *BookFestival*

You may wish to recommend that students read *Willie Mays: Young Superstar* by Louis Sabin in the Scott Foresman - Addison Wesley *BookFestival* program.

FYI
- Villa, a Newfoundland puppy, rescued a girl during a blizzard in New Jersey. After she found the girl in a snowdrift, Villa cleared a path and led the girl home.
- During an earthquake in California, Reona, a rottweiler, saved a child by pushing her out of the way of falling debris.

More Context Clues Complete the paragraph with these list words. The underlined words may help you.

debris compassionate extraordinary tremendous devastate

A powerful earthquake can <u>destroy</u>, or (6), a city. The <u>awesome</u>, (7) force of the earth moving can topple buildings. <u>Building materials, crushed automobiles, broken pipes, and other</u> (8) can block the streets. At times like this, <u>ordinary</u> citizens show (9) courage to help their neighbors. And <u>concerned</u> people from all over the country show their (10) nature by sending food, clothing, and money to aid the victims of an earthquake.

6. **devastate**
7. **tremendous**
8. **debris**
9. **extraordinary**
10. **compassionate**

■ SPELL WELL

Divide and Conquer Study the words below syllable by syllable. Then cover them and write them.

11. com • pas • sion • ate ______ **compassionate**

12. ex • traor • di • nar • y ______ **extraordinary**

Did You Know?

Courage comes from a Latin word that means "heart."

FOLLOW-UP

Critical Thinking

Recognizing Values In Quincy, Illinois, during the Great Flood of 1993, the mayor saw two young girls volunteering to help fill sandbags to build levees. Have students discuss the values the girls showed. Do they think the girls deserved special recognition?

MEETING THE NEEDS OF ALL STUDENTS

Kinesthetic Learners

Acting Out Courage Encourage students to find real-life tales of courage and dramatize them for classmates, using list words as appropriate.

Bilingual/ESL

List Word Demonstrations Have students choose one list word to explore and explain the meaning of. They can explain the word's meaning by drawing a picture or acting it out. Have them share their explanations in small groups.

LESSON PLAN

- Building Background
- Developing Concepts
- Practice on pp. 214–215
- Follow-Up

● Core ○ Optional

Link to Weekly Lesson

Before presenting this lesson, you may wish to teach Lesson 9, **Short e and Long e,** to introduce the spelling patterns that appear in *key, memory,* and *equals.*

BUILDING BACKGROUND

Ask students to recall situations when they have used a calculator. Have them name situations in which a calculator is a useful tool at home, at school, or on the job. Then work with students to list these on the board.

DEVELOPING CONCEPTS

Explain that the list words pertain to the parts and functions of a calculator. Ask volunteers to tell the definitions of the words they are familiar with.

Additional Practice
Everyday Spelling **CD-ROM,** Lesson 9

---

operation key
number keys
display
memory recall
memory plus
memory minus
key sequence
error
clear key
equals key
Words will vary.

1. **number keys**
2. **display**
3. **operation key**
4. **clear key**
5. **equals key**
6. **key sequence**
7. **error**

MATHEMATICS

The Calculator

Do you, your parents, or your friends use calculators? The words in the list tell all about these small, remarkable machines. Add your own words. Use the Spelling Dictionary for help.

■ **GETTING AT MEANING**

Understanding a Calculator   Read the paragraphs below. Then write list words to complete the sentences.

The **number keys** and each **operation key** are used to give information to the calculator. The order in which you press the keys is the **key sequence.** The answer to the problem appears in the **display** after you press the **equals key.**

Press the **clear key** once if you make a mistake entering numbers. An "E" will appear in the display if you make an **error** like trying to divide by zero.

Marta wanted to add the number of muffins she sold on Monday and Tuesday. She pressed the (1) 3 and 5, and the number 35 appeared in the (2). She pressed the "+" (3) before she entered 27. When 24 appeared in the display, she realized that she had pressed the 4 by mistake. She pressed the (4) once and then entered the correct numbers. The answer appeared after she pressed the (5). 35 ⊞ 27 ⊟ is the (6) Marta entered to solve her problem. If the answer to her problem had been greater than eight digits long, or she had tried to divide by zero, an "E" in the display would have told her that she had made an (7).

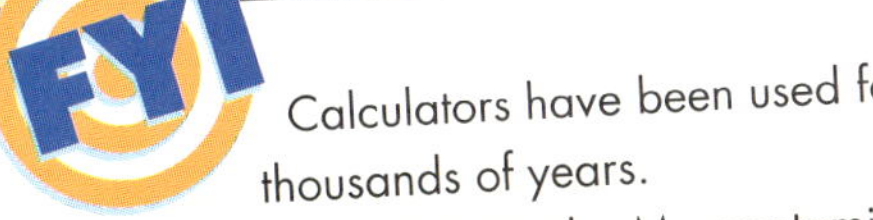

Calculators have been used for thousands of years.

• About 5,000 years ago, the Mesopotamians made furrows in the ground into which they placed ten pebbles. They calculated by moving the pebbles from one furrow to another.

• Not much later, the abacus was invented by the Chinese and Japanese for counting. It uses rows of beads on wires. It is still in use today.

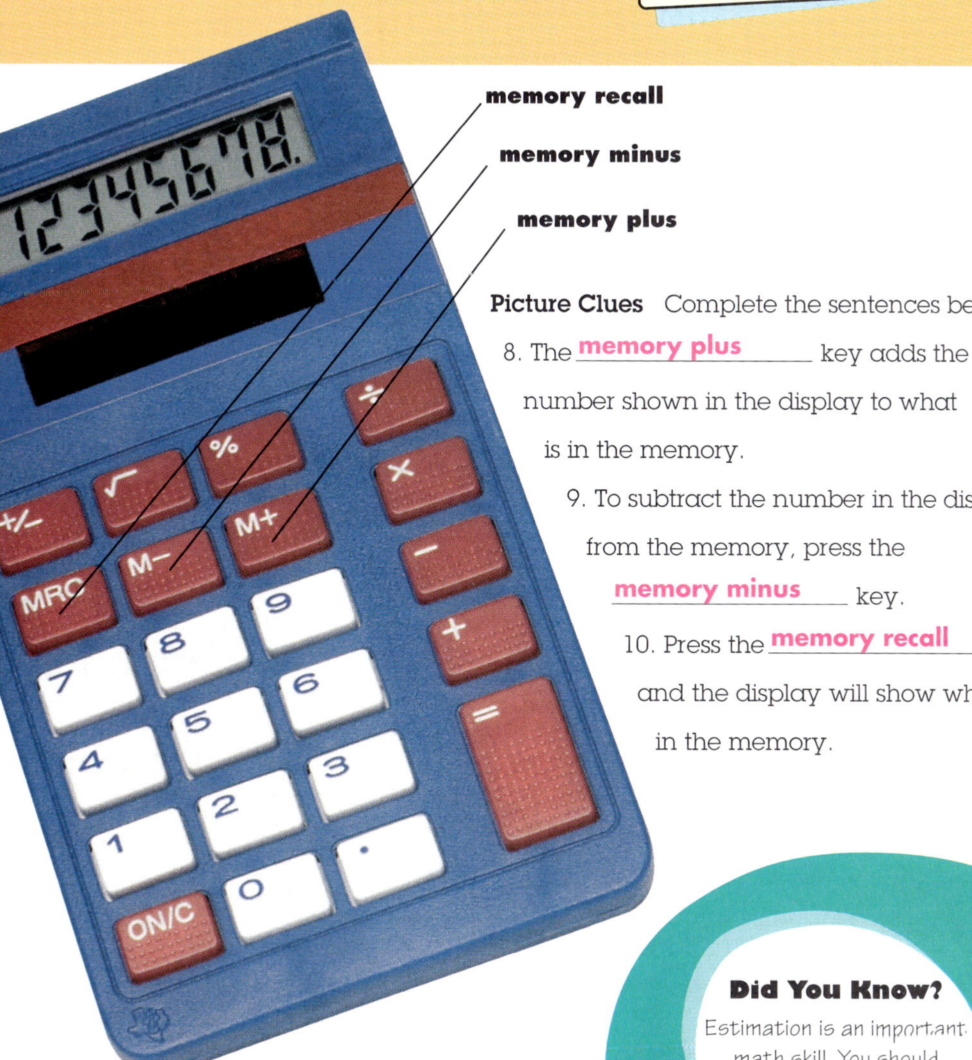

Picture Clues   Complete the sentences below.

8. The ___memory plus___ key adds the number shown in the display to what is in the memory.

9. To subtract the number in the display from the memory, press the ___memory minus___ key.

10. Press the ___memory recall___ key, and the display will show what is in the memory.

■ **SPELL WELL**

Pronouncing Words Correctly   We sometimes spell words wrong because we say them wrong. Write each word below. Then say each word. Be sure to pronounce the sound of the underlined letter.

11. mem<u>o</u>ry plus ___memory plus___

12. mem<u>o</u>ry minus ___memory minus___

13. mem<u>o</u>ry recall ___memory recall___

Did You Know?

Estimation is an important math skill. You should estimate the answer to a problem when you use a calculator. If your answer isn't close to your estimate, you may have entered some numbers incorrectly.

FOLLOW-UP

Critical Thinking

Applying Have students apply their knowledge of calculators as they complete the following activity with a partner: *Suppose you have just held a successful garage sale. Make up a math problem involving items sold and their selling prices. Have your partner use a calculator to solve the problem.*

MEETING THE NEEDS OF ALL STUDENTS

Kinesthetic Learners

Use a Calculator Students can use list words to make labels for the parts of a calculator key pad and then attach the labels to the correct parts of a real calculator.

Bilingual/ESL

Cultural Awareness If possible, show an abacus and point out that it has remained popular in China and Japan, even in the age of electronic calculators. Encourage students from these cultures to share with the class what they know about the abacus.

215

215

LESSON PLAN

- ● Building Background
- ● Developing Concepts
- ● Practice on pp. 216–217
- ○ Follow-Up

● **Core**   ○ **Optional**

Link to Weekly Lesson

Before presenting this lesson, you may wish to teach Lesson 5, **Adding -er and -est,** to introduce the spelling patterns that appear in adding endings to *length* (-y, -ier, -iest) and *weight* (-y, -ier, -iest).

BUILDING BACKGROUND

Ask students to suggest words they associate with measurement. Add their responses to a word web like the one below.

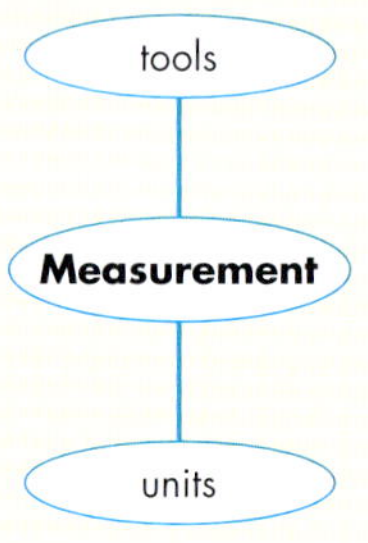

DEVELOPING CONCEPTS

Discuss the list words with students. Help them see that all the words name specific characteristics that can be measured. Encourage students to name tools that can be used to measure these characteristics. Volunteers can add the list words and tools to the web.

Additional Practice

Everyday Spelling **CD-ROM, Lesson 5**

length
width
height
weight
capacity
volume
area
perimeter
distance
temperature

Words will vary.

____

1. width
2. length
3. distance
4. area
5. perimeter
6. weight
7. height
8. temperature

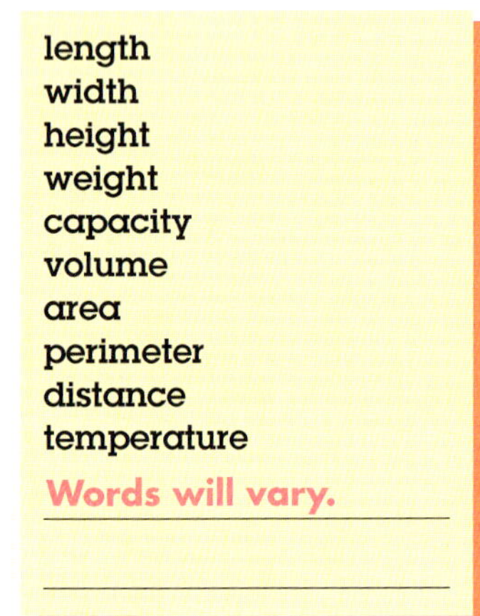

Measurement

How would you describe the size and shape of a soccer field? Words of measurement, like the ones in the word list, help you describe places or objects.

■ GETTING AT MEANING

Context Clues   Complete each sentence with the correct list word from those given in parentheses.

1. In youth soccer, the field is usually 100 yards in length and 50 yards in _____. **(width, length)**
2. The _____ of the field is divided by a halfway line. **(width, length)**
3. The _____ from one goal to the other is 100 yards. **(distance, area)**
4. The entire _____ of the field covers about 5,000 square yards. **(distance, area)**
5. White lines are drawn around the _____ of the field. **(perimeter, volume)**
6. Modern soccer shoes are light in _____ . **(height, weight)**
7. In soccer, the _____ and weight of a player are not as important as the player's speed and fitness. **(height, width)**
8. Soccer can be played outside whether the _____ is warm or cool. **(volume, temperature)**

216

Understanding Measurements   Study the figure to the right. Complete each sentence with the correct list word.

9. To measure volume, multiply length x width x height. The __volume__ of the box is 27 cubic feet.

10. When the box is filled to its __capacity__ it holds about ten soccer balls.

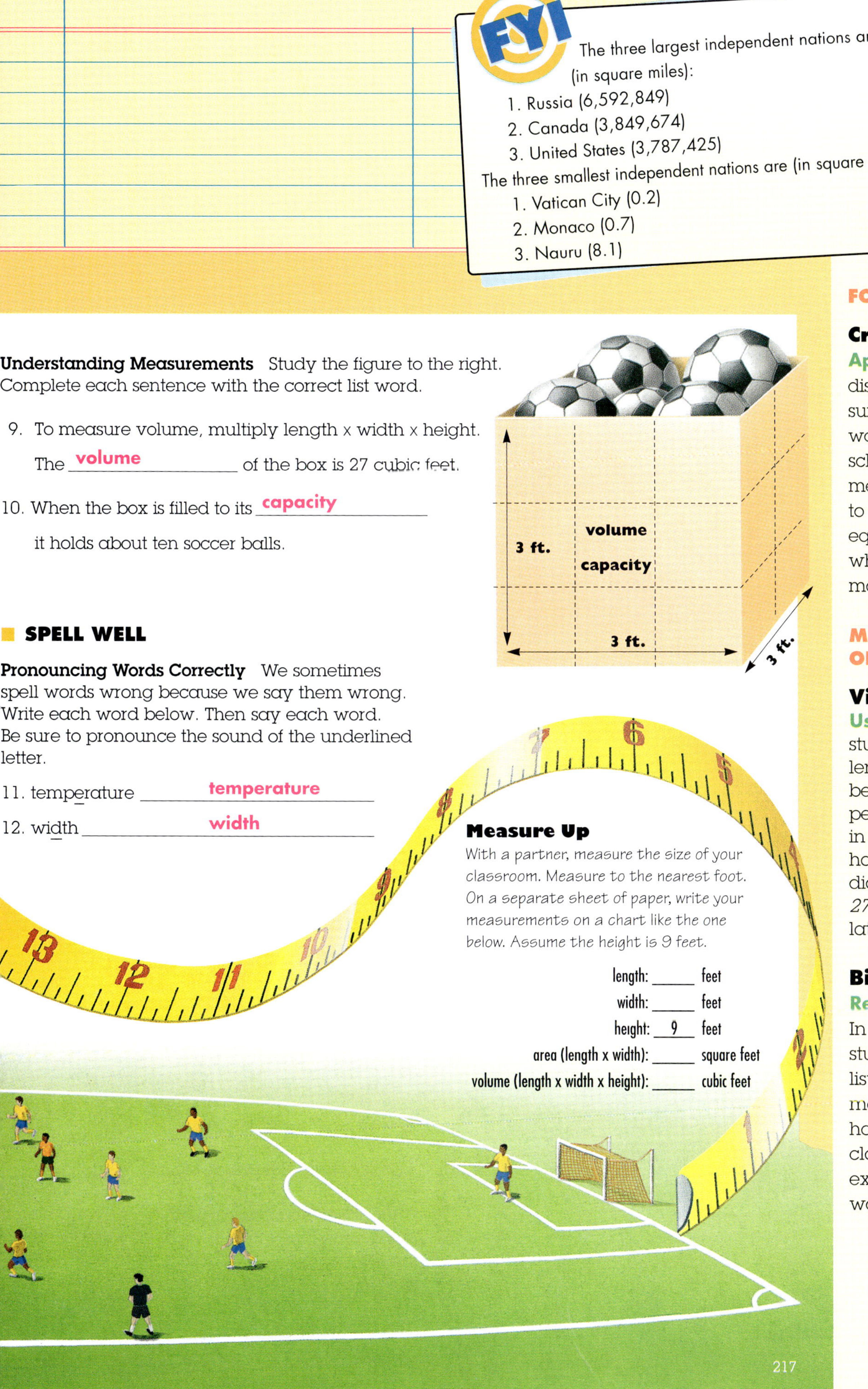

■ **SPELL WELL**

Pronouncing Words Correctly   We sometimes spell words wrong because we say them wrong. Write each word below. Then say each word. Be sure to pronounce the sound of the underlined letter.

11. temperature __temperature__

12. width __width__

Measure Up

With a partner, measure the size of your classroom. Measure to the nearest foot. On a separate sheet of paper, write your measurements on a chart like the one below. Assume the height is 9 feet.

FOLLOW-UP

Critical Thinking

Applying Have students discuss what units of measurement and tools they would use to measure the school's playground equipment. Assign small groups to choose one piece of equipment and apply what they have learned by making the measurements.

MEETING THE NEEDS OF ALL STUDENTS

Visual Learners

Using a Diagram Have students point out the length, width, distance between goals, area, and perimeter of the soccer field in the illustration. Then have them use the volume diagram to explain how *27 cubic feet* was calculated in question 9.

Bilingual/ESL

Real-World Measurement

In small groups, have students practice using the list words. Provide a tape measure or yardstick and have the groups measure classroom objects to find examples of as many list words as possible.

217

- Building Background
- Developing Concepts
- Practice on pp. 218–219
- Follow-Up

● Core ○ Optional

Before presenting this lesson, you may wish to teach Lesson 16, **Using Just Enough Letters,** to introduce words that are often misspelled when an extra letter is added, such as *family* (not *fammily*) and *remainder* (not *remmainder*).

BUILDING BACKGROUND

Work with students to build a word web like the one below. Point out that the four math operations are used to solve different problems. Encourage students to come up with examples of problems.

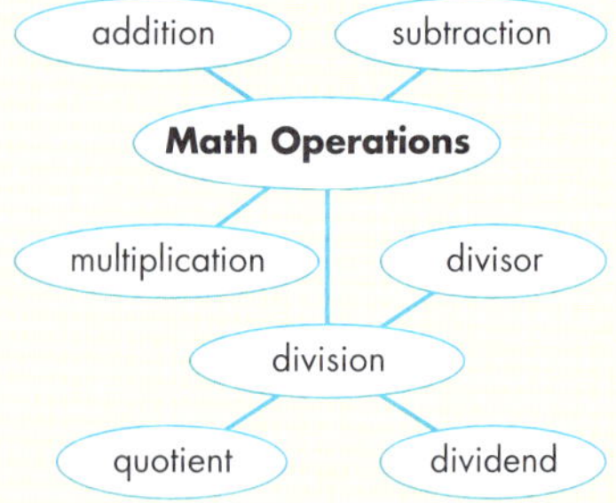

DEVELOPING CONCEPTS

Give students the following problem: *Suppose you and three friends order a pizza that has sixteen slices. If you want to share the pizza equally, how many slices should each person get?* (4) Have students write the problem in number form. Then point out that the list words are terms used in division but that some of the words are common to different math operations. Ask volunteers to use list words to name each number in the problem.

Additional Practice

Everyday Spelling CD-ROM, **Lesson 16**

family of facts
grouping
number sentence
divide
dividend
divisor
division
quotient
remainder
divisible

Answers

will vary.

Division

Division is one of the four basic math operations. Read the list of words that talk about division and add your own words. Look up unfamiliar words in the Spelling Dictionary.

■ GETTING AT MEANING

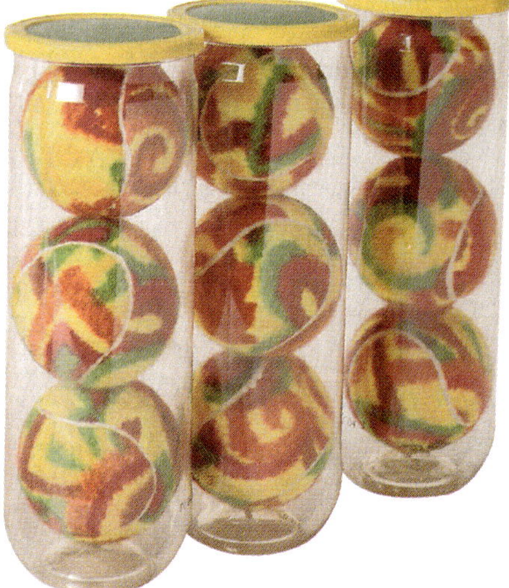

Understanding Math Terms When you have 12 tennis balls and want to put them into groups of 3, you **divide** to find the number of groups you can make. You may show the **division** problem in two ways.

$$3 \overline{)12} \qquad \frac{4}{}$$

$$\text{divisor} \overline{)\text{dividend}} \qquad \overset{\text{quotient}}{}$$

$$12 \div 3 = 4 \qquad \text{dividend} \div \text{divisor} = \text{quotient}$$

A **family of facts** can be used to represent the groupings of the tennis balls. Each **number sentence** in a family of facts tells about the **grouping.** Two of the number sentences show related multiplication facts and two of the number sentences show the related division facts.

218

Write the list word that describes each item.

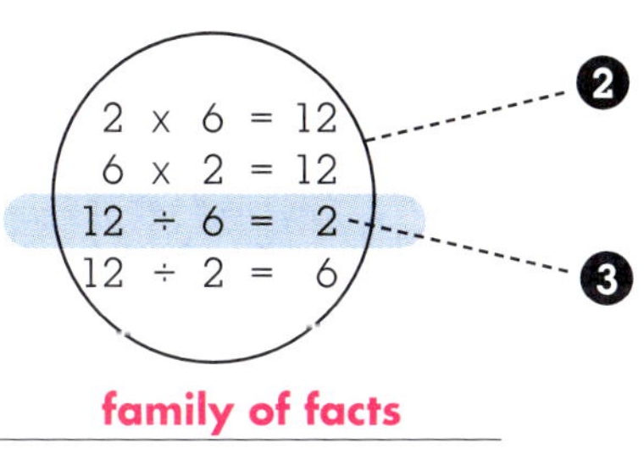

2. **family of facts**

3. **number sentence**

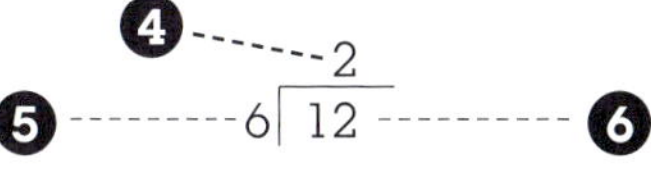

4. **quotient**

5. **divisor**

6. **dividend**

1. **grouping**

A number is **divisible** by another if it can be divided by that number with no remainder. When a number cannot be divided exactly by another number, the number left over is called a **remainder.**

Look at the examples below. Complete the sentences with list words.

$$2\overline{)8} = 4 \qquad 2\overline{)5} = 2R1$$

7. Eight is ______ **divisible** ______ by two.

8. One is the ______ **remainder** ______ in the second problem.

9. When you ______ **divide** ______ eight by two, the quotient is four.

10. The symbol ÷ represents the operation of ______ **division** ______ .

■ SPELL WELL

Problem Parts Say the words below. Notice that the last syllables of the two words sound alike but are spelled differently. Write each word and underline the last two letters.

Did You Know?
Division is repeated subtraction. To find how many groups of 3 are in 12 you can subtract 3 from 12 until your answer is zero. You can subtract 4 times, so there are 4 groups of 3 in 12.

11. divisor ______ **divisor**

12. remainder ______ **remainder**

FOLLOW-UP

Critical Thinking

Solving Problems Have students work in pairs to develop word problems for the following situation: *You are eating lunch in a restaurant with four friends. How much money should each person pay?* Help students decide which operations they should use to solve the problems.

MEETING THE NEEDS OF ALL STUDENTS

Kinesthetic Learners

Using Manipulatives Encourage students to use everyday objects like six-packs of soda to help them understand and practice the basic concepts of division.

Bilingual/ESL

Cultural Awareness Invite students to make up word problems that use items from their own culture. Students can write the problems in number form. They can then exchange papers, label the parts of the problems with list words, and solve the problems.

LESSON PLAN

- Building Background
- Developing Concepts
- Practice on pp. 220–221
- Follow-Up

● Core ○ Optional

Link to Weekly Lesson

Before presenting this lesson, you may wish to teach Lesson 35, **Easily Confused Words,** to introduce words that have similar pronunciations and spellings, such as *angle* (*angel*).

BUILDING BACKGROUND

On the board, draw a point, a line, a set of intersecting lines, a set of parallel lines, and a set of perpendicular lines. Name each drawing. Tell students that the branch of mathematics that studies lines and what a line is made of is called geometry.

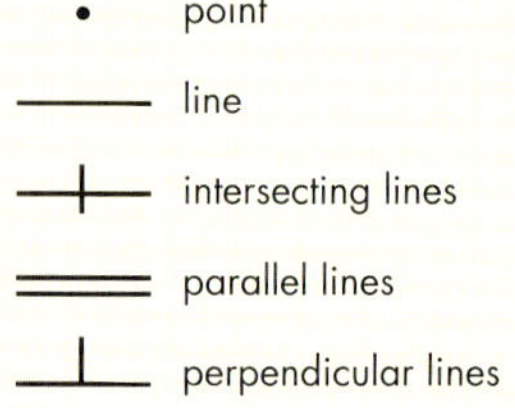

DEVELOPING CONCEPTS

Ask volunteers to read the list words. They can explain the terms, using the drawings as illustrations. It may be helpful to have students copy the figures from the board and label them.

Additional Practice

Everyday Spelling **CD-ROM,** Lesson 35

angle
vertex
endpoint
intersecting
line
parallel
point
ray
segment
perpendicular

Answers

will vary.

Geometry

Geometry is the branch of mathematics that studies and measures lines, angles, and shapes. The words in the list will tell you about geometry. Look up unknown words in the Spelling Dictionary. Add more words.

■ GETTING AT MEANING

Picture Clues Use the illustrations to help you write the list words that complete the sentences.

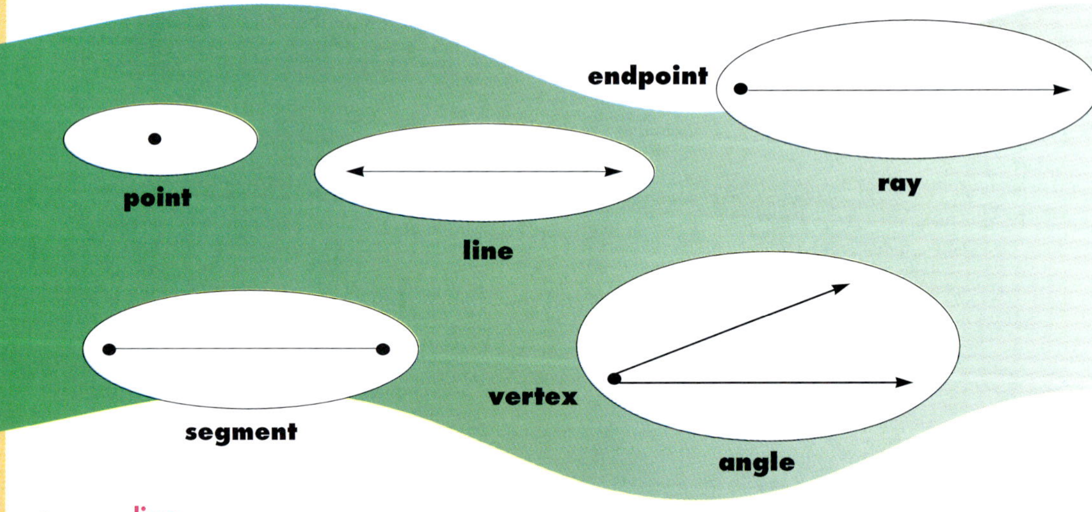

1. **line**
2. **segment**
3. **ray**
4. **endpoint**
5. **angle**
6. **vertex**
7. **point**

A (1) continues without end in both directions.

A (2) is part of a line. It has two endpoints.

A (3) is part of a line that has one (4) and goes on and on in one direction.

An (5) is formed by two rays with the same endpoint. The endpoint is its (6).

The sharpened end of your pencil could be thought of as a (7).

220

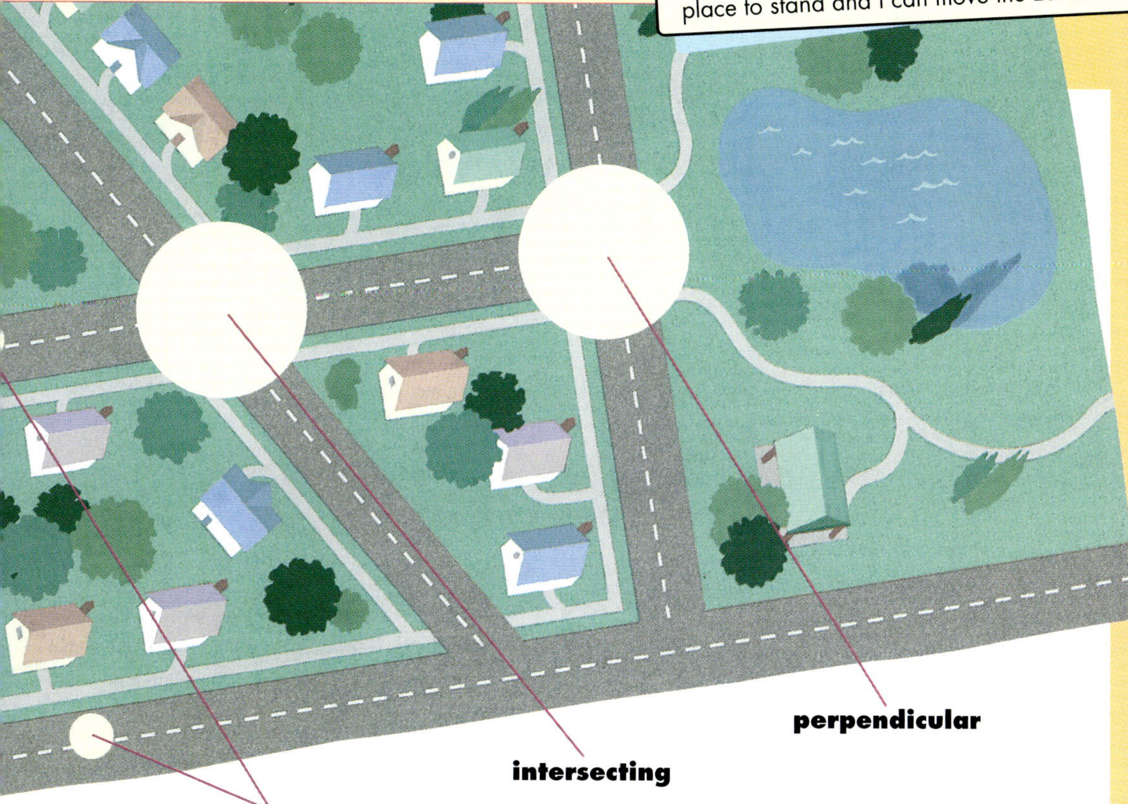

Sometimes lines meet, or intersect. Two lines that cross each other at one point are __(8)__ lines.

Lines that do not meet and remain the same distance apart are called __(9)__ lines.

Intersecting lines that form square corners are called __(10)__ lines.

8. **intersecting**

9. **parallel**

10. **perpendicular**

■ SPELL WELL

Divide and Conquer Long words are easier to spell when they are divided into syllables. Say the syllables in each word. Then write the words.

11. par • al • lel ______ **parallel**

12. in • ter • sect • ing ______ **intersecting**

Did You Know?

The word geometry comes from two ancient Greek words that mean "to measure" and "earth." The ancient Egyptians used geometry to figure out the boundaries of their farms every year after the Nile River's flooding washed away or covered landmarks!

SWIMMING

LESSON PLAN

- ● Building Background
- ● Developing Concepts
- ● Practice on pp. 222–223
- ○ Follow-Up

● Core ○ Optional

Link to Weekly Lesson

Before presenting this lesson, you may wish to teach Lesson 1, **Words with thr, scr, str, squ,** to introduce the spelling pattern that appears in *stroke.*

BUILDING BACKGROUND

Ask students to tell about their experiences with swimming. Then work with students to build a word web about swimming like the one below. Ask them to help you expand the web by suggesting words and phrases that fit the three categories shown.

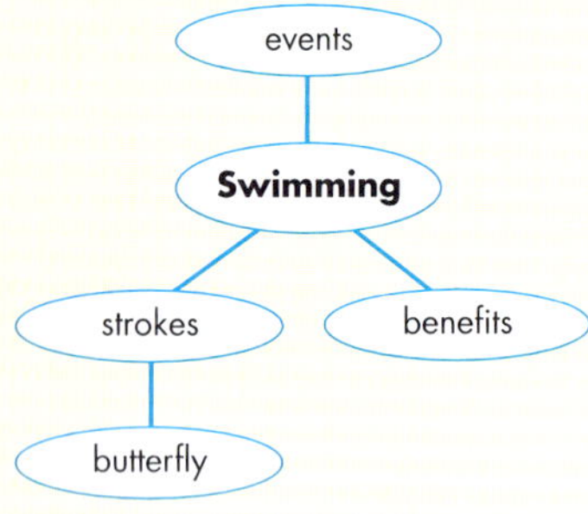

DEVELOPING CONCEPTS

Suggest that students read the list words and add to the web any that are missing. If students need help, point out that some of the list words describe the kicks and strokes used in swimming. Ask volunteers to explain the words.

Additional Practice

Everyday Spelling **CD-ROM,** Lesson 1

---

kicks
stroke
breathe
floats
treads
dive
dog paddle
backstroke
butterfly
freestyle

Answers will vary.

1. **kicks**
2. **stroke**
3. **breathe**
4. **dog paddle**
5. **floats**
6. **treads**

WORK AND PLAY

Swimming

Swimming is a sport that people of every age enjoy. What swimming skills do you have? Which are you working on? Add your own words about swimming to the list. Check unknown words in the Spelling Dictionary.

■ GETTING AT MEANING

Using Picture Clues Look at the illustration. Complete the sentences using list words.

treads floats stroke kicks breathe dog paddle

Jamal is practicing (1), moving his legs and feet.

An instructor shows students a new (2) with his arms.

As Sal raises his arm, he brings his head out of the water to (3)

Mailee does the (4) . Just like a swimming dog, she keeps her head above water and moves her arms in circles.

Robert (5) quietly nearby.

Julie (6) water by moving her feet up and down as if she were walking underwater!

222

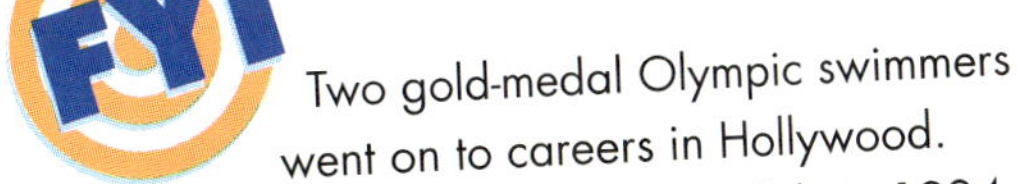

freestyle   dive   butterfly   backstroke

A good (7) will give Alma a super start.

Janice likes the (8) because it's easy to breathe swimming on her back.

Abe works on his (9) stroke. Moving both arms and legs together is tough!

Abe, Janice, and Alma compete in (10) meets. In these races swimmers are free to choose any swimming style.

7. **dive**

8. **backstroke**

9. **butterfly**

10. **freestyle**

SPELL WELL

Double Consonants The double consonants in the words below have only one sound. Remember to include both consonants when you write these words.

11. butterfly _______ **butterfly**

12. dog paddle _______ **dog paddle**

Did You Know?
American swimmer Mark Spitz has won more Olympic medals in swimming events than any other swimmer. Spitz has eleven medals: nine gold, one silver, and one bronze. He won seven of his nine gold medals in 1972.

FOLLOW-UP

Interpretive Thinking

Questioning Have students discuss the following statement: *It is important for everyone to learn how to swim.* Encourage students to formulate questions that explore the statement. For instance: *Why is swimming useful? Is it useful for everyone?* Students should decide whether or not they agree with the statement.

MEETING THE NEEDS OF ALL STUDENTS

Visual Learners

Picture Clues Remind students to match the numbered picture clues with the list word sentences.

Bilingual/ESL

Demonstrating Words

Ask volunteers to demonstrate each list word with an action. Have students repeat each word chorally as it is being shown.

223

LESSON PLAN

- ● Building Background
- ● Developing Concepts
- ● Practice on pp. 224–225
- ○ Follow-Up

● Core　○ Optional

Link to Weekly Lesson

Before presenting this lesson, you may wish to teach Lesson 17, **Contractions.** Point out to students that they will hear a lot of contractions being used if they listen to basketball games. For instance, "He's up for the shot. It's in!"

BUILDING BACKGROUND

Make a word web on the board centered around the word *Basketball.* Have students contribute words they associate with the game.

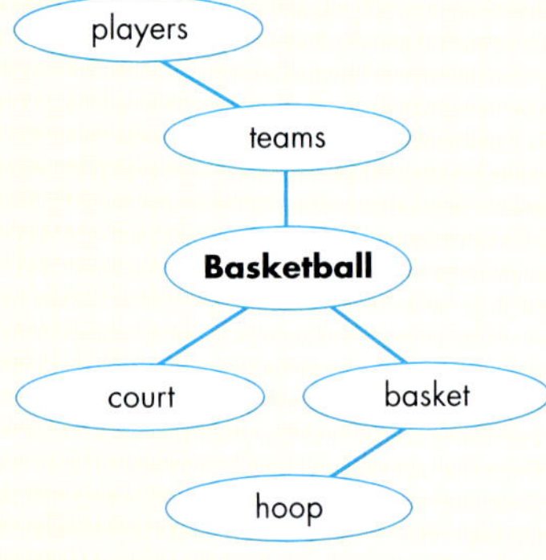

DEVELOPING CONCEPTS

Have volunteers read the list words. Point out that while all of the words are related to basketball, they describe different elements of the game. Some of the words describe the basketball court, some relate to rules, and others describe moves. Help students define and categorize the words and add any missing words to the web.

> ### Additional Practice
> *Everyday Spelling* CD-ROM, Lesson 17

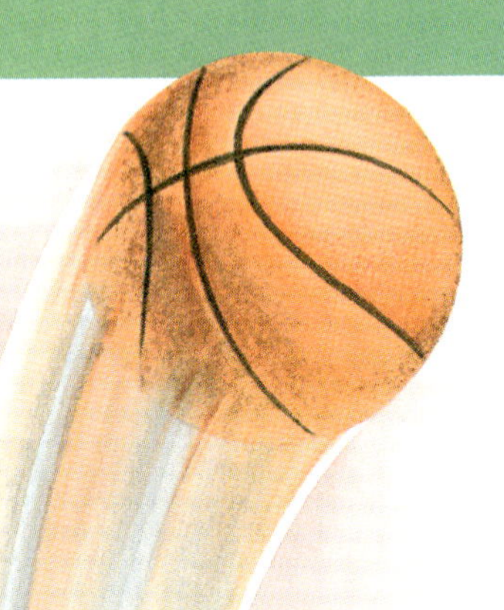

Basketball

Basketball is a fun, fast, and entertaining game. Knowing the list words can help you enjoy the game more. Read the sentences below. Add your own related words to the list. Check unknown words in the Spelling Dictionary.

backboard	A **backboard** with a basket hangs over each end of the court.
rim	A basket is made of a net hung from a metal **rim.**
dribble	Players can **dribble** the ball on the floor past an opponent.
rebound	A **rebound** is a ball that bounces off the backboard or rim.
foul	Hitting or pushing another player is a **foul.**
free throw	A player shoots a **free throw** from behind a free throw line.
field goal	A player can score a **field goal** from anywhere on the court.
lay-up	A player close to the basket can shoot a **lay-up** to score.
jump shot	A player jumps straight up to shoot a **jump shot.**
slam-dunk	In a **slam-dunk,** a player slams the ball through the basket from above.
Words will vary.	**Sentences will vary.**

■ GETTING AT MEANING

Rhyming Clues Complete these rhyming basketball cheers with list words.

Just (1) that basketball
down the floor!
Make a (2)
for two points more!

The ball bounces off the (3)
And rolls around the (4).
Get that (5) and put it in!

We'll all howl
If you (6).

1. dribble
2. field goal
3. backboard
4. rim
5. rebound
6. foul

Picture Clues   What kind of shot is each player trying to make? Write the list word that matches each picture.

lay-up   slam-dunk   jump shot   free throw

7.   **free throw**

8.   **jump shot**

9.   **lay-up**

10.   **slam-dunk**

■ **SPELL WELL**

Divide and Conquer   It helps to study some words piece by piece. Study the words syllable by syllable. Then cover them and write them.

11. re • bound _______ **rebound**

12. drib • ble _______ **dribble**

Did You Know?
The first game of basketball was played with two peach baskets and a soccer ball.

FOLLOW-UP

Interpretive Thinking

Making Inferences Have students study photographs of basketball players in action. Work with them to make inferences about what specific skills are used in playing the game. List the skills on the board. Then invite students to discuss what skills they have that would be useful in playing basketball. What skills could they learn or practice to become better players?

MEETING THE NEEDS OF ALL STUDENTS

Kinesthetic Learners

Play the Game Write the list words on cards and ask volunteers to act them out. Other students might enjoy drawing pictures to illustrate the words.

Bilingual/ESL

Basketball Terms Basketball was invented in the U.S., but it has become an international sport. Have students compare basketball terms in their first language with the English terms. Encourage them to make an international dictionary of basketball terms.

225

LESSON PLAN

- ● Building Background
- ● Developing Concepts
- ● Practice on pp. 226–227
- ○ Follow-Up

● Core   ○ Optional

Link to Weekly Lesson

Before presenting this lesson, you may wish to teach Lesson 11, **Long Vowels a, i, o,** to introduce the spelling pattern that appears in *headline* and *deadline*.

BUILDING BACKGROUND

Display a newspaper. Encourage students to think about all the elements that go into putting a newspaper together. Then have students help you create a word web like the one below.

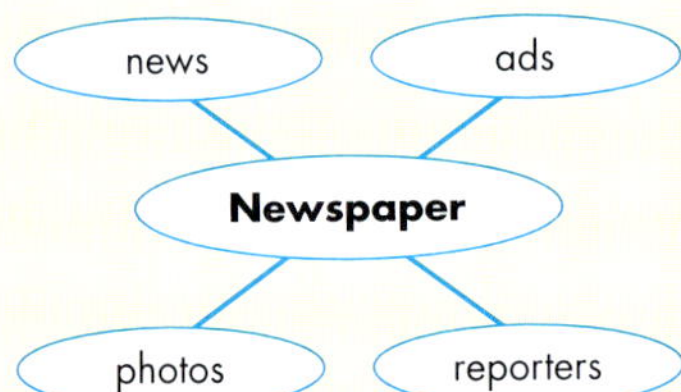

DEVELOPING CONCEPTS

If students have not already thought of it, add the word *reporter* to the web. Explain that reporters gather information and write newspaper and magazine articles, and that all the list words relate to the job of reporting. Have volunteers use a real newspaper to point out items from the word list. Then add any missing list words to the word web.

Additional Practice

Everyday Spelling **CD-ROM,** Lesson 11

articles
headline
deadline
byline
lead
details
interview
verify
sources
editors

Answers will vary.

1. **articles**
2. **headline**
3. **byline**

WORK AND PLAY

Reporter

Newspapers and magazines employ thousands of reporters. Knowing the list words will help you understand a reporter's job. Use your Spelling Dictionary to learn the exact meaning of the words or to find other words to add to the list.

■ GETTING AT MEANING

Using Picture Clues Look at the illustration below to help you finish each sentence with the correct list word.

Newspapers and magazines contain many (1) about important events and people.

A (2) in big, dark print tells about the article in a few words.

Many articles have a (3) that gives the writer's name.

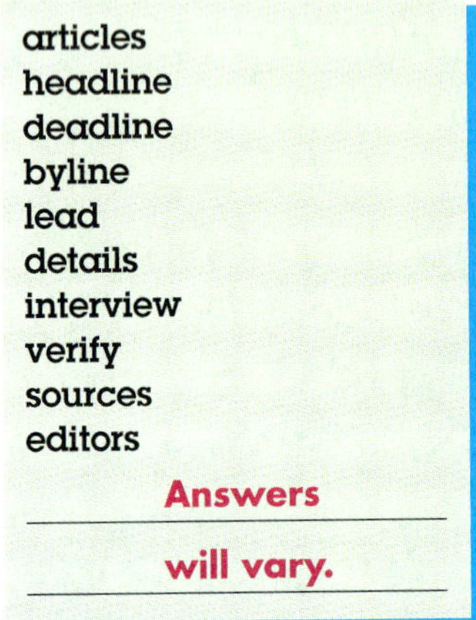

226

Connections to *BookFestival*
You may wish to recommend that students read *The Case of the Sabotaged School Play* by Marilyn Singer in the Scott Foresman-Addison Wesley *BookFestival* program.

FYI
- Before printing began, each copy of every book had to be written by hand. This made books very rare and expensive.
- The first people to print books were the Chinese and Japanese in the sixth century.
- The greatest advance in printing was the invention of moveable type. This innovation began in China in the eleventh century.

Using Definitions Use the definitions to help you complete the news article on the computer screen.

details	the facts of a news story that give more information about the news
editors	people who often write the headlines and add or rewrite the details of articles
sources	people, places, or written materials where reporters and editors get information
lead	the opening paragraph of a news story
verify	to be sure that a fact is true
interview	to ask people about their activities or opinions
deadline	latest time by which articles must be finished

4. **sources**
5. **interview**
6. **editors**
7. **lead**
8. **verify**
9. **details**
10. **deadline**

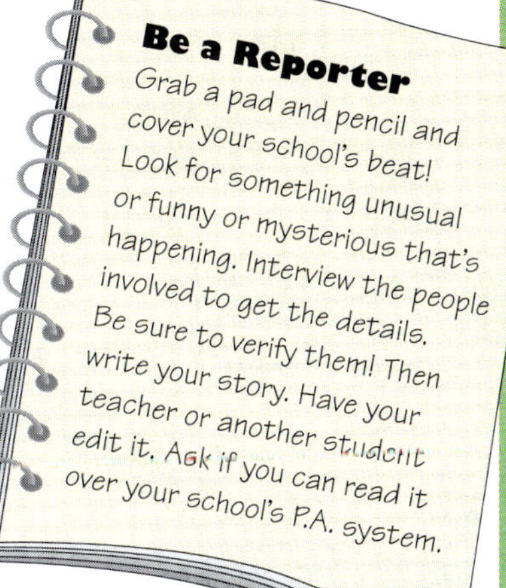

GETTING THE STORY TAKES WORK

Newspaper reporters get their stories from many (4). Some have a regular route called a beat. Some investigate politics or crime. Others report the news from overseas. Reporters sometimes (5) people to get their opinions. Once reporters "get the story," they quickly write it and give it to one of the (6). The most important information goes in the (7), or opening paragraph. The editors must (8) the (9) in the stories. They call people whom reporters have interviewed or check the details in books or magazines or special news services. All this work must be done quickly so that the newspaper can meet its daily (10). At deadline time, a story must go to the printing presses.

Be a Reporter
Grab a pad and pencil and cover your school's beat! Look for something unusual or funny or mysterious that's happening. Interview the people involved to get the details. Be sure to verify them! Then write your story. Have your teacher or another student edit it. Ask if you can read it over your school's P.A. system.

■ **SPELL WELL**

Problem Parts Sometimes the vowel sounds you hear in a word give you no clue as to its spelling. Pay special attention to the underlined letters below. Then write the words.

11. articles ___**articles**___   12. editors ___**editors**___

227

FOLLOW-UP

Critical Thinking
Generalizing Have students reflect on the information in the lesson and on their own experiences with newspapers. Then have them generalize about the traits of a reporter as they discuss the following questions in small groups: *What traits should a good reporter have? What traits do you have that would make you a good reporter?*

MEETING THE NEEDS OF ALL STUDENTS

Visual Learners
Study a Newspaper Give students pages from a newspaper to study. Have them label the pages with list words and other appropriate words from their newspaper word web.

Bilingual/ESL
Cultural Awareness Invite students to bring to class newspapers from their own culture. Have them share the newspapers with the class, using appropriate list words.

LESSON PLAN

- ● Building Background
- ● Developing Concepts
- ● Practice on pp. 228–229
- ○ Follow-Up

● Core ○ Optional

Link to Weekly Lesson

Before presenting this lesson, you may wish to teach Lesson 20, **Vowels with r,** to introduce the spelling patterns that appear in *portrait, shutter,* and *camera.*

BUILDING BACKGROUND

On the board, start a word web based on the word *Photography.* Have students contribute words that describe the process and equipment used in taking pictures, as well as words that describe the pictures themselves.

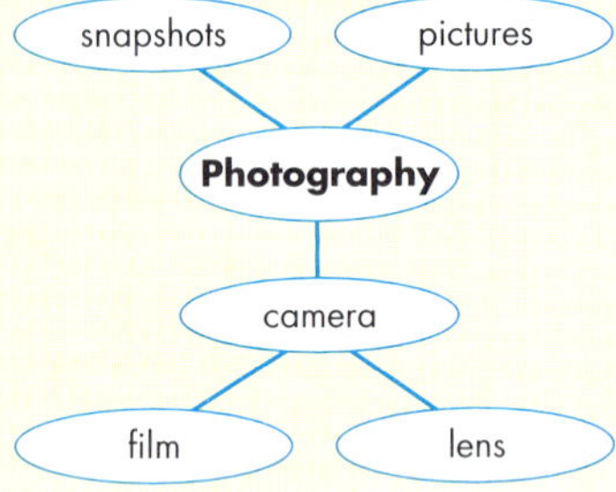

DEVELOPING CONCEPTS

Have students compare the list words with the word web on the board and identify any list words they did not name. Ask volunteers to suggest where those words belong in the web. Point out that some of the list words name pieces of photographic equipment, while others tell how a photograph is made.

Additional Practice

Everyday Spelling **CD-ROM, Lesson 20**

---

camera
film
lens
shutter
focus
portrait
snapshot
develops
negative
print

Answers will vary.

Photography

Photographs surround us everywhere we go. In newspapers, in magazines, on billboards, and in brochures, photographs give us glimpses of people, places, and events. The list words tell about photography. Look up unfamiliar words in the Spelling Dictionary. Add your own related words.

■ GETTING AT MEANING

Diagrams Complete the sentences with words from the labels and captions of the diagram.

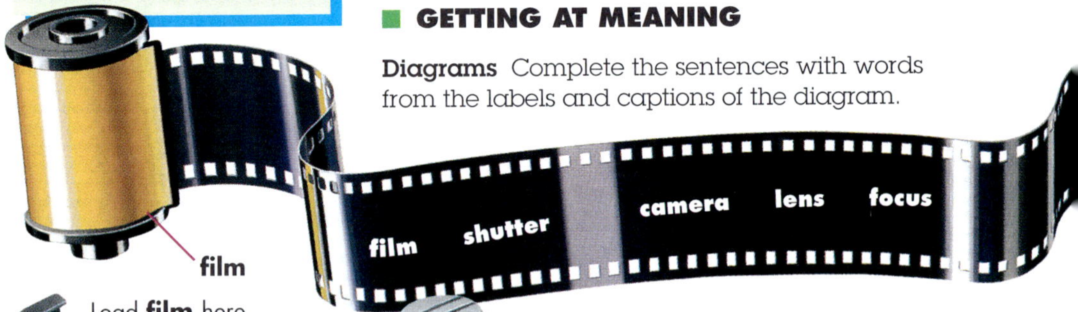

film
Load **film** here.

1. A _____**camera**_____ is a photographer's tool.

2. The glass _____**lens**_____ is the camera's "eye." You see your subject through the lens.

3. The lens also helps to _____**focus**_____ the picture so that it will appear sharp and clear.

4. The _____**shutter**_____ opens to let light through the lens. The shutter works like an eyelid.

5. As the shutter clicks, a picture is recorded on the _____**film**_____ inside.

228

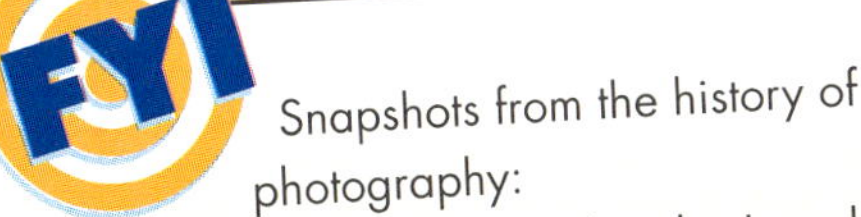

Snapshots from the history of photography:
- The first photograph was taken by Joseph Niepce in 1827.
- Early photographic equipment was bulky and heavy—it could weigh as much as 110 pounds!
- In 1888, George Eastman introduced a small camera that used film that came on a roll.

Analogies Use the words in dark type in the following sentences to finish the analogies.

- A special process **develops** the photographs on film.
- A **negative** photograph is developed first. A negative shows dark objects as light and light objects as dark.
- A **print** is made from each negative.
- A **portrait** is a photograph of a person's face.
- A **snapshot** is a photograph taken quickly with a small camera.

6. Cake is to cake mix as **print** is to negative.

7. Pattern is to sewing as **negative** is to photograph.

8. Fingerprint is to finger as **portrait** is to face.

9. Sketch is to drawing as **snapshot** is to photography.

10. Bakes is to cake mix as **develops** is to film.

SPELL WELL

Divide and Conquer Some words are easier to study in smaller parts. Study each word syllable by syllable. Then cover the words and write them.

11. cam • er • a   **camera**

12. neg • a • tive   **negative**

Did You Know?
A camera can take a picture faster than you can blink an eye!

FOLLOW-UP

Interpretive Thinking

Making Inferences Have students answer this question: *Where can you usually find photographs?* Then have students make inferences about the following in small groups:

- Think of reasons why photography has become such an important form of communication.
- How might you use photography in a career that interests you?

MEETING THE NEEDS OF ALL STUDENTS

Kinesthetic Learners

Using a Camera Display a camera and help students use list words to identify each part. If possible, allow each student to have an opportunity to use the camera. Develop the pictures and use them in a display.

Bilingual/ESL

Portraits from Home

Invite students to bring photographs from home that show aspects of their native culture. Have them share their photographs in small groups, using any list words that apply.

Writer's Handbook

INTRODUCTION

You can speak and even read well without knowing how to spell. However, knowing how to spell well is a skill that every good writer needs. This handbook will help you with some of the other skills good writers need.

CONTENTS

The Writing Process

This section answers questions that you might ask about the five steps of the writing process: prewriting, drafting, revising, proofreading, and presenting.

1. PREWRITING

What should I do before I start to write?

Think about and plan your writing before you actually put sentences on paper. Time you spend prewriting is time well spent. Follow these steps and suggestions.

- **Select a topic** by listing ideas; by browsing through books, magazines, or newspapers for ideas; or by reviewing a personal journal or diary.
- **Determine your purpose and audience.** Your purpose may be to express feelings, describe or explain, give or get information, persuade, or tell a story. Your audience could be classmates, your aunt in Tennessee, or a friend.
- **Narrow your topic.** To focus on one specific idea, you might brainstorm questions about the topic, create a word web or cluster, or list and classify key words to explore.
- **Find details** about your topic from a variety of sources and make notes. Make personal observations, interview people, or look up information in books and magazines.
- **Organize your information** to best accomplish your purpose for writing. Use time order, spatial order, or order of importance.

231

■ **WRITER'S HANDBOOK**

Step 2: Drafting

Facilitate student success:

- Have students discuss the ways they motivate themselves to begin writing.
- Provide a conducive setting in which to write.
- Write alongside students.
- Be supportive.

Step 3: Revising

Facilitate student success:

- Encourage students to read their drafts to themselves.
- Help students identify key words in the list of changes they might make as they revise. **(add, take out, move, substitute)**
- Make a chart of the questions to ask oneself and post it in the classroom.
- Work with students to establish guidelines for conferences with peers or with you.

2. DRAFTING

How do I actually begin to write the paper?

Take your writing materials and prewriting notes to a comfortable, well-lighted place. Plan on writing for at least twenty minutes. Try some of these strategies to get started.

- **Ignore** distractions like the telephone, and television.
- **Set a goal.** Decide how much that you *will* write now.
- **Review** your notes to find an idea for the first paragraph.
- **Start** with a direct, interesting sentence that states the main idea of the composition. Then let your ideas flow.
- **Push ahead** without worrying about perfect spelling, punctuation, or capitalization.

3. REVISING

How do I start revising?

Revising means to review what you've written and find ways to improve it. To begin, you might do the following:

- **Read your draft to yourself** to catch obvious errors such as unclear sentences.
- **Have a conference** with other students or your teacher.

What kinds of changes should I make?

You might do any or all of the following:

- **Add** words or ideas.
- **Take out** unnecessary words, sentences, or paragraphs.
- **Move** words, sentences, or paragraphs.
- **Substitute** words or ideas to improve your draft.

What kinds of questions should I ask myself?

The questions you'll ask depend on your purpose, audience, and type of writing. Here are some basic questions:

Ask yourself these questions!

- Did I say what I wanted to say?
- Are my details in the best possible order?
- Do I have a clear beginning, middle, and end?
- Does each paragraph have a topic sentence and stick to one idea?
- Can I take out extra words or choose better ones?
- Are all facts and figures correct?

4. PROOFREADING

Why should I proofread, and when and how should I do it?

Proofreading a paper means reading it carefully to find any mistakes in grammar, punctuation, and spelling. Proofread after you have completed revising your first draft to be sure that you have included all corrections. Proofread your final copy too.

Use proofreading symbols such as those at the right to clearly mark the corrections that are needed.

≡	Make a capital.
/	Make a small letter.
∧	Add something.
ℯ	Take out something.
⊙	Add a period.
⁋	New paragraph

What kinds of things should I look for when I proofread?

Use the following questions as a proofreading checklist:

- Do subjects and verbs agree?
- Is each sentence correctly punctuated?
- Have I avoided fragments and run-on sentences?
- Did I capitalize the first word of each sentence?
- Did I capitalize proper nouns and adjectives?
- Did I check spelling and meaning of unfamiliar words?
- Is my handwriting clear and easy to read?

Check for these possible errors!

5. PRESENTING

How should I present my final work?

Publishers have certain guidelines for writers. Teachers do too. The guidelines will vary depending on the assignment.

Here are some suggestions for **regular assignments.**

- Write neatly on the front side only of white lined paper. If you're typing your final copy on a computer, use plain white paper.
- Put your name, the class, and the date in the top right-hand corner of the first page.
- Center the title of your composition on the second line.
- Leave a one-inch margin on the sides of the paper and leave the last line blank.

Special ways to present writing include displaying it on a bulletin board, sharing it in a young author's conference, binding it in an illustrated book, publishing it in a newspaper, and reading it aloud.

Step 4: Proofreading

Facilitate student success:
- Model the process using an overhead transparency or the chalkboard.
- Make dictionaries and thesauri available.
- Provide examples for each bulleted item in the proofreading checklist.

Step 5: Presenting

Facilitate student success:
- Establish a writing center that includes materials writers may use to "publish": colored paper, binders, markers, colored pens, yarn, and so forth.
- Allow writers to choose work they wish to present.
- Provide bulletin board or table space for display.

233

Taking Writing Tests

Writing under pressure can be difficult. Improve your performance on writing tests by following these guidelines.

GENERAL GUIDELINES FOR WRITING TESTS

- **Listen carefully to test instructions.** Note how much time you have. Listen for whether to use pen or pencil.
- **Read the assignment and identify the key words.** Be certain that you are writing the correct type of answer. Look for key words like these and know what they mean.

Categorize or Classify: Sort ideas or facts into groups.
Compare or Contrast: Point out similarities (compare) or differences (contrast).
Defend: Give evidence to show why a view is right.
Define: Tell what something is or means.
Describe: Create a word picture with details and examples.
Discuss: State your ideas about what something means.
Evaluate: Give your opinion, with support, on whether an idea is good or bad, right or wrong.
Explain: Make something clear by giving reasons, examples, or steps.
Summarize: State main points, or retell important parts of a story or article.

- **Plan how you'll use your time.** Allow time for prewriting activities, actual writing, and revision.
- **Write a strong opening** to catch your reader's attention. It should address the topic directly.
- **Use specific facts, details, or incidents** to develop your topic.
- **Write an interesting conclusion** that sums up your ideas or brings your story to a satisfying end.

Taking Writing Tests

This section of the Writer's Handbook serves two purposes:

- It raises the comfort level of students facing a writing test by spelling out specific guidelines for taking one.
- It reviews the types of writing students will encounter in writing tests and provides specific information for handling each type.

Look for these key words!

WRITING A PERSONAL NARRATIVE

When you write about something you did or something that happened to you, you are writing a personal narrative.

KEY WORDS IN ASSIGNMENTS

- "Tell **what happened** to you. . ."
- "Write about how you **felt** when. . . "
- "What did you **do** when. . ."

SAMPLE ASSIGNMENTS

- Write about an experience you had when you were a child. Tell what you did and how you felt about your experience.
- Write about something you have done that makes you feel proud of yourself. Be sure to tell where you were when it happened and why it made you feel proud.

A PLAN OF ATTACK

- For both assignments, choose an occasion to write about that will be interesting and entertaining for the reader. If your topic seems too broad, narrow it.
- Jot down the details describing the event you are writing about. Think of strong verbs and colorful adjectives and adverbs to use to relate your story.
- Organize your story in **time order.** Make notes on what happened at the beginning, middle, and end of your experience. Then, when you write, use your time-order notes and list of details as a guide.

FOLLOW-UP CHECKLIST

- Did you tell your story in time order, from beginning to end?
- Did you tell both what happened and how you felt about what happened?
- Did you leave your readers with a clear sense of what kind of person you are?
- Is all capitalization, punctuation, and spelling correct?

235

Writing a Personal Narrative

Facilitate student success:

- Brainstorm a list of superlatives that may help students think of topics for a personal narrative: *biggest, tallest, fastest, scariest, most fun.*
- Let students make a chart in which they identify people, places, and things that are important to them and that may be the bases for personal narratives.
- Have students select one of the sample assignments. Establish a time limit during which they will plan, draft, and edit their writing. Have them evaluate each other's work.

Writing Model Transparency 1B

provides a model for the first sample assignment on this page.

WRITING A DESCRIPTION

Descriptive writing allows a reader to experience a scene by appealing to the senses of sight, sound, smell, touch, and taste.

KEY WORDS IN ASSIGNMENTS

- "**Tell** what you **see** (or **hear, smell, feel, taste**). . ."
- "**Describe** what it **looks** (or **sounds, smells, feels, tastes**) **like**. . ."

SAMPLE ASSIGNMENTS

- Thanksgiving is an American holiday celebrated with a traditional dinner. Describe a Thanksgiving dinner.
- Many people wear uniforms for their jobs. Visualize yourself wearing a uniform for a job you might enjoy. Describe what you are wearing.

A PLAN OF ATTACK

- Know exactly what you must write about. In the first assignment describe the sights, sounds, smells, and tastes of a Thanksgiving dinner. In the second, tell only about the uniform, not the job itself.
- Jot down specific details that tell about the color, shape, feel, sounds, smells, and tastes. Think of colorful, precise words. What comparisons can you use?
- Choose an order to use to describe details. You might use **time order** for the first assignment, describing the first course through dessert. Many descriptions use **spatial order.** You might describe the uniform from top to bottom.

FOLLOW-UP CHECKLIST

- Does the topic sentence state what you're describing in an interesting way?
- Do all the details focus on your topic?
- Do you follow the order you've decided upon?
- Does your ending tie your description together?
- Is all capitalization, punctuation, and spelling correct?

WRITING INSTRUCTIONS

Instructions tell a reader how to do or make something. Good instructions are written in step-by-step order.

KEY WORDS IN ASSIGNMENTS

- "**Explain how to. . .**"
- "**Describe the steps** you would take to. . ."
- "**Tell how you would**. . ."

SAMPLE ASSIGNMENTS

- Mmmm good! Explain how to make the best-ever ice cream sundae.
- Recycle it! Describe the steps you would take to make a book cover from a brown paper grocery bag.

A PLAN OF ATTACK

- Before you write, list the materials needed and the steps in the process.
- Organize the steps in time order, beginning with the first step and ending with the last.
- When you write, use time-order words like *first, next, then,* and *last* to show the correct order of steps.

FOLLOW-UP CHECKLIST

- Does the topic sentence state what the reader will learn to make or do?
- Are the steps arranged in correct order, and are all the steps there?
- Have you stuck to the topic—or have you put in extra information that you ought to get rid of?
- Are time-order words used to help the reader understand the order of the steps?
- Is all capitalization, punctuation, and spelling correct?

■ **WRITER'S HANDBOOK**

Writing a Fable

Facilitate student success:

- Retell familiar fables and discuss how the characters' actions and the consequences of those actions teach lessons.
- Have students select one of the sample assignments. Establish a time limit during which they will plan, draft, and edit their writing. Have them evaluate each other's work.

Writing Model Transparency 4B

provides a model for the first moral in the list under the first sample assignment on this page.

WRITING A FABLE

A fable is a very short story. The characters are usually animals, and the story states a moral, or lesson.

KEY WORDS IN ASSIGNMENTS

- "Write a modern **fable**. . ."
- "Choose a **moral,** or **lesson,** to **illustrate**. . ."

SAMPLE ASSIGNMENTS

- Choose a moral from this list. Then write a modern fable to illustrate it.
  Think how you will get out before you get in.
  Better safe than sorry.
  One good turn deserves another.
- We sometimes think of animals as having human traits— the fox as sly, the owl as wise, and so on. Choose several animals. What morals or lessons might they teach by their actions? Write an original fable that features one or more of these animals.

A PLAN OF ATTACK

- For either assignment, think carefully until you choose or decide upon the moral you will develop into a fable. Visualize animal characters that will teach the lesson well.
- Develop the plot of the fable. List what happens in the beginning, the middle, and the end. Organize the details of the plot in time order.
- Jot down possible dialogue that the animals might use to develop the story and to show character traits.
- End your fable with your moral.

FOLLOW-UP CHECKLIST

- Have you told your story in time order, with a beginning, a middle, and an ending?
- Are the animal characters well-chosen to teach the lesson you've chosen to illustrate?
- Does your fable really teach the moral that ends it?
- Is all capitalization, punctuation, and spelling correct?

238

WRITING COMPARISON/CONTRAST

Comparison tells a reader how two or more people or things are alike. Contrast tells how two or more things are different from each other.

KEY WORDS IN ASSIGNMENTS

- "**Compare** (or **contrast**) these two things (or people, places, ideas, and so on)."
- "Describe the **similarities** (or **differences**) between. . ."
- "How are . . . **alike?** How are . . . **different?**"

SAMPLE ASSIGNMENTS

- Like mother, like daughter. Like father, like son. Write a paragraph explaining how you and one of your family members are alike.
- What's that you're reading? Contrast the differences between reading for pleasure and reading a textbook.

A PLAN OF ATTACK

- Know the purpose of your paragraph. In the first assignment, you will tell about likenesses. In the second, you will tell about differences.
- List the likenesses or differences. Think of vivid, descriptive words to use for the comparison or contrast.
- Decide what order you will use to describe details. You may want to use **order of importance**—from the most important likeness or difference to the least important. If you are making a physical comparison or contrast, you may want to use **spatial order**—from head to toe, for example.

FOLLOW-UP CHECKLIST

- Does the topic sentence state what things are being compared or contrasted?
- Are the points of comparison or contrast arranged in the order you planned?
- Are words like *same* and *different* used to signal comparisons and contrasts?
- Is all capitalization, punctuation, and spelling correct?

**Writing
Comparison/Contrast**

Facilitate student success:

- Allow small groups to debate similarities and differences in things they know about, such as siblings, favorite sports, and so forth.
- Select two objects whose differences are obvious and brainstorm ways in which they are alike.
- Have students select one of the sample assignments. Establish a time limit during which they will plan, draft, and edit their writing. Have them evaluate each other's work.

**Writing Model
Transparency 5B**

provides a model for the second sample assignment on this page.

WRITER'S HANDBOOK

■ **WRITER'S HANDBOOK**

WRITING A PERSUASIVE PARAGRAPH

When you write a persuasive paragraph, your goal is to make the reader agree with your opinion. To do this, you must support your opinion with good reasons.

KEY WORDS IN ASSIGNMENTS

- "**Persuade** your parents. . ."
- "Write a paragraph to **convince** your principal. . ."

SAMPLE ASSIGNMENTS

- You have been eyeing the iguana in the pet store for months, and you are sure it would be a perfect pet. Write a paragraph for your parents to persuade them to let you buy it.
- Your home town's baseball team is playing in a championship game in a nearby town. Convince your teacher to allow your class to watch the championship game, which will be played on a school day.

A PLAN OF ATTACK

- Clearly state the opinion you intend to support.
- List at least three good reasons to support your opinion.
- Organize your reasons in **order of importance.** Usually writers save their strongest reason for last.
- Jot down convincing words to use to persuade your reader.

FOLLOW-UP CHECKLIST

- Does the topic sentence clearly state your opinion?
- Are the supporting reasons organized from least important to most important?
- Are the reasons logical and sensible?
- Does the conclusion summarize the opinion and reasons?
- Is all capitalization, punctuation, and spelling correct?

Writing a Persuasive Paragraph

Facilitate student success:

- Discuss what makes writing persuasive. Talk about occasions when you may want to persuade someone to accept your position.
- List two or three statements of position on the chalkboard. Have students support or dispute each position with reasons or examples.
- Have students select one of the sample assignments. Establish a time limit during which they will plan, draft, and edit their writing. Have them evaluate each other's work.

Writing Model Transparency 6B

provides a model for the first sample assignment on this page.

Models and Guidelines

FRIENDLY LETTER FORM

Study the five parts of the friendly letter below. Notice the capitalization and punctuation in the greeting and the closing. If you know the person you are writing well, omit your address from the heading, but include the date.

21 Juneway Terrace
Glenview, IL 60025
February 13, 19—

Dear Julie,

Thanks for inviting me to your Mardi Gras party! I'm really upset that I can't be there. We're going to be out of town that weekend. Take pictures so I can see all the costumes. Maybe we can get together over summer vacation.

Your friend,

Lizzie

Heading

Greeting

Body

Closing

Signature

State abbreviations:

AL (Alabama)	**LA** (Louisiana)	**OH** (Ohio)
AK (Alaska)	**ME** (Maine)	**OK** (Oklahoma)
AZ (Arizona)	**MD** (Maryland)	**OR** (Oregon)
AR (Arkansas)	**MA** (Massachusetts)	**PA** (Pennsylvania)
CA (California)	**MI** (Michigan)	**RI** (Rhode Island)
CO (Colorado)	**MN** (Minnesota)	**SC** (South Carolina)
CT (Connecticut)	**MS** (Mississippi)	**SD** (South Dakota)
DE (Delaware)	**MO** (Missouri)	**TN** (Tennessee)
FL (Florida)	**MT** (Montana)	**TX** (Texas)
GA (Georgia)	**NE** (Nebraska)	**UT** (Utah)
HI (Hawaii)	**NV** (Nevada)	**VT** (Vermont)
ID (Idaho)	**NH** (New Hampshire)	**VA** (Virginia)
IL (Illinois)	**NJ** (New Jersey)	**WA** (Washington)
IN (Indiana)	**NM** (New Mexico)	**WV** (West Virginia)
IA (Iowa)	**NY** (New York)	**WI** (Wisconsin)
KS (Kansas)	**NC** (North Carolina)	**WY** (Wyoming)
KY (Kentucky)	**ND** (North Dakota)	

241

Models and Guidelines

Friendly Letter Form

Facilitate student success:

- Let students discuss these questions in small groups: *What are some advantages and disadvantages of a letter compared with a phone call? When is it better to write rather than call? to call rather than write?*
- When writing friendly letters, students may want to use state abbreviations in addresses. Point out that both letters in each abbreviation are capitalized and no punctuation follows the abbreviation.
- Have students write a friendly letter to a friend or relative. Have them check that the five parts are included and are capitalized and punctuated correctly.

WRITER'S HANDBOOK

Capitalization

Facilitate student success:

- Set up a "Capitalizations Needed" box into which students put cards containing examples of sentences with words that need capitalization. In their spare time, students can take cards from the box and write sentences correctly.
- Let students take turns identifying the name of a movie or book and calling on classmates to write it, using correct capitalization.

Punctuation

Facilitate student success:

- Set aside a section of the chalkboard for sentences in which punctuation is missing. Students can proofread and write the sentences correctly in their spare time.

CAPITALIZATION

Besides letter parts, capitalize the following:

Names, initials, and titles used with names:
> Dr. Martin S. Alvarez, Jr.   Lieutenant Ann Jones

Proper adjectives:
> Midwestern values   Canadian bacon   African art

The pronoun *I*:
> Laura and I will interview the principal.

Names of cities, states, countries, continents:
> Glenview   Utah   Mexico   Australia

Names of lakes, rivers, mountains, structures:
> Fish Lake   Po River   Ural Mountain   Navy Pier

Names of streets and street abbreviations:
> Fir Street   Locust Ave.   Crown Rd.   East Spruce

Days, months, holidays, special events:
> Monday   Wed.   June   Dec.
> Labor Day   Olympics

First, last, and all important words in movie, book, story, play, and TV show titles:
> Tom Sawyer   The Cat in the Hat   "The Gold Bug"

First word in a sentence:
> We'll try harder.

First word inside quotation marks:
> Marcus said, "He's allergic to cats."

PUNCTUATION

Use **periods**

- to end declarative and imperative sentences:
  > Susan likes sunflowers.   Please listen carefully.

- after most **abbreviations**:
  > Ms.   Jan.   Sat.   Jr.   Ave.   P.M.   Dr.

Use **exclamation marks**
- after sentences that show strong feeling:
    We won the championship!

Use **question marks**
- after interrogative sentences:
    Where are the stamps?

Use **commas**
- between the day and the year in a date:
    April 15, 1994
- between the name of a city and state:
    Mendocino, California
- between series of words in a sentence:
    Mr. Lee grows tomatoes, peppers, and beans.
- before the word that joins a compound sentence:
    The sun is out, and the air is warm.
- to separate a noun after a direct address:
    Mom, where's my key?   It's on the desk, Amy.
- before quotation marks or inside the end quotation marks:
    Bob said, "I like soup."   "I prefer salads," said Zoe.

Use **quotation marks**
- around the exact words someone used when speaking:
    Vera asked, "What time is it?"
- around titles of stories, poems, and songs:
    "The Cat's in the Cradle"   "The Pit and the Pendulum"

Underline titles of books and movies:
    Anne of Green Gables   Aladdin

Use **apostrophes**
- to form the possessive of a noun:
    nurse's   brothers'   men's
- in contractions in place of dropped letters:
    wasn't (was not)   don't (do not)   I'm (I am)

Use **colons** between hours and minutes to indicate time:
    2:20   4:45

- Let students work in small groups to make up different examples for each type of punctuation identified on pages 242 and 243.

243

Spelling Dictionary

Parts of a Dictionary Entry

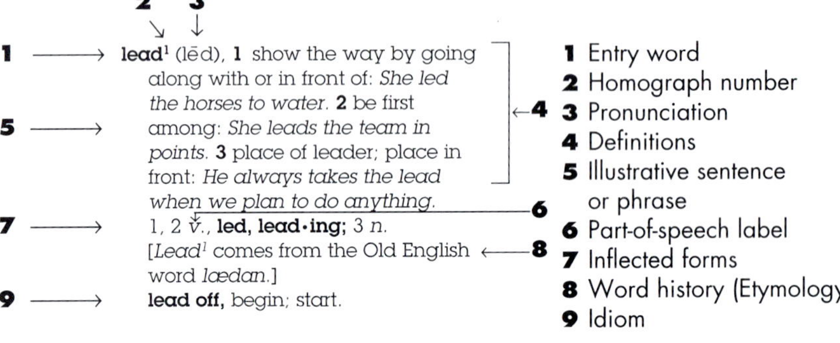

1 Entry word
2 Homograph number
3 Pronunciation
4 Definitions
5 Illustrative sentence or phrase
6 Part-of-speech label
7 Inflected forms
8 Word history (Etymology)
9 Idiom

Full Pronunciation Key

a	hat, cap	i	it, pin	p	paper, cup	v	very, save
ā	age, face	ī	ice, five	r	run, try	w	will, woman
ä	father, far			s	say, yes	y	young, yet
âr	care, hair	j	jam, enjoy	sh	she, rush	z	zero, breeze
		k	kind, seek	t	tell, it	zh	measure, seizure
b	bad, rob	l	land, coal	th	thin, both		
ch	child, much	m	me, am	ŦH	then, smooth		
d	did, red	n	no, in				
		ng	long, bring	u	cup, butter	ə	represents:
e	let, best			u̇	full, put		a in about
ē	equal, be	o	hot, rock	ü	rule, move		e in taken
ėr	term, learn	ō	open, go				i in pencil
		ȯ	all, saw				o in lemon
f	fat, if	ô	order, store				u in circus
g	go, bag	oi	oil, voice				
h	he, how	ou	house, out				

The contents of the dictionary entries in this book have been adapted from the *Scott, Foresman Intermediate Dictionary*, Copyright © 1993, 1988, 1979, 1974 by Scott, Foresman and Company or from the *Scott, Foresman Advanced Dictionary*, Copyright © 1993, 1988, 1983, 1979 by Scott, Foresman and Company.

Spellings of English Sounds*

Symbol	Spellings	Symbol	Spellings
a	at, plaid, half, laugh	ng	long, ink, handkerchief, tongue
ā	able, aid, say, age, eight, they, break, vein, gauge, crepe, beret	o	odd, honest
		ō	open, oak, toe, own, home, oh, folk, though, bureau, sew, brooch, soul
ä	father, ah, calm, heart, bazaar, yacht, sergeant	ȯ	all, author, awful, broad, bought, walk, taught, cough, Utah, Arkansas
âr	dare, aerial, fair, prayer, where, pear, their, they're	ô	order, board, floor, tore
b	bad, rabbit	oi	oil, boy
ch	child, watch, future, question	ou	out, owl, bough, hour
d	did, add, filled	p	pay, happy
e	end, said, any, bread, says, heifer, leopard, friend, bury	r	run, carry, wrong, rhythm
		s	say, miss, cent, scent, dance, tense, sword, pizza, listen
ē	equal, eat, eel, happy, cities, vehicle, ceiling, receive, key, these, believe, machine, liter, people	sh	she, machine, sure, ocean, special, tension, mission, nation
ėr	stern, earth, urge, first, word, journey	t	tell, button, two, Thomas, stopped, doubt, receipt, pizza
f	fat, effort, laugh, phrase	th	thin
g	go, egg, guest, ghost, league	TH	then, breathe
gz	example, exhaust	u	up, oven, trouble, does, flood
h	he, who, jai alai, Gila monster	u̇	full, good, wolf, should
hw	wheat	ü	food, junior, rule, blue, who, move, threw, soup, through, shoe, two, fruit, lieutenant
i	it, England, ear, hymn, been, sieve, women, busy, build, weird	v	very, have, of, Stephen
ī	I, ice, lie, sky, type, rye, eye, island, high, eider, aisle, height, buy, coyote	w	will, quick
		y	yes, opinion
j	jam, gem, exaggerate, schedule, badger, bridge, soldier, large, allegiance	yü	use, few, cue, view, vacuum
k	coat, kind, back, echo, ache, quit, account, antique, excite, acquire	z	zero, has, buzz, scissors, xylophone
		zh	measure, garage, division
l	land, tell	ə	alone, complete, moment, authority, bargain, April, cautious, circus, pageant, physician, oxygen, dungeon, tortoise
m	me, common, climb, solemn, palm		
n	no, manner, knife, gnaw, pneumonia		

*Not all English spellings of these sounds are included in this list.

ability | animal

adobe (definition 3)
an **adobe** village

almond blossom
The **almond blossom** is the national flower of Israel.

A

a·bil·i·ty (ə bil′ə tē), **1** power to do some special thing; skill: *He has great ability in making jewelry.* **2** special natural gift; talent: *Musical ability often shows itself early in life.* n., pl. **a·bil·i·ties.**

a·ble (ā′bəl), having enough power, skill, or means to do something; capable: *A cat is able to see in the dark. adj.*

ac·ci·dent (ak′sə dənt), something harmful or unlucky that happens: *automobile accidents. n., pl.* **ac·ci·dents.**

ac·com·plish·ment (ə kom′plish mənt), something that has been done with knowledge, skill, or ability; achievement: *The teachers were proud of their pupils' accomplishments. n., pl.* **ac·com·plish·ments.**

ac·tion (ak′shən), process of acting; doing something: *The quick action of the firemen saved the building from being burned down. n.*

a·do·be (ə dō′bē), **1** brick made of sun-dried clay. **2** building made of sun-dried clay. **3** built or made of adobe. 1,2 *n.,* 3 *adj.* [*Adobe* was borrowed from Spanish *adobe,* which came from Arabic *at-tūb,* meaning "the brick."]

ad·van·tage (ad van′tij), anything that is in one's favor, or is a benefit; a help in getting something desired: *Good health is always a great advantage. n.*

a·gain (ə gen′), another time; once more: *Come again to play. Say that again. adv.*

air mass (âr′ mas′), a large amount of air with the same temperature and humidity.

aisle (īl), passage between rows of seats in a hall, theater, school, etc.: *The teacher walked down the aisle between the rows of desks. n.*

a·lign (ə līn′), bring into line; arrange in a straight line: *The mechanic aligned the front wheels of our car. v.*

al·ley (al′ē), a narrow back street in a city or town. *n., pl.* **al·leys.**

al·low·ance (ə lou′əns), a sum of money given or set aside for expenses: *a household allowance for groceries of $50 a week. My weekly allowance is $1. n.*

al·mond blos·som (ä′mənd blos′əm), flower, especially of a plant that produces a peachlike fruit from a tree growing in Israel. *n.*

al·most (ȯl′mōst), very near to; all but; nearly: *It is almost ten o'clock. I almost missed the train. adv.*

a lot (ə lot′), **1** a great deal; much: *I feel a lot better.* **2** often, a great many: a great deal: *a lot of books.*

al·pha·bet (al′fə bet), the letters of a language arranged in their usual order, not as they are in words. *n.* [*Alphabet* can be traced back to the names of the first two letters of the Greek alphabet: *alpha* A and *beta* B.]

al·ways (ȯl′wāz or ȯl′wiz), at all times; every time: *Night always follows day. adv.*

a·mus·ing (ə myü′zing), causing laughter or smiles: *an amusing joke. adj.*

an·a·con·da (an′ə kon′də), a very large South American snake related to the boa that crushes its prey in its coils. Anacondas live in tropical forests and rivers and are the longest snakes in America, sometimes over 30 feet (9 meters). *n., pl.* **an·a·con·das.**

an·gel (ān′jəl), **1** messenger from God. **2** person as good or as lovely as an angel. **3** a replica used as a statue on a tree. *n.*

an·gle (ang′gəl), **1** the space between two lines or surfaces that meet. **2** the figure formed by two such lines or surfaces. *n.*

an·gry (ang′grē), feeling or showing anger: *I was angrier when you disobeyed me again. adj.,* **an·gri·er, an·gri·est.**

an·i·mal (an′ə məl), any living thing that is not a plant. Most animals can move about, feed upon other animals or plants, and have a nervous system. A dog, a bird, a fish, a snake, a fly, and a worm are animals. *n., pl.* **an·i·mals.**

an·nounce (ə nouns′), give public or formal notice of: *The teacher announced that there would be no school tomorrow.* v., **an·nounced, an·nounc·ing.**

an·nounce·ment (ə nouns′mənt), what is announced or made known: *The principal made two announcements. The announcement was published in the newspapers.* n.

an·oth·er (ə nuᴛʜ′ər), **1** one more: *Have another glass of milk (adj.). I ate a candy bar and then asked for another (pron.).* **2** a different: *Show me another hat.* 1,2 *adj.,* 1 *pron.*

an·ten·na (an ten′ə), one of the long, slender feelers on the head of an insect, scorpion, lobster, etc. *The antennas of the grasshopper can be long or short.* n., pl. **an·ten·nae** (an ten′ē) or **an·ten·nas.**

an·y·way (en′ē wā), in any case; at least: *I am coming anyway, no matter what you say.* adv.

an·y·where (en′ē hwer), in, at, or to any place: *I'll meet you anywhere you say.* adv.

a·pol·o·gize (ə pol′ə jīz), make an apology; say one is sorry; offer an excuse: *I apologized for being late.* v. **a·pol·o·gized, a·pol·o·giz·ing.**

a·pos·tro·phe (ə pos′trə fē), sign (') used: **1** to show the omission of one or more letters in contractions. **2** to show the possessive forms of nouns or indefinite pronouns. **3** to form plurals of letters and numbers. n.

ap·pear·ance (ə pir′əns), outward look: *a pleasing appearance.* n.

ap·point·ment (ə point′mənt), meeting with someone at a certain time and place; engagement: *an appointment to see the doctor at four o'clock.* n.

ap·pre·ci·ate (ə prē′shē āt), think highly of; recognize the worth or quality of; value; enjoy: *Almost everyone appreciates good food.* v. **ap·pre·ci·at·ed, ap·pre·ci·at·ing.**

A·pril (ā′prəl), the fourth month of the year. It has 30 days. n.

are (är; *unstressed* ər), form of the verb **be** used with *we, you,* and *they* and any plural noun to indicate the present tense. *We are ready. You are next. They are waiting.* v.

ar·e·a (âr′ē ə), amount of surface; extent of surface: *The area of this floor is 600 square feet.* n., pl. **ar·e·as.**

ar·gue (är′gyü), discuss with someone who disagrees: *He argued with his sister about who should wash the dishes.* v. **ar·gued, ar·gu·ing.**

ar·rive (ə rīv′), come to; reach: *You should arrive at school before nine o'clock.* v. **ar·rived, ar·riv·ing.**

ar·thri·tis (är thrī′tis), inflammation of a joint or joints of the body. n.

ar·ti·cle (är′tə kəl), a written composition on a special subject, complete in itself, but forming part of a magazine, newspaper, or book: *This newspaper has a good article on gardening.* n., pl. **ar·ti·cles.**

art·ist (är′tist), person who is skilled in any of the fine arts, such as sculpture, music, or literature. n.

ash·es (ash′iz), what remains of a thing after it has thoroughly burned: *Ashes have to be removed from the fireplace to make room for more wood.* n. pl.

ask (ask), try to find out by words; inquire: *Why don't you ask? She asked about our health. Ask the way.* v.

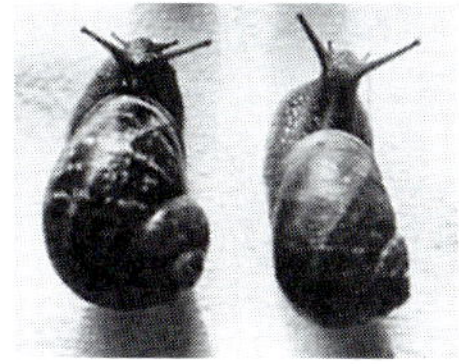

antenna

Snails have slender **antennae.**

a	hat	ī	ice	u̇	put	ə stands for	
ā	age	o	not	ü	rule	a	in about
ä	far, calm	ō	open	ch	child	e	in taken
âr	care	ȯ	saw	ng	long	i	in pencil
e	let	ô	order	sh	she	o	in lemon
ē	equal	oi	oil	th	thin	u	in circus
ėr	term	ou	out	ᴛʜ	then		
i	it	u	cup	zh	measure		

assign | beach

astronaut

An **astronaut** is trained to travel in space.

barometer

A **barometer** predicts changes in weather.

as·sign (ə sīn′), **1** appoint (to a post or duty): *We were assigned to decorate the room for the party.* **2** name definitely; fix; set: *The judge assigned a day for the trial. v.*

as·sign·ment (ə sīn′mənt), something assigned, especially a piece of work to be done: *Today's assignment in arithmetic consists of ten examples. n., pl.* **as·sign·ments.**

as·tro·naut (as′trə nȯt), pilot or member of the crew of a spacecraft. *n.*

At·lan·tic O·cean (at lan′tik ō′shən), ocean east of North and South America, west of Europe and Africa.

at·tack (ə tak′), **1** use force or weapons against; set upon to hurt; begin fighting: *The dog attacked the cat. The enemy attacked at dawn.* **2** act harmfully on: *Locusts attacked the crops. v.*

Au·gust (ȯ′gəst), the eighth month of the year. It has 31 days. *n.*

aunt (ant), **1** sister of one's father or mother. **2** wife of one's uncle. *My aunt's name is Sarah. n.*

au·to·graph (ȯ′tə graf), **1** a person's signature: *Many people collect the autographs of celebrities.* **2** write one's name in or on: *The movie star autographed my program.* *1 n., 2 v.*

Ave. or **ave.,** Avenue; avenue.

a·while (ə hwīl′), for a short time: *Stay awhile. adv.*

B

ba·by (bā′bē), **1** child too young to walk or speak; infant: *The babies' mothers took them to the park.* **2** the youngest of a family or group. *n., pl.* **ba·bies.**

back·board (bak′bôrd′), (in basketball) the upright, rectangular surface of wood, glass, or plastic, to which the basket is fastened. *n.*

back·pack (bak′pak′), a pack, often supported by a frame, that is worn on the back by hikers and campers to carry food, clothes, and equipment. *n.*

back·stroke (bak′strōk′), a swimming stroke made by a swimmer lying on his back. *n.*

ba·con (bā′kən), salted and smoked meat from the back and sides of a hog. *n.* **bring home the bacon,** succeed; win; earn a living.

band (band), group of musicians performing together, especially on wind and percussion instruments: *The school band played several marches. n.*

bare·foot (bâr′fu̇t′), without shoes and stockings on: *A barefoot child played in the puddles (adj.). If you go barefoot, watch out for broken glass (adv.). adj., adv.*

ba·rom·e·ter (bə rom′ə tər), instrument for measuring the pressure of air, used in determining height above sea level and in predicting probable changes in the weather. *n.*

bar·rel (bar′əl), container with a round, flat top and bottom and sides that curve out slightly. Barrels are usually made of boards held together by hoops. *n.*

base·ball (bās′bȯl′), **1** game played with bat and ball by two teams of nine players each, on a field with four bases. A player who touches all the bases, under the rules, scores a run. **2** ball used in this game. *n.*

bas·ket·ball (bas′kit bȯl′), **1** game played with a large, round ball by two teams of five players each. The players try to toss the ball through a ring into a net shaped like a basket but open at the bottom. **2** ball used in this game. *n.*

beach (bēch), an almost flat shore of sand or pebbles over which water washes when high. *n., pl.* **beach·es.**

beat | blubber

beat (bēt), **1** stroke or blow made again and again: *the beat of a drum.* **2** get the better of; defeat; overcome: *Their team beat ours by a huge score.* **3** mix by stirring rapidly with a fork, spoon, or other utensil: *I helped make the cake by beating the eggs.* 1 *n.,* 2,3 *v.,* **beat, beat·en** (bēt′n) or **beat, beat·ing.**

beau·ti·ful (byü′tə fəl), very pleasing to see or hear; delighting the mind or senses. *adj.*

be·cause (bi kóz′), for the reason that; since: *Because we were late, we ran the whole way home. conj.*

beet (bēt), the thick, fleshy root of a garden plant. Red beets and their green leaves are eaten as vegetables. Sugar is made from white beets. *n.*

be·gin (bi gin′), do the first part; make a start: *begin on one's work. When shall we begin? Begin at the third chapter. v.,* **be·gan** (bi gan′), **be·gun** (bi gun′), **be·gin·ning.**

be·go·nia (bi gō′nyə), a tropical plant often grown for its large, richly colored leaves and waxy flowers. *n., pl.* **be·go·nias.** [*The begonia was named after Michel Bégon, 1638-1710, a French patron of botany.*]

be·hav·ior (bi hā′vyər), manner of behaving; way of acting: *Her sullen behavior showed that she was angry. n.*

be·hind (bi hīnd′), **1** not on time; late: *The class is behind in its work.* **2** farther back: *The rest of the bikers are still behind. adv.*

be·lieve (bi lēv′), **1** think (somebody) tells the truth: *Her friends believe her.* **2** think; suppose: *I believe I will go. v.,* **be·lieved, be·liev·ing.**

bev·y (bev′ē), a small group or flock: *a bevy of quail. n., pl.* **bev·ies.**

bib (bib), cloth worn under the chin, especially by babies and small children, to protect clothing during meals. *n.*

bi·cus·pid (bī kus′pid), a double-pointed tooth that tears and grinds food. Adult human beings have eight bicuspids. *n.*

bi·cy·cle (bī′sik′əl), a lightweight vehicle with two wheels, one behind the other, that support a metal frame on which there is a seat. The rider pushes two pedals and steers with handlebars. *n.*

big (big), great in amount or size; large: *a big room, a big book. Making automobiles is a big business. An elephant is a big animal. adj.* **big·ger, big·gest.**

blan·ket (blang′kit), a soft, heavy covering woven from wool, cotton, nylon, or other material, used to keep people or animals warm. *n.*

bleach·ers (blē′chərz), section of wooden or plastic benches for spectators at baseball or other outdoor events. Bleachers are not roofed, and are the lowest priced seats. *n. pl.*

bliss·ful (blis′fəl), very happy; joyful: *blissful memories of a summer vacation. adj.*

block (blok), space in a city or town enclosed by four streets; square. *n.*

bloom·ers (blü′mərz), loose trousers, gathered at the knee, formerly worn by women and girls for physical training: *In the old days girls wore bloomers when playing sports. n. pl.* [*Bloomers were named for Amelia J. Bloomer, 1818-1894, an American magazine publisher who popularized their use.*]

blub·ber (blub′ər), fat of whales and some other sea animals. The oil obtained from whale blubber was formerly burned in lamps. *n.*

bicycle
riding **bicycles** in
the park

a	hat	ī	ice	u̇	put	ə stands for	
ā	age	o	not	ü	rule	a	in about
ä	far, calm	ō	open	ch	child	e	in taken
âr	care	ȯ	saw	ng	long	i	in pencil
e	let	ô	order	sh	she	o	in lemon
ē	equal	oi	oil	th	thin	u	in circus
ėr	term	ou	out	ŦH	then		
i	it	u	cup	zh	measure		

249

Blvd. | bruise

bridge

a **bridge** over the bay

broccoli

two stalks of **broccoli**

Blvd., boulevard.

bo·lo·gna (bə lō′nē), a large sausage usually made of beef, veal, and pork. *n., pl.* **bo·lo·gnas**. [*Bologna* was named for *Bologna*, Italy, where it was first made.]

boom (büm), a deep hollow sound like the roar of cannon or of big waves: *The big bell tolled with a loud boom. n.*

bor·row (bor′ō), get (something) from another person with the understanding that it must be returned: *I borrowed his book and promised to return it in a week. v.*

boss (bòs), person who hires workers or watches over or directs them; foreman; manager: *It was the boss's decision to hire the new construction worker. n., pl.* **boss·es.**

bot·tle (bot′l), container for holding liquids, made of glass, plastic, etc. Bottles often have narrow necks fitted with caps or stoppers: *drink a bottle of milk. n.*

bow¹ (bou), **1** to stoop; bend: *The old man was bowed by age.* **2** submit; yield: *She bowed to her parents' wishes. v.* **bow out**, withdraw. **take a bow**, accept praise or applause for something done.

bow² (bō), **1** weapon for shooting arrows. A bow usually consists of a strip of flexible wood bent by a string. **2** a slender rod with horsehairs stretched on it, for playing a violin, cello, etc. *n.*

bow³ (bou), the forward part of a ship, boat, or aircraft. *n.*

boy (boi), a male child from birth to about eighteen. *n.*

brain·storm (brān′stôrm′), INFORMAL. a sudden idea or inspiration. *n.*

brake¹ (brāk), **1** anything used to slow or stop the motion of a wheel or vehicle by pressing or scraping or by rubbing against. **2** slow or stop by using a brake: *The driver braked the speeding car and it slid to a stop.* 1 *n.,* 2 *v.,* **braked, brak·ing.**

brake² (brāk), a thick growth of bushes; thicket. *n.*

break (brāk), **1** come apart or make come apart; smash: *The plate broke into pieces when it fell on the floor.* **2** fail to keep; act against: *to break a promise. People who break the law are punished. v.,* **broke, bro·ken, break·ing.**

breathe (brēᴛʜ), stop for breath; rest; allow to rest and breathe. *v.,* **breathed, breath·ing.**

breath·less (breth′lis), out of breath: *Running upstairs very fast made me breathless. adj.*

bridge (brij), something built over a river, road, railroad, or other obstacle, so that people, cars, trains, etc., can get across. *n.*

bright (brīt), lively or cheerful: *There was a bright smile on his face. adj.* —**bright′ly,** *adv.* —**bright′ness,** *n.*

bring (bring), come with or carry (a thing or person) from another place; take along to a place or person: *The bus brought us home. Bring me a clean plate. v.,* **brought, bring·ing.**

broad·leaf (bròd′lēf′), of or about a type of tree with broad, flat leaves. An oak is a broadleaf tree. *adj.*

broc·co·li (brok′ə lē), vegetable with green branching stems and flower heads. It belongs to the cabbage family. *n., pl.* **broc·co·li.** [*Broccoli* comes from Italian *broccoli,* meaning "sprouts."]

broke (brōk), See **break.** *I broke my watch. v.*

bro·ken (brō′kən), separated into parts by a break; in pieces: *a broken leg, a broken cup. adj.*

brook (brük), a small stream; creek. *n.*

broth·er (bruᴛʜ′ər), son of the same parents. A boy is a brother to the other children of his parents. *I knocked on my brother's door. n.*

brought (bròt), See **bring.** *I brought my lunch yesterday. They were brought to school in a bus. v.*

bruise (brüz), injury to the body, caused by a fall or a blow, that breaks blood vessels without breaking the skin: *The bruise on my arm turned black and blue. n.*

bubble | canoe

bub·ble (bub′əl), **1** a thin, round film of liquid enclosing air or gas. The surface of boiling water is covered with bubbles. **2** plan or idea that looks good, but soon falls apart. *n.*

buf·fa·lo (buf′ə lō), the bison of North America. *n., pl.* **buf·fa·loes, buf·fa·los,** or **buf·fa·lo.**

build (bild), make by putting materials together; construct: *People build houses, bridges, and machines. Birds build nests. v.,* **built** (bilt), **build·ing.**

bunch (bunch), group of things of the same kind growing, fastened, placed, or thought of together: *a bunch of grapes, a bunch of flowers, a bunch of sheep. n., pl.* **bunch·es.**

bush (bush), a woody plant smaller than a tree, often with many separate branches starting from or near the ground. *n., pl.* **bush·es.**

bus·y (biz′ē), having plenty to do; working; active; not idle: *a busy person. adj.,* **bus·i·er, bus·i·est.**

busi·ness (biz′nis), thing that one is busy at; work; occupation: *A carpenter's business is building. n.*

butch·er (buch′ər), person who cuts up and sells meat. *n.*

but·ter·fly (but′ər flī′), **1** an insect with a slender body and two pairs of large, often brightly colored, overlapping wings. **2** a swimming stroke, a type of breast stroke, in which both arms are pulled upward out of the water and forward while the feet are kicking up and down. *n., pl.* **but·ter·flies.**

but·ton (but′n), **1** a round, flat piece of metal, bone, glass, or plastic, fastened on garments to hold them closed or to decorate them. **2** fasten the buttons of; close with buttons: *Button your coat.* 1 *n.,* 2 *v.*

by·line (bī′līn′), line at the beginning of a newspaper or magazine article giving the name of the writer. *n.*

C

cab·i·net (kab′ə nit), piece of furniture with shelves or drawers, used to hold articles for use or display: *a medicine cabinet, a filing cabinet for letters. We keep our very best dishes in the china cabinet. n.*

ca·ble (kā′bəl), an insulated bundle of wires which carries an electric current. *n.*

cac·tus (kak′təs), plant with a thick, fleshy stem that usually has spines but no leaves. Most cactuses grow in very hot, dry regions of America and often have brightly colored flowers. *n., pl.* **cac·tus·es, cac·ti** (kak′tī).

caf·e·ter·i·a (kaf′ə tir′ē ə), restaurant where people serve themselves. *n., pl.* **caf·e·ter·i·as.**

cam·er·a (kam′ər ə), machine for taking photographs or motion pictures. A camera lens focuses light rays through the dark inside part of the camera onto film which is sensitive to light. *n.*

Can·a·da (kan′ə də), country in the N part of North America, consisting of ten provinces and two territories and extending from the Atlantic to the Pacific. *Capital:* Ottawa. *n.*

ca·nal (kə nal′), waterway dug across land for ships or small boats to go through or to carry water to places that need it. *n.*

ca·noe (kə nü′), **1** a light boat pointed at both ends and moved with a paddle. **2** paddle a canoe; go in a canoe. 1 *n.,* 2 *v.,* **ca·noed, ca·noe·ing.**

butterfly (definition 1)
three colorful
butterflies

a	hat	**ī**	ice	**u̇**	put	**ə** stands for	
ā	age	**o**	not	**ü**	rule	**a**	in about
ä	far, calm	**ō**	open	**ch**	child	**e**	in taken
âr	care	**ȯ**	saw	**ng**	long	**i**	in pencil
e	let	**ô**	order	**sh**	she	**o**	in lemon
ē	equal	**oi**	oil	**th**	thin	**u**	in circus
ėr	term	**ou**	out	**ŦH**	then		
i	it	**u**	cup	**zh**	measure		

251

capacity | Chanukah

catcher

a **catcher** kneeling behind home plate

cattleya orchid

The **cattleya orchid** is the national flower of Costa Rica.

ca·pac·i·ty (kə pas′ə tē), amount of room or space inside; largest amount that can be held by a container. *n., pl.* **ca·pac·i·ties.**

care (kâr), **1** a troubled state of mind because of fear of what may happen; worry: *Few people are completely free from care.* **2** be concerned; feel interest. 1 *n.,* 2 *v.,* **cared, car·ing.**
take care of, watch over; be careful with: *Take care of your money.*

care·ful (kâr′fəl), showing care; done with thought or effort; exact; thorough: *Arithmetic requires careful work. adj.* —**care′ful·ly,** *adv.*

care·less (kâr′lis), not thinking what one says; not watching what one does; not careful: *I was careless and broke the cup. adj.*

car·i·bou (kar′ə bü), the North American reindeer. *n., pl.* **car·i·bous** or **car·i·bou.**

car·ni·vore (kär′nə vôr), any animal that feeds chiefly on flesh. Carnivores have large, strong teeth with sharp cutting edges. *n.*

cash (kash) money in the form of coins and bills. *n.*

cat (kat), a small, furry, flesh-eating mammal, often kept as a pet or for catching mice and rats: *The cat meowed for food. n.*

catch (kach), **1** grab or seize (something in flight): *Catch the ball with both hands.* **2** come upon suddenly; surprise; *Mother caught me just as I was hiding her birthday present. v.,* **caught, catch·ing.**

catch·er (kach′ər), a baseball player positioned behind the batter to catch the ball thrown by the pitcher. *n.*

ca·the·dral (kə thē′drəl), a large or important church. *n.*

cat·tle·ya or·chid (kat′lē ə ôr′kid), a tropical South American plant with showy flowers. [The *cattleya orchid* was named for William *Cattley,* died 1832, English patron of botany.]

caught (kot), See **catch.** *I caught the ball. v.*

cause (koz), **1** person, thing, or event that makes something happen: *The flood was the cause of much damage.* **2** make happen; make do; bring about: *The fire caused much damage.* 1 *n.,* 2 *v.,* **caused, caus·ing.**

cel·e·brat·ed (sel′ə brā′tid), much talked about; famous; well-known: *a celebrated author. adj.*

cel·er·y (sel′ər ē), vegetable related to parsley, with long, crisp stalks. Celery is eaten either raw or cooked. *n.*

Cel·si·us (sel′sē əs), of, based on, or according to the Celsius scale; centigrade. *adj.* [The *Celsius* scale was named for Anders *Celsius,* 1701-1744, a Swedish astronomer who invented it in 1742.]

ce·ment (sə ment′), a fine, gray powder made by burning clay and limestone. Cement is used to make concrete and mortar. *n.*

cer·e·mo·ny (ser′ə mō′nē), a special act or set of acts to be done on special occasions such as weddings, funerals, graduations, or holidays: *The graduation ceremony was held in the gymnasium. n., pl.* **cer·e·mo·nies.**

cer·tain (sèrt′n) without a doubt; sure: *It is certain that 2 and 3 do not make 6. I am certain that these are the facts. adj.*

chalk·board (chok′bôrd′), a smooth, hard surface, used for writing or drawing on with crayon or chalk. *n.*

cham·pi·on (cham′pē ən), person, animal, or thing that wins first place in a game or contest: *He is the swimming champion of our school. n.*

change (chānj), **1** make or become different: *She changed the room by painting the walls green. The wind changed from east to west.* **2** change one's clothes; *After swimming we went to the cabin and changed. v.,* **changed, chang·ing.**

Cha·nu·kah (hä′nə kə), Hanukkah. *n.*

chap·ter (chap′tər), main division of a book or other writing, dealing with a particular part of the story or subject. *n.*

charge (chärj), **1** put down as a debt to be paid: *We charged the entire dinner, so the restaurant will send a bill for it.* **2** a task, a responsibility: *The charge of the baby was given to my sister.* 1 *v.*, **charged, charg·ing;** 2 *n.*

Char·tres (shär′trə), city in N France. Its Gothic cathedral is more than 700 years old. *n.*

chase (chās), run or follow after to catch or kill: *The cat chased the mouse.* *v.*, **chased, chas·ing.**

check (chek), stop suddenly. *v.*

cheer·ful (chir′fəl), full of cheer; joyful; glad: *She is a smiling, cheerful girl.* *adj.*

child (chīld), **1** a young boy or girl: *games for children.* **2** son or daughter: *Parents love their children.* *n.*, *pl.* **chil·dren** (chil′drən).

child·hood (chīld′hùd), time during which one is a child. *n.*

Chi·nese New Year (chī′nēz nü′ yir′), a yearly event that begins between the dates of January 21 and February 19. It lasts four days, and on the last day people dress as dragons.

choc·o·late (chòk′lit *or* chòk′ə lit), **1** candy made of chocolate. **2** made of or flavored with chocolate: *chocolate cake.* 1 *n.*, 2 *adj.*

chop (chop), cut by hitting with something sharp: *You can chop wood with an ax. We chopped down the dead tree.* *v.*, **chopped, chop·ping.**

chore (chôr), an odd job; small task: *Feeding the dog is my daily chore.* *n.*, *pl.* **chores.**

Christ·mas (kris′məs), the yearly celebration of the birth of Christ; December 25. *n.*, *pl.* **Christ·mas·es.**

church (chèrch), building for public Christian worship. *n.*

cin·na·mon (sin′ə mən), spice made from the dried inner bark of a small tree of the East Indies: *Put cinnamon into the apple cider and heat it up.* *n.*

cir·cus (sèr′kəs), a traveling show of acrobats, clowns, horses, riders, and wild animals. The performers who give the show and the performances they give are both called the circus. *n.*, *pl.* **cir·cus·es.**

cit·i·zen (sit′ə zən), person who by birth or by choice is a member of a nation. A citizen owes loyalty to that nation and is given certain rights by it. *Many immigrants have become citizens of the United States.* *n.*

class (klas), group of students taught together: *The art class meets in room 202.* *n.*, *pl.* **class·es.**

class·mate (klas′māt′), member of the same class in school. *n.*

class·room (klas′rüm′), room in which classes are held. *n.*

clat·ter (klat′ər), a confused noise like that of many plates being struck together: *The clatter in the cafeteria made it hard for us to hear one another talk.* *n.*

clear key (klir′ kē′), the calculator key that enables the user to remove the number in the display window from the calculator's memory.

climb (klīm), **1** go up, especially by using the hands or feet, or both; ascend: *She climbed the stairs quickly.* **2** go in any direction, especially with the help of hands: *climb over a fence, climb down a ladder.* *v.*

cinnamon

different forms of the
spice **cinnamon**

a	hat	ī	ice	ù	put		ə *stands for*
ā	age	o	not	ü	rule	a	in about
ä	far, calm	ō	open	ch	child	e	in taken
âr	care	ò	saw	ng	long	i	in pencil
e	let	ô	order	sh	she	o	in lemon
ē	equal	oi	oil	th	thin	u	in circus
èr	term	ou	out	TH	then		
i	it	u	cup	zh	measure		

253

close¹ | conduct

close¹ (klōz), bring together or move the parts of so as to leave no opening; shut: *Close the door. The sleepy child's eyes are closing.* v., **closed, clos·ing.**

close² (klōs), intimate; dear: *We are close friends.* adj., **clos·er, clos·est.**

clos·et (kloz′it), a small room for storing clothes or household supplies. n.

clothes (klōz or klōₜₕz), coverings for a person's body: *I bought some new clothes for my trip.* n. pl.

cloud (kloud), **1** mass of tiny drops of water, water vapor, or ice particles floating in the air high above the earth. Clouds may be white, rounded heaps, streamers, or dark, almost black, masses. **2** mass of smoke or dust in the air. n.

coal (kōl), a black mineral that burns and gives off heat, composed mostly of carbon. It is formed from partly decayed vegetable matter under great pressure in the earth. Anthracite and bituminous coal are two kinds of coal. n.

col·lapse (kə laps′), fall in; shrink together suddenly: *Sticking a pin into the balloon made it collapse.* v., **col·lapsed, col·laps·ing.**

col·lec·tion (kə lek′shən), group of things gathered from many places and belonging together: *Our library has large collections of books.* n., pl. **col·lec·tions.**

co·logne (kə lōn′), a fragrant liquid, not so strong as perfume. n.

col·o·ny (kol′ə nē), group of animals or plants of the same kind, living or growing together: *a colony of ants. Coral grows in colonies.* n., pl. **col·o·nies.**

col·or (kul′ər), any color except black, white, or gray; red, yellow, blue, or any combination of them. The color green is a mixture of yellow and blue. n.

comb (kōm), take out tangles with a comb. v.

come (kum), move toward: *Come this way.* v., **came** (kām), **come, com·ing.**

com·mer·cial (kə mėr′shəl), **1** having to do with trade or business: *a store or other commercial establishment.* **2** an advertising message on radio or television, broadcast between or during programs. 1 adj., 2 n.

com·mon (kom′ən), **1** from all; by all; to all; general: *By common consent of the class, she was chosen president.* **2** often met with; ordinary; usual. adj.

com·mute (kə myüt′), **1** travel regularly to and from work by train, bus, automobile, etc. **2** the distance or trip ordinarily traveled by a commuter: *a long commute, an easy commute.* 1 v., **com·mut·ed, com·mut·ing;** 2 n.

com·pass (kum′pəs), instrument for showing directions, especially one consisting of a needle that points to the North Magnetic Pole. n., pl. **com·pass·es.**

com·pas·sion·ate (kəm pash′ə nit), wishing to help those that suffer; sympathetic; pitying. adj.

com·plete (kəm plēt′), **1** with all the parts; whole; entire: *We have a complete set of garden tools.* **2** make whole or entire; make up the full number or amount of: *I completed the set of dishes by buying the cups and saucers.* 1 adj., 2 v., **com·plet·ed, com·plet·ing.** —**com·plete′ly,** adv.

com·pose (kəm pōz′), **1** make up; form: *The ocean is composed of salt water.* **2** put together. To compose a story or poem is to construct it from words. To compose a piece of music is to invent the tune and write down the notes. v., **com·posed, com·pos·ing.**

com·po·si·tion (kom′pə zish′ən), thing composed. A symphony, poem, a school exercise, or painting is a composition. n.

con·cert (kon′sərt), a musical performance in which several musicians or singers take part: *The school orchestra gave a concert last night.* n.

con·duct (kən dukt′), transmit; be a channel for: *Those pipes conduct steam to the radiators upstairs.* v.

collection

a baseball card **collection**

compass

Compasses show directions.

confession | couple

con·fes·sion (kən fesh′ən), act of confessing; owning up; telling one's mistakes or sins. *n.*

con·fi·dence (kon′fə dəns), firm belief in oneself; self-confidence: *Years of work at school have given her great confidence. n.*

con·fuse (kən fyüz′), **1** throw into disorder; mix up; bewilder: *So many people talking to me at once confused me.* **2** be unable to tell apart; mistake (one thing or person for another): *People often confuse this girl with her twin sister. v.,* **con·fused, con·fus·ing.**

con·i·fer (kon′ə fər *or* kō′nə fər), plant that bears cones. The pine, fir, spruce, hemlock, and larch are conifers. *n., pl.* **con·i·fers.**

con·scious·ness (kon′shəs nis), condition of being conscious; awareness: *The injured woman did not regain consciousness for two hours. n.*

con·sti·tu·tion (kon′stə tü′shən *or* kon′stə tyü′shən), **1** way in which a person or thing is organized; nature; makeup: *A person with a good constitution is strong and healthy.* **2** system of fundamental principles according to which a nation, state, or group is governed: *The United States has a written constitution.* **3** the Constitution, the written set of fundamental principles by which the United States is governed. *n.*

con·sum·er (kən sü′mər), a living thing that has to eat to stay alive. Animals are consumers, but plants make their own food. *n., pl.* **con·sum·ers.**

con·test (kon′test *for 1,2;* kən test′ *for 3*), **1** trial of skill to see which can win. A game or race is a contest. **2** a fight, struggle, or dispute. **3** argue against; dispute about: *The decision was not contested.* 1,2 *n.,* 3 *v.*

con·test·ant (kən tes′tənt), person who takes part in a contest: *My sister was a contestant in the 100-yard dash. n.*

cool (kül), somewhat cold; more cold than hot: *a cool, cloudy day. adj.*

co·or·di·nate (kō ôrd′n it), any of a set of numbers that give the position of a point by reference to fixed lines or axes. *n., pl.* **co·or·di·nates.**

corn (kôrn), kind of grain that grows on large ears; Indian corn. *n.*

cor·rect (kə rekt′), **1** free from mistakes; right: *give the correct answer.* **2** change to what is right; remove mistakes or faults from: *Correct any misspellings that you find.* 1 *adj.,* 2 *v.*

cor·rec·tion (kə rek′shən), a change to correct an error or mistake: *Write in your corrections neatly. n.*

couch (kouch), a long seat, usually upholstered and having a back and arms; sofa: *She sat on the couch and read the newspaper. n., pl.* **couch·es.**

could've (kud′əv), could have.

coun·se·lor *or* **coun·sel·lor** (koun′sə lər), person who gives advice; adviser. *The counselor helped my brother select some courses for college. n.*

cou·ple (kup′əl), **1** INFORMAL. a small number; a few: *Give me a couple of those apples—about four of them.* **2** man and woman who are married, engaged, partners in a dance, etc. *n.*

constitution

(definition 3)

the **Constitution** of the United States

a	hat	**ī**	ice	** u̇**	put	**ə** stands for	
ā	age	**o**	not	**ü**	rule	**a**	in about
ä	far, calm	**ō**	open	**ch**	child	**e**	in taken
âr	care	**ȯ**	saw	**ng**	long	**i**	in pencil
e	let	**ô**	order	**sh**	she	**o**	in lemon
ē	equal	**oi**	oil	**th**	thin	**u**	in circus
ėr	term	**ou**	out	**ŦH**	then		
i	it	**u**	cup	**zh**	measure		

255

courageous | curfew

cou·ra·geous (kə rā′jəs), full of courage; brave; fearless. *adj.*

course (kôrs), **1** regular order: *the course of nature.* **2** a series of studies in a school, college, or university. A student must complete a certain course in order to graduate: *Biology is the course I will take to become a science teacher. n.*

court (kôrt), place marked off for a game: *a tennis court, a basketball court. n.*

court·room (kôrt′rüm′), room where a court of law is held. *n.*

courtroom

hearing a case in the **courtroom**

cous·in (kuz′n), son or daughter of one's uncle or aunt. First cousins have the same grandparents; second cousins have the same great-grandparents. *n.*

cov·er (kuv′ər), **1** put something over: *I covered the child with a blanket.* **2** anything that covers. Books have covers. A box, can, or jar usually has a cover. A blanket is a cover. **3** be enough for; provide for: *My allowance covers my lunch at school.* 1,3 *v.*, 2 *n.*

cov·er·let (kuv′ər lit), a covering, especially a covering for a bed. *n.*

cov·ey (kuv′ē), a small flock of partridges, quail, etc. *n., pl.* **cov·eys.**

cow·ard (kou′ərd), person who lacks courage or is easily made afraid; person who runs from danger, trouble, etc. *n.*

crash (krash) a sudden, loud noise like many dishes falling and breaking: *The lightning was followed by a crash of thunder. n., pl.* **crash·es.**

cra·zy (krā′zē), unwise or senseless; foolish: *It was a crazy idea to jump out of such a high tree. adj.,* **cra·zi·er, cra·zi·est.**

cred·it (kred′it), a trust in a person's ability and intention to pay: *This store will extend credit to you by opening a charge account in your name. n.*

cried (krīd), See **cry.** *The baby cried until its mother picked it up. v.*

crocodile

A **crocodile** is a large reptile.

croc·o·dile (krok′ə dīl), a large, lizardlike reptile with thick skin, similar to the alligator, but having a long narrow head and webbed feet. Crocodiles live in the rivers and marshes of the warm parts of Africa, Asia, Australia, and America. *n.*

cross·walk (krôs′wôk′), area marked with lines, used by pedestrians in crossing a street. *n., pl.* **cross·walks.**

crowd (kroud) a large number of people together: *A crowd gathered at the scene of the fire. n.*

cruise (krüz), **1** sail about from place to place on pleasure or business; sail over or about: *Freighters and tankers cruise the oceans of the world.* **2** a voyage from place to place for pleasure: *We went for a cruise on the Great Lakes last summer.* 1 *v.,* **cruised, cruis·ing;** 2 *n.*

crumb (krum), a very small piece of bread, cake, etc., broken from a larger piece: *I fed crumbs to the birds. n.*

crum·ble (krum′bəl), fall to pieces; decay: *The old wall was crumbling away at the edges. v.,* **crum·bled, crum·bling.**

crutch (kruch), a support to help a lame or injured person walk. It is a stick with a padded crosspiece at the top that fits under a person's arm and supports part of the weight in walking. *n., pl.* **crutch·es.**

cry (krī), call loudly; shout: *"Wait!" she cried from behind me. v.,* **cried, cry·ing.**

cuck·oo clock (kü′kü klok′), clock with a little toy bird that makes a sound like that of the European cuckoo to mark intervals of time.

cue card (kyü′ kärd′), words written out as to what to do or when to act: *He held up the cue cards to the actor so he could continue the play. n., pl.* **cue cards.**

cur·few (kėr′fyü), rule requiring certain persons to be off the streets or at home before a fixed time: *There is a 10 p.m. curfew for children in our city. n.*

cur·rent (kėr′ənt), **1** flow of electricity through a wire, etc.: *The current went off when lightning hit the power lines.* **2** of the present time: *We discuss current events in social studies class.* 1 *n.,* 2 *adj.*

cur·tain (kėrt′n), drapery that separates a stage from where an audience sits. *n., pl.* **cur·tains.**

cush·ion (kush′ən), a soft pillow or pad used to sit, lie, or kneel on: *I rested my head on a cushion. n.*

cuspid (kus′pid), the kind of tooth with a sharp point used to tear food. Adults have four cuspids. *n.*

cute (kyüt), pretty and dear: *a cute baby. adj.,* **cut·er, cut·est.**

D

dad (dad), INFORMAL. father: *Dad's new car is green. n.*

dahl·ia (dal′yə), a tall plant with large, showy flowers of many colors and varieties that bloom in autumn. It is related to the aster. *n., pl.* **dahl·ias.** [The *dahlia* was named for Anders *Dahl*, 1751-1789, a Swedish botanist.]

dai·ly (dā′lē), done, happening, or appearing every day, or every day but Sunday, day by day: *a daily newspaper, a daily visit. adj.*

dair·y (dâr′ē), room or building where milk and cream are kept and made into butter and cheese. *n., pl.* **dair·ies.**

dance (dans), move in rhythm, usually in time with music: *She can dance very well. v.,* **danced, danc·ing.**

dan·ger (dān′jər), chance of harm; nearness to harm; risk; peril: *The trip through the jungle was full of danger. n.*

dark (därk), **1** absence of light; darkness: *Don't be afraid of the dark.* **2** night; nightfall: *The dark comes on early in the winter. n.* —**dark′ness,** *n.*

dead·line (ded′līn′), the latest possible time to do something: *The teacher made Friday afternoon the deadline for handing in all book reports. n.*

deal (dēl), distribute playing cards: *It's your turn to deal. v.,* **dealt, deal·ing.**

dealt (delt), See **deal.** *The cards have been dealt. v.*

de·bris (də brē′), scattered fragments; ruins; rubbish: *The street was covered with debris from the explosion. n.*

Dec., December.

De·cem·ber (di sem′bər), the 12th and last month of the year. It has 31 days. *n.*

de·cide (di sīd′), make up one's mind; resolve: *She decided to be a scientist. v.,* **de·cid·ed, de·cid·ing.**

de·ci·sion (di sizh′ən), **1** a making up of one's mind; deciding: *I have not yet come to a decision about buying the property.* **2** judgment reached or given: *The jury brought in a decision of not guilty. n.*

de·com·pos·er (dē′kəm pō′zər), any living thing that puts materials from dead plants and animals back into soil, air, and water. *n.*

deed (dēd), thing done; act; action: *a good deed. Deeds, not words, are needed. n.*

deep (dēp), **1** going a long way down from the top or surface: *the deepest well. The pond is deeper in the middle.* **2** in depth: *a tank 8 feet deep. adj.,* **deep·er, deep·est.**

dance

dancing in a ballet

a	hat	ī	ice	u̇	put	ə	*stands for*
ā	age	o	not	ü	rule	a	in about
ä	far, calm	ō	open	ch	child	e	in taken
âr	care	ȯ	saw	ng	long	i	in pencil
e	let	ô	order	sh	she	o	in lemon
ē	equal	oi	oil	th	thin	u	in circus
ėr	term	ou	out	ŦH	then		
i	it	u	cup	zh	measure		

257

degree | didn't

desert[1]

exploring the dry
desert

diary

A **diary** is for writing
personal thoughts.

de·gree (di grē′), **1** unit for measuring temperature: *The freezing point of water is 32 degrees (32°) Fahrenheit, or 0 degrees (0°) Celsius.* **2** unit for measuring an angle or an arc of a circle. A degree is 1/90 of a right angle or 1/360 of the circumference of a circle. 45 degrees (45°) is half a right angle. *n., pl.* **de·grees.**

de·lay (di lā′), **1** put off till a later time: *We will delay the party for a week and hold it next Saturday.* **2** a putting off till a later time: *The delay upset our plans.* **3** be late; go slowly; stop along the way: *Do not delay on this errand.* 1,3 *v.,* 2 *n., pl.* **de·lays.**

de·liv·er·y (di liv′ər ē), a carrying and giving out of letters, goods, etc.: *There is one delivery of mail a day in our city. n., pl.* **de·liv·er·ies.**

dem·o·crat·ic (dem′ə krat′ik), of a democracy; like a government run by the people who live under it. *adj.*

dem·on·stra·tion (dem′ən strā′shən), a showing or explaining something by carrying out experiments or by using samples: *A compass was used in a demonstration of the earth's magnetism. n., pl.* **dem·on·stra·tions.**

den·im (den′əm), a heavy, coarse cotton cloth with a diagonal weave, used for overalls, sports clothes, etc. *n.* [*Denim* comes from French *serge de Nimes,* meaning "serge from Nimes," a town in France where the fabric was made.]

der·mis (dėr′mis), the sensitive layer of skin beneath the outer skin; derma. *n.*

de·scrip·tion (di skrip′shən) a telling in words how a person, place, thing, or an event looks or behaves; describing: *The reporter's description of the hotel fire made me feel as if I were right at the scene. n.*

des·ert[1] (dez′ərt), a dry, barren region that is usually sandy and without trees. The Sahara Desert is a great desert in northern Africa. *n.*

de·sert[2] (di zert′), go away and leave a person or a place, especially one that should not be left; forsake: *She deserted her old friends when she became famous. v.*

de·sign (di zīn′), **1** arrangement of details, form, and color in painting, weaving, building, etc.: *a wallpaper design in tan and brown.* **2** make a first sketch of; arrange form and color of; draw in outline: *design a dress.* 1 *n.,* 2 *v.*

de·tail (di tāl′ or dē′tāl), a small or unimportant part: *Her report was complete: it didn't leave out a single detail. n., pl.* **de·tails.**

de·ter·mi·na·tion (di tėr′mə nā′shən), great firmness in carrying out a purpose; fixed purpose: *His determination was not weakened by the difficulties he met. n.*

de·ter·mine (di tėr′mən), make up one's mind very firmly; resolve: *He determined to become the best player on the team. v.*

dev·as·tate (dev′ə stāt), lay waste; destroy; ravage: *A long war devastated the country. v.,* **dev·as·tat·ed, dev·as·tat·ing.**

de·vel·op (di vel′əp), **1** come into being or activity; grow: *Plants develop from seeds.* **2** treat (a photographic film or plate) with chemicals to bring out the picture: *A photographer develops film and makes prints.* **3** make or become known: *The lawyer's investigation did not develop any new facts. v.*

di·ar·y (dī′ər ē), a book for writing down each day of what has happened to one, or what one has done or thought, during that day. *n., pl.* **di·ar·ies.**

dic·tion·ar·y (dik′shə ner′ē), book that explains the words of a language or of some special subject. It is arranged alphabetically. You can use this dictionary to find out the meaning, spelling, or pronunciation of a word. *n., pl.* **dic·tion·ar·ies.**

did·n't (did′nt), did not: *I didn't hear you.*

dif·fer·ent (dif′ər ənt), **1** not alike; not like: *People have different names. A boat is different from an automobile.* **2** not like others or most others; unusual. *adj.*

di·rect (də rekt′ *or* dī rekt′), have authority or control over; manage or guide: *The teacher directs the work of the class. v.*

di·rec·tion (də rek′shən *or* dī rek′shən), a directing; managing or guiding: *the direction of a play or movie. The school is under the direction of the principal. n.*

dirt·y (dėr′tē), soiled by dirt; not clean: *Children playing in the mud get dirty. adj.*

dis·a·gree (dis′ə grē′), have unlike opinions; differ: *Doctors sometimes disagree about the proper method of treating a patient. Your account of the accident disagrees with hers. v.,* **dis·a·greed, dis·a·gree·ing.**

dis·ap·pear (dis′ə pir′), pass from sight; from existence; stop being seen: *The dog disappeared around the corner. When spring comes, the snow disappears. v.*

dis·ap·point·ment (dis′ə point′mənt), a being disappointed; the feeling you have when you do not get what you expected or hoped for: *When she did not get a new bicycle, her disappointment was very great. n.*

dis·cov·er (dis kuv′ər), see or learn of for the first time; find out: *discover a new drug, discover a secret. v.*

dis·hon·est (dis on′ist), ready to cheat; not upright: *A person who lies or steals is dishonest. adj.*

dis·like (dis līk′), not like; object to; have a feeling against: *He dislikes studying and would rather play football. v.,* **dis·liked, dis·lik·ing.**

dis·o·be·di·ence (dis′ə bē′dē əns), refusal to obey; failure to obey: *The child was punished for disobedience. n.*

dis·play (dis plā′), a showing of information in visual form, as on the screen of a computer or calculator. *n.*

dis·tance (dis′təns), space in between: *The distance from the farm to the town is five miles. n.*

dis·trust (dis trust′), have no confidence in; not trust; be suspicious of; doubt: *Many people distrust statements made in advertisements. v.*

dive (dīv), **1** plunge headfirst into water. **2** act of diving: *The crowd applauded the girl's graceful dive.* **1** *v.,* **dived** *or* **dove** (dōv), **dived, div·ing; 2** *n.*

di·vide (də vid′), to find how a total amount can be separated into an equal number of groups, or into groups of equal size. *v.,* **di·vid·ed, di·vid·ing.**

div·i·dend (div′ə dend), number or quantity to be divided by another: *In 728 ÷ 16, 728 is the dividend. n.*

di·vis·i·ble (də viz′ə bəl), able to be divided without leaving a remainder: *12 is divisible by 1, 2, 3, 4, 6, and 12. adj.*

di·vi·sion (də vizh′ən), operation of dividing one number by another: *26 ÷ 2 = 13 is a simple division. n.*

di·vi·sor (də vī′zər), number or quantity by which another is to be divided: *In 728 ÷ 16, 16 is the divisor. n.*

doc·tor (dok′tər), person trained in treating diseases or injuries. *Physicians, surgeons, dentists, and veterinarians are doctors. n.*

does·n't (duz′nt), does not.

dive (definition 1)

						stands for
a	hat	ī	ice	u̇	put	ə	in about
ā	age	o	not	ü	rule	a	in about
ä	far, calm	ō	open	ch	child	e	in taken
âr	care	ȯ	saw	ng	long	i	in pencil
e	let	ô	order	sh	she	o	in lemon
ē	equal	oi	oil	th	thin	u	in circus
ėr	term	ou	out	ᴛʜ	then		
i	it	u	cup	zh	measure		

259

dog paddle | earthquake

dog pad·dle (dȯg′ pad′l), a downward swimming stroke in which the arms and legs stay under the water and each limb paddles by turns, first one and then the other: *The child did the dog paddle in the pool.*

dol·phin (dol′fən), a sea mammal related to the whale, but smaller. It has a beaklike snout and remarkable intelligence. *n.*

don·key (dong′kē), a small animal somewhat like a horse but with longer ears and a shorter mane. *n., pl.* **don·keys.**

door·bell (dôr′bel′), bell that a caller may ring by pressing a button or pulling a handle on the outside of a door to a house. *n.*

down·stairs (doun′stârz′), on or to a lower floor: *Look downstairs for my glasses* (adv.) *The downstairs rooms are dark* (adj.).

Dr., Doctor.

drib·ble (drib′əl), **1** move (a ball) along by bouncing it or giving it short kicks: *dribble a basketball, dribble a soccer ball.* **2** act of dribbling a ball. 1 *v.,* **drib·bled, drib·bling;** 2 *n.*

dried (drīd), See **dry.** *I dried my hands. The dishes have already been dried. v.*

drive (drīv), **1** go or carry in an automobile or carriage: *We want to drive through the mountains on the way home. She drove us to the station.* **2** (in sports) hit very hard and fast: *drive a golf ball.* **3** make by drilling, boring: *drive a well. v.,* **drove, driv·en** (driv′ən), **driv·ing.**

drive·way (drīv′wā′), a privately owned road to drive on, usually leading from a house or garage to the road. *n.*

drove (drōv), See **drive.** *We drove two hundred miles today. v.*

drown (droun), die under water or other liquid because of lack of air to breathe: *We almost drowned when our sailboat suddenly overturned. v.,* **drowned, drown·ing.**

dolphin

a **dolphin** enjoying the water

dry (drī), make or become dry: *We washed and dried the dishes after dinner. Clothes dry in the sun. v.,* **dried, dry·ing.**

dry cleaner (drī′ klē′nər), person or business that does dry cleaning. *n.*

dry dock (drī′ dok′), dock built watertight so that the water may be pumped out or kept high. Dry docks are used for building or repairing ships. *n.*

dry run (drī′ run′), a practice test or session. *n.*

dud (dud), shell or bomb that fails to explode. *n.*

dune (dün or dyün), mound or ridge of loose sand heaped up by the wind. *n.*

dur·ing (dùr′ing or dyùr′ing), through the whole time of; throughout: *The children played inside during the storm. prep.*

E

ear (ir), part of the body by which people and animals hear. It consists of the external ear, the middle ear, and the inner ear. *n.* **be all ears,** INFORMAL. listen eagerly; pay careful attention: *The children were all ears while their teacher read them the exciting story.* **play by ear,** play (a piece of music or a musical instrument) without using written music: *She can't read notes but she can play any tune on the piano by ear.*

ear ca·nal (ir′ kə nal′), tunnel sound travels through to the eardrum. *n.*

ear·drum (ir′drum′), a thin membrane across the middle ear that vibrates when sound waves strike it. *n.*

ear·ring (ir′ring′), ornament for the ear. *n., pl.* **ear·rings.**

earth·quake (ėrth′kwāk′), a shaking or sliding of a portion of the earth's crust. It is caused by the sudden movement of masses of rock far beneath the earth's surface. Earthquakes are often related to volcanic activity. *n.*

edelweiss | equal

e·del·weiss (ā′dl vīs), a small plant that grows in high places, such as the mountains in Austria and Switzerland. It has heads of very small, white flowers in the center of star-shaped leaf clusters. *n., pl.* **e·del·weiss** or **e·del·weiss·es.**

edge (ej), **1** line or place where something ends or begins; side: *This page has four edges. We walked to the edge of the water.* **2** rim; brink: *The stag stood on the edge of the cliff. n.*

ed·i·tor (ed′ə tər), person who edits. *She is the editor of our school paper. n., pl.* **ed·i·tors.**

e·lect (i lekt′), choose or select for an office by voting: *We elect our class officers every autumn. v.,* **elect·ed, elect·ing.**

e·lec·tion (i lek′shən), a choosing or selecting for an office by vote: *In our city we have an election for mayor every four years. n.*

e·lec·tric·i·ty (i lek′tris′ə tē), form of energy which can produce light, heat, motion, and magnetic force. *Electricity makes light bulbs shine, televisions play, and cars start. n.*

el·e·phant (el′ə fənt), a huge, heavy mammal, the largest living land animal, with ivory tusks and a long, muscular snout called a trunk. *n.*

e·lev·en (i lev′ən), **1** one more than ten; 11. **2** a football or cricket team. 1,2 *n.,* 1 *adj.*

e·mer·gen·cy (i mėr′jən sē), **1** a sudden need for immediate action: *I keep a box of tools in my car for use in an emergency.* **2** for a time of sudden need: *The surgeon did an emergency operation.* 1 *n., pl.* **e·mer·gen·cies;** 2 *adj.*

e·nam·el (i nam′əl), the smooth, hard, glossy outer layer of the teeth. *n.*

end·point (end′point′), the point at the end of a line segment or ray. *n., pl.* **end·points.**

en·e·my (en′ə mē), a force, nation, army, fleet, or air force that opposes another; person, ship, etc., of a hostile nation. *n., pl.* **en·e·mies.**

en·er·gy (en′ər jē), capacity for doing work, such as lifting or moving an object. Light, heat, and electricity are different forms of energy: *A steam engine changes heat into mechanical energy. n., pl.* **en·er·gies.**

en·er·vate (en′ər vāt), lessen the vigor or strength of; weaken: *A hot, damp climate enervates people who are not used to it. v.,* **en·er·vat·ed, en·er·vat·ing.**

en·gine (en′jən), machine that changes energy from fuel, steam, water pressure, etc., into motion and power. An engine is used to apply power to some work, such as a car engine. *n.*

Eng·lish (ing′glish), the language of England. English is also spoken in the United States, Canada, Australia, New Zealand, the Republic of South Africa, and many other countries. *n. sing.*

e·nough (i nuf′), quantity or number needed or wanted; sufficient amount: *I had enough to eat. n.*

ep·i·der·mis (ep′ə dėr′mis), the outer layer of the skin. *n.*

ep·i·gram (ep′ə gram), a short, pointed or witty saying. EXAMPLE: "Speech is silver, but silence is golden." *n.*

e·qual (ē′kwəl), **1** the same in amount, size, number, value, or rank: *Ten dimes are equal to one dollar. All persons are considered equal before the law.* **2** the same throughout; even; uniform: *equal pieces. adj.*

edelweiss

The **edelweiss** is the national flower of Austria.

elephant

The **elephant** is the largest four-footed animal.

a	hat	**ī**	ice	**u̇**	put	**ə** stands for	
ā	age	**o**	not	**ü**	rule	**a**	in about
ä	far, calm	**ō**	open	**ch**	child	**e**	in taken
âr	care	**ȯ**	saw	**ng**	long	**i**	in pencil
e	let	**ô**	order	**sh**	she	**o**	in lemon
ē	equal	**oi**	oil	**th**	thin	**u**	in circus
ėr	term	**ou**	out	**ᴛʜ**	then		
i	it	**u**	cup	**zh**	measure		

261

equally | explosion

evergreen

the majestic **evergreen**

e·qual·ly (ē′kwə lē), in equal shares; in an equal manner: *Divide the pie equally. My sister and brother are equally talented.* *adv.*

e·quals key (ē′kwəlz kē′), key that supplies a result of a calculator's next calculation.

e·qua·tion (i kwā′zhən), statement of the equality of two quantities. EXAMPLES: (4 × 8) + 12 = 44. C = 2πr. *n.*

e·qua·tor (i kwā′tər), an imaginary circle around the middle of the earth, halfway between the North Pole and the South Pole. The United States is north of the equator; Australia is south of it. *n.*

Er·ie (ir′ē), **Lake,** one of the five Great Lakes; it borders Ohio, Pennsylvania, New York, and Canada. *n.*

er·ror (er′ər), a message that appears on a calculator when more digits are generated than can be displayed. *n.*

e·rup·tion (i rup′shən) a bursting or throwing forth: *There was an eruption of glowing melted rock from the mountain top.* *n.*

es·cape (e skāp′), get out and away; get free: *The bird escaped from its cage.* *v.,* **es·caped, es·cap·ing.**

es·pe·cial·ly (e spesh′ə lē), more than others; specially; particularly; principally; chiefly. *adv.*

etc., et cetera. *Etc.* is usually read "and so forth." *Etc.* shows that the definition applies to many similar items in addition to the ones mentioned.

eve (ēv), the evening or day before a holiday or some other special day: *New Year's Eve, Christmas Eve, the eve of my birthday.* *n.*

experiment

working on an

experiment with light

eve·ning (ēv′ning), the last part of day and early part of night; time between sunset and bedtime. *n.*

ev·er·green (ev′ər grēn′), a plant that has green leaves or needles all year round. *n., pl.* **ev·er·greens.**

eve·ry·bod·y (ev′rē bud′ē or ev′rē bod′ē), every person; everyone: *Everybody likes the principal.* *pron.*

eve·ry·one (ev′rē wun or ev′rē wən), each one; everybody: *Everyone in the class is here.* *pron.*

ex·act·ly (eg zakt′lē), accurately; precisely; just so; quite right. *adv.*

ex·cel·lent (ek′sə lənt), of unusually good quality; better than others; superior: *Excellent work deserves high praise.* *adj.*

ex·cept (ek sept′) leaving out; other than: *He works every day except Sunday.* *prep.*

ex·cess (ek ses′ or ek′ses), part that is too much; more than enough: *The tailor trimmed off the excess from the cloth being measured for the two sleeves.* *n.*

ex·cite (ek sīt′), **1** stir up the feelings of: *News of the wedding excited the entire family.* **2** arouse: *Plans for a field trip excited the students' interest.* *v.,* **ex·cit·ed, ex·cit·ing.**

ex·cuse (ek skyüs′), reason, real or pretended, that is given; explanation: *Sickness was his excuse for being absent from school.* *n.*

ex·hib·it (eg zib′it), an exhibiting; public showing: *The village art exhibit drew 10,000 visitors.* *n.*

ex·pect (ek spekt′), think something will probably come or happen; look forward to: *I expect to take a vacation in May.* *v.*

ex·per·i·ment (ek sper′ə mənt), trial or test to find out something: *a chemistry experiment. Scientists test out theories by experiments.* *n.*

ex·pert (ek′spėrt′), a very skillful person; person who knows a great deal about some special thing: *She is an expert at fishing.* *n.*

ex·plain (ek splān′), make plain or clear; tell the meaning of: *The teacher explained long division to the class. Will you explain this poem to me?* *v.*

ex·plo·sion (ek splō′zhən), a bursting with a loud noise; a blowing up: *The explosion shook the whole neighborhood.* *n.*

extra | fence

ex·tra (ek′strə), beyond what is usual, expected, or needed; additional: *extra fare, extra pay, extra favors.* adj. [*Extra* was probably shortened from *extraordinary.*]

ex·traor·di·nar·y (ek strôr′də ner′ē), beyond what is ordinary; very unusual; very remarkable: *Eight feet is an extraordinary height for a person.* adj.

eye (ī), the organ of the body by which people and animals see. n.
an eye for an eye, punishment as severe as the injury.
catch one's eye, attract one's attention: *The bright red sign caught my eye.*
see eye to eye, agree entirely: *My parents and I do not see eye to eye on my weekly allowance.*

eye·lash (ī′lash′), 1 one of the hairs on the edge of the eyelid. 2 fringe of such hairs. n., pl. **eye·lash·es.**

F

Fahr·en·heit (far′ən hīt), a scale for measuring temperature on which 32 degrees marks the freezing point of water and 212 degrees marks the boiling point. adj. [The *Fahrenheit* scale was named for Gabriel D. *Fahrenheit,* 1686-1736, the German physicist who introduced it.]

fair·ness (fâr′nis), a being fair: *Our teacher is known for fairness in grading pupils.* n.

fam·i·ly (fam′ə lē), 1 a father, mother, and their children: *Our town has about a thousand families.* 2 all of a person's relatives: *His family's reunion is an annual event.* n., pl. **fam·i·lies.**

family of facts, (fakts), related number sentences for addition and subtraction (or multiplication and division) that contain all the same numbers.

fat (fat), 1 having much flesh; fleshy; plump; well-fed: *a fat baby, a fat pig.* 2 large or larger than usual: *a fat contract, a fat salary.* adj., **fat·ter, fat·test.**

fa·ther (fä′тнər), a male parent. n.

fault (fôlt), a break in the earth's crust, with the mass of rock on one side of the break pushed up, down, or sideways. n., pl. **faults.**

fa·vor·ite (fā′vər it), liked better than others. adj.

fear·less (fir′lis), without fear; afraid of nothing; brave; daring. adj.

Feb., February.

Feb·ru·ar·y (feb′rü er′ē or feb′yü er′ē), the second month of the year. It has 28 days except in leap years, when it has 29. n.

fed·er·al (fed′ər əl), formed by an agreement between states establishing a central government to handle their business while the states keep separate their own affairs: *Switzerland and the United States both became nations by federal union.* adj.

feel·ing (fē′ling), 1 emotion. Joy, sorrow, fear, and anger are feelings. *The loss of the ball game stirred up much feeling.* 2 feelings, pl. tender or sensitive side of one's nature: *You hurt my feelings when you yelled at me.* n., pl. **feel·ings.**

fence (fens), railing, wall, put around a yard, garden, field, farm, etc., to show where it ends or to keep people or animals out or in. Most fences are made of wood, wire, or metal. n.

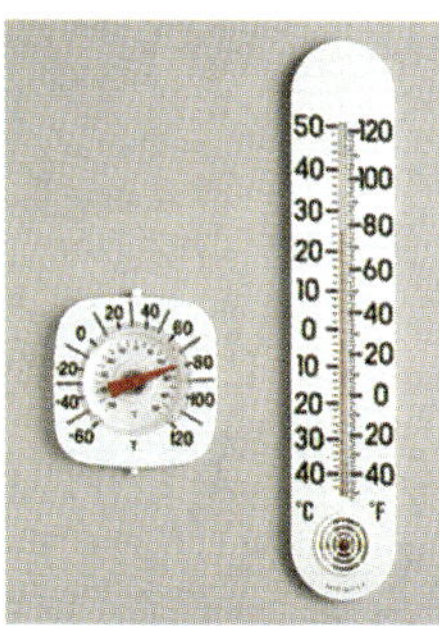

Fahrenheit
The **Fahrenheit** scale is used on these thermometers.

a	hat	ī	ice	u̇	put	ə stands for	
ā	age	o	not	ü	rule	a	in about
ä	far, calm	ō	open	ch	child	e	in taken
âr	care	ȯ	saw	ng	long	i	in pencil
e	let	ô	order	sh	she	o	in lemon
ē	equal	oi	oil	th	thin	u	in circus
ėr	term	ou	out	ŦH	then		
i	it	u	cup	zh	measure		

263

fern | forget

fern

two Boston **ferns**

fern (fėrn), kind of plant that has roots, stems, and feathery leaves, but does not have flowers or seeds. The plant reproduces by means of spores which grow in little brown clusters on the backs of the leaves. *n., pl.* **ferns.**

fer·ti·lize (fėr′tl īz), unite with (an egg cell) in fertilization; impregnate. *v.,* **fer·ti·lized, fer·ti·liz·ing.**

few (fyů), not many: *Few people attended the meeting. adj.*

field (fēld), piece of land used for crops or for pasture. *n.*

field goal (fēld′ gōl′), (in basketball) a basket scored while the ball is in play, counting two points.

fil·i·gree (fil′ə grē), very delicate, lacelike, ornamental work of gold or silver wire. *n.*

film (film), roll or sheet of thin, flexible material covered with a coating that is sensitive to light, used in taking photographs. *n.*

fi·nal·ly (fī′nl ē), at the end; at last. *adv.*

fin·ger (fing′gər), one of the five slender divisions that end the hand, especially the four besides the thumb. *n.*
put one's finger on, point out exactly: *The inspector was able to put his finger on the weak point in the suspect's alibi.*

fire·proof (fīr′prǔf′), very resistant to fire; almost impossible to burn: *A building made entirely of steel and concrete is fireproof. adj.*

first (fėrst), **1** coming before all others: *She is first in her class.* **2** person, thing, place, etc., that is first: *We were the first to get here.* 1 *adj.,* 2 *n.*

first aid (fėrst′ ād′), emergency treatment given to an injured or sick person before a doctor sees the person.

flash·light (flash′līt′), a portable electric light, operated by batteries. *n.*

flaw (flo), defective area: *There is a flaw in this shirt. n.*

football (definition 2)

flawed (flod), having a defect: *a flawed diamond. adj.*

float (flōt), stay on top of or be held up by air, water, or other liquid. A cork will float, but a stone sinks. *v.*

Flo·ri·da (flôr′ə də), one of the southeastern states of the United States. *Abbreviation:* Fla. or FL *Capital:* Tallahassee. *n.*

flow·er (flou′ər), part of a plant that produces the seed; blossom. It has modified leaves called petals. Flowers are often beautifully colored or shaped. *n., pl.* **flow·ers.**

fly (flī), any of a large group of insects that have two wings and make a buzzing sound, especially the housefly. *n., pl.* **flies.**

fo·cus (fō′kəs), bring (rays of light, heat, etc.) to a focus: *The lens focused the sun's rays on a piece of paper. v.* **fo·cused, fo·cus·ing,** or **fo·cussed, fo·cus·sing.**

food chain (fůd′ chān′), several kinds of living things that are linked because each uses another as food. Cats, birds, caterpillars, and plants eat the one named next.

food web (fůd′ web′), the flow of energy and materials through connected food chains. *n.*

foot (fůt), the end part of a leg; part that a person, animal, or thing stands on. *n., pl.* **feet** (fēt).
put one's best foot forward, INFORMAL. do one's best.

foot·ball (fůt′bol′), **1** game played with an inflated leather ball by two teams of eleven players each, on a field with a goal at each end. A player scores by carrying the ball over the goal line by a run or pass, or by kicking it through the goal posts. **2** ball used in this game. *n.*

fore·cast (fôr′kast′), what is coming; prophecy; prediction: *What is the forecast for the weather today? n.* **—fore′cast′er,** *n.*

fo·rest (fôr′ist), a large piece of land covered with trees; thick woods. *n.*

for·get (fər get′), fail to think of; fail to do, take, notice, etc.: *I forgot to call the dentist. v.,* **for·got, for·got·ten** (fər got′n) or **for·got, for·get·ting.**

264

forgot | **gang**

for·got (fər got′), See **forget**. *She was so busy that she forgot to eat her lunch.* v.

form (fôrm), **1** be formed; take shape: *Clouds form in the sky.* **2** piece of printed paper with blank spaces to be filled in: *We filled out a form to get a license for our dog.* 1 v., 2 n.

foul (foul), **1** (in football, basketball, etc.) an unfair play; thing done against the rules. **2** make an unfair play against. 1 n., 2 v.

four·teen (fôr′tēn′), four more than ten; 14. n., adj.

fourth (fôrth), next after the third; last in a series of 4. adj., n.

Fourth of July, Independence Day.

fran·tic (fran′tik), very much excited; wild with rage, fear, pain, or grief. adj.

freck·le (frek′əl), a small, light-brown spot on the skin, often caused by exposure to the sun. n., pl. **freck·les.**

free·style (frē′stīl′), a freestyle race or figure-skating contest. n.

free throw (frē′ thrō′), (in basketball) an unblocked shot from a line **(free-throw line)** about 15 feet (4.5 meters) away from the basket, awarded to a player fouled by a member of the opposing team, and worth one point.

friend (frend), **1** person who knows and likes another. *My friend's companionship is priceless.* **2** person who favors and supports: *She was a generous friend to the poor.* n.

front (frunt), the line where two air masses meet. n.

fruit (trut), a juicy or fleshy product of a tree, bush, shrub, or vine which consists of the seed and its covering and is usually sweet and good to eat. Apples and pears are fruits. n.

fuch·sia (fyü′shə), shrub with handsome pink, red, or purple flowers that droop from the stems. n., pl. **fuch·sias.** [The *fuchsia* was named for Leonhard *Fuchs,* 1501-1566, a German botanist.]

fudge (fuj), a soft candy made of sugar, milk, chocolate, butter, etc. n.

fu·el (fyü′əl), **1** anything that can be burned to produce useful heat or power. Coal, wood, and oil are fuels. **2** supply with fuel. **3** get fuel: *The ship will have to fuel at the nearest port.* 1 n., pl. **fu·els,** 2,3 v.

fun·ny (fun′ē), **1** causing laughter; amusing: *The clown's funny jokes and antics kept us laughing.* **2** INFORMAL. strange; queer; odd. adj., **fun·ni·er, fun·ni·est.**

fur (fėr), **1** the soft hair covering the skin of many animals. **2** skin with such hair on it. Fur is used to make, cover, trim, or line clothing. n.

fur·ni·ture (fėr′nə chər), movable articles needed in a room or house. Beds, chairs, tables, and desks are furniture. n.

fruit

Fresh **fruit** is good for your health.

G

gag (gag), **1** something put in a person's mouth to prevent talking or crying out. **2** INFORMAL. joke; amusing remark or trick. n.

gal·lant (gal′ənt), noble in spirit or in conduct; brave: *King Arthur was a gallant knight.* adj.

gal·lon (gal′ən), measure for liquids equal to 4 quarts. n.

gang (gang), group of people acting or going around together: *A whole gang of us went swimming.* n.

gallon

a **gallon** of milk

a	hat	**ī**	ice	**u̇**	put	**ə** stands for	
ā	age	**o**	not	**ü**	rule	**a**	in about
ä	far, calm	**ō**	open	**ch**	child	**e**	in taken
âr	care	**ȯ**	saw	**ng**	long	**i**	in pencil
e	let	**ô**	order	**sh**	she	**o**	in lemon
ē	equal	**oi**	oil	**th**	thin	**u**	in circus
ėr	term	**ou**	out	**ᴛʜ**	then		
i	it	**u**	cup	**zh**	measure		

265

gasoline | hand

giraffe
Giraffes are the tallest animals in the world.

grasshopper
a **grasshopper** and its surroundings

gas·o·line (gas′ə lēn′ or gas′ə lēn′), a colorless, liquid mixture of hydrocarbons that evaporates and burns very easily. It is made from petroleum or from gas formed in the earth and is used as a fuel to run automobiles, airplanes, etc. *n.*

gen·tle (jen′tl), not severe, rough, or violent; mild and soft: *a gentle tap. a gentle sound. adj.*, **gen·tler, gen·tlest.**

ghost (gōst), spirit of a dead person, supposed to appear to living people as a pale, dim, shadowy form: *A ghost was said to haunt the house. n.*

gi·ant (jī′ənt), like a giant; huge: *a giant potato. adj.*

gi·gan·tic (jī gan′tik), very large; huge: *a gigantic elephant. adj.*

gi·raffe (jə raf′), a large African mammal that chews its cud and has hoofs, a very long neck, long legs, and a spotted skin. Giraffes are the tallest living animals. *n.*

girl (gėrl), **1** a female child from birth to about eighteen: *The girl's face was young and pretty.* **2** a young, unmarried woman. *n.*

girl·friend (gėrl′frend′), INFORMAL. **1** boy's sweetheart or steady female companion. **2** a female friend. *n.*

glass (glas), **1** container to drink from made of glass: *I filled the glass with water.* **2 glasses,** *pl.* eyeglasses. *n., pl.* **glass·es.**

go (gō), move along. *v.* **went, gone** (gon), **going.**

good·ness (gud′nis), a being good; kindness. *n.*

grand·ma (grand′mä′ or gram′ə), INFORMAL. grandmother: *My grandma's cookies are delicious. n.*

grand·pa (grand′pä′ or gram′pə), INFORMAL. grandfather: *My grandpa's stories are very funny. n.*

grand·par·ent (grand′pâr′ent or grand′par′ənt), grandfather or grandmother: *Both sets of grandparents' letters arrived today. n.*

grass·hop·per (gras′hop′ər), a winged insect with strong hind legs for jumping. Locusts and katydids are grasshoppers. *n.*

grate·ful (grāt′fəl), feeling kindly because of a favor received; wanting to do a favor in return: *I am grateful for your help. adj.*

great·ness (grāt′nis), great mind or character. *n.*

group (grüp), number of persons or things together: *A group of children were playing tag. n.*

group·ing (grü′ping), putting a known number of objects into each group and making as many groups as you can. *v.*

guess (ges), form an opinion of something without really knowing. *v.*, **guessed, guess·ing.**

guest (gest), person who is received and entertained at another's home or staying at a hotel or motel. *n.*

H

ham·burg·er (ham′bėr′gər), ground beef, usually shaped into round, flat cakes and then fried or broiled and placed in a roll or bun. *n.* [*Hamburger* comes from a German word meaning "of Hamburg."]

ham·mer (ham′ər), hit again and again. *v.*

ham·ster (ham′stər), a small rodent with a short tail and large cheek pouches. Hamsters are used in scientific research and are often kept as pets. *n.*

hand (hand), the end part of the arm, below the wrist, which takes and holds objects. Each hand has four fingers and a thumb. *n.*
at first hand, from direct knowledge or experience.
by hand, by using the hands, not machinery: *embroidered by hand.*
lend a hand, help.
wash one's hands of, have no more to do with; refuse to be responsible for: *I washed my hands of that job when I discovered what I had done.*

hand signal | highway

hand sig·nal (hand′ sig′nəl), hand held to give a sign, notice, or warning, or to point out something: *The girl gave a hand signal when she turned. n.*

Ha·nuk·kah (hä′nə kə), a yearly Jewish festival celebrated in November or December. Candles are lighted on each of the eight days of Hanukkah. *n.* Also, **Chanukah.**

hap·pen (hap′ən), **1** come about; take place; occur: *What happened at the party yesterday?* **2** be or take place by chance: *Accidents will happen. v.,* **hap·pened, hap·pen·ing.**

hap·pen·ing (hap′ə ning), something that happens; event; occurrence: *The evening newscast reviewed the happenings of the day. n.*

hap·py (hap′ē), feeling as you do when you are well and are having a good time; glad; pleased; contented: *She is happy in her new work. adj.,* **hap·pi·er, hap·pi·est.**

head (hed), the top part of the human body containing the brain, eyes, nose, ears, and mouth. *n.* **lose one's head,** get excited; lose one's self-control.

head·line (hed′līn′), words printed in heavy type at the top of a newspaper article telling what it is about. *n.*

head·phone (hed′fōn′), earphone held against one or both ears by a band over the head. *n., pl.* **head·phones.**

heal (hēl), **1** make whole, sound, or well; bring back to health; cure. **2** become whole or sound; get well, return to health; be cured: *My cut healed in a few days. v.*

health (helth), condition of body or mind: *be in excellent health. n.*

hear (hir), **1** take in a sound or sounds through the ear: *We couldn't hear in the back row.* **2** receive news or information: *I heard from my parents. v.,* **heard** (hèrd), **hear·ing.**

heart (härt), **1** the part of the body that pumps the blood. **2** the part that feels, loves, hates, and desires: *a heavy heart, a kind heart.* **3** figure shaped like this: ♥ *n.*

heart·bro·ken (härt′brō′kən), crushed by sorrow or grief. *adj.*

he'd (hēd), **1** he had: *He'd had an accident.* **2** he would: *He'd come if he could.*

height (hīt), measurement from top to bottom; how tall a person is; how high a thing is; how far up a thing goes: *the height of a mountain. n.*

he'll (hēl), he will: *He'll tell us the story tomorrow afternoon.*

hel·met (hel′mit), covering made of steel, leather, plastic, or some other sturdy material, worn to protect the head. *n.*

help·less (help′lis), not able to help oneself: *A baby is helpless. adj.*

hem·i·sphere (hem′ə sfir), half of a sphere or globe, half of the earth's surface. The earth has four hemispheres: western, eastern, northern, and southern. *n., pl.* **hem·i·spheres.**

her·bi·vore (hèr′bə vôr), any animal that feeds mainly on plants. *n.*

her·self (hər self′), form of *she* or *her* used to make a statement stronger: *She did it herself. pron.*

hide (hīd), put or keep out of sight; conceal: *Hide it where no one else will find it. v.,* **hid** (hid), **hid·den** (hid′n) or **hid, hid·ing.**

high·way (hī′wā′), a main public road or route. *n.*

headphone

listening to music
through the
headphones

herbivore

A rabbit is a
herbivore.

a	hat	**ī**	ice	**u̇**	put	**ə** stands for	
ā	age	**o**	not	**ü**	rule	**a**	in about
ä	far, calm	**ō**	open	**ch**	child	**e**	in taken
âr	care	**ȯ**	saw	**ng**	long	**i**	in pencil
e	let	**ô**	order	**sh**	she	**o**	in lemon
ē	equal	**oi**	oil	**th**	thin	**u**	in circus
ėr	term	**ou**	out	**ᴛʜ**	then		
i	it	**u**	cup	**zh**	measure		

267

hippopotamus | iguana

hippopotamus

hip·po·pot·a·mus (hip′ə pot′ə məs), a huge, thick-skinned, almost hairless mammal found in and near the rivers of Africa that eats plants and can stay under water for a long time. *n., pl.* **hip·po·pot·a·mus·es, hip·po·pot·a·mi** (hip′ə pot′ə mī).

hob·by (hob′ē), something a person especially likes to work at or study which is not the person's main business or occupation; favorite pastime. *n., pl.* **hob·bies.**

hock·ey (hok′ē), game played by two teams on ice or on a field. The players hit a puck or ball with curved sticks to drive it across a goal. *n.*

ho·gan (hō′gän′), dwelling used by the Navajos. Hogans are built with logs and covered with earth. *n., pl.* **ho·gans.** [*Hogan* was borrowed from a Navajo word.]

hol·i·day (hol′ə dā), **1** day when one does not work; day of pleasure and enjoyment: *Labor Day and the Fourth of July are holidays in the United States.* **2** Often, **holidays,** *pl.* vacation. *n.*

home (hōm), place where a person or family lives; one's own house; where a person was born or brought up. *Her home is at 25 South Street. n.*

home·less (hōm′lis), without a home: *a stray, homeless dog. adj.* —**home′less·ness,** *n.*

hon·ey (hun′ē), a thick, sweet, yellow or golden liquid that bees make out of the nectar they collect from flowers. *n.*

hon·or (on′ər), great respect; high regard; *held in honor. n.*

hope·ful (hōp′fəl), feeling and giving or showing hope; expecting to receive what one desires: *a hopeful attitude. adj.* —**hope′ful·ly,** *adv.*

hope·less (hōp′lis), feeling or giving no hope: *He was disappointed so often that he became hopeless. adj.*

horn (hôrn), a hard, hollow, permanent growth, usually curved and pointed and in pairs, on the heads of cattle, sheep, goats, and certain other animals. *n.* **blow one's own horn** or **toot one's own horn,** INFORMAL, praise oneself; boast.

hos·pi·tal (hos′pi təl), place for the care of the sick or injured. *n.*

hot (hot), having much heat; very warm: *Fire is hot. The sun is hot today. adj.,* **hot·ter, hot·test.**

ho·tel (hō tel′), house or large building that supplies rooms and food for pay to travelers and others. *n.*

house (hous), building in which people live. *n., pl.* **hous·es** (hou′ziz).

how·ev·er (hou ev′ər), in spite of that; nevertheless; yet: *We were very late for dinner; however, there was plenty left for us. adv.*

huge (hyüj), very big; extremely large or great: *A whale is a huge animal. adj.*

hu·mid·i·ty (hyü mid′ə tē), moisture in the air: *On a hot, sultry day, the humidity is high. The humidity today is worse than the heat. n.*

hu·mor (hyü′mər), funny or amusing quality: *I see no humor in your tricks. n.*

hu·mor·ous (hyü′mər əs), full of humor; funny: *We all laughed at the humorous story. adj.*

Hur·on (hyùr′ən), **Lake,** one of the five Great Lakes; it borders Michigan and Canada. *n.*

hy·dro·e·lec·tric (hī′drō i lek′trik), developing electricity from water power. *adj.*

hogan

A **hogan** is a type of house.

I

I'd (īd), **1** I would: *I'd enjoy a vacation right now.* **2** I had: *I'd just finished dinner when she called.*

ig·nore (ig nôr′), pay no attention to; disregard: *The driver ignored the traffic light and almost hit another car. v.,* **ig·nored, ig·nor·ing.**

i·gua·na (i gwä′nə), a large tropical American lizard having a spiny crest along its back. *n., pl.* **i·gua·nas.**

I'll (īl), I will: *I'll call you tomorrow.*

I'm (īm), I am: *I'm going to the concert tonight.*

i·mag·ine (i maj′ən), suppose; guess: *I cannot imagine what you mean.* v., **i·mag·ined, i·mag·in·ing.** —**i·mag·i·na·ble,** *adj.*

im·pos·si·ble (im pos′ə bəl), not capable of being, being done, or happening; not possible: *It is impossible for two and two to be six. adj.*

in·ac·tive (in ak′tiv), not active; idle; slow: *Bears are inactive during the winter. adj.*

in·ci·sor (in sī′zər), tooth having a sharp edge for cutting; one of the front teeth between the canine teeth in either jaw. Humans have eight incisors. *n.*

in·com·plete (in′kəm plēt′), not complete; lacking some part; unfinished. *adj.*

in·con·ven·ient (in′kən vē′nyənt), not convenient; causing trouble, difficulty, or bother; troublesome: *Shelves that are too high to reach easily are inconvenient. adj.*

in·cor·rect (in′kə rekt′), containing errors or mistakes; not correct; wrong: *Today's local newspaper gave an incorrect account of the accident. adj.*

in·cred·i·ble (in kred′ə bəl), hard to believe; seeming too extraordinary to be possible; unbelievable: *The racing car rounded the curve with incredible speed. adj.*

in·de·pend·ent (in′di pen′dənt), **1** not influenced by others; thinking or acting for oneself: *an independent voter, an independent thinker.* **2** person who is independent in thought or behavior. 1 *adj.* 2 *n.*

in·jur·y (in′jər ē), hurt or loss caused to or endured by a person or thing; harm; damage: *She escaped from the train wreck without injury. n., pl.* **in·jur·ies.**

inner ear (in′ər ir′), the fluid-filled part of the ear that sends messages to the brain.

in·stru·ment (in′strə mənt), **1** a mechanical device that is portable, and usually operated by hand; tool: *a dentist's instruments.* **2** device for producing musical sounds: *wind instruments. n.*

in·su·late (in′sə lāt), keep from losing or transferring electricity, heat, sound, etc., especially by covering, packing, or surrounding with a material that does not conduct electricity, heat, etc.: *Telephone wires are often insulated by a covering of rubber. v.,* **in·su·lat·ed, in·su·lat·ing.**

in·ten·si·ty (in ten′sə tē), extreme degree; great vigor; violence: *intensity of thought, intensity of feeling. n., pl.* **in·ten·si·ties.**

in·ter·est·ing (in′tər ə sting *or* in′tə res′ting), arousing interest; holding one's attention: *Stories about travel and adventure are interesting. adj.*

in·ter·sect·ing (in′tər sekt′ing), crossing each other at a point: *intersecting lines. adj.*

in·ter·view (in′tər vyü), a meeting between a reporter and a person from whom information is sought for publication or broadcast. *n.*

in·to (in′tü; *before consonants often* in′tə), to the inside of; toward and inside: *Come into the house. We drove into the city. I will look into the matter. prep.*

In·u·it (in′ü it *or* in′yü it), the people living mainly in the arctic regions of the world; the Eskimo people. *n.*

instrument
(definition 2)
types of brass
instruments

a hat	**ī** ice	**u̇** put	**ə** stands for	
ā age	**o** not	**ü** rule	**a** in about	
ä far, calm	**ō** open	**ch** child	**e** in taken	
âr care	**ȯ** saw	**ng** long	**i** in pencil	
e let	**ô** order	**sh** she	**o** in lemon	
ē equal	**oi** oil	**th** thin	**u** in circus	
ėr term	**ou** out	**ᵀн** then		
i it	**u** cup	**zh** measure		

invade | kick

in·vade (in vād′), enter with force or as an enemy; attack: *Soldiers invaded the country to conquer it.* v., **in·vad·ed, in·vad·ing.**

in·va·sion (in vā′zhən), an invading; entering by force or as an enemy; attack. n.

in·ven·tion (in ven′shən), something new, thing invented: *Television is a modern invention.* n.

in·vis·i·ble (in viz′ə bəl), not visible; not capable of being seen: *Thought is invisible. Germs are invisible to the naked eye.* adj.

in·vite (in vīt′), ask (someone) politely to come to some place or to do something: *I invited some friends to a party. We invited them to join our club.* v., **in·vit·ed, in·vit·ing.**

i·ris (ī′ris), the colored part of the eye around the pupil. n., pl. **i·ris·es.**

i·ron (ī′ərn), **1** an implement with a flat surface that is heated and used to press clothing. **2** smooth or press (cloth, etc.) with a heated iron. 1 n., 2 v.

is·land (ī′lənd), body of land smaller than a continent and completely surrounded by water: *Cuba is a large island.* n.

is·sue (ish′ü), send out; put forth: *This magazine is issued every week.* v., **is·sued, is·su·ing.**

it'll (it′l), it will: *It'll be better soon.*

it's (its), **1** it is: *It's my turn.* **2** it has: *It's been a beautiful day.*

jai alai
playing the game of
jai alai

J

jai a·lai (hī′ lī′), game similar to handball, played on a walled court with a hard ball. The ball is caught and thrown with a kind of curved wicker basket fastened to the arm.

James (jāmz), a boy's name. *James's house is next door to mine.* n.

Jan·u·ar·y (jan′yü er′ē), the first month of the year. It has 31 days. n.

jewel
This **jewel** is a sapphire.

jay·walk (jā′wȯk′), walk across a street without paying attention to traffic rules. v. —**jay·walk·ing,** n.

jer·sey (jėr′zē), a close-fitting, pullover sweater made of a machine-woven cloth with a tight weave. n. [*Jersey* gets its name from the island of *Jersey,* where this cloth had been made for a long time.]

jew·el (jü′əl), a precious stone; gem. n., pl. **jew·els.**

juice (jüs), the liquid part of fruits, vegetables, and meats: *the juice of a lemon, meat juice.* n.

Ju·ly (jù lī′), the seventh month of the year. It has 31 days. n.

jum·bo (jum′bō), INFORMAL. a big person, animal, or thing; something unusually large of its kind: *a jumbo ice-cream cone.* adj. [*Jumbo* comes from the name of a large circus elephant.]

jump shot (jump′ shot′), (in basketball) shot made while jumping, especially at the highest point of the jump. n.

June (jün), the sixth month of the year. It has 30 days. n.

jur·y (jùr′ē), group of persons chosen to give a judgment in a court of law or to decide who is the winner in a contest: *The jury gave her poem the first prize.* n., pl. **jur·ies.**

K

Kan·sas (kan′zəs), one of the midwestern states of the United States. *Abbreviation:* Kans. or KS *Capital:* Topeka. n.

kay·ak (kī′ak), an Eskimo canoe made of skins stretched over a light frame of wood or bone with an opening in the middle for a person. n. Also, **kaiak.**

key se·quence (kē′ sē′kwəns), a connected series of keys on a calculator used in order to obtain a result.

kick (kik), strike out with the foot: *The boy kicked the soccer ball.* v.

kindergarten | lasagna

kin·der·gar·ten (kin′dər gärt′n),
school or class for children from
about 4 to 6 years old that
educates them by games, toys,
and pleasant occupations. *n.*
[*Kindergarten* is from German
Kindergarten, which comes from
Kinder, meaning "children," and
Garten, meaning "garden."]

kitch·en (kich′ən), room or area
where food is cooked. *n.* [*Kitchen*
comes from Old English *cycene*,
and can be traced back to Latin
coquere, meaning "to cook."]

knee (nē), the joint between the thigh
and the lower leg. *n.*

kneel (nēl), go down on one's knee or
knees: *She knelt down to pull a
weed. He kneels in prayer. v.,* **knelt**
(nelt) or **kneeled, kneel·ing.**

knit (nit), make (cloth or an article of
clothing) by looping yarn or thread
together with long needles, or by
machinery which forms loops
instead of weaving: *knit a pair of
socks. v.,* **knit·ted** or **knit, knit·ting.**

knob (nob), handle on a door,
drawer, etc.: *the knob on the dial
of a television set. n.*

knot (not), **1** a fastening made by
tying or twining together pieces of
one or more ropes, cords, strings,
etc.: *a square knot, a slip knot.*
2 tie or twine together in a knot: *He
knotted two ropes together.*
3 group; cluster: *A knot of students
stood talking outside the
classroom. 1,3 n., 2 v.,* **knot·ted,
knot·ting.**

know (nō), have knowledge, have
facts: *I know from experience how
to drive on icy roads. She knows
the poem. v.* **knew** (nü), **known,
know·ing.**

known (nōn), See **know.** *George
Washington is known as the father
of his country. v.*

Kwan·zaa or **Kwan·za** (kwän′zə),
a yearly African American
celebration celebrating various
African festivals. It lasts from
December 26 to January 1. *n.*
[*Kwanzaa* is from Swahili *Kwanza*,
originally meaning "first (fruits),"
which comes from *kuanza*,
meaning "to begin."]

Kwanzaa
a family celebrating
Kwanzaa

L

la·crosse (lə krós′), game played
on a field with a ball and long-
handled, loosely strung rackets by
two teams, usually of 10 players
each. The players carry the ball in
the rackets, trying to send it into
the other team's goal. *n.*

la·dy (lā′dē), **1** woman of good
family and high social position:
a lady by birth. **2** a well-bred
woman: *I borrowed the lady's
umbrella.* **3** a polite term for any
woman. "Ladies" is often used in
speaking or writing to a group of
women: *Ladies, please be seated.*
4 woman who has the rights and
authority of a lord. *n., pl.*
la·dies.

lamb (lam), a young sheep. *n.*

land·form (land′fôrm′), a physical
feature of the earth's surface.
Plains, plateaus, hills, and
mountains are landforms. *n., pl.*
land·forms.

large (lärj), of more than the usual
size, amount, or number; big:
*America is a large country. A
hundred thousand dollars is a
large sum of money. adj.,* **larg·er,
larg·est.**

la·sa·gna (lə zä′nyə), dish consisting
of chopped meat, cheese, and
tomato sauce, baked with layers
of wide noodles. *n.*

lasagna
lasagna topped with
grated cheese

a	hat	**ī**	ice	**u̇**	put	**ə** stands for	
ā	age	**o**	not	**ü**	rule	**a**	in about
ä	far, calm	**ō**	open	**ch**	child	**e**	in taken
âr	care	**ȯ**	saw	**ng**	long	**i**	in pencil
e	let	**ô**	order	**sh**	she	**o**	in lemon
ē	equal	**oi**	oil	**th**	thin	**u**	in circus
ėr	term	**ou**	out	**ŦH**	then		
i	it	**u**	cup	**zh**	measure		

271

lately | longitude

library (definition 2)
gathering information at
the **library**

late·ly (lāt′lē), a little while ago; not long ago; recently: *He has not been looking well lately. adv.*

lat·i·tude (lat′ə tüd *or* lat′ə tyüd), distance north or south of the equator, measured in degrees. A degree of latitude is about 69 miles (111 kilometers). *n.*

laugh (laf), make the sounds and movements of the face and body that show one is happy or amused: *We all laughed at the joke. v.,* **laughed, laugh·ing.**

lay-up (lā′up′), (in basketball) a shot from close under the basket. *n.*

la·zy (lā′zē), not willing to work or be active: *He lost his job because he was lazy. adj.,* **la·zi·er, la·zi·est.**

lead (lēd), the opening paragraph in a newspaper or magazine article. A lead often summarizes the information in the body of the article. *n.*

lead·er (lē′dər), person who leads, or is well fitted to lead: *an orchestra leader. That girl is a born leader. n., pl.* **lead·ers.**

least (lēst), less than any other; smallest; slightest: *Ten cents is a little money; five cents is less; one cent is least. I have the least work. adj.*

leg (leg), one of the limbs on which people and animals stand and walk. *n.*
on one's last legs, about to fail, collapse, or die.
pull one's leg, INFORMAL. fool, trick, or make fun of one.
shake a leg, hurry up.

length (lengkth *or* length), how long a thing is; what a thing measures from end to end; the longest way a thing can be measured: *the length of a room, an animal eight inches in length. n.*

lens (lenz), **1** a curved piece of glass which brings closer together or sends wider apart the rays of light passing through it. The lens of a camera forms images on film. **2** the part of the eye that focuses light rays upon the retina. *n., pl.* **lens·es.**

let's (lets), let us: *Let's go for a walk.*

lion
A **lion** can be 3 feet
high at the shoulder.

let·tuce (let′is), the large, crisp, green leaves of a garden plant, used in salad. *n.*

lev·el (lev′əl), **1** having the same height everywhere; flat; even: *a level floor.* **2** an instrument for showing whether a surface is level. 1 *adj.,* 2 *n.*

li·brar·i·an (lī brer′ē ən), person in charge of a library. *n.*

li·brar·y (lī′brer′ē), **1** collection of books, magazines, films, recordings, etc. **2** room or building where such a collection is kept for public use and borrowing. *n., pl.* **li·brar·ies.**

limb (lim), a large branch: *They sawed the dead limb off the tree. n.*

line (līn), a set of points continuing without end in both directions. *n.*

li·on (lī′ən), a large, strong, flesh-eating cat, with a dull-yellowish coat, and a loud roar. It is found in Africa and southern Asia. The male has a full, flowing mane of coarse hair. *n.*

liq·uid (lik′wid), **1** substance that is not a solid or a gas; substance that flows freely like water. **2** In the form of a liquid; melted: *liquid soap, butter heated until it is liquid.* 1 *n.,* 2 *adj.*

lo·cal (lō′kəl), of a place; of a certain place or places: *the local doctor, local self-government, local news. adj.*

lo·cate (lō′kāt), establish in a place: *They located their new store on Second Avenue. v.,* **lo·cat·ed, lo·cat·ing.**

lo·ca·tion (lō kā′shən), position or place: *The camp was in a bad location as there was no water near it. n.*

lock (lok), an enclosed section of a canal or dock in which the level of the water can be changed by letting water in or out, to raise or lower ships. *n., pl.* **locks.**

lon·gi·tude (lon′jə tüd *or* lon′jə tyüd), distance east or west on the earth's surface, measured in degrees from Greenwich, England. *n.*

loose | meet¹

loose (lüs), **1** not tight: *loose clothing.* **2** not firmly set or fastened in: *a loose tooth.* 1,2 *adj.,* **loos·er, loos·est.**

lose (lüz), **1** not have any longer; have taken away from one by accident, carelessness, parting, death, etc.: *lose a finger, lose a friend, lose one's life.* **2** fail to win: *lose the prize. v.,* **lost** (lòst), **los·ing.**

lo·tus (lō′təs), kind of water lily that grows in Egypt, India, and Asia. *n., pl.* **lo·tus·es.**

loud (loud), **1** making a great sound; not quiet or soft: *a loud voice, a loud noise.* **2** in a loud manner: *The hunter called long and loud. adj.*

love (luv), have such a warm liking or deep feeling for: *We love our parents. I love my country. v.,* **loved, lov·ing.**

lux·ur·i·ate (lug zhùr′ē āt *or* luk shùr′ē āt), **1** indulge in luxury. **2** take great delight: *The campers planned to luxuriate in hot baths when they came home.* **3** grow very abundantly. *v.,* **lux·ur·i·at·ed, lux·ur·i·at·ing.**

M

ma·chine (mə shēn′), arrangement of fixed and moving parts for doing work, each part having some special function: *Sewing machines and washing machines make housework easier. n.*

mag·net (mag′nit), stone or piece of metal that has the property of attracting iron or steel. A lodestone is a natural magnet. *n.*

mag·net·ic field (mag net′ik fēld′), space around a magnet or electric current in which its magnetic force is felt. *n.*

mag·net·ism (mag′nə tiz′əm), properties or qualities of a magnet; the showing of magnetic properties. *n.*

mar·ble (mär′bəl), **1** a hard rock formed from limestone by heat and pressure. It may be white or colored and can be polished to a smooth gloss. Marble is used for statues and in buildings. **2** made of marble. 1 *n.,* 2 *adj.*

March (märch), the third month of the year. It has 31 days. *n.*

mat·ter (mat′ər), importance; significance: *Let it go since it is of no matter. n.*

maul (mòl), beat and pull about; handle roughly. *v.,* **mauled, maul·ing.**

max·im (mak′səm), a short rule of conduct; proverb: *"Look before you leap" is a maxim. n.*

may (mā), be permitted or allowed to: *May I have an apple? v., past tense* **might.**

May (mā), the fifth month of the year. It has 31 days. *n.*

mean¹ (mēn), have as a purpose; have in mind. *v.,* **meant, mean·ing.**

mean² (mēn), not noble; petty; unkind; small-minded: *It is mean to spread gossip about your friends. adj.*

meant (ment), See **mean¹**. *She explained what she meant. v.*

meet¹ (mēt), **1** come face to face (with something or someone coming from the other direction): *Our car met another car on a narrow bridge.* **2** fulfill; put an end to; satisfy: *The campers took along enough food to meet their needs for a week.* **3** a meeting; a gathering: *an athletic meet.* 1,2 *v.,* **met** (met), **meet·ing;** 3 *n.* —**meet′er,** *n.*

lotus

The **lotus** is the national flower of India.

magnet

A **magnet** attracts iron or steel.

a	hat	ī	ice	ù	put	ə stands for	
ā	age	o	not	ü	rule	a	in about
ä	far, calm	ō	open	ch	child	e	in taken
âr	care	ò	saw	ng	long	i	in pencil
e	let	ô	order	sh	she	o	in lemon
ē	equal	oi	oil	th	thin	u	in circus
ėr	term	ou	out	ᴛʜ	then		
i	it	u	cup	zh	measure		

273

meet² | model

meet² (mēt), OLD USE. suitable; proper; fitting: *It is meet that you should help your friends. adj.*

Mem·or·i·al Day (mə môr′ē əl dā′), holiday for remembering and honoring members of the United States armed services who have died. In most states, it is observed on the last Monday in May.

mem·or·y (mem′ər ē), person, thing, or event that is remembered: *I was so young when we moved that our old house is only a vague memory. n., pl.* **mem·or·ies.**

memory mi·nus (mem′ər ē mī′nəs), the calculator key that enables the user to subtract the display from what is in the memory.

memory plus (mem′ər ē plus′), the calculator key that enables the user to add the display to what is in the memory.

memory re·call (mem′ər ē rē′kȯl′), the calculator key that enables the user to display what is in memory.

men·u (men′yü), list of the food served at a meal; bill of fare. *n.*

me·rid·i·an (mə rid′ē ən), an imaginary circle passing through any place on the earth's surface and through the North and South Poles. Meridians mark longitude. *n., pl.* **me·rid·i·ans.**

me·te·o·rol·o·gist (mē′tē ə rol′ə jist), a person who studies weather. *n.*

me·ter¹ (mē′tər), the basic unit of length in the metric system. A meter is equal to 39.37 inches. *n.* Also, **metre.**

me·ter² (mē′tər), **1** any kind of poetic rhythm; the arrangement of beats or accents in a line of poetry. **2** musical rhythm; the arrangement of beats in music: *Three-fourths meter is waltz time. n.*

met·ric (met′rik), of the meter or the metric system. *adj.*

Mich·i·gan (mish′ə gən), **Lake,** one of the five Great Lakes. It lies entirely within the United States. *n.*

middle ear (mid′l ir′), the three tiny bones that carry sound waves from the eardrum to the inner ear. *n.*

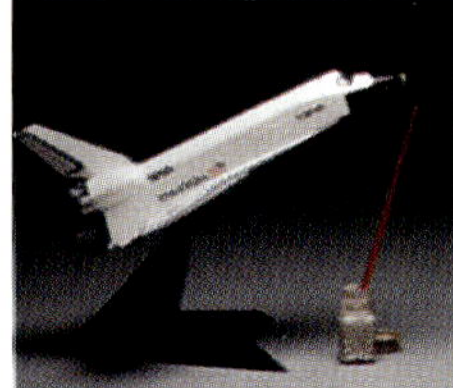

model (definition 1)

painting a **model** of the space shuttle

Middle English (mid′l ing′glish), period in the development of the English language between Old English and Modern English, lasting from 1100 to about 1500.

might (mīt), See **may.** *Mother said that we might play in the barn. v.*

might·'ve (mīt′əv), might have: *He might've been outdoors when you called.*

mis·be·have (mis′bi hāv′), behave badly. *v.,* **mis·be·haved, mis·be·hav·ing.**

mis·for·tune (mis fôr′chən), bad luck; unlucky accident. *She had the misfortune to break her arm. n.*

mis·lead (mis lēd′), cause to go in the wrong direction; lead astray: *Our guide misled us and we got lost. v.,* **mis·led, mis·lead·ing.**

mis·led (mis led′), See **mislead.** *We were misled on our hike by a careless guide. v.*

mis·place (mis plās′), put in a place and then forget where it is; mislay: *I have misplaced my pencil. v.,* **mis·placed, mis·plac·ing.**

miss (mis), **1** fail to hit: *I swung at the ball and missed it.* **2** fail to catch: *miss the train.* **3** notice the absence of; feel keenly the absence of: *I missed you while you were away. v.,* **missed, miss·ing.**

mis·sion (mish′ən), a sending or being sent on some special work; errand. An operation by one or more aircraft against the enemy is called a mission. *n.*

Mis·sis·sip·pi (mis′ə sip′ē), **1** large river in the United States. It flows south from N Minnesota to the Gulf of Mexico. **2** one of the south central states of the United States. *Abbreviation:* Miss. or MS. *Capital:* Jackson. *n.*

mis·spell (mis spel′), spell incorrectly. *v.*

mis·treat (mis trēt′), treat badly. *v.*

mod·el (mod′l), **1** a small copy: *a model of a ship or an engine.* **2** thing or person to be copied or imitated: *Your mother is a fine person; make her your model. n.*

moisture | mystery

mois·ture (mois′chər), slight wetness; water or other liquid suspended in drops in the air or spread on a surface. *n.*

mo·lar (mō′lər), tooth with a broad surface for grinding. A person's back teeth are molars. *n.*

mo·ment (mō′mənt), a very short space of time; instant. *n.*

mon·ey (mun′ē), coins of gold, silver, or other metal, or paper notes which represent these metals, issued by a government for use in buying and selling. *n., pl.* **mon·eys** or **mon·ies.**

mon·key (mung′kē), **1** animal of the group most like human beings. **2** person, especially a child, who is full of mischief. *n., pl.* **mon·keys.**

mood (müd), state of mind or feeling: *I am in the mood to play now; I don't want to study. n.*

morn·ing (môr′ning), the early part of the day, ending at noon. *n.*

moth·er (muᴛʜ′ər), a female parent. *I'll have to ask my mother. n.*

mo·tor (mō′tər), an engine, such as a gasoline or diesel engine, that makes a machine go. *n.*

mo·tor·cy·cle (mō′tər sī′kəl), a two-wheeled motor vehicle which resembles a bicycle but is heavier and larger. *n.*

moun·tain (moun′tən), a very high hill. *n.*

mouth (mouth), the opening through which a person or animal takes in food; space containing the tongue and teeth. *n.*
down in the mouth, INFORMAL. in low spirits; discouraged.

move·ment (müv′mənt), **1** act or fact of moving: *We run by movements of the legs.* **2** the moving parts of a machine; special group of connected parts that move together. The movement of a watch consists of many little wheels. *n.*

Mr. or **Mr** (mis′tər), Mister, a title put in front of a man's name or the name of his position: *Mr. Stern, Mr. President. pl.* **Messrs.**

Mrs. or **Mrs** (mis′iz), a title put in front of a married woman's name: *Mrs. Weiss. pl.* **Mmes.**

Ms. (miz), a title put in front of a woman's name: *Ms. Karen Hansen. pl.* **Mses.**

muf·fin (muf′ən), a small, round cake made of wheat flour, corn meal, or the like, often without sugar. *n.*

mul·ti·pli·ca·tion (mul′tə plə kā′shən), operation of multiplying one number by another. *n.*

mu·sic (myü′zik), beautiful, pleasing, or interesting arrangements of sounds. *n.*

music box (myü′zik boks′), box or case containing apparatus for producing music mechanically.

music hall (myü′zik hȯl′), hall for musical performances.

music vid·e·o (myü′zik vid′ē ō), a short musical film or videotape or videodisc. *pl.* **music vid·e·os.**

mus·tard (mus′tərd), a yellow powder or paste made from the seeds of the mustard plant, used as seasoning. *n.*

must·n't (mus′nt), must not: *You mustn't wake the baby.*

my·self (mī self′), form used instead of *me* or *I* in cases like: *I can cook for myself. I hurt myself. pron.*

mys·ter·y (mis′tər ē), something that is hidden or unknown; secret. *n., pl.* **mys·ter·ies.**

monkey (definition 1)

mountain

a	hat	**ī**	ice	**ů**	put	**ə** stands for	
ā	age	**o**	not	**ü**	rule	**a**	in about
ä	far, calm	**ō**	open	**ch**	child	**e**	in taken
âr	care	**ȯ**	saw	**ng**	long	**i**	in pencil
e	let	**ô**	order	**sh**	she	**o**	in lemon
ē	equal	**oi**	oil	**th**	thin	**u**	in circus
ėr	term	**ou**	out	**ᴛʜ**	then		
i	it	**u**	cup	**zh**	measure		

275

nation | number sentence

N

na·tion (nā′shən), people occupying the same country, united under the same government, and usually speaking the same language. *n.*

na·tion·al (nash′ə nəl), of a nation; belonging to a whole nation: *national laws, a national disaster. adj.*

na·tur·al gas (nach′ər əl gas′), a combustible gas formed naturally in the earth, consisting primarily of methane. It is used as a fuel.

Nav·a·jo (nav′ə hō), member of a tribe of American Indians living mainly in New Mexico, Arizona, and Utah. *n., pl.* **Nav·a·jo, Nav·a·jos,** or **Nav·a·joes.**

nee·dle·leaf (nē′dl lēf′), of or about a type of tree with thin, sharp needles. A pine is a needleleaf tree. *adj.*

neg·a·tive (neg′ə tiv), a photographic image in which the lights and shadows are reversed. Prints are made from it. *n.*

neigh·bor (nā′bər), someone who lives in the next house or nearby. *n.*

neph·ew (nef′yü), son of one's brother or sister; son of one's brother-in-law or sister-in-law. *n.*

nerve (nėrv), **1** mental strength; courage: *nerves of steel.* **2** INFORMAL. rude boldness; impudence. *n.*

net (net), an open fabric made of string, cord, or thread, knotted together in such a way as to leave holes regularly arranged. *n.*

news·cast·er (nüz′kas′tər *or* nyüz′kas′tər), person or commentator who gives the news on a newscast. *n.*

newspaper
We read **newspapers** for information.

news·pa·per (nüz′pā′pər *or* nyüz′pā′pər), a daily or weekly publication printed on large sheets of paper folded together, telling the news, carrying advertisements, and having stories, pictures, articles, and useful information. *n.*

nic·o·tine (nik′ə tēn′), poison contained in the leaves, roots, and seeds of tobacco. *n.* [*Nicotine* comes from Jean *Nicot,* about 1530-1600, a Frenchman who introduced tobacco to France in about 1560.]

night (nīt), **1** the time between evening and morning, especially when it is dark. **2** the darkness of night; the dark. *n.*

night crawl·er (nīt′ krȯl′ər), a large earthworm that comes to the surface of the ground at night.

night·gown (nīt′goun′), a long, loose garment worn by a woman or child in bed. *n.*

night·mare (nīt′mâr′), a very distressing dream or experience: *The hurricane was a nightmare. n.*

night·time (nīt′tīm′), time between evening and morning. *n.*

non·sense (non′sens), worthless stuff; junk: *a drawer full of useless gadgets and other nonsense. n.*

noon (nün), 12 o'clock in the daytime; middle of the day. *n.*

nose (nōz), the part of the face or head just above the mouth. The nose has openings for breathing and smelling. *n.*
lead by the nose, have complete control over.

No·vem·ber (nō vem′bər), the 11th month of the year. It has 30 days. *n.*

num·ber (num′bər), **1** the count or sum of a group of things or persons; amount: *The number of students in our class is twenty.* **2** figure or mark that stands for a number; numeral. *n.*

number key (num′bər kē′), a key on a calculator that shows one of the numbers 0 through 9. *n., pl.* **number keys.**

number sen·tence (num′bər sen′təns), a way to write a relationship between numbers. 18 + 27 = 45 and 9 > 6 are number sentences.

oak | orchestra

O

oak (ōk), several kinds of trees or shrubs found in most parts of the world, with strong, hard, durable wood and nuts called acorns. *n.*

oc·cur (ə kėr′), take place; happen: *Storms often occur in winter. v.*, **oc·curred, oc·cur·ring.**

o·cean (ō′shən), the great body of salt water that covers almost three-fourths of the earth's surface; the sea. *n.*

oc·e·lot (os′ə lot *or* ō′sə lot), a spotted cat somewhat like a leopard, but smaller, found from Texas through Mexico and into parts of South America. *n.*

o'clock (ə klok′), of the clock; by the clock: *It is one o'clock. adv.*

Oc·to·ber (ok tō′bər), the tenth month of the year. It has 31 days. *n.*

odd (od), strange; peculiar; unusual: *What an odd house; it has no windows. adj.*

of (ov *or* uv; *unstressed* əv), **1** belonging to: *a friend of my childhood, the news of the day, the driver of the car.* **2** in regard to; concerning; about: *think well of somebody. prep.*

off (ȯf), so as to stop or lessen: *Turn the water off. adv.*

of·fer (ȯ′fər), hold out to be taken or refused; present: *offer one's hand. She offered us her help. v.*

of·fice (ȯ′fis), place in which the work of a business or profession is done; room in which to work: *The doctor's office is closed. n.*

of·ten (ȯ′fən), in many cases; many times; frequently. *Blame is often misdirected. We come here often. adv.*

oil (oil), any of several kinds of thick, fatty or greasy liquids that are lighter than water, burn easily, and are soluble in alcohol, but not in water, such as mineral oils, kerosene, vegetable and animal oils, olive oils. *n.*

oil gland (oil′ gland′), gland of the skin that secretes oil. *n.*

Old Eng·lish (ōld′ ing′glish), period in the history of the English language before 1100.

om·niv·ore (om′nə vôr), a consumer that eats producers and consumers. *n.*

on·ly (ōn′lē), merely; just: *only on weekends. adv.*

On·tar·io (on ter′ē ō), **Lake,** one of the five Great Lakes; it borders New York and Canada. The water from Niagara Falls flows from Lake Erie to Lake Ontario. It is the smallest of the five Great Lakes. *n.*

o·pen (ō′pən), **1** not shut; not closed; letting (anyone or anything) in or out: *Open windows let in the fresh air.* **2** make or become open: *He is opening the window. The door opened.* **3** spread out or unfold: *open a book, open a letter.* 1 *adj.*, 2,3 *v.*, **o·pened, o·pen·ing.**

op·e·ra·tion (op′ə rā′shən), the way a thing works: *The operation of this machine is simple. n.*

operation key (op′ə rā′shən kē′), the key which tells the calculator what to perform. The symbols +, −, ×, and ÷ appear on the operation keys. *n., pl.* **operation keys.**

op·tic (op′tik), of the eye; of the sense of sight. The **optic nerve** goes from the eye to the brain. *adj.*

or·ches·tra (ôr′kə strə), group of musicians playing together on various stringed, wind, and percussion instruments. *n., pl.* **or·ches·tras.**

ocelot

An **ocelot** can be up to 3 feet long without the tail.

a	hat	ī	ice	u̇	put	ə stands for	
ā	age	o	not	ü	rule	a	in about
ä	far, calm	ō	open	ch	child	e	in taken
âr	care	ȯ	saw	ng	long	i	in pencil
e	let	ô	order	sh	she	o	in lemon
ē	equal	oi	oil	th	thin	u	in circus
ėr	term	ou	out	ᵺ	then		
i	it	u	cup	zh	measure		

277

other | perimeter

parallel (definition 1)
parallel stripes on a
piece of fabric

oth·er (uᵗH′ər), **1** additional or further: *I have no other place to go.* **2** other person or thing. 1 *adj.,* 2 *pron.*

our (our), of us; belonging to us: *We need our coats now. adj.*

our·selves (our selvz′), form used instead of *we* or *us* in cases like: *We cook for ourselves. pron. pl.*

out·cast (out′kast′), person or animal cast out from home and friends. *n.*

out·er ear (ou′tər ir′), the part of the ear outside of the head and the ear canal.

out·look (out′lùk′), way of thinking about things; attitude of mind; point of view: *a cheerful outlook on life. n.*

out·side (out′sīd′), **1** the side or surface that is out; outer part: *polish the outside of a car, the outside of a house.* **2** on or to the outside; outdoors: *Run outside and play.* 1 *n.,* 2 *adv.*

o·ven (uv′ən), an enclosed space, usually in a stove, for baking, roasting, and sometimes broiling food. *n.*

P

pack·age (pak′ij), bundle of things packed or wrapped together; box with things packed in it; parcel. *n.*

pad·dle (pad′l), row (a boat or canoe) with a paddle or paddles. *v.,* **pad·dled, pad·dling.**

pain·ful (pān′fəl), causing pain; unpleasant; hurting: *a painful illness, a painful duty. adj.*

pan·ic (pan′ik), a fear spreading through a multitude of people so that they lose control of themselves; unreasoning fear: *When the theater caught fire, there was a panic. n.*

Parthenon
the ancient **Parthenon**
in Greece

par·al·lel (par′ə lel), **1** straight lines or planes, lying or extending alongside of one another, always equidistant, but never meeting. **2** any of the imaginary circles around the earth parallel to the equator, marking degrees of latitude that run east and west. 1 *adj.,* 2 *n., pl.* **par·al·lels.**

par·al·lel cir·cuit (par′ə ləl sèr′kit), a circuit that connects several objects in a way that the current for each object has its own path.

par·ent (pâr′ənt or par′ənt), father or mother. *n., pl.* **par·ents.**

Par·the·non (pär′thə non), temple of Athena on the Acropolis in Athens, regarded as the finest example of Doric architecture. *n.*

par·tic·i·pate (pär tis′ə pāt), have a share; take part. *v.,* **par·tic·i·pat·ed, par·tic·i·pat·ing.**

pave·ment (pāv′mənt), a covering or surface for streets, sidewalks, etc., made of asphalt, concrete, gravel, stones, etc. *n.*

pay·ment (pā′mənt), amount paid: *a monthly payment of $10. n.*

peace (pēs), freedom from war: *work for world peace. n.*

peace·ful (pēs′fəl), **1** full of peace; quiet; calm: *It was peaceful in the mountains.* **2** free from trouble or disturbance. *adj.*

ped·al (ped′l), **1** lever worked by the foot; the part on which the foot is placed to move any kind of machinery. **2** move by pedals: *He pedaled his bicycle slowly up the hill.* 1 *n.,* 2 *v.,* **ped·aled, ped·al·ing** or **ped·alled, ped·al·ling.**

pe·des·tri·an (pə des′trē ən), person who goes on foot; walker. *n., pl.* **pe·des·tri·ans.**

peep (pēp), **1** the cry of a young bird or chicken; a sound like a chirp or squeak. **2** make such a sound; chirp. 1 *n.,* 2 *v.*

pe·o·ny (pē′ə nē), garden plant with large, showy red, pink, or white flowers. *n., pl.* **pe·o·nies.** [The *peony* was named by the Greeks for Paeon, physician of the gods (because the plant was used in medicine).]

peo·ple (pē′pəl), men, women, and children; persons. *n. pl.*

per·fect (pèr′fikt), without defect; not spoiled at any point; faultless: *a perfect spelling paper. adj.*

pe·rim·e·ter (pə rim′ə tər), the outer boundary of a figure or area: *the perimeter of a circle, the perimeter of a garden. n.*

perpendicular | point

per·pen·dic·u·lar (pėr′pən dik′yə lər), at right angles to. Perpendicular lines intersect to form right angles. *adj.*

per·son·al (pėr′sə nəl), of a person; individual; private: *a personal letter, a personal matter. adj.*

per·son·al·i·ty (pėr′sə nal′ə tē), the personal or individual quality that makes one person be different or act differently from another. *n., pl.* **per·son·al·i·ties.**

pet·al (pet′l), one of the parts of a flower that are usually colored. A daisy has many petals. *n.*

pho·to (fō′tō), picture made with a camera. A photograph is made by the action of light rays from the thing pictured passing through the lens of the camera onto the film. *n.*

pick·le (pik′əl), cucumber preserved in salt water, vinegar, or other liquid. *n.*

piece (pēs), **1** one of the parts into which a thing is divided or broken; bit. **2** portion; limited part; small quantity: *a piece of bread. n.*

pig·eon (pij′ən), any of a group of birds with thick bodies, short tails and legs, which makes a cooing sound, including doves and many varieties of domestic pigeons. *n.*

Pil·grim (pil′grəm), one of the Puritan settlers of Plymouth Colony in 1620. *n., pl.* **Pil·grims.**

pint (pīnt), unit of measure for liquids and dry things, equal to ½ quart; 2 cups; 16 fluid ounces. *n.*

pis·til (pis′tl), the part of a flower that produces seeds. It consists, when complete, of an ovary, a style, and a stigma. *n.*

pitch·er[1] (pich′ər), container for holding and pouring liquids, with a lip on one side and a handle on the other. *n.*

pitch·er[2] (pich′ər), a baseball player who pitches the ball to the batter. *n.*

piz·za (pēt′sə), a spicy Italian dish made by baking a large flat layer of bread dough covered with cheese, tomato sauce, herbs, etc. *n., pl.* **piz·zas.**

plain (plān), a flat stretch of land; prairie: *Cattle and horses wandered over the plains. n., pl.* **plains.**

pla·teau (pla tō′), plain in the mountains or at a height considerably above sea level; large, high plain. *n., pl.* **pla·teaus** (pla tōz′).

plate (plāt), a large section of rock that makes up part of the earth's crust. *n., pl.* **plates.**

play (plā), **1** something done to amuse oneself; fun; sport; recreation: *The children are happy at play.* **2** have fun; do something in sport. *The kitten plays with its tail. He played a joke on his sister.* 1 *n.,* 2 *v.*

pledge (plej), **1** a solemn promise: *they made a pledge to give money to charity.* **2** promise solemnly: *We pledge allegiance to the flag.* 1 *n.,* 2 *v.,* **pledged, pledg·ing.**

pluck·y (pluk′ē), having or showing courage: *a plucky dog. adj.,* **pluck·i·er, pluck·i·est.**

pock·et (pok′it), a small bag or pouch sewed into clothing for carrying money or other small articles. *n.*

pod (pod), a small herd of whales or seals. *n.*

po·et·ry (pō′i trē), poems: *a collection of poetry. n.*

point (point), (in mathematics) something that has position without length or width. *n.*

pitcher[1]
a **pitcher** of milk

a	hat	**ī**	ice	**u̇**	put	**ə** stands for	
ā	age	**o**	not	**ü**	rule	**a**	in about
ä	far, calm	**ō**	open	**ch**	child	**e**	in taken
âr	care	**ȯ**	saw	**ng**	long	**i**	in pencil
e	let	**ô**	order	**sh**	she	**o**	in lemon
ē	equal	**oi**	oil	**th**	thin	**u**	in circus
ėr	term	**ou**	out	**ᴛʜ**	then		
i	it	**u**	cup	**zh**	measure		

279

polar bear | pup

polar bear

pottery

ancient **pottery** made by North American Indians

po·lar bear (pō′lər bâr′) a large, white bear of the arctic regions.

pole (pōl), either of two parts where opposite forces are strongest. A magnet or battery has both a positive pole and a negative pole. *n., pl.* **poles.**

pol·len (pol′ən), tiny grains that make seeds when combined with a flower's eggs. *n.*

pol·lu·tion (pə lü′shən), anything that dirties the environment, especially waste material: *pollution in the air. n.*

pond (pond), body of still water, smaller than a lake. *n.*

pop (pop), make a short, quick, explosive sound. *v.,* **popped, pop·ping.**

pore (pôr), a very small opening. Sweat comes through the pores in the skin. *n.*

por·trait (pôr′trit *or* pôr′trāt), picture of a person, especially of the face. *n.*

pot·ter·y (pot′ər ē), pots, dishes, vases, etc., made from clay and hardened by heat. *n., pl.* **pot·ter·ies.**

pour (pôr), flow or cause to flow in a steady stream: *I poured the milk from the bottle. The rain poured down on the field. v.*

pow·er (pou′ər), **1** strength or force; might. **2** authority; influence; control; right: *Congress has power to declare war. n.*

pow·er·ful (pou′ər fəl), having great power or force; mighty; strong: *a powerful person, a powerful medicine, a powerful argument. adj.*

pred·a·tor (pred′ə tər), a consumer that hunts and eats animals. *n.*

pres·sure (presh′ər), a state of trouble or strain: *She has been working under pressure. n.*

prey (prā), animal hunted and killed for food by another animal: *Mice and birds are the prey of cats. n.*

prime me·rid·i·an (prīm′ mə rid′ē ən), meridian from which the longitude east and west is measured. It passes through Greenwich, England, and its longitude is 0 degrees.

print (print), **1** photograph produced from a negative. **2** produce a photograph by transmission of light through a negative. 1 *n.,* 2 *v.*

pri·vate (prī′vit), not for the public; for just a few special people or for one: *a private road, a private house. adj.*

prob·a·bly (prob′ə blē), more likely than not. *adv.*

pro·duc·er (prə dü′sər), a living thing that can use sunlight to make sugars. *n., pl.* **pro·duc·ers.**

prod·uct (prod′əkt), **1** that which is produced; result of work or of growth: *factory products, farm products.* **2** number resulting from multiplying two or more numbers together: *40 is the product of 8 and 5. n., pl.* **prod·ucts.**

proud (proud), feeling or thinking well of, showing satisfaction: *I am proud to call him my friend. adj.*

psy·chol·o·gist (sī kol′ə jist), an expert who is trained to help people with feelings, especially troubled feelings that last a long time. *n.*

pud·ding (pu̇d′ing), a soft cooked food, usually sweet: *rice pudding. n.*

pueb·lo (pweb′lō), an Indian village built of adobe and stone. *n., pl.* **pueb·los.**

pun·ish (pun′ish), cause pain, loss, or discomfort to for some fault or offense: *punish criminals for wrongdoing. v.* [Punish is from Old French *puniss-,* a form of *punir,* meaning "punish," which came from Latin *punire,* meaning "penalty."]

pun·ish·ment (pun′ish mənt), pain, suffering, or loss: *Her punishment for lying was not being allowed to watch TV. n.*

pup (pup), a young dog; puppy. *n.*

pu·pil[1] (pyü′pəl), person who is learning in school or being taught by someone. *n.*

pu·pil[2] (pyü′pəl), the opening in the center of the iris of the eye which looks like a black spot and where light can enter the eye. *n.*

pur·suit (pər süt′), a chase: *The dog is in pursuit of the cat. n.*

Q

quart (kwôrt), measure of capacity for liquids, equal to one-fourth of a gallon: *a quart of milk. n.*

queen (kwēn), woman who rules a country and its people. *n.*

ques·tion (kwes′chən), thing asked in order to get information; inquiry: *The teacher answered the children's questions. n.*

quick (kwik), fast and sudden; swift: *The cat made a quick jump. Many weeds have a quick growth. adj.*

qui·et (kwī′ət), making no sound; with little or no noise: *quiet footsteps, a quiet room. adj.*

quilt (kwilt), cover for a bed, usually made of two pieces of cloth with a soft pad between, held in place by stitching. *n.*

quit (kwit), **1** stop: *They quit work at five.* **2** leave: *quit one's job. v.,* **quit** or **quit·ted, quit·ting.**

quite (kwīt), **1** completely; entirely: *a hat quite out of fashion. I am quite alone.* **2** actually; really; positively: *quite the thing. adv.*

quo·tient (kwō′shənt), number arrived at by dividing one number by another. In $26 \div 2 = 13$, 13 is the quotient. *n.*

R

rain gauge (rān′ gāj′), a tool that measures precipitation. *n.*

rat·tle (rat′l), toy, instrument, etc., that makes a noise when it is shaken. *n.*

ray (rā), a set of points that has one endpoint and that extends without end in one direction. *n.*

Rd., Road.

re·act (rē akt′), act in response: *Dogs react to affection. v.*

re·al·ly (rē′ə lē), actually; truly; in fact. *adv.*

rea·son (rē′zn), **1** justification; explanation: *What is your reason for being so late?* **2** think logically; think things out: *Most animals can't reason.* **1** *n.,* **2** *v.*

re·bound (rē′bound′), (in basketball) a ball that bounds back off the backboard or the rim of the basket after a shot has been made. *n.*

re·build (rē bild′), build again or anew. *v.,* **re·built** (rē bilt′), **re·build·ing.**

re·call (ri kȯl′), call back to mind; remember: *I can recall stories told to me when I was a small child. v.*

re·ceiv·er (ri sē′vər), thing that receives: *Public telephones have coin receivers for change. n.*

re·cent (rē′snt), done or made not long ago: *recent events. adj.*

re·cess (rē′ses or ri ses′), time during which work stops: *There will be a short recess before the next meeting. n.*

rec·og·nize (rek′əg nīz), **1** know again: *You have grown so much that I scarcely recognized you.* **2** identify: *recognize a person from a description. v.,* **rec·og·nized, rec·og·niz·ing.**

quilt
a sampler **quilt**

a	hat	ī	ice	u̇	put	ə stands for	
ā	age	o	not	ü	rule	a	in about
ä	far, calm	ō	open	ch	child	e	in taken
âr	care	ȯ	saw	ng	long	i	in pencil
e	let	ô	order	sh	she	o	in lemon
ē	equal	oi	oil	th	thin	u	in circus
ėr	term	ou	out	ᴛʜ	then		
i	it	u	cup	zh	measure		

record | retina

record

re·cord (rek′ərd), a thin, flat disk, usually of vinyl or other plastic, with narrow grooves on its surface, used on a phonograph. *n.*

re·cov·er (ri kuv′ər), **1** get back (something lost, taken away, or stolen): *recover one's health, recover a lost purse.* **2** get well; get back to a normal condition: *She is recovering from a cold. v.*

rec·tan·gle (rek′tang′gəl), a four-sided plane figure with four right angles. *n.*

re·cy·cle (rē sī′kəl), to process or treat (something) in order that it may be used again. Paper, aluminum, and glass products are commonly recycled. *v.,* **re·cy·cled, re·cy·cling.**

red (red), the color of blood or of a ruby: *The jewel is redder than the sun at sunset. n., adj.,* **red·der, red·dest.**

re·flec·tor (ri flek′tər), a piece of glass or metal for reflecting light: *The motorist saw the reflector on the girl's bike and slowed down. n.*

re·late (ri lāt′), **1** give an account of; tell: *The traveler related her adventures.* **2** be connected in any way: *We are interested in what relates to ourselves. v.,* **re·lat·ed, re·lat·ing.**

rel·a·tive (rel′ə tiv), person who belongs to the same family as another, such as father, brother, aunt, nephew, or cousin. *n., pl.* **rel·a·tives.**

re·lax (ri laks′), loosen up; make or become less stiff or firm: *Relax when you dance. v.*

re·main·der (ri mān′dər), **1** number left over after subtracting one number from another. In 9 – 2, the remainder is 7. **2** number left over after dividing one number by another. In 14 ÷ 3, the quotient is 4 with a remainder of 2. *n.*

re·mem·ber (ri mem′bər), call back to mind: *I can't remember that man's name. v.*

re·mote (ri mōt′), out of the way; secluded. *adj.*

recycle

children **recycling**

paper, cans, and bottles

re·place (ri plās′), fill or take the place of: *A substitute replaced our teacher. v.,* **re·placed, re·plac·ing.**

re·ply (ri plī′), answer by words or action; respond: *She replied with a shout. The washing machine replied with a bang. v.,* **re·plied, re·ply·ing.**

rep·re·sent (rep′ri zent′), act in place of; speak and act for: *We chose a committee to represent us. v.*

re·pro·duce (rē′prə dūs′ *or* rē′prə dyūs′), produce offspring: *Most plants reproduce by seeds. v.,* **re·pro·duced, re·pro·duc·ing.**

re·pub·lic (ri pub′lik), nation or state in which the citizens elect representatives to manage the government, which is usually headed by a president. The United States and Mexico are republics. *n.*

res·cue (res′kyū), a saving or freeing from danger, capture, harm, etc.: *A dog was chasing our cat when your sister came to the rescue. n.*

re·search (ri sėrch′ *or* rē′sėrch′), **1** a careful hunting for facts or truth; inquiry; investigation: *cancer research.* **2** to hunt for facts or truth; inquire; investigate. 1 *n., pl.* **re·search·es;** 2 *v.*

re·sent (ri zent′), feel injured and angry at; feel indignation at: *I resented being called lazy. v.*

res·er·va·tion (rez′ər vā′shən), land set aside by the government for a special purpose: *an Indian reservation. n.*

re·source (ri sôrs′ *or* rē′sôrs′), **1** any supply that will meet a need. We have resources of money, of knowledge, of strength, etc. **2 resources,** *pl.* the actual and potential wealth of a country: *natural resources, human resources. n., pl.* **re·sourc·es.**

re·sult (ri zult′), good or useful effect: *The new medicine got results. n.*

ret·i·na (ret′n ə), layer of cells at the back of the eyeball that is sensitive to light and receives the images of things looked at. *n., pl.* **ret·i·nas, ret·i·nae** (ret′n ē′).

282

reunion | scrapbook

re·un·ion (rē yü′nyən), a coming together again: *the reunion of parted friends. n.*

re·use (rē yüz′), use again: *reuse the papers. v.,* **re·used, re·us·ing.**

Rhode Is·land (rōd′ ī′lənd), one of the northeastern states of the United States. Rhode Island is the smallest state. *Abbreviation:* R.I. or RI *Capital:* Providence.

Rich·ter scale (rik′tər skāl′), a scale for indicating the force or magnitude of earthquakes. On this scale, light tremors register 1.5, while highly destructive earthquakes measure 8.3.

rid·den (rid′n), See **ride.** *I had ridden my horse all day. v.*

ride (rīd), sit on a horse and make it go. *v.,* **rode** (rōd), **rid·den, rid·ing.**

rim (rim), an edge, border, or margin on or around anything: *the rim of a wheel, the rim of a basketball net. n.*

riv·er (riv′ər), **1** a large, natural stream of water that flows into a lake, ocean, etc. **2** any abundant stream or flow: *rivers of lava. n.*

rob (rob), take away from by force or threats; steal from; plunder; pillage: *Bandits robbed the bank of thousands of dollars. v.,* **robbed, rob·bing.**

rough (ruf), **1** not smooth; not level; not even: *rough boards, the rough bark of an oak tree, a rough, rocky hill.* **2** INFORMAL. unpleasant; hard; severe: *She had a rough time in the hospital. adj.*

run·way (run′wā′), **1** a paved strip at an airport on which aircraft land and take off. **2** way, track, groove, trough, etc., along which something moves, slides, etc. *n.*

S

sad (sad), not happy; full of sorrow: *You feel sad if your best friend goes away. adj.,* **sad·der, sad·dest.**

safe (sāf), free from harm or danger: *Keep money in a safe place. adj.,* **saf·er, saf·est. —safe′ly,** *adv.*

sage·brush (sāj′brush′), a grayish shrub that smells like sage, common on the dry plains of western North America. *n.*

said (sed), See **say.** *He said he would come. They had said "No" every time. v.*

salm·on (sam′ən), a large saltwater and freshwater food fish with silvery scales and yellowish-pink flesh. It appears in the northern Atlantic and northern Pacific, and it swims up rivers in order to spawn. *n., pl.* **salm·on.**

say (sā), speak; utter: *What did you say? "Thank you," she said. v.,* **said, say·ing.**

scar·y (skâr′ē), INFORMAL. **1** causing fright or alarm: *scary sounds, a scary movie.* **2** easily frightened. *adj.,* **scar·i·er, scar·i·est.**

school¹ (skül), place for teaching and learning. *n.*

school² (skül), a large number of the same kind of fish or water animals swimming together: *a school of mackerel. n.*

scis·sors (siz′ərz), tool or instrument for cutting that has two sharp blades so fastened that their edges slide against each other. *n. pl. or sing.*

scrap·book (skrap′bük′), book in which pictures or clippings are pasted and kept. *n.*

a	hat	ī	ice	u̇	put	ə stands for	
ā	age	o	not	ü	rule	a	in about
ä	far, calm	ō	open	ch	child	e	in taken
âr	care	ȯ	saw	ng	long	i	in pencil
e	let	ô	order	sh	she	o	in lemon
ē	equal	oi	oil	th	thin	u	in circus
ėr	term	ou	out	ᴛʜ	then		
i	it	u	cup	zh	measure		

283

scratch | she

scratch (skrach), **1** rub or scrape to relieve itching: *Don't scratch your mosquito bites.* **2** a mark made by scratching: *He had a large scratch on his arm.* 1 *v.*, 2 *n.*, *pl.* **scratch·es.**
from scratch, with no advantages; without help; without prepackaged ingredients.

scream (skrēm), a loud, sharp, piercing cry. *n.*

screen (skrēn), **1** wire woven together with small openings in between. **2** a glass surface on which television pictures, computer information, radar images, etc., appear. *n.*

scrub (skrub), **1** rub hard; wash or clean by rubbing: *I scrubbed the floor with a brush and soap.* **2** a scrubbing: *Give your hands a good scrub.* 1 *v.*, **scrubbed, scrub·bing;** 2 *n.*

seal (sēl), a flesh-eating sea mammal with large flippers, living usually in cold regions. *n.*, *pl.* **seals** or **seal.**

seal

Seals usually live in cold areas.

sea·son (sē'zn), **1** one of the four periods of the year; spring, summer, autumn, or winter. **2** any period of time marked by something special: *a holiday season, the harvest season. n.*

see (sē), be aware of by using the eyes; look at: *See that black cloud.* *v.*, **saw** (sȯ), **seen, see·ing.**

seed (sēd), the part of a plant from which another plant like it can grow. A seed has an outer skin or coat which encloses the embryo that will become the new plant and a supply of food for its growth. *n., pl.* **seeds** or **seed.**

seen (sēn), See **see.** *Have you seen Father? v.*

seg·ment (seg'mənt), two points and the part of a line between them. *n.*

seismograph

A **seismograph** records sudden movements of the earth's crust.

seis·mo·graph (sīz'mə graf), instrument for recording the direction, strength and length of earthquakes. *n.* [*Seismograph* comes from Greek *seismos,* meaning "earthquake," and the combining form *-graph.*]

sep·a·rate (sep'ə rāt'), **1** keep apart; be between; divide: *The Atlantic Ocean separates America from Europe.* **2** divide into parts or groups: *separate a tangle of yarn.* *v.*, **sep·a·rat·ed, sep·a·rat·ing.**

sep·a·ra·tion (sep'ə rā'shən), a being apart, being separated: *The friends were glad to meet after so long a separation. n.*

Sep·tem·ber (sep tem'bər), the ninth month of the year. It has 30 days. *n.*

ser·ies cir·cuit (sir'ēz sėr'kit), a circuit that connects several objects one after the other so that the current flows in a single path.

ser·i·ous (sir'ē əs), showing deep thought or purpose; thoughtful; grave: *a serious manner, a serious face. adj.*

serve (sėrv), **1** put (food or drink) on the table. **2** in tennis, a player's turn to start the play by hitting the ball. 1 *v.*, **served, serv·ing;** 2 *n.*

set (set), **1** put in the right place, position, or condition; put in proper order; arrange: *The doctor set my broken leg. Set the clock. Set the table for dinner.* **2** number of things or persons belonging together; group; outfit: *a set of dishes.* 1 *v.*, **set, set·ting;** 2 *n.*

sev·er·al (sev'ər əl), more than two or three but not many; some; a few: *gain several pounds (adj.). Several have given their consent (n.)*

sham·poo (sham pü'), **1** wash (the hair, the scalp, a rug, etc.) with a soapy or oily preparation. **2** a washing of the hair, the scalp, a rug, etc., with such a preparation. **3** the preparation used in this way. 1 *v.*, **sham·pooed, sham·poo·ing;** 2,3 *n., pl.* **sham·poos.**

share (shâr), use together; enjoy together; have in common: *The sisters share the same room.* *v.*, **shared, shar·ing.**

she (shē), anything thought of as female and spoken about or mentioned before: *She was my sister. She was a fine old ship. pron.*

sheep | skateboarding

sheep (shēp), mammal with a thick coat and hoofs that chews its cud, and makes a baaing sound. Sheep are related to goats and are raised for wool, meat, and skin. *n., pl.* **sheep.**

she'll (shēl), she will: *She'll help you with your problem.*

shel·ter (shel′tər), **1** something that covers or protects from weather, danger, or attack. **2** protection; refuge. *n.*

sher·iff (sher′if), the most important law-enforcing officer of a county. A sheriff appoints deputies who help to keep order in the county. *n.*

shoot (shüt), **1** send swiftly: *A bow shoots an arrow. She shot question after question at us.* **2** move suddenly and swiftly: *A car shot by us. Flames shot up from the burning house.* **3** take (a picture) with a camera; photograph. **4** send (a ball, puck, marble, etc.) toward the goal, pocket, etc. *v.,* **shot** (shot), **shoot·ing.**

short (shôrt), not long; of small extent from end to end. *adj.*

should·n't (shüd′nt), should not: *You shouldn't cross the street without looking both ways.*

show (shō), **1** make clear to; explain to: *Show us how to do the problem.* **2** a play, motion picture, etc., or a performance of one of these: *The show starts at 6:00.* **1** *v.,* **showed, shown** or **showed, show·ing;** **2** *n.*

show·er (shou′ər), bath in which water pours down on the body from an overhead nozzle. *n.*

shown (shōn), See **show.** *We were shown many tricks by the magician. v.*

shud·der (shud′ər), tremble with horror, fear, cold. *v.*

shut·ter (shut′ər), a movable cover, slide, etc., for closing an opening. The device that opens and closes in front of the lens of a camera is the shutter. *n.*

sign (sīn), **1** write: *Sign your initials here.* **2** an inscribed board, space, etc., serving for advertisement, information, regulations, etc.: *See the sign over the door. The stop sign is used by the crossing guard.* **3** motion or gesture used to mean, represent, or point out something: *talk to a deaf person by signs.* **1** *v.,* **2,3** *n.*

sig·nal (sig′nəl), **1** a sign giving notice, warning, or pointing out something. **2** make a signal or signals to: *She signaled the car to stop by raising her hand.* **1** *n.,* **2** *v.,* **sig·naled, sig·nal·ing** or **sig·nalled, sig·nal·ling.**

sil·ver (sil′vər), **1** a shiny, white, precious metal. **2** made of silver: *a silver spoon.* **1** *n.,* **2** *adj.*

sim·ple (sim′pəl), easy to do or understand: *a simple problem.* *adj.,* **sim·pler, sim·plest.**

si·ren (sī′rən), kind of whistle that makes a loud, piercing sound: *We heard the fire engine's siren. n.*

sis (sis), INFORMAL. sister. *n.*

sit (sit), rest on the lower part of the body with the weight off the feet: *She sat in a chair.* *v.,* **sat** (sat), **sit·ting.**

skate·board (skāt′bôrd′), **1** a narrow board resembling a surfboard, with roller-skate wheels attached to each end, used for gliding or moving on any hard surface. **2** to ride a skateboard: *The neighborhood children love to skateboard in the summer.* **1** *n.,* **2** *v.*

skate·board·ing (skāt′bôr′ding), the sport of riding a skateboard. *n.*

sheep
a **sheep** and its young

silver
a **silver** table setting

a	hat	**ī**	ice	**u̇**	put	**ə** stands for	
ā	age	**o**	not	**ü**	rule	**a**	in about
ä	far, calm	**ō**	open	**ch**	child	**e**	in taken
âr	care	**ȯ**	saw	**ng**	long	**i**	in pencil
e	let	**ô**	order	**sh**	she	**o**	in lemon
ē	equal	**oi**	oil	**th**	thin	**u**	in circus
ėr	term	**ou**	out	**ŦH**	then		
i	it	**u**	cup	**zh**	measure		

285

ski | somewhere

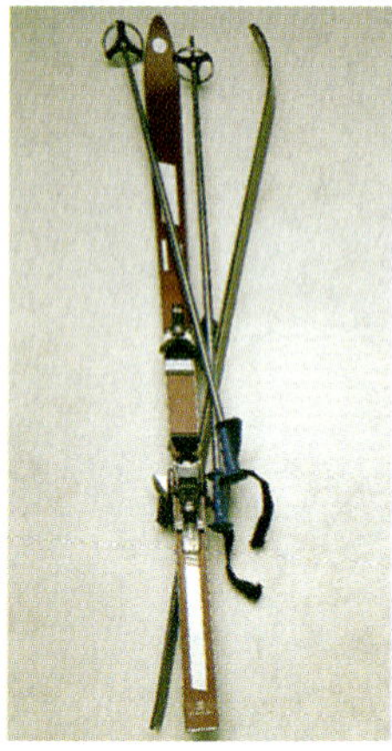

ski (definition1)
skis and ski poles

soccer

playing the game of
soccer

ski (skē), **1** one of a pair of long, slender pieces of hard wood, plastic, or metal, that can be fastened to the shoes or boots to enable a person to glide over snow. **2** glide over the snow on skis. 1 *n.*, *pl.* **skis** or **ski**; 2 *v.*, **skied**, **ski·ing**.

skirt (skėrt), **1** a woman's or girl's garment that hangs from the waist. **2** something like a skirt: *A skirt covered the legs of the chair. n.*

skulk (skulk), a group of animals that prey on game, as the fox or weasel. *n.*

sky·scrap·er (skī′skrā′pər), a very tall building. *n.*

slam-dunk (slam′dungk′), (in basketball) a shot made by leaping so that the hands are above the rim of the basket, and throwing the ball down through the netting. *n.*

slap (slap), put, dash, or cast with force. *v.*, **slapped**, **slap·ping**.

slip (slip), slide suddenly without wanting to: *He slipped on the icy sidewalk. v.*, **slipped**, **slip·ping**.

slip·per (slip′ər), a light, low shoe that is slipped on easily: *dancing slippers, bedroom slippers. n., pl.* **slip·pers**.

slow (slō), not fast: *Traffic is very slow during rush hour. I walked slowly home. adj.* —**slow′ly**, *adv.*

small (smòl), **1** not large; little; not large as compared with other things of the same kind: *A cottage is smaller than a house.* **2** not great in amount, value: *The cent is our smallest coin. adj.*, **small·er**, **small·est**.

smoke (smōk), the mixture of gases and particles of carbon that can be seen rising in a cloud from anything burning. *n.*

smug·gle (smug′əl), bring, take, put, etc., secretly: *I tried to smuggle my puppy into the house. v.*, **smug·gled**, **smug·gling**.

snack (snak), **1** a light meal, especially one eaten between regular meals. **2** to eat a light meal. *We snacked on fruit after school.* 1 *n.*, 2 *v.*

snail (snāl), a small, soft-bodied animal that crawls very slowly. Most snails have spiral shells on their backs into which they can move for protection. *n.*

snap·shot (snap′shot′), photograph taken quickly with a small camera. *n.*

snore (snôr), a harsh rough sound made in sleeping. *n.*

soc·cer (sok′ər), game played with a round ball between two teams of eleven players each. The players may strike the ball with any part of the body except the hands and arms. Only the goalkeeper may touch the ball with the hands and arms. Players score by knocking the ball into a net cage at either end of the field. *n.*

soft (sòft), **1** not hard; not stiff; yielding easily to touch: *a soft pillow.* **2** not loud: *a soft voice.* 1,2 *adj.* —**soft′ness**, *n.*

soft·ball (sòft′bòl′), **1** a kind of baseball that is played on a smaller field, with a larger and softer ball, and lighter bats. Softball must be pitched underhand. **2** the ball used in this game. *n.*

soft-boiled (sòft′boild′), (of an egg) boiled only a little so that the yolk is still soft. *adj.*

soft drink (sòft′ dringk′), drink that does not contain alcohol.

soft·en (sòf′ən), make or become soft: *Hand lotion softens the skin. Soap softens in water. v.*

soft soap (sòft′ sōp′), a liquid or semiliquid soap.

some·one (sum′wun), some person; somebody: *Someone is coming. pron.*

some·thing (sum′thing), some thing; a particular thing not named or known: *I'm sure I've forgotten something. n.*

some·times (sum′tīmz), now and then; at times. *adv.*

some·where (sum′hwâr), in or to some place; in or to one place or another: *She lives somewhere in the area. adv.*

source | steal

source (sôrs), person or place from which anything comes or is obtained: *The newspaper gets news from many sources. Mines are the chief source of diamonds.* n., pl. **sourc·es.**

south·ern (suᴛʜ′ərn), **1** toward the south: *a southern view.* **2** from the south: *a southern breeze.* adj.

speak (spēk), **1** say words; talk: *speak clearly.* **2** use (a language): *Do you speak French? v.,* **spoke** (spōk), **spo·ken** (spō′kən), **speak·ing.**

spe·cial (spesh′əl), more than ordinary; unusual; exceptional. adj.

speech (spēch), what is said; the words spoken: *We made the usual farewell speeches.* n., pl. **speech·es.**

spi·der (spī′dər), a small animal with eight legs, no wings, and a body divided into two parts. Spiders are arachnids that spin webs to catch insects for food. n.

spider web (spī′dər web′), the delicate, silken threads spun by a spider.

spore (spôr), a single cell capable of growing into a new plant or animal. Spores are produced by plants that do not have flowers, such as ferns or molds. n., pl. **spores.**

spot·less (spot′lis), without a spot: *a spotless white shirt.* adj.

square (skwâr), **1** a plane figure with four equal sides and four right angles. **2** having this shape: *a square box. A block of stone is usually square.* **1** n., **2** adj., **squar·er, squar·est.**

squash (skwäsh), press or be pressed until soft or flat; crush: *She squashed the bug. Carry the cream puffs carefully, for they squash easily.* v.

squeak (skwēk), make a short, sharp, shrill sound: *A mouse squeaks.* v.

squeal (skwēl), **1** make a long, sharp, shrill cry: *A pig squeals when it is hurt.* **2** such a cry. **1** v., **2** n.

squeeze (skwēz), **1** press hard; compress: *Don't squeeze the kitten; you'll hurt it.* **2** force out by pressure: *squeeze juice from a lemon.* **3** crush; crowd: *Six people squeezed into the little car.* v., **squeezed, squeez·ing.** **—squeez′a·ble,** adj.

squirm (skwėrm), turn and twist; writhe: *The restless boy squirmed in his chair.* v.

squir·rel (skwėr′əl), a small, bushy-tailed rodent that usually lives in trees. n.

squirt (skwėrt), force out (liquid) through a narrow opening: *squirt water through a tube, squirt water at the statue.* v.

sta·men (stā′mən), the part of a flower that contains the pollen. The stamens are surrounded by the petals. n., pl. **sta·mens, stam·i·na** (stam′ə nə).

stand (stand), be set upright; be placed; be located: *The box stands over there. Some food stood on the table.* v., **stood, stand·ing.**

state (stāt), of a state: *a state road, state police, state government.* adj.

state·ment (stāt′mənt), something stated; report; account: *Her statement was correct.* n.

sta·tion (stā′shən), a regular stopping place: *She met her at the bus station.* n.

steal (stēl), **1** take (something) that does not belong to one; take dishonestly. **2** move secretly or quietly: *She stole softly out of the house.* **3** (in baseball) run to (second base, third base, or home plate) as the pitcher throws the ball to the catcher. v., **stole, sto·len** (stō′lən), **steal·ing.**

spider
a crab **spider**

a	hat	**ī**	ice	**u̇**	put	**ə** stands for	
ā	age	**o**	not	**ü**	rule	**a**	in about
ä	far, calm	**ō**	open	**ch**	child	**e**	in taken
âr	care	**ȯ**	saw	**ng**	long	**i**	in pencil
e	let	**ô**	order	**sh**	she	**o**	in lemon
ē	equal	**oi**	oil	**th**	thin	**u**	in circus
ėr	term	**ou**	out	**ᴛʜ**	then		
i	it	**u**	cup	**zh**	measure		

steam | sugar

steam (stēm), give off steam: *The cup of coffee was steaming.* v.

steel (stēl), an alloy of iron and carbon. Steel has greater hardness and flexibility than cast iron and is used for tools and machinery. n.

stiff (stif), **1** not easily bent; fixed; rigid. **2** hard to move. adj.

St. Law·rence Sea·way (sānt′ lôr′əns sē′wā′), waterway that links the Great Lakes to the Atlantic Ocean by means of canals and the St. Lawrence River.

stole (stōl), See **steal.** *They stole my car.* v.

stom·ach (stum′ək), the large muscular bag in the body which receives swallowed food, and digests some of it before passing it on to the intestines. n.

stood (stůd), See **stand.** *She stood in the corner for five minutes. I had stood in line all morning to buy tickets to the game.* v.

stop (stop), leave off (moving, acting, doing, being, etc.); come to an end; cease: *The baby stopped crying. The rain is stopping.* v., **stopped, stop·ping.**

storm (stôrm), a strong wind often accompanied by rain, snow, hail, or thunder and lightning. In deserts there are storms of sand. n.

St. Pat·rick's Day (sānt′ pat′riks dā′), a holiday celebrated in honor of St. Patrick, who converted Ireland to Christianity; March 17.

strange (strānj), unusual; odd; peculiar: *a strange accident, a strange experience.* adj., **strang·er, strang·est.**

strat·e·gy (strat′ə jē), plan based on skillful planning: *We need some strategy to win this game.* n., pl. **strat·e·gies.**

straw·ber·ry (strȯ′ber′ē), the small, juicy, red fruit of a plant that grows close to the ground. Strawberries are good to eat. n., pl. **straw·ber·ries.**

street (strēt), place or way for automobiles, wagons, etc., to go. n.

strength (strengkh), **1** quality of being strong; power; force; vigor. **2** something a person is strong in or can do well. n.

strike (strīk), **1** set or be set on fire by hitting or rubbing: *strike a match.* **2** a stopping of work to get better pay, shorter hours, and so on. *The workers were home for six weeks during the strike last year.* **3** baseball pitched through the strike zone and not swung at, any pitch that is swung at and missed, or any pitch that is hit foul. After three strikes, a batter is out. 1 v., **struck** (struk), **struck** or **strick·en** (strik′ən), **strik·ing;** 2,3 n.

stroke (strōk), a single complete movement to be made again and again: *He rowed with a strong stroke of the oars. She swims a fast stroke.* n.

stud·y (stud′ē), try to learn: *She studied her spelling lesson for half an hour. I am studying to be a doctor.* v., **stud·ied, stud·y·ing.**

stuff (stuf), belongings; goods: *What will we do with all this stuff?* n.

suc·cess·ful (sək ses′fəl), having success; ending in success; prosperous; fortunate. adj.

sud·den (sud′n), happening without warning or notice; not expected: *a sudden stop, a sudden rainstorm, a sudden rise to power.* adj.

sud·den·ly (sud′n lē), in a sudden manner. adv.

suf·fer (suf′ər), **1** have or feel (pain, grief, etc.): *I suffered sunburn from being at the beach all day.* **2** bear with patiently; endure: *I will not suffer such insults.* v.

suf·fix (suf′iks), syllable or syllables put at the end of a word to change its meaning or to make another word, as -ly in *badly,* -ness in *goodness,* and -ful in *spoonful.* n., pl. **suf·fix·es.**

sug·ar (shůg′ər), a sweet substance obtained chiefly from sugar cane or sugar beets and used extensively in food products; sucrose. n.

storm

a lightning **storm**

suit (süt), set of clothes to be worn together. A man's suit consists of a coat, pants, and sometimes a vest. A woman's suit consists of a coat and either a skirt or pants. *n.*

Sun., Sunday.

su·per·i·or (sə pir′ē ər), above the average; very good; excellent: *superior work in school. adj.*

Su·per·i·or (sə pir′ē ər), **Lake,** the largest of the five Great Lakes. These lakes form the largest group of freshwater lakes in the world. *n.*

sup·per (sup′ər), the evening meal; meal eaten early in the evening. *n.*

sup·ply (sə plī′), **1** provide (what is lacking); furnish: *Many cities supply books for children in school.* **2 supplies,** *pl.* the food, equipment, etc., necessary for an army drive, or the like. 1 *v.,* **sup·plied, sup·ply·ing;** 2 *n., pl.* **sup·plies.**

sup·port (sə pôrt′), **1** give strength or courage to; keep up; help. **2** be in favor of; back; second: *She supports the amendment.* **3** help or assistance: *They need our financial support.* 1,2 *v.,* 3 *n.*

sup·pose (sə pōz′), **1** consider as possible; take for granted; assume. **2** believe, think, or imagine: *I suppose he will come at noon.* *v.,* **sup·posed, sup·pos·ing.**

sur·prise (sər prīz′), cause to feel surprised; astonish: *The victory surprised us. v.,* **sur·prised, sur·pris·ing.**

sus·pense·ful (sə spens′fəl), characterized by or full of suspense. *adj.*

swarm (swôrm), group of bees settled together in a hive. *n.*

sweat gland (swet′ gland′), gland of the skin that secretes sweat. A sweat gland is connected with the surface of the skin by a tube or duct that ends in a pore. *n.*

swim (swim), move along on or in the water by using arms, legs, fins, etc.: *Fish swim. Most boys and girls like swimming in the lake. v.,* **swam** (swam), **swum, swim·ming.**

sword (sôrd), weapon, usually metal, with a long, sharp blade fixed in a handle or hilt. *n.*

swum (swum) See **swim.** *We have swum in that lake many times. v.*

T

Taj Ma·hal (täj′ mə häl′), a famous white marble mausoleum in northern India, built in the 1600s.

take (tāk), **1** lay hold of; grasp: *I took her hand when we crossed the street.* **2** indulge in: *take a nap, take a vacation. v.,* **took, tak·en** (tā′kən), **tak·ing.**

tax (taks), money paid by people for the support of the government and services; money regularly collected from citizens by the government. *n., pl.* **tax·es.**

teach·er (tē′chər), person who teaches, especially one who teaches in a school: *We entered the teachers' lounge. n.*

team·mate (tēm′māt′), a fellow member of a team. *n.*

tear (tir), drop of salty liquid coming from the eye. *n., pl.* **tears.**

tem·per·a·ture (tem′pər ə chər), **1** degree of heat or cold. The temperature of freezing water is 32 degrees Fahrenheit (0 degrees Celsius). **2** a body temperature higher than normal; fever: *A sick person may have a temperature. n.*

swim

swimming the backstroke

a	hat	**ī**	ice	**u̇**	put	**ə** stands for	
ā	age	**o**	not	**ü**	rule	**a**	in about
ä	far, calm	**ō**	open	**ch**	child	**e**	in taken
âr	care	**ȯ**	saw	**ng**	long	**i**	in pencil
e	let	**ô**	order	**sh**	she	**o**	in lemon
ē	equal	**oi**	oil	**th**	thin	**u**	in circus
ėr	term	**ou**	out	**ŦH**	then		
i	it	**u**	cup	**zh**	measure		

289

temple | tomb

thrill

The roller coaster gave us

a **thrill**.

tiger

The **tiger** is about 9 feet

long with the tail.

tem·ple (tem′pəl), building used for the service or worship of a god or gods. *n.*

ten·sion (ten′shən), **1** a stretching. **2** mental strain: *Tension may be brought on by overwork. n.*

Tex·as (tek′səs), one of the southwestern states of the United States. *Abbreviation:* Tex. or TX *Capital:* Austin. *n.*

than (ᴛнan; *unstressed* ᴛнən), **1** in comparison with. **2** compared to that which: *You know better than I do. 1,2 conj., 1 prep.*

that's (ᴛнats), that is: *That's a beautiful picture.*

their (ᴛнâr), of them; belonging to them: *I like their house. adj.*

them (ᴛнem; *unstressed* ᴛнəm), the persons, animals, things, or ideas spoken about: *The books are new; take care of them. pron.*

then (ᴛнen), **1** being at that time; existing then: *the then President.* **2** soon afterwards. 1 *adj.,* 2 *adv.*

there (ᴛнâr), in or at that place: *Finish reading the page and stop there. adv.*

they (ᴛнā), the persons, animals, things, or ideas spoken about: *I had three books yesterday. Do you know where they are? They are on the table. pron. pl.*

they'd (ᴛнād), **1** they had: *They'd arrived late.* **2** they would: *They'd come if they could.*

they'll (ᴛнāl), they will: *They'll be a few minutes late.*

they're (ᴛнâr), they are: *They're going to be leaving soon.*

thirst·y (thėr′stē), **1** feeling thirst; having thirst: *The dog is thirsty; please give it some water.* **2** having a strong desire or craving; eager. *adj.,* **thirst·i·er, thirst·i·est.**

thought·ful (thôt′fəl), full of thought; thinking: *He was thoughtful for a while and then replied, "No." adj.*

thou·sand (thou′znd), ten hundred; 1000. *n., adj.*

threat (thret), sign or cause of possible evil or harm. *n.*

thrill (thril), a shivering, exciting feeling. *n.*

throat (thrōt), the passage from the mouth to the stomach or the lungs. *n.*

throne (thrōn), chair on which a king, queen, bishop, or other person of high rank sits during official ceremonies. *n.*

through (thrü), **1** from end to end of; from side to side of; between the parts of; from beginning to end of: *march through a town, cut a tunnel through a mountain.* **2** here and there in; over; around: *stroll through the streets of a city. prep.*

throw (thrō), **1** send through the air; toss; hurl. **2** bring to the ground: *His horse threw him.* **3** put by force: *throw someone into jail. v.,* **threw** (thrü), **thrown, throw·ing.**

thrown (thrōn), See **throw.** *She has thrown her old toys away. v.*

thumb (thum), the short, thick finger of the hand. It can be moved against any of the other four fingers to grasp things. *n.*

ti·ger (tī′gər), a large, fierce, flesh-eating mammal of Asia, that has dull-yellow fur striped with black. It is related to the cat and the lion. *n., pl.* **ti·gers.**

ti·tle (tī′tl), **1** the name of a book, poem, picture, song, etc. **2** name showing rank, occupation, or condition in life. King, duke, lord, majesty, highness, captain, doctor, and Miss are titles. *n.*

to (tü; *unstressed* tu̇ *or* tə), **1** in the direction of; toward a destination: *She came to school.* **2** *To* is used with verbs. *I like to play the piano.* **3** on; against: *Nail the shelf to the wall.* **4** *To* is used to show action toward. *Give the book to me. prep.*

toe (tō), one of the five divisions that end the foot. *n., pl.* **toes.**

tomb (tüm), grave, vault, mausoleum, etc., for a dead body, often above ground. *n.*

290

tomorrow | unheard

to·mor·row (tə mor′ō), **1** the day after today. **2** on the day after today. 1 *n.*, 2 *adv.*

tongue (tung), the movable fleshy organ in the mouth. The tongue is used in tasting and, by people, for talking. *n.*

too (tü), **1** in addition; also; besides. **2** beyond what is desirable, proper, or right; more than enough. *adv.*

took (tůk), See **take.** *She took the car an hour ago. v.*

toot (tüt), sound of a horn or whistle. *n.*

tot (tot), a little child. *n.*

touch·down (tuch′doun′), score of six points made in football by putting the ball on the ground behind the opponent's goal line. *n.*

tough (tuf), **1** hard to cut, tear, or chew. **2** strong; hard: *a tough team. adj.*

track (trak), **1** a double, parallel line of metal rails for cars to run on: *railroad tracks.* **2** a course for running or racing. *n.*

trash (trash), **1** broken or torn bits, such as leaves, twigs, husks, etc.: *Rake up the trash in the yard.* **2** worthless stuff; rubbish: *That magazine is trash. n.*

tread (tred), **1** set the foot down; walk; step: *Don't tread on the flower beds. They trod through the meadow.* **2** move the legs and feet as if walking: *Everyone in swimming class treads water for five minutes.* **3** act or sound of treading: *We heard the tread of marching feet.* 1,2 *v.*, **treads, trod** (trod), **trod·den** (trod′n) or **trod, tread·ing;** 3 *n.*

treat (trēt), **1** entertain with food, drink, or amusement: *treat some friends to ice cream.* **2** anything that gives pleasure. 1 *v.*, 2 *n.*

treat·ment (trēt′mənt), way of treating: *This cat has suffered from bad treatment. n.*

tre·men·dous (tri men′dəs), INFORMAL. very great; enormous: *That is a tremendous house for a family of three. adj.*

tri·an·gle (trī′ang′gəl), a plane figure having three sides and three angles. *n.*

trou·ble (trub′əl), **1** cause trouble to; disturb. *The lack of business troubled the grocer.* **2** extra work; bother; effort: *Take the trouble to work.* 1 *v.*, **trou·bled, trou·bling;** 2 *n.*

truth·ful (trüth′fəl), telling the truth: *He is a truthful boy and will tell exactly what happened. adj.* —**truth′ful·ly,** *adv.*

tun·dra (tun′drə), a vast, level, treeless plain in the arctic regions. The ground beneath its surface is frozen even in summer. Much of Alaska and northern Canada is tundra. *n.*

two (tü), one more than one; 2. *n.*, *pl.* **twos;** *adj.*

track (definition 2)
running on a **track**

U

ug·ly (ug′lē), very unpleasant to look at. *adj.*, **ug·li·er, ug·li·est.**

un·con·test·ed (un′kən tes′tid), undisputed; unopposed: *The referee's decision was uncontested. adj.*

un·for·tu·nate (un fôr′chə nit), not lucky; having bad luck. *adj.* —**un·for′tu·nate·ly,** *adv.*

un·friend·ly (un frend′lē), not friendly; hostile. *adj.*

un·heard (un hėrd′), not listened to; not heard: *unheard melodies. adj.*

a	hat	ī	ice	ů	put	ə *stands for*	
ā	age	o	not	ü	rule	a	in about
ä	far, calm	ō	open	ch	child	e	in taken
âr	care	ò	saw	ng	long	i	in pencil
e	let	ô	order	sh	she	o	in lemon
ē	equal	oi	oil	th	thin	u	in circus
ėr	term	ou	out	ŦH	then		
i	it	u	cup	zh	measure		

291

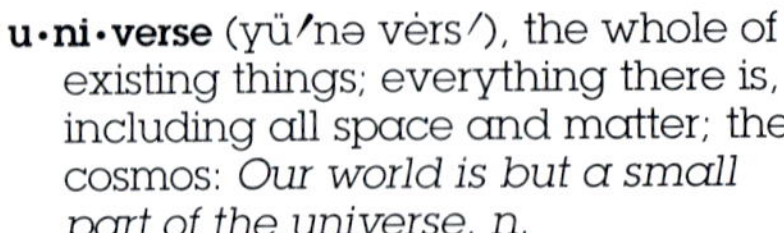

universe | watch

u·ni·verse (yü′nə vėrs′), the whole of existing things; everything there is, including all space and matter; the cosmos: *Our world is but a small part of the universe. n.*

un·known (un nōn′), not known; not familiar; strange. *adj.*

un·til (un til′), up to the time when. *conj.*

un·u·su·al (un yü′zhü əl), not usual; not ordinary; not in common use; uncommon; rare. *adj.*

up·on (ə pon′), on. *prep.*

up·set (up′set′), an unexpected defeat: *The hockey team suffered an upset. n.*

up·stairs (up′stârz′), on or to an upper floor: *She lives upstairs (adv.). He is waiting in an upstairs hall (adj.).*

use·less (yüs′lis), of no use; worthless: *A television set would be useless in a house without electricity. adj.*

u·su·al (yü′zhü əl), commonly seen, found, or happening; ordinary; customary. *adj.*

u·su·al·ly (yü′zhü ə lē), according to what is usual; commonly; ordinarily; customarily; often: *We usually eat dinner at 6. adv.*

walrus

The **walrus** has ivory tusks.

V

va·ca·tion (vā kā′shən), **1** freedom from school, business, or other duties: *There is a vacation from school every summer.* **2** take a vacation. 1 *n.,* 2 *v.*

Val·en·tine's Day (val′ən tīnz dā′), a holiday in which cards or small gifts are given to friends and loved ones; February 14.

val·ley (val′ē), low land between hills or mountains. *n., pl.* **val·leys.**

van·ish (van′ish), disappear, especially suddenly: *The sun vanished behind a cloud. v.*

ver·i·fy (ver′ə fī), test the correctness of; check for accuracy: *You can verify the spelling of a word by looking in a dictionary. v.,* **ver·i·fied, ver·i·fy·ing.**

ver·tex (vėr′teks), the point where two sides of an angle meet. *n., pl.* **ver·tex·es, ver·ti·ces** (vėr′tə sēz).

vil·lage (vil′ij), group of houses, usually smaller than a town. *n.*

vol·ca·no (vol kā′nō), an opening in the earth's crust through which steam, ashes, and lava are forced out in periods of activity. *n., pl.* **vol·ca·noes** or **vol·ca·nos.**

vol·ume (vol′yəm), space occupied: *The storeroom has a volume of 800 cubic feet. n.*

W

waist (wāst), the part of the human body between the ribs and the hips. *n.*

wal·rus (wol′rəs or wol′rəs), a large sea mammal of the arctic regions, resembling a seal but having long tusks. It is hunted for its hide, tusks, and blubber oil. *n., pl.* **wal·rus·es** or **wal·rus.**

want (wänt), wish for; wish: *We want a new car. I want to become an engineer. v.*

wash (wäsh), clean with water or other liquid: *wash one's face, wash clothes, wash dishes. v.,* **washed, wash·ing.**

wash·a·ble (wäsh′ə bəl), able to be washed without damage: *washable silk. adj.*

wash·cloth (wäsh′klòth′), a small cloth for washing oneself. *n.*

was·n't (wuz′nt or wäz′nt), was not.

waste (wāst), **1** make poor use of; spend uselessly; fail to get full value or benefit from: *Though I had much work to do, I wasted my time doing nothing.* **2** poor use; useless spending; failure to get the most out of something: *Buying that suit was a waste of money.* 1 *v.* **wast·ed, wast·ing;** 2 *n.*

watch (wäch), **1** look attentively or carefully. **2** device for telling time, small enough to be carried in a pocket or worn on the wrist. 1 *v.,* 2 *n., pl.* **watch·es.**

water fountain | whirl

wa·ter foun·tain (wȯ′tər foun′tən),
1 water flowing or rising into the air
in a spray. 2 place to get a drink.

wa·ter·way (wȯ′tər wā′), river,
canal, or other body of water
that ships can go on. n.

weak·ness (wēk′nis), a weak point;
slight fault: *Putting things off is her
weakness. n., pl.* **weak·ness·es.**

weave (wēv), make out of thread,
strips, or strands of the same
material. v., **wove** (wōv), **wo·ven**
(wō′vən) or **wove, weav·ing.**

we'd (wēd), 1 we had: *We'd left
the party early.* 2 we would:
We'd love to see you again.

Wed., Wednesday.

week·end (wēk′end′), Saturday and
Sunday as a time for recreation,
visiting, etc. n.

week·ly (wēk′lē), of a week; for a
week; lasting a week: *a weekly
wage of $150. adj.*

weight (wāt), how heavy a thing is:
the amount a thing weighs. n.

weight·less (wāt′lis), being free from
the pull of gravity. adj.

weird (wird), 1 unearthly or
mysterious; wild; strange: *They
were awakened by a weird shriek.
It was the weirdest noise I had
ever heard.* 2 odd; fantastic; queer:
*The robin made a weirder sound
than the sparrow. adj.,* **weird·er,
weird·est.**

wel·come (wel′kəm), 1 greet kindly;
give a friendly reception to: *We
always welcome guests at our
house.* 2 a kind or friendly
reception: *You will always
have a welcome here.* 1 v.,
wel·comed, wel·com·ing; 2 n.

we'll (wēl), we will: *We'll be arriving
at about 6:00.*

went (went), See **go.** *I went home
promptly after school. v.*

we're (wir), we are: *We're all looking
forward to your visit.*

were (wėr), form of the verb **be** used
with *you, we, they* or any plural
noun to indicate the past tense.
The officer's orders were obeyed. v.

we've (wēv), we have: *We've had a
wonderful time.*

whale (hwāl), mammal shaped like a
huge fish and living in the sea. Oil
from whales used to be burned in
lamps. *n., pl.* **whales** or **whale.**

what·ev·er (hwot ev′ər or hwut
ev′ər), anything that: *Do whatever
you like. pron.*

what's (hwots or hwuts), 1 what is:
What's the latest news? 2 what
has: *What's been going on here
lately?*

wheat (hwēt), the grain of a common
cereal grass, used to make flour. n.

when (hwen), 1 at what time: *When
does school close?* 2 at the time
that: *Stand up when your name
is called.* 1 adv., 2 conj.

when·ev·er (hwen ev′ər), when; at
whatever time; at any time that:
*Come whenever you wish (conj.).
I'll come whenever possible (adv.).
conj., adv.*

where (hwâr), in what place; at what
place: *Where do you live? Where
is he? adv.*

wher·ev·er (hwâr ev′ər), where;
to whatever place; in whatever
place: *Sit wherever you like (conj.)
Wherever are you going? (adv.).
conj., adv.*

whirl (hwėrl), 1 turn or swing round
and round; spin: *The leaves
whirled in the wind.* 2 move
round and round: *whirl a lasso.
We whirled about the room. v.*

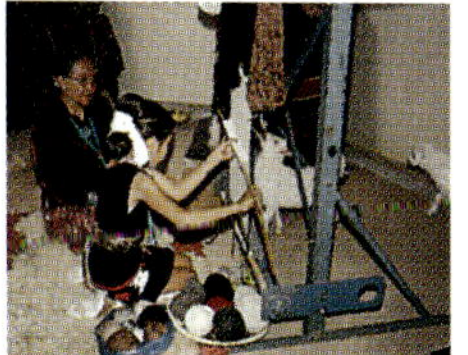

weave

weaving on a large loom

a	hat	**ī**	ice	**u̇**	put	**ə** stands for	
ā	age	**o**	not	**ü**	rule	**a**	in about
ä	far, calm	**ō**	open	**ch**	child	**e**	in taken
âr	care	**ȯ**	saw	**ng**	long	**i**	in pencil
e	let	**ô**	order	**sh**	she	**o**	in lemon
ē	equal	**oi**	oil	**th**	thin	**u**	in circus
ėr	term	**ou**	out	**ŦH**	then		
i	it	**u**	cup	**zh**	measure		

293

whole | wrench

whole (hōl), **1** having all its proper parts; complete: *whole egg, whole milk.* **2** full; entire: *He ate the whole melon. adj.*

whole milk (hōl′ milk′), milk from which none of the natural elements have been removed.

whole note (hōl′ nōt′), (in music) note to be played four times as long as one quarter note.

whole-wheat (hōl′hwēt′), made from whole-wheat flour: *whole-wheat bread. adj.*

who'll (hül), who will: *Who'll help me wash the dishes?*

who's (hüz), **1** who is: *Who's going with me?* **2** who has: *Who's seen the new wildlife documentary?*

whose (hüz), of whom; of which: *The girl whose work got the prize is very talented. Whose book is this? pron.*

width (width), how wide a thing is; distance across; breadth: *The room is 12 feet in width. n.*

wild (wīld), not in proper control or order: *wild hair. adj.*

will (wil), am going to; is going to; are going to: *We will go to the beach on Saturday. v., past tense* **would.**

win (win), be successful over others; get victory or success in: *We all hope our team will win. v.,* **won** (wun), **win·ning.**

win·dow (win′dō), an opening to let in light or air set into an outer wall or roof of a building or into a vehicle. *n.*

wind sock (wind′ sok′), device somewhat like a large sock, mounted on a pole and open at one end to catch the wind and show its direction.

wind vane (wind′ vān′), a tool that shows wind direction.

wish·y-wash·y (wish′ē wäsh′ē), lacking strength of character; indecisive: *a wishy-washy person. adj.*

wisp (wisp), a flock of birds, especially of marsh birds called snipe. *n.*

wrench

A **wrench** holds and turns bolts and nuts.

with (wiᴛʜ *or* with), *With* shows that persons or things are taken together in some way. **1** in the company of: *Come with me.* **2** by means of: *The man cut the meat with a knife. prep.*

with·draw (wiᴛʜ drȯ′ *or* with drȯ′), draw back; draw away. *v.,* **with·drew, with·drawn, with·draw·ing.**

with·hold (with hōld′ *or* wiᴛʜ hōld′), refrain from giving or granting. *v.,* **with·held, with·hold·ing.**

with·stand (with stand′ *or* wiᴛʜ stand′), stand against; hold out against; resist; oppose, especially successfully. *v.,* **with·stood, with·stand·ing.**

wood (wůd), trees or parts of trees cut up for use in building houses, making boats and furniture, etc. *n.*

wor·ry (wėr′ē), **1** feel anxious; be uneasy: *Don't worry about little things. They will worry if we are late.* **2** make anxious; trouble: *The problem worried me. v.,* **wor·ried, wor·ry·ing.**

worth·less (wėrth′lis), without worth; good-for-nothing; useless: *Throw those worthless, broken toys away. adj.*

would (wůd), See **will.** *Would you help us, please? v.*

would·n't (wůd′nt), would not.

would've (wůd′əv), would have.

wow (wou), exclamation of surprise, joy, etc. *interj.*

wreath (rēth), a ring of flowers or leaves twisted together. *n., pl.* **wreaths** (rēᴛʜz).

wreck (rek), **1** what is left of anything that has been destroyed or much injured. **2** cause the wreck of; destroy; ruin: *Raccoons wrecked our campsite looking for food.* **1** *n.,* **2** *v.*

wren (ren), a small songbird with a slender bill and a short tail. Wrens often build their nests near houses. *n.*

wrench (rench), tool for turning nuts, bolts, etc. *n., pl.* **wrench·es.**

wrestler | zinnia

wres·tler (res′lər), person who wrestles, especially as a sport. *n.*

wrist (rist), the joint connecting hand and arm. *n.*

write (rīt), make letters or words with pen, pencil, or chalk: *You can read and write. v.,* **wrote** (rōt), **writ·ten, writ·ing.**

writ·ing (rī′ting), literary work; a book or other literary production: *the writings of Benjamin Franklin. n.*

writ·ten (rit′n), See **write.** *He has written a letter. (v.) a written note. (adj.). v., adj.*

Y

yes·ter·day (yes′tər dē), the day before today. *n.*

you'd (yüd; *unstressed* yəd), **1** you had: *You'd already left.* **2** you would: *You'd love this book.*

young (yung), without much experience or practice. *adj.*

your (yùr; *unstressed* yər), belonging to you: *Wash your hands. adj.*

you're (yùr; *unstressed* yər), you are: *Tell me where you're going.*

Z

zin·ni·a (zin′ē ə), a garden plant grown for its showy flowers of many colors. *n.* [The *zinnia* was named in honor of Johann G. Zinn, 1727-1759, a German botanist.]

wrestler
wrestlers during
a match

a	hat	**ī**	ice	**ù**	put	**ə** *stands for*	
ā	age	**o**	not	**ü**	rule	**a**	in about
ä	far, calm	**ō**	open	**ch**	child	**e**	in taken
âr	care	**ò**	saw	**ng**	long	**i**	in pencil
e	let	**ô**	order	**sh**	she	**o**	in lemon
ē	equal	**oi**	oil	**th**	thin	**u**	in circus
ėr	term	**ou**	out	**ŦH**	then		
i	it	**u**	cup	**zh**	measure		

Writer's Thesaurus

Many of your spelling words have synonyms, which are words with same or similar meanings. This thesaurus lists those spelling words alphabetically, defines them, and provides synonyms. For many words, you can also look up antonyms, which are words with opposite meanings. A thesaurus can even introduce you to new words.

Understand a Thesaurus Entry

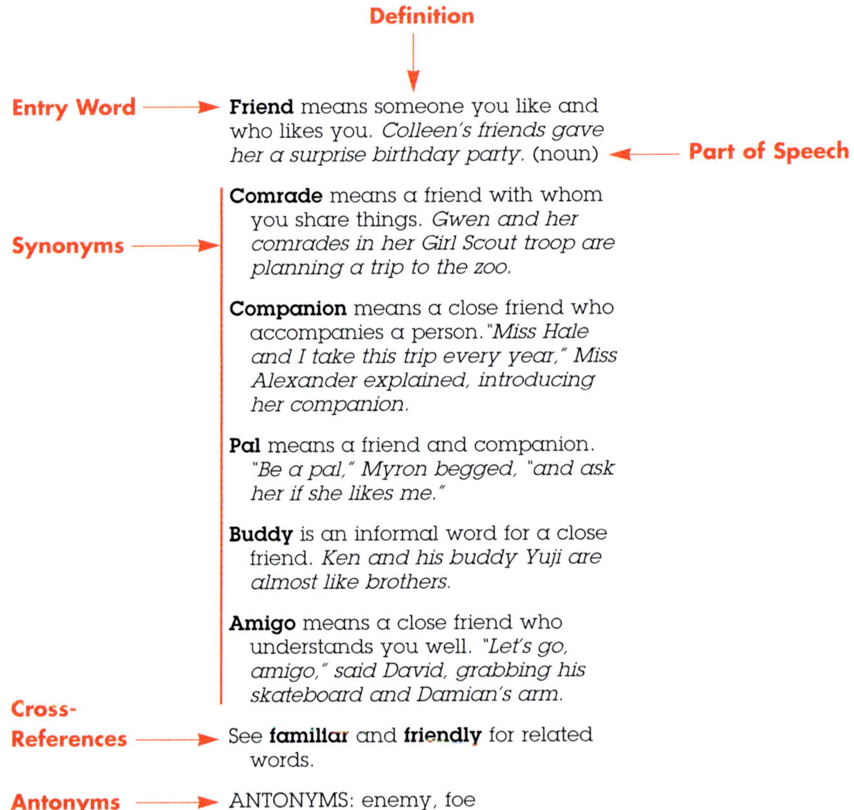

A a

Ability means the power to do something well. *Renee's ability to make her own clothes has saved her a lot of money.* (noun)

Talent means an inborn ability. *Julio's drumming shows real musical talent.*

Capacity means an inborn ability. *Bob has a great capacity for foreign languages and speaks three.*

Skill means an ability gotten by means of training and practice. *Michiko's skill in cooking has improved.*

Announce means to make something known to the public. *The manager announced that the team had traded two pitchers.* (verb)

Broadcast means to make something widely known by radio or television. *Warnings of the approaching hurricane were broadcast to residents of the coast.*

Advertise means to make something known to the public by paying for it. *The sale was advertised in the local newspaper.*

Publicize means to make something known to as many people as possible. *The kids publicized their car wash by posting signs.*

Ask means to try to get information by using words. *Ask Marcy where she got that great jacket.* (verb)

Inquire means to ask in order to get detailed information. *Yukio inquired about the hours that the video store is open.*

Quiz means to ask questions about what has been learned. *Our science teacher always quizzes us on last night's homework.*

Question means to ask over and over again, in a systematic way. *The police questioned several suspects about the bank robbery.*

ANTONYMS: answer, reply

Attack means to begin fighting someone or something with actions or words. *A mother bear may attack anyone who gets close to her cubs. A group of parents has attacked the plan to close the schools early.* (verb)

Assault means to attack suddenly, usually with weapons. *The enemy assaulted our fort with bombs and cannons.*

Charge can mean to attack by a sudden rush. *An elephant opens its ears wide when it charges.*

ANTONYM: defend

B b

Beat means to hit over and over. *José and his friends spend Saturday mornings beating conga drums at the Caribbean Cultural Center.* (verb)

Winds howled, and waves **pounded** the little ship.

Hammer can mean to beat. *"Why can't I remember?" said Shirley, hammering her head with her fists.*

Pound means to hit hard, over and over. *Winds howled, and waves pounded the little ship.*

Bang can mean to beat noisily. *Liza's little sister loves to bang on pots and pans.*

Beautiful means very pleasing to the senses or the mind. *These beautiful rugs were made by hand in Turkey 100 years ago, but they still look almost like new.* (adjective)

Pretty means pleasing to see or hear. It is often used to describe girls and women. *Mariko looks really pretty in that hat.*

Handsome means pleasing to see. It is often used instead of beautiful or pretty to describe a man or boy. *Candace thinks Mr. Walking Bear, the science teacher, is awfully handsome.*

Lovely means especially beautiful and fine. *The rose garden in the park is so lovely, I could stay there for hours.*

ANTONYMS: ugly, unattractive

297

■ WRITER'S THESAURUS

Beginning means the time when something first happens or first exists. *The Declaration of Independence marked the beginning of the United States.* (noun)

Start can mean a beginning. *Jason led the sack race from start to finish.*

Creation means the act of making something that did not exist before. *Since the creation of the Cafeteria Committee, we've had better desserts.*

Opening can mean a beginning, especially of a story, music, or other works of art. *The opening of the musical, with its great song and fabulous dancers, really grabbed Mike's attention.*

Introduction can mean a beginning in common use. *Since the introduction of the microwave, cooking habits have changed greatly.*

ANTONYMS: conclusion, end, finish

C c

Care means an unhappy, nervous feeling, with fear of pain or loss. *After weeks of struggle and care, the refugees have escaped from the fighting.* (noun)

Concern can mean an uneasy feeling because something or someone important to you is in trouble. *Marcia's parents feel a lot of concern because she wants to quit school.*

Worry means repeated, nervous thought about possible pain or loss. *Our worry about Billy Don's safety turned to anger when he strolled in two hours late.*

Anxiety means strong worry and fear. *Every time Coach Petrangelis tells us how important this next game is, my anxiety gets worse.*

Tension can mean worry and emotional upset, especially lasting a long time and using up much strength. *After the tension of waiting for the audition, White Bird felt that actually performing was almost easy.*

SEE **worried** for related words.

Careful means paying close attention to what you say and do. *I feel safe in the car with Mrs. Gomez, who is a very careful driver.* (adjective)

Cautious means careful to avoid danger. *Pia has been very cautious about riding her bike in the street after seeing the bike safety movie.*

Wary means very careful and expecting danger. *Mice have to be wary of cats and owls.*

Guarded can mean cautious. It is used especially to describe someone's way of talking. *The scientists are very guarded about their invention, and they say it needs more tests.*

ANTONYMS: careless, negligent, thoughtless

Careless means not paying attention to what you say or do. *Tom was careless, and now his shoes are all wet.* (adjective)

Thoughtless means not thinking before doing or saying something. *Those thoughtless girls talk loudly while everyone else is trying to study.*

Inconsiderate means thoughtless of other people's feelings. *Taking a parking space reserved for the disabled isn't just inconsiderate, it's illegal.*

Reckless means not thinking about possible danger. *Reckless driving frequently causes accidents.*

Rash means dangerously careless, often because of haste. *Maryanne now regrets her rash decision to quit school.*

ANTONYMS: careful, cautious

Change means to make or become different. *Jermayne changes her nail polish every couple of days. Inside its case, the pupa changes to a butterfly.* (verb)

Alter means to change slightly. It suggests limited change of a particular sort. *The pilot altered her flight plan to avoid a bad thunderstorm.*

Vary means to change in a number of ways. It suggests change for the sake of difference, or change according to circumstances. *The form of government varies from country to country.*

Turn can mean to change. It often describes change in color or form. *The sun turned Alan's face red. Water turns to steam when it boils.*

IDIOMS

Change is a key word in several idioms. Here are some of them:

Change hands means to go from one owner to another. *The gas station changed hands twice in one year before Mr. Ortega bought it.*

Change off means to take turns. *Mariolet and I change off doing the dishes and setting the table.*

Change your tune means to say something very different from before. *Cassie thinks she's a better cook than I am, but she'll change her tune when she tastes my barbecue.*

Climb means to move upward, most often by using feet or hands or both. *The squirrels climb the pole to get the birdseed.* (verb)

Ascend means to move upward toward the highest point. *The Japanese mountaineers will try to ascend one of the highest peaks in the Andes.*

Mount means to go up or climb up. *Mrs. Vargas slowly mounted the stairs to her apartment.*

Scramble means to climb where climbing is especially hard and awkward. It may suggest climbing on all fours. *An otter will scramble up a steep, muddy riverbank and slide down again, over and over, just for fun.*

ANTONYM: descend

Clothes means covering for a person's body. *Miguel has grown so much he needs new clothes.* (noun)

Clothing means clothes. It is a slightly more formal word. *New-to-You Fashion Shop sells both women's and men's clothing.*

poncho

kimono

caftan

Wardrobe means all the clothes a person has. *Most of Ray's wardrobe came from his older brothers.*

Outfit can mean clothes that go together. *Mom has a plaid skirt and a red blouse that she wears as an outfit with her velvet blazer.*

Uniform means the clothes worn by some special group while at work. *When Aunt Phyllis goes to her Army Reserve training, she looks strong and proud in her uniform.*

Common means happening often or often met with. *"It's just a common cold," Dr. Wu told Jerome.* (adjective)

Ordinary means like most others. *Since the note was written on ordinary paper, the police concentrated on tracing its rare purple ink.*

Average can mean like most others. It is often used with numbers. *On an average day, the store sells two dozen sponges.*

Normal means like most others. It suggests that this is a good way to be. *It is normal for people to want to be liked and respected.*

Popular can mean widespread and done, had, or known by many people. *Grandpa and Grandma like to do popular dances from years ago.*

SEE **usual** for related words.

Confused means unable to think clearly or act correctly. *Alan's directions got us so confused that we arrived more than an hour late.* (adjective)

Bewildered means confused, especially by many parts or items. *On his first day at school, Luis was bewildered by all the long halls, doors, and hurrying students.*

Puzzled means unsure or unable to understand. *The ranger was puzzled by the strange tracks he found.*

Perplexed is a formal word that means very puzzled. *Perplexed by the new disease attacking the sheep, the vet sent for experts from the university.*

Mixed up means confused. *Our waiter got mixed up and brought baked potatoes instead of the rice we had ordered.*

■ WRITER'S THESAURUS

There are many words that we use to describe people and things that are strange, abnormal, senseless, or just plain silly. You and your friends might call each other "crazy" or names like that and then laugh together about them. But it is not polite to use *crazy*, *mad*, or *lunatic* in describing sick people. *Insane* is used for legal purposes. Otherwise the phrase to use is "mentally ill."

Crazy means senseless and foolish. *Whose crazy idea was it to walk all the way home?* (adjective)

Lunatic means crazy. *It's lunatic to take foolish risks.*

Mad means very crazy and possibly dangerous. *Mr. Brady may look like a mad scientist, but he's actually a lot of fun to talk to.*

Insane means mentally ill and not legally responsible. *The murderer was insane, and he was sent to a mental hospital.*

ANTONYM: sane

Crowd means a large group of people together. *Huge crowds arrived on the day of the big game.* (noun)

Mob means a crowd, especially a noisy and violent one. *The mob made so much noise that the governor returned to her helicopter.*

Flock can mean a crowd. *A flock of preschoolers ran out the door.*

Swarm can mean a crowd moving together. *Every weekday morning and evening, swarms of commuters pour through the train station.*

D d

Danger means a chance of harm or injury. *The approaching tornado brought danger to everything in its path.* (noun)

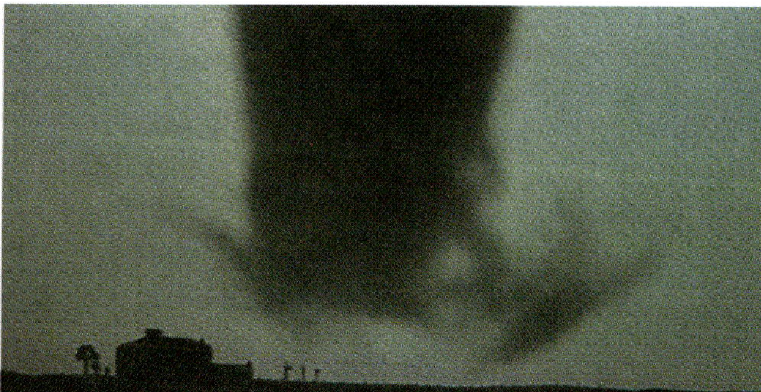

The house was in great **danger** as the tornado approached.

Risk means a chance of harm or loss. *Lynn wonders if the view would be worth the risk of the climb.*

Hazard means a likely cause of injury or misfortune. *The hazards of mining include cave-ins, explosions, and flooding.*

Threat can mean a possible cause of injury or misfortune. *The weather forecaster warned of the threat of a statewide blizzard.*

ANTONYM: safety

Deal means an arrangement for trade or exchange. This meaning is informal. *Lucy thought that trading three cat's-eye marbles for a circus ticket was a pretty good deal.* (noun)

Bargain means a deal. *William Penn made a fair bargain with the Indians.*

Agreement means an arrangement to act in certain ways. *I thought we had an agreement: you'd vacuum and do the bathroom, and I'd do the laundry and wash the kitchen floor.*

Contract means a legal agreement. *The third baseman has signed a contract for a total of $6,000,000.*

Decide means to make up your mind. *It was such a hot day that we decided to go to the city swimming pool.* (verb)

Determine means to decide firmly, often from several choices. *Jolene is still trying to determine which hairdo looks best on her.*

Conclude can mean to decide after thinking it over. *The police concluded that the driver who caused the accident had been reckless.*

Rule can mean to decide publicly and with authority. *The referee ruled that the ball was out of bounds.*

Different means not alike. *Edgar and Edwin try hard to be different, because they don't want to be known as "the twins."* (adjective)

Various means different. It is used when there are many different things. *The recreation center offers various classes and activities.*

Miscellaneous means of many sorts, not all the same. It may suggest no effort to choose. *My sister collects only clear marbles, but she keeps some miscellaneous ones to trade.*

Mixed means of many kinds combined together. *Connie thinks "Mixed Nuts" would be a good name for our comedy act.*

ANTONYMS: alike, same, similar

300

Disappear means to go from sight. *Arlene turned off the TV, and the picture disappeared.* (verb)

Vanish means to disappear, usually suddenly and often mysteriously. *The magician will now make her assistant vanish from the stage.*

Evaporate can mean to disappear the way water does when it turns to vapor. *The bad feelings between Lana and Crystal evaporated when Lana broke her arm.*

Fade can mean to disappear slowly. *As the sun rises, stars fade away.*

ANTONYM: appear

Dishonest means willing to lie, cheat, or steal. *A dishonest accountant stole $4,000 from the business.* (adjective)

Crooked can mean dishonest. It expresses contempt. *That man was so crooked his own dog didn't trust him.*

Lying means not telling the truth. *The lying witness tried to mislead the jury.*

Untruthful can mean not telling the truth. *Since she is known to have been untruthful many times in the past, people tend not to believe her.*

ANTONYMS: honest, truthful

Dislike means a feeling of not liking someone or something. *Teresa has a real dislike for long bus rides.* (noun)

Distaste means a strong dislike. *Tanya's distaste for cold weather is even stronger now than when she first came to Chicago.*

Disgust means an extreme dislike of something physically unpleasant. *The smell of the garbage truck filled us with disgust.*

Disapproval means dislike of something because it is bad. *The students showed their disapproval of the movie by protesting outside the theater.*

ANTONYM: fondness

E e

Edge means the line or place where something ends. *Zena planted marigolds around the edges of the class garden.* (noun)

Margin means an area next to an edge. *In the margin of my paper, my teacher wrote a few comments about my work.*

Rim means the edge of something round. *The rims of these plates are decorated with flowers.*

Border means an edge or the area along the edge. *The white linen tablecloth had pink daisies embroidered all around the border.*

Boundary means an edge of a place or the area along the edge. *When the two countries merged, the boundary lines between them were left off the new maps.*

Excellent means having very high quality. *When it was Barry's turn to cook dinner, he made excellent tacos.* (adjective)

First-class means excellent. *"Why, Daniel, this drawing is wonderful!" the art teacher cried. "You're becoming a first-class artist!"*

Superior means having very high quality, especially compared to others. *"Now that you have seen the others," Mr. Bartholomew murmured, "I will show you a truly superior diamond."*

Outstanding means so excellent as to stand out from others. *You have to be an outstanding athlete to be considered for the Olympic team.*

ANTONYMS: bad, poor, terrible

Explain means to make something easier to understand by talking or writing about it. *This book explains the background of the war in Vietnam.* (verb)

Interpret means to explain the meaning of something. *Rob interprets the movie as a comedy, but Tara thinks it was serious.*

Clarify means to make something clearer and easier to understand. *Celia could not understand the diagram and asked her teacher to clarify it.*

Spell out means to give a careful, detailed, and easy-to-understand explanation. *Roger had trouble setting the VCR until Marissa spelled out the process for him, one step at a time.*

ANTONYMS: confuse, misinterpret

WRITING TIP: SLANG

There are lots of slang words that mean "excellent." Here are just a few of them:

bad	icy
boss	keen
chill	neat
cool	nifty
dandy	righteous
dynamite	swell
fab	tough
groovy	

Remember that slang gets old very quickly. Some of the words in this list may already be so out of date that you have never heard them used to mean "excellent." When you see in this book or in your dictionary that a word is slang, be careful about using it in your writing. In dialogue, slang can help suggest a character through conversation, but in description, it can make your story sound old.

HAVE YOU HEARD...?

You may have heard people say that someone has "shed light on the question." This means to provide information about a subject, especially a subject in doubt—as if shining a light into darkness. "My next witness," said Ms. Ortega, "can shed some light on the question of the defendant's whereabouts at that time."

■ WRITER'S THESAURUS

Extra means more than usual or more than necessary. *Every student should bring an extra pencil to the exam. Rodney always carries extra batteries for his tape player.* (adjective)

Spare can mean extra. It suggests that something will probably not be needed. *Ms. Healy checks her spare tire every few weeks.*

Surplus means extra. It suggests that there is a lot more of something than necessary. *The bakery sends its surplus bread to the church's shelter for the homeless.*

Additional means added to something else. *"Will you stop now," asked the TV host, "or risk all your prizes for an additional five thousand dollars?"*

F f

Friend means someone you like and who likes you. *Colleen's friends gave her a surprise birthday party.* (noun)

Comrade means a friend with whom you share things. *Gwen and her comrades in her Girl Scout troop are planning a trip to the zoo.*

Companion means a close friend who accompanies a person. *"Miss Hale and I take this trip every year," Miss Alexander explained, introducing her companion.*

Pal means a friend and companion. *"Be a pal," Myron begged, "and ask her if she likes me."*

Buddy is an informal word that means a close friend. *Ken and his buddy Yuji are almost like brothers.*

Amigo means a close friend who understands you well. *"Let's go, amigo," said David, grabbing his skateboard and Damian's arm.*

ANTONYMS: enemy, foe

H h

Hide means to put out of sight. *We quickly hid the birthday present we were making for Mom when we heard her at the front door.* (verb)

Conceal means to hide something on purpose so that it won't be found. *Ugo conceals his comic books, but I always find them.*

Camouflage means to hide something by giving it a false appearance. *This caterpillar's dull colors let it camouflage itself as a twig.*

Stash is an informal word that means to hide something for safekeeping or future use. *Everything the gang stole was stashed in a hiding place under the floor.*

Bury can mean to hide something by covering it. *When Tana saw the teacher coming, she quickly buried Michelle's note under her books.*

ANTONYMS: expose, reveal, show

Hopeless means without any feeling that something good will happen. *Mr. Cho stared at his flooded home and felt more hopeless than ever before in his life.* (adjective)

Desperate means hopeless and reckless. *The mountain climbers made a desperate effort to get back to camp through the raging storm.*

Pessimistic means ready to believe that bad things will happen. *Patrick is too pessimistic even to try out for the swim team.*

ANTONYMS: confident, hopeful

Huge means very big. *A huge oak tree in the park blew down in the storm last night.* (adjective)

Enormous means much larger than normal. *We're celebrating the hundredth anniversary of the founding of the town with an enormous parade and picnic.*

Giant means much larger than other things of the same kind. *That's the Happy Cow Dairy with the giant milk carton on the roof.*

Gigantic means giant. *At the county fair, Richie saw a gigantic pumpkin weighing 150 pounds.*

Colossal means tremendously large. *The colossal head of Washington on Mount Rushmore is as high as a five-story building.*

Mammoth means colossal. *Mammoth Cave has miles of passages and is hundreds of feet deep.*

ANTONYMS: little, small, tiny

I i

Interesting means making you feel like paying attention and knowing more. *To a chameleon, any insect is interesting.* (adjective)

To a chameleon, any insect is **interesting.**

Fascinating means so interesting that it's hard to stop. *Damien finds computer programming so fascinating that he'll sit at his keyboard for hours.*

Spellbinding means so interesting that it is impossible to stop paying attention. *Both pitchers have no-hitters going into the eighth inning of this spellbinding game.*

ANTONYMS: dull, boring, uninteresting

K k

Know means to have knowledge of something or someone. *Marina knows a beautiful spot in the state park.* (verb)

Realize means to understand that something is true. *Watching Mr. Brigano work in his garden, we never realized he was almost 90.*

Recognize can mean to realize. *Matt recognizes now that he was wrong to make fun of his sister's singing.*

Understand means to get the meaning of something. *After years of work, scientists understand something about the writing carved on this stone by an ancient people.*

L l

Loud means having or making a big sound. *The thunder was so loud, it seemed the storm was right over our house.* (adjective)

Noisy means with a lot of loud, harsh sounds. *Elora ran past the noisy street repairs as fast as she could.*

Roaring means making a loud, deep sound. *This is no place for kids to play, with broken glass and roaring traffic.*

Thunderous can mean very loud, like thunder. *"Just listen to that thunderous applause from these hockey fans!" said the announcer.*

Blaring means making a very loud, harsh sound. *The blaring stereo in the upstairs apartment kept Pavel's family awake.*

ANTONYMS: quiet, silent, still

M m

Misfortune means bad luck or an unfortunate happening. *Josleen had the misfortune to race against the city's best sprinter in the first round of the girls' 100-meter dash.* (noun)

Accident means an unfortunate happening, usually a sudden one. *Traffic is backed up because of the auto accident.*

Misadventure means an accident, usually not a serious one. *James and his friends were covered with mud after their misadventure while feeding the pigs.*

Mishap means a misadventure. *"Keep practicing the dance," the director said, "and it will go without any mishap."*

O o

Often means many times. *Casimir often earns a few dollars helping people carry groceries.* (adverb)

Frequently means often and at short intervals. *Rain falls frequently in the tropical forest.*

Repeatedly means many times and the same each time. *Juana must go repeatedly to the stream for her family's water.*

Regularly means often and at the same interval. *"Buses should arrive at this corner regularly," said Mr. Crankshaw, "but I haven't seen one yet."*

ANTONYMS: infrequently, rarely, seldom

IDIOMS

There are many idioms that mean to know something fully and thoroughly. You can **know** something

by heart
like the back of your hand
inside out
backwards and forwards
like a book

There are also many ways to say that someone understands the situation. You can be **in the know,** and you can **know**

the dope   the score
the ropes   what's up
the scoop   what's what

Do you have other ways of saying this?

■ WRITER'S THESAURUS

Most ants have enough **strength** to lift ten times their own weight.

P p

Perfect means having no faults or being the best. *The swimmer made a perfect dive. Vladimir found the perfect gift for his grandmother.* (adjective)

Ideal means perfect, or as wonderful as you could imagine. *When Saturday came, it turned out to be an ideal day for the carnival.*

Flawless means not having any defects. *On the slender fingers of her right hand, the princess wore two flawless diamonds.*

Pure can mean perfect. It suggests that something contains no bad parts. *Ronald prides himself on his homemade candy, made with pure chocolate and fluffy coconut.*

Foolproof means made so that nothing can go wrong. *The prisoners thought that their escape plan was foolproof—until they found the guards waiting in the tunnel.*

SEE **excellent** for related words.

ANTONYM: imperfect

Piece means a small part of something larger, or one thing among others like it. *Della swept the pieces of the broken glass into a pile. The platter was the largest piece of china on the Serra's dinner table.* (noun)

Bit means a small piece of something larger. *Caroline tore the letter into bits.*

Scrap means a little piece, especially a piece left over. *Andrea cut the picture to fit into the frame and then threw away the paper scraps.*

Lump means a small, solid piece of material. *Darryl gave the carnival pony a lump of sugar.*

Slice means a thin, flat, broad piece cut from something. *Franklyn wants a sandwich with one slice of cheese and three slices of ham.*

Power means the ability to do something or to make something happen. *Senator Hughes has the power to get that law changed.* (noun)

Energy can mean power. It often suggests power stored up, ready to be used. *The creative energy of the students really comes out in the school's Festival of Brazil.*

Force means active power. It suggests effort and work. *The force of the blast destroyed the building and took out the side of the mountain.*

Strength means the amount of power that someone or something has. *Most ants have enough strength to lift ten times their own weight.*

Might means great power or strength. *Janek took a deep breath and flung himself at the locked door with all his might.*

ANTONYM: weakness

Proud means pleased with yourself and with what you have done. *Congresswoman Martinez told her election workers that they should all be proud of themselves.* (adjective)

Conceited means having too high an opinion of yourself or your good qualities. *The conceited actor stopped bragging after he forgot his lines.*

Boastful means fond of talking about yourself and how good you are. *The boastful man went on and on about what a great fisherman he was.*

Stuck-up is an informal word that means conceited. *Patricia is so stuck-up that she has no friends at all.*

ANTONYMS: humble, modest

Punish means to cause pain or loss to a person who has done something wrong. *The soldiers were punished for sleeping on duty.* (verb)

Discipline can mean to punish, especially to control people. *Mr. Berman disciplines his students fairly.*

Correct can mean to punish, in order to make someone better. *Mom says she must correct our new puppy so he'll stop chewing furniture and shoes.*

Fine means to make a person pay money for doing something wrong. *Our library fines people five cents a day for late books.*

Ground can mean to punish a young person by not letting him or her go out for fun. This meaning is informal. *When he came home two hours late, Chung-Ho knew his parents would ground him.*

Q q

Quick means moving, happening, or done in a short time. *Graciela made a quick grab and got her purse back from the thief.* (adjective)

Fast means moving with much speed. *Young Raven hurled his fish spear, but the salmon was too fast.*

Swift means very fast. *This train is so swift that we'll be in Los Angeles tomorrow.*

Speedy means very quick. It is often used to describe things that you want to happen or be finished. *The bank robbers could not make a speedy getaway because of the parade.*

Hasty means quick and with not enough time or thought. *Courtney's hasty reply started a quarrel.*

SEE **suddenly** for related words.

ANTONYM: slow

Quiet means to make someone or something less noisy and more peaceful. *Desi quieted his younger brothers when they were frightened by the thunderstorm.* (verb)

Calm means to make someone less excited or nervous. *Following the bomb scare, the police officer calmed the crowd.*

Soothe means to make quiet and comfortable. *Mrs. Benson soothed the crying child.*

Hush means to make someone or something less noisy or silent. *As the mailman approached, the owner hushed his barking dog.*

ANTONYMS: disturb, excite, stir up

R r

Reason means an explanation of why something happened. *Doug says his reason for quitting the job is that he didn't respect the boss.* (noun)

Cause can mean a reason. *The "A" on Jaleel's history final was cause for celebration!*

Motive means a thought or feeling that makes someone do something. *The high cost of city living was Mr. Poole's motive for moving to a small town.*

Rough means having a surface that is not smooth. *Frank snagged his sweater on the rough wall of the basement.* (adjective)

Uneven means not smooth or level. *Our car bounced along the uneven gravel road.*

Bumpy means having a lot of bumps. *The sidewalk was too bumpy for good skateboarding.*

Rugged means having a rough, uneven surface. *The slope looked easy, but the ground became rugged toward the top.*

Coarse can mean rough and heavy. *Silas used coarse sandpaper to smooth the sides of the bookshelf.*

ANTONYMS: even, level, smooth

S s

Separate means to keep things apart or take something apart. *The highway separates these apartment buildings from the neighboring houses. Separate the dark from the light clothes before you wash them.* (verb)

Divide means to separate. It is often used about equal parts or sharing. *Ms. Polanak divided the class into teams for a softball game.*

Split can mean to divide something as if by cutting. *Tom and Dave split the money they got for the empty cans.*

Segregate can mean to separate people of different races. *The people of South Africa were the last in the world to remain officially segregated.*

ANTONYMS: unite, join

Serious means showing deep thought and purpose. *"I am the man of the family now," said Tom in a serious voice.* (adjective)

Earnest means serious and full of strong feeling. *The governor made an earnest appeal for help from the federal government after his state was struck by a hurricane.*

Solemn means serious, formal, and impressive. *The President takes a solemn oath to uphold the Constitution.*

ANTONYMS: lighthearted, cheerful, carefree

305

WRITER'S THESAURUS

Shelter means something that covers or protects from the weather or from danger. *During the rain, the church picnic continued under the shelter of the tents.* (noun)

Cover can mean shelter. *The baby crane took cover between the long legs of its mother.*

Refuge means a shelter or place of safety. It suggests escape from trouble. *The first National Wildlife Refuge was created by Theodore Roosevelt to protect pelicans.*

Sanctuary can mean a refuge or place of protection, especially one where animals are protected from hunters or other dangers. *Behind the zoo is a bird sanctuary, closed to people.*

Preserve can mean a place where animals and plants are protected. *This whole area within the bend of the river is a wildlife preserve.*

Short means taking only a small amount of time. *"This was supposed to be a short assignment, but it's taking forever," Regina sighed.* (adjective)

Brief means taking a small amount of time. *Ken gave a brief talk about collecting beetles.*

Thumbnail means very short. *Dario gave a thumbnail description of the baseball game: "They got the runs; we didn't."*

Summary means brief and limited to main ideas. *Mr. Perrera has his classes hand in summary outlines of each week's reading.*

ANTONYMS: lengthy, long, wordy

Sign means an indication of something that will happen. *The first red and yellow leaves are a sign that summer is over.* (noun)

Symptom means a sign, especially of illness or suffering. *Symptoms of the flu include a fever and nausea.*

Omen means a sign or something believed to be a sign. *Daniel thinks it's an omen of good luck if he sees an all-white pigeon.*

Warning means something that tells of possible trouble or danger to come. *"Let that be a warning to you," Alejandro told the sobbing bully.*

Soft means easy to bend or push into; not hard or stiff. *After two weeks of sleeping on a hard camp cot, Phil is glad to get back to his own soft bed.* (adjective)

Floppy means easy to bend and hanging or swaying in a loose way. *After a long week in her squad car, Mom spends Saturday morning in her floppy old bathrobe, reading and relaxing.*

Fluffy means as soft as fluff. *The young swan has short, fluffy feathers.*

The young swan has short, **fluffy** feathers.

Limp means so easy to bend that it cannot stay straight. *The noodles were limp when Tessa lifted them from the boiling water.*

ANTONYMS: firm, hard, rigid, stiff

Steal means to take something that belongs to someone else. It suggests secret, usually nonviolent taking. *"I saw the robbers steal the money," the witness stated.* (verb)

Rob means to take money or property from a person or place. *The convenience store over on 27th Street was robbed twice last weekend.*

Shoplift means to steal things from a store while pretending to be a customer. *Since the Trans installed a lot of mirrors and cameras, nobody shoplifts from that store.*

Hold up means to stop by force and take money or property. *Bandits held up the stagecoach outside Bitterroot Springs.*

Stick up is a slang expression that means to rob. *She stuck up a couple of banks, so she's in jail for fifteen to twenty years.*

WORD STORY

Sanctuary comes from a Latin word meaning "a holy place." In the Middle Ages, people could avoid arrest by staying in a church. Because a church is a holy place, the laws at that time said that a person could be protected there.

WATCH IT !

Steal and *rob* have related meanings, but they are not really synonyms because of the way they are used. The object of *steal* is the thing that is taken. The object of *rob* is the person or place that something is taken from. They *robbed* the store and *stole* the money.

306

Stiff means not easy to bend or move. *Grandpa prefers a hairbrush with stiff bristles.* (adjective)

Rigid means very stiff. *The wet clothes became rigid overnight in the frosty air.*

Firm means hard. *The butter is still cold and too firm to spread.*

Tense means stretched tight. *Every muscle was tense as the runners waited for the race to start.*

Suddenly means quickly and without being expected. *Suddenly the sky became dark, and a fierce storm began.* (adverb)

Unexpectedly means without any sign that something is going to happen. *The phone rang unexpectedly in the middle of the night.*

Immediately means instantly. *When he missed the bus, Gavin immediately called his mother to let her know he would be late.*

All of a sudden and **all at once** mean suddenly. *All of a sudden, Korinne realized that she was falling. All at once, Tony jumped up and caught her arm.*

SEE **quick** for related words.

ANTONYM: gradually

Surprised means filled with wonder because of something unexpected. *"Marceea, I'm surprised to find you here!" exclaimed Grandpa.* (adjective)

Amazed means greatly surprised. *His parents were amazed when Eldred began composing music at such an early age.*

Startled can mean caused to jump in surprise and fright. *Kazuo is such a light sleeper that once he woke up, startled by a noisy goldfish.*

Shocked means surprised and very upset. *Jamaine was shocked to find her ordinarily quiet dog barking and snapping at the mail carrier.*

T t

Thoughtful means careful of other people's feelings. *"How thoughtful!" said Angelique. "You brought my favorite flowers!"* (adjective)

Considerate means thoughtful. It suggests thinking of people's feelings without having to be told. *They were considerate of the downstairs neighbors by walking quietly in the hallway.*

Sympathetic means thoughtful, kind, and able to understand how someone else feels. *When he saw my braces, Emilio showed his own in a sympathetic smile.*

Caring means attentive. It suggests that someone else's feelings are important to you. *Everyone in class made a fuss when Jacob first broke his leg, but only Amanda was caring enough to visit him often.*

ANTONYMS: inconsiderate, thoughtless

U u

Ugly means unpleasant to look at. *Vandals have covered the wall with ugly spray paint marks.* (adjective)

Homely means not good-looking. It is also not as strong a word as ugly. *Amid the crowds in the railway station, Lise was delighted to see the smiling, homely face of her beloved Uncle Frank.*

Hideous means very ugly and horrible to look at. *Butch loves movies with hideous monsters, but I think they're mostly boring and stupid.*

Monstrous can mean hideous. *The monstrous faces stared at Mr. Williamson and chanted, "Trick or treat!"*

ANTONYMS: beautiful, good-looking

Useless means not worth using or doing, or not able to be used. *It's useless arguing with Bill, because he never admits it when he's wrong.* (adjective)

Worthless means having no use or value. *If the broken leg on that table can't be fixed, the table is really worthless.*

Needless means useless and without purpose. It suggests a waste of time. *Take a safer route to avoid any needless risk.*

Inefficient means not worth using or doing because work is wasted. *Copying whole pages of the textbook is an inefficient way to study the lesson.*

ANTONYM: useful

WORD STORY

Ugly comes from an old Scandinavian word meaning "fear." *Hideous* comes from an old French word meaning "fear." One reason we have synonyms is that sometimes the same idea came into English from different languages.

Usual means most commonly seen, found, or happening. *In Chicago some snow is usual in winter. We'll meet for lunch at the usual time.* (adjective)

Traditional means customary because it has been handed down from generation to generation. *Thanksgiving is a traditional American holiday.*

Regular means usual and according to custom or rule. *Sarah was late and missed her regular bus.*

Ordinary means usual and regular. *Visiting and helping out friends who are sick is an ordinary part of my grandmother's life.*

SEE **common** for related words.

ANTONYMS: peculiar, rare, unusual

W w

Want means to feel an urge to have or do something. *Peter wants a pair of in-line skates for his birthday.* (verb)

Wish means to want or hope for something. *"If you wish to become a ballerina," Madame Claire told Ramona, "you must work as hard as you can."*

Desire is a formal word that means to wish seriously and very much. *Many people desire to conserve the environment but wonder what they personally can do.*

Long means to desire. It suggests thinking about something over and over. *The Navajo children longed to hear more stories about their ancestors.*

Watch means to keep your eyes on something carefully for a period of time. *The burglars tied up the guard, so all he could do was watch as they emptied the warehouse.* (verb)

Look means to turn your eyes to something. *"Look at the sea lions!" Darseea called to her mother.*

Eye means to look. *Mustafa eyed each camel carefully as it approached the starting line.*

Gaze means to watch steadily. It suggests a strong attraction to what is watched. *Mr. Thurman gazed fondly at his newest grandchild.*

Stare means to watch steadily and directly, usually without blinking. *The first time Rachel got a pimple, she felt that everyone in school was staring at her.*

Weird means very strange and mysterious. *From deep in the forest, She Walks Away heard a weird croaking rumble.* (adjective)

Spooky is an informal word that means strange enough to make you nervous. *It's spooky how quiet the street gets at night when traffic stops.*

Creepy can mean weird and frightening. *The heroine of the movie has to save her friend from some creepy villains.*

The heroine of the movie has to save her friend from some **creepy** villains.

Ghostly means like a ghost. *Sometimes, when Obadele walks homeward across the fields at evening, mist rises in ghostly shapes around him.*

ANTONYMS: natural, normal

Welcome means to be glad to let someone or something in. *The Drama Club welcomes new members.* (verb)

Accept can mean to let in with approval. *Raquel's sister has been accepted by a medical school.*

Admit can mean allow to enter. *One hundred lucky contest winners will be admitted early and introduced to the band.*

Take in means to admit, especially as part of business. *The animal shelter takes in stray dogs and cats.*

308

Whole means with all its parts and with nothing left out. *Adam watched the whole movie, but Bert left when it got scary.* (adjective)

Complete means whole. *Consuela gave complete instructions for making a piñata.*

Entire means whole. *Did Lucy and Calvin eat the entire batch of cookies?*

Total means all added together. *The total bill was $81.16.*

ANTONYM: partial

Wild means extremely excited and out of control. *When Rita scored the goal that won the championship, the fans went wild.* (adjective)

Frantic means wild with rage, fear, pain, or grief. *From the burning building came frantic cries for help.*

Disorderly can mean wild and causing trouble, especially in public. *Ushers asked the disorderly group to be quiet or leave the concert.*

Unruly means hard to control. *Lamar's puppy has so much energy that she is sometimes unruly.*

ANTONYM: calm

Worried means uncertain what will happen and afraid of what may happen. It suggests thinking about something over and over. *Willie Don is worried because his dog won't eat and might be sick.* (adjective)

Uneasy means having a strong feeling that trouble is coming. It suggests not knowing for sure what the trouble will be. *Changes in the Earth's atmosphere make scientists uneasy about possible climate changes.*

Nervous can mean afraid that things will not go well. It suggests restlessness. *Before the race, Emma was nervous and wheeled her chair around the block to calm herself down.*

Anxious means convinced that something bad will happen, and busy thinking about it. It suggests painful excitement. *After an anxious search, Nancy found her contact lens under the seat of the car.*

SEE **care** for related words.

ANTONYMS: calm, relaxed

Y y

Young means in the early part of life. *Some young birds can walk and swim soon after they hatch from eggs.* (adjective)

Youthful means young or like young people. It suggests hope, energy, and imagination. *Grandma Salazar dances with a youthful enthusiasm that makes her seem half her age.*

Immature means not completely grown. It is often used to suggest that feelings or behavior are not grown-up enough. *Justin apologized to the substitute teacher for his immature behavior.*

Teenage means in the years of life from thirteen to nineteen. *With two teenage sons, a job, and night school, Mrs. Chee is always busy.*

ANTONYMS: adult, elderly, mature, old

IDIOMS

There are many idioms meaning *worried* and *nervous.* They describe a restless, uncertain feeling by comparing it to being on top of something that keeps you from being comfortable.

on edge: *It's been two months since Dad had any work, and he's on edge most of the time now.*

on pins and needles: *Afraid of missing the fireworks, the children were on pins and needles until they reached the park.*

like peas on a hot griddle: *When the cat appeared at the window, the birds at the feeder were like peas on a hot griddle.*

The Word List in English and Spanish

A

ability (13)	habilidad
able (13)	capaz, poder
accomplishments (CC)	logros
action (27)	acción
adobe (CC)	adobe
again (19)	otra vez
air mass (CC)	masa de aire
alley (9)	callejón
almost (16)	casi
a lot (16)	mucho, mucha
alphabet (3)	alfabeto
always (16)	siempre
angel (32)	ángel
angle (32, CC)	ángulo
animals (31)	animales
another (32)	otro, otra
anyway (26)	de todos modos
anywhere (7)	dondequiera
appearance (CC)	apariencia
appreciate (CC)	apreciar
April (11)	abril
are (35)	eres, son, somos; estás, están, estamos
area (CC)	área
arrive (11)	llegar
articles (CC)	artículos
artist (CC)	artista
ashes (15)	cenizas
asked (19)	preguntar; pedir (pasado)
assign (2)	asignar
assignments (CC)	tareas
Atlantic Ocean (CC)	Océano Atlántico
attack (3)	atacar
August (31)	agosto
aunt's (34)	de la tía
aunts' (34)	de las tías
Ave. (33)	avenida
awhile (7)	un rato

B

babies' (34)	de los bebés
baby's (34)	del bebé
backboard (CC)	tablero
backpack (10)	mochila
backstroke (CC)	brazada de espalda
bacon (11)	tocino
band (10)	banda
barometer (CC)	barómetro
barrel (32)	barril
baseball (26)	béisbol
basketball (26)	baloncesto; balón
beaches (15)	playas
beat (9, 23)	batir; tocar; vencer
beautiful (27)	bello, bella
because (3)	porque
beet (23)	betabel; remolacha
beginning (25)	comenzando
behind (11)	detrás
believe (19)	creer
bicuspid (CC)	primer molar
bicycle (CC)	bicicleta
blanket (10)	manta
block (10)	cuadra
blubber (CC)	grasa
borrow (8)	tomar prestado
bottle (8)	botella
boy's (34)	del muchacho
boys' (34)	de los muchachos
brainstorm (CC)	torrente de ideas
brake (3, 23)	freno; frenar
break (23)	quebrar; faltar
breathe (CC)	respirar
breathless (28)	sin aliento
bridge (14)	puente
brightness (28)	claridad
broadleaf (CC)	hoja ancha
broke (11)	quebrar (pasado)
broken (32)	quebrado, quebrada
brook (21)	arroyo
brother's (34)	del hermano
brothers' (34)	de los hermanos

310

ENGLISH/SPANISH WORD LIST

brought | cover

brought (19)	traer *(pasado)*
bruise (22)	magulladura
bubble (8)	burbuja
buffalo (31)	búfalo
build (19)	construir
bunches (15)	montones; racimos
bush (21)	arbusto
business (28)	asunto, negocio
butcher (21)	carnicero
butterfly (CC)	mariposa
button (32)	botón; abrochar
byline (CC)	renglón con nombre de autor

C

cable (11)	cable
cactus (CC)	cacto
cafeteria (CC)	cafetería
camera (25, CC)	cámara
Canada (31)	Canadá
canal (CC)	canal
canoe (31)	canoa; ir en canoa
capacity (CC)	capacidad
care (3)	preocuparse por; preocupación; cuidar
carefully (27)	cuidadosamente
careless (28)	descuidado, descuidada
caribou (CC)	caribú
carnivore (CC)	carnívoro, carnívora
cash (10)	efectivo
catcher (7)	receptor
cathedral (CC)	catedral
caught (25)	agarrar *(pasado)*
celebrated (CC)	célebre
Celsius (CC)	celsius
cement (31)	cemento
ceremony (CC)	ceremonia
certain (20)	seguro, segura
chalkboard (26)	pizarra
change (14)	cambiar
chapter (7)	capítulo
charge (14)	cargar
Chartres (CC)	Chartres
chased (4)	perseguir *(pasado)*
chasing (4)	persiguiendo
cheerful (27)	alegre
childhood (CC)	niñez
children (CC)	niños
Chinese New Year (33)	Año Nuevo Chino

chocolate (7)	chocolate
chop (10)	cortar
chores (CC)	quehaceres
Christmas (33)	Navidad
church (7, CC)	iglesia
circuses (15)	circos
classes (15)	clases
classmate (26)	compañero, compañera
classroom (26)	salón de clases
clear key (CC)	tecla de borrar
climb (2)	escalar
close (23)	cerrar
closer (5)	más cerca
closest (5)	el más íntimo, la más íntima, el más cerca, la más cerca
closet (10)	armario
clothes (23)	ropa
cloud (21)	nube
coal (CC)	carbón
collections (CC)	colecciones
color (32)	color
comb (2)	peinarse; peine
coming (16)	viniendo
common (32)	común
compass (CC)	brújula
compassionate (CC)	compasivo, compasiva
compose (13)	componer
composition (13)	composición
concert (CC)	concierto
conduct (CC)	conducir
confidence (CC)	confianza
confuse (22)	confundir
conifers (CC)	coníferas
Constitution (CC)	constitución
consumers (CC)	consumidores
contest (9)	concurso
cool (22)	fresco, fresca
coordinates (CC)	coordenadas
corn (CC)	maíz
correction (27)	corrección
could've (17)	pudiera haber
counselor (CC)	consejero, consejera
couple (10)	par
course (20)	curso
court (20)	corte
cousin (10)	primo, prima
cover (3)	tapar; cubierta

■ ENGLISH/SPANISH WORD LIST

crazy | epidermis

crazy (16)	loco, loca
credit (9)	crédito
crosswalks (CC)	cruces de peatones
crowd (21)	multitud
cruise (22)	crucero; hacer un crucero
crumb (13)	migaja
crumble (13)	desmigajar
curfew (22)	toque de queda
current (8, CC)	actual; corriente
curtains (CC)	cortinas
cushion (21)	cojín
cuspid (CC)	colmillo

D

Dad's (34)	de papá
daily (27)	diario
danced (4)	bailar (pasado)
dancing (4)	bailando
danger (11)	peligro
darkness (28)	oscuridad
deadline (CC)	plazo
deal (13)	repartir; tratar con; trato
dealt (13)	repartir; tratar con (pasado)
debris (CC)	escombros, desechos
Dec. (33)	dic.
December (25)	diciembre
decide (11)	decidir
decision (CC)	decisión
decomposer (CC)	descomponedor
deeper (5)	más profundo, más profunda
deepest (5)	el más profundo, la más profunda
degrees (CC)	grados
delays (15)	demoras
democratic (CC)	democrático, democrática
demonstrations (CC)	demostraciones
dermis (CC)	dermis
desert (CC)	desierto
design (2)	diseño; diseñar
details (CC)	detalles
determination (CC)	determinación
devastate (CC)	devastar
develops (CC)	desarrolla
didn't (16)	no (pasado)
different (8)	diferente
dirty (20)	sucio, sucia
disagree (29, CC)	estar en desacuerdo

disappear (29)	desaparecer
disappointment (CC)	desilusión
dishonest (29)	deshonesto, deshonesta
dislike (29)	tener aversión a
display (CC)	representación visual
distance (CC)	distancia
distrust (29)	desconfianza
dive (CC)	clavado
divide (CC)	dividir
dividend (CC)	dividendo
divisible (CC)	divisible
division (CC)	división
divisor (CC)	divisor
doctor (32)	doctor, doctora
doesn't (17)	no
dog paddle (CC)	chapotear
dolphin (3)	delfín
donkey (9)	burro
doorbell (26)	timbre
downstairs (26)	piso de abajo
Dr. (33)	Dr.
dribble (CC)	driblear
dried (4)	secar (pasado)
driveway (26)	camino de entrada
drove (11)	conducir (pasado)
drying (4)	secando
dune (CC)	duna
during (16)	durante

E

ear canal (CC)	canal auditivo
eardrum (CC)	tímpano
earrings (26)	aretes
earthquake (CC)	terremoto
edge (14)	borde
editors (CC)	editores
elected (CC)	elegido, elegida
electricity (CC)	electricidad
elephant (3)	elefante
eleven (16)	once
emergency (CC)	emergencia
enamel (CC)	enamel
endpoint (CC)	punto final
enemies (15)	enemigos, enemigas
energy (CC)	energía
engine (9)	motor
enough (3)	suficiente
epidermis (CC)	epidermis

ENGLISH/SPANISH WORD LIST

equal | grasshopper

equal (14)	igual	
equals key (CC)	tecla de resultado	
equator (CC)	ecuador	
error (CC)	error	
especially (31)	especialmente	
evening (25)	tarde	
evergreens (CC)	árboles de hojas perennes	
everybody (25)	todos	
everyone (25)	todos	
excellent (14)	excelente	
except (14)	menos	
excited (14)	emocionado, emocionada	
excuse (22)	excusa	
exhibit (CC)	exhibición	
expect (14)	esperar	
experiment (CC)	experimento	
expert (CC)	experto, experta	
explain (14)	explicar	
extra (14)	extra	
extraordinary (CC)	extraordinario, extraordinaria	
eyelashes (15)	pestañas	

F

Fahrenheit (CC)	Fahrenheit
fairness (28)	imparcialidad
families' (34)	de las familias
family (CC)	familia
family of facts (CC)	familia de operaciones básicas
family's (34)	de la familia
father (16)	padre
fatter (5)	más gordo, más gorda
fattest (5)	el más gordo, la más gorda
faults (CC)	fallas
favorite (31)	preferido, preferida
Feb. (33)	feb.
February (25)	febrero
federal (CC)	federal
feelings (16)	sentimientos
fence (9)	cerca
ferns (CC)	helechos
fertilize (CC)	fertilizar
few (22)	pocos
field (19)	campo
field goal (CC)	gol de patada
film (CC)	película

finally (25)	finalmente
finger (10)	dedo
first (20)	primero, primera
first aid (CC)	primeros auxilios
flashlight (7)	linterna
floats (CC)	flota
Florida (20)	Florida
flowers (15)	flores
focus (CC)	enfocar
food chain (CC)	cadena alimentaria
food web (CC)	red alimentaria
football (21)	fútbol americano; balón
forecast (CC)	pronóstico
forest (20, CC)	bosque
forgot (10)	olvidar *(pasado)*
form (20)	formulario; formar
foul (CC)	falta
fourteen (20)	catorce
fourth (20)	cuarto
free throw (CC)	tiro libre
freestyle (CC)	estilo libre
friend (19)	amigo, amiga
friend's (34)	del amigo, de la amiga
friends (15)	amigos, amigas
front (CC)	frente
fruit (22, CC)	fruta
fudge (14)	dulce de chocolate
fuel (22)	combustible
fuels (CC)	combustibles
funnier (5)	más gracioso, más graciosa
funniest (5)	el más gracioso, la más graciosa
fur (CC)	piel
furniture (CC)	muebles

G

gallon (32)	galón
gasoline (CC)	gasolina
giant (31)	gigante
giraffe (3)	jirafa
girlfriend (20)	amiga
girl's (34)	de la muchacha
girls' (34)	de las muchachas
glasses (15)	anteojos
goodness (28)	bondad
grandma's (34)	de la abuela
grandpa's (34)	del abuelo
grasshopper (8)	saltamontes

313

■ ENGLISH/SPANISH WORD LIST

greatness | **Kwanzaa**

greatness (28)	grandeza
grouping (CC)	agrupación

H

hamster (16)	hámster
hand signal (CC)	señal de mano
Hanukkah (33)	Hanukkah
happened (4)	pasar (pasado)
happening (4)	pasando
happier (5)	más feliz
happiest (5)	el más feliz, la más feliz
headline (CC)	sumario de noticias
heal (13)	sanar
health (13)	salud
heard (19)	oír (pasado)
heart (19)	corazón
he'd (17)	él + (condicional)
height (19, CC)	altura
he'll (17)	él + (futuro)
helmet (CC)	casco
helpless (28)	desamparado, desamparada
hemispheres (CC)	hemisferios
herbivore (CC)	herbívoro
herself (20)	ella misma
hide (11)	esconderse
highway (26)	carretera
hobbies (15)	pasatiempos
hobby (8)	pasatiempo
hockey (9)	hockey
hogans (CC)	hogans
holidays (15)	días de fiesta
home (CC)	hogar
honey (9)	miel
honor (CC)	honor
hopefully (27)	esperanzadamente
hopeless (28)	desesperado, desesperada
hospital (19)	hospital
hotel (16)	hotel
hotter (5)	más caliente
hottest (5)	el más caliente, la más caliente
house (21)	casa
however (21)	como quiera que; sin embargo
huge (22)	enorme
humidity (CC)	humedad
humor (CC)	humor

hydroelectric (CC)	hidroeléctrico, hidroeléctrica

I

I'd (17)	yo + (condicional)
I'll (17)	yo + (futuro)
I'm (17)	soy, estoy
inactive (29)	inactivo, inactiva
incisor (CC)	incisivo
incomplete (29)	incompleto, incompleta
incorrect (29)	incorrecto, incorrecta
independent (29)	independiente
inner ear (CC)	oído interno
insulation (CC)	insulación
interesting (25)	interesante
intersecting (CC)	cruzando
interview (CC)	entrevista
into (10)	en, por
Inuit (CC)	inuita
invention (27)	invento
invisible (29)	invisible
invite (11)	invitar
iris (CC)	iris
iron (31)	planchar; plancha
island (25)	isla
it's (17)	es

J

January (10)	enero
jaywalking (CC)	cruzar la calle imprudentemente
jewels (CC)	joyas
juice (22)	jugo
July (21)	julio
jump shot (CC)	lanzamiento con salto
June (33)	junio

K

Kansas (3)	Kansas
kayak (CC)	kayac
key sequence (CC)	secuencia de teclas
kicks (CC)	patadas
kitchen (7)	cocina
kneel (2)	arrodillarse
knit (2)	tejer
knob (2)	tirador
knot (2)	nudo
know (2)	saber
known (25)	conocido, conocida
Kwanzaa (33)	Kwanzaa

314

ENGLISH/SPANISH WORD LIST

ladies' | mysteries

L

ladies' (34)	de las damas
lady's (34)	de la dama
Lake Erie (CC)	lago Erie
Lake Huron (CC)	lago Huron
Lake Michigan (CC)	lago Michigan
Lake Ontario (CC)	lago Ontario
Lake Superior (CC)	lago Superior
lamb (2)	cordero
landforms (CC)	accidentes geográficos
larger (5)	más grande
largest (5)	el más grande, la más grande
lately (27)	últimamente
latitude (CC)	latitud
laughed (3)	reír (pasado)
lay-up (CC)	(en baloncesto) lanzamiento desde abajo del aro
lazy (16)	perezoso, perezosa
lead (CC)	párrafo introductor
leaders (CC)	líderes
least (9)	el menos, lo menos
length (CC)	largo
lens (CC)	cristalino; lente
let's (17)	vamos a
lettuce (8)	lechuga
librarian (CC)	bibliotecario, bibliotecaria
library (CC)	biblioteca
limb (2)	rama
line (CC)	recta
lion (11)	león
liquid (14)	líquido
local (CC)	local
location (27, CC)	localidad
lock (CC)	esclusa
longitude (CC)	longitud
loose (35)	suelto, suelta
lose (35)	perder
loud (21)	fuerte
love (CC)	amar

M

machine (31)	máquina
magnet (CC)	imán
magnetic field (CC)	campo magnético
magnetism (CC)	magnetismo
marble (CC)	mármol
March (7)	marzo
matter (8)	importar
May (33)	mayo
mean (13)	tener la intención; malo, mala; querer decir
meant (13)	tener la intención (pasado)
Memorial Day (33)	Día de conmemoración de los caídos
memories (15, CC)	recuerdos
memory minus (CC)	tecla de memoria para el signo menos
memory plus (CC)	tecla de memoria para el signo más
memory recall (CC)	tecla de llamada de la memoria
menu (22)	menú
meridians (CC)	meridianos
meteorologist (CC)	meteorólogo, meteoróloga
meter (13)	metro
metric (13)	métrico, métrica
middle ear (CC)	oído medio
might (25)	poder
misbehave (29)	portarse mal
misled (29)	engañar (pasado)
misplace (29)	extraviar
missed (16)	perder; echar de menos (pasado)
misspell (29)	deletrear mal
mistreat (29)	maltratar
model (32)	ejemplo; modelo
moisture (CC)	humedad
molar (CC)	muela
moment (31)	momento
money (9)	dinero
monkey (9)	mono, mona
monkeys (15)	monos, monas
mood (22)	humor
morning (20)	mañana
motor (32)	motor
motorcycle (26)	motocicleta
mountain (21)	montaña
mountains (CC)	montañas
movement (28)	movimiento
Mr. (33)	Sr.
Mrs. (33)	Sra.
Ms. (33)	Srta., Sra.
muffin (3)	panecillo
myself (26)	yo mismo, yo misma
mysteries (15)	misterios

ENGLISH/SPANISH WORD LIST

natural gas | punishment

N

natural gas (CC)	gas natural
Navajo (CC)	návajo
needleleaf (CC)	hoja de aguja
negative (CC)	negativo
neighbor (19)	vecino, vecina
nephew (22)	sobrino
nerve (20)	nervio
newspaper (26)	periódico
nighttime (26)	noche
November (33)	noviembre
number (32)	número
number keys (CC)	teclas de números
number sentence (CC)	expresión numérica

O

oak (CC)	roble
October (32)	octubre
odd (8)	raro, rara
of (35)	de
off (35)	apagado, apagada; de
offer (8)	ofrecer
office (CC)	oficina
often (25)	a menudo
oil (CC)	petróleo
oil gland (CC)	glándula sebácea
omnivore (CC)	omnívoro
only (19)	sólo
opened (4)	abrir *(pasado)*
opening (4)	abriendo
operation key (CC)	tecla de operación
optic nerve (CC)	nervio óptico
orchestra (CC)	orquesta
other (32)	otro, otra
our (35)	nuestro, nuestra
outer ear (CC)	oído externo
outside (21)	afuera
oven (32)	horno

P

paddle (8)	remar; canalete
painful (27)	doloroso, dolorosa
panic (CC)	dejarse llevar por el pánico
parallel (CC)	paralelo, paralela
parallel circuit (CC)	circuito paralelo
parallels (CC)	paralelos
parents (CC)	padres
Parthenon (CC)	Partenón
participate (CC)	participar
pavement (28)	pavimento
payment (28)	pago
peace (23)	paz
peaceful (27)	pacífico
pedestrians (CC)	peatones
people (32)	gente; personas
perfect (20)	perfecto, perfecta
perimeter (CC)	perímetro
perpendicular (CC)	perpendicular
photo (3)	foto
pickle (19)	pepino
piece (19, 23)	trozo; pedazo
pint (11)	pinta
pistil (CC)	pistilo
pitcher (7)	lanzador, lanzadora
plains (CC)	praderas
plateau (CC)	meseta
plates (CC)	placas
pocket (3)	bolsillo
point (CC)	punto
polar bear (CC)	oso polar
poles (CC)	polos
pollen (CC)	polen
pollution (27)	contaminación
pond (10)	charco
pore (CC)	poro
portrait (CC)	retrato
pottery (CC)	loza
pour (20)	verter
power (21)	poder; fuerza
powerful (27)	poderoso, poderosa
predator (CC)	depredador, depredadora
pressure (CC)	presión
prey (CC)	presa
prime meridian (CC)	línea de Greenwich
print (CC)	impresión
probably (31)	probablemente
producers (CC)	productores, productoras
products (CC)	productos
proud (21)	orgulloso, orgullosa
psychologist (CC)	sicólogo, sicóloga
pudding (21)	pudín, budín
pueblo (CC)	pueblo
punish (7)	castigar
punishment (28)	castigo

ENGLISH/SPANISH WORD LIST ■

pupil | skyscraper

pupil (22, CC)	alumno, alumna; pupilo, pupila

Q

quart (14)	cuarto
queen (14)	reina
quick (14)	rápido, rápida
quiet (35)	silencio; quieto, quieta
quilt (14)	colcha de retazos
quit (35)	abandonar
quite (35)	muy
quotient (CC)	cociente

R

rain gauge (CC)	pluviómetro
rattle (19)	sonaja
ray (CC)	rayo
Rd. (33)	ruta
react (29)	reaccionar
really (25)	verdaderamente
reason (9)	razón
rebound (CC)	rebote
rebuild (29)	reconstruir
recall (29)	recordar
record (3)	disco
recover (CC)	recobrar
reflector (CC)	reflector
relate (13)	relacionarse; contar
relative (13)	pariente
relatives (31)	parientes
relax (14)	relajar
remainder (CC)	residuo
remember (25)	recordar
remote (11)	remoto, remota
replace (29)	reemplazar
represent (CC)	representar
reproduce (CC)	reproducir
republic (CC)	república
rescue (CC)	rescatar
research (CC)	investigar
reservation (CC)	reservación
result (CC)	resultado
retina (CC)	retina
reuse (29)	reusar
Richter scale (CC)	Escala Richter
ridden (8)	montado
rim (CC)	aro
river (10)	río
robbed (4)	robar (pasado)
robbing (4)	robando

rough (3)	desigual; difícil; áspero, áspera

S

sadder (5)	más triste
saddest (5)	el más triste, la más triste
safely (27)	con toda seguridad
sagebrush (CC)	artemisa
said (19)	decir (pasado)
scarier (5)	más espantoso, más espantosa
scariest (5)	el más espantoso, la más espantosa
school (22)	escuela
scrapbook (CC)	libro de recuerdos
scratch (1)	rascar; arañazo
scream (1)	grito; gritar
screen (1)	biombo
scrub (1)	fregar
seal (CC)	foca
season (9)	estación
seed (CC)	semilla
segment (CC)	segmento
seismograph (CC)	sismógrafo
September (33)	septiembre
series circuit (CC)	circuito de series
serve (20)	servir
set (35)	poner
several (25)	varios, varias
shampoo (22)	champú
shared (CC)	compartir
she'll (17)	ella + (futuro)
shelter (7)	refugio
shoot (22)	tirar; sacar una foto
short (7)	corto, corta
shouldn't (17)	no deber
shower (21)	ducha
shown (7)	mostrado
shudder (8)	estremecerse
shutter (CC)	obturador
sign (2, 13)	señal; letrero; seña
signal (13)	señalar; señal
silver (CC)	plata
simple (32)	sencillo, sencilla
siren (CC)	sirena
sit (35)	sentarse
skateboarding (CC)	patinaje
skirt (20)	falda
skyscraper (1)	rascacielos

317

■ ENGLISH/SPANISH WORD LIST

slam-dunk | they'll

slam-dunk (CC)	(en baloncesto) lanzamiento desde arriba del aro
slipped (4)	resbalarse *(pasado)*
slippers (8)	zapatillas
slipping (4)	resbalándose
slowly (27)	despacio
smaller (5)	más pequeño, más pequeña
smallest (5)	el más pequeño, la más pequeña
smoke (11)	humo
snack (3)	bocadillo
snapshot (CC)	fotografía instantánea
soft (13)	suave; blando, blanda
softball (26)	sóftbol
soften (13)	suavizar; ablandar
softness (28)	suavidad
something (26)	algo
sometimes (26)	a veces
somewhere (7)	en alguna parte
sources (CC)	fuentes
speak (9)	hablar
special (CC)	especial
spider web (CC)	telaraña
spores (CC)	esporas
spotless (28)	inmaculado, inmaculada
square (1)	cuadrado
squeal (1)	chillido; chillar
squeeze (1)	exprimir
squirm (1)	retorcerse
squirt (1)	dejar salir a chorros
stamen (CC)	estambre
state (CC)	estado
statement (28)	declaración
station (11)	estación
steal (9)	robar; marcharse furtivamente *(pasado)*
steel (CC)	acero
stiff (3)	tieso, tiesa
St. Lawrence Seaway (CC)	Ruta marítima de San Laurencio
stole (11)	robar
stomach (31)	estómago
stood (21)	pararse *(pasado)*
stopped (4)	cesar; parar; detenerse *(pasado)*
stopping (4)	deteniéndose; parando
storm (20)	tormenta
strange (1)	raro, rara
strategy (CC)	estrategia
strawberry (1)	fresa
street (1)	calle
strength (1)	fuerza
strengths (CC)	fuerzas
strike (1)	golpe; golpear; prender un cerillo
stroke (CC)	brazada
studied (4)	estudiar *(pasado)*
studying (4)	estudiando
successful (CC)	exitoso, exitosa
sudden (32)	imprevisto, imprevista
suddenly (27)	de repente
suffer (8)	sufrir
suffixes (15)	sufijos
suit (22)	traje
Sun. (33)	dom.
supper (8)	cena
supplies (15)	provisiones; materiales para escuela
support (31)	apoyo
suppose (31)	suponer
surprised (25)	sorprendido, sorprendida
sweat gland (CC)	glándula sudorífera
swimming (25)	nadando

T

Taj Mahal (CC)	Taj Mahal
taxes (15)	impuestos
teacher's (34)	del maestro, de la maestra
teachers' (34)	de los maestros, de las maestras
tears (CC)	lágrimas
temperature (CC)	temperatura
temple (CC)	templo
Texas (14)	Texas, Tejas
than (35)	que
that's (17)	eso es
their (23)	su (de ellos, de ellas), sus (de ellos, de ellas)
them (9)	ellos, ellas, los, las, les
then (35)	entonces; luego
there (23)	ahí, allí
they (25)	ellos, ellas
they'd (17)	ellos + *(condicional)*, ellas + *(condicional)*
they'll (17)	ellos + *(futuro)*, ellas + *(futuro)*

318

ENGLISH/SPANISH WORD LIST ■

they're | worried

they're (23)	ellos (ellas) son, ellos (ellas) están
thirsty (20)	tener sed
thoughtful (27)	considerado, considerada
threat (1)	amenaza
thrill (1)	emoción
throat (1)	garganta
throne (23)	trono
through (1)	por, a través de
thrown (1, 23)	tirado, tirada
thumb (2)	pulgar
tigers (15)	tigres
title (32)	título
to (23)	a, hacia
toes (19)	dedos de los pies
tomb (CC)	tumba
tomorrow (8)	mañana
too (23)	también; demasiado, demasiada
took (21)	tomar; llevar (pasado)
tough (10)	duro, dura
track (3)	vía; pista
trash (7)	basura
treads (CC)	pedalea en agua
treat (9)	convidar; tratar; gusto
treatment (28)	tratamiento
tremendous (CC)	tremendo
trouble (10)	preocupar; dificultad
truthfully (27)	verdaderamente
tundra (CC)	tundra
two (23)	dos

U

ugly (16)	feo, fea
unknown (2)	desconocido, desconocida
until (16)	hasta
upon (16)	sobre
upstairs (26)	arriba
useless (28)	inútil
usual (22)	usual
usually (31)	usualmente

V

vacation (11)	vacación
Valentine's Day (33)	día de San Valentín
valley (9)	valle
verify (CC)	verificar
vertex (CC)	vértice

village (14)	pueblo
volcano (CC)	volcán
volume (CC)	volumen

W

walrus (CC)	morsa
want (16)	querer
washed (16)	lavar (pasado)
wasn't (16)	no era, no ser, no estar (pasado)
watch (7)	observar; reloj
water fountain (CC)	fuente de agua
waterway (CC)	vía fluvial
weaknesses (CC)	debilidades
weaving (CC)	tejido
Wed. (33)	miér.
weekend (26)	fin de semana
weekly (27)	semanal
weight (19, CC)	peso
weird (19)	raro, rara
welcome (31)	bienvenido, bienvenida
we'll (17)	nosotros + (futuro), nosotras + (futuro)
went (9)	ir (pasado)
were (35)	ser; estar (pasado, subjunctivo)
we're (35)	somos, estamos
we've (17)	hemos
whale (CC)	ballena
what's (17)	qué es
whatever (7)	todo lo que
wheat (7)	trigo
when (35)	cuando, cuándo
whenever (7)	cuando sea
where (35)	donde, dónde
wherever (7)	donde sea
who's (35)	quien es, quien está
whole (11)	entero, entera
whose (35)	de quien
width (CC)	anchura
wild (11)	salvaje
win (35)	ganar
wind vane (CC)	veleta
window (10)	ventana
with (10)	con
wood (21, 23)	madera
worried (4)	preocupado, preocupada; preocuparse (pasado)

■ ENGLISH/SPANISH WORD LIST

worry | your

worry (8)	preocuparse
worrying (4)	preocupándose
worthless (28)	sin valor
would (23)	*(condicional)*
would've (17)	*(condicional)* + haber
wouldn't (17)	no + *(condicional)*
wreath (2)	guirnalda
wreck (2)	restos (de un auto); accidente
wren (2)	reyezuelo
wrench (2)	llave inglesa
wrist (2)	muñeca
writing (2)	escribiendo
written (8)	escrito, escrita

Y

yesterday (31)	ayer
you'd (17)	tú + *(condicional)*, usted + *(condicional)*
you're (23)	eres, estás
young (10)	joven
your (23)	tu, tus, su, sus

PROGRAM TESTS

Test-Study-Test

Research studies indicate that the test-study-test approach to teaching spelling is the most effective because it allows students to concentrate on words they can't spell.

Early in the year, have students set up a Spelling Notebook. One section of this notebook should be set aside for pretests.

Pretest

Context sentences for a pretest are provided on the second page of the weekly planning guide of each lesson in the Teacher's Edition.

Administering the Pretest First read the underlined word, then read the sentence, and finally repeat the underlined word. Students are to write the underlined word only.

After the pretest, have students put a check mark next to each word they think is spelled correctly and a question mark next to each word they are not sure of.

Self-Correcting the Pretest It is important to work with students as they self-correct their pretests.

- Say each word and then spell the word aloud. As you spell, students should use a pencil to guide the checking of each letter.
- Students should then write each misspelled word correctly. They might also circle parts of words they find troublesome.

Following this procedure will help students develop a spelling "consciousness" about which words they know and which words they need to pay special attention to.

Cooperative Midweek Test

An effective way to be certain that a "practice" test has been taken is to provide time for pairs of students to test each other informally. The cooperative midweek test is optional.

Posttest

A posttest can be administered in four different ways.

- Have students write the <u>list words</u> only. For this kind of test, use the posttest sentences in the Teacher's Edition. Read the underlined words, then read the sentence, and finally repeat the underlined words.
- Use the <u>auditory posttest</u>. An auditory posttest is available as an alternate testing format on the *Everyday Spelling* CD-ROM.
- Have students write a <u>dictation sentence</u>. For this test, read the dictation sentence slowly and repeat it if necessary. All words used in the dictation sentences have been previously taught in the program. Dictation sentences are found on pages T37–T42.

- Use a <u>standardized test format</u>. For each lesson a Standardized Test Master is available in the *Practice for Standardized Tests* book as an alternate form of assessment.

Review Test

- Every sixth lesson is a review lesson and contains a review test. Each review lesson includes half the words taught in the five basic lessons that precede it.
- The review words taught in a unit are also included in the *Practice for Standardized Tests* book. These formats are based on the most widely used standardized tests and help students become accustomed to different ways spelling can be tested.
- For students studying the modified word list, dictation sentences that test the words studied on the Review masters are provided on the second page of the weekly planning guide.

Midyear and End-of-Year Tests

Lists appropriate for midyear and end-of-year testing are included here for teachers who wish to administer them.

Midyear Test

1. cover	11. fence	21. paddle
2. slippers	12. larger	22. they'd
3. invite	13. ability	23. drove
4. washed	14. closet	24. enough
5. strike	15. skyscraper	25. funniest
6. equal	16. sign	26. holidays
7. whenever	17. shouldn't	27. trouble
8. signal	18. church	28. wasn't
9. danced	19. hobbies	29. change
10. steal	20. knob	30. studying

End-of-Year Test

1. different	18. July	34. they'll
2. incorrect	19. drying	35. heard
3. classes	20. recall	36. flashlight
4. mood	21. bacon	37. December
5. with	22. close	38. heal
6. spotless	23. usually	39. treatment
7. aunt's	24. Mrs.	40. tough
8. morning	25. first	41. curfew
9. engine	26. always	42. attack
10. another	27. knot	43. house
11. thrill	28. carefully	44. remote
12. welcome	29. basketball	45. their
13. fattest	30. matter	46. studied
14. muffin	31. powerful	47. hotter
15. than	32. composition	48. alley
16. tigers	33. Chinese New	49. expect
17. know	Year	50. downstairs

PLACEMENT TESTS

You can make sure that your students are placed in the correct level of *Everyday Spelling* by using the group dictation test on page T35. The test consists of a list of twenty words for each grade level, drawn from the list words in each student book.

Administering the Test to Your Class

1. **Where to start.** Start with the list that is two grade levels below that of your students. For example, you should begin with the first-grade spelling list for third-grade students, the second-grade spelling list for fourth-grade students, and so on. Begin with the first-grade spelling list for first- and second-grade pupils.
2. **Where to stop.** Stop testing after you have dictated three spelling lists, ending with the list for your students' grade level.
3. **What to do.**
   - Say the word.
   - Use the word in a sentence with a clue to its meaning.
   - Say the word again.

4. **How to do it.** It is imperative that you provide the best possible test-taking conditions for students. This will ensure their most accurate performance.
   - Provide each student with paper and pencil.
   - Direct students to write their names on their papers and number the papers from 1 to 20.
   - Make clear that students are to remain quiet and listen very carefully. Explain the procedure outlined in Step 3. Tell students that after you say the word the last time, they should think about its spelling and then write it.
   - Speak slowly and clearly.
5. **How to determine grade placement levels.** Each correctly spelled word is worth 5 points. Multiply the number of correct words in each list by 5. Use this score to determine the independent level, the regular instruction level, the modified basic level, and the frustration level. Use the following chart of Spelling Placement Test Levels to determine these levels.

SPELLING PLACEMENT TEST LEVELS

Number of Words Correct	Percentage Score	Achievement Level	What to do about placement or further testing
18–20	90–100%	Independent Level	Test at the next higher level. Continue testing until you find the regular instruction level* or assign the basic word list, challenge list, and Cross-Curricular Lessons.
10–17	50–85%	Regular Instruction Level	Assign the basic spelling list at grade level and the Cross-Curricular Lessons.
6–9	30–45%	Modified Basic Level	Test at the next lower level. Continue testing until you find the regular instruction level,* or assign the top half of the total basic list.
0–5	0–25%	Frustration Level	Students are unlikely to succeed if required to work at this level. Therefore, the best option is to test students at the next lower level. Continue testing until you find the regular instruction level.

* Many schools discourage or prohibit placement at book levels other than a student's grade level. For this reason a single grade-level book may be used for total class instruction, supplemented by materials that provide enrichment or remediation.

SPELLING PLACEMENT TEST WORD LISTS

GRADE 1

1. big
2. up
3. rode
4. class
5. end
6. at
7. two
8. like
9. going
10. had
11. led
12. kite
13. try
14. mop
15. ripe
16. what
17. day
18. sister
19. park
20. would

GRADE 2

1. first
2. egg
3. bath
4. I'm
5. table
6. dress
7. kick
8. special
9. read
10. swimming
11. myself
12. baseball
13. grade
14. because
15. part
16. soon
17. streets
18. that
19. before
20. walk

GRADE 3

1. secret
2. hungry
3. unsafe
4. smash
5. stalk
6. bedroom
7. circle
8. America
9. sight
10. cried
11. happiness
12. spray
13. inventor
14. balloon
15. instead
16. sugar
17. house
18. people
19. point
20. wrestle

GRADE 4

1. peace
2. comb
3. health
4. pond
5. giraffe
6. who's
7. outside
8. common
9. sadder
10. honey
11. interesting
12. teachers'
13. worthless
14. Canada
15. coming
16. court
17. March
18. suddenly
19. fudge
20. could've

GRADE 5

1. journey
2. opened
3. first aid
4. trunk
5. arrow
6. planet
7. practical
8. easier
9. civil
10. plumbing
11. leaves
12. accurate
13. preparation
14. chimney
15. pollute
16. python
17. knead
18. reversible
19. haircut
20. downtown

GRADE 6

1. connect
2. question
3. sensitive
4. distance
5. resignation
6. schedule
7. something
8. council
9. portable
10. ceiling
11. men's
12. stereos
13. koala
14. irrational
15. satisfied
16. forty
17. personnel
18. distraction
19. forgotten
20. precaution

GRADE 7

1. substitute
2. all-around
3. discourage
4. aircraft
5. exempt
6. physician
7. publicity
8. horrified
9. pendant
10. appreciate
11. mosquito
12. vacuum
13. generous
14. commitment
15. enterprise
16. funeral
17. afghan
18. identical
19. auditorium
20. unique

GRADE 8

1. available
2. pressure
3. referral
4. karate
5. embargoes
6. invasion
7. substantial
8. hideous
9. rationale
10. embarrassment
11. kayak
12. gentleness
13. susceptible
14. initiation
15. judicious
16. interfere
17. subsection
18. cooperate
19. monstrous
20. assistance

Name _________________________________ Date _________________

■ SPELLING PRETEST LESSON _____________

- Write each list word as you hear it read.
- Place a check in the box for each word you're sure is spelled correctly.
- Place a question mark in the box for any word that you're not sure is spelled correctly.
- In the second blank, write each misspelled word correctly.

		Spelled Correctly	Not Sure	
1.	_______________	☐	☐	_______________
2.	_______________	☐	☐	_______________
3.	_______________	☐	☐	_______________
4.	_______________	☐	☐	_______________
5.	_______________	☐	☐	_______________
6.	_______________	☐	☐	_______________
7.	_______________	☐	☐	_______________
8.	_______________	☐	☐	_______________
9.	_______________	☐	☐	_______________
10.	_______________	☐	☐	_______________
11.	_______________	☐	☐	_______________
12.	_______________	☐	☐	_______________
13.	_______________	☐	☐	_______________
14.	_______________	☐	☐	_______________
15.	_______________	☐	☐	_______________
16.	_______________	☐	☐	_______________
17.	_______________	☐	☐	_______________
18.	_______________	☐	☐	_______________
19.	_______________	☐	☐	_______________
20.	_______________	☐	☐	_______________

UNIT 1

LESSON 1

1. A scream came from his throat when he got scared.
2. The threat that the cat might strike made the mouse scratch and squirm.
3. The skyscraper was on the first street.
4. An orange may squirt you if you squeeze it.
5. The fly came in through a hole in the screen.
6. I have thrown the strawberry back into the garden.
7. It can take strength to scrub the dirt off a house.
8. The fast train ride gave him a strange thrill.
9. I heard you squeal when the square dance began.

LESSON 2

1. Writing for one hour made his wrist hurt.
2. We know our teacher will assign us homework.
3. She hurt her thumb when she hit it with a wrench.
4. We use paint to make a sign with a pretty design.
5. Cats climb into our tree house and wreck it.
6. A wren flew from the limb of a tree.
7. You can knit socks from the coat of a lamb.
8. She can comb the knot out of her hair.
9. The man had to kneel to reach the knob under the chair.
10. An unknown person gave us a pretty wreath.

LESSON 3

1. We listen to the alphabet on an old record.
2. That dolphin will not attack you.
3. I have a photo of a farm in Kansas.
4. We laughed because the clown was funny.
5. An elephant is not as tall as a giraffe.
6. My brother had a muffin for a snack.
7. Jane took care to cover her head in the rain.
8. The bark on the tree was stiff and rough.
9. I have enough pennies in my pocket to buy an apple.
10. The brake made the train stop on the track.

LESSON 4

1. She was worried about slipping as she ran.
2. I happened to be studying when my friend came over.
3. They were chasing the man who had robbed the house.
4. He had a cold drink after he stopped dancing.
5. She slipped outside to see what was happening.
6. He opened the box of dried oranges.
7. The dog chased the rabbit through the opening in the forest.
8. She was worrying she might fall as she danced.
9. The squirrel was robbing us of our lunches while we studied.
10. After stopping to put away the dishes, he started drying the pots and pans.

LESSON 5

1. The smallest clown was the funniest one.
2. He got sadder as his shoe went deeper into the mud.
3. The scarier monster was the funnier one.
4. I wear a larger cap when the sun is hottest.
5. I am happiest in the sunshine and saddest in the rain.
6. The largest and fattest cat eats the most.
7. The smaller baby was the happier one.
8. The sun grew hotter the closer we got to home.
9. I will tell my deepest secret to my closest friend.
10. The fatter monster was the scariest one.

UNIT 2

LESSON 7

1. A short pitcher will throw the ball to the catcher.
2. Grandfather will punish me whenever I do wrong.
3. We went to watch a ball game in March.
4. It took him awhile to read the first chapter.
5. Somewhere in the kitchen is a flashlight.
6. She was shown where to find the wheat bread.
7. A church is a kind of shelter.
8. I like whatever is made with chocolate.
9. I did not sit anywhere near the trash can.

LESSON 8

1. Ken gave her a bottle of bubble bath.
2. Tomorrow it will not matter.
3. She has a different hobby every week.
4. My mother will offer him some supper.
5. I shudder from the cold and put on my slippers.
6. Jan has written a letter to her current teacher.
7. Grandmother had to borrow a paddle for the boat.
8. My sister will worry if I suffer from a cold.
9. The grasshopper is an odd kind of bug.
10. She has ridden to the store to get lettuce.

LESSON 9

1. That monkey might try to steal a treat.
2. It is better to use money instead of credit.
3. Our hockey team beat the one from out of town.
4. Winter is the season I like the least.
5. I have a good reason to think that I won the contest.
6. Tom rode the donkey across the valley.
7. I will speak to them tomorrow by the fence.
8. Mother went to the kitchen to get honey.
9. We found a toy train engine in the alley.

LESSON 10

1. Grandma put the blanket in the closet.
2. Part of the town river runs into a small pond.
3. The food was too tough to chop.
4. A couple down the block play in a band.
5. My young cousin had trouble with his homework.
6. Meg almost shut the window on her finger.
7. Bill will use cash to buy a backpack.
8. I forgot that school is out on the first day of January.

LESSON 11

1. The lion stole through the trees.
2. We drove to a remote farm for our vacation.
3. You have a place to hide if you are in danger.
4. Smoke came out of the cable after it broke.
5. Soon our train will arrive at the station.
6. He will use two cups to make a whole pint.
7. Grandma will decide if she wants bacon or toast.
8. Do not stand behind a wild horse.
9. I will invite Tom to my party in April.

UNIT 3

LESSON 13

1. She is <u>able</u> to make muffins when she uses a <u>metric</u> cup.
2. A nurse has the <u>ability</u> to help <u>heal</u> sick people.
3. Today he will write a <u>composition</u> for <u>health</u> class.
4. The bread began to <u>soften</u> and <u>crumble</u>.
5. I <u>meant</u> to <u>compose</u> a letter to a friend.
6. The cat <u>dealt</u> the kitten a <u>soft</u> strike.
7. It is fun to use a <u>signal</u> to <u>relate</u> a secret.
8. Tim made a <u>deal</u> to help a <u>relative</u> with homework.
9. I saw no <u>sign</u> of a <u>crumb</u> on the clean rug.
10. Do you <u>mean</u> that a <u>meter</u> is about three feet?

LESSON 14

1. One <u>quart</u> of <u>liquid</u> is <u>equal</u> to four cups.
2. We <u>expect</u> our mom to make a pretty <u>quilt</u>.
3. Everyone <u>except</u> the <u>queen</u> must kneel.
4. I want to bring an <u>extra</u> <u>change</u> of clothes.
5. I am <u>excited</u> about our trip to <u>Texas</u>.
6. Let me <u>explain</u> how I <u>relax</u> after school.
7. The <u>fudge</u> was <u>excellent</u>.
8. The <u>bridge</u> led to the <u>edge</u> of the <u>village</u>.
9. Grandfather was <u>quick</u> to <u>charge</u> our lunches.

LESSON 15

1. My <u>eyelashes</u> hit the edge of my <u>glasses</u>.
2. You see <u>monkeys</u> and <u>tigers</u> at many <u>circuses</u>.
3. We pick <u>bunches</u> of <u>flowers</u> for the <u>holidays</u>.
4. <u>Supplies</u> got here after many <u>delays</u>.
5. We study <u>suffixes</u> in our spelling <u>classes</u>.
6. I have <u>memories</u> of going to many <u>beaches</u>.
7. In <u>mysteries</u> some people may be <u>enemies</u>.
8. I am happy that we don't have to pay <u>taxes</u> on <u>hobbies</u>.
9. My <u>friends</u> saw their barn burn to <u>ashes</u>.

LESSON 16

1. <u>Father</u> is not <u>coming</u> <u>until</u> tomorrow.
2. You might hurt his <u>feelings</u> if you call him <u>ugly</u>.
3. I <u>missed</u> you a lot when you stayed at the <u>hotel</u>.
4. My <u>hamster</u> is a <u>crazy</u> little animal.
5. I <u>almost</u> <u>always</u> feel <u>lazy</u> during summer.
6. We <u>washed</u> our clothes after <u>eleven</u>.
7. My sister <u>didn't</u> <u>want</u> to go to the picnic.
8. Peg <u>wasn't</u> going to sit <u>upon</u> the ground.

LESSON 17

1. I'm sure <u>they'd</u> like to go to the movie.
2. We <u>would've</u> come over if <u>he'd</u> said yes.
3. She <u>doesn't</u> think <u>she'll</u> go to the picnic.
4. <u>We'll</u> go for a walk if <u>he'll</u> come with us.
5. <u>I'll</u> go to the beach if <u>it's</u> a nice day.
6. Let's see if <u>they'll</u> play baseball with us.
7. <u>That's</u> the way <u>I'd</u> like to paint a picture.
8. I <u>could've</u> come if <u>you'd</u> wanted me to.
9. He <u>wouldn't</u> tell them <u>what's</u> going on.
10. <u>We've</u> walked home even if we <u>shouldn't</u> have.

UNIT 4

LESSON 19

1. My neighbor asked me to take him to the hospital.
2. Grandma said she wants a piece of pickle.
3. My best friend has a heart of gold.
4. I heard a weird noise from the field.
5. The school nurse checks our height and weight.
6. Father brought the rattle over to the baby.
7. I believe we will build a new house again.
8. She can reach it only if she stands on her toes.

LESSON 20

1. I was certain my girlfriend went to Florida.
2. It began to pour rain in the morning.
3. She made a skirt for herself when she was fourteen.
4. We did not have the nerve to camp in the forest.
5. He will serve the ball across the court.
6. The first course was very good.
7. After my fourth drink I was still thirsty.
8. The form got dirty after I dropped it in the mud.
9. The day was perfect until the storm hit.

LESSON 21

1. The butcher will cut the turkey however you want.
2. My sister was proud of the pudding she made.
3. The brook runs behind the large bush.
4. Use a power saw to cut the wood.
5. We saw a dark cloud over the house.
6. The mountain is so pretty in July.
7. I stood in the hot shower.
8. Grandma took a cushion to the football game.
9. The crowd outside was very loud.

LESSON 22

1. Our teacher did not want to confuse the new pupil.
2. I am not in the mood to wear a suit today.
3. I have a huge bruise on my arm.
4. A few of my friends want to go on a cruise.
5. I used my usual shampoo to wash my hair.
6. Fruit is a favorite thing on the menu.
7. There is no excuse to stay out after curfew.
8. My nephew drove to the station to get fuel.
9. After school I will shoot some pictures.
10. Ben had two cool glasses of juice.

LESSON 23

1. Sam has beet juice on his clothes.
2. He uses the brake to stop the train.
3. Close the window if you're cold.
4. From her throne the queen asked for peace.
5. The ball was thrown into their yard.
6. The wood chair was too old to put in the new house.
7. I would like to see your new puppy.
8. They're going to beat us at the football game.
9. I get two tries to break the swimming record.
10. There is a piece of muffin on the rug.

UNIT 5

LESSON 25

1. I took an <u>interesting</u> picture with my <u>camera</u>.
2. It gets cold <u>beginning</u> in <u>December</u>.
3. Last <u>evening</u> we <u>caught</u> <u>several</u> fish.
4. Our family <u>might</u> camp on an <u>island</u> in <u>February</u>.
5. <u>They</u> <u>finally</u> saw the new movie.
6. <u>Everybody</u> <u>really</u> wants to go to the <u>party</u>.
7. <u>Everyone</u> had <u>known</u> that Uncle Tim would come.
8. I <u>remember</u> how <u>surprised</u> I was on my birthday.
9. We <u>often</u> go <u>swimming</u> during the summer.

LESSON 26

1. Lin wants to buy a <u>motorcycle</u> and a new pair of <u>earrings</u>.
2. We will play <u>softball</u> this <u>weekend</u>.
3. <u>Sometimes</u> we play <u>basketball</u> after school.
4. It might be hard to see the <u>highway</u> at <u>nighttime</u>.
5. We might go to see the <u>baseball</u> game <u>anyway</u>.
6. <u>Downstairs</u> you will find the <u>newspaper</u>.
7. <u>Upstairs</u> is our new <u>classroom</u>.
8. She wrote <u>something</u> funny on the <u>chalkboard</u>.
9. I will ring the <u>doorbell</u> <u>myself</u>.
10. My new <u>classmate</u> walked up our <u>driveway</u>.

LESSON 27

1. He <u>suddenly</u> got very <u>cheerful</u>.
2. He speaks <u>hopefully</u> about ways to stop <u>pollution</u>.
3. The <u>powerful</u> tigers jump into <u>action</u>.
4. Our <u>thoughtful</u> <u>invention</u> won the <u>contest</u>.
5. <u>Lately</u> my mother has been running <u>daily</u>.
6. The beach was a <u>peaceful</u> <u>location</u>.
7. We <u>slowly</u> and <u>safely</u> walk across the street.
8. I <u>carefully</u> made a <u>correction</u> to my homework.
9. He tells her <u>truthfully</u> that she is <u>beautiful</u>.
10. Her <u>weekly</u> visit to the hospital is never <u>painful</u>.

LESSON 28

1. His <u>greatness</u> came from his fair <u>treatment</u> of people.
2. You could get hurt if you are <u>careless</u> in the <u>darkness</u>.
3. A <u>punishment</u> is <u>worthless</u> if you do not learn from it.
4. She was <u>breathless</u> after she ran across the <u>pavement</u>.
5. Our house looks <u>spotless</u> in the <u>brightness</u> of the sun.
6. My arm was <u>useless</u> and <u>helpless</u> after I broke it.
7. He made a <u>payment</u> to the new <u>business</u>.
8. He made a <u>hopeless</u> <u>statement</u>.
9. There was <u>softness</u> in the <u>movement</u> of the cat.
10. My father is known for his <u>goodness</u> and <u>fairness</u>.

LESSON 29

1. <u>Dishonest</u> people might have <u>misled</u> you.
2. He uses <u>invisible</u> paint that will <u>disappear</u>.
3. I <u>dislike</u> people who <u>mistreat</u> animals.
4. I <u>distrust</u> those who <u>misbehave</u>.
5. Her spelling homework was <u>incorrect</u> and <u>incomplete</u>.
6. You must <u>recall</u> where you <u>misplace</u> something.
7. I <u>disagree</u> that cats are very <u>independent</u>.
8. He will <u>replace</u> a ball player who is <u>inactive</u>.
9. They will <u>reuse</u> engine parts to <u>rebuild</u> the train.
10. My teacher might <u>react</u> if I <u>misspell</u> a word.

UNIT 6

LESSON 31

1. My favorite relatives are my aunt and uncle.
2. The old machine is made with iron parts.
3. I was sick to my stomach yesterday.
4. The giant cement truck rode down our street.
5. We will probably go on a canoe trip.
6. We especially like to go to Canada in the summer.
7. I suppose we will welcome our new neighbor.
8. It took Dad a moment to support what he said.
9. Bill usually goes to camp in August.
10. Buffalo are very large animals.

LESSON 32

1. We made a model of a motor in class.
2. A barrel and a gallon both hold liquid.
3. Some people are afraid to go to a doctor.
4. The house number was at an angle.
5. His oven was broken.
6. There was another sudden rain shower.
7. I like the color of the trees in October.
8. The book title was a common one.
9. It is simple to button a shirt.
10. The other child looks like an angel.

LESSON 33

1. Hanukkah, Christmas, and Kwanzaa are in Dec.
2. Memorial Day is in May.
3. Mr. and Mrs. Lopez lived on River Rd.
4. Dr. Ling has a house on Fourth Ave.
5. Valentines' Day is in Feb.
6. Chinese New Year is on Wed. this year.
7. Ms. Jones has a birthday the first Sun. in June.
8. September and November are in the fall.

LESSON 34

1. The boys' and girls' teams both won.
2. Grandma's scarf and grandpa's coat were on the chair.
3. The teacher's favorite was the girl's story.
4. The lady's child was the boy's friend.
5. Our families' houses were visited by our aunts' friends.
6. My aunt's dog stole the baby's rattle.
7. Our brothers' team beat the teachers' team.
8. My Dad's cat sat on my friend's coat.
9. My family's truck ran over my brother's toy.
10. The babies' blankets were knitted by the ladies' team.

LESSON 35

1. We're going to win the game.
2. They were quiet in class.
3. It is better to stay in school than to quit.
4. I know where we will sit at the play.
5. Find out whose toy it is and then give it back.
6. They are quite happy with their new puppy.
7. A friend of his got off the train.
8. He doesn't know when the dog got loose.
9. Our team might lose the game.
10. I know who's going to set the table.

SPELLING GENERALIZATIONS

Sound–Letter Associations

Consonant Sounds

/f/ spelled **gh**	22–25
/f/ spelled **ph**	22–25
/j/ spelled **dge**	70–73
/j/ spelled **ge**	70–73
/k/ spelled **c**	22–25
/k/ spelled **ck**	22–25
/k/ spelled **k**	22–25
/ks/ spelled **x**	70–73
/kw/ spelled **qu**	70–73
/m/ spelled **mb**	18–21
/n/ spelled **gn**	18–21
/n/ spelled **kn**	18–21
/r/ spelled **wr**	18–21

Double Consonants

	44–47, 203, 223

Consonant Digraphs

/ch/ spelled **ch**	40–43
/ch/ spelled **tch**	40–43
/hw/ spelled **wh**	40–43
/sh/ spelled **sh**	40–43

Consonant Blends

/skr/ spelled **scr**	14–17
/skw/ spelled **squ**	14–17
/str/ spelled **str**	14–17
/thr/ spelled **thr**	14–17

Vowels

/a/ spelled **a**	52–55
/e/ spelled **e**	48–51
/i/ spelled **i**	52–55
/o/ spelled **o**	52–55
/u/ spelled **ou**	52–55
/ā/ spelled **a**	56–59
/ē/ spelled **ea**	48–51
/ē/ spelled **ee**	170
/ē/ spelled **ey**	48–51
/ī/ spelled **i**	56–59
/ī/ spelled **i-e**	56–59
/ō/ spelled **o**	170
/ō/ spelled **o-e**	56–59
/ėr/ spelled **er**	96–99
/ėr/ spelled **ir**	96–99
/ôr/ spelled **or**	96–99

/ôr/ spelled **our**	96–99
/ou/ spelled **ou**	100–103
/ou/ spelled **ow**	100–103
/u̇/ spelled **oo**	100–103
/u̇/ spelled **u**	100–103
/ü/ spelled **oo**	104–107
/ü/ spelled **ui**	104–107
/yü/ spelled **ew**	104–107
/yü/ spelled **u**	104–107
/yü/ spelled **u-e**	104–107

Schwas and Syllabic Consonants

/ə/ spelled **a**	144–147
/ə/ spelled **e**	144–147
/ə/ spelled **i**	144–147
/ə/ spelled **o**	144–147
/ə/ spelled **u**	144–147
/əl/ spelled **el**	148–151
/əl/ spelled **le**	148–151
/ən/ spelled **en**	148–151
/ən/ spelled **on**	148–151
/ər/ spelled **er**	148–151
/ər/ spelled **or**	148–151

Word Structure

Abbreviation and Capitalization	149, 152–155, 211, 241, 242
Compound Words	39, 122–125
Contractions	82–85, 243
Greek/Latin Word Parts	43, 127, 189
Inflectional Endings	26–29, 30–33, 45, 74–77, 97
Possessives	156–159, 243
Prefixes	39, 95, 134–137
Related Words	66–69, 195
Suffixes	39, 95, 126–129, 130–133
Syllables	38–39, 42, 101, 119, 142, 153, 175, 179, 187, 191, 197, 199, 213

Words from Other Languages

	25, 41, 53, 77, 103, 105, 127, 149

COMMON SPELLING ERRORS

SPELLING STRATEGIES

SPELLING AND WRITING

Writing Forms

Writing Modes

Writing Process

Spelling and Writing continued

Writing Tests

Proofreading

Capitalization Errors

Careless Errors

Handwriting Errors

Punctuation Errors

Spelling Errors

Usage Errors

SPELLING AND VOCABULARY

Vocabulary Development

This list shows all the words in *Everyday Spelling*, grades 1–8. The words from this grade level are highlighted in color. The numbers after each word indicate the grade and lesson in which that word appears. The key explains the letter designations.

Key

Core Lessons
F . . . Frequently Misspelled Words
EW . . Everyday Words
Ch . . Challenge Words

Cross-Curricular Lessons
SS . . . Social Studies
He . . Health
Sc . . . Science
Rd . . Reading
Ma . . Math
WP . . Work and Play

A

a 1–15EW
abandon 7–13
abbreviate 8–33
abbreviation 7–3
abduct 8–33
abduction 7–20
ability 4–13
able 4–13
abnormal 8–33
abolish 5–SS6, 8–33
abolitionist 8–SS4
about 2–26F
abrasive 8–33Ch
absolute magnitude 6–Sc8
absolute value 7–Ma4
absolutely 6–4
absorb 8–33
abstain 8–14Ch
abstention 8–14Ch
absurd 5–21Ch
academic 7–8
academy 7–8
acceleration 8–Sc1
accept 5–34, 6–14
acceptable 7–13
access 6–14
accessible 7–33Ch
accessory 8–2
accident 2–He4, 5–9
accidentally 7–23
accidents 4–15Ch, 5–He2
acclaim 7–32Ch
acclamation 7–32Ch
accommodate 7–3
accompaniment 6–9Ch
accompanist 7–21Ch
accompany 5–14Ch, 8–2
accomplice 7–16Ch
accomplish 6–9
accomplishment 7–3
accomplishments 4–Rd1
according 6–9
accordion 8–35Ch
accountant 7–21
accumulate 5–11Ch, 8–2
accuracy 8–28
accurate 5–14
accuse 5–14
achieve 6–3
achievement 8–25Ch
acid rain 7–He4
acknowledgment 8–25
acne 7–He1
acquaintance 8–31
acquiesce 7–35Ch
acquisition 7–9Ch
acquittal 7–13Ch
acre 5–19
acreage 8–10Ch
acropolis 8–20Ch

across 2–13
action 2–14Ch, 4–27
activate 6–26
activity 3–8Ch
actor 3–34
actually 5–13
acute triangle 5–Ma4
adapt 5–34Ch, 7–22
add 2–19, 2–Ma1
addition 8–33
additives 6–He3
address 6–9
adequate 6–2Ch
adherent 7–21Ch
adhesive 8–33
adjacent 8–33
adjourn 8–31
adjust 5–1
adjusted 6–1
administration 6–22Ch
admiral 8–35
admiration 3–Rd4, 5–28
admire 6–2
admiring 6–Rd6
admit 5–Rd6
adobe 4–SS6
adolescence 7–4Ch
adolescent 7–35
adolescents 7–4Ch
adopt 5–34Ch, 7–22
adopted 5–13Ch
advantage 4–14Ch, 8–33
advantageous 8–25Ch
advent 8–32
adventure 5–9, 5–Rd4
adventures 2–Rd6
adventurous 5–Rd3, 8–3
adverse 7–22Ch
adversity 8–33Ch
advertise 7–16
advertisement 8–32
advice 7–22
advise 7–22
advisory 7–19
advocate 8–15
aerial 8–19
aerobics 8–7Ch
aesthetic 8–7Ch
affect 7–22
affectionate 6–26
affective 8–16
affirmative action 8–SS9
afford 6–9
afghan 7–35
afraid 3–9
Africa 6–SS2
after 2–34
afternoon 3–31
aftershocks 6–Sc5
afterthought 6–34
afterwards 8–22Ch
again 2–35F, 3–23F, 4–19F, 5–8F, 6–29F

against 5–8
aggravate 8–28
aggression 8–SS8
aggressive 8–2
aghast 5–3
agility 6–He2
ago 3–10
agrarian 7–SS9
agree 2–SS1
agreeable 5–27
agreement 3–Rd4, 6–Rd2
agriculture 5–SS2
ahead 5–8
aim 3–9
air conditioner 6–11
aircraft 3–1Ch, 7–10
air mass 4–Sc4
airplane 2–31, 2–SS4
air pollution 5–He3
aisle 4–23Ch, 8–23
Alabama 5–33
à la carte 8–22Ch
alarm 2–27Ch, 2–WP1
Alaska 5–33
alcohol 8–31
algebra 7–29
alienate 6–26Ch
aliens 5–10
align 4–2Ch
a little 6–29
all 2–33
all-American 8–22Ch
all-around 7–17
allergens 6–He4
allergic 5–14Ch, 8–29
allergy 6–He4
alley 4–9
Allies 8–SS8
alligator 5–Sc3, 6–23
allot 8–22
allowance 4–8Ch, 6–9
allowed 5–23, 8–23F
all ready 8–22
all right 8–35
all together 8–22
allude 8–16
all ways 6–29
almost 3–13F, 4–16
alone 3–13
a lot 2–13F, 3–13F, 4–16F, 5–7F, 6–29F, 8–22F
aloud 5–23, 8–23
alphabet 4–3
already 5–8, 8–22
also 2–13
alternate 7–26
alternative 7–26
although 5–2Ch
altogether 8–22
alumni 7–10
always 2–13, 3–13F, 4–16F, 5–7F, 6–29F
am 1–7EW

amasses 7–SS4
amateur 8–17
amazed 3–5Ch
amazing 3–5Ch
amber 6–Sc3
ambidextrous 8–29Ch
ambitious 5–28Ch
ambulance 5–13Ch, 8–28
ambulances 5–4Ch
America 3–29
American 6–31
amino acids 7–He1
among 5–2
amount 5–20
amphibian 2–Sc1, 3–Sc1, 7–13Ch
amphitheater 6–SS3
amused 5–5
amusing 5–5
an 1–7
analyses 8–5
Anasazi 3–SS6, 5–SS2
anatomy 6–SS6
ancestor 7–13
ancestors 7–SS4
anchor 8–35
ancient 8–3
and 1–7EW, 2–4F, 3–9F, 5–9F
android 6–Rd5
anemia 7–Sc7
angel 4–32
angle 4–32, 4–Ma4
angrier 4–5Ch
angriest 4–5Ch
angry 3–13
animal 3–33
animals 4–31, 5–Sc2
animism 7–SS9
annex 8–SS6
annihilate 8–7Ch
anniversary 7–19
announce 6–9
announced 4–21Ch
announcement 4–28Ch
announcer 3–34Ch
annoy 5–20
annual rate 8–Ma5
anorexia nervosa 7–He1
another 2–34F, 3–33F, 4–32F, 5–32F
answer 5–13
answered 3–25Ch, 6–5
answering 6–5
antecedent 7–33Ch
antelope 5–10
antennas 4–8Ch
anthropology 7–15Ch
antibiotic 7–Sc4, 8–27
antibodies 6–He4, 7–Sc4
antibody 8–27
antidote 6–25Ch, 8–27
antifreeze 8–27

antihistamine 8–27Ch
antiseptic 8–27
antisocial 8–27
anxious 6–15Ch
any 3–8
anymore 8–22
any more 8–22
anyone 3–31
anything 5–16
anyway 4–26, 8–22
any way 8–22
anywhere 4–7
apart 8–22
a part 8–22
apartment 5–21
apiece 6–3
apologize 4–11Ch, 6–31
apologized 6–Rd2
apparent 6–33
apparent magnitude 6–Sc8
appear 3–29Ch, 5–22
appearance 4–He1, 6–33
appendix 7–20
appetizer 6–20
applause 5–11Ch
apple 2–34
appointment 4–28Ch
appreciate 4–He1, 7–29
appreciation 5–28Ch, 5–Rd2
appreciative 6–26Ch
apprehend 8–14Ch
apprehensive 7–Rd1, 8–14Ch
apprentice 7–16
apprenticeship 6–26Ch
appropriate 8–2
approximate 5–Ma1
approximately 7–3
April 2–35Ch, 4–11
April Fools' Day 7–11Ch
apropos 8–7Ch
aptitude 6–4Ch
aquarium 6–19
aqueduct 7–20Ch
Arabic 7–SS3
arc 6–Ma1
archaeologist 6–SS1
archaeology 6–31Ch, 8–19
architecture 6–SS6, 8–Ch10
arctic 8–31
are 1–22, 4–35F
area 4–Ma2
arena 6–SS4
aren't 3–32
argue 5–21
argued 4–4Ch, 7–5
arguing 4–4Ch, 7–5
argument 8–25
argumentative 7–29Ch

COMPLETE WORD LIST

COMPLETE WORD LIST

COMPLETE WORD LIST

K

kaleidoscope 8–1Ch
kangaroos 7–SS8
Kansas 4–3
karate 8–17
kayak 4–SS7, 8–35
keelboat 8–SS2
keep 2–14
Kentucky 5–33
kept 3–25
kernel 8–23
keyboard 8–Sc7
key sequence 4–Ma1
khaki 8–35
kick 2–2
kicks 4–WP1
kickstand 5–16
kiln 3–WP4
kilogram 7–Ma2
kiloliter 7–Ma2
kilometers 5–Ma2
kimono 8–35
kimonos 7–SS7
kind 2–2
kindergarten 4–25Ch, 6–20
kindness 3–27
kind of 8–22
kingdom 5–Sc2, 7–Sc3
kisses 5–4
kitchen 4–7
kite 1–21
kites 1–21
kitten 1–23
kiva 3–SS6
knapsack 5–3
knead 5–3, 5–23
knee 3–16
kneel 2–20Ch, 4–2
knew 2–17F, 5–3F
knickknacks 5–3Ch
knife 3–16
knight 3–16
knights 6–SS5
knit 4–2
knitting 5–3
knives 6–16
knob 4–2
knock 3–16
knock-knock joke 5–WP4
knot 4–2
know 1–33EW, 2–29F, 3–16F, 4–2F, 5–3F
knowledge 3–16Ch, 5–3
knowledgeable 5–27Ch, 8–21
known 4–25
koala 6–23
koalas 7–SS8
kookaburra 7–SS8
Kwanza 4–33

L

label 5–32
labels 3–Ma6
laboratory 7–23
labor unions 5–SS7
ladder 3–19, 3–Rd2
ladies 3–4
ladies' 4–34
lady's 4–34
lagoon 7–25
Lake Erie 4–SS3
Lake Huron 4–SS3
Lake Michigan 4–SS3
Lake Ontario 4–SS3
Lake Superior 4–SS3
lamb 4–2
lamppost 3–31Ch
land 2–4
landfill 3–He3
landfills 5–He3
landforms 4–Sc5, 5–SS1
language 3–SS4, 7–2
lantern 7–29
large 3–3
larger 4–5
largest 4–5
lariat 5–Rd3, 8–SS5
lasagna 4–2Ch
last 3–9
late 1–14
lately 4–27
later 6–14
latitude 4–SS1, 6–Sc1
latter 6–14
laugh 3–35
laughed 4–3
laughing 2–Rd1
laughter 5–WP4, 6–31
launch 5–11
laundry 3–22Ch, 5–11
lava 3–Sc4, 6–Sc2
lawn 3–22
lawn mowing 5–WP3
laws 3–WP3
lawyer 3–22Ch
lay-up 4–WP2
lazy 4–16
lead 4–WP3
leaders 4–SS5
leadership 6–26
league 6–8
learn 2–28
learned behavior 7–Sc9
least 2–20Ch, 4–9
leaves 5–17
led 1–8
ledge 5–14
left 3–1
leg 2–7
legalize 7–16
legend 5–14
legislative branch 5–SS5
legislature 8–10
leisure 6–3
lemon 3–33
lemonade 6–2
length 3–Sc2, 4–Ma2, 5–13
lens 4–Sc6, 4–WP4
lesson 3–19
less than 2–Ma3
let 2–7
let's 3–32, 4–17F, 5–15F, 6–10F
letter 3–19
lettuce 2–13Ch, 4–8
leukemia 7–He1, 7–Sc7
level 6–20
lever 3–Sc3
liable 8–16
liaison 8–19
libel 8–16
liberal 8–31
liberate 8–Rd2
liberation 8–SS8
librarian 2–Rd4, 4–Rd2
libraries 4–15Ch
library 3–25Ch, 4–Rd4, 5–13
license 6–1
lieutenant 7–1
lifeguard 7–He3
life jacket 2–Rd6, 7–He3, 8–11
life span 5–Sc2
ligaments 7–Sc5
light 2–16
lighter 5–5
lightest 5–5
lightning 3–11Ch, 5–2, 7–He3
light-years 6–Sc8
like 1–16, 2–2F
likely 6–Ma5
limb 4–2
limelight 7–Rd1
limestone 6–Sc2
limousine 8–19
line 4–Ma4
line drive 3–WP1
line of symmetry 7–Ma1
lines of latitude 6–Sc1
lion 4–11
lions 2–5
liquid 2–Sc3, 4–14
listen 3–16
listening 5–3
liter 3–Sc2, 3–Ma4
literal 7–14
literature 6–SS6
litter 3–He3
little 1–23EW, 2–34F, 3–19F
Little Rock 5–33
lived 2–13
lively 3–13
liver 7–Sc6
lives 5–17
living room 5–35
load 3–10, 3–Sc3
loaves 5–17
lobster 5–9
local 4–SS5
locate 3–SS1
location 4–27, 4–SS1
lock 4–SS3
locker 3–15
locker room 6–11
locomotion 7–33
lodge 5–14
logging 3–SS3
logical 7–13
lonely 3–27Ch, 5–19
long 3–2
longhorn 5–Rd3, 8–SS5
longhouse 5–SS2
longitude 4–SS1, 6–Sc1
long-term memory 7–Sc9
look 2–10
looking 2–10
looms 8–Rd4
loose 4–35
loquacious 8–15
lord 6–SS5
Los Angeles 5–33
lose 3–21, 4–35
lost 1–27
loud 4–21
Louisiana 5–33Ch
Louisiana Purchase 8–SS2
love 4–Rd3
low-pressure system 6–Sc7
loyal 5–20
loyalty 7–9
luckily 8–7
lucky 3–8
lucrative 7–SS4
luggage 8–17
luminous 8–Sc5
lunch 2–15Ch
lunches 2–5
lungs 2–He3, 3–Sc1
luxurious 7–7Ch

M

macaroni 6–23
machete 8–17
machine 4–31, 5–SS7
machinery 7–19
macramé 8–17
made 1–14
magazine 6–31
magic 6–28
magician 6–28
magma 3–Sc4
magnate 8–16
magnet 4–16Ch, 4–Sc3, 8–16
magnetic compass 7–SS6
magnetic field 4–Sc3
magnetism 4–Sc3
magnificent 8–28
magnified 5–5Ch
magnify 6–2
magnifying 5–5Ch
magnitude 6–Sc5
mah-jongg 8–17Ch
mail 2–15
mailbox 5–16
mailboxes 3–4Ch
main 5–10, 5–23
Maine 3–9
maintain 7–32
maintenance 7–32
majestic 5–Rd2
major 5–14, 6–17
majority 6–17
make 1–14EW, 2–15
make-believe 7–17
malicious 6–13Ch
mammal 2–Sc1, 3–Sc1
man 1–7
manacle 8–26Ch
management 8–26
manager 3–34Ch, 5–31
mandatory 7–19
mane 5–23
maneuver 7–1
manicure 8–26
manifest destiny 8–SS6
manipulate 8–26
manipulative 8–26Ch
mannequin 8–7Ch
mannerism 8–10
manor 6–SS5
man's 6–10
mantle 3–Sc4, 6–Sc4
manufacture 8–26
manuscript 8–15
many 3–8

map 2–SS3
map key 3–SS1
mapmakers 5–SS1
maraca 8–35Ch
marathon 8–28
marble 4–Rd5, 6–Sc2
march 2–27
March 4–7
marches 3–4
margarine 5–21Ch
marimba 8–35Ch
Mars 3Sc–5
marshal 6–7Ch
marshmallow 3–19Ch
marsupials 7–SS8
martial 6–7Ch
marvelous 5–28
Maryland 6–31
mass production 5–SS7
masterpieces 6–SS6
matches 5–4
material 7–14
materialism 8–10Ch
math 3–9
mathematical expression 8–Ma4
mathematics 7–7
matinee 8–19
matter 2–Sc3, 4–8
mattress 8–35
may 1–14EW, 2–15
May 4–33
Mayas 6–SS7
maybe 5–13F, 8–22F
may be 8–22
mayonnaise 7–3
me 1–15
meadow 5–8
mean 4–13, 7–Ma3
meant 4–13
meanwhile 7–2
measles 6–16
measure 5–8
meat eater 2–Sc2
mechanic 3–9Ch, 5–14
mechanical clock 7–SS6
medal 6–14
medalist 7–21Ch
media 7–10
median 7–Ma3
medicine 7–14
mediocre 6–1Ch, 8–1
megalopolis 8–20Ch
megaphone 6–35
meiosis 7–Sc2
melancholy 8–Rd3
melanin 8–He2
membership 6–26
mementos 8–5
memorable 8–28
memoranda 8–5Ch
Memorial Day 4–33
memories 4–15, 4–Rd3, 5–Rd6
memorize 7–16
memory 7–7, 7–Sc9
memory minus 4–Ma1
memory plus 4–Ma1
memory recall 4–Ma1
Memphis 5–33
men 2–7
men's 6–10
mention 6–13
menu 4–22

COMPLETE WORD LIST

suspended 7–20
suspense 8–Rd2
suspenseful 4–27Ch
suspension 8–34, 8–Sc3
suspension bridges 7–SS6
suspicious 6–19Ch, 8–25
sustain 8–14
sustenance 8–14
sweat gland 4–He3
sweatshirt 6–11Ch
sweet 2–3, 8–23
swim 2–11
swimming 2–11F, 3–25F, 4–25F, 6–2F
swing 2–3
sword 4–19Ch, 6–21
swung 5–9
symbol 3–SS1, 5–23Ch, 5–Sc4, 8–23
symmetric 7–Ma1
symmetry 8–4
sympathetic 8–Rd1
sympathize 7–16
symphony 6–35
synchronize 8–4

T

table 2–34
tackle 3–15Ch
tail 3–9, 3–17
Taj Mahal 4–Rd5
take 2–15
tale 3–17
talent 5–Rd6
talk 3–22
tall 2–19
tallies 3–Ma6
tally chart 3–Ma6
tambourine 8–17
tap 1–20
tape 1–20
tape measure 3–WP2
tape recorder 6–11
tariffs 8–5
tar pit 6–Sc3
task 5–1
Tasmania 7–SS8
taught 5–11
taxes 4–15
tea ceremony 7–SS7
teacher 1–21EW, 7–Rd2
teacher's 4–34
teachers' 4–34
team 2–14
teammate 4–26Ch, 6–11
tears 4–He1
technicality 7–9Ch
technician 7–21
technology 6–Rd5, 7–15
teenage 6–11
teeth 2–14
telecast 6–35
telecommunication 6–35Ch
telegram 6–35
telegraph 6–35
telephone 6–35
telescope 6–35
telethon 8–28
television 6–22
tell 2–7
temperamental 6–31Ch, 8–7

temperature 4–25Ch, 4–Ma2, 5–SS1, 6–25, 8–Sc4
temple 4–Rd5, 6–SS2
temporary 7–19
ten 1–8
Tennessee 6–9
tentacles 5–Sc3
tepee 5–SS2
tepees 3–SS6
term 6–Ma4
terminating decimal 8–Ma2
terraces 6–SS7
terra cotta 7–SS4
terrapin 7–25Ch
terrible 5–31
tessellation 7–Ma1
Texas 4–14
textbook 5–16, 5–WP2
than 4–35
thank 3–1
Thanksgiving 2–SS5, 5–2
that 1–31EW, 2–8
that'll 3–32Ch
that's 2–32F, 3–32F, 4–17F, 5–15F, 6–10F
thaw 3–22
the 1–31, 2–20
their 1–34, 2–25F, 3–17F, 4–23F, 5–19F, 6–7F, 7–4F
theirs 7–11
them 2–7F, 4–9
thematic map 7–SS1
themselves 5–17, 6–11F
then 1–20EW, 2–20F, 3–7F, 4–35F, 5–2F
theory 5–Sc1
therapist 6–He2
therapy 8–7
there 2–20F, 3–17F, 4–23F, 5–2F, 6–7F, 7–4F
therefore 6–21
there's 2–32F, 5–15F, 6–10F
there've 5–15Ch
thermal 8–4
thermodynamic 8–4Ch
thermometer 8–4, 8–Sc4
thermonuclear 8–4Ch
thermos 8–4
thermosphere 6–Sc6
thermostat 8–4, 8–Sc4
these 2–22
they 1–31, 2–20F, 3–2F, 4–25F, 5–2F
they'd 4–17
they'll 2–32Ch, 4–17
they're 2–32F, 3–17F, 4–23F, 5–15F, 6–7F
they've 3–32
thick 3–2
thief 5–8
thieves 6–16
thing 2–9
think 3–1
third 3–28
thirds 2–Ma5
thirsty 4–20
thirteen 6–1
thirtieth 7–1
thirty 2–8Ch
this 2–9
Thomas Jefferson 8–SS2

thorough 6–21
thoroughly 8–1
those 1–19EW, 2–22
though 5–2
thought 2–33F, 3–23F, 5–2F
thoughtful 4–27
thousand 4–21Ch, 6–1
threat 4–1
threatening 3–Rd3, 7–23
three 1–11
three-dimensional 8–Ma3
threw 5–11, 5–23
thrill 4–1
thrive 8–Rd2
throat 2–22Ch, 4–1
throne 4–23
through 2–25F, 3–25F, 4–1F, 5–23F, 6–1F, 7–1F, 8–1F
throughout 5–16Ch, 8–11
throw 2–16
thrown 4–1, 4–23
thumb 4–2
thumbtack 5–16Ch
thunderstorm 6–2Ch, 8–11
Thursday 3–28
ticket 3–15
tickling 6–15
tigers 4–15
tight 3–11
time 1–16
time machine 6–Rd5
times 3–Ma2
time zones 6–Sc1
timid 8–Rd1
timpani 8–35Ch
tired 3–23
tissue 6–2, 7–Sc1
title 4–32
to 1–17EW, 2–29F, 3–17, 4–23, 5–23F
toast 3–10
tobacco 5–SS4
toboggan 6–20Ch, 8–17
today 3–9
today's 5–29
toes 4–19
together 3–7, 6–29
Tokyo 7–SS7
tomato 6–23
tomatoes 5–17, 6–SS7
tomb 4–Rd5, 5–3, 6–SS2
tomorrow 4–8, 6–29
tone 6–Rd1
tongue 4–19Ch, 6–1
tonight 6–29
too 1–32EW, 2–17F, 3–17F, 4–17F, 5–17F
took 2–2F, 3–20F, 4–21F
tooth 3–2
toothbrushes 5–4Ch
top 1–10
topographic map 7–SS1
tornado 6–Sc7, 7–25
tornadoes 5–17
torpedo 3–8Ch
torpedoes 7–10
touch 2–9
touchdown 4–7Ch
tough 4–10
tourist 3–34, 3–SS2
tournament 6–SS5, 7–7

toward 6–31
towel 5–20
town 2–26
toxin 7–Sc4
toys 3–20
trachea 5–He1
track 4–3
tractor 6–20
traditional 8–Rd3
traditions 3–SS4, 5–Rd2, 8–Rd4
traffic signal 2–He4
tragedy 7–29
trail 3–9
trail drive 8–SS5
Trail of Tears 8–SS3
train 1–26, 2–SS4
traits 5–Sc2, 7–Sc2
trajectory 7–20Ch
trampoline 8–7
tranquil 8–8Ch
tranquillity 8–8Ch
transaction 8–13
transcript 8–13
transfer 8–9
transferred 7–5Ch, 8–Sc4
transferring 7–5Ch
transformation 7–Ma1
transfusion 8–13
translate 8–13
translation 7–Ma1
translucent 8–13Ch, 8–Sc5
transmit 8–13
transmitted 7–33
transoceanic 8–13Ch
transparent 8–13, 8–Sc5
transport 6–35
transportation 8–13
trapezoid 6–Ma2
trash 4–7
travel 3–33
traveled 7–5
traveling 7–5
treads 4–WP1
treasure 3–Rd2, 5–SS3, 7–14
treasurer 5–8Ch
treat 4–9
treatment 4–28
treatment plant 5–He3
treaty 8–SS6
tree 1–15
trembling 6–15, 6–Rd6
tremendous 4–Rd6, 6–1Ch, 8–1
trench 6–Sc4
trespass 8–2
trial-and-error learning 7–Sc9
trials 6–Ma5
triangle 2–Ma6, 7–27
triangular prism 8–Ma3
trick 3–15
tried 2–35F, 3–23, 5–5F
tries 3–4
trigonometry 7–27Ch
trillion 7–27
trip 2–11
triple 7–27
triplets 7–27
tripod 7–27
tripped 2–11
trophies 5–4Ch
trophy 3–8Ch

troposphere 6–Sc6
trouble 2–34Ch, 2–Rd3, 4–10
truck 3–21
true 3–21
truly 7–29
trunk 5–2
trustworthy 6–21Ch
truth 2–9Ch
truthfully 4–27
try 1–26
trying 5–5
tsunami 6–Sc5
Tuesday 3–25
tumble 5–19
tundra 4–SS7, 7–25
tunnel 6–20
turbines 5–Sc6
turkey 3–28
Turkish 7–SS3
turmoil 5–20Ch
turn 2–28
turquoise 8–19
turtle 2–28
turtleneck 6–11Ch
tutoring 5–WP3
tuxedo 8–29
TV 5–7F
twelfth 6–25
twenty-one 7–17
twins 2–15Ch
twirl 3–28Ch
twittering 6–Rd3
two 1–11, 2–29F, 3–17F, 4–23
typewriter 5–35
typhoon 7–25
tyrant 8–SS3

U

ugly 4–16
ukulele 6–4Ch, 8–17
umbrella 5–9Ch, 8–17
umbrellas 7–SS6
unable 5–26
unbelievable 5–19Ch, 7–31
unbreakable 7–34
unbuckle 5–26
unbusinesslike 7–34Ch
uncertainty 5–26Ch
uncle 3–21
unclear 5–26
uncle's 5–29
uncles' 5–29
unconscious 3–26Ch, 7–34
uncontrollable 7–31
undaunted 8–Rd2
undefeated 3–26Ch, 7–34
under 2–34
underachiever 6–27Ch
undercover 6–27
underground 3–Rd5, 8–11
Underground Railroad 8–SS4
underneath 6–29Ch
undernourished 6–27
underrated 8–11
understand 6–19
understanding 8–Rd3
understood 3–20Ch
underweight 6–27
undoubtedly 8–31Ch

COMPLETE WORD LIST